D0793554

A Landscape of Hawaii by Jules Tavernier. *(Honolulu Academy of Arts)*

"Old San Jose." Artist Unknown. *(Courtesy of N. Eric Oback)*

"Dog Team" by Ted Lambert. *(University of Alaska Museum)*

"Louisiana Marsh" by William H. Buck.
(Courtesy of Issac Delgado Museum of Art)

"Rainy Season" by Peter Hurd. *(The Brooklyn Museum)*

"A View of the Brooklyn Bridge" by Robert Lebron. *(Courtesy of Robert Lebron)*

"Map," 1963, by Jasper Johns. *(Private Collection)*

USA

An American Record

"Winter in New England" by George Durrie. *(The British Museum of American Art)*

USA

An American Record

Paul Goodman
University of California, Davis

Frank Otto Gatell
University of California, Los Angeles

Holt, Rinehart and Winston, Inc.

New York   Chicago   San Francisco   Atlanta   Dallas   Montreal   Toronto

Library of Congress Catalog Card Number: 70-167812
ISBN: 0-03-077435-7
Printed in the United States of America
2 3 4 5   071   9 8 7 6 5 4 3 2 1

Preface

This volume joins a growing number of new textbooks surveying the history of the United States. It offers students and instructors a text intermediate in length between the standard one- or two-volume surveys and the brief summary books. It provides students with a basic narrative and body of information, but it also permits greater use of collateral readings to enrich the course. More important than length, we have given greater attention than is customary in most survey texts to explaining *why* events occurred as they did. Readers will find, for example, following the narrative of events culminating in major developments such as the American Revolution or the Civil War, an analysis of causation that aims to make the preceding narrative more understandable. We believe that by viewing the narrative and the data within sharper analytical focus students will derive more that is meaningful from their study of history.

In still another way we have sought to overcome the tendency of survey texts that confront students with a grab bag of historical information. Survey textbooks supply the necessary chronology of events and highlight the central facts of the nation's history for the beginning student. But students often get so lost in the forest of textbook information that they lose sight of a principal reason for studying history: to achieve that greater self-knowledge which comes through understanding the paths to the present. Introductions preceding each Part of the book delineate major historical developments to be described and analyzed in the next Part. We hope that with this carefully spelled out framework the narrative detail and analysis will make more sense and that we have presented a serviceable guide to the American past.

El Cerrito, California   P. G.
Los Angeles, California   F. O. G.
January 1972

Contents

Maps and Figures

USA *An American Record*

Part One
A New Society, 1607-1760

Introduction

Sometime before the American colonies became the United States, perceptive Europeans noted that "a new race of men" inhabited England's North American provinces. By the time these colonies won independence, a widespread sense already existed among the citizens that they differed from the English, Irish, Scotch, Dutch, Germans, and other nationalities they had left behind in their home lands. This transformation of the European into the American occurred during America's colonial period, the 175 years after the first settlement early in the seventeenth century until the declaration of nationhood in 1776. Those formative years laid the foundations for a powerful nation.

The distinctive characteristics of colonial America later became common characteristics of modern society. Here in the New World material abundance and the diffusion of wealth enabled the majority of white citizens to live in relative comfort and to aspire to improve their condition. Government in the colonies was far more sensitive to the wishes and interests of the people at large than in Europe at that time. Here a sizable percentage of adult males could vote, and though people generally deferred to the wisdom, judgment, and leadership of the "better" sort—the colonial elite—the terms of political participation were broadening and pointing in the direction of popular government, at a time when kings and aristocrats monopolized power elsewhere. America also was the birthplace of religious freedom. By the end of the colonial period, not only were men free to worship as they wished, but the ties between church and state had weakened, pointing to the separation of the sacred from the secular during the revolutionary era. Finally, birth counted for less and individual achievement for more in determining a family's status than was the case in Europe. Here there were no hereditary, privileged classes but a relatively fluid social structure with extensive opportunities for upward mobility.

America, wrote the French visitor to the colonies, Hector St. John de Crèvecoeur, in *Letters from an American Farmer,* displays "one diffusive scene of happiness reaching from the sea-shores to the last settlements on the borders of the wilderness." The most striking difference between the Old World and the New was that most colonists were freeholders. The ownership of property gave men pride and independence as well as the right to vote. In the words of Crèvecoeur's American farmer: "The instant I enter on my own land, the bright idea of property, of exclusive right, of independence exalts my mind. . . . On it is founded our rank, our freedom, our power as citizens, our importance as inhabitants."

Out of their experiences as colonists, Americans formulated the revolutionary principles on which to found a new nation. Their belief in individual liberty, the equality of man, and freedom of thought distinguished the Americans from other nations. In the eighteenth century it provided the basis of their identity as a people. In our own time as in the past, the gap between the republic's professed ideals and such realities of American society as racial injustice and poverty amid plenty creates a dynamic tension. The way Americans have resolved the conflict between their beliefs and their behavior has shaped their history and will determine their future.

The first Americans: "Noble savage" or obstacle to civilization? *(New York Public Library)*

Landing of the pilgrims at Plymouth, December 22, 1620. *(Library of Congress)*

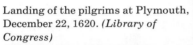

The Great God who is the power and wisdom that made you and me Incline your hearts to Righteousness Love and peace. This I send to Assure you of my Love, and to desire your Love to my friends, and when the Great God brings me among you I Intend to order all things in such manner that we may all live in Love and peace one with another whilst I hope the Great God will Incline both me and you to do. I seek nothing but the honor of his name, and that we who are his workmanship, may do that which is well pleasing to him. The man which delivers this unto you, is my special friend Sober wise and Loving, you may believe him. I have already taken care that none of my people wrong you, by good Laws I have provided for that purpose, nor will I ever allow any of my people to sell Rumme to make your people drunk. If anything should be out of order, expect when I come, it shall be mended, and I will bring you some things of our Country that are useful and pleasing to you. So I rest In ye Love of our god yt made us I am

England 25 : 2 : 1682
mo

Your Loveing freind

I send this to the Indians
by an filter pr to the
6 mo 1682   Tho. Holme

WM PENN

GOV. STUYVESANT'S HOME,
"THE WHITEHALL," 1658.

New York beginnings. *(Library of Congress)*

William Penn buys some land, 1682.
(Library of Congress)

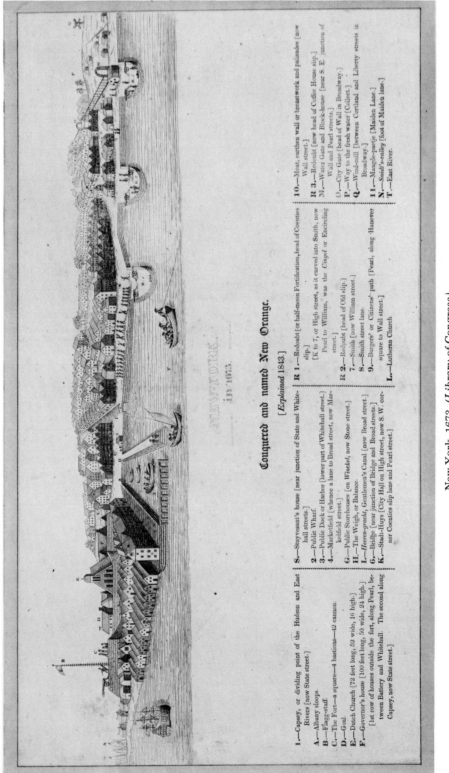

New York, 1673. *(Library of Congress)*

View from Bushongen Tavern 5 miles from York Town on the Baltimore road.

Colonel Hay

Colonial farmers: "Nature's noblemen." (*Library of Congress*)

Old Bruton Parish Church, Williamsburg, Virginia, and a Sunday gathering in colonial times. This church was completed in 1715. *(Library of Congress)*

Harvard College, 1739:
Culture in the wilderness.
(Library of Congress)

Chapter 1
The Expansion of Europe

For thousands of years the Western Hemisphere lay hidden from the great civilizations of East and West. But toward the end of the fifteenth century Europe discovered a New World. During the next hundred years the Spanish, Portuguese, French, English, and Dutch spilled blood and gained treasure exploring this new continent and staking out imperial claims. Almost overnight Western Europeans broadened their horizons. For centuries following the collapse of Rome, European civilization had contracted, hemmed in by newly risen and hostile forces, first the Arabs, mobilized by the faith of Islam, later by the Ottoman Turks, and always by the impenetrable barrier that the ocean placed in the way of Europe's westward thrust.

All that changed during the century after Columbus discovered America. Christians repelled the Turkish threat at the gates of Vienna in 1529, and Europeans gained a foothold in North Africa from which Islam had launched its invasion of Christendom. The rough waters of the Atlantic now carried European vessels to the far reaches of the globe. It was no accident that ships bearing the flags of Spain, Portugal, and other European kingdoms, and not those of China, Japan, or other Eastern nations found a new world; nor was the timing of America's discovery accidental. The Western Hemisphere became Europe's prize because what had been happening in the Old World long before Columbus set sail in August, 1492, prepared Europeans for the role of successful colonizers and empire builders.

THE PRECONDITIONS OF EXPANSION

In the vanguard of European expansion stood Portugal and Spain. The Iberian peninsula had played a minor role in European affairs until the Age of Columbus when its soldiers and sailors carved out great empires. The Spaniards and Portuguese were first in the race for empire be-cause they possessed the necessary resources and expansionist attitudes which other colonizing kingdoms did not acquire until later.

Overseas expansion was the work of strong, unified states. Internal unity gave Spain and Portugal a head start, just as, on the other hand, Germany and Italy lagged behind in the scramble for foreign possessions until their own unification toward the end of the nineteenth century. During the Middle Ages many great and lesser nobles shared political power and the king was rarely master of his kingdom. In the modern state which began to emerge in the fifteenth century, the king increasingly centralized power in his own hands. Spain, as did other parts of Europe, comprised some large and many small feudal principalities recognizing no supreme secular power.

Necessity, however, compelled Spaniards to unite behind a strong king before other countries saw the need. For seven centuries all or part of Spain lay under Arab rule. Christian reconquest proved slow and difficult. It ended the same year Columbus sailed west under the patronage of the dynasty that succeeded in expelling the Moors. This was the work of Isabella of Castile and Ferdinand of Aragon who joined forces against the Moors and subdued their Spanish rivals in the name of Christian unity and national liberation. Until England and France overcame their internal disunity, they were not ready to compete.

Portugal took the lead in organizing public and private resources for expansion. This small kingdom, unified even earlier than Spain, and inspired by a Catholic faith nourished in centuries of struggle with the Moslems, conquered the city of Ceuta in North Africa (1415) and planned further assaults against Arab power. The weakening or destruction of Moslem control of the Mediterranean also offered rich material rewards to Europe's merchants and trading companies once they gained more direct access to the oriental spices which were then staples in international trade. The strategic shortcut, the Portuguese believed, lay not in assaulting Islam directly in the Mediterranean but in sailing down the west coast of Africa to attack the enemy from the rear.

During the fifteenth century, the Portuguese colonized the Azores and Canary Islands far out in the Atlantic, trafficked in gold and slaves, and explored the African coastline. In 1488 Bartholomeu Dias reached the Cape of Good Hope at Africa's southernmost tip and ten years later, Vasco da Gama completed a voyage around Africa to India and back. These and other expeditions, not all of them successful, cost money. But by mobilizing a small portion of the national wealth for exploration the Portuguese crown eventually profited enormously.

The crown did more than finance exploration; it attempted to solve technical problems that impeded long ocean voyages into strange and dangerous seas. During the later Middle Ages, navigational advances had been made but ships were still designed for short, relatively safe voyages, and scientific aids were often inadequate for the ambitious, dangerous undertakings Portugal contemplated. Prince Henry the Navigator (1394–1460), son of John I, established an institute where scholars and experienced seamen pooled their knowledge and applied it to solving practical problems. By the sixteenth century European vessels were the best in the world. Capitalizing on cumulative scientific advances in shipbuilding and navigation, the Portuguese built superior and better-armed vessels. With cannons mounted on their vessels, Portuguese captains enjoyed an overwhelming advantage over slower, clumsier, and undergunned enemy fleets. Portugal thereby undermined Arab control of the spice trade and gained command of the Indian Ocean, establishing naval bases and fortresses at the sources of supply in India, China, and the East Indies. Its success foreshadowed the next four centuries during which Europe's scientific and technological advantages made it the dominant continent.

For Spain, as for Portugal, exploration and expansion were outlets for the energy and enthusiasm created by success in the reconquest campaign against Islam. The methods of reconquest at home—mobilizing power against the enemy, securing strong points, staking out claims, and acquiring dominion over defeated populations—all could be used to carry the flag abroad as well. Spain's seven hundred year crusading tradition led it to press into North Africa, but Spaniards also dreamed of finding newer areas to provide lands and booty to seize and "infidels" to convert.

Columbus

Christopher Columbus (1451–1506), the son of a Genoese wool weaver, was an experienced seaman who believed that he could reach the East Indies by sailing west. Neither Portugal nor Spain, whose patronage he repeatedly sought, were willing to back him. The western seas were uncharted and Columbus thought the voyage practical only because he grossly underestimated the distance. His persistence finally paid off. After the fall of Granada, the last Moorish fortress, the Spanish crown, flushed with victory, appointed him Admiral of the Ocean Sea, viceroy and governor of whatever land he might discover. Jealous of Portuguese success, the Spaniards hoped to compete by finding a new route to the Orient via oceans yet unknown to their rivals.

With a fleet of three ships and a crew of ninety, Columbus, a superb sailor, sailed west. Nine weeks later, he sighted land in the Bahamas and soon discovered Cuba and Santo Domingo. In the next ten years he made three more voyages to America, believing each time that further exploration would bring him to the Indies. He died insisting that the large land mass he had found was an island, never realizing that he had discovered a fourth continent. Yet within his own lifetime this truth was gaining recognition, although for the next century explorers of many nations persisted in the quest for a passage to India through the Western Hemisphere.

The discovery of a new world shattered the medieval Christian belief in a static and finite universe with a fixed habitable portion of land, an island surrounded by hostile seas. Believing in the Fall of Man, the Christian perceived the world as a prison in which he must suffer and labor, destined by God to "take possession of the earth so far as he is able to do so by his own efforts" and to transform "it to meet his own needs." Columbus was driven by a mystical vision that he could conquer the unknown. After his voyage the universe no longer appeared so fixed or finite. For some it was now no longer a prison but instead a constant challenge to human courage, intelligence, and imagination.

European expansion rested on many interrelated foundations. Christian belief in the imperfection of the present sent restless men into the world to search for El Dorado and spread the faith. The powerful new nation-states provided political and administrative structures which harnessed scientific and technical knowledge, surplus capital, and the desire for material gain in the cause of exploration and empire. As nations pushed through the geographical limits that had once confined medieval Europe, they were entering a new era in the history of the West. The birth of modern science was unlocking the secrets of the universe. The centralized modern states were rationalizing government. And economic development was creating new wealth and possibilities for material achievement. The expansion of Europe was thus an expression of the dynamic forces transforming the West from a medieval to a modern civilization.

VARIETIES OF COLONIZATION: THE SPANISH EXAMPLE

Each European nation entering the race for empire had a unique colonization experience. A nation's internal development prior to expansion, as well as opportunities and obstacles encountered in the New World, influenced the timing, direction, and methods of settlement. Latin America in the middle of the twentieth century still awaits modernizing revolutions that will transform outdated and unpopular social orders, which are in part legacies from colonial experience under Spain. Canada, first settled by the French, but acquired by England through military victory over France in 1763, still struggles to harmonize two antagonistic ethnic traditions, English and French, and to develop vast resources not yet exploited. Like the former Spanish colonies, Canada

had its national development shaped in part by its colonial history. Similarly the United States' experience as English colonies helped produce a nation decidedly different from its neighbors to the north and south.

The Spanish empire was a vast estate whose economic, political, and religious life lay under royal control. Though the crown employed private adventurers to finance initial conquest and settlement, it carefully prevented them from acquiring too much power. Superior organization and military technology, coupled with strong faith in their cause, enabled a handful of Spaniards to gain mastery over several Indian civilizations. Hernando Cortes, with only 600 soldiers and sixteen horses, quickly subdued the Aztecs in Mexico. Francisco Pizarro, with 180 soldiers and thirty-seven horses, conquered the Incas in Peru. Once the Spaniards broke the power of the most advanced Indian cultures, they were free to construct a new social order.

Faithful soldiers received grants of land and the command of Indian labor, while the merchants of Seville enjoyed a monopoly of the transatlantic trade. The Church undertook vast campaigns to convert the Indians, thus helping to make them more resigned to Spanish rule, and in the process acquired valuable grants of land and taxing powers. The crown, however, controlled the Church, its revenues, and appointments. It also carefully limited the rights of large planters, denying them representative institutions in order to stifle the rise of a powerful aristocracy. Madrid, the center of all political authority, made decisions, leaving little initiative to local functionaries who could not lay out a new town or even decide on the width of a street without orders from home.

Farming took place on large estates controlled by the crown, the Church, and Spaniards who migrated to form the local elite. During three centuries of Spanish rule, only 300,000 Europeans came to America; a great many of them were fortune seekers, minor nobility, and gentry who regarded manual labor as degrading. Since the crown desired to keep its colonies free of alien racial and religious elements, it barred Jews, Moors, and any except Spanish Catholics. It also excluded Spanish commercial interests other than the Sevillian monopoly. The Spanish peasantry

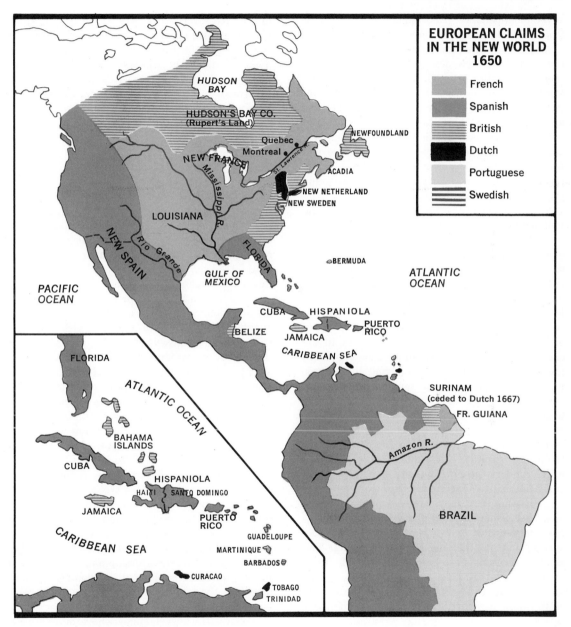

EUROPEAN CLAIMS IN THE NEW WORLD 1650

- French
- Spanish
- British
- Dutch
- Portuguese
- Swedish

HUDSON BAY

HUDSON'S BAY CO. (Rupert's Land)

NEWFOUNDLAND

Quebec
Montreal

NEW FRANCE

St. Lawrence R.

ACADIA

NEW NETHERLAND
NEW SWEDEN

Mississippi R.

LOUISIANA

NEW SPAIN

Rio Grande

FLORIDA

BERMUDA

ATLANTIC OCEAN

PACIFIC OCEAN

GULF OF MEXICO

CUBA

HISPANIOLA

PUERTO RICO

BELIZE

JAMAICA

CARIBBEAN SEA

SURINAM (ceded to Dutch 1667)

FR. GUIANA

Amazon R.

BRAZIL

FLORIDA

ATLANTIC OCEAN

BAHAMA ISLANDS

CUBA

HISPANIOLA

HAITI   SANTO DOMINGO

JAMAICA

PUERTO RICO

CARIBBEAN SEA

GUADELOUPE

MARTINIQUE

BARBADOS

CURACAO

TOBAGO
TRINIDAD

had not yet undergone an agricultural revolution which elsewhere forced farmers off the land and created a large reservoir of potential immigrants. Lacking a displaced peasantry or numerous religious dissenters, since the Protestant Reformation did not make much headway in the Iberian peninsula, the Spaniards relied on Indian and later on African labor, either as slaves or as peons tied to the land by debt and obligations which guaranteed planters a stable work force.

Spain extracted great wealth from America. For a century, New World mines yielded gold and silver in abundance. And plantations produced tropical staples such as tobacco and sugar. But mining and agricultural technologies were primitive and there were few incentives to improve them. A wealthy colonial elite preferred to live comfortably, or return to Spain, rather than reinvest capital and exercise initiative to increase productivity. An American merchant class did not flourish because Seville monopolized imports and exports, and the principal market for imports was a small luxury-consuming elite. Most of the population remained impoverished. Economic growth consequently lagged.

The Spaniards erected impressive public buildings and founded universities which had no equals in size or importance in the English colonies, but their principal legacy was an exploitative social system that enriched crown, Church, and a small European elite at the expense of Indians and Negroes held in peonage or slavery. Much of the wealth of Latin America is still concentrated in a few hands, and the great mass of impoverished peasants have little stake in the existing social order. The ruling elements seem unwilling or incapable of modernizing and reforming their societies before revolutionary forces sweep them away as happened in Communist Cuba. Today's concentration of wealth in the hands of a few repeats the colonial past. The average standard of living is low and there are few strong representative governments, a condition which hinders the development of stable, democratic societies in Latin America.

Spaniards established their American empire a century before England planted its first permanent settlements in the New World, but their example did not become England's model. The English methods of colonization, though influenced in the beginning by Spanish experience, differed because English society on the eve of colonization bore little resemblance to imperial Spain.

THE EXPANSION OF ENGLAND

England's internal condition long delayed its entrance into the competition for empire. While Spain came under control of a powerful dynasty in the fifteenth century, England was torn apart by civil war among rival claimants of the throne—the Wars of the Roses. Finally, in 1485, a new dynasty under the leadership of Henry Tudor methodically restored order, subdued resisting noblemen, and made the monarchy master of England.

Political Modernization

The Tudors accumulated power by undermining the authority of potential rivals and by building a broad base of support among newer elements whose prosperity depended, in part, on royal favor. The crown forced great nobles to disband their private armies. A reformed system of royal justice penetrated the countryside and the king forced his will upon the local notables. The financial weakness of other monarchs had severely restricted their freedom of action by making them dependent on others. The Tudors avoided expensive wars and otherwise managed their revenues carefully, lessening dependence on the nobles or Parliament. By the time of Henry VIII (1509–1547), the Tudors had stabilized their rule. Eager to perpetuate the dynasty, Henry VIII sought a male heir whose succession, he thought, was less likely to stir opposition than a female's. The king hoped that a new wife would produce a male heir but the pope refused to grant him a divorce. He then joined Martin Luther and other Protestants in rejecting Rome as the authentic voice of Christianity.

The English Reformation gave the crown control over the resources and influence of the dispossessed Roman Church. Many Englishmen whose spiritual needs no longer found adequate expression in Catholic worship and who resented Rome's influence applauded the change. By confiscating the monasteries and granting their lands to supporters, the Tudors encouraged the rise of wealthy new families whose interests became identified with those of the royal dynasty. The crown shrewdly worked through Parliament and these rising elements could usually be counted on to support the crown there, further strengthening its resources and influence. By strengthening Parliament, the monarchy gave its subjects the privilege of participating in decision-making, a privilege that was, in the next century, ultimately expanded at the expense of royal authority.

Economic Development

At the same time that England experienced political modernization which consolidated power in the hands of the monarchy and broadened the terms of participation, its economic system likewise underwent change. England became more productive but also more unstable as economic development brought major dislocations.

Most Englishmen lived on the land and labored to satisfy their own wants. But now production for markets at home and abroad became increasingly important, as did commercial and industrial enterprise. In the sixteenth century, population swelled from three to four million inhabitants and the city of London more than doubled in size, reaching a population of 200,000 by 1600. This growth depended in part on a surge in national wealth which came from more efficient methods of agriculture and the development of new sources of wealth in industry and commerce. The more enterprising landowners, large and small, found it profitable to acquire and consolidate the lands of poorer grain farmers. On the enclosed, larger holdings they raised sheep and marketed their wool abroad where it was manufactured into cloth. The enclosure movement, which had begun in the late Middle Ages, increased in tempo in the sixteenth century, pushing farmers off their lands without providing them alternative employment. As a result, "sturdy beggars" roamed the English countryside, often drifting into London in search of jobs. They gave vivid and tragic proof that English agriculture was more and more a way of making money rather than a way of life. Unemployment led some to believe that England was overpopulated and could profitably employ surplus labor in overseas colonies.

The export first of raw wool and then cloth to the continent of Europe had long been the principal item in English commerce. England led all Europe in cloth production and during the first half of the sixteenth century exports boomed, stimulating both wool production and cloth manufactures. As the English economy became more commercialized, regions began to specialize economically. Consequently, domestic markets for food, fuel, and clothing broadened in urban centers involved in overseas trade, and villages and rural communities concentrated on the production of exports. At the same time new industries developed. Armaments made England self-sufficient in the implements of war and coal mining provided fuel in place of depleted woodlands for the growing towns.

Social Instability

Although growth in foreign trade and industrial enterprise produced greater national prosperity, they also sensitized the economy to frequent unpredictable changes in the marketplace. High prices encouraged farmers and merchants to expand production. Eventually supply exceeded demand and forced prices down. Currency manipulation by the crown to increase revenue altered the terms of trade, sometimes, but not always, to England's advantage. Political turmoil abroad and the growth of foreign competition wiped out traditional markets. Unfavorable weather meant poor harvests which reduced the income of farmers and, consequently, their purchasing power, hurting merchants, manufacturers, and those they employed. Recurrent changes in the level of business activity disrupted the productive system, though hopes for striking it rich in a boom year encouraged risk taking and entrepreneurial activity.

The crown attempted to cushion the impact of these changes which left some permanently, others temporarily, unemployed, and which endangered the public order by creating unrest and riots among the needy. The state provided relief for the destitute, restricted labor mobility, and attempted to slow down the progress of enclosure but it did not halt economic change. Nor did the Tudors wish to do so. As national income grew, their wealth and power grew accordingly, especially their power to defend England against foreign enemies.

Depression in the wool trade encouraged British merchants to diversify their activities and seek new outlets for investment capital. British merchants squeezed out foreign merchants who had once controlled Britain's overseas trade. The English began to import goods from faraway places for reexport to the Continent. Hoping to avoid antagonizing Spain, England did not initially compete with her rival in the New World. Henry VII gave only halfhearted support to John and Sebastian Cabot who explored the North American coast for England in 1497 and 1498 and his successors were too preoccupied with maintaining internal order and with defending England against foreign attacks to undertake colonial expansion. By the middle of the sixteenth century, however, the crown chartered companies to discover new trade routes without conflicting with Spanish colonial claims. The Cathay Company (1552) sought a northeast passage to the Indies through the Arctic Ocean. Its failure led another group of adventurers to charter the Muscovy Company (1553) which opened trade with Russia. At the same time the Eastland Company traded in the Baltic countries and the Levant Company (1580) penetrated the Mediterranean, finding new markets for British cloth and metals in Italy, Turkey, and along the Barbary coast of North Africa.

The trading company, a medieval institution, gained increasing importance and became more complex in the sixteenth century. Those organized as joint-stock companies sold shares, enabling them to raise substantial amounts of capital. New and risky enterprises in distant places which required convoys, forts, and warehouses were too dangerous to attract investors without political support, so the crown granted monopoly charters to these companies. The growing number of joint-stock companies testified to the vitality of commercial enterprise, the availability of investment capital, and the shrewd patronage of the state. The greatest prize, however, remained beyond England's reach as long as Spain barred the way to India and America. England's more advanced economy, however, enabled it to develop

the productive potential of colonies far more successfully than did Spain, once Britain acquired overseas settlements.

Like her predecessors, Queen Elizabeth (1558–1603) had to guard against internal disorder and sought therefore to avoid, or at least to delay, war with Spain. The wealth gathered from America made Catholic Spain the most powerful nation in sixteenth-century Europe and a formidable enemy for Protestant England. Instead of reinvesting their new-found wealth in the colonies or in Spain itself, the Spaniards used it to finance grandiose wars of conquest in Europe. Officially England remained at peace until 1586, but Elizabeth permitted attacks on Spanish shipping by Sir Francis Drake and Sir Walter Raleigh while developing warships that were tougher and more maneuverable than Spain's. In 1588, the English defeated Spain's mighty invasion armada off the southeast coast of England, ending Spanish maritime supremacy and clearing the seas for Britain's thrust across the Atlantic.

By the beginning of the seventeenth century, England was ready for empire in Asia and America. A strong and ambitious monarchy ruled over a unified and prosperous kingdom, flushed with the victory over Spain. At the same time, economic development created new resources, incentives, and institutions for carrying the flag across the ocean. Self-confident and expansive, Englishmen looked forward to conquering new worlds far from home. In the same year in which the King James Bible appeared, the English court attended a performance of William Shakespeare's new play, *The Tempest*. Expressing the spirit of the age, the drama was set in a distant, unknown and remarkable land—

O, wonder!
How many goodly creatures are there here!
How beauteous mankind is! O brave new world,
That has such people in't!

Chapter 2
Plantations in the Wilderness

Early in the seventeenth century thousands of Englishmen emigrated to North America, the start of a European exodus which lasted 300 years. By the end of the seventeenth century a quarter million people inhabited twelve colonial settlements between French Canada and Spanish Florida. The methods of settlement varied, because England, unlike Spain and France, adopted no systematic, uniform, centrally administered plan for expansion. The crown played a limited role at first. Heavy reliance on private initiative and enterprise produced a distinctive pattern of origin and settlement for each colony. From the beginning, diversity and a capacity to adapt to unexpected and challenging circumstances colored the development of American society.

Despite the diverse origins of these first settlements, they shared assumptions about how to proceed, assumptions based on common traditions and familiar experiences. People who ventured abroad in search of gain or a better life did not anticipate the social disorganization they encountered. They expected to transfer intact to the New World, as Spaniards and Frenchmen did, patterns of social organization similar to those they left behind. Few imagined that they would create a radically new society. Yet the English, much more than their rivals, modified early colonization plans, at first in order to survive and later to prosper. Dependence upon voluntary, rather than state-controlled enterprise, facilitated this willingness to adjust. Political instability in England during the first colonizing century and social disorganization within Britain also contributed. The crown was relatively inattentive to colonial affairs, and civil war (1641–1660) at home turned many Englishmen toward the attraction of new opportunities in North America.

VIRGINIA

Twenty years after Sir Walter Raleigh discovered Virginia, the English established their first permanent colony in North America. Initial attempts to settle on Roanoke Island had failed because of insufficient resources. However, the three ships dispatched by the Virginia Company which sailed into Chesapeake Bay and founded Jamestown on May 24, 1607, came better prepared.

The Virginia Company, chartered by the crown in 1606, was the first of eleven major companies which invested heavily in the settlement of North America and the West Indies during the first two decades of the century. Begun as a commercial venture, it raised money and recruited managers and laborers to engage in exploration and trade. The leading investors were rich London merchants led by Sir Thomas Smyth (active in the East India Company about 1600), others who had engaged in privateering during the war with Spain, and country gentry of small means willing to speculate while simultaneously supporting a patriotic enterprise. The charter gave the company title to the lands and resources it discovered, placed it under protection of the crown, and established orderly means for administering the enterprise in England and in Virginia.

For two decades the company poured men and money into Virginia, hoping like other trading companies to earn profits on its investment. When by 1624 it realized that its assumptions and expectations did not fit the situation, it went bankrupt. Though it had failed as a business enterprise, it was the beginning of one of England's largest and most influential settlements in America.

The company had hoped to find as much precious metals and minerals as Spain had stumbled upon. It also had intended to profit by trading with the natives. Diligent explorers hoped to reach the Indies via a passage through the North American continent. Expectations of quick riches evaporated in the face of repeated disappointments and the difficulties of survival. There were no readily accessible surface resources such as the gold and silver of Spanish America, nor did the passage to the Indies materialize; and the Virginia Indians, who barely survived under a primitive social and economic system, offered neither markets for English goods nor exports that could be sold in Europe.

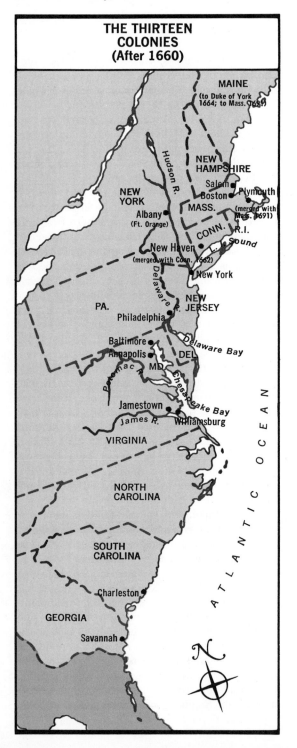

THE THIRTEEN COLONIES (After 1660)

MAINE
(to Duke of York 1664; to Mass. 1691)

NEW HAMPSHIRE

NEW YORK

Hudson R.

Albany
(Ft. Orange)

Salem
Boston
Plymouth
(merged with Mass. 1691)

MASS.

CONN.

R.I.

L.I. Sound

New Haven
(merged with Conn. 1662)

Delaware R.

New York

PA.

NEW JERSEY

Philadelphia

Baltimore
Annapolis
DEL.
MD.

Delaware Bay

Potomac R.

Chesapeake Bay

Jamestown
James R.
Williamsburg

VIRGINIA

NORTH CAROLINA

ATLANTIC OCEAN

SOUTH CAROLINA

Charleston

GEORGIA

Savannah

N

The company's emphasis on exploration and trade jeopardized the venture's survival. Time and resources spent in searching for the northwest passage or digging for gold might better have been devoted to providing food and shelter. In the first seven months, famine and disease killed two-thirds of the original adventurers. Food was so scarce that men ate dogs, cats, rats, snakes, toad-stools, and horsehides, and fed on the carcasses of the dead; one man killed his wife, ground her into powder, and ate her.

The company sent additional supplies but, in the long run, the settlers had to feed and clothe themselves. The iron-handed Captain John Smith, who took charge of the outpost in 1608, ruled by martial law, and forced men to work at growing food.

The realization that Virginia offered no quick road to wealth started a search for profitable staples but, since no one knew what could be raised, the company experimented with silk, wine, and iron, and in 1612, tobacco. Though tobacco eventually became the basis of Virginia's economy, at first it lacked a ready market in England. Smoking had not yet become habitual and many, including King James, regarded it as a vice. Tobacco production proved profitable but it came too late to save the company from bankruptcy. Moreover, the decision to grow staples posed new problems.

Though the company at first permitted no private enterprise, owning all land and employ-ing the entire labor force, it experienced difficulty in making the venture profitable. There were enough settlers to dig for gold, explore, and op-erate a trading post but not enough to establish a settlement in the wilderness. Because the In-dians were neither numerous nor willing to work for the English, additional labor had to be re-cruited from England. John Smith instructed the company to choose recruits carefully. Many of the first settlers were gentlemen, transients in search of quick gain, unaccustomed to hard work, and lacking in necessary skills. Virginia needed carpenters, farmers, fishermen, blacksmiths, and most of all "diggers up of trees' roots." The company sent over some children and felons as well as ninety "maidens" to meet the needs of the male population. However, it also dispatched skilled farmers who received shares of stock that entitled them to land grants after seven years of service. This arrangement increased the company's labor force only temporarily since settlers moved to their own plantations once their term of service expired.

Virginia Company's Failure

Between 1619 and 1625, twice as many settlers arrived in Virginia as in the preceding dozen years. Recruitment of an adequate labor force, though essential for the colony's development, strained its resources. It was expensive to transport and supply new settlers whose labor did not yield immediate returns. Moreover, by 1616, the company had spent its initial capital. The London directors found ways to attract additional investment but only by renouncing some of their authority and opportunities for profit. In the end, they failed to obtain adequate financing. They wasted much capital in efforts to make quick initial gains. These failures discouraged additional investment, without which the company could not survive. It did not estimate realistically its capital needs, because it had never intended to establish a new society. The capital required to furnish a settlement with the necessities of survival—food, water, housing, government, and defense—exceeded those of an ordinary trading company. Nor could it attract sufficient additional investment by promising immediate returns.

From the start the company could not solve its administrative problems. Beginning as a trading venture and only gradually tackling the problems of settling a wilderness thousands of miles from London, it necessarily made mistakes. Many migrants died before reaching America because the ships lacked enough food and water for the voyage; and adequate housing was not available because carpenters were scarce. Nor did the company provide sufficient supplies of guns, clothing, tools, utensils, cattle, and seed, as it was ignorant of conditions in Virginia and had difficulty obtaining accurate and timely information.

The failure to earn profits led to dissension among the stockholders and officers in London. A reform group gained control in 1619 and attempted to prevent collapse. To make Virginia more attractive both to those already there and to prospective immigrants, the company abandoned martial law, granted lands to migrants, and established a local assembly composed of two representatives from each town, "hundred," or plantation. The House of Burgesses met in 1619, giving settlers a semblance of participation in decision-making, though the London authorities retained the right to approve all legislation. The company hoped to enlist greater cooperation from the colonists as well as to rely on their knowledge of local conditions to improve management.

The reforms failed. The Virginia Company could become profitable only with time. Efforts to adjust to reality came too late. An Indian massacre in 1622 killed 300 colonists and hastened the crisis. As settlers whose terms of service expired left the barracks on the company estate, and as new migrants immediately carved out private plantations, its control over the colony as well as its ability to defend it diminished. In 1624 the crown revoked the charter, making Virginia a royal colony.

The Virginia Company had modeled its enterprise on the experience of earlier English companies that had traded with developed societies in Russia, India, and the Mediterranean, and on the example of Spanish conquistadors who had seized the accumulated wealth of America's most advanced Indian civilizations. But the experience of others was no reliable guide in Virginia or elsewhere in North America. The company could survive only by modifying its objectives and methods and by substituting colonizing for commercial enterprise. As it did so, it found the tasks of labor recruitment, capital formation, and efficient administration well beyond its capacities. Adjustment to American conditions came too late, but the Virginia Company was England's first permanent settlement in North America.

MASSACHUSETTS

Five hundred miles north of Jamestown, a generation after Virginia's "starving time" (1608–1609), another group of Englishmen established settlements in an even more forbidding part of the

North American wilderness. In one decade (1630–1640) 20,000 persons crossed the Atlantic to New England, more than double the number inhabiting Virginia after thirty years of settlement. Like the colonization of Virginia, the Great Migration to Massachusetts Bay was no ordinary business enterprise. Utilizing a royal charter as the legal basis for a new society, and the corporate form of organization as a convenient means of accomplishing its ends, the company intended to establish a permanent settlement from the outset and reckoned success not in profits but in how well it built a Zion in the Wilderness: a haven for souls stirred by new visions of God's design. New England would provide a refuge from the corruptions of Old England. Thus the Bay Company came better prepared than the Virginians to found a colony.

From the beginning it concentrated on the major problems of survival, providing food and shelter, recruiting capital and labor, and searching for crops which would sustain life, rather than looking for a passage to India or for precious metals. Hence, no conflict existed, as in Virginia, between the commercial goals of the company and the survival needs of the adventurers.

Also, the Massachusetts Bay Company tapped resources and enterprise unavailable to a trading company. Planning a permanent settlement, it realized, was expensive especially since migrants expected to stay and to maintain a living standard roughly comparable to what they had enjoyed in England. It sold shares of stock, attracting funds from both prospective emigrants and from others remaining in England yet sympathetic to its social and religious objectives. But it did not have to finance settlement entirely from its own resources. Immigrants traded possessions they could not carry abroad for what they would need in their new homes. Once in America, settlers could call upon relatives and friends at home to assist them.

The Bay colony was not only more adequately financed than Virginia was, but it also had less of a labor problem. The many settlers included persons with all the necessary social skills—ministers, lawyers, merchants, and officials as well as artisans, mechanics, shopkeepers, servants, and farmers who were good "diggers up of trees' roots."

Possessing extensive capital and commanding large numbers of settlers, the Bay Company was also better able than its Virginia counterpart to master administrative problems. Its plan for a permanent settlement prepared it to deal with the difficulties of such an enterprise. It did not need to resort to martial law or to monopolize natural resources since it relied on voluntary cooperation. The emigrants, united by shared suffering and expectations, were eager to promote the success of an enterprise on which everybody's life and fortune depended.

For six decades Massachusetts settlers worked under the authority of the original charter as the company merged into the society it was organized to create. Its success stemmed partly from the events in England which generated extraordinary energies and passions that found an outlet in America.

THE PROTESTANT REFORMATION IN ENGLAND

Those who migrated to New England believed they had been called to participate in an event of historical importance. Their settlement, one of them proclaimed, was "as a City set upon a hill, in the open view of all the earth; the eyes of the world are upon us, because we profess ourselves to be a people in covenant with God." They believed that God had kept America hidden until the day when it would provide mankind with one last chance for regeneration and salvation.

For over 1500 years Christianity had satisfactorily explained man's purpose and God's design to Europeans. The Church taught that men, though sinners, could choose between good and evil and hence each man determined his own fate —whether he would enjoy eternal life after death or suffer the eternal torments of Hell. The Church offered men models of holiness in the monasteries and rituals of worship in the churches. A Christian who observed God's commands, performed good works, kept his faith, and received absolution for his sins, expected to be saved.

By the sixteenth century, however, many Christians found their faith waning, their inner lives in turmoil. The Church's paths to salvation failed to bring spiritual peace. Fearing damnation, people looked for a new gospel of deliverance. It came in 1517. Martin Luther, a German Augustinian monk, denounced the pope and Church doctrines, thus touching off the Protestant Reformation. Luther received support from some German princes jealous of funds drained from their territories by Rome, and eager to strengthen themselves by appropriating the Church's wealth and power. Though the Protestant revolt could not have succeeded without such mundane political support, it spread rapidly, enlisting popular support among pious Christians alienated by the then notorious corruption within a church, supposedly universal but actually dominated by Italian politicians. Luther's message spread mainly, however, because thousands of Christians, like Luther himself, no longer found in Roman Catholicism an adequate interpretation of experience or a suitable guide to their lives.

Social Basis of the Reformation

The emergence of a modern social order involved not only the creation of powerful nation states and the increasing commercialization of the economic system but also the formulation of new beliefs and codes of behavior. Protestantism attempted to supply an ideology that would sustain people through the break up of an old social order and the painful emergence of a new one.

In England as on the Continent, Protestantism prospered, backed by the crown. The kingdom was growing richer, yet life seemed more uncertain; no one could be sure of the future. Life had once been more secure, even if the aspirations of most people were limited. Fewer opportunities for improvement had existed but there had been less danger of sinking below one's inherited station. But now England was changing. New economic opportunities enabled some to rise, though others were pushed off the land or speculated unsuccessfully in the commercial arena.

People in motion searched for ways to stabilize their lives. The unfortunate craved consolation and protection; the successful feared that fortune would turn against them. Those most afflicted by uncertainty were the groups somewhere in the middle of the social structure— farmers who owned some land, merchants on the way up, professional men who had positions to lose and expectations that might be frustrated in a society experiencing greater upward and downward mobility than in the past. Their life style distinguished them from the lower and higher classes whose positions were more firmly fixed and who consequently experienced less anxiety than those with more unpredictable futures.

The middling elements were self-conscious and individualistic. Better educated and more independent than most Englishmen, they actively tried to shape their lives, believing that men were not prisoners of fate but determined their own success or failure. Experience taught them that success stemmed from virtue, the capacity to work hard, save, and to seize economic opportunities. Yet men often found themselves unable to control the forces that shaped their lives. They turned for help and relief to the church and to the state but neither responded adequately.

Catholicism urged men to scorn the flesh in favor of other-worldly self-denial, but in practice tolerated worldliness among laity and clergy, offering sinners quick and easy absolution. Moreover, the faith was profoundly anti-individualistic. It encouraged acceptance and resignation since what counted was rebirth after death and it insisted that men approach God by rejecting the world. Though the Church acknowledged man's free will, it offered convenient intercession in case an individual's godly impulses proved too weak.

Calvinism

Little of this suited the needs of those perplexed by early modern society. These men were drawn to a faith which regarded sin not as a force pervading the world, a part of the air men breathe, but the result of an individual act. To find salvation, each man, whatever his calling, must actively strive for deliverance in the workaday world. No church or priest, no elaborate ritual, could relieve men of their personal responsibilities. John Calvin, a Swiss theologian, formulated a doctrine which claimed to recover an earlier, purer Christian faith and which powerfully appealed to men of his own day. Calvinism spread across Europe and into England where those who hoped to purify the Anglican church of Roman error embraced it.

English Puritans believed that man's original sin had left him totally depraved. All men were born with an irresistible propensity for evil: "In Adam's fall, we sinned all," Puritans taught their children. Since each child inherited this curse, man was incapable of saving himself. Neither good works, confession of sin, faithful church attendance, nor intercession by the clergy could offer redemption.

Man's only hope was faith. God had already picked His Saints, those He had chosen to save. Men wondered whether they were among the elect and waited for signs—an overpowering inner experience that told them they were among the regenerate. Though man could not will to be saved, he could strive to lead a godly life, an indication though not a certainty of sanctification. Good works did not save souls, but since Christian virtues expressed love of God they were a possible sign of election. Those who led model lives suspected that their ability to resist temptation better than most men derived from God's grace. But no one could ever be sure. Signs of salvation reassured men only of probable election for eternal life. Conversion thus became the Calvinist's preoccupying concern.

The new faith sanctified each man's calling, since every person had the same obligation and the same chance. Neither the priesthood nor the monastery offered an advantage. Because one could never be certain of salvation, an endless search for signs of grace, revealed by the capacity to act morally, imposed upon the Calvinist far greater internal discipline than the external rewards and punishments of the Catholic church. And with the denial of absolution from sin, compromises with evil could no longer be tolerated. This redefinition of the Christian pilgrimage offered no easy path, but at least it seemed to conform more closely to human experience and to satisfy the needs of changing conditions. "You must

not think to go to heaven in a feather bed," Calvinists learned, because "if you will be Christ's disciples you must take up his cross and it will make you sweat."

English Puritans, like Calvinists on the Continent, demanded a church reformation in line with these new doctrines. Since they believed in individual salvation, the role of the priesthood and the church changed. The church could neither absolve men of their sins nor save them; it could, however, preach the gospel and help men find signs of salvation. Elaborate rituals and lavish ceremony, architectural splendor and traditional worship, all departed from the simplicity of early Christianity. The Bible was the Christian's ultimate source of God's word; no pope or bishop, no prince or king took precedence over man's direct relationship with God or had the right to intervene.

This included the English monarchy. The Tudors had broken with Rome for political, not theological, reasons. Henry VIII substituted himself for the pope as head of the Church of England but he did not radically alter Catholic practices. Queen Elizabeth also wished to avoid alienating traditionalists but her precarious hold on the throne, early in her reign, forced halfhearted concessions to Calvinists. During the reign of her successor, James I (1603-1625), Puritans demanded abolition of hierarchy in the church, giving each congregation the right to govern its own spiritual affairs. They also insisted on "purifying" or simplifying church ritual and worship. The crown refused, fearful of turmoil and loss of control over an institution whose power and resources supported the dynasty.

The Puritans

James was the first member of the new Stuart dynasty and, like his successors, he tried to make the crown truly sovereign. Whatever stood in the way—an uncooperative Parliament or religious dissenters—had to be crushed. His son, Charles I (1625-1649), continued his father's quest for absolute power. When Parliament balked, Charles ruled without it for over ten years (1629-1641), taxing his subjects by decree rather than consent. Puritans had fought the crown in Parliament, in alliance with other disaffected groups, and they relentlessly pressed for reformation of the Church of England. Intent on crushing opposition, Charles appointed William Laud as Archbishop of Canterbury to wipe out religious dissent. Laud forced Calvinist clergy from their pulpits, required congregations to conform, imprisoned and tortured Puritan leaders, and suppressed their publications.

Puritan hopes had rested on the assumption that the Church of England could be captured from within. But widespread official persecution dimmed such hopes. A generation earlier, a Puritan congregation in Nottinghamshire, despairing of success, separated from the Anglican church and moved to Holland in 1608 seeking religious freedom. After a decade abroad, they decided to move again, fearful that further residence in the Netherlands would jeopardize the group's survival as English Calvinists. With a patent from the Virginia Company and financial support from England, the Pilgrims sailed to America on the *Mayflower* in 1620 and settled at Plymouth, Massachusetts, near Cape Cod.

During the decade that the Plymouth colony was gaining a foothold, many more English Calvinists became progressively more disheartened. Persecution caused increasing numbers to see no future within the Church of England, no escape from it except by migration. A depression that pressed hard on the centers of the cloth industry where Puritanism had many adherents added to the discontent and swelled the number of potential migrants.

THE CITY UPON A HILL

For several years the Puritans—ministers, country gentry, and merchants—thought of establishing a settlement in New England that would be both a commercial base for fishing and a refuge. After several false starts, they succeeded in 1629 when the king chartered the Massachusetts Bay Company. That same year twelve Puritan members of the company signed the Cambridge Agreement, declaring their intention to emigrate to America. They took with them the charter and with it the power to govern, thereby hoping to protect themselves against the crown or other outside control.

A Puritan State

Eleven ships sailed in 1630. Settlement started in Boston and Salem and a new society began to take shape. The charter called for a governor and assistants chosen by the freemen. These were the stockholders, but since there were only twelve among the original settlers it was necessary to elect others to freemanship. However, the first governor, John Winthrop, lawyer and country squire, and a leader of the group that launched the company, sought to preserve tight control over the settlement. In violation of the charter, he declared only church members eligible for freemanship, on the assumption that only the godly could be entrusted with power. Winthrop and his supporters also ignored the charter provisions that gave freemen the right to choose their governor and enact company—and hence colony—law. In 1632, one town objected to a tax levied by the assistants and after that the freemen regained the power to elect the governor and to choose deputies from each town to the General Court, or legislature. An elite ran the colony's politics, but without permanent tenure in office, and with its decisions subject to review. The Puritans thus attempted to balance the claims of individual freedom and the need for communal order. Only animals had natural liberty, John Winthrop reminded the people, the freedom to do whatever impulse dictated. Men who enjoyed the blessing of civic liberty in a covenanted community were free only to obey the righteous commands of godly authority as interpreted by upright rulers. Yet Winthrop, who served as governor for eleven years, was several times ousted from office by disgruntled freemen and rival leaders. In Massachusetts, as in Virginia, settlers resented efforts by a few to monopolize power and they demanded the right to participate in decision-making. Though the notion that government derived its power from the consent of the governed was foreign to this generation's thinking, people insisted that power be exercised responsibly. Tyranny would not be permitted. Rulers were bound to govern *under* law as faithfully as the ruled were obliged to obey authority.

The township dominated communal life in Massachusetts. Each group of settlers petitioned the General Court for land on which to establish a community. The town leaders then distributed it, in amounts according to the social status of the inhabitants. Local officials were chosen, village lots and roads laid out, and a church erected. In contrast with Virginia where individuals settled wherever they pleased, Puritans established and maintained well-regulated communities which enforced conformity to the Bay colony's rules.

In a colony committed to a religious ideal, the church proved a powerful source of discipline. Groups often migrated under the leadership of a minister who petitioned the General Court for a town charter and provided firm leadership in the early years of town building. Though Puritans asserted that they remained in communion with the Church of England, once free to do as they wanted, they organized their own kind of church life. Each congregation chose its own minister and adopted a confession of faith and style of worship in accordance with its interpretation of Calvinist teaching, although synods composed of neighboring churches, coordinated congregations. Every inhabitant had to attend services, support the church, and accept its discipline though only the elect, those who had experienced God's grace, were technically church "members." Every European became a church member at birth, but the Congregational churches in New England were select bodies, made up exclusively of "Saints" with full and exclusive power to run the church as they saw fit. These unplanned changes came about because Puritans in a wilderness were free to pursue the logic of their beliefs. They insisted, however, that their new model churches remain part of the Anglican communion.

Despite the importance of the church and the power of the ministers, the Bay colony was not a theocracy. Although freemen had to be church members, the clergy did not rule or generally hold office. However, laymen exercised political power in consultation with the ministers. John Winthrop and his fellow leaders made no distinc-

tion between the sacred and the secular; God ruled over every aspect of human affairs. Heresy was as much a crime against the state as theft or murder.

Yet men did not live by faith alone, not even Puritans. The colony supplied its material needs by raising food, and by trading furs, fish, and timber to finance imports from England. Though settlers had to work hard at their tasks, merchants were expected to charge "just" prices and artisans to receive "just" wages. Excessive pursuit of wealth marked one as a victim of the devil's snares and made one subject to punishment.

Begun as a community in covenant with God, the Bay colony successfully parried a series of dangers that threatened its success. The most formidable came from neither the Indian wars nor the attacks on the charter in England, but from internal dissension. Puritans were united in their spiritual commitment but men sometimes interpreted the Almighty's design differently.

Religious Dissenters

Early in 1635 the town of Salem chose a new pastor, Roger Williams, a Cambridge University graduate who had migrated four years earlier. Williams soon stated publicly that the colony charter was void because the crown could not grant land belonging to the Indians. He considered the colony's invasion of the rights of conscience even worse, and argued that the church should exclude the unregenerate since their presence compromised the purity of the faith. Forced worship stank in God's and Williams' nostrils. As long as the community imposed orthodoxy, good Christians might be forced to accept erroneous doctrines promulgated by the church and enforced by the state. Each man, Williams believed, was a church unto himself, seeking God throughout his life. Since the search never ends, men must be free to follow wherever conscience leads, for there was no other path to God.

Williams challenged the foundations of the Massachusetts experiment. Most Puritans believed they had discovered the Truth and hence it was their duty to uproot error before it spread.

Winthrop and others insisted that the magistrates had a responsibility to reclaim those who strayed and to prevent them from infecting others. Consequently, the Massachusetts General Court banished Roger Williams in September, 1635. During the winter he fled Boston, taking refuge among the Indians from whom he purchased land on which he founded the city of Providence. Williams later obtained a royal charter for the Rhode Island colony and granted freedom of conscience to all.

Like Williams, Anne Hutchinson also threatened the authority of the church and magistrates and the survival of the Bible Commonwealth in Massachusetts. Uncertain of her own election, Mistress Anne claimed that God spoke to her directly. The revelation brought her peace and spread the word that the only valid sign of election was a mystical experience. She denied that outward godly behavior was a reliable indication of one's inner condition since one could easily play the pious hypocrite. But if each individual relied exclusively on mystical experience, neither the church nor the state could enforce uniform standards of behavior. A thousand heresies would spring forth from a thousand mystics and if good works were no sign of election, people would have little incentive to behave morally.

Hutchinson was a greater threat than Williams because she found powerful support in Boston. Once again John Winthrop mobilized the forces of orthodoxy. The General Court convicted Hutchinson of sedition and banished her and another follower. Together with her husband and children, she found temporary refuge in Roger Williams' new settlement. She was later murdered by Indians.

The Williams and Hutchinson cases revealed the precariousness of a covenanted community in the face of individual interpretations of God's intent. Without firm control by an elite, John Winthrop and others feared that the City on a Hill might disintegrate into a hundred petty sects each with its own vision of a Wilderness Zion. So persistent were the disruptive tendencies within Massachusetts Puritanism, that six years after the first settlement, a group of orthodox Calvinists in several towns around Boston, led by Thomas Hooker, one of the colony's leading preachers, moved to Connecticut. Hooker and his followers claimed they wanted more room in which

to settle but they also sought freedom from the rulers of Massachusetts who, they believed, governed with too little regard for the wishes of the majority as required by the charter. In 1639 the Connecticut migrants adopted the Fundamental Orders, a charter they hoped would legalize their settlement and define its terms of government. As in Massachusetts, towns elected deputies to an assembly but freemen need not be church members, and the magistrates had less freedom of action. These modifications had religious origins but political repercussions. Hooker believed that since one could never be sure that those claiming to be regenerated had indeed received grace, they should not exercise too much power. The magistrates' powers should therefore be restricted. In 1662, the sixteen towns of Connecticut received a royal charter legitimatizing the authority assumed by the colonizing generation.

The Virginia Company measured success in terms of return on investment. The New England Puritans judged their efforts by how close they came to building a godly community. But even before the passing of the first generation of Saints, some began to doubt that man could escape the past in the New World. Toward the end of his long life, Roger Williams warned John Winthrop, Jr., son of his great antagonist: "Sir, when we that have been the eldest and are rotting a generation will act, I fear, far unlike the first Winthrops and their Models of Christian Charity: I fear that the common trinity of the world— Profit, Preferment, Pleasure—will be here as in all the world besides: that Prelacy and Popery too will in this wilderness predominate; and that God Land will be as great a God with us English as God Gold was with the Spaniard." Only time would test the accuracy of Williams' prophecy.

MARYLAND

In addition to the chartered trading company, the English had another flexible instrument of overseas expansion, the proprietary grant. Maryland was the first of the proprietary colonies, and its founding illustrates an alternate method of English expansion.

The joint-stock company appealed most

strongly to merchants seeking overseas opportunities; the proprietary attracted aristocrats and politicians with close ties to the crown who saw in landed estates a means of increasing their wealth. In 1632, the crown made Cecilius Calvert, second Lord Baltimore, proprietor of Maryland, a colony carved out of land formerly held by the Virginia Company. Calvert's father was a Catholic and a faithful servant of James I. That monarch's son, Charles I, rewarded the Baltimore family with extensive territory in America.

The proprietor had had tremendous authority in the past. The English crown had granted special privileges to noblemen willing to subdue the rebellious Scots and Welsh. These grants were models for later proprietary charters. Lord Baltimore owned all the land in Maryland, controlled its government, and sought to develop his colony as a great manorial estate. Expecting to profit principally from the land, the proprietor reserved 12,000 acres in each county and established manors to be farmed by tenants, granted manors of 1000 to 3000 acres to others, and sold small farms to freeholders who paid a modest yearly rent. The proprietor also had the power to tax, command the militia, and establish courts and an assembly, though he retained the ultimate power to make and enforce law. Secondarily, the Baltimore family also intended Maryland to become a shelter for fellow Catholics seeking refuge from persecution at home.

Medieval feudal arrangements strongly influenced the colonization design for Maryland. The first settlers, mostly craftsmen, servants, and farmers, were better prepared than those in Virginia and thus escaped a "starving time." As Maryland grew and proprietary authority weakened, the original settlement plan needed modification. As long as people could obtain land elsewhere without accepting manorial obligations, Maryland could not compete for new migrants. The small farm, raising tobacco and food, not the manorial estate, predominated. The proprietor never used his right to establish manorial courts. As in Virginia, counties and hundreds administered themselves. Despite the proprietor's legal monopoly of political power, he found it convenient to create an assembly and concede it a voice in decision-making.

Nor did Maryland become a Catholic settlement. Since few English Catholics were willing to migrate, most of the settlers were Protestant.

Profitable settlement by Protestant farmers coupled with a declared haven for Catholics meant that both groups would enjoy religious tolerance. Expediency, not principle, led to the Toleration Act (1649) which granted religious freedom to Maryland Christians. (Jews did not share in the blessing.) The Baltimores' economic interests led them to modify policies even at the expense of rights and authority granted in the original charter. As in Virginia and Massachusetts, colonizers soon learned that success in the New World placed a premium on the ability to adapt to new conditions.

FROM NEW HAMPSHIRE TO GEORGIA

In the century following the birth of Maryland, nine other English colonies completed the foundations of English settlement in North America. Most were proprietaries and except for Georgia they were established between 1660 and 1680. The popularity of the proprietary reflected the growing regard of English landed interests for America's virgin lands, which, properly developed, offered generous opportunities for profit. By relying on settlers themselves to supply most of the initial developmental capital, proprietors did not need to invest much of their own money. Since they risked only small amounts and had no stockholders to please or fear, they were willing to wait until they could sell land to immigrants for annual rents or until real estate values rose.

England acquired New York and New Jersey from the Dutch, then a powerful maritime and commercial rival whom the British fought several times during the middle of the seventeenth century. In 1623 the Dutch West India Company established a permanent settlement in New Amsterdam to trade in furs. The English seized the Dutch forts in 1664 and the king granted his brother the Duke of York (later James II) extensive proprietary powers. The duke hoped to profit from New York, and treated the conquered Dutch liberally, permitting religious freedom and eventually granting freeholders an assembly. When the duke was crowned King James II, New York became a royal colony. In 1664, the duke granted New Jersey to proprietors but the crown regained control in 1702.

Carolinas and Pennsylvania

The well-connected nobility also founded the Carolinas. In 1663 a group with close ties to the crown and strong overseas interests received a charter. They invested little capital, expecting migrants to come from older colonies such as Virginia, the British West Indies, and Europe. In 1669, the proprietors issued the Fundamental Constitutions mapping out an aristocratic social structure for the Carolinas. A hereditary aristocracy would receive 40 percent of the land in each county. The scheme proved unworkable since manorial estates without tenants to work them had little value. The Carolinas faced difficulties enough attracting settlers without discouraging land-hungry farmers by the prospect of working another man's estate. Instead, the proprietors, like those elsewhere, found it necessary to sell freeholds to farmers, who paid annual rent, grant them religious freedom, and establish an assembly. As Carolina grew, the proprietors had constant difficulty governing. In 1721 South Carolina became a royal colony as did North Carolina in 1729 when the proprietors finally sold their claims to the crown.

The impulses behind the founding of Pennsylvania combined the religious zeal that inspired the New England settlement with the personal interests of a proprietary family. William Penn, the son of an admiral to whom Charles II was financially indebted, rejected an easy aristocratic life. The young Penn became a Quaker, spreading the faith energetically, suffering temporary imprisonment in the Tower of London. The king discharged his debts to the Penns by granting William a large tract that became Pennsylvania. In 1682, he also acquired the nearby Delaware territory from the Duke of York.

Penn's offer of religious freedom and land on liberal terms attracted Quakers from England, Wales, Ireland, and Germany. He assumed a paternalistic attitude toward the well-being of the colony but did not anticipate that immigrants whom he treated generously would insist on a substantial voice in governing Pennsylvania. As proprietor, Penn controlled the land, appointed the governor, and established an assembly chosen by freeholders. Under constant pressure from settlers during the first twenty years, he finally granted the assembly the power to initiate laws, though he had originally created it as an advisory body. As Pennsylvania prospered, populated by a variety of ethnic and religious elements, a powerful native Quaker elite emerged that competed with the Penn family for control. Penn governed neighboring Delaware through the same authority that controlled Pennsylvania until 1701 when the small colony established its own assembly though a single governor chosen by the proprietor ruled.

Georgia

Georgia, the last colony established during the colonial period, originated in humanitarian impulses that shaped a noble colonizing purpose thoroughly inappropriate to American conditions. James E. Oglethorpe led a group of prominent individuals who thought a new settlement in America could absorb thousands of the English poor. Though settling people abroad would be costly, the trustees of Georgia, chartered in 1732, expected that the colony would soon become self-supporting. Hard-working Georgia farmers would no longer be public charges as they were in England. Moreover, Georgia would strengthen the Southern defenses of the American colonies against the Spaniards in Florida and would produce silk for export to Britain to lessen dependence on foreign sources.

The key to success, the trustees thought, lay in transforming shiftless people into enterprising yeomen by controlled development. Since the settlers were too poor to finance migration and settlement, the trustees, with generous support from Parliament, provided the capital. To make Georgia easily defensible against the Spaniards, settlements were compact and population relatively dense. Hence farms remained small, and to prevent speculation and dispersal of migrants, land could neither be alienated nor sold. The trustees also barred Negro slaves for fear that whites would prefer to import them rather than work themselves, and that availability of slaves would attract speculative and absentee landowners. To discourage production of staples such as tobacco and rice which had proved profitable elsewhere, Georgia farmers had to grow silk to validate their claims. Finally by prohibiting alcohol, the trustees expected to promote sobriety and discourage indolence.

After twenty years, the trustees abandoned the noble experiment. Their rigid controls discouraged migration and private investment. Military obligations antagonized the farmers. Also, they could not expand their lands or sell them, and had little incentive to work hard. Moreover, silk production soon proved impractical. Without representative institutions, a bureaucracy that was at best paternalistic, and sometimes corrupt and arbitrary, governed Georgia. The company attempted to rescue the scheme from failure by allowing farmers slaves and liquor, and the right to pass on their properties to their heirs. Settlers bitterly complained that "the poor inhabitants of Georgia are scattered over the face of the earth; her plantations a wild; her towns a desert; her villages in rubbish; her improvements a byword, and her liberties a jest; an object of pity to friends and of insult, contempt and ridicule to enemies." In 1752 the crown took control and Georgia became another royal colony rather than a humanitarian refuge for England's poor.

During the century-and-a-quarter between the founding of Virginia and the establishment of Georgia (1607–1732), English colonizers discovered that settlements planned at home often had to be modified abroad. None could predict that the wilderness would force men to abandon preconceptions and adjust to strange and often threatening circumstances. An English trading company became a permanent settlement, producing tobacco; another joint-stock company established a City on a Hill only to find that distance from kings and bishops did not eliminate dangers threatening a Christian commonwealth. And proprietary grants to noblemen with feudal intentions had to be modified in the face of laborers, short in supply but long in demands for land of their own and increased political and religious liberties. The long-term growth and prosperity of each settlement depended on the ability of the founding generation to grapple intelligently and practically with the difficulties of setting up new societies. None was more important than developing a productive system for profitably exploiting America's resources.

Chapter 3
Roots of Expansion

Though the American continent contained enormous untapped wealth, hunger and disease claimed over half of Virginia's first settlers. The "starving time" took a heavy toll of human life but only briefly because people discovered in Virginia and elsewhere how to survive, and eventually how to prosper.

By the end of the colonial period most Americans enjoyed a standard of living higher than that of most Europeans. Visiting foreigners frequently noted the healthfulness and prosperity of the people. They saw few paupers and found a mass of property owning farmers, artisans, and shopkeepers whose high levels of material achievement and expectation radically altered perceptions of human possibilities.

From the beginning of time, most people had been poor. Food, clothing, and shelter were so scarce that except for a fortunate few, the masses suffered material deprivation. Nor could it be otherwise. The world's wealth was limited, and when it increased, it did so slowly; few could hope for more than subsistence. Consequently peasants and laborers, the majority of the population, fatalistically accepted the fact that their children would be peasants and laborers just as their ancestors before them had been. Some might improve their lot and even fewer live in relative comfort, but most people expected to endure along the margins of survival.

It was different in the American colonies. By the end of the colonial period, a French visitor announced that "from involuntary idleness, servile dependence, penury and useless labour," man in America had "passed to toils of a very different nature, rewarded by ample subsistence." Unlike colonists in other times and places who looked to national independence to free them from foreign exploitation, backwardness, and widespread poverty, the American colonists embarked on independence with a productive system already generating rising and substantial levels of individual welfare. When industrialization began in the nineteenth century, Americans enjoyed per capita incomes well above that of most present-day underdeveloped nations. Thus the roots of the affluence which make the elimination of poverty a realistic national goal stretch back deep into America's colonial past. As a *society*, America has never been poor, although many Americans have known poverty.

RECRUITMENT OF LABOR

Americans had to develop a new productive system in a virgin continent. They left behind European societies which, over many centuries, had slowly accumulated capital, grown in population, cleared and drained lands and brought them under cultivation, and built cities into busy commercial centers. In America, settlers found none of the factors of production except natural resources; and before they could be productively exploited, a labor force of sufficient size and quality had to be recruited.

By the end of the first fifty years of settlement, about 75,000 people lived in the colonies. On the eve of the American Revolution, their numbers had grown to over two and a half million, or ten times more than in 1700. Doubling every twenty or twenty-five years, population grew so rapidly that by the middle of the eighteenth century, the American colonies, only recently settled, had almost a third as many inhabitants as England.

Though the flood of migrants from Europe and slaves from Africa were important, they do not entirely explain why population grew at a rate higher than in England during the eighteenth century. Americans tended to marry at a younger age than Englishmen, thereby increasing a woman's period of childbearing. They married earlier because couples could easily establish and maintain independent households. England's land shortage encouraged people to limit family size and delay marriage for economic reasons. But America had land aplenty. Young couples could readily acquire farms which needed the labor of large families. Moreover, an abundant food supply sustained the health of women, particularly during the childbearing years, and kept the infant mortality rate well below England's.

Immigration

Heavy immigration further accounts for the high growth rate. Fortunately for the colonies, economic dislocation and religious unrest in Europe compelled people to find a refuge across the ocean. At first most immigrants were members of persecuted religious minorities as well as English farmers, laborers, craftsmen, and tradesmen who found it increasingly difficult to make a living. Those who came were usually neither very rich nor very poor. Lacking the means to migrate, the poorest often accepted their lot as decreed by fate; the well-to-do had too much to risk and too little to gain by migrating. But young farmers and artisans from families accustomed to owning some land or practicing a craft had unfulfilled expectations. Narrowing opportunities made it doubtful that if they remained at home they would enjoy a position comparable to that of their fathers. Economic change was squeezing the smaller landholders off the land. In the towns and cities, old crafts were declining, unable to compete with more efficient methods of industrial organization. Yeomen farmers found that

rising land values priced them out of the market, making it impossible for fathers to help their children acquire land. Journeymen laboring for master craftsmen, intending someday to open shops of their own, found it harder than ever to escape from wage labor. In these circumstances, many young men decided to strike out on their own by going to America. Since many migrants were religious dissenters, who left home with groups of coreligionists and were received by brethren in America, the hardship and pain of removal and resettlement were lessened.

From the late seventeenth century to the end of the colonial period, immigrants came from increasingly diverse ethnic and religious backgrounds. Though the English predominated, substantial numbers of Scots, Scotch-Irish Presbyterians from Northern Ireland, Irish Catholics, Germans, and Dutch gave the colonies a varied ethnic composition. These groups brought with them a culture which persisted and since they often settled together, they were better able to perpetuate their traditions, though there was a good deal of intermingling and intermarriage. Instead of scattering evenly through the colonies, non-English immigrants favored particular regions, avoiding New England, flowing toward the more hospitable Middle and Southern colonies. Germans and Scotch-Irish particularly

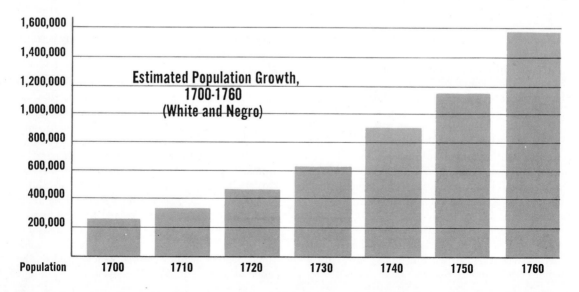

Estimated Population Growth, 1700-1760 (White and Negro)

favored Pennsylvania with its liberal land and religious policies. In the eighteenth century, declining emigration from England, which now needed labor, led the crown to welcome immigrants from other lands to the colonies. Thus from colonial times, America's population has been ethnically diverse, the dominant English majority confident that it could absorb people from other nations.

Colonial economic development could not proceed without recruitment of an adequate labor force, and although Europe contained thousands willing to leave home, a way had to be found to organize and finance such a vast migration. Some could pay their own way across and establish themselves in America by saving money and selling property in England, and others received help from companies and proprietors in the early stages of colonization, but many had to rely on other means.

The colonies themselves possessed the resources necessary to finance recruitment. By offering grants of land (headrights) to individuals who paid another immigrant's passage to America, colonies induced ship captains, anxious over empty hulls on the return voyage to America, and farmers and planters eager to enlarge their work force, to import labor. In turn, emigrants agreed to work a number of years for a master who financed passage. Indentured servitude adapted the familiar principles of the English apprenticeship system to American needs. In England a youngster entered the service of a master in return for training, protection, and the initial capital to establish himself independently. Those who went to America and for several years entered the service of a farmer, planter, or artisan, learned a skill in the New World. During their term of service, they could own property, serve in the militia, sue in court, and at the expiration of their contract they received "freedom dues," providing them with resources to start on their own. Some became farmers, others artisans, though many died in service or later returned home.

The planter or yeoman farmer who aided the migration of indentured servants to America, thereby acquired more land, but even more im-

portant, he recruited additional workers who enabled him to expand production. The more farmers prospered, the more capital they accumulated to recruit still more labor to work more land. But indentured servants could easily run away, if mistreated or if restlessly ambitious; and when their terms of service ended, they had to be replaced by others. By these means, the colonies used land, which was abundant, to induce private capital to finance the flow of labor, which was scarce.

Not everyone came voluntarily. Economic dislocation in England increased the incidence of crime. Jobless people in motion roamed the countryside and crowded into the cities, intensifying the difficulty of maintaining law and order. The state defined many petty acts of lawbreaking as felonies but mitigated the harshness of the legal code by permitting individuals to escape imprisonment by going to America. Though many Americans objected to receiving English felons, some welcomed their cheap labor.

THE BEGINNING OF SLAVERY

Another important source of labor came from Africa. Unlike the indentured servants, blacks came involuntarily. Twenty Negroes arrived in Virginia in 1619, part of a Dutch ship's "cargo." Thereafter the number of blacks grew slowly. There were fewer than 3000 in 1660 but after 1690 importations rose rapidly. By the time Americans founded a new nation on the principle that all men are created equal, a quarter million Africans labored in slavery. Comprising 20 percent of the population in 1776, slaves existed in all colonies but were especially important for the prosperity of the Southern colonies.

The origin of American Negro slavery lies shrouded in obscurity, although its tragic results are all too clear. Slavery as it existed on the eve of the Civil War did not come to America with the first cargo of Africans. Slavery was unknown in English law, and some of the Africans arriving during the first half of the seventeenth century were treated as indentured servants. In England servants often renewed their contracts repeatedly, since they could find no other employment.

Though a few Negroes were freed at the end of a term of service, most were not. Eventually the gap between white and black servants widened. Because white servants came voluntarily, colonies found it wise to improve the conditions of service to attract them; but since Africans came in chains, their terms of labor did not have to be liberalized. The sharp rise in Negro population complicated the task of managing them. Informal methods of control gave way to laws, the black codes, that permanently fixed the Negro's status as chattel labor, human property with few privileges and no rights. The degraded Negroes' condition, their loss of control over their own persons, and sometimes over life itself, ruffled few feelings among white Americans who regarded blacks as inferior, a "degraded" race well suited to enslavement. At the same time, slavery's dehumanizing process cultivated racial prejudice among people who might have been inclined to regard Africans as fellow human beings and who might have reacted accordingly. Thus racism justified slavery and slavery intensified racism.

Slavery flourished because it was profitable for the Northern merchant who imported slaves and the Southern planter who bought and employed them; profitable, that is, for everyone except the blacks. Torn from their families and homeland in Africa, Negroes were marched to the coast where ships waited to take them to the New World. Herded into cramped, filthy, stinking quarters, with hardly room to stand or lie down, manacled one to another, poorly fed, and victims of epidemic disease, Africans died in great numbers. "Their wailings were torturing beyond what words can express," confessed a slave trader. Some killed themselves rather than submit to the white man's brutality.

By the end of the colonial period labor, free and slave, white and black, spread across the coastal plain fronting the Atlantic and into the hill country further west, reaching and sometimes piercing the Appalachian Mountain chain, the first great barrier to the interior. Settlers tended to push into the valleys carved over the centuries by many rivers and streams. The valley floors had rich soils and the waterways kept settlers in touch with coastal ports, giving them access to markets and sources of supply.

THE INDIANS

The Indians, the French, and the Spaniards were obstacles to the westward movement. In the long run, the Indians proved no match for the colonists' superior technology and more advanced social organization. In the short run, however, the process of Indian removal was slow, tedious, and bloody. The colonists negotiated treaties under which tribes gave up lands in exchange for supplies. But Indians did not share the white man's conception of private property and disputes inevitably arose, especially since colonists ruthlessly cheated the red men. As whites continually encroached on hunting lands, the natives grew alarmed and fought to protect their way of life. Costly warfare erupted on each new frontier. Because the Indians were divided among numerous tribes, each independent of the other, English victory over one did not subdue the rest. Repeatedly, therefore, during a period of three centuries, Americans fought the red man until the last resistance ended in the late nineteenth century.

The Americans were ambivalent toward the Indians. They coveted their lands yet they regarded them as "noble savages," children of nature who possessed rare courage and skills for surviving in the wilderness. From them the English learned how to grow maize, or Indian corn, an important crop for survival during the early stages of settlement. At the same time the colonists regarded them as uncivilized heathen and attempted to enslave them and convert them to Christianity. The Indians resisted. Their culture was of such fragile nature that Indians disintegrated when removed from their tribes. They thus proved unsuited to enslavement and, at best, conversion to Christianity was superficial and short-lived. "For, take a young Indian lad," wrote a French traveler, "give him the best education you possibly can, load him with your bounty, with presents, nay with riches; yet he will secretly long for his native woods . . . and on the first opportunity he can possibly find, you will see him voluntarily leave behind him all you have given him, and return with inexpressible joy to lie on the mats of his fathers."

White attitudes toward Indians were a mixture of paternalistic benevolence and fear of savagery; whichever attitude prevailed at a given time depended on whether the interests of the two groups clashed. But no comparable ambivalence existed toward the black man. Torn from their homeland, the blacks could neither resist effectively nor threaten their white masters to the extent that the Indians did. Whites found no nobility in the Negro's "savagery."

The French and Spaniards encouraged Indian resistance to block English expansion and to maintain a balance of power in the New World. Spanish control of Florida slowed development of Georgia and the Carolinas. The Indians thwarted the settlement of South Carolina back country until the 1760s.

THE FRENCH

The French were England's chief rival. From Canada they contested for control of the Ohio Valley. Engaging in the western fur trade, erecting forts and forming alliances with Indian tribes, the French sought to confine the English to east of the Appalachians. The contest proved protracted. From time to time the competition escalated into warfare. The struggle for mastery of North America was a side show of a far greater struggle in Europe. France, under Louis XIV (1638–1715), was the most powerful nation in Europe. Britain sought to maintain a balance of power in Europe, in part, by denying France the resources and wealth of the New World.

From the end of the seventeenth century until the 1750s, England fought a series of inconclusive intercolonial wars. France and England, with their Indian allies, attacked one another's weak points, destroyed villages, impeded settlement, and exchanged territory, but neither side committed themselves sufficiently to achieve decisive victory. The outbreak of fresh fighting in 1754 led to "The Great War for Empire" (1754–1761). This time England, under the effective leadership of William Pitt, mobilized her wealth and power to dislodge the French from North America, thus opening the interior to American settlement. The elimination of the French and the enlargement of Britain's North American em-

pire created new problems that eventually led to revolution. At the time, none foresaw the consequences. For half a century the English and the Americans had coveted the west as an arena for advancing the power of the kingdom and the wealth of its subjects. The wealth of the colonies depended largely on the development of agriculture.

COLONIAL AGRICULTURE

The economic development of the colonies hinged on the production of agricultural surpluses. Many farmers, however, were unable to advance beyond subsistence. Inefficient technology, labor shortages, isolation on the frontiers, difficulties in transporting goods to markets, all combined to hinder commercial agriculture. Establishing a farm was a formidable undertaking. European soils though less fertile had been tilled for generations; forests had been cleared and swamplands drained for many centuries. In America yeomen first had to clear the land of trees and shrubs, build homes and farms, and lay out roads. But they did this expectantly. Even subsistence farmers hoped eventually to produce surpluses and frontier farmers sought to make a profit by selling their homesteads to the next wave of settlers.

Land Systems

The farmer's entrepreneurial (or businessman's) outlook owed much to the ease with which he could acquire good land. Colonies offered settlers the abundant lands on liberal terms, usually free from the manorial obligations that oppressed the European peasantry. The New England colonies granted land to each newly created town whose original proprietors parceled out acreage to settlers. The New England system encouraged compactness of settlement since the legislatures controlled town creation. Designed to establish tightly knit communities whose members would never stray from the influence of the Puritan clergy and magistrates, this system did not survive intact in the eighteenth century, when speculators, unconstrained by reli-

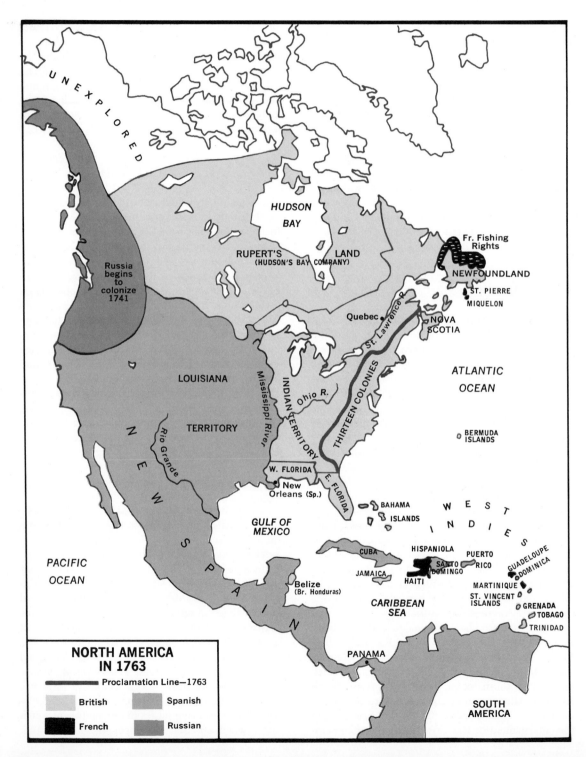

NORTH AMERICA IN 1763

Proclamation Line—1763

British

French

Spanish

Russian

UNEXPLORED

HUDSON
BAY

RUPERT'S LAND
(HUDSON'S BAY COMPANY)

Fr. Fishing
Rights

NEWFOUNDLAND

ST. PIERRE
MIQUELON

Quebec

NOVA
SCOTIA

St. Lawrence R.

ATLANTIC
OCEAN

Russia
begins
to
colonize
1741

LOUISIANA

TERRITORY

Mississippi River

INDIAN TERRITORY

Ohio R.

THIRTEEN COLONIES

BERMUDA
ISLANDS

N
E
W
S
P
A
I
N

Rio Grande

W. FLORIDA

E. FLORIDA

New
Orleans (Sp.)

GULF OF
MEXICO

W
E
S
T

I
N
D
I
E
S

BAHAMA
ISLANDS

PACIFIC
OCEAN

CUBA

JAMAICA

Belize
(Br. Honduras)

HISPANIOLA

SANTO
DOMINGO

HAITI

PUERTO
RICO

GUADELOUPE
DOMINICA

MARTINIQUE

ST. VINCENT
ISLANDS

GRENADA
TOBAGO

TRINIDAD

CARIBBEAN
SEA

PANAMA

SOUTH
AMERICA

gious scruples, induced colonies to grant them huge tracts of undeveloped lands far from settled communities.

Elsewhere farmers acquired lands through different means. Outside New England, acquisition was more informal. In the absence of a township system, individuals could locate wherever they pleased and hence settlement was generally less compact. In Virginia abuse of the headright system, whereby false claims enabled speculators to acquire land illegally, led the crown to sell land cheaply. The Maryland proprietors followed suit. For five shillings or one hundred pounds of tobacco, husbandmen could acquire fifty acres. Those who owed rents of a couple of shillings per acre found it easy to evade payment. Neither the crown nor the proprietors possessed efficient collection machinery and the local gentry, themselves large landowners, controlled government and connived with farmers to avoid payment.

Instead of satisfying land hunger, the availability of land intensified the desire and encouraged widespread speculation. Investments in more land than one could farm appealed to both urban and rural folk as well as to ordinary farmers and large-scale speculators. Rapid growth and shifts in population led people to expect land values to rise; a well-located purchase might yield considerable profit. Virgin land appealed to farmers who wanted to abandon soil worn out by wasteful methods of farming as well as to acquire surplus acreage for later sale. Except for commerce and farming, practically no other outlets for savings or opportunities for speculation existed —no banks or insurance companies, few government securities, and no corporate stocks and bonds. Moreover, in a society where wealth defined social position and land was the principal form of wealth, the ambitious understandably sought large estates.

Yet despite the colonists' land speculations, and despite the formation in the mid-eighteenth century of large speculative land companies, those who wanted land found it easy to obtain. Large-scale speculation often proved unprofitable because absentee owners lacked resources to develop their holdings and could not afford to bear the expenses until purchasers arrived and demand developed. Though some obtained large tracts, there was too much good land available for a few to monopolize it. Yet there were exceptions. In New York's Hudson River Valley the Dutch first, and the English later, granted large manorial estates whose owners rented or leased but did not sell the land. As a result many immigrants preferred to settle elsewhere and become freeholders rather than tenants owing obligations to a manorial lord, as in Europe. Because of this Hudson River Valley situation, New York's population and economic development lagged.

Crops

Climate, soils, and markets determined the kinds of crops farmers raised. Tobacco and wheat provided the bulk of export staples, making up almost half the value of exports in 1770. Tobacco, grown largely in Virginia, Maryland, and North Carolina, was the leading export, accounting for about one-quarter of the value of exports in 1770. When tobacco production began in Virginia early in the seventeenth century, the weed's potential market had hardly been tapped since it was native to the Western Hemisphere. The Spaniards acquired it from the Indians and introduced it into Europe where the habit spread. Demand grew beyond Spain's ability to supply it, offering English producers markets which they eagerly exploited. By the end of the colonial period, however, many tobacco growers found it profitable to switch to wheat because chronic overproduction of tobacco depressed prices on the world markets. During the eighteenth century wheat production rapidly rose in importance, notably in Pennsylvania, New York, and parts of Maryland and Virginia. By 1770 wheat, flour, and bread accounted for 22 percent of the value of exports to the West Indies and Europe. The swampy lands of Georgia, North Carolina, and especially South Carolina were suitable for growing rice and indigo (a textile dye) which together accounted for 14 percent of the value of colonial exports in 1770. Not all farmers, however, could raise these major staples. Less favorable soils and climate led many, particularly in New England, to produce a variety of foodstuffs for markets in the cities and the West Indies.

Farmers unable to grow the major export

staples could supplement income by engaging in industries related to agriculture. Those living near uncleared forests and with access to streams cut timber, some of it for export, some for shipbuilding, urban construction, and barrel manufacture. The forests also contained animals whose furs and hides were valuable enough to support transportation costs from the trading posts to cities where consumers sported warm beaver hats.

The most important extractive industry, however, was fishing. Centered in New England, fishing became a major source of the region's income because farming was less profitable here than elsewhere. Fishing towns dotted the New England coastline affording employment for sailors and those who processed the catch. Fish accounted for 12 percent of the value of colonial exports in 1770.

Agriculture and related industries were the foundations of colonial welfare. A European agricultural revolution that had increased efficiency and expanded production had also radically reorganized rural society. Enlightened landlords and the well-to-do farmers improved methods by consolidating holding and pushing the less efficient off the land. With opportunities in England shrinking, many of the excluded migrated to America where abundant land enabled most men to acquire their own farms. Some farmers prospered unusually well and expanded the scale of their operations without, as in Europe, forcing others off the land. The most successful developed plantations largely in the Southern colonies, which required considerable investment of capital, employed slave labor supervised by overseers, and produced much more than was possible on family farms.

Plantations

Plantations developed because larger units of production were more efficient and some farmers were able to acquire capital with which to enlarge their scale of operations. Rice growing, for instance, used a great deal of back-breaking labor. The coastal swamps of the Carolinas and Georgia had to be drained and dammed; mills had to be constructed; and all this required capital and labor beyond the means of small farmers. Tobacco, however, could easily be raised on a family farm with a slave or two. But here, also, plantations had superior advantages. Tobacco prices fluctuated violently because growers were unable to adjust supply to demand. Producers expanded production, hoping that a big crop would bring a fair return even at lower prices since distribution costs tended to be fixed. Selling more tobacco lowered a planter's fixed cost per hogshead. Moreover, those who grew tobacco on a large scale hoped to make a fortune when prices were high.

The key to expansion lay in acquisition of additional land and slaves. Farmers could enlarge their landholdings cheaply; a successful planter might obtain tens of thousands of acres, holding some of it as reserve to replace fields depleted by soil-exhausting methods of tobacco culture, and the rest as speculation for later sale. By purchasing additional slaves, the planter could clear fresh land and expand acreage under cultivation.

The planter financed expansion by plowing back profits into his operations and by borrowing. British merchants invested in American agriculture by extending credit to planters who could then expand operations and buy luxuries from England. Concentrating on tobacco, Chesapeake planters scorned commerce and urban life; dispersed settlement patterns, moreover, retarded the growth of market centers. South Carolina rice planters maintained residences on their plantations as well as in Charleston. Successful Southern merchants usually invested in plantations and became full-fledged planters. English and Scottish merchants therefore came to dominate tobacco marketing even though the bulk of the crop went to European markets after passing through British ports and paying heavy crown taxes.

In the eighteenth century, planters became chronic debtors. The planter lacked direct control over the sale of his crop, and sometimes two years passed before settlement of accounts. Without a precise idea of how much he could afford to spend on himself and on expansion, he indulged his appetite for luxuries and his ambitions to expand. Merchants encouraged these tendencies because once they had a planter in debt, he mortgaged the next year's crop and became firmly tied to the creditor. As planters raised larger crops, middlemen earned more for their marketing services. In these ways, British merchants provided credit for American expansion but at a price. In contrast, farmers, who raised crops such as wheat not marketed by English merchants, did not have access to British credit on the same scale as did Southern planters. Wheat farming, therefore, remained dominated by yeomen farmers, until the mid-eighteenth century when some planters, finding tobacco unprofitable, turned to grain farming. Planters mined the soil with one crop, often neglecting to grow enough food to feed their slaves.

Commerce and Cities

The profits from agriculture, whether carried on through family farms or large plantations, financed American economic growth, made possible a relatively high average standard of living, and paid for the goods Americans purchased abroad. The production of surpluses for sale at home and abroad also stimulated commercial development in growing port cities along the Atlantic seaboard and countless smaller towns that collected the farmers' produce and retailed foreign imports. Boston, New York, Philadelphia, Providence, and Charleston were the principal ports whose rapid growth mirrored expansion in the hinterlands they served. By the time of the American Revolution, Philadelphia, with 25,000 inhabitants, had as many people as any city in England except London.

Most American produce went to Britain, the West Indies, and southern Europe. The first important native merchant community developed in New England. Lacking staples for the English market, New Englanders financed development and imports from Britain by selling foodstuffs to West Indian sugar planters. At the outset the New Englanders acted as agents for London firms which financed the early fishing industry. Eventually, as traders accumulated capital, they gained direct control of the fishing business and the profits formerly shared with the Londoners. Americans sold their cargoes for bills of credit on London or for sugar and molasses which they profitably manufactured into rum. They thus paid for manufactures imported from England. Trading patterns were complex, because merchants roamed all over the Atlantic basin sailing from port to port seeking favorable markets, exchanging one cargo for another, and always with the object of earning credits in London.

Though Americans obtained most of their imports from Britain, they had to find markets elsewhere for many of their exports. Until 1740 they maintained a rough balance of payments for imports and exports with England sufficient to pay for manufactured goods and luxuries. During the last thirty years of the colonial period, however, the colonies chronically imported considerably more than they sold to Britain. Increasingly, they had to earn foreign exchange elsewhere, outside the British empire. These they found in the French West Indies and in southern Europe which consumed vast quantities of wheat, fish, and timber which paid for the rapid increases in American consumption of British goods.

The export of American staples led to urban growth everywhere except in the tobacco colonies. There, British and Scottish merchants (called "factors") dominated marketing because planters preferred to specialize in tobacco growing and because British traders offered easier credit than Boston or Philadelphia merchants. Moreover, the river system that penetrated the tobacco coast enabled British ships to sail to the planter's wharf thwarting the concentration of marketing activity in a few places.

Elsewhere commerce stimulated urban development in various ways. Overseas trade gave employment to those who built and serviced ships and shipping became one of the most important colonial industries. Access to raw material enabled Americans to build vessels cheaply for sale to British as well as to American merchants. The artisans, laborers, and seamen employed by the maritime industries created markets for retailers, mechanics, and nearby farmers.

Though merchants prospered and cities grew, English merchants and shippers controlled the lion's share of transatlantic trade. The American merchants were enterprising in gathering cargoes from far-flung reaches of the colonies, parlaying one cargo into another, scouring the Atlantic for profitable exchanges, but they lacked sufficient capital to displace British houses. They did, however, dominate the coastal trade.

British subjects, wherever they lived, were not free to do business and pursue profits as they saw fit. Americans were part of an empire in which an elaborate body of law regulated and constrained economic activity according to widely shared beliefs about how nations grew rich.

THE MERCANTILIST SYSTEM AND AMERICAN ECONOMIC DEVELOPMENT

The emergence of the modern state which monopolized power in the hands of kings and parliaments rested in part on the ability of central authority to control revenue—the Power of the Purse. Overseas empires offered statebuilders new sources of wealth and power. Spain's emergence from obscurity to become the colossus of Europe in the sixteenth century stemmed primarily from wealth gained abroad. Spain then translated the new wealth into power in Europe. Other kingdoms followed her example.

Mercantilism was the body of assumptions which directed statesmen in pursuit of national interest. Mercantilists believed that without wealth a nation could not be secure nor could it advance its power. Gold financed armies and expansion which brought added territories with valuable resources. New sources of wealth further enlarged a nation's capacity for both war making and expansion. Mercantilists believed that the sum of the world's wealth was fixed; a nation, therefore, could grow richer and more powerful only at the expense of another. The application of these principles varied from country to country and from time to time but governments did not hesitate to intervene directly in the economic life of the kingdom.

English mercantilism took many forms. The chartered trading companies receiving a monopoly of trade with Virginia, Bermuda, or the East Indies were typical instruments of national policy. During the first five decades of American colonization, England left the settlements fairly free to develop on their own. The end of civil war in England, the need for additional revenues, the growing importance of the colonial economies, and intensification of rivalry with the Dutch for naval supremacy led to the development of mercantilist legislation that attempted to maximize the colonies' value to the mother country.

The Navigation Acts, first adopted in 1651 and elaborated in 1662, gave British built and owned ships a monopoly of the carrying trade into which the Dutch had intruded, especially in the tobacco colonies. Certain enumerated colonial exports such as sugar, tobacco, rice, and naval stores had to be shipped directly to England for domestic consumption or reexport. The Plantation Duty (1673) attempted to prevent American merchants from evading the acts of enumeration. The Staple Act (1663) required that goods imported into the colonies from Europe come via England. Together with enumeration, this measure gave British middlemen tighter control of American trade. By funneling colonial goods through England, the crown taxed them and made the mother country the distribution center, to the advantage of British subjects *in England*. British mercantilists also sought greater self-sufficiency by providing bounties for the production of such items as naval stores and indigo which otherwise were purchased outside the empire. The mother country also encouraged the production of tropical staples consumed at home and reexported abroad through Britain by protecting colonial producers from foreign competition and giving them a monopoly of the home market.

Mercantilism was more than a system by which the mother country exploited its colonies. Conflicts among the various interests affected by British policy for the West Indies sugar islands illustrate its complexity. Sometimes two groups of colonists clashed, as did North Americans who preferred to buy sugar in the French West Indies where the terms of trade were more favorable than in the British islands, and the English sugar planters anxious to exclude the Americans from foreign sources. The sugar planters also clashed with British merchants and refiners who preferred to import the cheaper French sugar. Through political influence, the West Indies planters obtained passage of the Molasses Act (1733) placing a prohibitive duty on French sugar imported into the American colonies. For many decades, however, the law went unenforced because the Northern and Middle colonies relied on illegal trade with the French islands to finance English imports, a trade which Britain permitted. The necessity to evade the Molasses Act arose because colonies not producing staples had to find markets outside the empire.

Increasingly in the eighteenth century, Britain valued the colonies not only for their raw materials but as markets for industrial products. The growth of industry in Britain made the protected American market one of the foundations of national prosperity. With a large and growing population of freehold farmers who could afford English goods, the American colonies became England's most important overseas customer, outdistancing the West Indies in the late colonial period. Thus as Britain was industrialized, the colonies—which had failed to conform to the mercantilist ideal as producers of staples desired in the mother country—became valuable as customers for the industry of the mother country.

The growing importance of colonial markets led to British restrictions on the development of colonial industry. The Woolen Act (1699), the Hat Act (1732), and the Iron Act (1750) sought to discourage manufacturing. Iron production, for instance, grew rapidly in the eighteenth century, the Americans producing a seventh of the world's iron supply, manufacturing it into nails and axes, pots and pans, that otherwise would have come from England. The Iron Act encouraged colonial production of pig iron but discouraged fabrication into finished goods, hoping thereby to lessen the dependence of English manufacturers on foreign sources but assuring them a monopoly of the American market for finished iron goods.

The crown also regulated colonial efforts to provide an adequate supply of currency and credit. There were no banks in the colonies nor did Britain provide Americans with an adequate money supply, but when colonists resorted to local expedients they faced British disapproval and prohibition. Until the 1750s they managed to evade English restraints designed to protect British merchants from receiving in payment of debts cheap colonial paper money, though the paper money was often a stable medium strongly favored by American merchants.

Benefits and Burdens

The mercantilist system, like any other, had advantages and disadvantages. The Navigation Acts benefited colonial shipbuilding and shipping interests, eliminating foreign competition, and bounties subsidized certain producers. Though the colonists were not free to import goods from outside the empire, England as the most advanced industrial nation could undersell foreign competition and cater to colonial tastes; even after independence, the Americans continued to buy English manufactures. Enumeration favored British merchants and raised the distribution costs of staples which had to pass through England on their way to the Continent. But English merchants provided valuable services, developed foreign markets, and extended credits to planters whose exports enjoyed preferential treatment in the English market. Though American merchants had to accept a makeshift supply of currency and credit, they had access to English capital, enjoyed the protection of the British navy and, in wartime, government contracts made many American fortunes. Where mercantilism most pinched, as in the West Indies sugar trade, lax enforcement opened loopholes through which Americans scrambled.

Restraints on American industrial development were premature. The preconditions for industry did not exist in the colonies nor did they appear until forty years after independence. Labor and capital, in short supply, flowed into agriculture, and the domestic market for factory products was limited by the thinly distributed population, poorly linked by inefficient means of communication. Americans possessed limited purchasing power to support their own industries. A high degree of self-sufficiency limited the market for manufactures. Crude technology and high transportation costs moreover constricted industrial possibilities. In contrast, British manufacturers had large domestic markets, supplemented by additional outlets throughout the world.

British mercantilists regarded the colonies as a means of advancing the wealth and power of the kingdom. Britain prospered from its overseas dependencies but so too did the colonists who flourished economically despite the mother country's restrictions. By 1776 Americans were materially prepared for independence. A century long policy of British regulation aimed at keeping them subordinate had failed.

THE PROSPEROUS AMERICANS

American welfare rested on the productivity of its farms and plantations. Surpluses collected by merchants enabled farmers to buy things produced elsewhere. The natural resources of a rich unexploited continent provided the foundation of American economic development. An enterprising people, able to acquire land easily and accumulate or borrow capital, produced commodities that found eager buyers in world markets. By the time Americans separated from England, they had developed an agricultural system—owned and operated by colonials rather than by absentee proprietors in Britain—and an indigenous and experienced urban business community. In the formative years of American settlement, the necessity to recruit laborers from England and the willingness of the colonies to attract people by offering them land created a numerous body of freehold farmers, except in parts of the Southern colonies.

Though England profited extensively from its North American provinces, much wealth remained in the hands of colonists who produced it. Colonies in other times and places fared less well. In Africa and Asia, Europeans enslaved and ex-

ploited native populations, foreigners owned and managed most enterprises, enjoying the profits and determining the course of economic development. The Americans were more fortunate. Settling a continent populated sparsely by Indians, the British developed their North American colonies by attracting free labor and offering wide scope for the enterprise of diverse individuals and many groups. At the same time that opportunities in farming were diminishing in England, as a limited supply of land became increasingly concentrated in the hands of a few, America was becoming a land of independent yeomen whose numbers rapidly multiplied. Colonial prosperity, moreover, was less vulnerable to sharp fluctuations in the marketplace than was the case in the nineteenth century when the disappearance of subsistence farming and home manufacturing gave way to the growth of specialization of production for foreign and domestic markets. Regional interdependence and specialization then locked citizens in the grip of the business cycle, with its alternating periods of boom and depression.

During the 175 years of the colonial period, people discovered that the mass of men, at least in America, need not be poor. Natural resources were so abundant that, if appropriately distributed, most whites could be decently fed, clothed, and sheltered. Shrewd and hard-working individuals could improve their lot in life and their children might realistically entertain aspirations for social advancement that few sons of farmers and artisans in Europe could expect. This revolution of rising material and social expectations inevitably affected the forms of government under which Americans lived.

Chapter 4
From Plantations to Commonwealths

Democratic government, unknown in Europe since the collapse of ancient Greek democracy, was rediscovered in the New World. Colonists brought political ideas and practices from Europe where kings and aristocrats monopolized political power. They did not intend to innovate, yet during the colonial period Americans achieved a large degree of self-government and managed their own affairs in ways that pointed toward popular rule. Though colonists did not know full-scale democracy nor did they possess the political parties through which modern democracies govern themselves, they were laying the foundations for both. In the half century following independence, Americans completed the transformations in government begun during the colonial period.

European Assumptions

Throughout the colonial period, Europeans shared common assumptions about the uses of power. Governments existed to establish order among men whose passions, if left unchecked, would create chaos or anarchy. By protecting the peace, establishing and upholding a rule of law to guide individual behavior, the state made civilized existence possible. The responsibilities of wielding power fell to that small element in society fit to rule. The mass of men were no more capable of governing themselves than of existing without government. Power was the privilege of the wealthy, educated, and intelligent elite. Peasants, artisans, and laborers should work at their occupations, jobs which they could perform well, and leave decision-making to their superiors. In this way the various elements in society performed those functions for which each was best suited.

The politically responsible strata were thus identical with the social elite; power flowed down from the top of the social structure, from the king and the great nobility and lesser aristocracy down to the merchants, shopkeepers, farmers, and laborers subject to their authority. Furthermore, by the seventeenth century, the new nation-states lodged ultimate power in some central institution, the monarchy, or the monarchy and Parliament, as the best way of maintaining order and promoting the country's interests.

Though a few governed, they were not at liberty to tyrannize. In theory, the king and nobility must promote the well-being of all. They were no more free to do as they pleased than those they governed. Theoretically, the welfare of society mattered more than the claims of individuals, high or low in the social structure, and the state could rigorously discipline dissidents if necessary. Government gained its legitimacy from still another source, especially in England where a long medieval tradition established the principle that rulers must govern in accordance with their responsibilities as Christians and within limits established by their subjects through custom and law. Parliament became the principal instrument through which representative government developed in England.

American Realities

By the end of the colonial period Americans had transformed traditional political ideas and arrangements. The need for order in a wilderness society was at least as great as in the Old World. But Americans managed their public affairs differently. Legally, power in the empire flowed from the top down, since supreme authority centered in the crown and Parliament which made and administered the laws governing the colonies.

But from the beginning, power in America drained away into the local units of governments —the towns, the counties, and the provincial legislatures—and power flowed from the bottom up as well as from England to America. Compared to those who ruled in England, native American leadership came from socially inferior classes, often men who had risen from obscurity to positions of wealth and power. The American governing classes also had to pay much more attention to the interests and wishes of those they governed than their counterparts in England. Whereas the great majority of adult males could not participate in English politics, in the colonies generally a majority of adult white males could vote in local and provincial elections, though many did not exercise this privilege.

In America rulers found it increasingly difficult to impose a conception of the general welfare that constrained the various groups and interests. By the end of the colonial period, colonists were far more likely to question and even oppose authority than was the case in England, as a bewildering variety of elements competed for advantage. Increasingly, people came to view the state as the individual's servant, not his master. Government, many believed, must allow citizens to pursue their interests even at the expense of the welfare of others, though few explicitly repudiated the community's right to limit individual freedom for the common good. In America, however, it was harder for men to agree on what *was* the common good, and still harder for any one group to make others accept its particular version.

THE BEGINNINGS OF GOVERNMENT

Three thousand miles away from the courts, the king, and the Parliament that had governed them at home, settlers had to frame laws and establish governments in a wilderness. Disorder threatened civilized existence in the New World as it did in the Old. Political authority had to develop in the colonies without central direction or plan. Since the crown delegated colonization to private enterprise, it removed itself in the beginning from direct responsibility for governing. Internal conflict within England between Puritans and Anglicans, and king and Parliament until 1660 left the colonizing groups free to proceed as they wished. Yet despite the absence of central control or uniformity in the methods of settlement, political development followed a common pattern.

At first, the founders of each settlement—whether the Puritan elite in Massachusetts, the officers of the Virginia Company, or the proprietor of Maryland—attempted to concentrate power in their own hands. In every case events thwarted their plans. None had the power to impose his will on the settlers for long; prudence and neces-

sity led to a dispersal of power. The Virginia Company created the House of Burgesses to enlist greater cooperation from the settlers and to make the colony more attractive to immigrants. The crown, when it took control, also recognized the need for the legislature to regulate tobacco production, encourage the development of other staples, finance government, and defend the colony.

Similarly, John Winthrop's clique could not govern Massachusetts without enlarging the terms of political participation. Town leaders refused to cooperate unless they had a share in the government. And Lord Baltimore likewise discovered that though the charter gave all power to the proprietor, he was too far away, and too ignorant of affairs in Maryland to enforce his will. He too had to solicit support from the settlers through a legislature.

Government intruded on the lives of most people mainly when it punished crime, levied taxes, settled disputes over land and debts, laid out roads, and constructed public facilities. As the population dispersed from the original points of settlement, local bodies arose to govern beyond the control of the authorities in Jamestown or Boston. Towns and counties administered by sheriffs and justices of the peace became the instruments of local government. In practice, local leaders were the men of wealth and standing in the neighborhood who had either enjoyed positions of prominence in England or, more likely, acquired them in America. The representatives of the counties and towns chosen to attend the legislature linked communities to the central government.

At the provincial capital sat the governor, appointed by the crown as in Virginia, by the proprietor as in Maryland, or elected by the freemen as in Massachusetts. A council, usually drawn from the most powerful local leaders, aided the executive, participated in law making as part of the assembly, and also served as a court of appeals. Harmonious relations between the governor and his council, and between both of them and the legislature required accommodation on all sides. A governor who antagonized the council and the local elite usually did not last. Secure tenure rested on the ability to win over powerful local men by giving them lucrative appointments, land grants, control of the fur trade, and other privileges. Governors learned that they needed the support of local officials to obtain cooperation from the legislature and council.

Local government assumed far greater importance and authority than in England where organs of central administration, developed over many centuries, had encroached upon local authority. In the absence of professionally staffed royal courts, county courts in America assumed broad jurisdiction, dispensing justice tempered by common sense and local political circumstance rather than in strict accordance with legal precedent or complex legal practices. The English sheriff, the king's man, had had his power curbed by a Parliament jealous of royal authority; in the colonies the sheriff owed his office to the local elite who sat as justices on the county court. In England serving as sheriff was often regarded as a burden, but in the colonies it was a lucrative post which the justices rotated among themselves. Town and county cliques influenced appointments to local government, thereby enabling them to perpetuate their power. Represented by one of their members in the legislature and sometimes in the council, controlling the militia and other offices, they had extensive autonomy, with little fear of intrusion from royal government.

As the governor learned to work with the most powerful native elements, incorporating them into his council, demands arose to remove the councillors from the assemblies into a separate house. Bicameralism, or a two house legislature, grew out of distinctions arising among governing groups and the desire to check the power of the governor and his supporters in the council.

For the most part, provincial authority remained remote whereas local government more closely affected people's lives. As long as settlers had to invest most of their energies in carving out settlements, clearing the land, cultivating new farms, setting up shops, developing trade, and relying on their own efforts, government played a lesser role in their lives than it did later. During the last quarter of the seventeenth century, how-

ever, widespread civil disturbances disrupted the peace and brought turmoil to colonial America, as people violently challenged established authority.

SOURCES OF INSTABILITY

Between 1676 and 1688 rebellions erupted in half a dozen colonies from Massachusetts to North Carolina. These explosions occurred both because of pressures building up within colonial society and from external sources. As societies matured, rivalries among colonists intensified and compromise became increasingly difficult. At the same time, England, which had earlier paid little attention to the colonies, now attempted to tighten control.

Bacon's Rebellion

Bacon's Rebellion in Virginia (1676) grew out of internal conflicts with a long-entrenched faction around Governor William Berkeley which enriched itself through control of numerous offices, grants of land, and domination of the fur trade. Planters excluded from the governor's favored circle were resentful over poor tobacco crops and low prices. The governor's handling of the Indians increased the discontent and touched off the explosion.

Virginians had broken the power of the local Indians a generation earlier and, by the 1670s, whites greatly outnumbered the nearby tribes. The Indians living along the edges of white settlements were pacified and friendly, encouraging planters to encroach further on Indian territory. As tension mounted, the whites became more aggressive in the face of Indian weakness, an experience repeated on countless frontiers for almost three centuries. When a planter stole some Indian property and Indians retaliated by stealing some hogs, both sides began murdering one another.

The stage was set for war. Eager to keep the peace, Governor Berkeley ordered whites to withdraw from exposed plantations behind a line of forts at the falls of the rivers. Friendly Indians were disarmed but supplied with necessities, and the sale of arms and munitions to Indians was banned. Accusing the governor of being "soft" on Indians, of appeasing bloodthirsty savages, abandoning frontier plantations, and preventing the westward expansion of whites, a group of planters, led by Nathaniel Bacon, attacked the friendly Indians.

Bacon had recently fled from England in disgrace. A cousin-in-law of Berkeley, he became a councillor and received a land grant on the frontier to which he retreated, becoming the champion of anti-Berkeley elements. When the governor refused to approve the actions of Bacon and his followers, they marched on Jamestown and forced a commission from him at gun point. Civil war broke out. Bacon captured the capitol and burned it to the ground. When he died suddenly in August, 1676, Berkeley crushed the resistance and executed twenty-three rebels.

The crown dispatched commissioners to restore peace, hoping to assure a continued flow of revenue from tobacco taxes. Believing that the Baconians enjoyed popular support, the commissioners insisted on leniency for the rebels. Many of the laws adopted by the legislature under rebel influence remained in force, reducing the influence of Berkeley's faction and opening new opportunities for those previously excluded by the dominant elite.

Bacon's rebellion proved that no group could hold power indefinitely unless it accommodated and admitted ambitious newer elements. The clique that formed around Governor Berkeley had become dominant during the second generation of settlement. By the 1670s, as population grew and settlement expanded, new families demanded a share in government. Recognition of their demands restored peace to the colony for another century.

Dominion of New England

Massachusetts, like Virginia, also overthrew a royal governor. Rebellion in the Bay colony grew out of new pressures from England that sharpened existing divisions within the province. After twenty years of civil war which saw the execution of Charles I and the establishment of a republic (1649–1660) headed by Oliver Cromwell, the Stuart dynasty reclaimed the throne. After the Restoration, the crown took an increasing interest in its American empire. It discharged obligations to followers by chartering new proprietary colonies in the Carolinas and Pennsylvania and it enacted mercantilist legislation to drive the Dutch from imperial commerce and channel trade to England.

The Puritan colonies in New England attracted particular attention because they had sympathized with Cromwell's regime and had persecuted Anglicans. In 1664 four commissioners arrived in New England to obtain aid against the Dutch, insure enforcement of the navigation acts and compliance with other English laws, and to stop Puritan persecution of religious dissenters. Chronic defiance by Massachuetts eventually led to the annulment of the original charter in 1684. The crown replaced Puritan government with the Dominion of New England (1685–1688) which brought Massachusetts, Rhode Island, and Connecticut under the control of a royal governor and contemplated the inclusion of New York, New Jersey, and Pennsylvania to centralize colonial defense against the French and to enforce the Navigation Acts.

At first the new regime enjoyed support from merchants, moderate Calvinists, and dissenters excluded from power by the Puritan elite. They looked to the crown to protect their interests, to give them a share in governing, and to relieve them from religious disabilities. In 1686, King James II dispatched Sir Edmund Andros to take command of the dominion. The governor and a handpicked council of sympathetic merchants and dissenters ruled in place of the Massachusetts assembly. Furthermore, Andros declared that all land titles had to be reconfirmed subject to quit-rent. He moved against illegal trade, permitted town meetings to be held only once a year, levied new taxes, seized control of the militia, and eliminated the religious privileges of Puritans.

In 1688 the Glorious Revolution in England overthrew the Stuart dynasty. James II's Catholicism alienated powerful interests who replaced him on the throne with William of Orange, a Dutch Protestant. Massachusetts Puritans seized the opportunity to denounce Andros as a supporter of James II and an intriguer with the pope and the French to deliver English Protestants to Catholic tyranny. When Bostonians took up arms, Andros found himself isolated. The moderates who had once welcomed the intrusion of English authority deserted him, since the governor had ignored them in favor of a small clique that monopolized privilege and threatened the property and commerce of others. Those remaining loyal to Andros were mostly new arrivals from England, and many joined him in jail.

Though the Puritan elite regained power, the crown refused to restore the old charter. It issued a new one in 1691 which gave the king power to review legislation and appoint the governor, authorized the Massachusetts legislature to elect the council subject to the governor's veto, substituted a property qualification for voting in place of church membership, and required toleration of all Protestants. Under this new arrangement peace returned to the Bay colony. The Puritan elite lost its power monopoly but still remained the dominant element and English authority gained a foothold. The crown abandoned the dominion scheme, permitting Rhode Island and Connecticut to be governed under their original charters and relied thereafter on persuasion and cajolery to obtain colonial cooperation against the French. Over sixty years passed before England made another attempt to unify the administration of the colonies.

Maryland and New York

The Glorious Revolution in England touched off rebellion elsewhere in the colonies. Maryland Protestants had long nursed complaints against the proprietors who, together with their Catholic relatives and favorites, monopolized offices, the Indian trade, and accumulated vast land holdings. Discontent in Maryland drew support from respectable "outsiders," merchants, justices of the peace, militia leaders, and planters in the newly developed regions where proprietary influences were weakest. When the Baltimore family failed to rush to the support of the new Protestant line in England, their Maryland antagonists overthrew them in the name of William of Orange. They established the Anglican church and Maryland became a royal colony for almost

twenty-five years. In 1715 the crown restored the colony to the fourth Lord Baltimore, a Protestant.

The revolt in Boston against the Dominion of New England also inspired rebellion in New York in 1689. Jacob Leisler, a Dutch merchant, organized discontented elements and overthrew the Andros regime. Leisler found support among New England settlers on Long Island and among the Dutch who were restless under English rule. Leisler appealed to a broad spectrum of artisans, merchants, and farmers alienated by an office-holding elite and their mercantile and landed allies who governed the province for their own benefit.

The Leislerians, not a rabble, included local leaders, church elders, merchants, and militia officers. They established order, removed Catholics from office, raised taxes, opened the courts, reestablished the assembly, and fought the Indians and the French. In 1691 a new royal governor arrived but Leisler resisted until finally forced to surrender. He and a lieutenant were convicted of treason and were executed.

The rebellions of the late seventeenth century revealed the growing complexity of colonial society. First and second generation settlers who were most successful at accumulating wealth and entrenching themselves in positions of privilege antagonized the ambitious but excluded elements. The disgruntled were unwilling to permit a few to use the state to secure permanent advantage. They came from diverse social origins — Anglicans in Massachusetts, Dutch and New Englanders in New York, Protestants in Maryland, frontier gentry in Virginia, and farmers, merchants, and artisans bound together by a growing sense of exclusion and disadvantage.

Long-standing European patterns of privilege seemed illegitimate in America; those enjoying them were unable to justify them. In the colonies preferment was something achieved through hard work, rather than by inheritance. Others willing to work just as hard demanded an equal opportunity to participate in government. The ease with which rebellious elements overthrew governments demonstrated the fragile nature of political authority in America. Its control rested more on the willingness of people to obey than on the use of force. Rulers learned they must accommodate the governed, if they wished to retain power and preserve peace.

The fate of the Dominion of New England taught similar lessons in England. In addition to the internal tensions generating rebellion, new pressures came from a crown eager to establish a tighter grip on its colonies, extract more wealth, and make defense secure. The new bands of royal officials sent to America quickly discovered that they lacked power to impose their will. Few in number, isolated from all but a favored clique of colonists, without military forces to back them up, royal officials eventually had to come to terms with American leaders.

In a fit of centralizing zeal, the crown in the late seventeenth century attempted to set aside the proprietary and corporate charters and turn them into royal colonies. These efforts failed. Both the proprietaries and corporate colonies fought back and with concessions managed to preserve a large degree of private power. In the course of defending themselves against English encroachment, Americans learned how to manipulate the levers of power in London and how to enter into satisfactory and profitable relationships with royal officials. The tendencies of this political system took clearer shape in the last seventy-five years of the colonial period.

THE STRUCTURE OF COLONIAL POLITICS IN THE EIGHTEENTH CENTURY

On a Sunday in midwinter (1750), the 101st anniversary of the execution of King Charles I, the minister of a fashionable Boston church advised his parishioners "that no civil rulers are to be obeyed when they enjoy things inconsistent with the words and command of God" nor should men submit to government "at the expense of that which is the great and sole end of government, the common good and welfare of society." A quarter century after Jonathan Mayhew preached his sermon against "unlimited Submission and Nonresistance to the Higher Power," Americans took up arms against their king, defending, they believed, their rights and human liberty. Justifying their revolution as a struggle to perserve self-

government, the colonists thought they were upholding freedoms established during a century and a half of settlement.

Mayhew's sharp warning against tyranny underscored the fact that the colonists enjoyed unusual scope in governing themselves. The distance and weakness of British authority enabled Americans to develop working institutions and traditions of self-government. But these arrangements evolved without plan and were outside the sanction of the formal constitution which supposedly governed England and its colonies.

Imperial Control

From the beginning, the king had primary responsibility for colonial government. He granted and annulled charters, appointed royal governors, and had to supervise colonial development. Though the crown had relied initially on private enterprise to plant colonies, by the middle of the eighteenth century it had assumed control of all but five of the thirteen colonies. Parliament regulated trade according to mercantilist principles but the king enforced the laws. During the Restoration, Charles II (1660–1685) and James II (1685–1688) attempted to centralize administration. The Privy Council, the king's chief administrative body, established fact-finding committees to advise the crown on colonial affairs.

Because of more pressing matters at home and in Europe, no permanent government body administered the colonies. In 1696, the Board of Trade was created. Pressure to establish the Board of Trade came principally from those interested in a colonial economic development which would assure the primacy of British interests. The board advised the Privy Council on commercial questions, helped frame instructions to royal governors, and reviewed colonial legislation. But it did not have executive power. Moreover it had to compete with other agencies of the royal bureaucracy, such as the Admiralty, the Treasury, and the Secretary of State, for control of colonial affairs. The board's effectiveness varied with the involvement and competence of its membership. Many of its members showed little interest in its business, ignoring conditions in the colonies. This failure of the board to develop into an effective organ for imperial control reflected a general indifference in Britain to strengthening control over the colonies, despite the wishes of the crown and some political leaders. Prosperity, at home *and* in the colonies, provided the best measure of success for a mercantilist empire. The empire's growing wealth confirmed the wisdom of allowing a loose rein to distant but profitable settlements. Tightening British control might provoke controversy in Parliament or in the colonies, reactions neither the king nor his ministers desired. It was much easier and cheaper to let colonists control their own affairs, just as it had seemed wise to employ private rather than public enterprise to establish colonies in the first place. Effective English control would have required the creation of a large expensive colonial bureaucracy in America and England, and a permanent commitment of troops to defend the colonies.

Americans themselves shouldered these responsibilities in peacetime, through the militia, relying on British regulars in time of full-scale war. Financing an adequate civil service and military force raised some difficult questions. The king could not tax, but Parliament had never taxed colonists in the seventeenth century either and to do so after they had grown accustomed to self-taxation was politically dangerous. Nor could the Americans be counted on to contribute voluntarily to the royal treasury. So long as the colonies grew rapidly, and their increasing exports enabled them to remain Britain's best customer, prudence dictated to "let sleeping dogs lie," a maxim favored by Sir Robert Walpole, the king's "prime minister," and a leading figure in British government between 1721 and 1742. After the turbulence of civil war, Restoration, and a Glorious Revolution, England enjoyed political stability and rapid economic growth, and none wished to disturb things.

In these circumstances politicians preferred peace to reform. Moreover, few entirely appreciated the extent to which the Americans had chipped away at British power in America. The colonial elites and their instruments of government grew in influence and self-confidence, often silently undermining British authority. Americans did not challenge directly the theory of the constitution under which king and Parliament were sovereign. This was unnecessary so long as colonists succeeded in a long war of attrition and evasion against external control.

Until the 1760s not even the Americans, let alone Britons, realized how much their conceptions of sovereignty had diverged. Consequently, lack of royal control during the formative years of settlement, compounded by the ineffectiveness of later attempts to strengthen it, left king and Parliament supreme only in theory. As long as Americans could get their way by manipulation they did not challenge the notion of British supremacy. But well before the revolutionary crisis they were aware that government rests on the consent of the governed.

Rise of the Assemblies

The principal instruments of self-government were the colonial legislatures. Their rise illuminates the process of political development in America. In the seventeenth century the councils, the local elite, together with the governor, usually dominated provincial politics. As colonial society became more complex and as additional settlements opened up, new fortunes were made and new families became prominent. The council could not find places for all these ambitious aspirants. Many looked to the lower house as the arena in which they could best advance their interests. As a result, the governors found it increasingly difficult to manage affairs by reaching accommodations with councillors' cliques, who in turn were losing their influence over the lower house. From advisory bodies without the power to initiate law—established initially on the sufferance of the crown or the proprietors—the lower houses persistently enlarged their influence until by the end of the colonial period they had become the most powerful branch of government.

Britons regarded the colonial legislatures as subordinate bodies created by higher authority and subject to external control, but Americans ran assemblies like miniature parliaments. Through persistent effort they assumed the power to control provincial finance and taxation, to pay the salaries of royal officials, and to issue paper money and like Parliament they regulated their own membership and internal business. Assemblies sometimes went beyond Parliament's power, encroaching further on the executive jurisdiction by appointing certain important officials and depriving the governor of patronage.

The Royal Governor

The legislature's chief antagonist in their quest for power was the governor, the king's or the proprietor's stand-in. As the colony's chief executive, he lacked both the power and the prestige which enabled the king and his ministers in England to manage Parliament. The governor had formidable responsibilities: to defend the royal interests and enforce British law, protect his colony against attack, and at the same time promote harmony among the colonists. These tasks proved virtually impossible because he lacked the power to impose his will, nor could he count on colonial cooperation short of bowing to local pressures and demands that violated his instructions.

Governors, like other royal officials in America and England, expected to make money. Some purchased their offices, at a high cost, from persons unwilling to emigrate. Officials soon discovered that cooperation with the colonists was the surest way to profit from an office and accumulate fees and land grants. The governor's fear of removal should he antagonize powerful interests intensified the tendency to seek accommodation. In England enemies and rivals schemed to oust him. Disgruntled colonists sent agents to London to undermine the governor's position and to cooperate with the rivals who wanted his job. A governor unable to administer his colony smoothly, one who stirred up opposition in America and England, became a political liability and was presumably unfit to handle his job.

Self-interest thus encouraged governors to give way to colonial demands. His lack of sufficient power to resist made a virtue of such a course. Britain relied on the colonists to pay the governors but no colony established adequate salaries. Governors and legislatures haggled chronically, but the colonists had the advantage because the executive could not force them to vote

acceptable compensation and the crown proved unwilling to assume the burden.

Lacking financial independence, governors also lacked enough patronage to control influential colonial politicians. Officials in England filled many of the most lucrative American positions and the colonists also encroached on the governor's appointive power. Thus a governor responsible for enforcing the navigation laws had no power over customs officials chosen in England; and customs collectors who honestly attempted to enforce the trade laws encountered colonial judges and juries who repeatedly acquitted violators. Governors and collectors thus found it more prudent and profitable to ignore smuggling of French sugar into the colonies. American traders preferred to bribe royal officials rather than pay the tax, thus modestly increasing business expenses but maximizing profits.

Some governors learned their lessons slowly and only after much difficulty. For instance, Francis Nicholson, governor of Virginia (1698–1705), who was reputed to be "so abusive in his words and actions as not only to treat our best gentlemen with scurrilous names of dogs, rogues, villains, dastards, cheats, and cowards," but also "our best women with the names of whores, bitches, jades, etc.," obviously had lost the confidence of his people. Although a governor *appeared* to have the ability to rule independently, his lack of financial security, the uncertainty of tenure, and a desire to profit from office taught him that accommodation was the path to success. A broadening of political participation which enabled a growing percentage of adult males to participate in government compounded his difficulties. Politics became more turbulent and democratic than in Britain.

The Electorate

In Britain the landed aristocracy and some of the most successful representatives of the merchant class dominated politics. Property qualifications kept most people from voting and facilitated parliamentary control by a few. Some of the titled families with extensive estates had several parliamentary seats in their pockets ("pocket," or "rotten," boroughs) and could also count on the support of friends and relatives among the gentry. Farmers, artisans, and tradespeople either played no role in elections or passively deferred to rule by their landlords and customers. Thus a small and controlled electorate enabled a landed and mercantile elite to rule.

The electorate in America was, relative to the total population, much larger. Many farmers had enough land to satisfy the property qualification for voting, which in England disfranchised most citizens. American voters also inclined toward deference to the large planters, wealthy merchants, and professionals, but it was much harder to control elections. The enlarged electorate retained the power to defy local magnates and once aroused it was too numerous to manipulate easily.

The structure of representation posed further obstacles. Members of Parliament represented counties and boroughs as they existed in medieval times when Parliament emerged. Areas that lost population over the centuries still kept their seats whereas other growing parts of the country that had not been represented in the Middle Ages sent no one to the House of Commons. For this reason families controlling rotten boroughs with few voters retained their power while expanding and important parts of the country remained unrepresented.

Such inequities were less common in America. There, legislative districts had to be created repeatedly. In Massachusetts each town, and in Virginia each county, sent delegates to the assembly. New towns and counties were usually represented along with the old. As the older counties and towns grew in population, they often split, each entitled to representatives. Representation roughly followed the distribution of population, and hence rotten boroughs did not develop, although in the eighteenth century newly settled areas complained of underrepresentation. Rapid growth in population and the extension of settlements into new areas regularly increased the size of the colonial assemblies as new members came from freshly created districts. The size of the body and newness of its members often made the assembly difficult to manage. A governor or a fac-

tion that attempted to buy off opposition found that the numbers that had to be appeased steadily grew.

No modern political parties existed in colonial America to arouse the voters or to nominate candidates espousing rival programs and appealing for mass support. Because average citizens had not voted in Europe, many of those eligible in America showed no interest in politics. Most worked their farms or at their trades, leaving the management of public offices to their "betters."

Without parties, colonial ruling groups formed factions, loose groups of individuals temporarily allied to pursue immediate political advantage by obtaining lucrative offices, land grants, and contracts.

Politics of Faction

The governor had to navigate the dangerous waters of factional politics. He tried to win the support of the most powerful factions, thereby hoping to influence the council and the legislature. But every time he made a friend, he also made an enemy. The governor could never accommodate everyone, nor could his supporters be certain of maintaining control. Factions out of power harassed the governor and his allies. The tendency of dominant factions to quarrel among themselves over the spoils created instability, and new alliances were formed. Moreover, as successful new groups emerged in trade, farming, or the professions, they too demanded political recognition. An apathetic electorate saw little opportunity for ordinary citizens to gain anything through politics. From time to time, however, voters reacted to threats to their interests or saw ways to benefit themselves politically. Baptists suffering religious disabilities in Virginia or Massachusetts, frontiersmen anxious over Indian depredations, farmers and merchants desiring paper money, Scotch-Irish Presbyterians jealous of Quaker political control in Pennsylvania— these and other varied interests periodically entered politics. When interest groups engaged actively in politics, more people went to the polls contesting elections hotly, and campaigns involved issues, not simply rival personalities. But political involvement seldom lasted. Once a group had obtained a specific objective, it gave up the struggle, lapsed back into traditional apathy and left politics to the intrigue of factions.

The clash of factions and the periodic outbursts of aroused socioeconomic interests made colonial politics turbulent. More often than not, however, elections went uncontested; some communities even declined to be represented in order to save money. In most, self-perpetuating cliques of leading families held office and filled vacancies. "Go into every village in New England," John Adams once observed, "and you will find that the office of justice of the peace, and even the place of representative, which has ever depended only on the freest election of the people, have generally descended from generation to generation in three or four families at most." Ambitious and talented newcomers found it more prudent to serve an apprenticeship under the dominant gentry than to challenge it directly. Loyalty and faithful service usually earned advancement up the officeholding ladder. Sometimes, however, the ruling groups quarreled among themselves, or aspirants lacked patience to wait for recognition. If a county courthouse ring failed to repulse the challengers, a new faction took over.

Politics was more competitive in some colonies than in others. Politics in a colony whose population grew rapidly, pushing into new regions, and which was divided by ethnic, religious, and sectional interests, tended to be competitive. Pennsylvania politics, for instance, was competitive because it had a diverse social order with a great commercial center in Philadelphia balancing a large and rapidly growing rural hinterland. And numerous Quakers, Scotch-Irish, and Germans fought for political advantage. The division between supporters and opponents of the proprietors further heated up the colony's politics. In contrast, South Carolina politics remained relatively uncompetitive. There a planter-merchant elite of large rice and indigo planters and Charleston merchants, mostly slave-owning Anglicans, ruled the province. Until 1760, the Indians kept whites from filling up the back country and bring-

ing sectional, ethnic, religious, and economic diversity to the colony.

Where politicians competed, attitudes toward authority began to change. Government, originally conceived as an instrument to control human passions, became the object of contests for power. People began to view the state as an instrument for self-advancement. Those wielding power had triumphed at the polls or behind the scenes; they made no claim to a divine right to rule. The seed was being sown for the day when revolutionary Americans declared that "governments derive their just power from the consent of the governed."

The seed bore strange fruit in the case of John Peter Zenger, a New York newspaper editor, prosecuted in 1734-1735 for criticizing the governor but freed by a jury which disregarded English law. The law held that criticism of government was seditious since governments supposedly could not survive public attack. The New York jury insisted that because Zenger published the truth he was immune from punishment. This decision did not bind future courts and the American tradition of freedom of speech has roots much more complex than Zenger's case, but it pointed to the future when freedom of press came to be regarded as an indispensable condition of free government. English governors, fearful of antagonizing powerful local politicians, initiated few successful attacks on the press. Colonial legislatures, however, without similar restraints, were the principal enemies of a free press and often punished critics for contempt.

Though before the 1760s colonists had not yet defended popular sovereignty and freedom to criticize government, they were much less respectful of authority than were the first generations of settlers or their contemporaries in eighteenth-century Europe. Tradition required that the humble members of society defer to rule by their social superiors. For the most part, Americans conformed. Subtly and slowly, however, habits of deference fell away in a social order lacking either a nobility or other familiar ruling elements. With wealth so abundant in America, shrewd and enterprising newcomers constantly climbed the ladder, forcing their way into prominence and edging aside established families. When members of the gentry competed for the votes of farmers and artisans, it became increasingly difficult to know to whom deference was due.

THE SILENT REVOLUTION

In 1645, John Winthrop, recently defeated for reelection as governor of Massachusetts, lectured his people "about the authority of the magistrates and the liberty of the people." "It is you yourselves," he reminded them, "who have called us to this office, and, being called by you, we have our authority from God, . . . the contempt and violation whereof hath been vindicated with examples of divine vengeance." A century later, a Scottish physician traveling through the colonies reported that in Pennsylvania "their government is a kind of anarchy," in New Jersey "the House of Assembly . . . was chiefly composed of mechanicks and ignorant wretches, obstinate to the last degree" and in Rhode Island, government "is somewhat democratick" with royal officials afraid to "exercise their office for fear of the fury and unruliness of the people."

Slowly but steadily Americans fashioned political arrangements that differed from those brought from Europe or those which persisted in the Old World. King and Parliament remained supreme in theory, but the working constitution of the empire permitted Americans to carve out areas in which they were virtually self-governing. Yet few in England or America realized before the 1760s the tenuous nature of English authority or how much independence Americans actually enjoyed. Within the colonies, small groups of leading citizens held power but with less security than their English counterparts. A larger electorate and unstable ruling groups, more easily penetrated and challenged, weakened authority whether exercised by the English or Americans and gave individuals greater scope to shape their own lives.

By the end of the colonial period white Americans were not only the most prosperous but also the freest people in the world. Men did not transplant intact the ways of the Old World to the New. In America they found freedom from English control and an abundance of resources that liberated individual energies, raised the level of aspiration, and enabled people to mold the world in which they lived. These efforts evolved into a new material and political order, as well as into a social order that became distinctly American.

Chapter 5
Sources of American Nationality

In the spring of 1790, almost fifteen years after the American colonies declared their independence, sadness gripped the capital of the young republic. Twenty thousand Philadelphians paid their respects to an individual who had come to symbolize all that was distinctively American. Benjamin Franklin was dead, after a life that had spanned the last seventy years of the colonial period. This son of a Boston soapmaker had prospered and won fame both in America and Europe as a statesman, inventor, scientist, and philanthropist. His career provided an example to all enlightened men that genius in the humbly born flowered in a New World which rewarded talent and enterprise. Franklin's life dramatically confirmed a growing conviction that in America man might realize his fullest potential.

Franklin, a self-made man, had little formal schooling. As an apprentice he quarreled with his elder brother, a Boston printer, and moved to Philadelphia. Starting without connections or capital, his talents quickly won both. Franklin was wealthy enough at forty-two to retire. Although isolated from the centers of scientific learning, his experiments in electricity earned the acclaim of Europe's leading intellectuals. Franklin believed in a benevolent God who expected men to do good to others and throughout his life he promoted many schemes for public betterment. Yet Franklin remained always a shrewd politician with a keen instinct for self-advertisement. Fame, money, and position allowed him to instruct others on the path to success, preaching all the godly virtues, such as temperance, silence, order, moderation, chastity, and humility. Franklin attributed success to mastery of them, though his fathering an illegitimate son left questions about his chastity, his ambition and self-promotion raised doubts about his humility, and silence was as unnatural to him as was order.

More revealing than the discrepancies between Franklin's personal ideals and his behavior was the assumption that in America virtue received its just rewards, that man had a real chance to improve himself. America seemed exempt from the infirmities that debased mankind elsewhere. "The Divine Being," Franklin wrote, "seems to have manifested his Approbation . . . by the remarkable Prosperity with which He has been pleased to favor the whole Country."

As his fame spread on two continents Franklin came to symbolize "the new race of men" which some saw springing from the New World, people free from the tyranny, ignorance, poverty, and injustice that hindered mankind's pursuit of happiness elsewhere. Franklin's career suggested that the American social order was an environment uniquely hospitable to the individual's search for fulfillment.

THE SOCIAL STRUCTURE

The ease with which Franklin climbed the colonial social ladder represents a specific instance of a common experience in America. Men were not permanently tied to the social class of their birth. Through their own efforts and luck, they could improve their position. American society, like Europe's, was stratified with elites at the top, but the forms and extent of stratification differed in the New World.

A clear and measurable gradation of status, one that determined men's positions in the social hierarchy, existed in Europe. Those at the top usually possessed wealth, good family, and power. At the apex stood the royal family and the greater nobility, followed by the lesser nobility and landed gentry who ruled over the lower orders. Despite some vertical mobility, law, custom, and limited opportunity fixed most people's station at birth. The sons of peasants expected to remain peasants just as the nobility expected to bequeath their privileged status to their children. Tradition and social custom legitimized this arrangement. So long as men labored at their callings faithfully, there might be peace and order; rebellion brought anarchy. And the great mass of people in the lower strata fatalistically accepted their lot. To be sure, a few aspired to a better life, and even fewer actually achieved an improvement of their condition, but most labored at their tasks "bowed by the weight of centuries."

The first settlers in America intended no great social transformations. But from the beginning American society diverged from Old World patterns. Since few of England's wellborn migrated, the colonies lacked both royalty and nobility, that is, a hereditary aristocracy, to occupy the top of the social order. Nor among the white population was there a large mass of permanently landless folk such as comprised the bulk of English society. The typical white American was a landowner and, even if in possession of a small holding, it was far easier to acquire and keep property than had been the case in England where the numbers of farmers declined in the seventeenth and eighteenth centuries. Without either upper or lower strata comparable to Europe's, the colonies developed a large middle class that included propertied farmers, artisans, merchants, and professionals.

American Elites

There were colonial elites, however. Neither wealth, nor honor, nor power were equally distributed. But the upper strata in America differed markedly from their peers in Europe. In the first place, the American elite was self-created, not hereditary, recruited from individuals who made the most of opportunities in America. Though some of the elite stemmed from English gentry who migrated armed with advantages, even they had to work hard at securing and maintaining a superior position in the colonies.

Wealth, rather than birth, became the principle source of differentiation in American society, and even inherited property had to be safeguarded. The sons of successful men could not maintain their family's social standing unless they carefully managed their inheritance. The colonial elite, no leisured aristocracy, were usually hardworking estate managers or merchants. Also, a position of dominance brought insecurity with it. Competitive newcomers eagerly seized opportunities, made their way up the social ladder, and pushed to the top. Without strong legal or institutional barriers to hamper them, and since wealth

determined eminence, opportunities for rising were readily available.

Southern planters came closest to achieving a way of life resembling the English upper classes. Operating large estates worked by slaves, building impressive, elegantly furnished homes, the Southern gentleman imitated the English squirearchy. Yet for all their cultural pretensions, the planters remained provincials. These speculators in land, producers of tobacco, rice, and indigo, and drivers of slaves had their ranks penetrated often by newcomers. Their inheritance laws (primogeniture and entail) resembled those by which the English aristocracy made certain that the eldest son received and bequeathed the family fortune intact. In America, however, fathers could generally endow their younger sons with land and status, making such practices unnecessary or impractical.

Urban elites were even more unstable. In cities and towns trade afforded the principal means to wealth but a merchant's success involved risks. Overseas trade required heavy investments in long voyages and speculation in unstable markets. Such fortunes could be quickly made but they could be lost just as quickly. Equally uncertain were the profits dependent on political favor, such as contracts to supply the British army and navy. Keen competition for these favors meant that a merchant enjoying them one day might lose them in the shifting winds of patronage politics. Nor could those who made money in trade safely withdraw it for reinvestment elsewhere. No corporate bonds or stocks, and few government securities, existed; land speculation was tempting but risky. Yet if he remained in trade the successful merchant exposed himself anew to the uncertainties of business. As a result shrewd newcomers pushed aside older merchants. Thus the roster of leading urban families in the late colonial period differed from those of earlier generations.

Instability similarly affected the professions. With no clear qualifications for becoming a preacher, lawyer, or doctor, few men received formal training except clergymen. Thus no widely accepted professional standards of practice developed. American doctors, observed a welltrained Scottish physician, were "all empyricks, having no knowledge of learning, but what they have acquired by bare experience." Medicine had not yet become a lucrative occupation. Many doctors took "care of a family for the value of a Dutch dollar a year, which makes the practice of physick a mean thing and unworthy of the application of a gentleman." Professional schools, voluntary regulatory associations, and public licensing systems rarely existed. Consequently people had little protection against charlatan doctors or shyster lawyers. As a result the status of these occupations suffered and membership in them did not assure public respect.

Most white Americans, however, were farmers, and this group was also mobile and unstable. Landowners constantly bought and sold property, abandoning a developed farm to establish themselves on fresh lands, investing in mills, cutting timber, operating taverns—always looking for the main chance that meant admission into the elite. A thin and often-breached line separated the aspiring from the established. As a result, European titles designating a person's social status lost their meaning in America. In Connecticut, a traveler noted that his innkeeper used the title "Lady" and observed: "No, I cannot tell for what for she is the homeliest piece both as to mien, make, and dress that ever I saw, . . . but it is needless to dispute her right to the title since we know many upon whom it is bestowed who have as little right as she." Confusion in the use of titles revealed ambiguities in the status hierarchy and the difficulty of determining rank. One consequence was, in the words of Gilbert and Sullivan:

> When everyone is somebody,
> Then no one is anybody.

Inequality

As colonial society matured in the eighteenth century, opportunity for advancement narrowed. In the more densely settled seaboard, the best land passed into private ownership and its value rose accordingly. The sons of large families had difficulty finding attractive sites for farms near their homes. One could always migrate to less-developed areas with abundant land. Many did but others hesitated to leave family, friends, and a familiar environment and preferred a dependent

status or took up marginal lands. Likewise, those who stayed in the older areas found it harder to penetrate the community's upper strata of well-established families whereas newer settlements had more room at the top.

In the eighteenth century, wealth became increasingly concentrated. In Boston, for instance, the top 15 percent of the taxpayers owned 66 percent of assessed taxable property in 1771 compared to 52 percent in 1687. Similar stratification occurred in a rural community such as Chester county, Pennsylvania. Both areas experienced economic expansion and population growth, which offered the shrewd and enterprising opportunity to accumulate fortunes, whereas the less enterprising or less lucky became tenant farmers, laborers, servants, or seamen. Thus the percentage of those without property but not dependent on others doubled in Boston between 1687 and 1771. At the same time, the relative standing of the moderately well-off artisans, mechanics, and shopkeepers declined, though their absolute welfare probably improved as the community as a whole became more prosperous.

Foreign travelers in the colonies noticed the absence of the very poor so prevalent in Europe. Though poverty claimed fewer victims in America, the poor were still numerous enough to require public assistance. New York City's poorhouse sheltered 423 paupers in 1772—not many however out of a population of 25,000. Even in the prosperous colonies, there were orphaned children, blind, aged, and handicapped persons in need of public support. And Negroes, free and slave, in the North and South, remained permanently trapped in a degraded and exploited condition. Yet, for most whites, America offered greater opportunity than was available elsewhere.

RELIGION IN THE NEW WORLD

Unexpected circumstances not only altered traditional social relationships, they also transformed established religious forms. In the seventeenth century no man could publicly reject religion. The church helped the state maintain order, giving aid considered essential to the governing process. Until the Protestant Reformation shattered the religious monopoly of Catholicism, Europeans shared a single faith, embodied in one established church. People were born into the Church, accepted its doctrines, rituals, and discipline, and provided for its material support. In return, the Church offered to help men find salvation.

Even after Luther and Calvin broke with Rome, people remained convinced that their church—whether Lutheran, Presbyterian, Congregationalist, or Catholic—embodied the true faith. Religious error, or heresy, must be checked. Heretics sinned against their own souls by denying spiritual truth, and they endangered the souls of others. This obliged the state and the church to repress dissent as a threat to all men and to the peace of the community.

Both Massachusetts and Virginia acted on these principles when they established state churches, one Calvinist, the other Anglican. Massachusetts zealously suppressed heresy, exiling Roger Williams and Anne Hutchinson, and executing several Quakers who would not flee. Yet initial denials of religious freedom, though in keeping with accepted European practice, collapsed in the face of pressures that in the eighteenth century produced a gradual victory for the still novel principle of toleration.

Religious Toleration

Toleration spread because religious persecution proved impractical. New settlements in need of labor could ill afford to turn away immigrants who worshiped differently. Profit-hungry trading companies and proprietors discovered that it made more sense to welcome the able-bodied whatever their beliefs. But New England stood in no such need since the Puritan colonies received large numbers of coreligionists fleeing from persecution in England. Outside the closely knit townships of New England, settlements were dispersed and often without churches to enforce uniformity. Should a colony attempt to suppress dissent, those persecuted could easily find refuge elsewhere in other more tolerant communities. The wilderness always offered an escape. England depended on private enterprise to establish colonies in America, and paid little attention to the

colonizing group's religious inclinations. This enabled Catholics in Maryland and Puritans in New England to worship as they pleased despite the fact that in England tolerance of nonconforming Protestants did not come until after 1689.

Officially the Church of England was the established church in Britain, and other denominations, though tolerated, suffered disabilities. Anglicanism was likewise established in Virginia, Maryland, the Carolinas, and Georgia. But elsewhere it existed in competition with other churches, and in New England at the sufferance of the Congregationalist establishment. For these reasons religious diversity came to America very early, and the passage of time strengthened it. Thus, the crown unintentionally promoted religious variation.

New sources of immigration in the eighteenth century contributed to the diversity as Scotch-Irish Presbyterians, English Quakers, German Lutherans, and Pietist sects poured into the colonies. At the same time that the religious character of the Americans became more varied, new colonies appeared which from the beginning treated all religions alike, favoring none with state support. Pennsylvania was the most notable haven for dissenters but they also found a tolerant spirit in New Jersey and New York.

Pennsylvania tolerance rested on more than expediency. Quakers, like other Pietists, and like Roger Williams, held that religious belief was a private matter between man and God; the state therefore had no right to intrude. Toleration was necessary so that each person could commune freely with God. They insisted that the state respect man's conscience. Quakers and other Pietists thus added the force of principle to the lure of expediency that had strengthened the idea of toleration.

As toleration spread, so did diversity in belief. And as many Americans became more concerned with their lives in this world than the next, it became harder for the state to persecute dissent. Ultimately, the sheer number of competing denominations—Congregationalists, Anglicans, Presbyterians, Baptists, Quakers, Lutherans, German and Dutch Reformed, to mention only the leading groups—prevented any one from enjoying a monopoly. Catholics, however, feared and hated by all Protestant denominations were subject to discrimination.

An even more radical change than the spread of toleration was a steady erosion in the ties between church and state. Some colonies such as Pennsylvania and Rhode Island did not establish churches. Contrary to orthodox expectations, these communities remained peaceful and prosperous. Elsewhere religious establishments failed to achieve or maintain the influence of European state churches. In the South, dissenters often outnumbered Anglicans and the Church of England was the established church in name only. Establishments remained strongest in New England because of weaker pressures from dissenting sects. Yet even in the Puritan colonies, growing numbers of Anglicans, Quakers, and Baptists forced the acceptance of change. They refused to contribute to the Congregational churches. The Congregationalists preserved establishment by grudgingly permitting dissenters to allocate their church taxes for support of their own sects. Thus Massachusetts in the eighteenth century acquired multiple establishments.

The separation of church and state in some colonies, and the weakening of traditional ties between the two elsewhere, were the roots of an American tradition according to which religious concerns are private matters. Already in the colonial period, a new mode of organizing religious life—denominationalism—began to replace the idea of established churches. In the absence of state support, churches became voluntary associations, enjoying legal equality with all other sects. Lacking state compulsion to enforce membership and provide financial support, denominations depended on lay support and had to recruit adherents. Nevertheless, the absence of state aid had advantages. In order to grow, denominations had to serve public needs, involve citizens actively in their affairs, and compete for members. The voluntary principle conformed to the Pietist belief that exalted personal religious experiences over formal belief and ritual. Even the established Anglican church in the South reflected the powerful forces transforming the churches in America. Theoretically controlled by the Bishop of London, Anglican churches fell under the control of prominent laymen in the parish and had to rely on voluntary support.

Revivalism

The power of the voluntary principle in nurturing a vigorous religious life became strikingly clear in the 1730s when an upheaval called the Great Awakening took place. During the final forty years of the colonial period, Americans experienced recurrent religious revivals that reached a peak in the 1740s but reappeared for over a century. Revivals were intense, emotional reawakenings among people racked with the guilt of sin, the fear of damnation, and the desire for rebirth. Revivalism was also a technique for saving souls by shaking men out of their indifference and filling the hearts of sinners with terror. Yet they also offered a chance for salvation. The message of the Awakening spread in the colonies through the powerful oratory of preachers, such as Jonathan Edwards of Massachusetts, and the English revivalist George Whitefield. The signs of sin, they proclaimed, were everywhere: Sabbath breaking, abstention from church services, intemperance, a love for luxury, and, of course, loose morals.

During the second half of the seventeenth century, New England ministers endlessly noted and lamented a decline of piety since the days of the founding generation. Yet denunciations, however vivid or powerful, could not hold back change. The children of the Calvinist first settlers, born in America, had not shared the experiences of the founders. Their lives and aspirations were defined, not by the covenant with God, but by the prospects of settling a new land. The Puritan creed sanctioned hard work and perseverance, and urged men to pursue their callings energetically; but later generations found it increasingly difficult to subordinate worldly ambitions to spiritual duties. Life in the New World demonstrated that on earth men were not prisoners of a prearranged fate. They possessed a free will, and the ability to advance their earthly fortunes. Deviation from the original mission of the first settlers generated tension and guilt because although later generations no longer entirely believed in the ancient faith, they could not totally abandon their spiritual heritage. Instead, men sought ways of purging their guilt.

New Englanders attempted to halt the decline in piety by loosening church membership standards. Before 1648 only children of those who had experienced conversion, the "Saints," were baptized into the church. Subsequently children of the unconverted could become halfway members, if they led outwardly pious lives. Eventually, most congregations abolished the distinction between halfway and full members, no longer requiring a specific conversion experience for admission.

In the 1690s, alarm spread through Massachusetts when several hysterical teen-age girls in Salem convinced authorities that they were the victims of witchcraft. The craze led to the arrest of over 400 alleged witches and warlocks and the execution of twenty persons. Following four months of frenzy the colony regained its senses and the imprisonments and executions stopped. Though belief in witchcraft was widespread throughout the Western World, the outbreak in Massachusetts at that time provided a way to acknowledge that sin flourished, and that the agents of the devil lurked about everywhere, even among close neighbors. By identifying and punishing the witches, the preachers, with the state's aid, felt they were battling spiritual decline. By destroying the "forces of evil," the Puritan clergy briefly resumed the great power they had enjoyed during the founding generation.

But faith continued to decline. Conversions were fewer, church attendance dropped, and in New England and elsewhere people became increasingly absorbed in this world, not the next. As men mastered their environment, the supernatural concerned them less. Man, rather than God, became the center of their universe.

This secularization of outlook occurred slowly and unevenly. People, only a few generations removed from a time when salvation was regarded as man's first concern, did not easily shake off centuries of belief. From time to time they encountered ill-fortune. When affairs did not go as they hoped or intended, they doubted their capacities and found refuge in the supernatural. The revival offered hope. By confession and reliance on God's mercy, one might be saved. Though the ministers preached that only God could save, they also demanded that their listeners repent and actively seek forgiveness. In an extraordinary intellectual and emotional enterprise, Jonathan Edwards, among others, attempted to update Calvinist theology and the forms of Christian worship to reverse the decline of faith and piety.

The religious revival was a communal experience. People gathered at the riversides and in the public squares in throngs, praying, singing, and writhing together. For a moment they found fellowship among other sinners.

The revival also offered temporary release from the pressures of everyday existence, as men joined with their neighbors, high and low, in a common demonstration of piety and community solidarity. Paradoxically, the increased religiosity of the revivals further weakened the hold of orthodox religion. Benevolence toward fellowmen became more important than doctrines or rituals. And since every man could be saved, this equality of spiritual opportunity matched the abundance of worldly opportunity in America. Self-confidence about earthly matters bred self-confidence about salvation. A century earlier orthodox Puritans had preached that salvation came only through selection by a sovereign and unpredictable God. The revival thus adjusted religious life to the American experience.

The Great Awakening had far-reaching consequences. Stress on ethical behavior as a sign of conversion gave impetus to a broad range of humanitarian concerns for the condition of the drunkard, the slave, and the helpless. The Awakening further weakened the hold of established churches, dividing many congregations. Some ministers resented the intrusion of itinerant preachers more gifted than they at exhorting crowds, and many Christians rejected the appeal to emotions which provoked the crowd to convulsions and wild shouting. As churches divided into pro- and anti-revival factions, the minority often withdrew to form new congregations. In this way dozens of new churches appeared in New England, some remaining Congregationalists, others becoming Baptist.

The inclination of antirevivalists to use state power to curb revivalism, and especially itinerant preachers, increased hostility to state control over spiritual affairs. Moreover, by further fragmenting the structure of American Christianity, by insisting that the churches must actively seek out sinners, and by involving people in a Christian crusade, the Great Awakening strengthened already existing tendencies toward denominationalism.

Yet its most important function was to relieve men temporarily of the guilt of secularism, the subordination of spiritual values to worldly ones. Through confession and rebirth, people found momentary relief and gained new psychological strength to resume the struggle for earthly happiness. The revival thus offered a continuing opportunity for intense but occasional spirituality that did not reverse the trend toward secularization.

By the end of the colonial period a distinctive American pattern of religious life had emerged, based on tolerance, church-state separation, and denominationalism. The particular needs of religion in the wilderness and the growing proliferation of sects helped to shape a distinctively American culture whose characteristics are further revealed by developments in education and science.

EDUCATION IN A NEW WORLD

Universal literacy and free public schooling for all did not arrive until the nineteenth century. In Europe and in the American colonies of the seventeenth and eighteenth centuries the upper classes enjoyed the luxury of formal education. Most children learned the skills they would need in life, acquired the values and attitudes of the adult world, and were taught to read by a literate relative or neighbor. Many remained illiterate.

The family and the church were the principal instruments by which society transmitted its standards of behavior from one generation to the next. The children of peasants learned how to work at home and in the fields. Those who became artisans learned their trade as apprentices in the households and shops of master craftsmen.

Schooling remained the preserve of the more fortunate members of society, those expected to provide leadership. In English preparatory schools young men trained for the professions. Those becoming lawyers, doctors, or merchants received further training from established members of the professions; others, especially aspiring clergymen, enrolled at the universities of Oxford and Cambridge. Since most occupations did not require formal education, and few needed the skills it developed, conditions which led to the democratization of educational opportunity did not then exist.

The situation in the colonies was similar, though the American environment subtly altered the character of education there. Settlers established schools and colleges but English patterns were not entirely appropriate to colonial conditions. The first generation of settlers, conscious that they shared an untamed wilderness with Indian tribes, considered uncivilized, did not stray far from European cultural norms. Colonists feared that the wilderness would engulf them, unless some of them were literate and trained in the professions. The pressure to establish schools was greatest in the Puritan colonies, especially Massachusetts. In the Bay colony, government forcefully attempted to achieve communal goals through state action. In 1642 the legislature required all towns with fifty families or more to maintain an elementary school and towns with 100 families had to establish a grammar school as well. Support for the schools became the responsibility of each town under threat of fines for noncompliance.

The hopes of the first generation went unfulfilled. Later generations, especially those living in the country, were reluctant to support schools, preferring instead to pay fines for noncompliance. As religious fervor declined, one of the principal impulses spurring the creation of public schools weakened. Furnishing a steady supply of ministers and teaching people to read the Bible became less urgent. In other colonies, where the initial religious impulses had been weaker and where formally educated leaders were more rare, government was even less disposed to establish schools and education became largely a voluntary effort. Moreover, the low density of population, an inclination to invest capital in farms and businesses rather than in social services, created additional obstacles. The well-to-do could hire tutors or pay fees at private schools; others did not need schooling to prosper.

Colonial Colleges

Higher education received greater support. Massachusetts founded Harvard College in 1636, but until the end of the seventeenth century Harvard stood alone. Those who did not attend the Puritan college had to journey to England, an alternative preferred by the sons of Southern planters. Eventually, however, sufficient pressure developed in Virginia to establish the College of William and Mary (1693) and fresh needs in New England led to the founding of Yale in 1701. After 1745 the number of colleges grew rapidly. By the end of the colonial period ten institutions of higher learning existed, compared with only two in England, although the American colleges could not yet be compared with the universities of Oxford and Cambridge.

The growth of colleges resulted from both sectarian and secular pressures. Over 100 college graduates arrived in New England during the Great Migration (1630–1640), many of them ministers. Thus from the beginning Massachusetts possessed educated leaders, lay and secular. To assure a constant supply of trained clergy and officials, Puritans established educational institutions that would transmit and perpetuate their values. Other groups followed: Anglicans created William and Mary, Baptists founded Brown, and Presbyterians established Princeton.

The weakening of the ties between church and state, and the acceptance of the voluntary principle in religious life, intensified the pressures for denominationally sponsored colleges. More than any other institution, the church became the center of communal life and a source of group identity. People thought of themselves as Massachusetts Congregationalists, Virginia Anglicans, or Pennsylvania Quakers. Sects which had to compete with one another for members, and which could not rely on state support, made special efforts to perpetuate their group in a religiously open society. The college became a vital foundation of denominational survival and growth.

Though sectarian energies established the colleges, they served more than the needs of the controlling denomination. The colonial colleges trained students in the liberal arts and sciences preparing them for a variety of callings, not solely the ministry. In the eighteenth century the percentage of graduates who became ministers declined as men found more rewarding careers in trade, government, law, and medicine.

While the colleges served the needs of sectarians, they also represented self-conscious efforts to maintain English cultural standards in America and to furnish society with an educated leadership that would maintain order. Without the existence of Harvard, a commencement orator warned in the 1670s, "The ruling class would have been subjected to mechanics, cobblers, and tailors; we would have no rights, honors or magisterial ordinances worthy of preservation, but plebiscites, appeals to base passions, and revolutionary rumblings." College-educated leaders, in turn, received training that fitted them for the responsibilities of their position in society, helping to preserve them from the "vice of a certain class, by giving them easy access to more refined pleasure and inspiring the mind with an abhorrence of low riot and contempt for brutal conversation." At least that was the theory.

The increasingly secular mission of the college gained strength in the eighteenth century. Though diverse sects established such new institutions as Columbia and Princeton, it was necessary to enlist support from other groups in order to obtain charters of incorporation from the legislatures. Conditions for such support were the admission of students regardless of creed and instruction that did not offend the sectarian sensibilities of the several groups that backed and attended the college. Colleges increasingly came to serve society's needs, rather than that of a single sect. The growing tendency among those entering college in the late colonial period to seek nonministerial careers further weakened denominationalism in higher education. College curricula began to reflect an interest in science and modern languages as well as the traditional emphasis on the classics, philosophy, and theology.

Despite the proliferation of colleges in America, and the vast labor invested in them, they achieved their original aims only partially. In England higher education remained a monopoly of the established church but in America the variety of sects prevented one group from dominating higher education. American colleges were less under the sway of the church, but they became more dependent upon community support, especially the newer institutions which lacked the extensive endowments of European universities. Whereas the faculties controlled European universities, American colleges fell into the hands of the trustees who represented the supporting community.

Thomas Jefferson and John Adams were college graduates, but Benjamin Franklin and George Washington were not. Because the American social order was open, talent, hard work, and genius counted for more and the possession of a college degree for less than in England. A college education was not so valuable in the competition for wealth and position as it later became; it was not yet a professional "union card."

TOWARD AN AMERICAN CULTURE

The Americans, a French visitor observed near the end of the colonial period, were "the western pilgrims . . . carrying along with them the great mass of arts, sciences, vigour, and industry which began long since in the east; they will finish the great circle." In less than two centuries, as British colonial subjects, the Americans developed a style of life that distinguished them from the rest of mankind. The attitudes and institutions people brought to America from Europe changed as settlers adapted themselves to a new environment. America appeared different from Europe because its people were generally more prosperous, freer to govern themselves, to worship as they pleased, and advance their individual position in society. Above all, the American was optimistic, confident of his power to control his destiny and reap earthly rewards.

Though the colonists transformed the nature of the state, the church, and the social structure,

they took only halting steps in the development of a native culture that expressed American imagination in the arts and sciences. From the beginning, the workings of nature aroused colonial curiosity. Scientific inquiry reflected American expansive opportunities and circumstances. Americans showed most interest in natural history. The wilderness was full of unfamiliar and unclassified specimens which colonists supplied European scientists. Those with scientific curiosity could make distinctive contributions in a field that required relatively little professional training, whereas the physical sciences demanded greater technical knowledge.

Ben Franklin, however, made important contributions to the understanding of electricity precisely because little was known about it in Europe. As an amateur, out of touch with Europe's learned world, Franklin could let his scientific imagination freely wander along original paths which those operating within the conventional boundaries of European scientific opinion did not follow. Moreover, Franklin's mind had a practical bent. Though his investigations originated in curiosity about the natural world, he also sought to make scientific knowledge useful.

Similarly, American medicine lacked professionalization at a time when the healing arts were still rudimentary. European doctors had little understanding of the causes and cure of disease. Learning their trades as apprentices, rather than through formal schooling, American doctors were less prone to perpetuate the mistaken theories that dominated much of European medicine. They were also more inclined to rely on natural cures and treatments developed from practical experience. Thus the first large-scale use of inoculation against smallpox occurred in Boston because professional medical opinion, which was skeptical, was not powerful enough to block the experiment. Subsequently the success of inoculation encouraged its spread throughout Europe.

The arts in America, like science, developed far from the centers of cultural life. The first American painters lacked the technical skills possessed by European artists. Their portraits, anything but sophisticated, were still simple and realistic renderings of their subjects. As the colonies matured, eighteenth-century painters acquired more skill and some American patrons demanded portraits more like those which flattered Europe's highborn. Artists, in imitating English styles, departed from the earlier colonial preference for pictures that were direct and honest.

The same ambivalence marked colonial architecture. Many styles influenced colonial buildings, reflecting the cultural diversity of the times. German, Dutch, and English, Anglicans and Puritans, erected the type of structures with which they were familiar. As the colonies prospered, public buildings and private residences became more costly and elaborate. American elites imitated the Georgian style favored by eighteenth-century English leaders. This was a pretentious, highly derivative and imitative architectural style. At the same time a distinctively American building form developed. The American colonial cottage, the home of the middle classes, was a simple yet graceful rectangular dwelling, notable for its light frame construction, its use of wood which in Europe was scarce, and its numerous windows.

For all their interest in the arts and sciences, the life of the mind and the play of the imagination remained remote from the center of colonial concern. These isolated provincials had to establish a society far from the centers of learning and culture. Americans concentrated on taming the wilderness and advancing their individual fortunes. Someday, they would paint pictures, write stories, and erect buildings at which others would marvel. But they would first have to create an American nation.

THE COLONIAL LEGACY

In less than 200 years a new society took shape in British North America. On an undeveloped continent European colonists established the foundations of a great nation. They came to the New World hoping to improve their lot, not to transform institutions or to establish a new civilization. Even the Puritans, driven by a vision of establishing a Zion in the Wilderness, sought to re-establish an archaic Christian commonwealth

they thought had once existed. Instead, Americans created something new, less by design than as the result of the interaction of traditions and values, largely English, which they brought with them, and strange, unanticipated circumstances with which they were confronted in the New World.

Vast, open spaces, material abundance, and weak English control played havoc with the transit of familiar social patterns. By the middle of the eighteenth century, enlightened circles in Europe regarded America as a social laboratory of human happiness. Americans also came to believe that, once freed from religious superstition and oppressive institutions, man could use intelligence to reform society and improve his lot. The Abbé Raynal saw America "as the asylum of freedom, . . . the cradle of future nations, and the refuge of the distressed." "In America," wrote another admiring Frenchman, Hector St. John de Crèvecoeur, "every thing is modern, peaceful, and benign." Elsewhere "misguided religious tyranny, and absurd laws, . . . depress and afflict mankind." In the New World, however, laws were "simple and just" and mankind had "regained the ancient dignity of our species."

Americans also began to perceive themselves as "a new race of men" well before they embarked on the road to revolution and nationhood. They still considered themselves Englishmen but they were also Americans. One became an American, not simply by being born in the colonies, but by experiencing its blessings. Whoever set foot in America and shared its bounty became an American, regardless of previous national origin. "*He* is an American," Crèvecoeur explained, "who, leaving behind him all his ancient prejudices and manners, receives new ones from the new mode of life he has embraced, the new government he obeys, and the new rank he holds." America knows "properly speaking, no strangers; this is every person's country."

The image of America taking shape in the colonies and spreading through Europe was of a society which had liberated man from the forces that enslaved people in the Old World. The state was no longer man's master but his servant. Wealth and power were no longer concentrated in the hands of a hereditary elite but were widely diffused. In the New World man experienced "a sort of resurrection," wrote Crèvecoeur. Previously he had "simply vegetated; he now feels himself a man, because he is treated as such. . . . The laws of his own country had overlooked him in his insignificancy; the laws of this country cover him with their mantle."

Widespread distribution of land provided the dynamic force behind this social transformation and principal form of wealth. A freehold gave a man dignity, independence, and the right to vote. "He is become a freeholder, from perhaps a German boor—he is now an American. . . . From nothing to start into being: from a servant to the rank of a master; from being the slave of some despotic prince to become a free man, invested with lands to which every municipal blessing is annexed." Crèvecoeur believed that a fundamental change occurred in personality. The American yeoman farmer forgot "that mechanism of subordination, that servility of disposition which poverty had taught him." The result was a liberation of human aspiration and energies.

Rising in the world, once the accomplishment of a few, now became a possibility for many. "No sooner did Europeans breathe American air," Crèvecoeur insisted, "than he forms schemes, and embarks in designs he never would have thought of in his own country," because "human industry has acquired a boundless field to exert itself in." Opportunity unleashed ambition as men discovered that hard work, sobriety, and honesty brought rewards that no king, nobleman, or bishop could thwart or tax collector confiscate. A life of active enterprise bred among "the highest and the lowest a singular keenness of judgment, unassisted by any academic light." Common sense, based on practical experience, rather than "shining talents and university knowledge" was the source of truth. The farmer who perched his son atop the plough as he drove through his fields taught him the way to success: "I am now doing for him . . . what my father formerly did for me," said Crèvecoeur's American farmer. The child learned the simple lesson: "Here men are workers." Above all America offered salvation through work, salvation through individual enterprise.

Through work people acquired property and with property they achieved worth: on "land is founded our rank, our freedom, our power as citizens, our importance as inhabitants." Yet Crèvecoeur sensed the danger of wealth as the measure of man's worth, as the means of liberation from the constraints of institutions.

FREEDOM OF THE INDIVIDUAL

Freedom was a two-edged sword. Corrupt institutions enslaved; weak or nonexistent ones could unleash the darkness as well as the light in man. America was not only a land of sober, decent farmers and merchants but of frontiersmen governed only by their passions, who preferred to drink and live by the gun than become industrious yeomen. Without the restraining influence of government or religion, man in the wilderness could descend into a state of war, each pitted against the other.

Crèvecoeur saw on the frontier the dark possibilities of the free individual. But he need not have looked to the outer edges of organized society for doubts. Ben Franklin, that living embodiment of the "new race of men," celebrated on two continents as the quintessential American —peaceful and benevolent, industrious and frugal, learned yet practical, democrat yet man of genius—found it possible to reconcile his conviction that man exists to do good with his belief that nothing must thwart Americans in their quest for wealth. Concerning the Indians, he once said: "If it be the design of Providence to extirpate these savages in order to make room for the cultivators of the earth, it seems not improbable that rum may be the appointed means. It has already annihilated all the tribes who formerly inhabited the sea coast."

Certain that God was on his side, the First American could sanction the destruction of one race for the "benefit" of another. The same incongruity touched Crèvecoeur when he visited Charleston, South Carolina. The richest colony in America, South Carolina was the home of the rice and indigo planters who cultivated large plantations with numerous slaves, dividing their time between their plantations and their mansions in Charleston, a city of wealth and luxury, "of joy, festivity, and happiness." No less than other Americans, colonial South Carolinians would some day revolt against Britain because they preferred to believe that "all men are created equal," "endowed by their Creator with certain unalienable rights," including "life, liberty, and the pursuit of happiness." Yet the basis of South Carolina society was slavery, an institution unknown in Britain itself. Crèvecoeur reported that in Charleston the "horrors of slavery are unseen" though they abound everywhere. People had become deaf to the cries of the suffering: "their hearts are hardened; they neither see, hear, nor feel for the woes of their poor slaves, from those whose painful labours all their wealth proceeds."

Herein lies the ambivalence of the colonial experience. Most Americans were in fact freer and materially better off than people anywhere else. The state was relatively weak and the individual enjoyed enormous scope within which to move, act, and think as he wished. The church also had lost much of its influence. Many lived remote from houses of worship, the state often failed to buttress the church, and growing confidence in human ability weakened dependence on the supernatural. Even the family lost some of the cohesive and stabilizing force it possessed in Europe. Children left home at an early age, set out on their own, as Ben Franklin did, often settling far from parents and relatives. They lived apart, among others like themselves, relying on their own exertions to sink or swim. The open spaces offered both escape and opportunity, escape from constraints that annoyed, opportunity to test one's powers against the environment.

Beginning in the 1760s Great Britain, required by its victory over the French in the Great War for Empire (1754–1761) to reorganize the empire, restricted American freedom. Threatened from without, the colonists perceived more clearly than before the extent to which their society had diverged from their English model. Forced to defend their way of life, the colonists identified the American cause with the cause of human freedom. They boasted, in the words of Crèvecoeur's farmer: "We have no princes, for whom we toil, starve, and bleed; we are the most perfect society now existing in the world. Here man is free as he ought to be." They went to war, they said, to remain that way.

When Crèvecoeur's countrymen read his glowing, idealized account of America, 500 abandoned their native land for the wilderness, settling in the Ohio country where they died of famine and disease. Other newcomers, before and since, fared better. But none found in America an escape from history. Crèvecoeur himself recognized the paradox of America. Nowhere were men as well off, yet even in the New World "one part of the human species are taught the art of shedding the blood of the other." The country where man was freest enslaved 20 percent of its population.

Throughout most of their history since becoming an independent nation, Americans have been torn between their vision of the free individual and the gnawing realization that unrestrained individualism crushes the weak and debases the strong. Yet out of the colonial experience grew a vision of human liberty and equality that found expression in a revolution and a new nation. "Almost everywhere," Crèvecoeur concluded, "liberty, so natural to mankind, is refused, or rather enjoyed but by their tyrants; the word slave, is the appellation of every rank who adore as a divinity, a being worse than themselves."

SUGGESTIONS FOR FURTHER READING

Suggestions for further reading are highly selective. Works available in paperback are starred (*). Students should consult Clarence Ver Steeg, *The Formative Years, 1607–1763* (1964) and Curtis P. Nettels, *Roots of American Civilization* (1938) for additional references.

INTRODUCTION

General Works on the Colonial Period

Clarence Ver Steeg, *The Formative Years* (1964); Curtis P. Nettels, *Roots of American Civilization* (1938); Daniel Boorstin, *The Americans: The Colon-*

ial Experience (1958)*; Paul Goodman, ed., *Essays in American Colonial History* (1967)*; W. F. Craven, *The Colonies in Transition, 1660–1713* (1968)*.

Contemporary Accounts

J. Hector St. John de Crèvecoeur, *Letters from an American Farmer* (1782)*; Gottlieb Mittelberger, *Journey to Pennsylvania,* O. Handlin and John Clive, eds. (1960); Peter Kalm, *A Journey to North America* (1770); Andrew Hamilton, *Gentleman's Progress,* Carl Bridenbaugh, ed. (1948); William Bradford, *Of Plymouth Plantations,* S. E. Morison, ed. (1952); Andrew Burnaby, *Travels through North America* (1775)*; Charles Woodmason, *The Carolina Backcountry,* R. J. Hooker, ed. (1953)*; Hugh Jones, *The Present State of Virginia,* R. L. Morton, ed. (1956)*.

CHAPTER 1

European Background

Myron P. Gilmore, *The World of Humanism* (1952)*; J. H. Parry, *The Establishment of the European Hegemony* (1961)*; J. H. Parry, *The Age of Reconnaissance* (1963)*; Howard M. Jones, *O Strange New World* (1964)*.

Spain

J. H. Elliott, *Imperial Spain, 1469–1716* (1963)*; Clarence H. Haring, *Spanish Empire in America* (1952)*; J. H. Parry, *The Spanish Seaborne Empire* (1966); Silvio Zavala, *New Viewpoints on the Spanish Colonization of America* (1943); Charles Gibson, *Spain in America* (1966)*; S. E. Morison, *Admiral of the Ocean Sea,* 2 vols. (1942); S. E. Morison, *Christopher Columbus, Mariner* (1955)*.

France

Sigmund Diamond, "An Experiment in 'Feudalism': French Canada in the Seventeenth Century," *William and Mary Quarterly,* 3rd series, vol. 18 (1961), pp. 1–34.

England

Geoffrey R. Elton, *England under the Tudors* (1956); A. L. Rowse, *The England of Elizabeth* (1950)*; *The Expansion of Elizabethan England* (1955)*; Howard M. Jones, *O Strange New World* (1964)*; Wallace Notestein, *The English People on the Eve of Colonization* (1954)*; *Crisis in Europe, 1560–1660,* Tre-

vor Aston, ed. (1965)*; E. Lipson, *Economic History of England,* vol. 2 (1931); Lawrence Stone, "State Control in Sixteenth-Century England," *Economic History Review,* vol. 17 (1947), pp. 103–120; F. J. Fisher, "Commercial Trends and Policy in Sixteenth-Century England," *Economic History Review,* vol. 10 (1946), pp. 95–117; R. H. Tawney, *The Agrarian Problem in the Sixteenth Century* (1912)*; Barry E. Supple, *Commercial Crisis and Change in England, 1600–1642* (1959); Richard H. Tawney, *Religion and the Rise of Capitalism* (1926)*; Michael Walzer, *The Revolution of the Saints* (1965)*; Carl Bridenbaugh, *Vexed and Troubled Englishmen, 1590–1642* (1968)*.

CHAPTER 2

General Works on the Seventeenth Century

Oscar Handlin, "The Significance of the Seventeenth Century," J. M. Smith, ed., *Seventeenth-Century America* (1959)*; W. F. Craven, *The Southern Colonies in the Seventeenth Century* (1949)*; C. M. Andrews, *The Colonial Period in American History,* vols. 1–3 (1934–1938)*.

Virginia

Sigmund Diamond, "From Organization to Society: Virginia in the Seventeenth Century," *American Journal of Sociology,* vol. 63 (1958), pp. 457–475; Wesley F. Craven, *The Southern Colonies in the Seventeenth Century* (1949)*; Wesley F. Craven, *Dissolution of the Virginia Company* (1932); Bernard Bailyn, "Politics and Social Structure in Virginia," J. M. Smith, ed., *Seventeenth-Century America* (1959), pp. 90–115*; Louis B. Wright, *First Gentlemen of Virginia* (1964)*; Thomas J. Wertenbaker, *The Planters of Colonial Virginia* (1922).

New England

Perry Miller, *Errand into the Wilderness* (1956)*; *Orthodoxy in Massachusetts* (1933)*; *Nature's Nation* (1967); *The New England Mind: The Seventeenth Century* (1939)*; *The New England Mind: From Colony to Province* (1953)*; Edmund S. Morgan, *The Puritan Dilemma* (1958)*; Clinton Rossiter, *Seedtime of the Republic* (1953); Sumner C. Powell, *Puritan Village: The Formation of a New England Town* (1963)*; Edmund Morgan, *Visible Saints* (1963)*; Samuel E. Morison, *The Intellectual Life of Colonial New England* (1956)*; H. W. Schneider, *The Puritan Mind* (1930)*; *Puritanism in Seventeenth-Century Massachusetts,* David D. Hall, ed. (1968)*;

The Puritans, Perry Miller and Thomas H. Johnson, eds., 2 vols. (1938)*; Perry Miller, *Roger Williams: His Contribution to the American Tradition* (1962)*; Alan Simpson, *Puritanism in Old and New England* (1955)*; Ola E. Winslow, *Master Roger Williams* (1957)*; Emery J. Battis, *Saints and Sectaries: Anne Hutchinson and the Antinomian Controversy* (1962); Darrett Rutman, *Winthrop's Boston* (1965)*; S. E. Morison, *Builders of the Bay Colony* (1930)*; Richard S. Dunn, *Puritans and Yankees* (1962).

Other Colonies

Thomas J. Condon, *New York Beginnings: The Commercial Origins of New Netherland* (1968); S. G. Nissenson, *The Patroon's Domain* (1937); M. Eugene Sirmans, *Colonial South Carolina* (1966).

CHAPTER 3

Colonial Economic Development

Stuart Bruchey, *Roots of American Economic Growth, 1607–1861* (1965), chaps. 2, 3*; George R. Taylor, "American Economic Growth before 1840," *Journal of Economic History*, vol. 24 (1964), pp. 427–444.

Westward Movement

Ray Billington, *Westward Expansion* (1949); Verner W. Crane, *Southern Frontier, 1670–1732* (1928)*.

Immigration and Labor

Mildred Campbell, *The English Yeoman under Elizabeth and Early Stuarts* (1942); "Social Origins of Some Early Americans," J. M. Smith, ed., *Seventeenth-Century America* (1959), pp. 63–89*; Abbott E. Smith, *Colonists in Bondage* (1947); Richard B. Morris, *Government and Labor in Early America* (1946)*; Marcus Lee Hansen, *The Atlantic Migration* (1940)*; Oscar Handlin, *The Uprooted* (1951)*; Ian C. Graham, *Colonists from Scotland* (1956); Carl Bridenbaugh, *The Colonial Craftsman* (1950).*

Slavery and Indians

Oscar and Mary F. Handlin, *Race and Nationality in American Life* (1957), chap. 1*; Carl Degler, "Slavery and the Genesis of American Race Prejudice," *Comparative Studies in Society and History*, vol. 2 (1959), pp. 49–66, 488–495; David B. Davis, *The Problem of Slavery in Western Culture* (1966)*;

Stanley Elkins, *Slavery: A Problem in American Institutional and Intellectual Life* (1959)*; Winthrop D. Jordan, *White over Black* (1968)*; Kenneth Stampp, *The Peculiar Institution* (1956)*; J. H. Franklin, *From Slavery to Freedom* (1947)*; *The Indian and the White Man*, Wilcomb E. Washburn, ed. (1964)*; Alden T. Vaughan, *New England Frontier: Puritans and Indians, 1620–1675* (1965)*; Roy H. Pearce, *The Savages of America* (1953)*; Allen Trelease, *Indian Affairs in Colonial New York* (1960).

The Struggle for North America

Howard H. Peckham, *The Colonial Wars, 1689–1762* (1964)*; Max Savelle, *Origins of American Diplomacy* (1967); Walter L. Dorn, *Competition for Empire* (1940)*; Stanley M. Pargellis, *Lord Loudoun in North America* (1933); Robert C. Newbold, *The Albany Congress and Plan of Union of 1754* (1955); Lawrence H. Gipson, *British Empire before the American Revolution*, vol. 5 (1942); John Shy, *Toward Lexington* (1966)*, chap. 1.

Colonial Agriculture

L. C. Gray, *History of Agriculture in the Southern United States to 1860* (1933), vol. 1; Jacob Price, "The Economic Growth of the Chesapeake and the European Market, 1695-1775," *Journal of Economic History*, vol. 25 (1964), pp. 496-511; Aubrey C. Land, "Economic Behavior in a Planting Society: The Eighteenth-Century Chesapeake," *Journal of Southern History*, vol. 33 (1967), pp. 469-485.

Land System

Roy H. Akagi, *Town Proprietors of New England* (1924); Shaw Livermore, *Early American Land Companies* (1939); Roy F. Robbins, *Our Landed Heritage* (1942)*; Marshall Harris, *Origin of the Land Tenure System in the United States* (1953).

Currency

Curtis P. Nettels, *Money Supply of American Colonies before 1720* (1934); E. James Ferguson, *The Power of the Purse* (1961)*, chap. 1; Bray Hammond, *Banks and Politics in America* (1957)*, chap. 1.

Mercantilism

Jacob Viner, "Power versus Plenty as Objectives of Foreign Policy in the Seventeenth and Eighteenth

Centuries," *World Politics,* vol. 1 (1948), pp. 1-29; Lawrence A. Harper, *The English Navigation Laws* (1939); Oliver M. Dickerson, *Navigation Acts and the American Revolution* (1951)*; George L. Beer, *The Origins of the British Colonial System, 1578-1660* (1908); G. L. Beer, *The Old Colonial System, 1660-1668* (1912); Robert P. Thomas, "A Quantitative Approach to the Study of the Effects of British Imperial Policy upon Colonial Welfare," *Journal of Economic History,* vol. 25 (1965), pp. 615-638; Viola F. Barnes, *The Dominion of New England* (1933); Richard B. Sheridan, "The Molasses Act and the Market Strategy of the British Sugar Planters," *Journal of Economic History,* vol. 18 (1957), pp. 62-83; Charles M. Andrews, *The Colonial Period in American History: England's Commercial and Colonial Policy,* vol. 4 (1938)*; Curtis P. Nettels, "British Mercantilism and the Economic Development of the Thirteen Colonies," *Journal of Economic History,* vol. 12 (Spring, 1952).

Colonial Commerce

Bernard Bailyn, *The New England Merchants in the Seventeenth Century* (1955)*; Stuart Bruchey, ed., *The Colonial Merchant* (1967)*; W. T. Baxter, *The House of Hancock* (1945); James B. Hedges, *The Browns of Providence Plantations* (1952); Richard Pares, *Yankees and Creoles: The Trade between North America and the West Indies before the American Revolution* (1956); Richard Pares, *Merchants and Planters* (1960); Leila Sellers, *Charleston Business on the Eve of the Revolution* (1934).

Colonial Cities

Carl Bridenbaugh, *Cities in the Wilderness* (1938)*; Carl Bridenbaugh, *Cities in Revolt* (1955)*; Carl and Jessica Bridenbaugh, *Rebels and Gentlemen: Philadelphia in the Age of Franklin* (1942)*; Sam B. Warner, Jr., *The Private City: Philadelphia in Three Periods of Its Growth* (1968), chaps. 1-2; Charles N. Glaab and A. Theodore Brown, *A History of Urban America* (1967)*, chap. 1.

CHAPTER 4

Political Development

Bernard Bailyn, *The Origins of American Politics* (1968)*; J. R. Pole, *Political Representation in England and the Origins of the American Republic* (1966); Jack P. Greene, *The Quest for Power; The Lower Houses of Assembly in the Southern Royal Colonies, 1689-1776* (1963); Leonard W. Labaree, *Royal Government in America* (1930); Charles S. Sydnor, *American Revolutionaries in the Making*

(1965)*; *The Glorious Revolution in America,* Michael G. Hall, et al., eds., (1964)*; L. W. Labaree, *Conservatism in Early American History* (1948)*, chap. 1; J. R. Pole, "Historians and the Problem of Early American Democracy," *American Historical Review,* vol. 67 (1962), pp. 626-646; *Politics and Society in Colonial America,* Michael G. Kammen ed. (1968)*.

The South

Leonidas Dodson, *Alexander Spotswood: Governor of Colonial Virginia* (1932); Julian P. Boyd, "The Sheriff in Colonial North Carolina," *North Carolina Historical Review,* vol. 5 (1928), pp. 151-181; Wilcomb E. Washburn, *The Governor and the Rebel* (1957)*; Robert and B. Katherine Brown, *Virginia, 1705-1786: Democracy or Aristocracy?* (1964); Eugene Sirmans, *Colonial South Carolina: A Political History* (1966); Louis Morton, *Robert Carter of Nomini Hall* (1964)*; Aubrey C. Land, *The Dulanys of Maryland* (1955)*; David Mays, *Edmund Pendleton,* 2 vols. (1952); W. W. Abbot, *The Royal Governors of Georgia* (1959).

The Middle Colonies

Lawrence H. Leder, *Robert Livingston and the Politics of Colonial New York, 1654-1728* (1961); Jerome Reich, *Leisler's Rebellion* (1953); Stanley N. Katz, *Newcastle's New York* (1968); Milton M. Klein, "Democracy and Politics in Colonial New York," *New York History,* vol. 40 (1959), pp. 221-246; William S. Hanna, *Benjamin Franklin and Pennsylvania Politics* (1964); Theodore Thayer, *Pennsylvania Politics and the Growth of Democracy, 1740-1776* (1952).

New England

Oscar Zeichner, *Connecticut's Years of Controversy* (1950); Robert E. Brown, *Middle Class Democracy and the Coming of the Revolution in Massachusetts* (1955)*; David S. Lovejoy, *Rhode Island Politics and the American Revolution* (1958); Mack E. Thompson, "The Ward-Hopkins Controversy and the American Revolution in Rhode Island," *William and Mary Quarterly,* 3rd series, vol. 16 (1959), pp. 363-375; John A. Schutz, *William Shirley: King's Governor of Massachusetts* (1961); Jere R. Daniell, "Politics in New Hampshire under Governor Benning Wentworth, 1741-1767," *William and Mary Quarterly,* 3rd series, vol. 23 (1966), pp. 76-105; Charles S. Grant, *Democracy in the Frontier Town of Kent* (1961).

British Colonial Administration

Oliver M. Dickerson, *American Colonial Government, 1696-1765* (1921); Thomas C. Barrow, *Trade and Empire* (1967); Viola F. Barnes, *The Dominion of New England,* (1923); Alison T. Olson, "The British Government and Colonial Union, 1754," *William and Mary Quarterly,* 3d series, vol. 17 (1960), pp. 22-34; Michael Kammen, *Rope of Sand* (1968); Dora M. Clark, *The Rise of the British Treasury: Colonial Administration in the Eighteenth Century* (1960); Michael G. Hall, *Edward Randolph and the American Colonies* (1960).

Freedom of the Press

Leonard Levy, *Freedom of Speech and Press in Early American History* (1960).*

CHAPTER 5

Social Structure

Carl Bridenbaugh, *Myths and Realities: Societies of the Colonial South* (1963)*; Arthur M. Schlesinger, "The Aristocracy in Colonial America," *Proceedings of the Massachusetts Historical Society,* vol. 74 (1962), pp. 3-21; James Henretta, "Economic Development and Social Structure in Colonial Boston," *William and Mary Quarterly,* 3d series, vol. 22 (1965), pp. 75-92; Jackson T. Main, *Social Structure of Revolutionary America* (1965)*; Emory Evans, "The Rise and Decline of the Virginia Aristocracy in the Eighteenth Century," Darrett B. Rutman, ed., *The Old Dominion* (1965), pp. 62-78; Kenneth Lockridge, "Land, Population, and the Evolution of New England Society, 1630-1790," *Past and Present,* no. 39 (April, 1968), pp. 62-80; Edmund Morgan, *The Puritan Family* (1966)*; Edmund Morgan, *Virginians at Home* (1952)*; John Demos, *A Little Commonwealth: Family Life in Plymouth Colony* (1970)*; John Demos, "Families in Colonial Bristol, Rhode Island: An Exercise in Historical Demography," *William and Mary Quarterly,* 3d series, vol. 25 (1968), pp. 40-57; Philip J. Greven, Jr., *Four Generations: Population, Land, and Family in Colonial Andover, Massachusetts* (1969); Philip J. Greven, Jr. "Historical Demography and Colonial America: A Review Article," *William and Mary Quarterly,* 3d series, vol. 24 (1967), pp. 438-454; Frederick B. Tolles, *Meeting House and Counting House: The Quaker Merchants of Colonial Philadelphia* (1940).*

Religion

Evarts B. Greene, *Religion and the State* (1959)*; Perry Miller, "The Contribution of the Protestant Churches to Religious Liberty in Colonial America," *Church History,* vol. 4 (1935), pp. 57-66; Sidney E. Mead, *The Lively Experiment* (1963)*; William W. Sweet, *Religion in Colonial America* (1942); H. Richard Niebuhr, *The Kingdom of God in America* (1959)*; *Religion in American Life,* J. W. Smith and A. L. Jamison, eds., vol. 1 (1961); *American Christianity,* H. Shelton Smith et al., eds., vol. 1 (1963); Allen Heimert, *Religion and the American Mind* (1966); Perry Miller, *Jonathan Edwards* (1967)*; Conrad Wright, *The Beginnings of Unitarianism* (1955)*; Edwin S. Gausted, *The Great Awakening in New England* (1957)*; Ola A. Winslow, *Jonathan Edwards* (1940).*

Education

Bernard Bailyn, *Education in the Forming of American Society* (1960)*; Frederick Rudolph, *The American College and University* (1962)*; Lawrence A. Cremin, *American Education: The Colonial Experience* (1970); Beverly McAnear, "College Founding in the American Colonies, 1745-1776," *Mississippi Valley Historical Review,* vol. 42 (1955), pp. 24-44; Richard Hofstadter, *Academic Freedom in the Age of the College* (1955)*; Samuel E. Morison, *Three Centuries of Harvard* (1936); Edmund S. Morgan, *The Gentle Puritan: A Life of Ezra Stiles* (1962).

Colonial Culture

Max Savelle, *Seeds of Liberty* (1965)*; Louis B. Wright, *The Cultural Life of the American Colonies* (1957)*; Brooke Hindle, *The Pursuit of Science in Revolutionary America* (1956)*; Oliver W. Larkin, *Art and Life in America* (1959); Richard M. Gummere, *The American Colonial Mind and the Classical Tradition* (1963); Frederick B. Tolles, "The Culture of Early Pennsylvania," *Pennsylvania Magazine of History and Biography,* vol. 81 (1957), pp. 119-137; John Clive and Bernard Bailyn, "England's Cultural Provinces: Scotland and America," *William and Mary Quarterly,* 3d series, vol. 14 (1957), pp. 200-213; Peter Gay, *A Loss of Mastery: Puritan Historians in Colonial America* (1966)*; Frederick B. Tolles, *James Logan and the Culture of Provincial America* (1957); Michael Kraus, *The Atlantic Civilization* (1949)*; Dirk J. Struik, *Yankee Science in the Making* (1948).*

Part Two
Birth of the Republic, 1760-1815

Introduction

America became a nation through revolution. For a century and a half, the settlers had accepted colonial status. Then in the 1760s, with a swiftness that past acquiescence made surprising, Americans began a struggle with Britain ending in independence. In little more than a decade (1764-1776), American colonists became convinced that they could no longer promote their welfare without full power to govern themselves. American revolutionaries had to fight hard against a powerful empire. As some had foreseen, victory brought challenges and vexing responsibilities especially in establishing a nation on the principle that all men are created equal and free to engage in the pursuit of happiness. It proved easier to formulate inspiring goals than to assure the new republic's survival. In a world of hostile forces at home and abroad, the dreams of the revolutionary generation seemed utopian at times.

The founding fathers were both visionaries and realists. Unlike later generations, they could not take for granted that the new nation would become strong and free. The lessons of history and their own experience taught them that liberty was a perishable commodity. Few nations had ever enjoyed it for very long. In 1776 kings and aristocrats ruled almost everywhere, proof to many that hereditary rulers and control by the few were the only guarantees that nations could enjoy internal peace and security from foreign dangers. Why should the United States be an exception? Thoughtful Americans feared that their country might share the fate of other republics, which since the time of ancient Greece had succumbed to aggression from without and internal decay and class conflict from within. Yet Americans remained confident that they could demonstrate both the desirability and practicality of popular government.

For three decades following independence, Americans attempted to lay the foundations of a strong, free, and stable republic. They wrote and rewrote constitutions which defined the rules of the political game, and sought a workable balance between personal liberty and governmental authority; they worked to assure material prosperity; and they tried to avoid war with other nations. By 1815 Americans had passed the first test. The state and federal constitutions proved to be viable instruments of popular rule. The country kept out of war until 1812 and then emerged from the second conflict with Britain with greater self-confidence, convinced that it could defend its national interests against a powerful foe. Despite sharp conflicts among themselves, Americans in 1815 were more united than ever before. They had settled their major internal differences without resorting to arms against one another. No longer preoccupied with threats of war, nor entangled in foreign conflicts, confident of the stability of their own institutions, Americans after the War of 1812 turned their eyes westward to the

Mississippi Valley and to the Gulf Plains that awaited an army of frontiersmen and farmers.

Since Americans won their independence in the first modern war of national liberation, other peoples throughout the world have created new nations which, like the United States, are products of revolutionary struggle. And like the Americans over two centuries ago, the inhabitants of new nations in Africa and Asia, once colonies of Europe, have found that independence brings serious problems of nation-building. The ways in which Americans met these challenges were influenced by their experiences as colonists and by the hopes that inspired the revolutionary generation to found a new republic deriving its identity from a commitment to the rights of man. Their successes and failures in matching their goals with their achievements helped define more clearly what it meant to be an American.

The Boston "Massacre": Street violence as a revolutionary weapon (1770). *(Culver Pictures)*

The British army comes to Boston
(1768), seedbed of American resistance.
(Culver Pictures)

Direct action in Boston Harbor: The Boston Tea Party. *(Culver Pictures)*

General Washington with his soldiers, ending a camp brawl. *(New York Public Library)*

Supplying the Revolutionary army at Boston, 1775. *(New York Public Library)*

The shot heard round the world: Lexington, Massachusetts, 1775. *(New York Public Library)*

American soldiers in retreat, Long Island, 1776. *(New York Public Library)*

Raising the Liberty Pole, 1776. *(Library of Congress)*

Federal Hall, New York, 1789, first capitol of the United States. *(Library of Congress)*

An American victory at sea during
the War of 1812. *(New York Public
Library)*

Chapter 6
The American Revolution

In 1760, Benjamin Franklin, the Pennsylvania philosopher, philanthropist, and politician who generally kept his ear close to the ground, wrote a friend: "I will venture to say, a union among [the colonies] for such a purpose [as revolution] is not merely improbable but impossible." Events soon proved Franklin dead wrong. For over a century the American colonies grew and prospered as part of an empire that stretched from London to Calcutta. Though the interests of the colonists and the mother country did not always coincide, these differences seldom led to dangerous clashes. Parliament possessed supreme legal authority but it permitted the Americans a large measure of self-government. Accustomed to making and administering many of the laws under which they lived, the colonists accepted English authority even as they chipped away at the power of royal officeholders. As long as they could influence English policy and manipulate crown officials, they accepted in theory the supremacy of the mother country.

In the 1760s and 1770s, however, most Americans rejected British authority, and in little more than a decade the ties that had bound them to Britain for five generations shattered beyond repair. By 1776 Americans came to believe they could no longer remain Englishmen and retain their freedom, and in choosing to remain free they created a new nation. During the decade of agitation that led to revolution, few realized that they were traveling the road to independence. But changes within the British empire had disrupted the equilibrium that prevailed before 1763. This produced in Americans new perceptions of their interests and a heightened sense of identity as a distinct people—a nation in the making. These attitudes ultimately destroyed the common loyalty binding the colonists to England.

THE NEW EMPIRE

The American colonies were part of a mercantilist empire which aimed at increasing the wealth and power of Britain through the development of overseas outposts. As long as colonies grew and prospered, providing markets and raw materials that enriched Britain, they met imperial expectations. While the American colonies fulfilled their purpose and enriched the mother country, mercantilists were ready to permit them substantial self-government, especially since contented colonists were likely to be more productive and less troublesome than oppressed dissidents. By delegating extensive power to American colonial governments, England spared itself the cost of maintaining an army in America during peacetime, as well as an expensive bureaucracy in the colonies and in London.

After 1760 these policies no longer worked. Britain's victory over France in the Great War for Empire (1754-1761) gave it control over most of the North American continent. From a string of coastal settlements, British North America had become a great territorial empire, continental in scope, and including Canada and the Mississippi Valley. The transformation, which no one had foreseen and few in America or England clearly understood, confronted the British with new political problems. Their attempt to reform imperial government in response to new conditions ended in the disruption of the first British Empire.

Since coming to the New World, Englishmen had encountered formidable competition in the race for empire. Conceding most of the Southern Hemisphere to the Spaniards, whom they could not dislodge, the English staked out claims in the Caribbean but focused their main energies on North America. After seizing New Amsterdam from the Dutch, England's chief rival became France, which controlled Canada and the Mississippi Valley, threatening English expansion westward from the seaboard settlements that stretched from Maine to Georgia.

In the long contest with France each side claimed the Ohio and Mississippi valleys, seized strong points, erected forts, and made alliances with the Indians. From time to time, the competition escalated into warfare. Yet the struggle for mastery of North America remained the sideshow of a far greater contest in Europe. Louis XIV, "The Sun King" (1638-1715), had made France the most powerful nation on the European continent. Britain sought to maintain a balance of power in Europe as the best defense against French domination. It was therefore essential to deny France the resources and wealth of the New World.

From the end of the seventeenth century until 1763 England fought a series of intercolonial wars on two continents. King William's War (1689-1697), Queen Anne's War (1702-1713), and King George's War (1740-1748) all ended inconclusively. France and England, with their Indian allies, attacked the other's weak points, usually exposed frontier or coastal positions that might easily be captured. Villages were destroyed, settlement impeded, and bits of territory changed hands, but in America neither side committed sufficient resources to achieve a decisive victory.

A French attempt to seize the Ohio Valley, the gateway to the interior, provoked the outbreak of another war with England in 1754. This time England, under the effective war leadership of William Pitt, committed sufficient wealth and power to dislodge the French. Pitt exploited England's mastery of the sea and numerical superiority in America. After several initial setbacks, the British forces, troops from both England and the colonies, established their mastery. The French surrendered Canada in 1760. This permitted England to concentrate on the Caribbean and the capture of France's sugar-producing islands, Martinique and Guadaloupe. By the Treaty of Paris (1763) which ended this Seven Years' War, France ceded Canada to Britain but regained her West Indian possessions, restored European territory captured from England, and compensated losses suffered by its ally Spain by transferring the territory west of the Mississippi, including New Orleans, to the Spaniards.

Pitt, in deciding to keep Canada instead of the French West Indies, made a strategic decision that altered the nature of the British Empire. From a strictly mercantilist point of view the sugar islands were preferable since they produced a staple commodity which was in great demand.

The French islands, together with Britain's own sugar-producing West Indies, would have given England control of American sugar production. Canada, in contrast, remained largely undeveloped, a wilderness valuable chiefly for the fur trade. Yet English politicians and merchants appreciated the long-range value of Canada. Possession of Canada ended the French threat against Britain's North American colonies and permitted their further unfettered development.

By the mid-eighteenth century these colonies had become England's most valuable overseas possessions. England was becoming an industrial power, increasingly dependent on the export of manufactured goods. The American colonies provided one of Britain's best markets, surpassing by mid-century, the British West Indies. With their population doubling every twenty years, and their farmers producing cash crops that created purchasing power to buy English goods, the American colonies were far better markets than the French and British islands, inhabited mainly by slaves. Britain's landed gentry, the dominant group in Parliament, joined merchants, manufacturers, and imperial strategists in favoring the retention of Canada. Those who raised sheep for wool manufacturing, England's most important economic interest, stood to benefit from the growth of a large, protected market within the empire, especially since competition from European wool producers cut into established markets on the Continent.

Imperial Problems

Few realized that the acquisition of Canada changed the character of Britain's North American empire. An immense territory, continental in scope, could not be governed by the same methods applicable to a chain of isolated Atlantic settlements. The war had clearly revealed serious weaknesses in the old empire. Success in battle required the mobilization and coordination in England and the colonies of sufficient resources to defeat the French. The lax system of imperial government that had grown haphazardly for over a century did not meet the nation's new needs.

Before the 1750s Britain had delegated to each colony responsibility for the defense of its frontiers in peacetime against Indians and hostile foreigners. The Royal Navy patrolled the seas, a job vital to British and American commerce. Whenever war broke out between England and France or Spain in the New World, Britain sent troops. But victory in the Seven Years' War had required a large commitment of colonial troops who could be recruited more quickly, cheaply, and in greater numbers than mercenaries from Europe. However, money for war financing was not readily available. Though the British planned to pay the major part, they also expected the Americans to contribute a good part. England, however, had never raised revenue in the colonies, relying instead on voluntary contributions in response to requests by the crown. Furthermore, no way existed to assure that colonies would contribute men and material when needed or would coordinate their own resources to permit effective military operations. Finally, illegal trade, notably with the French West Indies, overlooked in peacetime, became in wartime trading with the enemy.

In 1754 delegates from the New England and Middle colonies met at Albany, New York, to negotiate an alliance with the Iroquois tribes. Sensing the need for imperial reorganization, the delegates adopted a plan, drafted by Benjamin Franklin, a Pennsylvania delegate. The Albany Plan of Union called for a grand council elected by the colonial assemblies and a president general chosen by the crown to supervise Indian affairs and westward settlement and to raise money. The colonies unanimously rejected the proposal, however, refusing to relinquish any of their powers. The British ministry, fearful of antagonizing the Americans and arousing opposition in Parliament, dropped the idea. England thus entered the Seven Years' War without a modernized structure of imperial administration, delaying such reorganization until after the French were beaten.

During the war, the necessity of obtaining American cooperation led the British to work as best they could under the existing system. A British commander-in-chief attempted to coordinate the military effort, the crown requisitioned support from the Americans while compensating them for part of their contribution, and royal officials generally overlooked violations of En-

glish laws. But all this began to change as the American phase of the war ended. No longer pressured by the exigencies of war, and forced to grapple with new problems inherited from the peace settlement, the British began to reorganize the government of North America.

Postwar problems were interrelated and pressing. The new territorial empire in North America had to be defended against the Indians, the French, and the Spaniards. The Indian danger intensified as white settlements moved further westward. A plan for the orderly settlement of the West thus became imperative, especially since fur trading and land speculating groups each favored opposing western policies that served their special interests. Policing the Indians, defending North America against foreign attack, regulating settlement and the fur trade, all required more soldiers and administrators. These in turn cost money. If some of the funds were to come from the colonies, royal authority in America needed strengthening to prevent further evasion of the revenue laws and frequent manipulation of royal officials and courts.

Neither the English nor the Americans clearly perceived the complexity of the problems, and to what extent solutions might lead to far-reaching departures in traditional policies. Like an iceberg, with but a small part visible, the dimensions of the imperial problem revealed themselves slowly or not at all. The British, however, faced a number of situations that required prompt responses, even without a carefully designed plan for meeting them. Moreover, the American problem intensified during a decade of uncertainty in England when a new unstable king, George III (1760–1820), upset the political equilibrium. Exercising his constitutional powers to choose his ministers, George dismissed the well-established politicians whom he distrusted, men who customarily commanded the parliamentary support necessary to govern. Ministry followed ministry—five in seven years— before the king finally selected Lord North, a middle-of-the-roader who enjoyed both His Majesty's support and could work reasonably well in Parliament. Ministerial instability before the naming of North in 1770 deprived English policy of consistency and coherence at a critical time when both were needed to make a successful transition from the old mercantilist to the new territorial empire.

REMODELING THE EMPIRE

The outbreak of Pontiac's rebellion in 1763, the bloodiest Indian war in American history, dramatized the need for new British policies. Indian discontent had smoldered for decades, kindled by the steady encroachment of English settlers on their lands. French defeat left the Indians at the mercy of the British who could raise the prices of goods in trade and cut off supplies of weapons and ammunition at will. The Indians decided to fight and caught the British by surprise, quickly destroying every post west of Niagara, until finally repulsed.

Victorious in the field, the British now prepared to introduce "system" in their relations with the Indians.

The Proclamation of October 1763 established a new policy for the West. It barred colonists from settling west of the Appalachians, an area that thus became a huge Indian reservation. New controls over the Indian trade sought to prevent abuses by permitting only royal officials to purchase additional lands from the Indians. Finally the crown established new colonies in east and west Florida and Quebec, spoils of the successful war for empire, where Americans could settle legally.

Implementation of western policy led Britain to station troops to defend the newly conquered territories, administer Indian affairs, and restrain white settlement. The Quartering Acts of 1765 and 1766 required that American colonists contribute to the care and feeding of British troops. The presence of a standing army in America, whatever its usefulness on the frontier, became potentially dangerous to the white colonists since troops could be used for other purposes than wilderness patrol.

Supporting an army of 10,000 soldiers cost over twenty times the amount Britain spent on the small garrisons maintained before 1754. This peacetime burden came on top of the cost of financing the long war. The British national debt had doubled during the war, and the interest on this debt constituted a major part of the government's annual budget. Taxes had to be increased and pressure from taxpayers for relief helped end the war. The landed gentry and other property owners who controlled Parliament expected relief. George Grenville, the chancellor of the exchequer, argued that the Americans, who would benefit from the conquest of Canada and from English protection, should shoulder some of the financial burdens of defending the new acquisitions. When Americans dragged their feet in this matter, Parliament quickly acted. By passing the Sugar Act (1764) which lowered the duty on foreign molasses, Parliament hoped to induce compliance from merchants who previously evaded paying the higher duty. But the act also raised the duties on other imports such as coffee, wines, and foreign goods purchased via England. Parliament next adopted the Stamp Act (1765), taxing newspapers, books, and legal documents. The British expected total American revenue to pay for about a third of the cost of maintaining the army in America, or what they thought was a fair but by no means oppressive share of the bill.

At the same time that the colonies had to pay new taxes, Parliament prohibited further issue of paper money as legal tender, and required that colonial paper money then circulating be retired. British merchants and creditors had long sought protection from payment in depreciated paper currency which colonies issued to overcome the shortage of gold and silver. Although not all colonial paper fluctuated wildly in value, the Currency Act (1764) deprived the credit-hungry colonists of the means of providing a more adequate circulating medium.

Perhaps as important as the new taxes themselves was the reform of administration, especially the overhauling of the customs service. This branch of the British bureaucracy was hopelessly understaffed and easily bribed. The revenues collected usually amounted to less than the costs of collection. Toward the end of the war the crown seriously attempted to suppress smuggling and trading with the enemy; absentee collectors were now required to reside in America, and the crown gave them greater financial inducements to enforce the laws of trade. Customs officials, using writs of assistance, could now search anywhere, whenever they were suspicious of illegal trade, and the Royal Navy stepped up enforcement on the high seas. The Sugar Act imposed elaborate and complicated regulations to prevent evasions, swelling the size of the customs service to meet its new responsibilities. Prominent colonial merchants such as Boston's John Hancock and Charleston's Henry Laurens found their ships seized and cargoes impounded, they claimed, by racketeering customs officials who entrapped honest merchants in the coils of bureaucratic red tape and legal actions.

Furthermore, vice admiralty courts, functioning without juries, had their jurisdiction enlarged, making it harder for colonists who violated British law to escape justice.

Within two years after the war's end, Britain had established the outlines and some of the details of a new system of imperial control. Colonists were no longer free to settle wherever they pleased; the fur trade had been made subject to new controls; a standing army guarded isolated outposts and settlements throughout the continent; and Americans now had to pay taxes imposed by Parliament and collected by a strengthened royal bureaucracy. These British initiatives triggered a sharp, sometimes violent, American response.

THE AMERICAN RESISTANCE

American resistance was sudden and determined. At first it centered in the cities under the leadership of disgruntled merchants; ultimately it drew support from many other elements of colonial society. By 1770 a widely held conviction spread that the colonists faced a conspiracy against their freedom. "A series of occurrences . . . afford great reason to believe," warned the Boston Town Meeting of that year, "that a deep-laid and desperate plan of imperial despotism has been laid and partly executed for the extinction of civil liberty." Sensing a "dreadful catastrophe" that threatened "universal havoc," Americans banded together to resist "being totally overwhelmed

and buried under the ruins of our most established rights."

The new taxes and controls fell heavily on a depressed economy no longer enjoying wartime prosperity. England stopped pouring large amounts of money into the colonies, Americans cut their spending, some defaulted on their debts, and merchants in turn found themselves overstocked and unable to pay off their English creditors. Peace thus brought an end to the profits of war contracting, privateering, and trading with the enemy. Eventually, the colonists recovered from the postwar depression but at the very time when they could least afford it—the mid-1760s—the mother country demanded a share of their income. Merchants accustomed to evading restrictive laws found that the old dodges no longer worked. Compliance with the letter of the law brought with it a wave of bankruptcies and hard times, especially in the cities. Though Parliament did not cause the postwar recession, the new taxes and regulations, Americans thought, made things worse.

The merchants, artisans, shopkeepers, sailors, and laborers in the ports were hit by depression and new taxes more quickly than the self-sufficient residents of the agricultural hinterland. The taxes particularly affected the business classes since they made the greatest use of the articles taxed. Thus urban communities became centers of resistance. Boycotts and demonstrations were the principal American weapons, and a nonimportation movement begun in Boston soon spread to other cities. Merchants promised not to purchase goods from England, while citizens pledged to find homemade substitutes. Secret organizations such as the Sons of Liberty attempted to enforce the boycott by intimidating royal officials, forcing stamp agents to resign, and unleashing mobs which destroyed the stores and homes of persons closely associated with royal authority.

The Stamp Act

The Sugar Act had disrupted the cities; the Stamp Act ignited the continent. Whereas the Sugar Act, though primarily a revenue measure, had also sought to regulate trade, the Stamp Act was exclusively a tax. Throughout the colonies, the legislatures assembled to confront the crisis. In the Virginia House of Burgesses, Patrick Henry, a young back-country lawyer, created a sensation with his inflammatory oratory. Denouncing the Stamp Act as tyrannical, Henry reportedly thundered: "Caesar had his Brutus—Charles the First, his Cromwell—and George the Third—('Treason,' cried the Speaker and other members) *may profit by their example. If this be treason, make the most of it.*" In October 1765, delegates from nine colonies met in New York City and denied the right of Parliament to tax the colonists without their consent. Since Americans were not represented in Parliament, they contended that the Stamp Act duties "have a manifest tendency to subvert the rights and liberties" of the colonists. This Stamp Act Congress strengthened the nonimportation movement. At first merchants refused to use stamps and business came to a halt; but by the end of the year, merchants resumed trading without stamps.

American resistance, including civil disobedience, could not be ignored by London since American markets were vital to British prosperity. The boycott stung English merchants and manufacturers, themselves recovering from a postwar depression. The volume of exports to the colonies plummetted, hurting especially those economic groups and regions that supplied the American market. They petitioned Parliament for repeal of the Stamp Act, citing unemployment and bankruptcies as the results of the American boycott.

Meanwhile the Grenville ministry, authors of the new measures, had fallen from office. The new Rockingham ministry, more sympathetic to the Americans and to the British merchants, preferred to repeal the controversial law rather than to send troops to enforce it and risk rebellion. Yet while Parliament appeased the Americans, for reasons of expediency, it passed a Declaratory Act which asserted its right to make laws binding on the colonies "in all cases whatsoever."

Repeal of the Stamp Act defused the crisis but settled nothing. Both sides misread the significance of the compromise. The Americans believed that resistance paid off and thought that the British realized the folly of trying to govern them without their consent. The British believed that concessions would cool things off and that the Americans would ultimately contribute their fair share of the costs of the empire, especially since some colonists insisted that they were not against paying taxes, only "internal taxes" such as the stamp duties.

Repeal did not change British policy fundamentally. The pressing problems of governing a territorial empire still awaited solution. Seven months after repeal, Parliament lowered still further the duty on molasses, applying it now to all molasses, British as well as foreign, hoping thereby to increase customs revenue by making it easier to collect. Parliament, looking for new ways to reduce land taxes in Britain, rebelled against the new ministry of Sir William Pitt, now Lord Chatham, and followed the lead of Charles Townshend, the unpredictable chancellor of the exchequer. The Townshend Acts imposed new "external," or import, duties. Significantly, part of the revenues could be used to pay salaries of royal officials, thereby lessening their dependence on the colonial legislatures. Like the Sugar Act, the new tax measure strengthened the customs enforcement machinery, now centralized in a resident American Board of Customs Commissioners at Boston, and aided the newly reorganized admiralty courts which were given wider authority to conduct searches.

In the face of this frontal assault, Americans went back to nonimportation, but this time American pressure had less immediate effect. English merchants and manufacturers had found new markets in Europe that made them less vulnerable to American pressure. Ultimately, however, the boycott made itself felt. Finally in 1770 a new ministry headed by Lord North repealed the Townshend duties on all articles but tea. By retaining this duty Parliament reaffirmed its right to tax the colonies, as proclaimed in the Declaratory Act. Though some Americans wished to hold out for repeal of *all* taxes, the boycott collapsed since most of its objectives had been achieved.

The prolonged crises over taxation and new

British controls created residues of tension and hostility not easily dispelled after the easing of each crisis. The continent had been aroused by common dangers as never before and had responded to them in collective acts of resistance. New leaders had emerged to defend the American cause. In Massachusetts the cousins Samuel Adams and John Adams emerged as powerful spokesmen of the American interest. Sam Adams, a failure in business, displayed a talent for politics, especially in managing the Boston town meeting. An organizer of the Non-Importation Association and the Sons of Liberty, he served in the Massachusetts legislature from 1765 to 1774. As a propagandist and leader of the rank and file he had few equals. John Adams exemplified another sort of revolutionary-in-the-making. A Harvard College graduate and a rising lawyer when the conflict with the mother country broke out in the 1760s, he thereafter made his mark with effective constitutional and legal arguments in defense of American rights. Elsewhere, up and down the Atlantic coast, men stepped forward to sound the alarm and coordinate resistance: John Dickinson and James Wilson in Pennsylvania, Patrick Henry and Thomas Jefferson in Virginia, Christopher Gadsden in South Carolina, to mention a few.

Into this explosive situation came substantial contingents of the British army. Until the 1760s the crown had never in peacetime maintained military forces in the colonies to sustain its authority. Now it posted ten thousand troops in America, deployed for defense of the continent, to be sure, but also to tame the colonists if necessary.

In 1765 and 1766 Parliament passed Quartering Acts which required that colonies furnish British troops with housing and supplies. When New York, the headquarters of the British army, refused, Parliament suspended the legislature. When a later legislature complied, New York's resistance leaders defiantly erected a liberty pole, and a riot followed between citizens and soldiers. The British army also made its presence felt in Massachusetts, the most rebellious colony. Denouncing the Townshend duties for taxing Americans without their consent, the Massachusets legislature sent a circular letter to other colonies calling for united resistance. Several colonies responded favorably, but Massachusetts was singled out for punishment. The crown dissolved its assembly, and when the next new legislature refused to renounce the circular letter, the governor dissolved it too. In Boston the populace was even more defiant. A mob rescued the sloop *Liberty*, owned by patriot merchant John Hancock, from the British officials who had seized it for alleged customs violations. Boston's military resistance ended when two regiments of infantry plus artillery moved in to uphold British rule.

In this tense atmosphere, clashes between the troops and the citizens became common. Citizens and soldiers traded insults and punches. On March 5, 1770, British soldiers killed five persons in a crowd which had been taunting them and pelting them with rocks and snowballs. Only the removal of the troops to an island in Boston harbor prevented further violence in the aftermath of this "Boston Massacre."

Despite increasing tension generated by the presence of British troops, the repeal of the Townshend duties temporarily cooled things off. Yet the new trade regulations and enforcement machinery remained a constant irritant. In 1772, a group led by Providence, Rhode Island, merchants burned the customs schooner *Gaspee*. The British threatened to ship the accused to England for trial. In 1772 and 1773 Americans established Committees of Correspondence, extralegal bodies that aroused people to defend American rights and united resistance leaders throughout the colonies.

Until 1773, American resistance had been triggered by British efforts, whether wisely conceived or not, to deal with pressing problems of imperial government. In 1773 Parliament accidentally provoked a new crisis while trying to aid the nearly bankrupt East India Company. The Tea Act of that year gave the company a monopoly of the American market where it began to sell off its huge surpluses. By seeming to discriminate against all American merchants, except a few favored by the company as its local distributors, the act sparked simmering American discontent. Though the measure actually lowered the cost of tea, Americans, sensitized by a decade of struggle to threats to their freedom and privileges, interpreted it as further evidence that England intended to oppress the colonies. Bostonians prevented three ships from landing their cargoes by dumping several hundred chests of tea overboard in the harbor.

Boston's Tea Party brought swift punishment. In 1774 Parliament adopted a series of coercive acts that virtually closed Boston harbor until the East India Company received compensation. British officials who were indicted for capital offenses in the course of repressing riots or collecting taxes could thereafter have their trials removed to England. Furthermore, the Massachusetts council, previously chosen by the assembly, would now be appointed by the crown, which also assumed the power to appoint and remove most local officials, including judges. Finally, town meetings could no longer be held without the consent of the governor. Self-government for the colony of Massachusetts was no more.

In the fall of 1774 twelve colonies sent delegates to attend the First Continental Congress at Philadelphia. The Congress declared the Coercive Acts illegal, labeling them the latest in a long succession of attacks on American liberty. The Congress then formed a Continental Association to revive the policy of nonimportation as a weapon against the crown. Finally, it encouraged Americans to prepare to defend themselves with arms, if their grievances went unredressed.

As men on both sides of the Atlantic searched for ways to settle differences peacefully, both sides prepared for war. Hoping to seize an important American supply depot at Concord, Massachusetts, General Thomas Gage, the British commander in America, secretly sent troops into the countryside. The Americans learned of the plan, and in April 1775 colonial militia, or "Minutemen," resisted briefly at Lexington and successfully at Concord, forcing the battered British troops to retreat to Boston. The Massachusetts revolutionary legislature thereupon moved to raise an army, and appealed to other colonies for help. In May 1775, the Second Continental Congress met in Philadelphia and appointed George Washington of Virginia to command the Continental Army. The Revolution had begun. For over a year, both sides tried to avert a final break

but, meanwhile, the fighting continued. On July 4, 1776, Congress finally declared American independence.

ROOTS OF REVOLUTION

Each year Bostonians commemorated the Boston Massacre with the solemnity and fervor appropriate to a people conscious that they were creating their history. In 1772, two years after the incident, Joseph Warren, the orator of the day, referred to the British as a "raging soldiery" who molested American women, causing them, "distracted with anguish and despair," to end "their wretched lives by their own fair hands." Warren's inflamed rhetoric revealed the deepseated emotions behind American resistance: the conviction that British tyranny endangered everything Americans cherished. "The voice of your father's blood," shrieked Warren, "cries to you from the ground, *my sons scorn to be slaves! We bled in vain, if you our offspring . . . [lack] valour to repel the assaults of her invaders. . . ."*

Many Americans believed, as did Warren, that Britain meant to destroy their way of life by draining their wealth, undermining self-government, and ultimately eliminating political and religious liberty. Some even believed that tyrannical forces within England plotted unceasingly against American liberty (sometimes with, sometimes without the king's support), and that each new British move formed part of a scheme to oppress Americans and then extinguish English liberty. This fear started as a mere suspicion; but each new clash turned the possible into the plausible, and then settled into a conviction regarding the alleged conspiracy. Although the new taxes and regulations did alter relations between Britain and the colonies, there existed no long-range plan for remodeling the empire, let alone for destroying American freedom. The new policies were no more than immediate, often improvised, responses to pressing emergencies growing out of the victory in the Seven Years' War in 1763.

While Americans misconceived English purposes, Britain failed to anticipate the extent of American resistance or to appraise it realistically

once it appeared. Convinced of their own reasonableness and of the fact that Americans had for
too long escaped their due portion of the burdens
of empire, Englishmen in turn invented American
plots aiming at independence. In the resulting
impasse neither side understood the other, and
without the ability to account for their opponents'
behavior rationally, both sides seized upon conspiratorial explanations.

Self-analysis, by an individual or a society,
is always difficult. Americans did not appreciate
the extent to which the Seven Years' War had
undermined the old basis of imperial relations.
They came to take for granted their effective and
loose-knit self-government. Having benefited
from British permissiveness for so long, Americans regarded it as a fixed part of the imperial
constitution, not acknowledging that Parliament
retained sovereign, though often unexercised,
power. Nor could they understand new policies,
especially the taxes that violated the principle
of mercantilist empire under which they and the
mother country had prospered for so long. Though
acknowledging that they received many benefits
from Britain, they thought that raising revenues
in America retarded the economy and amounted
to robbing the goose that laid the golden egg.

Neither side saw beyond its own immediate
interests. The British failed to understand the
far-reaching changes that triggered the crisis of
the 1760s. Britain had relied initially on private
enterprise to settle the colonies, and for many
decades had paid little attention to America. Even
after formalization of British control at the close
of the seventeenth century, the crown remained
distant, its local representatives unable or unwilling to resist American influence. As long as peace
and prosperity reigned overseas, few in England
wished to rock the boat. When circumstances
altered the character of the empire, the British
would not recognize or accept the extent to
which British sovereignty in America had eroded
or had failed to take hold. Nor did they fully
understand that America's institutions, traditions, and values differed from those prevailing
in England. The freedom the colonies had enjoyed
enabled them to depart from the original English
cultural models. The clashes of the 1760s made
people on both sides of the Atlantic uncomfort-

ably conscious of the fundamental changes that
had slowly transformed Englishmen into Americans.

The Challenge to Liberty

The external challenge heightened an already
growing sense of American identity. For the first
time, the colonies found a bond in common danger. Colonists, wherever they lived and whatever
their particular interests, began to expand con-
tacts with others who resisted English domination. Opposing what they considered threats to
their liberty, Americans believed in the defense
of freedom as their distinctive mission. No one
expressed this better than John Adams: "I always
consider the settlement of America with rever-
ence and wonder as the opening of a grand scene
and design of Providence for the illumination of
the ignorant, and the emancipation of the slavish
part of mankind all over the earth."

Throughout the controversy, Americans insisted that they were upholding the rights of
Englishmen to be governed only with their consent. The principle that governments derived their
just power from the assent of the governed, they
believed, had flourished in America, even when
power-hungry and corrupt forces in England
trampled on the nation's ancient and revered
tradition. Americans recalled that many of their
ancestors had fled from Britain when a tyrannical
monarch, Charles I, attempted to rule without
respect for religious conscience. The belief that
tyranny perpetually stalked liberty dominated
the thinking of Britons excluded from power, such
as religious dissenters and those without sufficient wealth to participate in politics. Americans
identified with the English dissenting tradition
which ceaselessly denounced assaults on freedom.
These views gained a fresh cogency in the 1760s,
and provided Americans with a ready-made explanation of events.

Perceiving their land as the best and perhaps
the last hope of freedom, Americans believed that
for this reason the colonies had become the prime
target of despotism. If freedom prospered and
endured in America, the days of tyranny were
numbered elsewhere. Yet at the same time that
Americans were suspicious of English power and

believed that eternal vigilance against external threats was the price of liberty, they also wondered if they possessed the strength and virtue needed to survive as a free society. Unless men respected their fellow men and subordinated private interests to the public good, unless people could restrain their impulse to amass wealth and power, the prospects for liberty would be no better in the New World than they had been in the Old. "We must return to that decent simplicity of manners, that sober regard to ordinances, that strict morality of demeanor, which characterized our plain forefathers," intoned a patriotic clergyman, one of the first of an immensely long line of Americans who would look back nostalgically to an America that never was. The resistance to England tested conviction, offering people the opportunity to take risks for what they regarded as a noble cause. Thus nonimportation exacted sacrifices from merchants and consumers alike. Some clergymen viewed the latest afflictions of Americans as divine punishment for their waywardness, another test of their devotion to that mission which had first sent them into the wilderness.

British policy apparently struck at civil and spiritual liberty, just as over a century earlier the kings of England had attempted to deprive Englishmen of both. If Parliament could tax Americans, self-government in the colonies would not long survive. Once the people lost the power to restrain their rulers by controlling the purse strings, nothing could prevent government from becoming tyrannical. The assemblies were the keystones of colonial self-government precisely because they controlled the purse strings. Americans also objected to the new taxes as economic burdens, though the amount of the taxes siphoned from American pockets into the royal coffers mattered less than the principle involved.

The colonists could see no reasonable basis for keeping a large army in America. The French were beaten; the Indians were only capable of mounting sporadic though bloody resistance. The colonies had not requested the presence of soldiers to protect them. Seeing no legitimate function for the army, many Americans believed it was yet another part of a master plan to undermine self-government. Should they resist taxa-

tion, should they refuse to quarter the king's troops, their assemblies could be suspended, as was New York's, with the Army there to enforce British commands. A knowledgeable British official explained why colonists feared the army: "Whilst their minds are oppressed with these doubts [about taxation] . . . they do think it is meant to throw a kind of military net over them."

British western policy seemed equally unreasonable. Americans had been free for generations to move west, to start over again in a new environment with greater chances for success. Now with the stroke of a pen, Britain dared to close enormous areas to settlement, depriving colonies of western lands claimed under their charters. Land speculators, settlers, and fur traders opposed to regulation saw their opportunities diminished, yet their local governments could not protect them.

As Parliament undermined the American legislatures, and the army stood ready to overawe them, the crown transformed the colonial civil service to render it immune to American influence. Before the 1760s, royal governors and their allies rewarded their supporters with multiple appointments. Now, this previously noncontroversial practice seemed an effort to prefer a few Americans who thereafter would act as servants of His Majesty. Above all, royal officials were no longer willing to connive with Americans in undermining British authority.

The reformed and strengthened customs service meant enforcement of new taxes and trade regulations, and rigorous enforcement often became arbitrary. Americans frequently committed technical violations of the new, complicated regulations since exact compliance was often impractical or unintentionally neglected. When the customs service prosecuted leading American merchants such as John Hancock and Henry Laurens of South Carolina, men prominent in the resistance enforcement, it seemed like persecution.

Americans had also lost confidence in the fairness of the courts. Before the 1760s, judges in America as in England had lifetime appointments, thereby shielding them from arbitrary removal. Now the crown insisted that new colonial judges be appointed, and old ones reappointed, at the pleasure of the crown. The reorganized vice-admiralty courts struck another blow at the English principle of fair trial. Americans attacked these courts—operating without juries, under English judges, and removed from local pressures—as "a most glaring and capital instance of tyranny." Some believed the courts were unconstitutional, violating the colonial charters and even the Magna Charta.

Religious Freedom in Danger

Paralleling the assaults on civil liberty, Americans saw new dangers to religious liberty. Most Americans were religious dissenters, that is, not members of the Anglican church. In England dissenters were second-class citizens, but not in America. This anomaly of "dissenting" churches enjoying the privilege of legal establishment in a nation where Anglicanism was the official religion, sharpened fears that English tolerance would not last. During most of the eighteenth century these fears lay dormant, surfacing occasionally when Britain intervened on behalf of Anglicans complaining of mistreatment. The great fear, however, appeared again in the 1760s and refused to die. The struggles in England in the seventeenth century convinced Englishmen that civil and spiritual liberty were inseparable, that tyrants bent on usurping political power also sought to control the church.

These anxieties gained fresh plausibility from renewed English concern with the religious condition of the colonies. The Church of England had long neglected its American responsibilities. In the 1760s the missionary zeal of a new Archbishop of London produced a campaign to strengthen colonial Anglicanism. Most needed were an American bishop who could remain on the scene to coordinate the work of distant parishes, and an effective mission to convert the dissenters. Calvinist colonies found the revival of the plan to create an American bishop most alarming. This scheme, John Adams noted, "spread a universal alarm against the authority of Parliament. . . . If Parliament could tax us, they could establish the Church of England."

But even the Anglicans, especially those in Virginia, were apprehensive. The plantation gentry who controlled their parishes did not want interference from either London or an American bishop. That danger became real when the local Anglican clergy successfully convinced the crown to disallow Virginia laws that altered their salaries, and then sued the colony for restitution. The Parsons' Cause thus threatened lay control over the clergy and struck at the authority of the Virginians to govern themselves. Appealing to a local jury to grant the clergy no relief, a young lawyer, Patrick Henry, denounced the ministers as "rapacious harpies [who] would snatch from the heart of their honest parishoner his last hoecake, from the widow and her orphan children their last milk cow; the last bed, nay the last blanket, from the woman in childbirth." Henry's oratory, once warmed up, knew no bounds.

Fears that England intended to disturb the religious life of the colonies added an additional emotional element to the growing crisis in the empire. Most Americans, whether Southern Anglicans, New England Congregationalists, Pennsylvania Presbyterians or Quakers had a common interest in preserving the religious status quo. Just as Americans believed in their mission to establish a society where men enjoyed civil freedom, so they viewed America as the home of spiritual freedom. Forgetting that their ancestors often had used their power to persecute religious minorities in America, as in seventeenth-century New England, they preferred to perpetuate the myth that men like John Winthrop had fled to America so that all might worship freely. In this way Americans claimed to defend the twin blessings of civil and religious liberty.

THE GREAT DEBATE

That defense took the form of a long, legalistic and far-ranging debate over the nature and meaning of liberty, of the British constitution and the colonial charters, of the rights of Englishmen and the rights of man. From this debate emerged principles that justified a revolution and shaped a new nation.

The central issue, whether limits existed on

British power over the colonies, had been precipitated by the Sugar and Stamp acts. Americans insisted on fixing such limits and the English countered with the notion of parliamentary supremacy. Their charters, Americans contended, gave them all the rights of Englishmen, including the right to approve the laws which governed them. Lacking representation in Parliament, local legislatures alone could speak with the authentic voice of the colonists.

If the charters did not protect them from arbitrary authority, the Americans insisted that the British constitution did. Since Britons could not be taxed without their consent, neither could Americans. The British insisted that the Americans were, in fact, "virtually represented" in Parliament, as were countless persons living in England who did not vote or whose communities lacked a seat in Parliament. Each member of Parliament represented every inch of British soil and every one of His Majesty's subjects.

Americans found this conception of representation incomprehensible. In the colonies, representation generally reflected the distribution of population. In theory, at least, every county or town, every group of people, expected to send delegates to the legislature. In Britain, however, representation reflected the distribution of population in the Middle Ages, when Parliament developed. As a result, by the eighteenth century—because of shifts in population and the development of new previously underpopulated regions—Parliament had become unrepresentative from the American perspective; according to American standards, it had no more right to legislate for disfranchised Manchester than for unrepresented Boston. How could Americans expect Parliament to tax them fairly, they asked, when its members would feel no burden from the revenues raised in the colonies?

The British could not compromise on the principle of virtual representation. It justified the disfranchisement of the great mass of Englishmen and rationalized the power of the governing elite. To put the American principle into action would require a major redistribution of power in England, a demand already raised within the realm by a few radicals. English reformers like John Wilkes sympathized with the colonists, and their campaigns for Parliamentary reform made clear that the American theory of representation threatened the authority of the ruling groups.

Throughout the debates, Americans searched for reasonable and trustworthy limits on British authority. A few were willing to concede Parliament the power to levy import, or external, taxes but not excise, or internal, taxes. Pennsylvania's John Dickinson argued that Parliament could regulate trade, since this was a matter beyond the competence of any single colony and that taxes incident to trade regulations were permissible, but taxes to raise revenue were not. But most writers denied that Parliament could tax the colonies at all.

As the Revolution neared and America failed to find acceptable limits to British authority, some suggested that Parliament had *no* right to legislate for the colonies. The ties that bound America to England were common traditions, common defense needs, and a common monarch to which all British subjects owed allegiance. In effect the Americans were groping toward a commonwealth solution of the imperial crisis, long before it became feasible in the nineteenth century.

Such a relationship was unthinkable then. It denied the sovereignty of Parliament, which the English regarded as the underpinning of the British constitution. Moreover, it was impractical as long as the monarch still actively participated in the executive and legislative branches. Loyalty to George III meant loyalty to the ministers, Parliaments, and policies for which the king still assumed responsibility. And England, then the world's superpower, victor in the Great War for Empire, had no intention of listening to lectures on political science from its colonial stepchildren.

Throughout the controversy, both sides claimed they were defending the British constitution. The British insisted that the constitution made Parliament supreme, its laws deriving from the will of the nation. The Americans slowly and often torturously, developed a novel conception of the constitution. Rejecting the traditional view that a constitution consists of the set of political arrangements that exist at a given time, they insisted instead that it embodies fundamental principles of natural law and justice. No legislative body or man-made law could violate those inalienable God-given rights to life, liberty, and property enjoyed by all human beings. The colonists argued that Parliament could govern only within the limits imposed by a higher law of natural rights. The English replied that the constitution was not a static set of commands but a living organism which Parliament interpreted. Its laws became part of the constitution and were man's best effort to embody natural rights in human law.

How to escape this impasse? By insisting on parliamentary supremacy, the British forced Americans to appeal to a higher law. The people were sovereign, the colonists concluded, not legislatures. They formed governments to protect their natural rights. When government betrayed its mission, it forfeited popular allegiance. For over a decade, Americans searched unsuccessfully for ways to reconcile their interests with those of the mother country. They insisted throughout that they accepted the British constitution, as they understood it. Their interpretation of the constitution and their vital interests, however, led them to adopt principles of government unacceptable in Britain.

When Americans first resisted British attempts to reorganize the empire after the Seven Years' War, no one anticipated or desired separation. Few on either side of the Atlantic saw irreconcilable differences. Some in England like William Pitt and Edmund Burke counseled moderation and patience, but appeasing the Americans did not pacify them. They remained just as uncooperative after repeal of the Stamp Act as before. Those arguing for a hard line gained increasing power. At the same time, Americans lost confidence in the mother country when the blunders of the Sugar and Stamp acts were repeated in the Townshend and Tea acts. The conviction spread that the colonists could no longer remain Englishmen and stay free.

Observing the Revolution from afar, a sympathetic English radical predicted that "next to the introduction of Christianity among mankind, the American revolution may prove the most important step in the progressive course of human improvement." Tom Paine, an English radical who arrived in America just in time to publish *Common Sense,* a powerful pamphlet in behalf of the American cause agreed. The Revolution, he prophesied, was not "the concern of a day, a year, or an age." All coming generations would be affected, "even to the end of time." The fulfillment of these forecasts depended on what Americans did with their independence.

Chapter 7
From Commonwealths to Nation

To declare independence from Britain was one thing, to win it was another. Even after the fighting began in 1775 some wished to reconcile differences with the mother country. But as the war dragged on, and the rebellious colonists set up their own governments, hopes for compromise faded. For six years Americans struggled against Britain's military might. Yet even before American victory had been assured, they began to build a nation. First they mobilized the resources to win the war; then they reconstructed sovereign governments in the states; and finally they created a national government. These political revolutions simultaneously altered the social order in important though not radical ways.

The former colonists knew that republican governments had almost always succumbed either to aggressive neighbors or to internal conflicts that ended in tyranny. No one could guarantee that the American republican experiment would escape that same fate. The United States comprised an extensive territory and a great diversity of people and interests. Northerners and Southerners, slaveowners and yeomen farmers, Congregationalists and Baptists, merchants and artisans, Germans, English, and Scotch—all had to cooperate to make one nation out of thirteen colonies. Cooperation assumed the existence of common interests strong enough to overcome the differences sure to emerge within such a diverse and dispersed society. It also assumed that men could find methods of decision-making that would command popular respect and support.

Within two decades Americans welded these varied elements into a nation, a potentially strong and stable republic. They created a democratic government, respectful of individual liberty, which offered citizens the means of advancing private interest and public welfare.

WINNING INDEPENDENCE, 1776-1783

The American Revolution, the first successful anticolonial struggle in modern history, foreshadowed the difficulties experienced by colonialist powers in our own times in repressing strong movements for self-determination. Americans won their war of national liberation against great odds. They had to establish new, untested governments and these fragile regimes had to put a citizens' army in the field, hoping that Americans would fight and pay taxes. The British, who had a powerful navy, a well-disciplined army, and extensive financial resources, rarely lost a battle. Yet they lost the war. Fifty to sixty thousand troops in the American colonies, generously supplied, and supported by the Royal Navy, failed to crush the rebellion.

British Strategy

The fighting began around Boston. In June 1775, the British forced the Americans to give up high ground overlooking Boston, but they took heavy casualties in the Battle of Boston Harbor. Ten months later the British had to evacuate Boston. The rebels had seized Dorchester Heights, and their artillery threatened the city. The first year of fighting ended inconclusively. The Americans attacked Canada, hoping that French-speaking Canadians would join the rebellion. Although they captured Montreal, Quebec held firm and the invaders got little support from the populace.

The British then made New York their center of operations. Their troops, which included several thousand German mercenaries, routed General Washington on Long Island, and occupied New York City in September 1776. Forced to flee south into New Jersey, Washington retreated across the Delaware as winter approached, while most of the British army returned to New York for the winter. Washington's army then took Hessian mercenaries at Trenton, New Jersey, by surprise and beat back the British counterattack at Princeton, freeing most of that state from enemy control.

The British planned to destroy American resistance in one major campaign that would cut off the New England colonies, regarded as the seedbed of rebellion. In June 1777 they launched the Hudson River Plan; General Burgoyne's main British force moved southward down Lake Champlain and the upper Hudson toward Saratoga. A smaller supporting army marched east from Lake Ontario, while a third army was expected to move north from New York City. The combined power of this coordinated triple pincer would supposedly crush the Americans and end the rebellion.

The plan failed. Burgoyne's large and cumbersome army moved slowly and was difficult to supply. An emergency expedition to capture supplies at Bennington, Vermont, met disaster at the hands of untrained American militia. As Burgoyne approached Saratoga, American forces gathered and dug in. Burgoyne's expected support from the other approaching forces never materialized. Surrounded by a vastly superior number of American troops "Gentleman Johnny" Burgoyne (who had no intention of meeting a hero's or any other kind of death) gave up the battle and surrendered.

The American victory at Saratoga decisively altered the course of the war. From the outset America had sought foreign aid. France was eager to weaken Britain and recover prestige and territories lost in the Seven Years' War. In the spring of 1776, secret French loans allowed the Americans to purchase essential military supplies. After Saratoga, France openly recognized the United States and in 1778 formed a military and commercial alliance. Sensing that it, too, might profit from Britain's troubles, Spain declared war in 1779, but without recognizing the independence of the United States, a potentially troublesome neighbor along the Florida and Louisiana borders.

Also after Saratoga, the new British commander, Sir Henry Clinton, abandoned the idea of crushing the Americans with one blow. He dispatched an army to the South to seize Savannah and Charleston, hoping to conquer the Carolinas and pacify other areas until American determination wore down. This strategy of attrition also failed. Pacification was slow and costly. Control of cities such as New York, Charleston, or Philadelphia did not give the British command of the countryside, the essential factor in a rural country. Guerrilla warfare in the Southern back country proved to be beyond the capacity of British troops sent to search out and destroy American forces. Convinced that control of the South required the capture of Virginia, in May 1781 British General Cornwallis invaded that poorly defended state. His command center was Yorktown, from which he could keep in touch with army headquarters in New York. Meanwhile, Washington and General Rochambeau, commander of the French forces, planned joint operations. Learning that the French naval squadron in the West Indies intended to sail for Chesapeake Bay, Washington and Rochambeau attempted to surround Cornwallis. At the end of August, the French fleet blockaded Yorktown as the Americans and French troops closed the trap. Caught by an army more than double the size of his own, his escape route to the sea cut off, Cornwallis fought hard but surrendered before Clinton could come to his rescue.

Yorktown proved decisive. The defeat destroyed Britain's will to fight in what seemed a hopeless cause, forcing Lord North out of office and paving the way for peace talks. The Continental Congress then appointed John Adams, Benjamin Franklin, and John Jay as peace negotiators. The resulting Treaty of Paris (1783) favored the United States. Britain recognized American independence, agreed to generous boundary settlements, and permitted Americans to fish off Newfoundland and Nova Scotia and dry their catch on British soil. In return the Americans promised to encourage the states to restore the rights and property of the Tories, the many colonists who had remained loyal to the crown, and both sides agreed to honor the claims of creditors against their citizens.

Why American Victory?

Americans owed their success as much to British failures as to their own efforts. Britain's best hope for victory lay in destroying the American army before French and Spanish power could influence the course of the war. This required mobilizing well-supplied men quickly and deploying them boldly. The British did neither. Their huge, unwieldy, eighteenth-century war machine greatly taxed London's ability to supply and coordinate the necessary resources. Armies and tactics designed for use in Europe often proved inappropriate to "the warfare of the woods." Thus the failure of the Hudson River Plan resulted from poor coordination. The British general who was supposed to proceed directly up the Hudson, captured Philadelphia instead, and the time lost in that campaign prevented him from reaching Burgoyne on schedule. Moreover, the strategy assumed that Burgoyne could move quickly down from Canada with adequate supplies for the entire campaign. These and other miscalculations doomed the plan and Britain's best chance for victory, and were representative of British military bungling.

The British commanders repeatedly missed tactical opportunities and failed to take risks that might have brought swift victory. Cautious men, their commands protected by political influence at home, they regarded their armies as too valuable to risk in daring campaigns. Political objectives further complicated the military goals. The British, who looked too far ahead to restoring their rule in North America, knew that ruthless and unrestrained use of force jeopardized the long-run chances for reestablishing harmony. The British expected those loyal to the crown would rally to the king's standard, but because the rebels controlled most of the continent, loyalist troops never materialized in the numbers anticipated.

Knowing that they could not match the British on the field, the Americans successfully fought a war of attrition. Washington avoided decisive encounters. His principal objective was to keep the army intact and keep patriot hopes alive. The limitless space into which Washington's army could flee, the absence of any strategic centers whose capture would doom the patriot effort, and widespread popular support he could count on, despite the failure of Congress to supply the army adequately, all strengthened the American cause. The British could not hold conquered territory without tying down troops needed for offensive operations. British victories often cost more in manpower, not easily replaced, than they were worth, whereas the Americans had a relatively inexhaustible reserve of citizen soldiers who could, if necessary, be quickly mobilized. As Americans learned, they could sustain defeats

on the battlefield; as long as they kept an army together, they gained confidence.

Once the failure of the Hudson River Plan led the British to adopt a counterstrategy of attrition, their chances for success faded. In England, political opposition to the war mounted as victory became more elusive. "Next year," the year of victory, never seemed to come. There were limits to which British taxpayers would sink money into what appeared to be a bottomless American pit, especially after the entry of France and Spain altered the balance of forces. Fearing a French invasion of England, the British deployed ships and soldiers at home that otherwise could have been sent to America. The French Navy contested British mastery of the Atlantic, forced the Royal Navy to protect the British West Indies, and made possible combined American and French land and naval operations, which caught the British in the trap at Yorktown. The American success against the world's greatest power stunningly demonstrated that a citizenry could be moblized for war and could defeat professional soldiers (with foreign help, of course), when it had nationhood as its aim. All Europe, not only Britain, watched this drama unfold with almost as much disbelief as attention.

THE SOCIAL CONSEQUENCES OF REVOLUTION

The great revolutions in France (1789), Russia (1917), and China (1940s) radically transformed those underdeveloped societies. In each country the revolution swept away old ruling groups and replaced them with new ones, fundamentally altering the distribution of wealth, power, and prestige.

No comparable transformation occurred in British North America. The Americans rebelled against foreign control, not against an oppressive social system. The leaders of the Revolution and of the new nation were often the same individuals who had dominated colonial society. Americans became revolutionaries less by intent than by circumstance. Wishing to retain their freedom, they had no choice but to separate from Britain. They chose independence yet shunned far-reach-

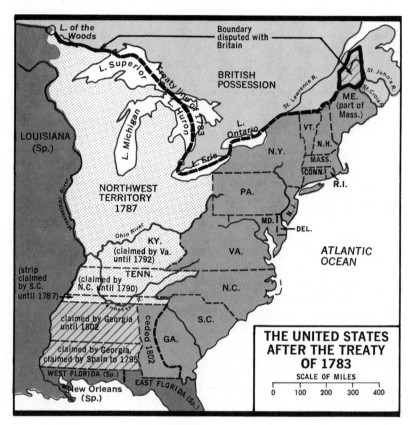

THE UNITED STATES
AFTER THE TREATY
OF 1783
SCALE OF MILES
0   100   200   300   400

ing plans for reorganizing society. The logic by which they justified and explained rebellion as necessary to establish a nation, nevertheless led to some unforeseen changes in American society.

The Revolution simultaneously intensified developments that had started in the colonial period while pushing America in new directions. Government, which in the colonial period had been more responsive to popular forces than in other countries, became *more* democratic; the economy and social structure, which had offered ambitious colonists extensive opportunity to improve their condition, now offered citizens even greater opportunities. The trend toward separation of church and state gathered momentum and became part of constitutional law. The Revolution, however, did more than accentuate changes already under way. Setting up strong and stable republican governments in a world of monarchies based on the belief that the people could not govern themselves represented an important innovation which kindled the flames of discontent among the lower orders of other nations.

THE SOCIAL STRUCTURE

Revolution altered the old structure of authority without destroying it. The colonists had shared power with the mother country, informally manipulated royal officials, and taken advantage of English negligence. But the crown always retained the final say, since London could veto colonial legislation and legislate for the colonies. Sovereignty—the whole range of governmental powers —now came to rest in American hands. Americans filled public offices once reserved for English placemen, and American ships sailed freely to all parts of the world, constructing complex trading patterns previously prohibited by the mother country's navigation laws.

The Revolution thus transferred to the Americans decision-making authority over matters that before the conflict had been English prerogatives. At the same time that Americans gained complete control over the political process, the Revolution eliminated from power and influence thousands of persons loyal to the crown. Upwards of 100,000 Tories fled, some to England, many to Canada; others retired into obscurity in the United States. The new revolutionary regimes required loyalty oaths of citizens, and punished prominent persons who had collaborated with the British by confiscating their property.

The Tories

Tories came from every walk of life. Most were farmers and shopkeepers, though loyalist ranks contained a disproportionate number of the wealthy professionals and officials. Those most closely identified with British power, such as royal officials, merchants doing business under government license, and Anglican churchmen outside of the South, were most likely to remain loyal. Others, recently arrived in the colonies, not yet integrated into the colonial social order, were less likely to feel their freedom endangered by British policy. On the contrary, groups alienated from local revolutionary elites often looked to the crown for protection and favor. Thus Hudson Valley tenant farmers who had rioted against their landlords in the 1760s were slow to join them in resisting the crown. Similarly, religious dissenters in Connecticut and Massachusetts restive under the Congregationalist establishment relied on Britain to preserve their religious freedom. Others became Tories or remained neutral because they simply could not bring themselves to join in rebellion. People accustomed to respecting authority in the family, the church, and the state frequently preferred to submit to unjust rule rather than follow a path that might lead to the gallows.

The incidence of Toryism varied considerably. The presence of the British Army encouraged loyalism, especially in New York City, which the British held for most of the war. But the fact that the dissident Americans controlled most of the country discouraged the spirit of loyalism.

The elimination of the Tories cannot be compared to the liquidation of ruling classes in other revolutions. For the most part the Tories were removed without aid of guillotine, firing squad, concentration camp, or brainwashing. Shortly after the war anti-Tory sentiment quickly subsided, and some loyalists who never constituted a hated ruling class returned. Though many loyalists were prominent officials, merchants, and professionals, most of the colonial elite had joined the revolutionary cause. They remained, therefore, to govern colonial society, though the loyalist exodus created wholesale social and occupational opportunities for newcomers to rise. Finally, the departure of antirevolutionary elements spared the new republic the dangers of a resentful counterrevolutionary faction waiting for a chance to regain power, a circumstance which in other revolutions, particularly in France, intensified hatred, bloodshed, and violence.

The American Revolution presented other opportunities for the ambitious. "I am weary to death of this dreadful war," ran a common complaint among the elite. "It is attended with such irregular distributions of property. People have been raised by the war from the lowest indigence to affluence." The new state and national governments had hundreds of positions to fill; the militias and continental army required numerous officers. Local politicians who left Virginia or Massachusetts to serve in national office opened the way for others at home. As a result, the recruitment of public officials became more democratic, especially in the new state legislatures. The wealthy and educated held a smaller percentage of posts, and farmers and others of moderate wealth held a greater percentage than before the Revolution.

The French and Russian revolutions radically redistributed wealth by expropriating the property of old ruling groups. The promise of land reform to satisfy the peasants' craving for his own soil has repeatedly mobilized the discontented throughout the world. But since most colonial Americans owned their own farms or expected to acquire them because land was cheap and abundant, no widespread attack on wealth took place, especially since the colonial elite generally supported the Revolution. So many had a stake in society that respect for private property, except that held by the crown or loyalists, universally prevailed. The revolutionary governments confiscated the ungranted lands belonging to the king and to the proprietors in Maryland and Pennsylvania; large Tory landowners, such as Lord Granville (who owned a third of North Carolina), lost all their holdings. But there it stopped.

These transfers of millions of acres from English to American hands helped the rebels finance the war. Governments paid creditors and soldiers in land, and sold large tracts to speculators to raise revenue. Confiscation thus enriched the public treasury and filled private pockets instead of appeasing the demands of the propertyless. Eventually persons acquiring public land hoped to resell it at a profit; but they had to compete with government, which still retained millions of acres of public domain. Those who profited most immediately from the redistribution of land, therefore, were persons with capital, merchants who had made money supplying the army with food and clothing, or engaging in privateering and currency speculation.

Though the Revolution did not radically redistribute landed wealth, it wiped out all traces of European landowning patterns. Quitrents, which some farmers had to pay annually to the crown or to proprietors, disappeared; states which applied the laws of primogeniture and entail to the inheritance of property abandoned them as remnants of aristocracy and inappropriate for a republic. But these changes, like so many during the revolutionary era, merely completed and formalized developments long in progress. Thus, neither quitrents nor primogeniture and entail played so important a role in the colonies before the Revolution as they did abroad. The Revolution hastened the disappearance of these anachronisms.

War and independence also altered the prospects of many farmers and merchants. The war created a boom market for supplies to maintain armies in the field. Farmers who produced surplus foodstuffs and could get their crops to market profited from inflation at the expense of urban dwellers, whose incomes did not grow rapidly enough to match rising prices. These groups demanded price controls and some states attempted to control inflation, but with little success.

The war also affected the fortunes of merchants. Many of the older merchants failed to adjust to new conditions. Though the war closed off older trade routes within the British empire, it became possible to explore alternate markets and establish new trading relationships. Merchants who quickly acquired supplies needed by government, who fitted out merchant vessels as privateers to prey on English shipping, and who bought up loyalist property cheaply and speculated in paper currency, easily acquired fortunes. With peace restored, merchants encountered new difficulties, but they now could use the state and national governments to advance their interests in ways not possible as colonials. They could charter banks and other corporations, develop natural resources, and obtain support for commercial and maritime enterprise.

In these ways—the displacement of the Tories, the transfer of land from British to American control, the war-born opportunities for making money—the American social order became more open and fluid than it had been in the colonial era, although its basic structure remained unchanged. New families acquired fortunes, gained office, and advanced their social standing; some older families, previously prominent, declined into obscurity. These changes, however, did not upset the stability of the established social order through the removal of an entire ruling class.

THE CHURCHES

The changes caused by the Revolution affected religious life as well as material circumstances. The Revolution further weakened the ties between church and state and gave fresh impetus to the spread of denominationalism. Almost every state guaranteed religious liberty in principle; the practice, however, meant different things in different communities. Most had religious tests for officeholders, on the assumption that unless officials believed "in one God, the Creator and Governor of the universe, the rewarder of the good and the punisher of the wicked," they could not be trusted to exercise power justly. Colonies without religious establishments wrote separation of church and state into their new constitutions. Others abandoned their state churches, the weak Anglican establishments in the South falling away easily, discredited by their ties with the crown. Massachusetts and Connecticut, however, preserved the Congregationalist establishments into the nineteenth century.

In one Southern state, Virginia, a prolonged struggle took place. During the war Virginia repealed discriminatory laws against religious dissenters. Anglicans, however, still had to support their church. Fearing complete disestablishment, they offered dissenters a multiple establishment that would give each denomination a share of religious taxes paid by all citizens. This proposal almost passed. For almost a decade Thomas Jefferson and James Madison had campaigned for complete separation in Virginia. Madison, while a member of the Virginia legislature, successfully rallied the dissenters against the compromise bill. In 1786 Virginia's Statute of Religious Liberty declared "that no man shall be compelled to frequent or support any religious worship . . . nor shall be burdened in his body or goods, nor shall otherwise suffer on account of his religious opinions and belief. . . ." The triumph of separation in Virginia over the oldest established church in America meant that for many Americans religious liberty required that churches receive no financial support from the state, a principle later applied to the national government.

Religion thus became a private matter. Citizens were free to join and support churches of their choice, if they wished, or to form new ones. The spread of denominationalism had its roots in the diversity of belief that made it difficult for any single group to maintain a privileged position or impose its will through government action. The Revolution strengthened the influence of religious dissent because Americans claimed

to be struggling against all forms of tyranny over the minds and bodies of man. The great fear of Anglican designs in the decade before independance gave the foes of religious establishments new arguments, and placed the Congregationalists in the peculiar position of attacking Anglican churches while maintaining their own establishments. Thus, revolutionary doctrine combined with the pressure of growing numbers of religious dissenters to make separation of church and state part of the American way. Proud of the triumph of religious freedom in Virginia, Jefferson expressed satisfaction to his fellow campaigner, Madison, that "after so many ages during which the human mind has been held in vassalage by kings, priests, and nobles," their state had the honor "to have produced the first legislature which had the courage to declare that the reason of man may be trusted with the formation of his own opinions."

RECONSTRUCTING GOVERNMENT: THE STATE CONSTITUTIONS

"How few of the human race have ever enjoyed an opportunity of making an election of government, more than of air, soil, or climate, for themselves or their children," noted John Adams. Revolutionary leaders proclaimed, perhaps a bit too smugly, that Americans were "the first people whom heaven has favored with an opportunity of deliberating upon and choosing the forms of government under which they should live."

The Revolution led to the reconstruction of government on republican foundations. No longer the subjects of a kingdom they considered corrupt, Americans could freely devise political arrangements that reconciled competing claims of liberty and authority, protecting individuals from abuses of power while restraining disruptive forces. For two decades Americans wrote and rewrote constitutions, confident that appropriate governmental mechanisms would control political divisiveness and lay the foundations of a strong yet free republic.

The outbreak of fighting in 1775 and the Declaration of Independence a year later had not produced anarchy. From the beginning, Americans regarded their resistance to England as a defense of local government against outside usurpation. The colonial dissidents before 1776 were not conspirators forced to operate outside of authority, but public officials and established political leaders accustomed to exercising power. Though they did resort to extralegal means, such as mobs and committees of correspondence, for the most part the resistance centered in such bodies as the provincial legislatures which sent delegates to the Stamp Act Congress and the Continental Congresses.

After the break with England, power devolved on provisional governments in the states, which quickly replaced British authority. Eventually citizens adopted new, more permanent governments. Between May and December 1776, eight states wrote constitutions and others soon followed. Soome of these constitutions went unchanged for generations. Other states experimented. By 1800 sixteen states had adopted twenty-six constitutions, some having produced as many as three.

According to revolutionary theory, government derived its powers from the consent of the people, the source of sovereignty. Independence from Britain, therefore, returned power once more to the sovereign citizens who could establish new governments that would protect their natural rights. But how were the sentiments of the people to be collected, articulated, and translated into practical instruments of government? And how could citizens protect themselves against future abuses of power that would make further revolutions necessary?

The Meaning of Constitutions

There were no easy answers, but Americans slowly perceived solutions. From the prerevolutionary debate over the nature of the British constitution and the limits on Parliament's power, they came to view a constitution as fundamental law, different from and superior to ordinary, statutory law. Constitutional law establishes government and places limits on it; all branches, the executive, legislative, and judicial, derive their authority from the constitution, and may not exceed constitutionally granted powers.

Americans assumed that constitutions were much more than prevailing political arrangements. The new state constitutions came to be regarded as fundamental law which could not be altered by the ordinary legislative process. Thus most of the new frameworks of government included bills of rights which specifically prohibited government interference with essential human rights such as freedom of speech and conscience, and which assured trial by jury according to due process. These restraints on government were not self-enforcing, but represented powerful expressions of men's belief in liberty to which citizens could appeal against arbitrary power.

As people came to accept constitutions as fundamental law, they also groped toward appropriate procedures for creating constitutions. At first state legislatures, the most conveniently available political bodies, framed constitutions. But if legislatures could write constitutions, they could also change them at will; a constitutional convention, chosen specifically to frame a new government, provided a solution to this potentially dangerous anamoly. Beginning with New York in 1777, it became customary to submit constitutions to the voters for ratification. In 1787, when some sought to alter the structure of the national government, ready-made procedures were available. They called a convention to meet at Philadelphia and sent the new federal constitution to the states for approval. Subsequent generations have remodeled state governments using most of the same procedures first devised by the revolutionary generation.

The new state constitutions retained many features familiar from colonial experience. They all included legislative, executive, and judicial branches, but with an altered relationship among the branches. The earliest state constitutions made the assemblies dominant. This ended the long contest for power between the royal governors and the popular branch. Constitution-makers stripped governors of independence, often had them elected by the legislature, and denied them patronage, the veto, and the right to dissolve the assembly. The legislatures, focal points of resistance to Britain, had long been the principal instrument of colonial self-government; the revolutionary constitutions formalized this historical development by making them the centers of power: the source of law, the dispenser of most patronage, and the place where local elites and interests made vital decisions. The need to establish new revolutionary governments quickly and the desire to remedy the defects of colonial government determined the forms the constitutions took.

But as men lived under these new governments and reflected upon problems of republicanism, constitutional principles and practices changed. Thomas Jefferson, a superb theorist who served, not too successfully, as governor of Virginia during the Revolution, reluctantly concluded that legislative supremacy was dangerous. "One hundred and seventy-three despots [in the legislature]," he warned, "would surely be as oppressive as one. . . . An elective despotism was not the government we fought for." Establishing republican governments that were free and stable proved to be a much more complicated task than many realized at the start.

Americans nevertheless felt that they could handle the task. As careful students of "the divine science" of politics, they knew that tyranny lurked only a few steps behind liberty. Nation-builders such as John Adams hoped to reconstruct government "on the simple principles of 'nature,'" without resorting to the "pretense of miracle or mystery" on which other governments rested. Diligent study might unlock the secrets of the political order, just as Newtonian science had laid bare some of the workings of nature for the eighteenth century. Government existed to promote human happiness, but usually ended by enslaving men. The struggles within the colonies among rival groups and the contest with Parliament reinforced the fears of governmental tyranny which Americans drew from the English radical and dissenting tradition. Nor could the people themselves be relied on always to choose rulers wisely, to reject the would-be tyrant, or to respect the rights of minorities.

Government and the Nature of Man

At bottom, the problem resided in the nature of man. If men were angels, they would not need government to protect one another from their predatory neighbors. In the best of all possible worlds, in Utopia, reason would always prevail; but, as John Adams noted, "it certainly never did since the Fall [of Adam and Eve], and never will till the Millennium." Adams, the foremost authority on constitution-making in the revolutionary generation, recalled the old adage, "the heart is deceitful above all things and desperately wicked." He insisted that "self-interest, private avidity, ambition, and avarice will exist in every state of society and under every form of government." Those in power should never forget these sobering realities.

American state-builders approached their task with a realistic view of the nature of man. They believed human beings capable of acting rationally and benevolently, but they also took baser impulses into account. A republican majority might oppress minorities, plunder the wealthy, and persecute men of differing religious faiths or unorthodox political beliefs. Minorities, however, also posed potential dangers to the liberty and stability of republics. They might corrupt elections and intimidate the poor and weak, and special interests might scheme to advance their fortunes at the expense of the common good. For these reasons neither majorities nor minorities could be trusted with uncontrolled power. "The fundamental article of my political creed," John Adams said, "is that despotism, or unlimited sovereignty, or absolute power, is the same in a majority of a popular assembly, an aristocratical council, an oligarchical junto, and a single emperor. Equally arbitrary, cruel, bloody, and in every respect diabolical."

According to Adams, without virtue—the capacity of citizens to restrain their "passions," to respect the rights and interests of others—man cannot achieve public happiness. Yet, given his nature, how can one expect men to be sufficiently virtuous. The "divine science" pointed the way. "We may hazard the conjecture," Adams suggested, "that the virtues have been the effect of a well-ordered constitution rather than the cause." Since man's character could not be changed, Americans put their faith in proper constitutional arrangements to restrain his baser impulses and liberate his nobler ones. The eighteenth-century conservative consensus held that:

For forms of government let fools contest,
That which is best administered is best.

Adams sharply disagreed: "Nothing can be more fallacious than this. Nothing is more certain from the history of nations and the nature of man, than that some forms of government are better fitted for being well administered than others." The main task was to discover the best forms.

Balanced Government

Britain's unwritten constitution provided a partial model. Theoretically, it divided power among the monarchy, the aristocracy (House of Lords), and the people (the House of Commons), in the hope that each would guard against threats to liberty from the other. In practice, however, the monarchial and aristocratic elements overwhelmed the popular branch. With no hereditary monarchial or aristocratic elements, the United States nevertheless contained sufficient groups whose influence had to be checked to maintain a balance between the rights of majorities and minorities, between the interests of a few and the good of the many.

A constitution that embodied the principle of "balanced government" carefully structured the legislative branch to make it an authentic voice of the people. The broad colonial franchise, carried over or in some states further liberalized, assured a mandate from a majority of the adult males for the legislatures. Attacks on virtual representation led to attempts to apportion seats according to the distribution of population, so that each man had one equally weighted vote. Some constitutions required that the makeup of the legislature reflect shifts in population by periodic readjustments, a stipulation that was not self-enforcing and often has been ignored by groups benefiting from overrepresentation.

Frequent elections, often every year, and instructions by constituents to guide representatives on vital issues provided other means of keeping the legislature close to the people. Electoral districts also had to be made sufficiently small and homogeneous so that voters could keep close tabs on their representatives, who in turn could have a clear idea of what the voters wanted. A small district in which the citizens had similar interests could more easily and accurately be represented than a large one containing many different and rival interests.

Most states had a second, or upper, house to balance the assembly. A carry-over from colonial times, when the governor's council usually served as the upper house, the senates created by the early constitutions often depended on the popular branch. The influence of councils had declined in colonial times, and the assemblies steadily cut into their power. Identifying them with the royal prerogative, the first constitution-writers made sure the senates would not rival the more popular houses. Subsequently, many came to regard strong, independent senates elected by the people as a valuable check on the majority. The senates, usually smaller bodies, often represented counties or reflected the distribution of wealth rather than population.

A strong independent executive also performed a balancing function. Although the early constitutions created a weak executive as a reaction against the royal governors, experience proved the value of a strong executive. A governor elected by all the voters of the state could help restrain factions in the legislature and, since he represented the entire state, was more likely to have a broad perspective. Legislators, on the other hand, reflected the particular interests and special outlook of their limited constituencies. By giving the governor short and fixed terms, a veto that could be overridden, and the right to appoint some officials with legislative assent, the executive could be made strong but not dangerous.

An independent judiciary provided additional ballast. Serving for long-term or even lifetime periods and at fixed salaries, the judges had no fear of the executive or legislative branches, and were nearly immune from popular pressure. Judges generally did not yet review the constitutionality of legislation, however, though a few began tentatively to assert that power. Judicial review eventually developed because the American conception of a constitution as higher law logically called for some body, relatively free from politics, to enforce limits on statutory power.

The theory of balanced government tried to prevent individuals or groups from acquiring undue power. Prohibition of plural office-holding served as a further precaution. Moderate salaries provided another: "Government is instituted for the common good," declared the Massachusetts constitution of 1780, "and not for the profit, of any one man, family or class of men." Therefore, judges, sheriffs, probate and deed registers, among others, could not serve in the legislature.

The new state constitutions generally worked well. Citizens accepted the new governments as legitimate and individual liberty seemed secure. The states, however, could not win the war on their own. Winning independence was a cooperative effort of the new United States of America.

General Washington remarked proudly on the high level of wartime cooperation among Americans: "Who . . . could imagine that the most violent local prejudices would cease so soon; . . . that men who came from different parts of the continent, strongly disposed by the habits of education to despise and quarrel with each other, would instantly become but one patriotic band of brothers?" But the long-term task of founding a stable republic strained the patriotic fraternity of the "band of brothers." Throughout a difficult decade, Americans searched for an appropriate framework of *national* authority by which to govern themselves.

Chapter 8
Founding the Union

In 1785, two years after the signing of the peace treaty that confirmed America's independence, Thomas Jefferson, serving in Paris as American minister to France, urged a friend back home to "find it convenient to come here. . . . It will make you adore your country, its soil, its climate, its equality, liberty, laws, people, and manners. My God how little do my countrymen know what precious blessings they are in possession of, and which no other people on earth enjoy." Residence and travel in Europe heightened Jefferson's sense of American identity. Seeing the mass of men in Europe trapped in perpetual poverty and in bondage to privileged aristocrats and a powerful church contemptuous of the rights of man made Jefferson value more highly his own country's experiment in freedom.

That experiment's survival was by no means assured. The Revolution had not automatically transformed thirteen colonies into a nation powerful enough to protect itself from foreign foes and internal strife. When Patrick Henry exclaimed in 1775 that "the distinctions between Virginians, Pennsylvanians, New Yorkers, and New Englanders are no more," and then went on to proclaim, "I am not a Virginian, but an American," he was indulging in patriotic exaggeration. Two centuries of provincial experience did not suddenly lead a people conditioned to local loyalties to abandon them for national loyalties. The union of states that banded together after declaring independence gave political form to America, but nationality depends on more than sudden outbursts of patriotic sentiment or the mere proclamation of shared ideals such as in the Declaration of Independence. Americans, like other people absorbed in nation-building, had to find ways to integrate diverse and numerous interests in a large republic and assure their participation in making decisions vitally affecting their lives; they had to create a central government which people would trust and which would command respect abroad; and finally, they had to balance all the elements in the Union to prevent local differences from threatening national harmony.

For over a decade Americans struggled with the tasks of nation-building. Colonial political experience provided few useful precedents, nor could Americans easily anticipate future problems and obstacles. The necessity to fight a long war for independence further complicated the job. Moreover, American fears of strong centralized power, such as they thought England had wished to impose, made them reluctant to grant extensive authority to the national government. The first efforts to create a satisfactory central government failed because each state insisted on retaining sovereignty. The Articles of Confederation, for all its faults, eventually generated forces and sentiments that produced a new framework for the Union. Convinced that unless they devised an adequate national structure, "the fate of an empire in many respects the most interesting in the world" would be jeopardized, and that Americans "by their conduct and example" would decide the question "whether societies of men are really capable or not of establishing good government," the founding fathers met in Philadelphia in 1787 to write a new constitution. The document they drafted became the foundation for a stable, powerful nation which met all the constitutional challenges that threatened its survival until the election of Abraham Lincoln in 1860, which precipitated an insoluble political confrontation ending in civil war.

THE CONFEDERATION, 1777-1787

During most of the Revolution, the Continental Congress served as a provisional national government pending agreement on a more permanent arrangement. It created an army and navy, negotiated with foreign powers, and requested funds from the states. Shortly after independence, Congress, like the provisional governments in the states, attempted to draft a constitution for the Union. In November 1777, it approved the Articles of Confederation and sent it to the states for ratification. Though Americans had early agreed upon the need for uniting the country, four years passed before all the states approved the Articles. The war for independence was thus nearly over before the American Union possessed a formal charter of national government.

The Articles of Confederation formalized the structure of the Union emerging during the war. The states surrendered very little power. They retained the authority to tax, regulate commerce, and police themselves internally. Congress had responsibility for waging the war and for conducting foreign relations, raising and administering military forces, settling boundary disputes among states, and managing the public lands not under state control. A Congress in which each state had one vote wielded the Confederation's limited powers, without separate executive or judicial branches, much like the wartime Continental Congress. Because Congress could only *request* money from the states, real power remained in state hands. The conduct of war and foreign affairs, the Confederation's principal administrative responsibilities, required an independent revenue which it lacked, and which the states very pointedly had no intention of turning over to the central government.

The framing and ratification of the Articles stirred up a controversy which revealed the difficulties of establishing an effective central government. The large, heavily populated states wanted representation in Congress in proportion to their numbers and importance in the Union. However, the smaller, less populous states feared their interests would suffer unless each state had an equal voice. The small states won out.

Although the Articles differed from state constitutions which tied representation to population, this departure did not violate constitutional theory because the Confederation government was not sovereign. It acted only through the states rather than directly upon citizens: it could not tax, and therefore representation need not follow population.

A second major controversy arose over the method of apportioning requisitions for money. The New England states, with relatively high land values, pushed for requisitions in proportion to population as the fairest measure of wealth and of ability to pay. Southern states, with populations including thousands of slaves and with relatively low land values, wanted taxes levied on the basis of property values. Southerners got their way with support from the Middle Atlantic states.

The last major dispute concerned disposition of western lands. The United States acquired extensive unsettled territory that had belonged to the crown and to English proprietors. Much of it lay outside of state jurisdiction and thus became the property of the Union. Some states, however, claimed extensive areas under colonial charters which would have extended their boundaries across the continent to the Pacific Ocean. The landless states, most notably Maryland, insisted that unsettled frontier regions belonged to all the citizens of the Union. If Virginia's or North Carolina's far-reaching claims were upheld, farmers and speculators in other states could not compete equally for these lands, since preference would probably go to Virginians and North Carolinians. Maryland refused to ratify the Articles until Virginia ceded most of its western land to the Confederation government.

These disputes between states large and small, landed and landless, those favoring requisitions based on land values or on population, pointed up the reluctance of Americans to lodge power in a strong central government. Their experiences as colonials, particularly during the stormy 1760s, taught them to distrust all concentrations of power. They believed that by vesting most power in the states, close to the people, citizens could more easily prevent abuses. And it was far easier to achieve agreement among the more homogeneous interests within a state than among the multiplicity of groups, often with conflicting views, spread throughout the Union. Thus confining sovereign power to a smaller, more socially uniform geographic area such as a state would presumably increase chances of obtaining a consensus on public policy and reducing the danger of factionalism. Dispersal of power among the states seemed to provide republican government's best chance for survival.

For these theoretical and practical reasons the Articles of Confederation differed in conception and structure from the state constitutions. The states were virtually sovereign governments, exercising all vital powers. The principles of balanced government, however, were inapplicable to the Confederation since Congress lacked sufficient power to use or abuse. Thus, no executive or judicial branches checked Congress, a task left to the states. Nor did the Articles contain a bill of rights because no one imagined that the Confederation, which did not operate on individuals, could jeopardize a citizen's civil or religious liberties. Furthermore, since Congress could not tax, its representation did not have to reflect the distribution of population.

CRISIS IN THE CONFEDERATION

As long as Americans believed that they could win independence and establish a workable national government without centralizing power, the Articles served as a reasonable arrangement for the Union. But the central government's weakness handicapped the war effort severely and cast doubts on its future. Gradually, many Americans became convinced that the states, despite their extensive power, could not satisfactorily promote the common welfare; nor could Congress, without a substantial increase in its authority.

Forced to rely on the states for revenue, Congress could not adequately supply Washington's army. The soldiers had suffered terrible privation in their winter camp at Valley Forge (1777); later mutinies among Continental troops in New Jersey (1780) and Pennsylvania (1781) expressed the pent-up frustration of soldiers of any nation when their food is rotten, their clothing threadbare, and their salaries unpaid. In March 1783, a group of officers threatened to defy Congress for failing to settle accounts and vote pensions previously promised. Washington had to step in, his restraining influence ending the danger of a military takeover.

Financial Problems

Peace brought no relief from financial problems, however. The United States financed the war by taxing, borrowing, and issuing paper money, relying most heavily on the latter two methods. Congress printed almost $200 million

in paper money called "continentals," currency which rapidly declined in value because the states failed to give Congress the funds to redeem the paper in hard money. By 1780, $40 in continental currency was worth $1 in gold or silver. Congress also borrowed from private citizens and from foreign countries, principally France, Spain and Holland. Government creditors who accepted payments in depreciating continental currency actually were speculating that someday the United States government would redeem the paper at face value.

Necessity drove the revolutionaries to finance the war for independence on credit. The new governments were fearful of taxing too heavily. Had they done so, the entire burden of funding America's revolution would have fallen on the shoulders of the citizens at that time. The benefits of independence, however, would be enjoyed by future generations. Deficit financing, used by the founding fathers, spread the cost over several decades, when the country was better able to pay off revolutionary obligations.

Domestic and foreign creditors, however, expected prompt repayment. When the Confederation government could not comply because the states failed to make their assigned contributions, Congress appointed Robert Morris as superintendent of finance (1781) to reform Confederation finances. But Morris and the *Treasury Board of three commissioners that succeeded him enjoyed limited success. Although the Dutch subscribed to new loans, interest on the foreign debt was paid, and accounts between the Confederation and the states straightened out, Congress rejected a comprehensive plan for funding the national debt. Some states, unwilling to vote money for Congress, funded part of the national debt for which they assumed responsibility. But others had contracted massive debts which they could not or would not cancel. Many public creditors, receiving no satisfaction from the small states or from Congress, came to support the idea of establishing an independent revenue that would permit the Confederation to tax and meet its financial obligations. Thus the Revolution created financial interests of national scope which would look to an invigorated central government to promote their welfare. Creditors, North and South, found they had common interests they could not promote within the framework of state politics.

Economic Depression

Other groups also experienced growing disillusionment and frustration over the Confederation, especially urban interests in the port towns, and increasingly became convinced that their welfare could be advanced only by a powerful central government. The end of the war brought a temporary economic boom. Eager to regain their dominant place in American markets, British merchants advanced credit generously, encouraging Americans to buy British goods unavailable during the war. Before independence, Americans had paid for British goods with exports to England, the West Indies, or to other markets. But the Revolution disrupted prewar trading patterns. The British refused to sign a commercial treaty, and imposed severe restrictions on American trade with their West Indian colonies. Other countries, following mercantilist principles, also refused to open their ports to American shipping. American expectations that independence would free trade from foreign restraints proved naive. Merchants could explore commercial opportunities in the Orient and elsewhere, but in the 1780s such new outlets could not immediately replace the older sources of profit.

When Americans had trouble paying their debts, the British cut credit and the boom collapsed. Prices, wages, and imports declined, threatening merchants, farmers, and artisans with bankruptcy or the loss of their property. The economic pressures on them mounted in states that levied new taxes to pay off the public debt. The combined weight of public and private indebtedness brought widespread distress and demands for action. In western Massachusetts, disgruntled farmers, failing to obtain relief from the state legislature, took up arms and under the leadership of Daniel Shays shut down the courts. The state mobilized the militia and easily routed the "rebels"; but the armed resistance indicated that a government insensitive to the vital interests of its citizens could expect further trouble.

The states responded to hard times in various ways. Because Congress lacked power over foreign commerce, some adopted mercantilist legislation that gave American shipping and merchants protection against foreign competition. But state navigation laws could not restore prosperity. Lacking uniformity, these efforts proved largely ineffective against foreigners and often served only to inconvenience fellow Americans from neighboring states. At best, the development of new markets would take time, but debtors and creditors needed immediate help.

Some states turned to the printing press. The colonies had been cronically short of hard currency and from time to time had resorted to massive emissions of paper money. If printed in limited amounts with adequate provision for redemption through additional taxes, paper money could serve the interests of all classes of society. During the war, however, governments issued excessive amounts and failed to redeem them promptly. People quickly lost faith in the notes, and their value just as quickly plummeted. After the war the states contracted the currency by calling in many of the notes. Recession worsened the impact of these measures, stimulating demands for yet more paper money. Although seven states responded, strong resistance also appeared. Many feared that unrestrained issue of paper money would produce an inflation similar to the wartime experience, enabling debtors to palm off nearly worthless paper to their creditors. Some states also enacted stay laws that gave debtors more time to pay. Though paper money and stay laws appeared to some creditors as an attack on property rights, they enabled citizens to weather hard times until they could discharge their financial obligations.

These state efforts did not eliminate the need to search for basic changes that would assure payment of the public debt and restore national prosperity. Even before the postwar recession revealed sharply the inadequacies of the central government, some Americans saw defects in the Articles. Efforts to amend them by giving Congress independent revenue and power to regulate foreign and interstate commerce began soon after adoption. But the amendments sent to the states failed to obtain the necessary unanimous approval. Though widespread agreement existed that Congress should possess greater authority, it proved impossible to revise the Articles.

Even those Americans who favored increasing the national government's powers disagreed over how best to strengthen Congress. Virginia was willing to let Congress assess duties on imports, but it wanted to collect them. New York at first approved the impost but later found that it could profitably tax imports, thus taxing citizens of New Jersey and Connecticut who received supplies via the port of New York. Several times amendments almost passed but one balky state could and did block change. In the absence of consensus over the best way to improve the Articles, and with the varied interests of the Union distrusting one another, unanimity was impossible.

National perspectives developed slowly. People accustomed to taking localist points of view were suspicious of "foreigners," and they worked together with similarly situated interests in other states only with difficulty. There was much diversity of opinion and chronic anxiety that the new powers would advance some interests at the expense of others. The danger of granting Congress additional authority lay in the fact that the Articles contained no checks on the use of power, and no assurances that it would be used to promote the general good. If some sovereign power were transferred from the states to Congress, the logic of revolutionary constitution-making required far-reaching changes in the structure of the national government to guard against abuses. Before 1787, few favored such a radical course.

Foreign Relations

Further unhappy experiences under the Articles modified opinion and intensified the demand for change. The Confederation proved unequal to the tasks of promoting national interests abroad and maintaining prosperity at home. Neither the persistence nor the skill of John Adams in London and Thomas Jefferson in Paris gained Americans access to British and French trade. England humiliated the fledgling republic by refusing to evacuate its forts in the western United States, thereby retaining control of the Indians and the fur trade in the West, until states allowed British creditors to collect American debts. Congress exhorted the Southern states, where planters had repudiated huge prewar debts, to honor these obligations, but it could not force them to abide by the terms of the peace treaty.

The United States was equally unable to protect vital national interests that conflicted with Spanish policy. The settlement of the trans-Appalachian West, in which the Southern states particularly had deep interests, depended on the free navigation of the lower Mississippi, then controlled by Spain. The Spaniards refused to open the water route from the interior to foreign markets to Americans and disputed the Florida boundary with the United States. Under pressure from Northern commercial interests eager for access to Spanish markets, John Jay, secretary of foreign affairs, was prepared to trade away the Mississippi claims for commercial concessions until vigorous opposition, organized by the Southerners, blocked the deal. Jay's negotiations revealed that a weak Confederation could only advance the legitimate interests of one part of the Union by sacrificing those of another. On this basis the Union could not endure, since those whose interests suffered had little incentive to remain part of the United States.

The cumulative experiences of the 1780s led some to doubt that the Articles could be patched up. The Republic could hardly survive unless a strengthened national government advanced those interests which the states were unwilling or unable to promote. The Articles of Confederation reflected initial fears of strong government and a deeply held conviction that the dispersal of power among the states afforded the surest safeguard against tyranny. At the same time, the difficulties of the 1780s created new dangers that frustrated citizens would turn against the Union and repudiate republican principles. Those who thought national government should be effective, looked around them and saw frustration at home and humiliation abroad. Observing America's experience as a new nation from his Virginia

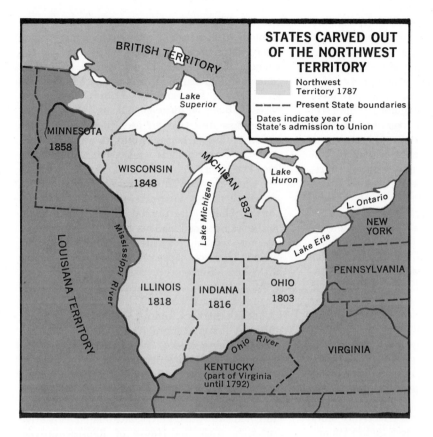

STATES CARVED OUT OF THE NORTHWEST TERRITORY

Northwest Territory 1787

– – – – Present State boundaries

Dates indicate year of State's admission to Union

plantation, George Washington confessed sadly: "To be more exposed in the eyes of the world, and more contemptible than we already are, is hardly possible."

Washington, like others, exaggerated the failures of the Confederation and overlooked its accomplishments. The Articles established a national government, although a defective one, and Congress created rudimentary administrative machinery to govern the nation. It succeeded in formulating far-reaching policies for the public domain. The Land Ordinance of 1785 established orderly procedures for surveying and selling the public domain, and the Northwest Ordinance (1787) guaranteed that new territories would enter the Union on an equal basis with the original states as soon as they had sufficient population to qualify for statehood. Congress banned slavery from the Northwest Territory (though not in the Southwest) and guaranteed basic civil liberties

and republican government to Western settlers. By 1787, although there were signs also of recovery from the postwar economic slump, a sense of crisis gripped many leaders and spread to Congress, which instructed the states to send delegates to a convention at Philadelphia for the purpose of revising the Articles of Confederation. "Would to God," George Washington sighed, "that wise measures may be taken in time to avert the consequences we have but too much reason to apprehend."

THE FEDERAL CONSTITUTION

During the spring and summer of 1787 fifty-five delegates met behind closed doors at Constitution Hall in Philadelphia. The average age of the delegates was only 42, but they brought with them extensive political experience and Washington, one of the "old guard," added his prestige by presiding. Most experienced delegates agreed that the central government needed strengthening, but they disagreed over how to achieve this. Some favored the New Jersey Plan which proposed a minimal reduction of state sovereignty, to give Congress power to tax and regulate commerce. This scheme involved limited structural changes in the Confederation. Each state would retain one vote in Congress and there would be a plural executive without a veto, as well as a supreme court. But the proposal, just as with earlier amendments to the Confederation, established no checks against congressional abuse of authority.

After about a month of deliberation, the convention made an all-important move. It decided against revising the Articles, as Congress had instructed, and drafted instead an entirely new frame of government for the Union. By adapting the principles of balanced government to central authority, the delegates hoped to strengthen the nation without jeopardizing liberty or diversity. After rejecting the New Jersey Plan, they reconsidered proposals advanced at the start of the convention by Virginia to create a two-house legislature with one chosen by popular vote. The proposed Congress would have the power to veto state legislation, and thus would effectively shift the locus of power from the states to the Union.

The delegates realized that whatever draft they proposed would have to command popular support and at the same time solve the country's constitutional problems. If they shifted the balance of power too heavily in favor of the nation, as the Virginia Plan contemplated, localist sentiment might block approval; but if the national government remained too weak, the defects of the Confederation would go unremedied. With one eye on popular opinion, the convention eventually found a way to redistribute power between states and nation: a federal system with divided sovereignty. Local and national governments each would have particular responsibilities and the necessary power to act effectively, including the ability to tax.

As one proponent of federalism later explained this fundamental and creative innovation: "The two governments act in different manners and for different purposes—the general government in great national concerns in which we are interested in common with other members of the Union; the state legislatures in our mere local concerns. The true distinction is, that the two governments are established for different purposes, and act on different objects." The framers further assumed that "If each power is confined within its proper bonds and to its proper objects . . . they can no more clash than two parallel lines can meet."

Once the convention agreed on a federal system, it moved to enumerate the new national powers. Unlike the Confederation, which could neither tax nor call citizens before a court of law, the new federal government acted directly on citizens. The voters therefore would have to elect lawmakers. Since Congress received extensive powers, the number of representatives each state sent to the House had to be proportional to population. Southerners wanted all slaves counted for purposes of apportioning representation; the convention compromised by counting every five slaves as three white persons.

To overcome the fears of the less populous states that Congress would ignore their interests, the framers also created a senate in which each state had two votes. The Senate shared legislative authority with the House of Representatives. Thus each chamber represented different constituencies. Congressmen owed their election every two years to the voters in their congressional districts, whereas senators, chosen by the state legislature, served six-year terms. Since members of the more popular branch had to stand for reelection frequently they would be expected to mirror more directly the particular interests of their districts. Senators, whose jobs were more secure, were freer from the pressures of localism and were expected to exert a stabilizing influence.

But these checks within the legislative branch did not entirely satisfy the Southerners. They feared that Congress would use its commercial power to favor Northern shipping interests at the expense of the planters, who relied on others to carry their goods. The convention, therefore, reached another compromise: Congress could regulate interstate and foreign trade but it could not place duties on exports or interfere with the international slave trade for twenty years.

Since Congress had the power to make war, raise an army, coin and print money, negotiate with foreign nations, and impose taxes, the framers designed an independent executive, with the veto to check the legislative branch. Deciding on a method for choosing the president proved troublesome. Alexander Hamilton, a conservative delegate from New York, favored hereditary rulers, but this was impractical in republican America. If Congress chose the president, the executive would be dependent on the lawmakers. There seemed no practical method of holding national elections through which the citizens would choose because there were no political parties or other institutions for nominating candidates and articulating popular preferences nationally. The framers therefore created an electoral college to which citizens in each state would send representatives to elect the president. They assumed that since each state would nominate prominent local favorites, no candidate would have a majority; the House of Representatives would then make the final choice from among the three highest vote getters in the electoral college.

Finally, an independent judiciary gave additional balance to the federal system. The judges had the power to interpret the Constitution and acts of Congress, and to settle disputes between states or between the states and the nation. Though the federal courts did not have explicit authority to review the validity of state or national legislation that might conflict with the Constitution, the power of judicial review could be inferred logically from its role as arbiter between local and central governments and as interpreter of the Constitution, which became the "supreme law of the land."

By the middle of September the framers had finished. All but three of the forty-two remaining delegates signed the document, and later that month Congress submitted it to the states for ratification. Though amendments to the Articles of Confederation had required unanimity among the states, Congress simply declared that the new Constitution needed approval of only nine of the thirteen states.

THE STRUGGLE FOR THE CONSTITUTION

Ratification proceeded slowly. No one could be sure that the Constitution would muster enough support. Some small states such as Delaware, New Jersey, Georgia, Connecticut, and Maryland ratified swiftly and with relatively little controversy. Elsewhere the Constitution generated intense excitement. Every state held elections for delegates to the ratifying conventions. For the first time, citizens cast ballots in what amounted to a national election. The conventions in Massachusetts, Virginia, and New York ratified, but only after closely fought contests and prolonged debate during which rejection of the document at times appeared likely. North Carolina and Rhode Island initially refused to ratify, entering the Union after the Constitution became the law of the land.

The Constitution in American History

For a long time Americans worshiped the framers as men acting under divine guidance, and the Constitution as a noble plan by which impartial statesmen secured liberty and order. By the end of the nineteenth century, a cult of Constitution-worship had developed among those who regarded it as a bulwark against majorities seeking to regulate railroads, corporations, and conditions of labor. While looking to the judges as guardians of the Constitution to protect their own interests, conservative Constitution-worshipers believed that the fundamental law enshrined unchangeable and objective principles without regard to class interest. "Our great and sacred Constitution," intoned one prominent corporation lawyer in the 1880s, "stretches its beneficent powers over our land—over its lakes and rivers and forests, over every mother's son of us, like the outstretched arm of God himself. . . . O Marvellous Constitution! Magic Parchment! Transforming word! Maker, Monitor, Guardian of Mankind! Thou hast gathered to thy impartial bosom, the people of the earth, Columbia, and called them equal. . . . I would fight for every line in the Constitution as I would fight for every star in the Flag."

Early in the twentieth century critics attacked the courts and the Constitution for blocking the will of democratic majorities by declaring unconstitutional laws favored by farmers, workers, and reformers. These Progressive-era (1900–1920) critics held that the courts and the Constitution had become instruments of special privilege, playthings of the banks, railroads, and large corporations.

Charles A. Beard, a leading Progressive historian, attempted to prove in *An Economic Interpretation of the Constitution* (1913) that the founding fathers, fearful of democratic majorities in the 1780s, pushed through the Constitution to favor the propertied elite, especially merchants and holders of government bonds. Beard suggested that the founding fathers' ownership of public securities whose values would rise under a strong central government that funded the national debt explained their actions in 1787. However, he argued, it was the great majority of Americans, the farmers, who would have to pay new taxes for the benefit of merchants and speculators in public securities.

According to Beard, the majority opposed centralization and wished to keep power in state hands where they could control it, but by clever manipulation, the elite triumphed. By insisting that the founding fathers were agents of elite economic interests, their *own* in most cases, rather than of Divine Providence, Beard and other progressive reformers hoped to give Americans of their generation a more realistic understanding of their own society. Just as the federal Constitution served the rich and well-born in 1787, they argued, so it was the tool of privilege in 1913. Once people realized this, the courts and the Constitution could be changed so they would no longer stymie necessary reforms.

Federalists v. Antifederalists

The founding fathers were indeed men, not demigods, politicians keenly sensitive to the country's complex interests, but neither a simple economic interpretation of the Constitution nor embalming the founding fathers as divinely inspired can adequately explain the ratification controversy. The framers came primarily from the social elite, but so did many of the leading anti-Constitutionalists (called Antifederalists), and though most members of urban interest groups, artisans and laborers, as well as merchants and public security holders favored the Constitution, farmers and planters, the vast majority, split sharply.

The framers were not opposed to popular government, nor were the Antifederalists its unquestioning champions. Both groups believed that tyranny, whether emanating from majorities or minorities, was equally arbitrary and unjust; both favored balanced government to prevent the abuse of power; and both acknowledged the need to strengthen the Union. Both recognized defects in the Articles of Confederation, but the Antifederalists felt no sense of alarm.

The Antifederalists believed, however, that the new Constitution lodged excessive power in a national government which would ultimately undermine the states. "From a well-digested, well-formed democratic [government], you are at once rushing into an aristocratic government," warned an Antifederalist delegate to the South Carolina ratifying convention. Protesting the insufficient checks against the abuse of power, they opposed dividing sovereignty between local and central government because the latter would ultimately swallow up the former. States are the "characteristics and the soul of a confederation," maintained Patrick Henry in the Virginia ratifying convention. "If the states be not the agent of this compact, it must be one great consolidated national government, of the people of all the states."

The pro-Constitutionalists disagreed. They viewed as exaggerated the ingrained fear of centralization which had produced the Articles of Confederation. Republican government, supporters of the Constitution argued, had a better chance to work in a large country than in a small one because so many competing interests would prevent anyone from usurping power. Each group would have to respect the interests of others whose support would be necessary in Congress. Thus citizens would compromise and bargain with one another to advance their mutual interests. The very size and diversity of the Union, therefore, with its multiplicity of economic, sectional, ethnic, and religious factions made it less likely that tyrannical majorities or sly manipulators could gain control. "In the extended republic of the United States, the . . . [federal] government would hold a pretty even balance between the parties of particular states," explained James Madison, "and be at the same time sufficiently restrained by its dependence on the community from betraying its general interests."

Critics of the Constitution found these notions novel, a departure from the assumptions that had made the states rather than the nation sovereign. Conventional republican theory held that the best protection against tyranny was to keep power close to the people. "The idea of an uncompounded republick, on an average one thousand miles in length, and eight-hundred in breadth . . . is an absurdity and contrary to the whole experience of mankind," ran a principal Antifederalist argument.

Antifederalists were equally alarmed by the proposed system of congressional representation. The Constitution envisioned a relatively small House of Representatives, at least initially, with perhaps 65 members. Each congressman would represent thousands of people and congressional districts would comprise extensive territory and diverse interests. The state constitutions, in contrast, made legislative constituencies small and homogeneous. In this way the electorate could keep closer control over their assemblymen, who, it was assumed, would faithfully advocate their interests. But could a congressman who represented 30,000 citizens spread out over hundreds of square miles including many different and often rival groups be as likely to know and advance the wishes of his constituents? The framers replied that elections every two years would make congressmen sensitive to local interests but not their prisoners, since in a large congressional district no single interest had sufficient power to determine elections.

Sharing the widespread suspicion of power held by all revolutionary-era Americans, Antifederalists declined to take a chance with such novel experiments. Like the pro-Constitutionalists, the critics had little faith in the benevolence of man or in his capacity to restrain base impulses. The advocates of the Constitution, however, had greater confidence in their ability to devise political arrangements that would check man's baser drives and liberate his nobler impulses. They could not, however, alter their opponents' pessimism nor their tendency to see countless dangers lurking in the new frame of government. Antifederalists saw the absence of a bill of rights, which most state constitutions contained, as evidence that civil and religious liberty would perish; the extensive power granted the president looked like the first step toward dictatorship; Congress, with power to legislate for the states, might usurp the authority of local government.

Those Americans more willing to experiment, less fearful of centralization, felt greater need for change. Georgia, which ratified unanimously, expected that a strong central government would curb the Indians, who blocked the state's expansion. New Jersey and Connecticut, largely rural states that imported goods taxed in New York City, would benefit from exclusive congressional control of foreign commerce. Moreover, congressional import duties would help to fund the national debt, in which both states had a stake, whereas New York's impost benefited only *its* citizens. Similarly in the urban centers artisans, merchants, shippers, and fishermen expected Congress to protect them against foreign competition and gain access to distant markets and fisheries. Public security holders were more divided. In states which funded their debts the pressure for the nation to assume responsibility remained weaker than in those states which neglected their revolutionary creditors.

In the larger states, notably New York, Virginia, Pennsylvania, and Massachusetts, the sharpest controversies took place. Their size and strength made many of their citizens confident that they could prosper without centralization. Entrenched public officials feared that they would lose importance and influence in a federal union. Persons suspicious of the dominant local elites were equally suspicious of the Constitution that these elites championed. Thus farmers in the Massachusetts back country, the men of Shays' "rebellion," feared any change that might upset the compromises that restored peace after the foray. Similarly, Virginia Baptists who had only recently won their long battle for religious liberty in 1786 feared a redistribution of power which might endanger religious freedom. On the other hand settlers on Virginia's western frontiers looked to a strong Union to force Spain to open the Mississippi to American navigation.

The Antifederalists, drawing on diverse sources of resistance to change, nearly prevailed. But their opponents, who included most of the country's leading public men, were better organized and seized the initiative. The adoption of the federal Constitution owed much to the zeal, ingenuity, and influence of men like Madison, Washington, Hamilton, and Franklin. Driven by a vision of America's republican mission, they perceived greater dangers in drifting along under the Articles of Confederation. As they watched the Confederation government stumble in defending American interests, unable to command respect at home or abroad, unable even to count on the attendance of delegates at Congress, their conviction hardened that the American republic needed a stronger national government.

The stakes were high, Madison realized, but if Americans succeeded, he predicted that "the cause of liberty will acquire a dignity and lustre which it has never enjoyed; and an example will be set which cannot but have the most favorable influence on the rights of mankind." On June 21, 1788, the ninth state, New Hampshire, ratified the Constitution, giving Americans a second chance to create "a more perfect Union."

Chapter 9
Experiment in National Sovereignty

A government had been reformed, in Jefferson's words, "by reason alone, without bloodshed." Americans could take pride in setting "the world a beautiful example," proving that "whenever the people are well-informed, they can be trusted with their own government," and to set things right. In 1788, Jefferson's mission to France neared its end, and new tasks awaited him at home where he would play a major role in the new government inaugurated a year later. In the next decade, however, his faith in the people's wisdom would be strained. Although George Washington had been chosen unanimously as president, agreement ended there. The political turmoil and turbulence of the 1790s lay ahead.

The Constitution provided a rough blueprint for republican government in an extensive and diverse nation. The founding fathers hoped that the federal system, varied methods of representation, and other integrating mechanisms would create a balanced government free from rivalry and corruption, but the first decade's experience under the new regime proved profoundly disillusioning. Many thought the Republic was about to split into warring factions, confirming the fears of the framers.

Enemies bent on subverting the structure of 1787 and overturning the social order seemed to lurk everywhere. Some imagined networks of aristocrats, monarchists, financial manipulators, religious bigots, and British agents plotting the country's destruction, while others were equally certain that demagogues, wild-eyed Jacobin revolutionaries, and atheistic French agents schemed to ruin the country. During the 1790s, as in the decade leading to the Revolution and periodically throughout their history, Americans thought that sinister elements at home and abroad endangered the nation's existence.

Happily by 1815 prospects had brightened. After twenty-five years, the federal Constitution proved itself as a practical political arrangement. The country defended its vital interests abroad and maintained order at home. Though citizens divided into political parties, a split the founding

fathers had hoped to avoid, the new Federalist and Jeffersonian Republican parties became vital elements in the success of the system inaugurated in 1789. The first American parties formulated national policy, put forward creative leaders, provided citizens with new means of participating in government, and also induced divergent groups to coalesce in order to gain power by pooling votes and influence. By these devices the first parties kept a fragile Union from being torn apart by provincial interests and prejudices.

Repeatedly in danger of being drawn into the European war that raged from 1793 to 1815, the United States remained neutral until 1812, profiting immensely by trading with belligerents. Resisting foreign pressures that threatened its sovereignty and that had stirred the fears of its citizens for two decades, the United States ultimately went to war with Great Britain to defend its sovereignty. By the war's end, three years later, Americans had gained fresh confidence in their experiment in republican government. The country stood free, prosperous, and independent, and, equally significant, divisive partisanship and political paranoia were on the wane.

THE FEDERALIST SYSTEM

From the outset, the new central government quickly fulfilled many of the framers' expectations. The nation swiftly tackled the problems that had bedeviled the Confederation. Prosperity returned in the 1790s, and by helping restore confidence, the new government stimulated enterprise. Additional foreign markets enriched American agriculture and commerce, while at the same time the nation funded the burdensome revolutionary debt.

Congress met in March 1789 to organize the government with Washington, a unifying symbol whom all Americans admired and trusted, the obvious choice as first president. Esteemed as the architect of the military victory that won independence, Washington's fairness, honesty, and integrity inspired confidence. With the general at the helm, citizens were confident that the chief executive would not abuse power or favor special interests at the expense of the common welfare.

If Washington's election inspired confidence, so too did Congress' prompt redemption of promises made during the ratification struggle to amend the Constitution and remedy defects listed by the Antifederalists. James Madison, now a Virginia congressman, steered a series of amendments through Congress meant to safeguard civil liberties. The first nine amendments formed the Bill of Rights (similar to those found in many state constitutions) prohibiting Congress from restricting freedom of speech, press, religion, and guaranteeing fair trials with due process of law. The tenth amendment reassured those who feared that the states would be swallowed up by an all-powerful central government. It explicitly reserved to the states all power not delegated to the national government.

The Hamiltonian Leadership

The president chose his wartime aide, Alexander Hamilton, as secretary of the treasury, heading one of the four executive departments established in 1789. Born in the British West Indies, Hamilton migrated as a youth to New York. At King's (now Columbia) College he warmly supported the revolutionary cause. He married into a leading family and gained entry into the New York elite. Brilliant, inventive, and ambitious, Hamilton fought for the creation of a powerful central government, one which would stand on equal terms with the European powers and one which he, Hamilton, would lead as Washington's "prime minister."

The Treasury Department gave Hamilton ample opportunity to display his talents. In a series of cogent reports to Congress, Hamilton designed a system for creating a powerful and united nation. He proposed to repay the national debt and take over the state debts to restore government credit, thereby binding creditors to the federal government, stimulating enterprise, and assuring the government's future revenue needs. Foreigners held one-fifth of the national debt, and speculators and investors had bought a large

part of the remainder cheaply. In Congress, Madison argued for compensating the original holders, including revolutionary veterans, who had sold their notes at far less than face value. Hamilton, however, insisted that the best way to create confidence in the new government was to pay the debt in full even if this meant windfall profits for creditors. Congress overwhelmingly agreed.

There was less agreement over Hamilton's plan for the federal assumption of state debts, a commitment he hoped would bind all creditors, state and national, to the central government and avoid competition with the states for revenue. States with large debts favored transferring heavy burdens from their taxpayers, but those which had small debts or had funded them in the 1780s with local taxes understandably opposed paying the burdens of others. Also, assumption, like funding, would benefit principally a handful of speculating capitalists who had descended on the Southern states and bought up discounted state securities.

As in the fight over the national debt, Madison and the Virginia delegation led the opposition, but this time other congressmen joined them to delay assumption. Hamilton, close to defeat, then enlisted the aid of Secretary of State Thomas Jefferson, whom he warned that the Union might split unless assumption carried. Jefferson, who was close to Madison, traded support for assumption in exchange for a promise to establish the national capital permanently on the Potomac River between Maryland and Virginia, a decision he later came to regret. Many Southerners believed they would have greater influence in national affairs if the capital were close to Virginia rather than in New York or Philadelphia, where merchants and bankers could besiege Congress. Following the "deal" with Jefferson, assumption passed in July 1790.

Congress now had to raise money. In 1789 it passed the first tariff act, imposing import duties to raise revenue rather than to protect American producers from competition. When these revenues proved insufficient, Congress in 1791 placed an excise tax on distilleries. This enraged frontier farmers accustomed to turning their grain into whisky, the most convenient and profitable way to get this bulky crop to market.

Hamilton's financial program achieved many of its aims. The value of public securities rose, and returning prosperity meant greater tariff revenue from increased imports. Congress also singled out the fishing and shipping industries for special favor. Goods imported in American ships and by American merchants paid lower duties than those brought in on foreign vessels or by foreigners. Within a few years American merchants gained the lion's share of foreign commerce.

Elated by success, Hamilton then recommended the creation of the Bank of the United States (BUS). Congress chartered the institution in 1791 (capitalized at $10 million, far more than all the few state banks combined) to provide a stable circulating medium to facilitate trade and stimulate economic development. A rush took place to buy shares of BUS stock which could be purchased with government securities. The bank was a semiprivate corporation, since the government owned only one-fifth of the stock and named one-fifth of the representatives on the board of directors. It made loans and issued notes to merchants and other businessmen, and served as the government's fiscal agent in holding public funds and disbursing them as the government ordered.

Hamilton designed the funding program and the BUS to meet the nation's immediate needs. His Report on Manufactures in 1791 planned for the future, recommending encouragement of American manufacturing through subsidies and protection from foreign competition. The United States, he hoped, would become less dependent on foreign supplies and steadily develop into a manufacturing nation. But the country was not yet ready, and Congress failed to respond to Hamilton's cue. Farmers and merchants prospered with capital and labor going into existing forms of enterprises. The American Industrial Revolution would have to wait.

Hamilton's program favored a system designed to ensure the stability of national government, but clearly at the expense of state sovereignty. At the Philadelphia convention, Hamilton spoke of turning states into administrative units under an all-powerful central government. The British constitution, he was reported to have said at Philadelphia, "forms the best model the world

ever produced," with its mixture of popular and hereditary features. Though Hamilton cherished *ordered* liberty, he feared anarchy more. Strong government, run by a shrewd and wise elite, provided the best safeguard in his opinion.

Failing to get his way at the convention in 1787, Hamilton pursued his goals indirectly. Funding and assumption, the tariff, the national bank and subsidies to manufacturing, all strengthened the federal government at the expense of the states and permanently attached parts of the propertied elite to the national government. But although Hamilton's system benefited some, it could not help but alienate many others, and this reaction produced divisions jeopardizing the survival of the Union.

THE BEGINNINGS OF PARTIES

The start of an effective central government in 1789 with enlarged powers and real responsibilities brought many of the country's leading politicians to the capital. All worked for the success of the new experiment, but naturally all did not agree on how to promote the general welfare. Madison and Hamilton, collaborators in the struggle to ratify the federal Constitution, split over how to fund the national debt. Madison, Jefferson, their fellow Virginians, and other Southern supporters had not expected that the new government would seriously threaten local interests. Hamiltonian finance, together with protection for American commerce and manufacturing, appeared to benefit bankers and capitalists in the Northern seaports. Southern planters charged that Hamilton exploited the power and prestige of President Washington, and that in league with speculators and merchants, the treasury secretary had gained undue influence over Congress. Hamilton, Jefferson believed, was "not only a monarchist, but for a monarchy bottomed on corruption." The Hamiltonian "system flowed from principles adverse to liberty, and . . . calculated to undermine and demolish the Republic."

While some congressmen, bitter over defeats on funding, assumption, and the bank proposal, attacked Hamilton's integrity, Jefferson and Hamilton battled inside the Cabinet for Washington's support. The showdown occurred in 1791 over the constitutionality of the national bank. Jefferson urged the president to veto the bank bill, arguing that Congress had no power to charter corporations. Hamilton's rebuttal insisted that only a liberal reading of the Constitution (what Jefferson called "loose construction") could strengthen the Union. Since Congress might pass all laws that were necessary and proper for carrying out its delegated powers, Hamilton argued for a bank as a useful means of exercising the taxing power, paying public debts, and promoting the general welfare.

Still Jefferson feared that loose construction through implied powers meant the end of constitutional limitations. Such interpretations would ultimately remove all restraints on national authority and violate states' rights. As spokesman for interests that had little use for a national bank that they did not control, Jefferson declared that the bank was not necessary. But Washington accepted Hamilton's view, increasing the budding opposition's sense of isolation and frustration.

Though Washington tried to restore harmony, the Cabinet feud between Hamilton and Jefferson and their partisans escalated. Jefferson retired from the Cabinet in 1793, and Hamilton resigned the following year, but the political divisions engendered by the two men persisted. Prosperity helped stabilize the Union, however. Funding and assumption relieved farmers from the burden of land taxes since duties on imports, collected primarily in the more prosperous cities and towns, covered most of the public debt.

The excise tax on whisky was another matter. Farmers in western Pennsylvania who refused to pay the impost were met with an overpowering show of military force. Hamilton bounded out of retirement to grab the opportunity to assert national power and crush the first organized resistance to its mandates. The armed and angry farmers melted away (their isolation left them little choice), but the incident convinced them that the national government meant them no good.

The first American party system began to grow as soon as the new federal government was established. The national capital (first in New York, and later Philadelphia) became an arena for partisan conflict. Reports of clashes in Congress and within the Cabinet filtered down to the countryside, and congressional elections, which would determine the strength of contending groups at the next session, took on added importance.

The second presidential election in 1792 reflected these emerging splits. Washington remained the unanimous choice for president, but Virginia and New York voted for George Clinton, governor of New York, as vice president rather than reelect John Adams who was identified with the Hamilton faction. Yet in 1793, as Washington began his second term, the conflict at the capital had not yet divided the nation into fixed, permanently opposed parties. Many congressmen won reelection with little or no opposition. But that situation changed after revolutionary events overseas threatened the country's prosperity, polarized its politics, and plunged the United States into a decade of fierce party warfare.

THE NEUTRALITY CRISIS, 1793-1795

Americans had always dreamed of escaping from Old World corruption, tyranny, and poverty, but though they crossed an ocean they remained bound to the larger civilization from which they had fled. Their initial experiences as an independent nation confirmed this. Although political ties with England had been cut, there was no avoiding European entanglements once war engulfed the Atlantic world in 1793. Reacting against centuries of oppression and exploitation, and partly inspired by the American example, Frenchmen rose in revolution in 1789, and in 1793 the new French republic went to war against a coalition of monarchies determined to crush republicanism and popular unrest. At first Americans cheered their fellow revolutionaries' efforts. War in Europe also created opportunities for Americans to profit from the turmoil, as the United States became the leading neutral trading nation. Americans gained access to business ordinarily denied them, especially in the West Indies. But since France and England both recognized

American trade as an important factor in the balance of power, complete neutrality proved impossible.

Geography and economics ultimately drew the United States into the struggle. Since the English dominated the oceans, they gained less from trading with the Americans than did the French, who relied extensively on American vessels for supplies. Americans could remain neutral only by refusing to trade with their two most important customers. Few were willing to sacrifice national prosperity and personal gain for the sake of absolute neutrality so long as hope remained of staying out of the war while profiting from it.

The initial enthusiasm for the French cause soon gave way to doubts and then to raucous divisions. Hamilton and the emerging Federalist party (generally the more nationalist-minded men who had demanded stronger central government) favored a pro-British neutrality. England provided America's most important foreign market, and import duties made up the government's largest source of revenue. The success of Hamilton's fiscal system and war with Britain were mutually exclusive. Also, French republicanism had degenerated by 1793 into a Reign of Terror. Radical forces (the Jacobins) took over the new government, liquidating the king, many aristocrats, and much of the political opposition, and expropriated property. Many Americans feared that the French had unleashed anarchic forces that threatened order, property, and the power of elites everywhere. When French armies marched into neighboring countries to set up satellite "radical" republics, American conservatives trembled over the Jacobin menace.

Jefferson and the emerging Republican party, though shaken by the Reign of Terror, stood by the French. For all its mistakes and excesses, the French Revolution, they believed, still represented the struggle of liberty against the despotism of corrupt monarchs. Executions were deplorable, admitted Jefferson, but the revolution must go on even if it meant seeing "half the earth desolated," and even if "but an Adam and an Eve [were] left in every country." Republicans favored a pro-French neutrality which avoided war with

England yet enabled Americans to help France as the French had done a generation earlier, during the American Revolution. Sympathy for France thus became a rallying cry for those who considered Hamilton and the Federalists enemies of republicanism at home and abroad.

Fearing involvement, Washington proclaimed American neutrality in April 1793. The United States thereby served notice that it would not let the treaty of alliance signed with France in 1778 draw the country into war. Washington warned against allowing sympathies for the belligerents to induce Americans to commit unneutral acts.

The arrival of a new French minister, "Citizen" Edmund Genêt, immediately tested the sincerity and effectiveness of the neutrality proclamation. Popularly acclaimed as he journeyed northward from Charleston, South Carolina, Genêt overplayed his hand. This undiplomatic diplomat commissioned privateers in American ports to capture British vessels, and authorized expeditions to march on Spanish and British territories. Genêt thus clearly made a mockery of American impartiality. Washington stopped Genêt's activities and demanded his recall. Jefferson agreed, though Republicans had been critical of the president's neutrality proclamation as anti-French.

The Jay Treaty

The next threat to neutrality came from Britain. In the summer of 1793, hoping to cut the lifeline of the French Empire, the Royal Navy began seizing American merchant vessels trading with France and its West Indian possessions. When outraged Americans demanded war, Washington refused to panic. He sent John Jay, chief justice of the U.S. Supreme Court, to England to negotiate a settlement of differences, including the evacuation of British army posts in the Northwest Territory. Jay bargained from weakness, however. Hamilton had told the British that Americans would do almost anything to avoid war. Thus undermined by the secretary of the treasury, Jay brought home a treaty so unsatisfactory that the president submitted it to the

Senate reluctantly. Although the English agreed to withdraw from the Northwest and to liberalize some commercial restrictions, Jay failed to stop impressment (the seizure of American seamen), or to obtain compensation for the thousands of slaves who had fled across the British lines during the Revolution. Nor had Jay received guarantees that American neutrality would be respected in the future. But the promise of compensation for recent shipping losses offered an honorable way of avoiding war. Washington seized it and the Senate ratified Jay's Treaty in June 1795 with more of a sense of duty than enthusiasm.

The treaty divided the nation more than ever. Republicans attacked it as a sellout to the country's old enemy and warned that France would regard it as an unfriendly act. Federalists considered the treaty, for all its faults, preferable to war. They depicted their opponents as lackeys of France, while Republicans responded by denouncing their rivals as Anglophiles.

The Adams Presidency

In this heated setting, Washington's retirement touched off the first struggle for the presidency in 1796. The Federalists backed Vice President John Adams, and the Republicans favored Thomas Jefferson. The two parties scoured the Union for allies and votes and ran rival candidates for most other offices. Although Washington's Farewell Address cautioned the country against blind partisanship and permanent foreign alliances, both sides indiscriminately accused the other of disloyalty and subversion. Adams won a close election, with seventy-one electoral votes to Jefferson's sixty-eight. Jefferson had a consolation prize, however, in the vice-presidency, since before 1804 and the Twelfth Amendment candidates for president and vice-president did not run on a single ballot.

Electing a new president did not improve the critical situation. Infuriated by the Jay Treaty, the French attacked American shipping and refused to receive the American minister. When French officials demanded bribes from a special three-man commission sent to try to reach an accommodation, the country was outraged by this crude attempt at blackmail. Following the epi-

sode, the "XYZ affair," many Federalists demanded war. The president decided to avoid it if possible, but fight if necessary. Adams hoped to vindicate the country's honor and defend its interests without bloodshed.

America began to rearm. The president named Washington commander of the army, the Congress established a Navy Department in the spring of 1798, preparations which proved timely. That fall undeclared naval war broke out between France and the United States. Though both countries went to the brink, they shied away from full-scale war. Informed in 1799 that France would receive an American minister, Adams was willing to go to the last mile. An agreement signed in September 1800 released the United States from the Alliance of 1778 and compensated Americans for lost vessels and cargoes. Preoccupied in Europe, the French wanted to avoid war but not until they had extracted as much as possible from the United States. By combining toughness with a readiness to negotiate, Adams kept the peace.

But the president paid a terrible political price. During the crisis with France the Federalists alienated large segments of the electorate and they themselves split. This lessened Adams' chances for reelection in 1800. Rearmament costs forced the government to float new, high-interest loans and to impose land taxes unpopular with farmers.

At the same time, anti-French hysteria led Congress to pass the Alien and Sedition Acts (1798) in order to repress political dissenters. The first law singled out aliens as a potential fifth column in the event of war. Congress tightened naturalization laws and increased presidential powers over foreigners. The Sedition Act went much further, making it a crime to publish "any false, scandalous and malicious writing" against the Congress and president. Twenty-five Republicans, many of them newspaper editors, were prosecuted under this law.

New taxes and infringements on freedom of expression rallied the Republicans to resist and gave them grievances to exploit, especially as the danger of war and anti-French feeling subsided. Jefferson and Madison drafted resolutions adopted by the Kentucky and Virginia legislatures which declared the Alien and Sedition Laws unconstitutional and upheld the right of the states to resist infractions of the Constitution.

Federalist divisions gave Republicans yet another advantage. Hamilton, resenting John Adams's ascension as Washington's heir, intrigued to dominate the administration from behind the scenes. The Hamiltonian faction thought war with France would eliminate the Republicans and forge an alliance with Great Britain. Adams' stubborn efforts to avoid war exasperated Hamilton, who in the election of 1800 schemed to drop Adams for the party's more reliable vice-presidential candidate, Charles C. Pinckney of South Carolina.

Although attacked from within his own party and of course from the Jeffersonian camp, President Adams ran surprisingly well in 1800. He lost to Jefferson by only eight electoral votes. A defect in the Constitution, however, blocked Jefferson's immediate election. He and his vice-presidential running mate, Aaron Burr of New York, received an equal number of electoral votes, throwing the election into the House of Representatives, where each state has one vote. Though Jefferson was clearly the popular choice, Federalists supported Burr and the House plodded through thirty-six ballots. Vague Jeffersonian reassurances to receptive and weary Federalists produced defections from Burr, finally clearing the way for Jefferson's election as third president of the United States.

ORIGINS OF THE FIRST AMERICAN PARTY SYSTEM

The peaceful transfer of power from Federalists to Republicans in 1801, despite the acrimony of a hard-fought election, represented a triumph for republicanism and party government. The Federalists and Republicans were the first modern political parties. Principles and techniques of party politics developed in the United States in the 1790s provided later generations with orderly means of establishing majority rule and settling differences among contending groups. As the political systems of other nations underwent modernization in the nineteenth and twentieth centuries, they too found political parties useful instruments of government. Some nations, as in

Western Europe, developed multiparty democratic systems; elsewhere as in Eastern Europe, Asia, and Africa, one-party authoritarian systems have emerged, but almost everywhere parties of some kind play a central role in contemporary society.

Parties developed in the United States in the 1790s because changing conditions made traditional methods of managing public affairs obsolete. Previously, local elite factions of merchants, planters, and officeholders monopolized power. Occasionally, voters became politically aroused over short-term objectives such as paper money, cheap land, or religious toleration. Discord within the elites also stimulated political competition, forcing challenging elements to appeal for popular support in order to displace rival cliques. But factions lacked permanence and were seldom well organized. In general, the electorate remained apathetic, seeing little to be gained by regular voting.

But the parties which emerged in the 1790s differed fundamentally from the factions. Relatively permanent organizations, they systematically engaged in the pursuit of power by nominating candidates and seeking votes. Parties also developed policies and programs, formed local, state, and national organizations, named leaders, recruited followers, and raised funds. In the quest for victory, they formed coalitions of diverse groups under one organizational umbrella. Parties thus developed a territorial range and social density that made them national in scope and function.

A National Political Arena

By creating a national center of decision making in which rival interests and viewpoints competed, the federal Constitution released new political energies. At first differences centered in Congress. Gradually, local leaders and citizens throughout the Union began to choose between Federalist and Republican policies and candidates. Decisions made at the capital (located in the 1790s in New York and Philadelphia and after 1800 in Washington, D.C.) now affected Americans wherever they lived. Recognition of this fact helped break down localist indifference. Groups with developing national perspectives—commercial farmers, merchants, public security holders—sought to influence public policy at the national level after 1789. They learned that they could effectively promote their interests only through national authority, and that rival groups could also thwart their desires through use of that same authority. Compromises, bargains, and deals with distant and often unfamiliar elements became necessary to obtain favorable legislation.

Often these attempts failed. Frustrated Virginians became exploited planters and Southerners; disappointed Bostonians became aggrieved merchants and New Englanders. Groups used to getting their way at home were unused to being thwarted in Congress. Their best hope lay in finding allies through party coalitions which could capture control of Congress and the presidency. National politics heightened conflict, but national parties also instituted orderly means of settling differences. The first American party system thus made leadership and public policy sensitive to the conflicting demands of diverse elements. Instead of vicious quarrels in the 1790s leading to disunion, parties offered a means for peaceful change.

The contest for the presidency, like the first clashes in Congress, promoted party development. Washington's two unanimous elections delayed the polarizing impact of the struggle for the presidency. In 1796 that consensus disappeared. Alliances to influence the choice of presidential electors or mobilize support behind particular candidates were formed in all the states. In addition, personal rivalries, old conflicts of state politics, enflamed party battle in the 1790s, the decade of Federalist domination. In some cases disappointed office seekers became national recruits for the Republican opposition.

The French Revolution

Yet these were minor sources of division compared with the ideological and diplomatic crises generated by the French Revolution. Party conflict in the mid-1790s revolved around fear for the Republic's future. The first Republicans opposed Hamilton's financial policies as departures from republican principles, which benefited the rich at the expense of the majority, while Federalists defended their policies as promoters of stability and prosperity, the only sure guarantors of the republican experiment. The neutrality crisis intensified anxieties over the thrust of internal politics. The Jay Treaty confirmed Republican suspicion that the Federalists were pro-British aristocrats; Republican willingness to risk war with England and to overlook French attacks confirmed Federalist suspicion that their opponents were pro-Gallic Jacobins. With each side defaming the other as disloyal factions in league with foreign powers, prospects for America's republican experiment looked dim.

There is no simple explanation of why some citizens became Federalists and others Republicans. Often, their attitudes toward national authority under the Washington and Adams administrations and the way it affected their vital interests determined party preference. Federalists drew their *leadership* mainly from elites who had achieved prominence before or during the Revolution and who felt threatened by challenges from below. Republican *leaders* were more often, but not always, ambitious newcomers, outsiders who had been held back from positions of prestige and power by the dominant "aristocratic" Federalists.

These alienated and ambitious Republican elements were galvanized, organized, and made politically self-conscious through the leadership of a Southern elite, at least as socially prominent as the Federalist elite. The Jeffersonian Virginians, and their colleagues elsewhere, felt disaffected because they believed that they were denied their rightful share of national power. The necessities of establishing a national political party required that they enlist support from among the discontented in all parts of the Union. Thus wealthy planters in the South joined forces with rising merchants and businessmen in the North, and with artisans and discontented ethnic and religious elements, to challenge Federalist rule. Both parties, however, received support from all segments of society. Federalists were strongest in New England, but Republicans developed support there too and after 1800 gained control of several of that region's states; Republicans were strongest in the South, but Federalists made inroads in the Carolinas and Maryland until 1800. The middle states, a political no-man's-land shifting between the parties, ultimately fell into the Republican column.

Just as the sections divided, so did occupational groups. Farmers split, with New Englanders tending towards Federalism and Southern yeomen towards Republicanism. During the 1790s urban interests were predominantly Federalist; artisans, merchants, security holders found much to admire in the Hamiltonian system. But toward the end of the decade, the Republicans made big gains in the cities and in 1800 carried most of them. The reasons for these shifting alignments and the consequences of party development became clearer after the Republicans assumed power in Washington, in March 1801.

REPUBLICAN ASCENDANCY

Jefferson, who had a keen dramatic sense, called his election a "revolution" in democratic government, and his career provides a study in paradox. As author of the Declaration of Independence, champion of religious liberty, and enemy of Federalist "monarchism," he was regarded by friend and foe alike as the nation's leading democrat, though he owned hundreds of slaves and thousands of acres, and lived in the style of the Virginia elite. More than most men of his generation, however, Jefferson attempted to transcend his class background. Like Franklin, he was an international personality whose wide-ranging intellectual curiosity and broad sympathies won him friends in enlightened circles at home and abroad. Above all, Jefferson symbolized a life committed to the promotion of human happiness through the application of reason to human affairs.

He believed in popular government, not because the people were infallible but because he thought them less likely to misgovern than kings or aristocrats. In the Jeffersonian vision, the ordinary American, a landowning farmer, sought only to live in peace with his neighbors, coveting neither undue power nor wealth. The independent yeoman was not subservient to the wealthy and

avaricious and therefore could cast his vote impartially for the common welfare. "Those who labor in the earth are the chosen people of God," Jefferson rhapsodized, "if ever He had a chosen people, whose breasts He has made His peculiar deposit for substantial and genuine virtue." Jefferson criticized the wealth and luxury generated by commerce, manufacturing and urban development. But even the yeoman farmer, for all the idealization, was actually more of a businessman than Jefferson realized or admitted, and Jefferson tempered his agrarianism with practicality. He knew that Americans of any class would not forgo the lure of profit, but he hoped to keep the temptations in check.

The chief danger to republican happiness came from the wealthy "upper crust," especially the commercial and financial speculators in the cities. Federalists toadying to this group, Jefferson argued, subverted the Republic. If unchecked, these elements would eventually control the country. Jefferson promised to return government to the people, or at least to the people's true interests, through rule by a *natural* aristocracy of talent and virtue. Luckily, Virginia had supplied the nation with the necessary leadership.

Jeffersonian Virginia

Virginia was the strongest and earliest foe of the Hamiltonian system, and had in Jefferson, Madison, and James Monroe produced a generation of able Republican leaders. As spokesmen for a plantation society, the Jeffersonian Republicans expressed the disappointment of Virginians over the performance of the federal government, which many had hoped would strengthen the Old Dominion. Since before the Revolution, Virginia's tobacco economy had been declining, while its slave population had grown dangerously. Blacks outnumbered whites east of the Blue Ridge Mountains by the 1790s. Though Virginians had supported the Revolution militantly, they could not transform their own society along purely republican lines. They disestablished the Anglican church and ended primogeniture and entail, but these reforms proved formalistic. Jeffersonians tried to go further by democratizing the state constitution, diversifying the economy, and improving agricultural methods. Jefferson dreamed of basic education for farmers which would enable them to act as responsible citizens, rather than as pawns in the hands of local elites.

In each case, the conservatism of Virginia's ruling gentry blocked effective change. Frustrated at home by their inability to make their institutions conform to republican ideals, realizing that thousands of Virginians were migrating to regions of greater economic opportunity, Jeffersonians in the 1790s blamed the federal government for their commonwealth's decline. The nation, they insisted, had been captured by a paper-money aristocracy whose manipulating schemes exploited agricultural interests, especially in the South.

The Jeffersonian Presidency

Victory in the presidential election of 1800–1801 gave the Republican party control of the central government for a generation, yet they did not repudiate all the Federalists had done. Jefferson moved to restore a balance between federal and state governments by reducing federal power, and he wished to remain aloof from entangling alliances overseas. For a few years, at least, the Republicans aim seemed on the way to fulfillment, but by the time Jefferson left office in 1809 the country again hovered on the brink of war and the federal government intervened in people's lives more obtrusively than ever.

The Republicans honored their party's commitment to reduce the national debt, which had grown steadily since the early 1790s until it consumed a third of the annual revenues. Republicans eased this burden by economizing and applying additional revenues toward debt reduction: in ten years the debt fell from $80 million to $53 million. Despite tax reduction, government revenues from import duties rose appreciably, enabling Republicans to cut taxes and eliminate the hated whisky excise. The Alien and Sedition Laws lapsed, and Congress repealed the Judiciary Act of 1800 by which Federalists had enlarged and packed the federal courts. As the last bastion of Federalist power, and not subject to popular election, the judiciary had to be brought into

line. Congress impeached an intemperate and insane Federalist judge who had persecuted Republicans, and it tried but failed to remove Justice Samuel Chase from the Supreme Court by the same impeachment process.

In these ways Republicans hoped to reverse the trend toward centralization. Jefferson wished above all to unite the country and solidify his power by winning over the rank-and-file Federalists. His moderate policy left intact the Bank of the United States and the Hamiltonian financial system, kept the country out of war, and thereby diminished Federalist fears of a Jacobin revolution. "We are all Republicans, we are all Federalists," the president proclaimed soothingly in his first inaugural, and within limits he observed this maxim. The Republican faithful demanded jobs, but Jefferson rejected a policy of wholesale removals. By filling all new and vacated positions with Republicans, the administration gradually paid off political obligations and strengthened the party. Jefferson's temperate course was rewarded by an easy reelection in 1804.

REPUBLICANISM IN THE STATES

The most important changes during the years of Republican ascendancy occurred in the states where party rivalry had unforseen consequences. By institutionalizing and legitimizing political competition, the first parties weakened habits of deference. Citizens accustomed to staying home on election day or voting dutifully for local elites became less manageable. Each party sought the largest possible turnout, and as a result a higher percentage of eligible voters began to participate in elections. To animate and influence the electorate, each party established newspapers, held rallies, and made popular appeals. With so many candidates competing for the citizen's support, parties made it difficult for voters to know who was supposedly entitled to deferential treatment. They also encouraged citizens to think of government instrumentally, or as an agency to advance their own welfare, thus making politics more relevant to their lives.

America was a land of many peoples with differing, often rival interests. Though most Americans were of English extraction, sizeable numbers of Germans, Dutch, Irish, and Scotch, often lived in compact, ethnic communities. Religion further fragmented the social order, dividing citizens among half a dozen major and countless minor denominations. Parties came to champion particular religious and nationality groups. Similarly, the parties capitalized on rivalries between established merchants and professionals in the cities who monopolized status and power in their communities, and aspiring rivals who sought access to power through political activity, since the prosperity of the 1790s created many new fortunes and claimants for social recognition. Sectional and geographical rivalries also promoted the development of a competitive party system. Not only were Northerners and Southerners rivals, but as cities grew and new regions increased their population these elements challenged older centers of control.

Thus religious minorities in Massachusetts and Connecticut, where Congregationalism remained the established church, turned to the Republican party to remove their disabilities. New York mechanics found that the dominant Federalist elite ignored their demands for state aid, so they switched to the Republicans. Many merchants who feared the effects of war with France on their pocketbooks deserted the Federalists in the late 1790s. Other entrepreneurs unable to acquire bank charters from Federalist-controlled legislatures worked through the Republican party to break these monopolies. Similarly emerging proto-elites in South Carolina's developing back country made the Republican party the instrument by which they overthrew entrenched, low-country planter domination.

As the Republicans consolidated their influence after 1800, especially in the state capitals, the groups to whom they appealed gained recognition and power. Jeffersonian legislatures chartered Republican-controlled banks, and a coalition of Republican state banking interests and party ideologists opposed to all banks prevented recharter of the Bank of the United States, thus leaving the field open to local institutions. Similarly, Republican victory in New England meant the end of the Congregationalist establishment. The Federalists resisted, mistaking demo-

cratic pressures for revolutionary insurgency, despite the fact that many Federalists were themselves self-made men who had climbed to the top a generation earlier. In an open and competitive society, with no group enjoying hereditary advantages, the elite had to expect pressure from those on their way up. On the other side, Republicans mistakenly assumed that Federalist resistance meant that the party favored monarchy or hereditary aristocracy.

When Republican rule did no more than broaden opportunities for newer elements, partisan fears subsided. Slowly Americans learned to accept the legitimacy of organized politics. The acceptance of parties, a process just beginning in Jeffersonian times, constituted a recognition that the forces which generated them were part of an open society. With this recognition came new views of freedom of the press and its right to criticize government. Though Americans were still inclined to accept government control of views they disliked, they *began* to perceive the necessity of a free marketplace of ideas in a democracy. As the parties spawned dozens of newspapers, repression became increasingly difficult, if not impractical, much the same way as the multiplication of religious denominations had aided in the growth of freedom of conscience.

The party system subtly but profoundly democratized American life. Parties increased the degree of popular participation, provided orderly means for the discontented to redress their grievances, and redistributed power peacefully. Above all, they helped keep the country reasonably united during crises when war and revolutionary unrest disrupted the rest of the Western world. In 1812 when the United States entered the international conflict, its experiments with responsible party government proved of immense value.

REPUBLICAN DIPLOMACY AND WAR

President Jefferson began by promising to maintain peace and to avoid entangling alliances. Napoleon's seizure of power all but ended Republican sympathy for France as the standard-bearer of Europe's oppressed. The establishment of the Napoleonic dictatorship in 1799 allowed Jeffersonians to revert to strict neutrality and concern themselves only with American interests. But in practice, Republican diplomacy mixed triumph with disaster. Jefferson acquired a vast new territory but he could find no way to defend national sovereignty without war.

Jefferson started triumphantly. His most dramatic achievement as president was the purchase of the immense Louisiana Territory (most of the land between the Mississippi River and the Rocky Mountains) from France in 1803. Napoleon's dreams of reestablishing a French empire in America had alarmed the United States. In 1802 western farmers were prohibited from sending exports down the Mississippi through New Orleans, the old problem of the 1790s, when Spain had owned Louisiana. Without access to markets, the western back country faced disaster. Jefferson sent James Monroe to France with authority to buy New Orleans and West Florida. Military reverses led Napoleon to give up hopes for North American dominions, and he decided

to sell all of Louisiana to the United States for about $15 million, a bargain even at that time.

Jefferson could find no authority in the Constitution for acquiring foreign territory, but he swallowed his scruples and seized the chance to double the area of the United States in one move. The Louisiana Purchase was too tempting to decline. The United States insisted that West Florida, claimed by Spain, was part of the Louisiana Territory and in 1812 forcibly annexed the area.

Jefferson's practical and aggressive diplomacy revealed that the apostle of limited government was also ready to use power boldly when national interests could be advanced. In another instance, the president, unwilling to pay further tribute as did other nations to Barbary pirates who controlled access to the Mediterranean, declared war against Tripoli. A concentrated use of naval power stopped the pirates' interference with American commerce. The expedition bolstered American morale and raised American prestige among European powers. But Jefferson remained practical. Other North African states

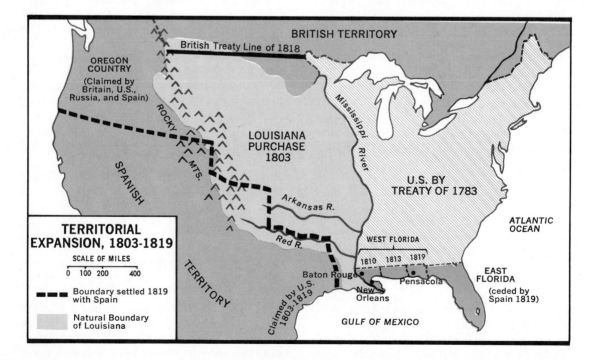

BRITISH TERRITORY

British Treaty Line of 1818

OREGON
COUNTRY
(Claimed by
Britain, U.S.,
Russia, and Spain)

ROCKY MTS.

Mississippi River

LOUISIANA
PURCHASE
1803

U.S. BY
TREATY OF 1783

SPANISH

Arkansas R.

ATLANTIC
OCEAN

TERRITORY

Red R.

WEST FLORIDA

1810   1813   1819

EAST
FLORIDA
(ceded by
Spain 1819)

**TERRITORIAL
EXPANSION, 1803-1819**

SCALE OF MILES

0   100   200   400

Boundary settled 1819
with Spain

Natural Boundary
of Louisiana

Claimed by U.S.
1803-1819

Baton Rouge

Pensacola

New
Orleans

GULF OF MEXICO

continued to disregard American rights. To fight them, along with Tripoli, would have been too costly, so the United States government continued to pay bribes selectively.

Renewed war between France and Britain in 1803 pushed the United States once again to the edge of involvement. As in the 1790s, Americans exploited neutrality for commercial gain. The volume of American imports swelled, largely because Americans imported many commodities from the British and French colonies and reexported them to Europe. France and England, attempting to break the military deadlock by engaging in economic warfare, put this trade in jeopardy. The British denied the right of neutrals to engage in trade in wartime prohibited in peacetime. Previously English admiralty courts had permitted Americans to trade with French colonies provided they imported enemy merchandise into the United States before continuing on to markets on the Continent. In 1805 a British court closed this loophole, hoping to choke off the lifelines of the French Empire. The following year the British proclaimed a partial blockade of Western Europe, further tightening the economic noose around Napoleon, who retaliated by declaring a blockade against the British. Both nations seized American vessels violating the regulations.

For Americans, England became the principal offender. Superior British seapower could enforce maritime policy far more effectively than could Napoleon. The British also seized or "impressed" seamen from American ships as alleged deserters from the Royal Navy, often rightly so, often not. Congress responded with a Non-Importation Act (1806) barring English goods available elsewhere or at home. Attempts to negotiate a settlement in London failed, and the crisis deepened as France and England intensified their economic warfare.

The president decided to try a radical experiment in peaceful coercion, hoping to vindicate America's neutral rights. Determined to avoid war, and remembering the effect of boycotts in the struggle against Britain in the 1760s, Jefferson applied economic pressure. In December 1807, Congress adopted the Embargo Act, virtually stopping all American overseas trade.

Jefferson's last months in office became a nightmare. The embargo failed to change British or French policy, but it created distress and dissension at home. Those who depended on foreign trade lost their livelihood. Widespread smuggling breached the embargo and eroded respect for law. Federalists capitalized on discontent to make a comeback, especially in the Northeast, shattering Jefferson's dream of one-party, Republican rule. The embargo also shattered Republican unity. Although James Madison, Jefferson's secretary of state, won the election of 1808, the party was divided and the administration befuddled.

War of 1812

The failure of peaceful coercion left two alternatives: war or submission. The country would not accept either. Madison and Congress adopted temporizing measures that only postponed the showdown. Congress tried to bar trade only with France and Britain, but later relented authorizing the president to reimpose an embargo on one nation if the other respected American rights. Napoleon pretended to comply, and Madison thereupon permitted trade with France. Eventually economic distress and political unrest forced the English to repeal their restrictive orders-in-council, a shift that came too late. Deceived by Napoleon, and ignorant of Britain's change in policy, Congress heeded Madison's request and declared war against England in June 1812.

For two decades the United States had struggled to stay out of war. The surest way of avoiding immediate involvement was total isolation. But this meant giving up the profits of foreign trade, and confessing the inability or unwillingness to defend American interests. The issues that led to war in 1812 were not new: impressment of seamen, interference with neutral trade, and British intrigue with Indians that hindered western settlement were all grievances of long standing. By 1812, however, the Republican party, exhausting peaceful means, and its patience ended, saw no alternative except national humiliation. The vote in Congress followed party lines, with outnumbered Federalists and a small group of anti-administration Republicans bitterly resisting. Pro-war sentiment was strongest in the South and West, the Republican bastions; anti-war sentiment concentrated in the Northeast where Federalists got most of their votes, but most New England Republicans voted with their party in favor of war.

Republican merchants and farmers supported war and blamed England for depressing the prices of American exports on world markets. Federalist merchants and farmers, equally strong in their convictions, preferred to turn the other cheek rather than give up whatever trade was still possible. Party loyalty shaped perceptions of economic interests and deep-seated fears reinforced them. Convinced that Napoleon menaced civilization, Federalists looked to England for salvation. Republicans with no love for Napoleon had even less for the English, who they believed still plotted against American independence.

A new, young generation of Republicans elected in 1810 to the Congress that declared war expressed the growing sentiment of the Republican majority that unless the United States defended itself, the cause of republican government would be discredited. "We have been long enough at peace," warned Elbridge Gerry, the Republican governor of Massachusetts, "we are losing our spirit, our character, and our independence. We are degenerating into a mere nation of traders, and are forgetting the honor of our ancestors. . . ."

The coming of war found the country unprepared and divided. Madison won reelection in 1812, yet Federalists and anti-war Republicans supporting New York's George Clinton carried all the states north of the Potomac except Vermont and Pennsylvania. The government had trouble raising troops and money for what many citizens called disparagingly "Mr. Madison's War," and when an American army invaded Canada it was thrown back. The navy did better on the Great Lakes, but victories there were indecisive. Napoleon's collapse in 1812 permitted the British to transfer veteran troops to America. They blockaded the American coastline and burned the White House, but their major campaigns in the Northwest failed. Tired, with little

prospect of achieving military victory, both sides gravitated toward peace. The Treaty of Ghent (1814) ended the war without settling any of the issues that had caused it.

Unaware that the war was over, General Andrew Jackson turned back a formidable British invasion force at New Orleans in January 1815 and won the war's greatest land battle. This needless encounter, like the decision to go to war, dramatically revealed the determination of the United States to assert itself as a sovereign nation. By war's end, Americans possessed renewed faith in their republican experiment.

ROOTS OF STABILITY

The embargo and war gave the previously disintegrating Federalists a short reprieve and prompted some of them to dream impossible dreams. Ever since Jefferson's triumph, some Federalists toyed with ideas of pulling the New England states out of the Union. At the Hartford Convention (1814), they denounced the war and proclaimed the right to resist laws which they thought violated the Constitution, the same stand Republicans had taken in their battle against the Alien and Sedition Laws. The end of the war and the victory at New Orleans undercut the Federalists and assured continued Republican supremacy. The Republican party's presidential candidate in 1816, James Monroe of Virginia, Madison's "right-hand man" during the war, won easily.

Monroe's triumph revealed the waning of older partisan divisions. During the heyday of Jefferson's presidency, many Federalists, despairing of making a comeback, simply gave up the fight. Young Federalists invested new energies in party activity without long-term success. The party exploited the crisis in foreign relations, but its gains proved temporary. By 1816 Federalism and Republicanism no longer divided the nation as they had for a generation. Party organizations withered, ideological and policy differences became blurred, and many Federalists in search of office joined the opposition. With each passing year, Jefferson's vision of a nonpartisan America approached reality. Many

Federalists had accepted Republicanism, and continued divisions between Adams and Hamiltonian wings further weakened the Federalist party after the defeat in 1800. Unable to unite, unwilling to adjust their ideology to an increasingly democratic society, and inept as popularity-seeking politicians, the Federalists were doomed.

The first political parties were fragile institutions, lacking deep roots in political experience, and short on party identification and loyalty. The parties, as loose alliances of individuals and groups, fell easily into factionalism, while party organization tended to atrophy. Before the 1790s, no one had been born a Federalist or Republican and thus most ordinary citizens and voters did not inherit an ancestral party loyalty, on which later parties have relied.

Party growth thrived initially on the tensions of the 1790s, which eased in the years after Jefferson's election. As Republicans assumed power, Federalists learned their fears of "Jacobinism" had been unfounded. Republicans paid the national debt, and discovered the advantages of a broad construction of the Constitution and a vigorous use of national power. Some even learned the usefulness of the national bank, though not enough to save its charter from expiration in 1811. Power also sobered the Republicans, who in office became less hostile to central government and less fearful of monarchical conspiracy.

The leaders of both parties had regarded themselves as statesmen, not as professional politicians. Politics was a duty, a responsibility of gentlemen whose primary commitment was to planting, trade, law, or medicine, and the good life. Unused to political combat, they preferred to remain at home than to become targets for mudslingers. Defeat had a shattering effect on Federalists, because they had no experience with the cyclical alternation of parties in and out of power. Failure, when it came, reduced them to the role of apprehensive bystanders.

Someday a new party system would emerge and with it professionals with but one occupation, politics. The founding fathers, however, were gifted amateurs in the art of governing. Winning independence did not so much create a nation as give men a chance to discover how to handle power. A republic founded on the principles that government derives its just power from the consent of the governed still had to prove itself more than a utopian dream. There were no magic solutions. The first effort to establish a stable central government, the Confederation, had failed. The Constitution of 1789 offered greater hope. The first American party system, which none had anticipated and many deplored, became the practical means by which Americans reconciled unity with diversity and liberty with order, and created models which later generations could build upon.

SUGGESTIONS FOR FURTHER READING

Suggestions for further reading are highly selective. Works available in paperback are starred (*). Students should consult the bibliographies in George A. Billias (ed.), *The American Revolution* (2d ed., 1970)*, and Paul Goodman (ed.), *The Federalists vs the Jeffersonian Republicans* (1967)*, as well as those in John C. Miller, *The Federalist Era* (1960)*, and Marshall Smelser, *The Democratic Republic, 1801–1815* (1968)*, for additional references.

INTRODUCTION

General Works on the Revolutionary and Early National Periods

Edmund S. Morgan, *The Birth of the Republic, 1763–1789* (1965)*; Benjamin F. Wright, *Consensus and Continuity, 1776–1787* (1958)*; Esmond Wright, *Fabric of Freedom, 1763–1800* (1961)*; Russel B. Nye, *The Cultural Life of the New Nation, 1776–1830* (1960)*: R. R. Palmer, *The Age of Democratic Revolution, 1760–1800* (2 vols., 1959–64)*.

CHAPTER 6

General

Charles M. Andrews, *The Colonial Background of the American Revolution* (1931)*; John C. Miller, *Origins of the American Revolution* (1943)*; Lawrence H. Gipson, *The Coming of the Revolution* (1954)*; Merrill Jensen, *The Founding of a Nation* (1968); Jack P. Greene, *The Reappraisal of the American Revolution in Recent Historical Literature* (1967)*.

The New Empire

Lewis B. Namier, *The Structure of Politics at the Accession of George III* (1929)*; Lewis B. Namier, *England in the Age of the American Revolution* (1930)*; Richard Pares, *King George III and the Politicians* (1953); Herbert Butterfield, *George III and the Historians* (1957); Robert L. Schuyler, *Parliament and the British Empire* (1929); Carl Ubbelohde, *The American Colonies and the British Empire* (1968)*; Harold H. Peckham, *The Colonial Wars* (1964)*; Thomas P. Abernethy, *Western Lands and the American Revolution* (1937); Jack M. Sosin, *Whitehall and the Wilderness* (1961).

Remodeling the Empire

Michael G. Kammen, *A Rope of Sand: The Colonial Agents, British Politics and the American Revolution* (1968); O. M. Dickerson, *The Navigation Acts and the American Revolution* (1951)*; Thomas C. Barrow, *Trade and Empire: The British Customs Service in Colonial America, 1660-1775* (1967); Carl Ubbelohde, *The Vice-Admiralty Courts and the American Revolution* (1960); John Shy, *Toward Lexington* (1965)*; Bernhard Knollenberg, *Origin of the American Revolution, 1759-1766* (1960)*.

American Resistance

Edmund S. and Helen M. Morgan, *The Stamp Act Crisis* (1953)*; Jesse Lemish, "Jack Tar in the Streets: Merchant Seamen in the Politics of Revolutionary America," *William and Mary Quarterly*, vol. 25 (1968), pp. 371-407; John C. Miller, *Sam Adams* (1936)*; Hiller B. Zobel, *The Boston Massacre* (1970); Benjamin W. Labaree, *The Boston Tea Party* (1964)*; Arthur M. Schlesinger, Sr., *Colonial Merchants and the American Revolution, 1763-1776* (1918)*; Carl Bridenbaugh, *Cities in Revolt: Urban Life in America, 1743-1776* (1955)*; Robert D. Meade, *Patrick Henry: Patriot in the Making* (1957).

Roots of Revolution

Max Savelle, *Seeds of Liberty* (1948)*; Clinton Rossiter, *Seedtime of the Republic* (1953)*.

The Great Debate

Bernard Bailyn, *Ideological Origins of the American Revolution* (1967); Bernard Bailyn, "Political Experience and Enlightenment Ideas in 18th Century America," *American Historical Review*, vol. 67 (1962), pp. 339-351; Bernard Bailyn, *Origins of American Politics* (1968)*; Edmund S. Morgan, "The Puritan Ethic and the American Revolution," *William and Mary Quarterly*, vol. 24 (1967), pp. 3-43; J. R. Pole, *Political Representation in England and the Origins of the American Republic* (1966); Philip Davidson, *Propaganda and the American Revolution* (1941)*; Arthur M. Schlesinger, Sr., *Prelude to Independence: The Newspaper War on Britain, 1764-1776* (1958)*; Bruce I. Granger, *Political Satire on the American Revolution, 1763-1783* (1960); Carl Becker, *The Declaration of Independence* (1922)*.

CHAPTER 7

General

John C. Miller, *Triumph of Freedom, 1775-1783* (1948)*; John R. Alden, *The American Revolution* (1954)*; Richard B. Morris, *The American Revolution Reconsidered* (1967)*.

Winning Independence

Howard H. Peckham, *The War for Independence* (1958)*; Piers Mackesy, *The War for America, 1775-1783* (1964); Carl Van Doren, *Secret History of the American Revolution* (1941)*; Eric Robson, *The American Revolution in Its Political and Military Aspects* (1955)*; William B. Willcox, *Sir Henry Clinton in the War of Independence* (1964); Samuel F. Bemis, *The Diplomacy of the American Revolution* (rev. ed., 1957)*; Richard W. Van Alstyne, *Empire and Independence* (1965)*; William C. Stinchcombe, *The American Revolution and the French Alliance* (1969); Richard B. Morris, *The Peacemakers: The Great Powers and American Independence* (1965)*.

Social Consequences of Revolution

J. Franklin Jameson, *The American Revolution Considered as a Social Movement* (1926)*; Evarts B. Greene, *The Revolutionary Generation* (1943)*; Jackson T. Main, *The Social Structure of Revolutionary America* (1965)*; Merrill Jensen, "Democracy and the American Revolution," *Huntington Library Quarterly*, vol. 20 (1957), pp. 321-341; Elisha P. Douglass, *Rebels and Democrats* (1955); Benjamin Quarles, *The Negro in the American*

Revolution (1961)*; William H. Nelson, *The American Tory* (1961)*; Wallace Brown, *The King's Friends* (1965); Paul H. Smith, *Loyalists and Redcoats* (1964)*.

The Churches

Alan Heimert, *Religion and the American Mind from the Great Awakening to the Revolution* (1966); Alice Baldwin, *New England Clergy and the American Revolution* (1928); E. F. Humphreys, *Nationalism and Religion in America* (1924); Carl Bridenbaugh, *Mitre and Sceptre* (1962)*.

State Governments

Allan Nevins, *The American States During and After the Revolution, 1775-1789* (1924); Walter F. Dodd, "The First State Constitutional Conventions, 1776-1783," *American Political Science Review*, vol. 2 (1908), pp. 545-561; Fletcher M. Green, *Constitutional Development in the South Atlantic States* (1930)*; Jackson T. Main, "Government by the People: The American Revolution and the Democratization of the Legislatures," *William and Mary Quarterly*, vol. 23 (1966), pp. 391-407, Jackson T. Main, *Upper House in Revolutionary America* (1967); Carl L. Becker, *History of Political Parties in New York, 1760-1776* (1909)*.

CHAPTER 8

General

Forrest McDonald, *E Pluribus Unum: The Formation of the American Republic, 1776-1790* (1965)*; Gordon S. Wood, *The Creation of the American Republic, 1776-1787* (1969)*; Cecilia M. Kenyon, "Republicanism and Radicalism in the Revolution," *William and Mary Quarterly*, vol. 19 (1962), pp. 153-182; E. James Ferguson, *The Power of the Purse: A History of American Public Finance, 1776-1790* (1961)*.

The Confederation

Merrill Jensen, *The Articles of Confederation* (1940)*; Merrill Jensen, *The New Nation* (1950)*; Richard B. Morris, "The Confederation Period and the American Historian," *William and Mary Quarterly*, vol. 13 (1956), pp. 139-156; Marion L. Starkey, *A Little Rebellion* (1955).

The Constitution

Carl Van Doren, *The Great Rehearsal* (1948)*; Clinton Rossiter, *1787: The Grand Convention* (1966)*; Charles A. Beard, *An Economic Interpretation of the Constitution* (1913)*; Robert E. Brown, *Charles Beard and the Constitution* (1956)*; Forrest McDonald, *We the People: The Economic Origins of the Constitution* (1958)*; Charles C. Thach, Jr., *The Creation of the Presidency, 1775-1789* (1923)*; Staughton Lynd, *Class Conflict, Slavery, and the United States Constitution* (1967)*; Clinton Rossiter, *Alexander Hamilton and the Constitution* (1964); Edward McNall Burns, *James Madison: Philosopher of the Constitution* (1938); Paul Eidelberg, *The Philosophy of the American Constitution* (1968)*.

Struggle for Ratification

Jackson T. Main, *The Anti-Federalists* (1961)*; Cecilia M. Kenyon, "Men of Little Faith: The Antifederalists," *William and Mary Quarterly*, vol. 12 (1955), pp. 3-43; Alpheus T. Mason, *The States Rights Debate: Antifederalism* (1964)*; Robert A. Rutland, *The Ordeal of the Constitution: The Anti-Federalists* (1966); Linda Grant De Pauw, *The Eleventh Pillar: New York State and the Federal Constitution* (1966); Staughton Lynd, *Antifederalism in Dutchess County* (1962).

CHAPTER 9

General

Marcus Cunliffe, *The Nation Takes Shape, 1789-1837* (1959)*; Morton Borden, *Parties and Politics in the Early Republic, 1789-1815* (1967)*; Curtis P. Nettels, *The Emergence of National Economy, 1775-1815* (1962)*.

The Federalist System

John C. Miller, *The Federalist Era, 1789-1801* (1960)*; Leonard D. White, *The Federalists* (1948)*; Marcus Cunliffe, *George Washington: Man and Monument* (1958)*; Broadus Mitchell, *Alexander Hamilton* (2 vols., 1957-62); Cecilia M. Kenyon, "Alexander Hamilton: Rousseau of the Right," *Political Science Quarterly*, vol. 73 (1958), pp. 161-178; Donald F. Swanson, *The Origins of Hamilton's Fiscal Policies* (1963); Leland D. Baldwin, *Whiskey Rebels* (1939).*

Crisis of the 1790s

Paul A. Varg, *Foreign Policies of the Founding Fathers* (1963); Felix Gilbert, *To the Farewell Address* (1961)*; Bradford Perkins, *The First Rapprochement: England and the United States* (1953)*; Alexander DeConde, *Entangling Alliance: Politics and Diplomacy under George Washington* (1958); Alexander DeConde, *The Quasi-War . . . with France, 1797-1801* (1966)*; Page Smith, *John Adams* (2 vols., 1962); Stephen G. Kurtz, *The Presidency of John Adams* (1957)*; Manning Dauer, *The Adams Federalists* (1953)*; Leonard W. Levy, *Legacy of Suppression: Freedom of Speech and Press* (1960)*; James M. Smith, *Freedoms Fetters: The Alien and Sedition Laws* (1956)*; John R. Howe, "Republican Thought and the Political Violence of the 1790's," *American Quarterly*, vol. 14 (1967), pp. 147-165.

First American Party System

William N. Chambers, *Political Parties in a New Nation* (1963)*; Joseph C. Charles, *Origins of the American Party System* (1956)*; Paul Goodman, "First American Party System," in William N. Chambers and Walter D. Burnham (eds.), *The American Party Systems* (1967)*; Norman K. Risjord, "The Virginia Federalists," *Journal of Southern History*, vol. 33 (1967), pp. 486-517; David H. Fischer, *Revolution in American Conservatism* (1965)*; Noble E. Cunningham, *The Jeffersonian Republicans: The Formation of Party Organization, 1789-1801* (1958)*; Eugene P. Link, *The Democratic-Republican Societies, 1790-1809* (1942); Charles A. Beard, *Economic Origins of Jeffersonian Democracy* (1915)*.

Republican Ascendancy

Marshall Smelser, *The Democratic Republic, 1801-1815* (1968)*; Noble E. Cunningham, *The Jeffersonian Republicans in Power* (1963)*; Charles M. Wiltse, *The Jeffersonian Tradition in American Democracy* (1935)*; Dumas Malone, *Jefferson and his Times* (4 vols. to date, 1948-); Merrill D. Peterson, *Thomas Jefferson and the New Nation* (1970); Merrill D. Peterson, *The Jeffersonian Image in the American Mind* (1960)*; Leonard W. Levy, *Jefferson and Civil Liberties* (1963); Adrienne Koch, *Jefferson and Madison: The Great Collaboration* (1950)*; Irving Brant, *The Fourth President: A Life of James Madison* (1970); Raymond Walters, Jr., *Albert Gallatin: Jeffersonian Financier* (1957)*; Linda Kerber, *Federalists in Dissent: Imagery and Ideology in Jeffersonian America* (1970).

Republicanism in the States

William A. Robinson, *Jeffersonian Democracy in New England* (1916); Paul Goodman, *The Democratic-Republicans of Massachusetts* (1964); Alfred F. Young, *Democratic Republicans of New York* (1967); Carl E. Prince, *New Jersey's Jeffersonian Republicans* (1967); Norman K. Risjord, *The Old Republicans: Southern Conservatism in the Age of Jefferson* (1965); Harry Ammon, "The Formation of the Republican Party in Virginia," *Journal of Southern History*, vol. 19 (1953), pp. 283-310; John H. Wolfe, *Jeffersonian Democracy in South Carolina* (1940).

Republican Diplomacy and War

Bradford Perkins, *Prologue to War: England and the United States, 1805-1812* (1961)*; Louis M. Sears, *Jefferson and the Embargo* (1927); Julius W. Pratt, *Expansionists of 1812* (1925); Reginald Horsman, *Causes of the War of 1812* (1962)*; Roger H. Brown, *The Republic in Peril, 1812* (1964); Bernard Mayo, *Henry Clay: Spokesman of the New West* (1937); Harry L. Coles, *The War of 1812* (1965)*; Patrick C. T. White, *A Nation on Trial* (1965)*; Reginald Horsman, *The War of 1812* (1969); Marquis James, *Andrew Jackson: The Border Captain* (1933)*.

Part Three
Liberty and Union, 1815-1877

Introduction

During the sixty years between the end of the War of 1812 and the end of Reconstruction, modern America was born. All aspects of American life underwent change, some of them fundamentally. A transportation revolution, itself a product of new forms of business entrepreneurship and a resurgent nationalism, transformed the structure of the economy. It knit the country together to create a large, national market, speeded the spread of settlement across the continent, and gave remote farmers access to faraway markets. At the same time the Industrial Revolution reached America. All segments of society felt these economic shock waves. Most Americans reaped immediate gains, but many others, most notably and alarmingly the working classes emerging in the new urban centers, did not.

Expanded economic opportunities and many new problems created by these changes raised significant political questions, casting doubt on the basic premises which underlay the American political system. The country moved from the Politics of Deference, in which the lower orders deferred to their betters, to the Politics of Egalitarianism, in which one man felt he was as good as any other, and said so. The previous political structure had worked effectively and comfortably within the accepted rules of a deferential society; but it had to yield in time to the democratizing forces then at work. Political adaptation required new rules of procedure, an abandonment of Jeffersonian gentility in favor of politics suitable to the "age of the common man." Jacksonians did not initiate all these changes, but they did fashion the period's most successful national party, and they held power for most of the time between 1829 and the Civil War.

The optimistic vision which could underwrite a massive technological feat like the Erie Canal also influenced thinking about man's relationship to God and society. If Americans could build roads and canals anywhere, they wanted to believe that the road to salvation was just as open to their efforts. Religion came to emphasize God's approachability. If God was ready for man, and vice versa, and if the American Adam might create a heaven on the American earth, then all Christians had to root out evil and corruption from American life. From this conviction sprang much of the reformist zeal of the years 1830–1860, during which Americans enlisted in as many crusades as there were evils to cure.

The greatest of these crusades almost ended in the permanent breakup of the Union. The existence of slavery mocked all the pretensions of a society which proclaimed itself free, cherished equality, and increasingly practiced what it preached for the white majority. The democratization of American society and the spread of humanitarian ideas in the nineteenth century made it more and more difficult to reconcile the contradictions between American ideals and American realities. Abandoning the attempt to reconcile these differences, abolitionists demanded the end of slavery, immediately and without compensation to slaveholders. Although abolitionists never gained effective political power (some of them boycotted the political system entirely), growing antislavery sentiment in the North eventually produced a sectional polarization which in 1861 became a civil war.

For four years the future of the American Union and its liberal-capitalist, national state hung in the balance. Northern victory in 1865 meant that the consolidation of the nation could proceed in earnest. America's black minority had been freed from slavery and relegated to second-class citizenship. Southern opposition to national consolidation had been crushed, and a major impediment to the growth of an industrial and urban nation into a mass society had been brushed aside.

Andrew Jackson: Democrat, man of iron. *(New York Public Library)*

A quiet day in Chicago, 1820.

Broad Way from the Bowling Green: Fashionable New York City, c. 1826.

From Albany to Buffalo on the Erie Canal, 1830–1831.

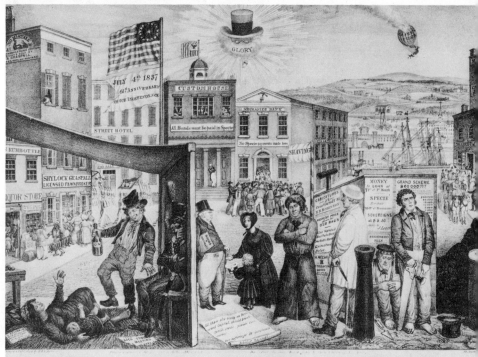

The American spirit, New York
1837. *(New-York Historical
Society)*

Abolitionist reading matter, 1839. *(New York Public Library)*

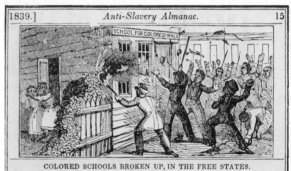

COLORED SCHOOLS BROKEN UP, IN THE FREE STATES.

When schools have been established for colored scholars, the law-makers and the mob have combined to destroy them ;—as at Canterbury, Ct., at Canaan, N. H., Aug. 10, 1835, at Zanesville and Brown Co., Ohio, in 1836.

IMMEDIATE EMANCIPATION.

Aug. 1, 1834, 30,000 slaves were emancipated in Antigua. Without any apprenticeship, or system of preparation, preceding the act, the chains were broken at a stroke, and they all went out FREE ! It is now four years since these 30,000 slaves were "turned loose" among 2,000 whites, their former masters. These masters fought against the emancipation bill with all their force and fury. They remonstrated with the British Government—conjured and threatened,—protested that emancipation would ruin the island, that the emancipated slaves would never work—would turn vagabonds, butcher the whites and flood the island with beggary and crime. Their strong beseechings availed as little as their threats, and croakings about ruin. The Emancipation Act, unintimidated by the bluster, traversed quietly through its successive stages up to the royal sanction, and became the law of the land. When the slaveholders of Antigua saw that abolition was *inevitable*, they at once resolved to substitute immediate, unconditional, and entire emancipation for the gradual process contemplated by the Act. Well, what has been the result? Read the following testimony of the very men who, but little more than four years ago, denounced and laughed to scorn the idea of abolishing slavery, and called it folly, fanaticism, and insanity. We quote from the work of Messrs. Thome and Kimball, lately published, the written testimony of many of the first men in Antigua,—some of whom were among the largest slaveholders before August, 1834. It proves, among other points, that

EMANCIPATED SLAVES ARE PEACEABLE.

TESTIMONY. " *There is no feeling of insecurity.* A stronger proof of this cannot be given than *the dispensing, within five months after emancipation, with the Christmas guards, which had been uninterruptedly kept up for nearly one hundred years*—during the whole time of slavery.

" I have *never heard of any instance of revenge* for former injuries." *James Scotland, Sen. Esq.*

"Insurrection or revenge *is in no case dreaded*. My family go to sleep every night with the doors unlocked. There is not the *slightest* feeling of insecurity —quite the contrary. Property is more secure, *for all idea of insurrection is abolished forever.*" Hon. *N. Nugent, Speaker of the House of Assembly.*

" There has been no instance of personal violence since freedom. I have not heard of a single case of even *meditated revenge.*" *Dr. Daniell, member of the Council, and Attorney for six estates.*

" Emancipation has banished the *fear of* insurrections, incendiarism, &c." *Mr. Favey, Manager of Lavicount's.*

" I have never heard of an instance of violence or revenge on the part of the negroes." *Rev. Mr. Morrish, Moravian Missionary.*

The call to conscience. *(Ohio Historical Society Library)*

LET THE NORTH AWAKE!

T. B. M'CORMICK

Will Discuss the Immorality, Illegality and Unconstitutionality of

AMERICAN SLAVERY,

And the Duty and Power of the General Government to Abolish it,

IN *Town Hall at Enton*

AT *7 OclK P.M. April 30th 1857*

Mr. M'CORMICK is the Clergyman for whom the Governor of Kentucky made a Requisition upon the Governor of Indiana, charging him with aiding in the escape of Fugitive Slaves. The Warrant was issued and Mr. M'Cormick is thereby exiled from his home. All are respectfully invited to attend.

The plantation police, or home guard, examining Negro passes on the levee road below New Orleans. *(Library of Congress)*

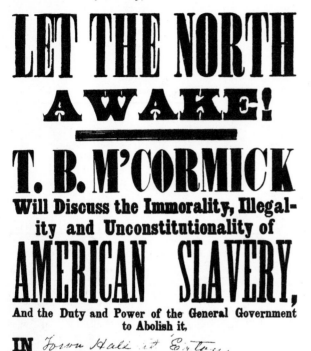

Detroit, 1832: The age of sailboats.

Senator Charles Sumner of
Massachusetts: The politician
as moralist. *(Negro History
Associates)*

The fifth generation: Slaves, Beaufort, South Carolina, 1862. *(Library of Congress)*

Atlanta, 1864: Future commercial capital of a new South.

"VERDICT", HANG THE D— YANKEE AND NIGGER".

Southern chivalry in defeat, *Harper's*, March 23, 1867. *(Library of Congress)*

The wages of war: Sherman's March to the Sea, 1864. *(Library Company of Philadelphia)*

"There's no place like home." *(Cook Collection, Richmond, Virginia)*

Black men for the Union: Battery A, 2nd U.S. Colored Artillery (light). *(Chicago Historical Society)*

Rehearsal for the bloodbath: Union ambulance and bearers, Army of the Potomac, 1862. *(Brown Brothers)*

Entertainment for the masses: Sand's, Nathan's & Company Circus comes to town, New York City, 1858. *(New-York Historical Society)*

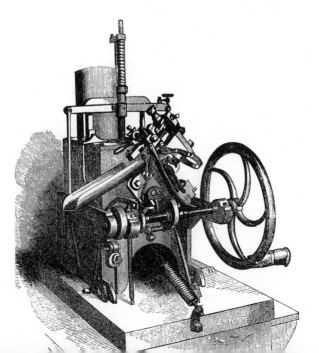

Type-casting machine.

General Jackson shortly before his death. *(Library of Congress)*

Rapid transit: Key to urban growth.
Proposed subway for New York City,
c. 1870.

Portland, Oregon, 1858.

Railroads span the continent, conquering the Great Plains. From *Harper's Weekly*, 1875.

Chapter 10
Roots of a Modern Society, 1815–1860

For most of their history, Americans lived off the land. Farming was more than a livelihood, it was a way of life, the principal source of national wealth. Settling a rich, undeveloped continent, Americans prospered but their wealth grew slowly, held back by shortages of labor and capital and by inefficient modes of production. Although independence transformed the political system, the structure of the economy remained largely unchanged. A half century after the Revolution, new forces began gathering the momentum which would transform the productive system, and by 1860 Americans had laid the foundation of a modern industrial society. Economic development produced a 50 percent growth in per capita income between 1820 and 1860, generated by new production methods far more efficient than those Americans had relied on for two centuries.

Behind this dramatic surge in per capita income lay many far-reaching and interrelated changes. The population more than tripled and spread across the great interior valleys and plains beyond the coastal mountain barrier. Agriculture remained the most important industry but mining, manufacturing, and construction accounted for almost 45 percent of output in 1860 as agriculture's relative importance declined. Manufacturing brought with it factories and urbanization. The percentage of the population living in cities in 1860 was three times as great as forty years earlier; New York became a metropolis of a million people.

In 1820, Americans had been isolated from one another. Rivers afforded the only efficient means of transportation and the difficulty of moving people and goods inexpensively impeded westward settlement and economic development. By 1860 an elaborate web of surfaced roads, canals and railroads, together with steamboats on inland rivers and lakes, knit the country together. Now farmers in the interior and manufacturers in New England could sell their goods to a large, national market. As markets expanded so did productive capacity; technological improve-ments vastly increased the productivity of labor, and new forms of business organization, especially the impersonal but efficient corporation, enlarged the scope and complexity of enterprise.

In 1820, the United States was a new country with economic resources far less developed than those of Britain, the leading industrial nation of the nineteenth century. By 1900, however, America had become the world's leading industrial power. The roots of this achievement go back to the decades before the Civil War when the American economy entered an era of sustained industrial growth.

The transformation from agriculture to industrialism, and from poverty to prosperity, remains the hope and necessity of three-quarters of the world's population, still struggling to discover the processes of economic development which Americans initiated long ago. During their first half century of national existence, Americans concentrated on establishing a stable government. By 1815 the experiment in republicanism had weathered repeated storms and appeared safe. During the next half century citizens turned inward to develop and people the continent.

IMMIGRATION

From about five million in 1790, American population grew sixfold to over thirty million by 1860. Most of the increase was homegrown, but immigration from Europe stepped up after 1820 and after 1840 it turned into a flood. Economic and political instability in America and war in Europe had interrupted the flow, but the return of peace in 1815 reopened the channels. Six million crossed the Atlantic between 1820 and 1860, nearly half of them Irish, a third from Germany, and a steady flow of Britons. In addition several thousand Canadians, many of them French-speaking Catholics, migrated each year, as did Scandinavians and Latin Americans—peoples whose great period of migration to America would come later. Not since "the encampments of the Roman empire, or the tents of the Crusaders," had such an army of humanity marched across continents, proclaimed the editor of the *Democratic Review* approvingly.

The newcomers came for the reasons that had sent previous generations to the New World: some to escape from political and religious persecution; most to find greater economic opportunity. The disruptive forces that had uprooted people in the past became stronger and more widespread, as industrialization in England and increased agricultural output combined to produce a dramatic increase in population. New crops, grown by new methods requiring less labor, meant that landlords could squeeze unwanted peasants off the land. Farmers who clung to their plots found themselves caught in perpetual debt and eventually gave up. Some peasants found employment in factories as did craftsmen whose tasks were now performed by machines, but others had to survive on public charity. As the poorhouses filled, fear of permanent destitution impelled peasants and laborers possessing some property to sell what they could and book passage for America. As the tempo of migration picked up, it developed its own momentum. Fathers and sons were the first to try their luck in America; they encouraged relatives and neighbors in their old villages to join them, and later sent money home that brought relatives across the ocean.

The stream of migration ebbed and flowed with changing conditions. Good times in the United States stimulated the influx, and depression and shrinking opportunity diminished it. Similarly, crop failures and political turmoil in Europe, such as the revolutionary insurrections in 1830 and 1848, intensified the desire to leave. Pressures once centered in England spread to Scotland, Ireland, and Germany. Landlords found it more advantageous to consolidate fragmented holdings into larger, more productive units. Ireland proved especially vulnerable. Thousands of peasants subsisted on tiny plots, surviving mainly because the potato had become by the eighteenth century their staple of life. Easily grown in large quantities on little land, the potato

was partly responsible for the surge in population. When the crop failed for several years in the late 1840s, famine stalked the Emerald Isle. Thousands starved to death, and thousands more left for America. In twenty years the number of poor Irish cottagers that remained shrank from half a million to less than a hundred thousand.

The immigration of 1840–1860 was primarily an Irish and German affair. In the 1820s Irish immigration, averaging about 10,000 a year, ran only slightly higher than immigration from the rest of the British Isles. But in the 1830s the figures for the Irish jumped appreciably, outstripping British immigration by two or three to one. Even before the Great Famine struck Ireland in the late 1840s, Irishmen were leaving for America at a rate of 40,000 to 50,000 a year. The potato famine pushed Irish immigration to record levels. In 1851, 380,000 immigrants came to America; nearly 60 percent were Irish.

That year Irish immigration reached its peak, but another mass migration soon replaced the Hibernian exodus. German immigration, which in the 1820s registered a yearly high of only 1,800, had been climbing steadily. Its peak came in 1854; out of a total immigration of 427,000, there were 215,000 Germans, or just over 50 percent. Thus in the decade before the Civil War, the 1850s, heavy immigration changed the character of the American population rapidly and sometimes painfully. The political consequences of the social tensions stemming from this immigration shaped antebellum America in many ways.

Mid-nineteenth century immigrants fled Europe in desperation and were generally poorer and less skilled than earlier newcomers. Cheaper transportation costs facilitated the flight as did the growing number of vessels that carried American products to Britain and returned with cargoes of immigrants. The newcomers found employment in the growing cities and on the farms, but the surge of population, native and foreign born, though it enlarged both the labor force and domestic markets, did not of itself produce the surge in national wealth. Neither did the settlement of the West, though both were important preconditions for industrial development.

THE SPREAD OF SETTLEMENT

Until the Revolution, most Americans lived along the seaboard and rolling uplands directly west of it; the Appalachian mountain chain blocked access to the valleys and plains of the interior. During the late eighteenth century, however, Americans began pushing across the mountains and by 1860 many had crossed the Mississippi River. By purchase and conquest, the United States rounded off its present territorial limits and carved twenty states out of the vast public domain, beginning with the admission of Kentucky in 1792 and reaching Oregon in 1859 and Kansas by 1861. An initial surge of settlers after the Revolution filled up western New York and Pennsylvania. Others pushed into Kentucky, Tennessee, and Ohio, and by 1820 these new states were among the most populous in the Union. During the next three decades farmers occupied the eastern half of the Mississippi Valley, completing American settlement from the Atlantic to the Mississippi River.

The Indians were ruthlessly swept aside. Regarding them as uncivilized and subhuman, Americans justified seizing their lands in the name of progress. Indians had no right to stop Americans from turning the Wilderness into a Garden. The process of Indian removal followed a grim pattern. As each wave of white settlers coveted the nearest Indian lands, the U.S. government negotiated treaties that opened new areas for settlement and promised the Indians perpetual control of the lands they still retained. But whites pressed on relentlessly. Each new removal treaty meant new betrayal.

Occasionally, Indians fought back but resistance only meant more certain annihilation. In the South, fifty thousand members of the Five Civilized Tribes—including the Cherokees and Creeks—were herded into concentration camps on their way to a barren reservation in the Indian territory set aside for the dispossessed, west of the Mississippi River. Four thousand Cherokees alone died on the "Trail of Tears" to their new homes beyond the Mississippi, known as "The Great American Desert," parched lands thought worthless for white settlement and therefore suitable as the red man's final resting place.

THE TRANSPORTATION REVOLUTION

The Indians were not the only physical obstacle to the westward movement of whites. Those Americans settling in the Ohio Valley after the Revolution found themselves isolated from the rest of the country. They cleared some fields, built a house and barn, and planted their crops, but it cost too much to ship goods to Eastern and European markets. As long as farmers could not produce for distant markets they grew little more than they needed for their own subsistence, trading off a small surplus for some gunpowder, salt, molasses, and cloth at a general store.

Eastern farmers also faced problems. After the Revolution, Southerners still relied on the colonial staples, tobacco and rice, but by the 1790s production fell off. Thousands abandoned worn-out plantations in the upper South for virgin lands in the South Carolina and Georgia back country and other thousands crossed the mountains into Kentucky, Tennessee, and Ohio. Yet remoteness from markets dimmed their prospects. Northern farmers continued to grow wheat, corn, and vegetables and raise livestock, but the self-sufficiency of most farm families limited domestic markets for these products, and overseas outlets were unpredictable. During the two and a half decades of war touched off by the French Revolution of 1789, Americans suddenly found large markets for foodstuffs in Europe and the Caribbean. Yet these were temporary and uncertain. Exports from the United States quintupled, mostly because Americans imported coffee and sugar from the West Indies, tea from China, textiles from India, and spices from the East Indies, and then reexported them to Europe. This trade lasted only so long as nations involved in war left the business to outsiders; in 1807 the carrying trade boom collapsed and never revived. Wartime prosperity had given the economy a temporary, artificial boost. It did not alter the structure of the economy nor solve the problem of American economic development. Nor could a factory system develop so long as farmers had limited purchasing power and were largely self-sufficient.

The bottleneck finally broke as the result of

a series of changes that knit the country together, creating national markets. These permitted different sections of the country to specialize in economic activities for which they were best suited, and they sharply increased productivity. A vital force in transforming the structure of the American economy was a transportation revolution that brought together distant markets and regions, promoting regional specialization and interdependence. Except for limited road building few improvements in internal communications occurred during the seventeenth and eighteenth centuries. But in the forty years preceding the Civil War a modern communications system took shape.

First came the steamboat. Operated successfully on the Hudson in 1807, the big river steamers spread to western waters after 1817. They linked farmers in the Ohio and Mississippi valleys with the lower South, and with the East and Europe via New Orleans, which became one of the nation's leading commercial centers. But the existing network of navigable rivers limited the usefulness of steamboats.

Canals and Railroads

These restrictions did not apply to canals. The period from 1820 to 1840 saw the construction of over 3,000 miles of canals. In twenty-five years the United States had built more canal mileage than Britain had in half a century.

New York led the way with the Erie Canal. The state possessed the only major break in the Appalachian Mountains, the Mohawk Valley, and this opening joined to the Hudson River could provide a water connection from New York City to the Great Lakes. New York also had DeWitt Clinton, an ambitious and sometimes successful politician who made the canal his pet idea. Sufficient private capital could not be attracted to do the job; government would have to step in. Initially, promoters hoped for a federal subsidy, but the Virginia dynasty's scruples over spending federal money on internal improvements (especially in a Northern state) ended that dream. New York would have to raise the money alone.

The Erie Canal project went on, by fits and starts. A triumph of determined amateurism,

it proceeded without benefit of a trained engineer, relying on several self-taught surveyors. In 1825 Clinton had the satisfaction of declaring the entire canal open. "Clinton's Ditch," originally forty feet across and only four feet deep, made already rich New York even richer. The greatest public enterprise yet undertaken in America, the Erie Canal opened markets for western farmers and eastern manufacturers and importers, raised land values along the right of way, provided thousands of jobs, and made money for the state. In just seven years canal tolls had paid off the cost of construction, and New York had a canal fund surplus to support education and underwrite further economic expansion.

New York's success stimulated other states to enter the race for the western trade. Pennsylvania built a huge, hybrid system (part canal, part railroad) that linked Philadelphia with the Ohio Valley. Several western states laid out canal networks that connected farmers to the main routes east. But no state matched the incredible returns of New York's Erie Canal.

Canals, however, were not feasible everywhere. Maryland turned instead to the railroad. The first major road, the Baltimore and Ohio (begun in 1828) connected that port city with the Ohio Valley. Massachusetts followed with the Boston and Albany (1842) and other roads that linked factories with raw material sources and markets. The canal building boom had ended and a railroad boom was under way. By the 1840s the United States had 3,300 miles of track, nearly twice as much as Europe, and by 1860 American railroad mileage had climbed to 30,000. It took only thirty years to lay out the basic rail network east of the Mississippi, including four major east-west trunk lines. Though railroads did not move goods more cheaply than canals, by 1860 the volume of merchandise shipped by rail began to exceed that going by canal.

Railroads spread rapidly because of their many advantages. They could move goods with greater certainty regardless of season, and they were faster. Railroads cut the travel time from New York to Chicago from over three weeks to under three days. Factories now could count on receiving raw materials on time and wholesalers could replenish stocks quickly, enabling businessmen to operate with less working capital. The second largest industry in America after agriculture, the railroads also generated the demand for iron and coal; but their greatest contribution was to accelerate western settlement.

Anticipating the extension of railroads, farmers in the more settled regions moved west, because they were confident of access to markets. As new construction pushed westward, the roads already found demand for their services. By bringing farmers in the older regions closer to markets and facilitating the opening of newer, more productive lands, the roads expanded agricultural capacity at a time when labor-saving machines had not yet dominated farming nor revolutionized agricultural productivity. Although the major contributions of railroads as promoters of economic development came after the Civil War, the prewar roads pointed the way to future growth.

As railroads were conquering the country, the telegraph spread with them, providing for the first time in history instantaneous communication. Pioneered by Samuel F. B. Morse, a New Yorker trained as an artist, the invention found no backers for several years, until Congress appropriated enough money to build the first telegraph line between Washington and Baltimore in 1844. Its usefulness established, private investors stampeded Morse and his partners (and those who ignored Morse's patent rights) to join in the new enterprise. It gained acceptance gradually and by 1860, 50,000 miles of telegraph wire spanned the Eastern part of the continent, and a year later came the first transcontinental line. Communication no longer depended on the speed of the messenger; the dissemination of news and data for businessmen and politicians had been revolutionized.

Steam engines which powered locomotives could also power ships and oceangoing steamships began to compete with sailing vessels. Each of these innovations had different consequences. Steamboats and canals dramatically broke through the communications barrier by substantially lowering shipping costs and promoting an integrated national market. Canals and railroads extended cheap and reliable transportation to areas not blessed with rivers; they also shifted the flow of trade. In the 1830s two-thirds of the

West's trade went down the Mississippi, giving New Orleans the lion's share of its business; but by the 1850s two-thirds of the West's exports flowed eastward, a direct result of the transportation revolution.

COMMERCIAL AGRICULTURE

Although America stood at the threshold of fundamental economic change, industrialization did not come automatically. The expansion of commercial agriculture in the South and West in the early nineteenth century played a leading role in stimulating manufacturing in the Northeast. Searching for a staple to replace tobacco and rice, planters found the answer in cotton. Eli Whitney's cotton gin (1794) gave them a cheap method of separating the green seed from the fiber, and a ready-made market for cotton existed in England where textile factories were transforming Britain into the first modern industrial society. The Southern Cotton Kingdom rapidly spread from South Carolina and Georgia into the Gulf Plains, expecially the dark, rich soils of the "Black Belt" of Alabama and Mississippi. Britain purchased all the cotton Americans could produce and paid high prices for it, providing capital and foreign exchange.

Cotton thus opened up the Southwest. By 1860 the United States grew two-thirds of the world's cotton compared to only 9 percent sixty years earlier. The upper South, which could not grow cotton profitably, found in the large plantations of the newer regions markets for foodstuffs and surplus slaves. The enormous expansion of cotton production not only enriched the large Southern planters (and many New York merchants), but also stimulated development in other regions. Between 1815 and 1860 cotton accounted for half the nation's exports, helped to finance imports from abroad and induced foreigners to invest in the United States.

As cotton became king in the South, wheat and corn gained mastery in the West. The Ohio and Mississippi rivers and their tributaries linked Western farmers to markets in the South, the East, and overseas once the steamboat made the western waters efficient arteries of commerce.

By lowering transport costs, especially on goods shipped upstream from New Orleans, the steamboat gave farmers an incentive to produce surpluses to exchange for other goods. So, too, did the spread of the Cotton Kingdom. Planters in the lower South specialized in growing cotton and sugar (in Louisiana) and purchased foodstuffs from the West. But the West found its best customers in the East. Beginning in the 1820s a series of canals and railroads linked the two regions and enabled Western farmers to reach growing markets along the coast.

Regional Interdependence

Those markets expanded as Easterners increasingly specialized in industry and commerce. Eastern farmers could not compete with Western grain or meat producers; thousands left for the Ohio Valley and others streamed into Eastern towns and cities, finding employment in the factories and service industries. In this way the three sections of the Union became increasingly specialized and economically interdependent.

Eastern merchants, especially New Yorkers, dominated the marketing of cotton because capital-hungry Southern planters reinvested most of their profits in more land and slaves to expand further their cotton culture. In addition, the planters disdained trade as a socially demeaning occupation for a gentleman. They relied on New Yorkers to buy and sell their crops, and left to the Yankees much of the profits from shipping, warehousing, insuring, and distributing the goods planters imported from Europe or bought in the Northeast.

The New Yorkers obliged by establishing the "Cotton Triangle." Their efficient coastal packet ships brought cotton and the other staples from the "colonial" Southern ports like Charleston, Mobile, and New Orleans, north to New York, where they were transshipped to Europe. Trade between the South and Europe was thus diverted by the need to break the voyages at New York, all for the greater profits of the New York merchants. Once established, the routine could not be changed, despite Southern protests that the New York break in the voyage meant a longer trip, costly delays, and extra charges for storage and reloading, for the Northern merchants needed cargo for their newly established and flourishing New York-to-Liverpool transatlantic packets. New York became the country's leading seaport, just as New York City led in urban development. By the 1820s, New York's leading export item was cotton—the same cotton which had been brought up from the South.

The Cotton Triangle had been well established even before completion of the Erie Canal. Afterwards, Southern dependence on Yankee credit and shipping became even more pronounced, as Southern agriculture expanded and New Yorkers, reaping the fantastic dividends of the canal, had more capital to invest in Southern trade. To protect this form of Yankee imperialism many New York firms sent agents to the Southern ports ("factors" they were called), as a kind of commercial carpetbaggers. Although in the two decades before the Civil War it became the custom to bypass New York in the cotton voyages, Southerners did not free themselves economically. On the contrary, so tightly were they enmeshed in economic arrangements with Yankee merchants, so high was their reliance on outside capital, that the Northerners who controlled the goods in transit could now allow the direct sailings while still skimming off their profits. The planters, like the South's sharecroppers of the second half of the nineteenth century, were caught in a maze of economic conveniences and liabilities from which they could not escape.

While the South helped to enlarge the national market for the goods handled by Eastern merchants, it also provided raw material for the textile factories of New England, America's first important manufacturing industry. In the half century before the Civil War manufacturing output increased ten times. This met the growing demand for cotton and woolen cloth, readymade clothing, boots and shoes, lumber and leather, iron and machinery. A third of the Southern cotton crop went to Northern textile mills and Southerners in turn bought Yankee-made shoes and clothing for their slaves. Western farmers in the Ohio and Mississippi valleys were even more important customers of northeastern industry, exchanging their wheat and hogs for Eastern manufactured goods.

As internal improvements lowered transportation costs and extended the market for Western surpluses, the farmer's purchasing power grew and the demand for Eastern manufactures also shot up. And as the national market widened, businessmen enlarged the scale of their enterprises, adopting more efficient techniques to produce goods more cheaply. By lowering the cost of factory products, they further broadened the market and discouraged household manufactures. Farmers now preferred to buy goods rather than make them at home. And as Eastern cities grew rapidly Westerners had an ever-enlarging market for farm products. Economic development thus involved a process of stimulus and response among sections and among different industries.

THE EMERGENCE OF INDUSTRY

Merchants became the architects of American industrial development. First they had to accumulate capital in overseas trade, a process that was highly risky and often disrupted by political turmoil. The Embargo (1807-1809) crippled foreign commerce, cut off the supply of English manufactured goods, and encouraged traders to invest in textile and iron factories. New England took the lead. Its commercial possibilities were less bright than New York's, but its merchants who possessed capital proved more enterprising. New England could also count on surplus labor from its declining rural areas, and it had numerous streams to power machinery. Yankees built the first factory towns and produced coarse cotton cloth that successfully competed with English fabrics.

The cotton mills at Lowell, Massachusetts, became the model, the showpiece for a new, American version of industrial utopia. A group of Bostonians, successfully adapting English technology, harnessed the falls of the Merrimack River at Lowell and combined spinning and weaving operations under one roof. Leasing land and water power to newcomers, and themselves manufacturing the machinery, the Lowell entrepreneurs later became industrial developers. Large profits attracted other investors as canals and railroads began to link the new factories with Boston, where merchants wholesaling English textiles now added American goods to their line.

Lowell attracted hundreds of visitors eager to inspect this marvel of American industry and to see for themselves that factory work need not bring the misery and pauperism of European industrialism. Founded in 1822, the Lowell mills employed mostly young, single girls, fresh from the farms of New England. They lived in well-kept boardinghouses run by the company, which kept as close an eye on their after-work conduct as during their long hours in the factory. Everyone seemed to benefit: the owners had dependable labor but no long-term responsibility for the girls; who after four or five years' work, or when ill, usually went back to the farm. The girls had a job under bearable working conditions, and the benefits of semiurban life. One prominent French visitor to Lowell reported that the town gave off the "peaceful hum of an industrious population whose movements are regulated like clockwork." The American environment had apparently worked a miracle, industrialism without exploitation.

Lowell's Golden Age proved short-lived, however. Within a decade, by the late 1830s, Lowell and later its sister mill town of Lawrence demonstrated that industrialism in America involved the same social dislocations experienced in Europe. Strikes, speedups, blacklists, and wage cuts all became a part of the labor scene. The native-born farm girls, increasingly employed as schoolmarms or joining the exodus of rural New Englanders to the West, stopped coming to work at Lowell. The mills then turned to Irish and French-Canadian labor, and slums—ethnic ghettoes—appeared in Lowell, together with female and child labor, and unprecedented poverty. As many had feared, and though the founders of Lowell tried to forestall it, the coming of the Machine proved incompatible with the hope that America would remain a Garden.

The Northeast was the natural home of American industry. Less suited for agriculture than the South or the West, it was the commercial center of the country and had an experienced merchant community accustomed to taking risks and in possession of considerable capital. The East was also the most densely settled region with the largest cities and the most accessible markets.

With capital and entrepreneurial talent available, the East could also recruit a labor force for industry from those who left the countryside or from the immigrants, most of whom arrived in the port cities of the Northeast and settled along the coast.

Though the East had most of the nation's factories, substantial industry, usually closely related to agriculture, developed in the West as well. Lumber mills, for instance, processed the timber from Western forests; meat packers prepared and distributed the hogs and cattle fattened on Western corn; millers ground wheat; and jobbers distributed Eastern manufactures to rural retailers. As a result, important urban centers such as Cincinnati and St. Louis emerged in the West. Again the South, where there was little industry or urbanization, fell behind. There, a planter elite that concentrated on cotton production owned most of the wealth, and poor whites and slaves, without buying power, could not provide adequate markets for local industry. In the West, however, a large and prosperous community of independent farmers predominated, men with considerable economic independence and purchasing power.

Once industry got started it developed an internal momentum. Textile factories for example produced the raw material for a ready-made clothing industry which in turn formed a market for sewing machines. Both textile and clothing manufacturers bought machinery and, together with other industrialists, created a market large enough for some to specialize in the production of machine tools. Machine builders then increased the demand for iron; iron producers, for lumber and coal to smelt the ore, and so on. Thus one industry forged links with another in an endless chain that ultimately expanded the production of goods and services and increased industrial output by 500 percent between 1810 and 1860.

FINANCIAL GROWTH AND THE ROLE OF GOVERNMENT

Financing these transportation and industrial revolutions required more capital than Americans had previously employed in either public or private enterprise. Considerable capital to finance state-sponsored canal systems flowed in from abroad, especially from Great Britain where industrial development had produced surpluses. By the early 1830s the United States had paid off its national debt and the country enjoyed a high credit rating. Foreign investors eagerly sought high returns in America, and the flush years before the panic of 1837 encouraged them. When the boom collapsed and several states defaulted on bond payments, foreigners who lost heavily became understandably wary about further investment in America.

Unlike canals, which were usually state enterprises, railroads were privately owned. Railroads were expensive and required far more capital generally than other businesses. They relied on private funds but they also received substantial state aid. By the 1840s railroads could sell securities which tapped pools of domestic capital generated by the profits in manufacturing and trade. State and local governments assisted with loans or guarantees of railroad bonds, and the federal government gave the first land grants in the 1850s, which also helped roads obtain private financing.

At the same time the nature of business organization underwent a fundamental change. In England and in colonial America the corporate charter had been regarded as a privilege, usually granted to those performing some acknowledged public service, a franchise not to be granted lightly. Men in business for profit alone were expected to rely on partnerships or unincorporated joint stock companies. This began to change in nineteenth-century America, especially in New England. States began passing general incorporation laws which gave investors the benefits of the anonymity, and eventually the limited liability, afforded by corporate organization. The "public service" aspect of chartering soon fell away, and by the Civil War even banks, the organizations most subject to legislative restrictions, could be created without special charter. Entry into business was thus "democratized" at the very moment that business was beginning to consolidate.

Government-chartered corporations played other important roles in economic development. Agencies of government participated in nearly every aspect of economic life. The federal government gave manufacturers a protective tariff and readily transferred public lands into private hands. The price of public lands fell after 1800 and the terms of sale were liberalized. In the 1840s farmers won the right to buy or "preempt" land they squatted on before it was put up for auction, and in the 1850s Congress lowered the price of unsold lands that had been on the market for some time.

Government Enterprise

State governments continued to regulate and stimulate economic activity. With the national government's role limited, constitutionally and politically, most economic initiative had to come from the states. Long-standing regulatory practices, dating back to colonial times, still remained in force. Towns and counties regulated the quality and price of many commodities and services, especially basic food items and transportation, through inspection and licensing. The states also promoted selected enterprises, usually of a semi-public character, through loans or bounties. A small army of state inspectors, weighers, appraisers, and the like looked after the public interest, and in the process their jobs became a patronage factor of considerable political importance.

In New York, where the state itself had built the Erie Canal, enormous profits from that enterprise were used as a fund to promote economic development. Also, New York became the first state to set up a permanent regulatory commission: under the Safety Fund Banking Act of 1829, all the banks in the state had to contribute to a fund to be used to reimburse those owning notes of a broken bank. This collective interest in the fate of individual banks meant the appointment of bank commissioners to inspect bank books twice a year and close down mismanaged institutions. In the half century before the Civil War, state courts imposed few judicial barriers to such interference in the economy by state legislatures and local governments.

Government also chartered banks. No banks existed during the colonial period, but after the Revolution they appeared rapidly. Congress chartered two national banks (the First and Second Banks of the United States, 1791–1811 and 1817–1837), but most banks were the creations of state legislatures answering the demands of credit-hungry entrepreneurs. These institutions provided most of the country's paper money in the form of state bank notes. Their fluctuating value added spice and uncertainty to much of American economic and political life. Many bank founders were essentially borrowers rather than lenders; that is, they wanted to bring together available but scattered capital through the sale of bank stock and reinvest it in commercial and land speculations. The early banks also served merchants needing short-term loans to finance overseas trade.

Eventually banking spread from the seaports into the countryside and to industrial towns. Some Southern states even established banks for planters, issuing notes based on land values. By regularly renewing short-term loans, and issuing notes and granting credit liberally, banks encouraged enterprise and promoted economic growth. Businessmen appreciated their value, but the general public never fully accepted banks. During bad times bankers became objects of hatred and were denounced as "rag-barons" and aristocrats, first by the Jeffersonians and then by the Jacksonians.

THE ROOTS OF ECONOMIC DEVELOPMENT

America in 1860 was still an agricultural nation, but it already had developed the economic network, the infrastructure, for a modern industrial society. A rapidly growing population had spread across half the continent and brought into production fertile lands in the Gulf and Lake Plains and had begun penetrating the prairies. An elaborate network of rivers, roads, canals, and railroads tied the country together and gave farmers, merchants, and manufacturers a larger, national market. As a result the gross national product (GNP) rose dramatically. "The Americans arrived but as yesterday on the territory which they inhabit, and they have already changed the whole order of nature for their own advantage," the French visitor Alexis de Tocqueville explained, because in the United States, unlike Europe, the spirit of enterprise was not confined to a few but "pervaded the whole people, enlisting their abundant energies."

Many marveled at America's growing wealth but not without concern: South Carolina's John C. Calhoun announced in 1817: "We are greatly and rapidly—I was about to say fearfully growing. This is our pride, and our danger; our weakness and our strength. . . . Let us then bind the Republic together with a perfect system of roads and canals." By 1860 a system far more perfect than Calhoun could have envisioned bound the country together—more securely than Southern secessionists who spoke in Calhoun's name on the eve of the Civil War had bargained for. At the same time geographic expansion and economic growth combined to produce profound changes in the conduct of American politics.

Chapter 11
Politics and the Promise of Equality

In the decades following the return of peace in 1815 the United States grew from a simple agrarian republic, most of whose citizens lived along the Atlantic seaboard, to a nation whose people spread across half a continent. This resulted from territorial expansion and economic developments such as the transportation revolution and the growth of a factory system. In addition, millions of foreigners came to America, many of them settling in the new cities that had recently been villages and in the sprawling metropolises that had once been stable commercial centers.

These changes helped to reshape American politics. For about a decade after the end of the second war with Britain, national party politics virtually disappeared. The dream of the founding fathers, that the Constitution would permit Americans to escape the factionalism that had torn other nations apart, seemed to have come true. Federalists stopped contesting elections in most states, and some slid over to the dominant Republican party. A blurring in ideological and programmatic differences also contributed to the decline of partisanship. Leading Republicans, including many Southerners, accepted such ex-Federalist measures as the tariff and a national bank. In the absence of contested elections, the prodding of active party organization, and the stimulus of hard-fought issues, many voters stayed home, indifferent to who won on election day. Without the conflicts generated a few decades earlier by the insecurity of living in an untested republic, menaced by innumerable and often imaginary dangers, Americans enjoyed a brief and rare degree of national harmony during the postwar years when James Monroe occupied the White House (1817-1825).

The Rebirth of Parties

Then in the late 1820s the consensus dissolved and political conflict revived, giving birth to the second American party system. By 1840, two competitive national parties, the Democrats

and the Whigs, each with support in all parts of the country, vigorously contested for control of the presidency and Congress as well as for state offices. After twelve years of Democratic supremacy, eight under Andrew Jackson (1829-1837) and four under Martin Van Buren (1837-1841), the Whigs finally captured the White House with William Henry Harrison in the election of 1840.

Party politics revived because once more Americans regarded political power as worth fighting for. Voter apathy in the 1820s gave way to intense interest that sent almost eighty percent of the eligibles to the polls in 1840, more than double the percentage who voted in 1828. Revisions in state law formally democratized the political process. Property qualifications for voting, already falling away before 1820, all but disappeared in the next two decades.

At the start of the nineteenth century, nearly all states had suffrage requirements tied to property holding. But because most white, adult males owned property and paid taxes, and because states enforced legal requirements laxly, large numbers of them could vote. In the decade following the end of the War of 1812, many states liberalized suffrage requirements. At some state constitutional conventions, diehard conservatives tried to hold the line against universal manhood suffrage, but by the late 1820s, universal suffrage generally prevailed. The debates on suffrage, and the quickening of the political pace in that decade, helped create a more egalitarian politics which further eroded the tendency of ordinary citizens to defer to a ruling class. More than ever, aspiring politicians had to sell themselves to the voting public if they wished to succeed.

The forms of political organization similarly changed, particularly regarding political parties. During the generation after independence, Americans organized into parties while fighting their political battles. Yet they continued to attack the *idea* of party, maintaining that in a good society community of interest should take precedence over personal interest or the political interest of one group. Such men as Hamilton and Jefferson thus acted as antiparty, party builders.

By the 1820s, however, a new generation of American politicians began to see the question more realistically and to square their professions with their actions. They rejected the charge that parties were no more than expanded cliques, arguing instead that they were popular, democratically run organizations, and a distinctively American innovation. Such new politicians clearly exaggerated the democratic aspect of parties, but the new, egalitarian politics required the mobilization of popular support, an end that could best be served through party organization. Parties no longer were the personal property of one individual or one family. Leaders became instruments of the organization ("good party men"), often at the expense of their own opinions. The transformation occurred most visibly in New York, where, for good or for ill, Martin Van Buren and the Albany Regency became the models for modern American party organization.

Older style, antiparty or personalist politicos tried to stem the tide. President Monroe had hoped to do away with parties in 1817, and in New York the organizer of the Erie Canal, DeWitt Clinton, fought the Albany Regency Republican machine by hurling anathemas on the party. But they failed; the reformers had the initiative and took the final step when they defended the *morality* of political parties, not merely their inevitability. "Organized parties," assured one member of the Albany Regency, "watch and scan each other's doings. The public mind is instructed by discussions of public measures, and acts of violence are restrained by the convictions of the people that the prevailing measures are the results of enlightened reason." Reasonable or not, parties had come to stay.

In other ways, too, citizens acquired a more direct voice and as a result gained a greater interest in electoral politics. Constitutional reforms made numerous offices, previously appointive, now elective; presidential electors, who in the past had been chosen by state legislatures, now were elected popularly. To nominate candidates for the plethora of offices and to mobilize the many more voters for recurrent campaigns, the parties constructed elaborate organizations. The political

convention became a vital instrument for conducting party business, enabling leaders to come together and agree on candidates at the same time that they gave parties greater claim to democratic legitimacy. Politics became so time-consuming and required such specialized skills that a new breed of professional politician emerged to replace the gentlemanly amateurs such as the planters and merchants who previously had assumed public office, often as a burdensome duty required of men of their station. Now politics offered a career open to men of talent, regardless of family prominence or wealth.

THE POLITICS OF NATIONALISM, 1816-1824

For almost a decade an Era of Good Feelings replaced the partisan rivalry that had raged for over two decades. The return of peace in 1815 delivered the final blow to the Federalists, and those who did not retire from politics sought advantage among the factions of the dominant Republican party. A consensus regarding national policies replaced the wrangling of the past. Wartime experience made Republicans appreciate the usefulness of a tariff and a national bank, confident now that such old Federalist measures could be introduced safely. And pressures from all parts of the country on federal government to promote economic development made the new measures hard to resist.

The second Bank of the United States (BUS) bill illustrated this clearly. Republicans had allowed the first bank's charter to expire in 1811, but five years later they replaced it with another. When, during the War of 1812, state banks proved unstable or inadequate in meeting the government's fiscal needs, Jefferson's successor, James Madison, shelved his former objections to the BUS. John C. Calhoun, Southern agrarian though he was, drafted a bill similar to Hamilton's plan of the 1790s. Calhoun later changed his views, but in 1816 he urged that constitutional scruples be put aside because of the need for a bank which could impose some central control over the currency. The bill passed and the fact that the handful of remaining Federalists opposed it showed the turnabout which had occurred in party attitudes as Republicans now took up and defended much of the old, Federalist program. The establishment of the second BUS in Philadelphia vindicated Hamilton temporarily. Little had changed, although the bank's capital had been increased from $10 million to $35 million, a reflection of the nation's growth in twenty-five years.

The tariff bill also drew support from unlikely sources. Newly established manufacturing companies clamored for protection of their "infant" industries, but national security considerations, especially the fear of a renewed war, were largely responsible for the Tariff of 1816. Widespread sentiment in behalf of American enterprise, a feeling which most Southerners in Congress shared, helped carry the measure. Men like Calhoun and other South Carolinians voted yes for patriotic reasons, not because of dreams of industrializing the South. Besides, they thought that the higher duties would be temporary. Southerners did not wish to abandon their plantation system, but they believed that as manufacturing grew in other sections, markets for the South's agricultural staples would also grow. Yet the protective tariff proved to be a Trojan horse. After 1816, protection of home industry, not revenue needs nor national security needs, became the chief arguing point of tariff advocates. Within four years, most Southerners reversed their stand on the tariff and they and their allies from other sections forestalled high protectionism until the Civil War.

A third nationalizing measure of national politics was federal sponsorship of internal improvements. As Americans settled the area between the Appalachian Mountains and the Mississippi River, the need for improved means of transportation became increasingly evident. The War of 1812 pointed up the fact that few all-weather roads existed. Waterways also needed improvement and the country was about to enter the canal era. In Jefferson's time, the absence of strong pressure for public works, commitment to economy in government, and constitutional objections had combined to prevent action. After the war, Madison favored improvements but he still nursed scruples about their constitutionality. When the new national bank paid the government a bonus of $1.5 million for its charter in 1816, Calhoun urged that the money be spent on internal improvements.

Westerners, hemmed in geographically and cut off from markets, favored the idea. But a divided South, unsure that it would benefit, and an unfriendly New England revealed that strong opposition existed in other sections. The bill barely passed. On his last day in office, Madison vetoed it. This defeat meant that the job would be left to the state governments and to private enterprise. It also showed the limits of postwar economic nationalism. Pressure for federally sponsored internal improvements continued for several decades, but the national government failed to adopt a comprehensive plan to further such projects.

THE MARSHALL COURT AND THE STATES

National powers also grew notably in another area, constitutional interpretation. This resulted largely from the work of John Marshall, Chief Justice of the Supreme Court (1801-1835) and one of John Adams's "midnight" appointments of 1801. Although by 1819-1824 most of Marshall's colleagues were Republicans, this Federalist politician-judge still maintained his leadership over the court. Only Justice William Johnson of South Carolina dissented with any regularity. Most justices lived then in the same Washington boarding house, and continuous contact with Marshall helped the Chief Justice convert some of his colleagues to his views, especially since he believed that the court should speak with one voice, preferably his.

Beginning in 1803, in *Marbury* v. *Madison*, Marshall wrote a series of opinions which put flesh on the bare bones of the delegated national powers created by the Constitution. This case involved another "midnight" judge, appointed to the minor office of justice of the peace in the District of Columbia, who had been denied his commission by the Jeffersonians. Marshall decided that although Marbury merited his appointment, the court could not act because of the illegality of part of the law under which the order favoring Marbury had to be issued. Thus, he declared a section of the Judiciary Act of 1789 unconstitutional, the first time the Supreme Court had voided an act of Congress.

Jeffersonians objected, realizing that if the *Marbury* case became a precedent it would shift much authority to the national government, and also upset the balance of power between branches of federal government. At the Constitutional Convention, nationalist delegates had urged that the Supreme Court be allowed to veto acts of Congress immediately after passage. Cooler but equally nationalist heads prevailed, however. Such a grant of power, even if passed at Philadelphia, would probably have failed to receive state ratification. Instead, they kept the Constitution's judiciary article purposely short and free of details. Although the problem of judicial review did not dominate the debates, many delegates shared the opinion of Oliver Ellsworth: "If Congress should at any time overleap its limits, the judicial department is a constitutional check. The federal judges will declare such a law void." And there the matter rested until 1803, when Marshall successfully employed the power described by Ellsworth. He and his colleagues thus took a giant step in creating a uniquely American institution: judicial review of legislation. Federal judicial power had increased enormously; by the end of the nineteenth century the Supreme Court would become the "balance wheel of federalism."

In several cases regarding contracts, Marshall continued to protect and expand national powers. The Constitution prohibits passage of state laws interfering with contracts, since from colonial and Confederation days debtor groups had tried to obtain legislation that granted relief from debt payments. In *Fletcher* v. *Peck* (1810), Marshall upheld the validity of land grants made by one Georgia legislature and revoked by another on grounds of fraud. He considered the original grants contracts which the state could not rescind. This was the first time the court invalidated a *state* law because it was in conflict with the federal Constitution, further extending its

power of judicial review. And in *Dartmouth College* v. *Woodward* (1819), Marshall disallowed New Hampshire's attempt to reorganize Dartmouth College, a private institution operating under a charter which was also deemed a contract. In both cases Marshall set a precedent, since he extended the application of the contract clause to include public contracts or charters, and not simply contracts between individuals, as originally intended. This curb on the states increased national power as well as the importance of the federal courts. It also assured businessmen operating with state charters that their privileges could not be revoked at the whim of the next state legislature.

Marshall argued in essence that the national government could act, if the Constitution did not explicitly prohibit the action. In *McCulloch* v. *Maryland* (1819), he ruled that the government might charter a national bank as a logical consequence of its power to coin money and regulate the currency, and that states could not tax this national institution. On the other hand, strict constructionists argued that the federal government could not act unless the Constitution had specifically delegated the necessary power to it.

In this fundamental debate, Marshall always favored enlarging national powers. He accordingly interpreted federal powers over interstate commerce broadly in *Gibbons* v. *Ogden* (1824) and ended a steamboat monopoly granted by New York. And Marshall also enlarged the power of federal courts, especially in *Cohens* v. *Virginia* (1821), maintaining that when a case arose under the Constitution, it could be transferred from the state courts to the federal courts on appeal. The courts of each state could not be allowed to be the sole judge of national rights, or the supremacy of the Constitution could be undermined. The Supreme Court therefore would render final decisions on the meaning of the "supreme law of the land."

Marshall's bold, nationalistic decisions removed many legal roadblocks in the way of strong central government and also checked the forces of state sovereignty and decentralization. But whether the national government would assert its power was subject to the discretion of politicians and depended on the outcome of party battles.

THE REVIVAL OF POLITICS

The near-monopoly which the Republican party enjoyed in national politics meant that the game of presidential politics was played differently than under a two-party system. In 1816, James Monroe of Virginia easily defeated the Federalist candidate, Rufus King, carrying all but three states. Many New England Federalists then approached Monroe, urging a coalition government. But Monroe believed that those Federalists who still had political ambitions would have to accommodate themselves to the fact of Republican rule. Four years later, the election of 1820 confirmed the wisdom of this judgment. Monroe was the only Republican candidate, eliminating the need for a congressional nominating caucus. Only one presidential elector voted against him.

National harmony and political reconciliation did not last long. Economic distress beginning in 1819, and sectional debates over the admission of Missouri to statehood, generated new conflicts. The Panic of 1819 arose from speculation and the inflated optimism of merchants and farmers after the second war with England. It hit the newer states west of the Appalachian Mountains hardest, and the new BUS became a convenient scapegoat; the bank had begun badly when its Baltimore branch fell into the hands of speculators who made illegal loans to its managers. Many of the new state banks went out of business almost as soon as they began. When general economic collapse followed, some state legislatures taxed heavily the operations of the BUS. Although the Supreme Court declared such measures illegal, the antagonism against the bank, both as a financial power and as a creation of the national government, lingered on. Debtor-versus-creditor "relief wars" erupted in both Kentucky and Tennessee. In these political struggles the "people" fought the "money power," foreshadowing the Jacksonian struggles that would occur in the 1830s.

At the same time, when residents of the Missouri Territory applied for statehood in 1819, a Northern congressman moved to prohibit slavery in Missouri, shattering the prevailing sectional truce. The Senate, where Southern strength equaled the North's, defeated the amendment. Next year, Congress again took up the Missouri question. Some Northerners argued that Congress could make the abolition of slavery a precondition for admission to statehood. Southerners fought this restriction, contending that state sovereignty meant that all states, including new ones, enjoyed the right to determine whether or not to exclude slavery. The request by Maine, then a part of Massachusetts, for separation and statehood, broke the deadlock. Congress admitted one slave state and one free state at the same time. The Missouri Compromise also prohibited slavery in the area of the Louisiana Purchase north of 36°30' latitude.

The Missouri debates were a prelude of things to come. Jefferson mused apprehensively: "But this momentous question, like a fire-bell in the night, awakened and filled me with terror . . . I considered it at once as the knell of the Union. It is hushed, indeed, for the moment. But this is a reprieve only, not a final sentence." Almost all of the issues and viewpoints involved in the great struggle of the 1850s that ended in civil war formed part of the Missouri controversy. The compromise, however, offered politicians from both sections a way out. Henceforth, most politicians observed an unwritten rule to keep slavery out of national politics, and for a quarter of a century they generally succeeded.

In 1823 the nationalistic temper found a fresh expression in America's foreign relations. Latin America was in turmoil. One after another the Spanish colonies declared their independence and after several years' warfare they defeated the Spanish and loyalist forces. Americans were sympathetic, but their government reacted cautiously. Prolonged negotiations for the purchase of Florida from Spain dictated restraint. Only after the United States acquired Florida did the president recognize the new Latin American states. Spain vowed to regain the lost colonies, and other continental European powers, known collectively as the Holy Alliance, offered to aid in the reconquest. Russia, a member of the Holy Alliance, simultaneously made claims to a portion of the Pacific coastline claimed by the United States.

Britain had the power to determine whether Spain would maintain its power in the Western

Hemisphere. The world's leading sea power could prevent attempts by the Holy Alliance to recolonize in Spain's name, or to transfer territories from one European power to another. Britain, an exporter of manufactured goods, wanted free trade in Latin America in order to enlarge overseas markets. The United States wanted European powers kept out, both for security and commercial reasons. Accordingly, the British and the Americans shared common interests in opposition to the potential threat of the Holy Alliance.

Monroe decided in December 1823 to take the initiative and proclaimed the Monroe Doctrine. He declared that the United States would regard further colonization by European powers in the Western Hemisphere as a threat to its safety. Existing European colonies would be left unmolested, but Monroe argued that the Western and Eastern Hemispheres differed fundamentally and should keep out of each other's affairs. Although the doctrine subsequently became the cornerstone of American hemispheric policy, in 1823 it had only as much standing as American power and British sea power could impose. British naval strength weighed most heavily; without British acquiescence and tacit support, the doctrine would have been an empty threat. Not until the end of the nineteenth century was the United States strong enough to enforce the Monroe Doctrine unilaterally and against all nations—including Britain.

THE SECOND AMERICAN PARTY SYSTEM

The contest for the presidency played a major role in the emergence of the second American party system. With the death of the leaders of the revolutionary generation and the breakdown of the discipline imposed on personal rivalries by strong parties, the 1824 presidential election became a free-for-all. Since no candidate polled a majority that year, the House of Representatives selected John Quincy Adams of Massachusetts. The defeated factions then rallied behind Tennessee's Andrew Jackson, the leader in popular and electoral votes.

Jackson provided a model for personal and political success in early national America—he became, in the words of a modern cultural historian, a "symbol for an age," personifying traits and aspirations which the majority of Americans responded to positively, blending reality and fantasy into a powerful political myth. Born in backwoods South Carolina in 1767 of Scotch-Irish stock, he fought briefly in the Revolution when he was only twelve years old. His father had died when Jackson was two, and his mother when he was fourteen. At age seventeen he began studying law, then migrated to Tennessee in 1788. Jackson became a successful lawyer and land speculator, with a pronounced interest in horse racing and a tendency to resolve quarrels on the duelling ground. By the end of the eighteenth century he had built a mansion (the "Hermitage") near Nashville, and had become a slave-owning cotton planter.

Jackson had also made important political friendships. He was a delegate to the convention which wrote the first constitution for Tennessee, and he served briefly both in the U.S. House and Senate at the turn of the century. But Tennessee was then his preferred scene of operations, in business as well as in politics. A local judgeship was followed by a general's commission in the state militia. The latter catapulted him to national fame after the War of 1812. His spectacular victory over the British at New Orleans, and subsequent campaigns against the Southern Indians, provided the basis for possible political advancement.

Jackson's image was precisely right. This "common" man had scaled uncommon heights, in a way that seemed natural to Americans fast abandoning the Politics of Deference and embracing the Politics of Egalitarianism in an age of economic expansion. Jackson identified with the average American, particularly the yeoman farmer. His opponents pointed out that the "comparison of the occupation of our hardy yeomanry to that of a man whose plantation is worked by slaves and superintended by an overseer . . . is almost too ridiculous to be seriously noticed," but voters and politicians did make such a comparison favorably, and with increasing seriousness.

Causes of Party Conflict

By 1828, the Jacksonians had formed a powerful enough coalition of state parties to sweep "The Old Hero" into the White House. As a candidate Jackson was all things to all men, but as president Jackson increasingly became identified with policies and an ideology that came to distinguish the Democrats from the Whigs, a new party formed to oppose the Jacksonians. The central issues in national politics during the second American party system involved the federal government's role in national economic development. By 1840 the Democrats championed lower tariffs and opposed federally funded internal improvements and the BUS. Behind these disputes over public policy lay more fundamental differences regarding the proper role of government. Democrats believed that it should play a modest role; otherwise the few would advance their interests at the expense of the many. Whigs countered that an activist government which stimulated growth would best serve the many, while at the same time aiding particular groups.

Party conflict stemmed in part from regional differences in the pace and direction of economic development. Though all agreed that government had important responsibilities, defining its role precisely produced endless disagreement. Many New Yorkers, for instance, whose state government had constructed the Erie Canal, giving them access to the West, opposed federal construction of roads and canals in other regions. Merchants fearful that high tariffs would injure foreign trade and planters who claimed that they would raise the cost of living, clashed with manufacturers demanding protection against English competitors. National party leaders faced the formidable job of reconciling such conflicting interests.

The expansion of the Union further weakened the stability of the second party system. Between 1816 and 1846, a dozen new states (all, except Maine, lying west of the Appalachians) entered the Union. Their votes in Congress and in presidential elections altered the balance of political forces and marked the emergence of an important new battleground of national politics. Beginning with Jackson in 1828, four of the next five elected presidents came from the new states. The emergence of the West further heightened the sense of sectional identity in New England and in the South, since in matters of vital interest to these older regions, Westerners could now play a decisive role.

Economic development and territorial expansion generated another kind of conflict which had political repercussions. A country with a mobile social order before 1815 became even more turbulent after that. Mobility brought a bewildering variety of groups and interests, fearful of threats to their status and dignity, into frequent contact, which often became group conflict. In the Old Northwest two streams of migration, one from the South and the other from New England, clashed frequently. In the cities, ethnically more scrambled than ever, Protestants and Catholics, native- and foreign-born, eyed each other warily. In addition, urban craftsmen and workingmen and small farmers demanded measures to reverse the economic and social slippage which eroded their status.

The product of the forces transforming America after 1815, the second American party system grew out of the problems and conflicts generated by rapid national expansion. For two decades the parties accommodated differences until expansion thrust the slavery question into the national political arena, a confrontation both parties had tried to prevent. When that happened, neither the parties nor the Union escaped unscathed.

THE REVIVAL OF PARTIES

Nothing revealed more clearly the end of political harmony and the collapse of the Republican party than the confused battle for the presidency in 1824. In the past the Republican congressional caucus had made the party's choice. But in 1824, the congressional caucus could not impose its will on a majority of republicans. Secretary of the Treasury William H. Crawford's rivals refused to recognize the legitimacy of the "aristocratic and undemocratic" caucus, and Crawford's subsequent paralytic stroke ended whatever chances he had.

The decline of the caucus still left a need for some method by which politicians could gather to nominate candidates. Conventions came to fill this vacuum. Unlike legislative caucuses, membership in conventions was not confined to legislators; they thus were generally more representative bodies. They gave a voice in party affairs to elements that were in the minority at home and therefore had no spokesmen in a legislative caucus. Politicians liked to boast that conventions were more democratic and though they often were, they also were subject to manipulation by political bosses who could more easily control convention delegates than legislators. However conventions worked in practice, in theory they symbolized more democratic methods of decision-making stemming from the grass roots.

Four ambitious politicians, all Republicans and all presidential aspirants, refused to be bound by the congressional caucus: Andrew Jackson, John C. Calhoun, Henry Clay, and John Quincy Adams. Jackson, the rapidly rising politician from Tennessee, did not have to rely on the power of the regular Republican organization. He was the hero of the Battle of New Orleans, and personal popularity sparked his campaign, though his candidacy had begun as an attempt by Tennessee politicians to use this popularity to further their own local schemes. The Nashville politicos who wanted to elect him governor lost control of the bandwagon they had gotten started. When Jackson showed great strength in other states, especially Pennsylvania, the general decided for himself to stay in the presidential race. His main rivals were Secretary of State John Quincy Adams and Crawford. Clay ran fourth and Calhoun soon dropped out, accepting the vice-presidency as a consolation and a possible springboard. With more votes than any of the others, Jackson still fell short of a majority. Thus for the second time the House of Representatives elected a president. Henry Clay, Speaker of the House, swung his support to Adams because he and Jackson were rivals in the West and he agreed more with Adams' nationalistic ideas than with Jackson's. The shift of Clay's 37 electoral votes decided the election.

The J. Q. Adams Presidency

The administration of John Quincy Adams proved to be a failure. He appointed the well-qualified Clay his secretary of state, but the opposition seized upon this as evidence of a "corrupt bargain." For the next four years, President Adams and Secretary Clay were on the defensive. Although Adams had the right to appoint anyone he wished to his Cabinet, political shrewdness should have restrained him. But Adams did what he thought right, in this and throughout his term, with little knowledge of and even less regard for the political consequences.

Adams was one of the more capable men to serve as president. But the four distressing years he spent in the White House demonstrated that success required special talents that he did not possess. Adams lacked personal magnetism and political skill. He was reserved to the point of coldness, undiplomatic to his many intellectual inferiors, and committed first to his own principles in a way which left little room for the backtracking and compromising familiar to all successful politicians. Adams's first message to Congress in December 1825 was a brilliant but vulnerable document. He took a broad view of national powers, calling for an increased role for the federal government in commerce, agriculture, and transportation. He also favored establishing a national university, an observatory, and other cultural projects under federal auspices. These proposals were visionary at the time, but few Americans shared Adams's belief that the national government should actively promote the general welfare through such enterprises.

Opposition began to crystallize in Congress. The Jackson men, already in league with the supporters of Vice-President Calhoun, then got the support of the Crawford forces, most importantly those who ran the state machines in New York and Virginia. Congress thus easily blocked the Adams administration at almost every turn, showing how little power Adams commanded. The Jacksonians who controlled Congress were master politicians, and in 1828 their leader appeared an easy victor over the dour New Englander.

THE JACKSONIANS

The outcome of the 1828 election seems now to have been predetermined in Jackson's favor. Jackson aroused popular enthusiasm in a way which was new in American politics. He claimed to be a man of the people, a poor orphan boy of limited education, self-made, whose manners were unpolished and who resembled Napoleon more than George Washington. The Jacksonians had also perfected the uses of political organization. Jackson won the support of two powerful machines in New York and Virginia and of a corps of active editors in many states who labored to turn pro-Jackson sentiment into Democratic votes. The general's campaign manager was Martin Van Buren, the New Yorker who had reestablished the Jeffersonian political alliance between his state and Virginia. The coalition promised a return to states' rights and Old Republicanism in opposition to the nationalism of Adams and Clay.

In Congress, Van Buren played a delicate game with the tariff, one of the few real issues of the campaign. He wished to combine Jackson's stand favoring a moderately lower tariff and the need for protection for some specific interests in New York and Pennsylvania. Because the resulting Tariff of 1828 maintained most of the high rates, Southerners called it the "Tariff of Abominations." Beyond the tariff controversy, the election remained essentially a battle between Jackson and Adams, with much mudslinging on both sides. Ironically, two of the most respectable public figures in American history were accused of gross immorality: Jackson because his marriage to Rachel Robards took place before her divorce became legally final; and Adams on the incredible charge that he had acted as a procurer for the Czar of Russia while on diplomatic service in St. Petersburg! The Adams forces, in a publication known as the Coffin Handbill, also accused General Jackson of arbitrarily executing militiamen.

Jackson won the election comfortably, 178 electoral votes to 83, despite close popular votes in many Northern states. Before 1828, relatively few among the Americans eligible to vote had participated in a presidential election. In 1824, only 26 percent of the eligibles voted; four years later, in the Jackson-Adams campaign, participation jumped to 56 percent. Jackson's strong personality, inspiring deep admiration or hostility, gave voters a clear-cut choice between two candidates, in contrast to the four-way race in 1824. The vote percentage in 1828 still fell short of record percentages in many state elections (in one New Hampshire state election, for example, 81 percent of eligible voters had cast ballots), but the turnout in 1828 showed that presidential elections were becoming as important as state elections as measures of popular sentiment and would ultimately surpass them. It provided another important advance in the nationalization of American politics.

The Jacksonian Presidency

During the campaign, the new president had not spelled out his policies. Even his inaugural address in 1829 remained noncommittal on key issues. But Jackson had promised reform, and part of this promise involved the status of officeholders. An entrenched elite, some in office since Jefferson's administration, and many of them anti-Jacksonian, ran the federal government. Jackson listened to the demands of his state leaders that changes be made. Political parties had finally gained acceptance and the importance of patronage to political organization became stronger. Although Jackson went further than Jefferson in causing "heads to roll," he removed only 10 percent of the federal officeholders the first year, and about 20 percent in his entire eight years as president. Yet the Jacksonians, in *declaring* openly the principle of rotation in office and justifying political preference in democratic terms, altered the atmosphere of politics. Jackson argued that public office should be open to all, that most citizens were competent to serve in some office, and that rotation would prevent the rise of a new Republican aristocracy. Jacksonian Senator William L. Marcy of New York's Albany Regency spoke for his party when he declared "to the victor belong the spoils," a policy which most politicians henceforth followed.

Jackson claimed to be a Republican of the "old school," a true Jeffersonian. This meant opposition to expansion of national power at the expense of the states. Many politicians ridiculed Jackson's moderate tariff views, but he refused to adopt an extreme stand favoring either pure revenue or pure protection. Also, Jackson lost little time in criticizing the BUS, questioning both its constitutionality and efficiency in his first annual message.

Public land policy was another important issue. In 1830, Thomas Hart Benton, a Jacksonian senator from Missouri, attacked proposals to slow down land sales. He charged that Eastern monied interests wanted to impede Western development by keeping land prices high. This led to a debate in the Senate between Daniel Webster of Massachusetts and Robert Y. Hayne of South Carolina over the nature of the Union. Webster, a nationalist, argued that the federal government had been created by the American people as a whole; Hayne, a states' rights man, contended that it was the creation of the constitutional compact among the sovereign states. Jackson sought a compromise between these two extremes.

The president best displayed his Jeffersonian orthodoxy in 1831, when he vetoed the Maysville Road bill. It called for the federal government to invest in a road to be built in Kentucky. Martin Van Buren, who helped prepare the veto message, could afford to be orthodox on internal improvements since New York had already completed the Erie Canal without federal help. Jackson argued that the proposed road was a local matter and that the federal government had no constitutional authority to grant such subsidies. It could assist only clearly interstate projects like the Cumberland Road. Jackson used the veto twelve times in all, three more than all his predecessors combined, and by this means and by "pocket vetoes" (withholding his signature when less than ten days remained in the congressional session) strengthened the power of the presidency.

The Maysville veto pleased Southerners, and so did Jacksonian Indian policy. For decades the federal government had tried to remove the southeastern Indians to land west of the Mississippi River, but carrying out this policy proved difficult. The Cherokees, largest of the "Five Civilized Tribes," were no longer nomadic hunters. They had set up a government complete with a written constitution. But Southern states, where these tribes lived, refused to permit them to stay, though the standard justification for removal was that Indians would not cultivate the land and therefore should not be allowed to stand in the way of white farmers. In 1828, Georgia assumed jurisdiction over the Indians, who then appealed to the federal courts for help. The Indians lost their first lawsuit for lack of federal jurisdiction, but a second case arose out of the arrest by Georgia authorities of Samuel Worcester, a New England missionary, who refused to leave the Indian territory. In 1832 the Supreme Court sided with the missionary (*Worcester* v. *Georgia*).

Legend has it that Jackson responded: "John Marshall has made his decision, now let him enforce it!" True or not, the statement summed up Jackson's feelings toward the Indians and toward that court ruling. The Supreme Court never issued the enforcing writ because Worcester finally agreed to accept his release on the promise to leave the state. The Cherokees succumbed to the inevitable in 1835 when they signed a removal treaty.

Nullifying Nullification

Jackson was by far a stronger chief executive than his predecessors, and one of the most forceful in the history of the presidency. The presidential office, after a good start, had lost influence with the other branches. But Jackson reversed that trend, especially toward the end of his first term, when he crushed South Carolina's attempt to nullify a federal law. The fight with South Carolina involved complex interests and strategies, but one essentially simple question remained: could a state decide for itself whether or not to obey a federal law? Jackson answered that it could not, revealing his basic attitude toward the Union and boldly pitting the power of his office and the nation against the will of a state.

For years South Carolina had denounced the tariff. In 1828, its legislature issued an "exposition," written by Calhoun but published anonymously, condemning the Tariff of Abominations. By 1831, Calhoun, one of the architects of Jackson's 1828 victory, had lost to Van Buren in the competition for Jackson's favor as Old Hickory's successor. Jackson believed that Calhoun, while secretary of war ten years earlier, had recommended punishing him for misconduct during the Seminole War. From then on, Calhoun's chances vanished and he no longer had any reason to conceal his switch from nationalism to states' rights, a stand popular in his native state. Jackson purged his Cabinet of Calhoun's friends, and the South Carolinian became an anti-Jacksonian leader of the nullification movement at home.

Jackson found some merit in Southern complaints about the tariff, and he backed a compromise bill to lower the rates. When it failed to pass in the summer of 1832, the South Carolinians called a state convention to nullify the tariff laws as unconstitutional. They refused to permit collection of federal duties in their state after February 1833. Jackson agreed to compromise on the tariff schedules, but not on federal sovereignty.

In December 1832, a month after his reelection, the president issued a Nullification Proclamation attacking South Carolina's stand as treason which he promised to crush with arms if necessary. At the president's request, Congress passed a Force Bill, authorizing the use of military forces against South Carolina. An armed clash seemed imminent. But a political solution became possible because South Carolina stood alone. Although other Southern states opposed the tariff, none would join in nullification.

South Carolina in 1832 was special; it had its own interests and special anxieties which set it apart from other states—even from other Southern states. The state had displayed a particular sensitivity to every question that touched or appeared to touch upon slavery. Specters of slave revolts and of outside interference tending toward emancipation combined to create a crisis psychology in South Carolina. Its leaders feared the tariff as an exercise of national power which might someday be used to weaken or destroy slavery. Coastal planters, relatively unharmed by the Tariff of 1828 and the agricultural depression of the 1820s, nevertheless espoused nullification ardently, probably because of the heavy concentration of slaves in their counties. In fighting against "abominable" tariff schedules, the nullifiers were also defending their system of slavery. Calhoun confided in 1830: "I consider the Tariff but as the occasion, rather than the real cause of the present state of things. The truth can no longer be disguised that the peculiar domestic institutions of the southern states [slavery], . . . has placed them . . . in opposite relation to the majority of the Union."

South Carolina's isolation defeated nullification, but Southern interests made some headway. Henry Clay, in cooperation with Calhoun, worked out a compromise which lowered the tariff over a ten-year period. The South Carolinians accepted the adjustment, at the same time pugnaciously "nullifying" the Force Bill. This saved face all around, but Jackson emerged with most to his credit: he proved that he had the personal courage and political skill to sustain his Unionist principles.

THE BANK WAR

Tariff reduction and the Maysville Road veto represented two backward steps from the policies of nationalism in the Era of Good Feelings. The assault on the BUS was a third, with even more far-reaching consequences than the other two. Under Nicholas Biddle, a young Philadelphian who took over as its president in 1823, the BUS weathered the political criticism blaming it for the Panic of 1819, but although Jackson had not campaigned against the BUS in 1828, he harbored a deep hostility toward it. Biddle's bank was both too large and too *national* to escape distrust and jealousy at a time when people feared concentration of political or economic power, especially in an institution enjoying special privileges granted by the federal government. Jackson opposed renewing the BUS charter, scheduled to expire in 1836. Biddle, aware of Jackson's hostility, accepted suggestions by Clay and Webster to push a recharter bill through Congress.

When the bill passed, Jackson returned it with a powerful veto message drafted by Amos Kendall, the leading member of the White House inner circle (the "Kitchen Cabinet") and a hater of the BUS. The veto message scored the bank as unconstitutional: ". . . some of the powers and privileges possessed by the existing bank are unauthorized by the Constitution, subversive of the rights of the states, and dangerous to the liberties of the people." Since many foreigners held its stock, "if we must have a bank with private stockholders, every consideration of sound policy, and every impulse of American feeling, admonishes that it should be *purely American.*" The message singled out the BUS as the principal means by which the rich oppressed the poor of America: "It is to be regretted that the rich and powerful too often bend the acts of government to their selfish purposes. . . . In the full enjoyment of . . . the fruits of superior industry, economy, and virtue, every man is equally entitled to protection by law. But when the laws undertake to add to these natural and just advantages, artificial distinctions, to grant titles, gratuities, and exclusive privileges, to make the rich richer, and the potent more powerful, the humble members of society, the farmers, mechanics, and laborers . . . have a right to complain of the injustice of their government." Thus, playing upon the patriotism, xenophobia, and egalitarianism of most Americans, the Jacksonians went into the election battle.

Jackson won again, but he polled a smaller percentage of the popular vote than four years earlier. Democrats lost some Southern support because of nullification, an issue not yet settled at election time. And some pro-BUS Democrats deserted, so forcing that issue may have cost Jackson votes. Also, a new, short-lived third party, the Antimasons, campaigning against an alleged conspiracy of the "establishment" to monopolize political offices and economic power, drew votes by employing the same kind of egalitarian rhetoric the Democrats used in 1828 and 1832. The Antimasons sprang up after the disappearance of William Morgan in western New York in 1826. Morgan, a former Mason, had threatened to publish the secrets of the Masonic order, and when he dropped out of sight permanently Masons were accused of murdering him. Several ambitious and astute New York politicians realized that the incident could serve as a vehicle for opposing the dominant Albany Regency and the Democrats, since so many public officials, including the president, were Masons. Masonry, they charged, was a secret society of

the ruling elite, a ruthless, aristocratic brotherhood, with its own laws, incompatible with republicanism. Antimasonry caught on in the Northeast and in 1832 nominated a presidential candidate, William Wirt, a Baltimore lawyer. Jackson's other opponent was the luckless Henry Clay, the candidate of the National Republican Party. The split in the anti-Jackson ranks favored the president, of course, as did an inept National Republican campaign and the fact that Wirt had never renounced Masonry. Biddle and the BUS backed Clay, but subsidies to friendly politicians and newspaper editors backfired and damaged the campaign.

After the election, Jackson moved again to punish the BUS in a campaign which tested all the powers of presidency and party leadership. Biddle's charter still had three years to run, and the BUS handled most of the federal government's money. It had performed this duty efficiently and without charge, its network of branches throughout the country ensuring that the government could draw funds wherever it wished. But by this time Jackson believed that the BUS was not only unconstitutional but so dangerous that it no longer should be tolerated.

Politics, not finance, became the ruling consideration. Despite strong opposition within his own party and cabinet, Jackson wanted federal deposits removed from the BUS. To accomplish this he had to shift one secretary of the treasury to a higher cabinet post and dismiss another. Jackson finally turned to his loyal Attorney General, Roger B. Taney. In October 1833, the new secretary of the treasury ordered federal officials to cease depositing government funds in BUS branches.

In place of a national bank, regarded by Jackson and his advisers as an encroachment on state rights, the president turned to the state banks. Most bankers had observed the Jackson-Biddle struggle warily, and some apprehensively. Very few attacked Biddle's bank before removal of the deposits, and in areas where Biddle had most influence, those bankers who took an open stand usually supported him. With removal accomplished, however, and with federal money available, the picture changed. State bankers came forward to accept the deposits, since they could use interest-free federal money to expand their loans. The selected banks quickly came to be known as "pet banks," and political favoritism dominated the selection process. Many pet banks were solid and well managed, and politically sound. Some were newly chartered and of questionable financial standing.

End of the Bank War

During the winter of 1833–1834, a recession threatened the pet bank system. Because he no longer held government funds, Biddle curtailed BUS operations, perhaps more so than necessary in order to increase economic distress and force Jackson to return the deposits or agree to a new charter. Despite strong pressure, Jackson held the line and by the spring of 1834 he defeated Biddle. The Second Bank of the United States was virtually dead. Biddle later obtained a Pennsylvania charter for a state bank in 1836, but by then it was only one among many state banks.

Jackson had launched the Bank War during a period of economic expansion. Speculation in Western lands sold on credit increased demands for bank loans and paper money. Dozens of new state banks were chartered to meet these needs. The Jackson administration had not intended to foster this runaway growth, but it took place nevertheless. First, the destruction of the BUS removed the single most important restraining force in the economy. It had curbed the more irresponsible bankers and speculators. Also, the national government possessed limited authority to direct the economy, especially with a president who rejected broad interpretations of national powers.

The economic boom so alarmed Jackson that in 1836 he issued an executive order, the Specie Circular, which required that all new purchases of government land be made in hard money. Jackson also obtained legislation regulating the pet banks, but his opponents in Congress channelled the federal government's treasury surplus to the states "on deposit." The additional funds in state hands intensified the inflationary spiral and directly counteracted the aim of the Specie Circular by encouraging speculation. Many observers warned that the pace of economic growth could

not be maintained indefinitely. But applying brakes to the economy proved more difficult than stimulating its growth.

In 1836, Jackson remained the political leader of the nation and chief of his party. Vice-president Martin Van Buren, chosen by Jackson to succeed him, won the presidential election despite dissatisfaction among Southern Democrats, distrustful of a Northerner. The opposition remained splintered. Borrowing from England the party name of those who opposed the royalist, or Tory, party, the Whigs were a coalition of ex-National Republicans (Adams-Clay men), Antimasons, and for a while the states' rights supporters of Calhoun. Unable to agree on a single choice, they ran candidates in each major section of the country, hoping to deny Van Buren a majority of electoral votes, and to force the election into the House of Representatives. But Jackson's political legacy proved rich enough to win the presidency for Van Buren.

Jackson had in eight years preserved the Union, destroyed the BUS, and installed a successor. He had immensely strengthened the presidential office, combining this constitutional position as chief executive with that of national party leader. By his use of patronage and the veto power, Jackson made the president the foremost American public man. And he established himself as the direct representative of the American people, the only important officeholder elected directly by the people as a whole. If a future president chose to act a weak part, it would be *despite* the precedents offered by Jackson.

VAN BUREN AND THE SOCIAL BASIS OF POLITICS

Within a month of his inauguration in March 1837, Van Buren had a business panic and then a depression on his hands. Jackson's Specie Circular, still in force, sharply curtailed land sales while simultaneously financial problems in Britain cut off credit from overseas. Planters with large stocks of cotton watched commodity prices tumble. Merchants with large inventories could not move their goods.

Van Buren called a special session of Congress in the summer of 1837 to propose retrenchment and the establishment of an independent treasury. Under this plan the government would keep its own funds in subtreasuries, no longer relying on banks, national or pet. The Democrats' antibanking policies thus culminated in a new, independent treasury scheme. The pet banks had been accused of becoming a new breed of baby "monsters" which differed little from Biddle's national bank. Van Buren now asked for a "divorce" of government and the banking system, arguing that the connection between them had caused the panic. Finance became the key issue of Van Buren's administration, but the Whigs and conservative Democrats prevented passage of the subtreasury bill for three years.

The attack on the BUS and the proposal to divorce government from banking through the subtreasury reflected the Democrats' increasing tendency to criticize moneyed interests. Jackson, in calling for the destruction of the BUS, had claimed that as the most powerful financial institution in the country, enjoying government favor, it violated the basic principles of republicanism: equal opportunity for all and special privileges for none. Yet the Jacksonian assault on the BUS was not an attack on either private property, businessmen, or banking as such, so much as an attack on special privilege—despite the fears of businessmen and the complaints of Whig politicians to the contrary.

The Jacksonian Coalition

The Bank War, unsettling though it had been, proved popular with different groups for different reasons. Some state bankers and most speculators resented the BUS connections with the government and the restraints it placed on their operations. Yet Jacksonian antibanking rhetoric appealed even more powerfully to those who blamed the BUS in particular, and accumulated wealth in general, for the dislocations accompanying economic growth. Jacksonian agrarians joined Jacksonian urban reformers in attributing their woes to the "money power." In the cities, artisans and their employees and apprentices, suffering displacement as a result of new manufacturing developments, came to

doubt that they could climb the business ladder from small shopkeeper to prosperous businessman. Two panics in less than twenty years had sent thousands of them into bankruptcy and economic dependency.

The emergence of an unskilled, urban working class, laboring for wages, intensified anxieties and conflict. An urban lower class had always existed in America, but not until the cities began to grow rapidly, as they did during the takeoff period of American industrialization in the second quarter of the nineteenth century (1825–1850), had the poor become so numerous and so noticeable. It appeared that the early years of such "happy experiments" as the Lowell mills would not be repeated, and that the United States would merely copy the grim example of European industrialism, with its slum cities and hopelessly impoverished laboring millions.

Such worries produced workingmen's parties in the major eastern cities in the 1830s. These organizations reflected the fears not only of laboring men, but also of an insecure middle class which shared the conviction that opportunity in America, though still abundant, was diminishing. Their demands focused on improving the common and "middling" man's chances by eliminating special privileges for the wealthy, establishing free public schools, and relying on "hard" currency based on gold and silver, one whose value would not fluctuate between the time the worker received bank notes and the day he tried to exchange them for goods. They also charged that "soft," or paper, money, lacking metallic backing, encouraged speculation which, in turn, produced panics, bankruptcies, and unemployment. Since Americans were just then beginning to experience the effects of the business cycle, money understandably preoccupied them. And since money came from banks, the banking system had to be controlled in order to regulate the currency.

In addition to demands for currency reform, hard-money Jacksonians, rural and urban, called for a halt or reduction in state-financed improvements in transportation. By 1837, many states had gone deeply into debt to build elaborate public works. The panic hit all states hard, and some defaulted on their bonds. This left citizens saddled with public obligations, which meant higher taxes in a society unaccustomed to paying very much for government services. Moreover, a road or a canal inevitably benefited some communities more than others. Those less well served by a state project responded with reduced enthusiasm than areas which had gained access to markets. Like the banking system, expensive, sometimes grandiose schemes of internal improvements seemed to serve special interests at the expense of the general welfare. Everyone paid taxes but not everyone benefited to the same degree from tax-supported enterprises. The Jacksonian call for retrenchment sought to put the brakes on the Transportation Revolution which was turning America from a simple and relatively stable agrarian society into a complex and far less stable commercial and industrial society.

The Fear of Monopoly

While the hard-money Jacksonians articulated their program and ideology, pro-business or "entrepreneurial" Jacksonians who had initially gone along with the Bank War, drew back. Those who opposed the subtreasury became known as Conservatives, and many eventually deserted the Democratic party for the Whigs. The Jacksonian attack on bank monopoly grew into a more general attack on all corporate monopoly. Many businessmen favored making corporate charters available to all who applied for them. Traditionally, the legislatures had granted corporate privileges guardedly. Incorporation required a special act of the legislature and this in turn depended on political favor. Those with friends in high places stood a better chance of obtaining a charter than those without such connections. As a result of the Jacksonian attack on the BUS and corporate monopoly, most states eventually adopted general incorporation laws which made charters easily accessible. This occurred even in banking, though "free banking" laws carried with them provisions for increased regulation.

The issue of corporate monopoly came to a head in the Charles River Bridge case (1837). The Supreme Court held that an old Massachusetts charter granted to a bridge company, giving it virtually a monopoly on transit between Boston

and Cambridge, did not invalidate a later legislative charter for a newer, competing bridge. The new Chief Justice, Roger B. Taney (the Jacksonian who had removed the deposits from the BUS in 1833), declared that the states must continue to exercise their police power "to promote the happiness and prosperity of the community." The Boston community, having grown so much since the first charter grant to the bridge company, needed the second bridge. Charter grants must be interpreted rigidly, and the original document had not guaranteed exclusiveness. Taney concluded that although "the rights of private property are sacredly guarded, we must not forget that the community also has rights, and that the happiness and well-being of every citizen depend on their faithful preservation."

This decision struck a severe blow at the doctrine and practice of corporate monopoly. After that, corporate charters no longer carried with them the assumption of exclusive privilege. This permitted a mushrooming of banks, bridges, canals, railroads, often competing in one locality for the same business. The Supreme Court in this case thus gave formal judicial recognition to irresistible political pressures from the many who would not permit the few to monopolize charter grants. The pressures generated by numerous would-be capitalists, plus the argument that monopoly conflicted with Republican egalitarianism, impelled the movement for democratization of business enterprise in Jacksonian times. Monopoly in business would develop later in the century through sheer size and consolidation.

Hard-money farmers and workers, Southern planters, and small businessmen comprised major elements of the Jacksonian coalition. But in addition, the Democrats could count on the votes from several ethnic groups to whom they catered, particularly among the Catholic immigrants from Ireland and Germany. Claiming to be friends of the common man, native- or foreign-born, and claiming also to be the most authentic heirs to America's republican tradition, Jacksonian leaders rejected nativism and won the steady support of the Catholic newcomers, many of whom had settled in cities amid Protestants resentful of competition from foreigners. Urban, native-born anxieties found an outlet in ethnic conflict. Riots sometimes erupted between the groups, and politicians running on anti-immigrant or nativist platforms soon appeared.

The Whig Party

Democratic influence among these immigrants could not help but alienate others. Antagonistic elements provided the materials out of which the Whig party sought to fashion a winning coalition. Whigs picked up votes from lower middle class and working people who feared immigrants and urban dislocation more than they feared the money power berated by Jacksonians. Also, as Americans from the older regions of the country migrated to unsettled areas, bringing with them established traditions and hardened attitudes, they often divided politically according to place of origin. Thus New England migrants into the Old Northwest (the Middle West of today) tended to become Whigs, while ex-Southerners in that region tended to vote Democratic.

The Whigs also picked up support from farmers and businessmen unimpressed with Jacksonian fears of the results of unregulated economic growth. The country needed more, not less, canals and highways, they argued, a strong central bank to channel growth, and ample encouragement to manufacturers in the form of a high tariff wall. They saw an activist government benefiting not a few but all Americans, since, as the nation as a whole grew richer, all its citizens would enjoy greater opportunities. These arguments appealed at once to the wealthier businessmen, yet the Whigs needed and eventually obtained support from farmers and workers. In the South, the larger planters, those directly tied in with commercial agriculture and international markets, allied with the business and professional classes of the cities and towns to provide the core support for Southern Whiggery.

VAN BUREN AND THE DELUGE

During the late 1830s, Democrats adopted a more "left-wing" or antibusiness position. The most radical Democrats, small groups in Eastern cities, were called "Locofocos," after the friction matches

they used to illuminate one of their New York meetings. The Van Buren policies of hard money and no government aid to business caused the opposition to smear all Democrats as Locofocos. Conservative Democrats overreacted to what they considered a threat to the social order from the Locos, and many deserted their party for the Whigs. At the same time, Calhoun supporters made an uneasy peace with Van Buren and returned to the Democratic side. These shifts meant that by the end of the 1830s the two major parties reflected differing attitudes toward business and finance to a greater degree than usual.

As the election of 1840 approached, two strong well-organized national parties prepared to battle. The Panic of 1837 had brought misery to thousands who blamed their condition on the Jacksonian Democrats, the party in power. Van Buren struggled to reverse the downturn, but neither the current state of economic knowledge, nor Jacksonian ideology with its emphasis on negative government, enabled him to do much. Van Buren had already lectured the country like a Dutch uncle: "All communities are apt to look to government for too much . . . especially at periods of sudden embarrassment and distress. But this ought not to be. . . . The less government interferes with private pursuits the better for the general prosperity."

The slavery issue added to his woes. From the beginning, the Jacksonians relied on strong Southern support. Northern Democrats like Van Buren as far back as the 1820s strenuously resisted the introduction of slavery into national politics. When Calhoun led his militant Southern following back into the Democratic fold in 1838, he recognized the Jacksonian party, with its respect for states' rights and a limited conception of federal authority, as the best available vehicle for defending Southern interests. But many other Southerners were not willing to accept Van Buren or any other Northerner.

The president's opposition to the annexation of the Republic of Texas complicated his Southern strategy. Texas was the creation of Southerners who had migrated with their slaves into Mexico's northeasternmost province. A successful revolution in 1836 prepared Texas for entry to the Union, but Van Buren would not go along for fear of injecting slavery into national politics and wrecking the Democratic coalition. On the other hand, his prosecution of the Seminole War in Florida, a territory still a haven for runaway slaves, and his refusal to support legislation outlawing slavery in the District of Columbia, alienated antislavery Northerners.

The Whigs did not promise Southern annexationists anything. Nor did they have to, riding into the White House on a wave of sentiment against the party in power. Moreover, by 1840, imitating the Jacksonians, Whigs had perfected their party organization and had achieved a hitherto elusive unity. A younger breed of party managers, many of them experienced in the Antimasonic crusade, dropped the wheelhorse Henry Clay in favor of the more marketable General William Henry Harrison. Here, as far as superficial images went, was a Whig version of Jackson, the Hero of New Orleans. Harrison was Southern by birth, Western by adoption, and a general by training, famed as an Indian fighter. Though no more a "man of the people" than Jackson, he could masquerade in that role. Like Jacksonians in 1828, the Whigs in 1840 preferred to keep silent on most issues for fear of antagonizing voters who would not like what the party stood for, and to emphasize instead Harrison's spurious claim to a log-cabin birth. Exploiting the egalitarian temper of the times, the Whigs went on to depict Van Buren as an aristocrat, though he actually was the son of a tavernkeeper and had dutifully worked his way up the political ladder.

Finally, they capitalized on Harrison's image as an honest, straightforward amateur in politics. Van Buren was painted as the scheming, wily, self-serving, professional politician as in the charge of Davy Crockett, a former Democrat turned Whig: "Van Buren is as opposite to General Jackson as cowdung is to a diamond. It is said that at a year old he could laugh on one side of his face and cry on the other, at one and the same time."

Whig propaganda, organization, and electioneering techniques paid off. Never before had parties made such sustained and frantic exertions to arouse voters and get them to the polls. Harrison won easily, many states voting Whig for the first time, and voter participation reached new highs. Since 1828 about 55 percent of those eligible had voted in presidential elections, but in 1840 the turnout surged to 78 percent. The average voter had finally become involved in presidential politics in electing the first Whig president. Measured in terms of popular participation alone the common man had arrived.

Yet whether the Whig victory would enable Americans to cope with the instabilities created by territorial and economic expansion, and by the Panic of 1837, remained unclear. Above all, the election of 1840 gave dramatic testimony to the revival of party politics. The second American party system had come of age. No one could foretell in March 1841, when William Henry Harrison became the first Whig president, how brief an existence the new party system would enjoy.

Chapter 12
A New Society, 1815–1860

Economic expansion and the democratization of politics nourished in Americans high expectations of individual achievement. Scarcity no longer condemned the mass of people to poverty, nor did a small elite monopolize political power as in Europe. American abundance sprang from the marriage of fertile land and industrial technology, and it gave birth to a particularly American brand of optimism. DeWitt Clinton, the governor of New York, declared proudly in 1828: "The great scourges of mankind have rarely visited us with destroying fury. Peace, plenty and health have presided over our land. War is a stranger, and famine, and the pestilence that walketh in darkness are never experienced. Instead of a scarcity, there is generally a superabundance of subsistence, an excess of production."

The United States was not the first industrial nation, nor even in the heyday of its agrarian prosperity had poverty been eliminated completely. Yet in the half century before the Civil War it seemed possible that a large society could expand without bringing economic deprivation to the masses. This expectation inevitably transformed the shape and direction of American thought and customs.

But rapid economic expansion came with a price tag. Growing wealth and social differentiation revived political conflict and resulted in the second American party system. The strains of growth and change penetrated every corner and level of life—politics, religion, education, and the arts. Americans embraced material progress, with its promise of greater comfort, affluence, and opportunity, while simultaneously sensing its dangers. A republic inhabited by virtuous, middling farmers might easily become a society of extremes, especially in the new cities with their few millionaires and many paupers. Once overwhelmingly British and Protestant, the country now admitted hundreds of thousands of Irish and German Catholic immigrants. Native Americans thought these newcomers' ethnic and religious traditions clashed dangerously with their own traditions of civil and religious liberty.

But the greatest danger came from within. Material accomplishments blinded man to his spiritual and temporal obligations; people subordinated piety and benevolence to acquisitiveness. "Here wealth is new and mainly in the hands of men who have scrambled for it," warned Boston's reformer-preacher Theodore Parker. "They have energy, vigor, and a certain generosity, but as a class are narrow, vulgar, and conceited." Parker concluded: "There is no country in Christendom where life is so insecure, hopes so cruelly dashed away in the manslaughter of reckless enterprise." The laboring classes, observed another Boston reform minister, William Ellery Channing, were equally infected by "their recklessness, their jealousies of the more prosperous, and subservience to parties and political leaders." This, he warned, "may turn all their bright prospects into darkness."

AMERICA'S MISSION

At issue was the country's destiny. Would America fulfill its mission as "the last best hope of mankind?" From the beginning Americans shared a sense of mission. Puritans established a godly commonwealth in the wilderness; the revolutionary generation sought to vindicate its natural rights and the Rights of Man. After 1820 a new generation for whom the revolutionary experience had become heroic history assumed the burden of fulfilling the national mission. The challenge was no longer one of mere survival, or mere example, but to see that material growth and territorial expansion did not deflect Americans from their chosen goals, or alter their character as a people.

This national ideal had received sharp definition in Jeffersonian thought. It projected a society of industrious, prosperous farmers living close to nature, democratic and public-spirited, seeking comfort but not luxury, jealous of individual freedom and suspicious of privilege. "Let us keep our workshops in Europe," Jefferson counseled, so that the United States could avoid the brutal-izing poverty and decadence of Europe's cities and factory towns. America would remain a bountiful garden so long as its people remained yeomen farmers and preferred a simple life to the reckless pursuit of wealth.

This vision—the Myth of the Garden—represented desires more than realities. Even Jefferson, late in life, had to alter his views and advocate increased national self-sufficiency through more manufacturing. And while people might idealize the yeoman farmer, more and more of those wielding power were aggressive business-men, restless and speculative. Farmers also fit this new prototype, speculating on the soil, mov-ing wherever greater opportunity called, and not much different in outlook from the commercial classes Jeffersonians had scorned. Indeed the very attacks on privilege of the Jeffersonians and Jack-sonians, by curbing national economic powers (and the power to regulate), created new oppor-tunities for entrepreneurs, especially merchants and market farmers. Still, people found the yeo-man ideal, the myth of a pastoral, simple, and un-competitive social order, powerfully appealing even as it receded from their actual experience.

Expansion and economic development sig-naled progress and provided the means of fulfill-ing the national mission. Americans felt destined to occupy a continent peopled by millions of free and prosperous citizens. Yet some sensed the dangers detected by the shrewdest foreign ob-server of their society, Alexis de Tocqueville, a French aristocrat who visited the United States in 1831 and 1832. "A native of the United States," he wrote, "clings to this world's goods as if he were certain never to die; and is so hasty at grasping all within his reach, that one would sup-pose he was constantly afraid of not living long enough to enjoy them." According to de Tocque-ville, Americans became wealthy by ignoring others. "They are nothing to any man," he ob-served, "they expect nothing from any man; they acquire the habit of always considering them-selves as standing alone, and they are apt to imag-ine that their whole destiny is in their own hands."

Yet the prevailing American mood remained optimistic. A generation which de Tocqueville described as infected by "a passionate, exag-gerated love of self," nevertheless enlisted in a dozen reform movements, flocked to countless religious revivals, and produced the first voices of a great national literature. Buoyed up by mate-rial achievement and political security, Jack-sonian America spawned schemes for human betterment. One professional reformer, Bronson Alcott, sounded the keynote: "Our freer, but yet far from freed land is the asylum, if asylum there be, for the hope of Man, and there, if anywhere, is the second Eden to be planted."

SALVATION FOR ALL

The churches, led by fiery revivalist ministers, claimed to hold the keys to the kingdom. "There is no country in the world," observed de Tocque-ville, "where the Christian religion retains a greater influence over the souls of men than in America," even though the law separated church and state. The pervasive influence of the churches which de Tocqueville observed in the 1830s re-sulted from a religious resurgence that went back to the beginning of the nineteenth century and beyond.

From the first settlements in America, even in the most outwardly pious communities such as Massachusetts, religious faith had to struggle against the secularism fostered by people's ability to improve their material lot. By the 1740s the tensions between the fear of God's wrath and the lures of the world burst forth in the Great Awak-ening. These fires of religious revivalism re-claimed souls for the churches only temporarily. In time, sinners lapsed into indifference, too busy with everyday affairs to worry much about their souls. The revivalists learned that their task was a continuing one, but public response waxed and waned unpredictably.

Americans in the late last third of the eigh-teenth century proved unreceptive. The revolu-tionary generation's triumphs strengthened con-fidence in man's ability to control his destiny and to find happiness on earth. Revolutionary leaders such as Franklin, Washington, Jefferson, and Hamilton were Christians whose religious beliefs, like those of elites elsewhere in the West-ern world, were shaped by the Enlightenment's rationalism and emboldened by the scientific triumphs of Galileo, Newton, and others in unlocking some secrets of the universe. Advocates of "natural" religion saw God as a benevolent deity who governed the world according to established laws which men could discover through use of reason. They thought that powerful churches, elaborate rituals, complex creeds, and divine mysteries had perverted Christianity. Institutionalized religion had become oppressive, corrupt, and maintained itself mainly through fear, force, and superstition. Enlightenment religion repudiated all this. Man need only believe what was reasonable, and the essence of faith lay in the ethical teachings of Christ.

Rational Religion

This religion of reason and benevolence, known as deism, spread from the upper classes to other elements in America. Unitarianism appeared in New England around 1800. The new denomination appealed to Congregationalists, especially to the urban upper classes, who rejected the Calvinist doctrine of predestination and insisted on the unity of God, his benevolence and rationality, and on the possibility of salvation for all.

A quiet revolution had taken place in eastern Massachusetts late in the eighteenth century, as church after church came into the hands of Unitarian preachers and parishioners. The appointment of a religious "liberal" to Harvard College's chair of divinity in 1806 confirmed the Unitarian triumph and broke the calm. Orthodox Congregationalists now fought back strenuously. But Boston and its environs remained Unitarian country, at least so far as Protestantism was concerned.

Unitarianism never became strong outside of Massachusetts, however. Churches were set up in the other large eastern cities, but penetration of the South and West proved minimal. It remained very much the church of the Boston Brahmin aristocracy. Yet despite their numerical insignificance, Unitarians ran Boston, and Boston counted for much in the economy and in culture. The Unitarian elite included powerful preachers, men like William Ellery Channing, noted not for their lung power but for their strong minds. And Unitarianism itself, soon lapsing into standpat orthodoxy, produced notable rebel ministers like

Theodore Parker and Ralph Waldo Emerson. Unitarianism, very much a religion of the individual, made an important contribution to the weakening of Calvinism and to rechanneling American religious fundamentalism.

At the same time that deism and Unitarianism were upsetting orthodox belief, established or government-supported churches were done away with by a campaign for separation of church and state launched during the revolutionary era. By 1833 even the entrenched Congregationalist establishments of Connecticut and Massachusetts had fallen due to pressure from increasingly numerous and powerful denominations that demanded an end to religious privilege and state support for one religious sect.

Evangelical Protestantism

In the face of these challenges, especially the persistence of widespread indifference toward religion, orthodox Christians fought back. In the 1790s New England Congregationalists warned that French Jacobinism was spreading atheism in Europe and that the Jeffersonians would do the same in America. The orthodox pointed to many frontier areas without ministers to preach the Gospel. As tens of thousands migrated westward and more thousands moved into the cities, the unchurched began to outnumber the faithful. A leading Congregationalist minister, Lyman Beecher of Connecticut, identified the dangers of "the extent of territory, our numerous and increasing population, from diversity of local interests, the power of selfishness, and the fury of sectional jealousy and hate." Never more than in a time of rapid growth did the country so badly need "a more powerful intellectual and moral fusion requisite to prevent the utter disorganization of society," warned another. The West in particular was "one immense field of moral desolation."

The tide began to turn against indifference and deism when the fires of revivalism kindled again in a Second Great Awakening that began around 1800 and flared again in the 1820s and 1830s and finally in the late 1850s. In camp meetings in the trans-Appalachian settlements beginning in the 1790s, and then in revivals in New England and the "Burned-Over" district of upstate New York in the 1820s, and eventually in the cities, sinners repented by the hundreds of thousands.

The power of Calvinism, waning since the first colonial settlements, all but died in the first half of the nineteenth century. During the Second Great Awakening, American religion definitely put aside the doctrines of predestination and election, in favor of a universal, salvation-for-all theology and a pietistic kind of church observance. The older churches had to adapt to changing conditions or wither. For example, they had to respond to the ever-increasing need to recruit new members, and accept multidenominational practices as members (and sometimes ministers) shopped around among the Protestant churches with remarkably little regard for denominational labels.

Hellfire revivalism, even more torrid than that of the First Great Awakening (1730-1750), provided a spectacular veneer partly obscuring a simple yet fundamental change in American religion. Each sect tried to maintain an exclusive appeal, to create the impression that it and it alone knew the road to salvation. But that effort failed. The Second Great Awakening democratized salvation. The era of the all-powerful ministry had ended and the dogmas of election became old-fashioned. Hellfire and damnation remained part of the revival preacher's stock-in-trade, however: salvation did not come automatically; sinners still went straight to Hell. But one could escape that unwelcome destination by accepting religion and the Word of God, and by obeying His commandments. In short, Christian commitment and behavior all but assured salvation. The agonizing over being damned in advance, whatever one's conduct in life, lost its relevance. Abundance—the chance of salvation for *all*—had come to religion; in affluent America it seemed only right that God should be as bountiful as the land.

The Spread of Revivalism

The unrestrained enthusiasm of trans-Appalachian revivalism set much of the tone for the religious upheavals of the Second Great Awakening. Settlers in Kentucky and Tennessee in the 1790s gave themselves to Christ with an abandon

that has since earned for some congregations the disparaging nickname, "holy rollers." One minister reported that when the worshipers became unruly and he went among them, some urged him to be more decorous and return to his pulpit. "I turned to go . . ." he admitted, but "the power of God was strong upon me. I turned again, and losing sight of fear of man, I went through the house shouting and exhorting with all possible ecstasy and energy." And this sort of ebullience went far beyond the tiny, evangelistic sects of trans-Appalachia, affecting such "respectable" denominations as the Presbyterians, the Methodists (who by the Civil War comprised the largest single sect in America), and the city revivals as well. All the denominations felt the influence, operational and doctrinal, of "enthusiastic religion." Those who sought a broad membership ignored it at their peril.

New York had a Burned-Over district (an area crisscrossed by waves of revivalism until it had been "burned over" by the heat of enthusiasm) in the central and western parts of the state. The crusades also produced the early nineteenth century's most noted revivalist, Charles G. Finney. An ex-lawyer who became a Congregationalist minister, Finney seared the Burned-Over district in the classic style in the 1820s. This master revivalist made explicit what was already implicit in the revivalist impulse, especially its rejection of the Calvinist doctrine that only God could save sinners, substituting the doctrine that men could save themselves with God's help. As long as preachers insisted on man's inability, Finney argued, sinners had little incentive to repent. "Be ye perfect," he countered, "even as your heavenly Father is perfect."

He designed his revival techniques, like those of other hellfire preachers, to make people fear for their souls. "Look, look," he shouted, "see the millions of wretches biting and gnawing their tongues as they lift their scalding heads from the burning lake of hell. . . ." Salvation was not easy but it was attainable. "Your prayers are so very cold," Finney complained, "they do not rise more than six feet high; you must strive hard and struggle—you must groan, you must agonize, why you must pray till your nose bleeds, or it will not avail."

Finney set out in the 1830s straight for the source of wickedness, the cities. His later sermons were free of cheap sensationalism, or simple-minded hellfire threats. In calling for regeneration of the human spirit, he ably blended the concepts of salvation by faith *and* works into a powerful rhetorical instrument. Finney was an all-out salvationist, so much so that in 1834 the Congregationalists expelled him from doctrinal deviation, or for taking too liberal a line on what man could do to be saved. Finney, who further antagonized church conservatives by embracing abolitionism, later moved to Ohio as president of Oberlin College, a radical and racially integrated institution.

Revivalism made theology less important than faith, and sectarian differences became less vital than the common desire to save souls. Above all the revivals responded to the need for continuing missionary work in a culture where religion was a voluntary matter and where the churches had actively to recruit members. At the same time, evangelical Christianity helped to define the character of the culture. America was "a missionary nation" whose example of piety would inspire other people and keep it on its destined course. "Commerce cannot be entrusted with the moral interests of mankind," warned the clergy. "She has no principle that can withstand a strong temptation to her insatiable cupidity." By ministering to a society undergoing growth and enjoying material progress, the churches catered to a people continually torn between chauvinistic pride and belief in Christian brotherhood, between personal self-satisfaction and a sense of Christian humility, between the profit motive and Christian selflessness. By enabling people to purge themselves temporarily of guilt the churches sent forth regenerate farmers, laborers, and businessmen with renewed strength to pursue material happiness.

The new religious currents also altered the institutional structure of American Protestantism. Though a variety of nondenominational organizations such as the American Bible Society and the American Sunday School Union fought against secularism, the most effective weapon remained the revival. Denominations that were quickest to adapt to the new methods tended to prosper; those slow to adjust theology and forms

of worship lagged in membership. By the Civil War, the Methodists and Baptists, the most ardent revivalists, comprised the largest denominations in the country. In contrast the two leading colonial churches, the Congregationalists and Episcopalians (Anglicans) had slipped in popularity.

At the same time new sects sprang up, since no single group could enforce its exclusive claims and since some troubled souls failed to find comfort in existing churches. Revivalism, by repeatedly stirring up sinners and encouraging them to seek direct access to God, stimulated the religious imagination. This produced dozens of new revelations of God's design. William Miller, for instance, preached that the world would end in 1843. Thousands waited expectantly but vainly for his proclaimed Day of Judgment.

The most important of the new sects was the Church of Jesus Christ of Latter-Day Saints, or Mormons, founded in 1830 by Joseph Smith, the son of a poor farmer in New York's Burned-Over district. Smith claimed to have received divine revelation and a new Gospel, *The Book of Mormon*. Like Miller, Smith preached the imminence of the millennium when only the Saints, those converted to Mormonism, would be saved. Within a few years, Smith commanded several thousand faithful and organized a tightly knit community ("a cooperative society ruled by an ecclesiastical oligarchy," it has been called) that controlled all aspects of Mormon life. Repeated persecution forced them to move to Ohio, Missouri, Illinois (Smith was murdered by a mob there in 1844), and finally near the Great Salt Lake in Utah, then outside the limits of the United States. There, under the extraordinary leadership of Brigham Young, the Mormons created the State of Deseret and grew to 200,000 in thirty years, free at last to worship God and practice polygamy in peace. The promise of salvation together with the authoritarian and communitarian features of Mormonism appealed to those Americans who wanted to escape from the uncertainties and instability of a fast-changing society in which many like Joseph Smith had fallen behind in the struggle for wealth and power.

Through the growth of new sects and the strengthening of the older denominations, through revivalism and interdenominational organization, American Protestantism attempted to save the souls of sinners as well as the soul of the nation. God blessed America and made it prosper, Theodore Parker explained, because He intended this land "to serve the great moral purpose of human life; to make the mass of men better off, wiser, juster, more affectionate and holy in all their life, without and within." Though church and state had been separated in America, the churches insisted that all institutions and communal practices be measured by Christian ethical standards and reformed if necessary.

THE REFORM IMPULSE

Abundance, optimism, belief in progress—all these shaped the American vision and pointed with renewed vigor to a glorious national future. There were naysayers, of course, some of them professional Jeremiahs reacting anxiously to rapid social change; others perceptive social critics who kept in mind how intractable and irrational human beings can be, even in the best of circumstances. But the central tendency in American culture remained positive, an optimistic faith that society's ills would be eliminated and that America could be perfected through reform. Reformers organized to rescue the drunkard, emancipate women and slaves, help the physically handicapped, and educate the masses. They set up the goal of an educated, sober citizenry, one which would act responsibly if the right measures were taken and the right values instilled.

Sources of Reform

Reform had both religious and secular roots. Revivalism sensitized Christians to social evils and inspired men to perform good works as a sign of their own repentance and godliness. "You ask why I cannot keep my religion to myself," explained a universal reformer and wealthy New York businessman named Lewis Tappan. "Because I see you are in danger of eternal damnation. As I love you then, and desire your happiness and usefulness, I urge upon you the obligations of faith in the Son of God. Were I not to do so your blood would be found on my skirts

at the Judgment Day." Evangelical Protestantism made men their brother's keepers.

Reform also stemmed from a pervasive optimism about the inevitability of progress. There seemed no limit to the power of the human mind and will. The secret of their success, Americans thought, lay in their freedom from oppressive institutions and authorities. Here, each man possessed a divine spark and could develop his potential. Yet even in America men had not yet fully realized themselves. The task of reform was to cut the bonds that still held people down.

For many reformers the principal demon was alcohol. They labeled it the root cause of immorality, and in the crusade against liquor the church played a leading role. Ministers urged temperance as evidence of conversion. Intemperance was sinful and led to other vices which brought on poverty and disease. Temperance reformers regarded sobriety as more than a personal virtue; it was a public necessity. In an age of popular democracy, citizens could hardly exercise their civic responsibilities in a besotted condition. Temperance also became a means of achieving social control. In a highly mobile society, one in which the majority prospered, some of the "failures" took up drink to escape from misery. Reformers, however, attributed failure to self-indulgence and urged the poor to imitate middle-class habits of self-control as the path to success. Also creating social concern were the hundreds of thousands of immigrants, beer-loving German immigrants and whisky-drinking Irishmen, who came to America after 1830. Alarmed by the influx of foreigners, the native born supported temperance and later prohibition movements partly to assert their cultural dominance over the newcomers.

Temperance reformers faced an uphill battle, however. Americans loved their liquor and until the 1820s they had expressed few qualms about heavy drinking. At first, reformers condemned only hard liquor and relied on moral suasion. In the 1840s ballyhoo also became part of the crusade, with mass meetings and parades of the "Cold Water Army," organized political action, and sentimental literature exposing the evils of quaffing the grape which included such tear-jerking songs as "Father, Dear Father, Come Home with Me Now." One group signed a new

Declaration of Independence: "We hold these truths to be self-evident; that all men are created temperate; that they are endowed by their Creator with certain natural and innocent desires; that among these are the appetite for COLD WATER and the pursuit of happiness."

The movement produced an outstanding leader, Neal Dow of Maine. In 1846, his state passed the first prohibition law, and a dozen other states followed. But the pre-Civil War movement went no further. Prohibition would have to wait sixty years for another reform wave, the Progressive movement, to gain its total but happily short-lived triumph through constitutional amendment (1919-1933). In both eras, however, temperance provided a mirror of society's hopes and fears. Many pre-Civil War prohibitionists still believed in a bright, sober future, but felt that drunkenness (which many of them unfairly blamed on the influx of non-British immigrants) had to be fought with government coercion. Social betterment became more than a personal responsibility; society should use government to promote progress by prohibiting evil.

Temperance was but one of a cluster of reform activities which enlivened the American scene during the four decades before the Civil War. Reformers, some gentle, some angry, but most of them dedicated, attacked such problems as the maltreatment of the insane and the handicapped, the abominable condition of jails and prisons, and the curse of war. They also championed women's rights, pushing demands for female civil and political rights then considered premature by the ruling autocrats, the men. Nevertheless the agitation produced increased educational opportunities for women, thus providing the basis for an educated, activist, and eventually successful suffragist movement a half century later. Lesser movements included, among many others, those believing that penny postage would usher in a new age of human brotherhood, or that phrenology, the study of configurations of the skull, brought scientific self-awareness.

Professional Altruists

A few persons devoted their lives to reform, thus becoming America's first professional altruists. Samuel Gridley Howe of Massachusetts longed for greatness and thought he could achieve it through some noble cause. As a young man, he had aided the Greeks in their battle for freedom from the Turks; but his true mission awaited him at home. Rejecting a career of moneymaking, he expressed instead "a desire to attack the Powers that be, Powers [which] I think from my soul have disgraced the country. . . ." Although many reforms interested him, Howe did his greatest work among the blind, deaf, and dumb. Convinced that no human being need live in darkness, he devised methods of teaching the handicapped which produced dramatic results.

His greatest success was with six-year-old Laura Bridgman. Sickness in infancy left Laura without sight, hearing, or the capacity to speak. Through Howe's patience and skill, Laura was the first such person to learn to read and communicate. Howe's life expressed the faith of a generation in perfectability, the belief that even those considered beyond help were salvageable. "Humanity demands that every creature in human shape," Howe insisted, "should command our respect; we should recognize as a brother every being upon whom God has stamped the human impress." Benevolence provided the road to genuine personal fulfillment. "Everything which brings out the hidden virtues of humanity," Howe considered worth doing. He was certain that God wanted "everybody to be happy all the time."

Some Americans doubted the sufficiency of simply remolding existing institutions. Perfectionism led them to withdraw from society and attempt to create new social orders. These communitarian experiments, such as Brook Farm, a transcendentalist colony led by New England intellectuals; New Harmony, a socialist colony founded by Robert Dale Owen, son of a reforming Scottish industrialist; several Shaker communities; and the Mormon State of Deseret involved relatively small numbers but they attracted the steady attention of the more conformist Americans. George Ripley explained the rationale of Brook Farm. Removed from a society based on competitive individualism, with its division of labor and class distinctions, man could now realize his greatest potential for unity and self-fulfillment. At Brook Farm, however, everyone would engage in both intellectual and manual labor, people would be thinkers as well as workers and they would perform tasks suited to their interests and abilities. The result, Ripley thought, would be "a society of liberal, intelligent, and cultivated persons, whose relations with each other would permit a more wholesome and simple life than can be led amidst the pressure of our competitive institutions." His experiment failed.

The communitarian settlements involved but a tiny portion of the American population, yet they stirred up an interest that went beyond mere curiosity or sensationalism in a nation largely convinced that humanity could shape its future, yet equally convinced that communistic separatism was not for them. The world, or at least the North American continent, offered too much for people to isolate themselves or abandon the hope of individual betterment. Freedom remained the byword, freedom to *do* things. Only a few Americans retreated from the world. Most reformers believed the challenge lay not in withdrawal but in commitment. For many, education seemed to hold the key to social transformation.

THE CRUSADE FOR PUBLIC SCHOOLS

"Preach, my dear Sir, a crusade against ignorance," Jefferson urged a friend in 1786. "Establish and improve the law for educating the common people. The tax which will be paid for this purpose is not more than the thousandth part of what will be paid to kings, priests and nobles who will rise up among us if we leave the people in ignorance." Many leaders of the revolutionary generation shared Jefferson's views, but because the elite could afford private education for their children, they refused to adopt his plan for free primary schools for the masses and higher education for a handful of the most talented common folk. Except in New England, whose poorly supported common schools had been established in colonial times, Americans accepted the principle that a republic required an educated citizenry, but they did not put it into practice. Some publicly aided schools for the poor existed; and many states subsidized higher education, but this benefited chiefly the sons of the well-to-do.

Yet in the thirty years after Jefferson's death in 1826, most states outside the South established free public schools. By 1870 over half the school-age population was receiving formal instruction in public schools and almost 90 percent of the white population was literate, a startling reversal. Support for common schools developed because of old dreams and new needs. Both Jacksonians and Whigs backed common schools, but this consensus obscures essential differences in motivation while it explains why public schools within one generation became a key, new institution in the United States.

Origins of Public Schools

The democratization of politics alarmed conservatives. Since politicians increasingly appealed to the masses for support, and since Jacksonians favored in theory if not quite in practice the appointment of ordinary citizens to public office, it was necessary to assure that all citizens were literate and indoctrinated with those moral and patriotic values which would induce them to exercise power wisely. "The great experiment of Republicanism," explained Horace Mann, a leading educational reformer from Massachusetts, "of the capacity of man for self-government is to be tried anew, which wherever it has been tried . . . has failed, through an incapacity in the people to enjoy liberty without abusing it." Mann warned the wealthy that unless they dropped their opposition to mass education there would be "no security for any class . . . nor for any interest, human or divine." Thus common schools appeared as a means of social control, especially in the cities where the children of the less fortunate knew nothing, according to Mann, "of the harmonies of their being with the being of others or with Nature." The only education they got was from the bustling life around them from which they learned that "each one seems to scramble to get the best morsel for himself."

Some people feared not only urban chaos but national catastrophe. America was an enormous continent, destined to absorb millions of immigrants as it developed. "To sustain an extended republic like our own," argued Calvin Stowe, "there must be a *national* feeling, a national assimilation." Yet the country contained diverse elements, divided by section, religion, and national origins, and the new immigration increased the dangers that America was becoming "a congeries of clans, congregating without coalescing . . ." Free schools, argued Protestant reformers, could instruct the children of Catholic peasants in the principles of republican self-government, principles alien to their Old World heritage of servitude and priestly domination. Schools would thus make sure that they did not "prove to our republic what the Goths and Huns were to the Roman Empire."

Workingmen, shopkeepers, and politicians also favored common schools to improve opportunities for those who felt threatened by rapid change and business fluctuations. Jacksonian era workingmen, and their allies, agreed that a monopoly of knowledge could be as dangerous as a monopoly in banking. Alarmed by "the glaring inequality of society," they argued that "until the means of equal instruction shall be equally secured to all, liberty is but an unmeaning word, and equality an empty shadow." Free schools would give the sons of the poor a better chance to compete with the sons of the well-to-do, not only by providing them with necessary skills but by inculcating "a just disposition, virtuous habits, and rational self-governing character." Children of the rich and poor would mingle together and be judged according to performance, not social class.

To overcome reluctance to finance public education, reformers argued that free schools would promote national prosperity, maintaining that the schools would cultivate industry and morality. While society would benefit, the common school was also an instrument for individual perfectability. "A mere bookworm is a worthless character," warned Governor Edward Everett of Massachusetts, "but a mere money-getter is no better." Schools would enlarge human possibilities for self-development among all ranks of society, enable people to act from ideas and principles rather than from blind impulse or imitation; they would cultivate the soul so people could resist the self-seeking, material drives so powerful in America.

Rising national wealth made it easier to finance public education and to overcome resistance from taxpayers. But religious obstacles also appeared, especially those raised by Catholics who opposed enrolling their children in institutions controlled by Protestants. Since the schools were supposed to teach morality and religion was considered the foundation of morals, the schools substituted for sectarian teachings nondenominational ethics which all groups could support. The schools utilized prayers and Bible reading but without sectarian emphasis, though Catholics disliked the use of the King James (Protestant) version of the Bible.

By midcentury the common schools had assumed their modern form. State-supported, and free to poor and rich alike, they replaced publicly aided charity schools to which most Americans had refused to send their children. The common schools provided instruction in the three Rs and preached morality and patriotism. They were sufficiently well run to attract middle-class children as well as those of the poor. Slowly the common schools came under the influence of professionalization. Increasingly the teaching staff became female, state boards of education set standards for local school boards, and teacher training institutions produced personnel specifically qualified for careers in education.

The performance of the common school fell far short of its promise. Though it did enlarge opportunity for the middle and lower classes, the quality of instruction was too often unimaginative, and the schools resembled factories rather than the gardens for the nurture of young minds which reformers had promised. The nation's per capita income grew significantly after 1840 but the level of financial support for education failed to keep pace. Nor did the schools halt the growing social stratification which increased as the tempo of industrialization gained momentum. They were most successful as instruments for social control: they diffused middle-class values and patriotic sentiment among the masses and strengthened the belief that society rewarded hard work and virtue. In time, the schools joined the church, the state, and the family as a pillar of the republic.

But not in the South. There neither the reform impulse nor the crusade for common schools made an impact comparable to the rest of the nation. Perfectionist individualism was hard to reconcile with Negro slavery. The equalitarian assumption that every human being was a child of God lay at the heart of the reformers' faith. As increasing numbers of Northerners identified slavery as the nation's deepest social evil, it became clear that reform ideology threatened the institution. Wealthy Southerners who dominated the region's politics also stood fast against common schools that would raise taxes and spread enlightenment and dangerous ideas among the poor whites, who were still willing to defer to their leaders. Yet even in the South most educated people felt the impact of the dominant ideology of mid-nineteenth-century America. The task of the Southern school reformer proved even more difficult than that of his Northern counterpart, and his accomplishments were even more limited.

Nevertheless, the idea of primary education for all won out, although it would take the rest of the nineteenth century to make it a reality. Education, even that minimum needed to escape the curse of illiteracy, had always been a privilege of the elite. In rejecting this notion, nineteenth-century Americans set the stage for a progressive democratization of education, which in the twentieth century would reach the colleges and universities. The belief that education was a "luxury," like so many other things, fell victim to American abundance.

CULTURAL FLOWERING

Shortly after the second war with Britain a hostile English writer asked the embarrassing question, "Who reads an American book?" Not many, it seemed. Americans were self-consciously sensitive about their cultural provincialism, yet they assumed that in time the republic would excel in the arts and learning just as it had in political thought and in producing material abundance. Twenty years later, Ralph Waldo Emerson, a young Harvard-educated minister who had abandoned Unitarianism for literature and philosophy, commanded Americans to stop imitating European artists and writers and produce a native culture rooted in American experience and feelings. Within a generation of Emerson's call, the country experienced a flowering of artistic imagination that produced America's "classic" period in the arts.

Architecture revealed graphically some of the dilemmas of cultural development. The colonists had adopted the Georgian style of architecture not only for its formal beauty, its sense of repose, and the ease with which it could be adapted, but also because the eighteenth-century English elite preferred it. American merchants and planters built Georgian mansions that evidenced their position in society and their imitative taste. But independence meant a rejection of the mother country. Though Americans still clung, of necessity, to their English heritage, they no longer thought slavish imitation of Georgian architecture appropriate in a new republic, especially for public buildings. They turned instead to antiquity. Greek revival state houses, churches, and banks began to appear. They seemed more suitable not only because the style was more grandiose than Georgian but because of its historical connection with a culture in which democratic republics had flourished. Americans insisted that architecture, no less than other forms of art, be morally uplifting; and "democratic" architecture was preferable to the Georgian which they associated with English aristocracy.

Eventually, however, the Greek revival ran its course as some questioned American imitation of those ancient republics as well. The Greeks, after all, were slave-owning pagans. The Gothic style had champions who insisted it was more appropriate in a Christian republic since it expressed an age of faith. The debate over building forms resulted in chaos once Americans abandoned the colonial consensus which had favored Georgian. Some advocated borrowing from a variety of traditions, Georgian, Greek, Gothic, and Renaissance, with the landscape and purpose of the building to determine the style. The consequences were sometimes bizarre—as in P. T. Barnum's mansion, Iranistan, a domed and minareted building fit for a Shah of Persia but located in stodgy Bridgeport, Connecticut. American society still lacked the confidence to risk originality in the fine arts. Patrons uncertainly pondered the meaning of "good taste." Imitation of European forms gave the best assurance that native works possessed "artistic merit."

Sculptors therefore turned out lifeless figures from antiquity. Patrons commissioned painters to go abroad and copy the great masters. Artists did utilize some native subjects, petrifying national heroes in marble busts and in romanticized portraits, but they avoided hinting at the rawness and terror of the wilderness. The greatest enthusiasm was for stylized pictures of rural life (such as prints by Currier and Ives) that ennobled and sentimentalized it at the very time that factories and cities were becoming the dynamic forces in American life.

Similarly, musical taste reflected both provinciality and a demand for the sentimental. P. T. Barnum earned a fortune when he persuaded soprano Jenny Lind, the "Swedish Nightingale," to tour America. Her appeal lay not only in her pure, sweet voice capable of considerable technical display but in her virginal image, reinforced by well-publicized and unspontaneous acts of charity. The most notable American musician of the day, Stephen Collins Foster, wrote songs for minstrel shows about supposedly contented slaves such as "Massa's in De Col', Col' Ground" and "Ol' Black Joe," as well as sentimental and popular lyrics like "Jeanie with the Light Brown Hair" and "My Old Kentucky Home."

Creation of Classic American Literature

Literature proved to be the most vital medium for the expression of the artistic imagination in America. Between 1830 and 1860 a classic American literature emerged from the writings of Emerson, Henry David Thoreau, Walt Whitman, Edgar Allan Poe, Nathaniel Hawthorne, and Herman Melville, and lesser lights such as James Fenimore Cooper and Henry Wadsworth Longfellow. In their poetry, essays, short stories, and novels they skillfully examined the new America and in their finest works they tried to understand the meaning of American experience. Most, like Emerson and Whitman, were optimistic; others, such as Melville and Hawthorne, were gloomy.

Though an essayist, poet, and social critic, Emerson reached an unusually large audience, especially on the lecture circuit, which became in the rural society of the nineteenth century one of the principal means of entertainment and adult education. Emerson's popularity stemmed in part from the ambiguity of his message. As a leading New England Transcendentalist, Emerson championed a vague romantic philosophy that preached that God inhabited every creature. Therefore man could fulfill his potential by following his heart and intuition, through which he could apprehend spiritual truth. "Standing on the bare ground,—My head bathed in the blithe air and uplifted into infinite space," Emerson wrote,

"all mean egotism vanishes. I become a transparent eyeball; I am nothing; I see all; the currents of the Universal Being circulate through me; I am part and parcel of God."

By exalting feeling over reason, insisting that every man could become "a transparent eyeball," Emerson advocated a philosophic individualism which at the same time united men through their common links with divinity. Despite his distaste for materialism and his recoil from the predatory values of the marketplace, Emerson regarded the acquisitive drive as one of the many manifestations of the divinity. "Money," he said, "is in its effect and laws as beautiful as roses," for he could not help but admire the practical achievements of businessmen and other men of the world. Consequently, many Americans interpreted Emerson's misty ideas as sanctioning the pursuit of wealth—though the philosopher of Concord believed that man's highest purpose was to cultivate his soul.

Emerson's younger friend and neighbor, Henry David Thoreau, shared his Transcendentalism but rejected his reforming impulse in favor of a philosophic anarchism. In 1845, Thoreau withdrew temporarily to Walden Pond near Concord, to live simply and alone, striving for communion with nature. He sought to "live deliberately, to front only the essential facts of life and see if I could not learn what it had to teach and not, when I came to die, discover that I had not lived." He eventually returned to town life, but later published *Walden* (1854), an eloquent and simple record of his life by the pond which later generations of America, even further removed from nature, would treasure. Never a conformist, Thoreau spent a symbolic night in jail when he refused to pay taxes to support the Mexican War.

Though his essays, which included the well-known piece on "Civil Disobedience," are among the stylistic glories of American literature, few of Thoreau's contemporaries read them. Whereas Emerson tended to assimilate everything within his philosophy, Thoreau battled American society head-on. When told that a cable was to be laid under the Atlantic between Britain and the United States, he wondered what they would have to say to one another. Railroads were "improved means to an unimproved end." An ecologist who was almost alone in his time, he worried over "making the earth bald before her time." Thoreau believed that the routine of daily life, of getting and spending, robbed men of their chance to live. "I see young men," he complained, ". . . whose misfortune it is to have inherited farms, houses, barns, cattle and farming tools. Who made them serfs of the soil? Why should they begin digging their graves as soon as they are born?" Thoreau's American did not bother to answer.

Like Emerson, Walt Whitman, the poet from Brooklyn, believed in the goodness of man, his capacity for improvement, and in a bright future for the United States. Whitman began writing as a newspaperman, a Jacksonian, reformist, antislavery editor, who loved the bustle of New York City and rejoiced in the egalitarianism of his times. Emerson's writings influenced him greatly, especially his call for an American literature. In *Leaves of Grass* (1855) and other poems Whitman adopted free verse forms to celebrate his rhapsodic faith in democracy, equality, and the American mission—and in himself: "Of every hue and caste am I, of every rank and religion." Americans were indeed a chosen people:

For we cannot tarry here,
We must march . . . we must bear the brunt
　of danger,
We the youthful sinewy races, all the rest on us
　depend.
　　　　　　　　　Pioneers! Pioneers!
All the past we leave behind. . . .

In Salem, Massachusetts, where he worked in the federal customshouse, Nathaniel Hawthorne, a descendant of old Puritan stock, wrote novels and stories which warned against the illusion that in America "All the past we leave behind." Hawthorne's theme was original sin, "the blackness ten times blackness" that infected and was inherent in all human experience. America, he warned, was no Eden, and the American was no Adam before the Fall. In his tales Hawthorne depicted how evil and sin destroyed people. His tragic view of life found expression in the first great American novel, *The Scarlet Letter* (1850), a psychological study of the disintegration of an adulterous Puritan minister under the burden of hidden sin.

No contemporary admired Hawthorne's stories more than Herman Melville. In a series of novels written in the 1840s and 1850s, notably in his greatest work, *Moby Dick* (1851), Melville also created art out of a tragic vision of human experience. In his epic of the great white whale, Melville portrayed the self-destructiveness of man's compulsion to subdue nature, "unable to resist the hypothetic attraction of the self with its impulse to envelop and control the universe." The result for those who succumbed was madness, isolation, and ultimately death. Melville's father had once said, "money is the only solid substratum on which man can safely build in this world." His son disagreed, describing his countryman as "intrepid, unprincipled, reckless, predatory, with boundless ambition, civilized in externals but a savage at heart." Yet these qualities were simply human, for no one could escape the reality of a dualistic world in which man is "caught . . . between opposites such as good and evil . . . God and Satan, head and heart, spirit and matter."

But few Americans then read Hawthorne or Melville and even fewer appreciated the strength of their work. Their preoccupation with the power of evil from which they insisted Americans were not immune, and their tragic, gloomy vision of human possibilities met with a cold reception in an age and in a country confident that Providence had chosen the United States for great and good things. Ralph Waldo Emerson spoke for American intellectuals and reflected Northern reformism. Although he detested much of the money-grubbing and bustle he saw around him, he proclaimed that man's power to mold his environment conformed to the natural scheme of things. In essays such as "Self-Reliance" he assured Americans that the world, spiritually as well as materially, was every man's oyster. He fashioned a critical but strongly affirmative view of life. And in a sense Emerson provided intellectual frosting for much of what he considered undesirable. Emerson and the other Transcendentalists, in their commitment to the ideal, automatically became critics of their age, but not the nihilistic critics who saw only corruption and doom. Emerson yearned for moral perfection, and since betterment necessarily comes before perfection, that yearning put him in the vanguard of American reform.

Chapter 13
The Dilemma of Slavery

Americans—*white* Americans—had created the freest, most prosperous society the world had yet known. Promising unaccustomed political liberties and bountiful material benefits, the openness and richness of the North American continent yielded enormous dividends to the citizens of the United States, especially for those in the North. However, noncitizens who lived within American society found themselves excluded from this civic and economic feast.

The American Indian, for example, was shouldered aside with relative ease. By the nineteenth century only the literary men of the Northeast viewed the red man as a "noble savage"; Western frontiersmen emphasized only the savage part. Pushing the Indian westward—peaceably if possible, forcibly if necessary—remained a constant feature of American history for three hundred years. The Indian was not even considered useful material for domestication in order to exploit his labor.

Such exploitation befell another noncitizen, the Negro. Slavery was the major flaw in the American system mocking the pretensions of a society which not only proclaimed itself free, cherishing equality, but increasingly practiced what it preached for its white majority. The existence of slavery meant that apologists had to argue for bondage for the black, while defending freedom for the white. The task was not impossible, but the democratization of American politics and the growth of humanitarianism in the early nineteenth century made it increasingly difficult to reconcile the contradiction between social ideals and racial realities.

Hard as they tried, white Americans could not shake off the "Negro problem." They had created it; many had benefited from it; and all Americans would ultimately have to confront it. The most penetrating foreign observer of nineteenth-century America, Alexis de Tocqueville, saw this clearly: "The Indians will die in isolation, as they have lived; but the destiny of the Negroes is in some way joined with that of the Europeans. The two races are linked to each other. . . . It is as difficult for them to separate completely as it

is for them to unite. The most fearful of all the ills which threaten the future of the United States grows out of the presence of a black population on its soil."

Freedom and slavery, equality and bondage—these comprised the irreconcilable elements challenging American democracy by midcentury. The short-run economic and political interests of white America demanded repressing controversy over slavery, a conflict which imperiled the Union. That strategy for preserving sectional harmony worked through the 1840s. The controversy would not die down, however, and in the congressional debates of the 1850s, the representatives of twenty-seven million whites spent most of their time quarreling over the fate of fewer than four million blacks. Fundamental national values and beliefs forced Americans to confront and try to resolve the contradiction between their public professions and private behavior. The result was a bloody conflict that destroyed chattel slavery but not the other forms of bondage spawned by racism.

THE PROBLEM

It is not possible—perhaps not even desirable—to be objective about American Negro slavery, even in retrospect. Slavery meant many things to many people, and reactions were as much the product of the beholder's mind and values as they were responses to the institution itself. A quick survey of writings on slavery demonstrates this. "In the so-called school of the plantation," wrote Francis Simkins, a white Southern historian, "the barbarian captive from Africa was Anglicanized. This was a type of training more effective than anything the South has experienced since. . . . The Negro imbibed the rich heritage of European folklore, and became so skilled in English handicrafts, and in the intricate practices of plantation agriculture, that he was perhaps better educated in the industrial arts than those Negroes who have lived since the time of Booker T. Washington." In contrast, the Northern historian Kenneth Stampp wrote: "To enjoy the bounty of a paternalistic master a slave had to give up all claims to respect as a responsible adult, all pretensions of independence. He had to understand the subtle etiquette that governed his relations with his master: the fine line between friskiness and insubordination, between cuteness and insolence."

For the South, slavery was intrinsic to its way of life. In effect, the only useful definition of the term "The American South" is that portion of the United States which permitted slavery after the Revolutionary period. It supplied the distinguishing feature of Southern society even though relatively few Southern whites owned slaves. For all white Southerners the American Dream included the possession of slaves or, at least, one slave. The white hill-country poor, who detested the wealthy tidewater planter, mixed disdain with an equal portion of envy, and felt no sympathy for the Negro's plight.

By the 1850s the classic forms of plantation slavery in the United States flourished principally in the lower South, the region producing cotton, sugar, and rice. In the fifteen slave states about six million whites lived with about half as many slaves and an additional quarter million free Negroes. The distribution of the slave population conformed to the requirements of Southern geography, so that in four states Negroes outnumbered whites. Slaves were scarce in the Appalachian uplands, but plentiful along the Atlantic coast and in the Black Belt of the Gulf states of the New South.

Although slaves made up one-third of the Southern population, only 6 percent of the whites owned slaves. And although most slaveowners held few bondsmen (the majority owned less than five), a significant minority held many slaves, as well as disproportionate political power and social influence. Without access to common schools, large numbers of Southern whites remained illiterate (illiteracy among slaves also was the rule). The large slaveowners thus enjoyed a virtual monopoly of education, leisure, and the opportunity for wielding power. In politics, the overrepresentation of plantation areas helped planters transfer their power from local areas to the state capitals, and from there to the national government.

To maintain white solidarity and effective control the large slaveowners stressed the identity of interest that supposedly existed among all Southern whites, especially the need to maintain white supremacy. A leading Southern journalist, J. D. B. DeBow explained that "the humblest white man feels that where there are slaves he is not at the foot of the social ladder, and his own status is not the lowest in the community." According to John C. Calhoun: "With us the two great divisions of society are not the rich and the poor, but white and black; and the whites, the poor as well as the rich, belong to the upper classes and are respected. They have a position and pride of character of which poverty cannot deprive them."

THE PLANTATION

The heart of the system was the large plantation. Owners with more than twenty slaves customarily employed a white overseer or manager, since in this way they might operate several plantations. But they had constant trouble finding reliable overseers, who were often incompetent or brutal, or both, and the turnover on most plantations was frequent. Overseers came from the poor white class, and were not accepted socially by their employers even though they relied on them to police, punish, and feed the slaves, and purchase supplies.

The overseer's task was not easy. Owners prohibited unnecessary cruelty toward the slaves, partly for humane reasons, and also because an injured or dead slave represented a loss of valuable property. But an overly permissive overseer soon received reprimands about not allowing the slaves to become unruly or lazy. It was the exceptional man, one of real strength of character and rare gifts of persuasion, who could extract an adequate amount of work from the slaves without the frequent threat or use of physical punishment.

A new trend set in as the Civil War approached, the substitution of Negro "drivers," themselves slaves, for white overseers where possible. The field hands worked in groups or gangs commanded by a driver. On the largest plantations, there might be a head driver, a kind of first sergeant who actually ran things. Plantation owners prized particularly intelligent and forceful head drivers even more than a good overseer, and they received relatively good treatment because of their value. Drivers could speak directly to the owner, and it was the head driver who gave all the signals which regulated the slaves' daily schedule.

Slaves got "room and board," though it was hardly first-class fare. For the most part slave quarters were little better than hovels of one or perhaps two rooms into which large families crowded. There was enough to eat, but the quality of the food was abominable and lacked variety, consisting primarily of pork fat (when an occasional trace of meat appeared it was euphemistically called bacon), corn meal, and molasses. In some areas cheap grades of fish, those without a market elsewhere, supplied some much-needed protein, all too rare in the slave's diet. In those days before the effects of imbalanced diets were known, the relationship between this unvaried fare and nutritional diseases went all but unnoticed. As bad as was the slave's standard of living, it was not much worse than the poor whites. Poverty, with all its resultant physical perils and psychological degradation, was the lot of many Southerners, white and black, since a few whites controlled most of the best land and wealth of the region.

The Black Man's Burden

Chattel slavery made family life almost impossible. Some planters required marriages and tried to abide by slave unions, but these ceremonies had no legal validity. One Louisiana planter staged an elaborate slave marriage, with bridesmaids and all the customary trappings, but instead of declaring the union "until death do ye part," they swore fidelity "unless we shall be unavoidably separated." As a result slaves were sexually promiscuous. Large planters discouraged "marriage" between slaves of different plantations as a threat to efficiency, but on farms with few slaves such unions were necessary. The woman remained at her master's place, and her children became the property of her master.

Promiscuity transcended the color line. The system produced over 600,000 mulattoes in the South by 1860. A few masters had the decency to send their mulatto children to free states, despite legal difficulties. But generally the mulatto offspring simply merged with the slave population. Racial gradations were clearly visible, but the American racial code recognized no subtle distinctions. Anyone with even a trace of Negro blood (1/16th in most slave states) was condemned to an "inferior" caste, and presumed to be a slave unless he could prove otherwise. As a troubled Jefferson had noted earlier: "The whole commerce between master and slave is a perpetual exercise of the most boisterous passions, the most unremitting despotism on the one part, and degrading submission on the other."

Slaveowners and their descendants liked to claim proudly that slave families were not broken up for public sale, but the South was as much prone to economic boom-and-bust as any other part of the country and during bad times sales of slaves were often unavoidable. A slave's value derived in part from the right of sale, and this proved a disruptive factor. The dread of being sold and separated from family and friends, to work in the plantations of Mississippi or Louisiana, terrified slaves. A slave mother could usually count on keeping her child for a while, but once past the age of six or seven, and certainly by age ten, the danger of separation through sale increased, especially if the owner needed cash. Although seldom admitted publicly, the practice of "slave breeding," or consciously raising slaves for sale at adulthood or even adolescence, proved a convenient way for families of sagging fortune to remain solvent. This was particularly true in the upper South, which had more slaves than could be profitably employed on worn-out soils unsuited to cotton or sugar. Thus the upper South provided slaves needed to till the virgin lands of the newer Southern states.

The slave lacked any claim to humanity which could be enforced at law. Whatever the rewards or incentives offered for good behavior and hard work (and on some plantations these could be considerable), the ultimate resort was always to punishment. The whip was an indispensable tool for establishing discipline, striking fear into the slave without incapacitating him. Floggings were as frequent as the master or overseer thought necessary, and the whip was sometimes used ingeniously. A North Carolina slave recalled that when he reached the age of ten, he had to pick fifty pounds of cotton a day; for each pound less he received a lash, for each pound over, a penny.

Although slaves were property, in theory they could not be slaughtered. Willful murder of slaves was illegal, but few Southern juries would convict an owner who had killed a slave. Thus, in the hands of the wrong master only the profit motive kept slaves alive. Slaves found no friend in the law, for they could not testify against whites in court or, of course, bring suit. Such a despotic system, by its very nature, could not be free of excesses. Any attempt by the slave to oppose the master's will resulted in severe retaliation. A slave who raised his hand against a white man could expect death.

Intricate and increasingly harsh slave codes became law in the nineteenth century, in order to clamp the bonds of slavery more firmly on the Negro and make manumission more difficult. Granting freedom to slaves at one's own death, a practice which in the late eighteenth century earned community approval for many planters, came to be scorned as treason to the Southern slave system, not merely a permissible way to dispose of private property. Some slave states by the 1850s would not allow emancipation; others required special legislative approval or required freed Negroes to leave the state.

THE SLAVE AS HUMAN BEING

Much self-serving nonsense has been written about slavery as a school in which Africans learned European ways and absorbed as much of an advanced and supposedly superior civilization as they were deemed capable of acquiring. Pro-slavery apologists such as William Grayson of South Carolina argued the point in verse:

Instructed thus, and in the only school
Barbarians ever know, a master's rule,
The Negro learns each civilizing art
That softens and subdues the savage heart.
. . . .
No happier system [can] wealth or virtue find,
To tame and elevate the Negro mind.

These apologists conveniently forgot or were ignorant of the fact that many slaves born in Africa were torn out of a civilized black culture. Moreover, by the late eighteenth century many other slaves were descended from four or five generations of black Americans, long removed from Africa. Nevertheless Southern publicists hammered away at the theme that the plantation was an educational institution, almost a charitable agency. But if the plantation was a school, it failed to provide any system of promotion, except for the chosen few, the mulatto servants who worked in the Big House and the drivers.

Rather than "civilize" the black man, slavery prevented him from developing a normal personality. Many became "Sambos," excessively meek, servile, and "happy-go-lucky" field hands, displaying exaggerated respect and affection for their masters. Unable to protect their women, preserve their families, or to head a household, black men could not assume normal male roles; and aggressive behavior courted certain punishment. Negroes learned that passive conformity and seeming contentment offered the surest way to accommodate to a system that treated them like animals, denied them elementary human rights, kept them from learning to read and write, and placed them at the mercy of whites who could beat, maim, and even kill them with impunity. The slave's passivity was a psychological defense mechanism which in turn reinforced the white Southerners' belief that Negroes were inferior, child-like creatures who needed "superior" white folk to care for them.

Not all Negroes conformed to this stereotype. Frederick Douglass escaped from slavery in Maryland to become a distinguished journalist, orator, and abolitionist; William Johnson was a respected and wealthy free barber in Natchez, Mississippi. These men were exceptions. The plantation system denied the Negro a future and forced him into dependence upon his master or overseer. The Negro had to resort to some psychic adjustments in view of the essentially terror-ridden nature of the society imposed on him.

Some modern writers have constructed an historical image of a rebellious, assertive, freedom-loving slave. But however strongly slaves cherished the idea of freedom, revolts occurred infrequently. There had been a revolt planned in Virginia in 1800, Gabriel Prosser's, and in the early 1820s Denmark Vesey's prospective rebellion in Charleston, South Carolina, had been betrayed by other slaves. This led to severe punitive measures although it is uncertain that an actual revolt had been planned. The most serious revolt, in terms of what actually happened and its psychological effect on white Southerners, occurred in Virginia in 1831, when a religious mystic and missionary, a Negro named Nat Turner, terrorized the county of Southampton as the leader of a slave revolt. With no real plan and little organization, the Turner rebels nevertheless killed over sixty whites before they were put down and Turner later executed.

Today many find it hard to understand why such an oppressive system produced so few revolts. Dispersed and surrounded by hostile whites, hounded by patrols that combed the neighborhood at night, and anxious over the likelihood that other slaves would warn their masters of an impending revolt, few slaves took up arms. Many of the insurrection scares proved to be figments of the imagination of guilt-ridden and apprehensive masters. Not one major outbreak occurred between the Nat Turner Revolt of 1831 and the Civil War. A few slaves like Douglass fled successfully from the border states, but escape was difficult and dangerous.

Passive resistance was more practical and more common. Slaves mishandled tools and farm animals, stole the master's goods, and worked as little as they could and still avoid punishment. These understandable acts fell far short of organized rebellion, although the frustration and resentment which produced them were real enough. Slaves seethed within at the permanent humiliation, degradation, and tyranny that denied their humanity. But controlled so tightly, most could do little else but break a hoe or run away for a few days.

Slavery attempted to rob the Negro of his humanity but it never succeeded in robbing him of a desire for freedom. When Union troops penetrated the South during the Civil War, the rush of slaves toward their lines demonstrated the true nature of the slaves' "loyalty" to their masters. Yet slavery left psychic wounds that ran so deep

into Negro personality that Samboism and habits of dependency survived long after slavery disappeared. This was not a permanent, biological condition, but slaves could not discard such habits at the very moment of emancipation. Slavery imprisoned the Negro far more than abolitionists believed then and far more than most Americans today will care to admit. The United States is still learning this in the black ghettoes of its cities where descendants of bondsmen find enormous difficulty overcoming the massive and cumulative deprivations of their past.

Try as they might to regard blacks as chattel property, little different from a horse or a mule, Southerners knew better. The Negro remained a human being; even the most rabid apologist for slavery recognized that fact. A slave who committed murder stood trial; but if executed, his master received compensation from the state for loss of property. A Tennessee judge reflected this ambivalence when he declared: "A Slave is not in the condition of a horse. . . . He has mental capacities, and an immortal principle in his nature."

The need to define slavery in both human and property terms led to long, learned debates on the innate capacities of the races of man. Needless to say, the outcome of the debates—affirmation of Negro racial inferiority—was never in doubt. Enlightenment philosophers, from John Locke to Thomas Jefferson, accepted and exalted human equality. But in the pre-Civil War period some American scientists discovered that some humans were more equal than others. This was not simply a Southern plot in pseudoscience, however, since some prominent Northern professors argued that the Negro was of a lower order, intellectually and culturally, than the Caucasian. This provided scholarly support for what most white Americans already believed. "There is a physical difference between the white and black races," declared Abraham Lincoln in 1858 in a speech attacking slavery, "which I believe will forever forbid the two races living together on terms of social and political equality. And inasmuch as they cannot so live, while they do remain together there must be the position of superior and inferior, and I as much as any other man am in favor of having the superior position assigned to the white race."

In essence the American Negro lacked all but

a technical humanity. Despite his contributions to the building of America, the slave was not allowed to dream the American Dream. Caught in this dead end, he might lapse into a sullen, zombie-like detachment, or he could giggle himself into that terrible state of false hilarity and dependence which seemed to amuse the lower forms of Caucasians so much. All Americans are still paying the price for this questionable form of entertainment.

THE ECONOMICS OF SLAVERY

American slavery involved more than a social system. Its prime function was to provide labor in an agricultural economy. Whether or not it operated efficiently and profitably has generated heated controversy ever since slavery became a leading issue in American politics. Participants in the disputes of the 1850s, and the historians who followed them, produced a bewildering number of variations on the theme, "Was slavery profitable?" Several elements have to be separated before the question can be answered. Was slavery simply a plantation-based business enterprise? Or should its profitability also be measured in terms of the economic growth of the South compared to the North?

Before the Civil War, proslavery apologists hesitated to argue that slavery made a few large planters rich for fear of alienating the many impoverished whites. On the other hand, antislavery writers contended that the South's economic backwardness resulted from slavery, and slavery alone. Hinton R. Helper, a North Carolinian who produced a best seller entitled *The Impending Crisis* (1857), insisted that Southern agriculture and industry lagged far behind the North because of slavery. Helper's book made him famous, but branded him a traitor to his section, and he had to leave the South. The proslavery men continued to assert that slavery, in addition to civilizing Negroes, produced economic blessings as well: Southern cotton provided America's principal export staple; Northerners, if they valued their own economic interests, should help strengthen Southern slavery, not attack it.

Popular mythology about the Old South has it that all planters were immensely wealthy. This was not the case, though some profited more from slavery than others. Southern planters were not generally experiencing poverty before the Civil War, although by the 1850s only the planters of the Southwest were making fabulous profits from new, rich lands. This accounts for the fact that slave prices continued to rise and a male field hand cost $1500 in 1860. Those wielding power in the South regarded slavery as a form of economic enterprise which reinforced social standing and political power, and its survival rested on more than simple economic self-interest.

The South was bound up in slavery, constricted by the myths of the institution and the requirements of the master-slave relation. A New England textile manufacturer might make larger profits on his investment of an equal amount of capital but the Southern planter did not want to own a cotton mill. The idea repelled him. As for his chronic debt, although farmers are usually in debt, the planter could pretend to believe that a further reduction in the tariff would ease his economic problems. Southern leaders enjoyed a good life and the fruits of toil, most of it other people's toil. The planter was clearly the lord of his small domain. He enjoyed a high standard of living made possible by the labor of others living in degradation. As one Southern historian puts it: "The plantation supplied its owner with many of the necessities of life, and the planter often had numerous house and yard servants to give a pleasurable distinction and dignity to his mode of life, and to relieve him and his family from physical labor."

Perhaps planters were purposely poor bookkeepers. Slaveowning in a plantation setting offered more to a socially conscious Southerner than economic rewards alone. Some wealthy Southern merchants purchased land and slaves, in the manner of eighteenth-century English merchants who bought country estates as a step up the social ladder. If slavery was a burdensome, decaying system (as later claimed), it showed few signs of internal collapse—certainly not in the 1850s when slave prices soared well in advance of the general price rise, and when railroads were opening up new cotton lands. Even the older slave states of the Eastern seaboard enjoyed a mild agricultural boom in that decade, creating a demand for more slaves.

Although slavery enriched a handful of planters, it retarded Southern economic growth. Slaves worked inefficiently and the low productivity of their labor contributed to Southern economic backwardness. Depleted soils required a more industrious and educated work force than that provided by most slaves. The slave system also created a contempt for manual labor among whites, especially the landless poor, hard pressed to find any distinction between themselves and slaves other than skin color. Charles Sumner, an antislavery man from Massachusetts, charged that under slavery "the whole social fabric is disorganized; labor loses its dignity; industry sickens; education finds no schools; and all the land . . . is impoverished." While Northern agriculture welcomed the introduction of labor-saving machinery and farm implements, the South, with a large and permanently bound unskilled work force, proved less receptive. And the heavy capital investment in slaves further impeded diversification and mechanization.

For decades the myth persisted that only the invention of the cotton gin saved a dying institution from extinction, since Southerners would quickly have abolished slavery as unprofitable. This claim ignores the fact that slavery and Southern agriculture were *not* declining at the time of the gin's introduction in 1794. Planters apparently had no idea that slavery was doomed. "Without Negroes," argued a South Carolinian, speaking for the proslavery Southerners of this early national period who are seldom quoted, "this state would degenerate into one of the most contemptible in the Union. Negroes are our wealth, our only natural resource." Southern agricultural production rose, and generally high farm prices made additional slave labor all the more desirable. The subsequent reign of King Cotton brought enormous change, but it did not put new life into slavery. It lifted the South's agriculture from one plateau to another.

But slavery did prevent widespread Southern industrialization. Instead of an agricultural revolution, a shift to urbanization, and the creation of a domestic market, slavery riveted the impoverished Southern peasantry, black and white, to the soil without purchasing power. Southern industry, where it existed, usually remained a servant of immediate plantation needs. These small-scale operations never seriously competed with Northern factories, even in basic items needed in the South. In 1860 only 7 percent of Southerners lived in cities and towns, while 35 percent of the population of the Northeast was urbanized. Export of two-thirds of the Southern cotton crop supported American foreign trade, but northeastern capitalists controlled that as well.

Whatever its dangers and economic drawbacks, slavery provided the foundation for Southern society. It knit together whites, rich and poor; it defined social aspirations and made some men rich and powerful; it gave whites control over a despised and feared black population; and ultimately it defined the region's identity, becoming the main source of Southern nationalism. Southerners considered slavery indispensable, although the years after the Civil War demonstrated that exploitation of Negro labor did not require the retention of slavery. By the middle of the nineteenth century, Southerners were ready to give their lives in its defense.

Though slavery retarded the Southern economy as a whole, Southerners never judged the peculiar institution strictly in terms of dollars and cents. Neither did the enemies of slavery.

THE WHITE MAN'S BURDEN

The early and successful introduction of Negro slave labor into the New World shaped the development of much of American history. An important labor problem had been solved, but the harmful effects of slavery on American society and politics would be felt for centuries. A chronic shortage of labor in colonial times meant that very few people cried out against the enslavement of one human being by another, and many biblical and historical precedents existed for those who wished to rationalize such enslavement. Before the Revolution, Quakers were almost alone in appealing to the consciences of their fellow Americans by calling for an end to slavery.

The Founding Fathers and Slavery

But slavery grew, and the institution, if not the black man, prospered in America. A sustained opposition did not appear until the last third of the eighteenth century, when some critics began to draw logical implications from the dominant natural rights philosophy of the time. The American elite, many Southerners included, agreed that slavery was evil, concentrating their condemnation on the slave trade. They felt that although it might not be possible to abolish slavery, at least its growth could be checked. In the quarter century after the Declaration of Independence had asserted that "all men are created equal," seven Northern states provided for immediate or gradual emancipation—even states like New York and New Jersey where slavery though minor was still profitable—and this took place because of a growing and dominant antislavery opinion in the North. Usually the children of slaves were freed at maturity. In the South masters could free their slaves, and some did, while further importation of slaves was generally banned, partly out of fear of the growing imbalance between the white and black populations along the coast.

The federal government's role had been carefully limited. At the Constitutional Convention in 1787, the founders made the protection of slavery an integral part of the compact. The debates at Philadelphia revealed the underlying reality of Southern politics, despite the challenge of Enlightenment philosophy. According to Madison, "the institution of slavery and its consequences formed the line of demarcation" between the contending groups of states at the convention. The Constitution counted three-fifths of the slaves as persons for purposes of congressional representation, thereby increasing Southern influence, and Congress could not interfere with the foreign slave trade for twenty years. The new federal government promptly adopted a fugitive slave law to help owners regain their lost property. Slavery thus was left primarily in state hands, enjoying the protection of the Constitution and federal law. Abolitionists who later burned copies of the Constitution in public, calling it a "covenant with the Devil," were attacked for fanaticism and lack of patriotism, but in fact the Union rested on an agreement which promised noninterference with slavery.

Yet at the same time that they demanded and received protection for their peculiar institution, some Southerners of the revolutionary generation criticized slavery. It was no accident that expressions of moral scruples, vague though they were, occurred at a time when Southerners expected to dominate the new Union and felt that their institutions were secure from attack.

Some of the South's revolutionary leaders, especially Virginians such as Jefferson and Washington, found it painful to reconcile the nation's commitment to the Rights of Man, the cause for which Americans justified their fight for independence, with the enslavement of millions. These Southern critics worried as much about the harmful effects of slavery on whites as the misery it inflicted on blacks. But though some toyed with schemes for gradual emancipation or wholesale removal of blacks, such plans proved impractical. The South's wealth and way of life seemed indissolubly linked to an institution which may have been evil, but which came to be regarded as a necessity. When faced with challenges, or apparent challenges, to the slave system, Southern politicians closed ranks (some still deploring the necessity for such action) in support of slavery. There thus existed side by side the theoretical agreement that slavery was evil and an insistence on resisting any moves which might jeopardize its future.

Virginia, the leading Southern state at the turn of the century, economically and intellectually, was not especially revolutionized by the introduction of cotton culture. Its leading men often referred to the evil of slavery, and in the 1780s the legislature prohibited the introduction of more slaves, making manumission easier than before. But a reverse trend soon set in. By the close of the Jeffersonian era slavery had as many vigorous defenders in Virginia as in the rest of the South. John Taylor, the philosopher of Jeffersonian agrarianism, devoted many pages in his long books to defending the institution. After the discovery of a slave plot by Gabriel Prosser and his followers near Richmond in 1800, Virginia enacted repressive measures to control its Negro population, slave and free. Virginians found slavery workable and feasible. They were able to keep their libertarian ideals and their authoritarian practices operating side by side. Racism provided the means and rationalization for maintaining a society which blended the incompatible elements of liberty and slavery.

The Travail of Southern Slavery

The Missouri Compromise crisis of 1820 again revealed Southerners' touchiness over any attempt to restrict slavery. As already noted, these debates included defenses of slavery as a positive good which benefited everyone concerned. Southerners would develop and extend this argument, especially during the 1850s. However, it existed long before William Lloyd Garrison and other radical abolitionists posed a direct threat to the slaveowners, and it had not been voiced frequently before because of the absence of sustained attacks on slavery.

Yet no matter how hard they tried, Southerners could never quite convince themselves, let alone Northerners, of the virtue of slavery. "We are human beings of the nineteenth century and slavery has to go, of course," admitted the wife of a planter. The creation of a closed society in the South after 1830—forbidding free discussion of slavery—was ostensibly designed to prevent abolitionist propaganda from infecting the blacks. But the illiterate slaves were unlikely readers of antislavery literature. The repression was aimed principally at stopping Southern whites from talking or even thinking critically about the institution.

As Americans, Southerners believed that "all men are created equal." And as human beings they could not avoid recognizing blacks as people. For example, an Alabama white woman pined after the death of her slave, a former nurse: "When I saw that Death had the mastery, I laid my hands over her eyes, and in tears and fervor prayed that God would cause us to meet in happiness in another world. I knew, at that solemn moment, that color made no difference, but that her life would have been precious, if I could have saved it, as if she had been white as snow." Such sentiments alarmed slavery's defenders. "What means the womanish qualms of conscience," scoffed a South Carolinian in 1831, "which we so often witness among many of our own citizens as to the justice and morality of keeping men in bondage?" Doubts plagued not only the upper classes but

also backcountry farmers such as the one Frederick Law Olmstead, a Yankee journalist touring in the South, encountered in the 1850s:

I wouldn't like to hev em free, if they gwine to hang around . . . because they is so monstrous lazy. . . . Now suppose they was free, you see, they'd all think themselves just as good as we. . . . Howd you like to hev a nigger steppin' up to your darter? Of course you wouldn't; and that's the reason I wouldn't like to hev 'em free; but I tell you, I don't think it's right to hev em slaves; that's the fact—t'aint right to keep em as they is.

Southern ambivalence toward slavery showed itself in many ways, including the efforts of some owners to emancipate their slaves and colonize them in Africa. Colonization was the most concrete expression of Southern antislavery feeling. The American Colonization Society (1817) called for gradual emancipation and transportation of free Negroes to Africa and the newly established colony of Liberia. It appealed to all Americans north and south to contribute, contending that slavery was a national problem.

But few Southerners were willing to sustain the loss of freeing their slaves. And those who did often could not afford the cost of transportation. Nor were Northerners willing to share these burdens. The ACS aimed at colonizing 50,000 free blacks a year, or slightly more than the annual natural increase of slaves, at a cost of $1 million. The most they raised in one year, however, was $43,000. The total number of blacks sent was probably around 4000 out of more than three million slaves. Southern states' rights principles prevented the federal government from playing an important role in these operations but the ACS did prove instrumental in selecting Liberia as the colonizing site on the west coast of Africa.

In addition to the cost involved, it proved difficult to convince free Negroes to migrate to Africa. America was their home, and Africa remained as unknown and forbidding to most black Americans as it was to whites. Supporters of colonization regarded themselves as antislavery men, yet they, like most white Americans, believed in the theory of a degraded black race, the idea that the free Negro could not be integrated into American society. The ACS was to be the instrument for ridding the country of free Negroes, regarded as potentially dangerous, and general troublemakers. "Colonization deals only with the free man of color," assured Henry Clay, president of the ACS, "and that with his own free, voluntary consent. It has nothing to do with slavery. It disturbs no man's property, seeks to impair no power in the slave states, nor to attribute any to the general government. All its actions . . . are voluntary, depending upon the blessings of Providence."

The ACS enjoyed a temporary popularity, especially in the 1820s and in the border slave states, but colonization clearly could not provide a solution. Some who had first accepted it began later to call for a more direct approach to the problem, to demand the end of slavery. The center of antislavery sentiment shifted to the North.

THE NONCOMPROMISERS

Even at the height of the ACS's popularity, a handful of Americans began to demand abolition of slavery. In 1829 a Boston free Negro, David Walker, published a pamphlet attacking colonization and urging slaves to revolt. Few slaves could have read or even heard of Walker's slim pamphlet, but Southerners reacted violently. Several states restricted the circulation of antislavery publications, calling them incendiary documents, but, by quoting abolitionists if only to denounce them, Southerners unwittingly spread the antislavery propaganda themselves. Many more Southern planters than slaves read abolitionist publications.

The most effective abolitionist propaganda came from a weekly newspaper, *The Liberator,* established in Boston in 1831 by William Lloyd Garrison. Garrison had helped a Quaker abolitionist publish an antislavery sheet in Baltimore three years earlier. An editorial, attacking a Baltimore city official, landed the young abolitionist in jail. Returning to his native Massachusetts, Garrison started his own radical abolitionist paper, scorning all compromise and intending to end the "conspiracy of silence" in the North regarding slavery. Garrison's first defiant editorial pro-

claimed his noncompromising stand: "Let Southern oppressors tremble . . . let their Northern apologists tremble . . . I will be as harsh as truth, and as uncompromising as justice. On this subject, I do not wish to think, or speak, or write with moderation. . . . I am in earnest—I will not equivocate—I will not excuse—I will not retreat a single inch—AND I WILL BE HEARD."

Garrison's enemies made him famous. Southern newspapers constantly reprinted his most vitriolic articles. The attempt to silence Garrison and restrict freedom of the press succeeded only in bringing him support from many otherwise hostile Northern sources. As abolitionism grew in the North, Southern fears of Garrison and other radicals intensified. Southerners always lived in fear of slave rebellion. Although few large-scale revolts had occurred, Southerners spoke and acted as if they lived under a constant threat. Abolitionist attacks heightened Southern paranoia just as they intensified guilt feelings. Most of all Southerners feared that attacks on slavery would undermine white solidarity, already strained by the contradition between slavery and liberal democracy.

Terror spread throughout the South. Nat Turner's uprising in Virginia in 1831 confirmed Southern fears that the writings of Walker and Garrison were indeed incendiary. Surely happy and contented slaves would never revolt unless instigated by outside agitators. Southern states tightened repressive slave codes, and a movement in the Virginia legislature for gradual emancipation collapsed. From that point on, Virginia, once the home of the leading Southern doubters of slavery, made it a crime for free Negroes to receive abolitionist papers through the mail.

The South was rapidly becoming a closed society. Southerners who dissented on slavery were persecuted, and the South demanded Northern cooperation to bar abolitionist tracts from the mail and antislavery petitions from being received by Congress, clear violations of civil liberties guaranteed by the Constitution. When abolitionists attempted to petition the federal government for an end to slavery, Southerners called upon Congress to refuse to accept the documents. Congress complied, adopting a regulation called the gag rule in 1836. In the House of Representatives, former President John Quincy Adams led the fight to repeal the rule and to maintain his constituents' right of petition. But politicians of both parties, hoping to keep slavery out of national politics, supported the gag rule and it remained in force for ten years.

Freedom of speech and the press, open use of the mails, and the right of petition were thus compromised in the interest of slavery. But abolitionism had become part of the powerful humanitarian impulse of the time, invigorated by the growth of the antislavery movement in Britain which resulted in the abolition of slavery in the British West Indies in 1833. Southern attempts at repression made plausible the abolitionist contention that white men could not keep their freedom so long as black men remained in chains.

Agreement on the wickedness of slavery did not unite American abolitionists, however. Abolition spawned a host of organizations, each employing different means to achieve their common end. In Boston, Garrison dominated the New England Anti-Slavery Society, the most radical group, demanding immediate, uncompensated emancipation, yet rejecting political action to bring this about. The American Anti-Slavery Society, formed in 1833, assumed a more moderate tone and was strong in New York and in the Midwest, which proved productive fields for abolitionist missionary work, especially those sections settled by New Englanders.

A leading antislavery missionary was the powerful revival preacher, Charles G. Finney. Finney and Theodore D. Weld successfully spread the abolition gospel throughout New York and Ohio. In 1839, Weld published *Slavery As It Is,* a compilation drawn from Southern newspapers, which depicted the brutality of the slave system by using the slaveowners' own testimony (such as runaway slave advertisements describing scars on the fugitive's back). Weld's book provided some of the inspiration and much of the detail for Harriet Beecher Stowe's great antislavery novel, *Uncle Tom's Cabin,* published in 1852. The high point of the blending of abolitionism and religious revivalism came in the mid-1830s. After the panic of 1837 funds for abolitionist causes were hard to raise, and popular interest declined.

Garrison and his followers began devoting time to other reforms as well. The futility of moral exhortation alone against slavery, and the tendency of some abolitionists to embrace wide varieties of mid-nineteenth-century reform (from temperance to women's suffrage) led to a split over tactics. The crisis came to a head in 1840 when Garrison tried to capture the national organization: the majority refused to allow the antislavery movement to become a sounding board for other, unpopular reforms, or to accept Garrison's dictation. The New Yorkers insisted on concentrating on the one great evil, slavery, and they entered politics by forming the Liberty party.

THE AGITATOR'S LOT

Regardless of tactics, whether moderate or intemperate in language, abolitionists frightened and repelled most Americans. Conservatives, many of them contributors to the ACS, were troubled by rapid changes in Jacksonian America which they felt threatened their power. They rejected abolition as a disruptive force in an already unstable society. The white working class feared the competition of the free Negro, and businessmen wanted nothing to disturb trade between the sections. A deep and widespread hostility to abolitionists existed, and showed itself spectacularly in the middle 1830s in a series of antiabolitionist riots and mobbings. Mobs in dozens of Northern cities and towns, usually led by the communities' leading citizens, broke up abolitionist meetings and sometimes destroyed their homes and the presses which had printed antislavery pamphlets. Garrison was led through the streets of Boston in 1835 with a rope around his waist and police took him into custody to protect him from the demonstrators. Two years later another mob murdered an abolitionist editor, Elijah P. Lovejoy, in Alton, Illinois—and in so doing provided the movement with a martyr.

Mob action also disrupted New York City several times, and for reasons that graphically revealed the response of Establishment America to antislavery agitation. New York abolitionists were led by Lewis and Arthur Tappan, New Englanders who had come to the city to make a fortune as importing merchants. They helped organize the American Anti-Slavery Society, and paid most of its bills.

This group, relatively moderate compared with the Garrisonians, still stirred up intense hatred among the general population. Many Negrophobes had joined the ACS in order to be rid of free blacks, and the abolitionist attack on slavery *and* colonization infuriated them. Moreover, the "printing revolution," the introduction of high-speed steam presses which could turn out tens of thousands of low-cost pamphlets in a day, allowed abolitionists to spread their unwelcome word far more effectively than ever before. The nation, North and South, seemed to be inundated with antislavery propaganda. Abolitionists further flaunted traditional standards by enlisting women and children in their work, and they allowed blacks to join the abolitionist societies.

Antiabolitionists denounced the reformers as dupes of a British plot to weaken America, claiming that any program which upset slavery would produce racial amalgamation, and they fanned popular prejudices until mobs took over, wrecking the Tappans' property and roaming New York's Negro districts in order to beat blacks. For the mob instigators, abolitionism had become a scapegoat, on which frustrations generated by a rapidly changing society could be conveniently vented.

Yet abolitionists refused to desert their cause even in the face of such hatred. Instead these attacks ultimately gained them fresh support, since assaults on the life or liberty of an abolitionist exercising his constitutional rights won the sympathy of some citizens who otherwise were antagonistic or indifferent to the attack on slavery itself.

Abolitionism and violence seemed to go hand in hand. Radical antislavery men and women spoke out against a moral evil which provoked violence against them, and the abolitionists, many of them pacifists, were blamed for the disturbance. In opposing slavery abolitionists were uncertain as to the best way to wage their campaign. During the 1830s when dozens of shortlived abolition societies appeared, all agreed in condemning violence. Garrison and the New Yorkers predicted that the bondsman would find freedom, but not by the sword. Unsuccessful slave revolts would only antagonize Northern whites, and abolitionists still believed that they would capture Northern public opinion. When abolitionists were mobbed, Garrison's advice was simple: turn the other cheek. Elijah Lovejoy, the martyred abolitionist editor, had taken up arms to protect himself. Eastern abolitionists mourned Lovejoy's death, but they regretted his resort to arms.

During the 1840s, the Garrisonians made pacifism and nonresistance cardinal points of their antislavery strategy. If these ideas still seem Utopian, many forms of Utopia, secular and religious, were then popular. The nonresistants believed that all government institutions were coercive and should be ignored. Most Americans considered such ideas eccentric, yet the perfectionist ideology helped sustain the fanatical faith of the abolitionists.

Other antislavery men decided to enter politics. Those who formed the Liberty party in 1840 feared identification of antislavery with perfectionist anarchism and embraced political action. By the later 1840s more and more leading abolitionists rejected nonresistance as impractical. In the next decade nonviolent abolitionism collapsed. The emergence of the slavery question at the center of American politics during and after the Mexican War undermined Garrisonian pacifism and his opposition to political action. At the same time, a new corps of antislavery leaders emerged in the late 1840s, men who had not engaged in the doctrinal debates of the preceding twenty years and who entered politics with a primary commitment to block the spread of slavery into the territories.

Nonresistance had not worked. By the 1850s most abolitionists had had enough of moral suasion. Many politicians were now willing to cooperate with antislavery men, but not along extremist lines. When political antislavery swallowed up abolitionism, it also diluted the extreme ideas of some abolitionists. Once antislavery began to compete directly with other political interests, noncoercion and perfectionism could not survive.

Abolitionism was but one part of the antislavery movement. The "fanatics" were never more than a small and usually disparaged minority. Yet the abolitionists, the vanguard in the fight against slavery, had to be tough. Whether caught helping runaway slaves to escape or distributing abolitionist literature, the antislavery militants faced social disapproval and physical danger. Most Americans, though troubled, simply wished to forget about slavery; the abolitionists would not let them. Keepers of the nation's conscience, they encountered hatred and violence because so many of their tormentors knew at heart that they were right. Americans, North and South, could not ignore abolitionism because it flowed from the mainstream of American thought, the belief in liberty and universal betterment. Abolitionism thus operated within a favorable, though not always readily apparent, consensus of progressive opinion. Despite powerful opposition to the Northern abolition societies, fear of disruption of the Union, and anti-Negro racism, most Americans recognized the evil of slavery.

Thus abolitionists drew the fire of society as much for the relentless and "antisocial" way in which they pursued their aims as for those aims themselves. They demanded the kind of America promised in the Declaration of Independence, and they demanded it right away, not at some distant point in time when brotherhood swayed the minds and hearts of men. They insisted that Americans face the fact that their commitment to liberty was irreconcilable with the existence of slavery. Given this contradition, and a free society, a radical antislavery movement was inevitable. What was surprising, and shameful, was that so few abolitionists appeared in a society of so many libertarians.

Chapter 14
The Politics of Slavery, 1841–1860

The emergence of two strong, nationwide parties in the Jacksonian era, parties committed to bridging sectional differences, did much to nationalize American politics. But in the mid-1840s the country learned that loyalty to local institutions and values still remained powerful enough to challenge the survival of the party system and the Union itself. Since the Confederation period Americans realized that the United States could not exist as a mere grouping of independent nation-states. To prevent this the Constitution had created a national government of strong powers, although within a federal system which left considerable power in the hands of the states. States' rights mattered then, much more so than today; yet the founding fathers hoped that the basic conflict arising from a division of power between the states and the nation had been resolved, and that the federal system could accommodate local differences within a strong, unified nation.

By the middle of the nineteenth century, the federal solution was in danger of foundering. Try as they might to keep slavery and sectionalism out of national politics, politicians felt the force of sectional pressures that made it harder than ever to reconcile states' rights with national sovereignty. Southerners, increasingly a minority in the Union, took refuge in states' rights as the best defense of minority interests, at the same time that growing numbers of Northerners looked to Washington to block the expansion of slavery. During these years national institutions could no longer cope with the disintegrating force of sectional interest. Private organizations, the churches, for example, split along sectional lines. Nationwide business organizations did not yet exist, but although merchants and manufacturers tried to continue business as usual, they too ultimately felt the divisive effect of sectionalism. Political parties tried especially hard to maintain the status quo. But the clear-cut, Democrat-versus-Whig division of 1840 soon disappeared. The Whigs went down first, expiring slowly during the 1850s. Democrats held on but they also split

sectionally on the eve of the Civil War. A new Northern party, the Republican, appeared to replace the Whigs, and attracted support from members of both older parties.

This all took place during a period of marked social instability, accompanying economic and territorial expansion. The population shifts of the early nineteenth century grew more intense as a result of improved transportation. As important as the shift of farmers from one state to another and the movement from east to west, was the growth of metropolitan centers. Americans were psychologically unprepared to face problems of urban growth and urban poverty. Most of the hundreds of thousands of immigrants who entered the United States each year were poor, and many of them crowded into cities. Tension between the native sons and newcomers produced political nativism in the 1850s, further weakening attempts to cope with sectional problems through established political channels.

Political consensus broke down when Americans felt that their fundamental interests and values were threatened by other Americans. Differences over the tariff, banking, or the public lands could be and had been adjusted through compromise; moral differences between those who upheld the morality of slavery and others, equally convinced, who denounced it, were not so susceptible to compromise. When the nation became morally polarized, as it did in the 1850s, the party system based on compromise disintegrated. The politics of morality then produced a new political alignment and organizations which could not preserve the Union without a civil war. The founding fathers and their Democratic and Whig successors in the next generation knew that once unleashed, moral passions can prevent men who differ from living together in peace. They failed to realize that a republic conceived in liberty and founded on the moral principle that all men are created equal yet which kept four million black people in bondage could not permanently postpone the day of reckoning, however sincere or artful the congressional compromisers might be.

A MONTH OF WHIGGERY

When the Whigs took over in 1841 a long and successful reign and a truly competitive two-party system seemed likely. The party finally made sense. Whigs were mainly former National Republicans, but during the 1830s a temporary coalition with Calhoun obscured their nationalist bias, creating the impression that Whigs were hybrids, united only by hatred of Jackson. In 1838, Calhoun rejoined the Democratic party, the true home of states' righters. In exchange, Whigs recruited support from Conservatives who feared the increasing Democratic hostility toward banking and commerce. Also, many Antimasonic leaders, such as Thurlow Weed of New York and Thaddeus Stevens of Pennsylvania, had become Whigs by 1840, bringing with them organizational talents and gut-fighter temperaments foreign to National Republican campaigns. Finally, the Southern Whigs were no longer a purely states' rights group. Many Southern merchants and large-scale planters cast their lot with the party and supported most of its nationalistic economic goals.

William Henry Harrison's inaugural address in March 1841 all but mortgaged the presidency to the Whig congressional leadership. He promised to use the veto only as a last resort, and he appointed a cabinet made up mainly of supporters of Henry Clay, the man who hoped to run the Harrison administration from the Senate. But within a month Harrison became the first president to die in office. Vice-president John Tyler, a states' rights Virginian who had been added to the Whig ticket as a supposed friend of Clay, then took over. Tyler insisted that he was the president and that he had full control over the executive branch. In pursuing his own policies he not only destroyed Clay's hopes, but he may have destroyed a political party as well. The Whigs' Golden Age lasted no longer than from the inauguration of Harrison to his death 29 days later. Despite its broad social base in the North and the South and among rural and urban constituents, the Whig party succumbed in the 1840s to internal divisions and sectional stress, a fate that would overtake the Democrats a decade later.

John Tyler, through conviction and tempera-ment, failed completely in the role of party leader. This failure arose partly from the unfulfilled expectations of Whig leaders. Harrison had indicated he might allow each cabinet member one vote on policy making. Tyler quickly scotched that idea. He also rejected the principal items of Whig legislation. Congress had prepared the way by repealing Van Buren's Independent Treasury in August 1841, and handing Tyler a bill chartering The Fiscal Bank of the United States, another thinly disguised national bank. Tyler vetoed the bill as unwise and unconstitutional. A second bill for a "fiscal corporation" met the same end. In September every member of the cabinet except Secretary of State Daniel Webster resigned and denounced Tyler for bad faith. A short while later, the Whigs officially read the president out of their party.

The Tyler administration marked an unhappy interlude in the history of American political parties. The turnover of personnel in Tyler's cabinet was frequent. This reflected his weakness and inability to draw on outstanding politicians, rather than the firm exercise of presidential power, as had been the case with Jackson's cabinet shifts. Tyler's tenure, moreover, was shaky because in the 1840s the two major political parties, the Whigs and the Democrats, enjoyed roughly equal strength and were well organized in all sections.

Thus under Tyler both parties treaded water, awaiting the next election in 1844. The dominant Whig politicians worked to recapture the nominal leadership of the party from Tyler who did his best to construct a personal political power base, but even heavy-handed use of federal patronage was no substitute for long-standing organization. Tyler, a Virginia states' rights Democrat, looked for intellectual support and for administrative manpower to his home state, then declining in influence. He could recruit only a weak "officeholders" party. Whig division and Tyler's ineffectiveness helped the Democrats win the congressional elections of 1842 and started them rebounding after the disaster of 1840. Returning prosperity helped the Democrats escape the onus for the economic collapse in 1837. As a result the "normal" Democratic majority reappeared.

POLK AND EXPANSION

The election of 1844 shaped up as a contest between ex-President Martin Van Buren and Henry Clay. Both men, subscribing to the gentlemen's agreement existing among professional politicians during the years of the second American party system that slavery be kept out of national politics, agreed to oppose the annexation of Texas, which had revolted from Mexico in 1836. The Whigs duly nominated Clay, but at the Democratic convention, Van Buren's enemies and those who supported Texas annexation used this opposition to prevent his nomination. A Democratic nominee needed a two-thirds vote of delegates, a rule which gave Southerners a veto. Van Buren could not muster the votes. In his place expansionists supported James K. Polk of Tennessee. Polk had the support of Jackson, who from his Tennessee retirement urged the selection of an annexationist. Polk was that and more. His slogan, "The Reoccupation of Oregon, and the Reannexation of Texas," won him the nomination on the ninth ballot.

Foreign affairs counted for more in that election than in any since the War of 1812. Americans still looked inward, or westward, but expansion now conflicted with the interests of other powers. Without a political accommodation, American expansion in Oregon (claimed by Britain) and in Texas (claimed by Mexico) would require the use of force. During the campaign, some expansionists demanded all of the Oregon Territory, chanting "Fifty-Four, Forty, or Fight," indicating the northernmost boundary of Oregon. Americans disagreed, however, over the proper limits of the nation's boundaries, and over how much diplomatic prestige and military force, if any, should be risked to back up their territorial claims. The closeness of the election results pointed up this national division. Had Clay carried New York he would have won. In that state the political abolitionist or Liberty party candidate, James G. Birney, received enough usually Whig votes to give Polk the state and the presidency.

Tyler, now a lame-duck president, wished to conclude his term with the annexation of Texas. He had supported Polk and considered the election an affirmative referendum on annexation. Tyler urged Congress simply to declare Texas annexed by resolution of both houses, thus avoiding the two-thirds Senate vote required for approval of treaties. A few days before leaving office, Tyler had his wish. Texas joined the Union as a state, bypassing completely the territorial stage.

Polk was a loyal Jacksonian who in a single but significant administration reestablished the Jacksonian programs. In 1846, the Democrats revived the Independent Treasury, an institution which continued to function until the Federal Reserve Act of 1913. And Congress lowered the tariff in 1846. Polk also used the veto to prevent expenditure of federal money for internal improvements. Thus he achieved three principal Democratic legislative objectives on the bank, tariff, and public works.

Despite this, Polk was most concerned with foreign affairs, first with the British over Oregon, then with the Mexicans over Texas. Only the second controversy brought war, but in both cases war threats circulated freely. During the early 1840s several thousand American settlers had gone to Oregon, and the United States (which had earlier offered to settle the boundary at the forty-ninth parallel) now claimed all of the disputed land. Polk called for an end to joint occupation of Oregon by Britain and the United States, and Congress agreed in April 1846.

Although the British initially adopted a tough attitude, there was no third war with Britain. In 1846 a new British ministry proved more conciliatory than its predecessor. Parliament's repeal of the Corn Laws meant greater British dependence upon foreign grain imports and gave added importance to good trade relations with the United States. A British declaration of noninterference in the Mexican-American dispute led the way to acceptance of an Oregon treaty. During the negotiations, Polk took the unusual step of seeking the Senate's advice before presenting the treaty for ratification. Under its terms both countries accepted a compromise boundary line drawn along the forty-ninth parallel. The slogan "Fifty-Four, Forty, or Fight!" had been more of an alliterative bargaining point than an actual threat. Both sides were prepared to accept the forty-ninth at the right moment. That moment came during the summer of 1846.

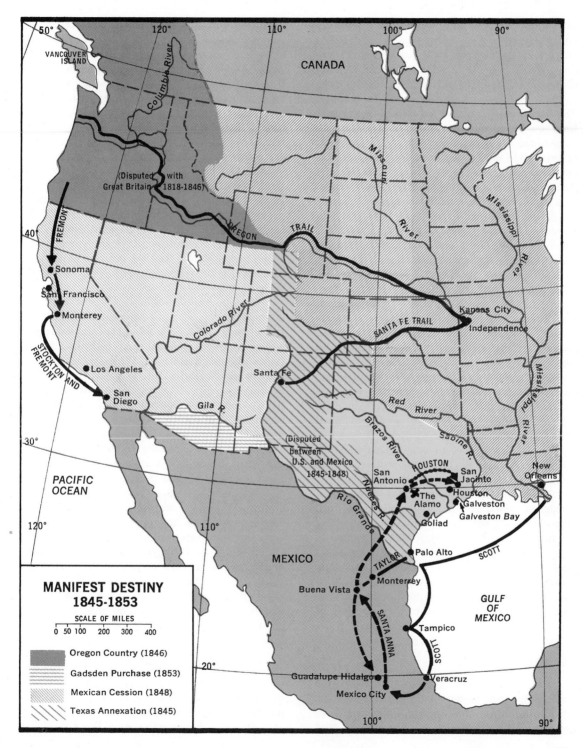

MANIFEST DESTINY
1845-1853

SCALE OF MILES

0 50 100 200 300 400

Oregon Country (1846)

Gadsden Purchase (1853)

Mexican Cession (1848)

Texas Annexation (1845)

VANCOUVER ISLAND

CANADA

Columbia River

(Disputed with Great Britain 1818-1846)

FREMONT

OREGON TRAIL

Missouri River

Mississippi River

Sonoma

San Francisco

Monterey

STOCKTON AND FREMONT

Los Angeles

San Diego

Colorado River

Gila R.

Santa Fe

SANTA FE TRAIL

Kansas City

Independence

Red River

Mississippi River

Sabine R.

PACIFIC OCEAN

(Disputed between U.S. and Mexico 1845-1848)

Brazos River

Nueces R.

HOUSTON

San Antonio

The Alamo

Goliad

San Jacinto

Houston

Galveston

Galveston Bay

New Orleans

Rio Grande

MEXICO

TAYLOR

Palo Alto

Buena Vista

Monterrey

SANTA ANNA

SCOTT

GULF OF MEXICO

Tampico

SCOTT

Guadalupe Hidalgo

Veracruz

Mexico City

While Congress had been debating the Oregon question, a New York paper published an article called "The True Title." Its editor, a Democrat named John L. O'Sullivan, argued that all of Oregon belonged to the United States. Its right to it was legally sound, and even sounder morally. The American claim, asserted O'Sullivan, sprang from "our manifest destiny to overspread, and to possess the whole of the continent. . . . The God of nature and nations has marked it for our own, and with his blessing we will firmly maintain the incontestable rights he has given." O'Sullivan was a booster, a salesman whose product was American territorial expansion. But although he tended toward bombast, his views were not isolated; many editors and politicians shared his vision and his territorial expectations.

The phrase "manifest destiny" caught on. Some leading publications began running separate columns under a "Manifest Destiny" headline. The doctrine reflected the already well-established American belief in their country's special mission. Some stressed the responsibility of setting a good republican example; others stressed democratic liberty. Most publicists tended to combine the two elements. Manifest Destiny in the 1840s reinterpreted the American mission. Now, for the first time, it became linked with the acquisition of new territory. It was further argued that expansion would guarantee freedom, by preventing the polarization of wealth and influence in the older parts of the Union.

Many, particularly the ruling Democrats, considered expansion inevitable, desirable, and even charitable, since those inhabiting the newly acquired areas would enjoy the blessings of American institutions. As James Buchanan, a loyal Democrat who later became an unhappy president, put it: "To talk of confining the American spirit of emigration within limits was like talking of limiting the stars in their courses, or bridling the foaming torrent of Niagara."

The Mexican War

Expansionism brought the nation to the brink of war with Britain, and pushed it over the brink with Mexico. In May 1846, Polk asked Congress to declare war. He falsely charged that Mexican troops had attacked U.S. forces on *American* soil, referring to a skirmish which actually took place in a disputed part of southern Texas. Mexico had warned that American annexation of Texas, her "stolen province," would be regarded as an act of war. At every point—Mexican failure to pay debts, and alleged mistreatment of Americans in California, among others—relations with Mexico had deteriorated. Perhaps a stronger Mexican government might have responded more effectively. But Mexican politics in the 1840s was chronically unstable. Those Americans coveting the slightly populated northern provinces of Mexico and the ports of the Pacific coast knew that little could restrain them. Following the failure of a last-minute diplomatic mission, Polk ordered United States troops under General Zachary Taylor to occupy territory up to the Rio Grande.

The Mexican War, like the War of 1812, did not gain the support of all Americans. But Whigs, though opposed, kept in mind the dangerous precedent of the Federalists and restrained themselves. Although nearly all Whigs voted for war, many sought to curb Polk by opposing increased military spending. The war issue never split the parties exactly, but antiwar feeling was stronger among Whigs, especially Northerners. New England Whigs comprised the antiwar vanguard, antislavery men especially condemning the venture as an alleged slave state conspiracy to extend Southern territory and political power.

Whatever the party division, the sectional consequence of the war soon became apparent. The acquisition of new territories might tip the sectional balance. A Northern congressman, David Wilmot of Pennsylvania, introduced a resolution to keep slavery out of new territories. The House agreed, but not the Senate, still balanced evenly between slave and free states. This Wilmot Proviso, reintroduced in several succeeding Congresses, revived the issue of slavery in the territories.

Despite harassment from Wilmot, a fellow Democrat, and despite Whig negativism, the war went well for Polk. The first campaign brought quick American victories. General Taylor routed numerically superior Mexican forces in a series of early engagements which made him both a war hero and a presidential candidate. In 1847 General Winfield Scott led an expedition to Vera Cruz, the chief Mexican port, and then inland to Mexico City. After a march of five months the Americans occupied the capital, climaxing one of the most successful campaigns in American military history. Polk had sent a peace negotiator along, a State Department clerk named Nicholas P. Trist. General Scott openly criticized the presence of the special envoy. Yet Trist persisted even after Polk had recalled him. A new Mexican government agreed to negotiate, so Trist came home early in 1848 without credentials but with a treaty containing most of the essential American demands, recognition of Texas annexation and cession of the northern Mexican provinces of New Mexico and California. The president, wisely deciding not to stand on ceremony, sent Trist's treaty to the Senate for approval.

The southern boundary had been expanded at a relatively small cost. Five years later another treaty, the Gadsden Purchase of 1853, completed the process. America's aggressive expansionism had paid off handsomely in the Pacific Northwest and in the Southwest. But the price of success was to reopen the question which would dominate and ultimately master the political processes of the 1850s.

THE TERRITORIAL TRAP

Neither the excitement of war nor the discovery of gold in California in 1848 could keep the slavery question out of national politics any longer. In Congress those who argued to exclude slavery from the territories anchored their stand on the constitutional right of Congress to provide for territorial government, as in the Northwest Ordinance of 1787 and the Missouri Compromise of 1820.

The chief Southern spokesman, John C. Calhoun, had opposed the war against Mexico, but acquisition of new territory required the protection of Southern rights. In denying federal sovereignty in the territories, Calhoun contended that they belonged to all the United States, as "tenants in common, or joint proprietors." Thus the federal government acted as the agent of the

states in administering territories, and all citizens should be able to enter them with their property, slaves included. To Calhoun, this went beyond constitutional quibbling, since to deny to the South the right to expand made it politically vulnerable. Half the states then allowed slavery, giving the South an equal vote in the Senate, although not elsewhere in the federal government. The new territories might be carved into a dozen states. If they were free, Southern power would be permanently destroyed. Calhoun demanded, therefore, that the territories be opened to slavery, and that in a territory ready for statehood the residents should decide the existence of slavery.

Between these polar positions lay a more moderate view, popular sovereignty. The principal early advocate of popular (or squatter) sovereignty was Lewis Cass of Michigan, the unsuccessful Democratic presidential candidate in 1848. He maintained that local institutions were exclusively state matters. Congressional power to regulate the territories did not extend beyond creating republican territorial governments and preparing the territories for statehood. Extremists rejected popular sovereignty, but those hoping for a workable political solution seized upon it. It seemed the democratic way of giving local inhabitants the right to decide, and it might also allow the federal government to escape the territorial dilemma.

Popular sovereignty seemed perfect from the Northern Democrats' point of view. They had to make an apparent concession to the South without actually permitting slavery to expand. Many Southern Democrats regarded popular sovereignty as a real concession to their section, while Northerners defended it as an even more effective exclusionary device than the Wilmot Proviso. There the matter rested. Each party interpreted and misinterpreted the tendencies of the many territorial proposals as it chose. But neither Whigs nor Democrats wanted to fight the issue. In 1848, Lewis Cass ran a dull Democratic campaign, and the Whig nominee, General Zachary Taylor, was innocent of any previous political involvement. A third party appeared when political antislavery and anti-Southern sentiment in the North burst the narrow confines of the abolitionist Liberty party to form the Free Soil party, promising no extension of slavery. Its candidate was ex-President Martin Van Buren. General Taylor won the election, and although Van Buren's Free Soilers could not carry a single state, they polled almost 300,000 votes. Many voters deserted the major parties to coalesce with Liberty party abolitionists in a broadly based anti-slavery political movement which would grow stronger in the 1850s.

Taylor became the first man elected president without political training, the first professional soldier in the White House. His limited knowledge of public issues inclined him to press for simple solutions to complex questions. Although he owned a Louisiana plantation, army life had given him a national outlook, and he showed no devotion to slavery. Since he had not committed himself to a set policy, Taylor took office with more than the usual amount of flexibility and freedom to maneuver.

THE COMPROMISE OF 1850

When Congress assembled in late 1849, Oregon had already been organized as free territory, but the former Mexican territories remained without political organization. The president wanted California and the other new territories to draw up constitutions allowing popular sovereignty. Because so few slaves lived in California, the proposal meant its admission as a free state. Southerners, knowing that California would tip the sectional balance northward, thought Taylor had betrayed them. But Taylor continued to favor this simple solution to the territorial question. He urged California and New Mexico to frame state constitutions, and Californians soon produced a document prohibiting slavery. They elected a state government, which petitioned Congress for immediate admittance, a demand supported by President Taylor.

The failure of Congress to provide civil government for the territories could be tolerated while their populations remained small, but the gold rush of 1849 changed that quickly. Over 80,000 Forty-Niners rushed to the goldfields of California, which at once had enough population to qualify for statehood. Yet many congressmen though

recognizing California's needs still resented President Taylor as a dangerous amateur in politics who acted without consulting them. Government for the territories was not the only issue. Northerners opposed the slave trade in the District of Columbia while Southerners demanded a tougher fugitive slave law, the boundary between Texas and New Mexico remained unsettled, and the Texas debt had not been paid.

Southerners increasingly felt that admission of California without slavery formed part of a widespread plot against their interests. The most radical Southern states' rights men, soon to be called "fire eaters," held a meeting in Nashville, Tennessee, to discuss means of preserving Southern political power and to plan for secession should that prove necessary.

Amid these pressures, political moderates turned their attention to framing a congressional compromise. Henry Clay, then 73 years old, submitted a plan to admit California as a free state, grant popular sovereignty to Utah and New Mexico, abolish the slave trade (but not slavery itself) in the District of Columbia, and give the South a stronger fugitive slave law as well as a congressional declaration of noninterference with slavery. Clay urged caution on all sides, telling Northerners that the restrictive Wilmot Proviso needlessly slapped at the South, and warning the South that secession meant civil war.

The proposals, introduced in January 1850, touched off a debate which lasted until September. John C. Calhoun, ill and near death, replied by calling for full minority rights. He demanded that the North either accept the South as it was, slavery and all, or allow it to secede in peace. On March 7, Daniel Webster, who previously had flirted with the Free Soil doctrine, sided with Clay, upbraiding abolitionists and Wilmot Proviso men as dangerous and misguided disunionists. Webster also ridiculed the notion, put forward by Calhoun, that secession could come about peacefully, but in calling on the North to accept the fugitive slave law, he knowingly faced the wrath of his own section, New England.

Most Senators favored compromise and the country was swinging in that direction. Businessmen, enjoying prosperous times, wanted to end the slavery controversy and get back to the serious matter of making money. But the compromise bill stalled in Congress, because of Clay's insistence on uniting the measures in one package. President Taylor wanted the admission of California to come first as a separate bill. He also spoke of using force should the South try to secede. The matter rested there until Taylor's sudden death in July which broke the logjam. The succession of Vice-president Millard Fillmore, a moderate Whig from New York and unlike Taylor a professional politician, meant that compromise bills would not be vetoed. Fillmore, who wanted a settlement, used his patronage power to force some Northern Whigs into line.

Democrats had not been a problem. Their Senate spokesman, Stephen A. Douglas of Illinois, had taken over leadership from Henry Clay, and Democrats in both houses loyally supported the compromise. Although Whigs delivered the major speeches, the Democrats made the compromise law. Despite Clay's initial action, Whigs in the White House and in Congress had created most of the obstacles. Democrats provided consistent support for compromise efforts, the most effective leadership coming from Douglas.

Support for the compromise and popular sovereignty became the hallmarks of the Democratic party in the 1850s. The man most identified with popular sovereignty by this time was Stephen Douglas. He pushed the compromise through, succeeding only after some Whigs abstained from voting against it. Their silence doomed the Whigs as a national party, undermining their Southern support. In 1850, Democrats wanted to strengthen the impression that the compromise was bipartisan, a national solution to the country's major problem. But during the next stormy decade the Democratic party sustained the politics of compromise and moderation, while the Whig party disappeared.

The North got the better of the Compromise of 1850. Southerners received little but the fugitive slave law, a provocative piece of legislation which did them tremendous political damage. The compromise offered a truce, under which the North temporarily gave up the Wilmot Proviso, and the South gave up the constitutional right of expanding slavery to all the territories. It represented a suspension of the Northern moral indictment against slavery. And it could be accepted by Southerners without shame, as a purely political deal between equals. The promise to enforce the Fugitive Slave Act was a symbolic act which the South hoped meant a firm guarantee for its way of life. Although only the slave trade had been abolished in the District of Columbia, in making this concession to national power the South gave up more than it bargained for.

Immediately after passage, the compromise seemed a huge success. A national propaganda campaign in its favor had gone well—especially in the North, where leading economic interests were weary of sectional strife. The South accepted less readily, although a second Nashville convention, hostile to the compromise, attracted only one-third as many delegates as the first. South Carolina remained intransigent, but the rest of the South agreed reluctantly to the compromise.

The presidential election of 1852 reflected this hopeful national mood. The two grand old men of the Whig party, Clay and Webster, died in that year. Their party reverted to its tested formula, hoping for success by nominating a war hero, General Winfield Scott, who straddled the compromise issue. Democrats countered with Franklin Pierce, an experienced but undistinguished politician from New Hampshire. Upholding the compromise, Pierce easily defeated Scott and demolished the Whig party, which could no longer count on holding its Southern members. They feared the growth of antislavery feeling among Northern Whigs, and preferred to trust the Democratic "doughfaces" who promised to uphold Southern rights. With political moderation in the saddle the Free Soil candidate, an abolitionist, received only half the number of votes cast for Van Buren in 1848. For the time being, moderation had triumphed.

THE FUGITIVE SLAVE LAW

During the compromise debates Southerners had insisted on a strong fugitive slave bill. This demand indicated their failure to understand the temper of the times. The permanent preservation of slavery was out of the question. Wisdom therefore dictated that Southerners settle for a long delaying action. Instead they decided to attack from a position of relative weakness, before the weakness became more pronounced.

The Fugitive Slave Act of 1850 was much stronger than its predecessor of 1793. Federal marshals had to execute the new law on penalty of heavy fines. After the arrest of an alleged slave, the marshal became responsible for the full value of the fugitive. The rendition or return became the job of a federal commissioner, and the slave owner needed only the commissioner's certificate to take the alleged runaway back to slavery. A fugitive could not testify in his own behalf, nor could he appeal to higher authority. Because of extra paper work, a commissioner received double the fee if he declared the detained person a runaway and sent him to slavery. Northern antislavery men called this differential a bribe, and the stringent provisions of the law made even conservative Northerners uncomfortable over it. As Abraham Lincoln put it, the fugitive slave law should have been written so that a free Negro was in no more danger of going into slavery than an innocent man would be of hanging because of laws punishing murder.

Thus the Compromise of 1850, adopted to calm sectional passions, included a law which ignited incidents that caused continued strife. Southerners had the legal right to reclaim their escaped property, but in 1850 only one thousand of the more than three million slaves in America had run away, most of them from border slave states into free states. And many of these escapees were ultimately caught and returned to their masters. The deep South, least affected by the problem, provided the hard-core support for the fugitive law and used it as an indicator of Northern sincerity in maintaining the sectional compromise. South Carolina, which lost but sixteen of its 400,000 slaves in 1850, seemed to regard itself in mortal peril from the threat of runaway slaves. Its politicians formed the vanguard of those Southerners fighting for the bill. Above all, Southerners valued the fugitive slave law because they believed it gave slavery the approval of federal law. If slavery was a sin, the fugitive slave law made Northerners accomplices in the South's crime.

Some Northerners refused to be implicated and during the early 1850s several rescues and attempted rescues occurred. In 1854, Anthony Burns, a Negro recently settled in Boston, was seized as a fugitive slave and hustled before a federal commissioner. Abolitionists plotted Burns's rescue but they could not act because of a heavy guard around the federal courthouse. Since Burns actually was a runaway, the outcome of the hearing was obvious. Rather than spirit him out of Boston at night, the federal officials decided on a public display. They paraded him through the main streets to the wharf, guarded by 5000 troops. The sullen crowd muttered threats, but Burns went back to Virginia.

The Burns rendition cost the federal government $40,000, yet much more than money was involved. As a Southern editor observed: "A few more such victories and the South is undone." Abolitionists, who later purchased Burns and sent him to Canada and to freedom, had a perfect issue to exploit. It appeared that the hotheads who had insisted on the new fugitive slave law deliberately wanted a raw nerve of sectional conflict to remain exposed. If so, the implementation of the fugitive slave law did the job. Such incidents as the Burns case, and "personal liberty" laws passed by Northern legislatures to make renditions of fugitives more difficult, pointed up the fragile nature of the compromise.

PIERCE AND KANSAS

Franklin Pierce was a mediocrity who won the Democratic nomination for reasons of party harmony. Although experienced politically, he was weak and the leading men of his cabinet easily dominated him. A New Englander who got along well with Southerners, Pierce hated abolitionists who, in his mind, were the true disunionists. He called for peace yet he helped to revive sectional strife.

Pierce began by promising to continue the Democratic policy of expansion. He hoped that by concentrating on foreign affairs and by exploiting expansionist sentiment he could deflect attention from pressing domestic problems. He failed because many Northerners viewed expansion as a means for annexing more slave territory. Pierce pursued a hard line with Britain regarding American fishing rights in the North Atlantic. In the Pacific, he tried unsuccessfully to annex Hawaii, and he also sent Commodore Matthew C. Perry with a fleet of warships to Japan in 1854. After threatening the use of force, Perry obtained trade concessions for the United States.

Pierce's Latin American policy provoked the most controversy. In Central America, the United States aimed at displacing Britain as the principal outside power. This gave encouragement to American soldiers of fortune, or filibusters. In 1855 when an American named William Walker declared himself dictator of Nicaragua, Pierce recognized his government. Walker later had to flee and was executed during a second filibustering expedition five years later. Northerners thought that Walker and other filibusters had been sent by Pierce to the Caribbean to form new slave states.

Cuba provided further substantiation for these fears. For years Southern annexationists had been greedily eyeing the fertile island, one of the few remaining Spanish colonies. Pierce appointed an annexationist, Pierre Soulé of Louisiana, as his minister to Spain, a man who acted as though he had been sent to Madrid to provoke war over Cuba. In 1854, several American diplomats, Soulé included, met at Ostend, Belgium, to formulate United States policy regarding Cuba; their "Ostend Manifesto" declared Cuba a vital interest of the United States. The United States should try to buy the island, but failing in that "then by every law, human and divine, we shall be justified in wresting it from Spain." Unfavorable Northern reaction to the manifesto obliged Pierce to disavow the ministers' unauthorized act. Antislavery men nevertheless charged Pierce with working for the South in seeking to bring more slave states into the Union, even at the price of war.

Kansas-Nebraska

Another hornet's nest, even more dangerous, soon appeared. Early in 1854, when Senator Stephen Douglas of Illinois introduced a bill for organizing the new territories of Kansas and Nebraska, he touched off an explosion over the extension of slavery. For decades most Americans considered much of the Louisiana Purchase unfit for settlement. But this myth of the "Great American Desert" soon gave way to reality as settlers moved in.

Speculators, developers, and settlers realized the advantages of railroad construction to hasten development of the new territories west of the Mississippi. Douglas became a key man in disputes over the location of railroad routes. Southerners and others opposing construction of a railroad over a Northern route terminating at Chicago argued that it would run through unsettled and unorganized territory, some of it still in Indian hands. Douglas then produced his bill to organize the Kansas-Nebraska Territory, and to placate the South he inserted a provision that territorial legislatures should decide on slavery. Theoretically this opened the territory to slavery.

But the South wanted more. So in a second bill, Douglas called for dividing the Nebraska Territory and for repealing the section of the Missouri Compromise prohibiting slavery north of 36° 30'. From this Southerners could infer that Kansas might become a slave state and that Nebraska would be free. Douglas's motives immediately became a hot political issue. He hoped that the bill providing for popular sovereignty would be nationally acceptable and carry him into the White House, at the same time solidifying his political position in Illinois if Chicago became the terminus for a transcontinental railroad.

Douglas's strategy required that he make concessions to the South on slavery. Though he regarded it as an evil, he viewed slavery unemotionally and felt that moralizing the issue, especially in the territories, would lead to national disaster. For the rest of the 1850s, Douglas sought to appeal to all sections, thinking that popular sovereignty would satisfy both Southerners and Northerners. His failure mirrored the failure of the Democratic party in that decade, and of other politicians who thought they could avoid confronting the moral issue of slavery.

The Kansas-Nebraska bill passed in the spring of 1854. Though it had not originated with the South, once Douglas pushed the legislation Southerners supported him. They knew that they lacked the manpower to win a race for settlement of new territories. A few may have thought that Missouri migrants would win Kansas for the

South and slavery. But with only 20,000 slave owners in Missouri, the South got little from the Kansas-Nebraska bill but the psychological victory of having the territories opened to the *possibility* of slavery. Like the fugitive slave law, also of little practical value to the South, Southerners grasped at any straw that appeared to give national sanction to their way of life. The great drawback, however, was that Southerners exposed themselves to the charge of senselessly reopening the territorial question.

Kansas-Nebraska put additional strain on the party structure. In the North, the Democrats began to split. Northwestern Democrats in particular complained that the South ran the party. The Whigs had collapsed beyond revival, and a new party of free soilers, the Republicans, appeared in 1854. Their principal objective was thwarting the Kansas-Nebraska bill's extension of slavery in the territories. Republicans did well in their first election tests, despite the fact that their party advocated only one basic idea.

In Kansas itself a small-scale war broke out. At first, after organization of the territory in 1854, violence had been sporadic. Intimidation seemed sufficient, as several thousand proslavery men from Missouri crossed over into Kansas to help establish a territorial government favorable to the South, but Northerners responded by forming a rival antislavery government. A succession of governors could not end the impasse, although President Pierce clearly intended to support the proslavery government. In 1856 the heaviest fighting occurred when proslavery men, including Missouri "Border Ruffians," destroyed the free soil town of Lawrence.

Within a few days a handful of antislavery men retaliated. A group of eight abolitionists, led by John Brown, perpetrated the Potawatomie Massacre, murdering five pro-Southern settlers chosen at random. Brown acted on no authority but his own, and free soil leaders in Kansas quickly condemned his deed. But Northerners had not pretended that pacifism would keep slavery out of the territory. Antislavery settlers, as well armed as their enemies, called their rifles "Beecher's Bibles," after Henry Ward Beecher, as Eastern minister, who raised money to purchase them for the "Good Fight" in Kansas. The antislavery

elements of New England had taken a particular interest in Kansas and keeping it free of slavery. They organized the New England Emigrant Aid Society which ultimately sent about two thousand free soil settlers to Kansas. After fighting which caused the deaths of several hundred men, a new territorial governor restored an uneasy peace.

NATIVISM FILLS A POLITICAL VACUUM

With the Whig party fast disintegrating, and the Democrats badly shaken by Kansas-Nebraska, a period of extreme political instability began. Frustration with traditional political leadership and fear of foreigners gave rise to a short-lived Native American, or Know-Nothing, party. This anti-Catholic and anti-immigrant movement was a mixture of honest conviction and ignorant prejudice, and for a few years challenged slavery as the principal issue in American politics, jeopardizing the growth of the fledgling Republican party. Nativism offered cynical politicians the possibility of rebuilding the national unity, shattered by sectional conflict, on foundations of bigotry.

Nativism first bloomed in the 1830s. During the next decade it invaded politics with modest success. Native Americans elected a mayor in New York City and several congressmen elsewhere. While immigration remained relatively light, however, nativism did not grow appreciably. A heavy rise in immigration in the late 1840s caused nativism to undergo a mushroom-like growth, and by 1854 the anti-immigrant party had acquired considerable political strength.

Many native Americans came to believe that one immigrant group in particular menaced them. To them, one ethnic strain seemed especially lazy, shiftless, and immoral. These newcomers lived in squalor and ignorance, and supposedly would never adopt American values. Nativists thought they lived as they did because they liked it that way, because they were "subhuman." The group singled out for such disparagement was the Irish, driven from their homeland to America by successive potato famines and British misrule. They, and many of the Germans (also arriving in large numbers in the mid-1850s), were Roman Catholics. Thus in an overwhelmingly Protestant country, nativism had religious roots, playing upon the ingrained Protestant antagonism toward the religion of Rome.

From a mere 25,000 in 1790, Roman Catholics in America numbered one million by 1850. Instead of blending into the population, they remained loyal to their church and to the customs of their homelands, establishing Catholic newspapers, benevolent societies, and over 400 parochial schools by 1840. Catholics chafed under Protestant efforts to mold their culture. They objected to Protestant control of public schools, demanding public support for their own schools. Germans insisted on drinking beer, even on Sundays, an affront to the Protestant sabbath, and the Irish were quick to resent any slur on their respectability or patriotism.

Native-born Americans became alarmed as the number of Irish and German Catholics continued to mount in the 1840s and 1850s. They felt that Catholics did not believe in either separation of church and state or in political democracy. Men like Bishop John Hughes, militant leader of American Roman Catholics, fed their fears when he admitted in 1850: "Everybody should know that we have for our mission to convert the world—including the inhabitants of the United States."

The anxieties of the native-born were sometimes irrational and paranoid. Some saw Catholic plots everywhere, hatched in the secrecy of convents where priests and nuns schemed against American freedom. Hundreds of thousands of copies of books and pamphlets circulated, combining nativism with pornography. They sought to expose a "Catholic Conspiracy" willing to resort to any means to achieve its subversive ends. The classic tales, such as one "Maria Monk's" revelations of clerical misbehavior in a nunnery, depicted virginal American girls captives of lascivious Catholic priests behind the shelter of convent walls. The lurid stories were all the more effective because the mid-nineteenth-century prohibition against explicit sexual writing made the authors rely on innuendo and suggestiveness. To break down those walls and rescue the innocent, a mob in Charlestown, Massachusetts, had in 1834 destroyed an Ursuline convent.

Repeatedly, violence between foreign-born Catholics and native-born Protestants supported by Protestant immigrants eager to prove their Americanism broke out in the ethnically mixed cities. In 1844 riots in Philadelphia left thirteen dead, fifty wounded, and thirty homes destroyed. "Throughout the city priests and nuns trembled for their life," a newspaper reported. In 1853, in New York City, the Hibernian Society parade led to a riot provoked by nativists. They used a runaway horse to scatter the marchers, and the enraged Irish retaliated by mobbing bystanders. Though respectable Protestant opinion condemned the savagery, many agreed with the nativist spokesmen who opined: "It were well if every Papist church in the world were leveled with the ground." The Irish responded in kind, matching Protestant bigotry with their own. The native-born, one Irish nationalist insisted, were "the very dregs and offal of the white population in America" and were even "lower than the race with black wool" on their heads.

Party politics also played an important role in the rise of nativism. In the Eastern cities the Irish and the Germans both participated in politics soon after arrival because of easy voting requirements. Democratic politicians had marshalled these immigrant votes effectively, making the Whigs receptive to nativist ideas. And since there was no real control of immigration, the many sick and indigent newcomers put an enormous strain on charitable facilities. One-half the paupers in New York City in 1835, for instance, were foreign born. Some upper- and middle-class Americans embraced nativism because they feared losing political influence to the "lower classes" whose numbers and power grew with the influx of the newly arrived and impoverished Irish.

The Know-Nothings

Several secret societies of nativists, usually organized by Whigs, sprang up to oppose the Catholics in politics. In 1853 they merged into the Order of the Star Spangled Banner, which became known popularly as the Know-Nothing party, since whenever asked about their societies they would profess ignorance and reply, "I know nothing."

Although Know-Nothings organized secretly, they nevertheless strongly resembled old-style reform groups. This was especially true on the question of temperance. As a group, the immigrant Irish were undeniably the hardest drinkers in America, a fact constantly remarked upon by the Yankee prohibitionists. And since Irish laborers were very antagonistic toward the Negro, his potential competitor for unskilled work whether slave or free, antislavery reformers had little sympathy among the Irish. German and Scandinavian immigrants, in contrast, were strongly antislavery and often settled on farms; this helped them gain more rapid acceptance.

The Know-Nothings enjoyed greatest success in the ethnically diverse Eastern states. They captured six governorships and elected seventy-five congressmen between 1854 and 1856. Their most startling victory occurred in Massachusetts, a state whose politics no single party had been able to dominate for almost a decade. In 1854, Know-Nothings elected all state officers, all the congressmen, and all but three members of the Massachusetts legislature. Yet for all the attempts at conspiratorial secrecy and bombastic rhetoric, the Native Americans made remarkably limited demands. They did not call for the end of immigration, only for a longer period (ranging from seven to twenty-one years) before an immigrant could obtain American citizenship and voting rights. They did not try to curtail the rights of American citizens of recent immigrant origin, although nativists asked their supporters to vote against all Catholic candidates.

Nativism, like antimasonry twenty years before, declined even more rapidly than it had risen. Most Americans remained confident of their country's ability to assimilate European immigrants and recognized the need for labor in a continent still only half-settled. Nativism cast doubt on the practicality of the American mission as an asylum for the oppressed and it violated American commitments to equalitarianism and democracy. None perceived this more clearly than the leaders of the Republican party. "I am not a Know-Nothing," declared the Illinois politician, Abraham Lincoln, in 1855. "How can anyone who abhors the oppression of Negroes be in favor of degrading classes of white people?"

Republicans could not reconcile nativism with their fundamental principles, yet they dared not oppose the nativists outright since both parties appealed for support among similar elements. In some states the two parties collaborated briefly, but everywhere Republicans hoped and waited for the Know-Nothing impulse to subside. The national Know-Nothing coalition was a loose grouping of proslavery and antislavery elements, North and South, and like the older parties this new one also split in 1856 on the rock of slavery. Republican patience thus paid off. Most Northern Know-Nothings drifted into the Republican party, which insisted, according to Horace Greeley's New York *Tribune*: "Neither the Pope nor the foreigners ever can govern the country or endanger its liberties, but the slave holders and slave traders do govern it." Democratic victory in 1856 lent added substance to these partisan charges.

JAMES BUCHANAN AND DRED SCOTT

The Democratic party in 1856 remained one of the few nationalizing institutions in America that had not been shattered by the slavery controversy. But in the next four years, America's oldest political party divided into irreconcilable, warring factions. Until then, the Democrats had found in the doctrine of popular sovereignty a formula for uniting Northerners and Southerners. But in 1856, the party nominated neither Douglas nor President Pierce who had been architects of the compromise politics that had prevented a rupture in the early 1850s. Instead, the party named James Buchanan, a mild and shopworn politician who had been overseas during the Pierce administration and thus had fewer enemies than the two principal aspirants.

The opposition did no better. Know-Nothings nominated the Whig ex-President Millard Fillmore, while the Whigs, then in the final stage of decay, endorsed the nativist candidates, avoiding as usual specific commitments other than a condemnation of sectional politics. The Republican candidate was as "safe" as those of other parties. John C. Frémont, a former soldier and Western explorer, had no political record. The Republicans remained primarily a one-idea party promising to block the expansion of slavery. But in addition to upholding the right of Congress to legislate for the territories, they began to broaden their appeal with such proposals as construction of a transcontinental railroad.

"Bleeding Kansas" dominated the campaign, the liveliest since 1840. Republicans generated much of the enthusiasm, claiming that Buchanan was a dupe of the slave power. Yet many Northern conservatives, fearing disunion, still rejected the Republicans' frankly sectional appeal, and this cut into their strength. Although nativism was waning, and Republicans benefited most from the shift of nativist votes, Buchanan and the Democrats won the election. Frémont carried eleven states, all in the North.

This contest marked the final transformation of the South into a one-party region. The Democratic party became dominant, creating a "Solid South" beyond any doubt. The election also signaled the end of the Whig party. Republicans, on the other hand, did well for their first outing, and they could look hopefully to 1860.

The new president, James Buchanan, had been in Democratic politics most of his life. He was a careful tactician who had always worked for the interests of his party. Though he had few outright enemies, he nevertheless became through weakness one of the least successful presidents. Buchanan's usual response to a crisis was first to delay making a decision, then to make a concession to the South. Peace at any price were his watchwords. In his inaugural address he pleaded for sectional conciliation. He supported popular sovereignty in particular, and condemned agitation of the slavery issue in general.

Hopes for sectional harmony received a jolt almost as soon as Buchanan took office. The Supreme Court was the only branch of government not yet badly tarnished by the slavery controversy. Two days after Buchanan's inaugural, however, the court entered the quarrel dramatically, and in a way which intensified the sectional conflict. Dred Scott, while a Missouri slave, had been taken to Illinois and to the Minnesota Territory in the 1830s. After his return to Missouri his master died. In 1846, Scott contended in court that the years he spent in free territory entitled him to freedom. The case finally reached the United States Supreme Court in 1854. By this time Scott's status was no longer the real issue. His former master's widow had married a New York abolitionist, assuring Scott freedom whatever the Supreme Court decided. The status of slavery in the territories was now at stake: did residence on free soil make a slave a free man?

The case attracted national attention and was not easily resolved. Each of the court's nine justices, seven Democrats (five from the South) and two Republicans, wrote a separate opinion. Initially, the majority intended to state simply that Scott, a free Negro, was not a citizen and therefore could not sue. But they learned that the two Republican justices were preparing wide-ranging dissents. The majority then decided to discuss the effect of Scott's stay on free soil and the constitutionality of the Missouri Compromise, not merely the court's jurisdiction.

Chief Justice Roger B. Taney argued that Scott was not a citizen, either of the United States or of Missouri, because a Negro descended from slaves could not become a citizen. The founding fathers had written the Constitution for white men, and Americans had always regarded Negroes as inferior beings. In the most controversial section of his opinion, Taney noted that colonial Americans denied that Negroes possessed "any rights that white men were bound to respect." He denied Scott's right to sue, and went on to declare a slave's residence in a free state or territory legally meaningless. Since the Constitution guaranteed the right of property by the Fifth Amendment, Congress could not restrict property rights in territories without due process of law. This ruling nullified the Missouri Compromise, a restriction upon the right of slaveowners to bring their property into certain territories. The two dissenting justices upheld the free soil stand.

Few judicial opinions have stirred so much excitement as *Dred Scott*. The South was elated, and its leaders urged fellow citizens throughout the country to uphold the law of the land, as expounded by the Supreme Court. In the North, Republicans reacted sharply, and with good reason, since the Court had just taken away their platform. Republicans denounced the seven majority justices as political hacks in the pay of the slave interest. And they announced that they would ultimately reverse the decision by packing the court.

President Buchanan had received *advance* notice of the decision. At his inauguration he declared blandly that he was willing to accept the court's decision, whatever it might be. According to Buchanan, the slavery controversy would be "speedily and finally settled" by the Supreme Court. This was wishful thinking. Even Northern Democrats were left unhappy, since popular sovereignty was as much threatened by the decision as the Republican's slavery restriction rule. If Congress could not prohibit slavery in a territory, how could a territorial legislature, a body Congress had created, do so? Obviously it could not, not within the confines of the court's interpretation in *Dred Scott* v. *Sanford*. The court thus deprived Northerners, Democrats and Republicans, of any constitutional means to limit the expansion of slavery. The next step, Republicans warned, was for the court to declare that no free state could exclude slaves since that too would deprive citizens of property rights.

THE FINAL CRISIS

The rest of Buchanan's administration was as luckless as its start. Despite widespread fraud by proslavery men in Kansas, the president accepted the constitution they framed, a stand which caused his territorial governor to resign in disgust. All knew that an honest vote in Kansas would bring the prohibition of slavery, but Buchanan was too deeply mortgaged to the South and too much under the influence of Southern cabinet members to alter his policy. Northerners attacked Buchanan as a "doughface"—a Northern man with Southern principles—and the Kansas problem awaited solution.

Economic troubles added to Buchanan's other woes. A business panic struck 1857, followed by several years of recession. The warning signs of former panics, as usual, went unheeded. The federal government still played a

"hands-off" role regarding regulation of national finance, and speculation remained virtually unchecked. The resulting downturn sharpened sectional conflict. Since cotton prices in Europe held firm, the South recovered quickly. Not only did this stimulate Southern feelings of economic self-sufficiency as a staple exporter ("Cotton is King," boasted the Southern nationalists confidently), but in the North, Republicans benefited by blaming the Democrats, clearly under Southern control, for the economic mess. Thus Northern economic interests previously allied to the Whigs moved toward Republicanism and political antislavery. Northern businessmen wanted high tariffs and internal improvements subsidies; Northern farmers wanted cheap land through passage of a homestead bill. With the South opposed, and while Democrats of the Buchanan persuasion held power, little chance existed of pushing these measures through.

These economic grievances and the sharpening sectional quarrel gave added importance to the off-year elections of 1858. The Douglas wing of the Democratic party, clinging to popular sovereignty as a safe way to keep slavery out of the territories, broke with Buchanan over Kansas. Douglas himself was up for reelection in Illinois, running against a lesser known but promising Republican, Abraham Lincoln. A former Whig, Lincoln had joined the Republicans only after much watchful waiting. He was a moderate, yet by 1858 he had accepted the chief Republican plank: no further expansion of slavery.

Although senators were then elected by state legislatures, the candidates campaigned throughout Illinois in a series of joint debates. Lincoln lost the election, but benefited from the encounters. The nationwide attention they received helped spread his name as a presidential possibility, and he forced Douglas to defend popular sovereignty in terms that antagonized the South. Without local police regulations positively upholding slavery, Douglas declared in the "Freeport Doctrine," the institution could not survive. This was the ultimate exclusionary technique. Southerners stamped it as heresy, and prepared to block Douglas's bid for the presidency in 1860.

The South's sense of betrayal was growing. It no longer could trust to Northern goodwill, or rely on pretended friends like Douglas or on the ability of the national Democratic party to protect Southern interests. The elections of 1858 cast in doubt continued Southern control of the federal government, supposedly the South's last defensive bastion. In addition to the equivocal position taken by Douglas Democrats in the North, Republicans had carried most Northern states. The House of Representatives, long controlled by Northerners, fell into free soil hands as well. Southern fire-eaters became more outspoken, making demands for protection which could not be met within the Union. Their new rallying cry was reopening of the African slave trade, a concession no Northern politician would or could accept.

Next year a bombshell exploded which seemed to confirm Southern fears. John Brown, the self-appointed avenger in Kansas, struck again. He and a score of men seized the federal arsenal in Harper's Ferry, Virginia, proclaimed a general slave insurrection, and then barricaded themselves in the building. Federal troops under Colonel Robert E. Lee quickly arrived to snuff out the uprising. Slaves knew nothing of Brown and his scheme, and this half-mystic, half-madman was hanged in December 1859. A few abolitionists had given Brown money, some with knowledge of his plan, but the South overresponded and blamed all Republicans for the raid. Because of his obvious sincerity and his desire to end slavery, Brown became a martyr in Northern antislavery circles. "You may dispose of me very easily . . . but this question is still to be settled," he warned shortly before his execution, "—this Negro question I mean."

The election of 1860 thus took place in a highly charged atmosphere. This time the Democrats split. Southerners demanded full guarantees for slavery and an acceptable candidate. Failing in this, Southern delegates to the national convention (held in fire-eater territory, Charleston, South Carolina) walked out. When a second convention of Northern Democrats nominated Stephen Douglas, Southern Democrats countered with their own nominee. The Democratic split opened the way to victory for the Republicans, still a minority and sectional party. Their convention rejected the best known Republican aspirant, Senator William H. Seward of New York, to name

Abraham Lincoln, who had a more moderate image on slavery than Seward. A fourth party of Constitutional Unionists appeared, made up of pro-Union conservatives, desperately hoping to hold the country together by denying the relevance of the issue then tearing it apart.

As expected, and as feared in the South, Lincoln won. He carried free states only, and had only 40 percent of the popular vote (60 percent of the votes in the free states); however, he far outdistanced his three rivals in the electoral college. Douglas obtained a heavy popular vote, but carried only one state. Southern extremists, growing in numbers and strength during the 1850s, had threatened secession if Lincoln or any other "Black Republican" was elected. The new president would take office four months later, in March 1861. Meanwhile, the Union hovered on the edge of civil war.

AND THE WAR CAME

On the eve of secession a shrewd observer reported that "the people of the North and of the South have come to hate each other worse than the hatred between any two nations in the world. In a word, the moral basis on which the government is founded is all destroyed."

Since the revolt against Britain, three-quarters of a century before, Northerners and Southerners had lived together, settling their differences peacefully, each tolerating the others' institutions. The Union had rested on common interests and common loyalties which led Americans to accommodate their differences, buoyed by the conviction that they were citizens of the world's leading republic.

But by the middle of the nineteenth century, Northerners and Southerners saw their fundamental interests and their deepest loyalties threatened by the other section. "We are two peoples," believed Horace Greeley. "We are a people for Freedom, and we are a people for Slavery." Lincoln declared what many in both sections had already come to believe: "A house divided against itself cannot stand." The Union, he predicted, "cannot endure permanently half slave and half free." Yet the Union had endured divided by

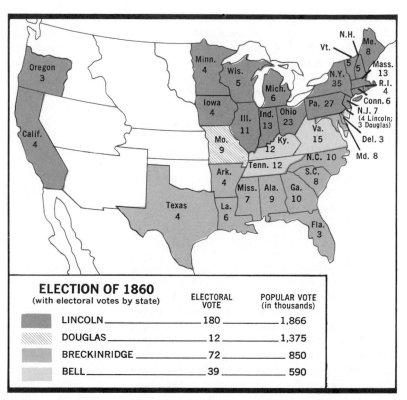

ELECTION OF 1860
(with electoral votes by state)

	ELECTORAL VOTE	POPULAR VOTE (in thousands)
LINCOLN	180	1,866
DOUGLAS	12	1,375
BRECKINRIDGE	72	850
BELL	39	590

slavery since its birth. Lincoln added: "I do not expect the Union to be dissolved; I do not expect the house to fall; but I do expect it will cease to be divided."

Territorial expansion and economic development triggered the confrontation. As long as each section had ample and undisputed room for expansion, sectional harmony could be preserved. But as the Cotton Kingdom spread through the lower South and as free white farmers settled the Old Northwest, pressures mounted for further territorial expansion. Southerners eyed Texas as a logical extension of the plantation economy and Northerners looked to California and Oregon for fresh opportunities. For millions, Manifest Destiny's appeal was more symbolic than real; few would move west but people wanted reassurances that American abundance was limitless, a need generated by the social disorganization accompanying urbanization, industrialization, and rapid economic growth. Expansion thus became the means by which many Americans hoped to

fulfill their destiny. Even Lincoln, who had opposed the Mexican War, explained during a later war that the Union was a government "whose leading object is to elevate the condition of men — to lift artificial weights from all shoulders . . . to afford all an unfettered start and a fair chance in the race of life." Only expansion, many believed, would assure that fair chance.

While the call for expansion was strong in the North it was even stronger in the South. The Democratic convention of 1844 proved a turning point that set the nation on a collision course. By dumping Van Buren, who opposed expansion because he feared the sectional animosities it would arouse, in favor of James K. Polk, an expansionist, Southerners and equally nearsighted Northern expensionists made the slavery question central to American politics, something the abolitionists had not been able to accomplish in two decades of agitation.

As long as slavery remained confined mostly east of the Mississippi and south of the Ohio

Rivers, most Northerners regarded it a strictly Southern matter. But when Southerners claimed the right to carry their slaves into the new territories acquired from Mexico and then into Kansas-Nebraska (from which slavery had been barred by the Missouri Compromise), growing numbers became convinced that an aggressive "Slave Power" threatened the interests of white labor. The Republican party became the vehicle for containing Southern expansion, for political antislavery. To understand the roots of America's Civil War, then, one must understand why Southerners insisted on expansion and why for the first time, millions of Northerners felt threatened by slavery.

THE SOUTH

Residents of the various sections had always nourished feelings of regional consciousness dating back to differences in colonial times. In the nineteenth century, the South became most acutely aware of its sectional identity and most determined to maintain its interests by preventing the growth of national power. Slavery, the South's most distinctive institution, was rapidly becoming an anachronism in the Western world at the very time that even those Southerners with qualms about slavery abandoned hope of getting rid of it. Yet despite the region's economic advances in the early nineteenth century, the South could not keep pace with the rest of the Union. In 1790 the South was the most populous region, and four of the first five presidents came from below the Mason-Dixon line. By 1860 Southerners felt themselves a beleaguered minority and were unwilling to accept the outcome of a free election in which the victorious candidate won without a single Southern electoral vote.

Southerners, increasingly anxious over the disparity in sectional growth, decided upon the expansion of slavery as the solution to their dilemma. In view of the South's failure to develop an industrial and commercial sector, its economic vitality depended on the expansion of plantation agriculture. But by the 1840s most of the best lands in the South had already lost much of their original fertility. Adding urgency to the need for fresh land were the wasteful methods of cultivation that exhausted the soil and the ever-present need of the upper South for new markets for their surplus slaves. Indeed, the solvency of the Southern economy as a whole, on which rested the unity of interests between Mississippi planters and Virginia slave breeders, was contingent upon expansion.

Only expansion could assure continued Southern prosperity. It was equally necessary to satisfy the psychological needs of a society at war with itself over slavery. "We must satisfy the conscience," pleaded Southerner Duff Green in 1833, "we must allay the fears of our people. We must satisfy them that slavery is of itself right, that it is not a sin against God. . . . In this way, and this way only, can we prepare our people to defend their own institutions." In the decades that followed, proslavery apologists desperately sought to convince Southerners that a just God had created slavery. By demanding that the Union approve the expansion of slavery, Southerners not only hoped to bolster their economy and their political influence but maintain their self-esteem as well.

Southerners needed these assurances because few could entirely repress the doubts that Duff Green recognized. Sensing their moral isolation, Southerners compensated by developing an elaborate myth of regional superiority. They claimed that slavery was "the greatest good of all the great blessings which a kind Providence bestowed upon our glorious region." They boasted, too, that their slave society had produced a superior breed of men—namely, themselves. Noble blood flowed in Southern veins for Southerners claimed descent from English aristocrats, whereas Yankees came from peasant stock. *They* had a keen sense of *noblesse oblige*, whereas Yankees were devoted exclusively to self. In short the true Southerner was a gentleman, the Yankee was a money-grubber.

Yet while Southerners boasted of their superiority, they envied and feared the Yankees. "Contrast the happiness and contentment which prevails throughout the North," a Virginia legislator once remarked soberly, "the busy and cheerful sound of industry, the rapid and swelling growth of [Northern population], . . . their enterprise and public spirit, the monuments to their commercial and manufacturing industry, and, above all, their devoted attachment to the government from which they derive their protection with the division, discontent, indolence and poverty of the Southern country." It was not a comforting comparison.

This ambivalence within the Southern mind could not be resolved or ignored. In desperation, Southerners created a closed and increasingly separate society, especially as they confronted attacks from antislavery elements in the North. Even religious denominations split along sectional lines. In 1843, Southern Baptists, refusing to accept criticism of slavery by Northerners, formed their own Baptist Convention. Southern Methodists and Presbyterians followed in their steps. In this way the South cultivated its own brand of Christianity, one which posed no danger to the white man's conscience.

Convinced of their superiority Southerners also created their own educational resources to resist assimilation by Northern customs and values. In university education especially, the South had always been dependent. Many planters sent their sons to New England colleges. Yale was one of their favorites (Calhoun graduated there, and he studied law in Connecticut as well), and other Northern colleges also had ample quotas of Southern students. When sectional tensions mounted, however, Southerners gave more attention to their own colleges and academies. Young Southerners began staying home, rather than mix with Northern students who were growing less tolerant of Southern institutions year by year. Such antagonism was very pronounced at the U.S. Military Academy, where Southern and Northern cadets carried rivalry almost to the point of warfare. Ultimately, even West Point became suspect in the South, as Southerners turned to founding their own military schools. "Patriotic" Southerners were even asked to spurn the vacation resorts of the North during the summer season.

Growing Southern nationalism took other forms. Literary nationalism had been part of the Southern scene for decades. The *Southern Quarterly Review* actively and truculently sought to foster esteem for all things Southern. But it was far easier to call for a distinctively Southern literature of value than to produce it. Although the South could and did boast of several excellent novelists and poets, the balance of literary achievement still leaned heavily on the side of the free states. Economic nationalism, the belief in regional self-sufficiency, also grew during the 1850s. The chief specific grievance remained the tariff and Southern political power kept it low, despite Northern complaints. But the network of credit and marketing arrangements, which made the South economically subordinate while its cotton exports provided most of American foreign exchange, came under increasingly heavy attack at Southern commercial conventions.

Despite the number of articles in Southern magazines arguing that separate civilizations existed in North and South, the objective similarities between Americans still outweighed their differences. Most of them spoke the same language, professed variations of the same religion, and shared a common culture. But however it may appear in retrospect, to Americans of the 1850s the differences between them were coming to mean more than the similarities. White Southerners had slavery to live with—their "wolf by the ears," as Jefferson termed it in 1820—and their inability to conceive of sharing their section with several million free Negroes made them cherish sectional differences all the more. "We can take no pride in our national character," warned one Southern editor, "because from our peculiar position we do not contribute to its formation." Sectional pride mounted in the South in equal proportion to criticism of all things in the North. Ominously, Southerners voiced particular pride in their ability and willingness to fight, while they ridiculed Yankee timidity. The Yankee poet, James Russell Lowell, put his finger on the problem when he argued that what seemed to bother the South most about the North was that it was free.

THE NORTH

Southern nationalists and Northern antislavery men agreed that fundamental sectional differences existed. Republicans looked upon the South in some ways as a foreign country whose institutions and attitudes clashed with those they regarded as truly American. The South was an undemocratic, hierarchical society dominated by a small group of planters. A society based on slavery, Republicans insisted, must remain hopelessly inefficient and economically backward. In contrast, the free North accepted Europe's millions, attracted by unmatched opportunity for self-improvement. The North honored free labor and rewarded it, whereas Southerners associated physical toil with slavery and degradation. "The great idea and basis of the Republican party, as I understand it," said a future Republican governor of Illinois in 1860, "is free labor. . . . To make labor honorable is the object and aim of the Republican party."

Northern fear that Southern expansion would force white labor to compete with slave labor, that the spread of slavery in the West would deprive white Americans of their birthright, gave the Republicans a powerful issue that appealed to millions who would never have joined a purely antislavery movement. Nonetheless, the dynamic leadership of the party came from such radical Republicans as Senator Charles Sumner of Massachusetts who thought slavery would crumble within the South unless it could expand, and sought full equality for the black man. Moderates like Abraham Lincoln believed slavery an evil but accepted its continuation in the South, and did not believe in racial equality. "All I ask for the Negro," Lincoln said, "is that if you do not like him, let him alone. If God gave him but little, that little let him enjoy." But he was quick to deny that he favored equality: "I am not, nor ever have been in favor of bringing about in any way the social and political equality of the white and black races. . . ."

Republican ideology thus mixed white racism with white idealism, joined by the commitment to block further expansion of slavery. By 1860 the doctrine had attracted a broad coalition of voters in the North, making the Republicans the dominant party in that region. This amalgamation of antislavery Democrats and Whigs, more of the latter than the former, enjoyed its greatest strength in New England and in areas from New York to Iowa settled by New Englanders. It was stronger in small towns and rural areas than in the cities, and among the nativeborn and Protestants than among the foreign-born and Catholics.

Republicans had to overcome Northern fears that their party's victory would break up the Union, a belief that led many businessmen and mid-westerners of Southern extraction to place their hopes on Stephen Douglas's brand of Democracy. Douglas believed that the American mission was to permit white majorities to prosper and rule as they wished, even if that meant degrading blacks. Lincoln and the Republicans disagreed; they insisted the Union rested on a moral ideal. Slavery was a system of organized robbery based on the maxim that "there is no right principle of action but self-interest," said Lincoln, a notion in "open war with the very fundamental principles of civil liberty." It had led Southerners to repudiate the Declaration of Independence and the nation's finest ideals. Democracy gave majorities the right to rule but equality required that they rule justly and respect the rights of other men. Slavery, moreover, deprived America "of its just influence in the world," Lincoln went on, and enabled "the enemies of free institutions, with plausibility, to taunt us as hypocrites. . . ."

Lincoln and most Republicans were willing to tolerate the taunts and allow slavery where it existed if only to preserve the Union. But when the slave states seceded in 1861, repudiating the democratic principle of majority rule and shattering the Union, Lincoln would resist. When the war came, he explained why: "This is essentially a people's contest . . . a struggle for maintaining in the world that form and substance of government whose leading object is to elevate the condition of men." No one, not even Lincoln, realized the stiff price Americans would have to pay to remain one nation.

Chapter 15
The Failure of Politics, 1861–1877

To find itself, the nation had first to split in two. The founding fathers had not permanently solved the problem of integrating diverse sectional interests. Decentralized politics, or the American federal system, respected local authority by dividing power between the states and the national government, and for almost seventy years this arrangement worked. But when rival elements in the free or the slave states tried to use federal power in ways that others regarded as intolerable threats to their values and interests, the system buckled under the strain.

For generations Southerners protected slavery through their influence in the national parties and in Washington. Losing that control in 1861, they claimed that the terms under which they had joined the Union had been violated. The Civil War which followed finally confirmed the superiority of national power and ended permanently the threat of secession. The Union survived, but only after a long and bloody war from which the nation finally emerged supreme, with its authority guaranteed by new nationalistic legislation and three constitutional amendments.

The cost was great. The Civil War cut a deadly swath across the center of the nation from the Atlantic to the Gulf of Mexico. Almost three million men served in the armed forces, a higher rate of participation than in any other American war, and more soldiers fell dead or wounded than in other wars. The conflict consumed enormous quantities of material and human resources, besides the six hundred thousand who died.

President Lincoln knew why the war came. In 1865 he reminded the nation: "One-eighth of the whole population were colored slaves, not distributed generally over the Union but localized in the southern part of it. All knew that this [slave] interest was, somehow, the cause of the war." Lincoln's initial aim was to preserve the Union, not to free the slaves; but in the end, the Union's preservation required freeing the black man. Lincoln thought that through the suffering of an entire generation, the Union had received "a new birth of freedom."

The Union intact, the curse of slavery lifted — all seemed favorable for the reunited nation. But the process of reconstructing the Union proved stormy. In less than a decade, the bright new day promised the black man turned to dusk. National power was available. The federal government *could* act with energy with the proper leadership and popular support. White Americans briefly committed themselves to guarantee political equality for blacks, but that commitment rested on shaky convictions about racial equality. Reconstruction became an unstable mixture of "politics, principles, and prejudice," with politics and prejudice easily winning out. In the end, Northerners deserted the Negro, restoring white supremacy and mocking the sacrifice of so many thousands of the "honored dead."

SECESSION

Thirty years before the crisis of 1860–1861, South Carolina had attempted to speak for the slave states in defense of their vital interests. But the rest of the South refused to go along with nullification of the Tariff of 1832. In 1860, South Carolina again led the way. This time, most of the South followed, although not unanimously or immediately.

The first wave of secession took place rapidly and peaceably. The South Carolina legislature called a special convention which unanimously voted to quit the Union, exercising its reserved sovereign right to withdraw from the compact with other states without submitting the question to a popular vote. The seceders condemned Lincoln, still two and a half months away from the White House, for his hostility to slavery. By early February six more states of the lower South joined the movement, and the South was ready for self-government. Representatives of the seven states, meeting at Montgomery, Alabama, adopted a constitution for the Confederate States of America and named provisional officers: Jefferson Davis, a Mississippi fire-eater, as president, and Alexander H. Stephens, a moderate Georgian, as vice-president.

A Southern nation had become a reality. Using the U.S. Constitution as a model, and often borrowing its phrases, the secessionists produced a document which also guaranteed states' rights and slavery. All this took place in a jubilant atmosphere. The fire-eaters established control over the deep South on the basis of the "threat" which Lincoln allegedly represented. But two major problems remained for the Confederates: Would the states of the upper South, especially Virginia, accept secession? And, equally important, what would the United States government do to prevent the dissolution of the Union?

The federal government did not respond until after Lincoln's inauguration on March 4, 1861. James Buchanan, the last of the "doughface" presidents, had neither the will nor the policy to meet the crisis. Secession almost froze this kindly, undynamic man into total inactivity. Although he denied the South's right to secede, he simultaneously appeared to deny his own right or duty to use force against secessionists. Even Confederate seizure of all but two federal military installations in the lower South did not provoke Buchanan to act. Instead the president prayed for the success of several last-ditch congressional compromises, including a proposed constitutional amendment extending the Missouri Compromise line to the Pacific Ocean. A special "peace convention" also met in Washington without positive result. Such expedients were sincere but fruitless; neither the fire-eaters nor the incoming Republican administration would compromise essentials. Southern radicals now had a functioning government; while Lincoln, as president-elect, rejected all proposals which might allow extension of slavery.

Lincoln denied the right of secession more forcefully than Buchanan, yet without belligerence. The new president's inaugural address rejected interference with slavery where it already existed, but at the same time Lincoln warned, "We cannot separate." The national government would not resort to arms unless "forced" to do so. The new president meant to maintain federal control where it still existed.

Specifically this meant Fort Sumter in Charleston harbor. Negotiations concerning the fort had been going on for weeks, ever since Major Robert Anderson retired with a small federal force into the garrison. Northern opinion divided on the issue, with some of Lincoln's cabinet urging abandonment of the fort. When Lincoln decided in April to send food, but not munitions, to the garrison, Confederate artillery opened fire. After a two-day bombardment, Fort Sumter fell. The president then called for 75,000 volunteers to put down an insurrection against the United States. By firing the first shot, the secessionists prepared the North for war. On the other hand, by resisting the rebellion, Lincoln helped to unite the South behind the Confederacy.

The secession movement soon spread to the border states of the upper South. On April 17, less than a week after Sumter's fall, Virginia, which had voted in November for the Constitutional Union candidate and had called the Washington Peace Convention, decided to leave the Union. In May, Tennessee, Arkansas, and North Carolina seceded. This time the secessionists acted in a restrained mood. North Carolina, where unionist sentiment had always been strong, joined the Confederacy reluctantly. But with Virginia out of the Union, North Carolina's isolation and its ties to the rest of the South decided the question. A prominent North Carolinian, originally an antisecessionist, summed up the feelings of many reluctant rebels: the conflict, he thought, was "groundless," but if no longer avoidable, Southerners should "fight like men for our own fire-sides." Quick federal action prevented secession in Maryland, Kentucky, and Missouri, however. Troops repressed prosecession tendencies in those states. And the northwestern part of Virginia broke away from the Old Dominion, to become loyalist West Virginia in 1863.

Did secession represent majority sentiment in the eleven states of the Confederacy? Delegates to most secession conventions were chosen by popular vote, or by mass meetings as in South Carolina. Yet the conventions exercised the effective power of decision: in only three of the Confederate states did the people later vote an acceptance of the secession ordinances themselves. But if secession represented a minority sentiment, if a minority of forceful Southern politicians provoked secession by presenting false alternatives,

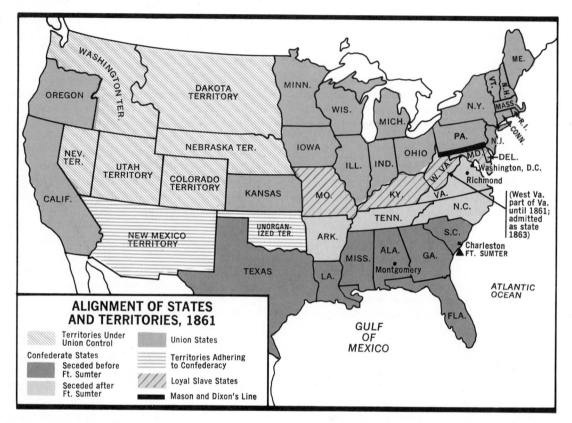

ALIGNMENT OF STATES
AND TERRITORIES, 1861

Territories Under Union Control

Confederate States
Seceded before Ft. Sumter
Seceded after Ft. Sumter

Union States

Territories Adhering to Confederacy

Loyal Slave States

Mason and Dixon's Line

(West Va. part of Va. until 1861; admitted as state 1863)

it should be remembered that Lincoln himself was a "minority" president, and that until secession the Republicans were outnumbered in both houses of Congress.

The country now moved from constitutional arguments and political maneuvering to bloodshed, with very few on either side realizing how much carnage lay ahead. In the South, secessionists believed that Yankees were too cowardly to fight. In the North, Lincoln called for volunteers for only ninety days' service. Thus each side regarded war as a sure means of gaining its ends through quick victory in the field. Both sides were wrong.

LINCOLN TAKES COMMAND

For the next four years, Lincoln, a man untested in offices of high responsibility, had to deal with problems so varied and so grave that even up to

the hour of Northern victory many of his countrymen doubted he could handle the job. Lincoln had to preserve the Union, not only by maintaining unity in the North and leading his own party, but also by shaping a successful diplomatic and military strategy. In the process he led the nation into its first modern war, a struggle of mass slaughter and mass conscription, one which approximated the total wars of the twentieth century. No one anticipated this at the start; the duration and range of the war surprised Americans as much as the strong performance of their president.

Lincoln's problems began well before his inauguration. Elected in November 1860, he did not take office until March 1861. During this long interregnum the South had seceded and the nation drifted without clear direction. Lincoln's party was still a loose coalition of many groups, and he had won only 40 percent of the popular vote. Many leading Republicans, moreover, barely concealed their disdain for the Illinois politician whom they considered a second- or third-rater, a political novice with only one previous term in Congress. Some Republicans as former Whigs still nurtured that party's fear of strong presidents, recalling with distaste such Democratic "usurpers" as Jackson and Polk. When Lincoln appointed several leading Republicans to his cabinet, including his rival for the nomination, William H. Seward, many thought that the president would play second fiddle to the stronger men.

But Lincoln refused to be dominated by his subordinates or panicked by the threat of secession. He rejected all proposals which subverted his party's principal plank: no further spread of slavery beyond where it then existed, and he tactfully ignored Secretary of State Seward's harebrained idea of reestablishing national unity by provoking war with one or more foreign countries. As the crisis deepened, Lincoln learned to make full use of the powers of the presidency, powers which in wartime can be enormous. A strong executive, Lincoln nevertheless sought whenever possible to avoid direct collisions with Congress.

The Confederates had attacked Fort Sumter in April 1861, but Congress was not due to reconvene until December. The recess allowed Lincoln to meet the emergency in his own way, and later to present Congress with accomplished facts, a practice he followed several times. With the country at war (whatever the constitutional and legal quibbles about the status of the rebellion), and with Republicans in control of Congress, Lincoln counted on having a free hand. He ordered the state militia to put down the rebels; he expanded the regular army and navy; he called for federal volunteers; and he declared a blockade of Southern ports. No specific constitutional authority existed for several of these actions.

The president pleaded necessity, admitting that the measures might not be "strictly legal." He could have called Congress into a hurried meeting within a few weeks, but decided instead convene a special session to meet, appropriately, on the Fourth of July. Congress, after showing some reluctance, approved all presidential orders issued after the fall of Fort Sumter, giving Lincoln his mandate and his operational precedents.

He wisely ignored the impulse to defend his course in detail.

Lincoln believed that some parts of the Constitution had to bend in order to preserve the republic. Throughout the war he acted accordingly, often running a step or two ahead of the established political process. The president, as commander-in-chief, suspended the writ of habeas corpus, or freedom from arbitrary arrest, several times and over large areas, though again he lacked constitutional sanction. When Congress acquiesced, the president's bold move was formally legitimized. Nor would Lincoln allow judicial interference, even when the Chief Justice of the United States Supreme Court ordered the release of a Confederate sympathizer in Maryland who had been jailed as a threat to military security. The Union general involved refused to obey, despite Chief Justice Taney's threat to hold government officials in Washington (the president included) in contempt. Lincoln said and did nothing, and Taney remained powerless.

Lincoln's Strategy

Lincoln moved swiftly to isolate the Confederacy from outside help, moral and material. He immediately imposed a blockade of Southern ports. Britain, a sea power with much experience in blockading, expressed doubts that three thousand miles of rebel-held coastline could actually be blockaded. Secretary of State Seward assured the British that the job would be done. Since the Confederates started with practically no navy, within a year the Union had established something approaching an effective blockade and had won the battle for control of the sea. The Union navy captured over 1500 vessels trying to slip in and out of the South. Several fast, low-hulled ships operated successfully as blockade runners, but the amount of cargo they could carry fell far short of the Confederacy's needs, both in marketing cotton and outfitting an army. Union forces seized much of the South's coastline, and in the spring of 1862, the Confederacy's most important port city, New Orleans, fell to the invading Northerners. The resulting naval stranglehold insured that Southern cotton would rot in warehouses and on wharves, and it gravely reduced the Confederacy's chances for survival. Meanwhile, the North bought munitions in England, and paid for them with enormously increased shipments of wheat.

Paralleling the blockade strategy, Lincoln sought to keep European nations neutral. The French emperor, Napoleon III, openly favored the Confederates for ideological reasons and from a desire to embark on expansionist ventures in the Western Hemisphere. Napoleon had sent French troops to Mexico, and he would later mastermind the futile installation of an Austrian Prince, Maximilian, as Emperor of Mexico. In 1861, he would have recognized the Confederate regime at once, but such a policy had to be worked out in unison with Britain, which declined to make a hasty commitment.

Britain held the diplomatic key. Many factors pushed it to favor the Confederacy: British power in the Americas would benefit by a permanent division of the United States; an independent South would become an ideal free trade market for English manufactured goods, while the supply of Southern cotton for English mills would grow; British commercial and political elites felt a closer affinity toward the South and its conservative civilization than for the brash egalitarianism of the North; and finally, government leaders, including the prime minister and the foreign secretary, believed that the North could never subdue the South.

Britain recognized early the belligerent status of the Confederacy, and almost intervened in its behalf in the fall of 1862. In October, British Chancellor of the Exchequer William E. Gladstone (later the prime minister several times) declared in public that Jefferson Davis and his confederates had "made a nation," a highly unneutral observation. But the British still would not grant full diplomatic recognition until assured that they were backing a winner. The indecisive Battle of Antietam (1862) upset British expectations. For the remainder of the war the British remained ambivalent about the South. They rejected a French proposal for joint mediation of the war, but their grant of belligerent rights gave Confederate vessels immunity from the laws of piracy.

Confederate diplomats counted on Southern cotton to win recognition abroad and to assure their nation's independence, since both Britain and France depended on foreign cotton for their textile mills. During the war's first year, the South held back cotton exports, waiting for the economic scarcity to work its political magic. But European stocks of cotton happened to be abnormally high (enough to last two and a half years), and when the South then tried to step up shipments, the Northern blockade kept most of the crop on this side of the Atlantic. Meanwhile, Europe turned to Egypt and India as alternate suppliers of cotton.

Confederate hopes for European intervention, diplomatic or military, faded quickly. Only a long war of attrition, one so costly that it would sap the North's will to fight, could assure the survival of the Confederacy. Here Southerners miscalculated again. The long, costly war severely taxed the Northern will, and though it faltered, that will never broke, thanks in part to Lincoln's leadership.

The Union War Machine

Having isolated the South by blockade and diplomacy, Lincoln concentrated on building an effective war machine. He had unilaterally expanded the regular army and had federalized the militia, but he also seriously underestimated manpower needs. The war dragged on, casualties were heavy, and inefficiency plagued the army. These experiences forced changes in recruitment policy. In March 1863, Congress passed the first national military conscription act, dramatically illustrating the growing shift of power from the states to the central government. During the Revolution, a few states had resorted to the draft, but in the War of 1812 and the Mexican War the federal government relied exclusively on volunteers and the small professional forces. Neither of these proved adequate during the Civil War. Voluntary enlistments could not provide the number of troops needed. As for the state militias, they were impressive on paper only.

Conscription seemed the only way to recruit a large army quickly and under federal control. The conscription law of 1863 made every male between 18 and 45 liable to be drafted. The wealthy, however, could hire substitutes for $300 to serve in their places. This first national draft provoked considerable opposition. Some citizens attacked its legality, but the courts, state as well as federal, refused to interfere with a measure deemed vital to national security. Northern judges held their peace, even those most concerned for states' rights and who thus might have been expected to question the law. The failure of legal attacks on the draft meant that opposition tended toward illegal forms. In New York City, antidraft rioters burned and looted for three days in 1863, venting their fury on the city's blacks, until put down by federal troops. But such opposition did not prevent the national government from exerting its power and filling the Union ranks.

Turning recruits into fighting men proved to be a formidable task. Equally difficult was devising a successful military stategy and finding a field commander capable of executing it. Lacking both a strategy and a general at first, Lincoln sadly watched the first major battle of the war, Bull Run (July 1861), where a disorganized Southern army routed even more disorganized Northern forces. The encounter demonstrated that the Yankees could not simply stroll to Richmond and crush the rebellion overnight.

In the wake of this setback, Lincoln thought he had found his military leader in General George B. McClellan, a mistaken conviction he nursed for too long. McClellan, a fine drillmaster and organizer, proved ineffective and hesitant in the field. He almost captured Richmond in June 1862 (seizing the rebel capital seemed more important to him than destroying the rebel army), but characteristically he pulled back at the moment a daring general might have made an all-out push. Later that year, though aware of the enemy's intentions to invade Maryland, he allowed the Confederate troops (now commanded by Robert E. Lee, the South's finest general) to escape unpursued after a savage, drawn battle at Antietam.

Lincoln dismissed McClellan in November 1862 and searched for a respectable replacement. Instead he found only several one-shot losers, Generals Burnside and Hooker, men who promptly led Union forces into shameful defeats; in both cases the Union forces far outnumbered and were more amply supplied than the Confederates. The

tactics of Lee and "Stonewall" Jackson proved too much for timid or inept Northern commanders. Lincoln refused to lose his head, however. Despite the sniping of his enemies (who now included ex-General McClellan), and despite rumors that the president might be deposed by the army, he kept cool, never doubting that Northern superiority in wealth, numbers, and technology would pay off, if it could be exploited effectively.

By mid-1863 it appeared that the Confederacy had fought the Union to a draw, but within a few months the tide turned decisively. In the West, a bold and ruthless Union general, Ulysses S. Grant, had been winning battles. In July 1863, after a long seige, his troops captured Vicksburg, Mississippi. The entire Mississippi River thus became Union waters, and the Confederacy was split in two. The same month, Lee invaded Maryland a second time, but at Gettysburg he failed to dislodge the main Union armies, falling back into Virginia with heavy losses. The South could no longer harass the North or outflank Washington. From then on it could fight a defensive war only. Lincoln later joined the two July victories together, when he named Grant general-in-chief and gave him command of the Army of the Potomac in March 1864. The president's long search for a winning field commander was over.

LIBERTY AND UNION

Neither the emergencies of wartime nor Lincoln's powerful leadership put a damper on political controversy, however. The most effective challenge to Lincoln came from within his own party. Radical Republicans wanted him to press the war more vigorously and expand its aims to include abolition of slavery. Lincoln insisted that his sole aim was to preserve the Union. He feared that abolition might weaken the government in the border states. In reply, the radicals formed a joint congressional committee, the Committee on the Conduct of the War, which quickly made itself a first-class nuisance, annoying both civilian leaders and military commanders. It could issue no orders, of course; Lincoln was commander-in-chief, but the committee used the political leverage of its members to undermine discipline and morale in the field. It consistently favored those Union generals who appeared most disposed to move against slavery, whatever their proficiency in battle.

Lincoln walked the political tightrope skillfully, as his handling of the emancipation question demonstrates. Early in the war, the national government abolished slavery in the District of Columbia and in the territories, but the president still emphasized the need to preserve the Union. At the same time he was considering an emancipation plan which included compensation to slaveowners.

Doubting that Congress could constitutionally emancipate the slaves, but with pressure mounting, and with radicals and abolitionists railing against his supposed tenderness for slave property, Lincoln decided to move in such a careful way that his enemies called it cynicism. Previously, he had rescinded actions by some field commanders who had freed slaves in occupied areas as "contrabands." By mid-1862, however, Lincoln was ready to declare free all slaves in rebel-held territory (still the major portion of the seceded states), as a war measure. In issuing the Emancipation Proclamation in September, following the battle of Antietam, Lincoln silenced just enough of his critics to ease the political crisis. The radicals obviously could not attack the proclamation, although they could and did point out that since it applied only to slaves in rebel-held areas it fell far short of indicting the sin of slavery itself.

But this bold stroke of executive power signed the death warrant for slavery in America. The proclamation went into effect on January 1, 1863, and within two years the Thirteenth Amendment to the Constitution ended slavery permanently in all of the United States. The proclamation also opened the way for large-scale recruitment of Negroes into the Union Army. By 1865, nearly 10 percent of the army was black. Despite discrimination (the black regiments had white commanders, received less pay at first, and were more poorly equipped than white units), they fought well when used in the line, distinguishing themselves in several battles. Through the proclamation, Lincoln had simultaneously strengthened his war powers and poliitical position, weakened the Confederacy, and won over world liberal opinion. He had stated candidly that he would free all or no slaves, depending on how it affected the Union. Emancipation represented, therefore, no departure from his earlier promise that he would adopt solely those measures which would save the Union. By late 1862, the president had become convinced that emancipation was necessary to achieve his main goal.

Lincoln's political savvy continued to guide his actions throughout the war. He handled the leading cabinet Republicans who felt superior to him kindly but firmly, like spoiled nephews. The president's views, once formed, always prevailed. In matters Lincoln did not consider vital, he avoided fights with Congress, using the veto sparingly and acting very much like the model Whig president, deferring to the wisdom of Congress (Lincoln had been a Whig in younger days). He wisely hoarded his political capital for the pressing issues of war and reunion.

Since Northern disenchantment with the war was extensive, Republicans tried to adopt a nonpartisan image as the party of the Union. Most Northerners opposed secession and supported the war effort, but war weariness and dissent grew, especially among Democrats. Denounced as "Copperheads," their loyalty suspect, Democrats remained openly critical of the conduct of the war. When they won several important elections, shaving the Republican majorities in Congress, Republicans responded by forming Union Leagues and by renaming their party the National Union party. Some wanted to suspend the presidential election of 1864; a few openly called for establishment of a dictatorship headed by someone other than Lincoln. The president brushed the ideas aside and proceeded to defeat handily the Democratic candidate, the same General McClellan whom Lincoln had picked to command the Union Armies. This was the second wartime presidential election in American history (Madison had been reelected in 1812), but the first held while the nation's survival stood clearly in peril. That the election took place at all counted as a victory for American democracy and Lincoln's faith in the system.

The War Ends

In the months following his reelection, Lincoln finally achieved his elusive goal. The war ground on relentlessly. Grant set as his primary target the destruction of Lee's army in northern Virginia. Meanwhile he sent General William T. Sherman southward from Tennessee into Georgia. Sherman captured Atlanta in September 1864 and then pushed to the sea, again splitting the Confederacy. In Virginia, Grant hammered at Lee's lines for months, accepting heavy casualties as the price of ultimate victory. The Confederate general fought brilliantly despite serious shortages in supplies and Union superiority in manpower. But Grant closed in, captured Richmond, and forced Lee to surrender at Appomattox Courthouse on April 9, 1865.

The American Civil War ended the era of "gentlemanly" warfare in which generals deployed their small-sized armies with care to fight limited, set-piece battles, rejecting ideas of total or exterminatory wars. The number of men involved between 1861 and 1865 dwarfed any previous military efforts in America: one-fifth of the adult male population (slaves excluded) joined the military, two million in the Union Army and Navy, and 800,000 in Confederate service; and one-fifth of these combatants died during the war. The Union lost 360,000 dead, one-third of them in battle; Confederate dead have been estimated at a quarter million, slightly less than a hundred thousand of them perishing in battle. Total casualties (dead and wounded) exceeded one million. The high proportion of deaths among the casualties (nearly 60 percent) testifies to the inadequacy of medical services in the field and in poorly equipped military hospitals, and to the lack of proper sanitation in the camps.

The battles raged over half of the country for four years. Supplying so many men meant, in effect, that most of the civilian population became part of the war effort, some of them to their enormous personal gain in war profits. The Civil War introduced the era of mass war, with tens of thousands, sometimes several hundred thousand troops fighting massive, prolonged battles. It also began the era of total war. General Sherman boasted: "My aim was to whip the rebels, to humble their pride . . . to make them fear and dread us." Old ways of fighting, devised half a century before when armies used short-range muskets, had to be abandoned in an age of long-range firepower. The concentrated, frontal assault had become a sure invitation to slaughter; it gave way to advances all along the line from a series of prepared positions. As war became more modernized, Northern advantages in manpower and resources made themselves felt and finally crushed the Confederacy.

Lincoln lived only five days to enjoy the victory. On April 14, 1865, John Wilkes Booth, an actor who sympathized with the South, cut him down in a Washington theater with a bullet through the head. Lincoln's death ended a remarkable politician's career at midpoint. Just as the war had absorbed all of the president's attention and talents during his first term, the second term, barely begun, would have been devoted to the larger task of restoration. Lincoln's leadership may not have been indispensable to the preservation of the Union, but his particular political skills and personal qualities greatly increased the likelihood of Union victory. In contrast, the Confederate president, Jefferson Davis, displayed few qualities of leadership. He did not inspire men, and his constant quarreling with cabinet members and governors of Southern states revealed both his personal limitations and the incompatibility between the Southern dogma of state sovereignty and the effective waging of a war for national survival.

Lincoln clearly emerged as the towering figure of the Civil War. He was at once eloquent and cagey. He could believe in high principles, yet he remained profoundly skeptical and cautious about ways to seek even the most desirable goals. Men who were committed partisans, those who scorned compromise within the political process, mistakenly confused Lincoln's low-keyed approach with timidity or even cowardice. But most Northern Americans sensed the president's honesty and they identified with his unpretentiousness. These qualities gave added force to his journeys into eloquence—at the Gettysburg cemetery, for example, or in his second inaugural address which rejected malice in favor of charity, and which promised to "bind up the nation's wounds." Those qualities would be especially needed after 1865. But Booth's bullet denied Lincoln the opportunity (and perhaps the failure) of Reconstruction, and put Andrew Johnson in his place.

JOHNSON AND CONGRESS

Never had a president taken office amid such a startling series of events. A four-year rebellion had grown into history's first modern war; the commander-in-chief had been murdered; and citizens of the Southern states stood on the brink of what they had always considered the worst possible calamity—their slave "property" had been made free by Yankee bayonets and would presumably demand full rights and privileges. Victory left the Union uncertain how to proceed. Northerners wanted reconciliation *and* retribution; they wanted justice *and* moderation in racial matters; they wanted the rule of law *and* a new politics to replace the older Southern way. Andrew Johnson's impossible task was to achieve all these contradictory goals.

The new president had been as loyal to the Democratic party as he was loyal to the Union. A self-educated tailor from the mountain country of east Tennessee, he steadily climbed the political ladder from mayor of a small town to U.S. senator, never forgetting his poor origins nor that he had little in common with the aristocratic planters and their retained lawyer-legislators, the men who had previously set the tone for Southern politics. When war came, Johnson did not "go with his state," as did Lee and so many others. His denunciation of secession earned him Lincoln's appointment as military governor of Tennessee. In 1864, Republicans, emphasizing the Union party label, nominated Johnson for the vice-presidency, despite his Democratic and Southern background.

Lincoln seemed more conciliatory toward the South than Johnson, who until the president's assassination had been denouncing the rebels harshly. Republicans advocating a punitive policy in the South—the Reconstruction Radicals—expected no trouble from tough-talking Presi-

dent Johnson. The day after Lincoln died, Johnson apparently reassured a leading radical that he would support measures granting voting rights to Negro freedmen.

The Radicals

A radical bloc existed among Republican congressmen, and it had already clashed with the White House. Radicals insisted on congressional control of Reconstruction, and that only a Republican Congress could assure the triumph of Northern war aims. Southern political power must be curbed, at a minimum, and rechanneled if possible by a solidly Republican black vote. Radicals also believed that continued Republican rule represented the Negro's only chance for fair treatment. From these premises evolved the first congressional attempt at Reconstruction, the Wade-Davis Bill (1864), which provided stiff terms for the readmission of ex-rebel states. Lincoln killed it with a pocket-veto.

Lincoln had been conciliatory toward the South, while declining to commit himself entirely. Avoiding abstract constitutional debates, he wished to restore the Union quickly. Late in 1863, he favored disqualifying leading Confederates but requiring a loyalty oath by only 10 percent of a state's voters as a precondition for readmission. He suggested to white leaders in Louisiana that they grant voting rights to literate Negroes and to Negro veterans, but he did not insist on enfranchising all the blacks. Lincoln appreciated the difficulties of framing a Reconstruction program which simultaneously met Northern political and emotional needs, while enlisting the support of the white South. Probably no one, not even Lincoln, could have worked that miracle.

A much less able politician, Johnson met disaster in the attempt. He quickly rejected the radicals' contention that secession had "destroyed" the Southern state governments. His Reconstruction plan proved slightly harsher than Lincoln's, and after Congress adjourned, Johnson proceeded on his own. First, he appointed governors for all Southern states and authorized constitutional conventions to set up civil governments. A majority of voters had to swear allegiance to the United States, and the Southern states had to repudiate slavery and Confederate war debts. Confederate officials and persons owning more than $20,000 worth of property had to apply to the president for pardon, but Johnson granted these liberally, despite his poor-white distaste for wealthy Southern leaders.

The president asked the white South to give up little but the formality of slavery. Like most Southerners, rich and poor, he wanted the Negro kept in his place, and he made no effort to guarantee the freed man's civil rights. Moreover, once readmitted, the South would *gain* congressional seats with the abolition of the three-fifths clause and thus regain a powerful voice in national politics.

When Congress reassembled in December 1865, civil governments were functioning in the South, and newly chosen Southern congressmen, some of them leading ex-Confederates, had come to Washington. Reconstruction under presidential initiative seemed complete. But if Johnson thought victory secure, the radical Republicans, apprehensive over the possible loss of the economic and party advantages gained during the war, prepared to fight back. Johnson's aggressiveness united the radicals, much more so than they had been under Lincoln, and more than they would be later under President Grant. And events in the South gave the radicals ammunition for transforming their anger into the domination of Reconstruction.

BLACK CODES AND FREEDMEN

Defeat on the battlefield had not reconciled white Southerners to the effects of emancipation. Nor had it taught them that good politics is the art of the possible. Still convinced that their cause, though lost, remained just, and encouraged by Johnson's leniency, Southerners restored white supremacy. Their major "concession" was the abolition of slavery, but beyond that it was to be business as usual. Most of the new Southern legislatures adopted Black Codes designed to keep the blacks at the bottom.

Johnson's Reconstruction plan left the condition of the Negro in state hands. If the freedmen had been treated fairly, reliance on local power would have been logical and desirable. But the Johnson governments discriminated blatantly. Though the Black Codes differed from state to state, all attempted to make the Negro more than a slave, yet less than a free man. Marriages between Negroes were legalized, but marriage between the races was prohibited. Such ambiguities ran through all the codes. The Louisiana laws prescribed that "every laborer shall have full and perfect liberty to choose his employer," *but* "once chosen, he shall not be allowed to leave his place of employment until the fulfillment of his contract." Children, even those born illegitimately, were to be supported by their parents, stated the South Carolina code, *but* the children of couples breaking portions of the code might be indentured involuntarily to work on plantations.

The codes aimed at keeping the Negro working and tied to the soil. The Alabama code and others barred Negroes from nonagricultural occupations without special permission. Some states also severely restricted Negro landowning rights. On the other hand, the codes protected Negro farmers from arbitrary eviction, and workers could leave the service of an employer who violated contractual obligations. Negroes also acquired their first civil rights. Some states permitted them to testify in court against white defendants. Yet whatever rights he received, the Negro remained at the mercy of the white Southerners wielding power. In a society where Negroes so recently had been chattels, there was no likelihood that a civil or social revolution would be engineered by the former masters in behalf of former slaves.

The black man's only hope lay in Washington. Toward the end of the war, Congress created the Freedmen's Bureau, the first federal welfare agency, to aid those persons—mainly but not exclusively Negroes—made destitute by war. The bureau's first job was to supply food rations to war refugees, white and black. The end of the fighting enlarged the bureau's tasks, since someone had to assist the freedmen in the transition from slavery to freedom. Realizing that the ex-slave needed to be prepared for his new role, the Freedmen's Bureau concentrated on education. Most Negroes were illiterate. Volunteer Northern school-marms went south to run many of the bureau schools, only to be damned as "carpet-baggers"—or Northern intruders—by the local whites. The bureau also supervised labor contracts to see that freedmen received just treatment.

Most Negroes stayed put. Immediately after the war, some fled to the cities and towns, enjoying the right to move freely for the first time. The movement was dramatic compared with the tight control formerly exercised over all Negroes, slave and free. In a short time, however, the perambulations ceased. Negro farm workers traded the communal slave quarters of the plantation for the rude cabins of the sharecropper.

Few Negroes became landowners. Some received land from the federal government under the Homestead Act, and with the Freedmen's Bureau aid others expected to receive "forty acres and a mule" from the government, as some Republicans proposed. But that dream never materialized. Instead, after working for wages for a year or two, Negroes became sharecroppers. The cropper supplied only his labor. The landowner furnished tools, seed, and loans for provisions during slack months. Cropper and owner divided the yield. The cropper usually found that the loans from owner or storekeeper barely covered the value of his share of the crop, and he remained in debt after the year's accounting. From these conditions arose the patterns of Southern rural life in the post-Civil War era. Sharecropping made a peon of the freedman, tying him to the soil almost as securely as had slavery. It also produced the rise of the country storekeeper, who was often the landowner as well, and who replaced the planter as the dominant figure in Southern rural society.

In 1866, only the Freedmen's Bureau agent stood between the Negro and the new peonage. Incensed by the Black Codes, Republicans extended the Bureau's life indefinitely and broadened its powers and jurisdiction. Johnson promptly vetoed the bill, singling out as unconstitutional a provision granting bureau agents judicial functions to protect Negroes from racial discrimination. Johnson felt that Southern state courts should handle such matters.

Johnson's veto message was as gruff and undiplomatic as the man who wrote it. He stated that a permanent Freedman's Bureau would "inevitably result in fraud, corruption, and oppression." In short, it would become a wasteful boondoggle and would require military force to make it work. The president vehemently opposed federal encroachment upon the traditional rights and responsibilities of the states. This meant that no realistic Reconstruction program was possible under Johnson, a position Republicans could not accept. Johnson not only sacrificed the Negro, but he also jeopardized the Republican party's power. Morally and politically, Republicans never doubted the need to respond strongly to the president's challenge to their party and to the Union.

THE RADICAL TAKEOVER

The radicals failed to override Johnson's veto of the first Freedman's Bureau bill. But after that setback they gained support among moderate Republicans and had little trouble. Refusing to seat the congressmen-elect from Southern states, they formed a Joint Committee of Fifteen which became a powerful instrument for developing and implementing radical policy. Although chaired by a moderate senator, its leading member was Thaddeus Stevens, a thoroughgoing radical congressman from Pennsylvania, the man who more than any other personified Radical Reconstruction. Stevens was as tough-minded about what should be done in the South as Johnson appeared to be at first; unlike the president, however, Stevens stuck to his views. Stevens did not "rule" Congress (in fact, he suffered several important legislative defeats), but Southern intransigence and Johnson's ineptitude increasingly brought Republican moderates into the radical camp.

Radicals responded to Johnson's challenge in April with a civil rights bill that defined national citizenship for the first time and promised protection to citizens against state infringements of their rights. Johnson promptly vetoed it as unconstitutional, despite massive counterpressure from his advisers including all but one member of the cabinet. This time the Republicans, radicals, and moderates united to override the veto. A short while later a new version of the Freedmen's Bureau bill passed, again over a Johnson veto. The Radical legislative program was under way.

Seeking a more permanent basis for Reconstruction than acts of Congress which could be repealed, Republicans decided to write their program into the Constitution. Slavery had already been abolished by the Thirteenth Amendment (1865), but radicals now pushed for a Fourteenth Amendment (written in 1866 and adopted in 1867) which expanded federal power. The proposed amendment disqualified Confederate leaders politically, repudiated the Confederate debt, denied compensation for slave property, and gave Congress the power to reduce a state's representation if Negroes were denied the vote.

The key section of the Fourteenth Amendment defined citizenship nationally. In other words, Americans were citizens of both their state and of the United States. States were forbidden to deny any of their citizens "the privileges and immunities of citizens of the United States"; nor could they deprive citizens of "life, liberty, or property, without due process of law"; finally, all were to receive "the equal protection of the laws." These constitutional guarantees though comprehensive were vague and it remained to be seen if they would be valid in the lesser world of politics and social relations.

Congress sent the Fourteenth Amendment to the states for ratification in 1866, an election year. This congressional contest took place in a tense atmosphere. Violence in the South, especially bloody race riots in Memphis and New Orleans, in which blacks suffered most heavily, alerted and alarmed the Northern electorate. President Johnson proved to be the *Republican's* most effective campaign speaker. Johnson toured the country blasting radical candidates and policies so violently that he simultaneously damaged his cause and lowered the dignity of the presidential office. The united Republicans fought the campaign as if the fate of the Union still hung in the balance, as if Grant were besieging Vicksburg. For them, all opposition bordered on treason. Even conservative Republicans, Johnson's only hope, went with the radicals, as did many Northern businessmen who feared Johnson's Democratic past. The voters returned massive Republican majorities in both houses of Congress.

Military Reconstruction

With this popular mandate, radical Republicans took the offensive, moving to impose Military Reconstruction on the South. Congress turned the clock back to April 1865, to Lee's surrender, dividing all the ex-Confederate states (except Tennessee, which had accepted the Fourteenth Amendment) into five districts under military commanders. Before civil government could be restored, the states would have to hold constitutional conventions to ratify the Fourteenth Amendment and male suffrage regardless of race. On another front, the fight with the president led Congress to seek greater powers at the expense of the executive. The Tenure of Office Act, for instance, prescribed Senate approval for presidential *removals* as well as appointments.

Johnson had no stomach for Military Reconstruction, but he appointed the commanders as required by law. This did not satisfy the radicals, who wanted him ousted. A squabble over the Tenure of Office Act soon provided the pretext. Secretary of War Edwin M. Stanton had been feeding the radicals information about Johnson's cabinet. Understandably, the president sacked Stanton, but without obtaining Senate approval. In March 1869 the House impeached the president for removing Stanton and opposing congressional Reconstruction. Benjamin F. Wade, the radical president of the Senate, waited hungrily in the wings to assume the presidency, once Johnson's head had rolled. But the count fell one vote short of the number necessary for conviction. Seven Republican senators voted not guilty, risking *their* heads while preserving their integrity and perhaps the presidential office itself.

The Republicans showed excessive malice in impeaching Johnson. The president had already been neutralized and would soon leave office. No one imagined that Johnson could be elected in his own right. Also, the judicial branch offered little effective opposition to Radical Reconstruction. A year after the war, the Supreme Court had denied the right of a military court to try a civilian Southern sympathizer (*ex parte Milligan, 1866*). This principle, if applied to Reconstruction after 1867, might topple the whole structure of the radical program. Congress had demonstrated its hostility to judicial interference by seeking to limit Supreme Court jurisdiction, and by reducing the number of justices in order to deny Johnson an appointment. When Southerners tried to test Reconstruction laws directly, the court would not accept the case. Although the Supreme Court actually enlarged its powers in this period (in other fields) it remained neutral on Reconstruction. Thus Congress, unhampered by strong executive or judicial politics, had its own way. In 1869, Republicans altered the Constitution a third time. The Fifteenth Amendment guaranteed voting rights for blacks. Radical Reconstruction had reached its high point.

BLACK RECONSTRUCTION

With Johnson read out of the party, Republican radicals and moderates elected General Ulysses S. Grant to the presidency. For eight years (1869–1877) Grant carried out the Radical Plan for reconstructing the Union. Military Reconstruction, the imposition of Republican-dominated civil governments on the ex-rebel states, and the Fifteenth Amendment gave Southern Negroes their first chance to participate in the political process. As slaves, each had counted as three-fifths of a man; emancipation and Reconstruction amendments made them theoretically first-class citizens whose votes politicians needed as much as those of others. In 1868 a half dozen Southern states reentered the Union under conditions set by Congress, including acceptance of Negro suffrage and disfranchisement of ex-Confederate leaders, inaugurating a new political order.

For generations since, Southern whites have looked back upon Reconstruction with horror. "Black Reconstruction" they call it, implying that incompetent and vengeful Negroes wielded all power. Reconstruction after 1868 certainly broke with the Southern past; how much horror it contained is in the eye of the beholder. Negroes generally voted and some held offices: two Negro senators and fifteen members of the House of Representatives were elected to Congress. Three blacks became lieutenant-governors; one was a judge of a state supreme court. Dozens more participated in state constitutional conventions, then sat in state legislatures organized under those constitutions.

Despite these significant changes, white domination of politics went on as before. Negroes never acquired a proportionate share of political power. Although they controlled one house of the South Carolina legislature for a short time (in a state where they comprised the numerical majority), no black became governor of a Southern state —an event that has yet to occur in any state. Negro officeholders were more numerous in local and county government. But even in Mississippi, which also had a black majority, there were only twelve Negro sheriffs. Radical Reconstruction did not bring black domination, although it created political regimes friendly to Negro interests for the first time. When the white coalition sustaining them withdrew support, the Reconstruction governments quickly collapsed.

Most Negroes holding office during Reconstruction realized how uncertain was their toehold on power. Black congressmen were generally undistinguished but able men who acted responsibly and quietly in their states' interest. Hiram B. Revels, for example, the first Negro senator (elected in Mississippi to the seat once held by Jefferson Davis), was a soft-spoken and college-educated former minister. He earned as much respect from his colleagues as the strangeness of his situation and the harshness of the American racial code would allow.

Revels, like many Negro politicians, initially worked to remove the political disabilities applied to thousands of ex-Confederates. Reflecting this conciliatory attitude, a Negro delegate to the South Carolina constitutional convention pleaded ". . . we are not prepared to vote. But we can learn. Give a man tools and let him commence to use them, and in time he will learn a trade. We recognize the Southern white man as the true friend of the black man." Such was the hope, but few Southern whites were ready for friendship and conciliation on the basis of racial equality. Those hearing the delegate's appeal needed no convincing that the Negro was "not prepared to vote" at that time; that they wanted him to learn a political trade was doubtful.

According to the myth, Radical Reconstruction brought not only black domination but exceptionally corrupt government to the South. In reality, politics in the Southern states conformed to no set pattern. South Carolina was the most corrupt of the reconstructed states. Its debt rose sharply and government costs skyrocketed. The state bought property from persons with political influence and paid more than market value. It sold public land at giveaway prices. Mississippi, on the other hand, although thoroughly "radicalized," suffered only three cases of embezzlement and a white Mississippian stole most of the money. Similarly, other Southern states did not approach South Carolina's record for outright corruption, or theft of public funds.

Reconstruction history—radical or otherwise—cannot be divorced from national history. The process of uncontrolled economic growth after the Civil War, together with the rapidity of urbanization (especially in the North), made political corruption a national, not a regional, problem. To blame four million Negro freedmen in the South for corrupting America, at a time when illiteracy and poverty were widespread among Southern whites and Northern immigrants, smacks more of race prejudice than rational analysis. No radical politician or carpetbagger came close to matching the dubious achievements in thievery of the Tweed Ring in New York City, or the Whiskey Ring during the Grant administration, crooks who were mostly native-born WASP Northerners.

Reconstructed state governments spent more money than their predecessors. The prewar Southern governments, under the control of rich planters, had been stingy about spending for public services that benefited the poor whites. Emancipation and civil equality required that the South, like the North earlier, provide basic education for its citizens. Illiteracy among whites was higher in the South than elsewhere in the nation because no common school system existed, and it had been illegal to teach slaves to read and write. Radical Reconstruction brought the first free public education to the South, for white and black. Similarly, Southern states had failed to invest sufficiently in transportation improvements. Several radical legislatures were overly generous to railroad builders, thus emulating many Northern legislatures' efforts to attract investment. Unlike the prewar regimes, radical governments were ready to spend public funds, even if at times too liberally, to promote economic development. Radi-

cal Reconstruction also gave Southerners progressive state constitutions—documents which were color blind. Besides abolishing slavery they did away with remaining undemocratic restrictions on the franchise and imprisonment for debt.

Despite these achievements, Radical Reconstruction failed. Although some Southern whites ("scalawags" they were called derisively) participated in the radical governments, many more than the myth of Black Reconstruction would admit, the mass of white Southerners remained hostile. Some resorted to the terror tactics of the night-raiding Ku Klux Klan to intimidate Negroes and cooperative whites. The Klansmen used whippings and even murder to enforce white solidarity. Several race riots occurred, including one in New Orleans in 1866 which resulted in forty-one deaths.

Growing white Southern resistance and waning Northern support eventually doomed Reconstruction. In view of what white Americans expected of Negroes, and of what they would permit them, regimes resting on the votes of people only recently freed and enfranchised could not enjoy public approval indefinitely in any part of the Union. After several years of Radical Reconstruction, Northern whites increasingly agreed with the South Carolina black orator that Negroes were "not ready." But unlike the South Carolinian, they did not see a better future ahead.

RECONSTRUCTION EXPIRES

The end of Reconstruction came slowly but steadily. Year by year, the political disqualifications imposed upon Confederate leaders fell away. In 1871, Congress repealed the ironclad loyalty oath, and a year later a general amnesty cleared all but a few hundred ex-rebels. The South was thus poised to resume native white rule. Tennessee led the way in 1869. Other states followed, and by 1876 only Flordia, South Carolina, and Louisiana remained under radical control. The grip of the radicals on the South loosened as their power waned nationally. The wartime union of Republicans disintegrated, and serious quarrels broke out among economic interests who differed over the protective tariff and currency policy, and over Grant's disappointing performance as president.

At the same time the Democratic party rebounded strongly. The Republican charge that the Democrats were the "party of treason" began to wear thin. As the North tired of its halfhearted crusade for the Negro, Democrats, especially Southerners, took heart and turned to effective poltical action. In 1874 they easily won control of the House and almost captured the Senate. Previously, white Southerners had used violence such as Ku Klux Klan night rides, but the federal government's "Force Bills" of 1870 and 1871 curbed Klan activities. This demonstrated, first, that force alone would not restore white Southern rule; and, second, that Washington *could* protect Negro civil rights in the South if it had the will. But disclosures of corruption in carpetbag governments provided further rationalization for abandoning the Northern determination to dominate the South.

A disputed presidential election in 1876 allowed the South a measure of freedom over its future and formally ended Reconstruction. The issue of corruption dominated the contest, and not solely in the South, since during the Grant administration high government officials plundered the federal treasury. More was at stake in 1876 than who would live in the White House. Republicans argued that all that had been won through civil war would be lost if Democrats regained power. Playing upon Northern patriotism, they "waved the bloody shirt," reminding Union army veterans of their fallen comrades, many of whom perished in Confederate prison camps.

Diverse economic interests, benefiting from Republican rule, might also be imperiled. The South had always been hostile to national economic programs, such as the high tariff and national banking legislation, that Northern businessmen had finally obtained during the Civil War while Southerners were out of Congress. Now, not only might the South upset the national balance of power (which since 1860 had clearly been an imbalance favoring the Republicans), but it could also bargain for special political and economic privileges.

Such speculations about the balance of power proved well founded. In an extremely close election, Democrat Samuel J. Tilden received more popular votes than Republican Rutherford B. Hayes, but his electoral votes fell one short of the necessary majority. Each party claimed the doubtful votes of the three Southern states still in Republican hands. Tilden seemed the victor as he had won beyond question some of the disputed Southern votes, but election boards under Republican control carefully "reviewed" the returns and fraudulently certified Republican electors.

Congress met in December 1876, while the country seethed with controversy over the "stolen" electoral votes. Reports circulated that Democratic veterans might resort to armed resistance should Hayes be declared president. The key question was who should count the electoral votes. The Constitution declares only that electoral votes shall be counted by both houses of Congress. The impasse continued for weeks. As inauguration day, March 4, approached, it appeared that the country might have no president, or that frustration might boil over into violence.

Significantly, most of the strong language came from Northern Democrats. Southern Democrats talked peace and compromise, convinced that Hayes would not harm the South and that the Republicans intended to abandon the vestiges of Reconstruction in favor of white home rule. Many Southerners who had been Whigs and had opposed Democratic leadership before the war favored railroad building and industrial development. These projects would require aid from Northern capitalists, most of whom were Republicans. The South desperately needed capital. Its waterways and harbors had not been dredged for fifteen years. And the South, lacking a comprehensive railroad network, eyed the congressional subsidies to the transcontinental railroads enviously. Its state governments, heavily in debt and further hit by the panic of 1873, looked to the federal treasury for aid.

Previous Southern requests for subsidies had been blocked. Retrenchment became the order of the day, and Northern Democrats were the worst penny pinchers. On the other hand, Republicans responded sympathetically in 1876. Most supported a subsidy bill for a Texas and Pacific Railroad as "justice to the South." Southerners repaid this favor when many of them accepted the report of an electoral commission which certified all the doubtful electoral votes for Hayes and thus made the Ohio Republican president.

President Hayes lived up to expectations. Calling for sectional reconciliation and federal aid for internal improvements in the South, he withdrew the remaining troops and the last radical governments collapsed. Hayes hoped to build a strong Republican party in the South, based on white votes, yet his policy failed to upset Southern voting behavior. The South, "redeemed" in white hands, remained Democratic. The accommodation of 1876-1877 succeeded only partially. But white Southerners could count on one thing: the Negro would no longer receive protection from Washington. The White South had been Redeemed; the Black South had been Reclaimed.

THE FAILURE OF RECONSTRUCTION

No episode in American history has left a more bitter legacy than the decade which followed the Civil War. Northerners eventually joined Southerners in rejecting Reconstruction as a tragically misguided effort to upset the natural order of things—white supremacy. Most Northerners had gone to war neither to uplift the black man nor to revolutionize Southern society, but to preserve the Union. "To the flag we are pledged,/ All its foes we abhor,/ And we aint for the nigger,/ But we are for the war," sang Northern troops as they marched off to battle.

The war, however, proved to have an inner logic and momentum of its own that none could foresee. Although anti-Negro sentiment in the North had been an important factor in the emergence of the Republican party, and although most Northern states still discriminated against Negroes and treated them as second-class citizens, the war set in motion new forces that produced a commitment to racial equality far exceeding the real convictions of most Northerners.

First, the war gave that small but well-organized and articulate group of radicals fully devoted to racial equality an influence over policy out of proportion to their numbers. They were the Union's most militant defenders and they capitalized on patriotic feeling unleashed in wartime. As the Northern investment in human life to preserve the Union mounted beyond early calculation, Lincoln and others felt compelled to justify the expenditure of so much blood. At Gettysburg, Lincoln explained, Americans died so that the Union could have "a new birth of freedom," so that popular government "shall not perish from the earth." By investing the Union cause with a providential mission to vindicate human liberty, it became easier for Americans to accept their losses. The radicals gained even more strength from the hatred for the South and all things Southern (including slavery) which then dominated the North.

But revenge did not provide a stable underpinning for a policy that required, to be workable, radical changes in attitudes and a revolutionary redistribution of power and wealth. As Northerners satisfied their initial need to punish the rebels, the shallowness of their commitment to racial equality became evident. Even during the heyday of Radical Reconstruction, Republicans met Democratic charges that they were "nigger lovers" by arguing that only a fair chance for blacks in the South could keep them from migrating northward. Thus in the 1860s, as in the 1850s, the Republican party staked a claim as a champion of free, *white* labor. Repeatedly, Northern states voted down proposals to give the black the vote until forced to do so by the Fifteenth Amendment.

As wartime emotions subsided, compassion for the black man also waned. The freedmen grasped their new responsibilities of citizenship eagerly and discharged them remarkably well. But racists and the fainthearted seized upon and exploited the blacks' shortcomings until they convinced most Northerners, and even some abolitionists, that blacks were not ready for equality. Few Americans realized that a workable program of Reconstruction required massive help to lift both blacks and poor whites from the conditions of ignorance, poverty, and dependence in which they had lived for so long. Yet Northerners never seriously considered confiscating rebel property wholesale (other than the slave property) and redistributing it among the poor. That would have been a revolutionary act, alien to American respect for property rights and to the purposes for which the war had been fought.

Reconstruction resulted in many tragedies. The Negro suffered most from its failure, of course, since the freedmen desperately needed comprehensive aid to make them a useful part of American society. The radical Republicans also contributed to the tragedies. Although political corruption disgraced the whole nation, the radicals, by their own promises, had more to live up to. Their program overstressed politics to the neglect of the economic and educational needs of their Negro wards, with predictable results. And the white South added to the tragedies through its inability to accept the Reconstruction amendments to the Constitution. Emancipation meant that new policies more in keeping with the freedmen's potential had to be devised. White Southerners responded in 1865-1866 only to their need for labor and racial security. They would not take the Negro seriously as a political factor. A limited franchise for Negroes (those who were veterans or literate, Lincoln's two minimum categories) might have prevented Military Reconstruction and much of the bitterness it left behind.

Radical Reconstruction was out of place because state matters were not in state hands. The South's "natural" leaders in 1865 were not carpetbag politicians from Vermont or Wisconsin (or their scalawag allies), but the men who had held office before the war. For them to regain power successfully in the immediate postwar period demanded magnanimity and vision. The white South did not respond to that challenge. Yet Re-

construction in some form had to come, and for compelling reasons. Most important, the Negro had to find a place in America as a person, not as an implement. Reconstruction tried to survive in an unreceptive social climate, but it was applied haphazardly, and Northern enthusiasm for it evaporated rapidly. Better to forget it and concentrate attention on the herosim of the war. Toward the end of the century, veterans of the Union and Confederate armies began meeting regularly to exchange war stories. But a reunion convention of carpetbagger and scalawag descendants has yet to assemble in a border state to swap yarns and chuckle over old times.

Without social reconstruction of the South, Military Reconstruction had to fail. Its downfall left many wondering whether the bloodbath had been worth it. Yet even as the last troops left the South, the lives of most Americans were being transformed by forces that within one generation would make America the world's leading industrial power. As the United States moved rapidly forward in the last quarter of the nineteenth century to become a modern, urbanized and industrialized nation, the era of the Civil War receded into the distance and became the stuff legends and romantic movies are made of.

SUGGESTIONS FOR FURTHER READING

Suggestions for further reading are highly selective. Works available in the paperback are starred (*). Students should consult Edward Pessen, *Jacksonian America: Society, Personality, and Politics* (1969)* and J. G. Randall and David Donald, *The Civil War and Reconstruction* (2d edition, 1961) for additional references.

INTRODUCTION

General Works on the Period

Glyndon G. Van Deusen, *The Jacksonian Era, 1828-1848* (1959)*; Arthur M. Schlesinger, Jr., *The Age of Jackson* (1945)*; Edward Pessen, *Jacksonian America* (1969)*; Elbert B. Smith, *The Death of Slavery: The United States, 1837-65* (1967)*; Roy F. Nichols, *The Stakes of Power, 1845-1877* (1961)*; Frank Otto Gatell, ed., *Essays on Jacksonian America* (1970)*; Irwin Unger, ed., *Essays on the Civil War and Reconstruction* (1970)*.

Contemporary Accounts

Warren S. Tryon, ed., *A Mirror for Americans: Life and Manners in the United States, 1790-1870, as Recorded by American Travelers*, 3 vols. (1952).

1820s and 1830s: Adam Hodgson, *Letters from North America, Written During a Tour in the United States and Canada, 1819-1821,* 2 vols. (1824); Bradford Perkins, ed., *Youthful America: Selections from Henry Unwin Addington's Residence in the United States of America, 1822-25* (1960); Karl Bernhard, Duke of Saxe-Weimar Eisenach, *Travels Through North America during the Years 1825 and 1826,* 2 vols. (1828); Capt. Basil Hall, *Travels in North America in the Years 1827 and 1828,* 3 vols. (1829); Frances Trollope, *Domestic Manners of the Americans* (1960)*; Alexis de Tocqueville, *Democracy in America* (1969)*; E. S. Abdy, *Journal of a Residence and Tour in the United States* (1835); Michael Chevalier, *Society, Manners and Politics in the United States* (1961)*; Harriet Martineau, *Society in America* (1962)*.

1840s and 1850s: James S. Buckingham, *America, Historical, Statistical, and Descriptive.* 3 vols. (1841); Sir Charles Lyell, *Travels in North America in the Years 1841–42,* 2 vols. (1845); Signe Alice Rooth, ed., *Frederika Bremer's American Journey, 1849–1851* (1955); "Misses Mendell and Hosmer," *Notes of Travel and Life, by Two Young Ladies (1854);* Nehemiah Adams, *A South-Side View of Slavery . . .* (1859); Charles Mackay, *Life and Liberty in America . . .* (1859); Frederick Law Olmsted, *The Cotton Kingdom: A Traveller's Observations on Cotton and Slavery . . .* (1953).

1860s and 1870s: William Howard Russell, *My Diary North and South* (1965)*; Walter Lord, ed., *The (Lt. Col. Arthur) Fremantle Diary* (1960)*; Charles A. Dana, *Recollections of the Civil War* (1963)*; Mary Boykin Chesnut, *A Diary from Dixie* (1961)*; Earl Schenck Miers, *A Rebel War Clerk's Diary* (1961)*; Ray Allen Billington, ed., *The Journal of Charlotte Forten* (1961)*; C. Vann Woodward, ed., *After the War: A Tour of the Southern States, 1865–1866* by Whitelaw Reid (1965)*.

CHAPTER 10

Immigration and Labor

Marcus L. Hansen, *The Atlantic Migration, 1607–1860 . . .* (1940)*; Oscar Handlin, *Boston's Immigrants: A Study in Acculturation* (rev. edition, 1959)*; Robert Ernst, *Immigrant Life in New York City, 1825–1863* (1949); Rowland T. Berthoff, *British Immigrants in Industrial America, 1790–1950* (1953); William F. Adams, *Ireland and Irish Emigration to the New World from 1815 to the Famine* (1932); Norman Ware, *The Industrial Worker, 1840–1860 . . .* (1924)*; Hannah Josephson, *The Golden Threads: New England's Mill Girls and Magnates* (1949)*; William A. Sullivan, *The Industrial Worker in Pennsylvania, 1800–1840* (1955).

The Spread of Settlement

John D. Barnhart, *Valley of Democracy . . . the Ohio Valley, 1775–1818* (1953)*; R. Carlyle Buley, *The Old Northwest: Pioneer Period, 1815–1840,* 2 vols. (1950); Stewart H. Holbrook, *The Yankee Exodus: An Account of Migration from New England* (1968)*; Richard C. Wade, *The Urban Frontier . . .* (1964)*; Everett Dick, *The Dixie Frontier* (1964)*; Ray Allen Billington, *The Far Western Frontier, 1830–1860* (1956)*; Bernard DeVoto, *Across the Wide Missouri* (1947)*; Henry Nash Smith, *Virgin Land: The American West as Symbol and Myth* (1950)*; Rush Welter, "The Frontier West as Image of American Society," *Mississippi Valley Historical Review,* vol. 46 (1960), pp. 593–614.

The Indians

Francis P. Prucha, *American Indian Policy in the Formative Years . . . 1790–1834* (1962)*; Reginald Horsman, *Expansion and American Indian Policy, 1783–1812* (1967); Robert Berkhofer, Jr., *Salvation and the Savage . . . Protestant Missions and American Indian Response, 1787–1862* (1965); Grant Foreman, *Indian Removal: The Emigration of the Five Civilized Tribes . . .* (1932); Marion L. Starkey, *The Cherokee Nation* (1946); William S. Hoffman, "Andrew Jackson . . . [and] the Georgia Indians," *Tennessee Historical Quarterly,* vol. 11 (1952), pp. 329–345.

Economic Developments

C. Douglass North, *The Economic Growth of the United States, 1790–1860* (1961)*; Stuart Bruchey, *The Roots of American Economic Growth, 1607–1861 . . .* (1965)*; Louis B. Schmidt, "Internal Commerce and the Development of a National Economy Before 1860," *Journal of Political Economy,* vol. 47 (1939), pp. 798–822; G. B. Hutchins, *The American Maritime Industries and Public Policy . . .* (1941); Morton Rothstein, "Antebellum Wheat and Cotton Exports . . . ," *Agricultural History,* vol. 40 (1966), pp. 91–100; Norman Sydney Buck, *The Development . . . of Anglo-American Trade, 1800–1850* (1925); Samuel Eliot Morison, *The Maritime History of Massachusetts, 1783–1860* (1961)*; Robert G. Albion, *The Rise of New York Port, 1816–1860* (1939).

Agriculture

Paul W. Gates, *The Farmer's Age: Agriculture, 1815–1860* (1960)*; Leo Rogin, *The Introduction of Farm Machinery . . .* (1931); Neil A. McNall, *An Agricultural History of the Genessee Valley, 1790–1860* (1952); Lewis C. Gray, *History of Agriculture in the Southern United States, to 1860,* 2 vols. (1933); Joseph C. Clarke, *The Tobacco Kingdom . . . 1800–1860* (1938); J. Carlyle Sitterson, *Sugar Country . . .* (1953); Avery Craven, *Soil Exhaustion as a Factor in the Agricultural History of Virginia and Maryland, 1606–1860* (1926); Charles S. Davis, *The Cotton Kingdom in Alabama* (1939); Paul C. Henlein, *The Cattle Kingdom in the Ohio Valley, 1783–1860* (1959).

Transportation Revolution

George Rogers Taylor, *The Transportation Revolution, 1815-1860* (1951)*; Louis C. Hunter, *Steamboats on the Western Rivers . . .* (1949); Carter Goodrich (et al.), *Canals and American Economic Development* (1961); Ronald E. Shaw, *Erie Water West: A History of the Erie Canal . . .* (1966); Robert W. Fogel, *Railroads and American Economic Growth* (1964); Edward C. Kirkland, *Men, Cities and Transportation . . .* , 2 vols. (1948); Merl E. Reed, *New Orleans and the Railroads . . .* (1966).

Industry

Victor S. Clark, *History of Manufactures in the United States,* 3 vols. (1929); Peter Temin, *Iron and Steel in Nineteenth-Century America . . .* (1964); Blanche E. Hazard, *The Organization of the Boot and Shoe Industry in Massachusetts Before 1875* (1921); Arthur H. Cole, *The American Wool Manufacture,* 2 vols. (1926); Caroline F. Ware, *The Early New England Cotton Manufacture* (1931); Paul F. McGouldrick, *New England Textiles in the Nineteenth Century . . .* (1968); Ernest M. Lander, Jr., *The Textile Industry in Antebellum South Carolina* (1969).

Financial Growth and the Role of Government

Fritz Redlich, *The Molding of American Banking . . .* , 2 vols. (1947-51); Bray Hammond, *Banks and Politics in America . . .* (1957)*; Harry E. Miller, *Banking Theories in the United States Before 1860* (1927); Joseph Van Fenstermaker, *The Development of American Commercial Banking . . .* (1965); Davis R. Dewey, *State Banking Before the Civil War* (1910); Oscar and Mary F. Handlin, *Commonwealth: A Study of the Role of Government in the American Economy, Massachusetts, 1774-1861* (rev. edition, 1969); Louis Hartz, *Economic Policy and Democratic Thought: Pennsylvania, 1776-1860* (1948)*; John W. Cadman, *The Corporation in New Jersey: Business and Politics, 1791-1875* (1949); Milton S. Heath, *Constructive Liberalism: The Role of the State in Economic Development in Georgia to 1860* (1954).

CHAPTER 11

The Politics of Nationalism

George Dangerfield, *The Era of Good Feelings* (1951)*; Norris W. Preyer, "Southern Support of the Tariff of 1816 — A Reappraisal," *Journal of Southern History,* vol. 25 (1959), pp. 306-322; Robert K. Faulkner, *The Jurisprudence of John Marshall* (1968).

The Revival of Parties

Glover Moore, *The Missouri Controversy* (1956)*; Richard Hofstadter, *The Idea of a Party System . . .* (1969)*; Shaw Livermore, *The Twilight of Federalism* (1962); Chilton Williamson, *American Suffrage: From Property to Democracy, 1760-1860* (1960)*; James C. Chase, "Jacksonian Democracy and the Rise of the Nominating Convention," *Mid-America,* vol. 45 (1963), pp. 229-249.

Jackson Takes Over

Robert Remini, *The Election of Andrew Jackson* (1963)*; Richard P. McCormick, "New Perspectives on Jacksonian Politics," *American Historical Review,* vol. 65 (1960), pp. 288-301; Erik M. Erikson, "The Federal Civil Service Under President Jackson," *Mississippi Valley Historical Review,* vol. 13 (1927), pp. 517-540; Leonard D. White, *The Jacksonians: A Study in Administrative History, 1829-1861* (1954)*; Richard P. McCormick, *The Second American Party System . . .* (1966)*; William W. Freehling, *Prelude to Civil War: Nullification in South Carolina* (1966)*.

The Bank War

Robert V. Remini, *Andrew Jackson and the Bank War* (1967)*; Thomas P. Govan, *Nicholas Biddle* (1959); Frank Otto Gatell, "Sober Second Thoughts on Van Buren . . . and the Wall Street Conspiracy," *Journal of American History,* vol. 53 (1966), pp. 19-40; Frank Otto Gatell (ed.), *The Jacksonians and the Money Power* (1967)*; Lynn L. Marshall, "The Authorship of Jackson's Bank Veto Message," *Mississippi Valley Historical Review,* vol. 50 (1963), pp. 466-477; Marvin Meyers, *The Jacksonian Persuasion* (1957)*; John W. Ward, *Andrew Jackson: Symbol for an Age* (1955)*.

Van Burenism

Reginald C. McGrane, *The Panic of 1837* (1924)*; Edward Pessen, *Most Uncommon Jacksonians: The Radical Leaders of the Early Labor Movement* (1967)*; James C. Curtis, *The Fox at Bay: Martin Van Buren and the Presidency . . .* (1970); Robert G. Gunderson, *The Log-Cabin Campaign* (1957).

CHAPTER 12

America's Mission

Paul C. Nagel, *One Nation Indivisible: The Union in American Thought, 1776–1861* (1964); Yehoshua Arieli, *Individualism and Nationalism in American Ideology* (1966)*; Edward M. Burns, *The American Idea of Mission . . .* (1957).

Salvation for All

William W. Sweet, *Religion in the Development of American Culture, 1765–1840* (1952); Catharine C. Cleveland, *The Great Revival in the West, 1797–1805* (1959); Whitney R. Cross, *The Burned-Over District . . . Enthusiastic Religion in Western New York, 1800–1850* (1965)*; Charles I. Foster, *An Errand of Mercy: The Evangelical United Front, 1790–1837* (1960); Timothy L. Smith, *Revivalism and Social Reform in the Mid-Nineteenth Century* (1965)*; David P. Edgell, *William Ellery Channing . . .* (1955); Barbara M. Cross, *Horace Bushnell . . .* (1958); Ralph H. Gabriel, "Evangelical Religion and Popular Romanticism in Early Nineteenth-Century America," *Church History*, vol. 19 (1950), pp. 34–47; William G. McLoughlin, "Pietism and the American Character," *American Quarterly*, vol. 17 (1965), pp. 163–186; Thomas F. O'Dea, *The Mormons* (1964)*.

The Reform Impulse

Alice Felt Tyler, *Freedom's Ferment: Chapters in American Social History to 1860* (1962)*; Clifford S. Griffin, *Their Brothers' Keepers: Moral Stewardship in the United States, 1800–1865* (1960) and *The Ferment of Reform, 1830–1860* (1967)*; Arthur M. Schlesinger, *The American as Reformer* (1968)*; John L. Thomas, "Romantic Reform in America, 1815–1865," *American Quarterly*, vol. 17 (1965), pp. 656–681.

John A. Krout, *The Origins of Prohibition* (1925); Joseph R. Gusfield, *Symbolic Crusade: Status Politics and the American Temperance Movement* (1967)*; Frank L. Byrne, *Prophet of Prohibition: Neal Dow and His Crusade* (1961); Harold Schwartz, *Samuel Gridley Howe, Social Reformer* (1956); Arthur E. Bestor, Jr., *Backwoods Utopias: . . . Communitarian Socialism in America, 1663–1829* (1950); Edward D. Andrews, *The People Called Shakers . . .* (1963)*; Edward R. Curtis, *A Season in Utopia: The Story of Brook Farm* (1961); William R. Waterman, *Frances Wright* (1924); Otelia Cromwell, *Lucretia Mott* (1958).

Education

Sidney L. Jackson, *America's Struggle for Free Schools . . .* (1941); Raymond A. Mohl, "Education as Social Control in New York City, 1784-1825," *New York History*, vol. 51 (1970), pp. 219-237; Timothy L. Smith, "Protestant Schooling and American Nationality, 1800-1850," *Journal of American History*, vol. 53 (1967), pp. 679-695; Mary Peabody Mann, *Life of Horace Mann* (1891); Maxine Greene, *The Public School and the Private Vision . . .* (1965)*; Michael Katz, *The Irony of Early School Reform . . .* (1968).

Cultural Flowering

Russel B. Nye, *The Cultural Life of the New Nation* (1960)*; F. O. Matthiessen, *American Renaissance: Art and Expression in the Age of Emerson and Whitman* (1968)*; R. W. B. Lewis, *The American Adam . . .* (1958)*; Stephen E. Whicher, *Freedom and Fate: An Inner Life of Ralph Waldo Emerson* (1961)*; Perry Miller, *The Raven and the Whale* (1956)*; Irving H. Bartlett, *The American Mind in the Mid-Nineteenth Century* (1967)*.

CHAPTER 13

Winthrop D. Jordan, *White Over Black: American Attitudes Toward the Negro, 1550–1812* (1969)*; David Brion Davis, *The Problem of Slavery in Western Culture* (1968)*; Philip D. Curtin, *The Atlantic Slave Trade: A Census* (1969); U. B. Phillips, *Life and Labor in the Old South* (1966)*; Kenneth M. Stampp, *The Peculiar Institution . . .* (1956)*; Stanley M. Elkins, *Slavery . . .* (2d edition, 1968)*; Allen Weinstein and Frank Otto Gatell, eds., *American Negro Slavery: A Modern Reader* (1968)*.

William Cohen, "Thomas Jefferson and the Problem of Slavery," *Journal of American History*, vol. 56 (1969), pp. 503-526; Robert McColley, *Slavery and Jeffersonian Virginia* (1964); Edgar J. McManus, *A History of Negro Slavery in New York* (1966); James B. Sellers, *Slavery in Alabama* (1950); Charles S. Sydnor, *Slavery in Mississippi* (1966)*; Joe G. Taylor, *Negro Slavery in Louisiana* (1963); William D. Postell, *The Health of Slaves on Southern Plantations* (1951); William K. Scarborough, *The Overseer: Plantation Management in the Old South* (1966); Richard C. Wade, *Slavery in the Cities: The South, 1820-1860* (1967)*; Benjamin H. Mays, *The Negro's God* (1939)*; Donald G. Mathews, *Slavery and Methodism . . .* (1965); Thomas E. Drake, *Quakers and Slavery in America* (1950).

Slave Resistance and Revolt

Charles H. Nichols, *Many Thousands Gone: The Ex-Slaves' Account of Their Bondage and Freedom* (1969)*; Raymond and Alice Bauer, "Day-to-Day Resistance to Slavery," *Journal of Negro History*, vol. 27 (1942), pp. 388-419; Herbert Aptheker, *American Negro Slave Revolts* (1963)*; Eugene D. Genovese, "Rebelliousness and Docility in the Negro Slave . . . ," *Civil War History*, vol. 13 (1967), pp. 293-314; William F. Cheek, *Black Resistance Before the Civil War* (1970); John Lofton, *Insurrection in South Carolina: The Turbulent World of Denmark Vesey* (1964); Richard C. Wade, "The Vesey Plot: A Reconsideration," *Journal of Southern History*, vol. 30 (1964), pp. 143-161; Edwin A. Miles, "The Mississippi Slave Insurrection Scare of 1835," *Journal of Negro History*, vol. 42 (1957), pp. 48-60.

Economics of Slavery

Thomas P. Govan, "Was Plantation Slavery Profitable?" *Journal of Southern History*, vol. 8 (1942), pp. 513-535; Harold D. Woodman, "The Profitability of Slavery: A Historical Perennial," *Journal of Southern History*, vol. 29 (1963), pp. 303-325; Eugene D. Genovese, *The Political Economy of Slavery . . .* (1968)*; Robert S. Starobin, *Industrial Slavery in the Old South* (1970); Alfred H. Conrad and J. R. Meyers, *The Economics of Slavery . . .* (1964).

The Antislavery Movements

Alice D. Adams, *The Neglected Period of Anti-Slavery in America, 1808-1831* (1908); Philip J. Staudenraus, *The African Colonization Movement* (1961); Louis Filler, *The Crusade Against Slavery, 1830-1860* (1964)*; Dwight L. Dumond, *Antislavery . . .* (1967)*; Gerald S. Henig, "The Jacksonian Attitude Toward Abolitionists in the 1830's," *Tennessee Historical Quarterly*, vol. 28 (1969), pp. 42-56; Leonard L. Richards, *"Gentlemen of Property and Standing": Anti-Abolition Riots in America in the 1830's* (1970); Robert P. Ludlum, "The Antislavery 'Gag Rule' . . . ," *Journal of Negro History*, vol. 26 (1941), pp. 203-243.

John L. Thomas, *The Liberator: William Lloyd Garrison* (1963); Bertram Wyatt-Brown, "William Lloyd Garrison and Antislavery Unity," *Civil War History*, vol. 13 (1967), pp. 5-24; James B. Stewart, "The Aims and Impact of Garrisonian Abolitionism," *Civil War History*, vol. 15 (1969), pp. 197-209; Aileen S. Kraditor, *Means and Ends in American Abolitionism: Garrison and His Critics . . .* (1969); Irving H. Bartlett, *Wendell Phillips . . .* (1961).

Joseph G. Rayback, "The Liberty Party Leaders of Ohio . . . ," *Ohio Historical Quarterly*, vol. 42 (1948), pp. 165-178; Betty Fladeland, *James G. Birney . . .* (1955); Benjamin P. Thomas, *Theodore Weld . . .* (1950); Bertram Wyatt-Brown, *Lewis Tappan and the Evangelical War Against Slavery* (1969); Merton L. Dillon, *Elijah P. Lovejoy . . .* (1961).

Black Abolitionists and the Free Negro

Benjamin Quarles, *Black Abolitionists* (1969)* and *Frederick Douglass* (1968)*; Philip S. Foner, *Frederick Douglass . . .* (1964); William Farrison, *William Wells Brown . . .* (1969); Earl Conrad, *Harriet Tubman* (1943); Leon F. Litwack, *North of Slavery: The Negro in the Free States, 1790-1860* (1965)*; E. Franklin Frazier, *The Free Negro Family . . .* (1932); Luther P. Jackson, *Free Negro . . . in Virginia* (1969)*; John Hope Franklin, *The Free Negro in North Carolina . . .* (1943).

CHAPTER 14

E. Malcolm Carroll, *Origins of the Whig Party* (1925); Glyndon G. Van Deusen, "Some Aspects of Whig Thought and Theory . . . ," *American Historical Review*, vol. 63 (1958), pp. 305-322; Charles G. Sellers, "Who Were the Southern Whigs?" *American Historical Review*, vol 59 (1954), pp. 335-346; John V. Mering, *The Whig Party in Missouri* (1960); Robert J. Morgan, *A Whig Embattled: The Presidency Under John Tyler* (1954).

James C. N. Paul, *Rift in the Democracy* (1961)*; Bernard DeVoto, *The Year of Decision, 1846* (1962)*; Albert K. Weinberg, *Manifest Destiny . . .* (1963)*; Otis A. Singletary, *The Mexican War* (1963)*; Eric Foner, "The Wilmot Proviso Revisited," *Journal of American History*, vol. 56 (1969), pp. 262-279; Charles G. Sellers, *James K. Polk: Continentalist . . .* (1966).

The Compromise and Its Aftermath

Holman Hamilton, *Prologue to Conflict: The Crisis and Compromise of 1850* (1966)*; Larry Gara, *The Liberty Line: The Legend of the Underground Railroad* (1967)*; Stanley W. Campbell, *The Slave Catchers: Enforcement of the Fugitive Slave Law . . .* (1970); Gerald M. Capers, *Stephen A. Douglas . . .* (1959); Alice Nichols, *Bleeding Kansas* (1954); Samuel A. Johnson, *The Battle Cry of Freedom: The New England Emigrant Aid Company . . .* (1954).

Nativism

Ray Allen Billington, *The Protestant Crusade, 1800–1860* (1964)*; David Brion Davis, "Some Themes of Counter-Subversion: An Analysis of Anti-Masonic, Anti-Catholic, and Anti-Mormon Literature," *Mississippi Valley Historical Review*, vol. 47 (1960), pp. 205–224; William G. Bean, "Puritan versus Celt, 1850–1860," *New England Quarterly*, vol. 7 (1934), pp. 70–89; W. Darrell Overdyke, *The Know-Nothing Party in the South* (1950).

The Road to War

Roy F. Nichols, *The Disruption of American Democracy* (1964)*; Vincent C. Hopkins, *Dred Scott's Case* (1967)*; Don E. Fehrenbacher, *Prelude to Greatness: Lincoln in the 1850's* (1964)*; Eric Foner, *Free Soil, Free Labor, Free Men: The Ideology of the Republican Party Before the Civil War* (1970)*; Harry V. Jaffa, *Crisis of the House Divided: . . . the Issues in the Lincoln-Douglas Debates* (1959); Avery Craven, *The Coming of the Civil War* (1963)*; David M. Potter, *The South and the Sectional Conflict* (1968).

CHAPTER 15

Secession

Dwight L. Dumond, *The Secession Movement* (1931); Steven A. Channing, *Crisis of Fear: Secession in South Carolina* (1970); Ralph A. Wooster, *The Secession Conventions of the South* (1962): Robert G. Gunderson, *Old Gentlemen's Convention: The Washington Peace Conference of 1861* (1961); Kenneth M. Stampp, *And the War Came: The North and the Secession Crisis, 1860–61* (1964)*; Richard N. Current, *Lincoln and the First Shot* (1963)*.

Lincoln in Power

John S. Tilley, *Lincoln Takes Command* (1941); J. G. Randall, *Constitutional Problems Under Lincoln* (rev. edition, 1964)*; Jay Monaghan, *Diplomat in Carpet Slippers: Abraham Lincoln Deals with Foreign Affairs* (1962)*; T. Harry Williams, *Lincoln and His Generals* (1967)*.

Liberty and Union

John Hope Franklin, *The Emancipation Proclamation* (1965)*; Mark Krug, "The Republican Party and the Emancipation Proclamation," *Journal of Negro History*, vol. 48 (1963), pp. 98–114; Benjamin Quarles, *The Negro in the Civil War* (1953)*; T. Harry Williams, *Lincoln and the Radicals* (1960)*; Frank Klement, *The Copperheads of the Middle West* (1960).

Clement Eaton, *A History of the Southern Confederacy* (1965)*; Charles P. Roland, *The Confederacy* (1960)*; David Donald, ed., *Why the North Won the Civil War* (1962)*; Ralph Andreano, ed., *The Economic Impact of the American Civil War* (1962)*; Richard N. Current, *The Lincoln Nobody Knows* (1963)*.

Johnson and the Freedmen

Kenneth M. Stampp, *The Era of Reconstruction . . .* (1967)*; Rembert W. Patrick, *The Reconstruction of the Nation* (1967)*; Kenneth M. Stampp and Leon Litwack, eds., *Reconstruction: An Anthology of Revisionist Writings* (1969)*; Eric L. McKitrick, *Andrew Johnson and Reconstruction* (1964)*; Lawanda and John H. Cox, *Politics, Principle, and Prejudice, 1865–1866: Dilemma of Reconstruction America* (1969)*; W. R. Brock, *An American Crisis: Congress and Reconstruction, 1865–1867* (1966)*; Theodore B. Wilson, *The Black Codes of the South* (1965); Forrest G. Wood, *Black Scare: The Racist Response to Emancipation and Reconstruction* (1970)*.

Radical Reconstruction

Hans L. Trefousse, *The Radical Republicans: Lincoln's Vanguard for Racial Justice* (1969); Willie Lee Rose, *Rehearsal for Reconstruction: The Port Royal Experiment* (1967)*; George R. Bentley, *A History of the Freedmen's Bureau* (1955); W. E. Burghardt Du Bois, *Black Reconstruction . . . in America* (1966)*; August Meier, "Negroes in the First and Second Reconstruction of the South," *Civil War History*, vol. 13 (1967), pp. 114–130; Robert Cruden, *The Negro in Reconstruction* (1969)*; Joel Williamson, *After Slavery: The Negro in South Carolina During Reconstruction . . .* (1967)*.

The End of Reconstruction

Stanley Horn, *Invisible Empire: The Story of the Ku Klux Klan . . .* (1939); C. Vann Woodward, *Reunion and Reaction . . .* (rev. edition, 1956)*.

Part Four
Industrial America, 1877 - 1900

Introduction

The triumph of industrialism in late-nineteenth-century America transformed the face of the country. Towns became cities, and cities metropolises which no one knew how to govern. Men accumulated new fortunes overnight in railroading, mining, and manufacturing, pushing aside older families that had once monopolized social and political power.

Industrialism made the United States rich and powerful but it also exacted a heavy price in social dislocation. Repeatedly the system faltered, and hard times stalked the land, bankrupting farmers, throwing thousands of factory hands out of work, and igniting smoldering antagonism between the native-born and the recently arrived foreigners. At time, men despaired of the future. Workers fought pitched battles with their employers, and farmers grasped at radical, sometimes fuzzy solutions to their predicament.

Yet throughout most of these years protest proved ineffective, rarely sustained by many or for long. The lures of industrialism, offering seemingly boundless opportunites, proved irresistible. As long as most men believed that hard work and enterprise (with a bit of luck) would eventually pay handsome rewards, they tended to blame themselves for failure. Few thought of seeking government help: the government should remain a policeman, maintaining the peace so that industrial progress could advance without interruption; politicians should help but not control the forces of economic growth.

For almost twenty-five years after the Civil War, both parties minimized government's role. They quarreled over the issues of the past, such as the war and Reconstruction, and they scrambled nimbly and hungrily for the spoils of power; but otherwise, the principles, programs, and performance of Republicans and Democrats differed little. Neither party dared confront the disruptions caused by industrialism; nor could they alleviate the suffering generated by rapid change. A generation of American politicians tried to ignore the accumulating stresses and dilemmas that ultimately exploded at the end of the century.

Politics instead became a grand entertainment, the hoopla of campaigns a source of excitement that relieved the monotony in the lives of millions, without television or movies, who wanted to believe that their votes and voices counted in a society increasingly under the sway of large, impersonal organizations. So the parties competed relentlessly and closely at the polls for the voter's favor, and until the mid-1890s neither won a safe majority.

From time to time, society's "losers" turned to government for help, but dissidents found the two parties deaf to their demands. Most Americans remained faithful to free enterprise and distrusted government, so the parties could ignore dissenters or appease them with minor concessions. The dissatisfied formed short-lived splinter parties or severed their traditional party moorings, but they failed to unite. Rapid and pervasive change, extensive social disorganization, and belief in the ultimate wisdom of unregulated industrialism kept protests disorganized, scattered, and disconnected.

Significant change came finally in the last decade of the nineteenth century. William Jennings Bryan's campaign for the presidency in 1896, explained Kansas editor William Allen White, was different: "It was the first time in my life and in the life of a generation in which any man large enough to lead a national party had boldly and unashamedly made his cause that of the poor and the oppressed." The effort was long overdue.

A grim army of factory workers in New England, 1868. *(Library of Congress)*

From slaves to share-
croppers, Virginia, 1890s.
(Library of Congress)

Stemming tobacco. *(Cook
Collection, Valentine
Museum)*

Europe's uprooted: Irish
immigrants for America,
1866. *(Library of Congress)*

Exporting the unwanted,
1879. *(Culver Pictures)*

2347. Tallyho Coaching. Sioux City party Coaching at the Great Hot Springs of Dakota.
Photo and copyright by Grabill, 1889.

No room on the stage coach, Great Hot Springs, Dakota, 1889. *(Library of Congress)*

The medicine man, taken at the battle of Wounded Knee, South Dakota, January 1, 1891. *(Library of Congress)*

Home of Mrs. American Horse, Deadwood, South Dakota, 1891. *(Library of Congress)*

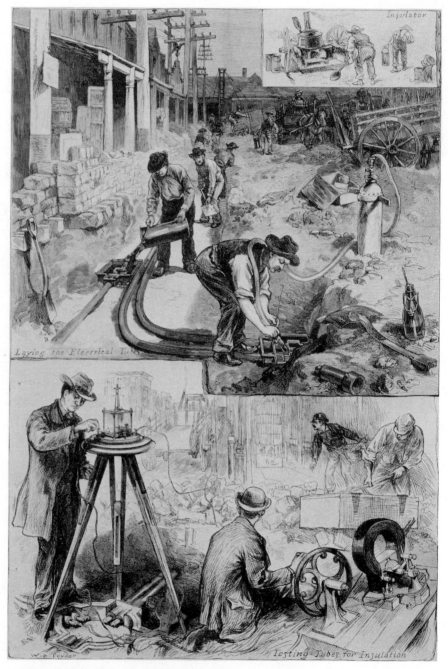

Lighting up America, New York, 1882. *(Library of Congress)*

Boston Jews in the Promised Land, 1899. *(Library of Congress)*

Chapter 16
The Emergence of Industrial America

In the forty years following the Civil War the United States seized the world's industrial leadership, overtaking Great Britain in the 1880s and forging far ahead of its other rivals. American production quadrupled and per capita income more than doubled. By the eve of the First World War (1914-1918), American factories turned out twice as many goods as Britain and Germany combined.

This extraordinary advance in national wealth after the Civil War occurred because in the preceding four decades (1820-1860) the United States had laid the foundations of a modern economy: population spread across the eastern half of the country, agricultural production boomed in the South and the Midwest, and manufacturing had emerged in the Northeast. The communications network had produced a transportation revolution, which made possible the creation of a large national market stimulating regional specialization and interdependence and using resources far more efficiently.

In 1860 agriculture still remained the leading sector of the American economy, but by the end of the century manufacturing topped farming and in 1900 it accounted for half of the country's gross national product (GNP). The farms generated more wealth than ever but they could not outproduce the factories in dollar value of goods. Older manufacturing industries expanded as new ones sprang up. Railroads reached the Pacific, further broadening the national market and bringing millions of acres of new farm land into production. The railroads themselves became a leading customer for heavy industry, thereby promoting growth in both the agricultural and industrial sectors.

Toward the end of the century, the cities replaced the railroads as the dynamic spur to economic growth. New factories and mines, together with an elaborate distribution network, created millions of jobs in the commercial and industrial sectors of the economy. New cities arose around mills and near mines, and older urban centers became densely packed metropolises. By 1885 a majority of American workers found employment outside agriculture and by the end of the century 40 percent of the population lived in cities or towns of over 2500 people.

Modern America thus took shape in the late nineteenth century. The United States became the richest nation on earth and one of the most populous. Its citizens increasingly lived in cities; those who remained on farms became the most productive agriculturists in the world. Its industrial machine spawned Big Business—powerful corporations which organized capital, labor, and enterprise on massive scales. In the international economy, the United States became a world leader. At home its citizens enjoyed the highest per capita living standard on the globe. This achievement of preeminence and affluence resulted from the efforts of the generation that had preserved the Union and then developed its productive potential during the decades after Grant and Lee made peace at Appomattox Court House, the final third of the nineteenth century.

THE LABOR FORCE

From the beginning, a shortage of labor had hindered American economic growth. Originally inhabited by small numbers of "uncooperative" Indians, the British North American colonies had relied for labor on white immigrants from Europe and black slaves from Africa. Though the native-born reproduced rapidly, the continent was so large and potentially so productive that Americans needed successive waves of newcomers to work on farms and in factories—and never more so than in the late nineteenth century. The responsive movement of people across the oceans dwarfed all earlier migrations. Fourteen million immigrants, mostly Europeans, poured into the United States between 1860 and 1900, more than twice the number entering during the preceding forty years. And the tide kept rolling: another fourteen million came during the first fifteen years of the twentieth century until war in Europe checked the flow. In all, forty million immigrants reached American shores during the century and a half after 1820.

The Irish and Germans, who had migrated in such large numbers before the Civil War, still came, but now other parts of Europe sent their sons and daughters, too. As Scandinavia and southern and eastern Europe began to modernize and feel the pinch of economic competition from other parts of the world, peasants and craftsmen found it harder to make a living. Millions of Swedes, Italians, Poles, and Russians set off for America and the prospect of a better life; among them were hundreds of thousands of East European Jews who regarded America as their Promised Land, a refuge from religious persecution and poverty. These new sources of immigration, and a heavy resurgence in German migration, made the population of the United States, already the most diverse on earth, still more varied ethnically.

Railroad operators, land speculators, and industrialists welcomed the newcomers and even helped to organize migration in Europe and at the ports of entry in America. The flow of newcomers seemed essential for America's rapid development. Immigrants with capital were potential customers for Western land, and as farmers they would also become customers for freight services. Those who remained in the cities assured industrialists of ample factory help and enlarged demands for the products of America's farms and factories. Between 1860 and 1900 the nation's population more than doubled, reaching 76 million, with newcomers contributing mightily to that growth. The labor force grew even more rapidly, however, since most immigrants were of working age.

THE END OF THE WESTERN FRONTIER

A tidal wave of internal migration within the United States paralleled the unprecedented movement of people across the Atlantic Ocean to America. As the millions of foreigners and more millions of the native-born poured into the towns and cities, others spread across the continent. By 1890, the federal government reported that the frontier—the continuous belt of unsettled land—was gone. In half a century Americans settled the areas west of the Mississippi and created fourteen new states, beginning with Kansas in 1861 and ending with Arizona and New Mexico in 1912.

The Trans-Mississippi West was a strange wilderness, unlike other environments Americans had encountered in the eastern half of the country. Prairies heavily matted with tall grasses but with few trees gave way beyond the hundredth meridian to a seemingly endless semiarid plain with even fewer trees. The plains stretched for hundreds of miles to the Rocky Mountains, a formidable barrier to the Pacific. Across the mountains lay a great desert, surrounded by the peaks of the Rockies to the east and the Sierra Nevada to the west. But beyond this forbidding country waited the lush valleys of the far West, the Willamette in western Oregon and Washington, and the fertile Central Valley of California.

Long before settlers moved into the Trans-Mississippi West, explorers and fur traders had penetrated the wilderness. Jefferson sent Lewis and Clark to investigate the far Northwest (1804-1805), and Zebulon Pike explored the Southwest (1806-1807). For generations the remote mountains, plains, and deserts remained the preserves of Indians and a few white fur trappers. As they entered unknown country, the traders tapped new sources of pelts, which they bought cheaply from the Indians; at the same time they traced the sources of the rivers, discovered mountain passes, and became familiar with Indian tribes. These activities prepared the way for permanent white settlement.

When descriptions of the Far West filtered back East, Americans concluded by the 1820s that most of the area west of the ninety-fifth meridian was a Great Desert punctured by impassable mountains. With plenty of fertile and empty land in the East to occupy the white man's mind, the Great Plains seemed destined to become an enormous reservation for dispossessed Indians, an outdoor concentration camp where native tribes could be left unmolested.

Washington policy reflected this smug conviction. In the 1830s the federal government set aside a large area as a "Permanent Indian Fron-

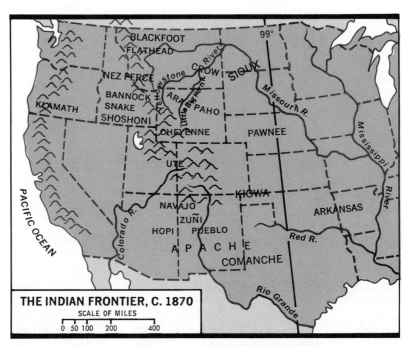

THE INDIAN FRONTIER, C. 1870

SCALE OF MILES

0 50 100 200 400

tier." It specified areas as reservations for tribes uprooted from the East and for those native to the Plains, and it established the Bureau of Indian Affairs in 1832 to teach farming and to license white traders.

Forced from their traditional hunting grounds, scorned by the Plains Indians who regarded them as intruders, and perplexed by a strange environment, the eastern tribes disintegrated economically and socially. The decline of the Indians, most Americans believed, was the price of advancing civilization. "What good man," asked President Andrew Jackson rhetorically in 1830, "would prefer a country covered with forests and ranged by a few thousand savages to our extensive Republic, studded with cities, towns, and prosperous farms, embellished with all the improvements which art can devise or industry execute, occupied by more than 12 million happy people?" Obviously, few white men would prefer the first choice.

By midcentury Americans once again shattered the peace of the "permanent" reservation. The discovery of gold in California in 1848 touched off a rush to the Pacific Coast. Lured by the prospect of quick riches, thousands scur-

ried to the Golden Hills of California. Requiring little capital, the prospector trusted to his luck and when disappointed in one place he tried elsewhere. In three years, as a result of the California Gold Rush, fifty thousand Indians perished, mostly from diseases against which they had no immunity. Although the fever of the 1850s began to subside in California it recurred elsewhere in the next decade. One hundred thousand miners pushed through Kansas in 1859 to Nevada and Arizona, Idaho and Montana, Colorado and the Dakotas. The permanent settlement of these areas by whites awaited the coming of cattlemen and farmers, but the advancing mining frontier brought Americans and Indians into conflict once more and helped prepare the way for settlers.

The construction of transcontinental railroads in the 1860s and 1870s, during the heyday of the mining boom, intensified Indian fears that the lands solemnly promised would be lost. The tough and proud Plains Indians, superb horsemen and warriors, fought back. The rush into Colorado and the Black Hills set the Plains afire with conflict. For two decades (1860–1880) white men and red men massacred one another, but the Indians never had a chance. A few initial victories encouraged them to continue the struggle, but the United States Army slowly ground them down. Troops deployed from Texas to North Dakota and from Kansas to California, fought over a thousand battles and taught the Indians, as one western commander put it, that "all who cling to their old hunting grounds are hostile and will remain so till killed off." The slaughter of thirteen million buffalo in less than twenty years by hide hunters and soldiers destroyed the basis of Indian range life and further broke their resistance. The government then herded the remaining Indians into continually shrinking reservations, opening more land for white exploitation.

By the end of the nineteenth century, the last pockets of Indian resistance had collapsed. After three centuries, the American continent belonged exclusively to the white man. In the process whites justified the dispossession of the red men by arguing that the Indians stood in the way of progress. Irked by their guilty consciences, whites also attempted to dehumanize Indians in order to legitimize their ill treatment of them. The Indians, according to popular attitudes, were "a set of miserable, dirty, lousy, blanketed, thieving, lying,

sneaking, murdering, graceless, faithless, gut-eating skunks . . . whose immediate and final extermination all men, except Indian agents and traders, should pray for." Much of the extermination took place without prayers.

AGRICULTURE AND ECONOMIC DEVELOPMENT

The neutralization and partial liquidation of the Indians opened the way for farmers and cattlemen who transformed the Trans-Mississippi West from a wilderness into a valuable addition to the country's agricultural economy. Before the Civil War the agricultural sector, the main source of the country's wealth, had played a leading role in economic development. Southern cotton growers and midwestern corn and wheat producers became steady customers for domestic manufacturers as well as the principal supplier of the raw materials and foodstuffs on which America's export trade and industrial development rested. Until the postwar expansion of the railroads, agriculture also provided the main market for

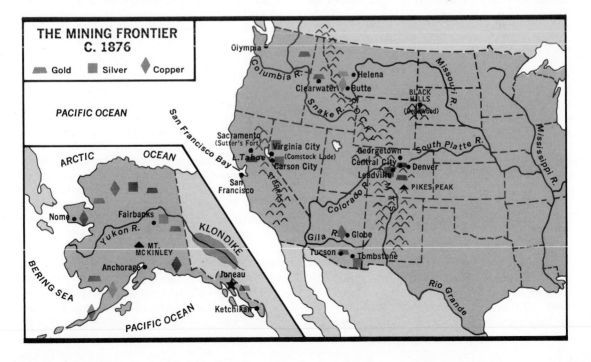

iron and steel as well as other products of American industry. In this way, rural America kept factories and workshops busy and growing; at the same time industrial cities also grew and consumed food and fiber produced on the farm. After the Civil War, though the manufacturing sector surpassed the agricultural sector in economic importance, the surge in farm output continued to play a major role in America's industrialization and in securing its newly won industrial preeminence.

Cotton remained America's leading export. The Civil War devastated much of the South but not the land itself. After a decade of peace cotton exports reached prewar levels. Cotton production expanded into new regions, especially in Texas, Arkansas, and the lower Mississippi Valley. Outside the cotton belt, tobacco and sugar remained the South's leading staples. But Southern agriculture no longer played so important a role as it had before the Civil War. Most of the South's best land had come under cultivation before the war, and sharecropping and tenant farming proved inefficient. Mechanization and improved methods of cultivation increased farm efficiency in the Middle West, but Southern farmers modernized slowly.

Corn and Wheat Belts

The dynamic center of the agricultural economy shifted to the corn and wheat belts in the Midwest. As the railroads spread into Illinois and spanned the Mississippi River millions of acres of virgin land, well-suited to cereal agriculture, came within reach of distant markets. Farmers quickly followed, spurred on by cheap transportation, generous federal land policy, new technology, and the boom spirit.

Aided by land grants and other forms of public support, railroads rapidly spread west of Chicago after the Civil War. A network of feeder roads linked farmers with the main lines to Chicago and St. Louis and with the eastern trunk lines. As a result, the amount of land under cultivation more than doubled between 1860 and 1900. The federal government contributed by liberally transferring the public domain to private hands. Until the Civil War farmers had had to buy land at auction at the minimum purchase price of $1.25 per acre. The Homestead Act (1862), blocked by Southern opposition during the 1850s, now offered 160 acres of free land to anyone settling a tract for five years. Under this law 400,000 families acquired farms in the late nineteenth century. But most still bought the best land either from the government or from speculators who had acquired huge tracts.

Advocates of land reform through a homestead law wanted the public domain reserved for actual settlers. They fought against its use as a source of revenue through land sales to capitalists. The 1862 law brought them apparent victory, yet the federal government still disposed of great quantities of public land—usually the choicest tracts—through sale and giveaways. Shrewdly manipulating the provisions of postwar land legislation, speculators purchased far more of the public domain than did homesteaders, and railroads received millions of acres as subsidies from Congress and from state and local governments. Though the government's generosity enriched a few and increased the cost of buying a farm, speculators, it should be noted, encouraged settlement and offered liberal credit. Subsidies to railroads also made commercial agriculture possible in areas that otherwise would have remained inaccessible and untouched.

Though land was abundant, the prairies and plains posed new problems. At the start, they baffled farmers accustomed to the well-watered and heavily forested areas to the East. The treeless prairies and plains lacked the timber that farmers needed to fence their land and build homes and barns. The railroads helped by bringing lumber from the forests of northern Michigan and Wisconsin, and the invention of barbed wired solved the fencing problem cheaply. Development of the Trans-Mississippi West depended upon advances in agricultural technology. Prairie sod was tough, not easily broken by conventional ploughs. Heavy, cast-iron ploughs pulled by large teams of horses or oxen made clearing land for the first crops expensive, until new and more efficient steel ploughs solved that problem too.

Machinery held the key to the rapid cultivation of the prairies and plains. Without it the farmer, relying on the labor of his family and perhaps a few hired hands, could plant only as much as could be harvested by old and inefficient methods. Farm machinery developed before the Civil War and perfected and widely distributed after 1860, changed that. As hundreds of thousands of farmers joined the Union Army, machines helped produce the food then bringing high prices in the East. The thousands of seed-planters, cultivators, harvesters, threshers, and binders turned out by farm equipment manufacturers dramatically increased agricultural productivity. Output per man-hour in wheat and oats by 1900 was four times that of 1840. Since the flat prairies and plains were well suited to mechanization, farmers quickly invested profits in machines that permitted further expansion. The emergence of a large market for farm equipment enabled manufacturers to reduce prices, which declined until the 1890s, thereby bringing the new technology within the reach of still more farmers.

Mechanization profoundly and permanently altered American agriculture. Before the distribution of machinery, most agricultural advances came through the westward spread of more farmers cultivating more land. Machinery, however,

enabled farmers to increase output dramatically without depending primarily on increased inputs of labor. As a result, American farmers vastly expanded productive capacity while the percentage of the labor force employed in agriculture declined, releasing the majority of the population for work in other sectors of the economy. This meant that a family farm, aided by machinery, could operate on a relatively large scale; thousands of highly capitalized and mechanized family farms became the backbone of midwestern agriculture.

Pioneer farm makers provided the cutting edge of agricultural advance. Infected by speculative fever, they established farms as going businesses and then sold them at a profit to latecomers. With additional capital, the speculative farmer bought land cheaply in the new territories further west, repeating the process. The restless, venturesome energies of the pioneer farmer, encouraged by the spread of railroads and the availability of new land and labor-saving machinery, speeded up the process of settlement and contributed to the high degree of geographic mobility in rural America. In 1910, for example,

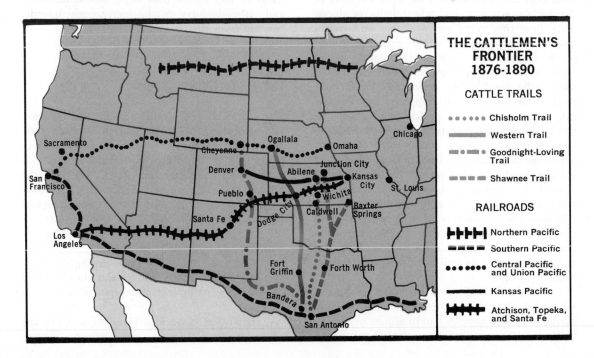

over half the farm population lived on land they had occupied for less than five years.

The prairies and plains became the nation's breadbasket; they also kept the country well supplied with meat. Before the Civil War the livestock industry was centered in the Ohio Valley; in the late nineteenth century it moved further west. The development of the corn belt stimulated hog production. The grasslands of the Great Plains became open range, which led to the development of an enormous cattle industry. By 1865, half a million longhorns roamed the Texas grasslands. As the transcontinental railroads pushed west of the Mississippi it became practical to corral cattle in Texas and drive them north to railheads for shipment to the East. Eventually, cattlemen established ranches near the railheads and grazed their herds on the public domain at no cost. Thus free or cheap grazing land, inexpensive range stock from Texas and elsewhere, and railroad connections to eastern markets created a western livestock industry that supplied much of the country with meat.

Agricultural expansion had its perils too, subjecting farmers, both in the newer and the older regions, to unforeseen hazards. Farmers in the midwestern corn and wheat belts produced more than they could sell at home and consequently they had to find outlets overseas. America had replaced Russia as the major wheat supplier for western Europe. Americans mechanized the handling of grain, developed bulk methods of storage and shipping, and erected grain elevators on the prairies and plains to create an efficient transportation system. Similarly, Americans became major meat exporters, achieving the status of a leading pork supplier of Europe. Foodstuffs thus became a leading export in the late nineteenth century, still far surpassing the growing volume of manufacturing exports. Although foreign markets brought unprecedented prosperity to American farmers, they also made them vulnerable to fluctuations in price levels on the world markets as well as to competition from foreign growers.

At the same time that western farmers had to adjust to rapidly shifting fortunes in international markets, eastern farmers had to adjust to competition from the newer regions. New York wheat farmers in the 1840s, for instance, were no match for Ohio Valley growers; a generation later, Ohio farmers found it hard to compete with the western prairies. Thousands abandoned eastern farms and moved west or streamed into the cities. Others adapted to nearby urban markets which provided a growing demand for dairy products, fruits, and vegetables. The shift to truck and dairy farming thus enabled older, rural regions to avoid a direct and ruinous competition with the West and to benefit from their proximity to local markets.

In the last forty years of the nineteenth century, American agriculture entered its modern phase. Important changes have occurred since 1900, but for generations Southern cotton and tobacco and midwestern grains and livestock have dominated the nation's farm output. The rapid spread of settlement across the prairies and plains, then into the mountain country and the Far West, and the dramatic surge in agricultural production came about because railroads gave farmers access to markets at home and abroad, and because new machinery improved farm efficiency. Farmers, however, also became important customers. Their rising productivity enabled them to buy goods that kept mines, factories, and railroads busy in the increasingly interdependent economy.

RAILROADS AND INDUSTRIALIZATION

The railroads spearheaded advances in industry and agriculture. "The generation between 1865 and 1895," wrote Henry Adams, "was already mortgaged to the railways, and no one knew it better than the generation itself." By 1900 the country had almost a half million miles of track, eight times more than in 1880. Capital investment in railroads exceeded the total investment for manufacturing. The roads consumed enormous quantities of iron, steel, coal, and lumber. They employed over 200,000 workers during the peak of construction in the 1880s; and they reduced the cost of distributing the output of farms and factories.

Expansion came in several ways. Until the 1870s the construction entrepreneurs concentrated on laying out the basic network and consolidating eastern roads into trunk lines running from the seaboard to the Midwest. The New York Central and the Erie connected New York directly with Chicago, and the Pennsylvania Railroad did the same for Philadelphia. At the same time transcontinental railroads, aided by enormous federal land grants, spanned the continent along northern, central and southern routes: the Union Pacific; the Texas and Pacific, which linked up with the Southern Pacific in California; the Atchison, Topeka and Santa Fe; and in the Northwest, the Northern Pacific and the Great Northern. After establishing the basic continental network, railroad men continued to build more intensively in search of more traffic. Financial buccaneers also stimulated expansion by building lines parallel to existing roads in order to force rivals to buy them out at inflated prices.

Huge investments of private capital and government aid, the rapid growth of demand for transportation by all sectors, and reckless speculative construction resulted in overbuilding. Self-destructive competition then jeopardized the solvency of even the best-managed roads. Because railroads were expensive to run, whatever the volume of business, roads tried to make full use of facilities and thus reduce the cost of moving freight. By juggling rates, roads tried to lure traffic away from competitors. But arbitrary rate setting benefitted no one. It disrupted the flow of traffic, proving unprofitable for the railroad that got the traffic and disastrous for the one which lost it. To balance low rates on competitive lines, roads charged what the traffic would bear in noncompetitive territory. They also allowed lower rates for carload lots than for smaller shipments and for bulk freights such as coal and lumber which could not bear heavy transportation charges. Competitive conditions created a rate structure that discriminated against some cities and towns, as well as against particular shippers and commodities in favor of others, thus multiplying grievances against the railroads.

The railroads sought to stabilize the industry by curbing competition and ending rate wars. First, they entered into pooling agreements, dividing the traffic. But since there was no way to enforce such agreements, the untrusting participants often violated them. The Interstate Commerce Act made such deals illegal after 1887. The real solution lay in consolidating several roads into fewer, stronger systems. A wave of railroad bankruptcies during the depression of the 1890s speeded up the process. The stronger roads leased, purchased, and merged with competitors; by 1904, ten major systems had come to dominate the American railroad network.

Despite internal difficulties, during these decades of expansion, railroad rates declined, though not rapidly enough for some people, and industry efficiency improved. The American railroads carried bulk freight over long distances more cheaply than foreign roads, enabling American farmers and manufacturers to tap the growing home market efficiently and to become one of the best customers for heavy industry. By the end of the century, with the roads built, they no longer played their previously dynamic role in stimulating growth. That role fell to cities and a national market, now extended in scope.

The Urban Boom

Industrial America inevitably became urban America. In 1900 five times as many Americans lived in cities than when the Civil War began. As electric trolleys replaced the horsedrawn variety, and as they in turn gave way to elevated lines and subways, people were able to live far from their jobs in the inner city. By adapting the railroad to urban needs, the cities could grow into metropolises. The resulting urban construction boom, like the railroad boom a generation earlier, provided the markets for heavy industry, which made possible the mass production of consumer durables in the twentieth century.

Before the Civil War light industry had turned out a considerable variety of consumer goods such as textiles, shoes, and clothing, but in the late nineteenth century heavy industry came into its own. Technological innovations and the discovery of new resources met the needs created by the railroads and the cities. By the 1890s the United States became the world's leading producer of coal and iron. The Bessemer converter and the open hearth process made it possible to mass produce steel of high quality at a low cost.

Other industries grew even more rapidly. The first commercially important oil strikes occurred in Pennsylvania in the 1850s. Overnight a new industry arose to make the United States the world's leading oil producer. Refineries sprang up to turn crude oil into kerosene, the most popular source of artificial light before 1890, then into the lubricating oil required to keep machines running, and later into gasoline. Toward the end of the century, electricity became a new source of power and light. As the country was becoming wired for electricity, copper found new uses and copper mining boomed. Growth in one industry thus promoted expansion in others. Metal manufacturing stimulated mining, which made new demands on the railroads, which in turn burned more coal and consumed more steel rails. Similarly, petroleum refiners shipped oil first by rail and then by pipeline, creating new uses for steel.

THE RISE OF BIG BUSINESS

This expansion of older consumer industries and new heavy industries eventually led to the rise of Big Business. Until the 1890s few large industrial combinations existed. The railroads pioneered in this respect. Other large businesses also emerged in mining and manufacturing in the late 1890s as competing firms merged into huge corporations which dominated American business enterprise. Companies that previously had specialized in one activity diversified, enlarging their scope in an effort to increase profits and stabilize business in an era of intense competition.

Special circumstances and opportunities in each industry determined the pattern of business consolidation. Manufacturers of sewing machines and farm equipment, for instance, developed their own marketing network because distributors on whom they initially had relied were not aggressive merchandisers, and did not offer customer credit. Manufacturers therefore awarded franchises to retailers, offered credit, and serviced equipment. In this way they acquired more customers and achieved economies through mass production.

A related process was at work in meat packing. Until Gustavus Swift revolutionized that industry, meat packing had been decentralized and firms remained small. Swift, who operated an eastern wholesale slaughterhouse, had to purchase meat in the Midwest because demand in his section outran supply. Instead of shipping livestock directly east, Swift concentrated meat packing in Chicago to achieve economies of scale and to reduce transportation costs. Refrigerated cars delivered meat to branch wholesalers, who then distributed to retailers in the major eastern cities. By lowering the cost of meat, Swift enlarged the market, already growing in the cities, and then established additional packing plants in the Midwest. The large packers boosted their profits further by finding ways of turning waste, such as bones and hides, into glue, soap, and other by-products. By 1900 a handful of packers dominated the industry.

Monopoly Making: Standard Oil

The most famous business consolidation was Standard Oil. John D. Rockefeller, a successful Cleveland commission merchant, invested in oil refining in the 1860s just as the fields of Pennsylvania were coming into full production. At first the business was highly competitive. It did not require much capital to drill a well or operate a refinery. Supply outpaced demand and prices tumbled. Rockefeller obtained a decisive advantage over his competitors through rebates from railroads. This enabled him to undersell, since transportation amounted to about 20 percent of final cost. With the power to drive his rivals out of business, Rockefeller easily bought them out. As Standard Oil grew, so did its bargaining power with the railroads. By the 1880s the company controlled 90 percent of the nation's refining capacity. It closed down most of the facilities it purchased, and concentrated production at the most efficient refineries, thereby further reducing costs.

When competitors built the first pipelines and threatened to undermine its transportation advantage, Standard laid its own pipelines, thus moving directly into the transportation business. Spurred by a desire to achieve greater stability, Standard eventually began to produce crude oil. It acquired extensive holdings in new midwestern fields, and thus assured control of supply as the

Pennsylvania fields dried up. Integrating forward into pipelines and backward into crude oil production gave Standard additional competitive advantages over its rivals. The increased cost of entry into an integrated industry also kept out potential rivals.

Eventually Standard Oil also moved into marketing. Producing more kerosene than the domestic market could absorb, Standard relied heavily on foreign outlets, especially in Europe. American oil dominated that market until new supplies from Russia provided tough competition. To meet the Russian threat, Standard developed more efficient methods of bulk distribution. As foreign competition cut into overseas business, Standard had to rely more on the domestic market. Here too, aggressive marketing and more efficient bulk methods of distribution paid off. Thus by 1900 Standard Oil had become a "vertical" trust, engaging in production, refining, distribution, and marketing.

As Rockefeller and his associates attempted to achieve control and impose their brand of stability on the industry, they ran into legal obstacles and public hostility. Consumers and independent oil producers feared that Standard was destroying competition and acquiring a monopoly even though the price of oil products generally declined. Standard's control of the companies that made up its large empire conflicted with state and federal law that prohibited combinations in restraint of trade. Eventually, New Jersey permitted firms incorporated under its laws to hold the assets of other corporations; this "holding company" concept thus made consolidations legal.

Despite its success, there were some limits to Standard's control. A few smaller firms that specialized in quality products and superior service survived, and the discovery of new oil fields in the South and Far West created new giants in the industry, though Standard Oil still retained a dominant position.

What Rockefeller did in oil and Swift did in meat packing, others repeated in sugar refining, machine tools, grain milling, tobacco, and steel. Andrew Carnegie, for example, manufactured steel which other companies fabricated. Eventually Carnegie assured a market for his steel by making rails and building railroad bridges. To guarantee a steady flow of raw materials at favorable prices, Carnegie also purchased coal and iron mines and shipping facilities to move raw materials to his mills. Others imitated, and the steel industry became plagued in the 1890s with price wars. When Carnegie sold out to the newly formed United States Steel Corporation (1901), many firms consolidated into a holding company powerful enough to impose stability and protect profits.

The rise of corporate Big Business was distinctively an American phenomenon. In Europe family firms survived much longer. European entrepreneurs could stabilize business through private, market-sharing agreements which were illegal in the United States. But American businessmen had to seek stability through corporate consolidation. They more quickly realized the opportunities in a large national market for higher profits through mass production and mass distribution, and they more readily adapted the latest and most efficient technology to economize on labor costs. Bigness gave them the resources to adopt new techniques and to integrate, thereby reducing prices through economies of scale. Above all, bigness proved profitable and it rescued business from the competition characteristic of the initial stages of industrial growth.

THE BANKERS

In the quest for greater stability and protected profits, bankers played an important role. The spread of corporations, first in railroads and later in manufacturing, required much larger amounts of capital than the earlier industrial enterprises. The process also required new methods of financing. Firms could no longer rely on investments by elite merchants, such as the Bostonians who earlier had put up the capital for textile firms established by members of their own group. By selling bonds and stock, however, corporations could tap the nation's growing volume of savings.

A securities market centering in Wall Street developed long before the Civil War, but it did not dominate the availability of capital until after midcentury when Wall Street bankers became the key intermediaries between investors and industry by mobilizing funds through their extensive connections with capitalists abroad and through their control of banks, trust companies, and insurance companies at home. Thus the development of an efficient capital market financed American industry by establishing mechanisms which transferred savings into investment capital. Consequently, foreigners, reassured by the rationality of the system, quadrupled their investments in the United States between 1860 and 1900.

Eventually bankers also became deeply involved in the corporations they financed. Ruinous competition, poor management, and industry-wide instability led bankers to intervene in order to safeguard the interests of investors. The firm of J. P. Morgan & Company became a principal overseer of the industrial system. During the depression of the 1870s, 40 percent of all railroad bonds were in default and many roads went bankrupt, a process that recurred in the depression of the 1890s. Morgan reorganized railroads to put them on a sounder basis. He reduced large bonded indebtedness, consolidated smaller lines into larger systems, and used his financial power to curb competitive building and to end rate wars.

By 1900 Morgan had brought order and profits out of chaos in the railroads. He did the same for steel after the creation of United States Steel. The bankers sold stock in the new giants in excess of the value of their assets on optimistic expectations of future earnings. They also handsomely compensated themselves for their services. But many Americans feared that banker control, no less than industrial monopoly, placed small stockholders and consumers at the mercy of a tiny, plutocratic elite.

INDUSTRIAL AMERICA, 1860-1900

During the late nineteenth century the United States assumed world industrial leadership, a position of preeminence it still holds. A rapidly multiplying population, enlarged by millions of immigrants, quickly spread across the continent and brought billions of new acres under cultivation. The United States became Europe's breadbasket. But the farmer's best market remained in America, in the cities and towns where millions found jobs in factories, warehouses, and shops created by the industrial machine.

Though agriculture remained important, industry contributed the lion's share of national wealth and fundamentally altered the American way of life. Railroads and telephones speeded up communications, electric power illuminated homes and businesses and ran machinery, steel frames supported buildings that scraped the skies, and large corporations institutionalized the process of growth and change. The United States became richer than ever before, but industrialism also created new strains that bewildered and threatened its people. Americans were supremely successful at creating wealth, yet many critics believed that the national genius for business was at bottom "anti-social . . . an education in self-seeking at the expense of others, and no society whose citizens are trained in such a school can possibly rise above a very low grade of civilization." Thus, even as the country emerged as the leading industrial nation, some Americans turned their thoughts to ways of making this newfound abundance better serve the welfare of man.

Chapter 17
The Politics of Drift

For two decades (1870–1890) the Republican and Democratic parties competed vigorously at the polls, with Republicans emerging the more successful of the two. Neither party could achieve majority status; presidential contests often turned on a few thousand votes; in only three Congresses did one party control both houses and in only two did the party controlling the legislative branch also capture the presidency. This near deadlock persisted despite the Republicans' seemingly impregnable advantage after the Civil War. Smeared with the brush of treason, the Democrats had to overcome the bitter heritage of the rebellion. Yet the party regained strength with amazing swiftness. The failure of Radical Reconstruction and the restoration of "home" rule brought the white South back into American politics as a solid Democratic bloc.

If the South always went Democratic, New England was just as solidly Republican; but in the rest of the country the two parties fought on nearly equal terms. Voting patterns, forged at midcentury in the heat of sectional division and civil war, lasted into the late nineteenth century. Each party had strong support among urban and rural voters, the wealthy and the poor, working class and middle class.

The most outstanding and long-lasting differences in party preference stemmed from ethnocultural and religious loyalties. Thus midwesterners of Southern ancestry tended to vote Democratic, while those of New England origin favored the Republicans. Among the foreign-born, both first and second generation, who were becoming an increasingly important element in in the electorate, Protestants from Germany and Scandinavia tended to enter the Republican fold, while Catholics from Ireland and Germany found a home in the Democratic party. As a party born out of a crusade against slavery, a movement rooted in evangelical, Protestant moralism which sought to purify public life, the Republican party became the party of Northern, Calvinistic Protestants, both native and foreign born, who were alarmed at the growing influence of Catholic and Lutheran immigrants with variant life-styles. Tension mounted as Protestants attempted to use government to impose their standards on unwilling minorities. The Democratic party, with its commitment to negative government and states' rights, seemed the safest bet for Catholics, and on this basis they joined with Southern Protestants to form a powerful coalition. Thus two very different groups united in one party to protect their "gut" interests.

The parties therefore represented coalitions of mixed, sometimes contradictory elements. Political organization brought them together in a common cause and gave some cohesion to an otherwise fragmented society. Americans divided along party and sectional lines far more than they did along class lines. Though each party drew its support from different constituencies, neither tailored its appeal to class interests; both agreed with the Reverend Henry W. Beecher that "a paternal government is an infernal government."

THE GAME OF PARTY POLITICS

For a generation Republicans exploited the legacy of the Civil War. To vote Democratic was to vote for the party of treason, GOP orators warned; a Democratic victory would deliver the Republic to an unrepentant slavocracy and its Northern cohorts. "Waving the Bloody Shirt" in the face of the hundreds of thousands of Union veterans and Northern patriots proved a potent weapon. Southern success in overthrowing Radical Reconstruction and subjugating the blacks on whom Republicans once counted gave the Democrats a good chance to regain power nationally. Such a catastrophe, Republicans predicted, would rob Northerners of their victory. To prevent this, the Grand Army of the Republic (G.A.R.) organized Union veterans into a powerful force supporting the Republican party in return for generous pensions, which by the 1890s went to many of the 400,000 members.

Republicans captured the presidency in five of the seven elections between Ulysses S. Grant's victory in 1868 and William McKinley's in 1896, but the presidential office itself declined in influence. Though the parties fought hard for the White House, and with it control of federal patronage, the chief executives did not give the country strong leadership. Presidents had difficulty controlling their party leaders and spent much of their time absorbed in patronage disputes, administering routine business, and performing at ceremonial occasions. Though Lincoln had stretched presidential powers to the limit, his successors did not follow his example. Andrew Johnson's attempt to dominate merely divided the Republicans. An enraged Congress impeached and nearly ousted him, discrediting presidential leadership in the process and producing a lowered status which Grant and his immediate successors did not contest.

The late-nineteenth-century presidents, moreover, were weak personalities, with the partial exception of Democrat Grover Cleveland (1885–1889, 1893–1897), and even he had a narrow conception of the office. With presidents little more than patronage dispensers, administrative caretakers and ceremonial heads, they rarely entered office with legislative programs to push through Congress. Since the parties did not divide on ideological or socioeconomic lines, and since most Americans resisted enlargement of the federal government's responsibilities, limited purposes and conventional imaginations characterized the era's leading politicians.

From Grant to Cleveland, 1868–1892

For eight years Ulysses S. Grant, architect of military victory over the Southern rebels, occupied the White House but not the presidency. The Old Soldier's presence reassured Northerners at the same time that Republicans began quietly to abandon Reconstruction in the South. Unsuited for and uninterested in his job, Grant confessed, "I never wanted to get out of a place as much as I did to get out of the Presidency." He had good reason. Repeatedly betrayed by cronies to whom he gave jobs and who misused power, Grant's administration became a synonym for the political corruption of the Gilded Age. According to Henry Adams, the history of the presidency from Washington to Grant cast doubt on Darwin's theory of evolution and on the idea of progress.

The stench of official corruption in Washington and growing desires among Northern Republicans for sectional reconciliation split the Re-

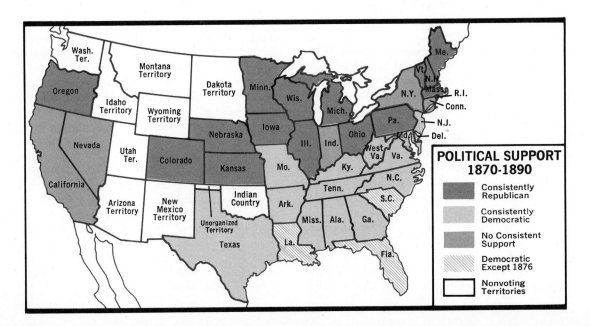

POLITICAL SUPPORT 1870–1890

Consistently Republican

Consistently Democratic

No Consistent Support

Democratic Except 1876

Nonvoting Territories

publican party in 1872. "Clean government" Republicans bolted to unite with the Democrats in the Liberal-Republican party which nominated Horace Greeley, but Grant won reelection to a second term which proved as undistinguished as the first.

Disgust with corruption led both parties in 1876 to nominate candidates with brighter public images. Samuel J. Tilden, a New York Democrat, attracted attention as dragon-slayer of the Tammany Hall machine in New York City. Rutherford B. Hayes, Republican governor of Ohio, was noted for sobriety and piety. Hayes won the disputed contest, though Tilden obtained more popular votes. But rival Republicans in Congress soon challenged Hayes's leadership, grumbling over the president's denial of their customary patronage. After a year in office Hayes sadly confessed: "I am not liked as a president, by the politicians in office, in the press, or in the Congress."

Hayes refused to run for a second term, thus clearing the way for a fight over the Republican nomination. The Roscoe Conkling faction of New York opposed the backers of Representative James G. Blaine of Maine. When the Republican convention deadlocked, "Stalwarts" and "Half-Breeds" engaging in dubious battle, the prize went to party workhorse James A. Garfield of Ohio, who picked a Conkling henchman, Chester A. Arthur, as his running mate. Garfield beat Democrat Winfield S. Hancock narrowly and held office briefly, until an assassin's bullet cut him down. President Arthur, identified as a spoils system politician, surprised many by his support of civil service reform.

After twenty-five years of unbroken Republican rule, the Democrats recaptured the presidency in 1884. Grover Cleveland was an ideal choice to run against Republican James G. Blaine whose reputation, never spotless, had been further sullied by Grantism. As mayor of Buffalo and governor of New York, Cleveland made a name as an incorruptible enemy of political machines who was dedicated to restoring dignity and honor to the presidency. "A public office," he intoned, "is a public trust." In those days, the truism needed repetition.

Cleveland entered office apprehensively: "I look upon the four years next to come as a dreadful self-inflicted penance for the good of the country." The New Yorker had energy and drive, however. He did his job honestly, though he could not resist demands from hungry Democrats for rewards. He reasserted executive leadership, battled Congress for repeal of the Tenure of Office Act (the legislative club Congress had used against Andrew Johnson), opposed giving the public domain to cattlemen, and launched a campaign to lower the tariff, an issue most politicians avoided for fear of losing votes. "What is the use of being elected or re-elected," Cleveland asked, "unless you stand for something?"

Cleveland based his reelection campaign in 1888 on tariff reform. The Republicans predictably stood for protection. The injection of a significant policy difference between the parties still did not break the deadlock of presidential politics. Benjamin Harrison, teetotalling Republican from Indiana, lost in the popular vote but won an electoral majority. The Republicans jacked up the tariff in 1890, and Cleveland came back to win decisively in 1892. Although pledged to tariff reduction, Cleveland failed to get his way with a Congress controlled by his own party. Even a relatively strong president had difficulty overcoming the long-term shift in the center of political gravity from the executive to the legislative branch.

CONGRESSIONAL GOVERNMENT

The House of Representatives, huge and badly organized, conducted its business poorly. Its rules permitted interminable obstruction until Speaker Thomas B. (Czar) Reed brought order out of chaos in the 1890s by imposing his iron-fisted rule. Until then the House, according to one observer, was "a disintegrated mass of jarring elements." The Senate emerged as the more purposeful and powerful branch of Congress. A much smaller body, with only 76 members compared to the House's 325 in 1890, it contained many of the state party leaders who bargained with the White House for patronage and influenced presidential nominations.

The composition of the Senate also reflected changes in the country. Most Senators were self-made men with backgrounds in law or business.

But increasingly, Big Businessmen entered the body; twenty-five millionaires served between 1870 and 1900. Dubbed a "millionaire's club," the Senate fell in public esteem as it rose in power. Senators, chosen by state legislatures, not by popular election, came under attack as mouthpieces of powerful business interests. They were "growing more and more aristocratic, more and more regardless of public opinion, and some people say more and more corrupt," charged a Republican newspaper in Massachusetts.

Neither the presidency nor Congress gave coherence to late-nineteenth-century politics. That was the task of party organization and party loyalty. In the absence of sharp policy differences between the parties, politics became largely a struggle for preferment. Success at the polls often went to the party with the most efficient machine rather than the most attractive program or candidate. Both parties were collections of local machines in the cities, towns, and counties where a local boss and faithful retainers delivered the votes. Politics in America had become a profession attracting individuals who devoted most of their time and derived most of their income from its practice, in contrast with England, where a leisured class still managed public affairs. Lawyers, merchants, and saloon keepers, and others who came into contact with many people formed political organizations and joined with others across the state to seek power. The victorious party gained control of lucrative jobs and other patronage, including public works contracts, with which to reward the faithful. In return the party regulars worked to elect the ticket.

Americans perfected the organization of politics in the late nineteenth century. The close division between the parties and the absence of sharp ideological or programmatic differences placed a premium on organizational efficiency. This resulted in heavier voter turnout at elections and tighter party loyalty than at any time before or since.

The increasing professionalization of politics, well under way in the Jacksonian era, gained impetus from frequency of elections, from the numerous elective offices for which candidates had to be recruited, and from the voter's need for direction in casting his ballot, given the diffi-culty of making rational choices between candidates. Although the machines were self-serving, by helping people to find jobs, by providing coal and food for the distressed (especially recently arrived immigrants in cities), by helping businessmen obtain valuable privileges from government, and by doing countless other favors, they performed a vital function that made government more responsive to the needs of various groups.

In return politicians exacted their stiff price. Since the results of the next elections were unpredictable, particularly during the late-nineteenth-century party deadlock, those in office were under pressure to make the most of their opportunities. Controlling railroad charters, land grants, government contracts, tariff schedules, and streetcar franchises which others wanted and were willing to pay for, public officials often sold their influence and votes to the highest bidder, especially when there was little reason to prefer one group of favor-seekers over another. Nor did social pressures restrain them. People unashamedly entered politics for gain and politicians rarely had social positions to forfeit in the event of scandal. Besides, Americans during the Gilded Age were usually indulgent toward grafters who were only engaged in the national pastime of getting rich regardless of the means. "Nothing has been lost save honor," wisecracked one cynical spoilsman, caught with his hand in the till. Why should politicians be held to a higher standard than businessmen, who flagrantly flouted the law? "Every man at present may be said literally to live by his wits," lamented E. L. Godkin, puritanical editor of *The Nation,* and "the result is a kind of moral anarchy."

Corruption reached into the highest places. Congress, for example, chartered the Union Pacific Railroad (1862) to span the continent, and according to Massachusetts Senator George F. Hoar, a descendant of Puritans, "every step of that mighty enterprise has been taken in fraud," including the bribery of dozens of congressmen. "The only product of [America's] institutions in which she surpassed all others beyond question was her corruption," Hoar moaned. In 1875, for instance, a St. Louis newspaper exposed the Whisky Ring, a conspiracy of distillers and government revenue collectors to defraud the federal treasury. Over 200 persons were indicted, including Grant's private secretary, but the president stuck by his friends in this and in other scandals.

Graft enriched the politicians and financed their organizations. Since voters saw little difference between the parties or the candidates, many sold their votes. The parties poured thousands of dollars into critical districts they needed to win. Through the wholesale purchase of votes, the Republicans virtually bought the presidency in 1888. Eventually, though, blatant corruption and betrayal of democratic ideals generated pressures for reform.

THE CONFLICT OF INTERESTS: SPOILS

The parties did little to cope with the political pressures building up in industrial America. They remained generally unreceptive to groups that felt threatened or injured by rapid social change. But the chronic corruption and extreme partisanship of late-nineteenth-century politics ultimately produced a reaction politicians could not ignore.

First came demands for restoration of honesty in government. A coalition of eastern upper-class elements and older established businessmen, mostly seaboard financiers and merchants, led the protest movement. These groups harked back to an earlier age when men of good family and good breeding ruled as supposedly disinterested public servants. The upheavals of mid-century—the disruption of the pre-Civil War party system, the creation of the Republican party, the emergence of powerful men whose wealth came from railroading, mining, and manufacturing—had brought new men to power, especially in the North. Partisanship and political professionalism, reformers warned, elevated unprincipled individuals who sought power only for personal gain. Reformers demanded an end to the spoils system of patronage, which sustained the political bosses and their machines. They wanted federal jobs to go to qualified persons, men selected through competitive examinations and promoted according to merit. Civil service reform, they promised, would cleanse government and increase efficiency by eliminating the corrupt

and incompetent. They also hoped it would weaken unscrupulous elements then dominating the parties and thus enable "gentlemen" to regain influence.

Professional politicians in both parties resisted bitterly. When reform sentiment first surfaced in the late 1860s and early 1870s, it was met by hostility from Democrats who looked forward to eventual return to office and *their* control of the spoils. Republican leaders proved equally hostile, believing that reform threatened the party's survival. Fearful of Democratic resurgence, and sensing their shaky hold on the national government, Republicans regarded a free hand with patronage as indispensable to their continued rule. Since the promise of jobs galvanized party organization, civil service reform portended disaster for the pros. "What are we here for except for the offices?" shouted a candid delegate to the 1880 Republican convention. Without the armies of party hacks, who would provide the money obtained through assessments on officeholders to finance party activities? New York boss Roscoe Conkling contemptuously reminded reformers "that parties are not built up by deportment, or by ladies' magazines or gush."

Not only did reformers have to overcome resistance from entrenched spoilsmen, but they also proposed abolishing a system of rotation that rested on a deep-rooted democratic tradition that the elite should not monopolize public officeholding. Whatever the defects of the spoils system, it made civil service a channel through which men with limited education or wealth could advance themselves, if only for the four years of a presidential administration.

Gradually reformers made headway. They won increasing support from businessmen disgusted with the inefficiency and the expense of the spoils system, especially importers at the mercy of corrupt customs collectors. Both Grant and Hayes made concessions in the hope of appeasing reformers and keeping them loyal to the Republican party. But some bolted in 1872 and by the 1880s the danger of massive defection mounted. Reformers were not numerous but they were influential and strategically located, with access to the press and aware of the value of organization. With political parties divided so evenly, even a few thousand votes might decide an election. Garfield's assassination by a disappointed officeseeker, coming on the heels of a decade of exposures of corruption in high places, dramatically discredited the spoils system. In 1883 Congress finally passed the Pendleton Act establishing a Civil Service Commission. The law authorized competitive examinations for recruitment, and protected some officeholders from the threat of political removal.

The Pendleton Act did not end the spoils system immediately. Yet the number of positions covered by civil service protection increased, as succeeding presidents attempted to protect their own appointees from removal when they left office. However, most federal and even more state and local positions remained outside civil service at the end of the nineteenth century. Modest success nonetheless encouraged reformers to increase their efforts. When the Republicans nominated spoilsman James G. Blaine in 1884, many reformers voted for Cleveland. These independents, called Mugwumps, made good on their claim of loyalty to principle being superior to party loyalty.

THE CONFLICT OF INTERESTS: THE TARIFF

While Mugwumps worked for civil service reform, they increasingly identified the high tariff as another primary evil, and the tariff reform movement attracted more generalized support than did the campaign against spoils. Through it, widely divergent interests voiced discontent stemming from the social dislocations which accompanied unregulated industrial growth.

Tariff reform, like the civil service crusade, was a reaction against the consequences of mid-century crisis in the Union. The Republican victory of 1860 ended two decades of Democratic supremacy which had kept tariff schedules low, in deference to the interests of Southern planters and northern and western Jacksonians who favored a tariff for revenue only. The Republicans, once in office, honored their promises to protect American manufacturers from foreign competition. With the Southern Democrats gone and a

war to be financed, Congress passed the Morrill Tariff (1861), the first of a series of measures that pushed rates up to new highs. Moderate downward revision in 1870 and 1872 did not survive the new rates of 1875. Protection remained firmly in the saddle.

In the 1880s, however, the tariff came under increasingly heavy attack from many directions. Mugwumps made it a moral issue. "Protectionism," opined the Reverend Henry W. Beecher, "is the jugglery of the Devil." Tariffs transferred money out of the pockets of consumers into the hands of a few privileged producers, and unwisely injected the government into the marketplace; protection violated the reigning ethic of free enterprise, rugged individualism, and laissez faire. Mugwumps received backing from merchants who believed their businesses suffered from restraints on international trade and from some manufacturers who did not need protection but who wanted to purchase foreign raw materials cheaply. Some farmers also joined the attack. They blamed tariffs for raising the prices of commodities they bought without reciprocal protection in the home market. Recurrent farm crises from falling agricultural prices caused farmers to blame the tariff for retaliatory trade barriers against American agricultural exports in needed foreign markets.

Protectionists responded that the tariff ensured the country's industrial progress by stimulating economic growth. As factories spread across the land and workers poured into cities, the internal market for American farm products grew proportionately. The tariff thus supposedly scattered its blessings on farmers and on workers, who received protection from cheap foreign labor, as well as on manufacturers assured of their domestic markets. Many farmers and workers, including the head of the Knights of Labor, accepted these arguments and their votes provided mass support for high-tariff businessmen.

Until the mid-1880s both parties shied away from tariff reform. The well-organized protectionists could pour money into pro-tariff campaigns, and Republicans depended particularly on contributions from protectionists. The Democratic party, although historically committed to a revenue tariff only, also included other powerful protariff elements. They feared jeopardizing their return to power from the political wilderness by supporting a cause long identified with the Southern slavocracy. Toward the end of his first term, Cleveland belatedly called for tariff reduction, citing the large federal treasury surplus as an additional reason for action. Cleveland made the tariff the central issue of the 1888 campaign. Cautious politicians attributed his defeat to this clearcut stand, though actually Cleveland ran better in industrial areas than he had four years earlier. Still, Cleveland's experience confirmed the consensus among politicians who thought it unwise for candidates to confront controversial issues.

The Republicans interpreted their victory as a mandate for increasing the tariff. They did so with the McKinley Tariff of 1890. Likewise, when Cleveland returned to power in 1892 he pushed hard to achieve tariff reduction, but pro-tariff elements in his own party combined with Republicans to defeat meaningful reduction; the wishy-washy Wilson-Gorman Tariff (1894) became law without the president's signature.

For over three decades since the adoption of the Morrill Act (1861) the country had fought over tariff schedules. Protectionism still reigned in the 1890s despite repeated attempts at reduction, and the issue remained divisive though not decisive. Mugwumps continued to blame the tariff for enriching a few persons while creating new fortunes that threatened their status. By the 1890s, the attack on protection intensified as many Americans assaulted the tariff as responsible for the growing and dangerous concentration of economic power in fewer and fewer hands. The tariff, they concluded, spawned business monopoly.

THE CONFLICT OF INTERESTS: CORPORATE POWER

Americans reacted ambivalently to the large corporations taking shape in the late nineteenth century. They wanted the benefits of concentrated capital: rigged but lower prices, greater efficiency, and increased national wealth, but they still feared that Big Business destroyed competition and exploited the public. The rail-

roads, the earliest example of large-scale enterprise, revealed the contradiction in public attitudes. At first, cities and towns, western farmers and eastern merchants welcomed rail connections that would expand economic opportunities. The spread of commercial agriculture into the prairies and the Great Plains depended on rail links that would take corn and wheat to eastern markets. Towns and counties went into debt to bring roads to their doorstep and during the 1870s and 1880s the railroad network spread across the country linking farm to factory.

As long as times were good, people regarded the railroad as a blessing. But when prosperity gave way to depression, as it did periodically, many blamed the roads for charging excessive rates, favoring some shippers over others, and corrupting politicians in order to avoid regulation. Most railroad rates fell during the last three decades of the century, but not so much as the general price level. Farmers singled out the roads for attack because transportation costs, especially from west of the Mississippi, often consumed their profits. They also complained that grain elevator operators cheated them by undergrading the quality of their wheat.

The first major national farm organization, the Patrons of Husbandry, or National Grange (1867), spearheaded a midwestern push for railroad regulation, a movement which received powerful support from local businessmen threatened by railroad practices that put them at a competitive disadvantage. In the 1870s states such as Illinois and Wisconsin established railroad commissions with power to regulate rates and prohibit discriminatory practices. These controls proved difficult to administer, however. The railroads ingeniously evaded them and the U.S. Supreme Court in 1886 barred states from regulating roads operating in interstate commerce.

Railroad critics then demanded federal legislation. Ironically, New York City interests, believing that rates unduly favored businessmen in Philadelphia and Baltimore in the competition for midwestern business, played a leading role in the movement. Another problem came from stock market manipulators who gained control of roads only to milk them for short-term gain. America watched in fascinated horror as Commodore

Cornelius Vanderbilt, owner of the New York Central, battled with the unscrupulous Wall Street plunger, Daniel Drew, for control of the competing Erie Railroad. "Both these men belonged to a low and degraded moral and social type," charged Charles F. Adams, Jr., speaking for an old elite unable or unwilling to compete with the Vanderbilts and Drews for power or wealth in a society that regarded "failure as the one unpardonable crime, success as the all-redeeming virtue, the acquisition of wealth as the single worthy aim of life."

In the face of widespread and irresistible pressure for regulation, many railroad owners accepted the use of federal authority to stabilize the industry and free it from cutthroat competition. Others, however, feared and fought federal control. After more than a decade's discussion, Congress adopted the Interstate Commerce Act (1887), requiring that rates be "reasonable," banning discriminatory practices that favored some shippers at the expense of others, and outlawing longhaul-shorthaul differentials. The act also created the first federal regulatory agency, the Interstate Commerce Commission. But the new commission lacked the power to fix rates and federal courts soon further weakened its limited authority. The law was thus mainly a symbolic gesture to appease voters, and not a realistic attempt to grapple with the problems of transportation monopoly.

The attack on industrial monopoly suffered the same fate. Business consolidation, led and symbolized by the mammoth Standard Oil Company, smothered competition and left consumers helpless before giant combinations such as the "Sugar Trust," the "Beef Trust," or the "Whiskey Trust." Though pressures within some industries made competition among many small firms obsolete, many Americans did not understand the forces behind change. Fear of monopoly power over essential commodities made them turn to government for help. In 1890 Congress adopted the Sherman Anti-Trust Act which outlawed "every contract, combination in the form of trust or otherwise, or conspiracy, in restraint of trade" in interstate or foreign commerce.

This law gave the federal government power to dissolve unlawful combinations but, as some congressmen admitted, it was little more than a pacifier. Congress had as little interest in dismembering corporations as it had in effectively regulating railroads. However, enactment of ineffective, declaratory laws temporarily relieved some of the anxieties generated by the growth of corporate power, and also enabled Americans to express the wish for a return to the lost world of small-scale competitive enterprise without reversing the trend toward Big Business. As the consolidation movement in industry and transportation gained new momentum in the 1890s, despite the Interstate Commerce and Sherman acts, that nostalgic wish became little more than a dream.

THE MONEY QUESTION

In seeking civil service reform, tariff reduction, and the regulation of Big Business, Americans tried to reassert control over matters seemingly in the hands of political cliques allied with corporate monopoly. From the end of the Civil War until the close of the century, many believed that the root of the country's problems lay in the condition of the currency.

Periodically, Americans focused attention on the currency supply to explain the cycles of boom and bust. In the late colonial period, during the 1820s and 1830s, and in the three decades following the Civil War the money supply became a central political issue. "Soft" money advocates believed in expanding the money supply through the issue of paper notes without gold or silver backing. This would stimulate business, expand opportunity, guarantee high wages, and increase the economy's growth rate. In short, it would do everything the pro-tariff men claimed for *their* panacea. "Hard" money interests, however, feared that an inflated currency would encourage runaway speculation and overheat the economy, inevitably producing a crash that would devastate wage earners and creditors alike.

Until the Civil War the federal government backed its currency with gold and silver. Wartime necessity, however, forced the Union to issue $450 million in "greenbacks," paper money declared to be legal tender. After the war hard money interests demanded contraction of the currency and retirement of the greenbacks. The Treasury began to withdraw them until a business recession in 1868 aroused soft money interests to block further deflation. Political parties were caught between two powerful coalitions. Expansive industrialists, speculators, and western merchants and bankers, resenting the concentration of capital in the East, generally favored cheap money and easy credit. Soft money businessmen found allies among ex-Jacksonian antimonopoly elements who regarded greenbacks as a means of scaling down the national debt that enriched capitalists.

The hard money interest included eastern investors and financiers with access to ample credit, owners of the older and more established eastern industries which were growing slowly and in less need of capital, and merchants engaged in foreign trade who conducted their business in gold and silver. Additional moral weight for the hard money cause came from several "noneconomic" interests. Ministers regarded paper currency as a cause of fraud, dishonesty, and extravagance; Mugwumps, most of whom descended from older prewar elites, blamed cheap money for helping to create a new unwholesome class of wealthy men ("a set of mere money getters and traders") who pushed aside more scrupulous gentlemen.

The Panic of 1873 touched off a prolonged recession and renewed demands for induced inflation. Now the soft money forces found powerful support among many farmers who abandoned a hard money faith that went back to Jacksonian times. When Grant vetoed a bill to increase the supply of greenbacks in 1874, Democrats capitalized on widespread discontent over the move. They won control of Congress in the 1874 midterm election and soft money forces gained influence in both parties. The lame duck Republican Congress moved swiftly to defuse the explosive currency issue and preserve party unity. The Resumption Act (1875) postponed the withdrawal of greenbacks and the return to a purely specie currency until January 1, 1879.

Inflationists remained unsatisfied but they could not gain control of either party. Businessmen who had previously backed paper money began to fear that continued controversy might foster business instability and hinder economic revival. Repulsed by the major parties, militant soft money forces established a Greenback-Labor party (1876) which united a diverse group of farm leaders, labor reformers, unorthodox businessmen, and marginal politicians. The party ran poorly in 1876, but in the 1878 midyear elections it polled a million votes and sent fourteen men to Congress.

By the mid-1870s soft money forces took up the banner of free coinage of silver, rather than greenbacks, as the final solution to the currency problem. Until 1873 the United States maintained a bimetallic monetary standard, coining both gold and silver. But the Treasury bought little silver because it commanded a higher price on the private market than the official price paid by the government. Congress, therefore, made gold the sole monetary standard. Though demonetization of silver evoked little opposition or controversy at the time, within a few years inflationists attacked it as the work of a "gold conspiracy." A gold dollar, they argued, was an expensive, bondholders' dollar.

The opening of new silver deposits in the Far West produced a powerful coalition in favor of remonetizing silver. Champions of soft money believed that the free coinage of silver would restore prosperity by increasing the money supply and pushing up the level of prices and wages. Silver coins enjoyed greater popular acceptance than paper money and thus offered a tempting method of expanding the currency supply with "hard" money. Western silver-mine owners, hurt by sagging prices for their metal, readily joined the soft money crusade. Congress finally bowed and passed the Bland-Allison Act (1878) which required the Treasury to purchase at market price between $2 million and $4 million worth of silver monthly for coinage into dollars. Three months later Congress renewed the life of the greenbacks indefinitely. The amount of silver purchased by the government did not significantly expand the currency, but as prosperity returned toward the end of the decade the currency question lost much of its force. In 1878, in accordance with the terms of the Resumption Act, the Treasury offered to exchange greenbacks for gold, using gold reserves accumulated for this purpose, but by that time restored confidence in the value of the paper money made it as good as specie-backed currency.

For about a decade after 1878 the currency question slumbered as the return of prosperity touched off a boom which quieted the discontented. By the end of the 1880s, however, hard times returned to thousands of American farmers and after 1893 one of America's worst depressions hit the country. As in the 1870s, currency again became the central issue of American politics.

This time hard (gold) and soft (silver) money forces prepared for the final struggle. The battle split the country more sharply than at any time since the Civil War, and the widespread suffering of the new depression, coming only a generation after the deprivations of the 1870s, undermined belief in an unregulated economic and social order. Some way had to be found to ensure material progress without paying an unacceptable price in human suffering every twenty years.

Chapter 18
The Crisis of Industrialism

Americans, reported Lord Bryce, the shrewdest foreign observer of the United States in the late nineteenth century, "are satisifed with the world they live in, for they have found it a good world, in which they have grown rich. . . ." Material progress inspired confidence that man could master his fate and improve the world. No other country had so many millionaires, or so many morals-improvement societies. Ambitious men might rise from rags to riches. Millions flocked to America to partake of the horn of plenty and the country welcomed them, proclaiming itself a mecca for the world's poor, oppressed, and enterprising.

Yet beneath the prevailing mood of optimism lurked considerable fear and doubt. Industrialism unsettled everything. A land of farmers living close to nature was becoming a land of factories and propertyless workers living in disorganized, slum-ridden, and corruptly governed cities. Corporations controlling vast wealth easily put smaller entrepreneurs out of business, dictating the prices consumers paid and the wages labor earned. Perhaps as bad, industrialism was unpredictable. Three times in twenty years prosperity gave way to depression. Economic interdependence brought hard times and uncertainty for millions when the industrial machine faltered. Yet even in boom years, many lived in deprivation, and the disparity between industrial workers, farmers, and the lower middle class barely scraping by, on the one hand, and the few who piled up fortunes they could not spend in ten lifetimes, on the other, produced envy, puzzlement, and anger. Equally disturbing were the millions of immigrant strangers in the land, who clustered together preserving customs and beliefs alien to the American tradition.

The anxieties generated by rapid industrial development produced sporadic violence. "Land of opportunity, you say," a Chicago laborer scoffed, "You know damn well my children will be where I am—that is, if I can keep them out of the gutter." The frightened middle class joined employers to suppress the challenge to property. "Hand grenades should be thrown among those union sailors," recommended the Chicago *Times* when seamen on the Great Lakes stopped work to go out on strike. Some had easy explanations for industrial unrest: "Year after year," as the good Dr. James Weir pointed out, "Europe pours into the United States multitudes of degenerate human beings, who . . . immediately . . . plunge into anarchy and lawlessness; . . . these people are savages and should not be treated as civilized beings."

Rural America was also deeply troubled. Agriculture, complained a Mississippi farmer, was "the biggest fraud on earth. . . . No wonder Cain killed his brother. He was a tiller of the ground." Farmers, like miners, worked from dawn to dusk to get "one day older, and deeper in debt." Their children abandoned the farm for the lures of the city. If honest labor on God's green earth did not yield a decent livelihood, then sinister forces, agrarians argued, such as the railroads, the bankers, and the industrialists must be to blame. When farmers turned to government for relief, President Cleveland lectured them: "Though the people support the Government, the Government should not support the people." Eight years later, southern and western farmers read Cleveland out of the Democratic party and launched an agrarian crusade led by William Jennings Bryan.

The capture of a major party frightened conservatives and confirmed suspicions that, according to one conservative lawyer, in "the secret conclaves of socialism, agrarianism, and anarchism," men were hatching a "conspiracy for the subversion of our American institutions." Good citizens regardless of party united to turn back the challenge. A future president, young Theodore Roosevelt, suggested lining up a few radicals against the wall and shooting them. Despite such histrionic remarks, in the stormy years preceding Bryan's defeat in 1896, conservatives turned for protection to the courts which rushed to erect new barriers against the power of popular majorities to regulate and control private property.

When workers, farmers, and small businessmen, supported by some dissident elements in the middle class, banded together, the well-to-do overreacted and mistook the challenge for revolution. Though millions of Americans turned for help to trade unions and farmers' organizations, few embraced genuinely radical responses such as socialism which repudiated private ownership. Reformist demands did not include abandonment of capitalism. Most critics wanted no more than adjustments favorable to them. But the dissenters were so divided over remedies that they never formed an effective force for social change. Their failure originated in the complexity of a nation of farmers and city folk, native born and immigrants, Protestants and Catholics, eastern and western businessmen. This diversity forestalled a direct confrontation between the haves and the have-nots. At the same time, defenders of the existing system formulated a powerful ideology that justified things as they were, one that discovered cosmic virtue in the *status quo*.

THE GOSPEL OF WEALTH

Industrial productivity, according to the Gospel of Wealth, provided conclusive evidence of the American system's soundness. True, a few acquired great fortunes, but most Americans still shared in the prosperity. The poor, Andrew Carnegie insisted, were doing better all the time, and living standards steadily improved as Big Business reduced costs and spread the benefits of modern industry. Big Businesses were agents of progress and large fortunes were signs of that progress; therefore both deserved encouragement and praise.

Conservative professors, ministers, and businessmen, explaining the system's operations, hoped to discourage dangerous tampering. Economists argued that the profit motive stimulated people to invest capital which rapidly developed the nation's resources. Competition in the marketplace acted as a constant force promoting economic welfare. It forced railroads, manufacturers, and other producers to lower prices, increase variety, and improve quality. Best of all, the relentless pressure of the marketplace forced out the inefficient and unenterprising. Only the able,

the socially useful, survived. Competition thus rewarded those best suited to own and manage the nation's business. As each individual struggled to advance his fortune, society as a whole benefited from the investment of capital and the application of entrepreneurial talent. Such dynamic forces spurred the economic development.

Mid-nineteenth-century science added the weight of its growing authority to the teachings of the economists. The English naturalist, Charles Darwin, formulated a theory of evolution which replaced the biblical account of Creation with a naturalistic version. Organisms, Darwin contended, evolved from simple to more complex forms in the course of adapting to their environment. Evolution worked through a mechanism he termed natural selection. Man, like any other organism, had evolved over hundreds of centuries from primitive ancestors such as the ape by the process of natural selection, during which the "fittest" biological strains survived.

Some, like the English philosopher Herbert Spencer and his American admirer, William Graham Sumner, argued that evolution governed the development of society as well as the natural world. Social Darwinism appealed to certain circles in the United States for it provided conservatives with scientific sanction for existing institutions and the privileged position of the rich. Men prospered in America more than anywhere else, conservatives argued, because they adapted to their environment more successfully. The government left Americans freer than people elsewhere to develop their potential, to accumulate wealth, and to enrich society. Big Business supplied the most dramatic evidence that natural selection ruled the social order. Standard Oil survived, and most of its competitors collapsed, because Standard's managers were shrewder, more enterprising, more clever—in short, *fitter* than their less efficient rivals.

The clergy chimed in. Russell Conwell, a Baptist minister who preached a sermon called "Acres of Diamonds" thousands of times, told his listeners: "I say that you ought to get rich, and it is your duty to get rich." A man did God's work in diligently following his calling in the marketplace. "In the long run," added Episcopalian Bishop William Lawrence, "it is only to the man of morality that wealth comes. . . . Godliness is in league with riches."

Economics, science, and religion joined forces to promulgate a Gospel of Wealth. Its doctrinal hero became the successful businessman such as Carnegie and Rockefeller whose career attested to what man could do when turned loose by belief in competitive individualism, the struggle for survival, and the godliness of material accumulation. This ideology achieved popularity because it seemed to conform to experience. Most people agreed with Russell Conwell "that the opportunity to get rich is within the reach of every man."

A danger to the "gospel" lay in demands by the unsuccessful, or unfit, that the government interfere to soften the rigors of natural selection. Businessmen, for example, who sought protective tariffs or railroad regulation, farmers who demanded cheap money, workers who agitated for shortening their hours of labor—all threatened freedom of enterprise and the rights of the propertied classes. Conservatives warned that it was both wrong and futile to interfere with laws of competition and evolution. Since men could not repeal natural laws, the weak deserved neither sympathy nor help. "There is not a poor person in the United States," intoned Conwell, "who was not made poor by his own shortcomings." How, then, could one "sympathize with a man whom God has punished for his sins . . ."?

Conservatives insisted that government must leave men alone, simply maintaining order and protecting property. A few doctrinaire social Darwinists opposed public schools, and even anti-drug laws. Yet most Americans, including businessmen and professionals, were inconsistent in practice. Railroad men preached competition in principle while preferring the security of monopoly, and they accepted federal subsidies in the form of land grants. Manufacturers denounced labor unions while joining combinations to shelter themselves from competition, and demanding high tariffs. Blinded by self-interest, and soothed by the sophistries of the Gospel of Wealth, the "fittest" were unaware of these contradictions. Some called it hypocrisy.

The conservative ideology reassured men that "whatever is, is right," but many remained disturbed by the staggering wealth of the super-rich. Andrew Carnegie, impressed equally by Spencer's social Darwinist arguments *and* the need for Christian fellowship, scolded his fellow millionaires who lived conspiciously and spent lavishly. Recognizing an obligation to use wealth for the benefit of society, Carnegie, Rockefeller, and others organized large-scale philanthropic activities, under the guidance of professional managers, out of which emerged the private foundation. This doctrine of stewardship, part of the "Gospel of Wealth," partially humanized the results of competitive struggle without violating the alleged laws of nature and national prosperity. It was moral for individuals voluntarily to aid the less fortunate; but it was wicked for the state to confiscate private property through taxes to support the weak.

Conservatives admitted that evolution sometimes produced cruel results. Even Lord Bryce, a sympathetic foreign observer of American society, noted the strains. Everything in America, he observed, "tends to make the individual independent and self-reliant. He goes early into the world; he is left to make his way alone; he tries one occupation after another, he gets to think that each man is his own best helper and adviser." This contributed to the rootlessness, almost nomadic quality of Americans, constantly on the move and seeking economic betterment. Increasingly, some Americans balked at paying the crushing price evolutionary "progress" demanded. They began to question conservative ideology and wonder why people in a self-styled Age of Progress must remain passive observers, or sometimes become the victims, of evolutionary "progress." They insisted that men should use government to direct social development in more satisfying ways than allowed by the doctrine of rugged individualism. Ultimately the Gospel of Wealth failed to block social reform, but first came a struggle that left many Americans fearful for the Republic's future.

MIDDLE-CLASS DISSENT

Dissent arose because the new industrial order did not benefit, but rather victimized many Americans. The Gospel of Wealth increasingly appeared to many as a cheap rationalization of the unrestrained power of the almighty businessman and his dollars. Moreover, conservative ideology repudiated an older American tradition which, in Lincoln's words, put man before the dollar and gave government the responsibility to curb individual freedoms that endangered the common good.

Dissent came from many quarters and for varying reasons. Some attributed the success of the new arrivals to unscrupulous methods. A Boston Brahmin assumed that those entrusted with other people's money, such as railroad or corporation managers, held a public trust to guard the investors' interests. Horrified, they watched a new breed of businessmen turn corporations into speculative playthings. Yet those who gained wealth through fraud and deceit became pillars of their communities because Americans honored "wealth more than honesty." At the same time that the new rich corrupted business, they polluted politics, since their schemes needed government protection. As industrialization disrupted the lives of Americans, fear of unbridled wealth and of large corporations spread to other groups who rejected Darwinian explanations of their misery.

The railroads, America's first Big Business, drew the heaviest fire. As the railroad network expanded, new towns appeared, often at the expense of older distribution centers. Towns served by two competing roads enjoyed the benefit of competitive rates; communities served by one, consolidated line paid monopoly rates. Discriminatory rates led to demands for government supervision in contradiction of the Gospel of Wealth. But advocates of rate regulation did not repudiate free enterprise in principle; they wanted simply to curb the railroad's absolute freedom in order to protect their own particular interests. As long as many areas still needed railroads, as did the Midwest and Far West, proposals for control bogged down because the have-not communities feared discouraging capitalists from building new lines out of fear of government regulation.

The growth of industrial combinations intensified attacks on Big Business. Oil producers unable to compete with Standard Oil went bankrupt or sold out, blaming their failure on the unfair and illegal advantages Rockefeller had obtained from the railroads and the government. The recurrent panics and depressions which wiped out many small-scale businesses further weakened belief in the justness of free enterprise, since hard work often ended in poverty.

Competition and individual enterprise, previously unquestioned catalysts of economic progress, were being eliminated. Trusts and combinations destroyed competition and virtually excluded new firms. In a detailed exposé of Standard Oil, *Wealth Against Commonwealth* (1894), Henry Demarest Lloyd charged: "Nature is rich; but everywhere man, the heir of nature is poor," echoing the sentiments of Rosseau's *Social Contract* that man was born free, but that everywhere he was in chains. Lloyd blamed this condition on monopoly capitalism. Competition, he argued, resulted in callousness and the triumph of evil for "business success is won by a sort of predatory, over-reaching, down-treading quality." The inventors, the pioneer entrepreneurs who enriched society, rarely benefited because latecoming business buccaneers always grabbed the profits. Standard Oil gained mastery of the oil industry, Lloyd argued, not because it was the fittest producer, but the most unscrupulous. "The Standard," he observed sarcastically, "has done everything with the Pennsylvanian legislature except to refine it."

While men like Lloyd frontally attacked the Gospel of Wealth, other more representative expressions of middle-class anxiety appealed to people who did not consider themselves social critics. The novels of Horatio Alger, all best sellers, celebrated the rise of young men from rags to riches. Success, according to the lowbrow wisdom purveyed in these stories, went to the thrifty, honest, industrious, and self-reliant. Yet Alger's heroes, though models of virtue, succeeded ultimately because of luck; they did good deeds, to be sure, but their real break came with marriage to the boss's daughter. Alger nostalgically attempted to evoke an earlier time when virtue was rewarded, but although he still preached the merits of frugality, faithfulness, and diligence, virtuous people could no longer count on automatic rewards. Experience taught many Americans that no matter what they did, they sometimes fell victim to the fickle finger of fate, to crop failures, to business depressions and speculative frenzies.

Yet the moral foundation of the Gospel of Wealth rested on the conviction that the prosperous deserved their good fortune. Conflict between experience and inherited moral values found expression in the Alger stories, which tried to shore up belief in the ethic of success. "The delusions of the time ought to be exposed," wrote a conservative apologist, "and young men should be taught that *principle* wins, in the long run, instead of luck or unscrupulous scheming." The careers of a John D. Rockefeller or a Jay Gould, however, strained the credulity of many Americans.

None spoke for the doubters more eloquently then Henry George, a California journalist whose powerful critique of American industrial society, *Progress and Poverty* (1879), became a best seller on two continents. George denied that free enterprise rewarded the principled or benefited the majority. Why, he asked, did so much poverty exist amid unprecedented wealth? Why did the existing system fail to reward the producers? Wealth, according to George, resulted from the labor of workers and entrepreneurs, but both paid tribute to landowners who received unearned increment in the form of rents. The *rentier* did nothing, yet he appropriated riches that rightly belonged to the producing classes. Rent was responsible for most social problems: "it takes little children from play and from schools and compels them to work before their bones are hard . . . it robs the shivering of warmth; the hungry of food; the sick of medicine. It debases, and embrutes, and embitters . . . it makes lads who might be useful men candidates for prisons . . . it fills brothels with girls who might have known the pure joy of motherhood."

By imposing a "Single Tax" on land alone, George argued, the state could reclaim the unearned income of landowners. He did not reject capitalism or private property, or demand a radical reconstruction of society; he offered, rather, one simple solution which aroused new hope for those dreaming of success in a capitalist society. When George ran for mayor of New York in 1886, he received strong support from labor and even some middle-class votes. Though a loser, his strong showing revealed that discontent with the Gospel of Wealth was spreading.

Edward Bellamy expressed even deeper alienation in *Looking Backward* (1888), a popular novel that proposed a socialist solution. He branded competition in the race for wealth the cause of social problems. The cure required a society based on love, but capitalists set man against man in a ruthless struggle for survival. Bellamy envisioned a utopia set in the year 2000. The state owned the means of production, wealth was socialized, and every man worked and enjoyed a decent life. Bellamy's vision found a receptive audience because it appealed to Christian belief in the brotherhood of man and to the American tradition of equal opportunity. Best of all, Bellamy's socialism was vague. No Marxist, he neither preached class struggle nor explained *how* to reach utopia. *Looking Backward* offered an escape from the harsh rigors of the Gospel of Wealth, a nostalgic invitation to dream about how life might be in a society that respected the worth of *all* men. Bellamy himself had failed in business in New York City; he fled to the hills of western Massachusetts where he pondered the advantages of an America governed by middle-class moralists like himself rather than industrial freebooters.

Though these widely read social critics voiced the discontent and anxieties of millions of Americans, most people remained ambivalent about reform. Despite disappointments which dimmed faith in the Gospel of Wealth, hope still lingered that one's luck would improve and that expectations would be fulfilled. When workers and farmers challenged the system and threatened social stability, many middle-class people became frightened. Some interpreted strikes and agrarian dissent as proof that injustice was generating unrest and committed themselves to social reform. But most sought refuge in the conservative camp as the best way to resist disorder and repress protest, especially dissent emanating from working people who revolted against the socially oppressive by-products of an industrial economy.

THE CHALLENGE OF LABOR

The new factories, mines, and railroads employed millions of workers who became the largest occupational group in late-nineteenth-century America. From rural America and from across the oceans, peasants streamed into the older cities and the hundreds of new ones spawned by industrialism. Men, women, and children worked long and hard under conditions set by employers. People accustomed to living on the land, or working as skilled craftsmen in small shops, found the new industrial system bewildering and often menacing. Their labor had been reduced to a commodity which employers bought as cheaply as possible. New technology wiped out old skills; labor became a cog in a machine, subject to disturbing impersonal forces. Periodically, thousands lost their jobs as factories cut production or shut down; competition and recurrent hard times reduced wages and ate away at the worker's slim margin of comfort. Above all, millions felt that their individuality went unrecognized, their needs ignored; yet they were powerless to alter conditions.

Occasionally discontent surfaced. Workers periodically put down their tools, hoping to gain some control over their lives. Helpless against powerful corporations, some joined unions. But these initial efforts failed, since early organizations were weak, their methods and objectives often impractical, and employers hostile.

Workers were confused. Many could not or would not perceive themselves as a permanent proletariat whose best hope lay in accepting industrialism and improving their lives within the system. Like other Americans, many accepted the Gospel of Wealth and hoped to move up through hard work. Some did, and their success encouraged others to believe that opportunity would come their way eventually. But many despaired. "There is an industrial problem," a Bellamyite warned, "which, if it be not soon solved by ballots, will be settled by bullets." The explosion never came. Conservatism and divisions within the working classes, the resistance of employers and the middle classes, and the emergence of practical, modern trade unionism prevented it.

Ever since the first factories threatened craftsmen with competition from machines, and business fluctuations after 1819 periodically threw able men out of work, workers experimented with collective action to bargain with employers. But the early unions established in the 1820s and 1830s collapsed when business slackened and employers replaced the unionized men with non-union workers. Workers then turned to political remedies such as banking and currency reform, free public schools, or land reform. In the 1850s and 1860s a few skilled crafts such as the iron molders and the typographers reestablished trade unions but as late as the 1870s unionism had made little headway. In 1877, desperate railroad workers spontaneously struck the nation's railroads to resist wage cuts. When the state and federal governments called out troops to get the railroads moving, workers battled police and troops. In Pittsburgh twenty-six people died while mobs destroyed millions of dollars of railroad property.

Knights of Labor

Suddenly, in the mid-1880s, the Knights of Labor, an organization founded in 1878, became the hope of hundreds of thousands. A victorious strike on Jay Gould's western railroads sent workers flocking into the new organization. The Knights tapped a deep-seated and widespread discontent, since workers were ready to support leaders who offered hope. From 100,000 in 1885, the membership grew to over 700,000 in a year. The Knights of Labor preached that workers could achieve social justice without resorting to violence. They rejected strikes and collective bargaining because their aims, as their leader Terence V. Powderly said, were to abolish the wage system, to make each man his own employer by establishing producer's cooperatives. Powderly agitated for political reforms that would destroy "monopoly" and restore opportunity for small-scale enterprise. With these goals and means, the Knights generally did not organize along industry or craft lines but geographically, taking in all who wished to join.

The success of the Knights on the railroads was largely accidental, not the result of careful planning. Workers began those strikes without authorization and thrust leadership on Powderly's reluctant shoulders. The railroads, caught unprepared, had to buy a quick peace. But a year later they smashed the union, revealing the Knights' weakness. Ideological aversion to strikes, violence, and the accumulation of economic power for bargaining purposes left the Knights unprepared to wage a wider struggle. Theirs, too, was a utopian response to industrialism; they dreamed of restoring small individual enterprise.

Within the Knights of Labor, however, as well as outside its ranks, some workers discovered a more practical alternative. The Cigar Makers International Union under the leadership of Samuel Gompers offered a new model, that of "pure-and-simple" unionism. Skilled workers banded together to control the supply of labor in a craft or industry; the unskilled were ignored as unorganizable. If unions controlled the labor supply they could bargain with employers to improve wages, hours, and working conditions. In the event employers resisted reasonable demands, the workers struck, but only after they had accumlated a strike fund through monthly dues payments; and strikes were reserved for times when the union had a fair chance to win, such as during the busy season. By stressing job consciousness, seeking limited but immediate gains, and shrewdly deploying slender resources, the cigar makers and other unions of skilled workers slowly built stable and successful organizations. In 1886, twenty-five craft unions with 150,000 members formed the American Federation of Labor.

American Federation of Labor

The AFL, with Samuel Gompers as president, grew and replaced the Knights as the country's leading labor organization. It was more successful because it accepted industrialism and adapted to it. Concentrating on collective bargaining, rather than on political reform, "business unionism" rejected radical proposals for social change. Some unions, under socialist control, denounced Gompers as a sellout to capitalism, an advocate of "wage slavery." They preached the class struggle and backed the Socialist Labor party, which sought to abolish capitalism. Socialism found little support among American workers, however, and the socialist-run unions languished until they abandoned politics for the methods and aims of "pure-and-simple" unionism. Gompers fought the socialists within the AFL, insisting that unions could not gain public sympathy or make headway with American workers unless they shunned radical political commitments.

By 1904, the trade unions had organized about two million workers—mainly in the railroads, in the highly skilled building trades, and in coal mining. The Gompers formula proved most successful in industries composed of small firms, those with limited resources and heavily dependent on skilled labor. In heavy industry and against large corporations, such as United States Steel, unions made no headway.

Employers resisted unions in order to maximize control over wages and internal management. When unions were new and untried, businessmen cultivated exaggerated fears about collective bargaining. "I have talked with the stockholders," a railroad manager told the union, "and they say we cannot accept your wage schedule, because it would allow labor to dictate to capital." Experience later taught employers that collective bargaining did not produce union domination but usually resulted in agreements acceptable to both sides. Until employees learned that lesson, they resisted dilution of their control with all their might. Though Andrew Carnegie had once upheld the right of workers to form unions, in 1892 the iron and steel workers unions were smashed in the bloody Homestead Strike. The company hired a private army of 300 Pinkerton Detective Agency men to protect strike breakers from union workers who tried to keep the Homestead works shut down. The forces fought a battle in which three Pinkertons and ten strikers died. Peace returned only after the state militia moved in and enabled Carnegie to reopen with nonunion, or "scab," labor.

The same violent story occured again on a much larger scale in 1894 when the American Railway Union struck and halted service in the Midwest in support of the efforts by Pullman Company workers to roll back a wage cut. This time President Cleveland sent federal troops to break the strike on the grounds that workers interfered with the mails, and that violence threatened to disrupt the flow of interstate commerce. A federal court injunction against all union activity led to the arrest of Eugene V. Debs, the ARU's leader. The appearance of troops triggered riots, and the strike collapsed.

With the power of government thrown on the side of capital the deck was stacked against unionism. Management could resort to intimidation and the use of spies; it could blacklist union workers; and it could force employees to sign yellow-dog contracts promising not to join a union on pain of losing their jobs. According to the Gospel of Wealth, workers did not need unions because as Andrew Carnegie maintained, anyone "who can handle a pick or a shovel, stands upon equal terms with the purchaser of his labor," such as corporations like Carnegie's. Behind such a nonsensical view of the individual worker's bargaining power lay fierce opposition to anyone who threatened the employer's power. Frightened by industrial violence, the middle classes went along with the efforts of business and government to resist unionization.

The Haymarket Massacre (1886) startled the nation and also tarred unions with the brush of anarchism. In 1886 workers were campaigning nationally for an eight-hour day. In Chicago, anarchists who advocated revolution held a meeting to support striking workers at the McCormick Reaper plant. When police attempted to break up the assembly, someone threw a bomb which killed several policemen. An outraged public demanded revenge. Seven anarchists involved in the eight-hour-day campaign were convicted of murder, and four were executed though no proof existed that any was responsible for the tragedy. When the Governor of Illinois, John Peter Altgeld, later freed those unfairly imprisoned, he ruined his political career. This miscarriage of justice sent innocent men to their deaths and revealed the extent to which turbulence in industrial society strained the American sense of fair play.

Unions thus faced hostility from government, employers, and the public. In addition, millions of American workers shunned them. Many were immigrants to the cities, native and foreign born,

and as bad as conditions were in the mines and mills, they were often an improvement over rural life. Many immigrants were Catholic, and the Church was suspicious of unionism, which in Europe was identified with socialism and atheism. Divisions among ethnic groups, such as the Irish and Italians, as well as between native- and foreign-born workers further weakened labor's solidarity as a class, never very strong in America in any case. The existence of large numbers of unskilled immigrants enabled native-born workers who moved into skilled and supervisory positions to feel superior and to identify with management. Most of all, millions of workers believed they could get ahead without joining unions. Real wages (earning power) rose during the last forty years of the nineteenth century, and though most of the sons of workers remained in the working class, many workers accumulated savings and owned their own homes, proof that people could progress and that the Gospel of Wealth worked. Not until that faith died did unionism win the allegiance of the majority of American workers.

STRANGERS IN THE LAND

Several of the Haymarket affair anarchists were German born, and foreigners figured prominently in socialist and other radical organizations. Gompers was an English-born Jew, and Terence Powderly was a Catholic. The new Italians, Poles, Russians, and Jews seemed even stranger than the Germans and Irish who had flooded the land before the Civil War and who kept coming afterward. These earlier arrivals eventually lost many of their alien qualities, but they still stuck together and the second generation began to compete with older stock for power and prominence. Thus the children of the second generation of immigrants who had arrived before the Civil War, together with the millions of newcomers from eastern and southern Europe who had never before come in large numbers, generated unprecedented ethnic and cultural tension.

Originally most Americans had welcomed the newcomers, not in their neighborhoods, of course, but at least in their country. The open door was a source of national pride, a means through which the country fulfilled its destiny as a home for the oppressed. The immigrants also supplied a rapidly growing industrial society with inexpensive labor and swelled the number of consumers. Though strangers brought with them alien customs and beliefs which many Americans disdained, ethnic diversity had not weakened the nation. Newcomers embraced American values and the native-born remained confident that they could absorb and remake foreigners into their own American image.

Under the strains of industralism and rapid urbanization, this confidence weakened. The spread of nativism and racism expressed fears and anxieties of older stock who blamed the newcomers for the country's social ills. The cities were corrupt, some believed, because depraved immigrants sold their votes to machine politicians. By 1890, sixty-eight towns and cities in Massachusetts came under the control of the Irish, who in 1885 elected their first mayor in Boston. Yankees, rich and poor, no longer felt that the land their fathers had settled still belonged to them. They blamed the newcomers for industrial violence. When hard times left thousands unemployed, immigrants added to the misery of labor and hindered unionization by serving as strike breakers.

Millions of immigrants were Catholic. The Know-Nothings in the 1850s had contended that a Catholic could not become a good American because of the Church's hostility to democracy. As the numbers of Catholics increased in the late nineteenth century, anti-Catholic sentiment flared up again, especially when Catholics began to occupy public office and the Church sought public aid for its schools and charities. Immigrants thus became identified with industrial unrest and radicalism, urban squalor, and a powerful religion allegedly hostile to American ideals. Native-born workers exploited by industrialism, the middle class bewildered by social instability and rapid change, and elites displaced by men of new wealth and of new ethnic stock turned on the alien.

In such an atmosphere, racism and a policy of exclusion easily found supporters. Many Americans embraced theories of Anglo-Saxon superiority. Anglo-Saxons, racists argued, had carved a great republic out of a wilderness because of inherent industriousness and devotion to liberty. Germans and Irish, Italians and Russians, Catholics and Jews, on the other hand, were unassimilable because an inclination to crime, drunkenness, laziness, and pauperism supposedly ran in their bloodstream.

Nativist tension expressed itself in several ways. Some Americans became genealogy worshipers, gaining reassurance and comfort from public recognition that their ancestry entitled them to membership in the Sons or the Daughters of the American Revolution, organizations from which newcomers were automatically excluded. But nativism also took uglier forms. In Pennsylvania a sheriff's posse slaughtered twenty-one Polish and Hungarian coal miners on strike; in the South, mobs lynched Italians and burned Jewish stores. An important nativist organization, the American Protective Association, grew to a half million members in the mid 1890s.

Inevitably, nativism infected politics. Because most Democratic strength outside the South centered in the cities and among immigrants and their children, Republicanism became the channel for Northern nativist sentiment. Presidents Grant and Hayes had attacked the Catholic Church in the 1870s; in the states, Protestants struck at Catholic schools and responded to the immigrants' fondness for liquor by reviving the temperance crusade.

But the most promising remedy was exclusion. Anti-Chinese agitation in California led the federal government in 1882 to close the door to immigrants from China. By 1880, over 100,000 Chinese lived in the western United States. Though most did not compete directly with white labor, California workers—the chief force behind the anti-Oriental movement—reacted hostilely. Most whites had come to California to get rich quick, or at least to get rich; many were Irish immigrants, themselves members of an exploited and downtrodden group. Inevitably, inflated expectations concerning "Golden" California turned to bitterness. When the depression of the 1870s hit the state, anti-Chinese agitation mounted. In 1877–1878 mobs rioted in San Francisco against Orientals. Businessmen, who still wanted Oriental labor, could not stem the tide. With national parties evenly balanced, both catered to the demands for Chinese exclusion. "The Asiatics," proclaimed Republican orator James G. Blaine in 1878, "cannot go on with our population and make a homogeneous element," for according to the man described by Democrats in the election of 1884 as "James G. Blaine—James G. Blaine/ the Continental Liar from the State of Maine," the Chinese do "not recognize the relation of husband and wife," nor "have in the slightest degree the ennobling and civilizing influence of the hearthstone and fireside."

Also in 1882, Congress barred convicts, mental defectives, and lepers. In 1890 Congress had proposed a literacy test aimed at excluding peasants from southern and eastern Europe but President Cleveland vetoed it.

For another generation the doors remained open to Europeans. Despite the growth of nativism and racism, especially during the depression of the 1890s, an older faith in America as a refuge for the world's oppressed, and the conviction that newcomers could be assimilated and were a source of economic strength, persisted. Most businessmen opposed restriction and the return of prosperity in the late 1890s, together with a return of confidence that industrial America would not collapse, weakened the nativist impulse. A far greater challenge to stability in the 1890s came from rural America, where "nature's nobleman," the American farmer, repudiated the Gospel of Wealth and challenged control by Big Business and its allies.

Chapter 19
The Politics of Crisis

American agriculture boomed during most of the late nineteenth century, as an army of farmers spread across the continent, borrowing capital to create new farms and bringing millions of acres of virgin land under mechanized cultivation. The world's most efficient transportation and distribution network made the farmer part of a world market. Agriculture as a whole prospered; but not all farmers, at all times and in all places, shared in the prosperity. The gap between expectations and rewards, between the age-old isolation of rural life and the novel excitement of the cities, between the wealth piled up by Big Business and the comparatively meager returns for farmers, generated much unrest.

Like industrial workers, farmers wondered why hard work ended in failure for so many. Finally, they too organized to advance their interests. In the 1870s, the National Grange and the Greenback movement arose to advocate currency inflation and to express rural discontent. In the next two decades agrarian insurgency intensified. New Farmers' Alliances in the South and West first agitated for reform, then proposed radical solutions, and finally merged into the Populist party. Ultimately agrarians, supported by other reformers, captured the Democratic party and in the election of 1896 challenged the business elements then dominating both parties. The roots of this agrarian challenge and the reasons for its failure grew out of the difficulties farmers experienced in adjusting to industrial society. Most farmers managed to adapt; those who did not protested.

THE FARM PROBLEM

From the 1870s until the end of the century, agricultural prices declined less rapidly than did railroad rates or the price of manufactured goods. At the same time agricultural production expanded enormously. Since farmers still cleared a profit, they felt encouraged to increase production for a steadily growing home market and an in-

creasingly important international market. They cultivated more and more acreage, encouraged by the availability of free public land, farm machinery, and reductions in freight costs. Farmers, as has ever been their custom, financed expansion by going into debt, mortgaging property to obtain loans from local bankers and eastern investors who regarded western mortgages as excellent investments. Captivated by the spirit of optimism and speculative gain that swept late-nineteenth-century America, rural communities overextended themselves. "Do not be afraid of going into debt," preached a Kansas newspaper in the 1880s, "Spend money for the city's betterment as free as water. But judiciously. . . . Do all you can for Belle Plaine regardless of money, and let the increase of population and wealth take care of the taxes." On the prairie and plains new farming communities shared the faith of the Kansans who imagined that "in less than a decade the inhabitants of Ninescah valley will roll in luxury and wealth."

The most vulnerable of these optimists were midwestern producers of wheat, corn, and hogs, and Southern cotton growers. Their prosperity depended on foreign markets. As production expanded, supply outpaced demand, and as other countries such as India, Australia, and Argentina competed with America in the world markets, prices fell. Farmers, however, did not curtail production or adjust it to demand, as manufacturers had done. While prices declined, farmers produced more, depressing prices still further. They failed to gear production to demand because the individual farmer could not offset supply and no way existed to get all farmers to cut back. Government controls might have helped, but such federal interference was visionary at the time. With land and credit freely available, new producers constantly expanded output, contributing further to overproduction. Moreover, farmers, with no control over weather, could not accurately predict the size of crops. And whether a farmer produced a small or a large crop, his interest payments and taxes remained the same. So he took his chances and planted as much as he could in the hope of profits if prices rose. When the gamble paid off, the farmer went more deeply into debt to expand production, for a bigger killing expected the following year.

Eventually, disaster came. From the 1870s until the end of the century, farm prices fluctuated sharply. The general trend was downward, however, as supply outpaced demand and competition on the world market intensified. Drought and unusually harsh winters in the mid-1880s increased agriculture's natural hazards. When prices hit bottom in the late 1880s and the 1890s, many overextended farmers failed. The hardest hit were the wheat, corn, and livestock producers in newly settled areas west of the Mississippi, and cotton farmers in the South. Kansas, for instance, lost 180,000 people between 1887 and 1891, as "busted" farmers fled the state. "The idea seems to have obtained in the minds of thousands of farmers," wrote one, "that every man's hand is against them and, hence, there is a kind of war spirit pervading their entire being."

THE FARMER'S EXPLANATION AND RESPONSE

Distress left the farmer confused and angry. Living in the midst of rapid and radical changes, they had difficulty understanding that dependence on international markets subjected them to unpredictable price fluctuations and heavy risks. Many farmers denied that the source of their difficulties lay in overproduction. For 250 years American farmers, infused with a speculative outlook, had concentrated on expanding production. During the first half of the nineteenth century, foreign markets for cotton and home markets for foodstuffs seemed limitless. Experience thus offered few guides for adjusting to changing conditions.

Acceptance of the concept of overproduction would have placed the blame on the farmers themselves. They thought they knew better, and saw themselves as the victims of exploitation by railroads which charged excessive rates, warehouse owners who cheated them, industrial trusts that rigged prices, lenders who exacted usurious interest payments, and a government which ignored them. The farmer's explanation had some merit, but the exploitation was not nearly so stark as they pictured it. Railroad rates in the Southwest and west of the Mississippi were discriminatory and higher than in the East and older Midwest. But rates reflected, in part, competitive conditions and costs. The newer Western states were less densely settled, coal was more expensive there, traffic lighter, distances to Eastern markets greater, and trains returned from the East half empty. With the roads built, people who had to pay for them became critical, especially after expectations of selling all their wheat or cotton failed to materialize.

Manufacturers provided another convenient scapegoat. Farmers complained that they paid dearly for everything bought in a protected market while they sold cheaply in unprotected markets. Actually, the price of industrial goods fell more rapidly than farm prices from 1870s to the late 1890s, yet the cost of farm machinery and consumer goods appeared outrageous to those deeply in debt. Farmers did lack adequate sources of credit; the banking system was not geared to their needs. But Eastern moneylenders and their agents did not charge undue interest rates considering the risks involved and the rate of return they earned.

Ultimately, farmers put the blame on government. Agrarian discontent arose not only from the hazards of farming as a business, but from its privations. For over a century Americans had lauded the yeoman farmer as the cornerstone of the Republic, imputing to him virtues of independence, honesty, goodness, and industriousness. Yet the gap between rhetoric and reality widened steadily. The city, not the farm, became the mecca for the new America. Far more people abandoned the country for urban life than settled on the land, even though vice and corruption allegedly ran rampant in the cities, or perhaps because of it. Young people who craved the more interesting and varied experiences of the cities proved the least faithful to rural America. Life on the plains and prairies and in the South was dull; farm life was drudgery with little to relieve the boredom and loneliness. "I hate farm life," cried the wife in one of Hamlin Garland's stories of the Midwest. "It's nothing but fret, fret, and work the whole time, never seeing anybody but a lot of neighbors just as big fools as you are." Farmers complained that city slickers patronized them as bumpkins, crude and unsophisticated rubes. Having lost out in the marketplace, a shift in values crushed the farmer's self-esteem. William Jennings Bryan of Nebraska, better than anyone else, articulated the despair of rural America with compliments that began to sound patronizing: "Burn down your cities and leave our farms," he assured, "and your cities will spring up again as if by magic; but destroy our farms and the grass will grow in the streets of every city in the country."

Grangers and Populists

Holding others responsible for rural America's troubles, farmers organized to obtain justice. The Grange campaigned for regulation of railroad and grain elevators, set up producers' manufacturing and purchasing cooperatives to reduce middleman costs, and built Grange Halls where farm families gathered for educational and social activities. The Grange enjoyed a modest success, working with business to regulate the

railroads, but their cooperative enterprises failed. As the Grange movement passed its peak by the mid-1870s, some farmers put all their hopes on currency reform, the Greenbacker party's demand for more paper money, and later on the campaign to enlarge the currency supply through unlimited coinage of silver. Yet as the nation began to recover from the depression of the 1870s, agrarian enthusiasm for monetary reform waned and unrest subsided.

Grangerism had centered in such states as Ohio and Illinois. In the 1880s, agrarian protest shifted west of the Mississippi and also erupted in the South. Farmers' Alliances sprang up, demanding that the government aid producers by lowering the tariff and regulating Big Business, especially the railroads. Agrarians also demanded low-cost credit and an inflated currency so farmers could pay their debts in dollars worth less than the dollars they originally had borrowed. Southern cotton farmers pressed for government loans on commodities that would enable them to hold crops off the market, selling when prices rose. Western farmers urged government ownership of the railroads to lower freight rates and end regional discrimination.

At first the Alliances established coopera-

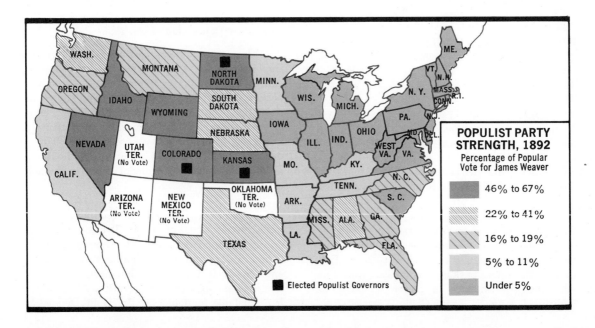

POPULIST PARTY STRENGTH, 1892
Percentage of Popular Vote for James Weaver

46% to 67%

22% to 41%

16% to 19%

5% to 11%

Under 5%

■ Elected Populist Governors

tives and tried to work through the existing party system. Their businesses usually failed, however, and the old parties proved unresponsive. Farmers then turned to independent political action, forming the Populist, or People's, party. In 1892 the Populists nominated a former Greenbacker for president and campaigned for unlimited or "free" coinage of silver, a federal income tax, and regulation of business. To assure popular control of government, Populists demanded direct election of U.S. senators, the secret ballot, and the initiative and referendum which would enable voters to legislate directly, thus theoretically preventing professional politicians from thwarting the people's will. In a bid for support from workers and middle-class reformers, Populists called for a reduction in the hours of labor and restrictions on immigration.

Populist rhetoric was strong. "A vast conspiracy against mankind has been organized on two continents," declared the Populist platform, "and it is rapidly taking possession of the world. It boldly steals the fruits of the toil of millions to build up colossal fortunes for a few." Populists polled over a million votes and sent a dozen men to Congress, also gaining control of several state legislatures. Some predicted the end of the old parties; next time, the People's party would do even better. Certainly the depression which followed the Panic of 1893 provided ample material for the Populists' arguments.

1896: THE CRISIS

Between 1870 and 1890 party battles had involved competing personalities, sectional and ethnic divisions. Neither party advocated clear-cut policies to deal with the disruptions of industrialization; and neither won a safe majority. But in the mid-1880s, the Republicans started to slip. They lost the presidency in 1884, and although Harrison regained it for the GOP in 1888 they failed to poll a popular majority.

Realizing the precariousness of their position, in 1890 Republicans pushed through Congress a legislative package they hoped would assure their continuance in power. Looking for additional support from Civil War veterans,

the Republicans added 300,000 names to the pension rolls. To appease antimonopoly and antiinflationist sentiment, especially among farmers and silver mining interests in the West, Congress adopted the Sherman Anti-Trust Act and the Sherman Silver Purchase Act. Finally, the Republicans enacted the McKinley Tariff, which raised duties in the hope of winning votes from workers and businessmen. But when a Force Bill to protect Southern Negro voters failed to pass, chances for the party's revival in the South disappeared.

The overall Republican strategy failed as well. Farmers flocking to Populism had lost faith in the GOP. The Sherman Silver Purchase Act did not satisfy inflationists, who gained increased political power with the admission to the Union in 1889–1890 of North and South Dakota, Montana, Washington, Idaho, and Wyoming. These defections proved especially damaging because Populists and Democrats sometimes pooled their votes to win elections. The mountain and plains states, once Republican strongholds, were no longer safe. At the same time, Republicans met with trouble in the East. Sound money men, or deflationists, objected to the party's flirtation with inflation; and growing anti-immigrant and anti-Catholic sentiment among Republicans alienated the newer ethnic groups.

The Great Depression of the 1890s

The 1890 midterm elections produced the Republicans' worst defeat. For the first time in a generation, Democrats seemed relatively sure of becoming the majority party. But no sooner did they recapture the presidency in 1892 under Grover Cleveland, with massive majorities in Congress, than disaster overtook them. The industrial machine faltered, panic swept the money markets, and the government faced a financial crisis.

Blame fell upon the Democrats, those in power, and the Republicans rebounded in the midterm elections of 1894. Traditional Democratic strongholds crumbled, especially in the urban centers and among immigrants and workers. President Cleveland's handling of the economic crisis split the Democratic party into two irreconcilable factions: (1) the Gold Democrats, who opposed currency inflation; and (2) the Silver Democrats, who insisted that expanding the currency would cure the country's ills. The struggle ended with the silver wing in control, but with the divided party headed for disaster in the 1896 presidential campaign. The convulsions within the Democratic party enabled the Republicans to gain a long-term majority which they held until the 1930s, the decade of Franklin Roosevelt and the New Deal.

Although the depression of the 1890s caused the Democratic debacle, the party had not created the downturn. After years of industrial expansion, production had outpaced demand, profits sagged, and investors were less inclined to finance further expansion. Contraction had already hit agriculture; eventually it spread to railroads and the industrial sector. Almost 500 banks and 15,000 businesses failed in 1893; by 1897 a third of the country's railroad mileage was in bankruptcy and 20 percent of the labor force was out of work. Armies of the jobless inspired by "General" Jacob Coxey tramped across the country to dramatize their plight; a few marched on Washington and landed in jail. Why hard times engulfed the land, few understood. Some passively accepted the depression as a phase of national readjustment needed to weed out unsound enterprises and to lay firm foundations for the next boom. They believed that nothing could be done except to wait patiently for the return of prosperity. A critical minority pointed out that masses of Americans lacked adequate purchasing power to pay for all the goods and services the country produced, but few listened to these voices.

Financial problems became President Cleveland's chief concern. In April 1893, the U.S. Treasury's gold reserves dropped below $100 million, the sum regarded as necessary for the government to meet its obligations without going off the gold standard. Cleveland struggled to protect this standard, believing its perservation necessary to restore business confidence and encourage investment. He blamed the country's troubles on Republican fiscal policies. The McKinley Tariff cut import revenues, the soldiers' pensions were expensive, and government ran a deficit. Summoning a special session of Congress, and squandering enormous amounts of his politi-

cal capital, Cleveland forced through repeal of the Sherman Silver Purchase Act. But gold reserves continued to decline. The president then persuaded J. P. Morgan and other Wall Street bankers to float a series of loans that replenished the Treasury's gold reserves (and earned the bankers handsome profits).

Election of 1896

In saving the gold standard, Cleveland lost control of his party. Its southern and western wings rebelled in response to agrarian distress and the president's reliance on Wall Street. They championed free coinage of silver to inflate the currency. Silverites controlled the Democratic national convention of 1896, repudiating Cleveland and nominating an active, eloquent, and ambitious advocate of Western agrarianism and free silver, William Jennings Bryan of Nebraska. The Democrats also attacked monopolies, the high tariff, and the use of injunctions to break strikes, but Bryan campaigned chiefly for free silver.

Bryan's crusade was unprecedented. Carrying his message directly to the people, he toured the country longer than any previous candidate. He appealed to the have-nots in language that had seldom been heard from the candidate of a national party. Never before had a presidential candidate made such a blunt and repeated appeal to class interest. Bryan set the revivalistic tone of the campaign in a powerful speech at the Democratic convention. "Upon which side will the Democratic party fight," he asked rhetorically, "upon the side of the idle holders of capital or upon the side of the struggling masses?" The sympathies of the Democratic party, he answered, "are on the side of the struggling masses" who needed, above all, free silver and inflation to rescue them from the clutches of creditors and international bankers profiting from the gold standard. Just as Andrew Jackson sixty years earlier had fought "the bank conspiracy" and saved America, Bryan called on the Democratic party to renew the battle. He told the cheering Democrats, "having behind us the producing masses of the nation and the world, supported by the commercial interests, the laboring interests and the toilers everywhere, we would answer their demand for a gold standard by saying to them: You shall not press down upon the brow of labor this crown of thorns; you shall not crucify mankind upon a cross of gold."

The Populists abandoned independent politics and supported Bryan. Here was a major party leader whom farmers could understand; some Populists feared that fusion with Democrats would destroy their party and that to campaign primarily on the currency question diverted attention from other vital reforms. But Bryan's magnetism swept objections aside; most Populists thought "the Commoner" had a good chance to win, and so did Bryan.

The Republicans nominated William McKinley governor of Ohio on a platform favoring the gold standard, adding vague promises in favor of eventual restoration of a bimetallic currency. The Silver Republicans from the western mining states bolted to back Bryan.

The battle of the standards was on.

While Bryan exhausted himself touring the country, McKinley sat home and greeted visiting delegations, trusting to the well-oiled and well-financed Republican organization, under the expert direction of Mark Hanna, an Ohio industrialist, to carry the election. Republicans spent money like water; over 200 million pieces of literature flooded the country and convinced millions that free silver was a hoax: the way to restore prosperity, Republicans agreed, was to raise the tariff against foreign goods that stole business from American workers and employers. McKinley, the party's tariff expert, was the man to do it.

Why Bryan Lost

Never before had so many Americans gone to the polls. Outside of the South, over 85 percent of the eligible voters participated, the highest turnout in the history of presidential elections. McKinley won with over a half million more votes than Bryan, but the Democrat had also polled more votes than any previous candidate. The Republicans swept every state east of the Mississippi and north of the Mason-Dixon line; Bryan carried the traditionally Democratic South, silver

mining areas, and he also ran well in the Great Plains, which usually went Republican. But the Democrats suffered defections elsewhere. Middle-class, old-stock Democrats felt that the Silver wing had read them out of the party and had adopted a crackpot money policy.

Thousands of workers, especially immigrants and members of certain ethnic groups, also deserted. They blamed the Democrats for hard times and remembered Cleveland's ruthless use of force to break the Pullman strike. Catholics, rural and urban, traditionally pillars of the Democratic party, bolted in great numbers, repelled by Bryan's Protestant moralism that smacked of nativism (he was a teetotaller and flirted with temperance politicians). They feared that the use of government power to achieve social controls— the heart of Bryan's message—might lead to renewed efforts by a Protestant majority to impose its ways on Catholic minorities. And finally, many were repelled by the free silver campaign which seemed to promise that the state would intrude more deeply into people's lives.

Bryan's free silver rhetoric, agrarian ethos, and revivalistic manner thrilled many Protestant dirt farmers, however, and thousands of Republicans bolted, including those who already had deserted the GOP for the Populist and Prohibition parties. But Bryan's message fell like a lead balloon on the ears of the AFL (which refused to endorse him) and of businessmen, professionals, and most leaders of public opinion, who denounced free silver as dangerous and impractical. Some employers warned that Bryan's dangerous schemes made the election a test of national loyalty and might cost workers their jobs. A vote for Bryan was tantamount to treason. "National honor is above party fealty," chimed in a newspaper editor.

The Democrats under Bryan failed to fashion a winning coalition because they could not build a sufficiently broad political power base. Bryan repelled many urban Democrats and failed to unite all of rural America behind him. That failure revealed the limits of agrarian unrest and the impracticality of building a campaign around protesting farmers and on revivalistic emotions.

Populism enjoyed localized and limited support. Its greatest strength lay in the South, where declining cotton prices in the 1880s infuriated farmers already impoverished and cronically in debt. Since the Civil War Southern whites had repressed differences among themselves to unite against the reality of Yankee domination and the myth of Negro rule. The end of Reconstruction and restoration of local white supremacy unleashed pent-up economic conflict between the ruling elite and long-suffering white farmers. Whites and blacks worked together in their separate alliances for common goals. "They [the blacks] are in the ditch just like we are," admitted a white farmer in Texas. But interracial cooperation was fragile. Conservative white politicians exploited fears of Negro resurgence and at the same time intimidated and purchased thousands of black votes to defeat the Populist challenge. By embracing free silver and Bryan, Democratic politicians in the South undercut their rivals.

In the midwestern corn and wheat belts lay the main hope of Democratic Populist coalition, but here too Bryan miscalculated. In areas that had been settled a generation earlier, such as Illinois, Wisconsin, and eastern Kansas, farmers were *relatively* prosperous. Many had paid for their farms, accumulating savings to carry them through hard times. Even in Kansas, Nebraska, the Dakotas, and Minnesota, Populist strongholds, support came from the less well-established farmers, those recently arrived and heavily in debt. Many who failed on the western plains returned East instead of staying and becoming Populists or Bryanites. Moreover, Catholic farmers, traditional Democrats, generally shunned Populists, who were Protestants and, in the North, ex-Republicans often tainted with nativism.

With rural voters split, Bryan relied mainly on a minority of alienated farmers, supported by the silver interests which helped to finance the campaign, some middle-class and laboring elements disenchanted with the Gospel of Wealth, and the loyalty of Democratic voters (who deserted him in droves). Yet even the Populists regarded the Gospel of Wealth ambivalently, though anticapitalist rhetoric and their statist solutions such as government ownership of the railroads made them appear radical. In fact, those who rallied to Populism and Bryan were not the advance guard of an American socialist movement but small entrepreneurs who wanted government to shelter them from storms in the marketplace that jeopardized their prosperity and survival.

Free silver became an obsession because it offered a simple explanation of their troubles and an even simpler solution. It was an apparent escape from the harsh results of overproduction, of excessively rapid expansion and too much speculation, the farmer's chief problems. Though the money supply had not contracted in the late nineteenth century, agrarians thought otherwise; though bimetalism was impractical unless other countries followed suit, Bryan and millions of his followers insisted that the United States could remonetize silver unilaterally; though the farmer's plight resulted from impersonal forces, such as low prices in competitive world markets, they preferred to personify the sources of trouble by blaming a conspiracy of international bankers and the British; and though the future of the country lay with the cities and industry, the Bryanites preached the restoration of the good life—the rural life. Denied a decent reward for their labors, millions turned in desperation to a one-track diagnosis and remedy, soothingly dispensed by the greatest orator of the day.

When prosperity returned after 1896, Populism vanished almost overnight. But for a few years rural insurgency frightened the country's established leaders. Just as the insurgents believed that Bryan and free silver would save the country from plutocracy, conservatives were equally convinced that a Democratic-Populist victory meant social upheaval. Fearing defeat at the ballot box, conservatives turned for protection from popular majorities to the judges and the courts.

JUDGES MAN THE BARRICADES

Sober, middle-class citizens denounced Bryan as an anarchist. Theodore Roosevelt, among many others of his class, thought the Populists were "plotting a social revolution." The Haymarket Massacre and the Pullman and Homestead strikes made labor violence a seemingly integral part of American industrial relations. More workers went on strike in the 1890s than ever before; and close to 700,000 left their jobs in 1894, a tense depression year. Increased union activity, agrarian unrest linked to political organization, and dislike of Big Business among some elements of the middle class, all combined to create the demand that government regulate wealth in the public interest.

Conservative thought moved from uneasiness to fear. "Government interference is proclaimed and demanded everywhere as a sufficient panacea for every social evil to protect the weak against the shrewdness of the stronger," a leading lawyer complained. Conservatives lived "in constant fear of the advent of an absolutism more tyrannical and more unreasoning than any before experienced by man, the absolutism of a democratic majority." The people, described by Alexander Hamilton a century earlier as a "great beast," seemed at the point of toppling the pillars of civilization.

Beginning in the 1880s the courts rushed to the rescue. Repudiating a century-old tradition of judicial restraint, and ignoring long-accepted precedents and public policies, judges proclaimed legal doctrines that protected corporations and employers from the efforts of government and citizens to cushion the impact of industrialism. In the past judges had rarely declared state or federal legislation unconstitutional. Unless a law clearly violated constitutional standards, the courts were reluctant to veto the decisions of legislative majorities. Judges had no right to substitute their views on public policy for the electorate's. A judge, therefore, generally did not invalidate statutes because he personally deemed them unwise. American tradition and legal practice allowed for reasonable public regulation of private rights. The tradition extended from the mercantilist controls of colonial days to the numerous laws regulating business passed subsequent to independence.

The Supreme Court reaffirmed this view in the 1870s in the Granger cases (*Munn* v. *Illinois*, 1877), which upheld the right of the state to regulate rates charged by grain elevator and railroad companies since the industries were clothed with a public interest. Within a decade, however, the court abandoned this principle and its earlier restraint, formulating new principles that made it a virtual third branch of every legislature, one which wielded veto power.

The Lawyers

In the movement to overturn the *Munn* decision, the legal profession played a key part through newly adopted organization forms. During the last three decades of the nineteenth century, an inner circle of lawyers from leading cities figured prominently in fostering a constitutional revolution. The conservatism of these groups, members of large bar associations, can be gauged by the associations of the men. Most belonged to the elite Republican clubs, such as New York's Union League, where they associated with the businessmen of this Golden Age of Industrial Enterprise. Since the tycoons paid the highest legal fees, these lawyers were not only flattered by the attentions of the corporate leaders, but were well paid for their legal services. The era of the corporation lawyer had arrived.

The consolidating tendencies of post-Civil War American life affected the lawyers as well as other professionals. Bar associations formed in several cities, and in 1878 the American Bar Association (ABA) appeared. A legal consensus on the important judicial questions of the day also developed. Lawyers could usually approach the bench with assurance of general agreement on fundamentals. Although the bar associations disclaimed any intention of passing officially on questions of constitutional law, the nature of their programs and discussions, and the widespread conservative consensus growing among the upper strata of both bench and bar, greatly influenced reactions to constitutional problems.

The bar came to regard itself as a priesthood ordained for the purpose of saving the Constitution. One president of the ABA declared: "Constitutional law is the most important branch of American jurisprudence, and the American bar is and should be in a large degree that priestly tribe to whose hands are confided the support and defense of this Ark of the Covenant of our Fathers."

The leading operative principle became the doctrine of constitutional limitations. The Constitution was above politics, ran the argument, and the courts, being nonpolitical, had to give proper shape to constitutional interpretation which could not be allowed to fall into the hands of "pothouse politicians, dung-hill editors, or pseudo-scholars in the science of government." Such exclusions seemed to eliminate everyone but the lawyers.

In its reports and proceedings, the ABA's propaganda hammered away at the themes of limited government, laissez-faire, and judicial review. They emphasized rights rather than powers, the ideas of contract and property rather than public policy. During the crisis of the 1890s, with American conservatives quivering in fear, Association president, John Dillon warned that the law was not what the agitated mass thought it was at any given, unstable moment. The Constitution existed independently, and it effectively protected the people against themselves. Lawyers had to protect fundamental law, and thus protect society from the demands of interested parties and the incursions of ignorant multitudes.

The Judges

In the end, of course, individual judges, not high-blown rhetoric, made constitutional decisions. Between 1877 (the year of the *Munn* case) and 1890, seven of the Supreme Court's nine justices either died or resigned. All of these seven men had been constitutional traditionalists, usually abiding by the previously established patterns of American judicial power. But nearly all their replacements came from the new, corporation-oriented legal circles, and all of them, whatever their party affiliation, were extremely property-minded. Under their leadership a new brand of Supreme Court conservatism began to crystalize, one more concerned with protecting property rights than with preserving long-standing patterns of federal-state relations and judicial restraint.

Under steady pressure from lawyers, legal scholars, and judges imbued with the Gospel of Wealth, the courts wrote the philosophy of laissez-faire conservatism into the law of the land.

The Fourteenth Amendment (1868), which prohibited the states from depriving persons of "life, liberty, and property without due process of law," proved usable for their purposes. Though this Reconstruction amendment sought to protect the rights of Negroes, the Supreme Court held in 1886 that Congress regarded corporations as "persons" entitled to protection.

The courts, furthermore, redefined the meaning of "due process." In the past, due process meant only that government must abide by fair procedures when infringing upon private rights. The courts in the 1880s now claimed the right to determine whether government policy itself was fair, which in practice meant whether the judges thought the laws were wise. Thus, although admitting that government had the right to regulate railroad rates, the courts assumed the power to rule on the fairness of the prescribed rates. During the 1890s the judges completed the process, striking down a series of state laws aimed at regulating business in which the public had a vital interest. In almost every case the Supreme Court ruled that the offending laws violated the corporation's "due process" guarantee.

Judges also curbed the states' police power, under which they had traditionally protected the health and safety of citizens. A New York court struck down a law banning the manufacture of cigars in filthy and overcrowded tenement houses. The judges ruled that the state had violated the Fourteenth Amendment by denying employers and workers freedom of contract, or the liberty to engage freely in business and sell one's labor. On the same grounds, the United States Supreme Court, in *Lochner* v. *New York* (1902), invalidated another New York law which prohibited more than ten hours' daily labor in bakeries.

The judges also crippled the exercise of the federal regulative power. The Supreme Court in the *E. C. Knight* case (1895) gave manufacturers immunity from the Sherman Anti-Trust Act on the grounds that Congress had only prohibited combinations in restraint of trade in interstate commerce and that manufacturing, an intrastate activity, did not form part of the stream of national commerce. This novel, narrow, and self-interested construction of the commerce clause came at the same time the Supreme Court redefined the power to tax by invalidating the modest income tax included in the Tariff of 1894. The tax, meant to make the wealthy bear a larger share of the tax burden, touched off hysterical cries that it opened a wedge for "communism." In order to strike down the law, the judges had to reverse constitutional doctrines that stretched back a century, as well as a decision of 1882 upholding the Civil War income tax.

The courts further displayed their conservative bias by fashioning new weapons to aid employers against unions. Beginning in the 1890s, courts issued injunctions that crippled labor's right to strike. The strike, said one judge, was "a serious evil, destructive to prosperity, destructive to individual right, injurious to the conspirators [the workers] themselves, and subversive of republican institutions." The judges demonstrated their power in the Pullman strike, issuing a sweeping injunction that prohibited all effective activity by Eugene Debs' American Railway Union. Conservatives regarded strikes as revolutionary threats to society, endangering the process which had built up America's splendid industrial system. They were rebellions that attempted "to put the bottom on top, to put the intelligent under the ignorant. . ."; judges were eager to crush them.

By 1900 the courts had erected strong barricades against the regulation and control of private wealth. Judges, men with lifetime appointments, struck down protective labor legislation, hampered effective regulation of railroads and Big Business, blocked the equitable taxation of wealth, and obstructed unionization through injunctions. No branch of government served the short-term interest of the upper classes so well, and no branch seemed so immune to change from outside pressure.

THE SHOCK OF INDUSTRIALISM

A new, modern America took shape during the last four decades of the nineteenth century. By 1890 the frontier was no more, and the best land had come under cultivation. Workers toiled in the factories and mines of the world's leading industrial power. More mobile than any other people, Americans crisscrossed their land ceaselessly, yet the general pattern of movement was primarily to the cities and industrialized towns. Opportunities were there, but the gap between desires and rewards was hard to endure for the many who did not "make it." Equally important, the gap seemed immoral because it was unnecessary.

Although the country had never been more prosperous, the productive system repeatedly faltered. The Gospel of Wealth taught that hard work brought quick rewards. Thus economic misfortune left people who had followed the rules susceptible to scapegoat or devil-theory explanations of their troubles. Rapid social changes and a highly competitive social order threatened security. Farmers responded by constructing a conspiracy of bankers and monopolists; small businessmen blamed Big Business; conservatives attributed labor unrest to the malignant influence of revolutionary agitators and also pictured rural and middle-class critics as anarchists, socialists, and communists.

A dread of upheaval spread through every level of society, generating tensions which came to a head in the 1890s, as hard times led to industrial violence and the agrarian radicalism which produced the political movement for free silver. This battle over money possessed a deep symbolic significance as well. Conservatives equated gold with stability; silverites identified *their* metal with salvation. Happily, the social order proved far less fragile than the extremists of the 1890s thought. Bryan, who had captured the Democratic party in the name of the countryside and silver, lost badly and Populism faded quickly. Socialism, though much stronger then than now, never became a mass working-class movement. Instead, trade unionism, the Gompers-AFL brand, grew slowly and conservatively. When prosperity returned after McKinley's election, the industrial system, as it had in the past, continued to "deliver," further strengthening the appeal of the Gospel of Wealth.

Conservatism's triumph resulted to a great extent from the dissenters' lack of unity. The Grange section of the Midwest (north of the Ohio and east of the Mississippi rivers) turned conservative during the Populist revolt. And much of the dissent was too nostalgic to be effective. Men like Bryan could and did celebrate a golden age in American's agricultural past, but Americans could not halt or even divert the forces changing their lives. Ahead lay an industrial America, like it or not. Many of the factory workers, native-born ex-farmers, had bettered their status by moving to the city, and they hoped for still further improvement in their new setting. Ethnic and religious divisions diluted working-class solidarity and class feeling, and impeded the growth of organizations which might naturally have sprung from such feelings.

But it was at the top that the upper classes fought ruthlessly and often effectively to keep a lid on the social system. Self-interest had long since become sincere belief on their part that the country's continued prosperity depended on them, "the rich and the well-born," especially the rich — precisely those whom Hamilton, a century before, had called on to lead. Such leadership depended upon forestalling plans for governmental restriction of freedom of enterprise, or "unnatural" redistributions of wealth through devices such as the income tax. The arguments were very smug; but the stakes were high. Not until the dominant groups regained self-confidence, after the ebbing of the crisis of the 1890s, not until the middle classes joined the quest for social justice, not until the emergence of a new generation unwilling to accept as inevitable the crushing human toll exacted by industrialization, did the nation begin to cope with the social disorders plaguing the new America of the late nineteenth century.

SUGGESTIONS FOR FURTHER READING

Suggestions for further reading are highly selective. Works available in paperback are starred (*). Students should consult the bibliography in John A. Garraty, *The New Commonwealth*, cited below, for additional references.

INTRODUCTION

General Works on Industrial America

Samuel P. Hays, *The Response to Industrialism, 1885–1914* (1957)*; Ray Ginger, *The Age of Excess . . . 1877 to 1914* (1965)*; Robert H. Wiebe, *The Search for Order: 1877–1920* (1967)*; Fred A. Shannon, *The Centennial Years* (1967); John A. Garraty, *The New Commonwealth, 1877–1890* (1968)*; Bernard A. Weisberger, *The New Industrial Society, 1848–1900* (1969)*; C. Van Woodward, *Origins of the New South, 1877–1913* (1951)*.

CHAPTER 16

General

Edwin Frickey, *Production in the United States: 1860–1914* (1947); Rendigs Fels, *American Business Cycles: 1865–1897* (1959); Arthur M. Schlesinger, *The Rise of the City, 1878–1898* (1933); Blake McKelvey, *The Urbanization of America, 1860–1915* (1963); Seymour Mandelbaum, *Boss Tweed's New York* (1965)*; Sam B. Warner, Jr., *Streetcar Suburbs: The Process of Growth in Boston, 1870–1900* (1962)*.

The Labor Force

John A. Garraty (ed.), *Labor and Capital in the Gilded Age* (1968)*; Clarence D. Long, *Wages and Earnings in the United States: 1860–1890* (1960); Stephan Thernstrom, *Poverty and Progress: Social Mobility in a Nineteenth Century City* (1964)*; Roland T. Berthoff, *British Immigrants in Industrial America: 1790–1950* (1953); Charlotte Erickson, *American Industry and European Immigration: 1860–1885* (1957); Donald B. Cole, *Immigrant City: Lawrence, Massachusetts, 1845–1921* (1963).

End of the Western Frontier

Ralph K. Andrist, *The Long Death* (1964)*; Dee Brown, *Bury My Heart at Wounded Knee: An Indian History of the American West* (1971); William H. Leckie, *The Military Conquest of the Southern Plains* (1963); Paul W. Gates, "The Homestead Act in an Incongruous Land System," *American Historical Review*, vol. 41 (1936), pp. 652–681; Walter P. Webb, *The Great Plains* (1931)*; Edward E. Dale, *The Range Cattle Industry* (1930); Lewis

Atherton, *The Cattle Kings* (1961); Rodman W. Paul, *Mining Frontiers of the Far West* (1963)*.

Agriculture and Economic Development

Everett Dick, *The Sod-House Frontier* (1937); Allan G. Bogue, *From Prairie to Cornbelt: Farming on the Illinois and Iowa Prairies* (1936)*; Leo Rogin, *The Introduction of Farm Machinery* (1931); H. M. Drache, *The Day of the Bonanza . . . Bonanza Farming in the Red River Valley* (1964); James C. Malin, *Winter Wheat in the Golden Belt of Kansas* (1944); Edwin G. Nourse, *American Agriculture and the European Market* (1924).

The Railroads

George R. Taylor and Irene D. Neu, *The American Railroad Network, 1861-1890* (1956); Robert W. Fogel, *Railroads and American Economic Growth* (1964); John F. Stover, *Railroads of the South, 1865-1900* (1955); Robert E. Riegel, *The Story of the Western Railroads* (1926)*; Robert W. Fogel, *The Union Pacific Railroad* (1960); Julius Grodinsky, *Transcontinental Railway Strategy, 1869-1893* (1962); Thomas C. Cochran, *Railroad Leaders, 1845-1890; The Business Mind in Action* (1953); Leslie E. Decker, *Railroads, Lands, and Politics* (1964).

Rise of Big Business

Ida M. Tarbell, *The Nationalizing of Business, 1878-1898* (1936); Edward C. Kirkland, *The Coming of the Industrial Age* (1960); Edward C. Kirkland, *Industry Comes of Age . . . 1860-1897* (1961); Victor S. Clark, *History of Manufactures* (1929); W. P. Strassmann, *Risk and Technological Innovation: American Manufacturing Methods during the Nineteenth Century* (1959); Peter Temin, *Iron and Steel in Nineteenth Century America* (1964); Theodore A. Wertime, *The Coming of the Age of Steel* (1962); Harold F. Williamson and Arnold R. Daum, *The American Petroleum Industry . . . 1859-1899* (1959); Arthur M. Johnson, *The Development of American Petroleum Pipelines* (1956); Harold C. Passer, *The Electrical Manufacturers, 1875-1900* (1953); Alfred D. Chandler, Jr., "The Beginnings of 'Big Business' in American Industry," *Business History Review*, vol. 33 (1959), pp. 1-30; Matthew Josephson, *The Robber Barons* (1934)*; Allan Nevins, *Study in Power: John D. Rockefeller* (2 vols., 1953); Matthew Josephson, *Edison* (1959)*; Sigmund Diamond, *The Reputation of the American Businessman* (1955)*.

The Bankers

Margaret G. Meyers et al., *The New York Money Market* (4 vols., 1931-32); Henry Clews, *Fifty Years in Wall Street (1908);* Robert Sobel, *The Big Board: A History of the New York Stock Market* (1965)*; Frederick Lewis Allen, *The Great Pierpont Morgan* (1949); Arthur S. Dewing, *Corporate Promotions and Reorganizations* (1914); Morton Keller, *The Life Insurance Enterprise, 1885-1910* (1963).

CHAPTER 17

General

Matthew Josephson, *The Politicos, 1865-1896* (1938)*; Leonard D. White, *The Republican Era, 1869-1901* (1958)*; H. Wayne Morgan (ed.), *The Gilded Age* (1963)*; H. Wayne Morgan, *From Hayes to McKinley* (1969).

The Game of Politics

William B. Hesseltine, *Ulysses S. Grant* (1935); Harry Barnard, *Rutherford B. Hayes and His America* (1954); Stanley P. Hirshon, *Farewell to the Bloody Shirt, 1877-1893* (1962)*; Allan Nevins, *Grover Cleveland* (1932); Horace S. Merrill, *Bourbon Leader: Grover Cleveland* (1957)*; Harry J. Sievers, *Benjamin Harrison* (3 vols., 1952-1968). Geoffrey Blodgett, *The Gentle Reformers: Massachusetts Democracy in the Cleveland Era* (1966); Alexander B. Callow, Jr., *The Tweed Ring* (1966)*; Horace S. Merrill, *Bourbon Democracy in the Middle West: 1865-1896* (1953).

Congressional Government

Woodrow Wilson, *Congressional Government* (1885)*; Robert D. Marcus, *Grand Old Party: Political Structure in the Gilded Age* (1971); David J. Rothman, *Politics and Power: The United States Senate, 1869-1901* (1966); William A. Robinson, *Thomas B. Reed: Parliamentarian* (1930); David M. Jordan, *Roscoe Conkling* (1971); David S. Muzzey, *James G. Blaine* (1934); Mark D. Hirsch, *William C. Whitney: Modern Warwick* (1948).

Spoils and the Tariff

Paul P. Van Riper, *History of the United States Civil Service* (1958); Ari Hoogenboom, *Outlawing the Spoils . . . Civil Service Reform* (1961)*; Frank W. Taussig, *The Tariff History of the United States*

(8th ed., 1931)*; Fred B. Joyner, *Davis A. Wells: Champion of Free Trade* (1939); Festus P. Summers, *William L. Wilson and Tariff Reform* (1953).

The Money Question

Milton Friedman and Anna J. Schwartz, *A Monetary History of the United States, 1867-1960* (1963); Irwin Unger, *The Greenback Era* (1964)*; Walter T. K. Nugent, *Money and American Society, 1865-1900* (1968); Allen Weinstein, *Prelude to Populism* (1970).

CHAPTER 18

General

Thomas Beer, *The Mauve Decade* (1926)*; Fred C. Jaher (ed.), *The Age of Industrialism in America: Essays in Social Structure and Cultural Values* (1968); Sidney Fine, *Laissez Faire and the General-Welfare State . . . 1865-1901* (1956)*; Paul F. Boller, Jr., *American Thought in Transition: The Impact of Evolutionary Naturalism, 1865-1900* (1969)*; R. Jackson Wilson, *In Quest of Community* (1968)*.

The Gospel of Wealth

Richard Hofstadter, *Social Darwinism in American Thought* (rev. ed., 1955)*; R. Jackson Wilson (ed.), *Darwinism and the American Intellectual* (1967)*; Louis M. Hacker, *The World of Andrew Carnegie* (1968); Joseph F. Wall, *Andrew Carnegie* (1970); Irvin G. Wyllie, *The Self-Made Man in America* (1954)*; John G. Cawelti, *Apostles of the Self-Made Man* (1965)*; John Tebbel, *From Rags to Riches: Horatio Alger, Jr., and the American Dream* (1963).

Middle-Class Dissent

Henry Adams, *The Education of Henry Adams* (1918)*; Edward C. Kirkland, *Charles Francis Adams, Jr. . . . The Patrician at Bay* (1965); John G. Sproat, *"The Best Man": Liberal Reformers in the Gilded Age* (1968)*; Arthur Mann, *Yankee Reformers in the Urban Age . . . Boston, 1880-1900* (1954)*; Sylvia E. Bowman, *The Year 2000* (1958); Charles A. Barker, *Henry George* (1955); Lee Benson, *Merchants, Farmers, and Railroads . . . New York Politics, 1850-1887* (1955); Gabriel Kolko, *Railroads and Regulation: 1877-1916* (1965); Hans B. Thorelli, *Federal Antitrust Policy: The Origination of an American Tradition* (1955).

The Challenge of Labor

Norman J. Ware, *The Labor Movement in the United States, 1860-1890* (1929)*; Gerald N. Grob, *Workers and Utopia . . . Ideological Conflict in the American Labor Movement, 1865-1900* (1961)*; Robert V. Bruce, *1877: Year of Violence* (1959)*; Henry David, *The History of the Haymarket Affair* (1936)*; Donald L. McMurry, *The Great Burlington Strike of 1888* (1956); Almont Lindsey, *The Pullman Strike* (1942)*; Stanley Buder, *Pullman: An Experiment in Industrial Order* (1967)*; Gerald G. Eggert, *Railroad Labor Disputes: The Beginnings of Federal Strike Policy* (1967); Philip Taft, *The A.F. of L. in the Time of Gompers* (1957); Bernard Mandel, *Samuel Gompers* (1963).

Strangers in the Land

John Higham, *Strangers in the Land: Patterns of American Nativism, 1860-1925* (1955)*; Oscar Handlin, *The Uprooted* (1951)*; Barbara Miller Solomon, *Ancestors and Immigrants: A Changing New England Tradition* (1956); Donald E. Kinzer, *An Episode in Anti-Catholicism: The American Protective Association* (1964); Thomas N. Brown, *Irish-American Nationalism, 1870-1890* (1966)*; Moses Rischin, *The Promised City: New York's Jews, 1870-1914* (1962)*; Gerd Korman, *Industrialization, Immigrants, and Americanization* (1967); Harry Barnard, *Eagle Forgotten . . . John Peter Altgeld* (1938)*; Gunther P. Barth, *Bitter Strength; a History of the Chinese in the United States, 1850-1870* (1964).

CHAPTER 19

General

Harold U. Faulkner, *Politics, Reform, and Expansion, 1890-1900* (1959)*; J. Rogers Hollingsworth, *The Whirligig of Politics: The Democracy of Cleveland and Bryan* (1963); Charles Hoffmann, "The Depression of the Nineties," *Journal of Economic History*, vol. 16 (1956), pp. 137-164; Samuel Rezneck, "Unemployment, Unrest, Relief . . . during the Depression of 1893-1897," *Journal of Political Economy*, vol. 61 (1953), pp. 324-345; Paul Kleppner, *The Cross of Culture: A Social Analysis of Midwestern Politics, 1850-1900* (1970).

The Farm Problem

Fred A. Shannon, *The Farmers' Last Frontier: Agriculture, 1860-1897* (1945)*; Gilbert C. Fite,

The Farmers' Frontier, 1865–1900 (1966); Allan G. Bogue, Money at Interest (1955)*; Earl W. Hayter, The Troubled Farmer, 1850–1900 (1968).

The Farmers' Response

Solon J. Buck, The Granger Movement (1913)*; John D. Hicks, The Populist Revolt (1931)*; Norman Pollack, The Populist Response to Industrial America (1962)*; R. V. Scott, The Agrarian Movement in Illinois: 1880–1896 (1962); Walter T. K. Nugent, The Tolerant Populists: Kansas Populism (1963); Martin Ridge, Ignatius Donnelly (1962); Frederick E. Haynes, James Baird Weaver (1919); C. Vann Woodward, "The Populist Heritage and the Intellectual," American Scholar, vol. 59 (1959), pp. 55–72; C. Vann Woodward, Tom Watson: Agrarian Rebel (1938)*; Theodore Saloutos, Farm Movements in the South (1960); Jack Abramowitz, "The Negro in the Populist Movement," Journal of Negro History, vol. 38 (1953), pp. 257–289; Agricultural History, vol. 39 (1965), is devoted to a debate on the meaning of Populism.

1896: The Crisis

Stanley L. Jones, The Presidential Election of 1896 (1964); Robert F. Durden, The Climax of Populism: The Election of 1896 (1965)*; Margaret Leech, In the Days of McKinley (1959); H. Wayne Morgan, William McKinley and His America (1963); Herbert Croly, Marcus Alonzo Hanna (1912); Paul W. Glad, The Trumpet Soundeth: William Jennings Bryan (1959)*; Paolo E. Coletta, William Jennings Bryan: Political Evangelist, 1860–1908 (1964).

Judges Man the Barricades

Charles G. Haines, The American Doctrine of Judicial Supremacy (2d ed., 1932); R. L. Mott. Due Process of Law (1926); Walton H. Hamilton, "The Path of Due Process of Law," in Conyers Read (ed.), The Constitution Reconsidered (1938); Benjamin R. Twiss, The Lawyers and the Constitution (1942); Alan Jones, "Thomas M. Cooley and Laissez-Faire Constitutionalism," Journal of American History, vol. 53 (1967), pp. 751–771; Howard J. Graham, Everyman's Constitution . . . Essays on the Fourteenth Amendment (1968); Carl B. Swisher, Stephen J. Field, Craftsman of the Law (1930); Charles Fairman, Mr. Justice Miller (1939); C. Peter Magrath, Morrison R. Waite (1963); Arnold M. Paul, Conservative Crisis and the Rule of Law, 1887–1895 (1960)*; Gerald G. Eggert, "Richard Olney and the Income Tax Cases," Mississippi Valley Historical Review, vol. 48 (1961), pp. 24–41.

Part Five
The Search for Stability, 1900 - 1920

Introduction

From the beginning, America promised individual fulfillment. Millions left the safety and security of the familiar in Europe for the risks and possibilities of the unknown in America. Confident of a reasonable chance to improve their fortunes, they embraced the Gospel of Wealth. "Through all grades," reported Jay Cooke, a leading banker, "I see the same all-pervading, all-engrossing anxiety to grow rich, to snatch from the unwilling hand of fortune that which her caprice will never permit her to grant them. This is the only thing for which men live here." Some failed, others succeeded, but most kept the faith in the promise of American life.

Eventually, inevitably, industrialism challenged and shook that faith. In the late nineteenth century the United States became the richest country in the world, but millions paid a heavy price for the advance. At first, Americans welcomed railroads, factories, and urban sprawl as sure signs of progress, sources of new wealth, and boundless opportunity. Experience, however, turned hopes to ashes. Men worked all day in unsafe factories and mines for wages that allowed their families to subsist, but little more. Farmers and merchants spent lifetimes building up a farm or a business only to lose it when forces beyond their control sent them into bankruptcy. Even those fortunate enough to escape economic disaster still felt troubled by the enormous power of Big Business, the lopsided distribution of national wealth, the crime-breeding and disease-infested cities.

The defeat of Populism and William Jennings Bryan in 1896 did not end the search for stability. In the years between the election of 1896 and the onset of the Great Depression in 1929, the search took new forms and preoccupied every stratum of society. Some businessmen relied on bigness—the consolidation of competing firms into corporate giants—to control the uncertainties of the marketplace. Others looked to government and to voluntary association for protection of small and medium-sized enterprise. Farmers turned to cooperatives and adopted scientific methods of cultivation as well as more practical political schemes than the currency panacea of the 1890s. Workers joined labor unions in unprecedented numbers and benefited from welfare legislation that protected women and children from some of the worst hazards of urban and industrial life.

The crisis of industrialism taught Americans that they no longer could rely exclusively on personal efforts to achieve their goals, that organized endeavors, public and private, were also necessary. A minority embraced socialism in the conviction that wars among nations and conflict among social classes stemmed from private property and capitalism. But the great majority rejected government ownership of the means of production, convinced that moderate adjustments could achieve stability and establish social harmony without forcing citizens to abandon the incentives of private gain. A group of middle-class reformers—professionals, white-collar workers, and businessmen who regarded social justice as an indispensable precondition for peace among social classes—led the drive for the assumption of public responsibility for the welfare of the disadvantaged. People who had suppressed the uprising of farmers and workers in the 1880s and 1890s now worked to lessen conflict and exploitation in a variety of progressive crusades.

By the 1920s the progressive formula seemed to work. Prophets claimed that Americans had entered a new era of permanent prosperity and predicted the quick extinction of poverty. With the doors closed to immigration, with the consumption of alcohol—reputed source of all evil—prohibited by law, and with businessmen and citizens groups relentlessly suppressing "troublesome" elements, Americans anticipated unprecedented social stability and material fulfillment. These illusions collapsed with the stock market in October 1929. The Crash paralyzed the industrial machine, shattering the glib assumptions of the Prophets of Prosperity, and ushered in America's longest and severest depression.

In the 1890s—with the frontier gone—the United States began to emerge from its preoccupation with internal development. As a strong nation, it began to assume its place among the world's major powers, acquiring colonies and protectorates in Latin America and Asia and trying to mediate conflict among the other great powers. The search for a more stable world order led the country into war in 1917 to prevent England and France from being crushed by a decisive shift in the balance of power in favor of Imperial Germany. But the peace fashioned in 1919 sowed the seeds for a second world war more destructive than the first. The search for equilibrium abroad thus ended even more tragically than the quest for stability at home, and the reasons for that failure are locked in America's history during the first three decades of the twentieth century.

Saving the damned: The Salvation Army, 1880. *(Culver Pictures)*

Pioneer ingenuity:
Settlers in the state of
Washington, 1900.
(Library of Congress)

Kansas farmers at
home, 1902. *(Library
of Congress)*

"Workers of the World Unite": The Socialists run for president, 1904. *(Library of Congress)*

City crowd, New York, 1904. *(Library of Congress)*

Theodore Roosevelt on the way to his inauguration, 1905. *(Wide World Photos)*

At the State Fair, Concord,
New Hampshire, 1904.
(Library of Congress)

Selling the products of
American industry: The
first annual Advertising
Show, New York City,
1906. *(Museum of the City
of New York)*

The automobile takes over: Main Street, Stuttgart, Arkansas, 1914. *(Library of Congress)*

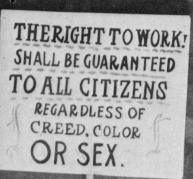

A family picnic, Minnesota, 1919. *(Minnesota Historical Society)*

The unemployed demonstrate in the world's richest nation, 1909. *(Library of Congress)*

Chapter 20
Imperial America

America's remarkable industrial growth during the second half of the nineteenth century made it a world power whose influence inevitably spread beyond its continental limits. Nineteenth-century American "isolation" had been less a conscious rejection of overseas expansion than a concern with more pressing and immediate opportunities close at home. Americans were busy taming the fattest part of the North American continent, a task nearly accomplished by the end of the century. But the dynamic forces of expansion and economic growth continued to make themselves felt and began to seek new outlets abroad at the end of the nineteenth century.

America found itself poised for overseas expansion during the height of the scramble for African and Asian colonial dependencies by the "Great Powers" of Europe. European expansionists hoped that since the Monroe Doctrine—backed now by the physical power of the United States—kept European countries from carving up Latin America into spheres of influence, the Americans would in turn stay out of the Eastern Hemisphere. During the decade from 1895 to 1905, however, the United States made clear its rejection of a policy of self-denial. Not only did American power expand relentlessly into Latin America, especially in the Caribbean Sea, but Washington intended to play an active role in the Far East as well.

As opposed to the earlier examples of European imperialism, the American variety differed significantly in procedure and outlook. The United States, for the most part, shunned the dubious rewards of outright annexation of foreign peoples. Although arriving late on the scene of imperialist scramble, the Americans' tremendous power might still have gained them far more "real estate." Instead, Americans favored the "open door," the assurance of commercial opportunities on a nondiscriminatory basis. This policy rested on the optimistic assumption that American production and efficiency gave it competitive advantages over other imperialist powers, and thus made the burdens of formal empire unnecessary.

In one respect, however, American foreign policy and its consequences deviated from open door commercialism. The spread of American power in the Caribbean became an extension of continental expansion. Construction of the Panama Canal across the Central American isthmus brought the Atlantic and Pacific coasts of the United States closer together, and also gave impetus to its imperial designs across the oceans. Defense of the canal made it necessary for the United States to dominate the Caribbean, and that tropical sea soon became an American lake, just as Great Britain had turned the Mediterranean into a British lake, the gateway to its Asian empire. During three decades of expansion in the Western Hemisphere (1890–1920) America faced several major crises, fought a minor war and a world war, and acquired a mini-empire. The United States became the colossus of the Americas, a position maintained (despite frequent Latin American challenges) for fifty years, until the rise of Fidel Castro in Cuba.

EXPANSIONISM: NEED AND RATIONALE

When President Grover Cleveland delivered his first inaugural address in 1885 he reaffirmed America's traditional foreign policy, which he described as "honest friendship with all nations, entangling alliances with none." Cleveland's views, widely accepted in the 1880s, gave no hint of the stormy new departure American diplomacy could take in the 1890s. Yet American "isolation" had never meant total withdrawal from the world, ostrich-fashion. Instead, Americans had been reluctant to make foreign *political* commitments, except for the alliance with France (1778–1800), which had been accepted in order to achieve the supreme goal of independence.

Until the end of the nineteenth century most

Americans believed that their country's wealth and spaciousness removed the temptation to profit at the expense of other nations. A few, however, thought differently. Starting at mid-century, at the same time that continental expansion was proceeding at full speed, some began to preach in favor of commercial expansion. Instead of searching for land abroad, Americans should seek markets. The chronic economic instability of industrial America in the post-Civil War era, when the number of depression years almost equaled the number of prosperous years, gave new urgency to the argument that since domestic markets could not absorb all the output of agriculture and industry, the United States must find customers abroad.

With each recession, business leaders renewed the demand for new foreign markets. Since with each passing decade industrial goods comprised a growing percentage of total exports, the problem of "overproduction" could be met only by exporting surpluses. Thus within the business community—the influential top strata of Big Business and finance capital—powerful voices favored American expansion, though not necessarily through outright annexation of overseas territory. And they did so for the same reason that many businessmen also supported domestic reforms in the Progressive era—in order to stabilize and rationalize the economic system.

From other quarters, too, came voices favoring expansion. In the same year that President Cleveland rejected imperialism, two men, Josiah Strong, an author and evangelist, and John Fiske, a historian and popular philosopher, argued in books and lectures for the unique genius of the Anglo-Saxon race, whose destiny it was to influence if not control the world. Thus at the very time that old stock Americans felt threatened by the influx of foreigners from Europe, they sought to bolster their self-esteem by enlisting in a crusade to export American democracy and Protestant Christianity to the "backward" peoples of the world.

By the 1890s the Anglo-Saxon cult had become a strong element in American thinking. From the beginning, Americans had believed in their mission to mankind, but now their nativist anxiety and their interpretation of Darwinian social science produced claims of racial superiority for those of English ancestry. If strength meant "fitness," then expansion of superior cultures was not only inevitable, but vital to the survival of civilization's higher forms. Those such as Josiah Strong did not explicitly favor the use of force to impose their will on "inferior" peoples, but they would not shrink from using it if they thought it necessary to fulfill the American mission. Thus began the "imperialism of righteousness." Although Great Britain had been America's traditional foreign rival, the two nations shared the myth of Anglo-Saxon superiority. And in Rudyard Kipling, Britain provided the North Atlantic world with its poet laureate of imperialism, the author of imperial verse such as "The White Man's Burden." Theodore Roosevelt called it "rather poor poetry, but good sense," as indeed it was for an Anglo-Saxon expansionist seeking literary gilding for his aims. In the speeches of Senator Albert J. Beveridge of Indiana, Americans came as close as they could to creating their own imperial poetry. "God has not been preparing the English-speaking and Teutonic peoples for a thousand years for nothing but vain and idle self-contemplation," Beveridge intoned. "No! He has made us the master organizers of the world."

Expansion required more than rhetoric; it required a navy. The movement for a modern navy began in the early 1880s, but despite authorization of two dozen new vessels, the Navy still had to pretend that it contemplated coastal defense only. Behind that facade, the outstanding advocate of a "Big Navy" policy was Alfred T. Mahan, a career naval officer whose influence increased year by year. Mahan, a professor at the Naval War College, published lectures in 1890 under the title "The Influence of Sea Power on World History." Predictably, Mahan argued that naval power had been the decisive element in settling national rivalries. His fame spread to Europe especially to Britain, long a naval power, but also to Germany and Japan, which were then in the process of becoming naval powers themselves. Kaiser Wilhelm II made Mahan's book required reading for all his naval officers.

Mahan's views appealed to expansionists of every stripe. He argued that commercial imperialism required a navy powerful enough to support such ventures. A large fleet in turn needed overseas bases for refitting, and coaling stations for refueling. More than the words of men such as Strong and Fiske who preached the evangelical export of American ideas and institutions, Mahan's ideas influenced men close to the centers of power. His converts included a generation of key movers in American foreign policy, such as Theodore Roosevelt, Senator Henry Cabot Lodge, and Secretary of State John Hay. Congress could hardly debate expansion and naval power without hearing quotes from Mahan.

During the 1880s and 1890s, the United States began to assume the prerogatives of an imperial power. Viewing American vital interests as extending beyond continental boundaries, few public leaders defended isolation. The "closing" of the agricultural frontier in the 1890s, together with the crisis of industrialism, pointed toward overseas expansion as a means of expanding opportunity, economic and moral. President Benjamin Harrison's secretary of state, James G. Blaine, organized the first Pan American Congress (1889), an instrument for spreading American influence in the Western Hemisphere. The United States nearly intervened militarily in Chile in 1891, following the death of two American sailors in a riot, foreshadowing future intervention in Latin America.

Cleveland's Foreign Policy

President Cleveland confirmed this trend during his second term (1893-1897). The president, though anticolonialist, opposed isolationism with equal force. Struggling with the depression of the 1890s, Cleveland joined with business leaders in believing that foreign markets offered a practical solution to domestic economic problems. Arguments pivoted on the problem of overproduction, since few Americans addicted to the Gospel of Wealth and the Rags-to-Riches myth realized or would admit that *underconsumption,* due to widespread poverty and the concentration of wealth in a few hands, might be the prime culprit. Cleveland insisted instead that foreign

markets would reverse the downturn by providing new customers for American factories, especially since American manufactures had a better chance of competing overseas than American agricultural products, historically the nation's main source of exports. This required more trade with underdeveloped, nonindustrial nations to compensate for reduced food exports to Europe.

Latin America offered the greatest opportunities. The depression had also slowed down capital investment at home, leaving funds available for investment abroad. Americans, particularly Southern textile producers, began investing heavily in Latin American ventures, competing with long-dominant British interests. In 1895 businessmen founded the National Association of Manufacturers (NAM), the organization which today speaks most authoritatively for American Big Business, and they did so partly in response to the push for Latin American markets.

Cleveland's commercial expansionism, aimed at economic penetration rather than territorial acquisitions, took a strong anti-British turn during the first Venezuelan crisis in 1895. The boundary between Venezuela and the British colony of Guiana was in dispute. Reports of gold finds in the area led Britain to use force to back up its claims. Republican Senator Henry Cabot Lodge argued that Britain had violated the Monroe Doctrine. In a widely read article attacking Cleveland's "do-nothingness," he charged: "The supremacy of the Monroe Doctrine should be established and at once—peaceably if we can, forcibly if we must." Cleveland, buffeted by depression, domestic unrest, and charges of a flabby foreign policy, decided to act. He demanded that the British submit quickly to arbitration. Britain, realizing that the United States meant business, and rejecting the idea of war over such a trivial matter, agreed to an accommodation along lines laid down by Cleveland.

As a result of this crisis the Monroe Doctrine received a new and enlarged interpretation: the United States declared that nonhemisphere powers could not settle disputes in America by the use of force. Washington also made explicit what was already implicit: "Today the United States is practically sovereign on this continent," Secretary of State Richard Olney boasted, "and its fiat is law upon the subjects to which it confines its interposition." In short, the United States warned other nations harboring designs on Latin America: Hands Off!

CUBA: CRISIS AND OPPORTUNITY

Throughout the nineteenth century, Cuba figured prominently in American diplomacy and in plans for territorial expansion. The fate of the island, the last major vestige of Spain's American empire, concerned every president from Jefferson to McKinley. The United States could never ignore Cuban affairs, and when the islanders began a war of independence against Spain in 1868, a conflict which lasted ten years, the American government offered to mediate to bring about Cuban independence. Spain refused the offer, finally put down the rebellion, and the United States acquiesced temporarily.

Although Spain promised reforms for Cuba, its harsh rule continued. The Spaniards repressed Cuban nationalism and forced the Cubans to pay the cost of the ten-year civil war. Cuban sugar, the mainstay of the island's wealth, had found a market in the United States on a favored basis, but the Tariff of 1894 put a duty on sugar imports. The American depression of the 1890s made a bad situation intolerable. Worsening economic conditions in Cuba led to another revolutionary outbreak in 1895. This war, like its predecessor, dragged on indecisively. Cuban rebels scorched the earth, particularly the sugar plantations, hoping to make the island worthless to Spain. The Spaniards responded by herding Cuban civilians, allegedly in sympathy with the rebels, into concentration camps established by General Valeriano "Butcher" Weyler. Poor food and lack of sanitation and medical facilities made death camps of these *reconcentrados*.

Americans sympathized with the Cuban rebels for humanitarian and other reasons. In the 1890s, as the expansionist impulse created new channels for expressing shock over the thousands of deaths in the Cuban concentration camps, an independent Cuba also offered the United States new possibilities for economic penetration overseas. American investments, though a small part of total overseas commitments, were still significant, and Cuba's strategic importance increased with the growth of American domination of the Caribbean. In 1896, Congress passed a resolution calling for recognition of Cuban belligerency, but President Cleveland ignored the request. Rumor had it that he would not mobilize the armed forces even if Congress declared war against Spain.

During the election campaign of 1896, Republicans called for expansion, demanding American control of Hawaii and construction of a canal across Central America. They also expressed sympathy for Cuban independence. But domestic issues—depression, Bryan, and free coinage of silver—dominated the election. William McKinley, the Republican candidate, did not favor territorial expansion. His party's foreign policy platform consisted largely of window-dressing to attract "jingo," or extreme expansionist, votes. Thus McKinley's inaugural address in 1897 touched traditional bases in dealing with foreign affairs and warned that "we must avoid the temptation of territorial aggression." There would be no "jingo nonsense under my administration," this easygoing conservative assured apprehensive Republican leaders.

Jingoism soon infected American politics, however. After the presidential election, the American press began to headline Spanish atrocities. Cuba became the pawn of a circulation war among leading New York newspapers, each one outdoing the other in sensational reporting, and sometimes in the manufacture of "news." These papers in turn influenced press opinion throughout the country.

The Cuban civil war ground on as cruelly as ever. With no end in sight, demands for American intervention increased. Expansionists saw the Cuban crisis as an opportune means to achieve full-scale United States expansion in the Caribbean, and to turn the sea into an American lake. Others insisted that America assume moral responsibilities. Agencies for Cuban relief sprang up throughout the country, and some Americans blended self-interest and idealism into a common cause. Both groups became convinced that something had to be done.

Despite the growth of sentiment for Cuban

intervention, American business and financial circles wanted to wait and see. Businessmen were fearful of a war which would upset the 1897 economic recovery from the panic of 1893. Even Americans with specific economic interests in Cuba were divided, and although Cuban investors wanted to end fighting on the island, most favored continuation of some form of Spanish rule. American businessmen first opposed, then stalled as the country drifted toward war with Spain. They wanted overseas markets for American goods, but thought that unrestricted foreign trade (the commercial open door) would be enough. Henry Cabot Lodge complained to another Massachusetts man: "The old merchants of New England from whom you and I are descended would be pressing Congress to take vigorous action instead of trembling with fear lest we should do anything, as the present money power does."

Spain vs. the United States

Early in 1898, the United States moved from involvement in Cuba to direct intervention. Spaniards offered the islanders increased home rule, but by then Cuban rebels would accept only independence. The Spanish government remained too weak to impose its will on Cuba, yet too proud to abandon the war. As tension mounted between Washington and Madrid, Cuban rebels stole and published a private letter written by the Spanish minister to the United States to a friend in Cuba. The letter referred disparagingly to President McKinley as a weak man and a demagogue. The leading jingo newspaper, William Randolph Hearst's New York *Journal,* ran provocative headlines such as: "THE WORST INSULT TO THE UNITED STATES IN ITS HISTORY." Then in mid-February the U.S.S. *Maine,* an American battleship sent to Havana as a show of interest and strength, blew up with heavy loss of life.

Spain expressed regret over the *Maine* tragedy, but reaction in the United States was almost hysterically anti-Spanish. Most Americans believed that the Spaniards had murdered 260 American sailors. The United States rejected participation in a joint inquiry commission. The explosion's cause remains undetermined, but Spanish foul play was unlikely with Spain then desperately trying to prevent American intervention. A few weeks later, a respected American

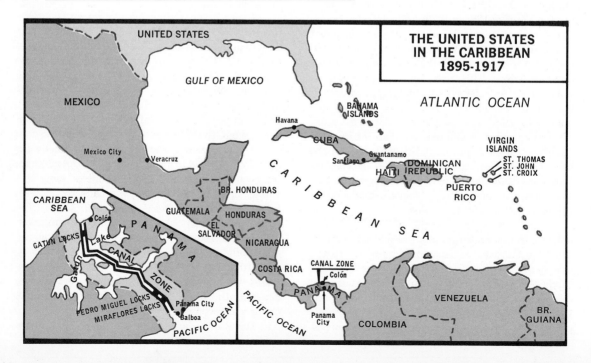

THE UNITED STATES IN THE CARIBBEAN 1895–1917

senator returned from Cuba to report on the horrors of the concentration camps. The new information further inflamed American opinion. Hearst's *Journal* proclaimed: "The flag of Cuba Libre ought to float over [Havana's] Morro Castle within a week."

National pressures for action converged upon President McKinley. Sensing a popular feeling for war, Congress had appropriated $50 million for defense without even waiting for a complete report on the *Maine* disaster. Late in March, McKinley sent Madrid an ultimatum: Spain must declare an armistice, end the concentration camp policy, and negotiate directly with the Cubans. Later, Americans insisted upon Cuban independence as the only solution.

Spain tried unsuccessfully to round up supporters in Europe, then agreed to some of the American demands. But Madrid would not accept outright independence for Cuba or allow the United States the right to arbitrate. "Spanish pride" was how the U.S. minister to Spain explained this impasse to Washington.

The United States had the power to rule the Caribbean; Cuba provided a chance to demonstrate that power. In April, McKinley asked Congress for authority to use the armed forces to impose peace in Cuba. Congress gave him that and more, declaring that Cuba was free and, in the Teller Resolution, disclaiming any American designs, territorial or otherwise, over the island. By April 25 both nations were formally at war.

The United States had decided to flex its muscles, to prove itself as a world power. Since national self-interest dictates that countries provoking confrontations do so only with weaker opponents, McKinley had little to lose on that score. Spain, weak and growing feebler all the time, was a ripe victim for the American imperial experiment.

WAR AND EMPIRE

The war with Spain, a three-month affair, brought a quick succession of easy, though by no means bloodless, American victories. The U.S. Pacific squadron, in Hong Kong when war began, quickly obliterated Spanish military power in the Philippine Islands. On May 1, 1898, American warships demolished Spanish ships still at anchor in Manila Bay in what was more a turkey shoot than a battle. That ended hostilities in the Pacific. What remained of the Spanish navy steamed slowly and dutifully across the Atlantic to the Cuban port of Santiago, where the U.S. Atlantic fleet promptly bottled it up. A later attempt to break out cost the Spaniards most of their ships and many men. On land, Americans met stiffer resistance, but Cuba fell to the invaders by July. Another American force quickly occupied the nearby island of Puerto Rico after meeting token resistance. Spain's American empire was no more.

The military victories gave momentum to the expansionist impulse, which now engulfed Hawaii. For decades American expansionists had tried to turn Hawaii, an American protectorate since 1875, into a possession. In 1881, Secretary of State Blaine included Hawaii within the orbit of the Monroe Doctrine. Toward the end of the century Hawaii had become an enormous sugar plantation, financed and managed by Americans, and worked by Oriental laborers, many of them Japanese. In 1893 Americans, who controlled commerce and the legislature, engineered a successful revolt against the Hawaiian queen and confidently awaited annexation to the United States. The American minister in Honolulu had improperly used American armed forces to aid the rebels a month before Grover Cleveland began his second administration. Cleveland, a commercial expansionist but a staunch anti-imperialist, would not send the annexation treaty to the Senate, though he recognized the new Hawaiian republic diplomatically.

President McKinley, Cleveland's successor, proved less reluctant. American expansionists, aware of the strategic importance of the Hawaiian Islands, feared Japan's rising power in the Pacific. They also thought Japanese intervention in Hawaii probable because so many Japanese workers had migrated to the islands. Soon after taking office, McKinley negotiated a new annexation treaty, but it too stalled in the Senate. War with Spain decided the issue. In July 1898, Hawaii came under American sovereignty. This, together with seizure of Manila Bay, made the United States one of the leading imperial powers in the Pacific and Far East.

When Spanish and American peace negotiators met in Paris late in 1898, the United States demanded the Philippine Islands. Hawaii had been the first major prize in Pacific expansion, and the Philippines, with the great harbor of Manila Bay, would ensure America's position in Asia. Playing upon fears that either Germany or Japan, or both, would move into the Philippines if the United States pulled out, American imperialists sought control of the entire archipelago, even though before the war President McKinley coyly pretended that he could not locate the Philippines on the map. But in sending American troops even before confirmation of the victory at Manila Bay, McKinley assured continued American presence there. Seizure of the Pacific island of Guam gave a sure sign that the Philippines would not be abandoned.

Republican business interests also wanted the islands. Many were entranced by the myth of a great market in China for American goods. At the same time American churchmen stressed the need to convert the Catholic Filipinos to the "true," Protestant faith. On the eve of the war, Protestant spokesmen joined the saber-rattlers to demand action. "Wherever on pagan shores," declared one, "the voice of the American missionary and teacher is heard, there is fulfilled the manifest destiny of the Christian Republic." Catholic editors protested, but with little effect. A month before the armistice, representatives of several Protestant denominations met in New York to coordinate their missionary plans, and to carve out religious "spheres of influence." Christian duty, they said, demanded that the nation embark upon what Protestants proudly called "the imperialism of righteousness."

McKinley's initial treaty demands involved American control of Manila, freedom for Cuba, and the cession of Puerto Rico to the United States. During the war, the president noted, "we must keep all we get; when the war is over we must keep what we want." His plans soon expanded to include control of the island of Luzon and finally all of the Philippines. When Spain balked, a compensation payment of $20 million and a threat of renewed fighting ended further discussion. The president, whose initially modest war aims did not include all the Philippines, later

charmed clergymen whom he told that after several sleepless nights, he fell to his knees seeking divine guidance. The answer soon came: the United States could not abandon the Filipinos to the Spaniards, to another imperialist power, or to themselves, "unfit" as they were for self-government. Therefore, "there was nothing left for us to do but to take them all, and to educate the Filipinos, and uplift and civilize and Christianize them. . . . And then I went to bed, and to sleep, and slept soundly." But McKinley was not so reluctant or so uninformed an expansionist as he wished to appear; he was instead a shrewd, conservative politician who seldom tipped his hand, recognizing that imperialism was a new path for the United States, along which he could better lead the country if he pretended to be a mere follower of fate and divine ordinances.

Debate over American Imperialism

Not all Americans went along, however. Anti-imperialist feeling cut across party lines, but Democrats were more likely to oppose expansion than Republicans. And they were joined by such strange bedfellows as the industrialist Andrew Carnegie and the labor leader Samuel Gompers. Leading writers and intellectuals, William Dean Howells and Mark Twain, for example, bitterly opposed the war and territorial expansion. The Anti-Imperialist League, founded in Boston in 1898, included many distinguished leaders, especially from the middle class in New England, but it failed to arouse popular enthusiasm.

The Spanish treaty touched off a significant though one-sided debate in the Senate. Ironically a Republican senator, George F. Hoar of Massachusetts, spoke most effectively for the anti-imperialist minority, attacking the establishment of colonies as unconstitutional. Americans could be citizens only, not subjects, and autocratic departures overseas might doom democracy at home. Hoar warned that the Philippines would prove hard to defend in a future Asian war. The treaty's defenders responded that the United States possessed full rights (plenary powers) to acquire territories. The form of government in such territories should always conform to the state of civilization of the inhabitants. And although imperialists usually employed moral arguments for expansion, they normally reverted to explanations of the strategic and commercial advantages of extending the American empire. Senator Albert J. Beveridge of Indiana, the most eloquent expansionist, declared simply that nothing could stop the march of the American flag.

The day before the vote on the treaty, its fate still in doubt, news reached Washington that Filipino insurgents had proclaimed independence. This direct challenge to American authority and pride helped to push the treaty through. Even William Jennings Bryan supported the treaty, urging other Democrats to follow suit in order to end the war. It passed by two votes.

The Filipino revolt raised the issue of imperialism squarely, but there was no turning back. Before the battle of Manila Bay, Filipino leaders mistakenly thought that if they aided the Americans against Spain, they would obtain independence for their country. The Filipinos therefore beseiged Manila while Commodore Dewey waited for U.S. troops to arrive. When they came, Filipino forces were not allowed to participate in the capture of Manila, presumably to avoid reprisals. The Spanish-American treaty gave the United States full control over the Philippines and touched off a three-year guerrilla war of national liberation. American public opinion overwhelmingly favored putting down the rebellion before discussing the Philippines' future. "These Filipinos must be taught obedience," counseled the Washington *Star,* "and must be forced to observe, even if they cannot comprehend, the practices of civilization." The resulting struggle, or "insurrection," was cruelly waged. Thus the United States practiced in the Philippines what it said it had gone to war to prevent in Cuba.

The United States acquired an empire in 1898, and William McKinley won reelection in 1900. One event did not necessarily produce the the other, but the voters clearly did not repudiate expansionism, which Bryan, the Democratic candidate, made the main issue of the campaign. The United States had annexed Hawaii, occupied Guam, and seized the Philippines. In the Caribbean, Cuba had become a protectorate as the self-denying promises of the Teller Resolution gave

way to the Platt Amendment (1901), which asserted the right of the United States to intervene in Cuba at will. Puerto Rico, with its nearly one million inhabitants, had been absorbed without debate.

Soon the Supreme Court put icing on the imperialist cake by approving the existence of "nonincorporated" territories, American colonies where most but not all of the Constitution was in force. Back in 1857, Chief Justice Roger Taney had declared that the federal government had no constitutional right to establish colonies "to be ruled and governed at its own pleasure; nor to enlarge its territorial limits . . . except by the admission of new states." But a half century later, in *Downes* v. *Bidwell* (1901), a case involving the status of Puerto Rico, the Supreme Court argued that territories under American control were not necessarily an integral part of the United States. Residents of Puerto Rico, and other nonincorporated territories, were entitled to "certain natural rights" but not all "artificial or remedial rights." Congress would decide which rights fell into which category. America's favorite turn-of-the-century comic commentator, "Mr. Dooley," summed it up: "Whether the Constitution follows the flag or not, the Supreme Court follows the election returns."

OPEN DOOR TO CHINA

The Philippines' main value lay in their strategic location as a stepping-stone to the Asian mainland. By 1899 Secretary of State John Hay, a leading expansionist, edged the country toward even greater involvement in Asia. The vehicle was the Open Door doctrine. It aimed at commercial penetration of China without the burdens and embarrassments of formal empire—at least not beyond the island stepping-stones already acquired.

The China market had long fascinated American businessmen, even though in the 1890s only 2 percent of American exports went to China. Yet during that decade, especially after 1897, Chinese trade increased substantially. This increase, part of a general upswing in foreign trade during the recovery of 1897, had a tremendous psychological effect. With the financial and industrial communities arguing that because of overproduction, prosperity depended on the expansion of overseas markets, China beckoned all the more. But there would be no happy hunting for American traders in China if Europeans (whom Americans believed they could outsell in an open situation) carved the country up into exclusive protectorates. Thus the desire for Chinese markets, but a reluctance to employ military power in the area, made the United States an advocate of Chinese territorial integrity. Partition among "great powers" (the Europeans, the United States, and Japan) would bring the Americans at best a small slice of territory; at worst, if the United States spurned colonialism in China, it would bring nothing. When Japan, Russia, and Germany moved to tighten their grip on *their* Chinese spheres of influence, America cooperated with Britain as the means of keeping China open.

It appeared at first that Britain and the United States might announce a joint policy. Britain suggested combined action to McKinley on the eve of war with Spain, but the president shelved the question. A year later, in the fall of 1899, Secretary Hay decided on an American declaration of policy. He asked the Great Powers to agree on equal trading privileges and nondiscriminatory harbor duties and railroad rates for all nations within the spheres of influence in China. Rejecting the idea of guaranteeing the political integrity of China, Hay hoped the power balance and European fear of a general war would keep China intact and open to American trade. The powers, eyeing each other warily, accepted Hay's notes but with many qualifications.

In less than a year, the unconsulted party, the Chinese, tried to slam the Open Door shut. In 1900, Chinese patriots and nationalists, known as Boxers, attacked foreigners and laid siege to the diplomatic compounds in the capital city, Peking. Troops from several nations, including Americans stationed in the Philippines, rushed to rescue their nationals, and perhaps to use the uprising as a pretext for partitioning China. In July, Secretary Hay sent out a second round of notes stressing Washington's wish to preserve Chinese territorial integrity, and to keep the trade lanes open. America had declared a policy which

would have fateful consequences. Hay's second note extended beyond a commercial Open Door. How far the United States would be prepared to go to assure Chinese territorial integrity remained the key question in Far Eastern politics for decades.

Initial American reaction to the Open Door notes was favorable. Even anti-imperialists who attacked American colonialism in the Philippines supported the apparent self-denial in China. The Open Door later came under criticism as unworkable moralism in American foreign policy. Yet American conviction that free trade in China would result in American domination, and belief in the myth of the China market, provided strong underpinning for the policy. "We believe that 'a fair field and no favor' is all we require," explained Hay, "and with less we cannot be satisfied. . . . We believe our interests in the Pacific Ocean areas as great as those of any other power, and destined to infinite development." In view of this presumed necessity to trade with China, and in view of American military reluctance (unlike Britain the United States would not go to war over China in 1900), the Open Door provided the only feasible alternative to withdrawal.

Everything depended on the power balance and on restraining the ambitions of intervening nations. At the time, Japan seemed the best bet to counterbalance growing Russian power in north China. But the Japanese had no intention of playing the game by American rules forever; in 1941 they would attempt to junk the Open Door even though it brought war with the United States.

FINAL PHASE: CANAL AND COROLLARY

Although the Far East captured the attention of the more imaginative expansionists, the country's most pressing diplomatic problems at the turn of the century concerned the nearby Caribbean and its conversion into an American lake. The job took a decade (1895-1905) and it proceeded with little difficulty.

First, the United States dislodged Great Britain, the leading Caribbean power for two centuries. The process began with the Venezuelan boundary dispute of 1895, and gained momentum after the war with Spain. Directly challenging Britain, America decided to dig a canal across Central America. The Clayton-Bulwer Treaty (1850) stood in the way of a canal under United States domination. In 1900, Secretary of State Hay negotiated a new treaty giving the United States control but still prohibiting fortifications. But the Senate would not approve a treaty under which the United States, immediately after a successful imperialist war, could build a canal but enjoy no special advantages even in wartime. A second treaty (Hay-Pauncefote, 1902) gave the United States full control, operational and strategic. The British acquiesced in this United States take-over because they found themselves isolated diplomatically. New powers had appeared to challenge traditional British prestige and privilege. In need of allies, the British could not afford to antagonize the United States in the Caribbean —where the Americans already had superior power. The British also wanted American cooperation in Asia. Thus when pressed, they agreed to the American demands.

Anglo-American agreement cleared the way for a battle over canal routes. There were several possibilities but the Nicaraguan route seemed most likely. An earlier French effort to build a canal through Panama had failed despite seven years' labor and the leadership of Ferdinand De Lesseps, the builder of Egypt's Suez Canal. Theodore Roosevelt, who became president in 1901 after McKinley's assassination, favored the Nicaraguan route because although a Panama Canal would cost less to build, the French company demanded over $100 million for its franchise. The French interests, represented by a clever lobbyist, Phillipe Bunau-Varilla, soon dropped their price to $40 million. Roosevelt and Congress reversed themselves in favor of Panama.

One major obstacle remained. Panama was then a province of Colombia, and after months of haggling the Colombian government agreed to allow American construction of the canal for $10 million plus an annual payment, but the Colombian Senate, in a nationalistic mood, rejected the terms, hoping to bid up the price when the French contract expired. Roosevelt exploded,

sputtering about the "bandits of Bogotá," and the "foolish and homicidal corruptionists" who had rejected the treaty. The president prepared to intervene under terms of a treaty with Colombia (1846) which gave the United States the right to guarantee transit across the Panamanian isthmus.

This transparently illegal maneuver became unnecessary after the unspontaneous outbreak of a revolution in Panama organized by Bunau-Varilla and a New York lawyer, with full knowledge of the president. Roosevelt helped by ordering the U.S. Navy to prevent the landing of Colombian troops, should they attempt to put down the "revolt." On November 3, 1903, the Panamanians declared independence; the United States quickly granted recognition · and within two weeks signed a treaty with the Panamanian representative in Washington, none other than the Frenchman, Bunau-Varilla. The document created the Canal Zone, under perpetual lease, where the United States was permitted to act "as if it were sovereign."

Roosevelt's actions had been "irregular." But he was willing to bend international law, and ignore the niceties of international relations in order to achieve this strategic objective. Criticism of Roosevelt continued for years, but he never backed down. Every action taken, he later declared, had been "in accordance with the highest, finest, and nicest standards of public and governmental ethics." On the eve of the First World War, when the canal opened, Roosevelt spoke more frankly: "I took the Canal Zone and let Congress debate; and while the debate goes on, the canal does also."

Roosevelt Corollary

At the same time that Roosevelt was acting on Panama, acquiring a canal route, an incident elsewhere in the Caribbean produced an important reinterpretation of the Monroe Doctrine. A second Venezuelan crisis erupted (1902–1903) when Germany and several other European powers bombarded and blockaded the chief port of Venezuela because of unpaid debts. Many nations had similar claims on Venezuela, but an international court ruled that the blockading powers should be paid first, thus apparently putting a premium on the use of force in such situations. Germany assured the United States of its limited objectives in Venezuela, but the Germans really used the incident to probe how far the American government would permit intrusion in the Western Hemisphere. With Britain pulling out of the Caribbean, the Germans hoped to fill the vacuum.

Roosevelt moved quickly to consolidate the United States' newly acquired status of Caribbean superpower. Another unstable government, the Dominican Republic, also unable to pay its debts, caused Roosevelt to step in. American troops arrived and American officials supervised the Dominican customshouses to put the Caribbean nation on the road to temporary solvency. The United States thus embarked on a policy of outright intervention in Central America and the Caribbean which lasted twenty years.

The president announced the new policy in a message to the Senate in 1904, a policy known as the Roosevelt Corollary to the Monroe Doctrine. "Chronic wrongdoing" on the part of a Latin American state, he said, made it necessary for the United States to become an international policeman in this hemisphere. In other words, since the Monroe Doctrine prohibited European intervention, Americans were responsible for seeing that Latin countries met their foreign obligations as the "only possible way of insuring us against a clash with some foreign power." This calculated misreading of the Monroe Doctrine's original meaning tried to disguise a basic change in American foreign policy. As the power which had ousted imperial Spain, seized Puerto Rico and Cuba, pushed aside the British, and acquired the Panama Canal Zone, the United States warned the world that the Western Hemisphere was henceforth its exclusive sphere of influence.

The ease with which the United States assumed its place among the world's great powers at the turn of the century obscured the dangers it would confront in the coming decades. Few fully perceived the significance of the revolution in American foreign relations, which ended a century of relative isolation from the international struggle for power. And paralleling the emergence of Imperial America was the emergence of Progressive America, a time when equally important changes were transforming the internal life of the nation.

Chapter 21
The Progressive View

The rapid changes of the late nineteenth century bewildered and frightened many Americans. The challenges posed by discontented groups aroused fear among the dominant elements in American society that their wealth and position were in danger. Resistance seemed the safest way to maintain order.

But by 1900, the crisis atmosphere subsided. The return of prosperity after 1897 ushered in a long period of economic growth, marred only by minor recessions in 1907 and 1914. The outbreak of war in Europe in 1914 touched off another wave of American prosperity. Those who remembered the hard times of the 1870s and 1890s and the unsettling strikes and rural protest regained confidence, especially after Bryan's defeats in the elections of 1896 and 1900, which served to channel protest into peaceful political outlets, destroyed Populism, and left the Republicans in control for most of two generations.

Billed as "the advance agent of prosperity" in 1896, President McKinley lived up to campaign propaganda. The country's easy victory in the war with Spain, marking its formal emergence as a world power, further bolstered the return of confidence. Even Bryan had rallied to the flag, eager to fight in Cuba. The return of confidence unleashed reform impulses among powerful groups previously opposed or silent, those who had been fearful of tinkering with the system while under radical attack. The middle classes, no longer apprehensive, began criticizing America.

Progressives believed that American humanitarianism, intelligence, and expertise could harness the productive energies of an industrial society in the interests of all and thus create a more just and stable order. Progressivism was as complex and many-sided as the problems reformers tackled. Politicians and social workers, farmers and businessmen, trade union leaders and scientists, each responded to problems of industrial society in ways which emphasized different themes in the progressive impulse. Yet despite the variety of responses, by the 1920s the important changes in institutions and values which distinguished Progressive America from an older America were clearly visible.

Fewer Americans believed that uncontrolled individual enterprise always produced the greatest good for the greatest number or that most individuals were able through individual effort to achieve the promise of American life. In place of rugged individualism, people began to accept the need for some social controls that would protect individuals and society from some of the perils of the marketplace. They would end child labor, protect workers from starvation wages, urban dwellers from slum housing, consumers from impure food and dangerous drugs, farmers from excessive and discriminatory railroad charges, railroads and manufacturers from cutthroat competition, native stock from "immigrant hordes," small bankers from big bankers, whiskey drinkers from "demon rum," and natural resources from monopoly and predatory exploitation. Progressivism promised something for everyone.

The Progressive view moved toward a shift in values and beliefs, a reconstruction of institutions, and a redistribution of power. Likewise, the Progressive impulse led down many different sometimes divergent roads, and it arose from many different sources. Only examination of the *varied* manifestations of Progressivism reveals its essential nature. Yet for all its diversity one thing remained clear: Progressives rejected the Gospel of Wealth in favor of a new Gospel of Reform.

THE GOSPEL OF REFORM

The gap between the country's ideals and the realities of lower-class life shocked Americans into questioning their most cherished and accepted assumptions. That doubting process had begun with the social criticism of Henry George and others; by the 1890s the volume of criticism mounted and the public displayed increasing receptivity to reformist voices of dissent. By 1900 dissent was becoming respectable.

According to the Gospel of Wealth, America, the richest country in the world, was "one helluva success." Reformers recognized the material achievement but insisted that the price paid in human suffering was excessive and dangerous. To the conservatives, warning that any restrictions on freedom of enterprise or aid to the weak at the expense of the strong would destroy history's most productive economic system, Progressives replied that man must master the industrial system, assuring a fairer distribution of wealth, and harnessing technology to serve the "common good." Otherwise, the country faced chronic conflict between the haves and the have-nots, and the possibility of social revolution.

None voiced the anxieties and hopes of the Progressive view more forcefully than the preachers of a new Social Gospel.

In 1896 Charles Sheldon published *In His Steps,* a novel destined to become one of the largest best sellers in American publishing history. It told the story of Raymond, Kansas, its minister, and a congregation deeply troubled by the state of society. "What had the multitude been to him during his ten years in the First Church," the minister mused, "but a vague, dangerous, dirty, troublesome factor in society, outside of the church and of his reach, an element that caused him occassionally an unpleasant twinge of conscience." One Sunday, he confessed his guilt to the congregation and summoned them to walk in the steps of the Saviour and treat other people as Jesus would have. Suddenly the townspeople were reborn: a businessman treated his workers more generously; a newspaper editor refused to run liquor ads; a railroad manager quit because his superiors flouted the Interstate Commerce Act; leisured women went into the slums and established a mission. "This is a terrible spot," confessed one do-gooder, "I never realized that Raymond had such a festering sore." The tale could be dismissed as pure fantasy, and many did so; but many others took seriously its call to action, its demand that Christian Soldiers mobilize.

The Social Gospel was American Protestantism's response to industrialism. At first the churches had blessed unregulated capitalism, sanctified the businessman, and ignored the demands of labor, organized or unorganized. "Excessive poverty, actual suffering for the necessities of life, terrible as it is, is comparatively rare," soothed the Rev. Phillips Brooks of Boston. And it *was* rare if not nonexistent among *his* prosperous Boston congregation. Since Brooks and other clergymen saw few working people in their churches, they neither knew nor understood their problems. The unemployed, according to one minister, were "social pests"; striking railroad workers, suggested another, should be disciplined with clubs if possible, with bullets and bayonets if necessary.

Some new voices spoke out in the last two decades of the century. "We are driving toward chaos," warned Washington Gladden, pioneer Social Gospeler. Walter Rauschenbusch, another leading theologian of the Social Gospel, explained his conversion. He went to work in the slums of New York in the 1880s "and there, among the working people, my social education began. When I began to apply previous religious ideas to the conditions I found, I discovered they didn't fit." Chronic industrial violence and widespread suffering eventually penetrated the consciousness and consciences of the churches. Alarmed by the religious indifference of the working classes and the influx of millions of Roman Catholics, the Protestants, for whom religion was a source of legitimacy and respectability, hoped to strengthen themselves by making their church more relevant to the needs of the lower class.

The Social Gospelers formulated new ideas that would answer modern needs. Traditionally, Protestantism stressed individual salvation. The Social Gospel insisted that alone man could not save himself in a corrupt society. Thus social reform became an indispensable precondition for individual salvation. Christian morality must govern both social relations and individual behavior. The "existing competitive system," charged a Social Gospel minister, "is thoroughly selfish, and therefore thoroughly unchristian." Business had become "the science of extortion, the gentle art of grinding the faces of the poor." The country was run on "the principle upon which Cain slew his brother . . . the assertion of self against God and humanity."

Gladden, Rauschenbusch, and their followers believed they had rediscovered the authentic message of Christian brotherhood. Some concluded that socialism, in collectivizing wealth and placing man before the dollar, offered the best hope for creating a Christian order. But most Social Gospelers favored more moderate solutions. They supported trade unions, favored curbs on female and child labor, and worked to alleviate the misery of the urban poor. Most important, the Social Gospel created a climate favorable to reform. Religion made reform respectable, just as it made regeneration imperative.

Social Christianity remained vague about how to achieve its goals, however. It preached goodness, but produced no systematic, practical plan for reconstructing society. Thus by expressing noble aspirations the Social Gospel also enabled the more fortunate middle classes to purge their guilt over the fact that they lived comfortably while others did without. "I want to do something that will cost me something in the way of sacrifice. . . . I am hungry to suffer for something," admitted one of Sheldon's characters. Yet at the same time ministers preached that "intelligent unselfishness ought to be wiser than intelligent selfishness," because laborers treated with kindness would be better workers.

Though some denominations were less receptive than others and though a few remained hostile, the Social Gospel penetrated deep into American Protestantism. In 1907 the Federal Council of Churches gave it national organization. Social Christianity's popularity owed much to the vagueness of its message, its blending of sacrifice and reassurance. Despite this limitation, the Social Gospel put complacency on the defensive. The Gospel of Wealth taught people that society was "not to blame for the poverty and misery. There have always been rich and poor. . . ." The Social Gospel upheld the quest for social justice as a Christian duty and thus reasserted American Protestantism's historic claim to act as the nation's moral guide.

THE INTELLECTUAL REVOLUTION

The ministers had help in attacking the justifications of free enterprise. Scholars and intellectuals, many of them based in the emerging universities, joined in sapping the intellectual foundations of conservative thought. The intellectual revolution also arose from a growing awareness of the gap between conservative ideology and social reality. Under the pressure of prolonged tension, and out of a desire to reduce conflict and promote stability, sociologists, economists, historians, and legal scholars laid the basis for a Gospel of Reform.

Conservatives believed that unfettered competition accorded with the teachings of science. Classical economics taught that to maximize national wealth each citizen should have freedom to maximize private profit. And the social interpreters of Darwinian science taught that survival of the fittest was nature's design for evolutionary progress. Both ideas came under heavy fire.

Sociologist Lester Frank Ward insisted that human evolution did not result from passive acquiescence to blind forces but from the application of human intelligence to nature. Nature was not *inherently* efficient or progressive or humane. It was full of wastefulness and brutality. But intelligence gave man the power to "put an end . . . to the wasteful economy of nature and to the blind operations of natural forces." Just as men bred animals to improve on nature, so too they could control the evolution of human affairs. Ward spoke for a generation of social scientists unwilling to accept the mechanistic determinism by which conservatives prevented tampering with "natural" law and sanctified their greed.

The so-called laws of economics, said Richard T. Ely, a leader of the younger economists rebelling against the Gospel of Wealth, were no more natural or lawful than the dogmas of Social Darwinism. Trained, like many of the younger scholars, at a German university, Ely was less culture-bound than the older generation, and he had seen the emerging welfare state in Germany at first hand. Ely regarded classical economics as a bundle of abstractions divorced from reality. He denied that the economy was a machine— "harmonious, self-regulating completely and governed by natural law." Competition, for instance, supposedly the dynamic force behind economic progress, had in the United States rapidly lost out to monopoly. The individual worker and the factory owner were supposed to meet as equals to determine terms of labor that would be *mutually* beneficial, clearly an absurd proposition.

Ely and others insisted that the new economics study the actual functioning of the productive system. Behind this search for reality lay a conviction that science could solve social problems. The interests of the individual and those of society no longer coincided, since unrestricted competition benefited employers but not their workers. Economics had to discover how to harmonize, through government intervention if necessary, the interests of the individual and of society. The younger economists, supported by Social Gospel ministers, formed the American Economic Association in 1882. At the same time, like scholars in other fields who also organized, they hoped to gain status by enlisting in the quest for social justice. From that point on, neither the university nor the world of scholarship could remain isolated from the pressing issues of the day.

The most brilliant exponent of the new economics was a maverick named Thorstein Veblen. In a series of savagely witty and probing books, Veblen sought to lay bare the inner workings of American society. America was above all a business culture, Veblen argued. The businessman's claim to dominance rested on a belief that he and he alone produced the nation's wealth. According to Veblen, however, the profit system often came in conflict with technology, the principal source of material prosperity. Thus businessmen sought to maximize profit, not the production of goods and services; if the two interests clashed, the entrepreneur would invariably choose profits over production. Moreover, most of the system's material rewards fell into the lap of an inherently wasteful leisured class. "Conspicuous consumption" and "conspicuous waste" gave them a sense of superiority over their "inferiors." America, Veblen concluded ironically, worshiped those most successful in injuring others.

Legal and Historical Realism

Though the legal profession stood as a bastion of conservatism, a man who was to become the greatest jurist of his generation brilliantly attacked the conventional wisdom. Though hardly a social reformer, Oliver Wendell Holmes, Jr., carried the search for reality into the courts and legal profession. Repelled by a predictable career in corporate law, where success according to Veblen required "a large endowment of . . . barbarian astuteness" and mastery of "the details of predatory fraud," Holmes preferred the bench, serving first on the Massachusetts Supreme Court and later on the United States Supreme Court (1903–1931). Experience and reflection taught Holmes that the roots of the law were in history and experience, and not in moral absolutes or abstract logic. Men make laws to serve their needs; therefore they can alter laws to meet changing needs. Holmes's legal relativism struck a blow against conservative insistence that laws embodied immutable and fundamental ethical principles, a doctrine used by conservative lawyers and judges to declare social legislation unconstitutional. Though Holmes personally opposed much reform legislation, more from skepticism than conservative commitment, he denied that judges had the right in a democracy to substitute their preferences for those of the legislatures. Unwittingly, Holmes aided reform because he exposed judges as interested parties in interpreting the Constitution, men with irresistible urges to read their personal philosophies into the law. Finally, by revealing the sociological basis of law, Holmes made it imperative for courts to consider the circumstances that moved legislators to interfere with free enterprise in order to protect women, children, and other workers from degrading social conditions.

Holmes's legal relativism applied the evolutionary idea to the law. Historical relativism bore the influence of science on the study of the past. "Scientific" history, like "scientific" economics, came to America via the German universities. The first generation of professional historians sought to discover the origins of existing institutions by studying primary sources. Thus most of them traced the foundations of American self-government back to European and English institutions, rather than explaining American democracy, as did earlier generations, as the work of Providence. Frederick Jackson Turner, a student in the 1880s at Johns Hopkins University, then the leading center of "scientific" history, accepted the methods of the new history but insisted that the American environment, notably the frontier experience of abundant cheap land, more than any other single factor accounted for American democracy.

As a midwesterner from a region in Wisconsin not far removed from the frontier era of settlement, Turner was profoundly impressed by the influence of environment on man.

Charles A. Beard, the most influential American historian of the twentieth century, challenged the prevailing view that abstract principles and noble men were the dynamic forces that shaped the country's development. Instead, he argued that history was the clash between competing economic interests and social classes. He wrote of the American Revolution as a struggle between British merchants and landowners on one side, and American merchants and planters allied temporarily with the lower classes on the other. Once the English had been beaten, clashes with yeoman farmers and town laborers led the conservative monied groups to write the federal Constitution in 1787 in order to protect and promote the interests of bondholders, merchants, creditors, and large slaveowners. Similarly, Beard dubbed the Civil War the "Second American Revolution" and claimed it resulted from conflict between Northern industrial capitalism and Southern agrarianism, not from any clash over the morality of slavery. The South's defeat cleared the way for the reign of Big Business that still governed in Beard's time.

By unmasking the "real" forces of history, Beard hoped Americans could see through the patriotic slogans and campaign speeches that kept them from confronting the problems of industrial society. Thus, if people understood that the Constitution was a class document, designed to protect the wealthy against the masses, rather than the work of unbiased patriots, they would be more inclined to modify the fundamental law, if necessary. Only such a realization could clear the hurdles that blocked the way of social reforms such as the federal income tax or social welfare legislation invalidated by the Supreme Court. Conservatives denounced Beard's work as historical slander, the product of Marxist philosophy. President Nicholas Murray Butler of Columbia University, Beard's boss, when asked if he had read the young professor's last book, replied: "I hope so." But the economic interpretation of history became a forceful and influential approach to the American past for over a generation.

Conservative ideology assumed that truth was fixed and absolute. Most philosophers in the colleges and universities taught it that way. Harvard's William James disagreed. His philosophy of pragmatism asserted that only experience would validate truth. The universe was open-ended, not closed, and intelligence could creatively manipulate the environment. John Dewey, a professor at the University of Chicago and later at Columbia, agreed. Ideas, he said, are plans of action, not mirrors of reality; and philosophers should engage in social engineering, not in fruitless speculation. Applying his instrumentalist philosophy to American education, Dewey charged that the schools did not train people for life, but imprisoned them in unrealistic abstractions. They transmitted useless learning that trained people to become cogs in the industrial machine instead of liberating their potential for self-realization.

The search for reality penetrated not only into the world of scholarship and the universities, but it also ignited the literary imagination. Most American writers, especially popular novelists, ignored the brutalities of industrial society. They wrote prissy tales about untroubled middle-class people who lived in a world where virtue always triumphed over evil. The "Genteel Tradition" in literature sentimentalized life, ignored its harsher aspects, and falsified experience. In the 1890s new voices began to revolutionize literature. Such men as William Dean Howells, Frank Norris, Stephen Crane, Jack London, and Theodore Dreiser wrote searing stories of thwarted hopes and crushed lives, re-creating for their middle-class readers vivid if one-dimensional portraits of women driven to sell their bodies, farmers forced to sell their land, and businessmen who corrupted everything they touched. (For a fuller treatment of literature, see Part Six, Chapter 27)

By 1900, the ministers, intellectuals and writers had developed a theory for a Gospel of Reform. They sapped the credibility of the conservative ideas that justified free enterprise. As long as most Americans believed in unrestrained individualism as part of eternal truth, people were helpless and foolish to try to control society. But under steady criticism, this grim doctrine lost its stranglehold on the American mind. Complacency toward those denied the promise of American life gave way to nagging concern; the Social Gospel made the righting of injustice the individual Christian's responsibility; the new economics argued that since "pure" competition did not promote human welfare, government would have to step in; legal realists and historians showed that the government and law served the interests of dominant groups; and the novelists, in creating characters who, though good men and women, were "losers" in industrial society, completed the indictment.

The intellectual revolution encouraged people to look for ways of harnessing the machine to serve common interests. This search led Americans to confront reality, no matter how sordid, unpleasant, and shameful, and to link "scientific" investigation and the new social morality as powerful weapons of reform. Finally, the reform impulse developed organizations to channel the energies of social reconstruction. In the process, reformers clashed with establishment politicians, businessmen, and upholders of the Gospel of Wealth, forcing them to make some room for those who believed more in the dignity of man than the pursuit of the dollar.

THE MAKING OF A PROGRESSIVE

In the vanguard of progressivism stood the professional reformers. They awakened conscience, mobilized public opinion, organized humanitarian sentiment, and proposed remedies. Their careers reveal the wellsprings of progressivism more so than those of their followers or others whose commitment to reform was more transient, or less deep rooted.

No one was born a Progressive. People became reformers through conversion. Leading Progressive politicians such as Presidents Theodore Roosevelt and Woodrow Wilson, Senator Robert M. La Follette of Wisconsin, settlement workers like Jane Addams, and urban reformers like Tom Johnson and Frederic Howe began their careers as conservatives. Wilson was a Gold Democrat who supported Cleveland; Roosevelt and La Follette were standpat Republicans; Tom Johnson was a millionaire who knew all the busi-

ness tricks; Jane Addams grew up with little awareness or understanding of the urban poor among whom she would spend her adult life. Yet each in different ways proved receptive to new experiences, testing assumptions against perceptions, and eventually redirecting their lives away from conventional paths.

The career of Frederic C. Howe illustrates the making of a Progressive. As part of a small-town Pennsylvania manufacturing family that was Republican, Methodist, and middle class, Howe was expected to become one of "the guardians of morality, respectability, and standing." He went off to college with thoroughly conventional ambitions and values. "Life meant business," he recalled, "getting on in the world; the business one was in determined one's social position. My ambition was to make money and enjoy the pleasures that possessors of wealth enjoyed." Success required conformity: "The important thing was to live as other men lived . . . to avoid any departure from what other men thought. Nonconformity endangered one's reputation."

Howe found college life dull and irrelevant. He wanted "to be admitted to the secrets of life," but not until he went on to graduate work at Johns Hopkins University was his imagination stirred. At Hopkins, he reported, "I came alive, I felt a sense of responsibility to the world. I wanted to change things." Richard Ely taught him that employers exploited workers; Woodrow Wilson exposed politics as "a struggle of vulgar interests, of ignoble motives, of untrained men" who were as "abandoned to money-making" in the conduct of government as Americans were in their personal relations; and from Albert Shaw he gained an enthusiasm for cities that were orderly, efficient, beautiful, and run by "university men, trained as I."

Full of desire to serve society upon leaving Hopkins, Howe found no adequate outlet for his talents. He joined the anti-vice crusaders in New York City but discovered that the Irish immigrants and the machine politicians had a more realistic understanding of government than respectable gentlemen of his own class who wanted to reform them. He "began to lose distrust for the poor and uneducated" and began to think "that maybe the state should promote the happiness of man, not be merely a policeman." New York got badly needed public baths, playgrounds, and parks because the masses, not the anti-vice crusaders, wanted them and because the politicians responded.

Before finding his life's work, Howe still dabbled at conventional careers. A job with the Pittsburgh Tax Commission gave him a bird's-eye view of corruption, which revolted him. Finally, he joined a settlement house, one of the new community centers springing up in the central cities to aid the urban poor. There he gained "a certain distinction" from performing good works as an authority on immigrants. Growing recognition brought him membership in the Charity Organization Society, a coordinating agency for urban philanthropy. Then one day the society received a letter that altered the direction of Howe's life. "Your society," wrote a minister, "with its board of trustees made up of steel magnates, coal operators, and employers is not really interested in charity. If it were, it would stop the twelve-hour day; it would increase wages and put an end to the cruel killing and maiming of men. It is interested in getting its own wreckage out of sight. It isn't pleasant to see it begging in the streets."

Howe resigned and went to work for Cleveland's reform mayor, Tom Johnson. Until then he had fought in the "good government" circle of his own class and had won a seat on the city council after a campaign financed without his knowledge by the local gas company. Johnson, a former streetcar and steel magnate who deserted business for reform, told Howe that respectable middle-class citizens, like those he left behind in Meadville and lived among in Cleveland, claimed to support good government but were unreliable because the banks, businessmen, lawyers, and preachers had a stake in corruption. Johnson had run for mayor as a Democrat and appealed to workers and the lower middle classes on a platform of municipal ownership of transit and utilities, and a low streetcar fare. Howe's friends had opposed Johnson because "good government" forces were unwilling to pay taxes to support necessary public services. Increasingly, Howe found himself isolated, but he also found a new vision on which to build a career. The city,

he thought, had enormous potential as "a social agency"; at small cost it "could fill the lives of people with pleasure." But a city must be planned, built, and run as a *community*, with the well-being of all its citizens preeminent, not the profit of a few. "Here democracy would show its possibilities," he thought, and "the city would become our hope instead of our despair."

Howe's career reveals the process which turned many conservative, middle-class Americans into Progressives. The generation that came of age between 1880 and 1900 looked critically at industrial America; an earlier generation had its moral fling in the great crusade against slavery. Those who gravitated toward the Progressive view questioned business values which justified political corruption and widespread suffering and misery. To conservatives, Howe wrote, "business was the most important thing in the world. . . . They had no other enthusiasm. They talked business, loved business, judged all men and measures in business terms. The political state existed for their benefit. Lawyers, ministers, teachers were employees, vassals. Farmers and working men were a servile class."

In contrast the Progressives felt a compulsion to serve others, to ease suffering and clean up politics—in short, to redeem their country and save themselves. Firsthand experience with the disadvantaged, such as Howe's contact with New York immigrants, Theodore Roosevelt's inspection of working conditions in slum tenements, and Walter Rauschenbusch's ministry to the poor, shook complacency and led to demands for change. Public service offered new possibilities to achieve individual fulfillment and promote social stability. The reform impulse also grew out of a sense of guilt among middle-class Americans. A career devoted to reform involved risks and sacrifice but it also offered enormous scope for self-realization.

THE PROCESS OF REFORM

Goodwill and noble aspirations alone did not bring about reform. Progressives had to generate public support and channel it constructively. Both tasks required new techniques and new organizations.

Publicity became one of the reformer's prime weapons. Through books, newspapers, magazine articles, and government investigations Progressives exposed injustice and stirred the public conscience. Combating indifference and educating a public either ignorant of how "the other half" lived or accustomed to looking the other way proved a full-time job. Conservatives accepted poverty and suffering for others, blaming the poor themselves for these conditions. Reformers had to teach people to blame the environment, or the system's manipulators, not the victims.

Professional journalists developed a kind of reporting known as muckraking—the recurrent exposure of public corruption and scandal—which made it increasingly hard for Americans to ignore unpleasant realities. Muckraking journalism effectively utilized the far-reaching changes in communications media. Toward the end of the century mass-circulation magazines and newspapers developed in response to new printing technology and the growth of advertising. Advanced technology reduced production costs and allowed for the use of lively illustrations, further stimulating mass appeal. Newspapers discovered that they could sharply increase circulation by championing popular causes. The magazines permitted the growing middle class, bent on uplift and self-improvement, to differentiate itself culturally from the working classes.

Magazines also catered to the anxieties of Americans who feared that industrialism, with its business giants and social unrest, jeopardized their chances to get ahead. Exposure of injustice and calls for reform reassured those who believed that orderly remedying of social ills offered the best hope. At the same time the growth of advertising as a means of selling products in a national market gave newspapers and magazines an incentive to boost circulation, since the more readers they had, the more valuable they became as advertising media. Advertising revenue also helped lower the sale price of newspapers and magazines.

Sometimes public catastrophe or a single, dramatic event helped reformers awaken the public conscience. A violent strike revealed to millions the shocking conditions that led workers to protest; Upton Sinclair's novel, *The Jungle* (1906), exposed unsanitary conditions in the meat-packing industry and awakened people to the need for government control; a fire at a New York sweatshop, the Triangle Shirtwaist factory (1913), which sent dozens of working girls leaping to their deaths from tenth story windows, educated the public to the need for factory safety legislation.

Maintaining the public clamor aroused by muckraking was a continuing task. Because exposure focused concern on a particular evil and galvanized support for a specific reform, the public might always revert to complacency. Piecemeal exposure and sudden clamor for short-term reform enabled Americans to reassure themselves that theirs was a decent and humane society, without attacking social problems comprehensively and systematically. Thus muckraking and short bursts of reform served cathartic ends, and brought about some changes as well.

Sustained reform required permanent organization. A galaxy of organizations sprouted up, each concerned with a particular evil. The National Consumer's League, the National Child Labor Committee, the Municipal Reform League of America, the American Association for Social Legislation, the Women's Christian Temperance Union, the Immigration Restriction League—each concentrated on a specific problem or issue. The National Council of Churches and the National Civic Federation reflected more generalized concern. Reform organizations, though undermanned and underfinanced, nevertheless exerted considerable influence. They claimed "scientific," expert knowledge of a problem; and they offered ready-made solutions. They learned how to stimulate widespread support by exploiting public shame and embarrasement at the gap between the country's democratic ideals and its class-ridden social realities. And finally, they gained the ear of powerful politicians and businessmen who controlled the levers of power and who could not ignore public unrest.

Most reform activity took place in the city. There, social injustice showed its meanest face, suffering was greatest, and middle-class reformism consequently strongest. The cities, said a muckraking journal, were "full of filth, poverty, and vice. They graduate thieves, murderers, and panderers as naturally as universities graduate scholars. A city is Moloch; the fagots of its fires are human bodies and souls." The quest for social justice thus centered fittingly in urban America, where unrestrained industrial growth and social problems went hand in hand.

THE QUEST FOR SOCIAL JUSTICE

"I regard my work people just as I regard my machines," boasted a factory manager in the 1890s, "so long as they can do my work for what I choose to pay them, I keep them, getting out of them all I can." In 1920 some employers still treated their workers as commodities; but by then an elaborate body of social legislation protected a small yet growing part of the labor force from unrestrained exploitation. The quest for social justice thus produced the beginnings of a welfare state, the attempt by government to protect people, especially the weak and dependent, from degradation. During the Progressive era some states curbed child labor, imposed safety standards on industry, limited the number of hours women could work and guaranteed them a minimum wage, insured laborers against industrial accidents, and regulated the housing of the poor.

Even before government assumed these new responsibilities, private voluntary efforts had tried to help victims of industrialization. Settlement workers and social workers in the ghettos aided the immigrant poor in improving their condition. These first steps were slow, uncertain, and woefully inadequate, but they opened the way for more comprehensive and effective measures a generation later, during the New Deal of the 1930s. They represented a fundamental change in attitudes toward social disorganization, a change originating in the rediscovery of poverty and the acceptance of new explanations of why people fail and how they should be helped.

Poverty was nothing new in late-nineteenth-century America. Even in the colonial period many dependent persons required private charity and public assistance. But the scale and character of poverty had changed markedly. A rural society could more easily take care of its relatively fewer dependent persons, but industrialization and ur-

banization seemed to produce the *visible* poor as quickly as it manufactured factory goods. People first became aware of the growth of slums in the 1830s when the increasing tempo of urbanization and industrialization produced a working class, many of whom were recently arrived immigrants. By the late nineteenth century, Americans took fright at the ghettoes that existed and spread in almost every city. Slums, said the Reverend Josiah Strong, were "a commingled mass of venomous filth and seething sin, of lust and drunkenness, of pauperism and crime of every sort."

The Causes of Poverty

Poverty repelled Americans who either tried to ignore it or accept it as inevitable, the result of the supposed moral defects of the poor, and definitely "Un-American." Residential segregation according to income enabled the middle classes to leave the older, run-down central city neighborhoods to the poor, and escape to more pleasant suburban neighborhoods. They thus had little day-to-day contact with the poor, who in their eyes became dehumanized. The cult of success preached that all men enjoyed equal opportunity; poverty therefore became a sign of inherent inferiority and at the same time a condition against which the successful could proudly measure their own achievement. Even in our times, some Americans retain this egocentric view of poverty—but thanks in part to the Progressives, a new, more humane understanding began to displace it. The Progressives identified poverty with environmental conditions. It was a prison that trapped people. As long as the disadvantaged were ignored, most could not escape from conditions that stunted mind and body and which had made one's parents poor and would condemn one's children to poverty.

Poverty had spread to an alarming extent. In 1900, according to Robert Hunter in his exposé, *Poverty* (1904), one out of every ten New Yorkers was buried in potter's field; about 30 percent of the city's population sought relief in 1897; and in 1903, 60,000 families were evicted from their homes. As hard as the middle class tried to ignore it or escape from it, poverty remained a cancer in the body of urban America, endangering everyone. Epidemics that started in the slums menaced the city's health. Criminals bred in the ghetto threatened middle-class neighborhoods.

As people came to believe that many of the rich had "obtained wealth by predatory methods . . . by the practice of vast extortions . . . by manifold arts that tend to corrupt the character and destroy the foundations of the social order," they began to blame the greed of the few for the misery of the many. In a country as rich as the United States no one need be poor. Finally, millions of middle-class Americans learned personally especially during the great depression of the 1890s that their own hard work often ended in failure and disappointment. Environment, "the system," not personal defects, they concluded, trapped people.

Better knowledge about poverty dispelled notions of the inherent inferiority and alleged laziness of the poor. That knowledge came from firsthand observation, especially by private charitable agencies. As poverty spread, the cost of keeping poor people alive soared, straining private resources. Moreover, periodic unemployment added able-bodied men to the ranks of the needy.

In order to curb "spendthrift" philanthropy and cope more efficiently with the problem, benevolent societies adopted "scientific" methods. Charity organization societies introduced modern efficiency, coordinated philanthropy, hoping to reduce waste and duplication. The societies discouraged "laziness" among the recipients of alms and tried to distinguish between the worthy and unworthy poor by sending social workers, at first volunteers but later professionals, to investigate applications. From this emerged professional social work and the case method as well as efforts to reform the moral character of the poor. Similarly, schools and hospitals employed social workers because teachers and doctors learned that they could not perform their jobs efficiently without altering the home environment.

This more realistic if sometimes meddlesome understanding of poverty based on firsthand observation soon led to social action programs. People learned that most of the poor preferred work to handouts. Low wages and periodic unemployment, not cultural attitudes, produced destitution. Thousands more became dependent as the result of industrial accidents. During the last twenty years of the nineteenth century over 100,000 persons were killed and almost 600,000 injured by the railroads. Many mishaps could have been avoided had the roads been willing to invest in available safety devices. The same was true in manufacturing and mining. Unsanitary tenements and factories sapped the health of millions; tens of thousands annually contracted tuberculosis, "The White Death," a disease largely preventable and produced by unhealthy living conditions. Conservatives blamed the poor for their poverty without considering their own outmoded individualism, and lack of social responsibility. "No other country as much as has our own permitted individuals to disregard, to a criminal extent, the health and welfare of employees," charged Robert Hunter.

THE ATTACK ON POVERTY

The assault on poverty took many forms. Since slums developed because builders did not construct decent housing at prices poor people could afford, one attack centered on housing. The homebuilding industry, a loose association of small entrepreneurs with limited capital, used inefficient production methods. They preferred to build new housing for the middle classes moving out of the central city. The poor were left with old housing or cheaply built new tenements cleverly designed to squeeze in as many people as possible. Overcrowded, poorly ventilated, without running water or indoor toilets, the homes of the poor were breeding grounds for pests and disease.

New scientific developments in medicine spurred housing reform. The discovery in the late nineteenth century that germs caused disease led physicians to denounce unsanitary housing. Without public sanitary controls even personal cleanliness had limited value. Eventually the scientific viewpoint linked up with humanitarian impulse. Reformers launched a public health movement to educate people in the principles of sanitation and brought some of the benefits of modern medicine into the slums through clinics and health stations. New building codes also required indoor plumbing, better ventilation, and protection against fire hazards in construction. The reform-minded middle class also viewed such efforts as a means of social control. Middle-class values sanctified the home, the well-kept home. More than just a place to live, it was a moral influence: a good home cemented the family; a bad one destroyed it. Reformers believed that by improving the housing environment, the poor would abandon their erring ways (drinking, laziness, gambling, and promiscuity) in favor of the virtues of middle-class life: sobriety, industriousness, frugality, and sexual moderation.

Housing reform had to overcome the resistance of the real estate interest and its political allies. The reformers, however, became housing experts. Investigations followed by publicity and legislation led to bureaucratization of reform, a pattern repeated in other Progressive crusades. The states established commissions to enforce the new building codes, for reform was a constant process of regulating private enterprise in the public interest. The reformers also organized the Public Health Association and the National Housing Association to propagandize nationally and to coordinate reform activities.

Like other Progressive attacks on poverty, results fell far short of hopes; and like other middle-class reforms, convictions outran commitment. Some of the worst conditions in the slums were eliminated but enforcement of building codes was slow, costly, and difficult. Nor did it strike at the root cause of bad housing; the poor could not *afford* decent homes. Reformers nonetheless had unwarranted faith that private enterprise, appropriately regulated, could solve the housing problem. Public housing was a notion too "radical" for serious consideration in the Progressive era. Today, almost a century since the beginning of housing reform, the United States still fails to provide all its citizens with decent, inexpensive housing. Private enterprise will not or cannot provide it and public housing has fallen short of its possibilities, producing the high-rise ghettos that stack the poor on top of one another in urban beehives.

THE SETTLEMENT WORKERS

Housing reformers soon discovered that the total tenement environment, not just housing, needed reconstructing. That task became the work of the settlement houses which sprang up in the ghettos. From a half dozen in the early 1890s, they grew to over 400 within twenty years. The settlement house experience reveals many of the strengths and weaknesses of Progressivism.

The settlement workers, typically middle class, college-educated, young adults from native, WASP (White Anglo-Saxon Protestant) families, acted as secular missionaries to the poor. Often the children of ministers, their families inclined toward reform and charity work. Poverty presented a challenge and an opportunity. Jane Addams, the "saint" of Progressive settlement workers explained that her generation constantly heard of "the great social maladjustments, but no way [was] provided . . . to change it." The would-be reformers' "uselessness hangs about them heavily." The settlement house offered people, especially educated women, meaningful lives through helping others "to do something about social disorder." Like the housing reformers, the settlement workers hoped to train the poor and the working classes in middle-class lifestyles.

The settlement houses offered temporary escape from ghetto misery and boredom. They brought culture to the poor by setting up art galleries, giving music lessons, and producing plays to awaken the sense of beauty and to civilize and humanize. The settlements taught people to be clean, neat, and well mannered. People learned handicrafts and acquired hobbies to relieve the drudgery of factory work. The settlements pioneered in vocational guidance and adult education, taught immigrants English, established kindergartens, and gave free medical care and lunches to children, functions later assumed by the public schools and adult extension courses.

Above all the settlements tried to build a sense of community among people from different classes and ethnic backgrounds. They hoped to bridge the gulf between the poor and the comfortable by turning dreary rows of tenements into clean, lively neighborhoods; and they demanded that the city increase public services, improve the schools, build playgrounds and public baths, and remove garbage regularly.

Living among the poor, the settlement workers learned that low wages and unemployment were the major problems. They sympathized with trade unions but with reservations, because union leaders distrusted the middle-class reformers and sought benefits only for their own members. The settlement workers preferred protective labor legislation for all workers. The settlement houses produced a generation that formed new organizations to combat every known social ill. As an instrument of organized conscience, they bridged two worlds: the nineteenth-century reliance on charity and voluntarism and the twentieth-century recognition that in an industrial society only the power of government can cope with social disorganization. But they failed to convince enough of their own generation of the truths they had learned from experience. Their individual efforts helped many people but barely made a dent in ghetto problems, since government would not then shoulder increased responsibilities.

Thorstein Veblen concluded sardonically that the settlements' main impact was "to enhance the industrial efficiency of the poor" and to help reconcile them to their lot.

The quest for social justice had to end in politics. Progressives insisted that government must aid the poor and prevent outright exploitation. They expressed that faith in new legislation that regulated the labor of children and women, promoted industrial safety, compensated working men injured in accidents, and improved housing. Progressive middle-class Americans also turned to politics to curb the influence of Big Business, protect the consumer, clean up political corruption and, as Woodrow Wilson promised in 1912, "free the average man of enterprise in America, and make ourselves masters of our own fortunes once again. . . ."

Chapter 22
The Politics of Progressivism

The Progressive view transformed American politics. For over a generation the political system had avoided a confrontation with industrialism's social dislocations. The uprisings of farmers and workers and the fears of Big Business in the 1890s made the social question the center of American politics. But the rhetoric and programs of Populists and Bryan Democrats seemed both impractical and frightening to many who longed for stability. The return of confidence by 1900—especially among the middle classes who feared radicalism but acknowledged the need for change—created a favorable climate for the politics of reform. Funneling upward, first from the cities, then the states, and finally nationally, a new civic spirit and a new breed of politicians appeared, a breed committed to making government more sensitive to society's needs.

THE URBAN CRISIS

The fight began in the cities. "Government of cities is the one conspicuous failure of the United States," concluded James Bryce, an astute British observer, in the 1880s, and the situation had not improved by the turn of the century. City government was corrupt government; it failed to provide adequate public services, and cities seethed with ethnic and class tensions.

The urban crisis began during the first decades of rapid urban growth before the Civil War. Cities grew as the result of unplanned commercial and industrial expansion. From the outset, the American city was "a community of private money makers," and its "successes and failures have depended upon the unplanned outcomes of the private market." The cities neither anticipated nor knew how to cope with the problems flowing from the influx of new millions from the farms and villages of America and Europe. Although private enterprise built housing and provided mass transit, gas, electricity, and telephone service more rapidly than in European cities, sanitation, police and fire protection, schools and hos-

pitals, parks and playgrounds remained public responsibilities.

Building the physical and institutional civic structure proved expensive and complex, far beyond the resources of the preindustrial city. Citizens balked at paying heavy taxes, and though tax rates soared in the late nineteenth century, municipalities lightened the immediate burden by going heavily into debt. State government had built and financed such large enterprises as canals, but Americans now preferred to rely on private enterprise. Of necessity, the cities became the largest government spenders in the nineteenth century, appropriating wastefully and building without plan. New services such as professional police forces developed in response to crisis situations. Uncontrolled growth and the crowding together of Catholics and Protestants, whites and blacks, immigrants and native-born produced conflicts that often led to rioting. Soaring crime rates understandably created grave anxieties among the more established and prosperous elements of the city population.

Without public planning and social control, thousands of uncoordinated private decisions shaped the city's development. From the outset, the industrial city dwellers became segregated along lines of income and ethnic origins. Previously, people had lived and worked together within the heterogeneous confines of the "walking city." But mass transit enabled the prosperous to buy housing in the more attractive suburban areas and commute to work. The old buildings of the central city housed the newcomers—the immigrants, the poor, and the blacks—while middle- and upper-income groups fled. Flight to new neighborhoods may have been evidence of "success," but in the process the city fragmented.

People became isolated from one another and even the newer neighborhoods were hardly communities. They lacked a coordinating focus for group activity. Churches, schools, and other public buildings were scattered about at random, and there were few public squares and shopping centers. Those enjoying modern plumbing in the newer housing felt little concern for those who lived without indoor water or toilets in older houses. Neighborhoods with paved streets opposed paying higher taxes to pave streets elsewhere. The shape of the cities thus reflected the individualism prevalent during the nineteenth century. As a result, public needs were either ignored or provided in a slipshod manner at the lowest cost and with little imagination.

Cities presented a dreary and monotonous physical appearance as builders repeated the same design on street after street. Children had few parks, playgrounds, or open spaces. The water supply became safer to drink but less palatable because of purifying chemicals. Schools, run as cheaply as possible, resembled factories rather than institutions devoted to developing youth's highest potential. The poor paid the heaviest price for urban neglect in schools geared to educating native-born, middle-class children, not coping with the ghetto. "Education," one reformer pleaded, "should treat children as individuals, not as an indiscriminate mass who must be put thru a certain routine, wholly regardless of the past of the child." Yet education remained the poor's best hope for helping themselves; its inadequacies meant that they would have to wait longer and work harder before some of their children rose out of the urban ghettos.

THE CITY BOSSES

As cultural centers and moneymaking emporia the cities were vital and exciting. But as places to live they left much to be desired, and their politics became the shame of the nation. Corrupt politics became the hallmark of urban government. The preindustrial city had been run by interested citizens; leadership came from the professional and business elites that regarded public service as a duty. Eventually, full-time politicians pushed them aside and monopolized local government. The democratization of politics and the revival and acceptance of parties in the Jacksonian era made urban politics highly competitive at the same time that rapid growth placed new stresses on city government. Prominent businessmen were unable to compete with the emerging bosses who

had influence among the varied interests and ethnic groups. The merchants returned to their countinghouses, leaving politics to specialists. As businesses grew in size and complexity, and as businessmen came to regard the nation rather than their city or region as their principal arena, they lost interest in local problems.

The bosses' power rested on the number of votes they controlled. Commanding a ward or neighborhood by catering to the special needs of their constituents and by buying votes, the bosses flourished because they performed vital functions. Their machines gave citizens ethnic recognition, got them jobs, and did numerous favors which voters remembered on election day. The more successful ward bosses parlayed their local power into citywide machines by forming alliances with other chieftains. But often no one could establish full control, and factionalism plagued city hall. The successful machines became one of the few cohesive and coordinating forces in civic life and tended to bring order out of chaos, although at a stiff price.

City charters, imitating state and federal constituions, placed checks and balances on local officials. They divided power, left mayors weak, and reserved final authority in the hands of the state legislature, making it impossible to govern municipalities effectively. In the 1860s in New York City, for instance, four agencies could tear up streets but none had responsibility to repave them. The political machines, through informal means, centralized decision-making. Thus under the notorious Tweed Ring, New York literally *bought* from the legislature a new charter that centralized power and launched an impressive building program to provide the city with vital facilities. In Philadelphia, professional politicians consolidated many small jurisdictions into one large unit so that a newly created professional police force could end rioting.

Machine government, however, was inefficient, wasteful, and had limited social vision. The politicians regarded government as a business to be milked for their own enrichment. Since the cities provided citizens with more services than any other level of government, and spent more money in the process, they presented enormous opportunities for graft. The machines determined who received city contracts, often channeling them to friends or to their own firms. Machines also granted valuable streetcar and utility franchises. In return successful streetcar and gas and electric companies paid bribes and provided jobs for the bosses to distribute among the hirelings. With the cities farmed out to private enterprise, public services which yielded great profits provoked fierce competition among rival capitalists for contracts and franchises. In the absence of rational, bureaucratic standards for awarding these prizes, politicians preferred friends, relatives, business associates, and those who paid the highest bribes. The more the city spent, the greater the graft potential. In favoring expansion of services and construction of new facilities, the politicians thus served to counter the middle-class taxpayer's reluctance to spend for community needs.

The system was not an efficiency expert's dream. Without an orderly, systematic method of expanding services, government costs skyrocketed, while politicians remained indifferent to the poor quality of services. Most citizens remained equally indifferent. The working class, especially the immigrants, appreciated the bosses' favors since there were no public agencies to find them jobs, or tide them over when unemployed or during an emergency. And the more prosperous were too occupied with their own affairs to pay much attention to maladministration and too deeply implicated in corruption to oppose it. Bribery became simply another item in the cost of doing business, a part of everyone's cost of living.

URBAN REFORM

Periodically, however, people revolted. When the stench of corruption became too strong, and taxes and debts rose too rapidly, reform movements emerged to conduct periodic housecleanings and belt-tightenings. Thus reformers exposed and prosecuted the Tweed Ring of New York in the 1870s, but they offered no alternative system for governing the city. Eventually reformers became tired and voters became disillusioned. As taxes and debts continued to mount, the political pros slipped back into city hall.

Beginning in the 1890s, however, urban reform gained new momentum, moving in new directions under the impetus of the Progressive spirit. Lincoln Steffens, a leading muckraking journalist, exposed "The Shame of the Cities" (1904) in a series of documented magazine articles. Steffens challenged the view widely held by native, middle-class Americans that foreigners who sold their votes and a few businessmen who neglected their civic duties caused urban corruption. "The spirit of graft and of lawlessness is the American spirit," Steffens charged. Politicians had thoroughly assimilated the values of the nation: "the commercial spirit is the spirit of profit, not patriotism; . . . the highway of corruption is the road to success in the United States." Without bribe givers there would be no bribe takers. Steffens insisted that "In all cities, the better classes—the businessmen—are the sources of corruption." He searched for the reality of urban life, found it sordid, but professed not to despair. "The purpose of these articles," he said, was "less to expose evil than to awaken conscience." The country could "stand the truth," he thought, because "there is pride in the character of American citizenship and . . . this pride may be a power in the land."

By 1900, Steffens found urban reform stronger and better organized than ever before. Crusades swept New York, Chicago, Minneapolis, Jersey City, Cleveland, Toledo, Detroit, and other major cities. The reform impulse found strength in several sources. When cities were young and raw, people were more willing to pay any price for growth. As the cities matured, becoming larger and more complex, people became more dissatisfied with poor services at excessive cost. By 1900 many concluded there must be better ways to run a metropolis than through machine politics. Businessmen wanted services that directly benefited them and many were tired of a system that put them at the mercy of unmerciful politicos. Reform movements often began when the thieves fell out and disappointed groups pointed accusing fingers at former "associates."

In some cities leading businessmen and professionals dominated and defended reform, championing structural changes that would undermine the ruling politicians' power. Decentralized and fragmented authority, they believed, enabled bosses, backed by the lower classes, to dominate. The parochial views of the ward bosses and the amateur approach to city problems deprived municipalities of badly needed expertise, managerial efficiency, and a broad, citywide outlook. Businessmen or their hand-picked representatives could bring efficient and expert management to city government. By eliminating ward elections and requiring aldermen to run citywide, ethnic and other minority groups lost power to well-financed, prominent local citizens. And by replacing weak mayors with strong city managers and commissions, businessmen hoped to bring professional, honest, and nonpartisan government to the cities. With power centralized in the hands of unbiased experts, the quality of services would improve at reasonable cost.

This approach to urban reform made its greatest impact on smaller cities where machines were weak and where elites were more homogeneous and influential. Reformers adopted democratic rhetoric to gain popular support, charging that the bosses subverted democracy, but centralization was actually a device to shift control from professional politicians (with their base among the lower classes) to experts attuned to the needs and desires of businessmen and professionals. Reform could also express nativist hostility to the political power of ethnically oriented political machines. Irish and German Catholic bosses winked at drinking on Sunday; old-stock Protestant reformers, when they got power, closed down the saloons. Culture conflict thus compounded the task of urban reform because the native-born, feeling threatened by the immigrants whose votes the bosses relied upon, blamed them for civic corruption.

In a few cities, such as Tom Johnson's Cleveland, Hazen Pingree's Detroit, and Sam "Golden Rule" Jones's Toledo, Progressives blamed social injustice, not immigrants, for the shame of the cities. Tom Johnson insisted that as long as private enterprise ran the streetcars and the utilities, rates would be excessive and corruption would flourish among businessmen competing for special privilege. Instead, he advocated municipal ownership and reduced streetcar fares and sought to provide the lower-income groups with expanded recreational facilities. Backed by the working and lower middle classes, Johnson encountered hostility from businessmen and the

upper middle class in general. With the aid of the state legislature, his program of "municipal socialism" gave Cleveland a much more honest and enlightened government than it had known before.

Limits of Urban Reform

Urban reform in the Progressive era improved city government but did not solve the problem of the cities. Reform was a process constantly requiring renewal; lethargy and complacency alternated regularly with militant cries for civic improvement. As long as Americans regarded the city primarily as an arena for moneymaking, they could not overcome the fragmentation and group conflicts that blocked a comprehensive, rational attack on urban problems. Businessmen and middle-class reformers wanted honest and efficient government, but they resisted controls on private enterprise and would not spend the money needed to make the cities more livable, especially for the working classes.

The immigrants clung desperately to the political machines which gave them a voice and some protection. But the machine politicians were as opposed to municipal socialism and as devoted to the pursuit of private wealth as the middle-class reformers who challenged them. Allied with rising ethnic business interests, the machines often opposed social legislation and were hostile to organized labor. Jane Addams discovered in Chicago that garbage went uncollected because the local ward boss allowed the garbage contractors to provide poor service though "his" people suffered.

In the Progressive era some Americans were beginning to glimpse a vision of a new city. The battle for municipal ownership eventually made headway; the more astutely run political machines became socially conscious; and businessmen learned that improved services required more money and that city planning could be good for business. The first efforts to control land use in New York City arose from the desire of the fashionable Fifth Avenue merchants, banks, and insurance companies with large investments in real estate to stabilize land values threatened by sudden shifts in the character of neighborhoods. But zoning a city to make optimal use of the land and to protect residential areas from the blight of undesirable industrial and commercial development interfered with free enterprise, and thus ran counter to a century of American urban experience.

The Progressives were the first to perceive the need to transform cities from marketplaces in which individuals merely earned money into communities whose environments graced, dignified, and respected human needs. Their vision remains unfulfilled half a century later.

STATE PROGRESSIVISM: LA FOLLETTE AND JOHNSON

The reform impulse went beyond the city limits. Urban reformers discovered that unreformed state government hindered all progress. At the same time some farmers and businessmen outside the big cities supported a new breed of politicians who promised to restore government to "the people" and campaigned against the corrupt alliance of political bosses and corporations then dominating the state houses, still the centers of most political power in America.

Robert M. La Follette of Wisconsin set the pace. He rescued his state from the grip of the railroads, timber barons, and their political henchmen, and tried to turn Wisconsin into "a laboratory of democracy." La Follette, son of a pioneer farmer from Indiana, attended the state university where as "a boy right from the farm" he felt self-conscious and socially inferior to the fraternity boys from upper middle-class families. He soon led a fight against fraternity power on campus, read Henry George, and followed the Grange and antimonopoly campaigns. While at the university, La Follette developed an interest in politics which, for a poor boy with ambitions, offered an attractive career outlet. Bucking the local political machine, he won election as district attorney and later a seat in Congress.

La Follette thus entered politics as an outsider successfully challenging the dominant Republican organization but, as he later admitted, with few "general political ideas" except those of orthodox Republicanism itself. During three terms in Congress (1885-1891) he remained a loyal party man, in 1896 backing McKinley, who he thought was "on the side of the public and against the private interests."

The turning point, La Follette explained, came in 1893. Senator Philetus Sawyer of Wisconsin, a lumber baron, tried to bribe him to protect the state treasurer, a Sawyer crony on trial for misusing public funds. When La Follette spurned the money and exposed Sawyer, he broke the rules of the political game, as Sawyer was used to playing it. The senator had not violated his own conscience, La Follette later acknowledged, because "he regarded money as the chief influence in politics" and he "bought men as he bought sawlogs," assuming "that every man in politics was serving, first of all, his own personal interests—else why should he be in politics." La Follette rejected a morality which held that "railroad corporations and lumber companies, as benefactors of the country, should be given unlimited grants of public lands, allowed to charge all the traffic would bear," because "anything that interfered with the profits of business was akin to treason."

La Follette worked closely with the University of Wisconsin, employing its resources to bring expertise into the management of public affairs. Ultimately, his achievements rested on his success in forming a winning political coalition. Starting almost without organization, and forced to buck a powerfully entrenched Old Guard, he obtained enthusiastic help from the university community. He also developed a following among the state's numerous Norwegian farmers who felt that the Republican organization denied them adequate recognition. As a congressman, he cultivated the veterans' vote by paying close attention to pension claims and he worked hard to gain support among influential citizens. "Get and keep a dozen or more of the leading men in a community interested in and well-informed upon any public question," he once explained, "and you have laid the foundation of democratic government." He also benefited at critical times from splits among the regular Republicans. But his power rested ultimately upon his appeal to the poorer farmers, with their normally Republican votes, plus the backing of the university community and elements in the middle class—"the younger and more independent" members of the Republican party.

La Follette demanded regulation of business and he first launched a campaign against those politicians who served corporations. By 1900 he had captured the state Republican party, the dominant political force in Wisconsin. To keep control, he sponsored a primary law giving voters the right to nominate candidates directly. Until then, party conventions, easily controlled by machine politicians, selected the nominees, and their grip was so tight that it took La Follette six years to break it.

Railroad regulation followed. For years the roads had recived favored treatment in tax assessments. La Follette equalized taxation but only after a prolonged struggle during which he mobilized support from farmers, shippers, and manufacturers, convincing them that they were paying exorbitant freight rates. The struggle to lower rates proved even fiercer. Rate-making, La Follette insisted, was a "scientific" question. A railroad commission, composed of experts, including engineers, accountants, and statisticians, determined "fair" rates, lowering them where possible, raising them when necessary. Though the railroads had fought reform, they actually benefited from state supervision. The state banned secret rebates and free passes which cost the railroads millions annually, and though rates fell the volume of business and revenues rose. The same thing occurred in the electric utilities industry; lower rates increased business, earnings, and spurred new investment. Another state commission regulated working conditions, protecting women and children in particular. New safety standards and workmen's compensation laws insured workers against the pauperism sure to follow a disabling accident. La Follette made Wisconsin Progressive, and his crusade for Progressive state government became a model for the nation.

Progressivism, California Style

Hiram Johnson did the same for California. Enormously rich but underdeveloped, California lay in the grip of the Southern Pacific Railroad.

The railroad controlled the key to the state's growth, opening up its rich lands and linking it with the rest of the country. Because California was young and had developed rapidly, no economic forces could yet compete for power and influence with the railroad. It had a virtual monopoly of transportation, was the biggest landowner, and controlled enormous timber and mineral holdings. To protect its empire, the railroad also bought control of state government. "They swindle a nation of a hundred million and call it Financiering," wrote Frank Norris in *The Octopus* (1901), a novel about railroad domination of California, "they levy blackmail and call it Commerce; they corrupt a legislature and call it Politics; they bribe a judge and call it Law . . . they prostitute the honor of a state and call it Competition."

In California, an urbanized state from the outset, reform began in the cities. First in San Francisco and then in Los Angeles businessmen and newspapers campaigned for clean government. A reform administration attacked corruption in San Francisco and opposed the mounting power of the trade unions. Gradually middle-class reformers in other cities joined to oppose Southern Pacific domination and to stop the drift toward class conflict between militant labor and reactionary employers. "Nearly all the problems which vex society," wrote the *Progressive California Weekly* in self-congratulation, "have their sources above or below the middle-class man. From above come the problems of predatory wealth. . . . From below come the problems of poverty and pig-headed brutish criminality." The Fresno *Republican* echoed the Progressives' longing for a new order:

Where none were for a class and all were for the
    state,
Where the rich man helped the poor and the poor
    man loved the great.

That day would come only if the "unbiased" middle classes mediated. "Every great reform," a Progressive congressman asserted, "has been taken up and worked out by those who are not selfishly interested. I believe altruism is a bigger force in the world than selfishness."

Hiram Johnson, appealing to both motives, captured the Republican party for Progressivism and then the state house in Sacramento. A lawyer active in the urban reform in San Francisco, yet also a friend of organized labor, Johnson shrewdly capitalized on antirailroad sentiment to unite a diverse coalition behind his leadership. His initial victory rested on the support of rural voters who complained of excessive freight rates and who responded to his single-issue campaign against the railroads. This also won him backing from businessmen fighting for clean government. Urban workers were at first lukewarm, since they did not directly suffer from railroad exactions and were suspicious of the antiunion bias of many Progressives. But Johnson eventually captured the labor votes by championing protective labor legislation, though Republicans, especially those from southern California, blocked legislation to foster unionization.

The Progressive Republicans initiated reforms meant to weaken machine politicians: the direct primary (through which voters nominate candidates); the referendum (through which voters themselves legislate); and the recall (by which voters remove public officials from office). Commissions regulated the railroads and utilities; an Industrial Welfare Commission fixed working hours and wages for women and children. The commissioner of corporations guarded against fraudulent securities issues. The Johnson regime extended civil service tenure, and modernized public administration with a businesslike budgeting system.

Ultimately, Johnson's coalition fragmented. Increasingly, the southern half of the state drifted away from Johnson after his success with railroad reform, for it defined Progressivism more in cultural terms and wanted to control gambling and the liquor interests and to repress the Japanese. And "rather than let Los Angeles be thrown under the sort of tyrannical domination of labor unions that exists in San Francisco," admitted a southern California Progressive, he would abandon the entire reform movement.

STATE PROGRESSIVISM IN THE SOUTH

Progressivism in the states was a nationwide phenomenon which spread to all parts of the country, though the forms it took depended on each state's social structure and special problems. Southern politics, for so long shaped by unique sectional and racial circumstances, also felt the impact. Southerners, like other Americans in the late nineteenth century, had given businessmen almost free reign to encourage investment and develop resources. Because of the region's relative poverty and the destruction caused by the Civil War, Southern economic advance depended heavily on Northern capital. By 1900, however, Southerners began to revolt against the outside domination that made their region a colonial dependency of the Northeast. A new urban middle class that had grown up with the Southern economy led the fight against railroads and other powerful business interests.

The collapse of Southern Populism removed the radical stigma from reform and strengthened Democratic reform elements. At the same time, the black disfranchisement in the 1890s allowed white reformers to challenge the Old Guard without worrying over a revival of Negro power because of divisions among whites. With blacks barred from voting, the Republican party had little future. The important contests took place within the Democratic party. The direct primary came into use first in the South because it was a one-party region in which white voters wanted the right to choose Democratic nominees directly. This structural change made it easier than in other parts of the country for Southern Progressives to challenge existing machines.

Southern Progressives, like those elsewhere, campaigned for railroad regulation. They strengthened ineffective regulatory commissions established a generation earlier and controlled rates, seeking also to improve safety and end discriminatory practices. Texas Progressives attacked the oil interests. Elsewhere, insurance companies came under review, and tobacco farmers fought the monopoly of the American Tobacco Company, which they blamed for depressing prices.

Southern Progressivism's support came from urban middle-class reformers and from farmers who backed the attack on plutocracy and Northern exploitation. Thus regional pride and a sense of grievance helped to unite the discontented. Southern Progressives also fought for prohibition of liquor to protect the poor and weak from its "debasing" influence and to strike at the corrupt alliance between liquor interests and machine politicians.

But Progressives in the South worked under several handicaps. The prohibition drive diverted them from more productive reforms, although it reflected the belief that "demon rum" helped to keep the South backward. The rise of a new variety of demagogue further weakened reform. Georgia's Senator Tom Watson, an ex-Populist gone sour, Mississippi's James K. Vardaman, South Carolina's "Pitchfork Ben" Tillman, and other racists inflamed rural whites with anti-Negro diatribes that diverted Southerners from dealing constructively with the problems of economic retardation and lopsided income distribution. Yet despite these obstacles to reform, humanitarian sentiment, as elsewhere in the country, produced the first tentative measures to protect working people, especially child laborers—a problem that steadily grew as textile factories brought industrialization to the South.

STATE PROGRESSIVISM: A BALANCE SHEET

By the first decade of the twentieth century, Progressive politicians had become powerful forces in state after state. In New York, Charles Evans Hughes's exposure of insurance companies' malpractices won him the governorship. Joseph W. Folk, attorney general of Missouri, prosecuted municipal grafters in St. Louis and went on to become governor. In New Jersey, Progressives led by Mark Fagan, Republican mayor of Jersey City, and later by Woodrow Wilson, Democratic governor, fought for equal taxation of business, limitations on the charters of franchised monopolies, and protective labor legislation.

Progressivism infiltrated both the Republican and Democratic parties. Since Progressive leaders were usually younger than the Old Guard politicians they challenged, and had less political experience, they found their ambitions thwarted by well-entrenched machines. Usually without attachment to corporations and conservative politicos, they were freer to voice the discontents of the time. They spoke for a younger generation,

more critical of the price the country was paying for industrial growth and convinced of the need for social controls. For over a generation Americans had worshiped the go-getting businessmen. Now they had second thoughts. Cities which had granted "sweetheart" streetcar franchises to obtain mass transit, for instance, awakened to "find their streets mortgaged for all time, future generations impoverished and themselves heavily taxed, while the corporations are enjoying special privileges and profits beyond a fair return on the capital invested."

In the states, Progressives concentrated on regulating business and "purifying" politics. By 1915 every state had adopted the secret ballot, statewide direct primaries spread to over a dozen states outside the South, and many others adopted the initiative, referendum, and recall. Before ratification of the Seventeenth Amendment (1913), some twenty states had already adopted popular election of United States senators. In state after state commissions tightened regulations of the railroads and by 1915 twenty-five states protected workers against industrial accidents, nine provided minimum wages for women, and several limited court injunctions against labor unions.

Progressives were not hostile to business, La Follette claimed. They insisted that it must operate within the law and serve the common good, but they saw no irreconcilable conflict between fair profits and social responsibility. For proof of this they could point to Massachusetts, a state that resisted organized Progressivism. The home of the industrial revolution in the United States, Massachusetts had long regulated freedom of enterprise and was a center of civil service reform and Mugwump attempts to clean up politics. It established the nation's first railroad commission in 1869, a Board of Gas and Electric Light Commissioners fixed rates, and it was the first to adopt the secret ballot.

Industrial development came early to Massachusetts but it spread out over several generations, the work of local elites investing Massachusetts capital with a greater sense of social responsibility than elsewhere. In other states industrialization came more quickly, often financed by outside entrepreneurs who lacked roots in the communities they developed and who operated without the social constraints that existed in Massachusetts. The Bay State was no paradise: its workers engaged in violent strikes; its rival ethnic groups, especially the Protestants and Irish Catholics, fought each other; and its businessmen sought profits and privilege; it too had a younger generation of reformers who exploited popular discontent in order to attack the entrenched machines. Thus no state went completely untouched by the Progressive impulses which fused into a drive to transform national politics as well.

Chapter 23
Progressivism and National Politics

The upheavals of the 1890s made a lasting impact on the party system. The deadlock between the two parties broke in 1896, making the Republicans the majority party until the 1930s. Thousands of Democrats, especially in the populous northeastern states, had been driven into the opposition party or into the political wilderness by the Bryan campaign. Each party still retained its centers of strength—the Democrats in the South, and the Republicans in the Northeast and Midwest—but now more than in the past, one party ruled large areas of the country. As party competition declined, participation at the polls also fell from the highs reached in the late nineteenth century. Members of the minority party saw little hope of electing their candidates. By the 1920s, about half of the electorate did not bother to vote in presidential elections.

As participation diminished, party loyalty loosened. More people split their tickets or voted for third parties. The Republicans captured a solid majority of the two-party vote, but between 1896 and 1916, parties won the presidency with an average of only 50.3 percent of the popular vote, and about 6 percent voted for a third party, usually the Socialist. Yet many more voters, dissatisfied with the major parties, simply ignored elections. This was especially true in the South where Democratic politicians who battled in the primaries—the deciding elections—failed to confront the economic problems afflicting Southern farmers and workers, and erected formidable legal obstacles such as the poll tax to keep poor whites and nearly all blacks from the polls.

Apathy prevailed elsewhere as well. Millions of immigrants preoccupied with adjusting to American life and working people chained to the treadmill of long hours and low wages found the rhetoric and programs of the two parties irrelevant to their needs and aspirations. They stayed home, or in the factory, on election day. The large ethnic and working-class vote in the cities remained a sleeping giant, awakened only occasionally by men like Tom Johnson in Cleveland, or the newspaper tycoon William Randolph Hearst in New York. These men campaigned for measures to improve working conditions but avoided the stigma of radicalism, which repelled those struggling for respectability.

Following McKinley's election in 1896, Republicans controlled Congress most of the time and won the presidency every four years until 1912. Then a divided GOP gave the Democrats, under Woodrow Wilson, a brief chance. Although Wilson occupied the White House for eight years, Republicans remained the majority party. In 1920 they recaptured the presidency and held it for another twelve years.

These shifts in party fortunes obscure remarkable stability in voting behavior, often dating back generations, a continuity rooted in ethnic, regional, and religious identity. The loyalty of Southerners to the Democratic party was paralleled by the loyalty of New England Yankees to the Republican. In a midwestern state such as Iowa, for instance, native-born Methodists and Presbyterians usually voted Republican, as did Scandinavian Lutherans and German Protestants; in contrast, German and Bohemian Catholic immigrants voted Democratic. Similarly, in the big Eastern cities, Irish Catholics were mainstays of the Democratic party, just as native-born Protestants of Yankee ancestry kept the Republican faith.

Such ethnocultural, historic attachments stabilized party alignment, yet at the same time, more so than in the past, voters began to switch parties or split their tickets, according to how candidates and party programs responded to the new demands made on the political system by the Progressive view. Conservatives resisted and fought to maintain control of both parties. The struggle ended inconclusively, but by 1914 the federal government had assumed broader responsibilities to promote order and stability.

TR AND THE REPUBLICANS

As the dominant party nationally, the Republicans became the vehicle of Progressive reform during the first decade of the twentieth century. Since Progressivism largely expressed the aspirations and anxieties of the native-born middle classes outside the South, these found logical outlet in the GOP.

In Theodore Roosevelt, who was president from 1901 to 1909, Progressive Republicans had a leader who effectively voiced their hopes and shrewdly tried to make his party responsive to new impulses. In the end, TR failed to reshape his party, and Progressive Republicans became prisoners of a narrow, standpat version of party orthodoxy. But during the strenuous, exciting years of the Roosevelt presidency, Progressivism gained national definition and broad bipartisan support, and it redefined the mission of the federal government.

Born into an old Dutch patrician family of New York, Roosevelt began with the advantages of money and social prominence. Yet from the start he came to believe that life meant to "work, fight, and breed." A sickly child, he struggled to overcome physical handicaps that left him permanently scarred emotionally; he never lost the need to dominate, to assert himself, to prove his manhood. Neither business nor the law provided a suitable arena for his extraordinary zest, his desire for power, his passion for leadership and service.

Politics was his natural element. But could the Gilded Age find a place for the descendant of an aristocratic family with a strong sense of *noblesse oblige?* Men of Roosevelt's set looked upon politics, as then practiced, as sordid and unfit for gentlemen, the province of ill-educated, ill-mannered, and greedy men, and certainly not for Roosevelt, a man of wide-ranging interests and even some culture. Few presidents equaled his love of literature, art, and nature, or had his intellectual curiosity.

Few surpassed him in political skill, either. Roosevelt began in the 1880s as assemblyman from Manhattan's upper-crust "silk-stocking district," where one faction of New York City machine politicians used him to oust another. Roosevelt learned early to work with professional politicians to advance his career, and to satisfy himself that he was not sacrificing his own integrity or goals. Party regularity, he believed, held the key to power. In 1884 he held his nose but voted for scandal-tarnished James G. Blaine, while thousands of his own class became Mug-

wumps, voting for Cleveland and "good government." The party rewarded TR's loyalty with appointments to the Civil Service Commission and the New York City Police Commission. He worked at both jobs with vigor and amid controversy, since Roosevelt loved to attract attention. In 1897 President McKinley made him assistant secretary of the navy.

When war with Spain broke out, Roosevelt led a volunteer cavalry unit called "The Rough Riders" to Cuba. The war, he later wrote, was "my chance to cut my little notch on the stick that stands as a measuring rod in every family"; he would have deserted his "wife's deathbed to have answered that call." The Rough Riders' exploits (some of them real) were well reported, and their colorful leader became a celebrity overnight. "I rose over those regular army officers like a balloon," he boasted. But the battlefield offered more than a chance to gain glory or to give Spaniards lessons in *machismo;* for TR, as for other Americans, it was a chance to bring "freedom" to the long-suffering Cubans, to demonstrate devotion to some higher, nobler cause than the pursuit of personal profit and power. It also gave him much free publicity.

New York's Republicans drafted the hero of San Juan Hill to save the 1898 gubernatorial election. Roosevelt won, and gave New York Progressive government without *publicly* breaking with the party organization he soon antagonized as a reform governor. As in the past, he explained, "I had to work with the tools at hand." He insisted on appointing able men to office, pushed for higher taxes on corporations and stricter control of utility franchises, consulted experts in the universities, and sought advice from trade unionists and social reformers. He also backed tenement house reform, industrial safety laws, and limitations on the hours women and children could work.

Roosevelt had no clear-cut philosophy of reform but he sensed the need for social controls to avoid explosion and he was out to learn from experience. As an assemblyman he had shown little sympathy for the plight of labor, but when Samuel Gompers of the Cigar Workers Union gave him a tour of working conditions in the slums, TR acknowledged the need for government control that would curb free enterprise. "I am a good deal puzzled over some of the inequalities in life, as life now exists," Governor Roosevelt admitted. "All I want to do is cautiously to feel my way to see if we cannot make the general conditions of life a little easier—a little better."

Roosevelt's cautious Progressivism cost him the support of the New York Republican organization. The disgruntled politicians worked to swing his nomination as McKinley's running mate in 1900 and thus remove this disturbing personality from New York politics by kicking him upstairs to the vice-presidency. Unwittingly, the standpatters gave him the chance to bring Progressivism to Washington when an assassin murdered McKinley and elevated the Rough Rider to the presidency.

TR as President

Although the new president promised to carry on in the conservative path of McKinley, he immediately began striking out on his own. By the time he left the White House seven years later, he had revived the moral and political preeminence of the presidency and had begun to remake his party. During his first term, Roosevelt tempered Progressive impulses with caution, to avoid pushing too far ahead of his party. From the beginning, however, he tackled some problems dodged by a half dozen predecessors.

None proved more vexing than the growing concentration of corporate power. The merger movement reached its peak when TR assumed office. Roosevelt sympathized with public anxiety over "the trusts," but he considered bigness irreversible and socially advantageous if the great wealth-producing capacity of industry could be socially controlled. Corporations that did "their honest duty to the public," should be encouraged; those "organized in a spirit of mere greed or for improper speculative purposes" should be curbed, he declared with all the imprecision of a moralist.

Roosevelt would be the judge, and the Sherman Anti-Trust Act of 1890 provided him with a convenient weapon. None of Roosevelt's predecessors had shown much interest in enforcing that law. The new president thought its total ban on "combinations in restraint of trade" unrealistic, but since a modernized, more workable law was not to be had, he had to act with the old one.

Progressives cheered when Roosevelt dissolved the Northern Securities Company. Morgan, Rockefeller, and other leading financiers had formed the giant railroad holding company in violation of the law. This suit, the first of over forty prosecutions, put new life into antitrust policy. Roosevelt did not reverse the trend toward consolidation, but he made government a restraining force at a time when business enjoyed virtual immunity from public accountability. "Wall Street is paralyzed at the thought that a President would sink so low as to try to enforce the law," reported the Detroit *Free Press*. Railroad magnate James J. Hill was furious that men like himself "should be compelled to fight for our lives against the political adventurers who have never done anything but pose and draw a salary." But millions of Americans, including many businessmen especially in the South and West, cheered the president. "He brought in a stream of fresh, pure bracing air from the mountains to clear the fetid atmosphere of the national capital," wrote one admirer euphorically. In 1903 TR prodded Congress to establish a Bureau of Corporations, a permanent investigating agency to gather data on business practices and to disclose business malpractices, if necessary. Yet at the same time that TR won acclaim as a "trust buster," he privately reassured J. P. Morgan that "good" trusts had nothing to fear.

Conceiving his role as an "honest broker" in a neutral state, Roosevelt also intervened in the long coal strike of 1902, as national fuel supplies dwindled with the approach of winter. The United Mine Workers of America had won public sympathy because the strikers avoided violence and had offered to arbitrate. The mine owners, however, scorned negotiations, counting perhaps on government to help them break the strike as it did during the labor crisis of 1894. But the climate of opinion had shifted. Threatening to send troops to run the mines, and enlisting aid from J. P. Morgan, TR forced the owners to settle. In the past, government had helped business to suppress labor. Now for the first time the president supported the workingman.

Although Roosevelt remained ambivalent toward unions for fear of intensified class conflict, in the face of employer intransigence he agreed that workers had no alternative but to organize and sometimes to strike. "The friends of property," he lectured conservatives, "must realize that the surest way to provoke an explosion of wrong and injustice is to be shortsighted, narrowminded, greedy and arrogant. . . ." It was the duty of those "with whom things have prospered to be in a certain sense the keeper of his brother with whom life has gone hard." His unique intervention on the side of labor had little lasting impact and did not shift the balance of power in favor of trade unionism, but Roosevelt began the process of persuading middle-class Americans to live with organized labor.

By the time Roosevelt ran for reelection in 1904 he controlled the presidential wing of the party tightly. Ruthless use of patronage reassured his renomination, and he established himself as a strong executive who could chastise Big Business without losing its confidence or its financial support. The secret of his strength, he explained, was his "genuine independence of the big monied men in all matters where I think the interests of the public are concerned and probably I am the first President of recent times of whom this could be truthfully said. . . ." Vaguely but effectively, Roosevelt promised a "Square Deal" for all Americans. Trouncing his Democratic opponent, Judge Alton B. Parker, a political unknown nominated by the conservative anti-Bryan wing of the Democratic party, Roosevelt began his second term with a promise that it would be his last, yet determined to advance Progressive policies more boldly now that he was president in his own right.

TR AND REFORM

Personal vindication accomplished, effective railroad regulation became Roosevelt's next major goal. For over thirty years, first the states and then the federal government had tried to end discriminatory practices and regulate rates that favored some businessmen at the expense of others. But the railroads and shipping interests successfully resisted public controls, aided by the judiciary and easygoing regulatory agencies. By 1900, however, with the railroad network built, demands for effective controls intensified, and respectable politicians like Roosevelt led the fight to achieve them.

Roosevelt made regulation a moral issue. "The standard of profits and business prosperity is insufficient in judging any business or political question," he warned. Reform was essential to restore equal opportunity: "We do not intend that this Republic shall ever fail as those republics of olden times failed, in which they finally came to be a government by classes, which resulted either in the poor plundering the rich or in the rich exploiting the poor." Equally important, Roosevelt calculated that the political prospects for railroad reform were relatively good, although some Republicans would give him trouble. In the Senate, a conservative Republican clique stood ready to protect vested interests. One of their leaders, Senator Nelson W. Aldrich of Rhode Island, believed that "most people don't know what they want." Therefore, Aldrich and likeminded colleagues would decide what was best for the country.

First, TR pushed for an antirebate law. Since the railroads themselves wanted to stop paying large rebates to preferred shippers, the Elkins Act (1903) sailed through Congress. But the roads fought Roosevelt's proposal to give the Interstate Commerce Commission power to fix maximum rates. That struggle ended with passage of the Hepburn Act (1906), giving Roosevelt most of what he wanted, but not until the president had compromised several points, and had indicated to conservatives that he would softpedal tariff reduction. The Hepburn Act disappointed advanced Progressives like La Follette because it did not establish "scientific" standards for determining rates. TR, however, willingly accepted half a loaf. The president, gathering support from powerful farming and business interests, especially in the West and South, defeated the conservative Republicans, the railroads, and the eastern shippers who benefited from the existing rate structure. Now for the first time a government agency to which all interested parties could appeal had responsibility for setting rates that were "fair" to the roads, shippers, and the consumer. In the past, the most powerful private forces in the marketplace set rates; now government assumed a responsibility to assure equity.

Washington also undertook to protect consumers from unhealthy food and unsafe drugs. Muckrakers had exposed businessmen who sold fraudulent drugs and spoiled food. In his novel about the Chicago stockyards, *The Jungle* (1906), Upton Sinclair wrote of diseased hogs being turned into lard, of workers in the cooling rooms falling into vats and being cooked for days, and of people urinating on the floor, where scraps of meat, pigskins, and rope were collected to become "potted ham." The president made the taste test and then recommended federal meat inspection. The big packers, livestock interests, and ideological conservatives fought effective controls, but Roosevelt got the Meat Inspection Act (1906) through, as usual a compromise that gave the government some powers to enforce sanitary standards in packinghouses selling meat in interstate commerce. The new and favorable climate of opinion also allowed for passage of a Pure Food and Drug Act in 1906.

In each of these campaigns, Roosevelt brilliantly coordinated the efforts of Progressive forces. He exploited muckraking exposures and subsequent public outrage; he made sure he had accurate information and enlisted expert opinion. He mobilized particularly concerned interests and put the opposition on the moral defensive, and he patiently and shrewdly outmaneuvered obstructionists in his own party.

Conservation

In the battle for reform legislation, TR lost no sleep over the need to compromise. In the fight for conservation, however, the president used all of his exceptionally broad executive powers, and his conservation record became his greatest legacy. "In the past," TR announced, "we have admitted the right of the individual to injure the future of the Republic for his own personal profit. The time has come for a change. As a people we have the right and the duty, second to none other, to protect ourselves and our children against the wasteful development of our natural resources." The president created enormous forest reserves, withdrew coal and mineral land from public entry, curbed excessive grazing on public lands, set aside water power sites for future development, and initiated irrigation projects to bring water to the parched far western states.

The conservation movement joined together

a variety of forces in the Progressive period. Conservationists asserted the primacy of the democratic distribution and rational use of resources instead of rapid and wasteful private development. Professional conservationists like Gifford Pinchot, TR's chief forester, brought expert knowledge into the management of natural resources. They aimed not at blocking development, but assuring efficient use through "large-scale, long-term planning and management." Sustained-yield forest management cost more than indiscriminate cutting but it replenished forests. Without price stability, lumbermen would favor cheaper more wasteful methods. Pinchot thought the solution lay in opening federal timber reserves to companies following sustained-yield or conservation procedures. The largest lumber firms and furniture manufacturers realized that conservation of timber favored their long-term interests. But the smaller, less well financed companies resisted.

The experts and big cattlemen similarly joined to protect the public range from overgrazing. Cattlemen looked to controls as a means of stabilizing the industry and protecting the range from the intrusion of homesteaders and sheepmen. Western farmers in need of water also turned to the federal government to harness rivers and redistribute water from areas of surplus to areas of shortage. The Newlands Act (1902) allocated the proceeds from the sale of public lands in the West to finance irrigation in arid states. The experts insisted that each particular resource was linked to another in nature's ecological chain. Thus, water conservation required forest conservation. They also argued for multipurpose public projects, such as giant dams which harnessed streams to manufacture electricity, to prevent floods, and to irrigate arid land, an idea that did not gain acceptance until the New Deal.

The conservation movement, though launched by experts and supported by certain economic interests that stood to benefit, gained increasing support from people critical of the consequences of uncontrolled industrial development. Freewheeling businessmen were destroying nature and ignoring moral and esthetic values in their lust for quick wealth. Conservation thus offered another means of resisting plutocracy, which plundered public resources for private gain, and of substituting public control based on scientific and democratic values.

Acting without congressional approval, on the advice of experts and with the certainty that he knew better than others how to serve the public interest, Roosevelt's conservationism aroused plenty of controversy. Standpat Republicans opposed the enlargement of federal power and the sweeping use of executive power, and businessmen and farmers resented restrictions on their free enterprise imposed by bureaucrats and scientists. Westerners in particular reacted inconsistently. They wanted federal money and help to develop resources rapidly, but they feared a loss of local control. Some favored subsidized water projects to irrigate their land while opposing charges for the use of grazing land or the removal of water power sites from public entry. Able to cloak their private goals under the mantle of Progressive rhetoric, many Americans overlooked the larger significance of conservation. Still, the conservation movement expressed the Progressive faith that Americans could rationally and democratically plan the future for the greatest happiness of the greatest number. But this belief that government, through scientific knowledge and public planning, could best promote the common welfare conflicted with an older tradition that placed the highest value on private decision-making in the pursuit of profit. The Progressives never reconciled the two.

Roosevelt's Record

Roosevelt's failure as a patron of the welfare state, a role he played with increasing vigor toward the end of his presidency, reveals this even more sharply. He proposed to make the District of Columbia a model city by enforcing the eight-hour day in the civil service, and proposing anti-child labor, factory sanitation, and slum clearance laws. Nor did he intend to stop with the capital. "We Progressives believe," he asserted, "that human rights are supreme, that wealth should be the servant, not the master, of the people." Before he left the White House, TR recommended increased income and inheritance taxes on the rich, workmen's compensation, a national child

labor law, restrictions on the use of injunctions against labor unions, and stricter regulation of the railroads and Big Business, a reform agenda that would take another decade to clear, and then only partially. Conservative Republican opposition stymied the president; his best hope was to choose a successor who would carry on the battle for Progressive government.

Theodore Roosevelt, a patrician reformer, believed that men of wealth and position must try to reconcile hostile social groups, handing down justice from above and thereby promoting the interests of all Americans. He respected businessmen, but neither worshiped nor stood in awe of great wealth. Increasingly, TR came to understand that those who "regarded power as expressed only in its basest and most brutal form, that of mere money," menaced the country.

More than any American of his generation including Bryan (to whom many refused to listen), TR educated the country to the dangers of "predatory wealth." Before he left office, *The Wall Street Journal* acknowledged a shift in public opinion. Acquiescence in acceptance of business leadership and the Gospel of Wealth had given way to criticism "of the eager pursuit of sudden wealth, the shameless luxury and display, growing and corrupting extravagence, the misuse of swollen fortunes, the indifference to law, the growth of graft, the abuses of great corporate power. . . ." For this shift, Roosevelt deserves a good share of the credit.

INSURGENCY, 1908–1912

Roosevelt settled on William Howard Taft of Ohio to succeed him. The Democratic nominee, William Jennings Bryan, was running for the third time. Although Taft won easily, this did not foreshadow a successful administration. Taft had faithfully served in the Roosevelt administration and had supported Progressive policies more out of loyalty and necessity than out of conviction. His personal ties were with the Old Guard and temperamentally this three-hundred-pounder was inclined to passivity. He preferred an administrative or judicial career to the presidency, which Roosevelt had remade into a dynamic office, the fulcrum of the American political system. The lethargic and unimaginative Taft once admitted: "I don't like politics." He never wanted to be president, but tapped by TR and nagged by his wife, Taft went along.

As president, Taft tried to follow a Progressive course. A stickler for law enforcement, he initiated twice as many antitrust suits as his predecessor, including one against the Morgan-controlled United States Steel Company (to which TR had previously promised immunity). In 1911 the Supreme Court upheld the government in two major cases, ordering reorganization of the American Tobacco Company and dissolution of the Standard Oil Company as then organized. Though Taft enforced the antitrust laws more consistently than Roosevelt, he did not arouse public enthusiasm on the issue as Roosevelt had done, nor of course did he reverse the trend toward concentration of economic power. The president also campaigned for railroad regulation. In 1910 Congress passed the Mann-Elkins Act, which gave the Interstate Commerce Commission added powers.

Despite these and other achievements, Taft lost the support of the Progressive Republicans and fell in line with the standpatters. He proved unable to prevent the GOP from fatally splitting apart. Early in his administration, the growing number of Progressive Republicans in Congress forced him to choose sides between them and the Old Guard. A band of House Progressives led by Nebraska's George W. Norris sought to curb the dictatorial powers of Speaker Joseph ("Uncle Joe") Cannon, who personified the reactionary obstructionism TR had encountered. At first Taft encouraged the insurgents but then suffered an attack of cold feet, or fear that if he bucked the regulars he might lose and thus face a Congress controlled by hostile leadership. With Democratic help, the insurgents stripped the Speaker of power, but they bitterly resented the president's retreat.

The Tariff Fight

Taft's role in the struggle for tariff reform confirmed their suspicions. Since the triumph of protectionism during and after the Civil War, traditionally low-tariff Democrats and antimonopoly agrarians had fought for tariff reduction without much success. After 1900 the pressure for reform mounted and recruited powerful new backing. The proliferation of mergers between 1897 and 1904 gave new credibility to the argument that the tariff was the mother of trusts. Consumers began to blame the rising cost of living on protection. Manufacturers who turned semifinished imports into finished products or who looked abroad for raw materials also favored lower duties. So did merchants in foreign trade. Midwestern and southern farmers joined the campaign, hoping that if the United States lowered the barrier on foreign imports, other countries would reciprocate by opening their markets to American agricultural commodities.

But most Republican leaders feared that tampering with the tariff might endanger the economy and the party. The Republicans blamed the Wilson-Gorman reductions of 1890 for the depression of that decade and they proudly asserted that prosperity followed adoption of the higher Dingley Tariff in 1897. Roosevelt supported tariff reform in principle, but he thought the tariff was mainly a question of expediency and not of morality. Needing the support of the standpatters, such men as Senator Aldrich and the Republican congressional leadership, TR had traded tariff reform for support on matters he considered more vital.

Taft, however, could not juggle the issue. He publicly committed himself to reduction as pressure for change steadily mounted. As in the fight against Speaker Cannon, the president first encouraged then deserted the Progressive Republicans. Roosevelt's style of cajoling his party, appealing to the country, depicting opponents as public enemies, yet always managing to leave room for compromise with the conservatives on Capitol Hill, was not for Taft. Lacking TR's political flair, he chose instead to make peace with Aldrich, accepting what he could get. The result was the Payne-Aldrich Tariff (1909), denounced by Progressive senators as a mockery of reform. Aldrich's idea of tariff reform was to put on the free list such vital items as curling stones, false teeth, canary bird seed, and silkworm eggs. Taft made matters worse by describing the new act as "the best bill that the Republican party ever passed."

Another controversy, the Pinchot-Ballinger

dispute, drove the president and the Progressives further apart. Progressive Republicans became convinced that Taft opposed a strong conservation policy. As a legalist, Taft doubted the validity of Roosevelt's sweeping withdrawal of lands and water power sites from public entry without congressional approval. When his interior secretary, Richard A. Ballinger, reopened some public lands to private interests, Chief Forester Gifford Pinchot led the conservationist forces in denouncing this "giveaway" to business. A drawn-out dispute erupted, one involving charges that Ballinger had conspired to turn over valuable Alaskan coal lands to private control. A congressional investigation led to the resignation of both Pinchot and Ballinger and the disclosure that the president, in order to protect his administration, had predated a letter, thus misleading the public.

The Progressive Revolt

When TR returned from an African safari in June 1910, he found his party divided and the prestige of the presidency fading rapidly. Many of TR's friends charged that Taft had betrayed the Progressive legacy. Roosevelt agreed. In August he proclaimed the "New Nationalism," a program reaffirming the goals of Progressive government: "to equalize opportunity, destroy privilege, and give to the life and citizenship of every individual the highest possible value." This required curbing the power of Big Business, regulating corporations in the public interest, and encouraging the organization of farmers and workers. Like Lincoln before him, TR affirmed that if he had to choose, he was for "men and not property!" The New Nationalism put the "national needs before sectional or personal advantage" and looked to the president "as the steward of the public welfare."

Progressive Republicans attacked Taft, none more vigorously than Senator La Follette. The Wisconsin senator emerged as the leading dissident, or Insurgent. The Insurgents were strongest in the Midwestern corn and wheat belts where farmers and some businessmen in Iowa, Wisconsin, Minnesota, and the Dakotas responded to antimonopoly and tariff reform appeals. With the bulk of the party leadership behind him, Taft

attempted to purge the Insurgents, but they won renomination in state after state. Democrats also beat enough conservative Republicans to win control of the House in 1910, and with Insurgent help gained a working majority in the Senate.

Buoyed up by their victory of 1910, the Insurgents formed the National Progressive Republican League, hoping to win the presidential nomination for La Follette. But the latter's appeal did not extend beyond the Midwest, and his campaign faltered. Early in 1912, Roosevelt decided to challenge Taft, his own hand-picked successor. With most of the party organization in Taft's corner, and with the president controlling federal patronage, TR faced an uphill fight. His main hope lay in convincing the party that Taft could not win, and that only Roosevelt's kind of leadership had kept Republicans in power.

Despite TR's offer to drag the Old Guard to victory again, they preferred to take their chances with Taft. With TR, they would have had to swallow his unpalatable policies, his newfound "radicalism," and risk letting the party slip into Insurgent hands.

The candidates battled ferociously for convention delegates. "I am a man of peace," Taft insisted, employing a curious figure of speech, "and I don't want to fight. But when I do fight I want to hit hard. Even a rat in a corner will fight." TR called the president a "fathead" and Taft described the Rough Rider as a "demagogue," a "dangerous egotist." TR won the primaries and the hearts of the rank-and-file, but Taft collected a majority of the delegates. At the Republican convention, the controlling Taft forces won most of the disputed seats. Roosevelt cried fraud, his supporters bolting to nominate him as the candidate of a new Progressive party on a comprehensive platform of reform. A whole generation of Americans who had rejected laissez faire and the Gospel of Wealth, veterans in many a battle for reform, joined him. The new party, particularly strong in the cities, embodied many of the different threads in the fabric of Progressivism: the attack on plutocracy and machine politics, the insistence that government promote justice and stability among social classes, and reliance on planning to solve problems and on dynamic leadership to direct the force of social reconstruction.

For years the Republican party had been divided between Progressive and conservative wings. Only a politician of unusual skill like TR could keep it together and make it an effective vehicle of reform. But not even TR could maintain unity indefinitely. As demands for reform increased, internal divisions grew greater, and the entrenched Old Guard became more stubborn. The Republican split offered the Democrats, for the first time in a generation, a chance to prove that they too could provide Progressive government.

PROGRESSIVISM, DEMOCRATIC STYLE

For sixteen years after Bryan's defeat in 1896, Democrats had wandered in the political wilderness. The party, a patchwork of warring factions, could not impose internal discipline or win national elections. The Bryanites who controlled the presidential wing during most of this period stubbornly resisted challenges from eastern and southern conservatives, and from eastern city machines. Time vindicated Bryan: not his free-silver panacea, but his identification of plutocracy as the party's key political issue. Progressive Republicans, however, reaped most of the political benefits. Taking up the cause of antitrust, railroad regulation, tariff reduction, and other elements of the Populist and Bryan programs, they made reform respectable among the urban middle classes. By 1908, style and personality more than policies distinguished TR from Bryan.

Eventually the political tides began to shift toward the Democrats. Between 1904 and 1910 the party gained over ninety seats in Congress, with most gains coming in large states such as New York, Illinois, Pennsylvania, and Ohio. In 1910, Democrats regained control of the House for the first time in eighteen years. All signs pointed toward victory in 1912.

The Democratic revival resulted from several factors. In the major industrial states, where the party advanced most impressively, Progressive Republicanism was weakest. There standpatters could count on backing from businessmen and rural voters who elsewhere were more divided and inclined toward Progressivism. In Massachusetts, for instance, such Progressive proposals as tariff reduction and railroad reform threatened to deprive the state's economy of competitive advantages it enjoyed over other underdeveloped regions. Many workers and middle-class elements went along with the Old Guard, to protect the local economy. As a result Progressive sentiment, when blocked in the GOP, often sought an outlet through the Democratic party. And in New Jersey as well, where Progressivism first developed within the Republican party but ran into stiff opposition, the Democrats became the vehicle of reform.

The process worked differently in New York, however. The Tammany Hall machine in Manhattan, the most powerful organization in the country, was led by Irish-Catholic politicians who could count on the votes of the city's immigrant working class. But Tammany, like most other big city machines relying on the ethnic vote, remained indifferent, if not hostile, to a social justice movement dominated largely by Republican, Yankee, Protestant, middle-class men who also enlisted in "good government" crusades. Tammany Hall discovered, however, that reform could be made to pay off. In New York, rising young Tammany politicians like Alfred E. Smith and Robert F. Wagner became converts to the moral necessity and the political advantages of the welfare state. Not only would their own working-class constituents benefit from such measures as factory inspection and workmen's compensation laws, but by championing Progressive ideas, these men broadened their political base and won some Progressive middle-class and Republican support.

Woodrow Wilson: The Road to the White House

No one learned these lessons better than Woodrow Wilson, chief exemplar of Progressivism, Democratic style, the party's first president since Grover Cleveland. Born in Virginia, Wilson spent his early years in the South and imbibed the traditional Southern Democratic credo of laissez faire, weak government, and Negrophobia. He went to Princeton and then practiced law but, like Roosevelt, a conventional career repelled him. The law, he explained, was a profession akin to business, in which "money cannot be made except by the most vulgar methods." Rejecting business values for the more genteel academic life of a professor of political science, he taught and wrote about American government. Though he criticized corruption and the dispersal of power in late-nineteenth-century America (a weak presidency on one hand, and a strong Congress incapable of governing effectively on the other), he slighted the economic basis of politics, which Progressive social scientists were soon to rediscover. The United States Senate, he wrote in *Congressional Government* (1885), "is . . . separated from class interest," though at no time before or since was the upper house as subservient to the rich and powerful. He supported the war with Spain and American imperialism because he believed "the way to perfection lies along these new paths of struggle, of discipline, and of achievement."

Yet for all his conservatism and conventionality, Wilson remained troubled. In 1902 he became president of Princeton and called for rule by a disinterested elite devoted to the common good. He entitled his inaugural address "Princeton for the Nation's Service," and during the next eight years, he sought to make the university a counterpoise to the business world and its crass values. It should send forth young men "untouched from corrupt influences" who would become "a force in the life of a great nation." Seeking to transform Princeton from an anti-intellectual social club for young snobs into a university, and its students from "dilettantes into reading and thinking men," he backed far-reaching reforms in graduate and undergraduate education.

At first faculty and alumni supported him, but increasingly Wilson ran into opposition. Conservative alumni did not share Wilson's conception of the university and the ensuing battle made him more critical of standpatters. Wilson saw himself as a martyr in a fight for a new, more democratic university. "The great voice of America does not come from seats of learning," he said during his Princeton struggles; "it comes in a murmur from the hills and woods and the farms and factories." But his celebration of the common man stemmed primarily from the frustration of being thwarted by the same powerful elite which he felt was shirking its civic responsibilities.

Wilson had an extraordinary ability to sense and reflect the popular mood, and to express the hopes and fears of Progressive America. He was a man of limited interests, without TR's far-ranging involvement in science, art, and ideas; in 1916 Wilson admitted that he had not read a serious book in fourteen years. Yet he had a keen intelligence, enormous ambition, and a deeply religious nature. All these qualities proved serviceable. Raised as a Presbyterian, he possessed a strict Calvinist sense of duty and a belief that God had chosen him for great works. Yet beneath the stained-glass veneer, Wilson himself acknowledged there raged within something "like a fire from a far extinct volcano. . . ." To get along with Wilson, noted Edward House, his closest adviser in the White House, "never begin by arguing. Discover a common hate, exploit it, get the president warmed up and then start your business."

Unlike Roosevelt, Wilson entered politics late, but he also had backing from conservative party leaders. In 1906 he began speaking out on public questions as a conservative Democrat who opposed unions, accepted Big Business, and regarded government regulation as socialistic. Looking for a candidate to block Bryan's bid for a third nomination, a magazine publisher, George Harvey, and other New York businessmen adopted Wilson as their man. They arranged for New Jersey Democratic boss James Smith to back Wilson's nomination for governor, serving the triple purpose of giving the Jersey regulars a respectable candidate, one who could also turn back the rising Progressive challenge, and one who had a good chance to win.

Wilson became the first Democrat elected governor in a generation. His success in New Jersey and later his still greater triumphs nationally owed much to his overnight transformation from a conservative Democrat into a strong-talking Progressive. As early as 1908 he began to shift gears and call for "a new morality" that would achieve "social reunion and social reintegration." This required that privileged citizens, especially businessmen, "see to it that there be in his calling no class spirit, no feeling of antagonism to the people, to the plain men whom . . . to their great loss and detriment, [they] do not know."

As soon as he got the Democratic nomination for governor Wilson proclaimed his independence. "I am and always have been an insurgent," he boasted. Once elected, Wilson broke with Boss Smith, opposing his bid for election to the United States Senate, and boldly seized party leadership. Wilson adopted most of the program of the Progressive Republicans and through skillful leadership of his party and frequent soundings of public opinion, he succeeded where the Republicans had failed. Wilson's battle against the bosses and plutocracy quickly put him into the front ranks of Progressives, especially since his triumph came in an eastern industrial state, normally Progressivism's weakest ground. Wilson offered a coy explanation for his celebrity: "All of New Jersey . . . was tired of the game and was willing to try an unsophisticated schoolmaster because it was in search of somebody that didn't know how to play the old game." Wilson was, in fact, a shrewd, unsentimental practitioner of the new rules of the game that spelled political success in the Progressive era.

The 1912 Campaign

Wilson's goal, the White House, lay ahead. His shift to the left lost him the backing of the eastern conservatives and the machines, but these were waning forces. He had claims on Bryan supporters, since their man had withdrawn, and on southern Progressives, which he presented in successfully fighting his way to the Democratic nomination.

Wilson and Roosevelt, both Progressives, dominated the 1912 campaign. President Taft had to admit: "I think I might as well give up so far as being a candidate. There are so many people in the country who don't like me." Wilson campaigned for the "New Freedom" which would restore equality of opportunity. The Democratic party, he proclaimed, believed "that every man ought to have the interest of every other man at his heart . . . an ideal never before realized in the history of the world"—and still to be attained,

despite Wilson's two terms in office. He promised workers to advance their right to organize unions. And he promised the "great middle class . . . being crushed between the upper and nether millstones" of business and labor, who no longer originated or controlled economic activity, "to free the average man of enterprise in America, and make ourselves masters of our own fortunes once again. . . ."

Accusing Wilson of an unrealistic desire to turn the clock back to a simpler era when competitive small business had been practical, Roosevelt urged the country to accept the necessity of Big Business and allow government to regulate it. At the same time, he called for government welfare legislation to benefit women, children, and the working classes. When pressed by TR to explain how he would bring about the New Freedom, Wilson mentioned lower tariffs and increased competition in business. He warned that if government sanctioned and then tried to regulate monopoly, it would end in Big Business control of regulatory agencies. Competition must be restored, he insisted.

The Republican vote split and Wilson picked up support from Progressive independents and Republicans, holding traditional Democratic strongholds in the South. He won the election, though not a majority of the popular vote.

THE NEW FREEDOM

The next four years proved to be the high tide of Progressivism. Under Wilson, Democrats passed most of the programs Progressives had demanded for a decade. Even more than TR, Wilson dominated his party and made it an instrument of presidential leadership. The president benefited from the broad consensus on reform that had developed earlier. But he also displayed an astute sense of party leadership. His party controlled Congress, and there were no Democratic Aldriches or Cannons to water down White House demands. More than a third of the House Democrats were freshmen, the older leaders realized that the party had to demonstrate its capacity to govern, and the opposition remained divided.

Wilson made peace with the state and local machines that could deliver votes in Congress, and effectively mobilized public opinion.

Acting like a British prime minister who directly participated in managing the legislative branch, Wilson sent an ambitious program to Capitol Hill. He maneuvered it through in two years. First came downward tariff revision, a traditional Democratic goal. The president broke with precedent to deliver his tariff message in person, taking advantage of his skill as a public speaker. Resisting high-tariff lobbyists and protectionists in his own party, Wilson succeeded where other presidents had failed. The Underwood Tariff reduced duties, enlarged the free list, and made up the loss of revenue with an income tax authorized by the recently adopted Sixteenth Amendment (1913).

Financial reform followed. In 1911, Wilson had warned, "The great monopoly in this country is the money monopoly." The banking system, dating from the Civil War, had repeatedly revealed defects. The volume of currency and credit did not expand and contract according to business needs. Without a central bank, no way existed to mobilize reserves in times of crisis; capital tended to concentrate in a few large cities and the banking system served agriculture poorly. The Panic of 1907 sharply pointed up the problems and Congress created the National Monetary Commission (1909), headed by Senator Aldrich, to recommend changes.

But the bankers and politicians could not agree and reform remained an unresolved issue in 1912. It gained greater urgency as a result of the investigation of the "money trust" by a Senate committee. Louis D. Brandeis, a crusading lawyer who deserted Taft to become Wilson's leading adviser on economic questions, popularized its findings in a book called *Other People's Money* (1914). Brandeis argued that Morgan, Rockefeller, and a few other powerful financiers had a stranglehold over the economy through interlocking directorates and control of large capital. In the past, Brandeis argued, investment bankers —those who floated corporate securities—had performed useful functions by raising capital for business and inspiring confidence among in-

vestors. Not content with merchandising securities, a "financial oligarchy" had gained control of banks, trust companies, and insurance companies where they "manufactured" securities. According to Brandeis, "these banker-barons" created the trusts. They used "the people's own money" for their own ends and were able to "chill and check and destroy genuine economic freedom."

While most people agreed on the need for banking reform, they disagreed on its form. Wall Street bankers understandably favored a powerful central bank under private control. Big city bankers in the Midwest favored centralization but feared eastern domination, and rural bankers wanted a decentralized system that gave them a meaningful voice. The Bryan, or agrarian, wing of the party insisted on a publicly controlled system under which the government would issue currency. Wilson backed a compromise that set up twelve regional federal reserve banks to which all nationally chartered banks would belong. The district banks held reserves of member banks, which appointed a third of the directors. The Federal Reserve Board in Washington, appointed by the president, chose the other third and could expand or contract the credit supply. The Federal Reserve Act thus divided control between the regional banks and a central bank, between public and private central credit, and it created a money supply that expanded and contracted according to business needs. It did not, however, break up concentrations of financial power.

Country bankers in the South and Midwest and the leading Chicago bankers supported the president's scheme, as did some other businessmen. But the New York *Sun*, speaking for Wall Street, saw it as a "preposterous offspring of ignorance and unreason . . . covered all over with the slime of Bryanism." Despite such diehard opposition, Wilson united his party and Congress passed the Federal Reserve Act in December 1913.

Wilson and Big Business

The third major item on Wilson's legislative agenda was the trust question. Wilson wanted to help "the smaller businessmen and manufacturers . . . the men who ask only that they shall be given equal business opportunities with big trusts." His adviser, Brandeis, argued that competitive small business was more efficient and innovative than Big Business. The government should therefore promote efficient competition. At first Wilson inclined toward a new antitrust law, the Clayton bill, one which would define more precisely restraints of trade outlawed by the Sherman Act of 1890. But with prodding from Brandeis, he came to favor establishing a Federal Trade Commission with the mandate to prevent "unfair" methods of competition in interstate commerce.

The Federal Trade Commission Act (1914) emerged full of ambiguities. Brandeis conceived of it as an agency to police business and to curb the cutthroat competition which hurt small business; others thought Wilson had shifted to Roosevelt's position and accepted Big Business subject to federal investigation and control. Businessmen, as usual, divided. Some small businesses supported the act, hoping that government would allow voluntary efforts to end cutthroat competition. Others feared government collusion with Big Business, which in turn was uncertain how the new commission would act.

At the same time Congress passed the Clayton Anti-Trust Act (1914), shorn of its toughest provisions. The law left the burden of interpreting the Sherman Act to the courts. The Democrats also granted agricultural and labor organizations immunity from prosecution under the antitrust laws and restricted the use of injunctions against labor unions. The American Federation of Labor's Samuel Gompers hailed the bill as labor's "Magna Charta," though in practice it did little to curb issuance of injunctions (court orders against strikes and other union activities).

In 1914 Wilson announced that an era of reform had ended. "Ten or twelve years ago," he said, "the country was torn and excited by an agitation which shook the very foundations of her political life. . . ." Now as the result of Democratic reforms, he claimed, antagonisms between classes and the suspicions of businessmen were "done away with. . . . The future is clear and bright with promise of the best things." The most perceptive Progressives scoffed. The president, wrote

TR's friend Herbert Croly, had a mind which "is fully convinced of the everlasting righteousness of its own performances and which surrounds this conviction with a halo of shimmering rhetoric. He deceives himself . . . but he should not be allowed to deceive progressive public opinion."

Wilson's boasting tried to obscure a shift to the right which occurred partly in response to a recession late in 1913. Fearing that the voters would blame the downturn on the party in power and on reform, Wilson tried to reassure business. He made a series of pro-business appointments to the new regulatory bodies, and he resisted the demands for social welfare legislation to benefit farmers and workers. A federal child labor law, he said, would violate states' rights, and government credit for farmers was "class" legislation. The outbreak of war in Europe in 1914 ended the recession, and as the 1916 elections approached, Wilson leaned once more in a Progressive direction. Since the Democrats were a minority (winning but 42 percent of the 1912 vote), Wilson's chances for reelection hinged on his ability to assemble a broad-based Progressive coalition. He needed votes from Roosevelt Progressives, whose third party barely survived the 1912 defeat.

The president decided to shelve his traditional suspicions of welfare "class" legislation. He supported the Federal Farm Loan Act (1916), providing farmers with long-term loans at rates lower than available at commercial banks, and the Warehouse Act (1916) which helped them obtain short-term loans to finance crops. Wilson also went along with a national child labor law, the Adamson Act, establishing an eight-hour workday on railroads, and the much-needed Seamen's Act to improve working conditions in the American merchant marine. Finally the president appointed Louis Brandeis, "the People's Lawyer," to the Supreme Court. The Brandeis nomination raised a storm for two reasons: Brandeis was a symbol of Progressivism, and it stirred up latent antisemitism. He had spent twenty years fighting Big Business, was a leading exponent of sociological jurisprudence, and was certain to bring a liberal voice to the conservative court. And he was the first Jew to sit on the high bench.

Wilson's strategy worked. Leading Progressives like Jane Addams, Lincoln Steffens, and Washington Gladden supported his reelection, as did most farm and labor organizations. Wilson's Republican opponent, Charles Evans Hughes of New York, ran a poor campaign but a strong race, owing to the normal Republican majority and the return of many Roosevelt Progressives to the party fold. President Wilson won, barely, running well in the South, the West, and a few midwestern states. His failure to crack the populous Northeast revealed the precarious position of the Democratic party nationally and the divisions still existing within the ranks of Irish, German, and other traditionally Democratic ethnic groups. Their loyalty had been strained by Wilson's reaction to the outbreak of world war in Europe in 1914—a conflict involving their former fatherlands, and which ultimately would involve the United States as well.

THE PROGRESSIVE LEGACY

By the eve of America's entry into the First World War in 1917, the search for stability and social justice in industrial America had led many down new roads. Throughout most of their history Americans believed that a good society should give individuals maximum freedom to pursue their own interests. In the late nineteenth century, Americans insisted that government's proper role was to keep hands off the competitive race, allowing each man to succeed or fail according to merit or luck. In a simple, rural society, economic self-sufficiency insulated them from insecurity. But industrialism involved everyone—farmers, workers, businessmen—in a marketplace economy of uncertainty, insecurity and possible failure.

Businessmen were the first to cope successfully with the hazards of the new order. Corporations and trade associations dominated markets, suppressed competition, and commanded nationwide resources which assured their control and prosperity. But others found voluntary efforts less satisfactory. Labor unions and farm organizations in the late nineteenth century enjoyed limited success and ultimately both farmers and workers turned to government for help. By 1900,

middle-class Americans, together with patricians like Theodore Roosevelt, reacting to the economic misery of millions and the growth of class conflict, provided the impetus for reform.

Progressives came from rural as well as urban backgrounds. Some, like Wilson, longed nostalgically to restore a simpler society of small-scale competition, though they had no feasible way of doing so. Others, like TR, understood that they lived in an age of large organizations. But both strains of Progressivism despised plutocracy and fought to make government a counterweight, as TR put it, to "the dull, purblind folly of the very rich men, their greed and their arrogance."

Progressives wanted a government that favored neither particular classes nor sections, but which secured justice for all, and, strange to tell, they actually believed that they could reach that happy goal. Progressivism's hero was the disinterested citizen, public servant, or entrepreneur. Its vision was of a "community of interests," a society where "the welfare of each individual is dependent fundamentally upon the welfare of all of us." Its technique was to investigate and expose evils, call upon experts to formulate solutions, enact laws, and set up public agencies to curb private interests that threatened the general welfare. Fundamentally, the Progressives were moralists, political preachers reacting against an immoral world and a corrupt body politic.

Most Americans accepted the Progressive view as the best response to the problems of industrial America. A few dissented and embraced Socialism, which flourished more during the Progressive era than in any other period of American history. Under the direction of Eugene V. Debs, who led the Pullman Strike in 1894, the Socialist party steadily grew and in 1912 polled almost a million votes out of 15 million. Thereafter, its power waned. The party was a mixture of German and Jewish eastern working-class immigrants who brought their socialism with them from Europe, native-born members of the middle class deeply alienated by the results of unregulated capitalism, and some ex-Populists, notably in the Southwest. Socialists believed that only public ownership of the means of production could eliminate wars, depressions, and poverty.

They were most successful when they subordinated long-term plans for radical social change to immediate reforms, such as municipal ownership of transportation facilities or welfare legislation. But this smacked of Progressivism and opportunism and conflicted with the Socialists' contention that social justice and capitalism were incompatible. The more ideologically pure they remained, however, the less chance Socialists had to gain popular support. Most Americans, including poor farmers and workers, believed that they could improve their condition within the existing system. By ameliorating the conditions of the exploited and offering the discontented some prospects for reform, Progressives further weakened the Socialist appeal.

The First World War crushed the Socialists. The party split, with the majority opposing American intervention. Denounced as subversives, they became victims of government persecution, their presses seized, their leaders jailed or deported. The war, however, also transformed Progressivism. It unleashed an intolerant demand for national unity, and rehabilitated the prestige of the business community. Its outcome sapped faith in Progressivism and prepared the country for a decade—the 1920s—during which conservatives would steer the search for stability in new directions.

Chapter 24
Progressivism Overseas

During the first two decades of the twentieth century, Progressivism redirected American politics. Progressives seemed on the verge of creating a new society, one which would salvage the older values and virtues of agrarian America in a modern industrial nation, preserving individual freedom while securing social justice. Progressives also reshaped the conduct of foreign affairs, combining a commitment to promote national self-interest with idealistic notions of international relations and power politics. America, reforming itself, must also try to reform other societies, remodeling and uplifting international relations. In these ways Progressives would export American democracy, and thus shore up confidence in the worth and the universality of the American way of life.

With a mini-empire stretching from the Caribbean to the Philippines, and with overseas economic involvements growing rapidly, the United States became a Great Power, a position that rested on its industrial might. Theodore Roosevelt, the first president to grasp opportunities for world leadership, believed that the United States had the power to fulfill its mission to spread its influence around the world. His successor, Taft, emphasized economic penetration, but he lacked the diplomatic skill and leadership qualities of Roosevelt. In Woodrow Wilson, however, Progressive internationalism found its most authentic voice. As schoolmaster to the rest of the world, Wilson told other nations what constituted "right" conduct. He expected them to abide by his instructions, insisting that relations among nations be governed by moral criteria. After so many centuries of cynical and Machiavellian diplomacy, Wilson's views were at least refreshing. Inevitably, however, Wilson learned that ideals are the hardest commodity to export, especially when other people distrusted them as no more than a cloak for American self-interest.

Roosevelt used the big stick with small Latin American states, but he behaved differently toward major European powers. He thought that major powers had far greater responsibilities and must honor different codes. The United States could not dictate to Britain or Germany as it did to Cuba and Panama. And just as there were "good" and "bad" trusts, a policy appropriate for dealing with one Great Power might be useless or counterproductive with another. Wilson, on the other hand, wished to apply a single standard of behavior to all nations, though in the end he, like Roosevelt, favored Britain. Moreover, in Latin America, Wilson not only carried on TR's Big Stick policy, but he also spoke loudly in accents of benevolent paternalism, which South Americans took as a hypocritical cover for imperialist designs.

Predisposed to judge the morals of other peoples and nations, Wilson practiced the "diplomacy of righteousness." Despite its dangers, shortcomings, and ultimate failure, the president's insistence that foreign policy be shaped by a moral sense gave U.S. diplomacy a consistent rationale, and won for it much support both at home and overseas among those impressed by Wilson's eloquence and idealism. But eventually, perhaps inevitably, Wilson and his followers demanded too much. In leading the United States into World War I, as he said "to make the world safe for democracy," he set forth an impractical goal. The political aftermath of that war sowed the seeds for World War II, an even more devastating conflict twenty years later. Just as the Progressive view of America's domestic affairs collapsed in the 1920s, so too, Progressivism in foreign policy ended in disillusionment and disaster.

PROGRESSIVISM AND EXPANSION

Most Americans assumed that their country's imperialism differed from the European variety. Even many of those who initially opposed intervention in Cuba and annexation of the Philippines agreed that the American presence in overseas colonies would civilize backward peoples who came under their control. Americans would teach the "natives" through example and practice. By 1910, the imperial debate no longer centered on the right to rule others without their consent, but had shifted to a timid exchange over methods and timing. How long, for instance, Americans wondered, would it take Filipinos or Puerto Ricans before they could be left to their own devices?

The Progressive impulse thus helped Americans to justify imperialism. And many leading Progressives supported overseas missionizing, welcoming the acquisition of an empire of dependent communities. In 1898, such a stellar Progressive as Senator Albert J. Beveridge of Indiana dismissed the anti-imperialists: "The opposition tells us we ought not to rule a people without their consent. I answer, the rule of liberty, that all just governments derive their authority from the consent of the governed, applies only to those who are capable of self-government." The inhabitants of the new American colonies obviously had not shown such capabilities. And a year later, the man who personified the Progressive, small-town editor William Allen White of the Emporia, Kansas, *Gazette* declared: "Only Anglo-Saxons can govern themselves. . . . It is the Anglo-Saxon's manifest destiny to go forth as a world conqueror."

These were not isolated views. Many other Progressives, especially among the younger Republicans, shared them. Most either supported or acquiesced in Roosevelt's Big Stick policy. No Progressive senator opposed the Customhouse Treaty, which made the Dominican Republic a financial ward of the United States, and even during the Taft administration, Progressives did not mount a frontal attack on Taft's scheme of American penetration through Dollar Diplomacy. After 1912, ex-Republican Progressives, attacking the Wilson administration, became strident and jingoist upholders of American overseas ventures. The leader of the Vermont Progressives, bemoaning Wilson's alleged "weakness," longed for a leader "that will make Americans feel no matter where they go, no matter where they invest their capital, that they, their families, and their properties, will be respected and protected, and above all that our dear flag

will be honored." After 1914, Progressives increasingly emphasized the need for military preparedness and as the party's leaders drifted back into the Republican fold, domestic reform became submerged in demands for an aggressive foreign policy.

Progressives regarded themselves as men of extended vision. They called for an active, national government, one that would purify all it touched, whether at home or abroad. In the Western Hemisphere the need seemed clear. "In all probability," warned Herbert Croly, a leading Progressive intellectual, "no American international system will ever be established without the forcible pacification of one or more centers of disorder." He reminded his countrymen of the need "to introduce a little order into the affairs of the turbulent Central American republics," as had been done in Cuba.

After 1912, under Wilson, Progressive Democrats pursued a foreign policy similar in aims and methods to the Republicans. American imperialism became bipartisan. Both Taft and Wilson adopted precedents laid down earlier, yet each stamped American diplomacy with his own personality.

UNRULY LATINS

As in its domestic policies, so in international relations the Taft administration plodded along on the trail opened by Theodore Roosevelt. But everything Taft touched turned to trouble. The president and his secretary of state, an inept man with the improbable name Philander C. Knox, stressed the importance of economic penetration overseas, a policy which became known as "dollar diplomacy." In the Caribbean this became an economic counterpart to Roosevelt's hemispheric-policeman corollary to the Monroe Doctrine. As a form of preventive medicine, American bankers would displace European bondholders in the strategically sensitive but financially and politically unstable countries of Central America and the Caribbean (nations Americans disparagingly called "banana republics"). To forestall intervention by European investors, Taft urged Wall Street interests to take over the debt of Honduras in 1909, and of Haiti a year later. He wanted the "right to knock their heads together until they should maintain peace between them."

In Nicaragua in 1909, the president did some head-knocking. Trouble began when President José Santos Zelaya, an anti-American, tried to cancel concessions held by a U.S. mining corporation, and when rumors spread that Japan might receive a canal concession from Nicaragua, the dispossessed mining company instigated a revolt. Following the execution of two Americans who were aiding the rebel cause, U.S. Marines invaded, forcing Zelaya from power. A new president, formerly an employee of the mining company, took over with American blessing and Wall Street money, and served as an American puppet. With peace restored, a force of 2700 Marines stayed behind to guard the American legation and to prevent the rise of "Zelayism" in any form. The marines lingered in Nicaragua till 1933.

Roosevelt had moved cautiously in the Far East, but Taft and Knox blundered ahead with ambitious schemes and Wall Street dollars. TR had not paid much attention to American businessmen calling for stepped-up American investment in China and Manchuria. Knox proved more receptive, however. He favored full-scale American participation in such ventures as the European "consortium" to build railroads in China as one means of neutralizing Japanese and Russian power in Manchuria in order to maintain the Open Door. American bankers joined the consortium, but the project lapsed. When Knox further proposed internationalization of Manchurian railroads he antagonized the Japanese, threatening their sphere of influence on the Asian mainland and violating pledges TR had made to the Japanese. With ambitions that exceeded American power in the Far East, Knox had to retreat in the face of Japanese opposition.

American Imperialism, Democratic Style

The election of Woodrow Wilson seemed to promise new departures in foreign policy, since Taft had been a standpatter domestically and an interventionist overseas. Also, the Democratic party promised eventual Philippine independence and a reduction in naval spending. Wilson spoke eloquently as a voice of international liberalism, and chose as secretary of state William Jennings Bryan, a staunch anti-imperialist. Bryan immediately launched a campaign to cover the earth with bilateral arbitration treaties which would replace force with reason in international relations and abolish war. Though the American Senate placed limitations on arbitration, Bryan signed thirty treaties calling for settlement of disputes by nonbinding decisions of referees and for a one-year cooling-off period.

Despite these fine deeds and good intentions, and despite such qualified reversals in imperialism as increased autonomy for the Philippines and Puerto Rico and withdrawal from the Chinese consortium, Wilson did not abandon inherited policies. Democrats believed in the Panama Canal lifeline and the need for U.S. supremacy in the Caribbean as much as did the Republicans. Even Bryan favored the export of American capital to extend American influence, and vice versa. Ultimately Wilson and Bryan became champion interventionists themselves, driven by the missionary impulse and their desire to use America's great power to advance its interests; at the same time they thought they were promoting the good of all mankind. Desiring to enlighten, not to oppress, when they intervened, they gave themselves ample opportunities to spread the light.

Wilson continued Taft's Dollar Diplomacy in Nicaragua, and in 1915 extended it to Haiti and the Dominican Republic. Using the standby excuses of internal instability, failure to pay foreign debts, and alleged threats of European intervention, U.S. armed forces moved in, establishing American protectorates which lasted almost twenty years.

Mexico was another matter, one which created problems far greater than the limited vexations of Caribbean Dollar Diplomacy. Mexico, large and populous, cherished proud, nationalist traditions and was hostile to any outside interference. For four years (1913–1917) Wilson put himself and American power in the middle of the Mexican Revolution—for altruistic reasons, he thought—and aroused universal scorn and opposition from Mexicans.

Before the Revolution of 1910–1920, Mexico had been ruled for thirty-five years by dictator

Porfirio Díaz, while the Mexican upper class and foreign capitalists exploited the country. The United States had an investment of close to $1 billion in Mexico. Popular unrest toppled the aging Díaz's regime in 1911, and a liberal democrat, Francisco Madero, became president. But a new dictator named Victoriano Huerta murdered Madero in 1913, and expected to resume business as usual, in the fashion of Porfirio Díaz.

Although most nations recognized Huerta's government, Wilson found its butchery morally repugnant. Soon after becoming president, Wilson declared that he would recognize only those governments which had come to power through "orderly processes" and legal means, a clear break with the American, and world, precedent of recognizing governments in power, however dictatorial or revolutionary. Wilson's theory, abandoned by the U.S. government in 1930, applied to Huerta and represented a new form of American intervention in the affairs of Latin America. Wilson, the ex-professor, privately explained his purpose: "to teach the South American republics to elect good men."

Moral suasion and diplomatic ostracism failed to topple Huerta, however. A succession of new revolutions and counterrevolutions, with fresh parades of generals and would-be generals, bewildered Americans. In 1914, Wilson lost patience and overreacted over a trivial matter. When Mexican officials refused to apologize for briefly arresting several American sailors for firing a twenty-one gun salute to the U.S. flag, Wilson sents troops to occupy Vera Cruz for six months. Nineteen Americans and several hundred Mexicans paid with their lives for this nonsensical American desire to wave the Big Stick. In 1916, two years after Huerta's fall, Wilson's self-created troubles erupted again. Pancho Villa, hoping to ride to power on a wave of anti-Americanism, decided to provoke further U.S. intervention by killing Americans, first in Mexico, then across the border in New Mexico. Wilson dispatched the U.S. Army 300 miles into Mexico to hunt Villa, but the only result was a bloody skirmish with government troops. Happily, Wilson did not emulate President Polk, who seventy years before had gone to Congress following a

similar incident to declare that war existed "by act of Mexico."

Wilson's policy had helped to topple Huerta, though the era of Díaz-type dictatorship was over, whatever the American president did. In 1917 the Mexican Revolution entered a new phase. Under the leadership of Venustiano Carranza, Mexicans adopted a socialist path to modernization by attacking the immense wealth and power of the oligarchy and the Church. This time Wilson resisted pressures to intervene to protect American capital. He had learned that the diplomacy of righteousness was as risky as any other, and that direct military intervention in Mexico could become a quagmire if Mexicans, united at this time only in the belief that Mexican politics was *their* business, declined to become the pupils of the Schoolmaster of the North. Wilson, preoccupied with affairs in Europe, withdrew the troops from Mexico in February 1917. They would soon be needed elsewhere.

ROAD TO WAR

Europe's Hundred Years' Peace (1815-1914) created an illusion of permanent peace that blinded Americans as well as Europeans to the dangers of a general war. Plenty of danger signals had flashed, but most people in the Western world thought a balance of power assured the peace, and that neither diplomatic crises nor economic rivalry would explode into war. That dream ended in July 1914, when the assassination of the heir to the Austrian throne by a Serbian nationalist brought ultimatums, mobilizations, and finally declarations of war involving most of Europe.

Urging Americans to be "impartial in thought as well as in action," Wilson declared the United States neutral. Although most Americans clearly favored one side or the other, national sentiment stood overwhelmingly in favor of staying out of the struggle. Thus when Germany, ignoring treaty obligations, invaded unoffending Belgium for strategic reasons, and when American public opinion reacted in horror, the president made no official protest. And although the view that the war represented a struggle between Prussian militarism and British and French liberty gained increasing acceptance, Americans regarded it as a conflict which did not threaten their vital interests—it was a European war to be settled by Europeans.

These assumptions, together with American neutrality, became strained when Washington refused to embargo the sale of arms or food to nations at war. Consequently, Britain and France (the Allies), enjoying supremacy at sea, obtained vital supplies from the United States while denying them to Germany and its allies (the Central Powers). As the Allies exhausted their cash, Americans granted credits to maintain the flow of goods. Swelling to over $2 billion by the time the United States entered the war in 1917, these loans gave the United States an economic stake in the outcome of the struggle. Should France or Britain lose, American creditors would lose too.

Initially, Secretary of State Bryan had tried to prohibit or at least limit such loans to belligerents, calling such money as much "contraband" as guns. But war orders from Europe provided a needed spurt for the then sluggish American economy, and Bryan found little support within the administration for his stand. The United States simply could not remain neutral, however it acted. Embargoing all trade with Europe would benefit Germany, a land power which did not depend on foreign supplies. In claiming neutral rights to trade with all customers, the United States was in effect claiming the right to trade with the Western Allies. As the loans mounted, some observers believed that American involvement had become inevitable. As had happened more than a century before, when the United States sought to remain neutral during the Napoleonic Wars, so in 1914 most Americans favored the goal of neutrality but none could achieve it.

The Submarine Crisis

Wilson, however, tried, without abandoning his pro-Allied leanings. Controlling the surface of the sea, the British tried to blockade the Central Powers, Germany and Austria, by laying minefields in their harbors and seizing noncontraband materials. Wilson made halfhearted protests which the Allies promptly ignored, confident that the United States would not force the issue of defending its maritime rights to trade with *all* belligerents. As a result, America became an armory and warehouse for the Allies and upset the balance of power in Europe.

The German armies had been initially successful, but by 1916 the struggle became hopelessly stalemated, turning into a war of attrition. Germany sought to undermine Allied control of shipping lanes and cut off supplies from America by using the submarine, a weapon which revolutionized naval warfare. In February 1914, the Germans declared the waters around the British Isles a war zone, warning that vessels would be torpedoed without notice, and refusing to guarantee the safety of neutral ships. They hoped to starve out Britain, a food-importing nation, without pushing the United States into war. For two years the German high command was to argue over how most effectively to use the submarine without provoking American intervention.

Wilson warned Germany that it would be held to "strict accountability" for its acts. Britian and France were also expected to respect neutral rights, but since the Allies did not rely on submarines, they could seize property and impair the movement of U.S. ships without sinking American vessels or destroying American lives in violation of previously accepted rules of naval warfare. Submarines, however, struck from below the surface without warning at ships thought to be armed, and had little opportunity to rescue survivors. The spectacular sinking in May 1915 of the British passenger liner *Lusitania,* with over a thousand persons aboard (128 of them Americans), inflamed public opinion. It mattered little that the German embassy in the United States had warned against traveling on belligerent ships, or that the *Lusitania* carried war materials, not passengers alone. Americans reacted to the sinking with anger and horror. Wilson sent a note to Germany so stern that Bryan resigned from the cabinet in protest against what he regarded as a breach of neutrality and a step toward war.

Germany admitted neither guilt nor responsibility, but agreed to alter its submarine policy to avoid a showdown.

A final confrontation had been put off, but the United States remained terribly vulnerable to involvement. Wilson and his new secretary of state, Robert Lansing, insisted on the unrestricted right of U.S. citizens to travel on belligerent ships, a right of dubious value, yet one for which they seemed willing to commit the country to war. The impetuous or accidental act of a single German submarine commander could thus push America into the holocaust. Wilson realized the risk and at the same time he sent his personal adviser, Colonel Edward House, to Europe as a peace mediator. Allied leaders gave House some worthless encouragement for the sake of American public opinion, but both sides still hoped for military victory, with or without American aid. Until that notion exploded, mediation could not succeed. The bloodletting went on in Europe, as the United States watched warily.

Officially, Wilson continued to maintain his own neutrality. But an influential minority of Americans, especially persons of British ancestry, considered a British victory essential to the United States. If the Germans won, they argued, the world balance of power would shift in favor of an unfriendly and aggressive nation. The Anglophiles also argued that America's period of isolation had ended. Use of the submarine and the airplane convinced them that the old ways were gone. Within the interventionist minority only a few called for a U.S. declaration of war during the conflict's first two years; but they felt America could influence the outcome by providing all-out material aid to Britain and France, and it should do so in its own self-interest. Wilson admired British society and the British system of government but, unlike the interventionists, he feared the consequences of American involvement.

"Preparedness"

After the *Lusitania* crisis of 1915 fear of war spread in the United States. "Preparedness" became an American catchword which had varied meanings for different people. Some wanted to prepare for entry into the war in Europe; others wanted to prepare to defend the Western Hemisphere. Although preparedness groups like the American Security League had few members and were confined almost entirely to the Northeastern states, where Republican strength centered, they affected Wilson's thinking. The president, fearing Republicans would make political capital of the preparedness issue in 1916, shifted his course the year before, in favor of increased military spending, a navy eventually the equal of Britain's, and a larger regular army in place of the state-run National Guard.

Ex-President Theodore Roosevelt led the new jingoists and attempted to goad Wilson. Roosevelt, convinced that German victory menaced American interests, and believing all the reports of Germany "Hun atrocities" circulated by British propagandists, thought the country was shirking its duty by staying out of a war that was bleeding white the forces of "civilization." Those who disagreed, TR labeled "laggards" and "cowards," including the president.

Yet Wilson also came under powerful counterpressure from the other side of the political spectrum. Progressives and Democrats, especially in the Midwest, attacked the president's switch on preparedness. The antimilitarists, led by ex-Secretary of State Bryan, charged that Wilson would turn America into an armed camp. During the 1916 campaign, Wilson backtracked from his preparedness proposals in order to court the Progressive vote. The National Guard would not be scrapped. There would by an army increase, but the navy obtained the largest authorization for expansion. As always, it was easier to "sell" the navy to defense-minded congressmen than a standing army.

The Republicans bypassed Roosevelt to nominate Charles Evans Hughes, a moderate Progressive and Justice of the Supreme Court. Hughes, no fire-eater, rejected the interventionist demands, but Roosevelt insisted on campaigning for Hughes, much to the Democrat's delight and Wilson's benefit. The president, to be sure, talked up Americanism and patriotism, but he emphasized peace. Denouncing the GOP as the "war party," Democrats adopted the slogan, chanted at the nominating convention, "He kept us out of war." Wilson won reelection narrowly (277 to 254 electoral votes), with strong support in the South and West.

Within two months a change in German policy made a mockery of Democratic promises. At the urging of his military advisers, the Kaiser resumed unrestricted submarine warfare on February 1, 1917. All ships in the war zones, armed or not, belligerent vessels or not, were to be sunk on sight. Wilson broke diplomatic relations with Germany at once.

The president still hoped to avoid war, but diplomacy proved fruitless and further German sinkings presented the issue squarely. The drift toward war intensified as the result of two incidents. The British intercepted a German cable sent to Mexico City—the Zimmermann Telegram —proposing an alliance with Mexico in case of war with the United States, and promising the return to Mexico of Texas, New Mexico, Arizona, and California—territories Mexico lost to the Americans in 1836–1846. Meanwhile, on the other side of the globe, a revolution had toppled the Russian czar in March 1917 and had installed a short-lived democratic regime under Alexander Kerensky, to the delight of liberal opinion throughout the world. Since Russia was one of the Allies, the moral claims of their cause were no longer compromised by association with czarist oppression. On April 2, Wilson asked Congress to declare war on Germany, a country he accused of waging "warfare against mankind."

Wilson thought this step necessary to uphold vital American interests, but many at the time, and many historians since, have disagreed. The president justified going to war because he had previously warned, "I cannot consent to any abridgment of the rights of American citizens in any respect. The honor and self-respect of the nation is involved." Yet the patriotic and intolerant frenzy of war soon resulted in the abridgment of the fundamental rights of many American citizens to free speech and assembly.

Though Wilson stressed freedom of the seas in justifying the decision to go to war, the fundamental consideration was his belief that American and British security were closely linked. British naval supremacy and maintenance of a balance of power in Europe benefited the United States. But Wilson, a Presbyterian moralist in the White House, did not admit publicly that considerations of power politics had driven him to war just as earlier they had pushed him towards a pro-Allied neutrality. Since the defense of neutral rights seemed insufficient grounds, Wilson sold the war as a crusade to "make the world safe for democracy," a "war to end all wars." Catchy slogans and grandiose expectations evoked a powerful response from the American people, who now bent their energies to winning this "final" struggle.

THE NEW CRUSADE

At first the extent of America's commitment remained unclear. Some thought it sufficient for the United States to contribute only war materials to the Allied cause. But Britain and France, drawing on their final reserves, demanded men — millions of them. And even after forming sufficient divisions around the small regular army nucleus, massive problems of transportation and supply would have to be overcome.

First, America had to clear the sea lanes of enemy submarines. Germany had gambled that unrestricted submarine warfare would knock out the Allies before the United States could bring appreciable power to bear in Europe. German U-boats sank so many Allied and neutral ships in 1917 (close to a million tons in the peak month) that the gamble seemed about to pay off. British ships went down faster than British shipyards could build them, as one in four British sailings ended in a sinking. Germany appeared on the verge of achieving in the Atlantic what it could not accomplish on the fields of France.

American intervention, through the mobilization of massive American resources and a convoy system, upset the German plan. The U.S. Navy rushed to aid in antisubmarine warfare, particularly in convoying large groups of merchant vessels across the Atlantic, enabling a flood of American material and men to reach France. Only two troopships were torpedoed, and within six months overall losses in tonnage had dropped by two-thirds.

With the seas relatively safe the United

States transported an army of two million men to Europe, although skeptics still doubted that the unbloodied American infantry would prove effective. The Americans lacked military experience and began with inadequate and inferior equipment, but they came from an advanced technological society, well suited for modern warfare. And their huge numbers were bound to make a difference against a German army already drained by three years of total war.

To recruit a mass army, the United States relied on conscription for the first time since the Civil War. The system allowed no exemption for those wishing to buy their way out of military service, nor did widespread, violent opposition to the war erupt. The draft worked smoothly, and eventually almost five million men entered the armed forces. The draft age was set first at 21, not 19, as the Army wanted, and the areas surrounding military bases were to be kept clear of bars and brothels so as not to corrupt the innocent draftees. The troops, after several months training, shipped out to France, mostly in British transports. Thus during 1917, the first year of war for America, American soldiers trained and prepared for the struggle.

British and French generals welcomed the American troops but resented sharing the limelight with Americans. The American commander, General John J. Pershing, fresh from the Mexican border misadventure, would not allow his forces to be chopped up and thrown in the line wherever the Allied generals dictated. Although he permitted assignments of groups of Americans to Allied divisions in emergency situations, Pershing demanded that the U.S. Army fight as a unit, and he ultimately got his way.

The final German offensive of 1918 tested the wisdom of Pershing's determination and the mettle of the American army. Late in 1917, the Bolsheviks (Communists) seized control of the Russian government, heretofore an ally of France and Britain, and signed a separate peace treaty. No longer fighting on two fronts, Germany shifted military forces from the eastern to the western front. The attacks began early in 1918, long before the American army had grown to one million men, Pershing's minimum objective for an effective army. The Germans rolled the Allied line back at most points, including those held jointly with Americans, but by the summer of 1918 the force of the offensive had been spent. Meanwhile the British navy transported tens of thousands of American doughboys to Europe, and the A.E.F.—the American Expeditionary Force—became a reality while the German hope for victory faded. In August, Pershing launched his first offensive, lasting three months and involving over a million men. With German exhaustion becoming apparent, and with Allied strength growing from the infusion of American manpower, Berlin finally accepted armistice terms in November 1918.

It appeared that the virtuous power of the New World had offhandedly redressed the wickedness of the Old, and now Americans could retire, smug and serene, to the Western Hemisphere. American casualty rates among front line units ran high. But the American losses did not come close to matching the holocaust suffered by the European powers. Although Congress declared war in April 1917, a full year passed before an appreciable number of American soldiers were on the line. After six months of heavy fighting, the Americans had ended the war. It was perhaps a bit too easy, a bit too quick, for a nation now expected to play a role as a world leader. There was no time for war-weariness to develop, nor did the majority of American families suffer directly from the war. Instead the war evoked for Americans images of lighthearted songs, of patriotism and adventure, of pink-cheeked and innocent crusading doughboys, and of dashing pilots in their trim, French-built, Spad fighter planes. All of this obscured the horror of Europe's worst bloodbath in history, during which the toll for major battles had reached one million killed or wounded and the structure of modern Europe had been blasted away.

The Home Front

To support the American war effort overseas, the home front also enlisted in the crusade. The nation mobilized its abundant resources and retooled for war. To pay the cost of $44 million a day, the government depended on loans and taxation. Taxes provided about one-third of the money, and loans the rest. Since each method had its advocates, Treasury Secretary William G.

McAdoo, a good politician, mixed both alternatives. Besides selling government bonds to large investors, the treasury also tapped funds from ordinary citizens by pushing Liberty Loan drives. Parades and rallies (often attended by figures prominent in show business and professional sports) aroused the patriotic fervor of modest-income Americans who contributed their mite to the great crusade.

Mobilization strained the country's resources, but American abundance proved sufficient. Businessmen still regarded government regulation as suspect, if not socialistic. Yet modern warfare demanded government controls. Americans were reluctant, however, to coerce private enterprise. The War Industries Board, set up in July 1917 to allocate scarce materials and determine production quotas, failed because it lacked enforcement powers and had to rely on persuasion. Similarly, the head of the Food Administration, Herbert Hoover, a mining engineer who had supervised a food relief program in Belgium before America's entry into war, relied on voluntary cutbacks in domestic food consumption. Yet American farmers prospered during the war, as the government urged them to expand production and guaranteed commodity prices.

Good times extended to organized labor too. Although Wilson once told union members that they would either have to work or fight, he rejected the ideas of conscripting domestic labor. Instead, to keep men in the factories and avert strikes he set up the National War Labor Board under ex-President Taft. Higher wages proved the key to industrial peace; during the war real wages for organized workers rose 14 percent, despite inflation. Union membership almost doubled between 1914 and 1919 (reaching over four million), and the Wilson administration supported union demands for an eight-hour day and the elimination of child labor. In return, Big Labor (personified by Samuel Gompers of the AFL) promised cooperation with government and industry to maintain production, and watched approvingly as the government suppressed radical unionism, particularly the International Workers of the World (or "Wobblies") who were strong in the Rocky Mountains and Far West.

Americans suffered little during the war. The combination of heavy government spending and boom times produced inflation; but as prices climbed upward, wages followed in hot pursuit. The government did little to combat the inflationary spiral because it wished primarily to expand war production at any cost short of immediate economic deprivation. The war exacted a heavy price in taxes and a swollen national debt, yet the nation paid a still heavier price in the erosion of personal freedom.

PATRIOTS AND DISSENTERS

As often happens in war time, constitutionally guaranteed rights became one of the first casualties, since "during war, the laws are silent." The constitutional crisis of World War I took on several aspects, one relating to use of the general war powers by the federal government, the other to the problem of civil liberties in wartime.

On war powers, the Lever Act of 1917 gave the president almost unlimited leeway to assure uninterrupted production of war goods. The president by declaring an "extreme emergency" could take over factories and mines, and manufacturers and producers could not waste resources or limit production in food or fuel. The broad terms of the law, should he choose to enforce it, made Wilson virtual dictator over the economy and represented a radical departure from constitutional tradition in the direction of centralizing power in the national government. Congress, however, passed it with little delay or debate. The federal government also prohibited liquor in 1918, took over the railroads, and censored the mails. A few objected, but Elihu Root, a leading Republican, spoke for the majority when he condemned as unpatriotic "all attempts in Congress and out of it to hinder and embarrass the government . . . in carrying on the war with vigor and with effectiveness. Under whatever cover of pacifism or technicality such attempts are made, we deem them to be in spirit pro-German and in effect giving aid and comfort to the enemy."

Voluntarism proved the rule in industry, but in the field of civil liberties, dissenters suffered repression. Two months after Congress declared war, Wilson warned: "Woe be to the man or group of men that seeks to stand in our way." The president was as good as his word. Convinced that he had done everything humanly possible to keep America out of war, he now demanded uncritical support. He thought a united homefront should back up the sacrifices of the front-line soldiers. While preaching liberal internationalism abroad ("Peace without victory," he promised the world), at home he conducted the war with an intolerance that equated dissent with treason.

Although a majority supported the president, some minorities opposed American involvement. Many, especially midwestern Progressives led by La Follette, doubted that Germany threatened American vital interests. German-Americans and Irish-Americans found themselves in difficult situations. Both groups remained loyal to America, but one became suspect because of its attachment to the old country, Germany, and the other for its undying hatred of America's ally, Britain, at a time when Irish nationalists were battling for their independence from Britain. Besides ethnic dissenters, socialists and other radicals also opposed the war. To counteract the dissidence Wilson set up a propaganda machine, the Committee on Public Information, run by George Creel, a Progressive journalist, to manipulate public opinion in favor of the war and to suppress criticism. The president justified the suppression of seditious or even "negative" news in order to maintain wartime morale. Creel was extremely touchy about criticism of Allied nations. Thus any article friendly to Irish independence would affront Great Britain. The foreign language press, especially the German newspapers, had to be extra careful. Socialists or radicals, the strongest foes of the war, were hardest hit. Socialist papers, attacking the war as a capitalist struggle in which the workers died to enrich the bosses, were closed down.

Repressing Dissent

Creel first had to intensify fear and hatred of Germany. In 1917 the object of immediate danger became the Germanic "Hun." Allied propaganda had already shown the way by creating an image of Germans as Hun barbarians who violated all the rules of civilized behavior. The Germans were depicted as ruthless militarists, invaders of innocent Belgium who had shelled French cathedrals and committed unspeakable

atrocities as an everyday matter of policy. The propagandists grossly exaggerated, for the Kaiser's Germany was not Hitler's Nazi Germany. But Hun-baiting became popular and led Americans to rename sauerkraut "liberty cabbage," ban German music, prohibit German language teaching, and harass German-Americans in countless ways. Wilson encouraged intolerance by attacking "hyphenates," those naturalized Americans "who have poured the poison of disloyalty into the very arteries of our national life." Such persons had to be "crushed."

Congress obliged with the Espionage Act of 1917, and a year later added the Sedition Act. The laws established new categories of crimes: causing insubordination in the armed forces; obstructing the draft; and making false statements which impeded military operations. The government also received comprehensive powers to censor all subversive utterances. The Sedition Act, specifically directed at radicals, forbade Americans to "utter, print, or publish disloyal, profane, scurrilous, or abusive language about the form of government, the Constitution, soldiers and sailors, the flag, or uniform of the armed forces . . . or by word or act oppose the cause of the United States."

With or without legal authority, the administration quickly moved to stamp out dissent. In response, civil libertarians formed what was to become the American Civil Liberties Union (ACLU), trying to uphold free speech and defend the rights of conscientious objectors and political radicals. They failed, and by late 1917 the government had effectively banned any publications considered antiwar. Wilson blandly denied the existence of any reign of terror: "certain copies of certain newspapers were excluded from the mails because they contained matter explicitly forbidden by law." He did not question the constitutionality of that law. The president would not allow any actions or utterances which he thought stabbed American soldiers in the back.

Dissenters turned to the courts for help, but the Supreme Court turned a deaf ear to radical pleas. By the time the cases reached the Court in 1919-1920, the country writhed in the grip of the Red Scare, a time of intense fear of Russian Bolshevism and domestic sedition. Undoubtedly influenced by these fears, the court held unanimously (*Schenck* v. *U.S.*, 1919) that freedom of speech was not absolute and the right did not permit people to urge draftees to refuse induction. Justice Oliver Wendell Holmes wrote the unanimous opinion that those who advocated draft resistance presented a "clear and present danger" to the prosecution of the war. The war did not justify suspension of the Bill of Rights, but it did permit greater limitations on free speech than would be tolerated in peacetime. Holmes argued that just as no one could lawfully abuse free speech by shouting "Fire!" in a crowded theater, so too free speech had its limits, especially in wartime.

The "clear and present danger" doctrine, though applied in a case which limited free speech, provided a reasonably libertarian standard for determining when the state could limit this right. It thus afforded more potential protection for dissenters than the "bad tendency" doctrine to which the court reverted in *Abrams* v. *U.S.* (1919). When the court upheld the convictions of persons protesting the presence of American troops in Russia, it permitted the government to suppress acts and statements that even vaguely tended to impede the war effort. In aiding revolutionary Russia the defendants inevitably hindered the U.S. war effort against Germany, ruled the court, and "men must be held to have intended, and to be accountable for, the effects which their acts were likely to produce." In another case involving socialist leaflets, *Pierce* v. *U.S.* (1920), the court scored the "tendency to cause insubordination, disloyalty, and refusal of [military] duty." Justice Mahlon Pitney wrote, with apparent seriousness, of the "common knowledge" of all Americans, including the defendants, that the socialist version of America's entry into the war was false, and that President Wilson had explained the true reasons in his war message of April 1917!

Two justices, Holmes and Louis D. Brandeis, dissented in the *Abrams* and *Pierce* cases. Holmes now argued unsuccessfully that "the ultimate good is better reached by free trade in ideas; that the best test of truth is the power of the thought to get itself accepted in the competition of the market." But the court majority thought otherwise; the "bad tendency" doctrine determined civil liberties decisions for another twenty years.

WILSON'S DREAM OF PEACE

The more Americans suppressed liberty at home, the more anxiously they pursued it abroad. Wilson believed that competition among the Great Powers had produced the war, that balance-of-power politics was inherently unstable and must lead to conflict. He also held that a new international order could not achieve peace without granting freedom to oppressed peoples. To prevent future wars, the old methods of diplomacy, alliances and secret deals based on power, must give way to open agreements openly arrived at and based on justice. Colonial peoples must be put on the road to freedom; ethnic minorities must enjoy self-determination. Nations must disarm and respect freedom of the seas.

Well before America entered the war, Wilson tried to play the role of mediator and architect of a "peace without victory," one that would be lasting and just. America's entry into the war did not change his goals. In January 1918, Wilson laid down principles for a new international order in the Fourteen Points. The first thirteen dealt with general freedoms and specific territorial problems; the Fourteenth Point called for the establishment of an international peacekeeping body, the League of Nations. When Germany accepted the Fourteen Points, France and Britain, which had no intention of treating the defeated Central Powers liberally, gave qualified and reluctant approval to appease Wilson.

Germany hoped to base its surrender in November 1918 on the Fourteen Points. The flight of the Kaiser to Holland had broken what remained of German morale, and capitulation meant that an Allied showdown on war aims could no longer be postponed. Wilson sent Colonel House to Paris, and when Allied leaders professed ignorance of the Fourteen Points, House read them aloud. The British objected to blanket guarantees of freedom of the seas; the French demanded ironclad guarantees against Germany, which should be made to pay war damages (or reparations) for destruction in France. A Wilsonian peace without victory, let alone without vengeance, seemed a remote possibility.

Wilson, however, remained optimistic. He needed full support from the American people and from moderate Republicans as well as Democrats. But hard-line Republicans denounced him as "soft" on Kaiserism. Theodore Roosevelt spent the final year of his life running off at the mouth against Wilson, and this kind of harrassment pushed the president into a blunder. He made peace a partisan issue in the congressional elections of November 1918. "A Republican majority in either House of Congress," he warned "would certainly be interpreted on the other side of the water as a repudiation of my leadership." Wilson lost this gamble, not because Americans repudiated his leadership in foreign affairs, but because local and purely domestic matters such as discontent over inflation and high taxes largely influenced the outcome of the midterm elections. The president painted himself into a corner, staking his leadership at the peace conference on a vote of confidence at home. His failure to get that vote, on top of Allied resistance to the Fourteen Points, doomed the chances of achieving "Peace Without Victory."

Thereafter, Wilson's sense of political realities deserted him. He would need the votes of two-thirds of the Senate to approve whatever treaty he brought home. A political scientist, author of a book called *Congressional Government* (in which Wilson referred to the Senate as the president's "overlord"), he nevertheless antagonized potential supporters in both parties by his intransigence and excessive personal involvement. He decided to go to Paris as head of the American delegation, even though some advised that he could negotiate more rigorously by staying in Washington. Wilson also ignored the Senate and selected but one Republican, a second-line diplomat, instead of appointing a broadly based peace commission. He took the risk in order to exclude Henry Cabot Lodge, Republican chairman of the Senate Foreign Relations Committee, who was unalterably opposed to a Wilsonian settlement. Leaving Lodge at home, however, left the senator free to organize the domestic opposition.

The Treaty of Versailles, 1919

Wilson arrived in Europe armed with tremendous moral force and considerable, though lessened, political power. Before the conference began at Versailles, outside Paris, the president toured several Western European countries. The European "man in the street" hailed him as a savior, a flattering response which doubtless made Wilson overconfident. But the negotiating sessions with the leaders of the western Allies, David Lloyd George of Britain, Georges Clemenceau of France, and Vittorio Orlando of Italy, soon brought Wilson back to the realities of international geopolitics.

There was no way to reconcile Wilson's desires for a generous and thus presumably a lasting peace with the Allies' demands for security and reparations for war damage: Northern France lay devastated after four years of war, and Clemenceau and the French wanted none of "peace without victory"; in Britain, Lloyd George had just won parliamentary elections with the figurative promise the he would "Hang the Kaiser"; Italians wanted to complete their reunification by annexing Austrian land on their northern border, and they wanted an overseas empire as well. In east Central Europe, historically recognized nationalities—the Poles, the Czechs, and the Hungarians, among others—demanded independence from the now-defunct Austro-Hungarian, Russian, and Ottoman empires. "National self-determination," they chanted, and their slogan aroused the sympathy of Wilsonian idealists, while it clashed with the security demands and power pretensions of stronger states.

Germany, the principal Axis power, was the key to the Versailles deliberations. France required security against renewed German aggression: Clemenceau demanded the border provinces of Alsace and Lorraine, lost to Prussia in 1871, and he wanted to establish pro-French buffer states in the German Rhineland. Wilson agreed concerning Alsace and Lorraine. National self-determination seemed to sanction that, but he balked over the Rhineland buffer states. Clemenceau yielded, finally, when Wilson agreed to a U.S.-French security pact (never put into force), demilitarization of the Rhineland, and severe limitations on German armed forces.

Wilson fared worse on the disposition of colonies and on reparations. The Allies stripped Germany of African and Asian possessions and divided them among themselves, ignoring the wishes of the colonial peoples. With a nod to Wilsonianism, the Allies agreed to hold their newly won colonies as "mandates" under the League of Nations. The Allies demanded and got promises of staggering reparations payments that placed an impossible burden on Germany's economic recovery.

Wilson agreed to these compromises largely because he put supreme faith in the final section of the treaty: the covenant which established the League of Nations. From this, all good things would spring. The president made the league an inextricable part of the treaty and gave the league responsibility for enforcing the treaty. Clemenceau thought the league useless without its own armed forces, but having obtained the pledge of an American security treaty for France he allowed Wilson a free hand on the league article of the treaty. Lloyd George was not so negative about the league, thinking that it could serve a useful purpose with proper cooperation among the great powers. But all recognized the league as Wilson's child and knew that without the full support of the United States a League of Nations could not prosper.

The Treaty of Versailles, like any agreement touching so many vital world issues, could not please everyone, let alone conform strictly to Wilsonian ideals. It violated national self-determination several ways, as when Italy received territory inhabited by 200,000 German-speaking people. Wilson accepted these compromises because he felt that on balance the settlement represented a good start toward permanent peace. Most of the Fourteen Points had been honored, and the defeats over colonies and reparations he considered inevitable. A forceful American role in the league might repair much of the damage. Wilson thought he had come as close as possible to his goals, and all agreed that if Wilson had abandoned the negotiations to the Allies they would have imposed a far more punitive, or Carthaginian, peace.

Wilson's Agony

In joining the league covenant with the treaty, Wilson knew he risked losing all. Even as the president sailed home, opposition mounted.

Lodge circulated a Senate protest against the Versailles Treaty which obtained thirty-nine signatures. Still this did not rule out an accommodation. Only a handful of the protestors were dead set against *any* international league. The majority wanted substantive changes, such as a reaffirmation of the Monroe Doctrine, but not emasculation of the Wilsonian scheme. Yet Wilson did nothing to bring together the wide spectrum of internationalists, even though in the Senate more than the needed two-thirds favored some sort of treaty.

Wilson, after months of bargaining and compromise in Paris, now refused to bargain or compromise in Washington. Lodge, knowing he could not defeat the treaty outright, introduced fourteen reservations, and while his committee dawdled over the treaty, anti-league sentiment grew. Refusing to make meaningful concessions, the president decided instead to take his case to the people during an 8000-mile tour in September 1919. For several weeks he addressed enthusiastic crowds, but in Colorado a partially paralyzing stroke forced him to return to Washington and seclusion.

The Senate voted on the treaty, now a political orphan, in November 1919. Seventy-seven senators voted in favor of some kind of treaty. But neither those who favored the version with the Lodge reservations, nor those following the president's lead, could command the needed votes. At the showdown, the president lost touch completely. He would not release the Democratic senators to vote as they pleased on the reservations, would see no one, and Mrs. Wilson "censored" his mail and messages. One of the adamant anti-Wilson senators chortled: "We can always depend on Mr. Wilson. He never has failed us." On the second vote the treaty had lost by only seven votes. Wilson, as irreconcilable as his opponents, had committed what one historian labels "infanticide"; he had killed his own brainchild.

The treaty died, and so too did hope for American participation in the league. Wilson, though beaten, refused to give up. He called on American voters to make the presidential election of 1920 a "solemn referendum" on the league. The Democratic defeat of 1918 was a prelude to a debacle in 1920; the "solemn referendum" ended in a landslide victory for the GOP and Warren Harding, a triumph that dramatically confirmed the death of the Progressive view. For over two decades, Progressives had sought stability at home and security abroad. The quest would continue, but in the third decade of the twentieth century Americans followed new leaders who promised, in Warren Harding's ill-chosen words, "not nostrums but normalcy."

SUGGESTIONS FOR FURTHER READING

Suggestions for further reading are highly selective. Works available in paperback editions are starred (*). Students should consult the bibliographical pamphlet by Arthur S. Link and William M. Leary, Jr., *The Progressive Era and the Great War* (1969)*, for additional references.

INTRODUCTION

General Works on Progressivism and the First World War

Samuel P. Hays, *The Response to Industrialism, 1885-1914* (1957)*; Robert H. Wiebe, *The Search for Order, 1877-1920* (1967)*; Harold U. Faulkner, *The Quest for Social Justice, 1898-1914* (1931); Walter Lord, *The Good Years: From 1900 to the First World War* (1960)*; Otis L. Graham, Jr., *The Great Campaigns: Reform and War in America, 1900-1928* (1971)*; Richard Hofstadter, *The Age of Reform* (1955)*; Gabriel Kolko, *The Triumph of Conservatism* (1963)*.

CHAPTER 20

General

Foster R. Dulles, *The Imperial Years* (1956)*; H. Wayne Morgan, *America's Road to Empire* (1965)*; Ernest R. May, "American Imperialism," *Perspectives in American History,* vol. 1 (1967), pp. 123-286; John A. S. Grenville and George B. Young, *Politics, Strategy, and American Diplomacy . . . 1873-1917* (1966); Charles S. Campbell, Jr., *Anglo-American Understanding, 1898-1903* (1957); Bradford Perkins, *The Great Rapprochement: England and the United States, 1895-1914* (1968).

Expansionism: Need and Rationale

David M. Pletcher, *The Awkward Years . . . Foreign Relations under Garfield and Arthur* (1962); William E. Livezey, *Mahan on Sea Power* (1947); William D. Puleston, *The Life and Work of Captain Alfred Thayer Mahan* (1939); Thomas F. McGann, *Argentina, the United States, and the Inter-American System, 1880-1914* (1957); Walter LaFeber, *The New Empire . . . American Expansion, 1860-1898* (1963)*; Howard B. Schonberger, *Transportation to the Seaboard: The "Communication Revolution" and American Foreign Policy, 1860-1900* (1970); William A. Williams, *The Roots of the Modern American Empire* (1969)*.

The Cuban Crisis

Julius W. Pratt, *Expansionists of 1898* (1936)*; Ernest R. May, *Imperial Democracy* (1961); Joseph E. Wisan, *The Cuban Crisis as Reflected in the New York Press* (1934); William A. Swanberg, *Citizen Hearst* (1961)*.

War and Empire

Walter Millie, *The Martial Spirit* (1931)*; Richard Hofstadter, "Manifest Destiny and the Philippines," in Daniel Aaron (ed.), *America in Crisis* (1952); Christopher Lasch, "The Anti-Imperialists, the Philippines, and the Inequality of Man," *Journal of Southern History,* vol. 24 (1958), pp. 319-331; Fred H. Harrington, "The Anti-Imperialist Movement," *Mississippi Valley Historical Review,* vol. 22 (1935), pp. 211-230; Robert L. Beisner, *Twelve Against Empire: The Anti-Imperialists* (1968); Julius W. Pratt, *America's Colonial Experiment* (1950); David F. Healy, *The United States in Cuba, 1898-1902* (1963); Edward J. Berbusse, *The United States in Puerto Rico, 1898-1900* (1966); Merze Tate, *The United States and the Hawaiian Kingdom* (1965); Frank T. Reuter, *Catholic Influence on American Colonial Policies, 1898-1904* (1967).

Open Door in Asia

A. Whitney Griswold, *The Far Eastern Policy of the United States* (1938)*; William R. Braisted, *The United States Navy in the Pacific, 1898-1907* (1958); Thomas J. McCormick, *China Market: America's Quest for Informal Empire, 1893-1901* (1967)*; Tyler Dennet, *John Hay* (1933); Paul A. Varg, *Open*

Door Diplomat: The Life of W. W. Rockhill (1952); Paul A. Varg, *Missionaries, Chinese, and Diplomats* (1958); Raymond A. Esthus, "The Changing Concept of the Open Door, 1899-1910," *Mississippi Valley Historical Review,* vol. 46 (1959), pp. 435-454; Charles Vevier, *The United States and China, 1906-1913* (1955); Raymond A. Esthus, *Theodore Roosevelt and Japan* (1966); Charles E. Neu, *An Uncertain Friendship: Theodore Roosevelt and Japan* (1967); Roy W. Curry, *Woodrow Wilson and Far Eastern Policy* (1957).

Canal and Corollary

Howard K. Beale, *Theodore Roosevelt and the Rise of America to World Power* (1956)*; Dwight Miner, *The Fight for the Panama Route* (1940); Charles D. Ameringer, "The Panama Canal Lobby," *American Historical Review,* vol. 68 (1963), pp. 346-363; J. Fred Rippy, "Antecedents of the Roosevelt Corollary of the Monroe Doctrine," *Pacific Historical Review,* vol. 9 (1940), pp. 267-279; Seward W. Livermore, "Theodore Roosevelt, the American Navy, and the Venezuelan Crisis of 1902-1903," *American Historical Review,* vol. 51 (1946), pp. 452-471; Robert A. Hart, *The Great White Fleet: Its Voyage Around the World* (1965); David H. Burton, "Theodore Roosevelt's Social Darwinism and Views on Imperialism," *Journal of the History of Ideas,* vol. 26 (1965), pp. 103-118.

CHAPTER 21

The Gospel of Reform

Charles H. Hopkins, *The Rise of the Social Gospel in American Protestantism* (1940); Walter Rauschenbush, *Christianity and the Social Crisis* (1907)*; Aaron I. Abell, *The Urban Impact on American Protestantism, 1865-1900* (1943); Henry F. May, *Protestant Churches and Industrial America* (1949)*; Herbert A. Wisbey, Jr., *Soldiers Without Swords . . . the Salvation Army* (1955); Aaron I. Abell, *American Catholicism and Social Action* (1960)*.

The Intellectual Revolution

Henry S. Commager, *The American Mind* (1950)*; Morton White, *Social Thought in America: The Revolt Against Formalism* (1949)*; Benjamin G. Rader, *The Academic Mind and Reform . . . Richard T. Ely* (1967); Samuel Chugarman, *Lester Frank*

Ward (1965); Joseph Dorfman, *Thorstein Veblen and His America* (1934); George R. Geiger, *John Dewey in Perspective* (1958); Arthur G. Wirth, *John Dewey as Educator* (1966); Richard Hofstadter, *The Progressive Historians: Turner, Beard, Parrington* (1968)*; Bernard C. Borning, *The Political and Social Thought of Charles A. Beard* (1962).

David W. Noble, *The Paradox of Progressive Thought* (1958); Charles Forcey, *Crossroads of Liberalism: Croly, Weyl, Lippmann* (1961)*; Henry F. May, *The End of American Innocence . . . 1912-1917* (1959)*; Christopher Lasch, *The New Radicalism in America, 1889-1963* (1965)*; Fred C. Jaher, *Doubters and Dissenters: Cataclysmic Thought in America, 1885-1918* (1964).

The Making of Progressives

Frederic C. Howe, *The Confessions of a Reformer* (1925)*; Jane Addams, *Twenty Years at Hull House* (1910)*; Dorothy R. Blumberg, *Florence Kelley: The Making of a Social Pioneer* (1966).

The Process of Reform

David M. Chalmers, *Social and Political Ideas of the Muckrakers* (1964)*; Stanley K. Schultz, "The Morality of Politics: The Muckrakers' Vision," *Journal of American History,* vol. 52 (1965), pp. 527-547; Frank L. Mott, *A History of American Magazines* (4 vols., 1930-1957); Peter Lyon, *Success Story . . . S. S. McClure* (1963); Lincoln Steffens, *The Autobiography of Lincoln Steffens* (1931)*; Robert H. Wiebe, *Businessmen and Reform: A Study of the Progressive Movement* (1962)*; James Weinstein, "Organized Business and the City Commission and Manager Movements," *Journal of Southern History,* vol. 28 (1962), pp. 166-182.

Quest for Social Justice

Robert H. Bremner, *American Philanthropy* (1960)*; Robert H. Bremner, *From the Depths: The Discovery of Poverty in the United States* (1956)*; Gordon Atkins, *Health, Housing and Poverty in New York City, 1865-1898* (1947); Roy Lubove, *The Progressives and the Slums . . . in New York City* (1962); Roy Lubove, *The Professional Altruist: The Emergence of Social Work as a Career* (1965)*; Allen F. Davis, *Spearheads for Reform: The Social Settlements and the Progressive Movement* (1967)*; Lillian D. Wald, *The House on Henry Street* (1915).

Jeremy P. Felt, *Hostages of Fortune: Child Labor Reform in New York State* (1965); Elizabeth H. Davidson, *Child Labor Legislation in the Southern Textile States* (1939); Joseph A. Hill, *Women in Gainful Occupation, 1870-1920* (1929); Hyman Weintraub, *Andrew Furuseth: Emancipator of Seamen* (1959).

CHAPTER 22

The Urban Crisis

Lincoln Steffens, *The Shame of the Cities* (1904)*; Harold Zink, *City Bosses in the United States* (1930); Nancy J. Weiss, *Charles Francis Murphy . . . in Tammany Politics* (1968); Humbert S. Nelli, "John Powers and the Italians: Politics in a Chicago Ward, 1896-1921," *Journal of American History,* vol. 57 (1970), pp. 67-84; Zane L. Miller, *Boss Cox's Cincinnati: Urban Politics in the Progressive Era* (1968)*; William D. Miller, *Memphis during the Progressive Era* (1957); George M. Reynolds, *Machine Politics in New Orleans, 1897-1926* (1936); Walton E. Bean, *Boss Ruef's San Francisco* (1952)*.

Urban Reform

Roy Lubove, "The Twentieth Century City: The Progressive as Municipal Reformer," *Mid-America,* vol. 41 (1959), pp. 195-209; Samuel P. Hays, "The Politics of Reform in Municipal Government in the Progressive Era," *Pacific Northwest Quarterly,* vol. 55 (1964), pp. 157-169; J. Joseph Huthmacher, "Urban Liberalism and the Age of Reform," *Mississippi Valley Historical Review,* vol. 49 (1962), pp. 231-241; Frank M. Stewart, *A Half-Century of Municipal Reform . . . the National Municipal League* (1950); James B. Crooks, *Politics and Progress . . . Urban Progressivism in Baltimore* (1968).

State Progressivism

Richard M. Abrams, *Conservatism in a Progressive Era: Massachusetts* (1964); Robert F. Wesser, *Charles Evans Hughes: Politics and Reform in New York, 1905-1910* (1967); Irwin Yellowitz, *Labor and the Progressive Movement in New York State* (1965); Ransom E. Noble, Jr., *New Jersey Progressivism Before Wilson* (1946); Hoyt L. Warner, *Progressivism in Ohio* (1964); Robert S. Maxwell, *La Follette and the Rise of the Progressives in Wisconsin* (1956); Belle C. and Fola La Follette, *Robert M. La Follette* (2 vols., 1953); Forrest McDonald, *Let There Be Light: The Electric Utility Industry in Wisconsin* (1957); Stanley F. Caine, *The Myth of a Progressive Reform: Railroad Regulation in Wisconsin, 1903-1910* (1970); Arthur S. Link, "The Progressive Movement in the South," *North Carolina Historical Review,* vol. 23 (1946), pp. 172-195; Sheldon Hackney, *From Populism to Progressivism in Alabama* (1970); Louis G. Geiger, *Joseph W. Folk of Missouri* (1953); George E. Mowry, *The California Progressives* (1951)*.

CHAPTER 23

General

George E. Mowry, *The Era of Theodore Roosevelt, 1900-1912* (1958)*; Horace S. and Marion G. Merrill, *The Republican Command, 1897-1913* (1971).

TR and the GOP

Henry F. Pringle, *Theodore Roosevelt* (1931)*; John M. Blum, *The Republican Roosevelt* (1954)*; William H. Harbaugh, *Power and Responsibility . . . Theodore Roosevelt* (1961)*; Willard B. Gatewood, Jr., *Theodore Roosevelt and the Art of Controversy* (1970); Robert H. Wiebe, "The Anthracite Strike of 1902; A Record of Confusion," *Mississippi Valley Historical Review,* vol. 48 (1961), pp. 229-251; Robert H. Wiebe, "The House of Morgan and the Executive, 1905-1913," *American Historical Review,* vol. 65 (1959), pp. 49-60; Emma Lou Thornbrough, "The Brownsville Episode and the Negro Vote," *Mississippi Valley Historical Review,* vol. 44 (1957), pp. 469-493; Nathaniel W. Stephenson, *Nelson W. Aldrich* (1930); Richard W. Leopold, *Elihu Root and the Conservative Tradition* (1954)*; Dorothy Fowler, *John Coit Spooner* (1961).

TR and Reform

J. Leonard Bates, "Fulfilling American Democracy: The Conservation Movement," *Mississippi Valley Historical Review,* vol. 44 (1957), pp. 29-57; Samuel P. Hays, *Conservation and the Gospel of Efficiency* (1959)*; Elmo R. Richardson, *The Politics of Conservation* (1962); James Penick, Jr., *Progressive Politics and Conservation* (1968); Oscar E. Anderson, *The Health of a Nation: Harvey W. Wiley and the Fight for Pure Food* (1958); Arthur M. Johnson, "Antitrust Policy in Transition, 1908," *Mississippi Valley Historical Review,* vol. 48 (1961), pp. 415-434.

Insurgency

Kenneth W. Hechler, *Insurgency* (1940); James Holt, *Congressional Insurgents and the Party System* (1967); Stanley D. Solvick, "William Howard Taft and the Payne-Aldrich Tariff," *Mississippi Valley Historical Review*, vol. 50 (1963), pp. 424-442; William R. Gwinn, *Uncle Joe Cannon, Archfoe of Insurgency* (1957); Russel B. Nye, *Midwestern Progressive Politics* (1951)*; Richard Lowitt, *George W. Norris: The Making of a Progressive* (1963); George E. Mowry, *Theodore Roosevelt and the Progressive Movement* (1946)*.

Democratic Progressivism

Arthur S. Link, *Woodrow Wilson and the Progressive Era* (1954)*; Arthur S. Link, *Woodrow Wilson* (5 vols. to date, 1947—); John M. Blum, *Woodrow Wilson and the Politics of Morality* (1956)*; William Diamond, *The Economic Thought of Woodrow Wilson* (1943); Laurence R. Veysey, "The Academic Mind of Woodrow Wilson," *Mississippi Valley Historical Review*, vol. 49 (1963), pp. 613-634; Alexander L. and Juliette L. George, *Woodrow Wilson and Colonel House: A Personality Study* (1956)*; Alpheus T. Mason, *Brandeis* (1946).

The New Freedom

J. Laurence Laughlin, *The Federal Reserve Act* (1933); Thomas C. Blaisdell, Jr., *The Federal Trade Commission* (1932); Robert K. Murray, "Public Opinion, Labor, and the Clayton Act," *Historian*, vol. 21 (1959), pp. 255-270; A. L. Todd, *Justice on Trial: The Case of Louis D. Brandeis* (1964); Arthur S. Link, "The South and the New Freedom," *American Scholar*, vol. 20 (1951), pp. 314-324; Richard M. Abrams, "Woodrow Wilson and the Southern Congressmen," *Journal of Southern History*, vol. 22 (1956), pp. 417-437; Nancy J. Weiss, "The Negro and the New Freedom: Fighting Wilsonian Segregation," *Political Science Quarterly*, vol. 84 (1968), pp. 61-79.

CHAPTER 24

General

Julius W. Pratt, *Challenge and Rejection: The United States and World Leadership, 1900-1921* (1967); Arthur S. Link, *Wilson the Diplomatist* (1957)*; Harley Notter, *The Origins of the Foreign Policy of Woodrow Wilson* (1937).

Progressivism and Expansion

William E. Leuchtenberg, "Progressivism and Imperialism . . . 1898-1916," *Mississippi Valley Historical Review*, vol. 39 (1952), pp. 483-504; Herbert Ershkowitz, *The Attitude of Business Toward American Foreign Policy, 1910-1916* (1967); Merle E. Curti, *Bryan and World Peace* (1931).

Unruly Latins

Samuel F. Bemis, *The Latin American Policy of the United States* (1943)*; Wilfred A. Calcott, *The Caribbean Policy of the United States, 1890-1920* (1942); Dana G. Munro, *Intervention and Dollar Diplomacy in the Caribbean, 1900-1921* (1964); David A. Lockmiller, *Magoon in Cuba: A History of the Second Intervention, 1906-1909* (1938); George Baker, "The Wilson Administration and Cuba," *Mid-America*, vol. 46 (1964), pp. 48-74; Howard F. Cline, *The United States and Mexico* (rev. ed., 1963)*; Robert E. Quirk, *An Affair of Honor: Woodrow Wilson and the Occupation of Veracruz* (1962); Clarence C. Clendenen, *The United States and Pancho Villa* (1961).

Road to War

Daniel M. Smith, "National Interest and American Intervention, 1917: An Historiographical Appraisal," *Journal of American History*, vol. 53 (1965), pp. 5-24; Walter Millis, *Road to War* (1935)*; Ernest R. May, *The World War and American Isolation, 1914-1917* (1959)*; John Milton Cooper, Jr., *The Vanity of Power: American Isolationism and the First World War, 1914-1917* (1970).

Charles Seymour, *American Neutrality* (1935); Richard W. Leopold, "The Problem of American Intervention in 1917," *World Politics*, vol. 2 (1950), pp. 404-425; Daniel M. Smith, *Robert Lansing and American Neutrality* (1958); James M. Read, *Atrocity Propaganda, 1914-1919* (1941); Armin Rappaport, *The British Press and Wilsonian Neutrality* (1951); Clara E. Schieber, *The Transformation of American Sentiment toward Germany, 1870-1914* (1923); Fritz Fischer, *Germany's Aims in the First World War* (1967); Edward H. Beuhrig, *Woodrow Wilson and the Balance of Power* (1955)*.

The New Crusade

Seward W. Livermore, *Politics Is Adjourned: Woodrow Wilson and the War Congress* (1966); Ernest L. Bogart, *War Costs and Their Financing* (1921);

William C. Mullendorf, *History of the United States Food Administration* (1941); G. B. Clarkson, *Industrial America in the World War* (1923); Randall B. Kester, "The War Industries Board, 1917-1918," *American Political Science Review*, vol. 34 (1940), pp. 655-684; Margaret L. Coit, *Mr. Baruch* (1957); Daniel R. Beaver, *Newton D. Baker and the American War Effort, 1917-1919* (1966).

Arno J. Mayer, *Political Origins of the New Diplomacy, 1917-1918* (1959)*; N. Gordon Levin, Jr., *Woodrow Wilson and World Politics: America's Response to War and Revolution* (1968)*; George F. Kennan, *Russia Leaves the War* (1956)*; George F. Kennan, *The Decision to Intervene* (1958)*; Betty M. Unterberger, *America's Siberian Expedition* (1956).

Patriots and Dissenters

James R. Mock and Cedric Larson, *Words That Won the War: The Story of the Committee on Public Information* (1939); George Creel, *Rebel at Large* (1947); Ray H. Abrams, *Preachers Present Arms . . . Wartime Attitudes . . . [of] the Clergy* (1933); Sidney Kaplan, "Social Engineers as Saviors: Effects of World War I on Some American Liberals," *Journal of the History of Ideas*, vol. 17 (1956), pp. 347-369; Christopher Lasch, *American Liberals and the Russian Revolution* (1962).

Horace C. Peterson and Gilbert C. Fite, *Opponents of War, 1917-1918* (1957); Carl Wittke, *German-Americans and the World War* (1936); Michael Wreszin, *Oswald Garrison Villard: Pacifist at War* (1965); James Weinstein, "Anti-War Sentiment and the Socialist Party," *Political Science Quarterly*, vol. 74 (1959), pp. 215-239; Ray Ginger, *The Bending Cross: A Biography of Eugene Victor Debs* (1949)*; Howard H. Quint, *Forging of American Socialism* (1953)*; David A. Shannon, *The Socialist Party* (1955)*.

Zechariah Chafee, Jr., *Free Speech in the United States* (1941)*; John M. Blum, "Nativism, Anti-Radicalism, and the Foreign Scars, 1917-1920," *Midwest Journal*, vol. 3 (1950), pp. 46-53; Theodore Draper, *The Roots of American Communism* (1957)*; Harry N. Scheiber, *The Wilson Administration and Civil Liberties* (1960); Philip Taft, "The Federal Trials of the I.W.W.," *Labor History*, vol. 3 (1962), pp. 57-91; Donald D. Johnson, *The Challenge to American Freedoms: World War I and the . . . American Civil Liberties Union* (1963)*.

Wilson's Dream of Peace

Thomas A. Bailey, *Woodrow Wilson and the Lost Peace* (1944)*; Thomas A. Bailey, *Woodrow Wilson and the Great Betrayal* (1945)*; Ruhl J. Bartlett, *The League to Enforce Peace* (1944); Harold Nicolson, *Peacemaking, 1919* (1933); Arno J. Mayer, *Politics and Diplomacy of Peacemaking* (1967); Victor S. Mamatey, *The United States and East Central Europe, 1914-1919* (1957); Louis L. Gerson, *Woodrow Wilson and the Rebirth of Poland* (1953); Louis A. R. Yates, *The United States and French Security, 1917-1921* (1957); Russell H. Fifield, *Woodrow Wilson and the Far East . . . the Shantung Question* (1952).

Wolfgang J. Helbich, "American Liberals in the League of Nations Controversy," *Public Opinion Quarterly*, vol. 31 (1968), pp. 568-596; Joseph P. O'Grady (ed.), *The Immigrants' Influence on Wilson's Peace Policies* (1967); John A. Garraty, *Henry Cabot Lodge* (1953); Edwin A. Weinstein, "Denial of Presidential Disability: A Case Study of Woodrow Wilson," *Psychiatry*, vol. 30 (1967), pp. 376-391.

Part Six
The Big Changes, 1920-1930

Introduction

The common life-styles of present-day America emerged in the second and third decades of the twentieth century, the product of a hundred years of industrialization and urbanization. Turn-of-the-century Americans like William McKinley would have felt like aliens in the Roaring Twenties. By then the balance had shifted decisively from rural and small-town America to metropolitan America and the Mass Society that would shape the future.

In this new world, more than ever before, science and technology, applied by large organizations, became the masters. They produced unprecedented affluence and revolutionized older modes of living. America became a nation of consumers working to buy an endless variety of goods undreamed of by previous generations. The automobile, a triumph of mass production, came within the reach of a majority of American families in the 1920s. And other consumer durables, including an array of electric appliances from telephones to washing machines, promised to transform the American home.

The Age of Mass Consumption, spurred by a dramatic surge in national income, was also an Age of Leisure. Americans worked less, earned more, and played more often than in any time in their history. The advance and diffusion of technology meant also a simultaneous revolution in communications. Movies and radio brought inexpensive entertainment to the most remote places. And these new media, triumphs of the marriage between scientific research and Big Business, spread the culture of the city—its jazz and jokes, its folkways and foibles across a continent. This growth threatened to end regional, local, and ethnic diversity. Main Street no longer nestled in the hills or on the plains, safely isolated from Broadway.

For over half a century people had been abandoning rural America for the cities. Now the metropolis began to spread its tentacles into the countryside. By 1930 almost 60 percent of the population lived in towns of 2500 or more. The auto enabled urban Americans to build suburban subdivisions ringing the cities. At the same time movies and radio reduced the cultural isolation of the hinterland. At last the nation was becoming one.

As in the past the price of social change proved high. Americans were torn between traditional values and new standards quickly adopted by young people. Now more than ever, science rather than religion promised to unlock the secrets of the universe, and with waning faith came moral attitudes that transformed interpersonal relations. Women seeking first-class citizenship tried to work out more satisfying roles in society. The family lost cohesiveness as its members made greater demands for autonomy that weakened the authority of the once powerful patriarch. And men and women experimented with new attitudes toward sexuality which made sensual pleasure an integral part of the pursuit of happiness, not the occasion for the growth of guilt complexes.

Yet as greater affluence and new technology were standardizing their lives, Americans reacted uneasily and with a sense of loss. Society changed more rapidly than ever and the country seemed fragmented. The gulf between old and new ways strained relations among Americans, raising unsettling questions about the nature of the national mission.

Wilson's war "to make the world safe for democracy" had ended in bitterness and cynicism. America's allies had toyed with Wilsonian principles of self-determination for all peoples, but were unwilling to make a peace that had a reasonable chance of preventing another bloodbath. Having entered the war supposedly to fulfill a global mission, the Treaty of Versailles, so at variance with this high expectation, left Americans bewildered and frustrated. Full of doubts about their role in history, they began to doubt themselves. Many turned against their neighbors and against historic traditions of generosity, idealism, and tolerance. Convinced that in them alone reposed purity and virtue in a world dominated by corruption and evil, Americans sought to isolate themselves from sin.

This loss of confidence also bred distrust at home. Although Americans grasped at the fruits of modern society, especially its creature comforts, they felt threatened. Science undermined ancient faiths; new life-styles that emphasized leisure, consumption, and pleasure flouted the tried-and-true virtues of hard work, thrift, and self-denial. Metropolitan centers were now more than ever the wellsprings of the threatening forces of modernism. In the cities lived hordes of immigrants and their ambitious, second-generation offspring, all alien in religions and habits, and all pushing for equal opportunity. Cities also housed the offices of the country's most powerful banks and corporations; they nourished Bolshevism and other frightening radicalisms, such as bohemianism, agnosticism, libertinism—in short, every *ism* but Americanism.

Fear bred hate, and hate bred repression. For a while hysteria gripped the country. Government, employing police state tactics, ran roughshod over individual liberties, while courts acquiesced. Dissenters went to jail, aliens were shipped back to Europe, and the gates clamped shut to keep out immigrant foreigners. A constitutional amendment banned all alcoholic beverages, a measure Prohibitionist forces urged as a powerful blow against immorality, poverty, and urban vice of every imaginable kind. Some state governments forbade the teaching of Darwinian evolution in the belief that in so doing they struck a mighty blow against science and modernist threats to the Old-Time Religion. For some, however, legal means of repression were too slow and gentle. A revivified Ku Klux Klan spread across the country, north and south, instilling fear in Catholics, Jews, blacks, and nonconforming white folks whom the hooded vigilantes threatened with cross-burnings and beatings.

By the middle of the 1920s fear and anxiety were subsiding, due primarily to a very sharply improved standard of living. Americans became preoccupied with getting and spending, convinced more than ever that the business of America was business. The Progressive spirit faded; attacks on Big Business and cries for social justice for the poor and weak went unheeded. Organized labor declined in the face of hostility from public opinion and government, and sharp employer counterattacks stunted union growth. After two decades of prosperity, agriculture experienced a decline in the 1920s and farm organizations also encountered frustration in their fight for a larger share of national wealth.

For twelve years (1921–1933) the Republican party ruled the country— largely purged of its Progressive elements and dominated by its Eastern, business-oriented conservative wing. The GOP, accurately reflecting the national mood, met only token opposition from the disorganized and divided Democrats.

Millions of Americans did not share the comforts created by national affluence, but they were ignored. The complacent majority believed euphorically that the genius of American business would abolish poverty and assure permanent prosperity. Against these sentiments the skeptics and the distressed made little headway. Then, in October 1929, the Roaring Twenties ended. The Great Stock Market Crash ushered in the worst depression in American history, destroying confidence in business leadership and forcing Americans to search for new leadership and new directions. The pressures of intense crisis helped resolve many ambivalent attitudes toward modernity. Americans, even rural Americans, became more willing to discard repression, anti-intellectualism, bigotry, and businessmen's folk wisdom and to rely on science and expertise, centralized power and political bureaucracies, pluralism and tolerance to restore prosperity.

For two decades the Progressives had preached the gospel of a new social morality. They had tried to reduce conflict and promote social stability but rhetoric alone did little to alter the central tendencies in American life that alarmed them—the loss of individual initiative, the fragmentation of society, the specter of class warfare, and the concentration of power in large business bureaucracies. Many knew that they could not turn back the clock to a simpler time, yet they groped ineffectively to redistribute power, to harness business in the public interest, to protect the weak, and to promote social cohesion. The failures of the middle-class reformers in the first two decades of the century, particularly their unwillingness to risk substantial changes in the system, meant the surrender of the 1920s to the complacent. Standpatters held on until overtaken by events beyond their control, events few Americans could fully comprehend. But knowledgeable or not, all shared responsibility in the new national disaster that engulfed the country in 1929.

Mr. and Mrs. John Morton listening to the radio with earphones, 1924. *(Minnesota Historical Society)*

The crowd that gathered outside Warners' Theatre to see the opening of the first sound motion picture, August 6, 1926. (Culver Pictures)

The poet Robert Frost, 1921. (Yankee Magazine)

Calvin Coolidge campaign headquarters in Minneapolis, 1924. (Minnesota Historical Society)

Autos parked at Nantasket Beach,
Massachusetts, Fourth of July holiday,
early 1920s. *(Culver Pictures)*

Park guide changing tire for girl in
Minnehaha tourist camp, c. 1925.
(Minnesota Historical Society)

Two sailors on shore leave, Hawaii, 1925. *(Courtesy of W. H. Davis)*

Listening to auto radio, 1922. *(Culver Pictures)*

The battle of the century, 1927.
Alfred P. Sloan *(left)* and Henry
Ford. *(Culver Pictures)*

"It seems there was a negro and an Irishman and a Jew—"

(Above left) A lynching, 1920s. *(Above)* From *Judge* magazine, August 16, 1924. *(Left)* Tri-City Social Club. *(Culver Pictures)*

Sacco-Vanzetti sympathizers, Union Square, New York, August 9, 1927. (*Wide World Photos*)

The stock market slump, New York *Times* headline, October 29, 1929. (*Brown Brothers*)

Chapter 25
The Age of Mass Consumption, 1900–1930

The United States entered the twentieth century the world's richest nation. In the first thirty years of the new century (1900-1930), affluence transformed the daily lives of Americans more profoundly than in the preceding three hundred years. Technological advances created new industries and revolutionized existing ones. By 1930, Americans communicated by telephone, drove to work in cars, ate canned food, bought national brands under the hypnotic influence of multimedia advertising, and spent evenings beside the radio or in the movie theater. A generation earlier they had communicated by mail, traveled to work on foot or by streetcar, ate home-made food (even at lunch time), bought loose soap and crackers from the grocer's barrels, and looked forward to the infrequent visits of a traveling circus or vaudeville show. Good or bad, the Big Change had come.

This transformation of life-styles depended on enormous advances in basic industry in the late nineteenth century. In 1900 steel was the leading manufacturing industry; thirty years later, automobile making was king. But the mass production of consumer durables such as cars could not have come without existing capacity for the mass production of steel, rubber, glass, paint, and gasoline. Nor would the early car makers have found many customers had not rising family incomes created a mass market for their product. Yet new industries (like autos, electric power, and telephones) themselves generated growth in national income. Detroit created enormous demand for all the products that went into automobiles, and it employed thousands of workmen who became customers for cars, electric appliances, movies, and telephones. In this way technology, diffused by mass production at low cost, became a self-generating process that dramatically raised the standard of living in the United States.

These changes occurred unevenly. Periods of growth alternated with recessions, the most rapid advances coming after 1914. The outbreak of war in Europe generated a boom in the United States that lasted until a short, though severe postwar depression (1921-1922). Then the economy surged forward to new highs until toward the end of the decade the boom lost momentum and collapsed in 1929, plunging the country into a ten-year depression. Until then, people had marveled at a productive system that made Americans the first to enter the Age of Mass Consumption.

THE SOURCES OF GROWTH

For most of their history, Americans counted on a rapidly growing population to develop their virtually unpeopled but resources-rich continent. By 1900 there were seventy-five million Americans, making the country one of the world's most populous, and in the next thirty years the figure grew to almost 125 million. Until the outbreak of the First World War in 1914, immigrants kept flooding in. Then in the 1920s Americans abandoned unrestricted immigration. Henceforth, the country's growth would depend primarily on the birthrate of native-born stock, and that declined sharply between 1900 and 1930, falling by a third. Family size also shrank, the result of urbanization, the diffusion of new personal values, and the spread of birth control.

Output grew much more rapidly than population. In 1900 gross national product per person was $800; by 1930 it reached $1100. The 1920s, a decade of pronounced economic progress, saw 60 percent of this advance. Developments in technology, and their widespread diffusion through mass production techniques, account in part for the economy's high performance. Manufacturing output led the way, growing three times faster than population. By 1920 the manufacturing sector generated almost three times the percentage of national income originating in agriculture. Yet despite this dominance by manufacturing, industry employed about the same percentage of the labor force—a fifth—in 1930 as in 1900, a percentage held steady by remarkable

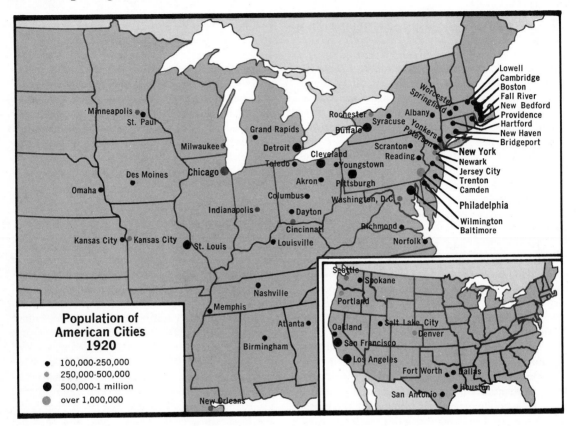

Population of American Cities 1920

- ● 100,000–250,000
- ● 250,000–500,000
- ● 500,000–1 million
- ● over 1,000,000

gains in labor productivity. A shift in occupational distribution became apparent in the 1920s, heralding future trends. By 1930 a smaller percentage of the work force found jobs in industry than a decade earlier, but expanded employment opportunities had emerged in various service industries—trade, finance, and government—industries which formed an increasingly large, lower middle class of white-collar workers.

Consumer durables and construction were the foundations of the boom in the 1920s. The dynamic role played by railroads and heavy industry in the late nineteenth century fell now to the cities. Urbanization continued to spark growth, with its endless demand for new residential housing, new office buildings and factories, sewage and water systems, and electric power. But in the Age of Mass Consumption, consumer durables—cars, household furnishings, appliances—also became one of the underpinnings of national prosperity, and automobiles led the way.

THE EMERGENCE OF DETROIT

In the 1890s a handful of companies began to manufacture automobiles powered by the recently developed internal-combustion gasoline engine. At first, cars were expensive playthings of the rich. Then in 1908, Henry Ford, an auto manufacturer who had begun by producing high-priced cars, reached out for the mass market with the famous Model T. Within a generation, autos had become America's leading manufacturing industry, transforming the national economy and its landscape.

At the outset, Ford explained his philosophy of building a car within the reach of the average family. "I will build a motor car for the multitudes," Ford announced. "It will be large enough for the family but small enough for the individual to run and care for. It will be constructed of the best materials, by the best men to be hired, after the best designs that modern engineering can devise. But it will be so low in price that no man making a good salary will be unable to own one—and enjoy with his family the blessings of hours of pleasure in God's great open spaces."

By exploiting the economies of standardization, division of labor, and mechanization through the introduction of the moving assembly line, Ford dramatically reduced the cost of manufacturing this highly complex product. By the 1920s, Ford made good his boast. The price of Ford's Model T had fallen from $850 to $310, and the Ford Motor Company became one of the most profitable business enterprises in history.

At the outset, many car manufacturers competed for the new markets. Initial capital requirements were small (Ford started with $28,000). Wall Street and Big Business all but ignored this small, unproved, risky business. By the 1920s, however, cars had become the biggest business of all. Three firms, then as now, dominated the industry—Ford, General Motors, and Chrysler—and Wall Street became deeply involved in their finance and management, especially with General Motors. The advantages of large-scale manufacture and enormous capital requirements now effectively excluded small manufacturers, a pattern that had developed earlier in heavy industry during the late nineteenth century.

Yet Ford's early methods proved inappropriate once the cars had become widely diffused. In the 1920s, General Motors seized the auto industry's leadership and has maintained it ever since. Founded in 1908 by William C. Durant, a manufacturer of horse-drawn carriages, General Motors started as a conglomeration of loosely integrated auto companies such as Buick, Oldsmobile, and Chevrolet, and of several auto parts suppliers. Durant was a master salesman and empire builder but, like Ford, he failed to weld his company into an effectively administered unit. The postwar recession (1921–1922) severely hurt General Motors and brought in new management with fresh strategies, infusions of Wall Street money, and methods which soon made General Motors the industry leader.

By the mid-1920s the market for new cars was becoming saturated at existing levels and distribution of national income. The problem then was to sell cars to people who already owned them. General Motors began innovations in mar-keting. It developed a wide line of cars appealing to different tastes and pocketbooks, from the phenomenally successful and low-cost Chevrolet to the luxurious Cadillac. It stressed style and comfort, relying heavily on advertising, and offered customers annual model changes, trade-in allowances and installment credit. And General Motors developed efficient structures and procedures for administering a large corporation, realizing that it could no longer depend on expanding output to lower costs and assure satisfactory profit margins.

Because General Motors was so large and complex, top management freed itself from day-to-day operational responsibilities. It concentrated on coordinating product flow, maximizing use of resources, developing statistical and financial controls vital to planning intelligently for the future. Operational responsibilities, however, were decentralized in the various divisions involved in the manufacture of parts and accessories or assembly under the overall supervision of the general offices. These reforms of internal management provided the solution for efficiently managing this giant enterprise and they became a model for other Big Businesses.

Innovation meant profits for General Motors. Ford's failure to adjust to changing conditions had made that company No. 2. Previously, Ford succeeded by building a simple, standardized single product, the Model T. When few persons owned cars, everyone wanted the utilitarian Ford flivver which came in only one color—black. Ford's strategy was to achieve maximum cost-savings through standardization. In the 1920s, however, Americans became increasingly willing to sacrifice economy and utility for styling and glamor, but Henry Ford refused to change: "We want to construct some kind of machine," he insisted stubbornly, "that will last forever. . . . We never make an improvement that renders any previous model obsolete." Ford ruled his great empire single-handedly, but severe losses ultimately convinced him of the obsolescence of his own strategy. Ford finally changed and brought out new models; but not until after he died did the Ford Motor Company in the 1940s undergo the basic transformation that had helped make General Motors one of the world's largest corporations.

Ford became the greatest of the businessmen heroes. An amused but impressed British traveler observed: "Just as in Rome one goes to the Vatican and tries to get audience of the Pope, so in Detroit one goes to the Ford Works and endeavours to see Henry Ford." People listened to Ford's opinions and indulged his crotchets even on subjects he knew nothing about; and there were many of these, since Ford's genius did not extend beyond auto mechanics. His enormous wealth and status as folk hero assured him an audience for whatever ideas he wished to propound—including anti-Semitism. Ford was both naïve and shrewd, simultaneously the architect of the new technological America *and* the high priest of the American cult of nostalgia for a simpler, rural America. He spent millions on constructing a mythical small town, Greenfield Village, which when contrasted with his mammoth River Rouge assembly plant reveals him as a man of divided loyalties, a cultural schizophrenic. More than any other single individual, Ford helped to modernize America, yet this supreme innovator could lament with apparent sincerity: "It was an evil day when the village flour mill disappeared."

The automobile industry provides a dramatic example of a common process of economic development. New technologies increased productivity, reduced costs, and expanded markets in a self-generating cycle. New machines powered either by gasoline engines or run by electricity intensified and diffused the advantages of mechanization. A new textile loom enabled a worker to tend three times as many machines; new machinery mechanized bottle production, put farmers on tractors, and drastically reduced the cost of steel and cement. Between 1900 and 1930 urban America also became electrified, as new inventions sharply cut the costs of electricity.

Developments in one industry revolutionized others. The internal-combustion engine, for instance, transformed oil, rubber manufacturing, and agriculture. Entrepreneurs now systematically began to finance research to develop new products and manufacturing methods. Companies in the more advanced industries were the first to appreciate the possibilities of institutionalizing technological progress. Thus General Electric which began primarily as a manufacturer of electric motors, generating equipment, and light bulbs developed electric appliances, plastics, and metal alloys. Du Pont moved from explosives into dyes, paint, and cellulose. In this way, divisions of research and development in the modern, large corporation systematized technological change upon which rapid economic growth depended.

THE STRUCTURE OF MASS MARKETING

With manufacturing output growing three times faster than population, business had to develop new techniques of distributing and advertising products and, just as important, new ways to finance consumer purchases. Chain stores began garnering larger shares of the retail dollar, especially in foods and drugs. Woolworth's and other "five-and-dime" stores took business away from specialty shops, and the mail-order houses opened large retail outlets in the new suburban neighborhoods, at the expense of downtown department stores. As in manufacturing, so in retailing, Big Business could undersell small business because it enjoyed economies of scale. Sears, Roebuck & Company, for instance, manufactured some of the merchandise it sold or put its own label on goods while dictating the price and quality to its suppliers.

When food, clothing, and rent had used up most of the consumer's budget, people needed little credit. By the 1920s, however, consumers were purchasing expensive, durable goods produced by the new industries, and they were buying them on time. Installment credit enabled people to buy now and pay later, instead of saving until they could afford a washing machine or a car. As people went into debt to acquire consumer durables, they had to allocate larger and larger portions of their income to pay their debts, rather than spend impulsively on small purchases at the grocery or clothing store.

Together with chain stores and installment credit, national advertising played a major role in creating a mass consumption society. Businessmen had begun to realize the advantages of advertising in the late nineteenth century but in the 1920s advertising expenditures tripled and

Madison Avenue assumed its present-day importance. Manufacturers initially used national advertising to reach consumers directly and to stimulate demand without having to rely on jobbers and retailers to push their products. By familiarizing shoppers with the alleged advantages of national brands, manufacturers broadened their markets and tried to stabilize the market by cultivating brand loyalty. As consumers came to desire Brand X, for instance, retailers began to stock it; the stimulation and the demand reinforced each other.

At first advertising appeals were simple, though exaggerated. "Not truth but credibility," claimed an ad man, was the key to success. One manufacturer informed an unsuspecting but believing public that it had bad breath; California lemon growers claimed their product cleaned teeth, shampooed hair, removed stains, polished glass, and loosened cuticles for manicuring. As advertising men became more sophisticated, they added irrational appeals to exaggerated claims. Cars, they insisted, gave people status, and toothpaste gave them sex appeal. The successful ad man, J. Walter Thompson, revealing a basic assumption of the industry, explained that the average consumer had the mentality of a "fourteen-year-old human animal," a creature of whim, infinitely gullible and infinitely capable of being manipulated. George Washington Duke, irascible and shrewd founder of the American Tobacco Company, acknowledged that his firm relied on repetitive and annoying advertising.

A few people, alarmed by dishonesty in advertising and the difficulty of getting one's money's worth because of a bewildering variety of merchandise, demanded regulation of the business. These anxieties led to an organized consumers' movement to test goods scientifically and help people spend their money more rationally, but most consumers remained indifferent to such efforts and businessmen were hostile. Business denounced any interference with free enterprise as un-American and a communist plot. The second charge proved a convenient though preposterous way to discredit critics of advertising; the first charge may have had much validity in the America of the 1920s.

National advertising had become vital in an age of mass consumption. It created new desires, informed the public about existing products, and most of all it persuaded people to buy a certain brand. Businessmen much preferred to compete through marketing appeals than through price wars, especially in industries such as soap, tobacco, cosmetics, and patent medicines in which little real difference existed among rival brands except the differences invented by the ad men.

Advertising served a larger function besides publicizing specific products. During the First World War the government used advertising to sell patriotism and Liberty Bonds, and in the 1920s Big Business turned to public relations to assure a favorable climate of opinion. Institutional ads depicted corporations as friendly, humane organizations, not soulless monsters. Americans learned that "Big Business is your Big Brother." But even more important, advertising trained people in new habits and values appropriate for a mass society. "Advertising," claimed one of its boosters, "is almost the only force at work against puritanism in consumption." It encouraged people "to live and enjoy—that is the basis of modern economics."

THE WELFARE OF THE AMERICAN PEOPLE

Economic growth produced remarkable improvements in the standard of living. The gains of productivity resulting from the achievements of basic industrialization and technological advance began to trickle down to working people. Real wages, which had grown slowly before 1914, surged ahead in the next fifteen years, while the average work week decreased from 60 hours in 1900 to just over 40 hours by 1930. As technology multiplied labor's efficiency, it simultaneously cut labor costs. Employers could improve wages and working conditions, and require fewer hours without cutting sharply into profits or raising prices. Both the climate of opinion generated by reformers and the pressure of unionization induced business to share more of the benefits of industrialization with the working classes.

No previous generation of Americans had experienced visible advances of such magnitude in its material well-being. Higher per capita income allowed people to spend a smaller portion of their income on food, clothing, and housing. They could now afford more expensive items such as meat, dairy products, and fresh fruits and vegetables; and they had more money for medical care, entertainment, and gadgets. By the late 1920s many Americans spent more on cars than on clothing. At the same time family size was shrinking so that a larger family income supported a smaller household.

The health of the American people improved dramatically. Life expectancy increased more in the first three decades of the twentieth century than in the preceding one hundred years. Males born in 1900 could expect to live forty-eight years; by 1930 life expectancy had reached almost sixty. Infant mortality dropped sharply especially in the 1920s, and infectious diseases such as tuberculosis, diphtheria, and pneumonia took a much lower toll. Improvements in health resulted largely from better diet, housing, and sanitation. Cities purified water supplies and enforced requirements for pasteurization of milk. But as people lived longer, the afflictions of aging, such as cancer and heart disease, became increasingly important causes of death. And by 1930 automobile accidents joined the list of major killers.

The quality of medical care also advanced, especially through mass vaccination against infectious diseases. Until the latter half of the nineteenth century medical science remained relatively primitive. Competing schools of medicine confused the public and created a field day for what later generations regarded as quackery. As medicine became more experimental and empirical, and less theoretical and speculative, breakthroughs in fundamental knowledge occurred with increasing rapidity particularly after Louis Pasteur demonstrated the germ theory of disease. Discoveries of the specific causes and cures of many infectious diseases such as tuberculosis, yellow fever, malaria, diphtheria, typhoid, and syphilis soon followed. At the same time the perfection of anesthesia opened up enormous new possibilities for the development of surgery. As the new knowledge seeped down, people became less inclined to accept disease and death as inevitable. They began consciously to conserve health, observe preventive measures, and seek professional care when illness struck.

An improvement in medical education had to precede the diffusion and wide application of this new knowledge. As medicine became more scientific, standards for practice tightened through tougher licensing requirements and radical improvement in the quality of medical schools. Although fewer medical schools and doctors per capita existed in 1930 than in 1900, the quality of medical care had advanced decisively. The number of hospital beds per capita almost doubled between 1900 and 1930, representing substantial investments in health facilities. And government, through city and county health departments, clinics and health centers, played a vital role. These agencies, together with philanthropic foundations and organizations such as the National Tuberculosis Association (1904), and the launching of industrial medicine by business, helped to diffuse new medical knowledge.

Yet advanced medical care remained too expensive or unavailable for most people. America, fast becoming a land of large-scale organizations of resources and services, still lived with a medical system largely in the hands of doctors maintaining individual practices—operating much like small businessmen. Health resources were unevenly distributed across the country, serving the city better than the country, the rich far better than the middle and lower classes. "We know how to do a lot of things which we don't do or do on a wretchedly small scale," complained Dr. William H. Welch, a medical reformer, in 1925. But organized medicine, speaking through the American Medical Association, fought, usually with success, the first, tentative steps toward bringing the benefits of modern medicine to all Americans regardless of wealth. Besides opposition from organized medicine to an adequate health care delivery system, millions of Americans were ignorant and even skeptical of modern medicine. "It's ridiculous to frighten people by talking about these millions of germs in our food, air, and water," said a midwesterner in the 1920s. "I went to school in a small room with lots of other children, and we were all rosy-cheeked and healthy and didn't know a thing about germs. There wasn't any of this foolishness of weighing children and frightening them to death because they may be underweight."

THE OTHER SIDE OF THE BOOM

Although most Americans fared better than ever before, economic gains had been distributed unevenly. Over half the income received by families and unattached individuals in 1929 went to the top 20 percent of the population, and only a quarter went to the bottom 40 percent. The Twenties produced *more* rather than less inequality in the distribution of income. Unemployment remained chronic. Between 1900 and 1930, the average annual rate of unemployment exceeded 4 percent (the currently "acceptable" minimum) in two out of every three years, and the average during the Twenties reached almost 5 percent. Since there was no unemployment insurance then, people thrown out of work often became destitute.

Millions of Americans lived below the poverty line. In 1915 the United States Industrial Commission reported that a third of the workers employed in mining and manufacturing lived at or below a subsistence level. A poor child was three times as likely to die before adulthood as a middle-class child. And poverty and disease took a still greater toll among blacks, the poorest of the poor, than among poor whites. Two decades of progressive reform and three decades of rapid economic advance had not eliminated serious imbalances in the distribution of wealth. The contrast between those few enjoying the delights of affluence and the millions left in squalor was sharper than ever.

Imbalance characterized most of the booming Twenties. Some of the older industries, such as agriculture, soft-coal mining, and textiles, experienced continuous hard times. In each case the markets for their products grew slowly in a maturing economy and an excess of supply over demand depressed prices. Nor were producers in these industries, made up of thousands of small units, able to adjust output to the market, whereas in steel and autos a handful of giants dominated and influenced supply and price.

The agricultural depression of the 1920s engulfed millions of Americans. The cities had been growing much more rapidly than rural America for decades but not until 1920 did the number of urban dwellers exceed the rural population. Although about 45 percent of the people still lived in rural areas in the 1920s, agriculture received only about 12 percent of the national income and its share continued to fall rapidly.

Farmers had traditionally lagged behind the urban sectors, where the *big* money could be made, but agriculture had enjoyed relative prosperity during the first two decades of the twentieth century (1900-1919). The depression of the 1890s and the closing of the frontier slowed the heady expansion of agricultural production that had resulted in supply outdistancing demand and plummeting prices. From 1900 to 1919 the terms of trade shifted. Domestic demand caught up with supply and pushed farm prices up more rapidly than the general price level. The outbreak of the First World War sustained and accelerated agricultural prosperity, as the United States became a major source of food for the Allies. Later, the government encouraged farmers to expand production with the patriotic slogan, "Food Will Win the War," and the even more convincing persuasion of guaranteed high prices.

Though rural America did not share in affluence to the same extent as urban America, agricultural productivity advanced in the early twentieth century. The gasoline engine promoted mechanization at a time when much of the countryside still had no electricity. By 1930 there were almost a million tractors and almost as many trucks on the farms, and the wealthier farmers had begun to buy grain combines, corn pickers, and milking machines. But low farm income deprived small-scale farmers of the benefits of such mechanization.

Modernization of the American farm received an additional boost from the diffusion of scientific research. The normally conservative farmers at first resisted new methods, fearful of risking their resources on the advice of government officials, university experts, and businessmen who were not themselves "dirt" farmers. But gradually, under prodding from the state agriculture colleges (which educated many of the farmers' sons) and businessmen who exerted economic pressure, the Agriculture Department officials gained their trust, and farmers began to innovate and achieve a modest growth in efficiency. Agriculture, however, did not benefit from lower prices, made possible by lower costs through expanded sales, to the same extent as other industries. Consumers who could already buy most of the food they wanted did not buy much more because prices fell.

Agriculture entered the 1920s with enlarged capacity but diminishing markets. Europe no longer relied as much on the United States as during wartime and the domestic market grew too slowly to take up the slack. The decline hit hardest the wheat growers, hurt by the shift in consumer preference for more meat, and the cot-ton growers who supplied raw material for the "sick" textile industry.

These imbalances in the productive system, the widespread poverty amid plenty, the prevalence of "sick" industries in a rapidly growing economy, paralleled conflicting American lifestyles. The ethic of production and work, the basis for the fast-receding rural society, now collided squarely with a new emphasis on consumption and leisure as mass society began to emerge in the 1920s.

Chapter 26
Emerging Life-styles in Mass Society

Greater affluence generated new life-styles. Mass society, rooted in an advanced, industrial economy and in urbanization, put its trust in large organizations and science rather than in individual enterprise and animistic religions. The process of constructing a secular "religion" began before the 1920s, but in that decade its consequences spread so widely that few Americans escaped its impact. New patterns of family life, interpersonal relations, and leisure, as well as new cultural directions and codes, reflected changes in American thought and life. Science and technology, schools and universities, movies and radio challenged the validity of older beliefs and the power of institutions nourished by them, especially the churches whose traditional pieties flourished in a rural society.

People left family farms and small towns for the exciting, impersonal city. They now lived far from relatives and old friends, working for unseen bosses, performing endlessly repetitive tasks as the clerks and production workers required by a complex division of labor. They thereby lost a sense of personal achievement, and the dignity and self-esteem that came from running a farm or small business, or practicing a craft.

Two decades of "reform" left unsolved the problems of humanizing an industrial society, and the disillusioning experience of the First World War left the United States and the rest of the world less safe than ever for democracy. Americans, in their pursuit of happiness, became confused and bewildered. Nothing seemed the same; even one's neighbors had changed. "I have no best friends," complained the wife of a working man in a medium-size midwestern town, one of thousands of such hamlets fabled in song and story for their friendliness. "It doesn't pay to be too friendly," warned another woman. People worked hard to buy things but, reported sociologists, they "seem to be running for dear life in the business of making money." Desires always outpaced means and "everyone seemed to run intent upon his own business as though one feared to stop lest those behind trample him down."

Artists, writers, architects, and musicians were the most sensitive barometers of change. They, more than others, lived at the intersection of old and new cultures. They probed critically and experimented ingeniously to find fresh ways of expressing authentically what life meant in an emerging mass society. They spoke for the silent millions experiencing the painful process of social change which undermined the old and nourished new life-styles, a process which betrayed the verities of the past yet seemed irresistibly attractive.

MEN, WOMEN, AND CHILDREN: SHIFTS IN INTERPERSONAL RELATIONS

The family underwent changes that altered its function and redefined the relations of its members. While most Americans lived on farms, the family functioned as a cohesive economic unit. On the farm, large families were an advantage, and women worked all day. The children's responsibilities in helping their fathers run the homestead made a strong patriarchal authority essential. Farm families before the age of automobile were isolated; they spent most of their time at home, working, with little but the visits of neighbors and peddlers to relieve the monotony.

Urbanization weakened the family's economic function. Men worked in factories and offices, and sometimes their wives and older children had to find jobs to supplement the breadwinner's wages. In the city large families became more of an economic burden than a blessing. A child a year meant more mouths to feed, whereas on the farm children enlarged the labor force. Living space was scarce and expensive in the city whereas on the farm there had always been room for more children and dependent, older relatives, such as aged grandparents. Though the urban working classes in the late nineteenth century continued to raise large families, the urban middle classes began to curb family size, and by the

1920s the limiting trend had spread to other groups. Between 1900 and 1930 the size of the average household fell from 4.6 persons to 3.8, though people now married younger. Contraception allowed for earlier marriage and smaller family size, and contributed to the rising standard of living. The middle classes, fearful of loss of status, were especially eager to ensure that their children had ample opportunity to "get ahead" by means of a "good education."

The reduction in the size of families depended on the adoption of birth control and of new attitudes towards sexuality. Some people approached sex with fear and guilt, most with ignorance. Conventional morality based on the teaching of the churches, Protestant and Catholic, insisted that procreation, not pleasure, was the sole legitimate function of sex, and urged the repression of sexual appetites. Sexual intercourse was moral only within marriage and for purposes of procreation. Sex itself was a forbidden subject, unfit for frank discussion among the decent and upright. "I believe children ought to be taught such things," said a midwestern mother of a sixteen-year-old in the 1920s but "I'm not much for talking about them. I've never talked to my daughter at all, though I suppose she knows more than I think she does. She's the only one I've got and I just can't bear to think of things like that in connection with her. I guess I wouldn't even talk to her if she was going to get married—I just couldn't!"

Yet birth control and new attitudes toward sex continued to spread, first among the middle classes, and then among the working classes. Techniques of contraception were as old as antiquity. Their widespread adoption, however, waited upon the industrialization and urbanization which made many people wish to limit family size. Self-appointed guardians of public morality, especially the Protestant clergy, tried to block change. In 1873 Congress barred contraceptives from interstate commerce and birth control information from the mails, and states such as Connecticut adopted repressive policies making it illegal to use contraceptives.

Court decisions eventually liberalized federal law, the medical profession encouraged birth control for reasons of health, and a militant movement led by Margaret Sanger organized to spread the new gospel and to fight government repression. Science lent the weight of its growing authority, especially the discoveries of Sigmund Freud, father of psychiatry. Freud's ideas, once popularized, undermined the view that sex was "dirty" or that a sensual appetite was normal among beasts but not among men. Freud interpreted the sex drive as natural and healthy, one that required satisfaction; repression of the sex drive only produced guilt, anxiety, and mental illness. The new outlook regarded sex as a means of expressing love and it needed neither the shelter of marriage nor the aim of procreation to give it moral legitimacy.

During the first three decades of the twentieth century, millions of Americans moved haltingly toward the new sexual morality. The continued decline of orthodox religion weakened the most powerful moral force standing in the way of such change. And the anonymity of urban life and the convenience of the automobile facilitated experimentation, especially among the young. Meanwhile the mass media, especially sensational magazines, newspapers, and movies, diffused and glamorized naturalistic attitudes toward sex. Hollywood particularly catered to the climate of opinion and produced movies like *Sinners in Silk, Women Who Give, The Price She Paid* and other films "with burning heart interest" such as *Alimony* about "brilliant men, beautiful jazz babies, champagne baths, midnight revels, petting parties in the purple dawn, all ending in one terrific smashing climax that makes you gasp." Popular magazines chipped in with stories of "The Primitive Lover" who "wanted a caveman husband," and advice about "How to Keep the Thrill in Marriage."

Thus began a sexual revolution stimulated by the availability of more leisure. People worked less hard and thus had more time and more energy to channel into other outlets. For millions this led to more premarital sexual activity and a consequent decrease in the frequency with which men resorted to prostitutes. For the first time, American women were becoming sexual partners, not merely sexual objects—a process of emancipation still largely uncompleted, but which was transforming the life of the American woman.

THE NEW WOMAN

American morality put women on a pedestal. The special function of females was to uphold virtue, serve as guardians of culture, and restrain the animal instincts of their mates. Men regarded wives as creatures not only "purer and morally better" than themselves, but as "relatively impractical, emotional, unstable, . . . incapable of facing facts or doing hard thinking." Man's arena was the factory and the marketplace, where aggressiveness and drive paid off. The home, the woman's responsibility, provided a refuge from the harsh, workaday world ruled by force and power. It was a civilized and genteel atmosphere. Women were so idealized that they faced the danger of becoming unreal. "There is a being," said one typical celebrator of womanhood, "the image and reflection of whom is ever present in the mirror of my soul. Her works are like charmed echoes in a beautiful dell and her laughter like the sweetness of the bursting magnolia and her beauty like the smiling violets and the laughing morning glory . . . heaven's divinest gift to the world—womanhood."

Until the twentieth century, nearly all women accepted their role. Child rearing and housekeeping in large families absorbed their energies. With both partners preoccupied with work, within and outside the home, marriage was less a setting for intimate companionship than a practical arrangement. Women regarded sex as an obligation, associating it with the endless cycle of child bearing that wore them out and killed thousands. Twentieth-century mores, however, redefined the role of women. A century earlier married women had almost no legal rights. During the nineteenth century they acquired rights to their own property, even after marriage, and in 1919 after almost a century of struggle they won the right to vote under the Eighteenth Amendment, a victory that symbolized the changes occurring in the status of women.

When the founding fathers in 1776 proclaimed that "all men are created equal" they did not see fit to include women. At the beginning of the nineteenth century wives were legal wards of their husbands and they had few legal rights over their property or their earnings. In practice, however, women were better treated in America than in Europe because there were relatively more men, and women were indispensable for running a farm household. But this demographic advantage did not immediately improve women's legal status or open educational opportunity. Regarded as inferior to men, in mind as well as in body, women were declared unsuited for intellectual development. Instruction in painting, music, and embroidery seemed sufficient. Women, unfit for "the turmoil and battle of public life," should merely exert a "mild, dependent, softening influence upon the sternness of man's opinion."

A few especially gifted women and their male sympathizers thought otherwise. "Remember," Abigail Adams reminded her husband John, the revolutionary leader who professed to oppose tyranny from whatever source, "all men would be tyrants if they could." Women, barely educated, appeared mentally inferior because—as Dr. Benjamin Rush, the scientist-statesman of the revolutionary era, explained—they were denied a chance to develop their minds and personalities; men were "taught to aspire, but women were early confined and limited."

Eventually a few women began to insist that a nation founded on the principles of human equality respect their humanity too. The early feminists established grammar schools, then colleges, so that at least a few women could develop their potential. A small cadre of educated women became the shock troops in the struggle for female rights, a struggle that flourished after the 1830s as one of the galaxy of reforms, including antislavery and temperance, that sought to rescue the weak and oppressed. Women advanced their own cause as they became prominent in crusades for the rights of others, especially the slaves. They forged alliances with males, learned skills in organization and in molding public opinion, and by expressing themselves on public issues, the reformers demonstrated their moral fitness for civic responsibility.

Women's entrance into man's world—schools, colleges, and finally the political arena—alarmed conservatives who saw a threat to society's most basic institution, the patriarchal family. Ignoring critics, feminists and suffragists by the middle of the nineteenth century had won improvements in their legal status, an advance achieved in part because the wealthy wished to protect female heirs from husbands who might squander their wife's inheritance. The struggle for freedom and equality for the black man in the 1860s encouraged women to press further but the Civil War enfranchised Negro males, not women.

Meanwhile, industrialization and urbanization more effectively changed the status of women than revolutionary ideology and protest, the principal forces of change until then. During the late nineteenth century in the cities of America and Europe, thousands of women left the home to work in factories and shops. By 1880 women constituted 15 percent of the American labor force, and by the 1920s over 20 percent. Mechanization created jobs which required less physical strength, jobs as suitable for women as men, and women were willing to work for less money. The growing importance of service industries and communications also created thousands of jobs for women as office workers, retail clerks, and telephone operators. At the same time the diffusion of mass education enlarged the demand for teachers; by 1890 a quarter million women were staffing the nation's schools. A few also began to find careers in other professions, including medicine and social work.

At the same time that women entered the labor force, increasing technological changes especially by the 1920s were revolutionizing housekeeping. Electric lighting, gas cooking, and new household appliances such as refrigerators, electric irons, and washing machines lightened household chores in middle-class and some working-class homes. So too did the shift to factory-made clothing, store-bought bread, and canned foods which came into wide use during the 1920s.

Once women became an integral part of the work force, they gained new status. As working wives they helped support the family, or they could be self-supporting though unmarried. Spending much of their time outside the home, economically they formed part of a previously all-male world. Eventually, they joined the reformers in demanding the political and social rights appropriate to first-class citizens.

The leadership in the movement for women's rights received fresh impetus from the growing number of educated, middle-class women who were the first to benefit from the new leisure and the newer permissible forms of female behavior. In the late nineteenth century women played a more important role than ever in national reform movements. The Women's Christian Temperance Union, for example, stood at the forefront of the crusade against liquor; and women were active in campaigns to clean up politics and improve living conditions in the slums.

The Battle for the Vote

During the Progressive period a favorable climate existed for renewal of the struggle for the right to vote. "Suffragettes" argued that women would strengthen the moral forces in American politics in the battle against the liquor interests, urban squalor, and political corruption. Their organizations, resembling professional political machines, won the vote in enough states by 1916 to create a female bloc vote in national elections. The final push came during the First World War. Reluctantly, President Wilson accepted the inevitable: "Democracy means that women shall play their part in affairs alongside men and upon an equal footing with them. . . . We have made partners of the women in this war; shall we admit them only to a partnership of suffering and not to a partnership of privilege and right?" Resistance stiffened, especially among Southerners, the liquor interests, the Catholic church, and Eastern industrialists who feared that women voters would strengthen the movement to curb business. To the charge that giving women the vote would rob them of femininity, Rose Schneidermann replied: "We have women working in the foundries, stripped to the waist, if you please, because of the heat. Yet the Senator says nothing about these women losing their charm. . . . Women in the laundries . . . stand for thirteen or fourteen hours in the terrible steam and heat with their hands in hot starch. Surely these women won't lose any more of their beauty and charm by putting a ballot in a box once a year. . . ."

The Amendment carried in 1919, but the outcome of the battle for the vote proved disappointing. Women's suffrage had little immediate effect on American politics since wives tended to be politically uninformed and few exercised a political judgment independent of their husbands. Nor did the vote resolve the tensions in the American family. Leisured, middle-class women wanted to be more than homemakers but they were not attracted to the physically tiring and intellectually unchallenging jobs then available to working women. These women insisted that they, no less than men, had a right to happiness through freedom for personal development and individual expression.

Women began to breach the double standard. They smoked and drank in public; they alternately shimmied and slithered as they danced the charleston and the tango; and they insisted upon greater satisfactions (even romantic love!) in marriage as well as liberation from the endless cycle of child rearing that birth control made possible. In the past women had suffered through unhappy marriages. Now couples separated more often when marriage failed to offer emotional fulfillment and companionship. At the same time that women were demanding more of marriage than in the past, many men were unable or unprepared to adjust to the women's new demands and attitudes. As a result the divorce rate soared. In the 1920s the United States had the highest divorce rate in the world, except possibly for the Soviet Union.

In the 1920s widespread anxiety existed over the stability of the American family. Not only the high divorce rate, but also the changing relationship between parents and children, generated those fears. "We seem to be drifting away from the fundamentals in our home life," a Midwesterner complained in the 1920s. "The home was once a sacred institution where the family spent most of its time. Now it is a service station except for the old and infirm." Members of the family spent less time with one another and more with their peers outside the home. Poverty had driven tens of thousands of children into the factories—almost 20 percent of the male population between 10 and 15 worked in 1900—but after 1910 child labor declined as rising family income levels eliminated some of the need.

Compulsory school attendance laws, longer school terms, and the diffusion of secondary education on a mass scale meant that children spent much of their time during their formative years in the classroom. The child's peer group—his fellow students and friends—competed with his parents for his attention and loyalty. In the densely packed cities, children were far less isolated from one another than they had been on the farm. As a result young people born into an urbanized, mass society began to form a "youth culture" with distinctive life-styles. Their parents still cherished many of the values and attitudes of the past and the Old World, but these youngsters were more prone to experiment. Especially among the middle classes, the automobile gave teen-agers new privacy and intimacy, and the telephone put them in instant communication with one another. Thus the young were more open in their attitudes toward sex and pleasure, and they often found themselves in conflict with the traditional mores of their parents.

The social life of the family centered around the evening meal but the rest of the time family members were off in different directions: children at school, fathers at their jobs, mothers doing the household chores. Not only did they work separately, they played separately as well. Each had his routine of leisure-time activities, especially clubs, sports, and other entertainment. "Folks today want to eat in a hurry," complained a butcher in the 1920s, "and get out in the car." The family car, a convenience and source of recreation, became something more, too. "I never feel as close to my family as when we are all together in the car," confided a Midwesterner in the 1920s. "We save every place we can and put the money into the car," another explained hopefully. "It keeps the family together." People mortgaged their homes to buy autos before they had acquired bathtubs. "I'll go without food before I'll see us give up the car," was a common attitude. The car became a family symbol, often a pathetic and counterproductive one, and since families without autos did not amount to much, people desperately sought them—but the car could not supply the cohesion missing in family life in mass society. As the family became less important in the urban setting, formal education came to mean more to young people.

THE EXPANSION OF EDUCATION

The coming of the common school during the two decades preceding the Civil War (1840–1860) made basic education available to most white Americans. But quality trailed far behind educational quantity and until this century few received more than eight years of primary schooling. During the first three decades of the twentieth century, however, developments already under way earlier began to bear fruit. Americans stayed in school longer. Over 80 percent of the population between the ages of 5 and 17 attended schools in 1930, a considerable jump since 1890. The school year lengthened, increasing almost forty days between 1890 and 1930, and compulsory school attendance laws began to ensure that potential pupils were not kept home or sent to work prematurely.

Advances in educational participation also came through the spread of high schools. In 1890 few but the children of the rich and upper middle class could study beyond elementary school. By the 1930s the sons and daughters of farmers and working people joined them. As the high school became nearly universal, colleges became the next target for the educational explosion. The percentage of people 18 to 21 enrolled in colleges and universities quadrupled in the period from 1890 to 1930, much of the growth occurring during the 1920s. At the end of that decade a million students attended institutions of higher learning, compared to half that number a dozen years earlier. While these extraordinary advances in the diffusion of education took place, other changes occurred which altered the style and substance of learning in primary and high schools and transformed the old colonial college into the modern university.

The expansion and extension of public education stemmed from several interrelated pressures. Urban growth shifted responsibilities for the so-cialization and education of children from the home to the school because city families counted less on the labor of their children than did rural families. The management of large numbers of children in crowded urban settings created problems. There was less room for play than rural children had, and overcrowding strained family life, producing demands that the state assume more of the burden of child rearing. Industrialization also made new demands on the schools to train a labor force in the habits and skills of factory and office. And in the late nineteenth and early twentieth centuries, social reformers looked to the schools to promote more equal opportunity for the disadvantaged, to equalized conditions of life, abolish child labor, and to instill social discipline in a society increasingly divided by the tensions of labor violence and urban unrest. The cities filled up with "exotic" immigrants with their different customs and beliefs, their "un-American" styles of life. Some thought they threatened the dominant position of the WASPS, the native-born Anglo-Saxon elements, and they expected the schools to Americanize the newcomers.

Until the twentieth century, high schools and private academies, catering mainly to more prosperous families, prepared adolescents for admission to college. By the 1920s the mission of high schools had changed as their enrollments soared and their doors opened to all income levels. High schools still prepared some for college, an ever-growing percentage, but most of their graduates went directly to work. Vocational training edged its way into the curriculum, under pressure from businessmen for practical courses in typing, bookkeeping, business English and arithmetic, homemaking, and the mechanical arts such as carpentry and auto repair. To make room for these new subjects, students spent less time studying the traditional classical curriculum which had emphasized Latin, mathematics, and history. By the 1920s science also had made heavy inroads into the academic course of study, reflecting the growing tendency for a society, so obviously enjoying the fruits of applied technology, to value scientific knowledge and its applications.

Progressive Education

The new curriculum was one of several changes instituted by educational reformers seeking to transform the beleaguered schools. In the 1890s discontent first emerged in sustained form in muckraking attacks on the quality of common schools. Overwhelmed by hundreds of thousands of students, inadequately financed, committed to a socially conservative mission of imposing on children "a life of order, self discipline, civic loyalty, and respect for private property," the nineteenth-century school system turned to the bureaucratic principles of centralization and standardization. The result was the graded school, frequent examinations, mass-produced textbooks, standardized buildings and salary schedules for teachers. School facilities were run-down, classes overcrowded, teachers overworked and poorly paid, and rote learning the norm. There was little regard for individual differences among children and little attempt to motivate learning by exploiting student interests and unleashing their imaginations. Above all, fear and repression pervaded the classroom. "Why should they look behind when the teacher is in front of them?" insisted a principal, explaining why his school did not permit students to move their heads during recitation. "How can you learn anything with your knees and toes out of order?" scolded another educator.

Educational progressives believed there were better ways the schools could serve the needs of an industrial society than as "grim factories deadened by routine." They attempted to break down the wall between the school and society by enlarging its functions. In addition to providing vocational instruction, incorporating the pioneering work of settlement houses in the urban ghettos, the schools broadened their mission and looked after children's health, instructed them in hygiene, cultivated taste for music and the fine arts, introduced nature study, and organized recreational activities. In these ways reformers thought education could better serve the needs of an urban society. The millions of immigrants arriving from Europe and the rural Americans who now lived in crowded cities had to be schooled in "proper"—that is, middle-class—standards of morality, behavior, and deportment. Reformers thus invested the schools with responsibilities for accommodating potentially disruptive elements into the existing order.

A philosopher, John Dewey, pioneered in constructing a theory of progressive education. The schools, he urged, must undertake what the family, neighborhood, shop, and farm had previously done. They must train citizens to assume civic responsibilities for improving society through the application of science and intelligence to social problems, while trying to cultivate the fullest potential for human development in every child. Exploiting new psychological insights, progressive educators insisted that children be regarded, not as miniature adults, but as a distinctive age group with needs which educators must understand and adapt to. Traditional educational doctrine held that subjects such as Latin and mathematics disciplined the mind and personalities of children. The progressives insisted that mathematics did not train people to think more logically, nor did memorization of Latin or English grammar teach students how to write and speak grammatically.

Dewey and other advocates of progressive education inspired dozens of experiments to exploit the student's natural curiosity and encourage learning as a means of self-gratification instead of arbitrarily imposing on children a body of subject matter which—like it or not—they had to assimilate. Thus a student's natural curiosity about experiences in his own life would provide a springboard into the study of nature and society, and the cultivation of the arts. At the same time, progressives tried to replace the coercive atmosphere of the classroom with a more informal, spontaneous environment that encouraged student initiative. Teachers were to become guides rather than taskmasters, and would pay greater attention to individual differences among children.

Progressive education promised more than it delivered. As Dewey's ideas became translated into popular practice only a few teachers had the knowledge, imagination, and training to make progressivism work fully. Nor would conservatives tolerate Dewey's idea that the schools should turn out citizens who would become social critics and social reformers, rather than conformists. And few communities were willing to finance the schools with the generosity necessary to implement a truly progressive system. Yet a marked improvement took place in the schools: the classroom atmosphere did become less repressive, the curriculum was broadened, and teachers received better training and better salaries. Education, if not revolutionized, had at least been revitalized —and the country spent a greater share of its income on education in 1930 than thirty years earlier.

THE EMERGENCE OF THE UNIVERSITY

A revolution in higher education paralleled the developments in basic and secondary education. Although in the 1930s only 12 percent of Americans between 18 and 22 were in college, enrollment between 1890 and 1925 had grown almost five times faster than the population. An advanced, industrial economy generating ever higher per capita income required more professionally trained people: doctors, lawyers, engineers, and teachers. The colleges and universities provided them, but to do so required an overhaul in the structure of higher education, a process that occurred in the half century after the Civil War.

Seven hundred colleges were founded in America before 1860, partly because of the competitive enterprise of the religious denominations which controlled most of them. Established to promote the interests of a particular denomination by training future ministers and providing an appropriate sectarian environment for the sons of the upper classes, the colleges served the few. As conservators and transmitters of traditional culture, the colleges relied on the classical curriculum and neglected science and other modern disciplines. Most also rejected free inquiry and expensive research, since these might threaten established doctrine. Their mission was to promote sound morals, not to stimulate intellectual inquiry or the advancement of knowledge.

The teachers, mostly clergymen, taught piety. But young men seemed more interested in "getting on" in the world, and in Greek letter fraternities. Originating in the 1820s and 1830s, these clubs filled a gap in college life and "institutionalized various escapes—drinking, smoking, card playing, and seducing" as well as "the new prestige values of worldly success, for they recognized good looks, wealth, good family, income, clothing, good manners." Officially, however, the colleges remained committed to the preeminence of spiritual values.

After the Civil War, science, secularism, and utilitarianism transformed the old liberal arts college into the modern university. Before that, the great scientific advances of the preceding two centuries had made limited inroads in higher education. The triumph of Darwinism in the late nineteenth century opened the way for change. Darwinism did more than substitute the theory of evolution for the biblical account of creation. It fostered the feeling that science held the key to the universe. This breakthrough in human knowledge also represented a triumph for the scientific method. It assumed that truth was not fixed, but something man discovered by formulating tentative explanations of puzzling phenomena and then testing the theories experimentally. At the same time that naturalistic explanations of creation were challenging supernatural accounts, medical science discovered the causes of several killer diseases such as tuberculosis. As a result, a dramatic, visible improvement in human welfare took place, giving science enormous prestige among ordinary Americans, further strengthened by such applications of scientific knowledge as the use of electricity in lighting.

In the late nineteenth century, Americans learned that science meant power, and the university became the center for the diffusion and advancement of scientific knowledge. Though some managed to reconcile religion and science, Darwinism convinced many that man, through the use of the scientific method, could understand the impersonal forces governing the world. This belief undermined the religious character of the American college and redefined its mission.

Foundations of the University

Leading colleges became universities by emphasizing the centrality of research and providing scholars with the resources and conditions to engage in free inquiry. Harvard led the way in 1869 when it chose a scientist, Charles W. Eliot, rather than a clergyman as president. Eliot placed science on an equal footing with the humanities in the curriculum, and he introduced the elective system, giving students considerable leeway in choosing their course of study. The elective principle proved revolutionary because it reawakened intellectual curiosity: undergraduates could pursue their interests and professors could offer specialized instruction in areas in which they did research and had gained expertise.

The old colleges had been financed on a shoestring but the new universities were far more expensive to run. The university required laboratories and libraries—and a large faculty, many of whom spent much of their time engaged in research and in training apprentice faculty. Increasing knowledge resulted in fragmentation and ushered in the age of the academic specialist. Science split into separate disciplines, such as physics, chemistry, zoology, and geology, and specialization eventually reached the more traditional disciplines as well. History, for example, also became "scientific" and specialized. Historians became experts by concentrating on a particular period such as ancient, medieval, or modern history, or the history of a particular country.

While science worked to transform the college, new wealth, generated by the industrial development of the late nineteenth century, provided the money. Tycoons such as John D. Rockefeller (benefactor of the University of Chicago) donated millions as tokens of their philanthropic spirit and as a means of winning public approval.

Paralleling an enormous increase in private support for higher education was the emergence of the state university. The first state universities were founded before the Civil War in the South and West, where private colleges were much weaker than in the East. The Morrill Act (1862) created the land-grant state university and provided federal funding for state institutions that offered instruction in agriculture and in the mechanical arts. As the state universities enlarged in the late nineteenth century, they imitated the older institutions but they also developed new functions to serve the people on whose support they depended. They engaged in agricultural research and also established professional schools. Free from sectarian control, the state universities were hospitable to science and to modern curriculums and together with the leading private universities they established graduate schools. Their special contribution was to make college available to thousands who could not afford private institutions and to make public service, together with research and the transmission of liberal education, one of the missions of the modern university.

A precondition of the modern university was academic freedom—the freedom of students and faculty to search for the truth, wherever it might lead. The old colleges had no room for such freedom, since truth was deemed fixed and already discovered, embodied in the theology of the sponsoring church and the values of influential laymen. In the new universities an accepted truth was never safe from critical scrutiny, for science had demonstrated that knowledge could advance only as men subjected all accepted beliefs to the test of scholarly inquiry. Inevitably scholars challenged many accepted beliefs and provoked criticism of the university by angry citizens and alumni. Some professors who espoused unconventional or unpopular views lost their jobs; others had to remain silent. The battle for academic freedom was hard-fought but by 1915 professors felt sufficiently strong to demand, through the newly organized American Association of University Professors, that universities voluntarily respect the need for free inquiry. At first college presidents and trustees refused, but by the 1920s the leading institutions accepted the principle of academic freedom though they sometimes violated it in practice.

By the 1920s the modern university had evolved. It still transmitted culture and moral values to undergraduates but at the same time it incorporated science into the curriculum and the scientific method into the spirit of the university. Graduate and professional schools trained the highly skilled personnel modern America needed, and large-scale private philanthropy together with public support of state institutions financed the expansion of higher education.

At the same time, the university engaged in a new activity, peripheral to its central concerns, but which provided entertainment for millions every Saturday afternoon—college football. The rise of football as a mass spectator sport in the 1920s satisfied the need of an emerging mass society for organized diversion that was inexpensive, frequent, and easily accessible. Spectator sports—college and high school football and professional baseball—and the new industries of movies and radio reshaped the way Americans spent their leisure time in the twentieth century.

ENTERTAINMENT FOR THE MASSES

Mass society created the mass media and mass entertainment. Newspapers were older than the republic, but in the twentieth century journalism took a new turn. Newspapers became big business and went after the largest market possible. Tabloids exploiting sensationalism catered to the urban masses and provided them with cheap, daily entertainment which they read to and from work each day. Magazine editors also learned the popular touch and found that there was more money in entertaining than in edifying. As in other businesses, the most successful entrepreneurs, such as newspaper magnate William Randolph Hearst, built huge publishing empires that made them a power in the republic. People looked to the press for information but they also insisted on being entertained—something the newspapers and magazines accomplished with great cleverness, through muckraking, comic strips, crossword puzzles, crimes of violence reported daily in gory detail, and gossip columns.

Mass entertainment was also the function of professional sports. The popularity of professional baseball and college football (which was amateur only in name) depended only partly on the skill of the athletes or the excitement of the games themselves. Professional sports had still another appeal: people identified with teams and athletic heroes. Cities rooted for the home club and basked in the glory of their victories. Following the exploits of a favorite team added interest and excitement to otherwise drab and dull lives. The triumphs of the baseball star "Babe" Ruth or a football hero like "Red" Grange enabled people who felt (and to a great extent were) like cogs in the industrial machine to identify with the individual achievements of heroic men. College football went even further in strengthening the loyalty of alumni to their alma mater, and inducing both alumni and state legislators to finance higher education more generously.

Professional sports thus catered to the need for entertainment and escape in an urban society but, like the theater and the circus, they were not readily accessible to or within the means of everyone; movies and radio were, however, and they transformed the way Americans spent the increasing leisure time created by affluence. These media relied on new technology and the marketing techniques and financial resources of Big Business to bring cheap entertainment into residential neighborhoods via thousands of local movie houses and into the homes through millions of radio receivers.

The Coming of the Movies

The commercial production and exhibition of movies began early in the twentieth century, first as peep shows and then with film projected on theater screens where many people could watch simultaneously. The first movies were primitive in technique, with inexperienced actors and directors. Shown in "nickleodeons," these short films depicted familiar scenes of city life—the pool hall, the ghetto, the pawnshop, and police and fire departments in action.

Crude though they were, the early films proved enormously popular. This attracted businessmen who built theaters and production companies turning out hundreds of short films. Fierce competition among producers and exhibitors, resembling the early competition in the railroad, steel, and oil industries, led to consolidation of many firms into a few powerful companies. The movie moguls gained control over the distribution system, acquiring hundreds of theaters across the country which assured them a steady outlet for their films. When movies became a profitable Big Business, Wall Street financiers in the 1920s and 1930s supplied capital and gained control.

At first New York City reigned as the center of movie-making, but by 1920 the industry had shifted to Hollywood, California. Independent producers located there so they could easily escape across the border to Mexico when the movie trust (located in New York) attempted to enforce its control over key patents. Southern California also offered a climate that made year-round production possible. The concentration of movie-making in Hollywood led to the development of a community of filmmakers which was highly competitive but which also encouraged the cross-fertilization of ideas.

The moviemakers repeatedly misjudged both the financial and artistic possibilities of the new medium. At first actors were ashamed to work in motion pictures. Those who did appeared anonymously in dozens of movies ground out like automobiles from a factory production line. When the public took a fancy to some of the early actors, producers feared that popular performers would demand higher salaries. Eventually, however, they realized the potential of the star system. Similarly, early movies were short, since no one thought people would watch a film for more than half an hour. The successful Italian full-length spectacle, *Quo Vadis* (1912), helped to convince them otherwise. Theaters could charge more for feature films and Hollywood thus made more money. The industry also resisted the advent of sound. In 1927, Warner Brothers introduced talkies in a desperate bid to stave off bankruptcy. Convinced that talkies were a fad that would pass, fearful that sound would undermine the huge investments in silent film stars, and reluctant to invest the millions of dollars conversion to sound would require, the leading studios held back until the popularity of talkies forced them to go along.

The star system, the feature film, and the sound track were three essential developments in the emergence of movies. In addition, the audience had broadened from the working classes to include the middle classes who caught the movie-going habit by the 1920s. The first movie houses were built in working-class neighborhoods but in the 1920s luxurious movie "palaces" rose in the big-city downtown districts, and impressive if less imposing theaters appeared in residential areas. In small towns the principal movie house was often the most impressive building in the community. By 1927 there were 17,000 movie houses and new plush theaters helped make moviegoing genteel and respectable. Finally, a shift in the thematic content of films captured the interest of the middle classes. The early silent films had realistically exploited scenes of urban life. They were crude social documents, sympathetically depicting the experiences of the poor and the downtrodden—as in the great films of Charlie Chaplin, who won the hearts of millions around the world with his portrayal of the tramp, the symbol of the underdog.

Middle-class audiences wanted something else. As the technical quality of movies improved, leading Broadway actors went to Hollywood. Films began to cater to the interests and anxieties of the new audience. Prewar movies, reflecting prewar optimism, assumed that love and honesty made for happiness, that poverty ennobled men because wealth corrupted them. In the 1920s, however, movies became preoccupied with the foibles of the rich, depicting them as restless, unhappy, and faithless—but glamorous. The audience sought vicarious pleasure for a few hours by escaping into a world inhabited by people who enjoyed luxury and who indulged in romantic exploits denied to most people. The movies thus exploited a fascination that derived from middle-class envy of the upper crust, ocean-liner set, an envy often accompanied by fear and disdain for those who repudiated conventional mores.

Movies could be more than a business and a form of mass entertainment. In the hands of creative people, movies became an art. Directors and cameramen slowly mastered their technique. They learned how to use the camera, edit film, and to light the set to create an aesthetic experience unique to films. D. W. Griffith was the great pioneer director whose films, such as *Birth of a Nation* (1915) and *Intolerance* (1916), explored the technical and artistic possibilities of the motion picture. But Hollywood never fully realized its potential. Movies remained first and foremost a business; commercial pressures, especially the need for rapid production of many movies, restricted the art of moviemaking. Some directors were little more than glorified foremen grinding out their prescribed footage, using formula actors whose box office appeal mattered much more than acting talent. Customers wanted to see their favorites play the same role in movie after movie. Hollywood obliged. In the 1920s the center of artistic filmmaking shifted to Europe, and there it has remained. The combination of mass production, new technology, and Big Business created the modern American movie industry, and made inexpensive entertainment available to millions every week (U.S. films were as popular overseas as at home), but the pressures of the marketplace stunted the film's development as an art.

Radio

Radio, like movies, represented a triumph of the new technology and Big Business. Radio broadcasting began in the early 1920s and quickly became popular. Mass production allowed millions to buy radio sets and stations multiplied to fill the air-waves with sound. At first, the financing of radio programming remained unclear. Set manufacturers might broadcast programs to stimulate sales or set owners might pay a fee. But the idea of government transmission smacked of socialism, and the notion of selling radio time to advertisers struck many as undesirable. Secretary of Commerce Herbert Hoover warned in the 1920s: "It is inconceivable that we should allow so great a possibility for service . . . to be drowned in advertising matter," and the code of the National Association of Broadcasters in 1929 banned radio commercials between 7 and 11 P.M.

But just as commercial pressures shaped the development of movies, advertising determined the destiny of radio. In the 1920s business had come to appreciate the power of advertising, and radio offered an unparalleled medium for selling brand-name products nationally. To attract large audiences radio stations hired leading entertainers. This raised costs but advertisers willingly bought expensive radio time because millions could be reached instantly and repeatedly across the entire country. The initiation of radio networks such as NBC (1926) and CBS (1927) hooked together hundreds of local stations and cleared prime evening time, nationwide, for popular programs originating from New York. The public quickly became addicted to radio. In millions of homes Americans tuned in their favorite weekly programs, at virtually no expense. Radio seemed like a free service, since the cost was hidden in the prices people paid for nationally advertised brands. Advertisers, wishing to reach the largest possible audience, geared programming to the lowest common denominator of popular taste. The public, however, seemed generally satisfied, and the addiction spread from the programs to the commercials, as consumers dutifully bought the products which the radio stars assured them "make this program possible."

CULTURE IN A MASS SOCIETY

At the same time that radio, commercial sports, and movies were providing entertainment for millions, writers, artists, architects, and musicians expressed the feelings of those sensing most keenly, often most painfully, the strains that altered people's lives in modern America. The first three decades of the twentieth century saw the birth of modern American "high" culture, following a generation of incubation. After 1900, a galaxy of great artists produced a distinctively American spirit in the creative arts. From provincials, American writers and artists became cosmopolitans, the best of them acknowledged world masters.

As in the first American Renaissance of 1830-1860—the burst of literary excellence that sprang from the pens of Hawthorne, Emerson, Whitman, and Melville—literature provided the most important vehicle through which Americans gave expression to their creative imagination. Emily Dickinson, Edwin Arlington Robinson, Robert Frost, Carl Sandburg, Ezra Pound, and T. S. Eliot, to mention a few, brought powerful, fresh voices to poetry. Among prose writers, Mark Twain, Henry James, and William Dean Howells in the last decades of the nineteenth century, followed in the next generation by Edith Wharton, F. Scott Fitzgerald, Theodore Dreiser, Ernest Hemingway, Sherwood Anderson, Thomas Wolfe, Sinclair Lewis, and John Dos Passos, transmuted experience into art in a series of classic modern novels.

Long in the making, modern American culture burst into full bloom in the 1920s, a decade of unprecedented vitality in the history of the creative arts in America, and of unprecedented alienation among intellectuals at odds with the ruling precepts and practices of their society. This achievement stands in sharp contrast to the situation thirty years earlier. In 1888 Matthew Arnold, an English man of letters and arbiter of culture, surveyed the American scene and delivered a negative verdict. "Let us take the beautiful first, and consider how far it is present in American civilization," he began. "Evidently, this is that civilization's weak side. There is little to nourish and delight the sense of beauty there. . . . What people in whom the sense for beauty and fitness was quick could have invented, or could tolerate, the hideous names ending in *ville,* the Briggesvilles, Higginsvilles, Jacksonvilles, rife from Maine to Florida. . . ." By 1930, European judgments on American small town culture had remained constant, but there was a new respect for American literature. In that year, the Nobel Prize for literature went, for the first time, to an American, Sinclair Lewis.

The Genteel Tradition at Bay

Yet this American cultural flowering, what Lewis called in 1930 a "second coming of age," differed from the awakening of the 1840s and 1850s. Before the Civil War, most important creative artists had been isolated; isolated from one another, from the literary world abroad, and from a large, appreciative audience at home. Their successors in the twentieth century, not only poets and novelists, but playwrights, architects, and musicians reached larger audiences and won recognition far beyond American shores. And most significant, they were artistic revolutionaries, rejecting established conceptions of the nature of art and its place in life. Despite intense hostility and, what was worse, indifference, they

ultimately overcame both, giving powerful expression to a counterculture which repudiated much of what most Americans cherished.

The imaginative writers reveal most clearly the roots of cultural modernity. In the late nineteenth century, literature, like the other arts in America, fell under the sway of the Genteel Tradition. Most Americans regarded the arts as artificial, far from the central concerns of a busy people. "Essentially we were taught to regard culture," explained the literary critic Malcolm Cowley, "as a veneer, a badge of class distinction—as something assumed like an Oxford accent or a suit of English clothes." The colleges where the young middle-class men and women received the finishing touches were "sales rooms and fitting rooms of culture," remote from real life, rather than "ground-floor shops" that opened one "to the life of the street." As custodians and transmitters of official culture, the colleges destroyed "whatever roots we had in the soil," setting up foreign aesthetic models and maintaining that whatever was sordid was unfit for a work of literature. Literature in general, and art and learning in particular, Cowley reminisced, "were things existing at an infinite distance from our daily lives."

"Good" literature, insisted the pundits of the Genteel Tradition, had to be ennobling and "pure." Dwelling on the sordid or anatomizing the underside of life had no place in books intended for the chaste living rooms of middle-class America or for the eyes of the female readers who dominated the fiction audience. The function of art was to adorn, uplift, and entertain. Against such socially imposed constraints, such narrowing limits that smothered vision and feeling, such prissiness, two generations of American writers struggled.

A few cracks were formed in the Genteel Tradition's Great Wall during the three decades after the Civil War which coincided with the heyday of industrialization. Writers, like other Americans, were alarmed by the social dislocations accompanying American growth. Eventually the malaise seeped into their work. Literary "realists" sought to discover in fiction life as it was. "Let fiction cease to lie about life," commanded William D. Howells, "let it portray men and women as they really are, actuated by the motives and the passions in the measure we all know." Howells led the way himself in *A Hazard of New Fortunes* (1894) writing about class conflict and the dilemma of the individual facing an increasingly collectivized society; Frank Norris described how corporations crushed the weak in *The Octopus* (1901); while Stephen Crane re-created, with extraordinary honesty the impact of war on a young man in *The Red Badge of Courage* (1895) and the impact of urbanization on a young woman in *Maggie, A Girl of the Streets* (1892).

Yet even before realism became a literary movement, Mark Twain was writing stories so deceptively simple and popular that many readers and critics never realized their real literary worth or their critical significance. Ernest Hemingway later described *Huckleberry Finn* (1884) as the source of all modern American fiction. Twain, one of a group of regionalist writers, wrote about the southern half of the Mississippi Valley, and about Americans everyone could recognize. He employed a vernacular style rooted in the speech of the people, and masked his savage satire and growing pessimism behind irresistible humor and a folk manner that won him huge audiences. Few puzzled over the larger meaning of the adventures of Huck Finn who runs away from civilization, befriends an escaped slave, and when the moment comes to decide whether to do his civic and Christian duty and turn the black man over to the law, decides otherwise. "All right," Huck declared, "I'll *go* to Hell"—hardly the destination American boys were supposed to prepare themselves for. Acclaimed in his own day as America's leading writer, Twain received the highest accolade his audiences could bestow, being classified as a writer of juvenile fiction by a generation that did not understand him. No wonder Twain died a bitter, old man with hardly a good thought for the human race.

Twain's contemporary Henry James was as different from the Hannibal, Missouri, master as one could imagine. The product of an Eastern, elite family of culture and means, James spent most of his career in Europe, the setting for many of his novels. Alienated from a society that deified self-made businessmen devoid of taste or refinement, James wrote a series of complex sto-ries that explore men's minds, striving for psychological realism in an effort to illuminate the human condition. Though he separated himself physically from the United States, James often wrote about Americans in Europe, all very rich, very impressed by a superior civilization, very uncultured, but sincere. In *Daisy Miller,* a young American girl, "an inscrutable combination of audacity and innocence," is victimized not by corrupt European suitors, but by her own innocence. Unlike Twain who employed vernacular style, James developed a highly self-conscious concern for form and language which made his work inaccessible to a wide audience.

Literary Realism

William D. Howells, Mark Twain, and Henry James, together with Stephen Crane, Frank Norris, and others, acted as pathbreakers preparing the way for the next generation that pushed into the promised land. Despite a desire to free artists to confront social reality, Howells, for example, could never fully escape from his middle-class gentility that insisted that the good in life was more real than the evil. The next generation of writers, for whom the chaos and brutality of industrial America were formative experiences, felt no such constraints.

Three outstanding "liberated" writers were Frank Norris, Jack London, and Theodore Dreiser, men whose novels had terrific impact though as literary stylists they fell far below the mark of James, Howells, or Twain. Influenced profoundly by the work of France's Émile Zola, the father of naturalism in literature, they strove to write objective yet searing accounts of American men and institutions, of a system crushing individuality, of an affluent society ignoring a hungry proletariat. Norris's *The Octopus* (1901) and *The Pit* (1903) laid bare two "monster" institutions, California's Southern Pacific Railroad and Chicago's grain exchange. Jack London achieved considerable popularity with novels that tried unsuccessfully to mix Social Darwinism with Marxism. The greatest of the naturalists was Theodore Dreiser.

Beginning with *Sister Carrie* (1900) and reaching the peak of his power in *An American*

Tragedy (1925), Dreiser spoke for the new generation of naturalists who lifted the curtain on every corner of American experience, especially the corrupting influence of the business world. Unlike the comfortable Howells, Dreiser came from the other side of the tracks: poor and Catholic, his parents had been crushed by the struggle for survival. Dreiser's method was to pile detail upon detail (sometimes too many), drawn from life both in the lower depths and at the heights, to re-create a thickly textured, believable picture of how life in America really was. Seeking a scientific objectivity without distortion of reality, Dreiser nonetheless could not hide his compassion for the victims of a society he found essentially self-destructive. At the heart of the American tragedy stood Clyde Griffiths, the hero whose material success required a girl's death, a price he was ready to pay until chance unexpectedly did the job for him. *An American Tragedy* is a Horatio Alger story with the morality turned around. Dreiser discovered that the truth hurt. Censorship temporarily silenced him; *Sister Carrie,* suppressed shortly after publication in 1900, did not appear again for twelve years.

Yet during the years of Dreiser's enforced silence, powerful underground forces were at work that were to burst forth by the 1920s and destroy the Genteel Tradition. Everywhere a young generation of writers, painters, and musicians was experimenting and creating something new in America: an artistic community. Little magazines, with tiny circulations but big ideas, opened their pages to experimental writers whose unorthodox works would not otherwise have seen publication. In 1913, a mammoth art show brought modern painting to America, not only from the studios of the young masters in Paris but from their counterparts in the United States. "Everywhere young men and women were coming up," reported John Butler Yeats, an Irish painter, "who felt themselves the appointed children of the twentieth century." One of those children, Mabel Dodge Luhan, who ran the most successful *salon* in Greenwich Village, later looked back with exhilaration to a time when it seemed "as though everywhere, in that year of 1913, barriers went down and people reached out to each other who had never been in touch before." Young artists

were most likely to meet in New York City's Greenwich Village. Creative people from all over the country flocked there to find a community inhabited by others like themselves who stimulated, supported, and often savaged one another.

Perhaps the greatest contribution of "The Village" was to house small, experimental theaters operating on shoestrings which gave unknown playwrights such as Eugene O'Neill a chance to present their works. On the eve of the First World War, the American theater had shown few signs of maturation. A dismal parade of mindless melodramas and insipid musical comedies monopolized the productions on Broadway. The theater had adopted the star system—producing a system duplicated later by the movie industry. Ignoring Shakespeare's dictum, "the play's the thing!" the handful of producers who controlled Broadway put all their energies (and their dollars) into showing off their stars. The general public seemed satisfied, unconcerned over the lack of a national repertory company, or of experimental theater. But American intellectuals could not allow so powerful a vehicle of communication as the theater to be lost by default. In 1915 the Provincetown Players shifted their yet unheralded operations from Cape Cod to Greenwich Village, producing among other things translations of European "new wave" drama and some short plays by Eugene O'Neill.

O'Neill, the son of an alcoholic, actor father and a drug-addicted mother, had wandered as a youth, working for a while as a merchant seaman and finding at last in theater a means for personal expression. When in 1920 a Village theater group moved "uptown" to perform his *Emperor Jones,* O'Neill had arrived, beginning a career without peer among American dramatists. He wrote extensively, and won three Pulitzer prizes for drama in the 1920s.

Though not a member of the Lost Generation of the 1920s, since his damnation was a *personal* problem, O'Neill nevertheless kept in tune with what was modern in literary experience. As much an interior and psychological writer as Henry James, O'Neill's dramas still employed the innovations of the realistic and expressionistic European drama masters. Far from painting a rosy picture of human nature and of life in America, this brooding and brilliant man always flirted with but kept a short step away from despair, as in his greatest play, produced late in his career, *The Iceman Cometh* (1947). Yet he did not blame "the system" for human tragedies, but human nature itself, an attitude which made him an ideological loner. A Nobel Prize in 1936 reconfirmed that with Eugene O'Neill the American theater had come of age.

The Emergence of Bohemia

The trail to bohemia started typically in the villages and small towns of mid-America. To the rebels who departed, according to Sinclair Lewis, Main Street was "an unimaginatively standardized background . . . a rigid ruling of the spirit by the desire to appear respectable." It was "contentment . . . the contentment of the quiet dead . . . prohibition of happiness . . . slavery self-sought and self-defended . . . dullness made God." Its inhabitants were "savorless . . . gulping tasteless food, and sitting afterward coatless and thoughtless . . . listening to mechanical music, saying mechanical things about the excellence of Ford automobiles, and viewing themselves as the greatest race in the world."

Bohemia was another world. Convinced that "each of us at birth," as Malcolm Cowley put it, affirmatively if a bit romantically, "has special potentialities which are slowly crushed and destroyed by a standardized society," it sought to liberate people from repression so that a new generation might arise where children could "develop their own personalities, to blossom freely like flowers. . . ." Anticipating the gospels of the Beatniks and Hippies, Bohemians rejected conventional careers and insisted that people could only achieve "full individuality through creative work and beautiful living in beautiful surroundings." They turned inward to proclaim that "the body is a temple in which there is nothing unclean, a shrine to be adorned for the ritual of love." One lived for momentary gratifications and broke "every law, convention or rule of art that prevents self-expression or the full enjoyment of the moment."

Whereas Main Street had been built on deferred gratifications, repressed feelings, and preoccupation with money-making, the new morality of Bohemia denounced all forms of puritanism as the enemy of life. It stunted the possibilities for human happiness, they charged. Its prototype— the successful American businessman—like others who became the victims of materialism, led in Bohemian eyes a life that was "joyless and colorless . . . tawdry, uncreative, given over to the worship of wealth and machinery." And none paid a higher price than women. The businessman's wife, Malcolm Cowley argued, "finds him so sexually inept that she refuses to bear him children and so driveling in every way except as a money getter that she compels him to expend his energies solely in that direction while she leads a discontented, sterile, stunted life," seeking compensation "by making herself empress of culture."

The First World War, which ended a hundred years of peace and material progress in the Western World, helped to intensify and crystallize the revolution against the old morality. War's brutality and irrationality made the charges of men like Dreiser and others more plausible. A young novelist of the 1920s, F. Scott Fitzgerald, recounted the shock of discovery: "Here was a new generation shouting the old cries, learning the old creeds, through a revery of long days and nights; destined finally to go out into that dirty gray turmoil to follow love and pride; a new generation dedicated more than the last to the fear of poverty and the worship of success; grown up to find all Gods dead, all wars fought, all faiths in man shaken." Ernest Hemingway was another of a group of young Americans who enlisted in the First World War as a volunteer ambulance driver in Italy to exchange the safe life at home for the danger, adventure, courage, and fatalism of men in war. "I was always embarrassed by the words 'sacred,' 'glorious,' and 'sacrifice,' and the expression 'in vain,'" Hemingway remembered. "We had heard them . . . and read them, on proclamations . . . for a long time, and I had seen nothing sacred, and the things that were glorious had no glory and the sacrifices were like the stockyards at Chicago if nothing was done with the meat except to bury it."

At war's end, a stream of intellectuals abandoned America, including Greenwich Village, convinced that a nation whose ideal was Warren Harding and which responded to the call to liberate the human spirit with Prohibition could not be redeemed. How could they stay, explained Malcolm Cowley, when "hardly anyone seemed to believe in what he was doing—not the workmen on the production line, or the dealer forced to sell more units each month to more and more unwilling customers . . . or the underpaid newspaperman kidding historians . . . and despising his readers—not even the people at the head of the system, the bankers and stock promoters and politicians in the little green house on K Street; everybody was in it for the money, everybody was hoping to make a killing and get away."

Exiles of the Lost Generation of the 1920s went to Europe, escaping to Paris, one of them explained, "to recover the good life and the traditions of art, to free themselves from organized stupidity, to win their deserved place in the hierarchy of the intellect." But they found that though America was richer than other nations, it was not much different: the spirit of Main Street and of George F. Babbitt was abroad in the capitalist nations of Europe, and the spirit of statist repression was abroad in the totalitarian dictatorships, fascist and communist. Nor could the artists and intellectuals of the Old World offer the eager Americans "stable intellectual leadership and esthetic values." Abroad as at home, Americans "found only chaos and shifting values." In the end, art became their only hope for personal salvation. "I know myself but that is all," said Fitzgerald. As for man's destiny, he concluded—"so we beat on, boats against the current, borne back ceaselessly into the past." In words such as these Fitzgerald and Hemingway forged a popular literary style that heightened then released the anguish and alienation of a generation that felt cut off from the past and without an acceptable future. All that remained was to perfect the craftsmanship of their art so that they might convince others and themselves, in Alfred Kazin's words, "that in writing the story of their generation, they were in some sense describing the situation of contemporary humanity. . . ."

MUSIC, ART, AND ARCHITECTURE

Like the English from whom they derived so much of their culture, nineteenth-century Americans showed only meager gifts for making music —except for American blacks who poured their souls into spirituals. When Americans tried their hand at composing symphonic music, their tepid imitations of European masters revealed both lack of inspiration and rudimentary technique. In the early twentieth century, however, Americans began making their own music. First, jazz began moving upstream along the Mississippi from New Orleans to Chicago, again relying on black musical genius for sustenance. Then came the rise of Tin Pan Alley, a professional stable of New York song writers that ground out new tunes weekly, but still created sounds that gave urban America an authentic and popular voice. American music, popular tunes and jazz, became exportable.

Popular music flourished by exploiting the musical heritage of the American Negro. The first such borrowings took place before the Civil War with the rise of minstrelsy. The minstrel show, *very* freely adapting plantation banjo music, remained popular throughout the nineteenth century. In the 1890s the combination of such banjo music and the minstrel's versions of black strutting rhythm, or the cakewalk, became known as ragtime and swept the country. The piano replaced the banjo as ragtime's characteristic instrument. An aggressive popular music industry turned out ragtime songs by the hundreds, forever changing the nature of American social dancing. After the turn of the century, the cocky, rapid-fire urban musical comedy triumphed, especially in the Broadway productions of George M. Cohan, establishing a particularly American form of musical culture which would flourish in the Twenties and beyond.

Despite their origins, ministrelsy and ragtime had had very little to do with Negroes. The more direct line of black music extended from the plantation spirituals and work chants and urban songs of blacks, elements fused together around 1890-1900 in blues. New Orleans, with its slightly freer racial mores, and its high concentration of black musicians, provided the setting. In the clubs and "houses" of the French Quarter, black groups played ragtime (and anything else popular in order to earn a living) while they began developing other forms much closer to Negro folk songs. The music began spreading slowly north from New Orleans, to St. Louis and then Chicago. By about 1915, the word jazz entered the national vocabulary.

White America found jazz attractive but "immoral." The word itself had sexual connotations, perhaps from its French Quarter origins, or from its association with supposedly sensual blacks. But the music could not be ignored, as proved by the success of W. C. Handy's *St. Louis Blues* (1912) and "Dixieland" jazz bands. White musicians quickly tried their hand at the jazz idiom, and large jazz bands (such as Paul Whiteman's) further tamed the music to make it more acceptable to the mass, white audience. Black jazz musicians responded to these pressures, as the solo (as opposed to continuous ensemble playing) and the bigger band began to predominate. The jazz influence was clear in the works of George Gershwin, *Rhapsody in Blue* and *An American in Paris,* as in his later opera *Porgy and Bess* (1935). What became popular in the Twenties was not authentic New Orleans jazz, but a new American music unmistakably influenced by jazz. It would maintain its hold on America, and most of the world.

At the same time that popular music took off, America produced its first major composer of "classical" music. Charles Ives, a Connecticut Yankee, was a partner in one of the largest insurance agencies in New York City. He also wrote strange music which employed American folk materials in a style that flouted the conventions of classical composition. Isolated from direct contact with the musical world, working alone and in his spare time, Ives attempted to forge a new musical language—in ways that anticipated the next wave of European masters of modern music. Ives's music remained unplayed for decades, too difficult for musicians to perform, too unconventional for audiences to comprehend. Yet he caught in sound, better than any other American composer, the sense of innocence and its loss, the nostalgic longing for a simpler past into which one could escape from the anguish, uncertainty, and confusion of the present.

Painting

America's painters could not match its music makers in originality. America exported music but it imported its art. What Americans lacked

in original creativity in painting they more than made up for in imitating the European masters and acquiring samples of their best work. Capitalists who accumulated fortunes in industrial America became avid collectors. With money to burn, they ravaged Europe for paintings by Rembrandt, Rubens, Titian, and other great masters. When they patronized American artists they preferred imitations of European masters to anything original. Most American artists obliged. Leading American painters received their training in Europe and some of the best of them such as James M. Whistler and Winslow Homer spent much of their career in the Old World, close to the centers of artistic creativity. The most original of the late nineteenth-century artists, Alfred Ryder, composed dark, mystical canvases which few understood and even fewer appreciated. Like Charles Ives, Ryder's work did not find an audience until after he was no longer around to bask in its admiration.

At their best, American artists skillfully imitated styles which were popular in Europe. When Impressionism became the vogue, some Americans joined the movement. When European painters turned to rendering realistically the seamier sides of life, Americans, too, turned their gaze on life in all its rawness. In the fifteen years before the First World War, this so-called "Ash Can" school rejected the false gentility, sentimentality, and social sterility of the older pictorialists and society portraitists who flattered the rich and comfortable.

In 1913 a bombshell exploded in the American art world. New York City became the scene of the "Armory Show," an exhibition of some 1600 works of art that included examples of the latest achievements of Europe's avant-garde—post-impressionists, cubists, surrealists, and futurists. The show attracted a large attendance and great public interest, and it generated heated controversy. But it did not immediately redirect American art. The traditionalists stood firm and conservative critics dismissed modern art as "unadulterated cheek."

In the 1920s the pace of American artistic activity cooled down after the fever-pitch of the pre-Armory days. Most American artists remained basically realists, despite considerable experimenting in abstract forms. Typically the decade produced Daniel Chester French's heroic statue of Lincoln, and placed it in its neo-classical setting in the Lincoln Memorial in Washington, D.C. Not until the 1950s did America become the center of an artistic vision—abstract expressionism—which became one of the central forces in contemporary art.

Between 1880 and 1930, American painting lacked originality but American architecture more than compensated for this failing. Like painting, architecture after the Civil War was at first imitative. Architects borrowed from the past and ground out pseudo-classical, Gothic, and Renaissance buildings which their patrons deemed "artistic," because they thought them appropriate monuments to their wealth and importance. Only rarely did an architect such as Henry H. Richardson take an old style—the Romanesque—and infuse it with new life through powerful simplicity and apt design.

The New Architecture

In the generation after Richardson, modern American architecture was born. The traditionalists still dominated, designing structures in which there was little relationship between form and function, whose façades were more important than the way they worked. Greek and Roman temples went up in the guise of customhouses and music halls, and twenty-five story office buildings sported gargoyles, flying buttresses, and Corinthian columns somewhere between the eighteenth and twenty-first floors.

But new forces redirected American architecture. Technology revolutionized building and enabled man to construct tall buildings made of steel and concrete, utilizing elevators. The skyscraper posed new artistic challenges and the technology that made them possible gave architects new materials with which to build. Not until after the Second World War did a new international architectural style become the norm in America's large cities, but already two generations earlier a group of first-rate architectural innovators were pointing the way. At their center was Louis H. Sullivan and his pupil Frank Lloyd Wright. In 1901 Wright told a Hull House audience in Chicago what he thought was wrong, namely, everything:

Chicago in its ugliness today becomes as true an expression of the *life* lived here as is any center on earth where men come together closely to live it out or fight it out. . . . We must walk blindfolded through the streets of this, or any great modern American city, to fail to see that all this magnificent resource of machine-power and superior material has brought to us, so far, is degradation.

Sullivan and Wright devoted their careers to designing buildings that authentically rendered in steel, concrete, and glass a modern architectural vision. What is the essence of an office building, Sullivan once asked? ". . . At once we answer, it is lofty. . . . It must be tall, every inch of it tall . . . It must be every inch a proud, soaring thing, rising in sheer exultation that from bottom to top it is a unit without a single dissenting line." This meant that a building's form must be adapted to its function and must express that function. "All things in nature have a shape," he proclaimed, "that tells us what they are. . . . Unfailingly in nature these shapes express the inner life . . . of the animal, tree, bird, fish, that they present to us." Buildings must do no less. Sullivan and Wright made good on their promise. Each commission they accepted proved a fresh problem to be solved according to the doctrine that form follows function. And they began designing structures that could be found nowhere else and which seemed a natural part of the landscape or cityscape.

In time, Sullivan and Wright won recognition as America's greatest architects but not in the decades between 1890-1930. Preferring the "imperial architecture" of traditional styles that supposedly made buildings impressive, the major patrons entrusted few commissions to Sullivan or Wright. Compare, for example, the Chicago *Tribune* skyscraper (1923-1925), with its Gothic towers, by Raymond H. Hood and John Mead Howells with the daring simplicity and beauty of Frank Lloyd Wright's design for the Press Building in San Francisco, a design that never came to life. Or compare the New York mansion Richard M. Hunt designed for William K. Vanderbilt with the bold but simple beauty of Sullivan and Wright's James M. Charnley House, or Wright's F. C. Robie House. Sullivan, who died destitute, once bitterly observed: ". . . the unhappy, irrational, heedless, pessimistic, unlovely, distracted and decadent structures which make up the bulk of our contemporaneous architecture point with infallible accuracy to qualities in the heart and soul of the American people."

The new music, the new literature, and the new American architecture, all gave expression to the feelings and dreams of sensitive and imaginative artists growing up in modern America.

Most Americans passed them by, preferring the familiar and the nostalgic. The artists of early twentieth-century America, however, were creating a modern High Culture in the United States out of their alienation from the prevailing values and the central tendencies of a nation whose folk heroes were successful businessmen like Henry Ford and popular politicians like Warren Harding and Calvin Coolidge.

Chapter 27
The Anxieties of Mass Society, 1900–1930

The shift from a rural society of individual entrepreneurs to an urban, mass society of workers, managers, and bureaucrats and the new life styles of mass society bewildered and frightened millions of Americans. They seemed powerless to check or control the unsettling forces of change which swirled around them. Rapid social change reawakened old anxieties and stirred new ones. The self-confidence that fueled the Progressives' earnest though ineffective attempts to achieve stability and social justice gave way to repressive apprehensions in the second and third decades of the twentieth century.

For those holding fast to the vision of an older America, the enemy lurked everywhere. The cities, they thought, were cancerous growths, spawning radicals, foreigners, and the sexually liberated Bohemians. In these cesspools of all that was "un-American," people danced to jazz music, raucous and lascivious new tunes created by black musicians in New Orleans. "Does Jazz put the Sin in Syncopation?" asked *The Ladies Home Journal* suggestively. Prominent clergymen rushed to denounce jazz as "a sensual teasing of the string of physical passion." Sinful or not, the people of urban America loved the new sounds.

Many traditionalists thought the disease of modernism so virulent and so widespread that only strong measures could save the country. The crusade to restore the old morality took many forms. Citizens banded together in mobs and private associations, such as the Ku Klux Klan, to intimidate and punish those regarded as dangerous, while government lent its powerful helping hand. Trampling on the civil liberties of radicals and aliens, especially after the country entered the First World War, and during the Red Scare of 1919, the government restricted free speech and imprisoned dissenters. A new federal agency—the forerunner of the Federal Bureau of Investigation (FBI)—emerged in the struggle for internal security through repression. Radical aliens became subject to deportation in 1919 and mass roundups clamped thousands of unoffending people in jail.

The temptation to blame Europe as the source of all trouble finally triumphed over America's traditional hospitality to newcomers, its confidence in its capacity to absorb people from Europe's many cultures. Oriental immigration had already been cut off as unassimilable, and in 1921 the open doors that had welcomed the Old World's "tired, poor and helpless" shut firmly, allowing only a trickle to enter. Immigration restriction, however, could not and did not discipline those already here, the millions whose life-styles clashed with 100 percent WASP Americanism.

After over a century of campaigning, anti-liquor forces, capitalizing on the patriotic and repressive mood of wartime America, finally succeeded in prohibiting the manufacture and sale of alcoholic beverages, and for over a decade the United States remained technically dry. Much of the Prohibitionist leadership came from the Protestant churches which were simultaneously fighting a rearguard action against the inroads made by secularism and science at the expense of religious authority. The churches counterattacked with dramatic efforts to restore "the old-time religion" and to prevent the public schools from instructing youngsters in scientific explanations of the earth's formation.

But repression could not hold back the uncertain future. For good or for ill, America had become an urban, pluralistic society. Its people worshiped in different faiths, came from different parts of the world, and clung to many badges of cultural identity imported from the Old World. Americans still quaffed illegal booze, hotly pursuing the creature comforts devised by advanced technology. Yet repression was not a total failure. It gave those frightened by mass society the illusion that they could block change without fundamentally altering the directions of American development. And poisonous repression produced its own antidote. Under the threat of attack, Americans gained a clearer understanding of the meaning of individual liberty, the strengths of a pluralist society, and the liberating possibilities and worth of the new modes of life. The immigrants, the "wets," the civil libertarians, the modernist clergy, all resisted fear and hate and ignorance. Their lost or drawn battles of the 1920s would be fought again another day, and more successfully.

THE DRIVE FOR INTERNAL SECURITY

During most of their history, Americans had maintained confidence in the durability of their way of life. Only rarely had hysteria gripped the country, bringing with it repression of unpopular elements, such as the Federalist drive against the Jeffersonian Republicans in the late 1790s, or Lincoln's suppression of militant opposition elements in the North during the Civil War. Three thousand miles of ocean secured the United States from foreign attack, and a tradition of settling differences among themselves peacefully seemed sufficient guarantee for the country's internal security.

In the twentieth century, however, many Americans lost their nerve. The appearance of radical revolutionary organizations, such as the anarchists, socialists, the Industrial Workers of the World, and after 1917 the communists, shook their belief in mutual trust. At the same time, America's involvement in the First World War dramatized the end of a century of isolation. For all the idealism with which Wilson had justified American participation, the overriding concern was fear of a German victory which would upset the world balance of power and endanger American interests. Postwar disillusionment, especially the failure to establish effective peace-keeping machinery in the League of Nations, betrayed Wilson's promise of a war to end all wars. None could foresee precisely how the Versailles settlement of 1919 sowed the seeds for the later rise of Adolph Hitler and the Second World War, but none could ignore the revolutionary crisis provoked by the war—especially not after the overthrow of the czar in Russia and his replacement, first by a short-lived democratic regime, but then by communist dictatorship. The emergence of Red Russia encouraged revolutionaries elsewhere, raising their hopes that the

Red Flag would someday fly elsewhere too. In this fearful atmosphere the American majority became prey to hysteria. John Lord O'Brian who worked in the Department of Justice during the First World War reported that people thought "a phantom ship sailed into our harbors with gold from the Bolsheviki with which to corrupt the country; . . . [German] submarine captains landed on our coast, went to the theater and spread influenza germs; a new species of pigeon, though to be German, was shot in Michigan. . . ."

American reaction to foreign and domestic radicalism exceeded all sensible views of the challenge it posed. The repression visited upon dissenters originated in an irrational feeling of insecurity springing from gnawing doubts about the stability and justness of the social order. Frustrated by intractable problems of adjusting to mass society, threatened by fears they had in part concocted themselves, committed wholly in a world war they wished to avoid, Americans sought to impose conformity on the weak minority of nonconformists who made attractive scapegoats.

The "Wobblies"

No group was more vulnerable than the Industrial Workers of the World founded in 1905. The "Wobblies," or IWW, inhabited the far left wing of organized American labor. Preaching revolution, not reform, as the only hope for working people, the Wobblies had a strong following in the mining, lumber, and migratory labor camps in the West. Several dramatic strikes gained for them a reputation (not wholly deserved) for violence, but their revolutionary ideology, their attack on organized religion, and their use of the red flag frightened people. Never before had the downtrodden developed an organization as visible and as potentially dangerous as the Wobblies. Worst of all, they scoffed at the view that America was the Promised Land. "You ask me why the IWW is not patriotic to the United States," explained one. "If you were a bum without a blanket . . . if your job never kept you long enough in a place to qualify you to vote; if you slept in a lousy, sour bunkhouse and ate food just as rotten as they could give you and get away with; if deputy sheriffs shot your cooking cans full of holes and spilled your grub on the ground . . . if every person who represents law and order and the nation beat you up, railroaded you to jail, and the good Christian people cheered and told them to go to it, how in hell do you expect a man to be patriotic?"

Repudiated by the AFL and the Socialist party, the IWW was too radical to attract the American masses, but businessmen, especially in the West, wanted to take no chances. Under their prodding, the state and federal governments began systematically to harass the Wobblies, seeking to drive them out of existence. "Hanging is too good for them and they would be much better dead," suggested the San Diego *Tribune* as early as 1912. "Now I would execute these anarchists if I could, for they are absolutely useless in the human economy, and then I would deport them," suggested a congressman with a talent for overkill, "so that the soil of our country might not be polluted by their presence even after the breath had gone out of their bodies." Since some Wobbly leaders were aliens, and Congress in 1903 for the first time had made radical beliefs grounds for deportation, the government used immigration laws to sanction mass roundups.

The repression of the war years did not end after the Armistice of November 1918. The postwar mania for internal security became an extension of the wartime spirit of intolerance, and the social dislocations accompanying demobilization intensified it. A fear of postwar mass unemployment set in as millions of soldiers returned home to look for jobs. Production levels held relatively firm, but the cost of living skyrocketed (increasing 20 percent between 1918 and 1920). This hurt Americans on salaries and fixed incomes, and contributed to the uneasiness which soon degenerated into hysteria.

Inflation produced a rash of strikes and stoppages which in 1919 involved four million workers. First the clothing workers, then the textile workers went out, demanding and winning shorter hours and substantial pay boosts. Next, the AFL decided to organize the virtually non-unionized steel industry. Half of these men worked from 11 to 14 hours a day for poor pay, so the union had little trouble signing up 100,000

recruits. But the companies, led by U. S. Steel, fought back. Company president Judge Elbert H. Gary would not negotiate, and the combination of injunctions, firing of union organizers, and armed protection for thousands of strike breakers caused the AFL organizing campaign to wither.

The company also spent heavily on propaganda to get across its side of the argument, and to discredit the strikers as "Bolsheviks." The coal fields witnessed labor unrest, too. The United Mine Workers (UMW), now led by the aggressive John L. Lewis, declared the wartime no-strike agreements dead. But Washington sustained their validity until 1920 and imposed the Lever Act to brand the strike illegal. Lewis, admitting that "we cannot fight the government," ordered his men back to the mines. Most of them continued to stay out, however, and as a result won pay increases from an arbitration board.

Another strike, though it involved few men, held the public's attention and fed its fears. Boston policemen, earning inadequate salaries, obtained an AFL charter in 1919. The police commissioner would not negotiate, and instead fired nineteen of the union leaders. The policemen walked out in September. Volunteer constables could not control the situation. When looting broke out the National Guard had to be called in. The striking police officers were fired, and new men took their jobs. Governor Calvin Coolidge had done little to avert the crisis and strike, but he gained national acclaim by rejecting Samuel Gompers' protests about repression of labor rights. Said Coolidge: "There is no right to strike against the public safety by anybody, anywhere, anytime." Most Americans agreed, and in that turbulent year, 1919, conservative America doubtless would have denied any right to strike.

Red Scare

Since Germany had been defeated in war, those concerned with alien dangers concentrated on domestic radicals. Communist revolts in Germany and Hungary, and the formation of the Communist Third International in 1919 stimulated such reactions, as did the communists' prediction of speedy world takeover. In America, the Socialist party (founded back in 1901) split in 1919, the more radical wing forming the Communist party. All unrest and all violence were then blamed on the Reds or the Wobblies, or both. A general strike in Seattle early in the year had been crushed by use of police and vigilantes. A short time later, Seattle's mayor received a bomb in the mail, but it did not go off. Another such lethal package did explode in Washington, D.C., at a senator's home. That same day, a New York City postal clerk held up sixteen parcels for insufficient postage. All of them contained bombs, and they were addressed to John D. Rockefeller and Postmaster General Burleson among others. The absurdity of waging revolution "through the mails" (and failing to buy enough stamps in the bargain) suggested that the sender was a psychotic who happened to be a radical, but the public was in no mood for fine distinctions. All left-of-center politics became tainted with the charge of terrorism.

One of the prospective bomb victims was the attorney general, A. Mitchell Palmer. Palmer, a Quaker, had a progressive record and had been appointed to the cabinet because of supposed friendliness to labor. Though a supporter of women's suffrage, anti-child-labor laws, and the League of Nations, as attorney general he set out to rid the country of radicals, thus becoming the prototype of the Wilsonian liberal gone sour. Although Congress refused to adopt a new, police-state sedition law sponsored by Palmer, he directed massive raids against radicals in late 1919. Hundreds of aliens, most with no criminal record, were deported, and several thousand U.S. citizens were held without charges, some for as long as a week, and then simply released. This was the police state in action, the worst peacetime violation of civil liberties since the Alien and Sedition Acts of 1798. Few Americans protested, however. Palmer became a temporary national hero with dreams of the presidency who esteemed the nickname, "The Fighting Quaker." But in 1919, Palmer was no joke.

Veterans' organizations such as the American Legion led the fight for 100 percent Americanism as did businessmen who hoped to weaken the labor movement by smearing it with the brush of radicalism. In the campaign against dissent

the Bureau of Investigation, predecessor of the FBI, played a major role. Established originally by the attorney general in 1909 to help curb interstate crime, in its early days the FBI concentrated on fighting organized vice rings. From its inception, the FBI tried to enlarge its jurisdiction and overcome traditional American hostility toward a secret police. Proclaiming itself the ears of the government against internal subversion, the bureau declared war against all disloyal and radical elements. Unable or unwilling to distinguish between the few radicals who were dangerous and the great majority employing peaceful means of protest, the FBI made indiscriminate arrests during the 1919 Red Scare. By the early 1920s, under the leadership of J. Edgar Hoover, it had secretly catalogued a half million Americans as dangerous. When Congress investigated the agency, it denied responsibility for searches and seizures which one U.S. senator described as "the lawless acts of a mob." And in the 1920s, as an arm of a corrupt attorney general, the FBI spied on congressmen seeking to expose scandal in the executive branch.

During the height of the Red Scare, Charles Evans Hughes, the Republican presidential candidate in 1916, and future Chief Justice of the Supreme Court, tried to rally moderates: "Perhaps to an extent unparalleled in our history," he warned, "the essentials of liberty are being disregarded." Hughes spoke for the classes which maintained their poise, as did New York's Governor Al Smith, an Irish Catholic, who spoke for the ethnic masses so often victimized by the hysteria. In his message vetoing a batch of repressive laws, Smith recalled Benjamin Franklin's warning: "They that can give up essential liberty to obtain a little temporary safety deserve neither liberty nor safety."

Fortunately, the Red Scare subsided. The cooling off process began in New York, where the legislature had expelled five legally elected members simply because they were Socialists. This time there was protest, and Charles Evans Hughes led a group of "blue-ribbon" lawyers who defended the rights of the expelled assemblymen. The scare psychology began to look increasingly ridiculous when supposed threats failed to materialize. Palmer then put all his hopes for radical unrest and personal advancement on May Day 1920. He called for extra police, and standby orders to National Guardsmen, but the revolutionary day went by peacefully. Not even an explosion outside the Wall Street office of J. P. Morgan & Co. which killed thirty-eight people several months later could revive the panic atmosphere of 1919. Palmer had been deflated, and in November Americans voted overwhelmingly for a man who promised relief from political intensity and social unrest. Warren Harding observed: "Too much has been said about Bolshevism in America."

The Supreme Court and Civil Liberties

The attacks on civil liberty led to efforts to protect the victims through the courts with the help of the newly formed American Civil Liberties Union. Founded originally by middle-class Progressives to defend the rights of conscientious objectors, the ACLU became the country's principal libertarian organization. It fought government censorship and defended opponents of the war and radicals caught in the net of the postwar Red Scare. Increasingly, the ACLU came to the aid of labor unions which became favorite victims of attacks on freedom of speech and assembly in the 1920s.

At the same time, the United States Supreme court upheld most state and federal prosecutions judges had to determine whether individual liberty could be protected in times of stress. The court upheld most state and federal prosecutions of radicals as legitimate restrictions on liberty in the interest of maintaining order. But to do so the antilibertarian justices (the "law and order" advocates) had to develop a legal rationale that squared repression with the American traditions of freedom and the guarantees of the Bill of Rights. This gave libertarians an opportunity to force the courts to weigh carefully the liberty of the individual against the state's need for security. The conflict produced a divided Supreme Court, although the majority usually upheld the government. However two dissenters—Justices Oliver Wendell Holmes and Louis D. Brandeis—

argued eloquently for judicial protection of civil liberties, a view which the Supreme Court eventually adopted a generation later, thus assuming for itself a new role as chief defender of weak and unpopular minorities.

In *Shenck* v. *the United States* (1919), Holmes had upheld the conviction of a socialist accused of obstructing the draft, but at the same time he defended freedom of thought and argued that "Persecution for the expression of opinions seems to me perfectly logical if you have no doubt of your premises and power. . . . But when men have realized that time has upset many fighting faiths, they may come to believe even more than they believe the very foundations of their own conduct that the ultimate good desired is better reached by free trade of ideas—that the best test of truth is the power of the thought to get itself accepted in the competition of the market. . . . That at any rate is the theory of our Constitution." That theory, he noted, is "an experiment, as all life is an experiment. . . . We should be eternally vigilant against attempts to check the expression of opinions that we loathe and believe to be fraught with death, unless they so imminently threaten immediate interference with the lawful and pressing purpose of the law that immediate check is required to save the country. . . ."

In a series of landmark decisions in the 1920s, the Supreme Court became the principal guarantor of individual liberty though it stumbled into this role reluctantly and haphazardly. The states posed the principal threat to civil liberty, especially after the war when federal wartime control lapsed. By 1920 thirty-five states had adopted legislation which restricted the free speech of radicals. Civil libertarians, therefore, searched for a constitutional basis that would enable the federal judiciary to restrain the states. That occurred in 1923 when the court struck down an Oregon law, backed by the Ku Klux Klan, that required Catholics and others who preferred to send their children to church schools to enroll them in the public school. This decision opened the way for further extension of the Fourteenth Amendment to protect citizens against state laws that limited freedom of speech and the press, and eventually to other provisions of the Bill of Rights *fundamental* to individual liberty. In 1927 Justice Brandeis, in a dissenting opinion, added his ringing voice to Holmes's earlier reasoned defense of freedom:

> Those who won our independence believed that the final end of the state was to make men free to develop their faculties. They believed liberty to be the secret of happiness and courage to be the secret of liberty. . . . They recognized the risks to which all human institutions are subject. But they knew that order cannot be secured merely through fear of punishment for its infraction; that it is hazardous to discourage thought, hope, and imagination; that fear breeds repression; that repression breeds hate; that hate menaces stable government. . . . Recognizing the occasional tyrannies of governing majorities, they amended the Constitution so that free speech and assembly should be guaranteed.

Fortunately for the liberties of Americans, the quest for national security through repression had ebbed by the mid-twenties, as Americans regained confidence amid unprecedented prosperity. Radicalism, of the socialist, communist, or Wobbly varieties, was weak; organized labor declined in strength; and wartime nationalism became a distant memory. In retrospect, the decision to get involved in Europe's woes in 1917 came under increasing attack from conservative and progressive opinion. But the hysteria did not wane until Congress ended unrestricted immigration, which champions of 100 percent Americanism had long insisted was the main source of subversive ideas and radical supporters.

THE HEYDAY OF RACISM

Bigotry and racism flourished in postwar America as never before. Racist ideology became respectable and widespread. Those Americans who crowned the Nordic "race" as the superior race relegated millions of Americans to a condition of hereditary inferiority, especially the newcomers from southern and eastern Europe, as well as the older proscribed and oppressed groups, Negroes and Indians. Hatred of Jews and Catholics reached a high point when millions of Americans—North and South—flocked to join a revived Ku Klux Klan. The Klan promised to suppress by force if necessary those who were turning America into an urban, secular, and pluralistic society. Xenophobia did begin to subside by the mid-1920s, but not before it had intimidated its intended victims, and debased those who had sought to conquer fears by organizing to hate.

By the 1920s, Congress finally gave in to the exclusionist pressure groups that had campaigned against foreigners for two generations. The imposition of a literacy test for immigrants in 1917 had not prevented the arrival of nearly a million foreigners in 1920, and millions seemed poised to abandon war-weary Europe in search of the American Dream. "America must be kept American," opined President Calvin Coolidge on signing the immigration bill of 1924, the National Origins Act, and he meant a very particular type of American. The new measure ended unrestricted immigration from Europe and established a quota system for the Eastern Hemisphere based on an ethnic group's proportion in the 1890 census, thus discriminating against the "new" in favor of the "old" immigration from northern Europe. It also limited immigration to no more than 150,000 persons per year.

This historic reversal of a policy that had welcomed men from all parts of Europe reflected a loss of faith in older ideals. Once the country had been confident of America's ability to assimilate Irish, German, Russian, or Italian peasants, and countless other strangers. The 1920s saw that commitment shelved. The First World War had increased doubts about the loyalty of the hyphenated Americans, and about the effectiveness of the "melting pot." The newcomers herded together in urban ghettos, formed ethnic churches and benevolent societies, they voted for friendly politicians, and they maintained many Old World customs—all understandable attempts to cushion the massive disruption in their lives caused by emigration to America.

The native-born mistook the immigrants' tendency to conserve their past and its traditions for hostility to American ways, though none had a more naïve faith in the promises of their adopted country than the newcomers. Immigrant adaptation and success in America, limited though it was, seemed threatening to the native-born. As the attacks mounted in the early 1920s, the immigrants found themselves too weak, too politically isolated, and too divided to influence public policy. A few of their leaders poured scorn on the racists. One such spokesman was Fiorello La Guardia, Republican congressman from a polyglot district in New York City. He, himself, was a second-generation hyphenated American—his father was Italian, his mother Jewish, and he an Episcopalian. La Guardia confessed impishly: "I have no family tree. The only member of my family who has is my dog Yank. He is the son of Doughboy, who was the son of Siegfried, who was the son of Tannhaeuser, who was the son of Wotan. A distinguished family tree, to be sure, but after all, he's only a son of a bitch."

The postwar Red Scare helped fuel the anti-immigrant nativist impulse. Most aliens were actually conservative or apolitical, but a handful of revolutionaries from eastern Europe made plausible the nativist identification of all "new" immigrants with subversion. Furthermore, the postwar disillusionment with the ability of Progressive reform to deal with social maladjustment left people open to irrational appeals. They blamed all problems on the "un-Americans." Middle-class Progressives regarded foreigners ambivalently, recognizing, as did businessmen, the economic advantages of unrestricted immigrant labor; but many still felt that the immigrants undercut wages, supported corrupt political machines, and preferred to live in squalor. A typical Progressive, a native-born Protestant, mingled a desire to help the downtrodden with a paternalistic distrust of those in need of benevolence.

On the whole, however, Progressives resolved their ambivalence in favor of the alien. The thrust of the Progressive impulse had been a conviction that rational social control would maximize equality of opportunity and restore cohesiveness and stability. "I now have one Catholic in my cabinet," boasted Theodore Roosevelt back in 1908, "and I now have a Jew in the cabinet; and

part of my object in each appointment was to implant in the minds of our fellow Americans of Catholic or of Jewish faith, or of foreign ancestry or birth, the knowledge that they have in this country just the same rights and opportunities as everyone else. . . ." But the collapse of Progressivism after the First World War convinced many Americans that only a coercive "100 percent Americanism" could assure stability at home. Instead of responding to the conditions that provoked thousands of steel workers to strike in 1919, they acquiesced as the government and the steel mill owners crushed the strike. That thousands of strikers were foreign born, and that they had a Communist leader, provided final proof that the country must act to stem the influx of un-American forces.

Under these pressures, businessmen, earlier opponents of immigration restriction, gave way before a coalition of racists who blamed the newcomers for their own relative decline in power and status, the American Federation of Labor which blamed immigrants for undercutting wages, and some ex-Progressives who argued that immigrants, not the conditions they encountered, produced squalor and corruption in urban America.

But bigotry did more than provide an outlet for expressing fears. Despite twisted efforts to justify racism scientifically, the insistence that ethnic groups and races differed in basic intelligence and morality remained at bottom irrational, catering to deeply felt needs of people "isolated from each other in strange places" who "could no longer recognize the brotherly gesture." The strain of living in a mobile society, a society in which neither tradition, the family, nor the church could adequately cushion an individual's struggle for success and self-esteem, led some to seek a racially defined nationalism. "It was an innermost necessity of their being," a historian has explained, "that they should come to recognize their brothers. If they could exclude or set apart the strangers, the outsiders, then they might somehow come to know each other." Yet long before the new immigrants from Europe, and in sharper ways, American Indians and blacks had suffered the consequences of racism.

THE INDIANS

In 1787 Congress pledged "utmost good faith" toward the Indians, and promised that "their lands and property would never be taken without consent." But in the century that followed, Americans repeatedly warred against the Indians whose effective resistance collapsed by 1880. First, Indians east of the Mississippi had been removed to the "Permanent Indian Reservation" in the West. But American settlers soon demanded those lands, once considered worthless. Then the Indians were herded into fixed reservations to free more land for white settlement. As white pressure mounted again, new treaties reduced the size of reservations, leaving the Indians with the poorest lands.

In the 1880s the reservation system itself came under attack. Whites who coveted the Indians' remaining lands wanted the reservations broken up. Eastern humanitarians and reformers expressed shock at the wretched living conditions on the reservations, arguing that Indians had no future as long as they lived in primitive, tribal societies. The reformers wanted to transform the Indians into farmers so that they could be assimilated into the national mainstream. The Dawes Act (1887) entitled each Indian head of household to 160 acres; the remaining undivided lands were to be sold and the proceeds used for Indian education.

The Dawes Act failed. White speculators easily cheated Indians out of their lands, and in the half century after its passage Indians lost 86 million of their 138 million acres. The more perceptive tribal leaders fought against the breakup of the reservations. The assimilationist policy reflected Americans' failure to appreciate the vitality of Indian culture or to foresee the devastating cultural shock Indians would experience when torn from their ancestral social organization. Boarding schools separated Indian children from their tribes and sought to turn them into aliens among their own people when they returned. Bureaucrats sent from Washington ordered Indian men to cut their long hair, ignorant or scornful of the importance Indians placed on preserving their native life-styles. Left with worthless lands, without capital or skills, Indians

sank into pauperism. As in the past, disease took a frightful toll. Not until 1910 did the Indian population, which had declined from between one and two million to a little over 100,000 after three centuries of contact with whites, begin to increase.

Despite recurrent efforts by white philanthropists and missionaries to aid the Indian, most Americans remained indifferent. "I suppose I should be ashamed to say that I take the Western view of the Indian," admitted President Theodore Roosevelt. "I don't go so far as to think that the only good Indians are the dead Indians, but I believe nine out of every ten are, and I shouldn't inquire too closely into the case of the tenth."

THE BLACK MAN IN THE AGE OF SEGREGATION

In the late nineteenth and early twentieth century, Americans also thought they had achieved a final solution in black-white relations. The end of Reconstruction and the withdrawal of federal troops from the South in 1877 left the blacks at the mercy of their white brothers. Without resources, the ex-slaves became tenant farmers or sharecroppers hopelessly tied to the soil by debt. Black political power withered in the face of terror and campaigns for Negro disfranchisement. During Radical Reconstruction, Negroes had gained some social equality, at least in public transportation and in such public places as theaters and restaurants. But the turn-of-the-century drive for segregation of the races proved irresistible. Public schools had always been segregated, and new "Jim Crow" segregation legislation passed in the 1880s and 1890s by nearly all-white legislatures formalized discriminatory practices that earlier had been extralegal and inconsistently applied. The Supreme Court permitted segregation by invalidating most of the post-war Civil Rights Acts and interpreting the Fourteenth Amendment narrowly. Then in *Plessy* v. *Ferguson* (1896) the court held that railroads could segregate passengers racially so long as they provided "separate but equal" facilities. The court later extended this principle to other public facilities, including schools. The new doctrine was a subterfuge, for everyone knew that facilities for Negroes were not equal. But Northerners, convinced of black inferiority, and eager to bind the wounds of the Civil War, had long before abandoned the rights of black people.

Assured of a free hand, white Southerners systematically robbed black people of their remaining rights in the two decades after 1890. Jim Crow legislation subjected Negroes to constant, everyday humiliation. Hotels, restaurants, and theaters refused to receive them, railroads relegated them to filthy "smoking cars," and they had to ride in the rear of streetcars. Shopkeepers served them last and denied them the courtesy titles of Mr. and Mrs. Through a variety of devices—poll taxes, discriminatory literacy tests, and the all-white primary election—blacks also lost the vote. Despite the effectiveness of legal pressures in condemning Negroes to second-class citizenship, Southerners also employed terror to keep Negroes in line. Lynch mobs became a part of the Southern way of life. Lynchings averaged a hundred a year in the 1880s and 1890s, and then tapered off; yet between 1918 and 1927, 416 blacks died at the hands of lynch mobs. They included a pregnant black woman who, in May 1918, was strung up by the ankles, soaked in gasoline, and burned alive as the fetus of her unborn child was cut out and smashed. A fusillade of shots then riddled her body.

The lynch mobs had revealed graphically racism's effects: fearful and guilt-ridden after three centuries of exploiting blacks and infected with the recurrent need to assert their supremacy, whites resorted to barbarism. They justified lynching as necessary to "protect the honor" of white women, though less than a quarter of the lynch victims were accused of rape. "Whenever the Constitution comes between me and the virtue of the white women of South Carolina," bellowed a senator from that state, "then I say 'to hell with the constitution'. . . ." With such blanket support from many leaders of Southern society, it is not surprising that the mass of whites periodically lost control.

By the twentieth century, white Southerners had perfected a system of white supremacy which kept blacks poor and subservient. The principal force behind this drive for racial domination was the need to find alternative means to slavery for controlling the blacks. But the timing and intensification of the trend toward a complete system of Jim Crow reflected increasing tensions within white society as well. As long as white Southerners had to defend themselves against a hostile North, they repressed their own differences, forming a united, Democratic front. But economic distress in the late 1880s and in the 1890s weakened white solidarity. Poor white farmers who found conservative white leadership unresponsive to their needs either became Populists or they backed Democratic, agrarian politicians. From time to time, poor whites cooperated with blacks to work for common economic goals, but such cooperation was short-lived, opportunistic, and fragile. Conservative Democrats bought black votes to turn back the challengers. This corruption enraged the agrarians, who demanded disfranchisement of blacks. The frustration and ultimate defeat of Populism in the late 1890s left agrarian politicians without effective issues.

Racist demagoguery filled the void. Mississippian James K. Vardaman, typical of the new breed, campaigned for governor in 1900 in a lumber wagon drawn by eight oxen, a visible symbol of his identity with the poor whites. "The Negro," he charged, was a "lazy, lying, lustful animal which no conceivable amount of training can transform into a tolerable citizen." "We should be justified," he argued, "in slaughtering every Ethiop on earth to preserve unsullied the honor of one Caucasian home."

Northerners were no strangers to negrophobia. In the early twentieth century, improved farming methods in the South reduced the planters' need for labor at the same time that Negroes were finding alternative employment in the North, especially after the First World War shut off European sources of cheap labor. In 1910, only 10 percent of American blacks lived outside of the South; by 1920, the figure rose to 20 percent.

As the number of Negroes in the urban, industrial centers grew rapidly, they competed with whites for jobs; and the participation of black soldiers in the First World War (fighting in segregated units, however) further raised Negro hopes for integration. Racial tensions mounted to an unprecedented level and erupted into race riots in Chicago, Philadelphia, Washington, and other cities between 1917 and 1919. Seventy blacks died at the hands of lynch mobs in the latter year, some of them uniformed war veterans. In Chicago, two weeks of rioting left the chief Negro district a shambles.

In the face of overwhelming white hostility, Northern and Southern blacks found both major political parties indifferent at best, hostile at worst. The Republicans had once courted the Northern Negro vote, but the party realignment of 1896 gave the GOP such a commanding majority in the Northeast and Midwest that it could ignore the black vote which earlier had possessed some strategic value. Theodore Roosevelt invited Booker T. Washington, the most prominent Negro leader of the day, to the White House in 1902, but this token gesture provoked so much criticism that he regretted making it. President Taft ignored blacks and cultivated white Southern Republicans, and Woodrow Wilson, a Southerner by birth, and heavily indebted to that region for his election, resegregated the federal civil service.

Black Accommodation vs. Black Power

In view of these realities, and the absence of anything resembling "Black Power," it is not surprising that Booker T. Washington adopted an accommodationist philosophy. An ex-slave, Washington became head of the Tuskegee Institute, a vocational training school in Alabama, from which he urged blacks to postpone their quest for political and social equality. They should instead place their hopes on self-help by learning skills that would uplift black people economically. The Negro, he reassured the country, was "fast learning the lesson that he cannot afford to act in a manner that will alienate his southern white neighbors." At the Atlanta Exposition in 1895, Washington won national acclaim for his philosophy. "No race can prosper," he proclaimed, "till it learns that there is as much dignity in tilling a field as in writing a poem. It is at the bottom of life we must begin." He exhorted whites to help Negroes help themselves economically by "casting down your bucket among my people . . . who will buy your surplus land, make blossom the waste places in your

fields, and run your factories." Blacks, Washington promised, would repay white benevolence tenfold: "You and your [white] families will be surrounded by the most patient, faithful, law-abiding and unresentful people that the world has seen."

White politicians and philanthropists responded enthusiastically. Washington acquired money and power with which he dominated the Negro community. He tirelessly preached his message of self-improvement. "It has been interesting to note," be boasted, "the effect that the use of the toothbrush has had in bringing about a higher degree of civilization among the students [at Tuskegee]." And despite overwhelming evidence to the contrary, Washington reassured blacks: "Every persecuted individual and race should get much consolation out of the great human law, which is universal and eternal, that merit, no matter under what skin found, is in the long run recognized and rewarded."

Though Washington publicly preached passive accommodation to white supremacy, privately he worked to oppose further erosion of the political and social rights of black people—but with little success, for his power came by virtue of his recognition by the white community. Operating from a position of black powerlessness, Washington thought his proposals offered the best hope under the circumstances. A small but growing black middle class, making money in businesses that served the black community—insurance companies and banks, shops, and mortuaries—agreed with him.

Eventually, however, some Negroes rose to challenge Washington's leadership. Led by W. E. B. Du Bois, a Northern-born sociologist and historian trained at Harvard, they argued that accommodation was doomed. "Is it possible and probable," Du Bois asked, "that nine million men can make effective progress in economic lines if they are deprived of political rights, made a servile caste, and allowed only the most meager chance for developing their exceptional men?" At a time when industry, not agriculture, was the economic wave of future, Washington encouraged blacks to become better farmers. At a time when Negroes needed above all to believe in themselves, Washington reinforced their self-doubts. "Manly self-respect," Du Bois insisted, "is worth more than lands and houses, and . . . a people who voluntarily surrender such respect, or cease striving for it, are not civilizing."

A brilliant, highly educated man, Du Bois gave voice to deep anguish. "One ever feels his twoness," he noted, "an American, a Negro; two souls, two thoughts, two unreconciled strivings; two warring ideals in one dark body, whose dogged strength alone keeps it from being torn asunder." The black man, he explained, did not want "to Africanize America, for America has too much to teach the world and Africa." Nor did he wish to "bleach his Negro soul in a flood of white Americanism, for he knows that Negro blood has a message for the world. He simply wants to make it possible for a man to be both a Negro and an American, without being cursed and spit upon by his fellows. . . ." Above all, Du Bois preached that Black is Beautiful: "the unknown treasures of their inner life, the strange rendings of nature they have seen, may give the world new points of view and make their loving, living, and doing precious to all human hearts."

In 1908 a small band of whites and blacks, including Du Bois, founded the National Association for the Advancement of Colored People (NAACP) to fight for political and social equality. Adopting a strategy of protest and resistance, in 1915 they won their first legal victory when the Supreme Court declared unconstitutional an Oklahoma law devised to disfranchise Negroes.

The new strategy of protest and the assertion of Negro pride found a receptive audience among the small, but growing, black middle class in the Northern cities. Thereafter the NAACP continued to work through the courts to protect the constitutional rights of blacks, and it also campaigned against lynching. In the 1920s the House of Representatives passed a federal antilynching law, but Southern senators talked it to death, denouncing the measure as an invasion of states' rights. The South, they claimed, could deal with lynching perfectly well without outside interference.

The northward migration of blacks from the South was creating black ghettos in the North. None could rival New York City's Harlem in importance or vitality. In the 1920s, it became a center for black artists, who found mutual support among one another and produced poems, novels, sculpture, and music expressing racial pride. For the first time, a cultural and intellectual black elite attracted white attention and admiration, helping to break down racist stereotypes. But more important, the Harlem Renaissance gave black intellectuals pride in themselves by restoring confidence in the black man's creative capacities, an indispensable precondition for Negro advancement. Calling themselves "The New Negro," they proclaimed that "the day of 'aunties,' and 'uncles,' and 'mammies' was gone." They were optimistic about the Negro's future in America and thought integration a realistic though distant goal. But they lacked a concrete strategy or an efficient organization for achieving that goal, and neither the NAACP nor the Negro intellectuals were able to sink deep roots among the Negro masses.

"Black Moses"

Marcus Garvey, founder of the Universal Negro Improvement Association, had both strategy and organization. A West Indian, Garvey migrated to Harlem during the First World War when the Negro capital was growing rapidly, as blacks poured in from the South. They nourished new hopes inspired by economic opportunity and the chance to escape the Southern caste system. When wartime prosperity gave way to unemployment, Negroes were the worst hit, and at the same time antiblack rioting erupted in many Northern cities. Garvey offered blacks new hope and built the largest Negro organization the country had ever seen. He preached black nationalism, instilling pride in race and demanding racial solidarity. "Black men, you were once great," this magnetic orator intoned, "you shall be great again." Garvey insisted that blacks could advance only by rejecting integration into white society—an impossible goal—and building instead a powerful black community. He organized black-owned businesses, including the ill-fated Black Star Steamship Line, which sold thousands of shares of stock to Negroes unaware of Garvey's incompetence as a businessman.

Given to grandiose visions and racism, Garvey placed his greatest hopes in the liberation of Africa from Western colonialism and its transformation into a Black Empire with Garvey as its leader. The Garveyites attempted to promote migration of blacks from America to Africa, where they would play a leading role in the struggle, but with no more success than in their business ventures.

None of Garvey's schemes materialized. Convicted of using the mails fraudulently, he went to jail in 1925 and the movement collapsed. Despised by most Negro leaders as a racist and a charlatan, this "Black Moses" held the affection of the Negro masses. Garvey did something new: he made the poor black "feel like somebody among white people who have said they were nobody," as a Negro sociologist explained. But such feelings were short-lived, for in the end Garvey merely sold escapism, and his ragtag program offered no realistic strategy in the struggle for racial justice.

The philosophy of protest enunciated by Du Bois and institutionalized by the NAACP and the surge of black pride in the Harlem Renaissance and in Garvey's nationalism laid the foundations for a revolution in race relations a generation later. But until white attitudes toward all ethnic, religious, and racial minorities changed significantly, blacks could not progress. In the 1920s, however, hatred of Jews and Catholics, blacks and Indians, Irish and Italians remained powerfully rooted in the tensions generated by the shift to mass society. The triumph of Prohibition and the attack on science by religious fundamentalism further demonstrated that Americans were at war with themselves.

RELIGIOUS CRISIS IN MODERN AMERICA

The Protestant churches entered the second half of the nineteenth century confidently. Despite the formal separation of church and state, Protestantism still helped to define American culture, and most people considered themselves Protestant, whether affiliated with a church or not. The denominations had met the challenge of national expansion between 1820 and 1860 with a prodigious evangelical and reformist effort. The church-

es followed settlers as they moved west and revivals rekindled enthusiasm when it lagged in the Eastern cities as well as in rural communities. Finally, the Civil War provided an unanticipated occasion for transcendence by sacrificing self-interest in a noble cause. The churches, North and South, claimed divine blessing for their respective sides: "As He died to make men holy/ Let us die to make men free," sang the Union armies in "The Battle Hymn of the Republic." Across the battle line, Southerners never doubted that God was on *their* side.

In the seven decades after Appomattox, however, the church in general, and the Protestant denominations in particular, faced serious challenges to their moral authority and institutional power. The growing percentage of Catholics and Jews in the cities undercut the Protestants' near-monopoly. The mounting prestige of science and the spread of secularism, both nourished in an increasingly urban society, weakened the hold of religion over minds and emotions. The churches attempted to meet these challenges by modernizing theology, by espousing a Social Gospel, by adapting revivalist techniques to new conditions, and by legislating Christian morality through politics. They also made frantic and ultimately unavailing efforts to impose the old-time religion (with its reliance on the supernatural) on a people who more than ever viewed the world through the eyes of science and acted on the assumption that God's only kingdom was here on earth.

The Challenge of Science

Darwin's theory of evolution popularized naturalistic explanations of phenomena that traditionally had been the province of the churches. Christians read in the Bible that God created the world in five days, and on the sixth he created man. Darwinism, however, maintained that evolution produced all forms of life, man included, in a long process during which organisms adapted to environmental demands. Species which successfully adapted survived; those that did not, like the dinosaur, died out. If man, like other animals, resulted from evolutionary chance, could people still consider him the final and crowning touch of a Divine Creator? Scientists dismissed the literal truth of the Bible, and after generations of biblical scholarship which had critically subjected the scriptures to the test of internal consistency, skepticism could no longer be brushed aside. If people could no longer trust in the authority of the Bible or rely on supernatural accounts of creation, they might then reject all of religion.

The churches responded to this threat in two ways. Those denominations with their roots deepest in the South and in the countryside among blacks, poor whites, and the less educated, among whom science and secularism had made little impression, rejected Darwinism and all Bible criticism as blasphemous. "Give me that old-time religion," they sang exuberantly, "that's good enough for me." But the more middle-class denominations, such as the Presbyterians, Episcopalians, and Congregationalists, with a tradition of a well-educated ministry serving constituencies deeply attracted by science and secularism, tried to reconcile science with religion. Evolution, after all, gave scientific approval to rugged individualism, the dominant social philosophy of the Gilded Age. Evolution, John Fiske had explained in the 1880s, was simply "God's way of doing things." Henry Ward Beecher, the leading minister in post-Civil War America, agreed: "Science is but the deciphering of God's thought as revealed in the structure of this world; it is merely a translation of God's primitive revelation." Accepting both evolution and biblical criticism, many ministers attempted to find a rational basis for Christian belief, since they saw little prospect of maintaining religiosity by appealing to blind faith.

Some went further and attempted to make the churches more relevant to human needs through the Social Gospel. By ministering to the temporal condition of the oppressed, Social Gospelers offered Christians the means of expressing their faith in daily life, and a tangible way of spreading Christ's message. In this way some thought Protestants could resist the secular trend that divorced man from God, and could win back to the churches thousands of backsliders among the urban working classes.

At first the modernist response appeared successful, but ultimately it weakened the authority of religion. Concessions to science to shore up religion endowed science with additional respectability and prestige. For a while the conflict between the scientific, secular world view and supernatural religion subsided. The modernist churches were complacently confident that the latest threat had been mastered when, in fact, religion suffered a continued, though often imperceptible, erosion in authority—especially among the educated. The modernist churches, however, were caught in a hopeless dilemma. They had become prisoners of their culture, servants of their congregations, and they could not resist science without risking shattering confrontations.

The Urban Challenge

Catholics and Jews, no less than Protestants, had to meet the challenge of modern science. The rise of the city, however, posed a special challenge for Protestant denominations. As millions of Protestants moved from farms to the cities in the late nineteenth century, they often left their fathers' religion far behind. In a rural society, Sunday churchgoing started a day in town, people mingled and visited with neighbors, and thus found escape from the routine and isolation of farm life. But in the bustling cities, neighbors were nearby; the ball park, the Sunday newspaper, the theater (and later the movies), and the saloon competed with churchgoing. In addition, the cities also housed many Catholic and Jewish immigrants, whose tendency to settle among their own kind facilitated the transfer of Catholic and Jewish worship to the New World. Protestantism thus faced for the first time a serious challenge to its near-monopoly. To reclaim Catholic and Jewish urban immigrants from heresy and native-born backsliders from apathy became one of the principal tasks of post-Civil War Protestantism, a task made all the more difficult by the scientific challenge to faith. The cities were the mainspring of modern society, and to lose them to the enemies of the Protestant God was unthinkable.

The Young Men's Christian Association (YMCA), founded before the Civil War, became a vital part of the crusade for the cities. The Y offered rural folk coming to the big city a temporary home suffused with a Protestant atmosphere, and it entered deeply into the lives of the cities by providing scarce recreational and charitable services. In many towns and cities, the Y was a tangible reminder that God had not forsaken the urban dweller. Its weakness, however, lay in the fact that people could use its services without joining a neighborhood church or abandoning secular attitudes.

The Y concentrated on winning back young people, and the same strategy lay behind the International Sunday School Union. Applying the technique of large-scale organization to the problem of religious education, the Sunday school movement proved the most effective means the churches devised to maintain their grip. So successful was the Sunday School Union in training teachers and providing educational materials that Bible classes were extended to adults as well.

In addition, the Protestant churches established missions to the immigrants, but these met with little success—for the foreign-born saw them as threats to their desire to re-create, in the urban ghettos and as best they could, the communal life of the Old Country. They preferred to cling to the faith of their fathers and establish a structure of their own associations including churches they controlled.

The Secularist Challenge

Protestants also poured new energy and resources into revivalism, adapting it to urban conditions. The leading late-nineteenth-century revivalist was Dwight L. Moody, a short, rotund former shoe salesman who first became active in the Chicago YMCA and later developed into a lay preacher of worldwide reputation. Moody succeeded in urban revivalism because he skillfully combined business methods of organization with sentimentality. Moody carefully planned his big-city revivals. He insisted on obtaining broad interdenominational cooperation in advance. This enabled him to raise large amounts of money, especially from businessmen who hoped that a supersalesman pushing the soothing consolation of life after death might curb lower-class unrest.

Moody had little patience with the notion that all men were brothers: "Show me a man that will lie and steal and get drunk and ruin a woman," he once asked, "do you tell me that he is my brother?" With large financial resources and a mastery of publicity, Moody built immense tabernacles in the large cities. As a layman, Moody had a knack for speaking simply. He avoided theological complexity for simple appeals to the heart. "The great truth we want to remember," he preached, "is that God loves the sinner. He hates sin, yea, with a perfect hatred; but he loves the sinner. God is love." Moody also had a keen sense of showmanship. His warm and friendly revivals had a carnival atmosphere, and he advertised them fittingly on the amusement pages of local newspapers. Huge, massed choirs sang sentimental hymns, and when Moody wept, the crowd wept with him. "Ah, it is that tender weeping power in dear Mr. Moody," reported a minister, "that is so overwhelming." The thousands who flocked to hear Moody seemed to prove the effectiveness of revivalism. Yet however much Moody succeeded in a city, the local ministers soon felt the need again for his services. The saved had become sinners again.

Yet faith in the effectiveness of revivalism persisted among the evangelical, antimodernist denominations. In each generation since Moody, another revivalist has risen to walk in his steps and adapt slightly the methods of the master. In the early twentieth century, the Reverend Billy Sunday established his primacy. Sunday endeared himself to big-city ministers, whose churches were losing worshipers and running at a deficit, because they thought, "He can deliver the goods." He perfected the bureaucratic organization of the urban revival, collecting money and putting together the Sunday party, a corps of experts in every phase of revivalism. When critics noted that Sunday had become a millionaire, the revivalist replied that "it cost him only $2 for every soul he 'saved' . . . less proportionate than other living evangelists."

Sunday's appeal was even simpler and more vulgar than Moody's. "What I want and preach," he said, "is the fact that a man can be converted without any fuss." Sunday adapted his message to the guilt-ridden consciences of people who feared secularism as they embraced it. "Let me tell you," he reassured them, "the manliest man is the man who will acknowledge Jesus Christ," who, according to Sunday, was "the greatest scrapper that ever lived." Turning to the women, Sunday promised: "Ladies, do you want to look pretty? If some of you women would spend less on dope and cold cream and get down on your knees and pray, God would make you prettier." But he warned youth: "A young man would not come to see a girl of mine in the parlor unless I had a hole cut in the ceiling with a Gatling gun trained through it."

Sunday also wrapped himself in the flag, preached racism, and told cheering crowds in the 1920s, "America is not a country for a dissenter to live in." The leading dissenter of the day, the Socialist Eugene V. Debs, regarded the evangelist as "a ranting mountebank, who, in the pay of the plutocracy, prostitutes religion to perpetuate hell on earth." But Sunday made no concessions to Darwin, modernist Christianity, or the Social Gospel. "The fatherhood of God and the brotherhood of Man," he sneered, "is the worst rot that ever was dug out of hell and every minister who preaches it is a liar."

The Fundamentalist Counterattack

In the 1920s, the conflict between modernist Christianity and conservative fundamentalist Christianity exploded, revealing the depth of the American Protestants' division. Outwardly the churches in the 1920s remained prosperous, with an upward growth trend. The percentage of the population with a church affiliation rose from about one-third in 1890 to about one-half by 1930. But these raw statistics can deceive. As the number of church members grew, the meaning of religious affiliation changed. "Even if going to church doesn't give us anything else," explained a Midwesterner in the 1920s, with charming logic, "it at least gives us the habit of going to church." People went because "it was the right thing to do," a sign of middle-class respectability, and all the while religiosity declined. "I guess I usually get something from church when I go," someone admitted, "but in summer, we mostly go out in the car Sundays." Ministers sensed the change. "My people seem to sit through the sermon in a

kind of dazed, comatose state," observed one, unhappily. "They don't seem to be wrestling with my thought."

Religious affiliation became an increasingly ritualistic act to many, devoid of piety or intellectual commitment, and the decline in belief infected the ministry itself. A comparison of the theological beliefs of Protestant seminary students with those of the older generation of ministers in the 1920s revealed that a majority of the younger generation did not believe in the literal truth of the Bible, the virgin birth of Christ, a final judgment, or the actual existence of heaven and hell. All this confirmed the claim of the fundamentalists—those who clung to orthodox, supernatural versions of Protestantism—that modernism had undermined the foundations of Christian belief. "The greatest menace to the Christian Church today," declared a leading fundamentalist theologian, "comes not from the enemies outside, but from the enemies within: it comes from the presence within the church of a type of faith and practice that is anti-Christian to the core." The fundamentalists, who launched a campaign to regain control of the institutional structure of American Protestantism, enjoyed a mass popularity, especially among country folk or those who had recently migrated to the cities. They reached millions struggling with the problems of adjusting to mass society, dependent on but fearful of science, frightened yet fascinated by the strangeness of city ways. Everything that people thought wrong with America—the new sexual mores, the evils of city life, drunkenness, political radicalism, or the assertion of women's rights—could be and was blamed on the loss of faith in old-time religion.

Not all, but most fundamentalists were socially conservative, and all believed that morality stemmed from belief in an omnipotent, miracle-working God, and on a literal reliance on the Bible. Above all, fundamentalists felt that any attempt to reconcile religious faith with scientific principles meant the end of faith. Fundamentalists protested against secularism and the reason and science on which it rested. They made their last stand in the 1920s because by then the new trend to the life-styles of secularized mass society had become unmistakably clear. Later, the fundamentalist crusade appeared a pathetic and anachronistic attempt to reverse the tide of history, and never more so than at the most famous trial of the decade in Dayton, Tennessee.

In the 1920s, fundamentalist pressures led several states to outlaw the teaching of Darwinian evolution in the public schools. Tennessee passed such a law in 1925; two years before six professors at the University of Tennessee were fired for teaching scientific evolution. John Scopes, a high school biology teacher in Dayton, decided to test the law. There then unfolded the dramatic "Monkey Trial," pitting William Jennings Bryan, the nation's leading fundamentalist layman, against Clarence Darrow, an agnostic Chicago lawyer who had made a career of championing unpopular causes. Bryan, three-time Democratic candidate for president and former secretary of state, who as spokesman for rural Protestantism in the South and West had spent a lifetime battling for social justice, believed that "some devitalizing force" was causing Americans "to forsake their spirituality for crass materialism." Scopes, the defendant, became almost forgotten in the battle between Darrow and Bryan, the one championing faith in science and reason, and the other in God and divine revelation.

The drama in the courtroom divided the country, especially after Bryan took the stand, confident he could defend the infallibility of the Bible against Darrow's famed skepticism. Bryan proudly professed belief in the literal truth of the Bible. The world went back to October 23, 4004 B.C.; the deluge came in 2438 B.C. He insisted that God created the sun on the fourth day, and that there had been evenings and mornings without sun. Women suffered at childbirth because Eve ate the forbidden apple. God, however, punished the serpent which tempted her by forever condemning it to crawl on its belly. "How do you suppose the serpent got along before that?" asked Darrow sardonically. Bryan rejected the theory of evolution because it lacked biblical support, and in his view it was only a scientific guess. "Apparently," wrote a scientist, "Mr. Bryan demands to see a monkey or an ass transformed into a man, though he must be familiar enough with the reverse process."

Though the big city press and the urban upper middle classes chuckled over Bryan's ignorance of science and his child-like faith in the Bible, he won the case and the plaudits of millions of fundamentalists. Scopes was fined $100. Prophetically, however, Darrow won the admiration of the youngsters of Dayton High School. They gave a dance in his honor, for, as one of Darrow's associates explained: "They seemed to recognize that this was their battle . . . it represented the issues between the eagerness of youth and the fear of age. Any pleasure unconnected with the church had been condemned by their elders. Smoking, dancing, free association between girls and boys, games and movies on Sunday had been their issues at home. Here were champions indeed." And a few days after the trial's end, Bryan collapsed and died suddenly—from overeating, his detractors claimed maliciously.

The attempt to legislate the theory of evolution out of existence did not succeed, but the fundamentalist impulse has persisted because there remain dwindling numbers of Americans who still have not made their peace with the modern world. (In 1969, the California State Department of Education ruled that Darwinian evolution should be taught as one of several theories of evolution along with the story in Genesis.)

PROHIBITION: "THE NOBLE EXPERIMENT"

Despite these deep divisions within Protestantism, most churches joined in supporting a new crusade against liquor early in the twentieth century. Almost a century after the launching of the first campaign for temperance, total prohibition triumphed. As in the past, the churches, particularly the fundamentalist ones, formed the vanguard. Liquor, the clergy argued, doomed millions of souls and signaled the spread of secularism and materialism. Social Gospelers and other Progressive reformers agreed, though for different reasons. Crusaders for social justice denounced liquor as a cause of poverty and urban disorder. The liquor interests, they argued, were a powerful "trust," growing rich by exploiting the poor and corrupting the politicians. Doctors and scientists added their voices. Little had been known about the precise effects of alcohol before 1860, but now scientific research concluded that alcohol, even in moderate amounts, harmed the body. Businessmen also joined the crusade; liquor, they thought, made workers less efficient and more prone to industrial accidents.

These arguments took on greater force as the cities, with their polyglot inhabitants from a dozen parts of Europe, appeared to threaten the dominance of native-stock Protestants of British extraction. By 1919, Roman Catholics, for instance, outnumbered other church members in fifteen states. The newcomers often drank heavily, and opposed temperance and prohibition movements. The consumption of alcohol reached an all-time high during the peak years of prewar immigration—further evidence that something had to be done. The insecure old-stock elements attempted to assert their superiority by imposing their standards on the newcomers. Prohibition thus became a means of banning an objectionable "un-American" habit, and coercing aliens into assimilation, another part of the campaign for 100 percent Americanism.

The Nineteenth Amendment to the Constitution, ratified in 1919, outlawed the manufacture and sale of intoxicating liquor. Its adoption resulted from skillful political pressure applied by the Women's Christian Temperance Union and the Anti-Saloon League. Founded in 1893, the League organized the "dry" Americans, and by 1915 it had a professional staff of 1500, with 50,000 field workers, many of them supplied by the churches. With the adoption of Prohibition, Billy Sunday predicted, "Hell will be forever for rent." William Jennings Bryan went further: "The reign of tears is over. The slums will soon be only a memory. We will turn our prisons into factories and our jails into storehouses and corncribs. Men will walk upright now, women will smile, and the children will laugh."

For fourteen years, the United States remained legally dry. In fact, however, the production and consumption of alcohol did not stop; it simply went underground. And in the end Prohibition turned into a nightmare. From the outset, millions refused to comply, including President

Warren G. Harding, though he campaigned as a staunch dry. The Yale University Club laid in a 14 year supply of liquor, and those with less foresight and cash bought illegal booze from bootleggers. Two thousand badly paid Prohibition agents had the impossible task of preventing drinking in a nation of 100 million people.

Production moved from the factory into the home. Eventually it became the special province of the underworld. Prohibition did not create organized crime—criminal syndicates already flourished in the big cities—but now gangsters, imitating Big Business, perceived the advantages of limiting competition, consolidating resources, and enlarging their take. Prohibition shifted an estimated $2 billion annually from the liquor manufacturers to the bootleggers and gave organized crime enormous sums of money for intimidating other businessmen. Big-time crime, like big business, was the achievement of powerful men such as Al Capone, the kingpin of the Chicago underworld. Unlike John D. Rockefeller, who bought out his competitors or drove them into bankruptcy, Capone cut them down with the Thompson submachinegun, or dropped them, weighted with chains, in Lake Michigan. At their height, the Chicago gang wars of the 1920s produced 400 murders in one year.

Enforcement proved impossible because the government would only devote a fraction of the resources necessary. President Herbert Hoover estimated that it would take a quarter of a million men to make America dry, but taxpayers would not pay that price, and Prohibitionists feared that stringent enforcement would arouse so much opposition that it might result in repeal. In many parts of the country, juries refused to convict offenders, and enforcement agents were hated. They did manage, however, to kill several hundred people during the decade, causing Jane Addams to insist that "what the prohibition situation needs first of all is disarmament." The drys, however, had no patience for such "gush stuff about murders by men who make mistakes once in a while." There were other kinds of mistakes, even more common. In October 1928, wood alcohol killed 25 New York guzzlers.

Prohibition did not stop all Americans from drinking, but it did dry up large parts of America, those inclined to be dry anyway. In 1932, 61,000 Americans were convicted of violating the Nineteenth Amendment and 45,000 got jail sentences; millions of gallons of booze were destroyed together with thousands of stills. But if small-town and rural America was drier than ever, urban America was as wet as ever. New York City for instance had 32,000 speakeasies in the 1920s, evidencing the widespread erosion of respect for law among the law-abiding, especially among Americans of immigrant stock. As for millions of native-born Protestants who accepted modernity, Prohibition was a reminder that an older, rural America still held power. Will Rogers, the country's leading satirical humorist, with a keen nose for hypocrisy, got to the heart of the matter: "If you think this country isn't dry, just watch 'em vote; if you think this country ain't wet, just watch 'em drink. You see, when they vote, it's counted, but when they drink, it ain't." Above all, Prohibition, like fundamentalism, represented a desperate effort to resist changes that were turning America into a pluralistic and secular society, in which no single culture ruled. In 1933, with the repeal of Prohibition, those who feared "the demon rum" because they doubted their own ability to resist it would now have to rely entirely on self-control.

THE WAGES OF FEAR

Fear of science and cities, fear of people different from the native-born Protestant majority (with radicals, Negroes, Catholics, and Jews the objects of particular scorn), fear that Americans, more than ever, were abandoning religious faith for worldly satisfactions, all these phantoms haunted America in the 1920s. The country luxuriated in the dizzying prosperity created by industrial technology, but though almost everybody wanted a new car and a radio and looked forward to visits to the movie palace or to the big city, many felt a sense of loss and betrayal.

Amid all the rapid change and after the disillusion of the First World War, people seemed isolated from one another and unable to find a larger meaning for their lives. On an unprecedented scale, the middle classes joined clubs:

country clubs, social service clubs, business and professional clubs. One Midwestern city, for instance, sported 458 clubs in the 1920s. With the church, the neighborhood, and the family no longer as important as before, the club filled a real need for fellowship. Club membership, people explained, "makes you realize the other fellow hasn't got horns on and ain't out to get you."

A more sinister response to the need for a sense of community and to the pervasive fears in postwar America among native-born, lower middle classes was a revived Ku Klux Klan. The Klan in the 1920s recruited between four and six million members, primarily in the WASP midsection of the country, North as well as South. It was not simply a rural phenomenon, but infested the cities, which were full of the most "threatened" people, the recent migrants from the countryside. "We want the country ruled by the sort of people who settled it," declared an Ohio Klan leader. "This is *our* country and we alone are responsible for its future." Above all, the Klan catered to a paranoid sense of deprivation which created a psychological state of siege. "Every criminal, every gambler, every thug, every libertine," claimed a Klan handbill, "every girl runner, every home wrecker, every wife beater, every dope peddler, every moonshiner, every crooked politician, every pagan Papist priest, every shyster lawyer . . . every white slaver, every black spider—is fighting the Klan." The Klan psychosis combined political animus against blacks, Jews, and Catholics with morbid sexual fears.

With its complicated ritual, its secrecy, and white robes and hoods, its burning crosses, its willingness to use violence, and its sense of solidarity, the Klan had undoubted appeal. It posed as a vigilante organization with the guts to fight evils ignored or underestimated by established institutions such as government. For a short time, the "Invisible Empire" became a powerful political force in several states. But by the mid-1920s the Klan suffered a decline. The top leaders fought among themselves for the profits, scandal tarnished their image (the Indiana Klan leader was convicted of murder), and respectable upper-class businessmen and politicians who had first encouraged the Klan pulled out. Most of all, the social anxieties that made millions of Americans susceptible to the Klan's appeal had begun to subside.

Not before, however, the Commonwealth of Massachusetts executed Nicola Sacco and Bartolomeo Vanzetti, two Italian anarchists convicted of murder in an armed robbery, and aroused liberal consciences throughout the Western world. Many doubted their guilt, and many more doubted that they had received a fair trial. The case made people wonder whether American justice had framed and executed two men because they were foreigners and radicals. "If it had not been for this thing," said the uneducated but eloquent Vanzetti in the courtroom after sentencing, "I might have to live out my life talking at street corners to scorning men. I might have died, unmarked, unknown, a failure. Now we are

not a failure. This is our career and our triumph. Never in our full life could we hope to do such work for tolerance, for justice, for man's understanding of man as now we do by accident. Our words—our lives—our pains—nothing! The last moment belongs to us—that agony is our triumph."

Whether Sacco and Vanzetti were guilty as charged remains uncertain. Yet one thing is clear: those who cheered their execution thought it a blow against dangerous foreigners and radicalism; and those who believed the Italian anarchists had been victimized found fresh proof that Americans had lost their nerve. Inevitably, the tensions of mass society which resulted in attacks on civil liberties, the rise of fundamentalism and the Klan, and the triumph of Prohibition also shaped American politics in the 1920s.

Chapter 28
The Politics of Normalcy

"Four-fifths of all our troubles in this life would disappear," mused President Calvin Coolidge in the Twenties, "if we would only sit down and keep still." For over five laconic years, "Silent Cal" sat still, confident that he had little to do in the White House, since as he put it tersely, "the business of America is business." Businessmen, untrammeled by government controls or labor unions, knew what was best for the country they had built, he thought, and therefore they deserved to run it. A generation earlier, another Republican president, Theodore Roosevelt, espousing the Progressive view, voiced contrary sentiments. "The more I see of the wealthy," he had maintained, "the more profoundly convinced I am of their entire unfitness to govern the country. . . ." By the 1920s Roosevelt's view became passe.

THE ECLIPSE OF PROGRESSIVISM

Progressivism declined in the 1920s, a victim of internal weaknesses. A vague, amorphous coalition, more a frame of mind than a movement, held temporary control of both political parties by catering to widespread fear that unchecked private power condemned millions to poverty, corrupted government, despoiled natural resources, and crushed the initiative of independent businessmen and farmers. The middle classes who cheered Roosevelt and Wilson feared social convulsions and backed politicians who promised to curb private power. Progressives claimed to have risen above class interest. They searched for ways to stabilize a turbulent society and replace group conflict, such as that which had burst forth so violently in the late nineteenth century, with more rational and equitable means of making decisions. They sought a more cohesive, peaceful, and just society—one in which, incidentally, they would have greater power.

Progressive results fell far short of Progressive aspirations. Despite modest successes, two decades of reform did not equalize power and end privilege. A few persons still monopolized the nation's wealth; Big Business had not been tamed; the economy remained vulnerable to the boom and bust cycle; and millions of Americans still lived in squalor with little prospect, no matter what they did, of improving their conditions. By 1916 Progressivism seemed exhausted politically. Wilson barely won a second term; the standpatters whom Theodore Roosevelt had checked regained control of the Republican party; and Progressivism floundered, lacking clear direction. The eagerness to achieve reform ebbed among the middle classes. Many believed their purposes accomplished with the adoption of Wilson's New Freedom in 1913 and parts of the New Nationalism in 1916. The much-feared explosion of the downtrodden never materialized and the humanitarians comforted themselves by believing that life for the have-nots was improving as a result of the Social Gospel, settlement work, labor legislation, and the slow growth of labor unions.

In the end Progressives failed to achieve reform because they did not understand clearly the realities of power, and they were not willing to push for fundamental changes in the structure of society without which stability, cohesion, and social justice were impractical goals. Regarding themselves as a disinterested class, eager to avoid conflict, Progressives failed to mobilize the underdogs, their "charges," the only effective way to counter the entrenched power of conservatism. Still wedded to individualism, still fearful of lodging too much power in the hands of government, and still suspicious of labor, Progressives relied excessively on private, voluntary instruments for reform and on goodwill to solve social problems. Progressives did enlarge the scope of government, but such characteristic Progressive goals as tariff reduction, antitrust laws, and the purification of politics were aimed primarily at increasing opportunity for themselves. Progressives took tentative steps toward welfare statism —such as workmen's compensation, tenement house reform, and minimum wage laws for women —but they failed to press for comprehensive measures that would assure a minimum decent standard of living for all Americans.

Nothing revealed the shallowness and confusion of Progressivism more graphically than its uncertain grappling with the trusts. In the campaign of 1912, Wilson had promised to destroy monopolies; as president he reassured businessmen by loading the Federal Reserve Board and Federal Trade Commission with pro-business appointees. La Follette, unsullied by power, remained a consistent crusader against "monopoly" but produced no alternative to the large corporation; and Theodore Roosevelt, who accepted bigness as inevitable and beneficial so long as the titans of industry consulted him or men like him, ended his career by returning to the party he had abandoned as a hopeless captive of reactionaries and a saber rattler in foreign affairs.

For Roosevelt, as for so many other Progressives, the First World War came as a great relief, and he rushed to offer his military services. "The American nation needs the tonic of a serious moral adventure," advised Herbert Croly, theoretician of the New Nationalism. Croly, like other Progressives, saw the war as an opportunity to provide new outlets for the reform impulse. Going to war to make the world safe for democracy enabled Progressives to substitute for the confusion at home a grandiose enterprise abroad.

THE ROLE OF WAR

At first the war justified Progressive expectations. Fighting a war required national unity. Americans would have to stop quarreling among themselves and cooperate to reach common goals. War offered the possibility, therefore, of achieving that long-sought sense of American community as people sacrificed personal interest to achieve the noble aims Wilson proclaimed in 1917.

The national emergency also justified resorting to coercive means for achieving unity, not only through propaganda and repression of dissenters, but through unprecedented direction and coordination of national resources by the government. The first step toward central economic planning arose from the need to make the nation's industrial machine serve the war effort more efficiently. Thus, following a gigantic bottleneck on the railroads, the federal government took over management of the industry. Shortages of food and raw material led to federally directed rationing. Private shipbuilders did not turn out ships rapidly enough so the government tried its hand. Wheat farmers received federal subsidies to stimulate production and relieve the shortage of grain, and coal producers got minimum-price guarantees that expanded output. Big Business no longer had to worry about the antitrust laws and the federal government encouraged unionization, especially in industries dependent on government contracts. In the short run, federal controls succeeded in gearing the economy to war production. The Wilson administration adjusted tax policy so that a proportionally greater burden fell on the more prosperous classes than on low-income families, though the new rates fell far short of "soaking the rich." Many people grumbled about wartime economic policy, but businessmen and other conservatives acquiesced to temporary controls during an emergency. Besides, the war meant prosperity.

The return of peace brought the immediate termination of government's wartime planning and control. The transition to a peacetime economy proved vexing. Demand declined and prices fell; the war boom gave way to an economic recession.

The war had stimulated an expansion in production in the United States but when peace returned overseas markets contracted. Since Europe no longer depended so heavily on the United States, a serious imbalance developed between supply and demand. Farmers were especially hard hit. A nationwide recession in 1921–1922 caused widespread unemployment and numerous bankruptcies. But eventually the economy adjusted and climbed steadily to produce prosperity during the rest of the decade.

The Democrats lost heavily in the 1918 congressional elections. Wartime controls and postwar economic distress turned voters against the party in power. All the anxieties generated by the war began to surface and people blamed the Democrats. Wheat farmers, mostly Midwestern Republicans, accused the Democrats of giving special favors to cotton farmers, mostly Southerners. Midwestern shippers charged that federal railroad rates discriminated against them in favor of the Northeast. Businessmen became alarmed by the rapid wartime gains of organized labor and the attempt to extend unionization to heavy industry which resulted in the Great Steel Strike of 1919.

At the same time, the peace settlement mocked the noble ideals for which Wilson said he led the country into war, and did much to discredit the Progressive view, even among the true believers. As the victors picked over the spoils at the Versailles conference, Wilson seemed helpless to bring about the magnanimous and lasting settlement he had promised. Progressives grew cynical and disillusioned. The war had made great fortunes at home and had ended in the triumph of imperialism abroad. And it had unleashed a spirit of intolerance and repression among Americans that divided the country more than ever.

The war, explained the middle-class professional reformer Frederic C. Howe, finally opened his eyes to reality, after a life spent trying first to reform Ohio and then the world. "My class did not see beyond its own interest. I had not been a realist but a moralist. I came to realize that reform was only possible from labor, not from my own class. I thought my class, its intelligence properly applied, would save the world. I wanted equal opportunity; my class did not."

Progressivism did not vanish altogether in the 1920s, however. The quest for social stability continued, but under the leadership of conservatives and the business community. The Progressives had singled out the power of concentrated wealth as the most acute social problem. By the 1920s, however, many came to accept the existence of mammoth corporations as necessary, inevitable, and beneficial. The first three decades of the twentieth century were relatively prosperous, marked only briefly by recessions. People enjoyed cars, radios, and movie houses—all proof of a rising standard of living created by the American business system. As long as most people shared in the gains, it seemed unimportant that a few reaped the largest share. Organized labor, after great gains during the war, declined as workers proved unresponsive to unionization and employers turned hostile. Farmers, who fared less well in the 1920s than other groups, remained politically too divided and weak to obtain anything but marginal government aid.

For a dozen years after 1918, conservative Republicans dominated American politics. But in 1929, "Republican Prosperity" collapsed, and with it faith in the leadership of businessmen and conservatives. The country plunged into the worst depression in its history and searched desperately for new leadership. For a decade, however, the Republicans had confidently ruled, unaware of what lay ahead.

REPUBLICAN SUPREMACY, 1920–1928

Despite the strains Progressivism placed on the party system, especially on the Republicans, the electoral patterns that had emerged in the 1890s remained largely intact through the 1920s. The South was still Democratic territory but the rest of the country went either solidly Republican or leaned toward the GOP. Wilson's two victories represented deviations from the norm and owed much to the split between conservatives and progressive Republicans. Since the Republicans were normally the majority party, control of the GOP proved crucial. By the 1920s the progressive Republicans became an isolated minority. Many had abandoned the party to follow Roosevelt into the Progressive party in 1912, but after its failure many drifted back to a GOP firmly in the grip of the standpatters.

Well before the 1920 presidential elections, the GOP smelled victory. A powerful group of conservative Republican senators blocked the candidacy of men they thought less pliable than their man, Senator Warren G. Harding of Ohio. "People are rather tired of great ability," explained a Midwestern businessman, "they've seen enough of that sort of thing in the Jews. What they want is a good, plain, common sense man of the people." Harding fit the bill perfectly. He climbed the ladder of Ohio politics with a devastating combination of a third-rate mind, laziness, and lack of ambition. His hard-working wife helped to make a success out of his languishing newspaper in Marion, and then a group of clever friends helped him win state office. Harding's success owed much to his lack of deep conviction and to his need to be popular, traits which led him to act as conciliator among the warring factions of the Ohio GOP. Harding himself had coined a word to describe his editorial and political approach, "inoffensivism." Later, as a member of the United States Senate, he preferred playing golf to attending roll calls, but when he did vote he generally sided with conservative Republicans and party regularity earned him choice committee appointments.

A handsome man with silver-grey hair and a good physical presence, Harding outwardly fit the presidential image, though some dismissed him as "a waxwork Adonis." Senator Boies Penrose, an architect of his nomination, made no great claims for the man. "Harding," he admitted, "is not as big a man as I thought he was; he should have talked more about the tariff and not so much about playing cymbals in the Marion brass band." Yet it was precisely his identification with an older America which preferred brass bands to jazz bands that so endeared the Ohioan to the average voter.

The same was true of his oratory, which said nothing but sounded eloquent to the ears of Main Street. "We have not only wrought the most liberty and opportunity for outselves at home," he once intoned with a straight face, "but the firmament of the earth, occident and orient, is aglow with shining suns of new republics, sped to the orbs of human progress by our example." The cynical journalist H. L. Mencken expressed a strictly minority view when he said that Harding's speechmaking reminded him of a string of wet sponges. Democrat William G. McAdoo claimed a Harding speech reminded him of "an army of pompous phrases moving over the landscape in search of an idea; sometimes these meandering words would actually capture a straggling thought and bear it triumphantly, a prisoner in their midst, until it died of servitude and overwork." But middle America ignored such criticism of their hero.

Saddled with the burden of defending the unpopular Wilson administration, and losers in the fight for American participation in the League of Nations, the gloomy Democrats sent James M. Cox, former governor of Ohio, and his running mate, Franklin D. Roosevelt, to an embarrassing defeat in 1920. Much of the big-city ethnic vote, traditionally Democratic, deserted the party. Irish-Americans, for instance, who supported Ireland's fight for independence against Britain complained that the peace settlement left the British Empire stronger than ever and thus Irish freedom even more remote. German-Americans, whose loyalty had been questioned, turned on the party that had declared war against the Kaiser. Only the South remained loyal. The basic issue of the campaign, Senator Penrose explained, was "Americanism," though when asked what that meant, the Pennsylvania Republican boss replied: "How the hell do I know! But it will get a lot of votes." Harding won 60 percent of the vote and entered the White House a hero, promising to return the country to "normalcy."

The Harding Presidency

Normalcy proved disastrous. Harding once confided to a journalist that he was just "a man of limited talents from a small town. . . . Often times, as I sit here, I don't seem to grasp that I am President." Many of the issues that came across his desk puzzled him. "I can't make a damn thing out of this tax problem," he confessed. "I listen to one side and they seem right, and then —God—I talk to the other side and they seem just as right. . . . I know somewhere there is a book that will give me the truth, but hell! I couldn't read the book." Though he sensed his many inadequacies, Harding surrounded himself with cronies from Ohio with whom he could indulge two of his favorite pastimes, drinking and poker playing. He appointed a few able men to his cabinet, such as Secretary of State Charles Evans Hughes and Secretary of Commerce Herbert Hoover, but he also named friends who proved his undoing. "The Ohio Gang, as they came to be known," writes one historian, "were a bunch of old-fashioned spoilsmen, political shysters, and just plain crooks who used public office for private gain." They sold protection to bootleggers, pardons to criminals, and favors to businessmen. The most notorious scandal involved the illegal transfer by Secretary of the Interior Albert B. Fall of the government's Teapot Dome oil reserves, worth millions, in exchange for bribes.

When facts began to leak out, some of the

guilty left immediately for Europe; a few committed suicide. Harding began to panic, although early in 1923 only a scandal in the Veterans' Administration had been made public. But he knew that further disclosures were coming, and his wife had learned about his relations with his mistress, Nan Britton. Looking none too well, the president left for a tour of Alaska and the Northwest. Ptomaine poisoning struck him in San Francisco, and he died soon after of pneumonia. The circumstances had been clouded enough to create rumors that his wife had poisoned him; but the specific infirmities and lack of the will to live were more than enough to kill him.

The Harding administration symbolized much more than it accomplished. Here was a man from the heartland of America, a "just folks" sort of person; a hand-shaking, good guy of average abilities, with whom millions of Americans could identify; someone like themselves who could be relied on to restore "normalcy" after two decades of exhausting crusades at home and abroad.

Calvin Coolidge: "Puritan in Babylon"

Though Harding disappointed his admirers, they did not give up their desire to restore the past. Vice-president Calvin Coolidge, the rock-ribbed and sour Yankee from New England who succeeded to the presidency, proved more reliable. Born in Vermont, he rose through the ranks of the Republican party in Massachusetts to become governor. He gained a national reputation in 1919 when he broke the Boston Police Strike. A man of considerable political skill, he had the confidence of Big Business without appearing to be their front-man. Coolidge was a man of few words and Spartan habits (Theodore Roosevelt's daughter said he had been "weaned on a dill pickle"). He refused for instance to buy an automobile. Editor William Allen White called him "a perfect throwback to the primitive days of the Republic." His conception of the presidency was that of a housekeeper who guarded the national treasury against undue expenditures, kept his administration free of scandal, and resisted efforts to enlarge the federal government's operations. He probably slept more than any other occupant of the White House and he kept healthy in a job

that broke Wilson and Harding physically, he explained, "by avoiding the big problems."

Coolidge moved swiftly to clean up Harding's mess. He sternly instructed the head usher at the White House: "I want things as they used to be—*before*." Coolidge thus undercut the corruption issue in preparation for his reelection campaign in 1924.

The Democrats approached the 1924 elections divided and at a loss to deal with the prosperity issue, which was Coolidge's strongest card. Disillusionment over the war and the campaign for 100 percent Americanism proved traumatic for the Democrats and brought the final collapse of Wilsonian Progressivism. The immigrant masses, mainly Catholic, dominated the Democratic party in the cities. But the party had also relied on the votes of rural Protestants in the South and West. Conflict in the 1920s between the old stock and the new, between urban and rural cultures that revealed itself in Prohibition, the resurgence of the Klan, Protestant fundamentalism, repression of aliens, and racist immigration legislation converged to tear apart the already weakened Democratic party. The Democrats, more socially heterogeneous than the Republicans, were more vulnerable to factionalism under the pressures of the 1920s.

Ethnocultural, sectional, and status rivalries have shaped the character of American politics and mitigated against extreme polarization along economic and class lines. Cultural conflict divided farmers and working classes and caused suicidal rifts within the Democratic party. For instance, Irish-Catholics had been loyal Democrats for generations; powerful in the inner councils of the party, they nevertheless rarely aspired to major public office except in overwhelmingly Irish constituencies. In the 1920s, the Irish and other groups began to seek greater political recognition. The issue exploded at the 1924 Democratic Convention. The big-city Democrats backed Al Smith, an Irish-Catholic who had risen from a clerkship in the Fulton Fish Market in Manhattan to the governorship of New York. Smith was the ablest politician the newer Americans had yet produced. Though a product of a big-city machine —New York's Tammany Hall—his was more than just an urban, Catholic candidacy. He supported labor and welfare legislation which bene-fitted his working class constituency, of course, but he also extended his appeal to old-stock Progressives by working for administrative re-form and defending civil liberties during the Red Scare.

Rural Democrats from the South and West backing William G. McAdoo blocked Smith's candidacy. Al Smith affronted the most cherished values of Democrats like William Jennings Bryan. Smith was a "wet" and he symbolized the metrop-olis which the small-town old stock sought to con-tain. The Smith forces demanded that the party publicly condemn the Ku Klux Klan; the South-ern and Western Democrats refused. The conven-tion deadlocked, after 95 votes, and as humorist Will Rogers warned the delegates: "New York invited you people here as guests, not to live." The exhausted party finally nominated John W. Davis, a Wall Street lawyer who stirred little en-thusiasm among either the urban masses or the Bryan Democrats in the South and West.

With neither of the two parties offering a choice, remnants of the Progressive coalition rallied behind Wisconsin's Senator Robert La-Follette who ran on the ticket of a new Progres-sive party. The eclipse of Progressivism left a small isolated minority in the Republican party with a voice in Congress through spokesmen like the aging La Follette, but with a power base con-fined largely to the Midwestern grain belt. La Follette tried to assemble a Progressive coalition by appealing to discontented farmers, labor, mid-dle-class reformers, and Socialists (whose candi-date in 1920, Eugene V. Debs, had polled nearly a million votes while in prison for antiwar protest activity). He also appealed to the postwar isola-tionist spirit and to the German-Americans, for he had been the most prominent opponent of American involvement in the First World War.

The Coolidge campaign concentrated its fire on La Follette and tried to smear the Progressive party as socialistic and a threat to prosperity. "If we could discover the three people who dis-graced our district by voting for La Follette," said the wife of a midwestern Republican businessmen, "we'd certainly make it hot for them." In a light turnout of only half the eligible voters, La Follette polled nearly five million votes, cutting into

Democratic strength in the Northeastern cities and running well in former centers of progressive Republicanism in the Midwest. Coolidge, how-ever, won with more votes than both his oppo-nents combined, further disheartening progres-sive Republicanism and making the Democrats even more cautious about disputing the reigning Republican philosophy that "the business of America is business."

BUSINESS SUPREMACY

As the American economy and stock market boomed, President Coolidge, who disapproved of gambling, became concerned about the specula-tion in securities. He summoned Harvard econo-mist W. Z. Ripley to Washington and listened to the expert describe how "prestidigitation, double-shuffling. honey-fugling, hornswoggling, and skullduggery" helped to sustain the Great Bull Market on Wall Street. In the end, however, the president declined to act to curb speculation or openly counsel moderation, since he thought busi-nessmen knew best. Government, the president insisted, must properly act as a servant, not a watchdog of business.

During the Progressive era, business had been on the defensive as a result of rivalry among business interests and widespread fears of con-centrated economic power. By the 1920s, however, banking, railroad, and tariff reforms had muted many of the differences which had previously divided businessmen. More important, the per-formance of Big Business, especially well-known firms like Ford and GM, did much to diminish popular hostility toward the large corporation. Now businessmen and their spokesmen explicitly claimed the right to rule. Free enterprise, they argued, made America great and had produced the highest standard of living in the world.

Driven by the profit motive, businessmen had supposedly done more for the good of man-kind than all the do-good reformers put together. "The Carnegie who made steel and millions of dollars was a hero," argued an advocate of busi-ness control, "but the Carnegie who gave medals to heroes and built libraries was just a sweet old lady." Another put it more bluntly: "The 100 percent American believes in the doctrine of self-ishness, although he is often ashamed to admit it." The majority of people had limited ability and were easily fooled by radical troublemakers and vote-seeking politicians. Power should be left in the hands of the nation's natural elite, the businessmen. The majority must be kept busy at work because leisure was dangerous. Any man who wanted a forty-hour work week "should be ashamed to claim citizenship in this great country." Inequality was inevitable, desirable, and necessary: inevitable because people differed in ability and talent, desirable because the chance to earn great wealth spurred creative energies, and necessary because the fear of destitution was the only thing that kept people working hard.

Government in the 1920s generally gave businessmen what they wanted: a free hand to run their own affairs and special privileges. The Wilson administration had granted businessmen virtual immunity from the antitrust laws. The Republicans in the 1920s expanded that policy to encourage the "New Competition." In certain industries, such as steel, autos, tobacco, and meat packing, a few firms dominated, divided the market, and fixed prices.

In industries with many small producers, however, cutthroat competition proved troublesome. The Federal Trade Act, designed to curb "unfair" competition, established a Federal Trade Commission which President Wilson staffed with pro-business commissioners. Republicans in the 1920s went further, turning the regulatory agencies into tools of the industries they were established to regulate. Government, especially the Department of Commerce, under Secretary Herbert Hoover, gave its blessing to this new method of limiting competition, thus legitimizing business practices that otherwise might provoke criticism.

The Transportation Act of 1920 represented yet another victory for business consolidation. The railroad unions demanded that government keep control of the railroads after the war. The railroads, aided by other businessmen and by Midwestern Progressives who complained that government control had discriminated against the interests of their region, defeated nationaliza-tion. Instead, the railroads received permission to consolidate into a few large systems with immunity from antitrust prosecution. At the same time, the ICC received greater power over rates. The booming new electric power industry also came under regulation by the Federal Power Commission (1920) but this agency proved an equally ineffective watchdog of the public interest.

Successful in making government "regulation" serve their interests, businessmen also pushed for lower taxes. During the war the government imposed personal and corporate income taxes that fell most heavily on those with the greatest ability to pay. In the 1920s, under the leadership of Secretary of the Treasury Andrew Mellon of the Aluminum Company of America (and a member of one of the country's wealthiest families), the federal government economized on expenditures and cut taxes. Progressive Republicans and Democrats fought to preserve the progressive tax structure, but by the mid-1920s Mellon pushed through Congress substantial tax relief for the well-to-do.

At the same time conservatives and businessmen fought welfare programs to help working people, such as health insurance and old-age pensions. They did so on the premise that only "rugged individualism" created prosperity, yet all the while they sought handouts and special favors for themselves. Secretary Fall gave away valuable federal oil reserves. Progressive senators, however, got wind of bribery in the executive branch and exposed the Teapot Dome corruptionists. Led by Senator George Norris of Nebraska, Progressives also blocked another giveaway to private industry of huge hydroelectric works built by the government during the First World War to produce nitrates at Muscle Shoals, Alabama. This preserved, for possible future public development, the water power resources of the Tennessee Valley.

Businessmen were more successful in increasing tariff rates. In 1921 and in 1922, Congress reversed the tariff reductions of the Progressive years. This satisfied businessmen who wanted protection against foreign competition, and it also pleased farmers caught in a postwar agricultural depression, though higher tariffs did them little real good. The high duty on imported reindeer meat, for example, did not help raise the price of wheat.

Despite conservative opposition to increased government spending, the budgetary trend moved markedly upward between 1900 and 1930. Government's share of national income in 1920 stood at just below 10 percent but it had grown 60 percent since the first decade of the twentieth century. Education took the largest share of public revenues, about 20 percent. While funding for other public services—welfare, sanitation, water, and police—lagged because of conservative opposition, ambitious, publicly financed highway programs made possible an automobile-based economy and represented a gigantic subsidy to industry which the public supported because it also benefited from better roads.

THE SUPREME COURT

As in the 1890s, the Supreme Court reflected the conservative temper of the twenties. Progressives had tried to promote social justice by adopting legislation on behalf of lower income groups. Reformers argued that industrialism subjected people to hazards they could not cope with individually. They therefore recognized the need for such collective protections as trade unions, and laws limiting child labor, setting maximum hours and minimum wages, and providing security against industrial accidents, unemployment, and impoverishment in old age. These ideas did manage to make inroads, but many businessmen reacted negatively to Progressive solutions to the labor question. In the 1920s the judiciary came to the aid of conservatives by declaring national welfare legislation unconstitutional and ruling repeatedly against labor unions.

One of the Progressives' strongest points of attack, the crusade against child labor, twice fell victim to judicial vetoes. Before the First World War the Supreme Court had allowed states to regulate the working conditions of certain types of laborers—women and children, or men with particularly dangerous jobs like miners. But judicial approval in a handful of cases did not create overall state policy. Progressives campaigned for a federal law which would outlaw child labor. In 1916 Congress barred the shipment of goods in interstate commerce made by children under the age of fourteen, or if made by children, between ages fourteen and sixteen who worked more than eight hours a day. Two years later, in *Hammer* v. *Dagenhart* (1918), the court used an extremely narrow definition of the federal commerce power to declare that Congress could not regulate manufacturing, a state concern, however laudable its intent to put an end to child labor.

Congress, refusing to give up, then placed a tax of 10 percent on the profits of any company using child laborers. Again the court, in *Bailey* v. *Drexel Furniture Company* (1922), declared the law void on the grounds that Congress could not use the federal taxing power to regulate a matter reserved to the states. Chief Justice Taft warned: "The good sought in unconstitutional legislation is an insidious feature, because it leads citizens and legislators of good purpose to promote it without thought of the serious breach it will make in [the Constitution] the ark of our covenant." Taft spoke for judicial restraint, but it should be noted that the Supreme Court's liberals, Holmes and Brandeis, both supported the Taft position in the *Bailey* case, though in the first child labor case Holmes had dissented, arguing that if the nation could prohibit alcohol, it could just as well prohibit "the products of ruined lives."

Previously, the court had upheld certain state limitations on the hours of labor on the grounds that a state could protect the health and safety of workers, and that limiting the workday might reasonably aid in achieving that desirable end. Progressives had hailed these decisions as landmarks, since they appeared to overrule the hated *Lochner* v. *New York* opinion (1905) which invalidated a New York law prohibiting a workday of more than ten hours' work for bakers. In that case the court held that the New York statute deprived both employers and employees of freedom of contract, a guarantee of the due process clause of the Fourteenth Amendment.

In the years after *Lochner* the court seemed to soften. Before joining it, Louis D. Brandeis, the country's leading Progressive lawyer, argued and won several regulatory cases before the Supreme Court. One involved Oregon's attempt to ease working conditions for women, and Brandeis in presenting his case observed wryly: "Experience has taught us that harsh language addressed to a cow impairs her usefulness. Are women less sensitive than beasts in these respects?" Tentative Progressive victories created the false impression that the court might enter a sustained liberal phase after World War I; but the court would soon agree with one of its staff members who snorted: "Brandeis has got the impudence of the devil to bring his socialism into the Supreme Court."

In 1923 the court struck another blow against the beginnings of the welfare state. It revived the doctrine of substantive due process in *Adkins* v. *Childrens' Hospital* (1923), declaring unconstitutional a minimum wage law passed by Congress for the District of Columbia. Felix Frankfurter had argued the case for regulation, presenting a Brandeis-type sociological legal brief, but this time the court would not accept it. Justice Sutherland, then starting his service to judicial conservatism declared: "We cannot accept the doctrine that women of mature age require . . . restrictions upon their liberty of contract." So the scrubwomen at Childrens' Hospital were "free" to accept whatever wages the trustees saw fit to pay them. Chief Justice Taft, this time one of the dissenters, protested that the majority wanted to "hold congressional acts invalid simply because they are passed to carry out economic views which the Court believes to be unwise or unsound." The cartoonist John Kirby was blunter: "This decision," he told working women, "affirms your constitutional right to starve."

At the same time that the Court invalidated legislation to protect unorganized workers, it made it harder for labor to protect itself through trade union activity. Unions had welcomed the Clayton Act (1914), thinking it had granted immunity from the antitrust laws, previously used to break strikes. In the 1920s, however, the Supreme Court interpreted the Clayton Act in a way which again brought unions under the provisions of the antitrust laws. The court also struck down an Arizona law which barred injunctions against picketers, claiming it denied employers equal protection of the law. Whatever the legal basis for this decison, and it was hotly debated, the justices had made their antilabor bias apparent. Chief Justice Taft explained that trade unions were dangerous institutions which "we have to hit every little while."

THE DECLINE OF ORGANIZED LABOR

During the Progressive era, unions had experienced their greatest growth up to that time, aided by prosperity and a favorable climate of opinion. During the First World War, with labor in short supply, unions almost doubled their membership, reaching five million in 1920. This union growth alarmed employers who launched counteroffensives through such organizations as the National Association of Manufacturers. In the 1920s employers stepped up their antilabor drive with considerable success. By the end of the decade union membership had fallen to less than three and a half million workers.

Employers capitalized on the postwar antiradical hysteria to smear unions as socialistic and un-American. The bosses' "American Plan" called for outlawing the "closed shop," a device which made union membership a condition of employment. Businessmen insisted that closed shops deprived workers of the right to work, and thus violated the tenets of rugged individualism, though in fact unorganized workers were powerless to influence the conditions of employment. The open-shop movement was an attempt to restore to employers a monopoly of power wherever unions had intruded. Aided by antilabor judges, politicians, and the press, resorting to the use of labor spies and hired toughs, employers created an atmosphere hostile to union growth. They were also helped by modest advances in real wages, tangible improvements in living standards, and substantial unemployment during the first half of the 1920s, which made workers more docile and less susceptible to unionization. The great citadels of the open shop were the mass-production industries, such as steel and automaking, which remained impervious to unionization.

At first, unions tried to fight back, but strikes against coal mines, railroads, and steel failed. The American Federation of Labor, therefore, altered its strategy on the assumption that labor could not grow through struggle as it had in the past. The AFL tried to convince business that unions were desirable because they promoted harmony and efficiency. The unions joined conservatives in attacking radicalism and supporting a high tariff in the hope of gaining respectability. But, although tariff rates went up, businessmen remained hostile.

Instead, some advanced "welfare capitalism" as a means of assuring labor peace. Leaders of big corporations such as Procter and Gamble, General Motors, and General Electric wanted a stable, pliable labor force. They recognized that labor had real grievances. Workers not only wanted decent wages, fair hours, and good working conditions, but protection against unemployment, the insecurity of old age, and arbitrary treatment in the factory as well. Welfare capitalism assumed that business could satisfy these needs through company unions controlled by employers which gave workers the illusion they could redress grievances. Several large corporations also tried to provide year-round employment, others established pension plans, built company housing, and offered employees stock purchasing plans.

But the most important legacy of welfare capitalism was the development of personnel administration as a "scientific" method of managing labor. The industrial relations movement of the 1920s was one of the main thrusts of "scientific management." As the modern, bureaucratic corporation evolved, businessmen rejected the older, informal methods of management, which relied heavily on trial and error. Corporations such as General Motors, Du Pont, Sears Roebuck, and Standard Oil of New Jersey found it necessary to develop new administrative techniques for more efficient production, planning, and marketing as well as the control of labor.

The father of "scientific management" was an engineer named Frederick W. Taylor. Taylor wanted to replace conflict between labor and management with rational cooperation. He thought it possible to determine scientifically the most efficient way to do a job through careful study. This in turn would permit engineers to determine rationally what constituted a fair day's work and would enable companies to reward workers according to performance. Taylor thought labor productivity would increase if employers shared profits with workers through a system of wage incentives geared to gains in efficiency. In theory, "scientific management," with its faith in "rational" solutions devised by "impartial" experts, was a typically Progressive approach to a social problem.

In practice, however, Taylor found employers unwilling to accept limitations on their authority, whether dictated by experts or by labor unions. But employers did see the value of adopting a philosophy of "industrial partnership" as a means of maintaining a docile labor force. They hired personnel officers to recruit loyal workers and weed out troublemakers. Industrial psychologists discovered that workers wanted to be treated like human beings, not as cogs in a machine, and that poor morale caused absenteeism, high turnover, and low productivity. The more sophisticated businessmen experimented with this "human relations" approach to labor. It also enabled businessmen to insist that voluntary programs eliminated the need for government action. Actually, very few workers received pensions or enjoyed stable employment, but as long as prosperity continued, welfare capitalism seemed plausible. The Great Depression (1929-1941), however, destroyed that illusion just as it convinced people that the basic problems of farm and factory required massive government intervention.

THE DILEMMA OF AGRICULTURE

In the two decades after the collapse of Populism, American farmers prospered. As urbanization enlarged domestic markets and the end of the frontier limited the amount of new acreage coming under cultivation, demand finally caught up with supply. This brought higher prices and a shift by farmers from protest to economic organization that would enable them to reap some of the advantages of new business methods. Like workers who joined unions and manufacturers who formed trade associations, farmers were learning that in modern America it was "organize or perish."

Agricultural cooperatives numbered 12,000 by 1921. Dairy farmers, for instance, found that it was more efficient to set up cooperatives to manufacture butter and cheese so they could concentrate on the production of milk. Grain farmers thought they could cut middlemen's costs and assure fair grading by marketing through cooperative grain elevators. Through cooperatives, farmers acquired better knowledge of markets and learned that scientific methods meant higher profits.

Farmers also established other organizations through which they hoped to advance their interests. The American Society of Equity limited output to raise prices but proved impractical without government control. The Farmers Union set up its own fertilizer and farm implement factories and went into the insurance business. In the winter wheat belt of the Dakotas and Minnesota, the Non-Partisan League emerged after 1914 with a program of state aid for agriculture. The League gained control of the dominant Republican party in North Dakota, elected its own candidates to office, and established state-owned grain elevators and a state bank to aid farmers.

But the most powerful farm organization proved to be the American Farm Bureau. The Farm Bureau grew out of efforts to encourage farmers to adopt modern scientific and business methods. Early in the twentieth century the boll weevil plagued Southern cotton growers. Backed by the Department of Agriculture and business, experts induced farmers to try new techniques of fighting the pest. Experimental farms convinced other farmers, a naturally conservative group who clung to old methods, to follow the advice of experts. A network of county agents, financed by the government and by businessmen, participated in agriculture extension programs in the state universities. When farmers stubbornly resisted new methods, local merchants and bankers refused them credit. Dominated largely by the wealthiest farmers, the bureaus were ostensibly private organizations, but they were often managed by paid government officials.

The American Farm Bureau solidified its position in the 1920s when agricultural prosperity gave way to a chronic agricultural depression. Dwindling overseas outlets after the war sent prices plunging, and farmers groped for solutions. Conservative Republicans offered higher tariffs but Midwestern farmers found that tariffs did not help, since few faced competition from foreign producers. Farmers placed increased emphasis on cooperatives, but these proved no more effective in shoring up sagging prices than tariff juggling.

Farmers then turned to the McNary-Haugen plan, under which the government would make up the difference between the market price and a politically fixed "fair exchange value." With support from farm implement manufacturers and other businessmen in the Midwest and Far West, farmers under the leadership of the American Farm Bureau eventually pushed the scheme through Congress. Eastern Republicans, however, opposed a subsidy to farmers and President Coolidge vetoed the bill. Yet despite defeat, the Farm Bureau and other such organizations had developed a powerful farm bloc that linked Southern and Western farmers to those businessmen such as farm machinery manufacturers directly dependent on agricultural prosperity in a common cause.

In the end, however, farmers found themselves too isolated from other interests to master the power necessary to obtain relief from government. Hostile to organized labor, seeking only to advance its own interests, the Farm Bureau was doomed to frustration until the Great Depression found allies for the farmers outside of agriculture. Confident of their political supremacy, Eastern Republicans ignored agrarian demands. President Coolidge, thinking perhaps about his native state's hard-scrabble agriculture, philosophized: "Well, farmers never have made money. I don't believe we can do much about it. But of course we will have to seem to be doing something; do the best we can and without much hope." Thus Coolidge accepted the politics of normalcy with its reliance on free enterprise and its hostility toward government intervention. But his successor, Herbert Hoover, caught in the crisis of the Great Depression, could not continue the Coolidge policy of avoiding the big problems and relying on the uncontrolled operation of the free market.

THE END OF NORMALCY

Perhaps Calvin Coolidge sensed that danger lay ahead when he announced he would not run for reelection in 1928. The Republicans then turned to Herbert C. Hoover, "the Great Engineer." Hoover was not the professional politician's choice but he seemed the best Republican available. An orphan, Hoover had a meteoric rise before the First World War as a mining engineer and a self-made millionaire. He then won fame directing relief efforts to Belgium and elsewhere during the war. To millions of Americans he came to symbolize the Progressive businessman, a man who had harnessed his administrative and organizing talents to humane purposes.

As secretary of commerce from 1921 to 1928 he brought advanced business thinking to Washington. In place of conflict between capital and labor, Hoover favored both welfare capitalism and unions; instead of cutthroat competition, he favored trade associations and business cooperation; in place of negative government, he believed government should actively encourage all economic sectors to organize into associations to promote prosperity and social stability. "We are passing from a period of extreme individualistic action," he once said characteristically, "into a period of associational activities." As one of the most articulate exponents of this "New Individualism," a man people regarded as a disinterested public servant rather than as a professional politician, Hoover seemed equipped with the vision and the technical expertise a complex modern society required. In this sense, Hoover symbolized a shift in American politics from figures like Harding and Coolidge whose popularity owed much to their ability to evoke nostalgia for an earlier, simpler time. In contrast, Hoover thoroughly identified with the idea that America had in the 1920s entered a New Era in which the genius of the American business system had created unprecedented affluence and permanent prosperity. Four more years of Republican rule, Hoover and his party promised, would bring the country near the day when it would achieve final victory over poverty. "The poor house is vanishing," he assured.

Hoover's Democratic opponent, Governor Alfred E. Smith of New York, ran with several handicaps. He was the first representative of the Newer Americans, the first Roman Catholic, and the first poor boy from the big city to run for president. He was also an open foe of Prohibition. In 1924 Southern and Western rural Democrats had blocked Smith's nomination. Four years later many deserted their party: "You *felt* with Smith or you *felt* with Hoover," recalled one observer. Feeling ran so high that for the first time since Reconstruction Republicans cracked the Solid South as Democrats voted for Hoover to save America, they thought, from a Catholic takeover following Smith's election. The more paranoid Bible-Belters thought Catholics would "hang, waste, boil, flail, strangle, and burn alive" Protestants and "rip up the stomachs and wombs of their women and crush infants' heads against the wall."

Conflicts between the two cultures which had divided the country throughout the decade dominated the 1928 campaign, though it is doubtful that *any* Democrat (even a Methodist bishop) could have beaten Hoover that year. During the campaign, old-stock Protestants met on the streets, wrote one of them, and told each other: "We cannot live if Hoover is not elected." And when Hoover won, they exulted: "We are saved! . . . this great Country, its presence lying out there in the vast darkness, like a soft thing enveloped in the sweet misty night, immense but one in purpose for the Clean Man, the Free Man,"—Herbert Hoover of West Branch, Iowa.

Hoover won the election of 1928 impressively. He benefited from continued "Republican prosperity" and from the normal GOP majority.

Yet the extent of Hoover's victory temporarily obscured important shifts in voting behavior which would have long-term consequences. Smith ran unusually well in the traditionally Republican Midwestern farm belt, a clear sign of farm discontent with the GOP. He proved even more popular in big cities with large ethnic populations. For the first time, newer Americans could identify with a candidate for the presidency. Smith's origins betrayed him with every word he uttered. His New York (Noo Yawk) accent and manners evoked laughter and contempt among the Protestant native-born but the immigrants accepted him as one of their own.

Newer Americans who had previously voted Republican or had not bothered to vote thus trooped to the polls for Al Smith and shifted many big cities to the Democratic column.

Hoover's triumph soon turned sour. In October 1929, the booming stock market collapsed, and for the remaining three years "the Great Engineer" wrestled unsuccessfully with the worst depression in American history. Even before the Wall Street debacle, several business indicators pointed to trouble. The auto and residential construction booms had leveled off and agricultural depression clouded the economy throughout the twenties. At first people minimized the stock market crash. "There has been a little distress selling on the Stock Exchange," explained a senior partner in the firm of J. P. Morgan & Co. "I see nothing in the present situation that is either menacing or warrants pessimism," opined Secretary of the Treasury Andrew W. Mellon. The American productive system, President Hoover reassured the country, remained sound; the difficulties in the stock market were temporary disturbances. Events soon turned these assurances into graveyard whistling.

THE ROOTS OF COLLAPSE

Hoover and most other hopeful experts proved dead wrong. The crash in Wall Street touched off a chain reaction that sent the economy spiraling downward and prostrated the nation. Within three years, 75 percent of the paper value of securities vanished. In 1929, 659 banks failed, wiping out $250 million in deposits; two years later another 2,294 banks and $1.7 billion dollars met a similar fate. Industrial production in 1932 dropped 50 percent from the 1929 level and unemployment grew from four million in October 1930 to seven million the next year and to eleven million by the fall of 1932. During the first three years of the Depression, farm income decreased by half, paralleling a decline in national income from $88 billion in 1929 to $40 billion in 1933.

Some pinned the blame on excesses in the stock market. Banks loaned funds for speculation too easily and the government had failed to control security issues. Investors, for instance,

could buy stocks without putting down much cash. The boom in securities rested in part on the solid performance of the economy in the latter half of the 1920s. But the lopsided distribution of national income that placed huge sums in the hands of corporations, banks, and wealthy investors fed the speculative impulse. The upper middle classes joined in the spree in unprecedented numbers, seeking a quick killing on Wall Street. As investors bid up the prices, security values reached levels far greater than warranted by reality. The speculative frenzy that had set the market soaring, tripling the values of stocks on the New York Stock Exchange between 1925 and 1927, was highly vulnerable to any unfavorable economic change. Millions of investors, sensing an inflated market, were likely to sell if they suspected a break. When that break occurred in October 1929, everyone rushed to sell before prices plummeted further and wiped out profits.

Yet the market crash would not have been so devastating had not profound structural weaknesses existed in the economy. The Federal Reserve System had only limited powers to control the shaky banking system and regulate the credit supply; and even these it failed to exercise energetically. The banks had gone into the securities retailing business and, by liberally extending credit for speculation, they had helped to create the Great Bull Market and the crash.

Equally serious was the precariousness of the international economy. The First World War made the United States the world's banker. European nations liquidated investments in the United States to finance war purchases and as they exhausted these resources the United States had to grant large loans. As a result Europe emerged from the war deeply in debt to the United States, a condition which placed heavy burdens on its economy.

The worldwide postwar economy depended on the export of American capital to enable other countries to meet their debt payments. American loans to Germany helped finance reparations payments to France and Great Britain, which were thus able to meet their obligations to the United States. Maintaining high tariffs and exporting more than it imported, the United States made it doubly difficult for foreign countries to pay their debts. And when the flow of capital from America to Europe tapered off in the later 1920s, the international financial structure crumbled. As the Depression engulfed Europe, it disrupted world trade and worsened conditions in the United States.

Yet even more important than the shakiness of the international economy were structural imbalances at home, where Americans sold most of their goods. The economy showed signs of sagging as early as 1927. National income was very unequally distributed. The top 20 percent of the nation's families and unattached individuals received 54 percent of the income, while the bottom 40 percent received only 12 percent. Had income been more equitably apportioned, millions of Americans would have had effective purchasing power. But instead of passing along gains in productivity to workers in the form of higher wages, or to consumers through lower prices, corporations increased their profits. Billions of dollars in corporate profits were either retained or went to finance speculation instead of being invested in productive activities that generated jobs and economic growth. Finally, the chronic difficulties of agriculture and other depressed sectors during the 1920s hung like a dead weight on the American economy.

The Grapes of Wrath

The richest country in the world now staggered through an economic catastrophe that reduced millions to destitution and many to despair. "We are the first nation in the history of the world," Will Rogers announced, "to go to the poor house in an automobile." In Kingstown, Ohio, the local newspaper reported:

FATHER OF TEN DROWNS SELF;
JUMPS FROM BRIDGE, STARTS TO SWIM
GIVES UP, OUT OF WORK TWO YEARS

"We are about to lose our home," sobbed the widow of the dead jobless steel worker who had worked for Republic Steel for twenty-seven years. In an Illinois coal town of 1350 people, only two miners still had jobs in 1931. By 1932 one out of every three wage and salary workers

was out of a job. In that year, 100,000 Americans applied for work in communist Russia, where they had heard everybody had a job.

Mass unemployment (12.6 million, or *25 percent* of the work force, was out of work by 1933) resulted in mass malnutrition and unprecedented hunger. New York City had an average of 31 breadlines a day in 1931. Near Danbury, Connecticut, in 1932, police found a mother and her 16-year-old daughter starving in the woods, huddled under a strip of canvas tied from a boulder to the ground; the woman had moved from town to town to seek work without success after her husband deserted her. Here and there food riots broke out. In Minneapolis in 1931, "Several hundred men and women in unemployment demonstrations late today stormed a grocery and meat market in the Gateway district, smashed plate glass windows and helped themselves to bacon and ham, fruit and canned goods." None suffered worse than children. In Pennsylvania 27 percent of the school children were undernourished. In a coal-mining town a teacher noticed that a little girl looked sick. "No, I'm all right," she explained, "only I'm hungry." The teacher told her to go home and get some food but the child refused: "It won't do any good . . . because this is sister's day to eat." In Philadelphia, a family lived exclusively on stale bread for eleven days. In the nation's richest city in 1931 the hospitals reported the deaths of dozens of persons weakened by malnutrition.

Tens of thousands lost their homes and farms. By 1933 a million men and women were on the road without a place to live. Dozens met their death stealing rides on the railroads. Because Chicago's city shelter was too small, hundreds of "women of good character," reported the Commissioner of Public Welfare, slept in the parks in the fall of 1931. Shantytowns sprung up around the cities on empty lots constructed of whatever flotsam and jetsam the homeless could find for a shelter, creating communities which the embittered residents called "Hoovervilles."

Some farmers took the law into their own hands to block foreclosure sales. In Iowa dairymen declared a milk holiday. "All roads leading to Sioux City were picketed," reported *Harper's* magazine. "Trucks by hundreds were turned back. Farmers by hundreds lined the roads. They blocked the roads with spiked telegraph poles and logs. They took away a sheriff's badge, his gun, and threw them in a cornfield. Gallons of milk ran down the road ditches. Gallons of confiscated milk were distributed free on the streets of Sioux City."

In the spring of 1932, nearly 12,000 veterans marched on Washington to demand immediate payment of a veterans' bonus not yet due. Building a shantytown near the Capitol, the Bonus Marchers sang:

> Mellon pulled the whistle,
> Hoover rang the bell,
> Wall Street gave the signal,
> And the country went to hell.

The president reacted nervously. A riot which resulted in two deaths, and reports of communist activity among the marchers, caused him to order the U.S. Army to evict the protesters. In an excess of zeal, the troops under General Douglas MacArthur used gas to disperse the veterans and burned down this newest Hooverville in the nation's capital.

Yet such outbursts and protests by the distressed were not the general rule. Most Americans silently, stoically accepted hard times, bewildered by the unexpected, paralyzed about how to respond. So many had believed in the myths of the New Era that their explosion left people dazed and floundering. Hoover realized that the country expected Washington to lead. "The Great Engineer" tried his best but failed, for Hoover like almost everybody else did not fully understand the causes of the Depression.

HERBERT HOOVER AND THE GREAT DEPRESSION

However people explained the collapse, they looked to President Hoover for leadership. Conventionally minded businessmen like Secretary of the Treasury Andrew Mellon advised a hands-off policy. They regarded depressions as natural phenomena which cured themselves after a period of belt tightening. In economics, as in physics, they said with well-heeled resignation, whatever goes up must come down. Hoover disagreed. Neither his social philosophy nor political realities would allow him to maintain a do-nothing policy as had earlier presidents confronting hard times. As leading prophet of the "New Individualism," Hoover believed that the cooperation of business, labor, and agriculture could turn the economy around without unduly enlarging the powers of government at the expense of individual freedom.

Restoring business confidence became his chief goal. Traditionally, businessmen cut expenses at signs of recession in hopes that by reducing prices and wages, and by cutting investment, they could insulate themselves from disaster. But retrenchment only worsened the deflationary spiral. Determined to avoid the mistakes of the past, Hoover summoned representatives of business and labor to Washington. Industry promised to maintain existing wage levels, stabilize employment, and expand investment. Hoover also urged the states and cities to speed up public works to offset the decline in private construction. To restore confidence in banking, Hoover called on the strong banks to help shore up the weaker ones and to loosen credit. Even before the Crash, Hoover had pushed through Congress the Agricultural Marketing Act (1929), his solution to the farm depression. The new law encouraged cooperative marketing and gave a Federal Farm Board $500 million to buy agricultural surpluses that were depressing farm prices.

None of Hoover's schemes worked. Relying on farmers voluntarily to curtail production, the Federal Farm Board kept on buying and prices kept on falling as farmers piled surplus on top of surplus. The board quickly suffered losses of over $350 million. Voluntarism worked no better with the bankers. The Federal Reserve Board loosened credit in the hope that banks would expand loans. Instead they used the new funds to decrease their indebtedness so they might survive should conditions worsen. The National Credit Corporation, established in 1931 by the bankers at Hoover's urging, proved a fiasco, since the strong banks refused to aid the weak ones. For a while, manufacturers made serious efforts to maintain employment and prices but as the Depression deepened these efforts also collapsed. The radio commentator Elmer Davis concluded that Hoover's strategy had failed: "It is easier to believe that the earth is flat than to believe that private initiative alone will save us."

The failure of voluntarism pushed the president reluctantly toward direct federal intervention. For a decade he had preached the theory of countercyclical finance: when business spending declined, government spending should increase to take up the slack. When the Depression hit, Hoover tried to follow his policy but the sharp drop in government revenue limited the funds available for public works. Hoover believed that a budget deficit due to greater public spending would undermine business confidence, the key to recovery. Under pressure from business for relief, the president agreed however to depart from voluntarism and establish the Reconstruction Finance Corporation (1932), a federal agency with another $500 million to lend to business and agriculture. When the RFC immediately went to the rescue of J. P. Morgan & Co. and other business giants, criticism mounted, especially in view of Hoover's failure to come up with a plan to help millions dependent for survival on public relief.

Ordinarily, private charities took care of the destitute. But mass poverty in the Depression revealed the hopelessness of relying on voluntarism despite efforts to raise more funds for charity. The burden of relief now fell on local government, whose resources were so strained that many cities and counties verged on bankruptcy. The president, despite his reputation for

humanitarianism, *seemed* indifferent to the plight of the unemployed. The administration had no accurate information on the number without jobs, the magnitude of the relief problem, or the financial ability of local government to shoulder the burden. Nor did Hoover present a realistic alternative to the collapse of local relief efforts. He ruled out federally funded relief because, said Senator David I. Walsh of Massachusetts, "Whatever the emergency, whatever the appeal, whatever the cry that comes from the suffering people of this country, he does not propose to levy one dollar more in increased taxes. . . ." But how could he, when informed opinion held that cutting government spending was the essential first step to restore business confidence?

Hoover found himself trapped by his own assumptions. Yet he was not alone. Most of the country's leaders agreed that government could or should do very little. "The main trouble," explained economist George Soule, "is not that business is in the saddle; the trouble is that nobody is in the saddle." The failure of voluntarism left Herbert Hoover without a policy and left the country without a leader. As unemployment grew worse and suffering spread, Will Rogers warned, "If our big men in the next year can't fix that— well, they just ain't big men, that's all." The "big men" failed and in 1932 the voters decided they "just ain't big men." In that year, Americans elected a new president, a physically handicapped man with an assured manner who made vague promises of a new deal.

SUGGESTIONS FOR FURTHER READING

Suggestions for further reading are highly selective. Works available in paperback editions are starred (*). Students should consult the bibliography in John D. Hicks, *Republican Ascendancy, 1921-1933* (1960)* and the footnotes in Burl Noggle's article "The Twenties," cited below, for additional references.

INTRODUCTION

General Works on the Twenties

Frederick Lewis Allen, *Only Yesterday* (1931)*; William E. Leuchtenberg, *The Perils of Prosperity, 1914-1932* (1958)*; John D. Hicks, *Republican*

Ascendancy, 1921-1933 (1960)*; Paul Carter, *The Twenties in America* (1968)*; Frederick J. Hoffman, "The Temper of the Twenties," *Minnesota Review,* vol. 1 (1960), pp. 36-45; Henry F. May, "Shifting Perspectives on the 1920's," *Mississippi Valley Historical Review,* vol. 43 (1956), pp. 405-427; Burl Noggle, "The Twenties: A New Historiographical Frontier," *Journal of American History,* vol. 53 (1966), pp. 299-314.

CHAPTER 25

General

George H. Soule, *Prosperity Decade . . . 1917-1929* (1947)*; Joseph Schumpeter, "The American Economy in the . . . Twenties," *American Economic Review*, vol. 36 (1946), pp. 1-10.

The Sources of Growth

Solomon Fabricant, *The Output of Manufacturing Industries, 1899-1937* (1940); Simon Kuznets, *National Income and Its Composition, 1919-1938* (2 vols., 1941); Harold Barger, *Outlay and Income in the United States, 1921-1938* (1942).

The Emergence of Detroit

John B. Rae, *The American Automobile* (1965)*; Keith Sward, *The Legend of Henry Ford* (1948)*; Allan Nevins and Frank E. Hill, *Ford: The Times, the Man, the Company* (3 vols., 1954-1963); Alfred P. Sloan, Jr., *My Years With General Motors* (1964)*.

The Structure of Mass Marketing

Adolph A. Berle, Jr. and Gardiner G. Means, *The Modern Corporation and Private Property* (1932); Peter Drucker, *The Concept of the Corporation* (1946); Harry W. Laidler, *Concentration of Control in American Industry* (1931); Alfred D. Chandler, Jr., *Strategy and Structure: Chapters in the History of Industrial Enterprise* (1962)*; Otis Pease, *The Responsibilities of American Advertising . . . 1920-1940* (1958).

The Welfare of the American People

Richard H. Shryock, *Medicine in America* (1966)*; Clarke A. Chambers, *Seedtime of Reform: American Social Service and Social Action, 1918-1933* (1963)*.

CHAPTER 26

General

Robert S. and Helen M. Lynd, *Middletown: A Study in Contemporary American Culture* (1929)*; Blake McKelvey, *The Emergence of Metropolitan America, 1915-1966* (1968); Roy Lubove, *Community Planning in the 1920's* (1963)*.

Men, Women, and Children

Arthur W. Calhoun, *A Social History of the American Family, From the Civil War* (1919)*; Sidney Ditzion, *Marriage, Morals, and Sex in America* (1953); Paul H. Jacobson, *American Marriage and Divorce* (1959).

The New Woman

Aileen S. Kraditor, *The Ideas of the Woman Suffrage Movement, 1890-1920* (1965); Anne Firor Scott, "The 'New Woman' in the New South," *South Atlantic Quarterly*, vol. 61 (1962), pp. 473-483; Anne Firor Scott, "After Suffrage: Southern Women in the Twenties," *South Atlantic Quarterly*, vol. 62 (1963), pp. 92-106; Carl N. Degler, "Revolution Without Ideology: The Changing Place of Women in America," in Robert Jay Lifton (ed.), *The Woman in America* (1967)*.

The Expansion of Education

R. Freeman Butts and Lawrence A. Cremin, *A History of Education in American Culture* (1953); Merle Curti, *Social Ideas of American Educators* (1935)*; Lawrence A. Cremin, *The Transformation of the School: Progressivism in American Education, 1876-1957* (1961)*.

The Emergence of the University

Richard Hofstadter and C. DeWitt Hardy, *The Development and Scope of Higher Education in the United States* (1952); Laurence R. Veysey, *The Emergence of the American University* (1965)*; Richard Hofstadter and Walter P. Metzger, *The Development of Academic Freedom in the United States* (1955)*.

Entertainment for the Masses

Albert McLean, *American Vaudeville as Ritual* (1965); Lewis Jacobs, *The Rise of the American Film* (1939)*; L. C. Rosten, *Hollywood* (1941); Arthur Knight, *The Liveliest Art* (1957)*; G. N. Fenin and William Everson, *The Western* (1962); Kelton Lahue, *Continued Next Week: A History of the Movie Serial* (1964); Paul Schubert, *The Electric Word: The Rise of the Radio* (1928); Eric Barnouw, *A History of Broadcasting in the United States* (2 vols., 1965-1968); Russel B. Nye, *The Unembarrassed Muse: The Popular Arts in America* (1970); Foster Rhea Dulles, *A History of Recreation: America Learns to Play* (1965)*.

Culture and Mass Society

Alfred Kazin, *On Native Grounds* (1942)*; Maxwell D. Geismar, *The Last of the Provincials: The American Novel, 1915-1925* (1947)*; Maxwell Geismar,

Writers in Crisis: The American Novel, 1925–1940
(1942)*; Frederick J. Hoffman, *The Twenties: Amer-*
ican Writing in the Postwar Decade (1955)*; Rod-
erick Nash, *The Nervous Generation: American*
Thought, 1917–1930 (1970)*; Carolyn F. Ware,
Greenwich Village 1920–1930 (1935)*; Ernest
Hemingway, *A Moveable Feast: . . . Life in Paris*
in the Twenties (1964); Arthur Mizener, *The Far*
Side of Paradise: A Biography of F. Scott Fitz-
gerald (1951)*; Mark Schorer, *Sinclair Lewis*
(1961)*; Edmund Wilson, *The American Earth-*
quake (1958); Matthew Josephson, *Life Among the*
Surrealists (1962); Malcolm Cowley, *Exile's Return:*
A Literary Odyssey of the 1920's (1934)*; Arthur
and Barbara Gelb, *O'Neill* (1962)*.

Oliver P. Larkin, *Art and Life in America* (19-
60); John Burchard and Albert Bush-Brown, *The*
Architecture of America (rev. edition, 1966)*; Irving
Sabolsky, *American Music* (1969)*; Sigmund
Spaeth, *A History of Popular Music in America*
(1948); Isaac Goldberg, *Tin Pan Alley* (1930);
Roland Gelatt, *The Fabulous Phonograph* (1955);
Barry Ulanov, *A History of Jazz in America* (1952);
Gunther Schuller, *Early Jazz* (1968).

CHAPTER 27

The Drive for Internal Security

William Preston, Jr., *Aliens and Dissenters: Federal*
Suppression of Radicals, 1903–1933 (1963)*; Melvin
Dubofsky, *We Shall Be All: A History of the Indus-*
trial Workers of the World (1969); Theodore Draper,
The Roots of American Communism (1957)*; Robert
K. Murray, *Red Scare: A Study in National Hys-*
teria, 1919–1920 (1955)*; Robert L. Friedheim, *The*
Seattle General Strike (1964); Stanley Coben, *A.*
Mitchell Palmer (1963); George L. Joughin and
Edmund M. Morgan, *The Legacy of Sacco and*
Vanzetti (1948)*; Paul L. Murphy, "Sources and
Nature of Intolerance in the 1920's," *Journal of*
American History, vol. 51 (1964), pp. 60-76.

The Heyday of Racism

John Higham, *Strangers in the Land . . . American*
Nativism, 1860–1925 (1955)*; William S. Bernard,
American Immigration Policy (1950); David M.
Chalmers, *Hooded Americanism . . . the Ku Klux*
Klan (1965)*; Charles C. Alexander, *The Ku Klux*
Klan in the Southwest (1965)*; Emma Lou Thorn-
brough, "Segregation in Indiana during the Klan
Era of the 1920's," *Mississippi Valley Historical*
Review, vol. 47 (1961), pp. 594-618; Kenneth T.

Jackson, *The Ku Klux Klan in the City, 1915–1930*
(1967)*.

The Indians

William T. Hagan, *American Indians* (1961)*; Henry
L. Fritz, *The Movement for Indian Assimilation*
(1963); Randolph C. Downes, "A Crusade for Indian
Reform, 1922-1934," *Mississippi Valley Historical*
Review, vol. 32 (1945), pp. 331-354.

The Black Man

August Meier, *Negro Thought in America, 1880–*
1915 (1963)*; Samuel R. Spencer, *Booker T. Wash-*
ington (1955)*; W. E. B. Du Bois, *Dusk of Dawn*
(1940)*; Francis L. Broderick, *W. E. B. Du Bois*
(1959)*; Elliott M. Rudwick, *W. E. B. Du Bois*
(1960)*; Louise Kennedy, *The Negro Peasant Turns*
Cityward (1920); James Weldon Johnson, *Black*
Manhattan (1930)*; Gilbert Osofsky, *Harlem: The*
Making of a Ghetto (1966)*; Allan H. Spear, *Black*
Chicago: The Making of a Negro Ghetto (1967)*;
Robert A. Bone, *The Negro Novel in America*
(1965)*; Stephen Bronz, *Roots of Negro Racial*
Consciousness: The 1920's (1964); E. David Cronon,
Black Moses: The Story of Marcus Garvey (1955)*;
Richard B. Sherman, "The Harding Administration
and the Negro . . . ," *Journal of Negro History,*
vol. 49 (1964).

Religious Crisis in Modern America

Paul A. Carter, *The Decline and Revival of the*
Social Gospel . . . 1920–1940 (1956); Robert M.
Miller, *American Protestantism and Social Issues,*
1919–1939 (1958); Donald B. Meyer, *The Protes-*
tant Search for Political Realism, 1919–1941 (1960);
Kenneth K. Bailey, *Southern White Protestantism*
in the Twentieth Century (1964); William G. Mc-
Loughlin, *Billy Sunday Was His Real Name* (1955);
Norman F. Furniss, *The Fundamentalist Contro-*
versy, 1918–1931 (1954); Ray Ginger, *Six Days or*
Forever? Tennessee v. John Thomas Scopes (1958)*;
Lawrence W. Levine, *Defender of the Faith, Wil-*
liam Jennings Bryan . . . the Last Decade, 1915–
1925 (1965)*.

Prohibition

James H. Timberlake, *Prohibition and the Progres-*
sive Movement, 1900–1920 (1963); Charles Merz,
The Dry Decade (1931); Andrew Sinclair, *Prohibi-*
tion, the Era of Excess (1962)*.

CHAPTER 28

General

Karl Schriftgiesser, *This Was Normalcy* (1948); Arthur M. Schlesinger, Jr., *The Crisis of the Old Order* (1957)*.

The Eclipse of Progressivism

Herbert F. Margulies, *The Decline of the Progressive Movement in Wisconsin, 1890-1920* (1968); Arthur S. Link, "What Happened to the Progressive Movement in the 1920's?" *American Historical Review*, vol. 64 (1959), pp. 833-851; Russel B. Nye, *Midwestern Progressive Politics* (1951); Paul W. Glad, "Progressives and the Business Culture of the 1920's," *Journal of American History*, vol. 53 (1966), pp. 75-89; Donald C. Swain, *Federal Conservation Policy, 1921-1933* (1963); Preston J. Hubbard, *Origins of the TVA: The Muscle Shoals Controversy, 1920-1932* (1961)*; George W. Norris, *Fighting Liberal* (1945)*.

The Role of the War

Selig Adler, "The War-Guilt Question and American Disillusionment, 1918-1928," *Journal of Modern History*, vol. 23 (1951), pp. 1-28; Harold and Margaret Sprout, *Toward a New Order of Sea Power . . . 1918-1922* (1940); D. F. Fleming, *The United States and World Organization, 1920-1933* (1938).

Foreign Policy

John Chalmers Vinson, *The Parchment Peace . . . the Washington Conference, 1921-1922* (1955); L. Ethan Ellis, *Frank B. Kellogg and American Foreign Relations, 1925-29* (1961); Robert H. Ferrell, *Peace in Their Time: The Origins of the Kellogg-Briand Pact* (1952); William A. Williams, "The Legend of Isolationism in the 1920's" *Science and Society*, vol. 18 (1954), pp. 1-20; Herbert Feis, *The Diplomacy of the Dollar* (1950)*; Joseph Brandes, *Herbert Hoover and Economic Diplomacy . . . 1921-28* (1962).

Republican Supremacy

Wesley M. Bagby, *The Road to Normalcy* (1962)*; Andrew Sinclair, *The Available Man . . . Warren Gamaliel Harding* (1965)*; Robert K. Murray, *The Harding Era* (1969); Burl Noggle, *Teapot Dome: Oil and Politics in the 1920's* (1962)*; William Allen

White, *A Puritan in Babylon . . . Calvin Coolidge* (1938)*; Donald R. McCoy, *Calvin Coolidge* (1967); Edmund A. Moore, *A Catholic Runs for President: The Campaign of 1928* (1956); Ruth C. Silva, *Rum, Religion, and Votes: 1928 Re-examined* (1962); Paul A. Carter, "The Campaign of 1928 Re-examined: A Study in Political Folklore," *Wisconsin Magazine of History*, vol. 46 (1963), pp. 263-272; Oscar Handlin, *Al Smith and His America* (1958)*; David Burner, *The Politics of Provincialism: The Democratic Party in Transition, 1918-1932* (1968); J. Joseph Huthmacher, *Massachusetts People and Politics, 1919-1933* (1959)*.

Business Supremacy

James Prothro, *Dollar Decade: Business Ideas in the 1920's* (1954)*; Morrell Heald, "Business Thought in the Twenties . . . ," *American Quarterly*, vol. 13 (1961), pp. 126-139.

The Supreme Court

Alpheus T. Mason, *William Howard Taft: Chief Justice* (1965); Stanley Kutler, "Chief Justice Taft, National Regulation and the Commerce Clause," *Journal of American History*, vol. 51 (1965), pp. 651-668; S. J. Konefsky, *The Legacy of Holmes and Brandeis* (1956); J. F. Paschal, *Mr. Justice Sutherland: A Man Against the State* (1951); Alpheus T. Mason, *Harlan Fiske Stone* (1956); R. G. Fuller, *Child Labor and the Constitution* (1929); Edward Berman, *Labor and the Sherman Act* (1930).

The Decline of Organized Labor

Irving Bernstein, *The Lean Years: A History of the American Worker, 1920-1933* (1960)*; Philip Taft, *The A. F. of L.* (2 vols., 1957-1959); David Brody, *Steelworkers in America: The Nonunion Era* (1960); Allen M. Wakstein, "Origins of the Open Shop Movement, 1919-1920," *Journal of American History*, vol. 51 (1964), pp. 460-475; Milton J. Nadworny, *Scientific Management and the Unions, 1900-1932* (1955).

The Dilemma of Agriculture

James H. Shideler, *Farm Crisis, 1919-1923* (1957); Gilbert C. Fite, *George N. Peek and the Fight for Farm Parity* (1954); Theodore Saloutos and John D. Hicks, *Twentieth Century Populism: Agricultural*

Discontent in the Middle West (1951)*; Robert L. Morlan, *Political Prairie Fire: The Nonpartisan League, 1915-1922* (1955).

The End of Normalcy

Giulio Pontecorvo, "Investment Banking and Security Speculation in the Late 1920's," *Business History Review,* vol. 32 (1958), pp. 166-191; Robert Sobel, *The Great Bull Market* (1968)*; John K. Galbraith, *The Great Crash* (1955)*.

Hoover and Depression

Harris G. Warren, *Herbert Hoover and the Great Depression* (1959)*; Albert U. Romasco, *The Poverty of Abundance: Hoover, the Nation, and the Depression* (1965)*; Carl N. Degler, "The Ordeal of Herbert Hoover," *Yale Review,* vol. 52 (1963), pp. 563-583; Robert H. Ferrell, *American Diplomacy in the Great Depression* (1957)*; Broadus Mitchell, *Depression Decade . . . 1929-1941* (1947)*.

Part Seven
The New Deal and the World Crisis,

1930-1945

Introduction

In the first three decades of the twentieth century contemporary America took shape. Government began assuming a larger responsibility for human welfare, a mass production economy stamped out millions of cars, telephones and appliances, the cities became the center of American life, and the mass media diffused a new popular culture and values rooted in urban life. Yet during these decades of change Americans remained ambivalent toward the new, longing nostalgically for an earlier, simpler, and presumably purer agrarian society which faded rapidly into memory. The anxieties generated by industrialism, the cities, and secularism came to a boil in the 1920s. Fear of Catholics, Jews, and blacks, fear of science and evolution, fear of alcohol and machines gripped millions of Americans as they plunged more deeply and irreversibly toward contemporary America.

Counterbalancing the fear of change were the benefits of change. Millions of Americans in the 1920s enjoyed unprecedented improvements in living standards, from better health care to new creature comforts their ancestors could not even imagine. American capitalism outproduced all the other countries of the world and gave Americans the highest standard of living. Then in 1929 a decade of prosperity ended in the worst economic catastrophe of the nation's history. Confidence in business leadership plummeted as fast as the stock market. The promise of American life turned suddenly into a cruel joke. There was no work for millions; there was no way to avoid foreclosure of home or farm; no matter where one turned for help, the doors soon slammed shut.

The nation, beset by self-doubt, wondered if it had lost control of its destiny. Franklin D. Roosevelt's New Deal (1933–1945) did not restore prosperity, but it did restore faith. The New Deal did not abolish capitalism, but it did place business under greater public control and made government responsible for assuring the material welfare of the American people. Even more important, the New Deal presided over a shift in values and attitudes that subdued the conflict between the village and the city, the Anglo-Saxons and the minorities, the old-time religion and modern science. The New Deal brought together in a grand coalition the have-nots, working people, farmers, and appreciable segments of the middle class. Mass unemployment and destitution forged common bonds among the down-and-out, bonds that transcended ethnic, religious, and cultural differences that for over a century had shaped American politics and blocked social reform.

The new coalition made the Democratic party the majority party, a party that broke the unwritten rule of American politics by appealing to voters on the basis of class interest. To farmers, the New Deal gave agricultural subsidies; to workers, it offered government protection for union organizations; for senior citizens, it provided old age pensions; for the unemployed and destitute, blacks included, it made sure no one starved. But the New Deal and its philosophy of reform liberalism which accepted private ownership never ended the depression though it alleviated the suffering. Committed to the preservation of private property, yet willing to experiment and throw overboard conventional notions that had paralyzed earlier generations in grappling with social dislocations, skeptical that there were indeed any "laws" of economics, the New Deal scrambled from one remedy to another without discovering a formula for economic recovery.

When full employment returned to America in 1941, outside forces were responsible. The United States became involved in a global war as Germany and Japan sought Fascist domination of the world. Not since the War of 1812 had the security of the United States been in serious danger from foreign enemies. But modern technology revolutionized warfare and not even 3000 miles of ocean could have protected America from the New Barbarians loose in the Old World.

After the First World War, Americans had turned their backs on a world they had hoped to make safe for democracy but which proved unwilling to follow the leadership of the United States under Woodrow Wilson. Though Americans expanded economically around the globe in the interwar years, they left the maintenance of a balance of power to others. By 1939, a rearmed Nazi Germany, under Adolph Hitler, challenged Britain and France for control of Europe. Meanwhile, the Rising Sun, the Japanese empire, had already carved out huge chunks of China as the first step along the road to imperial domination in Asia.

For almost twenty years the United States had assumed that if it minded its own business and remained neutral in the conflicts between other nations, it could avoid entanglement in a new world war. Neither isolationism nor neutrality proved workable. The world had become too small, too interdependent. Slowly the United States became enmeshed as it sought to stave off the defeat of Britain. Then in December 1941 a Japanese attack on Pearl Harbor swiftly ended American ambivalence.

For four years the United States made common cause not only with the democracies of France and Britain, but with Communist Russia and Nationalist China, to stop the spread of Fascism. The American arsenal proved decisive. Victory over Germany and Japan in 1945 imposed new responsibilities on the United States, since it had become the world's superpower. Americans could no longer retreat into isolation any more than they could rely blindly on American business and free enterprise to make them prosperous. Thus in the years between the Great Crash of 1929 and the end of World War II in 1945, Americans looked to reform liberalism at home and to liberal internationalism abroad to guide them through an uncertain future.

Fruits of American failure: Radicals demonstrate, 1930. (*Minnesota Historical Society*)

"We Want Justice": The Bonus Marchers in Washington, D.C., June 1932. (*Wide World Photos*)

Farmers take to direct action: Milk dumping to raise prices, 1930s. (*Minnesota Historical Society*)

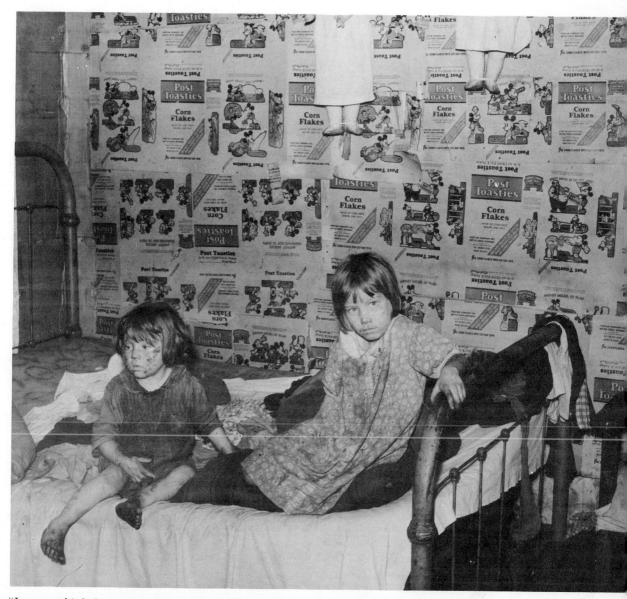

"I see one third of a nation ill-housed, ill-clad, ill-nourished."—FDR, 1938. *(Library of Congress)*

The hungry line up for a meal, New York City, 1932. *(Franklin D. Roosevelt Library)*

The forgotten Americans, Wyoming, 1930s. *(Franklin D. Roosevelt Library)*

On relief, Louisiana, 1930s. *(Franklin D. Roosevelt Library)*

Oklahoma migratory worker comes to California, 1930s. *(Franklin D. Roosevelt Library)*

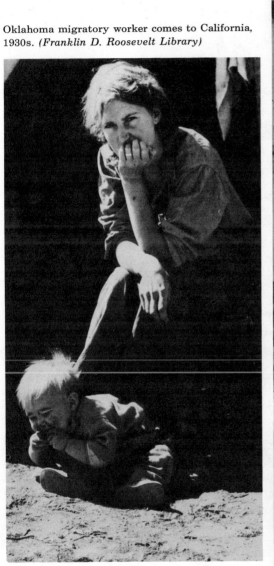

Young Indian "hunkering down," Sallisaw, Oklahoma, 1939. *(Library of Congress)*

Washington to the
rescue, 1934. *(Library
of Congress)*

The coming of the New Deal: FDR campaigning, 1932. *(Franklin D. Roosevelt Library)*

The New Deal's faithful, Orange County, California. Presidential campaign, 1940. *(Franklin D. Roosevelt Library)*

"Give us this day our daily bread," Washington, D.C., 1942. Free school lunches courtesy of Uncle Sam. *(Library of Congress*

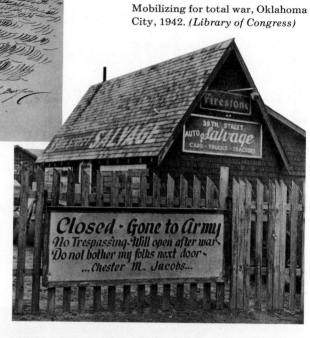

Mobilizing for total war, Oklahoma City, 1942. *(Library of Congress)*

(Library of Congress)

"A day that will live in infamy," the Japanese attack on Pearl Harbor, December 7, 1941. *(Wide World Photos)*

Allies in war: Americans, French, and Moroccans, Rabat, Morocco, 1942. *(Franklin D. Roosevelt Library)*

General Eisenhower and paratroopers on the eve of "the longest day"—D-Day, June 6, 1944. *(Wide World Photos)*

The Big Three at Yalta, February 1945: Churchill *(left)*, FDR, and Stalin. *(Franklin D. Roosevelt Library)*

"She'll Be So Nice to Come Home To." 1944. *(U.P.I.)*

Japanese children pledge allegiance, San Francisco, 1942. *(Library of Congress)*

Naturalized citizens attending "I am an American Day," Buffalo, New York, 1943. *(Library of Congress)*

The capture of Saarbrucken, Germany, 1945.
Population: 135,000 in 1939, 1000 in 1945.
(Wide World Photos)

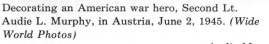

Decorating an American war hero, Second Lt.
Audie L. Murphy, in Austria, June 2, 1945. *(Wide
World Photos)*

Audie Murphy: An
American in war and peace.
*(Wide World
Photos)*

France salutes a young American liberator, First
Lt. Audie L. Murphy, September 9, 1945. *(Wide
World Photos)*

From war hero to Hollywood actor:
Audie Murphy with James Cagney.
(U.P.I.)

In *To Hell and Back. (U.P.I.)*

In *Gunpoint. (U.P.I.)*

(Above) Audie Murphy fund-raising for the American Cancer Society, 1968. *(Right)* After he was arraigned on charges of assault. May 28, 1970. A Congressional Medal of Honor winner, he was killed in a plane crash near Roanoke, Va., May 28, 1971. *(Above and below, Wide World Photos: right, U.P.I.)*

Chapter 29
The Emergence of the New Deal

The severity and prolonged duration of the Great Depression posed the most serious challenge faced by American democracy since the Civil War. American optimism and self-confidence, rooted in the nation's material abundance, were put to the test when American capitalism collapsed in 1929. America, the Land of Opportunity, became America, the Land of Mass Unemployment. After three years of steady decline the country looked for a change. Confidence in business leadership evaporated and the nation groped for new direction. Into this crisis stepped Franklin D. Roosevelt. Roosevelt put together one of the most successful political coalitions in the history of the United States, and went on to win four presidential elections between 1932 and 1944—a record which cannot be matched or surpassed, since the Constitution now limits presidents to two terms.

For eight of those years, Roosevelt attempted to make good on his promise in 1932 to give the American people a new deal. Fulfilling the promise proved difficult. Roosevelt had no clear idea of how to end the depression, and his programs were often hit-and-miss affairs. But he was willing to try any number of "solutions" so long as they did not conflict with private ownership of the industrial system. He sought to reform capitalism, not bury it.

The New Deal did curb some of the excesses of unregulated capitalism; it belatedly laid the foundation for a welfare state, and it forced businessmen to share power with organized farmers and workers. This changing power relationship involved long-term shifts in party allegiance. For the first time since before the Civil War, the Democrats became the majority party, Republicans having been saddled with the stigma of the "Hoover Depression." The New Deal Democratic coalition brought together the less affluent old-stock Protestants, the newer, ex-immigrant "ethnic groups," and the blacks, in an uncommonly broad-based coalition. The Democrats under Roosevelt took command of the main road

of American politics, and have dominated it ever since. In the process reform liberalism wrote an epitaph for unregulated capitalism.

THE ELECTION OF 1932

The outcome of the presidential election of 1932 seemed predetermined. Hoover had been discredited in the popular mind. All that remained was his defeat at the polls, and no one doubted that the repudiation would come in November. In the summer of 1932, the Republican convention renominated Hoover on the first ballot, but it acted with little enthusiasm. The president was apparently one of the few Republicans who thought he had a chance for victory and vindication.

The Democratic nomination was something else. Since they had won the congressional elections of 1930, the confident Democrats went to Chicago and their national meeting hungry for office. Al Smith, the previous candidate, remained the official head of the party. But by this time another New Yorker, Governor Franklin D. Roosevelt, had surpassed him as frontrunner. Roosevelt came from an urban state, yet was not identified with the city machines, and though an old-stock Protestant, he attracted ethnic votes. Thus he might unite the urban and rural Democratic factions whose feuding during the 1920s had all but wrecked the party.

Roosevelt had been campaigning effectively for over two years. He sent a hard-working political lieutenant, James A. Farley, crisscrossing the country, lining up support. When the convention met, Roosevelt had pledges from more than half of the delegates, although far fewer than the required two-thirds. Farley wisely held some Roosevelt votes in reserve during the first ballots, adding a few each time. After the third, John N. Garner of Texas, the Speaker of the House of Representatives, swung over to Roosevelt in order to avoid another prolonged convention battle, in the manner of the previous decade. The Garner switch pushed Roosevelt over the top.

Roosevelt immediately demonstrated a flair for the dramatic. He chartered a plane and flew to Chicago to accept the nomination in person. At the convention, Roosevelt promised to press for the Democratic platform, which included the repeal of Prohibition, but little else novel. Promising a balanced budget, he also pledged, "a new deal for the American people," a vague but catchy phrase which ultimately gave a name to a decade. What Roosevelt mainly accomplished was to project his personal magnetism, to demonstrate his superb sense of political timing, and to exude the strength and confidence which form part of the psychology of a winner.

In contrast, the Hoover outlook and campaign seemed peevish. The president worked hard at reelection, but to little effect. He warned gravely of further economic disasters should the Democrats win, predicting, in one of his rare graphic phrases (borrowed from William Jennings Bryan), that grass would grow in the streets of American cities and towns. But Hoover had nothing new to say. His party had taken credit for the prosperity of the 1920s and now it had to take the blame for the depression. The president was temperamentally incapable of either demagoguery or dynamism. His campaign never became more than an earnest but soft whisper on such themes as the tariff and rugged individualism. His crowds were silent and sometimes sullen. A hitchhiker made it from California to New York in five days with a sign warning: "Give me a lift or I'll vote for Hoover."

The Democrats campaigned vigorously and imprecisely. Roosevelt did not have to commit himself, and at first he was so vague that only criticism forced him to reply. Roosevelt made promises to all the major voting blocs, especially farmers and businessmen, but significantly he said little to organized labor, an interest group which later became one of the main beneficiaries of the New Deal. He pledged to cut government spending, promote conservation, and boost farm income. Yet in one significant speech, Roosevelt pointed toward the future, perhaps more than he then realized. At San Francisco's Commonwealth Club, he noted that America must adjust to the fact that its frontier had been closed for many decades. Unbridled economic activity no longer produced affluence. It brought instead economic catastrophe and therefore must be regulated in the public interest. Private economic power he declared to be a "public trust," and if the public good demanded it, private enterprise must submit to government controls.

Roosevelt's family and educational background, though conservative, prepared him for the role of reform leader. His branch of the New York Roosevelts had become Hudson River Valley squires. For them money was a means that enabled them to live as American aristocrats. Financially and socially secure, like his cousin TR, Franklin Roosevelt did not stand in awe of powerful businessmen. He never regarded the capacity to make money as the ultimate test of a man. Young Franklin went to the best private schools, and after graduation from Harvard he studied law at Columbia University but did not complete work for his degree. Politics interested him more than the law. Several years in the state legislature, where he acquired a progressive reputation as an opponent of "the bosses," set the stage for the jump to national politics. During World War I, Roosevelt used the minor office of assistant secretary of the navy as a springboard, just as his cousin Theodore had done twenty years before.

His reward came in 1920 when he received the Democratic nomination for vice-president. The honor had little immediate value, since the Republicans swept that election. But Roosevelt gained national publicity useful for the future. A year later, however, Roosevelt's political career seemed dead. He contracted polio (infantile paralysis) and a partial recovery left him in a wheelchair. Political ambitions had to be shelved for seven agonizing years during which Roosevelt fought to maintain his spirit and to master the use of half of his body. His chance to reenter politics came in 1928. Al Smith, the Democratic presidential candidate, persuaded Roosevelt, who needed little coaxing, to run for governor of New York to boost his own presidential chances. He won the election, and reelection two years later, victories which made him the nation's leading Democrat.

Roosevelt swept the 1932 election. He won all but six of the forty-eight states, with a whopping 57 percent of the popular vote. The Democrats also obtained large majorities in both houses of Congress. Although any respectable Democratic candidate probably would have won, Roosevelt's special political talents inspired confidence and helped make the election's outcome so one-sided. Strikingly, in the midst of their severest depression, the American people though dazed did not abandon hope in their social and political structure. The candidates of the Socialist and Communist parties, both of whom attacked the capitalist system, claiming that depression resulted from the "inherent contradictions" of that system, obtained less than a million of the forty million votes cast.

Reform liberalism received another chance, perhaps its last. Roosevelt came into office facing staggering problems, but also with an opportunity to exercise bold leadership. Political progressivism, in a state of suspended animation since the shattering of the Wilsonian coalition, awaited the appearance of a leader to fill the vacuum left by discredited conservatives. The opportunity was not of Roosevelt's making, but he accepted the challenge and revitalized American liberalism in the process. This time, reform liberalism became the dominant ideology, supplying Americans with the principles and programs with which they have since attempted to cope with the problem of mass society.

LAUNCHING THE NEW DEAL

When Roosevelt took office in March 1933, fear gripped the nation. The shock waves of depression were reaching new levels of intensity. Unemployment stood at nearly thirteen million (25 percent of the work force); local relief funds had been exhausted; and destitution spread as more families lost their homes, farmers saw their farms foreclosed, and businessmen had to shut down their enterprises. In addition, as inauguration day approached, the banking system hovered on the verge of collapse. Roosevelt realized that he

first had to restore hope that something could be done to reverse the spiraling downslide, hope that men still could control the system they had created. Roosevelt assured the country that it had "nothing to fear but fear itself." He was right— in the long run. America remained the world's richest nation. In the long run prosperity was bound to return. But as Harry Hopkins, Roosevelt's relief administrator, later remarked: "People don't eat in the long run. They eat every day." Curbing fear was essential, yet a brave front alone would not solve national problems.

The economy had to be put on the road to recovery, and the first step was to revive the nation's financial institutions, many of which had ceased to function, and all of which had been closed. Despite the creation of the Federal Reserve system a generation before, the American banking system remained in a chaotic condition. Many small, state banks had not joined the Federal Reserve, and during the 1920s several thousand of them had gone out of business. Many more banks had failed since the stock market crash of 1929, and others had been shut by order of state governments. In New York, the country's financial capital, the governor closed all banks pending federal action by the new president. Roosevelt responded by launching his "revolution" during the first three months of his administration, or the Hundred Days. Congress had been called into special session, and the heavy Democratic majorities gave the president nearly everything he asked for.

In finance and banking, the administration moved quickly and effectively. Roosevelt suspended all banking operations for four days. This breathing space gave time for Congress to meet. The president made it clear that he wanted action quickly, or he would assume extraordinary powers, as in wartime. The resulting Emergency Banking Act, which passed in four hours, aimed at driving small, unstable banks out of business by denying them licenses to reopen. Meanwhile the government bolstered the larger banks through loans made by the Reconstruction Finance Corporation (RFC). Wall Street approved. On March 12 Roosevelt took to the airwaves to assure Americans that bank deposits were safe, much safer than bills stuffed into mattresses.

This was the president's first radio "fireside chat," a means of mass communication which developed into one of his prime political weapons.

Depression Solutions

The end of the banking crisis solved nothing; it only bought needed time. The new administration had no master plan for dealing with the national emergency. Instead it improvised from day to day, hopeful that "bold, persistent experimentation" would pay off. Before and after taking office, Roosevelt received conflicting advice from different quarters, each with its own pet theory of the causes and cure of the depression. Leading businessmen, such as General Electric's Gerard Swope, insisted that cutthroat competition—"chiseling" they called it—was bankrupting business as the result of fierce rivalry for shrinking consumer purchasing power. The government, they said, should regulate competition, allow price fixing, and suspend the antitrust laws. Others, like Supreme Court Justice Louis Brandeis and Harvard Law Professor Felix Frankfurter (who became one of FDR's leading advisers), countered that monopoly, not competition, had created the problem. They blamed Big Business for piling up huge profits while denying the average American adequate purchasing power through higher wages and salaries. Still a third, small group of intellectuals, led by Rexford Tugwell, a Columbia University economics professor who became a member of Roosevelt's "brain trust," insisted that technology, not simply chicanery and political privilege, had created Big Business and only government planning could make it responsive to the public interest.

There were other, more specific remedies as well. Labor leaders like the mine workers' John L. Lewis insisted that all workers needed unions to acquire the purchasing power that would get the economy moving again. Similarly, farm spokesmen from the American Farm Bureau argued that in the restoration of farm income lay the key to revival. All these voices competed for Roosevelt's attention. As bewildered as most Americans, Roosevelt's understanding of economic affairs was rudimentary. But Roosevelt had to act, and

what distinguished him from the outset so sharply from Hoover was his determination to avoid becoming a prisoner of theory or consistency that inhibited action.

As a result a melange of depression remedies surfaced, some in conflict with the others, new ones adopted even before old ones were abandoned. He would try one thing, Roosevelt explained, and if that did not work, he would try another. When puzzled commentators sought to discover some guide to the president's shifting course, he characteristically explained that he was a Christian and a Democrat. He might have added that he was also firmly committed to preserving capitalism, a commitment that ruled out any *fundamental* redistribution of wealth or power. It also diminished the likelihood that the New Deal could lick the depression. But in the spring of 1933 no one, least of all reform liberals, knew that.

The first Hundred Days were above all a time of new hope. Beneath the discordant voices and conflicting advice ran a common assumption that reduced government spending and a balanced federal budget were indispensable preconditions for recovery. Roosevelt, like Hoover, accepted this soon-to-be-discarded axiom, and threw deflationists a bone by ordering cuts in ordinary governmental services and in the salaries of civil servants.

Yet at the same time Roosevelt typically fought the depression on a variety of fronts with many weapons: monetary inflation to raise prices, regulated competition to encourage business, production controls to boost farm prices, and vague assurances to workers guaranteeing the right to form unions.

Grasping for quick and easy solutions, Roosevelt listened initially to inflationists who urged that currency tinkering was the fastest road to recovery. A controlled inflation, if not a cure-all, would nevertheless provide the financial lubricant for economic recovery. Great Britain and other European powers, also in the grip of the worldwide Great Depression, had gone off the gold standard. In April the United States joined them. Public and private debts were now payable in paper money (silver certificates), and creditors could no longer obtain gold from the Treasury.

In May, Congress authorized the president to increase the currency supply in a further move to cheapen credit and stimulate business. Thus many years after their crusade, and for different reasons, the Populists' inflationary and silver-oriented ideas won a partial victory. Next year the country returned to a modified gold standard, but with a greatly devalued dollar designed to improve the country's ability to sell goods overseas.

To aid the inflationary push, the New Deal utilized the Reconstruction Finance Corporation (RFC), a creation of the Hoover years. The RFC, with more money to dispose of than before, made loans to businesses at lowered interest rates. And in order to reduce farm and home foreclosures, the federal government established agencies to grant cheaper credit to farmers and homeowners through refinancing of mortgages. The courts later declared some of these programs unconstitutional, but while they lasted they saved thousands from destitution.

NRA: THE BLUNTED SPEARHEAD

The spearhead of the New Deal recovery program, the National Recovery Act, a catchall incorporating elements of various depression remedies, was also improvised after Roosevelt came into office. Business and labor were then jockeying for advantage in the formulation of legislation to right the economy. In Congress, Senator (later Supreme Court Justice) Hugo L. Black sponsored a bill calling for a thirty-hour workweek, a reduction intended to spread available work among more men. Industrialists became alarmed because they thought the Black bill would be joined with a minimum wage bill for factory workers. At the same time, William Green, the usually mild-mannered president of the American Federation of Labor, denounced the employers' greed, complaining that the bosses only understood the language of force. He declared that if the Black bill failed, labor would resort to the general strike.

For two years the U.S. Chamber of Commerce had boosted a recovery plan based on holding prices stable through agreements made by trade associations. But in 1931 and 1932, President Hoover scotched the idea. His free enterprise principles were too rigid to allow him to give government permission for price fixing and to accept a suspension of the antitrust laws. Roosevelt proved more receptive. To head off Black's thirty-hour bill and yet win labor support, his Brain Trust devised a compromise supposedly satisfactory to both business and labor. Under government auspices, business could now make pricing and marketing agreements without risk of prosecution for antitrust violations, and labor received promises of minimum wages and collective bargaining.

The law set up the National Recovery Administration (NRA) whose main task was to draw up codes for each major industry, and many minor ones. Here, the businessmen who wanted to end "unfair" competition clearly had the upper hand. Many of the five hundred or so codes merely copied trade association agreements previously declared invalid by the Hoover administration. Government and consumer representatives formally participated in code formulation, but in practice the major industries wrote them as they wished. The codes became a kind of private law for each industry, determining the nature of its operation by dividing markets, limiting production, and restricting price competition. On the labor side, the model code suggested by the government outlawed child labor, fixed maximum hours and minimum wages, and guaranteed labor's right to organize.

To succeed, the NRA needed public support. Its head was a master of ballyhoo and former farm equipment manufacturer, General Hugh S. Johnson, who had served during the First World War under Bernard Baruch, the man who tried to mobilize American industry. Johnson, like Baruch before him, worked hard to maintain a good public relations image and had a talent for the salty phrase, the remark which would gain headlines for himself and the NRA. With a blue eagle as a patriotic symbol displayed by all participating businessmen in the battle for recovery, Johnson whipped up popular support through a series of parades and demonstrations, with extravagant promises and optimism.

If good public relations had only determined

indices of economic recovery, the United States would have shaken off the depression in Roosevelt's first year. The NRA Blue Eagle and its slogan, "We Do Our Part," could be seen everywhere. Even baseball players sported cloth eagles on the sleeves of their uniforms. General Johnson intoned solemnly: "When every American housewife understands that the Blue Eagle on everything she permits to come into her home is a symbol of the restoration of the nation's security, may God have mercy on the man or group of men who attempt to trifle with this bird."

Unfortunately, there were triflers aplenty. Johnson proved more adept at phrasemaking than efficient administration, and his agency lacked the enforcement machinery and personnel to make its decisions stick. Those who broke the code provisions, or those like Henry Ford who ignored them altogether, suffered verbal molestation only. Prosecutions were not numerous. NRA lawyers doubtless sensed what would happen if they took the offenders and their own agency into court. Many of its enabling provisions were of doubtful constitutionality.

The NRA came under attack from many sides. Small businessmen objected to the industry codes which had been framed by Big Business, and the government's winking at monopolistic practices which encouraged consolidation of business. Labor was disappointed, and accused General Johnson of allowing business to run the show. And Big Business, the prime beneficiary, began to chafe at even the limited role Washington bureaucrats played in running their companies, fearing greater encroachments once government got its foot in the door. The NRA, its early magic touch lost, came to be called the "National Run Around."

The squabbling became so bad that within a year Roosevelt had to appoint an investigating committee to look into NRA affairs. The committee, headed by Clarence Darrow, controversial Chicago lawyer who argued "for the Devil" against Bryan in the Scopes Trial of 1925, made quick work of Johnson's Blue Eagle. Darrow acted the part of prosecuting attorney. After four months of jousting with Johnson he submitted a negative report which termed NRA little more than a tool of Big Business. In

the fall of 1934, Johnson resigned under pressure.

The End of NRA

NRA limped along for another half year, but the bird had clearly been grounded. The Supreme Court put it out of its misery in May 1935. In a case appropriately nicknamed the "Sick Chicken Case," the court struck down the entire law because Congress had assigned legislative functions—codemaking—to the executive branch. The court also held that a New York City meat company, prosecuted for violating the code, had not been engaged in interstate commerce, the constitutional basis for NRA. The president had heralded the start of NRA with confident predictions, but its operation had been a trial to him. Publicly, Roosevelt objected to the court's invalidation of his recovery plan, especially the narrow view of the commerce clause, but in reality the administration welcomed the end of a measure which had not hastened recovery and which had become a political liability.

NRA produced disappointments for nearly everyone. Advocates of national planning saw business as capturing control of the planning process which they hoped would give primacy to government. Labor discovered that most employers hedged on their NRA commitments to grant workers collective bargaining rights. And opponents of bigness in business quickly saw through NRA arguments that curbs on competition would protect the small entrepreneur against the giants.

Above all, NRA did not cure the depression. Although the economy turned up from the rock bottom of 1933, NRA could not claim credit for unsteady improvements which still left massive unemployment. Proceeding on the assumption held by most businessmen that the economy had reached maturity, NRA saw only limited possibilities for future growth. It thus abetted economic conservatism and the tendency to restrict production, while the nation desperately needed new investment to prime expansion and return the jobless to work. Roosevelt himself had accepted the stagnation thesis—the American frontier was gone, he had noted, and with it an era of endless abundance fueled by territorial growth. Nor could the president resist the temptation to lick the depression by leading a "concert of interests"—business, labor, farmers, and consumers—from whom NRA asked little and to whom it promised too much.

In the end FDR discovered the limits of consensus leadership. Yet for a brief time, NRA had bouyed up hope. Most important, it marked a massive enlargement of federal responsibility and recognition that free enterprise was no longer workable. It also contained the seeds of new policies which Roosevelt came increasingly to rely on: public works and unionization. New Dealers learned much from the NRA experience; in the second round they would not try to blend so many contradictory elements in one package. Nor would they try to please all major economic pressure groups under the blanket of "national recovery."

A NEW DEAL FOR FARMERS

At the same time that the NRA sought through restrictions on production and restraints on competition to promote industrial revival, similar principles were adopted more successfully to rescue the farming sector from collapse. A month before Congress set up NRA, it passed the Agricultural Adjustment Act (AAA). Midwestern farmers, traditionally Republican, had switched to Roosevelt, despite the fact that Hoover had tried to rescue them by buying up surpluses to raise prices and encouraging farmers to curtail production. When they did not cut down and when surpluses mounted, many concluded that only government compulsion would help. Roosevelt appointed Henry Wallace, son of a Republican agricultural journalist from Iowa, to hammer out the details of a farm program with the major farm organizations.

Farm spokesmen had conflicting ideas. Some of the more radical farmers' groups, the National Farmers' Holiday Association for example, wanted no restrictions on production, insisting on inflationary policies to boost farm prices. But the large and more conservative farmers, organized within the Farm Bureau Federation, wielded the

deciding influence in drafting the AAA. The Triple-A granted special privileges to farmers, a status they still enjoy, by paying them subsidies for *not* planting part of their acreage. In this way, government hoped to curtail production and raise the prices of important staple crops, including cereals, meat, dairy products, and tobacco.

The AAA succeeded partially. Farm prices rose, but many farmers produced as much as before and they soon learned that they could plough up crops on their poorer lands and cultivate their best acreage intensively. For over a decade the government sought effective means of limiting production short of direct controls.

Farm subsidies were expensive and the brunt of the cost fell on the consumer. A processing tax financed Triple-A, but the food processors passed the cost on to consumers. Thus food buyers—especially the poor, who spend a large percentage of their income on food—paid more to help create artificial scarcity. When the program started, the creation of this scarcity made it necessary to plough under crops and slaughter livestock to keep them off the market, at a time when millions of Americans were hungry. Second, small farmers (especially tenant farmers) felt the squeeze of the New Deal policy of crop reduction, which forced them off the land.

As with NRA in the industrial sector, so in agriculture the principal beneficiaries of AAA were the most powerful, organized groups. AAA proved more successful because it enjoyed widespread public sympathy for the beleaguered farmer and could masquerade more plausibly as a savior of America's cherished small enterprise: the family farm. Moreover, government compulsion worked better in agriculture because with controls came a welcome sweetener, the subsidy payment.

Some New Dealers, like Rexford Tugwell, were not content with subsidizing prosperous farmers while squeezing out the poorer ones. They had visions of turning tenant farmers into proprietors, spreading the benefits of agricultural science and education to the backward and ignorant, and resettling those working barren soils on more fertile locations. In 1935 Tugwell became director of the Resettlement Administration, whose special mission was to help the poor of rural America—largely ignored by AAA. But he never received the funding necessary to help more than a few. The political power of organized agriculture saw to it that the lion's share of government aid to the farmers went to them, and in 1935 Secretary Wallace agreed to a purge of most AAA liberals.

Within a year the AAA conservatives had their victory cut short by a still more conservative group. The Supreme Court ruled the AAA unconstitutional, labeling the processing tax, one of the law's linchpins, a regulation of agricultural production instead of permissible taxation. Since Congress lacked such power to regulate under the Constitution's general welfare clause, according to Justice Roberts, down came another New Deal prop. This one, unlike NRA, had powerful support among farmers and seemed essential to agricultural recovery. Roosevelt was genuinely furious with the court and determined to resurrect AAA in another form.

Triple-A made the concept of "parity"—something farmers had been fighting for since the 1920s—public policy. Parity meant a federal commitment to restoring farm purchasing power to the level of the years preceding the First World War—years of agricultural prosperity. The concept remains in force today and sets the amount of government subsidies to farmers growing protected crops. The New Deal thus ended free enterprise in agriculture and speeded up the process of modernization. As in industry, small producers gave way to larger ones, and the percentage of Americans who made their living on the land continued to shrink, as it had for over a century.

THE BIGGEST CHANGE: FEDERAL RELIEF

For the millions of unemployed and destitute neither Triple-A nor NRA offered relief. NRA included $3.3 billion for a public works program, and created the Public Works Administration (PWA) to spend the money. But Secretary of the Interior Harold L. Ickes, a former Bull Moose Progressive named as PWA head, determined to

move cautiously to avoid waste and dishonesty. Ickes's new agency could not give immediate relief to the distressed during the dark days of 1933-1934. That task fell to the Federal Emergency Relief Administration, which had $500 million for direct relief to shore up bankrupt state welfare programs. To head the agency, FDR appointed Harry Hopkins, a social worker who had previously worked with the Roosevelt administration in New York. Since Hopkins strenuously opposed the dole, or cash handout, FERA's job was to put men to work, even if this often meant creating "make-work" projects which drew the fire of conservatives. Hopkins quickly became a controversial figure, a universal New Deal whipping boy, since a bureaucrat is always easier to attack than a popular president.

The sharp-tongued Hopkins returned the criticism, especially as Roosevelt's confidence in him grew. One colleague called the relief administrator a "high-minded holy roller in a semireligious frenzy." Conservatives were infuriated when Hopkins later boasted: "We shall spend, and spend, and spend; and elect, and elect, and elect." Much of the conservative fury stemmed from the fact that Hopkins proved right on both counts, in fact falling one "elect" short of Roosevelt's four presidential victories.

Whatever the drawbacks of federal relief projects in strictly economic terms, Hopkins' agency provided jobs at a time private enterprise could not. FERA worked in two ways: it granted funds to state governments to start work relief programs; and through the Civil Works Administration, it provided direct federal jobs to millions of unemployed. During its two-year lifespan, FERA disbursed $4 billion and had close to four million persons on its payroll.

PWA and WPA

Meanwhile the PWA moved into action, leaving a lasting legacy of new post offices, federal courthouses, Veterans Administration hospitals, schools, and parks. While building countless useful public projects, PWA gave a badly needed shot in the arm to the construction industry, prostrated by the decline of private building. Ickes tried to run a tight ship. His aim was to build only where an undeniable need existed, to disburse funds carefully. But in the face of intense political pressures for "pork barrel" projects, Ickes had to bow often to political realities.

Ickes and Hopkins battled for control of relief funds. Though FERA closed shop in 1934, early in 1935 Hopkins reappeared as head of a rival and even stronger relief agency, the Works Progress Administration (WPA). This bureau quickly spearheaded the New Deal program of relief and economic rehabilitation. To reach those not aided by PWA, Hopkins initiated makeshift work projects, when necessary, to "create" jobs, including remarkable aid programs for unemployed actors, artists, and scholars. Artists found employment as artists. Writers and painters could stop digging ditches and return to their professions. Historical societies and libraries received WPA funds to employ scholars to catalog and index collections, and prepare histories and guidebooks. And a Federal Theater brought live drama to many for whom it had never before been available.

Nor did the New Deal forget young people, especially hard hit when jobs were at a premium. The Civilian Conservation Corps (CCC), created in 1933 during the Hundred Days, put half a million young men to work on reforestation and flood control projects. A few objected to the paramilitarism of the CCC camps—they were run by the army—but most Americans favored giving city youth a chance to work in the bracing, and presumably morally purifying, outdoors. In 1935 Congress set up the National Youth Administration within WPA to provide work relief for young people between the ages of 16 and 25. By 1939 three quarters of a million college students were receiving benefits. The problem of idle youth remained far from solved, however; that same year three million persons in the 16-to-24 age group were neither working nor in school.

The New Deal's federal relief projects ended a long American tradition that had placed the responsibility for welfare on local government. Herbert Hoover never abandoned this principle, even when most counties and municipalities had bankrupted themselves trying to help the destitute. Like Hoover, Roosevelt was loath to in-crease federal spending, but unlike his predecessor he thought it more important to help the distressed (and keep their votes) than to balance the budget, a policy he could easily justify as a Christian who valued charity above frugality, and as a Democrat who preferred reelection to ideological consistency. Within eighteen months the New Deal had provided direct relief to twelve million Americans and had put another five million on work relief. And it did so primarily in the cities. Unemployment was higher and more visible in the cities and large towns, and with many rural hamlets suspicious of outside schemes—especially those proposed by Washington bureaucrats—most New Deal relief activities centered in urban areas.

THE MIRACLE WORKERS

Roosevelt entered office with a virtual free hand. Legislation whipped through Congress during the Hundred Days with unprecedented speed and a minimum of debate. The New Deal thus benefited from something akin to a feeling of wartime unity. This time the war was not against a foreign menace but against an internal enemy. The crisis atmosphere temporarily immunized the New Deal from attack.

Despite the slow pace of economic recovery, Roosevelt faced little effective opposition. After two years of the New Deal business had improved and more people had jobs, but millions of Americans still lived at the edge of survival, dependent on government handouts. American conservatives offered little beyond the complaints of businessmen and some conservative Democrats like Al Smith who formed the Liberty League. They charged the New Deal with destroying free enterprise and violating the Constitution by encroaching on states' rights by attempting to create an all-powerful federal bureaucracy controlled by "socialistic" visionaries such as Tugwell and Hopkins.

In a depression setting, these laments won few converts. The 1934 congressional elections gave the Democrats a tighter hold on Congress, reversing the historic tendency of the party in power to lose seats in off-year elections.

Yet if most Americans ignored the frightened wailings of the Liberty Leaguers, millions turned receptive ears to other voices that spoke in populistic accents. For millions of Americans the New Deal had proved better than the Old Deal, but it had not yet made good on its promises. Capitalizing on continued, widespread distress, and benefiting from waning faith in Roosevelt's brand of reform liberalism, a Catholic priest, a ruthless but brilliant Louisiana senator, and a crusading champion of America's senior citizens challenged the New Deal simultaneously.

Overnight a Detroit Catholic priest named Charles Coughlin acquired a radio audience of millions, proving that Roosevelt was not the only one who could master the political possibilities of the airwaves. Coughlin started from a left-wing position, urging currency inflation, attacking international bankers, and preaching a brand of Christian socialism heavily laced with Populist monetary doctrines. Though he had earned a doctorate at age 23, he preferred to cultivate the image of a "simple Catholic priest endeavoring to interject Christianity into the fabric of an economic system woven upon the loom of greed."

On the air and in his magazines, Coughlin gave Roosevelt strong support at first. But the moderate pace of the New Deal soon antagonized "the Radio Priest." Coughlin began moving further toward rightwing radicalism. He attacked the New Deal as the "Jew Deal," and Roosevelt as an aristocratic enemy of the masses. By the end of the decade, with his power much reduced, he helped organize the antisemitic Christian Front. Ultimately, higher church authorities silenced him. Yet in his heyday, Father Coughlin enjoyed a large following among those impatient with the slow process of reform.

In contrast to the slashing style of Father Coughlin, Dr. Francis Townsend was the mildest of men. In 1935 this California physician had an idea—super pump-priming. Economic stagnation, he argued, resulted simply from an absence of sufficient purchasing power. Government pensions of $200 per month for all persons over sixty would end the depression. The money could be raised through a national sales tax. By requiring old folks to spend their allotments within a month and infusing massive amounts of cash into the economy, Townsend felt that business would boom again from the proper "velocity of money." No matter that the pensions would use up half of the national budget; or that all Americans would pay taxes to subsidize 8 percent of the population. Ending the depression was more than worth the price.

Understandably, the Townsend Plan aroused most enthusiasm among old people. This panacea had a restricted but electric appeal. Townsend clubs sprang up everywhere, especially in California, and their national membership may have reached as high as two million. Whatever the exact number, with at least one million persons allied behind one political cause, such a formidable bloc could not be dismissed. Politicians began to give hurried but qualified endorsements to the scheme. Dr. Townsend became a national figure, for neither the president nor any other politician could match his promises, except, perhaps, "The Kingfish" of Louisiana politics, Senator Huey P. Long. Long posed a specifically political threat. He operated from a secure power base in Louisiana, where he had established iron-fisted control. And his wide appeal elsewhere in the South made him the most powerful of the extremists. The Long plan called for "Sharing Our Wealth" in a simple way: tax the rich heavily and redistribute income so that no American would earn less than $2000 annually. Long was dynamic, shrewd, flambouyant, and power-hungry. He appealed especially to the poor and barely employed, and he also proved attractive to those fed up with the compromise politics of FDR. His opponents ridiculed him as the "Cornpone Robin Hood," but Long gloried in that image.

When Long came to the Senate in 1932 he had already acquired a reputation for unorthodoxy and political toughness. In Washington he immediately established himself as the Bad Boy of Congress. A Democrat, he supported Roosevelt that year and campaigned well wherever the Democratic strategists allowed him to appear, establishing the fact that however much he played the clown, Huey Long was no fool. The early New Deal recovery measures were too namby-pamby for him. The NRA provoked his open opposition. Early in 1934 he started the Share Our Wealth Society. Every man could be a king; and "Kingfish" Long promised, if not the world, at least $2000 a year (much more than most workers were then earning). Democratic politicians reacted uneasily, fearing that on a third-party ticket Long might siphon off several million votes. Roosevelt, who considered Long a very dangerous man, had already tried but failed to tame him. The problem of Huey Long loomed starkly as the election approached. Roosevelt escaped that dilemma when an assassin killed Long in the fall of 1935 and dramatically terminated *his* threat to the New Deal.

NEW DIRECTIONS FOR THE NEW DEAL

The Democratic Congress responded to these challenges by enacting the most sweeping domestic legislation of the 1930s, legislation confronting two of the major problems of industrial society: the economic insecurity of the unemployed, aged, and dependent; and the quest by organized labor for greater power. Yet neither the Social Security Act (which launched the welfare state in America) nor the Wagner Labor Relations Act (which guaranteed workers the right to join unions) originated with the administration. These two fundamental pieces of New Deal legislation eventually won Roosevelt's support, but during his first three years the president concentrated on short-term recovery measures. The thrust of the 1935 legislation, however, extended in the direction of long-term structural reforms of American society.

TVA and Regional Planning

The New Deal had already shown some tendencies to go beyond recovery to reform. The Tennessee Valley Authority (TVA), established back in the Hundred Days, displayed a reformist streak that would grow in time. For over a generation, Senator George W. Norris of Nebraska and other Progressives had seen the possibilities of reconstructing the lives of the millions living in the huge valley created by the meandering Tennessee River. During World War I the federal government had built a dam at Muscle Shoals,

Alabama, to produce nitrates for munitions. Private electrical power interests tried to buy the facilities but Norris doggedly fought to keep it in government hands to permit multipurpose public development.

Like most rural Americans, the farmers of the Tennessee Valley were poor. Private power companies, complaining of unprofitability, refused to supply electricity, leaving most rural American homes badly lighted and most farmers unable to use many labor-saving machines and appliances. Backwardness and poverty also meant inefficient methods of cultivation, since most farmers could not afford to buy expensive fertilizer to replenish worn-out soils. Finally, periodic floods could destroy in a day a generation's labor. Floods, like economic depressions, seemed beyond human control. But Roosevelt was a strong conservationist. In eight years he removed more mineral land, timber stands, and power sites from private development than all his predecessors.

With a friend in the White House, Senator Norris easily got the Tennessee Valley Authority law through in the spring of 1933. Construction soon began on a network of twenty-four dams that transformed the valley. TVA produced cheap electricity and inexpensive fertilizer. It controlled floods and thus conserved the land at the same time that it sparked the economic development of the area. It did all this as part of a regional plan and sought, though with less success than had been hoped, to involve the people of the valley in directing its revival. TVA became a showcase for New Deal reform liberalism. When foreign VIPs visited the United States in the 1930s, a trip to TVA was a must. And since then this successful example of democratic social planning by government has been a model and challenge for underdeveloped countries struggling to modernize backward regions.

TVA elicited attacks from businessmen and ideological conservatives who cried "Socialism." They especially resented the "yardstick," TVA's low rates provided against the higher rates charged by nearby private companies. In the 1930s such scarewords as "socialistic" did not prevent most Americans from seeing the practical value and necessity for a project like TVA. It did something private enterprise would not or could not do. So successful was TVA that New Dealers later envisioned other TVAs, but by that time the New Deal had lost the impetus that had made TVA possible in 1933.

Though no other region felt the impact of such comprehensive regional planning, rural America finally got electricity. The president created the Rural Electrification Administration (REA) in 1935 to lend money to farm communities at low interest. By the end of the decade almost half the farms had been electrified and in the next decade the REA brought power to the rest.

TVA and REA represented government intrusion into an area once regarded as the exclusive concern of private enterprise. New Deal regulation of Wall Street marked another extension of federal authority over free enterprise. The Great Crash temporarily shattered American faith in Wall Street and the get-rich-quick attractions of stock market speculation. The fall of the market wiped out most small investors and put bankers and financiers in public disfavor. Congressional investigation of Wall Street revealed the extent to which investors had been victimized by dishonest and unethical financial schemes. There had been no way, for instance, for securities purchasers to verify information supplied by companies and brokers.

Regulating Wall Street

Roosevelt's inaugural address blamed the depression on the money changers, who had "failed through their own stubbornness and their own incompetence." But Richard Whitney, the president of the New York Stock Exchange, insisted that "the Exchange is a perfect institution," a claim of doubtful plausibility when made and thoroughly unbelievable after Whitney committed suicide as the truths behind the Great Bull Market became known. Congress during the Hundred Days passed the Federal Securities Act, requiring full disclosure to investors of information concerning new publicly marketed bonds and stock. The next year (1934) Congress created the Securities and Exchange Commission (SEC) to regulate the exchanges. New Dealers hoped that Ameri-

cans could now invest in Wall Street with greater safety. Though the purpose of the new controls was to strengthen one of the major props of the capitalist system, many businessmen resented this unprecedented intrusion of federal power in the marketplace.

Bankers shared an identical experience and responded similarly. Once the country had ridden out the banking emergency in the winter of 1933, the New Deal attempted to prevent its recurrence. Toward the end of the Hundred Days Congress passed a banking act (1933) which created the Federal Deposit Insurance Corporation (FDIC) to insure individual bank deposits, and which prohibited banks from adding securities marketing to their savings and checking deposit functions. Congress also strengthened the Federal Reserve System so that it could restrict excessive speculation on credit, a major factor in the rise and fall of the Great Bull Market of the 1920s.

No industry had become so tarnished by unethical financial practices and shaky business structures as the gas and electric utilities. Financial wheeler-dealers such as Chicago's Samuel Insull put together holding companies by parlaying control of one firm into control of many. A holding company, humorist Will Rogers explained, "is a thing where you hand an accomplice the goods while the policeman searches you." In the summer of 1935 the president demanded and got the Public Utilities Holding Company Act, which simplified and rationalized corporate structures in the utilities, and outlawed holding companies that could not be justified in terms of efficiency and public service.

Social Security

Regulation of the banks, the securities market, and the utilities disturbed many businessmen and angered others. But their anger and dismay were nothing compared to their reaction to new welfare and labor legislation adopted in the summer of 1935. The United States was the only advanced, industrial society to leave its citizens unprotected against the hazards of unemployment and old age. During the Progressive era, advocates of social insurance had argued that in a complex, urban society workers could not themselves provide for adequate health care, old age, or periodic employment. Except for workmen's compensation, backed by employers to rationalize and make more predictable their liability for industrial accidents, proponents of social insurance made little headway. Organized medicine defeated a health insurance plan supported by Governor Al Smith in New York. Businessmen opposed welfare programs that would raise labor costs.

Most Americans, whether Progressives or standpatters, rejected the welfare state ideologically. It was first of all a "foreign" idea, European in origin and socialistic in tendency. It denied a fundamental tenet of the private enterprise philosophy: that any industrious and prudent person could provide adequately for himself in an affluent America. Moreover, social security might make men lazy. Some argued or hinted that fear of unemployment and old age was necessary to assure a docile labor force and to maintain social order.

The depression destroyed these myths. It taught Americans truths that some Progressives, especially the settlement house workers, had learned a generation earlier: periodic unemployment was not the worker's fault but resulted from dislocations in the economic system, and low wages made it difficult for millions to save enough to see them through hard times. Moreover, in crowded cities, old people could not find homes with their children as they had when America was mainly a rural society.

The demand for social security became irresistible. A few progressive businessmen, proponents of welfare capitalism, had introduced private pension plans and continuous employment programs in the 1920s. But most of these schemes collapsed with the depression, and with them faded any lingering faith in "voluntarism," "The New Individualism," and other slogans adopted by those hoping to head off social security.

The Social Security Act (1935) gave persons over 65 pensions financed by a tax on earnings paid jointly by workers and their employers. Another payroll tax, paid entirely by employers, financed unemployment compensation administered by the states. The federal government also made grants to states to assist the blind, the disabled, and needy children. Conservative Republicans warned that social security was the opening wedge for a socialist America. A New Jersey senator predicted that "it would take the romance out of life." In reality, it took some of the uncertainty out of life. Far from meeting all the needs of the American people, the Social Security Act was a small step which could later be improved upon. Small pensions, inadequate unemployment compensation which varied from state to state, and lack of protection against the hazards of serious illness pointed to the need for future expansion of the program.

With one eye on Huey Long's Share the Wealth movement, Roosevelt proposed to shift a greater burden of taxation on the wealthy in whose hands, he claimed, lay "an unjust concentration of wealth and economic power." The president's "soak-the-rich" tax program, embodied in the Revenue Act of 1935, stemmed from the need for additional money to finance New Deal spending and reflected a growing conviction that the piling up of wealth in the hands of a relatively few corporations and private fortunes caused and prolonged the depression. As long as a few received an undue share of national income, New Dealers argued, most Americans would lack sufficient purchasing power to get the country moving economically. Billed as a move in the direction of massive income redistribution, the Revenue Act hardly warranted conservative fears. New Deal tax reforms did not shift income distribution significantly, partly because of the modesty of the president's recommendations and the skill with which conservatives watered down FDR's proposals in Congress.

The Wagner Act: A Law for Labor

Tax reform was one method of increasing consumer purchasing power. Many Americans believed that trade unions offered a far more effective method. NRA had recognized the right of workers to organize unions, but this vague guarantee lacked enforcement machinery. Eager as ever to head off unionization, employers set up company unions which they controlled but which sought to give workers the illusion of participation in management. During the euphoric early days of NRA business and labor leaders had joined government in a national crusade. The American Federation of Labor looked forward to a period of rapid recovery from the doldrums of the 1920s when employer hostility and working-class prosperity had blunted union growth. Even before the advent of the New Deal, signifying a pro-labor shift in public opinion, Congress had easily passed the Norris-LaGuardia Act (1932) which curbed the use of court injunctions against strikes and outlawed yellow-dog contracts. With Franklin Roosevelt in the White House, labor leaders expected even more help from Washington.

The first three years of the New Deal proved frustrating. Employers had agreed to NRA's labor clause only to get government sanction for price fixing, not because they intended to engage in collective bargaining. And as long as FDR put his faith in NRA, he felt he could not jeopardize his "concert of interests" by encouraging workers to strike. But Senator Robert F. Wagner of New York, a strong supporter of unionism, did not give up. In 1935 he introduced legislation that would make collective bargaining work and to his surprise the president in the summer of 1935 suddenly announced that the measure was one of his "must" bills, along with social security, tax reform, and utilities regulation. The Wagner Act ran into remarkably little opposition in Congress. The Great Crash had convinced many that organization among workers and farmers was necessary to assure a more equitable division of national wealth.

The National Labor Relations Act (1935) affirmed the right of workers to join unions, and set up the National Labor Relations Board (NLRB) with the power to supervise elections to determine by which union, if any, workers wished to be represented. The law also made it illegal for employers to fire workers for union activity or to commit other "unfair labor practices." Whether the Wagner Act would lead to unionization of the mass production industries — automotive, steel, rubber, for instance — would depend on the skill and determination of workers and their leaders. The law did not end management's hostility to unionization; it did, however, make resistance harder. But the showdown between labor and management did not occur until after the 1936 presidential election showdown between Franklin Roosevelt and those convinced that the New Deal, and especially the new directions taken in 1935, threatened the survival of their kind of America.

Chapter 30
Testing the New Deal

A few days before Americans went to the polls in November 1936, Roosevelt defined the central issue of the campaign to a roaring crowd in New York's Madison Square Garden: "Organized money," he said, "are unanimous in their hate for me—and I welcome their hatred. I should like to have it said of my first Administration that in it the forces of selfishness and of lust for power met their match. . . . I should like to have it said of my second Administration that in it these forces met their master." The 1936 contest was one of the most bitterly fought in American history. In the tradition of Jackson's Bank War of 1832 and Bryan's crusade against the Cross of Gold in 1896, Roosevelt tried to make the election a choice between government by the people and government by plutocracy. No American politician has ever been more successful.

The Republicans nominated Governor Alfred M. Landon of Kansas. A Progressive in advance of most of his party, Landon's corn belt origins and folksy manner, his obvious sincerity and lack of guile, might have had strong appeal against Roosevelt's sophisticated, self-confident Eastern aristocratic manner. No one—not even New Deal Democrats—would ever suspect that Landon harbored dictatorial ambitions or would resort to demagogic means. Republicans charged Roosevelt with both crimes.

Conservatives, businessmen especially, hated FDR passionately. He had successfully challenged their claim to act as the country's natural leaders. He had saddled them with blame for the depression and for the slowness of recovery. He had promoted counterorganization among farmers and workers, and subjected business to higher taxes and unprecedented federal controls. He had violated every tenet of economic orthodoxy by running the government in the red year after year, allegedly destroying business confidence and perpetuating the depression. Above all, conservatives regarded him a traitor to his class who had broken the unwritten law of American politics by building a political coalition through appeals to class interest. Government,

which had usually taken its cue from "practical" men of affairs accustomed to meeting payrolls, had become infiltrated by "bleeding-heart" do-gooders like Harry Hopkins, left-wing intellectuals like Rexford Tugwell, and power-hungry labor leaders like John L. Lewis. "It hurts our feelings" wrote a sympathetic member of the Wall Street financial community to Roosevelt, "to have you go on calling us money changers and economic royalists." In the 1930s as never before those used to running the country felt abused, displaced by outsiders.

Roosevelt's easy triumph over Landon, carrying every state except two, and polling an incredible 61 percent of the popular vote, only deepened conservative gloom. The 1936 campaign crystallized massive, long-term shifts in American voting alignments. The vote divided along class lines more than at any time in the past, with the bulk of the poor, the working classes and small farmers, and the lower middle classes overwhelmingly behind the president. The Democrats became the owners of the city vote as ethnic voters and Negroes flocked to the party of Roosevelt.

The Democratic slogan, "Four Years Ago and Now," touched the electorate at its most sensitive spot. "I would be without a roof over my head if it hadn't been for the government loan," one farmer explained. The crowds poured out to greet the president and millions looked to him as their savior. "God bless Mr. Roosevelt and the Democratic party who saved thousands of poor people all over this country from starvation," was a common sentiment. When a reporter asked a North Carolina mill hand how he could support a president who operated on crackpot theories that were bankrupting the country, he got an answer that might have come from millions of other workers: "Roosevelt is the only man we ever had in the White House who would understand that my boss is a sonofabitch."

Roosevelt coupled an appeal to those hardest hit by the depression with the claim that the New Deal had rescued the country from despair. New Dealers had not licked the depression but a substantial decline in unemployment accompanied by a significant rise in national income in the past four years gave Roosevelt four more years in office. The second victory laid the groundwork for a severe testing of the New Deal in the *next* four years. During Roosevelt's second term the welfare state expanded to provide some low-cost public housing and to guarantee workers minimum wages and maximum hours, unionism finally cracked the mass production industries, and the Supreme Court after a mighty struggle gave constitutional approval to basic New Deal legislation.

THE COURT FIGHT: VICTORY THROUGH DEFEAT

Acceptance of the New Deal required a far-reaching reinterpretation of the Constitution, since New Deal legislation stretched the taxing and commerce powers of the federal government far beyond their traditional boundaries. It delegated new authority to the president and it shifted power from the states to the federal government. Conservatives therefore looked to the courts, as they had in the past, to protect them against popular majorities that infringed on property rights.

Since the initial Progressive forays into government regulation of business, the Supreme Court had pursued an unpredictable, zigzag course, sometimes approving, at other times invalidating governmental regulation. In the 1920s the court revealed a pronounced conservative bias, ruling against child labor and minimum wage laws, and crippling the organizational activity of labor unions. It had not changed by the 1930s. Four of the nine justices—McReynolds, Butler, Van Devanter, and Sutherland (scornfully nicknamed "The Four Horsemen of Reaction" by New Dealers)—formed the nucleus of anti-New Dealism among the judiciary. Although in 1934 the court approved two significant cases of regulatory action by states, one giving aid to debtors, another fixing milk prices, it denied that the depression emergency had created new powers. Both sides readied for battle.

New Deal legislation reached the court on appeal early in 1935. In the next year and a half, eight of ten New Deal bills were struck down as unconstitutional uses of national power. NRA, AAA, a Railroad Retirement Act, and the Guffey Coal Act suffered identical fates. TVA, its constitutionality sustained, was one of two exceptions. The president responded by attacking the Supreme Court for its "horse and buggy" decisions, a reference to what he considered the majority justices' outmoded ideas of constitutionalism, their restricted view of federal power in interstate commerce and under the Constitution's general welfare clause.

Much more was at stake than the invalidated laws. While not entirely unhappy over the demise of NRA, for example, Roosevelt was more alarmed by the implication that the court would also strike down the "second round" of New Deal legislation passed in 1935. Congress had already approved Senator Wagner's Labor Relations Act, the Social Security Act, and a substitute for AAA. The controls imposed and powers delegated by some of these laws bore a close resemblance to those of the now-defunct NRA. They rested on constitutional foundations similar to those underlying the legislation invalidated by the court.

After the exhilarating reelection victory in 1936, Roosevelt felt in no mood to submit tamely to the court's backward glances. On the contrary, he came out of the contest cockier than ever, and overconfident that an overwhelmingly Democratic Congress would do his bidding. Roosevelt discarded as too cumbersome initial suggestions for a constitutional amendment to enlarge congressional powers, or to require a two-thirds vote of the justices to invalidate acts of Congress. Proper interpretation of the Constitution, he believed, not changes in the document, provided the answer. In other words, it all depended upon *who* handed down the decisions.

Court Packing

Roosevelt's scheme was legal, logical, and heavy-handed. Shortly after taking the oath of office for his second term (he was the first president sworn in on January 20 instead of March 4, under a new "lame-duck" constitutional amendment), he shocked the nation with a proposal for judicial reorganization—soon to be called "court packing." Roosevelt had not consulted with Democratic leaders in Congress, or with all of his advisers. Since most of the conservative justices were old men who definitely did *not* plan to retire (or as one New Dealer put it sadly: "The Supreme Court has declared the mortality tables unconstitutional"), and since they held office for life and could not be removed, Roosevelt concluded that their number would have to be increased. The president could then appoint "friendly" judges to rule favorably on New Deal laws.

A plea to rescue a supposedly overworked federal judiciary served as cover for this politically sound but ticklish maneuver. Roosevelt argued that not only the Supreme Court, but also the lower federal courts (which were also hampering New Deal operations) were so deluged with undecided cases and so behind in schedules that it was necessary to increase the number of judges without delay. Supposedly, elderly judges could not keep up the pace; but FDR's main complaint, one he dared not voice openly, was that they would not change their minds to fit modern ideas of government. When a Supreme Court justice reached age seventy and did not resign, the president might appoint an additional justice, up to the number of fifteen.

With unaccustomed unanimity, the justices denied that they were behind schedule. Justice Louis D. Brandeis, the court's staunchest liberal and then eighty years old, deeply resented the slurs about ineffectiveness due to advanced age. He cooperated with one of the court's conservatives to prepare a detailed denial of federal court inefficiency. Chief Justice Charles Evans Hughes, displaying a wit unfortunately rare in court annals, commented dryly on the prospect of a fifteen-member Supreme Court: "If they want me to preside over a convention, I can do it."

The number of Supreme Court justices had fluctuated between five and ten since the court's beginning. But the figure nine, unchanged since the end of Reconstruction, had been accepted by most Americans and apparently revered by conservative Americans. Court packing, even under the best circumstances, required much political legwork and delicate preparation. Roosevelt blundered ahead without support of the congressional leadership. The party whips did the best they could, but widespread congressional opposition doomed the effort. The plan proved a godsend to Republicans and conservative Democrats, then desperately seeking a handle for their opposition to the high-flying president.

A massive exercise of presidential power by Roosevelt, including use of the patronage axe, might have rammed the bill through, but the court itself made that unnecessary. In several anti-New Deal court decisions in 1935 and 1936, the court had split six to three. Chief Justice Hughes had sided with the conservative majority in these cases in order to avoid narrow negative splits of five to four, votes so close that the court's prestige might be further impaired. As counterpressure mounted, one uncertain justice, Owen J. Roberts, held the balance. Even before Roosevelt's bombshell threat, Roberts had agreed to validate a state minimum wage law, thus joining Hughes and three liberal justices in a new five-man majority. A few weeks later, in April 1937, the new "liberal" majority upheld the constitutionality of the National Labor Relations and Social Security acts. Chief Justice Hughes now spoke for a majority which no longer rode in a "horse and buggy," but had belatedly entered the twentieth century. The court now expansively interpreted the commerce and taxing powers. Reversing a long line of conservative precedents, it admitted the artificiality of its previous dividing lines between intrastate and interstate commerce, and revealed an awareness of the fact that the Supreme Court is never far removed from politics.

Roosevelt's plan thus lay in the rubble of victory. The court had not been reformed; it had reversed itself. The reversal came too suddenly and too obviously to have been accidental; as one Washington wit put it, "a switch in time saves nine." The court could not indefinitely defy public opinion or maintain judicial barricades against needed expansion in government authority and curbs on private power. One of the four conservative justices resigned soon after, and Roosevelt soon made other appointments that transformed the court's character. Henceforth when the judiciary reviewed the power of government over business, the watchword was self-restraint.

In the end, FDR had removed the judicial barrier but at considerable political cost. First, the court fight tarnished the president's image of near invincibility. Congress, its vigor restored since 1935 when it regained the legislative initiative, had flouted the president after the most smashing victory in the history of presidential elections. Second, the court fight crystallized latent opposition to the New Deal among conservative Democrats. Since even some firm New Dealers balked at the court packing scheme, conservatives felt safer resisting the president. They could now claim that they were merely upholding constitutional government and the integrity of the judiciary. The fight also made more plausible charges that the president was power mad, and would ignore traditional American fears of concentrated government power.

THE UNION REVOLUTION

Roosevelt's handling of the sit-down strikes and the outbreak of industrial warfare in 1937 confirmed these fears. The federal government's role in labor relations altered dramatically after 1935. Never more than an "honest broker," often an opponent of unionism, Washington now became an interested party on the side of labor. Starting with this bias, and armed with pro-union legislation, the federal government helped usher in the modern age of industrial relations.

Organized labor had not fared well in the 1920s, and initially the depression further affected unionism adversely. The labor surplus undermined union bargaining power, and employers were able to roll back some labor advances. Historically, unionism had been tied to the business cycle: good times meant labor scarcity, high profits, and union growth; on the other hand depressions normally reduced union strength. But after the lean years of the early 1930s unionism grew more rapidly than at any time in the past. From three million members in 1932, union strength expanded to ten million in 1941. Old unions like the mine workers and build-

ing-trades workers solidly organized their industries, and new ones like the steelworkers and auto workers finally broke the resistance to unionism in manufacturing.

The union revolution resulted from changing attitudes among workers, the collapse of employer resistance, and the helping hand of government. At first Roosevelt pursued a friendly but noncommittal labor policy. Although he appointed a liberal social worker, Frances Perkins, as secretary of labor, she was more oriented toward welfare legislation than to collective bargaining as the way to help labor. On the legislative front, neither the Norris-LaGuardia Act of 1932 nor the NRA had produced a union breakthrough, though they raised hopes for one among labor leaders.

The New Class Consciousness

These leaders correctly sensed a new militancy among workers. Repeatedly, spontaneous or "wildcat" strikes broke out, and union heads often found themselves behind the rank-and-file members. The AFL, for instance, could not resolve the problem of whether to organize the auto workers on a craft-skill basis, or into one big, industrial union. Leaders of this alliance of predominantly conservative, craft unions still spoke of preserving the legacy of Samual Gompers and abiding by his principles. So the AFL in the years 1932 to 1935 grew *in spite* of itself. Its leaders were either wary or openly hostile to organizing all workers in the major industries because of past failures, such as the steel strike of 1919. Attempts from within to prod the AFL into action failed, setting the stage for a bolt by some leaders and the eventual establishment of a rival movement.

Labor militancy grew out of a loss of faith in business leadership and business ideology. The Horatio Alger mentality that claimed every American had a chance to get ahead through hard work, coupled with the fact that *some* did move up from working-class to middle-class status, led most workers to pin their hopes on individual efforts rather than on collective action. Many had gone into the mines or factories from farms in Europe and America without the intention of spending the rest of their lives tending machinery or digging coal, but only for so long as it would take to gain needed skill to move on to a better job or to save money to open a business.

Few fulfilled these dreams, yet people still kept hoping, until the crash and depression turned millions of these modest visions into nightmares. By the mid-1930s American workers had come to realize that they would spend most of their lives in the same job. Thus it became imperative to make life in the factory more bearable. This meant more than simply raising wages and improving working conditions. Workers also wanted to end their employers' power to fire, promote, and discipline arbitrarily. As much as workers wanted more money, they also sought job security and a bilateral method of settling grievances.

Workers gave vent to their new militancy in a rash of strikes in 1934. Shutdowns occurred in Toledo, San Francisco (where efforts to organize longshoremen led to a citywide general strike), and Minneapolis (where the teamsters made a breakthrough in an antiunion stronghold.) But union victories there were matched by failure elsewhere. A strike in North Carolina's textile mills failed in 1934, just as previous efforts had collapsed in the 1920s.

Employers doggedly resisted. An exhaustive Senate investigation of antiunion methods detailed the lengths to which businessmen went to avoid unionization. They fired workers suspected of union activity and hired professional spies to spot troublemakers. They maintained private security forces, furnished with ample weapons and ammunition. Republic Steel Company's arsenal, for example, contained 552 pistols, 245 shotguns, and 4033 gas bombs. Employer attitudes encouraged the formation of professional strikebreaking agencies that supplied labor spies, strikebreakers, and roughnecks. One such agency advised employers: "To insure a prompt and early return of your employees, they should be confused, dissension should be spread among them and they should be urged to go back to their jobs by our own trained agitators." When necessary, some employers engaged thugs to intimidate and beat up workers. "A few hundred funerals," recommended a textile industry journal, "will

have a quieting influence." In many cities, the local police were at the service of union-busting employers. In the Minneapolis teamsters' strike, for instance, police shot down sixty-seven workers, killing two of them.

Despite continued hostility from employers, some labor leaders sensed that American workers were ripe for organization, especially since passage of the National Labor Relations Act meant that the federal government had moved from neutrality to positive encouragement of unionization. With workers now entitled to protection against discharge for union activity, it would be far easier to organize.

Unionizing Heavy Industry

No one had a clearer sense of labor's newly found opportunity than John L. Lewis, president of the United Mine Workers. Lewis had already capitalized on the new atmosphere to rebuild his own union, shattered in the 1920s, into one of the strongest in the country. Lewis supported the demands of coal mine operators for production controls and price stabilization backed by government sanctions in exchange for collective bargaining agreements that entrenched the union in the industry. Within the AFL, Lewis emerged as leader of a group that stressed labor's new opportunities to organize the mass production industries. However, a majority of craft unionists would not go along with Lewis's insistence that in industries like autos and steel it was necessary to organize all workers. Jealous of their jurisdictional rights, fearful of losing prospective members to new industrial unions or to rival craft unions, and remembering past failures to organize semiskilled workers, the dominant elements in the AFL forced Lewis and his allies to bolt and set up the Congress of Industrial Organizations (CIO), out of which grew such powerful new unions as the United Steel Workers and the United Automobile Workers. Armed with the protection of the Wagner Act, staffed with organizers and supplied with funds from the prospering unions that had created it, the CIO launched a series of organizing drives that ended the open shop in big industry, but not without a struggle. Employers had announced that they would not observe the Wagner Act since they regarded it as unconstitutional; not till 1937, well after the CIO had launched its drive, did the Supreme Court validate the act (*Jones and Laughlin Steel Co.* v. *NLRB*). The CIO had already tested its strength in Akron, Ohio, the year before in a strike against the Goodyear Rubber Company, protesting wage cuts and summary dismissals. Here for the first time it employed a new technique, the sit-down strike. Workers simply stood by their machines and refused to leave; production stopped and the introduction of strikebreakers became impossible.

The real test of the new technique came in the auto industry. At first the auto workers seemed to be dragging the CIO leaders along behind them. Then Lewis switched his strategy, which had called for organizing steel first. An AFL auto union had failed miserably, and in 1935 the United Auto Workers (UAW) appeared to fill the vacuum. Early in 1937 the UAW struck the industry giant, General Motors, using the sit down. Lewis, urged by President Roosevelt to get his men out of the GM plants, would not budge. Since neither Roosevelt nor the governor of Michigan wanted to use troops to clear the factories, Lewis held on until General Motors, eager to resume production, agreed to recognize the union. UAW membership immediately doubled.

The breakthrough in autos was soon matched in steel. The United States Steel Company "capitulated" in 1937 to an organizing drive mounted by Lewis's lieutenant, Philip Murray. But after these initial successes in steel and autos and elsewhere, the CIO campaign bogged down. A downturn in business made employers more resistant. The sit-down technique lost labor a good deal of public sympathy and the Wagner Act proved less of a boon than many had anticipated. Though the NLRB generally ruled in labor's favor, it took time to get decisions out of the board, precious time during which employers could defeat an organizing drive. Not until the approach of war in 1941 did the CIO solidify its position in the mass production industries. As defense and then war production finally brought economic recovery and full employment, profits zoomed to weaken employer resistance further.

And during the wartime emergency it became essential to avoid interruptions in production due to labor unrest.

The holdout smaller steel companies signed up with the United Steel Workers, and Ford Motor Company did likewise with the UAW. Old Henry Ford personified "rugged individualism" in business just as Herbert Hoover had in politics. He had fought unionization tenaciously, and at times viciously, employing hired toughs, the Ford "servicemen," to spy on and intimidate workers. In 1937 Ford's goons attacked a group of UAW organizers, including young Walter Reuther, severely injuring the future president of the UAW. Ford held the CIO to a stalemate for over two years until in 1939, with the quixotic suddenness that often characterized his actions, he agreed to full union recognition and even offered to "check off," that is to collect union dues for the UAW directly from wages.

The CIO, and with it, Big Labor, had come to stay. Although by 1940 membership had dropped below the figure of the heady months of 1937 when all seemed possible for the union organizers, the CIO's achievement in industrial unionism was undeniable. And the AFL had also benefited from the pro-union wave of the late 1930s, increasing its membership as well. Roosevelt enjoyed widespread, almost fanatical, support among union men. Some of the leaders were not happy over the president's caginess, however. Lewis broke with Roosevelt and supported the Republican candidate in 1940, but this time the coal miners did not follow their chief's lead, voting overwhelmingly for their "friend in the White House."

Yet most union leaders remained outspoken political allies of Roosevelt. The NLRB was still an arm of the government, and the NLRB, they all knew, was organized labor's strongest friend. It kept employers from interfering with legitimate union activities (sometimes reinstating workers discharged for union activities), and it certified the election of unions as bargaining agents. NLRB decisions were usually pro-labor, as was, of course, the Wagner Act itself, so much so that at times the federal courts had to curb the board's pro-labor rulings.

Roosevelt never entirely pleased any of his

supporters, and labor was no exception. But the president remained so popular among the union rank-and-file, and the administration's role had been so beneficial to labor that the "Union Revolution" became the heart of the New Deal's second phase.

THE ROOSEVELT DEPRESSION: LESSONS HALF LEARNED

The court fight and the union revolution severely tested the New Deal. The shift in constitutional interpretation and the newly won power of American workers came at a stiff political price. But when a recession occurred in the latter half of 1937, the president's leadership suffered its severest jolt. As during the days of smooth sailing in his first term, Roosevelt still remained cocky and glib and, though he loved to wisecrack with reporters, privately he was troubled. When the economy faltered, the New Dealers reached back into the past; like Herbert Hoover they tried to assure people that the economy was basically sound and that prosperity was just around the corner, meaningless words which were no more soothing in 1937 than they had been in 1929.

Roosevelt did not panic, but he was clearly apprehensive, and for good reason. Five and a half years of New Deal had not licked the depression. The administration always defended itself and the state of the Union by reminding voters of how bad things had been when Roosevelt took over. By that standard no administration could lose, since 1933 represented rock bottom. But in mid-1937 more than six million men still lacked steady employment; within a year the figure rose to ten million, or one-fifth of the work force. Wage rates did not drop, but the number of men on payrolls plummeted. Industrial production, which had finally topped 1929 figures, went down one-third. The social problems Roosevelt highlighted in his second inaugural address of 1937 ("I see one-third of the nation ill-housed, ill-clothed, and ill-fed") remained largely unsolved and worst of all a new depression, not prosperity, engulfed the country. The deprived one-third threatened to become two-thirds again.

Whereas Hoover's failings as a depression

fighter lay in what he did not do, Roosevelt's role in producing the depression of 1937–1938 stemmed from fiscal mismanagement. The president, one of the least attentive and least serious students of political economy (he hated statistics, graphs, and charts), had never made up his mind on the government's basic financial policy. This gave him tremendous flexibility. He could and often did switch from one course to another. But policy juggling became a method of trying to achieve recovery through the use of contradictory means. In the end, FDR learned that his kind of "bold, persistent experimentation" could become as much of a liability as Hoover's inflexible commitment to "sound money."

Spending vs. Trust-busting

The economic argument boiled down to a fight between the Spenders and the Belt-Tighteners. Roosevelt usually leaned toward the Spenders, but he never forgot his campaign pledge of 1932 to balance the budget. The promise now seems ridiculous and to many it appeared downright deceitful in view of the steady growth of the national debt under Roosevelt. Yet the president believed in the desirability of balanced budgets and in "sound" fiscal policy, a policy which contradicts enlargement of the public debt. Each rise in government spending therefore brought renewed Rooseveltian pledges to balance the budget "next year."

The Spenders had a philosopher who claimed to know how a modern nation could fight a depression. John Maynard Keynes, a widely respected British economist, urged massive government spending and lower taxes to increase investment and make up for the decline in spending by business. Eventually, government pump-priming, by pouring money into the economy and increasing consumer purchasing power, would theoretically revive private investment and achieve recovery. Keynes's ideas had already gained wide acceptance among economists, especially within the academic community. He had met the president, and they later corresponded (Keynes sent unsolicited advice, and Roosevelt replied with polite notes), but "Keynesianism" never became the operative philosophy of New

Deal economics, nor did any other "ism." Roosevelt went no further than alternating doses of "pump-priming" and "fiscal responsibility"—or government-stimulated inflation, followed by government-induced deflation.

New Deal spending was motivated less by Keynesian economics than by a humanitarian desire to help the distressed and by political calculations that relief was imperative. Not only did the government prime the pump on too small a scale to achieve the result Keynesian economics forecast, but it never did so consistently. In 1936, buoyed by substantial improvement in the economy, Roosevelt felt it was time to cut back on government spending and move toward a balanced budget. This proved fatal. Without the spur of government spending, the economy faltered.

Roosevelt called Congress into special session late in 1937. Once more he was ready to change course, this time in the direction of heavy doses of government spending. And as usual Roosevelt was responding to a specific emergency he hoped would prove temporary. Making no long-range commitment to economic theory, he asked Congress for new agricultural legislation, authority to reform government operations, and more money for the WPA. He also blamed the recession on the alleged shortsightedness and greed of businessmen. Privately he mused: "I get more and more convinced that most of them can't see farther than the next dividend."

The new depression of 1937–1938 was as much a national emergency as the crisis of 1933, but in the intervening five years, some of Roosevelt's magic had worn off. Big Business no longer willingly cooperated in national recovery schemes, and the administration, its alliances rearranged, welcomed the political mileage which could be gained by lambasting the businessmen—the "malefactors of great wealth," as Roosevelt called them.

The recession strengthened the influence of those advisers, following the lead of Justice Louis D. Brandeis, who argued that business monopoly was the chief problem. They charged that the large corporations had enough power to fix prices at unreasonably high levels, thus discouraging new investment. Only competition

could assure reinvestment and innovation, the antitrusters maintained, and only by breaking up concentrations of economic power could competition be restored. Roosevelt and most other New Dealers never accepted the argument that Big Business had to be broken up. Modern technology, they thought, inevitably created a few big corporations and caused a decline in competition. But frustrated by his inability to achieve permanent recovery, FDR was more inclined to listen to the antitrusters. The president recommended and Congress undertook a sweeping investigation of Big Business which produced shelves of scholarly studies but little else.

He also ordered the Justice Department to step up enforcement of the antitrust laws. The Department of Justice initiated more prosecutions than at any time in the past. Though New Deal trust-busters refined their techniques, employing consent decrees, or out-of-court settlements, to get companies to make changes, these efforts to reverse the trend toward concentration were no more successful than earlier ones. And at this late date in American industrial consolidation, even their symbolic value was questionable.

Roosevelt succeeded partially with Congress, gaining further extensions of the welfare state in the areas of housing and working conditions. Ever since the Progressives turned a spotlight on urban slums and publicized the obvious fact that decent housing was unavailable to the poor, reformers sought unsuccessfully to improve the housing of the American people. With the enormous expansion in government responsibility in the 1930s, housing reformers now proposed that the federal government finance and build low-income housing. Under the National Housing Act (1937) the federal government spent three quarters of a billion dollars on over 150,000 new dwelling units in the next four years. Though government-built ghettos for the poor came under attack a generation later, most of those who then moved into public projects acquired a decent home for the first time, homes whose value those accustomed to luxury housing had difficulty appreciating.

Another old Progressive cause also came to fruition in 1938 when Congress passed the Fair Labor Standards Act. This measure established a national minimum wage in businesses engaged in interstate commerce, fixed maximum hours at forty per week, and finally outlawed child labor. Opposition in Congress was intense from farm groups and the South and the measure squeaked through only by exempting large segments of the labor force from its protection. The chief beneficiaries were unorganized factory workers.

The president "muddled through" the second depression. Fortunately for the nation, and for Roosevelt, the economic pendulum swung upward again. But the New Deal could hardly take credit. And in the end Roosevelt joined a well-populated gallery of American politicians who have been confused and frustrated by the mysterious workings of the economy.

THE NEGRO'S NEW DEAL

To millions of black Americans depression was nothing new, and ironically the 1930s brought significant improvements in the status of the American Negro which foreshadowed the Black Revolution of the 1960s. The advances came less as a result of a planned campaign for racial justice than as the consequence of the nation's shift to the equalitarianism of the New Deal. Yet while on the whole Negroes benefited from the New Deal, some suffered.

NRA codes discriminated against black families, but with the bulk of Negroes at work on Southern farms rather than in industry, AAA had a greater impact on them. The depression had devastated Southern agriculture, especially in the cotton belts. Declining world markets, new technology, and New Deal agricultural policies combined to force out the marginal cotton farmer and tenant, many of whom were Negroes. The AAA, which sought to curtail farm production in order to raise prices, speeded up the process of removal. Landowners often kept the entire government subsidy for themselves, ignoring their tenants' legal rights. Ex-tenants, now working for wages, had no claim to government payments. With Southern agriculture overpopulated, any restriction of acreage inevitably worked against the tenant's interest, removing the need for his labor. New Dealers knew this, but the victims had

little political power whereas the landowners dominated their region's politics. Some official help came from the Farm Security Administration (FSA), which for a short while had a Negro director. The FSA, in a manner reminiscent of the Freedmen's Bureau after the Civil War, tried to help agricultural workers negotiate contracts, and it set up camps for migrant workers. But the agency never had a large budget, and it met strong and effective opposition, especially in the South.

As America's prime candidate for relief aid, the Negro fared a bit better at the hands of other New Deal agencies. Many displaced Southern Negroes migrated to Northern cities—as they still do today. Jobs were scarce in New York or Chicago or Detroit, but a black stood a better chance of obtaining a job or relief benefits in the North. There, too, blacks fleeing Southern peonage felt freer than under watchful white eyes in the rural South. In the 1930s, "Relief" became the American Negroes' third principal "occupation," after farm work and domestic service. At the end of the decade one million Negroes worked for the WPA, though relief administrators usually discriminated in apportioning funds. Sizable numbers of blacks benefited from the NYA and the CCC. Exclusion of farm and domestic laborers from the benefits of minimum wages and unemployment compensation laws, however, deprived Negroes of much New Deal aid, since black employment was concentrated precisely in those two categories.

The New Deal had trouble enough solving the nation's economic problems; it did not seek to transform the condition of the American Negro. Yet blacks made important gains in the 1930s. The new mood could be gauged by a growing self-assurance among Negro leadership. Even before Roosevelt's election there were strong indications of an imminent major switch in Negro voting patterns. Before 1932 most Negroes voted Republican, supporting "the party of Lincoln." The depression shattered that allegiance. Negroes turned against Hoover, just as did millions of other hard-pressed Americans. The benefits that blacks received from the New Deal convinced them that they, too, had a friend in the White House. As the poorest of the poor, blacks knew the importance of relief and welfare payments. The election of 1936 showed that slogans about the party of Lincoln meant little to Negro voters, now a solidly Democratic bloc.

Roosevelt did not neglect the psychological needs Negroes felt for political recognition and he moved to make visible the blacks who were part of the New Deal coalition. The president and Mrs. Roosevelt, who often served as "the conscience of the Administration," sought the advice of black leaders. Several dozen Negroes, not the customary one or two, received appointments to important, though second-line, positions. Unofficial Negro advisers became an informal "Black Cabinet," sometimes visiting the White House, causing outrage among white racists and stirring pride among blacks.

But the New Deal did little to end discrimination or segregation. The president appreciated the value of Southern Democratic votes, and among the most vicious racists on Capitol Hill were men who voted the straight New Deal line. In return FDR pursued a "moderate" line on race. Nor was there sufficient white liberal and black pressure in the North for civil rights legislation to force Roosevelt to make a choice. Americans, regardless of color, were preoccupied with economic survival in the 1930s. Roosevelt allowed several antilynching bills to die in Congress, despite close collaboration between Mrs. Roosevelt and the NAACP on the issue. Since lynchings had fallen to an average of ten a year (from a high of 200 per year in the 1890s), the president could rationalize his refusal to spend political capital in a campaign against this barbarity.

Under FDR, Negroes got less than they needed but more than they expected. As a result by the end of the decade, the Negro vote, growing with the migration of blacks from the South to the North, became firmly wedded to the Democratic party. This sleeping political giant would awaken a decade later and make possible greater strides toward equality in the next generation. But in the 1930s, bigotry was still respectable in educated white circles, North and South. When black singer Marian Anderson tried to use Washington's Constitution Hall for a recital, the old biddies of the Daughters of the American Revolution (DAR) who own the theater turned her down.

But Mrs. Roosevelt arranged for a massive open-air concert at the Lincoln Memorial and thousands came to hear the magnificent contralto on a Sunday in 1939. The concert was as much a rebuke to American racism as it was a testimonial to Miss Anderson's art.

In the end, Negroes benefited primarily from New Deal programs to help poor people. Just as the New Deal avoided radical changes in the economic system, so too it made no attempt to revolutionize race relations. Yet even when programs such as AAA hurt blacks in the short run, in the long run, by speeding up the process of black migration and urbanization, they advanced the day when a revolution in race relations would become possible.

THE AMERICAN LEFT AND THE NEW DEAL

The American Left took the New Deal's halfway policy toward blacks as confirmation of their charge that it was less committed to fundamental reform than determined to put the capitalist Humpty Dumpty together again. Yet for a quarter of a century, conservatives have falsely pictured the 1930s as the "Red Decade," a time when Socialists and Communists supposedly exercised unprecedented influence in American politics, infiltrating the top echelons of government and shaping policy. Time has gained acceptance for controversial New Deal measures such as social security, and resigned conservatives to the innovations. Today most criticism of the New Deal comes from those on the New Left, convinced that its failure to make fundamental structural reforms in American society, to redistribute wealth and power from the few to the many, and to make business socially responsible lies at the root of many of the problems Americans face today: racism, poverty, urban blight, pollution, and the bureaucratization of life in the factory, shop, and school. Yet while the American Left failed to push the country in the direction of Socialism in the 1930s, it gained a greater influence than it had enjoyed in the past. In the end, however, the New Deal exploited the Marxist Left, taking over some of its reformist proposals without accepting its anticapitalist goals, tapping its extraordinary organizing energies without surrendering real power to the left. At the same time, although neither Socialism nor Communism won over hordes of followers during the Depression Decade, American Marxism and Marxists gained a temporary respectability they had lacked in the past.

Recognizing Soviet Russia

First came diplomatic recognition of Russia in 1933. For sixteen years Washington had officially ignored Moscow. Initial moves by the Bolshevik government to gain recognition had been brushed aside. Woodrow Wilson's last secretary of state, referring scornfully to the "existing regime in Russia," read it out of the community of civilized nations since it negated "every principle upon which it is possible to base harmonious and trustful relations." Wilson's three Republican successors in the White House stood pat on that judgment. Yet American bankers and exporters (free to trade with the Soviets after 1920) did considerable business with this pariah nation, so much so that in the 1920s talk about the untapped possibilities of the Russian market resembled in miniature the old China Market Myth.

During the depression, professional anti-Communists like Father Coughlin railed at American Big Business for "subsidizing Bolshevism," but most business leaders who spoke out favored recognizing the Soviets as a prelude to trade expansion. They denied that diplomatic recognition had anything to do with approval of the Soviet regime; it would simply be good business. And early in the 1930s the country clearly could use any sources of new business. An American press lord, Roy Howard of the Scripps-Howard newspaper chain, urged recognition and quipped: "I think the menace of Bolshevism in the United States is about as great as the menace of sunstroke in Greenland or chilblains in the Sahara." A newspaper in Dallas editorialized that "after all, Sovietism is an experiment in a sort of democracy."

Roosevelt acted promptly to grant recognition in 1933. The rise of Fascist governments in

Germany and Japan posed a new threat to the Western world, one which might require full-scale cooperation with the Soviets. Although caught by surprise by Soviet-American reconciliation, the U.S. Communist party capitalized on it. The Communists (who had split from the older Socialist movement in 1919) had by the 1930s become the most active, militant, and successful of the Marxist groups. In 1932 their presidential candidate did badly, yet the Communist party captured the imagination and loyalty of many Americans on the Left. Communists had previously denounced the New Deal as papering over the "contradictions of capitalism," and had abused FDR as a "social fascist"—apparently the worst kind of scoundrel in their lexicon. But recognition of the USSR and Russia's call in 1935 for a Popular Front to unite all elements opposing Fascism forced American Communists to change their tune.

The Reds' qualified praise for Roosevelt, and the growing threat from Fascism made American liberals more tolerant of Communists. Some joined the Communist party and many were willing to cooperate with it. These flirtations created a corps of "fellow travelers" among the intellectuals. They adopted the slogan of the former Progressive muckraker-turned-radical, Lincoln Steffens, who on returning from Russia had proclaimed approvingly: "I have seen the future and it works." Many American intellectuals fell in love with the *idea* of a Communist Utopia where everybody had a job, where poverty was unknown, and where every citizen contributed to society according to his means and received according to his needs. Joseph Stalin's slaughter of peasants resisting collectivization of agriculture, and his execution of Old Bolsheviks whom he feared as rivals in the Moscow Purges (1934–1939), bothered sympathizers, but they chalked these off to the unavoidable bloodshed that accompanies any profound social revolution. And in the struggle against the horror of Hitler's Germany and the Fascist dictatorship in Italy and Spain, the Communists seemed the most dedicated and effective freedom fighters. Not all American intellectuals went Far Left, of course, but in literary, artistic, and academic circles, a left-of-center stance was fashionable. A right-of-center stance put one on the defensive.

American Communists also found the labor movement more receptive than in the past, especially the new CIO, which Communist party leader William Z. Foster described as "a great American People's Front against fascism and war." By deemphasizing their Marxist ideology and putting their considerable skills as organizers at the disposal of John L. Lewis, Communists worked their way into the burgeoning union movement. Lewis and other CIO leaders remained confident, and rightly so, that they could tap Communist energies while retaining control. "I do not turn my organizers or CIO members upside down and shake them to see what kind of literature falls out of their pockets," snorted Lewis. The Communists gained control of a few unions whose members were willing to ignore their leader's political views as long as they "delivered" the goods expected from "bread-and-butter" unionism. Besides, "in those days," a labor leader explained, "the Communists talked like democrats."

Communists made inroads among intellectuals, within organized labor, and also in government. A few Reds obtained positions in the Department of Agriculture, the State Department, and in the National Labor Relations Board, but their numbers were few and their influence slight. In 1939, the honeymoon between New Dealers and the Communists abruptly ended. The Nazi-Soviet treaty of that year made Russia and Germany allies and gave Hitler a green light to launch the Second World War. Stalin's deal, which divided up Poland between the two dictatorships, left the Communist party's "fellow travelers" dazed and feeling betrayed. Communist fortunes, never very bright even in the 1930s, went into eclipse.

The Communist experience highlights the limits of radicalism in the 1930s. Neither they nor the democratic Socialists won a mass following. As long as they attacked the New Deal from a fixed Marxist position, they remained isolated. When they consciously toned down their ideology, blurred their goals, and supported reform liberalism, their influence grew—but only because they had trimmed their sails to work within the system.

THE NEW DEAL SPUTTERS

The state of the economy, not political ideology or economic theory, had always been the New Deal's prime concern. America was an industrial nation (even its farms have been fittingly called "factories in the field"), and after the crisis following the Crash of 1929 the world's leading industrial society faced the possibility of a breakdown. Resources, machines, skilled labor were abundant to meet American needs, if they could be applied rationally and productively. But unwilling to move toward a planned economy, or to use the federal budget properly to prime the private sector, the New Deal failed to restore prosperity. Its greatest successes came in the new field of federal social welfare and in encouraging farmers and workers to organize.

But the New Deal, however uncoordinated, uncertain, and confused its policies during Roosevelt's first term, did pursue industrial reform. All eyes turned to Washington—even Wall Street seemed humbled by the Crash—and waited for the president to lead. Roosevelt's second administration never had the same control over events as during the emergency of 1933–1934. Many key developments after 1935 took place beyond the borders of Washington's power. In the case of the new industrial unionism, and the violence accompanying labor organization, Roosevelt appeared to be a follower, a course which antagonized businessmen and many farmers. On the political front, in so vital a matter as administration control of Congress, the president let his grip relax and never regained it fully.

Roosevelt made trouble for himself by not paying more attention to his friends. His string of victories after the Democratic convention of 1932 (many of them won with the help of conservative, Southern Democrats) lulled him into forgetting that political coalitions seldom last long. Roosevelt neglected to build up loyalty among the liberal, rank-and-file congressmen (many of them men of little seniority), those who gave him votes but received little recognition in return. Instead, the president never ceased trying to charm conservative, Democratic committee chairmen from the South, powerful men of long standing in Congress but skeptical of the New Deal and where it might lead.

Conservative Revival

The crisis atmosphere during FDR's first term obscured differences of interest and ideology within the Democratic party. Rural Democrats, for instance, went along with labor and welfare legislation in order to get support from urban Democrats for farm legislation. But as the emergency passed and as the administration moved leftward, cultivating support among the urban working classes, and as its relations with businessmen deteriorated, splits in the Democratic party became more open. The center of Democratic conservatism lay in the South. Wealthy Southerners, who dominated the party, opposed the New Deal's halting efforts to aid sharecroppers and tenants and regarded unionization as a threat to the South's belated industrial development, since cheap, docile labor was one of the region's principal attractions to manufacturers.

As a one-party region that repeatedly elected the same men to Congress, the South enjoyed power in Congress out of proportion to the number of Southern representatives. By virtue of seniority, Southern Democrats dominated the congressional committee system whenever their party gained control. Strategically positioned, conservative Southern Democrats in league with Republicans caused the president increasing grief. By the summer of 1937 many had clearly broken with Roosevelt, usually on the stated issue of the court-packing scheme. But obviously more than concern with judicial independence was at stake. The New Deal had become too liberal for them, it contained too many ways for upsetting Southern social and racial patterns, with such innovations as industrial unionism, informal "Black Cabinets," and Communist agitation. Led by Vice-president Garner of Texas, Southern Democrats (most Southern congressmen were both Democratic and conservative) joined in an informal coalition with the Republi-

cans. The coalition, explained another Texas Democrat, had the "support of nearly all small-town and rural Congressmen." They opposed "the men from the big cities which . . . [were] politically controlled by foreigners and transplanted Negroes, and their representatives in Congress . . . [who had] introduced insidious influences into the New Deal." All parties denied the existence of the coalition, but the voting records proved differently.

Roosevelt told the nation in June 1938 that these "Copperheads," or conservative Democrats, had to be retired from politics. He asked his party's voters to repudiate them in the 1938 primaries. The Southern voters, though still immensely loyal to Roosevelt as president, would not obey. Every major figure Roosevelt had tried to dump won renomination and reelection. And Congress began to reassert its authority after a half dozen years of passivity and presidential initiative. In 1938 the Republicans almost doubled their strength in the House and passed from the status of declining opposition to that of effective opposition.

New Deal liberalism still controlled the executive branch and it had just taken over the Supreme Court, but Congress now fought against dictation. With over eight million yet unemployed, relief and public works bills failed in the House or emerged badly trimmed by the amending process. Such "luxuries" as the WPA's Federal Theater went down the drain. Harry Hopkins anticipated this when he observed sadly in 1937 that America had become "bored with the poor, the unemployed, and the insecure." And the president tried to put the best face possible on the situation two years later: "We have now passed the period of internal conflict in the launching of our program of social reform. Our full energies will now be released to invigorate the processes of recovery in order to preserve our reforms."

Although the New Deal had clearly lost much of its punch, Roosevelt had helped create the modern presidency. Woodrow Wilson dreamed of becoming an American prime minister; Franklin Roosevelt came closest to achieving that position. In the 1930s the White House became the center of government as Roosevelt played a continuous role, sometimes welcome and sometimes unwelcome, in the legislative process. Presidential lobbyists worked on Capitol Hill to turn presidential wishes into legislation, often peddling draft bills prepared at the White House. Presidential power also grew through increased use of executive orders, the president's private "legislative" device. Some government departments closely watched by Congress, the Bureau of the Budget, for example, became parts of the Executive Office. The federal bureaucracy enlarged (became swollen, complained conservative critics), and although most of these jobs were not patronage appointments, their very creation tended to increase the power of the executive branch.

And, always, Roosevelt kept in touch emotionally with the "little people" through frequent press conferences and, most important, the incredibly successful "fireside chat" radio talks. The sense of personal warmth he exuded during these performances, and the sense of security it produced among many of his listeners, earned him dividends far beyond the dreams of most politicians.

A NEW DEAL BALANCE SHEET

The New Deal sharply divided Americans. Its meaning and legacy have sharply divided historians. Most historians agree on one point, however: Franklin Roosevelt and the New Deal aimed to strengthen, not destroy, American capitalism, though most capitalists did not then recognize or welcome the New Deal's rescue mission. Wall Street was made safer for investors, banks safer for depositors. New Deal lending agencies came to the aid of businessmen in trouble, rescued farmers from bankruptcy and homeowners from foreclosure. Massive government relief and social security offered people more security than they had enjoyed in the past. Triple-A and labor unions gave farmers and workers a boost up the ladder toward middle-class status. All of this came at the price of an enlarged federal government which placed more restrictions on freedom of enterprise than Americans had been accustomed to.

Beyond this, historians sharply disagree. "The New Deal however conservative it was in some respects," writes one, "marked a radically new departure." "The conclusion seems inescapable," writes another, "that traditional as the words may have been in which the New Deal expressed itself, in actuality it was a revolutionary response to a revolutionary situation." It was nothing of the sort, others insist. "In acting to protect the institution of private property," writes a critic, "and in advancing the interests of corporate capitalism, the New Deal assisted the middle and upper sectors of society. It protected them, sometimes, even at the cost of injuring the lower sectors. Seldom did it bestow much of substance upon the lower classes." "The story of the New Deal," another critic concludes, "is a sad story, the every recurring story of what might have been."

Theoretically, the New Deal might have nationalized the banks and imposed national planning on industry; it might have begun the socialization of American industry; it might have redistributed wealth from the haves to the have-nots; it might have ended private property; it might have cleared the slums, and provided every American with a decent home; it might have given a chance to sharecroppers and farm laborers; it might have rescued black Americans from impoverishment and discrimination. But the New Deal did none of these things; nor could it. Franklin Roosevelt, "magical persuader that he was," as one critical appraiser shrewdly observed, "probably could not have persuaded the people to accept any extreme measures." Though millions suffered as victims of the crisis in the capitalist system, few Americans gave up on that system. Had the New Deal *not* come to the rescue, had the suffering continued unrelieved, hawkers of radical solutions might have gained a hearing. And most likely a Fascist movement stood a better chance in exploiting despair in America than would have either democratic Socialism or totalitarian Communism.

The New Deal gave the system greater resiliency. It labeled as intolerable unregulated capitalism, with its periodic booms and busts. It provided a welfare floor for millions of the poor. It encouraged farmers and workers to organize and acquire the power with which to advance their interests. It did not, however, remake

America. And no one knew this better than the New Dealers themselves. A decade after Roosevelt became president, his vice-president, Henry Wallace, admitted: "We are children of the transition, we have left Egypt but have not yet arrived in the Promised Land." Yet though most Americans were grateful to the New Deal for leading them out of Egypt, few knew at the end of a decade of reform in what direction lay that Promised Land.

By then, however, the approach of war in Europe and the rising menace of Japan in the Far East began to loom as the principal dangers facing the United States. In 1941, as the country became engulfed in the Second World War, Roosevelt announced coyly that Doctor New Deal had gone home to make way for Doctor Win-the-War. Actually, Doctor New Deal departed some time before, even though the patient had not fully recovered.

Chapter 31
The Dilemma of Neutrality

The Great Depression had turned America inward, temporarily reversing the tide of its history. Domestic problems were so grave that many Americans easily forgot that other nations existed across the oceans. An isolationist sentiment swept across the land, at first confidently expressing a national consensus, until the realities of international politics insistently intruded upon the escapist dream of a self-sufficient America immune from the evils of the Old World.

In the 1930s Americans again watched Europe move slowly toward war, and then burst into flame. When traditional social systems collapsed in Italy, Russia, and Germany, people turned in despair to brown- or black-shirted Fascist demagogues and Communist dictators who replaced the emperors and kings. The cast of characters had changed, but the road to war resembled the death march which led to the First World War. Americans determined that *this* time they would not become involved. When war came in 1939, they swore they would not pull British and French chestnuts out of fires the Western democracies had foolishly helped to ignite by appeasing an aggressive Nazi regime in Germany. Europe had seemingly learned nothing from its first twentieth-century bloodbath. Having once wasted blood and treasure in an unsuccessful attempt to make the world safe for democracy, Americans now preferred to remain aloof from European power struggles. They denied that the survival of the United States depended upon what happened in Europe, for they were protected by 3000 miles of ocean.

Such was the theory. Its practice proved difficult early in the 1930s, and impossible by the end of the decade. No amount of nostalgic self-delusion that the United States might maintain its nineteenth-century isolation could erase the fact of America's world power or that events overseas threatened its vital interests. Events of the 1930s shattered America's innocence. At first most Americans viewed the outside world in traditional, moralistic terms. Accordingly, United States foreign policy was to be guided by righteousness and justice rather than concern for national self-preservation or national interest.

By 1941 these comfortable illusions had become largely outmoded. The transformation of American foreign policy reflected this change. Not all of the moralism had been discarded, to be sure, but self-interest stemming from the basic need for self-preservation increasingly dominated the thinking of government leaders and the responses of the citizenry. The threat of powerful Fascist regimes plotting world conquest made this clear to all but the most obtuse. By 1941, globe-spanning economic interests made American political isolation an impossible dream, and advanced technology left the United States physically vulnerable to aggression for the first time since the early years of the Republic. The challenges came first in East Asia, then Latin America, and finally Europe.

MANCHURIA AND MORALISM

The Kellogg-Briand Pact of Paris (1928) exemplified the operation of an earlier utopian idealism in foreign affairs. Having rejected the principle of collective security and membership in the League of Nations, the United States instead joined the fifteen nations signing a treaty designed to end war by making it illegal, but without enforcement machinery. Moreover, the major powers insisted on qualifications under which they might use their armed forces—Britain within its Empire, and the United States in the Western Hemisphere.

This declaratory judgment against force as an instrument of international politics quickly came under fire. Since the days of its victory over Russia in 1905, Japan had clearly become the leading Asian power, with compelling expansionist aims. Manchuria and parts of northeast China had come under Japanese domination, short of outright political control. In 1931, Japan decided to go beyond economic control. A new leader had appeared in China in the 1920s, young

General Chiang Kai-shek who had succeeded Sun Yat-sen as head of the Nationalist republican regime that overthrew the Chinese empire. With Chiang resisting Japanese domination of Manchuria, and with Russia bent on maintaining its sphere of influence in northern Manchuria, the Japanese civilian government bowed to military pressure. In September 1931 Japanese troops boldly invaded Manchuria. They quickly seized the cities, and a year later set up a puppet government in a new state they called "Manchukuo." This clearly violated the Kellogg-Briand Pact, inducing China to appeal to the League of Nations. But the League, lacking the will to use the weak enforcement machinery it had, and with its members preoccupied with a more pressing worldwide depression, did nothing but protest lamely.

This "Manchurian Incident," as the Japanese slightingly called it, put the United States on the spot. Japan had for years enjoyed special rights in Manchuria (in common with European powers in other parts of China), and Chinese sovereignty over the area had been more theoretical than actual. But the United States could not ignore the invasion since Japan seemed determined to try and turn the Far East into a private preserve, imperiling the international power balance in Asia, where the United States and its Western European allies had vital interests.

In Washington, President Hoover and Secretary of State Henry L. Stimson reacted, but not in unison. Although morally outraged by Japanese aggression, Secretary Stimson also appreciated its adverse effects on American national interests. He pressed Hoover for a firm response, perhaps in concert with the League of Nations. The president, however, who under no circumstances would consider using force or cooperate with the League except as a last resort, piously repeated American support for the principle of the Open Door in China, without indicating willingness to back it up if necessary with force. Under these circumstances, all that Secretary Stimson had left as a "weapon" was moral disapproval.

The American reaction—"Diplomacy by Condemnation"—proved ineffective. Equally unproductive was the League's response. Both the United States and the League refused to recognize the new puppet regime in Manchuria, calling for the return of Manchuria to China. Japan ignored the demand, flaunting world opinion by announcing its intention to withdraw from the League.

The "Stimson Doctrine" of nonrecognition was as far as the American public would then go. Hoover made little effort to resist the rising tide of isolationism. Nonrecognition meant a refusal to recognize the reality of Japanese conquest of Manchuria, and a retreat behind the ineffectual barrier of moral condemnation. This response, the basis for United States policy toward Japan until Pearl Harbor, angered but did not deter Japan from embarking on further adventures. The United States insisted upon conditions Japan would not accept: complete withdrawal from China and Manchuria.

ISOLATIONISM THROUGH "NEUTRALITY"

American isolationism reached its peak in the mid-1930s, at a time when the domestic economic crisis and the growing dangers of war in Asia and Europe evoked frequent and strident declarations that America alone stood for the Right, but that it would not use its power as a great nation to influence international affairs.

The worldwide depression put intolerable strains on the political settlements which followed the First World War. The old European monarchies and empires of many nationalities dissolved into shaky republics. After an initial wave of Communist gains, right-wing radicalism emerged as the main threat to stability. Benito Mussolini became Fascist dictator of Italy in 1922, and two months before President Franklin Roosevelt took the oath of office, in January 1933, Adolf Hitler, the Führer (leader) of the National Socialist (Nazi) party, became chancellor of Germany, dooming the postwar German republic. Hitler soon seized complete command, and denounced the Treaty of Versailles. His new Nazi state, the Third Reich, became the leading Fascist nation and the most dangerous threat to world peace.

From the beginning President Roosevelt appreciated the extent of the Nazi menace. But with isolationist feeling running so strong in the United States he had to proceed warily. At Geneva in 1932, Germany had demanded the right to rearm. Roosevelt responded a year later by indicating that with adequate guarantees the United States would support a general reduction of armaments as well as international consultation over threats to peace. Congressional leadership did not welcome this tentative move in the direction of collective security, and Hitler's withdrawal from both the Geneva disarmament conference and the League of Nations made the question academic.

Congressional legislation reflected the isolationist mood. In 1934 Congress prohibited loans to any nation which had defaulted on war debts still pending from the First World War, reducing the flow of capital from the United States to Europe. The United States thus attempted to legislate financial isolationism. In 1933, Roosevelt and Secretary of State Cordell Hull proposed a discretionary arms embargo law which would allow sales to countries under attack. Congress responded with the Neutrality Act in 1935, a law embargoing all arms shipments to *any* nation at war, aggressor or aggrieved. It also made a presidential proclamation of neutrality mandatory. Remembering the pre-World War I experience, Congress warned Americans that they traveled aboard belligerents' ships at their own risk.

The neutrality laws followed a series of important Congressional investigations that intensified isolationist sentiment. Congress did not have to prod Americans in this direction, however, since public opinion overwhelmingly opposed involvement in any foreign war. A Senate committee under Gerald P. Nye, a North Dakota Republican, investigated the origins of American involvement in the First World War. Concentrating his attention on the munitions industry and international bankers, Nye concluded that international capitalists seeking fat wartime profits had led the country into war for personal gain. The principal culprit was J. P. Morgan, who allegedly engineered United States intervention against Germany in order to protect his large loans to the Allied powers. The American busi-

nessman, the Wall Street banker especially, had fallen from his folk-hero niche. Having run the country in the 1920s, Big Business now received the blame for the depression, as well as for leading the country into a needless war to save their own skins financially.

The Nye Committee report was so effective that over two-thirds of Americans polled at the time thought that entry into World War I had been a mistake. Many New Dealers welcomed the Nye Committee's findings that "merchants of death," in league with Wall Street, were to blame.

The repudiation of Wilsonian principles seemed complete. The First World War now appeared as little more than a fight between rapacious powers, not a crusade for democracy. The Neutrality Act completely abandoned Wilson's defense of neutral rights, and made travel on belligerant ships illegal. When Mussolini conquered Ethiopia in 1936, Americans more than ever wished to avoid entanglements. That same year, as General Francisco Franco led a Fascist revolt against the Spanish left-wing republic, Roosevelt declared: "We shun political commitments which might entangle us in foreign wars. . . . we seek to isolate ourselves completely from war."

Neutrality, however, was a delusion. By refusing to aid the victims of aggression, the United States unavoidably gave an advantage to the well-armed aggressors and encouraged further threats to peace. Yet neutrality legislation did make one positive though unintended contribution. When the United States entered the Second World War in 1941, it did so for more important reasons than the questionable right to travel on belligerent vessels. That part of the Wilsonian baggage had been dumped overboard.

THE GOOD NEIGHBOR POLICY

As Americans disengaged from Europe and Asia, they paid more attention to affairs in their own hemisphere and reversed long-standing policies in Latin America. Roosevelt's inaugural address in 1933 dedicated the United States "to the policy of the good neighbor." The president meant this to apply to all nations, but the phrase "good neighbor" stuck, becoming the hallmark of Latin American policy.

The Good Neighbor principle meant an important shift in American policy. Ever since Theodore Roosevelt, the United States had asserted the right to act as policeman for the Latin American republics. The tendency had become an established practice, despite bitter Latin American protests against the actions of the Colossus of the North. During the Hoover administration signs of change appeared, including an official indication that Americans would soon give up the right of intervention. At the Inter-American Conference in Montevideo, Uruguay, in 1933, the United States moved further to improve relations with Latin America. Roosevelt's secretary of state, Cordell Hull, conceded that "no state has the right to intervene in the internal or external affairs of another." This became the working principle for Roosevelt's Good Neighbor Policy.

An early test of Roosevelt's sincerity took place in Cuba. The results were mixed. Shortly before the Montevideo conference, a revolution occurred in Cuba, but the United States refused to recognize the new government. Since the Spanish-American War, the United States by virtue of the Platt Amendment claimed a right to intervene in Cuba which made the island virtually an American protectorate. In 1933, Roosevelt preferred diplomacy to the use of force. A conservative government more friendly to established American interests replaced the revolutionaries, and the United States soon granted recognition, an apparent backward step. But a year later, the United States renounced the Platt Amendment, disavowing armed intervention, and restoring sovereignty to Cuba. Similarly, in 1934 American Marines pulled out of Haiti, another unofficial protectorate.

Besides nonintervention, the Good Neighbor Policy reshaped United States hemispheric trade and defense policy. American commercial penetration throughout the hemisphere had made many Latin American republics economically dependent upon selling commodities such as coffee and sugar to the United States. Under the Reciprocal Trade Agreements of 1934, the United States negotiated reductions in the high tariffs of the preceding decade, giving Latin Americans more open access to American markets. The threat of Fascist infiltration led Roosevelt to press for a new inter-American meeting in 1936. The president underscored his concern with the Good Neighbor Policy by traveling to Argentina for the meeting, where he reaffirmed renunciation of intervention; but at the same time he got the Latin nations to agree to take collective action to protect themselves against threats from outside the hemisphere.

The Good Neighbor Policy underwent its severest trial in 1938 when Mexico expropriated its oil industry, then largely under the control of British and American companies. The Mexican constitution of 1917 had provided for nationalization of subsoil resources, and during the 1920s the controversy between the oil companies and the Mexican government simmered.

In 1934, Lázaro Cárdenas became president of Mexico. A Socialist, he stepped up land reform and actively encouraged the organization of labor unions. As a champion of the Mexican revolution and its promise of social justice, Cárdenas pursued policies that paralleled many New Deal measures, and which made Roosevelt reluctant to bail out American oil interests through intervention. When the Mexican oil workers made stiff wage demands upon the foreign concerns, a government arbitration board sided with the workers. The oil companies rejected the terms. In March 1938, Cárdenas nationalized the oil industry.

A sincere desire to improve hemispheric relations and increased need for hemispheric security induced the United States to keep cool. Secretary Hull, treading warily, at first attempted to persuade Mexico to submit American claims to international arbitration. Cárdenas refused. The United States then agreed to negotiate over the value of American claims, thus acknowledging the legality of expropriation, an enormous concession by the old standards of economic imperialism. Unable to count on United States intervention, the American oil companies, which originally had made claims of over $260 million, settled with Mexico in 1941 for $24 million. Thus by the end of the 1930s the Good Neighbor Policy had begun to dispel some of the old and reasonably held suspicions of Latin Americans concerning the United States.

FORTRESS AMERICA

Isolationism rested on the assumption that the width of two oceans protected the United States from aggressor nations. Isolationists prided themselves in thinking they were hard-headed realists, whereas liberal internationalists were fuzzy-minded, sentimental do-gooders, with their faith in the exportability of democracy and the preservation of world peace through the League of Nations. Isolationists argued that American security lay in becoming a fortress, capable of defending itself in any contingency, instead of playing the balance of power game in Europe and Asia, or in relying for safety on Great Britain's naval power. Although many defenders of this Fortress Concept remained friendly to Britain, they did not believe that British policy had any real bearing on America's defensive capabilities.

Throughout the 1930s, American isolation faced a series of tests. After Italy invaded Ethiopia in 1935, the United States declared its intention to keep free of European entanglements, but the president also warned that the United States could not ignore aggression against other nations. Roosevelt hoped that the mandatory arms embargo would hurt Italy primarily. But Mussolini was sufficiently armed to wage war against the technologically backward Ethiopians, provided the Western powers did not cut off his oil supplies. The neutrality laws did not embargo oil—it was not considered armaments. Roosevelt could do no more than call for a voluntary halt of oil shipments, a plea ignored by the American oil industry. Ethiopia fell to the invaders, giving the Italian Fascist regime one of its few military victories. The Ethiopian emperor, Haile Selassie, made an eloquent and pathetic plea for aid for his country at the League of Nations in Geneva, and his presence provided Italy with a pretext for quitting the League.

America's policy of neutrality also contributed to another Fascist victory in Spain. While Italy and Germany supplied Spanish rebels under General Francisco Franco with arms, planes, and "volunteer" troops, Russia aided the left-wing Republican government, but on a lesser scale. The United States joined Britain and France in refusing to intervene and banned shipments of arms to both sides. Since Franco was already well supplied by his Fascist friends, Western nonintervention assured his victory. Still Americans and others insisted that nonintervention meant neutrality.

Although deeply troubled by Fascist aggressions, FDR dared not defy strong isolationist sentiment in the country. Another neutrality act in 1937 established cash-and-carry terms for shipments of nonmilitary goods to belligerents. Prepayment and shipment on foreign vessels were expected to remove the danger of United States involvement without embargoing American world trade altogether. Roosevelt accepted this reluctantly, fearful that open opposition might bring a total embargo of trade with belligerents. He did, however, get the right to issue a proclamation before the restrictive provisions went into effect, a concession which he later found valuable.

In 1937, Japan began the conquest of China, driving south from Manchuria and seizing the principal Chinese seaports. Japan's failure to declare war enabled Roosevelt to permit Americans to sell war materials to China at their own risk. Nor would the cash-and-carry embargo have hurt Japan, which had the resources to purchase and transport supplies.

Officially, America remained neutral, but the country overwhelmingly sympathized with the Chinese. Caught between a commitment to isolation and a growing realization that the world was drifting toward war, the president spoke out. In Chicago, in October 1937, Roosevelt warned against ignoring those forces in the world then creating a "state of international anarchy." Isolation and neutrality, he predicted, would not save the United States: "Let no one imagine that America will escape, that America may expect mercy, that this Western Hemisphere will not be attacked." He called on the peace-loving nations to "quarantine" the aggressors, but he did not spell out how this should be done.

Following a mixed reaction to the Quarantine Speech at home and a weak reaction by Britain and France, Roosevelt retreated. Moral support for China was one thing; material aid to China was another. The *Panay* incident in December 1937 highlighted the American dilemma. Japanese planes sank an American gunboat in the Yangtze

River. Claiming the affair was an unfortunate mistake, the Japanese government later apologized and offered to pay an indemnity. American reactions, official and popular, were surprisingly mild. The United States meekly accepted $2 million in damages.

Meanwhile, a new menace arose in Europe. Germany's new Nazi dictator, Adolf Hitler, repudiated the Treaty of Versailles, and in 1936 he sent German troops into the previously demilitarized Rhineland on the French border. German persecution of Jews and political dissenters shocked the world, incurring Roosevelt's personal condemnation. In 1938 Hitler annexed Austria and demanded the Sudetenland, the border areas of Czechoslovakia inhabited mainly by German-speaking Czechs.

Roosevelt did not hide his hostility toward Nazi Germany. According to rumor, he had declared privately that the frontier of the United States was in France, along the Rhine River. When Hitler demanded parts of Czechoslovakia at the Munich Conference in September 1938, Roosevelt asked the German Führer to guarantee that he had no aggressive intentions against thirty-one countries he listed in a letter. Hitler read the list to his rubber-stamp legislature, the Reichstag, and the Nazis roared with laughter.

THE INTERNATIONALIST COUNTERATTACK

Despite the threats to peace in Europe and Asia, most Americans remained isolationists. Some, however, began to dissent. They believed that Germany and Japan endangered American security, and that the preservation of free governments overseas was vital to the interests of the United States. At the same time liberal idealists became more realistic about the capacity of men and nations to live peacefully with one another. America, they thought, might not be able to make the world safe for democracy, but its great power and moral leadership could be used to defend the peace and protect other nations from aggression. Wilson's earlier failure, however, and the subsequent retreat into isolationism made it

difficult to persuade Americans to shoulder international responsibilities.

Few would listen until events overtook them and suddenly destroyed isolationism. Each Fascist victory in Europe and Asia helped convince increasing numbers of Americans that aggression abroad imperiled America as well. Many professionals and businessmen realized that the situation in the 1930s differed basically from the crisis that led to the First World War. For one thing, the tragedy of 1914 had erupted in a world that was complacent and even caught by surprise after almost a century of peace in Europe. But by the late 1930s only a hermit could have missed the signs pointing toward another catastrophe. The collapse of Western opposition to Hitler at Munich in 1938 troubled many persons who were previously unconcerned and who now wondered where a madman like Hitler would stop. Also, when the First World War broke out many Americans remained uncommitted; responsibility for that war was not so clear. The Kaiser's Germany was no Hitlerian nightmare, nor was it bent on destroying the accepted values of Western culture.

Hitler made clear that he declared war not only against nations but also against "decadent" civilization itself. Americans came to realize that the Atlantic was no longer the defensive shield it had been for over a century. Long-range military aircraft did not yet exist, but the thrust of military technology since 1918 made it likely that before long the major powers could wage war in any part of the globe. The Fascist coalition presented such a danger, and Hitler's ravings and demands created a sense of imminent peril.

The six fateful years of rising tension from Italy's seizure of Ethiopia to Japan's attack on Pearl Harbor (1935–1941) ultimately revolutionized American foreign policy. Terrifying realities forced basic alterations in American attitudes about national security. For the first time since the British navy threatened American security in 1812, national self-preservation became entangled in the course of events elsewhere, especially in Western Europe and in the Far East. Isolationism represented one of the gravest threats to American security, for national survival now required the United States to aid the Western democracies and others threatened by Fascist conquest.

Yet while the United States defended itself by helping others, internationalists affirmed that it was also upholding the ideals of freedom and national independence on which the country was founded, and which were now, more than ever, under attack. American civilization could not long survive in a world dominated by aggressive Fascist tyrannies. Moreover, Fascist brutality shocked the conscience of the world and shook the optimism of those who viewed mankind as basically good. The idea, long held by Americans, that the world was moving irresistably in the march of Progress could not survive the emergence of Hitler in one of the centers of Western Civilization. By 1940 the cherished illusions that fed the smug moralism which Americans had carried to war in 1917 were collapsing. The menace of Germany and Japan made prattling about neutral rights on the high seas absurd. In a world on the verge of a holocaust there could be no neutrals, certainly not among the great powers.

The End of Isolationism

American self-interest, which was not the same thing as national selfishness, became a prime consideration. At first most Americans believed that self-interest dictated isolation and withdrawal within Fortress America. Some never changed their minds. But the Nazis' spectacular success in disrupting the European balance of power pushed the United States, for its own sake, to support Great Britain. Americans from every part of the political spectrum had often acted as if the balance of power across the Atlantic did not matter. But the sight of Adolf Hitler dancing a victory jig in Paris (which fell to the Germans in 1940), and the prospect of a repeat performance in London, shocked Americans profoundly.

Appeasement had obviously failed. In 1939 France and England finally went to war when Hitler invaded Poland. After Germany quickly overran Poland and divided the conquered province with Russia, the result of an agreement between the two dictatorships, the pace of war slackened. Until the spring of the following year,

few Americans thought that Hitler could defeat the Western powers. American expectations and policy both changed, however, after the successful German *blitzkrieg* in the West, launched in April and completed by July 1940, had reduced France, the Low Countries, Denmark, and Norway.

From that time the United States abandoned, step by step, all vestiges of neutrality. After the fall of France in June 1940, interventionists became more vocal. Some called for repeal of the neutrality laws, while others favored entering the war. Germany had dealt a stunning blow to the concept of Fortress America by outflanking the presumably impregnable French defensive barrier, the Maginot Line. When the French republic collapsed, so too did much of American insularity—the belief that distance and strong defenses were enough to preserve American security.

The fall of France stiffened Roosevelt's determination to aid Britain, and gave the president greater public support. Since both isolationists and interventionists agreed on the necessity for rearmament as a first step, the administration had relatively little trouble in obtaining military "hardware" from Congress, especially for the navy. The president recommended building 50,000 warplanes, a number which sounded preposterous at the time, and Congress voted the largest peacetime military budget in American history. Supplying men to carry the guns was another story. But in September 1940, after a hot political battle, and by one vote, Congress passed the first peacetime draft law, conscripting a small number of men into service for one year.

Although aid to the Western Allies became popular, those wishing to enter the war remained a minority. Interventionists still had to argue that aid for Britain was the best way to keep out of war. Roosevelt cloaked his own clearly pro-Allied policies in the language of neutrality and nonintervention. But after France fell he announced that, having "learned the lessons of recent years," the United States must no longer "seek to appease aggressors by withholding aid from those who stand in their way." Such denial would "hasten the day of their attack upon us." To back up his words, Roosevelt established a joint defense board with Canada to promote hemispheric security and also to coordinate aid to Britain.

In 1940 FDR faced reelection. Roosevelt, good politician that he was, did not publicly commit himself to a third term. No president had served more than two terms. Although no constitutional prohibition then existed, the tradition and practice of a century and a half presented a formidable obstacle. Republicans approached the election hopefully. The New Deal had sagged badly, and earlier prospects that Roosevelt would step down offered the GOP a chance for a miraculous total recovery from the disaster of 1936.

Roosevelt's candidacy, clearly visible under the facade of his wish to be "drafted" by the Democratic convention, upset Republican strategy. The fall of France made foreign affairs the prime issue. On the eve of the election, Roosevelt delivered another blow. He appointed two Republicans to his cabinet to take charge of national defense. Henry L. Stimson, former secretary of state under Hoover, became secretary of war, and Frank Knox, Republican candidate for vice-president in 1936, became secretary of the navy. Not only were both men extremely capable, but their appointments were shrewd political moves, since Roosevelt crossed party lines to unite the country in time of peril.

Liberal internationalism unexpectedly took over the Republican convention. Most of the professional politicians were isolationists and favored Senator Robert A. Taft of Ohio, the son of President William Howard Taft. The nomination went instead to an internationalist businessman and lawyer, Wendell Willkie, a man who had been a declared Republican for less than six years. Willkie appealed to the moderate Republican and independent voter. He did not attack all aspects of the New Deal, concentrating his fire instead on bureaucracy, which has no friends, and on wasteful government spending. Willkie rejected the concept of Fortress America, and even criticized Roosevelt for timidity while the Western powers appeased Hitler, and for not rearming quickly enough. Willkie supported most of Roosevelt's foreign policy, favoring material aid to the

Allies, but he also expressed the hope, and made an implied promise, that the United States would stay out of the war if he won.

Although not a carbon copy, Willkie's campaign promises were too close to Roosevelt's for him to offer the voters a clear foreign policy alternative. The campaign started slowly. Roosevelt preferred to play the responsible statesman, too concerned with world problems to devote much attention to politics. Late in the campaign, Willkie grasped at the key issue. If Roosevelt's promise "to keep our boys out of foreign wars is no better than his promise to balance the budget," he gibed, "they're already almost on the transports." The remark struck home, and Roosevelt rushed to repair what he feared was serious damage. Before the election the president promised: "I have said this before, but I shall say it again and again and again: Your boys are not going to be sent into any foreign wars."

Roosevelt meant it. He did not think Americans would accept entry into the war without first being attacked. Nor did he consider a war declared in response to armed attack a *foreign* war. In November the traditional bar against more than two terms fell emphatically (until the revival of the two-term limitation by constitutional amendment in 1951). Roosevelt handily defeated Willkie, but the Republicans regained some of the congressional strength they had lost four years earlier.

THE FIGHT FOR PUBLIC OPINION

As Roosevelt moved more boldly to aid Britain, isolationists countered with an organized drive against involvement which proved to be their undoing. A Yale University law student established the America First Committee. Its leading supporters were conservative businessmen who contributed to a sustained isolationist propaganda campaign. The committee insisted that America was an impregnable fortress and it attacked Roosevelt's policy of all aid to the Allies short of war.

America Firsters correctly feared that increased aid would involve the United States in the war. They refused to become alarmed over the prospect of German domination of Europe, not even by Hitler's Germany. Nor did they believe that Hitler would destroy Britain, but rather would treat her as a junior partner; in any case, the Atlantic provided adequate security for America no matter what Hitler did in Europe. Entry into the conflict, they believed, would only increase Roosevelt's "dictatorial" tendencies and strengthen the power of the federal government, which would promote Socialism. These gloomy views were those of the more extreme, right-wing America Firsters. The committee generally stuck to the simple and popular theme that the United States had no business meddling in Europe's quarrels.

The voice of America First was Colonel Charles A. Lindbergh. "Lindy," idol of the 1920s for his solo flight across the Atlantic, burst again upon the public scene. Following the kidnap-murder of his son, Lindbergh had moved to Britain in 1936 to escape publicity. He became convinced of German invincibility, since it possessed the world's finest air force. Sincere repugnance to American overseas involvement, and little faith in British and French ability to contain Germany, induced Lindbergh to enter the debate on behalf of America First. "We must not be misguided," he warned, "to the effect that our frontiers lie in Europe. The ocean is a formidable barrier, even for modern aircraft." When Roosevelt later called Lindbergh an appeaser, the Colonel angrily resigned his reserve commission.

Unfortunately for America First, its message attracted the inhabitants of the lunatic fringes as well as conservative businessmen and folk heroes. American Communists, preaching anti-interventionism in the period before Hitler attacked Russia, tried to infiltrate the committee but failed. American Fascists had better luck. Their success tainted the committee with a pro-Fascist odor. The power of the radical right within the organization caused many who had joined simply as anti-interventionists to withdraw.

The interventionists also organized. William Allen White, a progressive Republican and nationally famous newspaper editor from Emporia, Kansas, led the Committee to Defend America by Aiding the Allies. Initially, this body called only for material aid to Britain. Then a significant

minority within the White Committee demanded entry into the war. This minority, the Century Group, included important leaders in business and government. The businessmen came from firms with an internationalist outlook, usually with headquarters in New York. These were the men the isolationists, whose most influential leaders were in the Midwest, called the "Eastern Establishment."

In September 1940, Roosevelt traded fifty World War I destroyers for British bases in the Western Hemisphere. His bitterest enemies, including the advocates of Fortress America, were hard pressed to attack the exchange since the acquisition of military bases on this side of the Atlantic fitted in with ideas of continental defense. Winston Churchill, who became British prime minister in the spring of 1940, termed the deal "a decidedly unneutral act," because it demonstrated that the president, on the eve of a presidential election, was prepared to use executive powers in a controversial matter. And from then on, Roosevelt increasingly linked United States national interest with British survival.

LEND-LEASE

In many ways Roosevelt was a spiritual descendant of Woodrow Wilson. He believed in high ideals. Yet his practicality, or what his enemies called his duplicity, saved him from the worst effects of Wilsonian moralism. In facing the world crisis of the late 1930s, Roosevelt had grasped one essential point: domination of either Europe or Asia by a hostile, aggressive power represented a serious threat to American security. Domestic politics, especially the strength of isolationism, induced Roosevelt to cloak many of his real intentions in silence or to entwine them in half-truths. His reputation for deviousness was thus not purely an invention of his opponents.

But Roosevelt felt that he had to keep several steps ahead of public opinion, which he hoped would then follow. At the same time he moved with warranted caution in view of the failure of the Quarantine Speech to rally public support in 1937. Yet Roosevelt may have been too timid, too wary of the force of traditional attitudes, and too inclined to underestimate the extent of the revolutionary changes then taking place in American thinking about world affairs. As always, he remained a cool and calculating politician.

During the election of 1940, Roosevelt obtained the draft law and engineered the destroyers-for-bases exchange. After reelection he moved with even greater decisiveness. The cash-and-carry provisions of the neutrality laws would have to be scrapped. Britain could neither pay for nor transport additional large-scale purchases. Repeal of the legislation meant a long fight in Congress, and since war loans provoked emotional responses, Roosevelt decided instead to lend the goods—"to eliminate the dollar sign," as he put it blithely.

At a press conference in December, Roosevelt compared his proposal to lending a neighbor one's garden hose to put out a fire next door. In a more formal radio "fireside chat" he declared that the United States must become the "great arsenal of democracy." Roosevelt still maintained that Lend-Lease meant full-scale commitment short of war. The bill (dramatically numbered H.R. 1776) started a spirited debate in and out of Congress. It proposed that in order to defend the United States, the president receive authority to transfer or have produced war supplies "for the government of any country whose defense the president deems vital to the defense of the United States." Repayment might come in the form of any "direct or indirect benefit which the president deems satisfactory." Isolationists, especially those who attacked the New Deal as a domestic dictatorship, balked at granting so much discretionary power to Roosevelt. Senator Burton K. Wheeler lamented that the president's foreign policy would "plow under every fourth American boy," a sarcastic reference to restrictive New Deal agricultural policies. Yet the bill passed fairly easily. It clearly signaled the end of neutrality and the beginning of the nonbelligerency period, which lasted through most of 1941.

Sympathy for the Allies and idealism helped the bill along, but the instinct of self-preservation, not altruism, lay behind the success of Lend-Lease. The congressional debate demonstrated how far the United States had come in this crucial transformation. Many leading Republicans, in-

cluding Wendell Willkie, supported Lend-Lease. Nebraska's Senator George Norris emerged as its champion. When questioned about his switch from isolationism, he replied that if England fell the United States would have to fight Hitler in the Western Hemisphere. Norris would not let previous convictions dictate his response to the crisis of 1939–1940. For him, and for many other Americans, changing world conditions required changes in American thinking. Roosevelt signed the bill in March 1941, and Congress promptly voted $7 billion in Lend-Lease money for him to spend.

THE FINAL STEPS

With the start of Lend-Lease, the United States moved steadily toward full participation in the war. First, American warships began escorting British convoys with war supplies halfway across the Atlantic. The navy did not yet have orders to join the fight, but it radioed information about the location of German submarines to the British. These patrols soon produced incidents. In May an American merchant ship became a victim of a German sub off the Brazilian coast. When in September the Germans attacked an American destroyer, the president ordered the Navy to "shoot on sight," calling the German submarines "rattlesnakes of the Atlantic." A month later the situation went beyond name-calling. The Germans sank an American destroyer, and nearly a hundred sailors lost their lives. The United States was now engaged in a "quasi-war," reminiscent of the undeclared naval war against France in the late 1790s.

By then Roosevelt had cemented the working agreements with Britain into an informal alliance. In the spring high-level meetings of British and American military men laid the basis for joint strategy, and in August 1941 Roosevelt traveled to Newfoundland to meet Churchill. A new factor complicated matters, but at the same time took pressure off the British: in June 1941, after a lightning campaign which subdued the Balkans, Hitler struck at Soviet Russia, his "ally" since 1939. Hitler thought that Russia could be conquered in three or four months, and early German victories seemed to bear this out. At Argentia, Newfoundland, Churchill called for aid to the Soviets, despite his long-time opposition to Communism. Roosevelt agreed, more confident of Russia's ability to hold off the Germans than were his military advisers.

Out of the Argentia conference came the Atlantic Charter. The document placed both governments unofficially in favor of a new world order based on national self-determination, freedom of the seas, and disarmament following the establishment of a workable system of collective security. These commitments could be dismissed as platitudes, or window-dressing for Roosevelt's policies. Many did so dismiss them, but the charter established the lines of American war diplomacy for the next five years, much more so than it did for the British. The conferences with Churchill also solidified the personal relationship between those two remarkable leaders. Roosevelt and Churchill got along well at their first meeting, despite some major policy differences. For example, Churchill feared that America meant to undermine the British Empire. Yet throughout the war, Roosevelt and Churchill cooperated as closely as two talented and egotistical individuals can.

The president resisted British suggestions that he press for immediate American intervention. Yet American cooperation with Britain soon became complete. British warships came to American drydocks for repairs. British pilots received advanced flight training at American bases. At the same time the United States began to move across the Atlantic. In April 1941, Roosevelt framed an agreement with Danish officials in exile allowing American occupation of Greenland, since Denmark was occupied by the Germans, as was most of Europe. In July, American troops reached Iceland, with the assent of the local government, and took over garrison duty from the British.

Roosevelt shared the hopeful, perhaps naive, attitude of the American people that massive involvement would not necessarily end in war. But as this illusion, too, vanished in late 1941 there was no exhilaration, no calls for crusades to purify the world. Roosevelt announced soberly that "our policy is not based primarily on a desire to preserve democracy for the rest of the world. It is based primarily on a desire to protect the United States and the Western Hemisphere from the effects of a Nazi victory."

Concerned principally with self-preservation, rather than acting as an international moral police force, the United States abandoned much of its earlier innocence and isolation. The country was not so well armed by late 1941 as it needed to be, but it had begun to balance ideals and realities, and thus was more prepared for whatever might come.

Chapter 32
The Superpower

After a decade of withdrawal and then hesitant involvement, the United States went to war totally. After two and a half centuries in which Americans had devoted their major efforts to taming the North American continent, the manpower and industrial might of the United States spread and were felt in most parts of the world. For nearly fifty years American economic power and business penetration overseas had been growing, but political commitments had not kept pace with the flag of commerce, despite such exceptions as the Philippines and the protectorates in the Caribbean. In general, however, the United States had not played a role in international affairs which corresponded to its actual responsibilities overseas or to its potential as a great power.

All this changed permanently during the Second World War. The United States emerged from the conflict as the world's first superpower. The country's economic might sustained a military effort unparalleled in history. Other countries had larger populations, but the productivity of the American labor force, combined with an advanced technology, gave the United States unmatched industrial and agricultural power. This material abundance made Americans optimistic, unwilling to believe in insoluble problems. The proper American efforts, they thought, could thwart any military threat from overseas. And in 1941 not only would America benefit, but with Germany and Japan crushed, the rest of the world could enjoy peace and independence.

Americans did not go to war in 1941 burdened with the same naïve assumptions their fathers held in 1917. There was no talk about neutral rights on the high seas, and little talk about making the entire world safe for democracy simply by the grace of American example. The Axis powers threatened American values and interests in a way that the Kaiser had not. The Japanese attack on Pearl Harbor made war unavoidable, whereas German attacks on shipping twenty-five years earlier had not. Although self-preservation became the foremost consideration, Americans still harbored some of the old missionary impulse. This time, however, the United States did not sit back and wait for other nations to progress along American lines. It moved to *lead* the world in that direction. In both cases the ultimate aim was a world made a bit more in the American image.

WAR WITH JAPAN

American global strategy during the Second World War dictated that Germany be considered the principal enemy. But the Japanese first attacked the United States, and during the early months of America's participation in the war the Japanese drove the Western powers out of most of Southeast Asia. Japan's intention to develop a so-called "East Asia Co-Prosperity Sphere" under its domination made a collision with European and American interests inevitable.

As relations between the two countries worsened, American leaders came to fear and expect a Japanese move. More than a year before the attack, U.S. intelligence had deciphered the Japanese diplomatic cable codes. In January 1941, the secretary of the navy predicted the surprise raid on Pearl Harbor, in Hawaii. At the same time the Japanese naval commander-in-chief, with great secrecy, began pushing the idea of striking at "Pearl," the main American Pacific base. However, throughout most of 1941 neither side wanted war. American strategists had already agreed that the main struggle must be in Europe against Hitler, should the United States have to fight all the Axis powers at once. And Japan still hoped that many of her strategic objectives could be gained without engaging in open hostilities against the United States.

Through unofficial diplomatic channels, the Japanese indicated that an accommodation might be worked out. Secretary of State Cordell Hull replied that the Japanese must respect the territorial integrity of all nations (which in this case meant China) and abide by the Open Door policy. This traditional American policy response proved unacceptable but useful to those Japanese militarists who had by late 1941 decided upon war. By then they ran the Japanese government, using civilians and diplomats as window-dressing. Their master plan was to subjugate China while moving into Southeast Asia for the establishment of a new Japanese empire. Although Washington had precise knowledge of the Japanese government's diplomatic maneuvers, the diplomatic cables interrupted by Washington did not carry military information. By September 1941 the Japanese navy produced a plan for the Pearl Harbor attack. Although many of their admirals considered it risky, Admiral Isoroku Yamamoto rammed it through, threatening to resign if it were not accepted.

In October the facade of civilian control came down. Prince Konoye's ministry collapsed and General Hideki Tojo came to power. But Emperor Hirohito insisted upon sending a special envoy to Washington in a last-ditch attempt to modify the American demand that Japan withdraw from China. The Japanese diplomat presented a final offer on November 20. Japan would take some troops out of Southeast Asia, but not from China, provided the United States ended its support of Nationalist China. Further the United States must unfreeze Japanese financial assets in America and resume normal trade. Hull at first favored a three-month cooling-off period, but none of America's allies agreed, so he replied negatively. The Japanese envoy had been told only that if no accommodation were reached by November 29, things were "automatically going to happen."

Washington knew that much from intercepted cables. A warning went out to all military commanders in the Pacific advising that negotiations had broken down and instructing them to put their installations on wartime alert. These precautions were not taken everywhere, however. The army commander in Hawaii merely acknowledged receipt of the warning and ordered greater vigilance against sabotage. He and most authorities, political and military, expected an attack exclusively on the Philippine Islands and in Southeast Asia. On November 26, 1941, a Japanese battle fleet left its home bases and began a fateful journey across the north-central Pacific

toward Hawaii. The naval commander at Pearl Harbor later testified: "I did not consider an attack on Hawaii anymore than a remote possibility." He was not alone in that belief.

This advantage of surprise made the attack successful. Japanese officers were amazed at the extent of their victory and at the lack of American preparation. They planned and executed the strike perfectly, the planes coming in from six aircraft carriers each with an assigned target. American battleships, then considered the backbone of a fighting fleet, were conveniently lined up at anchor. Eight battleships and many other smaller ships were sunk or heavily damaged. The massive raid inflicted over four thousand American casualties including more than two thousand dead.

Although much of the Pacific fleet had been knocked out, the base itself remained relatively intact. Before long it would become the focal point for the resurgence of American naval strength in the Pacific, the power which ultimately humbled Japan. And equally important, at that time the handful of American aircraft carriers—the prime offensive naval weapon of the Second World War—were luckily at sea. Yet Pearl Harbor added up to a staggering defeat for the United States. Two days later, December 9, President Roosevelt went before Congress to ask for a declaration of war. He called the seventh of December "a day that will live in infamy."

The attack ended the great debate on foreign policy. The problems of nonbelligerence and involvement short of war no longer existed. The task of defeating Japan, and soon Germany and Italy as well, united the American people as never before. The organized isolationist movement collapsed, most of its leaders rushing to offer their services to the government. Colonel Lindbergh, the leader of America First, requested assignment on active duty in the armed forces. Political isolationism also underwent a similar change. Senator Arthur Vandenberg of Michigan, a leading isolationist, became one among many who altered their views. He later reminisced: "My convictions regarding international cooperation and collective security for peace took firm hold on the afternoon of the Pearl Harbor attack. That day ended isolationism for any realist."

"Remember Pearl Harbor!" became the initial American rallying cry. The public wanted to know why this tragedy had occurred. Anti-Roosevelt forces accused the president of concealing knowledge of Japanese movements, either from stupidity or out of a desire to involve America in the conflict. Then, as now, some attempted to fix responsibility for the attack upon the Roosevelt administration, and particularly upon the machinations of the president who supposedly intrigued to force a Japanese attack. Actually, the irreconcilable positions of the two nations, not the president of the United States, created the conflict which ended in war. In supporting the Chinese government, and declaring support for the British and Dutch should Japan invade Southeast Asia, the United States squarely opposed Japan's strategic objectives. When Japan refused to back down, and decided upon expansion by force, all that remained to be determined was the time and the place for the first strike.

THE GRAND ALLIANCE

Before bombing Pearl Harbor, the Japanese had extracted Hitler's promise to honor the Axis Tri-partite Pact by declaring war against the United States. In keeping his word, the Nazi dictator committed one of his worst wartime blunders. Without such a declaration of war by Germany, the United States would have been in a dilemma, since American strategists thought that the battle against Fascism should be fought first in Europe against Germany, the stronger, industrial power. The German declaration of war allowed the United States to follow a Europe-first strategy, especially needed in view of the critical condition of the Old World. By December 1941, Hitler had already committed himself deeply in Russia, which he had invaded six months before despite the Hitler-Stalin pact of 1939. German troops reached the Moscow suburbs by late November. Perhaps the spectacular success of this initial German advance into Russia explains Hitler's foolhardy declaration of war against the United States.

That belligerent act created the Grand Alliance of all powers opposed to Hitler and the other Axis members. It was a coalition, and like any other, subject to many strains. From the beginning the Allies argued over military strategy. Although the United States and Great Britain had forged a close alliance, relations with the Soviets often proved difficult. But differences between the Western allies and the Soviets had to be accommodated because the Soviet Union was then engaging the main force of German military power. Two hundred German divisions were fighting on the Russian front. To allow a Soviet defeat would not only free those enemy troops, but give Hitler Russia's production of food and raw materials, and might decisively shift the balance of power in Germany's favor. Moreover, even if not defeated, a battered Russia might sue for peace and quit the war. On the other side of the alliance, Stalin remained wary, fearful that the Western allies would sit back on the British island fortress while Russian and German armies wore themselves out against each other. Then, he thought, the Western powers would force an end to the war, imposing a settlement on their own terms.

To ease these suspicions, Roosevelt assigned high priority to aiding the Soviet Union. By the end of the war Russia had received over $11 billion worth of arms and food, as part of the American Lend-Lease aid program to the Allies. At first, getting materiel to Russia posed an almost insurmountable problem. The Western allies had to rely upon suicidal Arctic convoys to the northern Russian ports of Murmansk and Archangel. In some cases very few ships got through. It was not until late in the war that a railroad linking Iran and Russia began to function effectively. Stalin took what he could get, but not always graciously. The head of the U.S. military mission to Russia once complained: "the Russians can't understand giving without taking, and as a result even our giving is viewed with suspicion. Each transaction is complete without regard to past favors. The party of the second part is either a shrewd trader to be admired, or a sucker to be despised." And despite the critical condition of his Soviet state, with German troops threatening the Russian capital, Stalin, like Churchill, always looked ahead to the postwar settlements. A shipload of tanks was important, of course, but

Stalin also wanted assurances that after Germany's defeat the Soviet Union would have a strong voice in the disposition of European affairs.

The memory of prewar measures to contain the Soviet Union stuck stubbornly in Stalin's mind. After the First World War, in order to isolate the "Bolshevik infection," French and British diplomacy constructed the *cordon sanitaire*, a tier of pro-Western, anti-Soviet states in eastern Europe, from the Baltic to the Black Sea. By the 1940s, however, Stalin was no longer willing to be surrounded by hostile elements. Winston Churchill, who had been one of the architects of Western Europe's anti-Soviet policy, appreciated the depth of these Russian desires and their explosive potential. But Roosevelt pushed insistently for military victory over the Axis first. Once that had been accomplished, the details of postwar geopolitics, he thought, could be worked out harmoniously by the Allies. Roosevelt's optimism finally wavered shortly before his death in April 1945, but throughout the war he insisted that he could work with "Uncle Joe" Stalin.

Roosevelt's hopes reflected American inexperience in foreign affairs, a relative lack of cynicism, and a naïve assumption that a hearty handclasp and a disarmingly frank attitude could dispel the ingrained suspicions of Old World diplomacy. Franklin D. Roosevelt, a shrewd politican at home, did not fully appreciate that methods which worked for him in domestic politics might not be useful in foreign relations.

The Liberation of Europe

From the beginning of the Grand Alliance, Stalin pressed for a second front in Europe. He insisted that a massive invasion of the Continent was the best way the Western allies could relieve German pressure on Russia. His contention was understandable. Russia was Germany's only major front after 1941. Except for Field Marshal Erwin Rommel's few armored divisions in North Africa, the bulk and the best of the German army remained in Russia. In the occupied countries of Western Europe inferior garrison troops, or men being rested after service in Russia, stood guard.

In view of these facts, the Western allies could not entirely ignore the Russian demands, though they resisted the idea of an early invasion.

Churchill had always been a leading anti-Communist, but during the Second World War he favored massive material aid to the Soviet Union. When Hitler began his drive eastward, Churchill quickly moved to ally Britain with Russia. He made a dangerous flight to the Soviet Union to establish a working agreement with Stalin. Churchill, despite his political past, explained that "If Hitler invaded Hell, I would make at least a favorable reference to the Devil in the House of Commons." Nevertheless, Churchill remained the principal voice counseling against a hasty venture across the English Channel. He never forgot World War I and the bloody four-year stalemate in the trenches of France. A supporter of the Anglo-French Dardanelles expedition against Turkey in 1916, Churchill, one world war later, still favored Mediterranean and Balkan campaigns against what he called the "soft underbelly" of the Axis.

Stalin thought that with the United States in the war the Allies might defeat Hitler by the end of 1942. He displayed little awareness of the difficulties of mounting a major attack across the English Channel. And while arguing for a second front, he always pointed to the enormous sacrifice of Russian blood then being spilled on the eastern front. The best Stalin could extract from the West in 1942 was an invasion of French North Africa late that year. This formed the basis for the Allied Mediterranean campaign and the subsequent invasion of Italy, but it hardly satisfied the Russians.

Despite Stalin's charges of Allied foot-dragging, the fact remained that the United States and Great Britain were not then ready to mount a major overseas offensive. During the first months of American involvement German submarines enjoyed open season. In a short time almost 500 Allied ships went down, some of them sunk a few miles off the Atlantic coast or in the Gulf of Mexico. In some cases the night lights of seashore resorts silhouetted the ships for the waiting German submarines. In that same period, the Germans lost only 22 submarines. Obviously, the Allies needed control of the Atlantic before

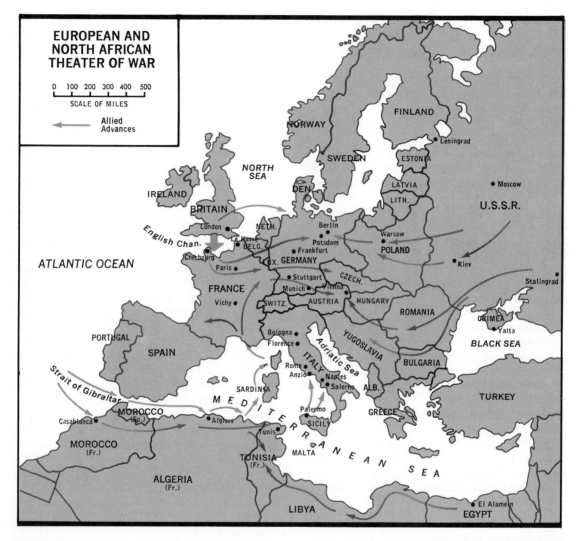

EUROPEAN AND
NORTH AFRICAN
THEATER OF WAR

0 100 200 300 400 500
SCALE OF MILES

Allied
Advances

they could transport and supply large numbers of fighting men for a major European offensive. Furthermore, some of the same problems which had prevented Hitler from invading Britain in 1940, in particular, shortage of landing craft for an invasion, stymied the Allies. Nor had air superiority yet been secured, and Allied strategists felt that to cross the channel prematurely might unnecessarily prolong the war three or four years.

Stalin made his initial demands for a second front during a period of false optimism after the German advance stalled before Moscow at the end of 1941. But during the spring of 1942 things

could not have gone worse for the Allies. In Asia, the Philippine Islands, the British stronghold at Singapore, and the Dutch East Indies (now Indonesia), all quickly fell to Japanese forces. These campaigns resulted in substantial naval losses for the Allies. On the other hand, in April the U.S. Navy held the Japanese to a draw in the battle of the Coral Sea, the first sea battle fought exclusively by aircraft, and a few months later effectively routed them in the central Pacific in the all-important battle of Midway. The painfully slow process of recapturing Pacific islands began when U.S. Marines landed at Guadalcanal in the Solomon Islands in August 1942.

But the Japanese still enjoyed almost un-molested use of the natural resources of South-east Asia. The Burma Road, the only reliable means of supplying China, had been cut and China's unhappy position became more perilous than ever. In Egypt, Marshal Rommel's Afrika Korps crossed Egypt and approached the Suez Canal, while the main German armies struck deep into southern Russia toward the oil fields in the Caucasus. The Allies could do little in mid-1942 but withdraw to new positions, count their losses, and plan for their inevitable victory.

For over three and a half years, the United States waged global war on a scale unprecedented in history. In the process, many proud chapters were added to the annals of American arms: in the Philippine Islands, out-gunned and out-manned Filipino and American troops held the Bataan Peninsula and the island fortresses in Manila Bay for several months early in 1942 until they could fight no longer; American pilots in slow-flying torpedo planes bravely gave their lives at the battle of Midway in successful attacks upon Japanese carriers; in Europe, the tank men of General George Patton's Third Army broke the enemy lines and raced across France, showing the Germans that other countries could master the *blitzkrieg* (lightning war) of tank warfare; and thousands of infantrymen, some with little train-ing, in the winter of 1944 held the line during the battle of the Bulge, the last German counter-offensive. Heroism alone, however, did not bring victory. Each major member of the Grand Al-liance made a particular contribution. Victory was the result of British stubbornness, Russian blood, and American production.

BRITISH STUBBORNNESS

The battle of Britain took place between the fall of France in 1940 and America's entry into the war a year and a half later. These months were Britain's most perilous time and, in the words of its wartime leader, Prime Minister Winston Churchill, also its "finest hour." American re-action to Britain's peril was powerful. "Away across the Atlantic," wrote Churchill later, "the prolonged bombardment of London, and later of other cities and seaports, aroused a wave of sympathy in the United States, stronger than any ever felt before or since in the English-speak-ing world. Passion flamed in American hearts, and none more than in the heart of President Roosevelt." The response was actually less unani-mous than Churchill depicted it. Although Ameri-can isolationism and the residue of anti-British feeling had been crippled politically by the fall of France and the battle of Britain, the force of these attitudes remained, working against in-volvement in the European power struggle.

A good case could have been made in June 1940 in favor of a British deal with Germany. Hitler described himself as a "victor speaking in the name of reason," and he suggested a "common sense peace through negotiation." Britain would not have been forced to accept unconditional surrender. Certain internal shifts would be neces-sary of course, including the removal of Churchill. The British would also have to recognize the su-premacy of Germany on the European continent, despite the fact that the prevention of such con-tinental supremacy by one land power had been the principal aim of British diplomacy for two centuries. And the Germans would have gained an increased role overseas, starting with the return of the colonies lost since the Treaty of Versailles in 1919.

German "reasonableness" could be also in-ferred from the fact that only half of France had been occupied by German troops. Hitler had al-lowed the establishment of a collaborationist French government in southern France at Vichy. Thus if the British were sensible they could es-cape the total destruction and subjugation which invasion would bring. Once the German army had successfully landed in Britain, no one imag-ined that it could be stopped. The British army had lost much of its heavy equipment in France and Belgium, and it was lucky that so many soldiers were able to escape the French disaster in the evacuation of Dunkirk.

But the British did not choose accommoda-tion. They did not trust Hitler. The lessons of Munich had taught them that he would never be satisfied with anything less than total control. A deal with Hitler would only give him time to pre-pare for the final kill. Despite their weak posi-tion, British hopes for ultimate victory became a national article of faith, and replaced rational analysis of immediate prospects. Britain's insularity, its partial isolation from continental Europe, became the country's chief asset. The English Channel gave no sure guarantee against invasion, yet in addition to the technical difficulties it posed for the Germans, it provided the British with substantial psychological security.

The best measure of the British response to this challenge lay in the fact that Churchill did not falter. He did not retreat within the home islands exclusively. Britain still had a powerful navy and a limited but effective air force, enabling her to keep imperial lifelines open. At home, much of the British preparation against invasion was busywork, undertaken to sustain morale. The real fight took place in the air, where the Royal Air Force denied the Germans air superiority and thereby ended the invasion threat. After this setback, a frustrated Hitler turned his attention eastward. If England could not be quickly vanquished, he thought, Russia could.

But before mounting the drive to the east Hitler decided to punish the British. This decision, more than any other single factor, helped spur American sympathy for Britain. The Battle of Britain, the daily bombing of London and other cities, became the leading story in the American press and on the American radio. Edward R. Murrow's vivid broadcasts from London during "the blitz" became an unforgettable experience for Americans, and helped strengthen resolves to aid Britain. At the same time British morale grew stronger. As Churchill put it: "I was glad that, if any one of our cities were to be attacked, the brunt should fall on London. London was like some huge prehistoric animal, capable of enduring terrible injury, mangled and bleeding from wounds, and yet preserving its life and movement. London could take it. . . . And at this time anyone would have been proud to be a Londoner." In the United States, many Americans shared the British pride.

RUSSIAN BLOOD

When the German army crossed the Russian border in June 1941, the Soviets had to trade manpower and land for time. This proved to be as true of their later advances as it did of their early retreats. The number of soldiers locked in combat on the eastern front ran into the millions. The Russians had a large, but poorly equipped army in 1941, and the Soviet government at first relied primarily on the Russian people's historic love for the motherland. Although in some areas, particularly in the Ukraine, the Germans received an initially friendly reception, most Russians fought against the German invaders (even behind the lines) with a determination that often bordered on fanaticism. Also the attempt by the German "master race" to subjugate the "inferior" Slavs rallied the Russians behind the Soviet government.

The Germans treated Russian prisoners of war like poor-quality cattle. Many of the hundreds of thousands captured in the initial campaign froze or starved to death during the first winter. German treatment of the civilian population in occupied areas proved equally harsh, especially after Soviet guerrillas began operating behind the lines. The Germans executed civilians in reprisals, sometimes at a rate of ten Russians for each dead German. This did not curb partisan activity. It merely made the peasantry and the villagers hate the Germans all the more. Any understanding of postwar Russian attitudes and policies toward Germany must take into account Russian fears of the recurrent German threat of invasion and the memories of German barbarism during World War II. Today, Russians remain determined to prevent the resurgence of German power.

It took several years, and millions of lives, for the Russians to adjust to the necessities of modern warfare. Eventually Russian war production reached a formidable level. Many factories were moved eastward to prevent capture by the Germans. Once Russian manpower could be fitted with a reasonable amount of firepower, the Red army began to fight the Germans in normal military terms. Reliance on superior numbers, however, remained constant. The manpower factor, the use of bodies as a substitute for armament, continued to influence the Red army's generals. General Eisenhower contrasted the American and Russian methods of clearing minefields: "Highly illuminating to me was [Soviet Marshal] Zhukov's description of the method of attacking through minefields. . . . It was always a laborious business to break through them, even though our [American] technicians invented every conceivable kind of mechanical appliance to destroy mines safely. Zhukov gave me a matter-of-fact statement of his practice: 'When we come to a minefield, our infantry attacks exactly as if it were not there. The losses we get from personnel mines, we consider only equal to those we would have gotten from machine guns and artillery if the Germans had chosen to defend the area with troops instead of with mines.' I had a vivid picture," continued Eisenhower, "of what would happen to any American or British commander if he pursued such tactics. And I had an even more vivid picture of what the men in any one of our divisions would have had to say about the matter if we attempted to make such a practice part of our tactics. Americans assess the cost of war in terms of human lives, the Russians in the overall drain on the nation."

Because the Russians heroically fought the Germans for three years before the Allies were ready to invade western Europe, the Russian army bore the brunt of the fighting against the Germans. For four years, the Nazis deployed over two hundred divisions on the eastern front. The Russians had more troops on the line than the Germans, probably at times twice as many. The major battles in Russia, the three-year seige of Leningrad, the fierce battles for the possession of the Crimean peninsula, and the massive decisive struggle at Stalingrad (now called Volgograd), all involved numbers of troops which dwarfed the size of Allied operations elsewhere, in North Africa and even in Italy. Not until the invasion of France in June 1944 did the American and British armies employ truly large numbers against the Germans, and that final campaign lasted ten months.

At the same time, Russia received considerable aid from the Allies. The importance of Lend-Lease supplies was undeniable, as even Stalin admitted. Yet the flow of war materiel in substantial quantities did not come until late 1943 and 1944. By that time the Russians had won the battle of Stalingrad late in 1942. And in the process Stalin had finally made a cohesive nation out of the Soviet dictatorship.

The eruption of the Cold War between the United States and Russia after 1945 should not blind Americans to the immense sacrifices the Russian people made, shedding oceans of blood to prevent Nazi victory until America was ready to commit its great might to the struggle. Total Russian casualties will never be known, but the nation lost at least ten million military and civilian dead. In addition, the Russians lost between twenty-five and thirty million population-gain in the process, if one includes the loss in natural growth due to wartime deaths. Only China matched Russia's high casualty figures, suffering even more than the Russians from lack of modern weapons. In short, the Russians made an essential contribution to the defeat of Hitler within three and a half years.

Bulldog British stubbornness led Hitler to turn east and make a fatal attack on Russia. Fierce Russian resistance stopped the Germans and cost them dearly. Thus Britain and Russia bought the time needed for full-scale rearmament by their American allies.

AMERICAN PRODUCTION

By the spring of 1942, the outlook for the United States appeared bleak. The Japanese had overrun much of Southeast Asia, and German submarines were sinking American vessels with impunity. But in retrospect it is clear that any attack on the United States which did not first cripple American industrial power amounted to national suicide. Once the productive capacity of the United States got into high gear, and once its young men could be equipped with modern weapons, an enemy who had not dealt an immediate knockout blow could expect retribution on an unparalleled scale.

Although the importance of the personal element in war is enormous, modern warfare is also a matter of machines and firepower. American factories and shipyards began producing military "hardware" at a fantastic rate. Since the government was the purchaser, few worried about cost. Many war contracts called for payment on a cost-plus basis. Thus rising wage rates and increased material costs not only were bearable, but a higher final cost increased the profit for the manufacturer. Organized labor, enjoying rising wages, agreed to a no-strike pledge and settlement of disputes with management by mediators from the government War Labor Board. Massive war spending from 1940 to 1945, not the deficit financing of the New Deal, in large part created an immense national debt which continued to grow because of the Cold War and Vietnam.

American industry had first to retool for war. Before Pearl Harbor some leading industrialists, doubting that the United States would become involved, did not convert their plants or make the necessary technical preparations for the rapid switch to wartime production. This was particularly true of the steel industry, which had not expanded facilities quickly enough. But by the end of 1942, American industry began pouring out war materiel in quantities which soon strained the ability of American military manpower to use it effectively. As a result the United States produced more than it needed and helped supply its allies, especially the British.

Much war production was too hasty and some of it was shoddy. Every factory tried to set a new production record. Some of the new cargo vessels, called Liberty Ships, cracked in half like eggshells in heavy seas. Some of the planes were clearly inferior to others, and American pilots quickly came to know which models they could rely on. Yet the staggering volume of so much production made the American fighting man the best supplied soldier in history. By the end of the war, whole communities of liberated people overseas were living on American discards and gifts, although only half of total American industrial production went to the war effort. The United States thus produced arsenals of guns, while Americans continued to enjoy considerable quantities of butter.

American production peaked in 1944. The United States turned out over 50 percent more in armaments than the Axis, and about half the total armament production of all fighting nations. Immediately after Pearl Harbor, the American Pacific fleet contained only a crippled battleship force and a half dozen aircraft carriers. But in the next four years the U.S. Navy amassed Pacific task forces of such magnitude and effectiveness that the Pacific became an American lake. Before entering the war, President Roosevelt had called for the yearly production of 50,000

planes. His critics ridiculed the figure as visionary. But from 2000 planes produced in 1939, American production jumped to an output of 92,000 fighting aircraft in 1944.

Americans did not simply turn out standard items in enormous quantity. American scientists had to develop synthetic products to meet shortages of raw materials. Rubber was particularly in short supply, and artificial varieties were developed to meet the enormous demand. Production of the first atomic bombs, an enterprise given the code name Manhattan Project, exemplified the union of advanced scientific thinking, economic might, and technological sophistication. In a short time, the Manhattan Project had installations throughout the country, employing large corps of scientists and technicians who worked on the construction of a nuclear bomb. In July 1945 the first bomb test proved successful, forever altering the nature of conflict among major powers.

The American cornucopia of war production provided the foundation upon which rested the cross-channel attack on France and the liberation of Europe. For almost two years the United States had been building up its forces in Britain. American and British planes bombed Germany day and night. By 1944 an entire American army, under the command of the General Dwight D. Eisenhower, waited in British camps. There were so many supply depots in Britain, the English quipped, that only their barrage balloons kept the island from sinking from the weight of American men and supplies. When D-Day came in June 1944, the English Channel appeared to contain more ships than it could hold, and more planes in the air than there were targets for them to strike. But enormous quantities of arms cannot prevent casualties entirely. Many men died that day and in the days that followed. The nature of the expedition and the tenacity of the German defense meant inevitable losses. But Allied firepower kept American and British casualties relatively light following the invasion of Normandy and throughout the war.

The Home Front

The Second World War became the most "popular" conflict in American history. The public supported the war effort almost unanimously, whereas in every previous conflict the country had been divided, divisions which sometimes hampered the government's conduct of military operations. But after Pearl Harbor, American men and women went to war if not gladly, at least readily. German and Italian Americans entered the armed forces and fought against the Axis powers with little consideration of former ethnic ties. The handful of Axis supporters within these groups were quickly silenced, some of the leaders being prosecuted for sedition. No general curtailment of civil liberties took place, nor did serious outbreaks of vigilantism occur. Americans did not stop listening to Beethoven or Verdi, nor did they give up sauerkraut or spaghetti for "patriotic" reasons. This confirmed the fact that assimilation of ethnic minorities of European origin had come faster than previous generations thought possible.

This sensible situation did not apply to Japanese Americans. Despite the fact that they had given no aid to the Japanese enemy, in early 1942 the army rounded up all Japanese in the Western states, United States citizens as well as aliens. Over one hundred thousand persons thus lost their constitutional rights, their liberty, their property, and were kept in "relocation" centers without regard to individual loyalty or past record of good citizenship. Although Washington had singled out Germany as the prime military threat, the Japanese remained throughout the war the principal psychological enemy.

Anti-Oriental prejudice, a sentiment with a long history in California, thus focused on Japanese Americans. Agricultural workers from Japan had been admitted back in the 1880s, since they were supposedly more docile than the Chinese, who had just been excluded as immigrants. But a strong reaction against the Japanese soon set in, producing discriminatory laws, school segregation, and finally total exclusion in 1924. When Japanese farmers started competing with other Americans as agricultural producers, Western states prohibited them from buying farmland. Racism bolstered the anti-Japanese campaign. According to the Los Angeles *Times* in the 1920s: "Japanese boys are taught by their elders to look upon American girls with a view to future sexual relations. . . . American womanhood is far too sacred to be subjected to

such degeneracy. An American girl who would not die fighting rather than yield to that infamy does not deserve the name." A group called the Native Sons of the Golden West promised to guard against the Yellow Peril. One nativist publication went all out, claiming that "the Japs pollute the communities like the running sores of leprosy. They exist like yellowed, smoldering, discarded butts in an over-full ashtray."

When war broke out in 1941 the nativist sickness soon became an epidemic. And the military situation during that first month of war was not conducive to cool, rational analysis. Hawaii had been bombed; rumors spread that the West Coast was vulnerable to Japanese attacks, perhaps even to invasion. The area military commander, General J. L. De Witt, ordered a curfew for all enemy aliens, but his real target was the Japanese. He told Washington that "the Japanese race is an enemy race, and while many second and third generation Japanese, born on United States soil and possessed of United States citizenship, have become 'Americanized,' the racial strains are undiluted." They constituted "112,000 potential enemies . . . at large." As for Japanese American passivity and apparent loyalty, De Witt had a theory: "The very fact that no sabotage has taken place to date is a disturbing and confirming indication that such action *will* be taken."

Washington agreed with this Alice-in-Wonderland "logic," giving De Witt a free hand. To the eternal shame of the United States, such decent men as Secretary of War Henry L. Stimson and President Roosevelt allowed the concentration camps to be filled, and most Americans felt more secure after the roundup in the Western states had been accomplished. They cited military necessity to justify the relocation, but this fooled no one. Most Japanese Americans on American soil lived not in California but in Hawaii, which was much more vulnerable to Japanese attack. Yet these U.S. citizens remained in their Hawaiian homes, subject to some security restrictions; and they remained loyal throughout the war, many of the young men fighting valiantly with the U.S. Army in Europe.

For the next three years, while the Japanese Americans remained imprisoned in camps in the Mountain States, the Supreme Court played with their fate. A case decided in 1943 upheld the curfew order. A year later in *Korematsu* v. *U.S.* (1944) the court divided over the case of a man who had refused to report for relocation. The majority supported the government, while one dissenter called it a case of "convicting a citizen as punishment for not submitting to imprisonment in a concentration camp"; another thought the government had gone over "the ugly abyss of racism." But since neither the presidential order nor a later act of Congress had mentioned *detention* of the Japanese Americans (the heart of the matter), the court could dodge the responsibility of ruling on the constitutionality of detention. The judicial evasiveness came on the heels of nearly a decade of liberalizing decisions which had expanded civil liberties dramatically. But the court's defenders could point out that it had generally upheld the president's use of war powers, and that the Japanese American cases were no exception.

After the war the government tried to erase the stain by apologizing and paying some compensation for lost property. The decline of anti-Oriental prejudice since 1945 has provided the best though belated recognition of the loyalty of Japanese Americans and has added a welcome final chapter to this human tragedy.

THE GRAND ALLIANCE CRUMBLES

Each major partner in the Grand Alliance made a singular contribution. Obviously all three displayed stubbornness in fighting, all shed their blood, and all produced war material. American bravery in battles at Iwo Jima or at Okinawa was as great as any nation could expect of its fighting men. And the United States also employed manpower in numbers far beyond any previous war effort. By the end of the war, close to fifteen million men and women served in the active armed forces of the United States. Yet the most important contribution of each partner lay in their specialized function: British stubbornness, Russian blood, and American production.

Together, they ended Hitler's dream of a thousand-year Third Reich, and destroyed Japan's self-serving "Co-Prosperity Sphere" in Asia. United, the Grand Alliance crushed the major threat to civilization in their time, Axis-Fascist expansionism in Europe and Asia. But Allied victory did not abolish the game of international power politics. After 1945 it resumed once more, but the game could no longer be played on the same terms.

The prospect of new conflicts became apparent even before the war's end, especially as a result of agreements made in the Crimean conference at Yalta in February 1945 by Roosevelt, Churchill, and Stalin. The Big Three had already met at Teheran, Iran, a year before, but after his reelection in 1944, Roosevelt requested another high-level meeting. Germany had been all but subdued by late 1944. Only the coming of winter postponed the final decision until the following spring. The postwar solution of the German question remained the key to a European settlement. Roosevelt, who also worried about the unfinished Pacific war, made an early mistake. He declined to meet Churchill privately for comprehensive pre-Yalta talks in order to approach the Russians with a single American-British stand. Still thinking that Stalin could be managed, Roosevelt kept many of his cards on the table with the Russian dictator. The military defeat of the Axis remained Roosevelt's primary concern, while Churchill had increasingly insisted on discussing the political consequences of military victory.

At Yalta, Stalin demanded that the Allies agree to divide Germany among them. Stalin would have gladly made the division then and there, but Churchill would not commit himself, although he accepted the principle of German partition. Churchill wanted France included as an occupying power in Germany since he feared the American army would not remain in Europe long. Stalin agreed, as long as the French zone came out of British and U.S. territory. All agreed that Germany should pay reparations for war damage. Stalin saw this as a method of permanently crippling German industrialism and militarism. His plan, subsequently carried out in the Soviet zone, was simply to cart away factories and the rest of the industrial apparatus which could be used in devastated Russia. But Roosevelt and Churchill did not want Germany to remain permanently enfeebled, though they favored reparations to help Germany's victimized neighbors to recover.

The future of Poland was another key issue.

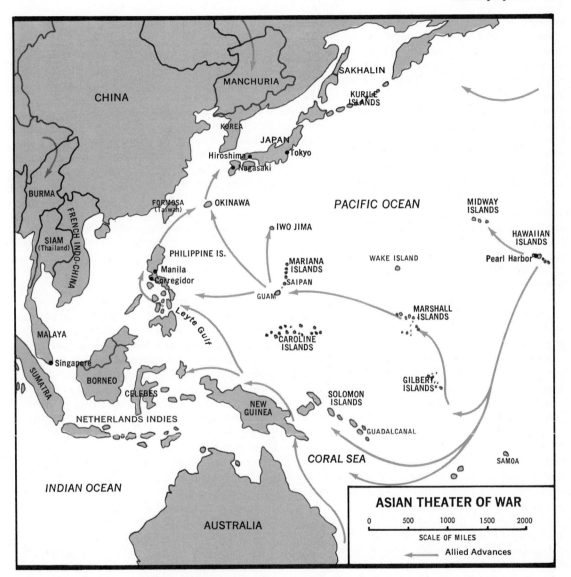

ASIAN THEATER OF WAR

SCALE OF MILES

Allied Advances

Two Polish governments, one in exile in London, and a Communist regime which the Russians had installed when they captured Poland from the Germans, vied for control. Roosevelt wanted to dissolve both provisional governments and set up a new, coalition regime, one which would not be hostile to the Soviets. Russia had made it clear that a friendly government in Poland was a necessity for security reasons. Stalin proposed broadening his puppet government by including some of the exiled pro-Western leaders. Then elections could be held. The presence of the Red Army in Poland had essentially settled the issue, however. With no alternative, Roosevelt and Churchill agreed but, significantly, Stalin brushed aside Roosevelt's suggestions for supervised elections. There was little Roosevelt could do but hope, by this time without much conviction, that Stalin would allow free elections. He did not.

Roosevelt desperately wanted the Soviets to enter the Pacific war, and cooperating with Stalin was the price. At that time Japan still appeared a formidable enemy. Japanese soldiers and airmen defended heroically each Pacific island, forcing American troops to take some of the heaviest losses in their history. The Japanese fighting man's code prohibited surrender. The prospect was for a long and bloody battle for the Japanese home islands themselves. Military men predicted that before the invasion most Japanese troops would be withdrawn from China and Southeast Asia for a final defense of Japanese honor on Honshu and Kyushu. The furious *kamikaze* attacks of suicide pilots on American warships off the Japanese islands substantiated this prediction. The long string of defeats since 1942 had not dampened the Japanese will to fight.

As early as 1943, Stalin indicated that he would enter the Pacific war, with the right inducements. His allies urged him to act after the defeat of Germany, despite the existence of a treaty between the Soviet Union and Japan. At Yalta, Stalin blandly asserted, and with a good deal of truth, "I only want to have returned to Russia what the Japanese have taken from my country, in the war of 1905." Roosevelt agreed to this and consummated the deal directly with Stalin, Churchill assenting later. These agreements meant that Russia would play an increasingly important role in Far Eastern affairs, especially in China, regaining special rights in Manchuria. But even without the agreements, Stalin would have turned eastward after Hitler's defeat. And because of the long border with China, Russian power would inevitably have been felt in that area before long.

The United States willingly made these paper commitments because of the presumed necessity of bringing Russia into the war. Russian help was expected to save thousands of American lives, in the event of an invasion of Japan. The first atomic bomb (which ultimately subdued Japan without an invasion) was not exploded until the summer of 1945. However well established the theory of atomic fission, as a weapon the bomb could not yet be counted on in February 1945. In May, Germany capitulated and Hitler committed suicide in his underground headquarters while above him Berlin burned. After two atomic bombs obliterated the cities of Hiroshima and Nagasaki, the Japanese surrendered in August.

Roosevelt had returned from Yalta worn out but optimistic. He told Congress, shortly before his death in April 1945, that he hoped Yalta would "spell the end of the system of unilateral action, the exclusive alliances, the spheres of influence, the balances of power, and all the other expedients that have been tried for centuries—and have always failed." The president felt, and most Americans then agreed, that he had gone far in laying the basis for a peaceful postwar world. Roosevelt reported: "We achieved a unity of thought and a way of getting along together. Never before have the major allies been so closely united." Events since 1945 made a mockery of that optimism. The transition from Grand Alliance to Cold War took but a few months. The changes had been coming for a long time. The United States could not become a major industrial power without becoming involved in world affairs. Americans were a world power whether they wanted to admit it or not. In the four years of the Second World War, Americans dropped the guise of noninvolvement and lost their innocence. Not only were they prepared to assume a major role in the postwar world, but the growing tension with the Russians and the start of the Cold War led the United States to forge a series of alliances which involved it in a worldwide struggle to curtail Soviet expansion. Americans no longer turned their backs on the outside world. A new era had arrived.

SUGGESTIONS FOR FURTHER READING

Suggestions for further reading are highly selective. Works available in paperback editions are starred (*). For additional references, students should consult William E. Leuchtenberg, *Franklin D. Roosevelt and the New Deal* (cited below), and A. Russell Buchanan, *The United States and World War II* (2 vols., 1964)*.

INTRODUCTION

General Works on the New Deal and the World Crisis

William E. Leuchtenberg, *Franklin D. Roosevelt and the New Deal, 1932-1940* (1963)*; Arthur M.

Schlesinger, Jr., *The Age of Roosevelt* (3 vols. to date, 1957—)*; James M. Burns, *Roosevelt* (2 vols., 1956-1970); Dennis W. Brogan, *The Era of Franklin Delano Roosevelt* (1950); Edgar E. Robinson, *The Roosevelt Leadership, 1933-1945* (1955); Dexter Perkins, *The New Age of Franklin Roosevelt, 1932-1945* (1957)*.

CHAPTER 29

General

Basil Rauch, *History of the New Deal* (1944)*; Frank Freidel, *Franklin D. Roosevelt* (3 vols. to date, 1952—); Rexford G. Tugwell, *The Democratic Roosevelt* (1957)*; Rexford G. Tugwell, *FDR: Architect of an Era* (1967); Daniel Fusfeld, *The Economic Thought of Franklin D. Roosevelt* (1955).

Election of 1932

Bernard Bellush, *Franklin D. Roosevelt as Governor of New York* (1958); Alfred B. Rollins, *Roosevelt and [Louis M.] Howe* (1962); Harold Gosnell, *Champion Campaigner: Franklin D. Roosevelt* (1952); Edgar E. Robinson, *They Voted for Roosevelt* (1947).

The First New Deal

Raymond Moley, *The First New Deal* (1966); Rexford G. Tugwell, *The Brains Trust* (1968)*; Bernard Sternsher, *Rexford Tugwell and the New Deal* (1964); Hugh S. Johnson, *The Blue Eagle—from Egg to Earth* (1935); Donald Richberg, *My Hero* (1954); Sidney Fine, *The Automobile Under the Blue Eagle: Labor, Management and the Automobile Code* (1963); Michael E. Parrish, *Securities Regulation and the New Deal* (1970).

    Van L. Perkins, *Crisis in Agriculture: The Agricultural Adjustment Administration and the New Deal* (1969); Dean Albertson, *Roosevelt's Farmer* (1961); Russell Lord, *The Wallaces of Iowa* (1947); Richard Kirkendall, *Social Scientists and Farm Politics in the Age of Roosevelt* (1966); Arthur Raper, *Preface to Peasantry* (1936)*.

Federal Relief

Josephine C. Brown, *Public Relief, 1929-1939* (1940); E. Wight Bakke, *Citizens Without Work* (1940); Donald Howard, *The WPA and Federal Relief Policy* (1943); Harry Hopkins, *Spending to Save* (1936); Searle F. Charles, *Minister of Relief: Harry Hopkins and the Depression* (1963); Betty and Ernest K. Lindley, *A New Deal for Youth* (1939).

The Miracle Workers

Donald McCoy, *Angry Voices: Left-of-Center Politics in the New Deal Era* (1958); David H. Bennett, *Demagogues in the Depression* (1969); Reinhard H. Luthin, *American Demagogues* (1954); Allan Sindler, *Huey Long's Louisiana* (1956)*; T. Harry Williams, *Huey Long* (1969); James Shenton, "The Coughlin Movement and the New Deal," *Political Science Quarterly*, vol. 73 (1958), pp. 352-373; Charles J. Tull, *Father Coughlin and the New Deal* (1965); Abraham Holtzman, *The Townsend Movement* (1963).

New Directions

C. Herman Pritchett, *The Tennessee Valley Authority* (1943); David E. Lilienthal, *TVA* (1944); Thomas K. McCraw, *TVA and the Power Fight: 1933-1939* (1971)*; Roy Lubove, *The Struggle for Social Security, 1900-1935* (1968); Edwin E. Witte, *Development of the Social Security Act* (1962); J. Joseph Huthmacher, *Senator Robert F. Wagner and the Rise of Urban Liberalism* (1968)*.

CHAPTER 30

General

George Wolfskill, *The Revolt of the Conservatives . . . the American Liberty League, 1934-1940* (1962); Otis L. Graham, Jr., *An Encore for Reform: The Old Progressives and the New Deal* (1967)*.

Court Fight

Edward S. Corwin, *Court Over Constitution* (1938); Robert H. Jackson, *The Struggle for Judicial Supremacy* (1941)*; Samuel Hendel, *Charles Evans Hughes and the Supreme Court* (1951); Alpheus T. Mason, *Harlan Fiske Stone* (1956); C. Herman Pritchett, *The Roosevelt Court* (1948)*; Wilfred E. Rumble, Jr., *American Legal Realism: Skepticism, Reform, and the Judicial Process* (1968).

Union Revolution

Irving Bernstein, *Turbulent Years: A History of the American Worker, 1933-1941* (1970); Milton Derber (ed.), *Labor and the New Deal* (1957); Irving Bernstein, *The New Deal Collective Bargaining Policy*

(1950); J. O. Morris, *Conflict within the AFL . . . Craft versus Industrial Unionism, 1901-1938* (1958); Walter Galenson, *The CIO Challenge to the AFL* (1960); Sidney Fine, *Sit-down: The General Motors Strike of 1936-37* (1969).

The Roosevelt Depression

Arthur W. Crawford, *Monetary Management under the New Deal* (1940); Allan S. Everest, *Morgenthau, the New Deal and Silver* (1950); John Morton Blum (ed.), *From the Morgenthau Diaries* (2 vols., 1959-1965); Kenneth D. Rose, *The Economics of Recovery and Recession . . . 1937-1938* (1954); Clay Anderson, "The Development of the Pump-Priming Theory," *Journal of Political Economy*, vol. 52 (1944); Arthur Burns and Donald Watson, *Government Spending and Economic Expansion* (1940); Henry H. Villard, *Deficit Spending and the National Income* (1941); Ellis Hawley, *The New Deal and the Problem of Monopoly* (1966); Gene M. Gressley, "Thurman Arnold, Antitrust, and the New Deal," *Business History Review*, vol. 38 (1964), pp. 214-231; James T. Patterson, *Congressional Conservatism and the New Deal . . . 1933-1939* (1968)*.

The Negro's New Deal

Raymond Wolters, *Negroes and the Great Depression* (1970); Leslie H. Fishel, Jr., "The Negro in the New Deal," *Wisconsin Magazine of History*, vol. 48 (1964); Gunnar Myrdal, *An American Dilemma* (2 vols., 1944)*; Dan T. Carter, *Scottsboro: A Tragedy of the American South* (1969); Robert L. Zangrando, "The NAACP and a Federal Anti-Lynching Bill, 1934-1940," *Journal of Negro History*, vol. 50 (1965); Frank Freidel, *F.D.R. and the South* (1965)*.

The Left

Robert P. Browder, *The Origins of Soviet-American Diplomacy* (1953); Frank A. Warren, *The Liberals and Communism* (1966); August R. Ogden, *The Dies Committee* (1945); Daniel Aaron, *Writers on the Left* (1961)*; James B. Gilbert, *Writers and Partisans: A History of Literary Radicalism in America* (1968); Irving Howe and Lewis Coser, *The American Communist Party* (1957)*.

New Deal Balance Sheet

Charles A. Beard and George H. E. Smith, *The Old Deal and the New* (1941); Paul K. Conkin, *The New Deal* (1967)*; Heinz Eulau, "Neither Ideology nor

Utopia: The New Deal in Retrospect," *Antioch Review*, vol. 19 (1959), pp. 523-537; Mario Einaudi, *The Roosevelt Revolution* (1959); Arthur M. Schlesinger, Jr., "Sources of the New Deal: Reflections," *Columbia University Forum*, vol. 2 (1959).

CHAPTER 31

General

Selig Adler, *The Uncertain Giant: American Foreign Policy Between the Wars* (1965); John E. Wiltz, *From Isolation to War, 1931-1941* (1968)*; Robert A. Divine, *The Reluctant Belligerent: American Entry into World War II* (1965)*; William L. Langer and S. Everett Gleason, *The World Crisis and American Foreign Policy* (2 vols., 1952-1953); Lloyd C. Gardner, *Economic Aspects of New Deal Diplomacy* (1964); Julius W. Pratt, *Cordell Hull* (2 vols., 1964); Henry L. Stimson and McGeorge Bundy, *On Active Service in Peace and War* (1947).

Manchuria and Moralism

William L. Neumann, *America Encounters Japan* (1963)*; Robert H. Ferrell, *American Diplomacy in the Great Depression* (1957); Richard N. Current, *Secretary Stimson* (1954); Armin Rappaport, *Henry L. Stimson and Japan, 1931-1933* (1963); Sadako N. Ogata, *Defiance in Manchuria . . . Japanese Foreign Policy, 1931-1932* (1964); Dorothy Borg, *The United States and the Far Eastern Crisis of 1933-1938* (1964).

Isolationism

Selig Adler, *The Isolationist Impulse* (1957)*; Herbert Feis, *1933: Characters in Crisis* (1966)*; Manfred Jones, *Isolationism in America, 1935-1941* (1966)*; Robert A. Divine, *The Illusion of Neutrality* (1962)*; Wayne S. Cole, *Gerald P. Nye and American Foreign Relations* (1962); John E. Wiltz, *In Search of Peace: The Senate Munitions Inquiry, 1934-1936* (1963); Brice Harris, Jr., *The United States and the Italo-Ethiopian Crisis* (1964); F. Jay Taylor, *The United States and the Spanish Civil War* (1956); Allen Guttman, *The Wound in the Heart: America and the Spanish Civil War* (1962).

Good Neighbor Policy

Alexander DeConde, *Herbert Hoover's Latin-American Policy* (1951); Bryce Wood, *The Making of the Good Neighbor Policy* (1961)*; Edward Guerrant, *Roosevelt's Good Neighbor Policy* (1950);

E. David Cronon, *Josephus Daniels in Mexico* (1960)*; Donald M. Dozer, *Are We Good Neighbors?* (1959).

Internationalist Counterattack

Robert E. Osgood, *Ideals and Self-Interest in American Foreign Policy* (1955)*; Charles A. Beard, *American Foreign Policy in the Making, 1932-1940* (1946); Charles C. Tansill, *Back Door to War: The Roosevelt Foreign Policy, 1933-1941* (1952); Donald F. Drummond, *The Passing of American Neutrality, 1937-1941* (1955); Basil Rauch, *Roosevelt: From Munich to Pearl Harbor* (1950); Wayne S. Cole, *America First: The Battle Against Intervention, 1940-1941* (1953); Walter Johnson, *The Battle Against Isolation* (1944); Mark Chadwin, *Hawks of World War II* (1968).

The Final Steps

Wayne S. Cole, "American Entry into World War II: A Historiographical Appraisal," *Mississippi Valley Historical Review*, vol. 43 (1957), pp. 595-617; T. R. Fehrenbach, *F.D.R.'s Undeclared War, 1939 to 1941* (1967); James V. Compton, *The Swastika and the Eagle: Hitler, the United States and the Origins of World War II* (1967); Saul Friedlander, *Prelude to Downfall: Hitler and the United States, 1939-1941* (1967); Alton Frye, *Nazi Germany and the American Hemisphere, 1931-1941* (1967); Warren F. Kimball, *The Most Unsordid Act: Lend-Lease* (1969); Raymond H. Dawson, *The Decision to Aid Russia, 1941* (1959); Paul W. Schroeder, *The Axis Alliance and Japanese-American Relations* (1958); Robert J. C. Butow, *Tojo and the Coming of the War* (1961).

CHAPTER 32

General

A. Russell Buchanan, *The United States and World War II* (2 vols., 1964)*; Robert A. Divine, *Roosevelt and World War II* (1969); Dwight D. Eisenhower, *Crusade in Europe* (1948)*; Omar H. Bradley, *A Soldier's Story* (1951); Douglas MacArthur, *Reminiscences* (1964); Henry H. Arnold, *Global Mission* (1949); Samuel Eliot Morison, *The Two-Ocean War* (1963).

Pearl Harbor

Herbert Feis, *The Road to Pearl Harbor* (1950)*; Roberta Wohlstetter, *Pearl Harbor* (1962)*; Charles

A. Beard, *President Roosevelt and the Coming of the War, 1941* (1948); Robert Ferrell, "Pearl Harbor and the Revisionists," *Historian*, vol. 17 (1955), pp. 215-233; Herbert Feis, "War Came at Pearl Harbor: Suspicions Considered," *Yale Review*, vol. 45 (1956), pp. 378-390; Ladislas Farago, *The Broken Seal: "Operation Magic" and the Secret Road to Pearl Harbor* (1967).

The Grand Alliance

John L. Snell, *Illusion and Necessity: The Diplomacy of Global War* (1963)*; Gaddis Smith, *American Diplomacy during the Second World War* (1965)*; Robert A. Divine, *Second Chance: The Triumph of Internationalism during World War II* (1967); Herbert Feis, *Churchill, Roosevelt, Stalin* (2nd ed., 1967)*; William H. McNeill, *America, Britain and Russia . . . 1941-1946* (1953)*; John R. Deane, *The Strange Alliance . . . Wartime Cooperation with Russia* (1947); Kent R. Greenfield, *American Strategy in World War II* (1963); Robert E. Sherwood, *Roosevelt and Hopkins* (1948)*; George F. Kennan, *Memoirs, 1925-1950* (1967)*.

American Production

Donald M. Nelson, *Arsenal of Democracy* (1946); Frederick C. Lane, *Ships for Victory* (1951); Walter W. Wilcox, *The Farmer in the Second World War* (1947); James P. Baxter, *Scientists Against Time* (1944); Leslie R. Groves, *Now It Can be Told* [the atomic bomb project] (1962); Francis E. Merrill, *Social Problems on the Home Front* (1948).

Imprisonment of Japanese Americans

Roger Daniels, *The Politics of Prejudice: The Anti-Japanese Movement in California* (1962)*; Dorothy S. Thomas, *The Spoilage* (1946)*; Morton Grodzins, *Americans Betrayed* (1949); Jacobus tenBroek, *Prejudice, War and the Constitution* (1954)*.

The Alliance Crumbles

Chester Wilmot, *The Struggle for Europe* (1952)*; John L. Snell, *Wartime Origins of the East-West Dilemma Over Germany* (1959); Anne Armstrong, *Unconditional Surrender* (1961); Gabriel Kolko, *The Politics of War . . . 1943-1945* (1968)*; John L. Snell (ed.), *The Meaning of Yalta* (1956)*; Athan G. Theoharis, *The Yalta Myths* (1970); Diane S. Clemens, *Yalta* (1971); Ruth B. Russell, *A History of the United Nations Charter* (1958).

Part Eight
Affluence and the Limits of Power

Introduction

In the decades following the end of World War II, Americans experienced unprecedented affluence and equally unprecedented anxiety over their national survival. The world's most powerful nation hung poised on a balance of terror that maintained the peace between the two superpowers, the United States and Soviet Russia. The Second World War altered the map of the world. Their resources drained, Britain and France reluctantly but unavoidably dismantled colonial empires and new independent nations arose in Africa and Asia to replace white colonial rule. The new Soviet colossus stood astride Eastern Europe as the area's number one power, determined to use its strength to spread Communism internationally but even more determined to guarantee its own security. The nations of Eastern Europe, seized from the Germans by the Red army, became Russian satellites; Germany underwent division between Russia and the West; two Germanies soon appeared, a "temporary" solution that now seems permanent. In Western Europe, the Communist parties grew rapidly after the war, feeding on the suffering of nations ravaged by four years of war, and came within striking distance of taking over Western governments in free elections.

Into this dangerous power vacuum stepped the United States, deploying its military and economic might as an umbrella under which Western Europe could recover from the war, get on its feet again, and its liberal capitalist politicians turn back the Communist challenge. By 1950, a tense power equilibrium maintained stability in Europe and defined the character of this Cold War. Both superpowers, armed with atomic weapons, as well as conventional forces, prepared to resist threats to their security, yet each remained wary of a self-destructive general war.

With Western Europe—second only to the United States in industrial development—safely protected behind the American shield, the zones of friction in the 1950s and 1960s shifted to Asia and then to the Middle East. Here the decline of open colonialism, and the emergence of often unstable new nations became entangled in the Cold War between the superpowers. First in Korea, later in Indo-China, the United States sought to contain Communist expansion, confident of duplicating in the Far East its success in Western Europe. But, in this case, experience proved to be a poor teacher. In 1949 China fell to a homegrown Communist movement that had been fighting a civil war there for over a generation. The United States refused to recognize Communist China, but nonrecognition did not exorcise the Red specter in Asia. And elsewhere in the Far East America met frustration. The United States successfully repelled an invasion of South Korea by Communist North Korea, but at a cost that left many Americans wondering whether they could or should afford another such "victory." Then, a decade later, it again intervened directly on the mainland of Asia— this time in Indo-China, where a Communist-led nationalist movement, centered in North Vietnam, threatened to gain control of the entire region.

The Indo-Chinese War turned into the longest, most inconclusive, and most brutal war in American history. It demonstrated that for all its military might, the United States was not all-powerful, and it set Americans to question whether the axioms of the Cold War and the containment policy it had generated were still applicable in the 1960s and 1970s. A split between Red China and the Soviet Union, together with the stabilization of East-West relations in Europe, altered the nature of the Communist challenge. Yet the world was not necessarily safer. Superpowers armed to the teeth with the most sophisticated and devastating weapons man had ever devised were still locked in an arms race that devoured national wealth on both sides of the Iron Curtain, and threatened the world with nuclear destruction. That danger became all the more possible when the Middle East joined Asia and Europe as a testing ground in the Cold War. As the principal ally of the new Arab nations, the Soviet Union supplied them with arms to conduct a prolonged war with Israel, a Zionist island in an Arab sea, whose existence depended on support from the United States. At stake was control of the Middle East, with its limitless oil reserves.

The balance of terror inevitably influenced Americans at home. The long struggle with Communist Russia and the difficulty of resolving conflicts among nations weakened American self-confidence. Unable to crush the threat of Communism overseas, some Americans hunted for Communist "subversives" at home. A new Red Scare made millions of loyal Americans afraid of being falsely accused by those who mistook democratic self-criticism for disloyalty. Full employment came back during the Second World War and continued afterwards. Unparalleled economic prosperity helped counterbalance the climate of fear generated by the Russian-American Cold War, however.

At first, Americans uncritically accepted the material comforts of affluence. A generation that had known the Great Depression was in no mood to examine too critically a system capable of putting two cars in many garages. But not all Americans shared in the affluence. Poverty persisted, especially in rural America and among blacks who had resumed the Great Migration from the South to the North during World War II when good-paying jobs beckoned. While the affluent took to the green suburbs, the cities of America filled up with poor people and became monuments to neglect. The environment, too, received little attention from a complacent majority ready to accept polluted air and water, urban blight, and a disfigured landscape as the price for enjoying the highest standard of living in the world.

Complacency could not hold the line forever. When the black ghettos in most of American major cities erupted in 1965–1967, when hundreds of thousands of college students rebelled against the American way of life, preferring drugs to chocolate sundaes, when a youth culture sprang up that repudiated the cherished values of the older generations—hard work and accumulation of money, respect for elders and repressed sexuality—the United States clearly faced a profound internal crisis.

The button business, 1960s. "You pays your money and you takes your choice." *(George W. Martin, dpi)*

"I have a dream." March on Washington rights, 1963. *(George W. Martin, dpi)*

Honoring the war dead, 1970. *(Tower News Service)*

"Keeping America free." *(Tower News Service)*

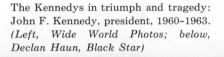

The Kennedys in triumph and tragedy:
John F. Kennedy, president, 1960–1963.
*(Left, Wide World Photos; below,
Declan Haun, Black Star)*

The longing for peace in a country at war, America, 1969. (*Hap Stewart*)

The Kennedys mourn: The death of Robert Kennedy, 1968. *(Werner Wolff, Black Star)*

"Nobody Knows the Trouble I've Seen." The family of Martin Luther King mourns his death, 1968. *(Harry Benson, Black Star)*

A dream denied. Demonstration after the assassination of Martin Luther King, 1968. *(Claus Meyer, Black Star)*

I·HAVE·A·DREAM

New York march against drugs, opiate of the alienated. *(Tower News Service)*

Students in revolt, Columbia University, 1970. *(Editorial Photocolor Archives, Inc.)*

President Johnson briefing Richard Nixon on foreign policy, 1968. *(Wide World Photos)*

Puerto Rican Day Parade, New York City, 1970. Banner: The Party of the Young Lords Serves and Protects Its People. *(Tower News Service)*

Saving America, 1970. *(Tower News Service)*

President Nixon delivering
his State of the Union
Message, January 23, 1971.
(Wide World Photos)

Chapter 33
The New Confrontation

After World War I, Americans had pulled back from the responsibilities of world power, confident that the defeat of German militarism left the world safe for democracy and left the United States secure. Immune from Europe's woes for most of their history, Americans relished the safety of their isolation, an illusion they clung to until engulfed, barely prepared, in the Second World War.

World War II permanently ended American isolation. Americans had learned at severe cost that in an interdependent world, made smaller by modern communications and made more dangerous by modern weaponry, no hiding places remained. In 1919, America's allies had quickly moved into the vacuum left by American withdrawal, and the great powers of Europe once more managed the volatile balance of power. In 1945, however, the war left Britain and France devastated and exhausted, unable to play their traditional great power roles. At the same time, the war also pushed another American ally, Soviet Russia—almost knocked out by Hitler in 1941–1942—into the unaccustomed position of the leading land power in the world; and in 1949 Russia also became the second atomic power. Determined to protect their national security, the Russians turned Eastern Europe, which they had captured from the Germans, into a region of Communist satellite states, standing as a buffer between them and the West.

Alarmed by Soviet expansion, its European allies enfeebled, the United States assumed responsibility for maintaining the balance of power. The watchword of American postwar policy was Containment, its aim to prevent the spread of Russian power into Western Europe as well as other parts of the world. Abandoning the precedents of seven generations of American leaders who had preached against foreign alliances, the United States spent billions of dollars to rebuild Western Europe and maintain the largest peacetime military force in its history. A prolonged struggle between the two superpowers

locked in a Cold War threatened to explode into a nuclear confrontation that would cover the planet with radioactive dust.

THE COLD WAR

Wartime cooperation between Russians and Americans had been a marriage of convenience based on mutual interests arising out of immediate *military* needs. Many nations had combined to defeat the Axis powers, but whenever the Allies discussed the postwar world, their unity dissolved. Each of the "Big Five"—Britain, France, Russia, China, and the United States—angled to advance its own interests. Roosevelt, however, sought to mediate, especially between Stalin and Churchill, two hard-liners whose belief in the primacy of national interests and the virtues of traditional balance-of-power politics conflicted with FDR's internationalist aspirations. Roosevelt declined to play the game. Committed to abstract principles of international justice and self-determination for all peoples, he concentrated on getting along with Stalin through fair and open treatment and insisted on giving top priority to winning the war. At war's end, this policy left a logjam of unsolved political problems whose settlement would determine the shape of the postwar world.

Although Roosevelt had entered the war asserting his preoccupation with American self-interest, in contrast to Wilsonian idealism, his conception of the peace settlement often resembled that of the president under whom he had served twenty-five years earlier as assistant secretary of the navy. Once again the United States sought a "universalist" solution which entrusted the task of keeping the peace to the United Nations, a new world organization founded in San Francisco in the spring of 1945 shortly after the death of FDR. Like Wilson before him, FDR groped for a substitute for the balance of power, a system which had always ended in war.

To avoid repeating Wilson's mistakes in the fight over the Treaty of Versailles, Roosevelt cultivated bipartisan Republican support for his foreign policy and he won GOP approval of the United Nations (UN). Yet the creation of the UN did not strip the big powers, Russia, and the United States, of their ability to protect their own interests. In the UN Security Council, the focal point of decision-making, each of five powers— the United States, Great Britain, France, Russia, and China—had a veto which could stymie action by the majority. This was a realistic and necessary arrangement, since no major power would agree to be bound by the votes of others, yet it also determined that the UN would become mainly an arena for debate, not action, in the Cold War.

Roosevelt's sudden death in April 1945 elevated to the presidency Vice-president Harry S Truman, a little-known former Democratic senator from Missouri. Truman personified the American Political Dream. In contrast to FDR's upper-class origins, Harry S (the "S" stood for nothing) Truman came from humble origins; his career had been so undistinguished that first his nomination for the vice-presidency and later his elevation to the presidency raised the eyebrows of most and the fears of many. After service in World War I as an artillery officer, Truman tried his hand as a haberdasher but failed. Short on formal education, he nevertheless attached himself to the ruling and corrupt Pendergast machine of Kansas City. A decade's obscure and loyal hard work earned him a seat in the Senate in 1934. Truman remained obscure during the New Deal decade, but made a reputation during the Second World War by his able handling of the Senate investigation of war production and profiteering. When Roosevelt, for reasons of political expediency, dumped Henry Wallace as vice-president in 1944 in favor of Truman, it seemed that the Missourian had advanced as far as he could or *should*.

Truman withstood the first shocks of diplomatic battle at the Potsdam summit conference, held in Germany in July 1945. Joined by Britain's Clement Attlee, who had just defeated Winston Churchill at the polls, the two inexperienced but tenacious Western leaders clashed with Stalin on all major issues. At Potsdam the Allies proved conclusively that they could not agree. Stalin demanded that the West accept Russian domination of Eastern Europe. The Western Allies refused and insisted on free elections in the Eastern European countries that were quickly becoming Russian satellites. But Stalin proved immovable. With Soviet troops in control of the area, no way existed short of war for the United States to wrest Eastern Europe out of Russian control.

Truman returned from Potsdam in a gloomy mood. No issues had been settled satisfactorily, and many had to be postponed. At the same time Truman became convinced of Soviet intransigence, agreeing with the earlier warning of the American ambassador to Russia W. Averell Harriman: "Words have a different connotation to the Soviets than they have to us. When they speak of insisting on 'friendly governments' in their neighboring countries, they have in mind something quite different from what we mean."

Roots of the Cold War

At the outset of the Cold War, most Americans regarded Russian control of Eastern Europe as part of a Communist design for worldwide expansion of its revolutionary ideology. In fact, both superpowers insisted first on protecting their national security. For the Russians this meant keeping a tight grip on Eastern Europe, territory conquered by the Red army. Alarmed by Russia's emergence as a superpower, and fearful that unless the West contained Soviet expansionism the balance of world power would shift adversely, the United States decided to apply counterpressure. Equally threatening for many Americans was the fact that Communist ideology preached world revolution and that Russia enlisted the aid of an international Communist movement. But for all its internationalist preaching about working-class solidarity and the need for revolutionary unity, Russia, ruled by its iron-fisted dictator, Joseph Stalin, sought above all else to build up its own power.

Stalin demanded regional security for Russia. He trusted no one, not even his closest advisers in the Kremlin, and certainly not the Western democracies. In 1919, with Soviet Russia weak, the West had created a *cordon sanitaire* along Russia's western borders, consisting of militantly anti-Bolshevik, Balkan countries. Now in 1945, with his armies in control, Stalin insisted on docile, pro-Soviet states in the area. In the Far East, Stalin had obtained concessions that restored Russian power as it existed before 1905 in exchange for a promise to enter the fight against Japan, a campaign cut short when the atomic bomb forced a quick Japanese surrender.

From the Russian point of view, this policy seemed logical and reasonable, but Americans thought otherwise. Some hoped for continued American-Soviet cooperation after the war and those hopes died hard. If only the Russians would permit free elections in Poland and the rest of Eastern Europe; if only they would accept reasonable reparations from Germany, an amount that would not denude Germany, leaving it industrially helpless (and powerless to attack Russia again); if only they would accept at face value American guarantees of Russian security. If these points were accepted, a liberal peace could be preserved. A majority of Americans, however, soon became convinced that Communists were never to be trusted, that the Russians would use any means, even war, to achieve world domination.

These fears, though plausible at the time, proved to be exaggerated. Of course, Stalin wanted to gain as much as he could without risk, in territory and in economic privileges. Yet the Soviet's main desire was freedom to expand into the rim of territories that surrounded Russia, the result of victory in war and the overriding need to assure Russian security. Once these gains were digested, Russia might look further afield to the industrial complex of Western Europe, or to the oil fields of the Near East, for example. The prospect of Soviet expansion into these areas alarmed Americans who interpreted Russian moves in Eastern Europe (always a marginal area in big power politics) as the prelude to world conquest.

So each side, Russia and America (East and West), girded for battle in a Cold War. Each went on the "defensive," convinced that the other side had taken the offensive and was threatening its vital interests. Fear fed fear, and hostility intensified, as Russia adopted a policy of *Consolidation and Probing* and America pursued a policy of *Containment*. The United States regarded any change in the status quo—in Greece, Iran, or Poland—as a threat to the balance of power, while the Soviets, possessing for the first time the power to act on their fears, would no longer tolerate being surrounded by hostile, capitalist nations.

CONTAINMENT IN PRACTICE

Containment meant the abandonment of universalism and the acknowledgment that the big powers, each with its own spheres of influence, sought to achieve a balance favorable to its interests. Although remaining within the United Nations (which never could play the role of impartial arbiter envisioned for it), the United States now sought to contain Soviet influence within the areas already occupied or dominated by Russia. Washington regarded any further expansion, especially into Western Europe, as a threat to American security. As George F. Kennan, the State Department's leading theoretician of Containment, epitomized American foreign policy: ". . . the main element of any United States policy toward the Soviet Union must be that of a long-term, patient but firm and vigilant containment of Russian expansive tendencies." Far from being a Bolshevik-hating hard-line ideologue, however, Kennan went on to argue that "the Kremlin is basically flexible in its reactions to political realities." The United States, he warned, must not force the Russians into a corner or provoke unwanted confrontations. But in 1947, Kennan's call for "firm and vigilant containment" received much more attention than the rest of his argument.

Thus, as conceived by Kennan and American foreign policy planners, Containment represented a compromise between the unattainable hopes of the liberal internationalists for friendlier relations with "Uncle Joe" Stalin on one hand, and the dangerous insistence by hard-line conservatives on a "roll back" of Russian power on the other. Instead America would hold the line, blocking further extension of Russian power, and hope that in time firmness would induce the Soviets to abandon aggressive designs and recognize that the West did not plan to launch a Holy Crusade for the eradication of Bolshevism in Russia.

Containment was contingent on the economic recovery of Western Europe. Left prostrate by the war's devastation, France and Italy saw the rise of powerful Communist parties, profiting from the economic catastrophe. The rebuilding task was enormous and complicated by the status of Germany—formerly the main Axis power, and now at the mercy of the Allies. Germany had been divided into four zones of occupation (the same arrangement also existed in Berlin, although the capital city lay deep in the Russian zone). It soon became apparent that Germany would not be reunified for many years, if ever. The weaker it remained, the more secure the Russians felt, and a demilitarized nonindustrial Germany offered the Soviets the greatest security short of genocide.

Late in the war some American leaders had toyed with the idea of "pastoralizing" Germany, but this view never became American policy. The start of the Cold War quickly snuffed it out. Early in 1946, the United States suspended further reparations payments to Russia from the Western zones of Germany. This ended cooperation between the former allies, and the Americans pushed for unifying the non-Russian zones, accomplishing the step a year later. By 1947, two Germanies existed and the United States counted on a revitalized West Germany to contribute significantly to the economic recovery of Western Europe.

Germany lay devastated, yet all Europe had been victimized by the war, winners as well as losers. Britain, clearly exhausted, seemed on the verge of collapse, and France, Italy, and the smaller nations of West Europe experienced economic deprivation and internal unrest compounded by the especially severe winter of 1946–1947. The British used up an American loan of several billion dollars much faster than anticipated, clearly indicating that the hope for European economic revival depended on American aid. The Russians were not responsible for the economic crisis in Western Europe, but they and the Communist parties of the West clearly stood to gain should the condition persist.

Truman Doctrine and Marshall Plan

The war left Britain so weak that after 1945 it could no longer play a big power role, especially in the eastern Mediterranean. Early in 1947, Britain informed the United States that after March of that year it would have to cut off military and economic aid to Greece and Turkey. The British decided in 1947 to pull back not only from Greece and Turkey but to abandon their Palestinian Mandate and to grant independence to India. With a civil war raging in Greece between Communist guerrillas and the Western-backed monarchy, unless the United States filled the vacuum created by Britain's departure, Greece might fall to the Communists, and Turkey would be hard pressed to withstand Russian demands for access to the Mediterranean. President Truman and his new secretary of state, General George C. Marshall, convinced congressional leaders of the gravity of the situation, and on the advice of Republican Senator Arthur Vandenberg, Truman addressed Congress in person, asking for $400 million in aid to Greece and Turkey.

Truman contended that the United States must "support free peoples who are resisting attempted subjugation by armed minorities or by outside pressures. . . . The free peoples of the world look to us for support in maintaining their freedoms." The Truman Doctrine of 1947 gave formal recognition to the fact that the United States and the Soviet Union were locked in a Cold War. Greece and Turkey, whose governments were antidemocratic, suddenly became part of that "Free World" which the United States pledged to defend against Soviet aggression. Playing on the threat of Communism rather than relying on a cool-headed analysis of strategic considerations, Truman got his way, demonstrating the effectiveness of Cold War rhetoric.

With the eastern flank of non-Communist Europe shored up, the United States now turned to strengthening Western Europe—always the area of key concern for the United States. In June 1947 Secretary Marshall called for a massive and long-range program of economic aid to rebuild Europe. The Marshall Plan's tone was positive and humanitarian rather than stridently anti-Communist, in contrast to the Truman Doctrine. The United States invited *all* Europe to participate—though its sincerity was not tested, since Russia would not join or allow its satellites to do so. Marshall, explaining the genesis of his plan, warned that "governments, political parties, or groups which seek to perpetuate human misery in order to profit therefrom politically or otherwise will encounter the opposition of the United States."

European recovery carried a high price tag. Truman asked Congress for almost $7 billion to get the Marshall Plan started, a sum which amounted to a revival of Lend-Lease—in peacetime. Congress debated the plan sharply, but though it meant reversal of America's traditional, peacetime foreign policy, approval came with surprising ease. Republican Senator Vandenberg assured it bipartisan support, as he did for the other major elements of Truman's foreign policy. A Communist coup which overthrew the coalition government of Czechoslovakia in 1948 and Russian economic pressure to cut off the Western zones of Berlin made the Marshall Plan, now called the European Recovery Program, even more urgent. It became law in late March 1948.

How near Western Europe would have come to Russian domination in the absence of American action is unclear. The Marshall Plan, however, made this question academic. As West Europe's economy recovered, the chances of Communist election victories in France and Italy receded. American capital goods and loans spurred a remarkable industrial recovery over the next decade and ended the danger of Communist takeover in Western Europe because of internal decay. The Russians boycotted the plan, after briefly hesitating, and attacked it as a plot on behalf of American imperialism. Yet they acknowledged its appeal among their satellite nations by starting a mini-program of their own, the Molotov Plan.

Berlin Blockade

Russia responded to the American initiatives in the Mediterranean and Western Europe with the Berlin Blockade. The immediate issue was the customary sore spot of East-West relations, Germany. The Russians, understandably fearful of any resurgence of German power, had fruitlessly argued for four-power control of the industrial Ruhr to block Western zone unification and prevent German economic recovery. The Western powers, however, now looked to the revival of West Germany, with its enormous industrial base, as a counterpoise to Russian expansion. When the three Western powers adopted one currency for their zones, moving an important step closer to unification, Russia retaliated by closing surface access to Berlin.

The crisis brought the world to the brink of war. The United States would not allow West Berlin to be lost by default, a victim of Russian strangulation. Although it had the right to supply Berlin by rail and river barge, the United States lacked the military strength to enforce its right at that time. In the two years after the war, the United States had demobilized 80 percent of its armed forces. And any hostilities, however limited, might touch off a larger fight. Washington decided on an airlift. For nearly a year, a city of two and a half million people received food and fuel by air. A bridge of American and British transport planes threaded the narrow air lanes, landing every three minutes at one of Berlin's clogged airfields. The city needed a minimum of 4000 tons of supplies a day. The airlift eventually brought in three times that amount, a tremendous logistical feat and a great propaganda victory for the West.

Both sides seemed to learn something from the incident. Neither pressed for total victory; each accepted a nonsolution which approximated the situation existing before the crisis began. Americans did not try to ram through an armored convoy; Russians did not try to interfere with the transport planes. Such limitation of aims and restraint prevented the Cold War from becoming a Hot War. When the Russians finally called off the Berlin Blockade in May 1949 it was clear that West Germany's anti-Communist, heavily populated, and industrialized areas would remain in the Western sphere and that American military strength in the center of Europe would continue to block Russian expansion. The Soviets would have to live with that fact, just as the West had had to accept the reality of Russian domination in Eastern Europe. The Cold War had a "front," the middle of Germany—and a "no man's land," the divided city of Berlin.

THE FAIR DEAL ELECTION

During his first three years as president (1945–1948), Truman sustained his forceful foreign policy despite a drastically reduced military establishment. Within a year and a half of war's end only 20 percent of America's fifteen million men under arms remained in uniform. The demand for rapid demobilization had been irresistible, since few Americans foresaw a Cold War between the two great wartime allies.

Millions of veterans became job seekers, competing with other millions formerly employed in war plants. Prices continued to shoot upward, because wartime restraints on consumer goods ended, but producers could not supply a public starved for goods unavailable during the war. Labor unions, no longer bound by the wartime no-strike pledge, reacted to the rise in living costs by demanding higher pay. It appeared that the conversion of the American economy to peacetime production could not be accomplished smoothly. Truman and the Democrats, the party in power, got the blame in the congressional elections of 1946, when the Republicans regained control of Congress for the first time in eighteen years, capitalizing on disgust with inflation, meat shortages, and fear of labor unrest.

The GOP, responsive to the business interests that controlled the party, moved to curb organized labor. Unions had come a long way since the stormy days of the late 1930s. With greater strength than at any time in its history, organized labor militantly defended its economic interests during the inflationary spiral of postwar conversion. Strikes in defiance of the government by railroad and mine workers aroused widespread public hostility toward Big Labor, which, some argued, had gained excessive power to interfere with vital production and services. President Truman himself denounced the railroad union leaders as irresponsible and unpatriotic, and threatened to draft striking workers. After the Republican victory in the 1946 elections Senator Robert A. Taft of Ohio, leader of the conservative Republicans, spearheaded a move to reduce the power of unions and particularly to curb strikes that created national emergencies. The Taft-Hartley Law thus put a brake on the growth and power of organized labor, giving employers new weapons with which to resist collective bargaining, particularly in the unorganized sectors.

Truman, recognizing that the union workers provided a major foundation for the Democratic coalition he hoped to sustain, vetoed the Taft-Hartley bill in a stinging message, and he later called the act a "slave labor" law. Congress overrode the veto but the president, year after year, demanded repeal. At the same time, with an eye to the approaching 1948 election, Truman tried to rekindle the New Deal by bombarding Congress with requests for more low-income public housing, national health insurance, and stronger civil rights guarantees to black Americans. Truman's program, which had no chance of passing through a hostile, Republican Congress, became the president's "Fair Deal," the platform on which he would base his reelection campaign. Truman refused to believe that liberalism was dead. Any other course would have left him without a constituency and without a program, though he knew that trouble awaited him no matter what he said or did.

The president's political problems grew each month as the election of 1948 approached. Despite a defiant State of the Union message to Congress ten months before the election, few gave him much chance for success. The doubters included leading Democrats, some of whom favored drafting General Dwight D. Eisenhower. Old New Dealers doubted Truman's liberal credentials from the time he entered office, nor did his first year in office restore confidence as one after another of Roosevelt's close advisers left the administration. In addition, Truman did not possess a commanding personality. He seemed a man of very limited talent, a second-rate political hack produced by a corrupt urban machine. Even the big city Democratic bosses wanted to dump him, convinced that he could not win. But Truman, though obviously worried, would not cave in. "I was not brought up to run away from a fight," he wrote later with pride. "Supposedly scientific predictions that I could not win did not worry me one bit." In control of the party machinery, and without a formidable rival for his party's nomination when Eisenhower refused to encourage a Democratic draft movement, Truman easily won the nomination.

Confident of victory, Republicans renominated their losing 1944 candidate, Governor Thomas E. Dewey of New York, who represented the party's moderate, Eastern establishment. Dewey was capable, he had made a good reputation as New York City district attorney and then as governor, and he had plenty of organizational help and money for his campaign. But he sorely lacked the personal touch, the ability to create an image with which voters wish to identify, or any of that magnetism which can transform a political campaign from farce into folklore. The colorless, slick, trimly mustached Dewey (once described by Theodore Roosevelt's daughter as "the little man on top of the wedding cake") multiplied his problems by assuming that he had the election won and that he could safely ride into the White House after a perfunctory campaign. Every political expert, including many Democrats, agreed.

Republican confidence seemed well founded, especially after rebellious Democrats broke away from both ends of the party's spectrum. First, left-wing Democrats under Henry Wallace formed a Progressive party. Wallace, a vice-president under Roosevelt, had been fired as secretary of commerce by Truman in 1946. Convinced that the Cold War had been started by the United States, that the Russians harbored no aggressive ambitions, and that Truman had abandoned FDR's policy of friendly relations with Stalin under pressure from imperialist-minded Big Business, Wallace found support among some radical labor leaders and intellectuals, and among the organized political left, including the Communist party. On the right, Truman faced defections from Southern Democrats who bolted to form a states' rights Dixiecrat party. Truman had gambled on retaining Southern support despite the strong civil rights plank pushed through over Southern opposition at the Democratic convention. Fearing that the Wallace Progressives would cut heavily into the Democratic vote in the vital urban-industrial states of the Northeast, Truman saw the civil rights issue as a means of keeping white liberal and black votes. When Dixiecratic Southerners, whose racist policies had never before been challenged in the national Democratic party, unexpectedly walked out, Truman's chances sank even lower.

The Truman Strategy

The underdog, with nothing to lose, Truman took the offensive. He called a special session of the Republican-dominated Congress to consider his party's convention platform, with every expectation that Congress would do nothing. The Republicans fell into Truman's trap, and the president then went to the country, scrappily denouncing the "do-nothing" Republican Congress, a charge that had potent popular appeal. Touring the country intensively, Truman reached directly almost six million people in hundreds of whistle-stops in small towns, and in the cities, where he poured forth his folksy, combative oratory that had the crowds shouting "Give 'em Hell, Harry!" Most of all Truman played on fears that a Republican victory would endanger the gains millions of Americans had made under the New Deal, and would "put Wall Street back in the saddle." His campaign proved particularly effective in the normally Republican farm belts, convincing prosperous farmers that renewed Republican rule would endanger their economic interests. Dewey, on the other hand, took the high road, declining to answer Truman's charges or exaggerations. As one observer wrote of Dewey: "The candidate, with his crisp executive manner and his rich commanding baritone, exuded so much confidence that he put his followers to sleep."

The election returns rudely awakened the Republicans. They proved that Truman had turned the tide during the campaign and achieved victory through a crazy-quilt electoral pattern. Each of the major candidates lost his banner section: Dewey carried the normally Democratic Northeast, and Truman carried the Republican farm belt. The president also carried the West and enough of the South to win with just slightly less than 50 percent of the vote. Progressive and Dixiecrat defections had hurt, but Truman squeaked through, thanks in part to Republican ineptitude, but mostly because of the continued loyalty of most of the elements that had made the Democrats the majority party since the New Deal.

Truman's victory also produced a Democratic Congress, but except for expansion of old programs such as public housing after 1948, the

Fair Deal never materialized. Southern Democrats who had stymied FDR in the late 1930s cemented their working coalition with conservative Republicans. The Southerners now had an additional goal: to defend white supremacy and block new demands for civil rights by the Northern wing of their party. Thus despite Truman's dramatic personal vindication, the 1948 election did not break the deadlock in American politics existing since the collapse of the New Deal in 1937. Moreover, the Cold War thrust domestic reform from the center of the stage. The Marshall Plan cost $5 billion between 1949 and 1950, or one-eighth of the federal budget, leaving little money to meet domestic needs. Truman gave top priority to Containment. The Cold War now became more dangerous than ever, as both sides entered into a full-scale arms race, which produced military alliances and Russia's first atomic bomb in 1949, and became a duel of thrust and counterthrust that ended in the limited Korean War of 1950–1953.

THE NATO ALLIANCE

The United States regarded European economic recovery as only one step in the restoration of a balance of forces in Europe that would contain Russian expansion. The Soviet takeover of Czechoslovakia together with the Berlin Blockade in 1948 made it imperative to strengthen quickly the West's military defenses. The North Atlantic Treaty Organization (NATO) provided the vehicle for achieving this strength. A multinational agreement, ratified in 1949, NATO represented as great a break with the American past as the Marshall Plan.

Since 1947, the United States had moved toward accepting long-range military commitments in Western Europe, since no one else could defend the area at the time. NATO formalized the shift. It became America's second military alliance, and its first in peacetime, since the alliance with France during the American Revolution. After that the United States had avoided "entangling alliances." During World War I it insisted upon "association," not alliance, with Britain and France. But under NATO, a dozen

nations in Western Europe and North America declared that "an armed attack against one or more [signatories] . . . shall be considered an attack against them all." The commitment to defend Western Europe with large American forces stationed in Germany warned Russia that any attack on West Germany meant war with America and its allies. In addition, the United States hoped that its monopoly on atomic weapons would further deter Russian expansion. Late in 1949, however, Russia exploded its first atomic bomb, ending the American monopoly. Now, both nuclear powers found themselves gripped in a "balance of terror," stockpiling atomic weapons that were useless except as retaliation. Since the United States could no longer frighten the Soviets by waving the Atomic Big Stick, a buildup of conventional forces in NATO became more urgent. Britain and France could not, or would not, supply sufficient troops to defend Europe, so the burden fell on the Americans, who insisted on the rearmament of West Germany with small-sized units integrated into the NATO command. Eventually West Germany would exact a price. From a conquered province it would quickly become a prosperous, sovereign ally, a transformation that alarmed the Russians, whose fears of German revival bordered on paranoia.

The Marshall Plan and NATO ended America's historic policy of avoiding peacetime *political* entanglements overseas. The United States became the West's international policeman, a role formerly assumed by Great Britain. Though far from American shores or immediate spheres of interest, Greece and Turkey became American protectorates (entering NATO in 1952), while the U.S. Navy patrolled the eastern Mediterranean to back up these commitments and take up the slack left by the British.

Also, the United States became the leading power in Western Europe, subsidizing the economies and rearmament programs of many nations. Reversing the rapid and large-scale demobilization after World War II, American armed forces in Europe were steadily rebuilt as part of NATO. In 1951 General Eisenhower returned to Europe as supreme commander of combined NATO forces. The Cold War had turned the clock back, but not to the happier days of the Grand Alliance. Europe as usual got first priority while Asian problems, many of them considered insoluble, mounted. The shaky stability achieved in Europe in the late 1940s provided no model for responding to challenges in the Far East.

THE ASIAN QUAGMIRE

Truman had responded effectively to the possibility of Russian military expansion in Western Europe. But the success of the Truman Doctrine, the Marshall Plan, and NATO in containing the Soviets offered little help in meeting the problems the United States faced in Asia. There, as in Europe, the Second World War fundamentally shifted the balance of power. It temporarily eliminated Japan, formerly the leading power in Asia, and left China weak and vulnerable to the revolutionary force of a local Communist movement that had been fighting for a generation to wrest control away from the Nationalist regime of Chiang Kai-shek. At the same time, European colonial empires were crumbling in the face of a surging Asian nationalism and the inability of the war-weary French, British, and Dutch to maintain their overseas outposts.

American Asian policy, the Open Door with a sprinkling of open imperialism, evolved in an earlier age. In 1900 Asians, except for the Japanese, did not participate in decision-making regarding their continent's fate. China then lay prostrate, saved from total partition among European powers only by the rivals' distrust for one another. Another large Asian country, Japan, had achieved industrial miracles in thirty years, but in 1900 it was not yet ready for full competition with the Western big powers. Nationhood for India seemed more remote than ever, and other smaller Asian societies simply did not count in the world of power politics. But in 1914 and 1939 the world's great Western powers went to war, touching off what Asians described as European civil wars. Europe's self-inflicted troubles generated Asian aspirations for self-determination.

One by one, Asian colonies gained independence. The United States, which had little formal empire to lose, finally granted independence to the Philippines in 1946, while maintaining economic arrangements and military bases that left the new Philippine republic within the American orbit. In 1947 Britain reluctantly granted independence to India, though many Britons nourished illusions that Great Britain could continue to hold its empire. The Dutch, victims of German occupation during the war, also thought they could hold on to their "East Indies." They were wrong, and in 1949, Indonesia, a nation of 90 million persons, was born. France proved more reluctant to abandon Indo-China. As a result, a Communist-led but nationalist guerrilla war against the French in Vietnam began in 1946, and eight years later the defeated French finally left North Vietnam to the Vietnamese. The southern half became an American protectorate in 1954.

American policy generally followed an anti-imperialist course. Washington normally favored the dismantling of European colonialism, realizing that the force of Asian nationalism was too powerful to resist, and that only the United States had the power to defend European imperial interests, a massive effort it was unwilling to make. It seemed far wiser to cultivate the new, independent nations, hopefully protecting American interests in the area and developing strong regimes that would resist Communist pressures.

Emergence of Red China

But that option was not available in China, where a fierce civil war raged, and where the United States had become hopelessly entangled as an ally of the regime of Chiang Kai-shek, a government whose days on the Chinese mainland were numbered. During the Second World War, the Chinese theater of action became an enormously bloody stalemate involving three forces: the invading Japanese, the Nationalist government of Chiang Kai-shek (who had American support), and the Communist troops of Mao Tse-tung operating in the northwest provinces. Under American prodding both Chinese groups finally devoted more of their energies to fighting the Japanese than one another. But civil war was sure to follow the defeat of Japan. The Japanese surrendered in 1945 to two victorious Chinese armies: the Nationalists, the official government of China; and the Red army, the military arm of the Communist revolution. Since Chiang ruled most of the country but could not crush the Reds in their strongholds, American advisers hoped to incorporate the Communists in the government. But neither Chiang nor Mao had any intention of forming a coalition regime; each side remained confident that it could crush the other on the battlefield.

Success for Chiang's Nationalists required immense American aid and the loyalty of the bulk of the Chinese people. America furnished aid but it could not manufacture popular support for a regime identified by Chinese peasants and workers with exploiting landlords and capitalists. Hopelessly mired in corruption, Chiang's Kuomintang party could not govern, nor did his generals fight well. The United States viewed Nationalist China as a sinking ship that could be salvaged perhaps only by a full-scale commitment of American troops on the Asian mainland. Though Republicans blamed the "fall of China" on Truman and the Democrats, alleging "softness" on Communism, a war to save the bankrupt Chiang regime was politically unthinkable. By late 1949 all China except the island of Formosa fell into Red hands.

The outcome of the Chinese civil war inevitably damaged American prestige and power. In contrast to the success the United States enjoyed in resisting Communism in Europe, Mao Tse-tung's triumph seemed to some Americans the result of political bungling, if not treason, in Washington. In fact, America could have assumed a much stronger position in Europe than it could in China, but many Americans, living under the anxiety and threat of war since 1941, and unable or unwilling to acknowledge that American power had its limits, insisted that China could have been saved.

The Korean War

When war broke out in Korea in 1950 the United States once more faced the danger of becoming bogged down in an Asian quagmire. Korea, a Japanese colony between 1895 and 1945, had been promised independence at the end of the war. But as with Germany, the Americans and Russians created two zones of temporary occupation which they refused to abandon. The result was two Koreas, one backed by the Americans and the other by the Russians. In June 1950 Communist North Korea attacked the South, which immediately looked to Washington for aid. United States ground forces had been pulled out of Korea the year before in compliance with the recommendations of American military advisers calling for a defensive perimeter off the Asian mainland. Secretary of State Dean Acheson had announced early in 1950 that neither Korea nor Formosa formed part of the American military commitment.

The North Korean invasion forced a hasty reconsideration. Truman hoped that a limited response, first military supplies for South Korea, then American air support, would stem the invasion, but only the American army proved able to stop the advancing Communists. The president called on the United Nations to brand the North Koreans the aggressors and authorize an international army to repel them. The Soviets, then boycotting the United Nations because it denied membership to Red China, were not present to veto the intervention resolution. The United States furnished nearly all of the foreign troops fighting in Korea, but the use of the United Nations' name and flag proved useful in the international propaganda war. Truman next ordered to Korea the only two American divisions stationed in Japan, a move considered safe since the Japanese had tamely submitted to American military government under General Douglas MacArthur since 1945. In addition, the U.S. Navy threw a protective shield around Formosa, insulating what was left of Nationalist China from attack by the mainland.

At first American forces in Korea found themselves backed into the Korean peninsula's southeastern corner, a bare foothold. But reinforcements poured in steadily, and General MacArthur (now both boss of Japan and UN commander in Korea) launched a spectacular amphibious assault near Seoul, Korea's capital, which sent the Communists retreating northward. Here, MacArthur made a fateful decision which Washington accepted: he did not stop at the 38th parallel, which divided the Koreas, but pushed forward, seeking to occupy all of North Korea. Disastrously miscalculating Chinese intentions, MacArthur ordered his troops to the Chinese border. Red China then attacked in force and sent the Americans reeling back south of the 38th parallel. The effect of this defeat on the American public was staggering, stirring memories of the gloomy months in early 1942. But in the case of Korea, Americans had not been convinced by their government of the need for a full-scale military commitment in a little-known Asian country.

The Chinese drive finally stalled, and MacArthur reestablished a front close to the original dividing line, the 38th parallel. There, the two forces remained deadlocked, with Koreans, Americans, and Chinese dying daily in a seesaw exchange of a few hills that altered neither side's military fortunes. Eventually both sides agreed to negotiate while the fighting continued sporadically.

General MacArthur, tied down by limitations set in Washington, and stung by his own blunder concerning Chinese plans, urged expansion of the war. At a minimum he wanted to bomb Chinese staging and supply areas in the Manchurian "sanctuary" and to blockade China. Truman refused, fearful of nuclear confrontation with China's ally, Russia, should the war in Asia expand. This further strengthened MacArthur's apprehensions over American overcommitment in Europe. Counting on Republican support, he then tried to sidestep the president by appealing openly to public opinion in the United States. Truman, though furious, tried to silence MacArthur privately. But the general, about whom it had been said, "There but for the grace of God, goes God," felt he could win the contest of wills. "I was operating in what I call a vacuum," he claimed haughtily. "I could hardly have been said to be in opposition to policies which I was not aware of even. I don't know what the policy is now."

No president could ignore such insubordination or allow the desires of a field commander in one area to govern United States global policy. In April 1951, Truman stripped MacArthur of his commands and ordered him home. Although the president's constitutional right to do so was

never in doubt, Republican right-wingers threatened to impeach the president. Without accepting all his ideas, Republicans used MacArthur (they made him the keynote speaker at the GOP convention in 1952), realizing he had considerable mass appeal and could hurt the Democrats. MacArthur had insisted that "in war, there is no substitute for victory"; but he failed to add that to achieve victory in Asia there could be no substitute for millions of American troops. His proposals boiled down to all-out war with China, and most Americans, Republicans as well as Democrats, found that unacceptable.

Korea presented a novel and trying predicament for the United States. Congress had not declared war, yet hundreds of thousands of Americans, most of them draftees, fought in an Asian "police action" as soldiers of the United Nations. Peace negotiators met almost daily while the armies continued to maul each other. Since 1941, American military doctrine placed increasing reliance on air power, yet the Air Force could not strike at enemy bases across the Yalu River in Manchuria. This rejection of total war in Korea contrasted with the World War II experience, and caused frustration among millions of Americans. In both world wars, the United States had entered the conflict "cleanly," with few clearly demarcated international interests and even fewer acknowledged international responsibilities. By 1950, however, America had made itself responsible for the defense of Western Europe, a pledge which compelled it to keep the Korean conflict limited. Russia pursued a similar policy, for both major Cold War powers saw the key to world power in the industrial base and advanced societies of Europe. Neither Korea nor China, therefore, were worth the unlimited commitment the United States had made in Western Europe.

THE NEW RED SCARE

The disappointing outcome of the Second World War, the constant tensions of the Cold War, and the gnawing frustrations of an undeclared but deadly stalemate in Korea inevitably infected American politics. Communists presented primarily an external military threat to the United

States; but to rally support for Cold War policies and the sacrifices they entailed, the Truman administration defined the issues for the American people not as an international power struggle, but as a battle between the Forces of Light and the Forces of Darkness, of liberty versus tyranny, of Western freedom struggling against Communist slavery.

Consequently many Americans came to believe that an International Communist Conspiracy threatened the very existence of their Free World. These oversimplifications ignored the fact that Russia, like America, had to protect legitimate security interests, and that Communism's main danger came not from a mystical, semireligious ideology, but from the industrial might of the world's second most powerful nation. To be sure, much truth lay behind the simplistic tenets of American Cold War rhetoric. The freedom people enjoyed in Truman's America was utterly foreign to Stalin's Russia, with its omnipresent secret police and labor camps for dissenters or mere suspects. Nevertheless, the exploitation of fear of Communism produced a paranoia in the United States which betrayed the nation's noblest traditions of individual freedom and resulted in a decade of hysteria and repression far worse than the Red Scare of 1918–1920.

The postwar anti-Communist hysteria began well before Senator Joseph R. McCarthy of Wisconsin perfected the techniques of Red witch-hunting and exploiting the nation's Cold War anxieties; and it has survived in muted form since McCarthy's death in 1957. President Truman led the way with the introduction of a federal loyalty-security program that investigated the political beliefs of government employees, touching off the New Red Scare. In 1947, stung by right-wing criticism and accusations that he and the Democrats because of softness on Communism had permitted many Reds and pro-Communist fellow-travelers to infiltrate the government, Truman ordered a loyalty check of all federal employees. Although any government has the right to demand loyalty of its workers, in practice the burden of establishing such loyalty shifted to those federal employees under suspicion. The difficulty of proving a negative became

more complicated when the government added a check on *security* as well as loyalty. Thus persons who might be subject to blackmail (such as alcoholics or homosexuals) lost their jobs as security risks. Since loyalty and security checks were administrative reviews, not court trials, suspects did not have the right to confront or cross-examine their accusers. Any damaging information, true or not, verifiable or ridiculous, could be and often was placed in the suspect's file. Such practices filtered down from Washington to state and local governments, school boards, and private employers. Defenders of the review programs claimed that loyal Americans had nothing to fear; but the use of innuendo, hearsay evidence, and intimidation of suspects proved otherwise.

The Fear of Subversion

The New Red Scare's central proposition was the myth that Communists, aided by uncounted thousands of American sympathizers in high places, were on the verge of taking over America. It gained plausibility from several spectacular cases of spying and disloyalty. A Justice Department employee was caught passing information to a Russian diplomat, and avoided jail only because the government had obtained evidence illegally through wiretapping, further angering those who felt that Communists were being "coddled." In 1950 Julius and Ethel Rosenberg were convicted and later executed for transmitting atomic secrets to the Russians during the war. Many ex-Communists appeared before congressional investigating committees to testify about their past activities and inform on their former comrades. Often unreliable and self-serving, the witnesses painted a lurid picture of a vast Red spy network extending into every aspect of American life, knowledge of which was the special preserve of the professional informer, making it harder than ever for an alarmed public to distinguish between accurate and inaccurate charges.

The outstanding postwar controversy over Communist infiltration involved Alger Hiss, a former State Department official. In 1948 Whittaker Chambers, an ex-Communist who had become an editor of *Time* magazine, told the House

Un-American Activities Committee that during the 1930s he and Hiss had belonged to a Communist cell and that Hiss had given him secret government documents. Hiss denied the charges under oath, challenging Chambers to repeat them without the protection of congressional immunity. The accusations shocked the nation, since Hiss had an impeccable background, and was head of the prestigious Carnegie Endowment for Peace. He had served in the New Deal during the 1930s and attended the Yalta conference in a minor capacity. He also worked in the group that founded the United Nations in 1945. Hiss's denials led to an indictment for perjury, and although many distinguished Americans, including several Supreme Court justices, testified as character witnesses in his behalf, the first trial ended in a hung jury. After a second trial jury found him guilty, Hiss went to jail for five years. Hiss's conviction lent substance to the long-standing charges of right-wingers and some Republicans that the New Deal had been tainted by Communism, and they used the outcome of the trial to discredit a whole generation of reformers.

Congress soon entered the picture in 1951 by passing the Internal Security Act and a new immigration law, the McCarran Act, sponsored by a conservative Democratic senator, which attempted to insure American security in ways which clearly jeopardized civil liberties. Aimed principally at Communist organizations and their members, the laws called for subversives to identify themselves by registering with the government and labeling their printed material; and it facilitated deportation of suspected aliens. Most of the provisions of these laws have since been declared unconstitutional by the Supreme Court, but while in force they clearly indicated the temper of the times during the New Red Scare.

The Cold War inevitably got into the courts, raising again the problems of sedition and political dissent. Several years before the repressive legislation of 1951 could be tested, other cases stemming from older laws arose. The Taft-Hartley labor law of 1947 required that union officials file affidavits with the NLRB avowing that they were not Communists or Communist supporters. In *American Communications* v. *Douds* (1950) the court's majority upheld the requirement,

arguing that Communist-led strikes were more political in nature than strikes called by "normal," bread-and-butter unions. The government might thus legally prevent such political interferences with interstate commerce. Justice Hugo Black, the only dissenter, retorted vainly: "No case cited by the Court provides the least vestige of support for thus holding that the commerce clause restricts the right to think."

The loyalty-security program also produced significant judicial twists. In 1951, the court ruled: first, that the public listing by the U.S. attorney general of organizations he deemed subversive, without notice and without a hearing, was unconstitutional; but, second, that the government had the right to fire an employee because of membership in one of the attorney general's blacklisted organizations. "So far as I recall," observed dissenting Justice Robert H. Jackson, "this is the first time that this Court has held rights of individuals subordinate and inferior to those of organized groups. It is justice turned bottom side up."

But the court majority felt otherwise and went on to sustain the most effective anti-Communist law, the Smith Act of 1940, which prohibited *advocacy* of the overthrow of the government. Passed hastily as a wartime anti-subversion measure, the statute lay dormant for eight years. But in 1948, eleven top leaders of the U.S. Communist Party were found guilty of violating the Smith Act after a marathon trial. Although no proof existed of an actual conspiracy, Communist leadership itself was deemed sufficient evidence of illegal advocacy. In *Dennis* v. *U.S.* (1951), Chief Justice Frederick M. Vinson tried to square his decision with the "clear and present danger" rule: "Obviously it cannot mean that before the government may act, it must wait until the *putsch* is about to be executed, the plans have been laid, and the signal is awaited." He felt that the gravity of the Communist threat justified "such invasion of free speech as is necessary to avoid the evil."

Thus the court upheld a law which made writing and speaking a crime. In that Cold War setting it appeared that the revolution in civil liberties, which had flowed from the Holmes-Brandeis dissents of the 1920s and had burst forth in the 1930s, might be abandoned. Justice William O. Douglas, who called the Red leaders "miserable merchants of unwanted ideas," nevertheless sustained their right to hold hated opinions: "To make a lawful speech unlawful because two men believe it, is to raise the law of conspiracy to appalling proportions." How appalling it might become, no one could then tell.

McCarthyism

Widespread fear of Communism invited exploitation by politicians. Richard M. Nixon, for example, first won election to the House of Representatives from California in 1946 by smearing his opponent as "soft-on-Communism," and he later played a prominent role in the Hiss investigation. But the master witch-hunter was Senator McCarthy. Few human beings can hope to contribute their names to the language, yet this honor fell to Joseph R. McCarthy. The frustrations of the Cold War created the temptation to blame a few individuals for "the mess." Some politicians seized on this and peddled the nonsense view that liberal, fuzzy-minded "pinkos" who had been taken in by the Soviets, and who in some cases had supposedly sold out to Russia, were responsible for the nation's woes. Senator McCarthy perfected the politics of anti-Communism and McCarthyism.

McCarthy grew up in a large and poor family in Wisconsin. He worked hard and educated himself with an intensity that paid off with election to the U.S. Senate in 1946. He made no mark at all for three years, but early in 1950 McCarthy decided to take the strong, anti-Communist road to prominence and reelection. He told a Republican Women's Club that the government, especially the State Department, was "thoroughly infested with Communists," and that Secretary of State Acheson, "that pompous diplomat in striped pants with a phony British accent," was covering it up. These accusations summed up the McCarthy approach: broad charges of Communist infiltration, combined with slashing attacks on the Eastern liberal establishment, in this case personified by Secretary Acheson, the haughty Ivy Leaguer of polished manners and a limitless self-assurance that McCarthyites

found infuriating. The McCarthy-Acheson confrontation became as much a clash of cultures as of politics. The senator, a Catholic, roused much enthusiasm among conservative Republicans, who relished his abrasive attacks on the Eastern establishment, and among Democratic "ethnic" voters in Eastern and Midwestern cities, who saw in anti-Communism a means of asserting their patriotism and their claims to 100 percent Americanism.

Despite McCarthy's national prominence and the frequency of his investigations (often conducted alone, as a one-man subcommittee), he turned up very little. He made specific charges, such as the claim that he knew of fifty-seven Communists in the State Department, but failed to substantiate them; the genuine revelations of Communist espionage were the work of others. Nevertheless, McCarthy pressed on and threw fear into other politicians and government bureaucrats. Few dared to speak out against his demagoguery, not even the Republican candidate in 1952, the war hero, General Dwight D. Eisenhower. Eisenhower, who had served under General George C. Marshall during the war, shared a campaign platform with McCarthy and agreed to delete some words of praise for General Marshall from his speech. McCarthy had charged Marshall, one of the most respected figures in American military and diplomatic history, with "selling out" China to the Reds. McCarthy, chanting his slogans of "twenty years of [Democratic] treason" and referring menacingly to "the Truman-Acheson gang," attempted to push American politics from the middle of the road into the gutter.

The Republican victory in 1952 temporarily increased McCarthy's power, but the Red-hunter had a tiger by the tail. When he began attacking the Republican administration, and even Eisenhower himself, he sealed his doom. A televised Congressional hearing turned into a verbal riot. It pitted McCarthy against the Department of the Army and enabled millions of Americans from the comfort of their homes to take a close look at the Wisconsin demagogue. Soon after, the Senate voted to censure McCarthy. The rebuke broke his spirit and the embittered, hard-drinking McCarthy died four years later, still remembered but no longer feared. A product of Cold War tensions, McCarthyism, whether the work of the senator or others, was one of several episodes in a series in American history when paranoid fears of enemies within momentarily gained sway over tolerance and common sense. This time, as in the past, political paranoia fed on frustrations. For most of their history, Americans had managed to have their own way, but a world power stalemate on the battlefields of Korea forced them to co-exist with a hostile Soviet Union in a world hanging in the balance of nuclear destruction. The United States proved susceptible to McCarthyism with its false but attractive explanation and easy remedy for the country's problems: clean out the traitors, and American greatness and invincibility would be restored. In the process McCarthy shook but did not destroy traditional institutions. He terrorized the civil service, the mass entertainment industries, parts of the press, and the foreign service. Yet most of organized religion, education, and the press—the very centers of establishment power McCarthy hoped to topple—held firm against him.

The elevation of Eisenhower to the presidency in 1953 doomed McCarthy. The average American had more confidence in the new grandfather figure who promised peace and security than in a shifty-eyed senator who specialized in manufacturing fear.

Chapter 34
The Affluent Society

By the end of the Second World War two of the goals that had eluded private enterprise and the New Deal during the 1930s had been achieved: full employment and economic prosperity. The American economy, prostrated in the early 1930s, recovered very slowly and eight million Americans still remained without jobs in 1940. For a decade the nation's productive capacity had not found enough customers to keep it working full time; then a new world conflict taxed it to the limit. The federal government became the biggest consumer, making insatiable demands for armaments, planes, ships, tanks, uniforms, and thousands of other items necessary to fight a global war. The economic might of the United States proved to be its greatest weapon in the struggle against the Axis powers.

As victory approached in 1945, most Americans, scarred by the experience of the Depression, feared that the end of the war would also mean the end of prosperity and a return to the economic stagnation and deprivation they had known in the 1930s, and that with the end of massive government spending for war business would sag, again throwing millions out of work.

Such gloomy forecasts proved mistaken. Instead, in the quarter century since V-J Day in August 1945, the American economy has achieved levels of prosperity and a degree of stability few had thought possible. It took Americans the three centuries since the Pilgrims landed at Plymouth in 1620 to develop an economy that produced goods and services worth $140 billion. In the next twenty years (1940-1960) the GNP swelled to over $700 billion. The *increase* alone exceeded the *entire growth* of national wealth in the preceding three hundred years.

America, the world's richest nation since the end of the nineteenth century, now became fabulously affluent. The age of mass consumption that it had inaugurated in the early twentieth century now fulfilled its potential for transforming the standard of living of the masses. Automobiles became the principal means of transportation and a powerful symbol of postwar affluence. As public transportation went into decline, government built thousands of miles of highways to accommodate the hordes of autos. Affluence enabled millions who had never before owned a car to acquire one. The same thing happened with other consumer durables, from washing machines to telephones, which became nearly universally available and no longer regarded as luxuries.

The new goods and expanded services transformed the American standard of living. Most students reading this book would hardly recognize the material world in which their parents grew up, and certainly not their grandparents' world. The previous generation did not own cars as teen-agers, nor could they watch television, eat frozen food (a dubious blessing), fly in a jet plane from city to city, wear clothing made of synthetic fibers, listen to transistor radios and stereo sound systems, or enjoy the comfort of air conditioners. Nor did they find their names transposed into numbers on computer punch cards.

Equally as important as these quantitative and qualitative material changes in mid-twentieth-century America was the stability of the productive system. Once locked in the seemingly unbreakable grip of the business cycle, with its periodic booms alternating with periodic busts, postwar Americans apparently had learned to tame major cyclical dislocations. Mass unemployment no longer haunted the United States; the much milder "recession" replaced the "panics" and depressions which had come every twenty years before 1929. Millions growing up in postwar America knew almost nothing of the fears of insecurity and deprivation which haunted their parents.

THE FOUNDATIONS OF AFFLUENCE

High-level consumer demand and continued government spending produced postwar economic prosperity. The Second World War put most Americans to work and for almost five years war production naturally took priority over civilian production. New cars, for instance, were not available because government commanded the resources of the auto industry to produce jeeps, tanks, and even planes. The same held true for countless other consumer goods, especially durable items. When the war ended an enormous pent-up demand burst forth for goods that people could not afford during the Depression and which were unavailable during the war. Consumer savings accumulated in the early 1940s became consumer purchases in the late 1940s as people rushed to buy what had been first unattainable and then unavailable. This kept manufacturers busy producing cars, washing machines, and refrigerators. At the same time the construction industry built millions of new homes, especially in the expanding suburbs. During the Depression, badly needed homes went unbuilt; after the war a construction boom exploded. Between 1946 and 1958 thirteen million new homes went up. Residents of the central cities, especially young couples starting new families, fled by the millions to suburbia. A million and a half New Yorkers left the nation's biggest metropolis for the suburban hinterlands between 1952 and 1962, creating a strange new world of bedroom communities and shopping centers.

The Baby Boom

Prosperity also contributed to a population boom. From 132 million in 1940 America grew to a nation of 180 million by 1960, a rate of growth unmatched by any other industrial nation, dramatically reversing the sluggish growth rate of the period between the two world wars. With millions of American males in the armed forces between 1941 and 1945, the rate of family formation fell. The postwar marriage and baby boom more than made up for lost time. The birth rate jumped 25 percent, holding at this new high level for most of the 1950s. Full employment after 1945 ended the negative pressure the Depression had exerted on early marriages and large families. Economic security enabled young people to marry earlier and encouraged couples to have more children. Americans were living longer too. Life expectancy of white males rose from 46 years

(1900) to 66 years (1958). Tuberculosis, historically the chief killer disease, proved no match for more hospitals and new drugs. By the 1950s auto accidents killed three times as many Americans as TB.

By the 1960s, the population boom began tapering off, though the rate of growth still remained relatively high. For one thing, the newly developed oral contraceptive quickly caught on with young women and facilitated birth control. As the postwar generation reached maturity in the 1960s, it proved more inclined than its parents to adopt family planning. Young wives went to work to boost family income before beginning to raise children. Young men and women in the 1960s, accustomed to the comforts of affluent homes, found that when they formed their own households they might not be able to afford to maintain the style of life they had known before leaving home. Their parents, in contrast, having lived through the Great Depression, had experienced a rapid improvement in living standards after 1945 which encouraged larger families.

As population and family formation grew rapidly, consumer demand kept pace. The resulting demographic surge sustained high levels of consumer demand in the 1950s even after the immediate postwar buying spree slackened. Millions of new families required millions of additional homes, cars, and appliances. This created jobs that filled the workers' pockets with cash to buy goods that in turn kept the factories humming.

Automobiles more than ever provided the basis for an affluent economy. By 1960 cars represented almost 10 percent of consumer expenditures, compared to 6.5 percent a dozen years earlier. In the late 1920s the auto industry had stagnated, after saturating demand at existing levels and distribution of national income. But by the 1950s family income had advanced so much that autos became almost universal. The replacement market alone now kept Detroit busy, while the new market for second cars for wives and third cars for teen-agers spurred production. In 1961 Americans junked five million cars and trucks.

Americans have always been in love with cars. In the postwar era they finally had enough money to prove their devotion. In the 1950s auto sales averaged 7 million a year, so that near the end of the decade 67 million cars and trucks were on the road. Consolidation within the industry had advanced so far that the Big Three—General Motors, Ford, and Chrysler—produced 95 percent of all autos manufactured in the United States. Detroit, and businesses allied to the auto industry, employed millions of workers. Service stations and motels sprang up everywhere, and the Auto Age reached maturity. In 1956 Congress authorized construction of a 40,000-mile interstate highway system. These multi-lane, limited-access, and high-speed roads would be used by both pleasure and commercial traffic, with the federal government paying 90 percent of construction costs.

Affluent America produced affluent cars. Models became longer, gaudier, and laden with decorative chrome. Ominously, they also became more powerful and dangerous. Detroit waged a horsepower war, enlarging its gas-hungry engines and stressing fast getaway and speed in its advertising, to produce what one writer called "The Insolent Chariots." As highway deaths rose, the National Safety Council began making holiday weekend predictions of the carnage and urging prudent driving, but to no avail. Intellectuals and social critics objected to these trends, and derided the tail fins sticking uselessly out of the car's rear end. But the average car buyer's infatuation with the chariot remained unshaken. Bigger and more expensive cars made the man behind the wheel feel bigger and more successful.

GIANT ENTERPRISE

At the heart of the business system stood giant corporations such as General Motors and American Telephone and Telegraph (AT&T). The average firm grew bigger and at a faster rate than before. Five hundred of the largest corporations by the 1960s produced half of all the country's goods and services. Three corporations—General Motors, Ford Motor Company, and Standard Oil of New Jersey—earned more income than all the farms in America, and GM's income amounted to eight times that of New York State and one-fifth of the federal government's.

The big corporations tightened their grip on the productive system, achieving unprecedented financial stability and autonomy. Small businesses continued to operate, but they were risky and suffered from a high rate of failure. Big Business, on the other hand, enjoyed virtual immunity from economic disaster. United States Steel, for example, has not sustained a loss in over twenty-five years, the same condition holding true for most leading corporations. For many of the giants, at least, America was no longer a profit *and loss* economy. Nor did the giants have to depend on outside sources for investment capital. Though securities markets provided some funds, the bulk came from undistributed profits, 60 percent of which were ploughed back into capital expansion in the late 1940s. This gave Big Business some measure of independence from Wall Street, and further increased its power.

Management became the undisputed top dog. Affluence increased the numbers of Americans owning corporate stock, and although shareholders in theory owned the enterprises, top management continued to run things. Both the highly dispersed shareholders and the boards of directors elected by stockholders to oversee their interests customarily deferred to the corporate managers. Secure in their control of the firm, management also achieved immunity from the danger of price competition in the marketplace and of effective enforcement of the antitrust laws in the courts. In the leading sector of industry, such as automobiles, steel, chemicals, or electronics, administered prices replaced prices set by competition in the market. In the steel industry, for example, when United States Steel raised prices, the other companies usually followed the price leader. Since administered prices did not require formal collusion to restrain competition, corporations avoided antitrust prosecution. And though periodic indictments of companies alleged to be in restraint of trade continued (Du Pont, for instance, had to sell its huge holdings of General Motors stock), such prosecutions served more to bolster the free enterprise myth—which businessmen and conservatives espoused to resist government controls—than to restrict seriously the autonomy of the business giants.

Business consolidations surged ahead in the 1960s, taking new forms. In the past, corporations had grown by swallowing up direct competitors and by integrating forward into distribution of the same or similar products, such as an oil company that owns its own retail outlets, or integrating backward into production, such as an auto manufacturer which produces its own paint. By midcentury the richest corporations had exhausted these means of expansion. Conglomerate mergers, the consolidation of firms engaged in unrelated industries, became a new growth strategy. Ford Motor Company, for example, acquired Philco, a huge home appliance manufacturer; the Columbia Broadcasting System (CBS) purchased Holt, Rinehart and Winston, the publishers of this book.

The investment of corporate savings became the principal mechanism of economic growth. Consumers spent most of their income, as the system required; business, however, accumulated two-thirds of all private savings. Business investment financed expansion of productive capacity to meet pent-up postwar demand and to modernize plant and equipment, moves which resulted in large gains in productivity. Automation and the use of computers, dramatic examples of the application of advanced technology in American industry, boosted production further. The replacement of men by machines capable of performing highly complicated tasks economized on the cost of semiskilled and unskilled labor. By the mid-1960s the auto industry employed almost 175,000 fewer workers than a decade earlier while producing a half million more cars. Consequently, the number of blue-collar workers stopped growing in the 1950s, but those in white-collar jobs increased markedly.

Controlling vast funds seeking profitable investments, corporations increasingly looked to overseas markets. A generation or more after America, Western Europe in the 1950s was entering the age of mass consumption. American manufacturers of cars, appliances, aircraft, and many other items vigorously competed for overseas markets and built factories abroad. Coca-Cola and English Fords were tangible evidences of the direct American penetration of Europe's economy. In 1940 U.S. assets overseas totaled $12 billion; by 1960 they had skyrocketed to $80 billion. American moviemakers took their cameras and actors to Europe and beyond to achieve greater realism and to use money earned overseas but unavailable in U.S. dollars.

Despite the enormous expansion, American business still had unresolved problems. The American economy, matured by the middle of the twentieth century, had generated enormous savings controlled mostly by a shrinking number of wealthy individuals and corporations. Because of the structure of income distrubution that still condemned a sizeable minority (perhaps 20 or 25 percent of the population) to poverty, and in the absence of fundamental new inventions and industries to spur economic growth, the postwar American economy failed to grow until the mid-1960s at a *rate* comparable to the historical average. Periodically, affluent America experienced recessions, first in 1949 as the postwar boom slackened, then in 1953-1954 as the end of the Korean War cut back government spending, and again in 1958, 1961, and 1969. Unlike America's major depressions—1837, 1857, 1873, and 1929— the postwar recessions proved *comparatively* mild, and unemployment went up but never reached the level of mass unemployment. Business activity briefly declined.

The postwar recessions revealed the limits of the giant corporations' ability to achieve stability. Business did all within its power to stimulate demand. It emphasized style and packaging; it introduced new variations of old products as well as brand-new merchandise. It benefited from planned obsolescence and from shoddy workmanship that forced customers to replace goods frequently. And it relied on advertising as never before. More families now had more discretionary income to use for impulse purchases. As per capita income surged, the affluent majority spent a smaller proportion on necessities—food, clothing, and housing—and became especially susceptible to suggestion for spending their growing discretionary income. Advertising outlays increased almost 250 percent in the 1950s, as businessmen expended millions to stimulate a high volume of consumer demand as well as to grab their "fair" share of the market.

Yet the giant corporations, controlling capital, markets, and prices, and with an ability to influence consumer preference, could not by themselves tame the business cycle. That difficult chore became the responsibility of government, which came to play a pervasive role in the American economy during the last quarter century, despite the accomplishments of business, and despite most Americans' aversion to the growth of Big Government.

THE NEW AMERICAN POLITICAL ECONOMY

For most of their history, Americans lived in a market economy in which the private decisions of buyers and sellers determined prices, profits, and employment. Orthodox economic theory upheld free enterprise as the best system for maximizing national wealth and individual freedom. But unregulated capitalism, even its staunchest champions admitted, exacted a heavy price in chronic instability and business busts that periodically threw millions out of work. Until the Great Depression, however, most Americans accepted the business cycle as inevitable, an uncontrollable phenomenon like death and taxes, something people complained about but could not influence. The severity and length of the Great Depression and the immense amount of suffering it inflicted on millions of Americans resulted in the first sustained attempts by government to counteract the business cycle. Americans lost confidence in the ability of businessmen to restore prosperity and few still believed in economic "laws" that condemned people to malnutrition, until an inevitable swing came from depression to recovery.

Throughout the 1930s, some had argued that only government spending could get the economy moving again, even if this meant massive deficits in the federal budget. Although Roosevelt only dabbled in planned deficits, conservatives denounced the experiments as dangerous and heretical. World War II clearly demonstrated the short-term advantages of large-scale government spending, however.

The experience of the 1930s and the lessons of the war produced a major shift in public policy.

Americans, rejecting both socialism and old-fashioned rugged individualism, favored instead a partially planned economy. Ownership and management of the means of production remained in private hands but government was to intervene in the marketplace to assure economic stability. The new strategy stemmed from a variety of government policies and programs that had developed piecemeal—some going back to the 1930s, others rooted in circumstances of the postwar years. The Employment Act of 1946, supported by both political parties, pledged the federal government to assure full employment and economic growth, but this vague statement of intent lacked blueprints for action. In the next twenty-five years, the economy experienced ups and downs but avoided depression, an uneven yet generally positive performance which postponed further hard thinking about such full-employment blueprints.

The federal budget provided Washington with a powerful tool of economic management. During the Second World War federal spending skyrocketed, and the Cold War kept government expenditures high. By the 1960s, government—state, local, and national—accounted for about 25 percent of the GNP, more than double the percentage in 1929. One out of every eight employees outside of agriculture worked for the government. Military spending created a new era of big federal budgets, with almost two-thirds going for defense. Uncle Sam became, for the first time in peacetime, a major market for American industry. Almost a tenth of the American labor force found employment in defense-related industry, and leading corporations and universities came to depend on federal contracts, especially for complex new weapons systems. The federal government employed two-thirds of the country's scientists and engineers on defense and space projects and spent three-quarters of all money going for research and development, most of it for military purposes. States such as California and Texas owed much of their phenomenal growth to federal spending, a third of nonagricultural employment in California, for example, being defense-related.

The military sector of the American economy

became a prototype of the new, partially planned economy. Government spending was far less volatile than spending in the private sector, since the federal budget went in only one direction—up. No matter how sincerely Republicans repeated conservative objections to government spending, and how often they promised to cut the federal budget, when they regained power in the 1950s defense spending continued to grow. Nor did the defense industry have to worry about shortages of capital. The government supplied it, financing research and development, and even built some factories. It often awarded contracts on a cost-plus basis—costs being difficult to predict in the manufacture of new weapons and a low-priority consideration in the Department of Defense, which wanted weapons quickly at whatever the price.

At the same time that military spending gave a boost to the economy, spending by state and local government shot upward in the postwar decades. As the result of the population boom and suburban growth, municipal expenditures during the 1950s increased twice as rapidly as the GNP. Local governments found themselves hard pressed to provide the schools, roads, streets, sewerage plants, and water systems required by burgeoning populations. Most states relied on increased sales and property taxes, burdens which fell more heavily on middle- and lower-income groups than on the affluent. The federal government, however, relied principally on the income tax, with rates set according to ability to pay, though numerous loopholes permitted the wealthy to weaken the progressive intent of the federal tax system. Yet despite the enormous increase in the dollars spent by government the proportion of GNP devoted to civilian needs increased only from 10 percent in 1929 to 12.5 percent in the early 1960s, half going to education and highways.

Government fiscal and tax policy exerted a stabilizing influence in two ways. When economic activity declined in the private sector, government spending remained strong and the millions employed by government—now 20 percent of the labor force—kept their jobs and helped to sustain consumer spending at a time when many factory workers were idle. The tax system also worked in a countercyclical fashion. As national income fell during the postwar recession, the federal tax revenue automatically declined, giving a shot in the arm to private spending; conversely, as income rose, the tax take rose to curtail private demand.

Recognizing the importance of tax policy, Congress during the 1954 recession gave a tax "break" to business investment and later under the urging of Presidents Kennedy and Johnson in the mid-1960s Congress adopted the biggest tax cut in American history in the expectation that a massive increase in consumer and corporate spending would speed up the sluggish rate of economic growth. Most businessmen supported this policy and called for a deliberately planned government deficit as a result of the tax cut. To do so meant the acceptance of government responsibility and assured a high level of aggregate demand, something beyond the power of Big Business.

INTEREST GROUPS AND AFFLUENCE

Federal fiscal and tax policies were only two weapons in the arsenal of economic planning, though the most important ones. Neither farmers, organized workers, nor homeowners—let alone businessmen—placed all their bets on the free market. Restrictions on production and government subsidies had rescued agriculture in the 1930s from economic collapse. The number of farmers steadily declined after the Depression (farm population dropped from thirty million in 1940 to twenty-one million in 1960), but because of mechanization, the use of fertilizers, and the intensive application of scientific knowledge agricultural productivity leaped ahead. Ten million farmers easily provided two hundred million Americans with most of the food for their tables and fiber for their clothing, and produced large surpluses as well. After the Second World War, these surpluses continued to mount, but farmers insisted on retaining government controls and parity payments. Farming became increasingly a large-scale operation. Small farmers were giving up, replaced by huge corporate farms which had the capital required to farm profitably. From a way of life which Americans celebrated nostalgically, agriculture had become agribusiness.

Unions in the Affluent Society

The sector of labor organized in unions also sought protection against the uncertainties of free enterprise. World War II had extended and solidified labor's advances of the 1930s. The basic rights of organization and collective bargaining even with unwilling employers had been secured. Union leaders cooperated with government and management to keep war production (and employment) at the highest possible level. Unemployment virtually disappeared, as even six million women found work during the war years. In exchange for a no-strike pledge, Washington encouraged unionization. Employers who were earning handsome wartime profits more willingly accepted collective bargaining and promised no lockouts. The War Labor Board settled disputes, some of which erupted into short, wildcat strikes. Labor did not benefit as much as other sectors, but with overtime pay and the start of emphasis on fringe benefits, labor came out of the war in infinitely better shape than when it began.

Nevertheless labor approached the prospects of postwar conversion apprehensively. Massive cuts in military spending and the return home of millions of servicemen caused a sharp rise in unemployment in late 1945. Just as important, rising prices, now free of wartime government controls, threatened to wipe out all of labor's wage gains. Most major unions went on strike (over four and a half million workers were out in 1946), making the two years between mid-1945 and mid-1947 a period of industrial unrest. Significantly, however, very little of the violence which characterized the organizing efforts of the late 1930s marred the struggles of 1945–1947. The federal government, no longer a wartime arbitrator, nevertheless often acted as mediator between business and labor, especially in strikes involving basic industries. Management proved cooperative, since profits held up. Successive rounds of wage increases could be justified on that

ground and because of increased output. Productivity per man-hour of labor doubled in some industries.

There seemed to be plenty to go around, despite periodic recessions which caused the unemployment index to shoot up. Union membership contintued to rise, steadily if not spectacularly. From nearly 15 million members in 1945, unions had enrolled 18.5 million in 1956. Labor made some gains in the South, the area which had always given union organizers most trouble. Unions also began fighting more strenuously for fringe benefits—company-financed pensions, longer vacations, health insurance—in addition to the old standbys, higher wages and shorter hours. Even the long-standing antagonisms between the two houses of labor, the AFL and the CIO, eased. In 1955 the two federations merged into the AFL-CIO, which spoke for 90 percent of America's 18 million organized workers.

But it no longer spoke in very militant terms. To be sure, union leaders still disparaged the bosses and Big Business; they railed against the restrictions of the antilabor Taft-Hartley Law of 1947; and they still banked as much as possible on the capital accumulated during the New Deal years. But much of the bite was gone, and with labor's enormous growth came a spiritual decline. During the war its social and political goals had been sidetracked. Afterward, a labor union bureaucracy of entrenched officials arose, making it difficult to tell the differences between the company executives and labor representatives at collective bargaining sessions. As a sociologist put it unflatteringly in the 1950s, labor was "taking on the grossest features of the business society." Rank-and-file workers took their cue from their leaders, readily accepting the precepts (and consumer habits) of the middle class in affluent America.

The bloody battles for union recognition in the 1930s now gave way to "maturing" relationships between labor and management. Employers accepted unions and unions fought for their share of corporate profits. Collective bargaining not only improved the worker's lot, but standardized industry's labor costs. Businessmen could now plan more confidently on the basis of contractual obligations with the unions. A few labor agreements included cost-of-living boosts which prevented employers making wage cuts during recessions. In the past these cuts had accelerated downward spirals in the economy. Now inflexible labor costs tended to stabilize the economy during recessions.

Though unions succeeded in reducing some of the uncertainty of working-class life, by the 1950s they had reached a plateau of growth. Unions remained strongest among blue-collar workers in manufacturing, construction, and transportation. But blue collars represented a declining element in the labor force and unions did not make substantial inroads among white-collar workers. Office workers traditionally enjoyed greater employment security. They jealously cultivated the social distance separating them from manual laborers by remaining aloof from unions and their working-class connotations. As a result white-collar workers failed to match the gains of unionized blue-collar workers, many of whom were entering the middle-income brackets. The especially hard-hit public employees began turning to unionization to help themselves. Traditionally government denied its employees the right to strike and refused to engage in collective bargaining with them. In the face of illegal but actual work stoppage by postmen, teachers, hospital workers, and others, officials had to accept for the public sector some aspects of labor-management relations already prevalent in the private sector.

And another major problem loomed for labor: automation. America had grown with machines. Man had invented them, tended them, and had prospered from them. But what of machines that dispensed with human labor or needed only a tiny number of dial-setting and button-pushing "masters"? Once machine tools had been programmed to computers the fascination of the automated assembly line turned to apprehension, then to horror in union halls. During the nineteenth century machines had reduced the need for large numbers of agriculture workers, so farmers headed for the cities to work in factories. But if displaced from the factory, or the office, where could they go? Certainly not back to the land, since twentieth-century agriculture had become even more mechanized than the factories.

The years of the cotton picker, the factory hand turning a nut with a hand-held wrench, and the filing clerk were clearly numbered. Organized labor's justified fears of automation made it a battle to protect jobs, even while agreeing to the gradual installation of automated equipment. Such overassignment of workers was called "featherbedding," and the railroads produced the classic case: firemen aboard locomotives powered by diesel fuel. This holding action on labor's part succeeded temporarily, and only among the strongest unions. Automation could not be prevented, and the union men knew it. Technological unemployment seemed bound to increase but this danger, though recognized in the 1950s, did not become that decade's prime economic concern.

Those not covered by union contracts had other sources of partial protection against economic insecurity. Unemployment compensation, adopted in the 1930s, became one of several built-in economic stabilizers. Workers laid off during a recession received weekly checks to tide them over until, hopefully, business picked up. Similarly the social security program sent out monthly checks to retired persons, which bolstered consumer spending during recessions. In both cases the payments were small, however, and unemployment insurance did not extend beyond twenty-six weeks, and less in some states.

As with farmers and workers, so too with homeowners. The federal government subsidized the cost of homeownership through low-cost loans, enabling millions to own their own homes — or at least their own mortgages. By 1960 about 60 percent of American families did so. By making mortgage money less expensive during recessions, the federal government hoped to stimulate residential construction and offset the decline in manufacturing. In this way Washington used control over interest rates to smooth the business cycle.

Through these and other "intrusions" into the marketplace — agricultural control and subsidies, the encouragement of collective bargaining, the built-in stabilizers and subsidies to the housing industry, together with the powerful impact of spending and tax policies — the federal government sought to achieve the objectives of the Employment Act of 1946: to promote maximum employment, production, and purchasing power. Though government fell short of reaching these goals, recessions did not become depressions, workers and farmers benefited from welfare programs, and Big Business obtained some security and greater ability to plan than it enjoyed in the days of freer enterprise.

The affluent society did not banish poverty, unemployment, or disease, nor did it improve the *quality* of American life in contrast to its impressive performance in producing greater *quantities* of goods and services. But to most Americans, veterans of the Depression Decade, the achievement of high-level employment and unprecedented advances in the standard of living for most families seemed impressive. Inevitably, complacency and contentment shaped American politics, producing in the 1950s the politics of abundance.

Chapter 35
The Politics of Abundance

The American productive machine functioned so spectacularly in the postwar era that the promise of the 1920s—the elimination of poverty—seemed again a realizable goal. The high level of prosperity inevitably altered American politics. Attitudes formed during the New Deal remained powerful, but in an age of abundance and renewed optimism, a time when Americans once again took sustained economic growth for granted, mass unemployment and the collapse of business leadership gave way to the politics of abundance. The business community regained prestige and the Republican party made a comeback. The Democrats remained the dominant party, but the GOP recaptured the White House for eight years.

The man who came to symbolize the 1950s politically, who won the presidency for the Republicans, and who won the hearts of the American people, was Dwight D. ("Ike") Eisenhower. Ike appealed particularly to Americans on the make: the suburban, managerial, and white-collar class, people who after twenty years of depression and war finally had a chance to accumulate, to become superconsumers. Eisenhower's fuzziness on most political issues, especially on economic and foreign policy, did not bother them. Americans in the Eisenhower era shared his uncertainties, his inability to forge a consistent policy, his barely concealed suspicion that politics itself was somehow unwholesome and essentially un-American. Political neophyte though he was, Ike symbolized his age as much as Andrew Jackson had symbolized another.

Eisenhower's election shifted American politics from slightly left to slightly right of center. From both sides of the political spectrum critics attacked the apparent equilibrium achieved by the genial general but with no immediate effect. The best of the politicians produced by either party—Robert A. Taft by the Old Guard Republicans, Adlai E. Stevenson by the New Deal Democrats—could not budge Eisenhower from the presidential chair he filled so unwillingly.

When John Kennedy won the presidency in 1960, this young, vigorous Democrat promised a political breakthrough, an end to the politics of deadlock and to the massive stalemate on domestic issues. When a sniper's shots cut down Kennedy after less than three years in office, he had still not shaken off the constraints of politics in the Eisenhower era.

"I LIKE IKE"

Politically, Dwight D. Eisenhower was an unknown, and this made him particularly attractive to a crisis-weary America in the 1950s. Democrats had ruled during twenty years of New Deal, World War II, and Fair Deal, and their reign generated a high level of acrimony because they pushed for changes strenuously resisted by conservatives. After twenty years most Americans wanted a rest, they wanted to enjoy the postwar economic boom, and they increasingly came to believe that the man who could best preserve what they had gained through a generation of reform, and what they expected to gain in an age of affluence, was General Eisenhower.

With that mood growing stronger, Eisenhower became unbeatable. Despite his refusal to accept nomination in 1948 by either party, some Eastern Republicans who had lost twice with Thomas Dewey would not give up. They needed a popular figure, they knew that America liked Ike, and they assumed that he, like them, was slightly right of center. Eisenhower had not yet chosen his political colors, but a remark made in the late 1940s—"if all that Americans want is security, they can go to prison"—reflected his hostility to the welfare state inaugurated by the Democrats. The principal hurdle to luring Ike lay in his status as professional soldier, since in 1950 he had been reactivated to head NATO forces. Ike himself expressed American ambivalence to military men in politics when he said earlier: "The necessary and wise subordination of the military to civilian power will be best sustained when life-long professional soldiers abstain from seeking high political office."

Yet the public's memory can be short and as

the election of 1952 approached Eisenhower's memory shortened as well. On the eve of the Republican convention Ike agreed to run. First he had to derail the candidacy of Robert A. Taft, the conservative Republican leader from Ohio. Ike's backers convincingly argued that Taft could not win. Taft, "Mr. Republican," duly went down fighting, but the resulting convention scars did not heal for some time. As vice-presidential nominee, the GOP selected a young California senator, more to the right than Ike, Richard M. Nixon.

Eisenhower's opponent, Governor Adlai E. Stevenson of Illinois, waged a strong campaign. Stevenson—articulate, probing, and witty—was also intelligent, a quality which had never been a necessary prerequisite for the presidency, and which in Stevenson's case hurt as much as it helped him. He spoke directly to the issues effectively and eloquently—attacking McCarthyism while addressing a right-wing veterans' organization, for example. Initially, Republicans had relied on their trinity of favorite issues, "Korea, Communism, and Corruption," and on Ike's personal magnetism to gain them an easy victory. But recalling the price of overconfidence in 1948, Republican strategists reshaped the Eisenhower campaign and made peace with Taft, probably at the cost of promising him free reign in Congress. Ike began to speak more strongly, decrying Stevenson's witticisms as irresponsible. A cultured man of aristocratic breeding, Stevenson was mockingly called an "egghead" as Republicans appealed to the ever-present current of anti-intellectualism among working and lower middle classes and to the fact that more Americans could identify with Ike's personality than Stevenson's. Ike's campaign picked up at once.

On that upbeat, sensational news broke concerning vice-presidential candidate Nixon. The revelations ultimately solidified the Republican campaign and demonstrated the enormous persuasive power in effective use of the mass media. Nixon had accepted $18,000 from a group of California businessmen, they claimed, so that he might "campaign against Communism and corruption in government." Democrats called the payment a slush fund, charging conflict of interest, and Eisenhower claimed to be on the verge of dropping Nixon from the ticket—"Dick must be as clean as a hound's tooth," Ike assured

as he prepared to look into the matter. To defend himself, Nixon went on TV and radio, pulling out all emotional stops. He talked about his family, his debts, his wife's "Republican cloth coat" (mink coats had figured in a Washington scandal involving Democrats), and about a family hound named Checkers. One journalist summed up perceptibly: "Dick Nixon stripped himself naked for all the world to see, and he brought in the missus and the kids and the dog and his war record into the act. . . . The nation saw a little man, squirming his way out of a dilemma. . . . This time the common man was a Republican, for a change." "Political soap opera," protested the doomed Democrats, but Nixon's tear-jerking performance worked. Supporting telegrams and letters flooded in and Ike reembraced his running mate.

Eisenhower and Nixon won all but nine states. They had six million more votes than Stevenson, and broke into the Solid South. Ironically, Stevenson also received more votes than any previous presidential candidate except FDR in 1936 (over twenty-seven million), showing that many persons who normally stay home on election day had come out to vote for Ike. Nearly 63 percent of eligible voters participated, 11 percent more than in 1948. The result clearly represented a personal victory for Eisenhower, who ran well ahead of most Republican congressional candidates, and pro-Ike voting patterns cut across class and geographical lines.

The nation seemed reassured. During the campaign Ike promised that he would go to Korea immediately after the election to wind up that unwanted struggle. Ike's election also promised to put a damper on politics and the controversy and anxiety that politics generated. Affluent Americans, and those aspiring actively to higher economic status, wanted to concentrate on the business of mass consumption. One Democratic politician moaned after the vote came in: "We ran out of poor people."

PRESIDENT IKE

No professional soldier who has gone on to the White House has proved to be a strong president. Dwight Eisenhower was no exception. His eight years in office provided an extended breathing spell following the contentious Roosevelt-Truman years, and most Americans welcomed this caretaker regime which put the presidency into a state of suspended animation. Ike's popularity and the prestige he gained outside of politics allowed him to keep normal political considerations and practices at arm's length for much if not all of his benign reign. He had brought the Republicans into power, not the other way around, and this gave him a degree of political independence which suited both his temperament and the mood of the voters. "The Eisenhower era," observed a journalist at the time, "is the time of the great postponement."

Postponement also meant consolidation, grudging acceptance of the major New Deal reforms. The failure of Taft's candidacy in 1952 hobbled right-wing Republicanism. Although Eisenhower might talk up free enterprise, and talk down government spending and centralization, the national consensus remained unshaken. The New Deal, though it would not be extended, would definitely survive, and Ike declared that he wanted "to take that straight road down the middle." Conservatives who harbored dreams of demolition, though disappointed, found the consensus of the 1950s more palatable coming from a Republican administration than from Democrats, and most came to accept, however reluctantly, the reforms of the Depression Decade.

Eisenhower was a genuinely modest man—perhaps too much so, since awareness of his limitations tended to immobilize him. He was not quick-witted or articulate, and during the campaign he turned his lack of intellectuality into a political asset, admitting it candidly and proudly. Nor did Eisenhower surround himself with a presidential Brain Trust to compensate for his own limitations. On the contrary, one of his most powerful cabinet members, Secretary of the Treasury George Humphrey, stepped right out of the pages of Sinclair Lewis's *Babbitt*. When asked if he had read Hemingway's powerful novel *The Old Man and the Sea*, Humphrey snorted: "Why would anybody be interested in some old man who was a failure and never amounted to anything anyway?" The New York *Times's* James Reston remarked sadly in 1957: "We are in a time when brain power is more important than

fire power, but in the last five years, the President has gradually drifted apart from the intellectual opinion of the country, filled up his social hours with bantering locker-room cronies, and denied himself the mental stimulus that is always available to any President."

Details bothered Ike. He preferred to be briefed in military staff fashion, with analyses of complex issues boiled down to a single page. Presidential assistant Sherman Adams and presidential press secretary James Hagerty acted as filters to conserve Eisenhower's time so that he had ample opportunity for his favorite pastime, golf. Two heart attacks while in office further cut Ike's work load. Critics charged that Ike favored golfing vacations to worrying over national problems. Few of these critics added, however, that so too did most Americans.

Eisenhower had a limited conception of the role of government. He rejected the example of the strong president set by his two predecessors, regarding himself as a "presiding" officer and little more. Presidential leadership, even in such vital matters as shepherding his budget through Congress, was conspicuously absent. Congress, relatively immune from White House arm-twisting, and usually in Democratic hands during the Eisenhower years, did not move into the vacuum created by the absence of presidential leadership because the conservative bipartisan coalition of Republicans and Southern Democrats shared Ike's immobilism.

The president's reluctance to push Congress reflected his desire to limit the expansion of the federal government. Ike believed that it should do little more than guarantee fair play and leave people alone as much as possible. During his first year in office he labeled government intervention in the economy "creeping socialism," and when asked to name an example of such creeping growth, he singled out TVA—the New Deal project which had become almost a holy cow among liberals. Although New and Fair Dealers reacted with horror, scoring the comment as an opening wedge for turning back the clock to 1929, Republicans did not dismantle TVA (though they tried to aid nearby private power companies at TVA's expense). And although the makeup of Eisenhower's first cabinet showed a decided pro-business bias—"eight millionaires and a plumber," someone called it—the president clearly sought an ideological middle ground.

The New Republicanism

This required modernizing the Republican party. Republican candidates had generally run far behind Eisenhower in 1952; the party could only hope to hold on to those voters who liked Ike by revamping its image. At first, congressional Republicans, stalwarts of the Old Guard, resisted change, and *had* Robert Taft been nominated in 1952, and *had* a union of old conservatives and McCarthyites been formed, the New Deal consensus might have shattered. But Taft died in 1953; Joe McCarthy was slapped down a year later; the White House espoused moderation; and with the coming of three successive Democratic Congresses during the last six years of Ike's tenure, accommodation to centrist politics was inevitable.

From time to time, Eisenhower called for a New Republicanism or "moderate progressivism," but he never matched the verbal calls to action with sustained organizational efforts. Professing to favor a conservative approach in economics, and a liberal approach in "human" affairs, Ike hoped to combine opposites. National welfare programs cost big money, however, money unlikely to come from an administration committed to large military spending as well as a balanced budget, and from a party deeply suspicious of welfare programs. During his first year in office, when Republicans in Congress all but ignored the White House, Eisenhower dreamed briefly of forming a new, middle-of-the-road party. Predictably, little was left in the end of his modernizing impulses but the moderation—the equilibrium of the Eisenhower era.

After twenty years occupancy (1933-1953), Democrats had come to regard Washington as their town. Thus the arrival of many Republican businessmen seemed to them an invasion by the Huns. But most incoming Republicans had more in common with the New Deal bureaucrats than it appeared on first impression. Men like George Humphrey and Secretary of Defense Charles Wilson of General Motors in some respects seemed throwbacks to the 1920s, especially in

their unguarded comments to the press. Yet these men of the managerial class knew that business and government needed one another. Government's inclination to interfere with business needed curbing, they felt, but there could be no rollback to the Coolidge era.

Thus, for example, Ike's secretary of agriculture, Ezra Taft Benson, proposed to cut farm subsidies and to reduce costly farm surpluses. But the farm organizations, their prosperous members having swung back to the Republican column with Ike, stymied the heretical Benson, and little happened. "Free enterprise," Republican watchwords, would not apply to agriculture. On another matter, Eisenhower reversed the Truman administrations's policy of keeping offshore oil drilling areas in the Gulf of Mexico and Pacific Ocean under federal jurisdiction. Liberals and conservationists feared that state control would mean unregulated exploitation, since oilmen had even more power in state capitals than in Washington. Eisenhower supported a bill granting the oil in the lands to the states, setting aside a Supreme Court decision upholding federal control. Oil companies then proceeded to build massive drilling towers in the ocean. (All was serene and profitable in the 1950s, but massive oil leaks from offshore wells in the Gulf and off California in 1969 and 1970 proved that the fears of conservationists had been well founded.)

Critics charged Ike and the Republicans with a pro-business, giveaway policy. The president's Dixon-Yates proposal confirmed some of the suspicions. The administration awarded a contract to a private company to supply power to Memphis, Tennessee, at the same time it denied the TVA authority to expand power production in that area. Despite this display of anti-TVA feeling, and despite Ike's popularity, the Dixon-Yates proposal failed. Moderation, or the status quo, triumphed here in the face of Eisenhower's efforts.

Ike was more conservative than many voters suspected, but his characteristic public posture remained that of a man full of good cheer and optimism, ready to approve increases in old-age pensions and social security coverage. The Eisenhower image worked its magic again in the election of 1956, when Adlai Stevenson again became his easy victim. Ike won all but seven Southern states, and even in that region he made significant gains. But his political independence carried a price tag for the Republican party: for the first time in over a century, a victorious president failed to carry with him a Congress controlled by his own party. The voters seemed to be saying that they did not completely trust the GOP on domestic matters, but they did desire more of Ike's brand of independent moderation.

FOREIGN POLICY: THE NEW LOOK

Eisenhower's limited achievements on the domestic front and his reluctance to grapple with major internal problems stemmed partly from the fact that the general had accepted the presidency in order to preserve the bipartisan foreign policy consensus. The Republican Eastern establishment supported him to block Taft and the isolationist wing of their party, since Eisenhower had been associated with the Roosevelt-Truman policies, and had last served as commander of NATO forces. Ike's election promised a continuation of Truman's key foreign policy—containment.

But during his first year in office, new tendencies appeared which, if pursued, would have altered the basic lines of that policy. First, Secretary of State John Foster Dulles indulged in loose and strong talk about the "liberation" of "captive nations," meaning the Communist regimes in Eastern Europe and the Balkans. The Republican platform of 1952 had attacked containment as "immoral," because it did not seek to roll back Soviet power in Eastern Europe, and had insinuated that Democrats were "soft" on Communism. Russia, obviously, would not allow its satellites to be "liberated" without war, but the slogans served the GOP's immediate purpose, especially in appealing for votes among Americans of East European descent. Dulles had Eisenhower's absolute confidence and ran the State Department almost without interference from the White House. A former Wall Street lawyer and the party's acknowledged foreign policy expert, he spoke of "seizing the initiative," of taking the offensive against World Communism.

Dulles did make one important shift in emphasis besides the shift in rhetoric. Republicans had charged Truman with being hypnotized over the defense of Europe while Asia went down the Communist drain. China had "fallen," they claimed, largely because of American neglect or subversion in the State Department, and Korea merely pointed up the failure of the Democrats' "too-little-too-late" policy. The end of the Korean War, six months after Eisenhower became president, revived the possibility that Asia would once more suffer neglect. To avoid this, Dulles negotiated defense treaties with Asian allies like South Korea and the Nationalist Chinese on Formosa, and in 1954 he organized what he hoped would become the Asian equivalent of NATO. The Southeast Asia Treaty Organization (SEATO) included Australia and New Zealand, and three Asian countries, the Philippines, Thailand, and Pakistan, plus several European nations with colonies in the area. The next year, Dulles masterminded another multilateral treaty, this one joining an anti-Communist "northern tier" of countries from Turkey to Pakistan. The United States stayed out of that organization, allowing Britain to play the leading Western role. Thus Russia and Red China had been ringed on all sides with America's allies. Dulles and other Republican critics of containment had not abandoned the policy but extended it on a global basis.

At the same time Dulles brought "massive retaliation" and "brinkmanship" into the foreign policy vocabulary. Massive retaliation meant a commitment to make atomic weapons the fundamental element in American military strategy, and it tied in nicely with Eisenhower's wish to reduce federal spending. The country could economize by cutting the size of its ground forces and strengthening the air force. American planes would soon be carrying hydrogen bombs, or H-bombs, first exploded in early 1954 and many times more destructive than the atomic bombs dropped on Japan. Aggressors should know, warned Dulles, that the United States possessed a "great capacity to retaliate, instantly, by means and at places of our own choosing." The air force's Strategic Air Command (SAC) would thus provide a "maximum deterrent" at a "reasonable" cost. The United States would be less dependent on its allies, who in turn enjoyed protection under the American nuclear umbrella. This also permitted reductions in foreign aid to build up the armies of America's allies. Eisenhower realized that placing more reliance on nuclear weapons reduced the flexibility of American foreign policy and military capability, but he thought the benefits outweighed the disadvantages.

Indo-China

The implications of massive retaliation and the pitfalls of brinkmanship became clearer during the Indo-Chinese crisis of 1954. Secretary Dulles stated that American policy must be forceful to be credible, and that shows of strength must be made even if they brought the nation to "the brink of war" when challenged by the Communists. The challenge came in Indo-China and proved perplexing. Of what use were thermonuclear weapons at the brink of a guerrilla war, with an enemy that was everywhere and nowhere? And how did one retaliate "massively" against limited aggression?

None of these questions received satisfactory answers in 1954, when the French asked the United States to save their fast-crumbling Indo-Chinese empire. A French colony since the 1880s, Indo-China had been occupied by the Japanese during World War II. As elsewhere in Southeast Asia, the Japanese invasion touched off a wave of nationalist, anticolonial feeling in Indo-China, which later split into three countries: Vietnam, Laos, and Cambodia. But when France, with the approval of Britain and the United States, re-established its Indo-Chinese colony after the Second World War, Ho Chi Minh, the Communist leader of the Vietnamese resistance to Japan, decided to fight. Beginning in 1946, Ho waged guerrilla war for eight years against the American-armed French troops. The installation of Bao Dai as "emperor" (he had served as a puppet for the Japanese during the war) confirmed the bankruptcy of French colonial policy.

The United States insisted that Ho Chi Minh was a tool of a worldwide Communist conspiracy, and that France, a NATO ally, had to be helped. The United States pressed France to achieve a military victory in Indo-China so that the French could then bring their regular army home and make a significant contribution to NATO defenses. But Ho and his Vietminh fought on, holding out during very lean years until after 1949 when the Red regime in China could support the Communist insurgents and transship supplies from Russia. French leaders repeatedly assured their people that military victory in Indo-China would come "next year." In 1953, Dulles again urged the French to reject a negotiated, political settlement, and fight on to military victory. Believing in the "domino theory," American leaders thought that if Indo-China fell to Communism, all of Southeast Asia, up to and including Australia, would eventually go Red.

A year later the Communists cornered the French in a network of forts in northern Vietnam. In this "Maginot Line in the jungle," the French had decided to stand fast, but as their situation deteriorated they pulled back within the fortresses. They asked for American aid—troops if possible, carrier-based aircraft at a minimum. Eisenhower agreed to the second request initially, taking the advice of the Chairman of the Joint Chiefs of Staff, Vice-president Nixon, and several cabinet members. But congressional hesitation, and the inability to bring the British into the scheme, killed it. The French forts fell, while Western diplomats assembled at the negotiating table at Geneva to salvage what they could.

The United States attended reluctantly, refusing to sign the final Geneva Accords. Laos and Cambodia became independent countries and Vietnam was "temporarily" divided into northern and southern zones. Within two years an election would choose a government for all of Vietnam. Few doubted that Ho Chi Minh would win that plebiscite, since he personified the nationalist spirit of Vietnam. But the election never came off. Instead the United States created and sustained a South Vietnamese regime headed by a Catholic, Ngo Dinh Diem. Since Dulles had not signed at Geneva, he felt free to ignore demands for an election that might turn all Vietnam over to the Reds. Years after the United States made this fateful decision to maintain South Vietnam within its sphere, the American people had to pay a terrible price to defend its puppet regime. For a while, however, until the outbreak of fighting in 1959, Dulles's policy seemed successful.

Latin America

Truman in 1950, and Eisenhower later, shifted some of the focus of United States foreign policy from Europe to Asia. Yet both all but ignored Latin America despite its proximity, skyrocketing birthrate, and massive poverty, because there seemed little threat of Communism in the Western Hemisphere. During the Second World War nearly all of Latin America joined the Allied side. This hemispheric solidarity stemmed largely from Latin dependence for markets on the United States and Britain, and obscured widespread Latin American discontent with United States policy.

Truman replaced the Good Neighbor Policy with regional security as the guiding principle of hemispheric policy. The United Nations Charter permitted regional alliances, and in 1947, the United States and the Latin American states signed a treaty at Rio de Janeiro, Brazil, calling for mutual aid should any of them be attacked. The next year the newly formed Organization of American States (OAS) established a political and economic framework for this agreement. Hemispheric defense against international Communism was the cornerstone of the new policy.

Central America provided an early test. In 1954, Guatemala had completed ten years of social change under a left-wing, reform government headed by a former military man, Jacobo Arbenz, who was trying to lead his poverty-stricken country out of the eighteenth and into the twentieth century. Reform efforts, halting though they were, inevitably stepped on the toes and the bank accounts of Guatemala's local economic elite as well as the powerful American enterprise, the United Fruit Company. The Guatemalan Communist party had been legalized in 1952 and Arbenz employed Communist organizers and bureaucrats, supplying a basis for accusations that Guatemala had gone Red.

At the Inter-American Conference of 1954, John Foster Dulles, citing a recent arms ship-

ment to Guatemala from a Communist nation, demanded action. The conference declared that domination of a Latin American nation by a Communist regime would threaten hemispheric security, without naming Guatemala. Dulles then moved alone, supplying arms to anti-Arbenz Guatemalans in neighboring Central American countries. In June 1954 they invaded Guatemala, and when Arbenz lost the support of the army, his government collapsed. Dulles called the coup "a new and glorious chapter to the already great tradition of the American states." In fact it was another chapter in the exploits of America's Central Intelligence Agency (CIA) which helped to restore oligarchic rule. The country got rid of its Communists, including a young Argentine named Ernesto "Che" Guevara, but in the bargain it also dispensed with agrarian reform, the voting franchise for illiterates (70 percent of the population), and taxes on foreign earnings.

Guatemala was 15,000 miles from Indo-China, but American policy in both places reflected similar tendencies. The invasion of Guatemala had occurred just two days after the United States installed the Diem regime in South Vietnam. By intervening in Southeast Asia, as in Latin America, and backing right-wing dictatorships, the United States hoped to promote the security of the United States. In Asia, Indochina became a bottomless pit; in Latin America, though Guatemala remains in the hands of the oligarchy, guerrilla war continues. And the United States became identified on both continents as the patron of any corrupt dictatorial regime that claimed to be anti-Communist.

BACK TO CONTAINMENT

Despite the grandiose phrases about liberating Eastern Europe from Soviet slavery and "unleashing" the Nationalist Chinese against the Red mainland, and despite Dulles's many pact-signing ceremonies, the Eisenhower-Dulles foreign policy worked no wonders. International Communism had not been "rolled back"; Korea had resulted in stalemate; Communists had gained the northern half of Vietnam; Arab nations had refused to make anti-Communist commitments; and the Soviets had reestablished the balance of terror by exploding *their* first hydrogen bomb. When Red China put a dozen captured American pilots on trial as spies, President Eisenhower, revealing once more the emptiness of his administration's belligerent rhetoric, rejected demands for a blockade of China, calling instead on Americans to have "the courage to be patient."

The twin crises of Suez and Hungary in 1956 confirmed the fact that Liberation was an idle and dangerous dream, that Containment (and its less pugnacious stepsister, Coexistence) continued to determine American policy.

Both trouble spots, the Middle East and Eastern Europe, had attracted Secretary Dulles's special attention, although they lay outside the orbit of effective American power. Republican talk of "captive nations" and "liberation" convinced the Russians that the United States harbored provocative intentions toward their satellites, despite America's failure in 1954 to aid East Berliners rioting against the repressive East German Red regime. In the Middle East, newly independent Arab states rebuffed Dulles. The French pulled out of Syria and Lebanon, and the British agreed to leave Egypt, but both European countries still controlled the Suez Canal. A new Egyptian nationalist regime under Colonel Gamal Abdel Nasser defied the British and French by nationalizing the canal in July 1956. Dulles, angry over Nasser's "positive neutralism" and his friendly overtures to Russia, canceled American loans to build a dam on the Nile River at Aswan, a project the Egyptians regarded as essential to their economic development. At the same time unrest against another colonial power, Russia, continued to grow in Eastern Europe, centering in Poland and Hungary. University students, who after Stalin's death in 1953 demanded more freedom of expression and less economic subserviency to the Soviet Union, led the agitation. The Communist satellites edged toward rebellion.

Suez and Hungary

The explosions occurred simultaneously in October 1956. The Jewish state of Israel, established by Zionists in 1948 out of part of the British mandate of Palestine, had been fighting border skirmishes with Arab neighbor states for years. In 1956, the Israelis attacked in force across the Sinai Desert and quickly reached the east bank of the Suez Canal. At the same time, students in Budapest touched off a general uprising in Hungary against their government and its Russian backers. The Soviets, caught by surprise, pulled their troops out of Budapest, as a new revolutionary regime promised reforms and hinted that Hungary would quit the Soviet bloc. A week later, British and French troops landed in Egypt, "to protect the canal" their governments claimed, but actually in collusion with the Israelis and with the hope of toppling the Nasser government.

The world reeled under the force of these events. Two superpowers, Russia and the United States, had been defied yet apparently had little control over the situations in which each had *declared* interests within the other's zone. The United States (especially in broadcasts of the privately owned but CIA-supported Radio Free Europe) had created the impression that it would actively aid liberation movements in Eastern Europe; and the Soviets had just begun a long-range effort to displace Western dominance in the Arab world. The emergencies thus created dangerous crosscurrents that could have swept the world into a nuclear war.

Both great powers moved to defuse the crises. The Soviets had much the better opportunity, since they could handle Hungary without fear of American armed intervention. Though Dulles and all Americans welcomed the prospect of a Hungary and other satellites free of Russian domination, such a goal was not vital to American interests, and in any case could not be achieved short of war with the Soviet Union. Consequently, the Russians simply reinforced their army in Hungary after the dramatic "pullout" from Budapest and then returned to crush the Hungarian insurgents. The installation of a new, hard-line Communist regime informed all Red satellites that partial liberalization following the death of Stalin would not be permitted to become de-Communization.

As for Egypt, the United States found itself in temporary alliance with Russia, issuing carbon copy condemnations of France and Britain, and demanding that Israel withdraw from Egypt. American leaders were furious with their Western allies for attacking Egypt without first consulting Washington. Faced with American displeasure that would have serious economic consequences, and with threats from Russia of nuclear missile attack if the invasion of Egypt continued, Britain prevailed on France to admit the failure of their venture. The Western and Israeli troops left Egypt. A small force of United Nations neutrals then took over in the Sinai Desert charged with the impossible task of keeping the peace between Arabs and Israelis.

From every point of view, American prestige had suffered. Its principal Western allies had been humiliated, and NATO would never again be the same. Nasser, humiliated militarily by the Israelis, nevertheless emerged as a national hero after the withdrawal of the British and French. The Soviets had waved the Atomic Big Stick, and had apparently forced the West out of Egypt; Russian stock in the area correspondingly rose, puncturing a gaping hole in the net of anti-Communist allies with which Dulles hoped to surround Russia. On the other hand, the savage repression of Hungarian desires for freedom and independence revealed, once and for all, especially for the new nations which might be harboring hopeful illusions, the true nature of Soviet imperialism and what Russia was prepared to do when it considered its vital interests threatened.

The Suez-Hungarian crisis coincided with the 1956 American election. Despite the reversals overseas, Eisenhower won again and he remained high in the confidence of the American public. This popularity in the face of adversity became the hallmark of Eisenhower foreign policy during his second term. The Dulles "initiative" petered out; the Communist world seemed to be calling the shots while Washington responded as best it could, but without a coherent pattern of action.

In no area was this more apparent than in the space race. Ever since the development of atomic weapons by the United States at the end of World War II, Americans assumed that no nation could match, much less excel, the United States in science and technology and their application to

warfare. Not even the explosion of atom and hydrogen bombs by Russia (and later by Britain) had diminished American overconfidence. In October 1957, Russia put a small artificial satellite (Sputnik I) into orbit around the earth. A month later a larger Sputnik, weighing 1300 pounds, went up. Most important for Cold War calculations, the powerful Russian rockets that had lifted the Sputniks into space meant that Russian intercontinental missiles could deliver hydrogen bombs to any part of the world.

As Soviet scientific and national prestige rose overnight, Washington reacted almost in panic. Eisenhower indicated that the cherished goal of a balanced budget might have to be sacrificed to space and security needs. Scientific education was to receive top priority, ranging from more federal funds for university laboratories to more science courses in junior high schools. World leaders rushed to congratulate the Soviets, exaggerating their accomplishment in a way that revealed how extensive anti-Americanism had become even among allies of the United States. Russian Premier Nikita Krushchev mockingly offered technical aid to the Americans, and when early in 1958 a new American rocket rose only a few feet off the ground before exploding, the United States' stock reached bottom.

These setbacks in diplomacy and the space race did not generate a new approach to American foreign policy. The United States continued to make limited responses to unexpected crises. The drifting became more pronounced after Secretary Dulles, near death, had to retire from office early in 1959. During the six years since the exuberant rhetorical beginnings of the Reign of Ike, world realities, rather than glib slogans, had inexorably shaped America's foreign relations. Washington stuck to the policy of Containment, but though Western Europe had grown strong and secure, new holes in the dike in the Middle East and Southeast Asia foreshadowed the sharpest points of conflict between East and West in the next decade.

In a last-ditch attempt to regain the initiative and leave office on a note of achievement, Eisenhower launched a campaign of personal diplomacy. In 1955, he had conferred with Russian leaders in Geneva, where he made a dramatic proposal for mutual aerial inspection by Russia and the United States and a start toward general disarmament. The Russians, suspicious of American motives, did not respond. And in 1959 Krushchev, by then the sole boss in Russia, visited the United States, but again without tangible results, though his trip confirmed the existence of a thaw in the Cold War. With pressure mounting for another summit meeting between Russian and American leaders, Eisenhower made several overseas tours, seeking friends for America and understanding for its policies. Welcomed almost everywhere, and wildly cheered by large crowds in some foreign capitals, Ike's trips proved a personal success, but they did not add up to a policy.

One last attempt at a summit meeting in the spring of 1960 ended disastrously. Eisenhower had reluctantly agreed to go, but two weeks before it was to start Russia announced that it had shot down an American spy plane deep within the Soviet Union. The U.S. government at first tried to deny all, then fudged, and after learning that the CIA pilot was alive in Russian hands, admitted the charge. Eisenhower, who had proposed "open skies" five years before, defended the use of spy flights as a necessary precaution against secret war preparations. Russia disagreed. When the president would not apologize for the incident, the heads of state left Paris without meeting.

Eisenhower came home, glad to be soon rid of the presidency. The debacle at the summit confirmed his inability to handle foreign affairs, and the recession of 1958 had created new pressures for domestic leadership. As much as Ike and the Republicans tried to steer America in conservative directions, events took matters out of their hands. After a generation of evasion the United States in the 1950s became more agitated than at any time since the Civil War by the problem of squaring the actual status of the Negro with the promises of the American creed. Thus during a time of conservatism and drift in American politics, a revolution in race relations exploded, triggered by an institution that had suffered a sharp decline in influence since the New Deal—the U.S. Supreme Court.

THE REVOLUTION IN RACE RELATIONS

The failure of Reconstruction and the triumph of segregation after the Civil War had condemned black Americans to second-class citizenship. Victims of poverty and illiteracy, subject to violence and constant humiliation, and denied the promise of American life, blacks constituted white America's number one domestic dilemma in the mid-twentieth century. In the 1950s, however, important changes occurred which pointed in the direction of long-denied racial justice. First, a new generation of blacks emerged, no longer willing to accept racism. Second, every Negro advance—and there were many—produced a white backlash. The world's leading multiracial society struggled to overcome deeply ingrained white racism that made a mockery of the country's historic commitment to human equality, a commitment on which its very identity as a nation rested.

Beginning in the 1940s and picking up momentum in the 1950s and 1960s the walls of segregation began tumbling down for black people. Millions who had not been able to vote entered the political process; racial segregation in public places—trains, buses, hotels, and at lunch counters, as well as in the armed forces—crumbled; a small but growing percentage of Negroes partook of the postwar affluence and escaped from poverty into the working and middle classes; and segregated, inferior education, which imprisoned black youth in a cycle of poverty and dependence and prevented them from developing either the aspirations, self-confidence, or basic skills necessary to get ahead in modern America, came under powerful attack.

These changes in race relations resulted from the converging force of new scientific views on race which discredited racism among educated Americans; a growing recognition that government must assume a responsibility to aid the disadvantaged (of whom Negroes made up a disproportionate share); the emergence of a more powerful Negro elite; and a consensus among most whites that racism threatened social stability and could lead a nation, as it did Hitler's

Germany, to the depths of barbarity and self-destruction.

The war, as it did for so many sectors of American society, provided a boost upward. For blacks it meant unprecedented job opportunity because of the labor shortage. As during the First World War, so too in the Second, tens of thousands of Negroes left the South for better paying jobs in the North. The flow of migrants continued after the war, given added impetus by mechanization of Southern agriculture, which reduced the need for farm labor. Residential segregation awaited the war workers, just as segregation awaited the blacks in the armed forces. Yet prosperity, continuing after the war, made for a dynamic economic situation for Negroes. These were still years of high employment for low-skilled workers, before the coming of the automation revolution reduced the need for semiskilled and unskilled labor. More and more blacks lived in cities, held jobs, and started to enter the mainstream of mass society. The young black was, to borrow the title of a novel about life in Harlem, "Manchild in the Promised Land."

In the postwar era the Negro vote became a major factor in American politics. Migration to Northern and Western states meant that previously disfranchised Southern blacks could vote without subjecting themselves to harassment by white officials or physical violence at the hands of racist vigilantes. Increasingly, Northern politicians courted the Negro vote and regarded it as a swing factor which might give the election to one party or the other in the major industrial states. Even in the South, despite white resistance, the black vote grew appreciably, especially in urban areas. Approximately three million Negroes voted in the election of 1948, three times as many as in 1940.

Since 1936, black voters had aligned themselves largely with the Democratic party. This connection proved invaluable to Truman in 1948. Although in close elections *any* recognizable group can claim credit for determining the outcome, Truman clearly needed and received the votes of Negroes in Northern, industrial cities. In Illinois, which Truman carried by only 33,000 votes, he received over 100,000 black votes. Four years later blacks committed themselves even more strongly to Stevenson, the Democratic candidate, declining to join Eisenhower's popularity bandwagon. Black opposition in 1952 did not unseat Eisenhower, of course, but the Negro vote's solidarity meant that it could no longer be discounted and that in the second half of the twentieth century white America would have to accept a growing and significant black role in American society. The Great Migration from the South thus set in motion a political and social revolution whose outcome is still uncertain.

The Negroes' new political home, the Democratic party, sought to capitalize on these developments. In 1946, President Truman set up a Civil Rights Commission and called for legislation to end racial discrimination in employment and housing, bills which, like the antilynching bill of the 1930s, could not get through a Congress dominated by a coalition of Republicans and Southern Democrats. But in the 1940s for the first time a president actively supported civil rights legislation and threw the weight of his moral leadership behind the struggle for racial justice—despite the Dixiecrat bolt in 1948 and despite the knowledge that support for civil rights would further cement the conservative Republican—Southern Democratic coalition. Defeated in his quest for fair housing and equal employment laws, Truman took the initiative in areas open to him. In 1948 the president ordered an end to job discrimination in the federal civil service and to racial segregration of the armed forces. Integration proceeded slowly at first, but speeded up enormously during the Korean War. In that conflict the military value of integration became clear—black morale rose and racial friction lessened. Men of goodwill hoped that the moral justice of integration would be equally clear.

RACE: SCIENCE AND SOCIOLOGY

A profound shift in ideas about race among the educated aided the black man's struggle. Until the 1940s racist attitudes prevailed in all levels of American society—Negrophobia dominated, and its harmful effects could be observed even among American Negroes themselves, as light-skinned Negroes lorded it over the blacks. Racism extended beyond white-black relations: Protestants regarded Catholics and Jews as their inferiors; the native-born disdained the foreign-born; and Americans whose ancestors came from northern and western Europe turned up their noses at the sons of immigrants from southern and eastern Europe—the "wops" and "kikes." The leading universities maintained quotas to restrict the entry of Jews and Catholics. Many large corporations would hire only WASPs in executive positions. And American whites, wherever they came from, and whatever their religion or ethnic identity, thought of Negroes as underlings.

Racial prejudice received powerful support from science, which lent it intellectual respectability. Arguing from Darwinian premises, and un-enlightened self-interest, white scientists contended that not only had some races evolved to a higher degree of civilization than others, but that these qualitative differences had become a biological component of racial makeup. Anthropologists and other social scientists affirmed the existence of innate differences among the races of mankind, with the northern European whites on top.

In the early twentieth century, however, a new generation of social scientists, many of them non-WASPs, reexamined the "pro-Nordic" views and concluded that available evidence did not support the theory of superior/inferior races or ethnic groups. Large-scale intelligence testing during the First World War provided additional evidence in the attack on scientific racism. Northern Negroes, for instance, tested out better than Southern whites. Differences among groups could best be explained by environmental variations: those from areas which afforded greater opportunity did better than those from regions with limited opportunities for individual development.

For over a generation these findings remained the property of a small sector of the academic world. Those whose prestige and power rested on scientific racism remained resistant or uninformed, and the victims of prejudice—blacks, Catholics, Jews, Italians, Greeks, Poles —did not need scientists to tell them they were equal. But their views, of course, hardly counted.

The New Deal and the Second World War prepared the way for a revolution in racial attitudes and the triumph of the view, now backed up by scientists, that the races of mankind are equal. The New Deal gave unprecedented political recognition to minority groups, Catholics and Jews, Poles and Italians, and to the other, newer immigrant groups. The Democratic majority depended on their big city votes, and it came as no surprise that they, like Negroes, would demand full equality of opportunity. The menace of Nazi Germany in the 1930s, with its psychotic racial theories and barbaric practices that condemned all but Germans to inferiority, and millions to cold-blooded slaughter, alarmed Americans. When the United States went to war against Nazi Germany in 1941, everything that regime stood for became America's enemy. Wartime propaganda emphasized that in contrast to racist Germany Americans believed in the brotherhood of man.

After the war minority groups demanded that the government eliminate discrimination. A coalition of white ethnic groups, plus blacks, now had in the Democratic party a powerful political base for achieving their goals. State after state outside the South adopted legislation that outlawed discrimination in employment and public housing. Colleges dropped their quota systems; big corporations now hired Catholics and Jews; resort hotels no longer labeled themselves "restricted" (meaning WASPs only). The inconsistency between discriminatory practices and the American commitment to equality of opportunity made it difficult for the prejudiced to resist reform, especially in an atmosphere of official propaganda on behalf of racial equality. The United Nations widely disseminated the findings of modern science disproving racial myths, and American schools were soon teaching the new doctrines.

Black leaders recognized the opportunity presented by the ideology of equality for a leap forward. Back in 1941 A. Philip Randolph, president of the Brotherhood of Sleeping Car Porters, a black union, threatened to lead a massive march on Washington unless President Roosevelt issued an executive order banning discrimination in federal employment, and FDR complied. This became a precedent for a flock of state fair employment practices laws pushed through by minority coalitions, as well as an important precedent for black assertiveness in presenting demands.

Negroes, however, received immediate benefit from the new racial consensus much less than did other minority groups. Second- and third-generation Americans of European extraction were already several rungs up the economic and social ladder, despite their groups' arrival in America much later than the blacks. The return of full employment during and after the Second World War made the newer Americans less willing to accept second-class citizenship—especially for their children who had greater educational advantages not available to their parents and who were determined to rise as far and as fast as their talents and ambition could take them. By the early 1950s the employment and educational barriers to all *white* Americans were crumbling.

THE SUPREME COURT AND SEGREGATION

Changes in the condition of American Negroes raised further expectations and produced important legal consequences. The ferment of the war years and their aftermath put an unbearable strain on the American racial caste system, a strain which the federal courts did much to intensify. At issue stood the Supreme Court's "separate but equal" rule, announced in *Plessy* v. *Ferguson* (1896). Under this doctrine, equality proved no match for separation. Public facilities—everything from schools to toilets—were labeled by race in the South, and in many Northern states as well, though usually extralegally. As long as segregationists could maintain the fiction that the separate facilities for blacks were as "good" as those provided for whites, the federal courts seemed satisfied that all citizens were enjoying equal protection of the laws.

Some blatantly racist practices failed to get the Supreme Court's approval, however. In 1915 the court ruled unconstitutional an Oklahoma "grandfather clause" meant to prevent Negro voting, and in 1927 the court voided "whites

only" primary elections, two early victories for the NAACP, the leading Negro defense organization. But on the whole, the system of legalized segregation seemed safe and as unshakable as white America's racial prejudices.

Nevertheless, the "impossible" began to happen. The NAACP had been fighting segregation on many fronts, including a campaign against restrictive covenants in housing—agreements signed by property owners to preclude sales of homes to nonwhites. In 1948, the court reversed rulings made in the 1920s, and declared state legal action to enforce such covenants unconstitutional. Whites might continue to sign covenants, either to express their inner feelings or because they mistakenly thought they could not purchase homes if they did not, but the documents were no longer legally binding.

Public transportation provided another field for changes. After 1941, Pullman berths on railroads had to be offered to all races. Not many blacks could afford to ride Pullman cars, however. In 1946 came a more far-reaching decision outlawing racial segregation on buses in interstate commerce. Four years later segregation in railroad dining cars ended (a curtained-off, Jim Crow section had previously been provided) when the court ruled that such practices violated the Interstate Commerce Act. By the mid-1950s all racial discrimination in interstate travel, including terminal and waiting room facilities, had been banned, although some localities continued to flout the law.

The fight against legalized segregation in schools understandably attracted more attention and created more acrimony. Whereas racial discrimination in interstate commerce or in voting rights operated in fields clearly subject to federal law, the operation of schools was a state matter. To intervene in education, federal courts would have to apply the Constitution's equal protection clause (among others) to state action through the Fourteenth Amendment, a step they had always been reluctant to take. Moreover school segregation appeared entrenched, with half the states of the Union either requiring separation of the races by law or allowing it at the discretion of local school boards.

In view of these somber realities, the process

of chipping away at school segregation began in higher education. Shortly before World War II, the Supreme Court sided with a Negro who had been denied admission to law school at the University of Missouri. Since Missouri ran no law school for blacks, the state offered to pay the student's tuition at a school in another state. The court ruled that this arrangement did not erase the original discrimination. The decision though significant did not overturn the "separate but equal" dictum.

By 1950, in another law school case, a Southern state had altered the situation, but not the court's decision. To maintain the University of Texas Law School lily-white by keeping Herman Sweatt out, the state established a separate law school for blacks. The persistent Mr. Sweatt sued again, and won his case. Chief Justice Vinson noted the glaring disparity in facilities between the two schools, which no one could pretend were equal. Vinson also spoke out sharply that year against racial segregation at a state university. A Negro admitted to Oklahoma State had been Jim Crowed: forced to dine at a separate table, and even put in an alcove of the classroom during lectures. Such restrictions, wrote Vinson, reduced the student's "ability to study, to engage in discussion and exchange views with other students, and, in general, to learn his profession."

These decisions had still not knocked down "separate but equal" as it applied to all public education, but that day was not long in coming. Five cases involving primary and secondary school segregation had been argued in the courts by the NAACP—two from Southern states, two from border states, and the fifth from the District of Columbia. One of the border state cases, *Brown* v. *Board of Education of Topeka, Kansas,* would soon lend its name to a breakthrough in American legal history. Although the school cases reached the Supreme Court in 1952, a two-year delay occurred before decision day. The cautious justices called for several rearguments of the cases, even going so far as to ask counsel how a decision against legalized segregation might best be put into action.

All sides sensed the historic nature of the case. Significantly, the U.S. attorney general filed a brief attacking segregation. Even the

battery of test cases may have been carefully chosen: the Kansas case involved primary school segregation in a Northern state which permitted but did not demand racial separation; the Virginia case involved high school segregation in a state where school integration was illegal. Also, the five cases showed a good geographic spread, including Washington, D.C. Thus the Supreme Court if it accepted the NAACP arguments would have to rule out school segregation in all public schools in all parts of the country.

The End of "Separate But Equal"

In May 1954, the court in a unanimous opinion written by the new chief justice, Earl Warren, concluded that "in the field of public education the doctrine of 'separate but equal' has no place. Separate educational facilities are inherently unequal." In upsetting *Plessy* v. *Ferguson,* Warren noted that its doctrine had not been decided until 1896, though the Reconstruction amendments had been passed a generation before, and that *Plessy* had concerned transportation not education. Warren's chief concern was the effect of segregated public education on children of both races, but especially on young blacks. Segregation, even in districts with roughly equal physical facilities, deprived minority children of equal educational opportunity, since it generated feelings of inferiority.

The court had ranged far afield in seeking information to guide its judgment, listening to arguments and accepting written material into the record from sociologists and psychologists, among other scholars. The defenders of segregation branded the *Brown* opinion "sociology" not law, a charge which ignored the fact that the *Plessy* decision had also been an example of "sociological" law, but the reflection of an earlier generation's racist "sociology." "In these days," observed Warren, "it is doubtful that any child may reasonably be expected to succeed in life if he is denied the opportunity of an education. Such an opportunity, where the state has undertaken to provide it, is a right which must be made available to all on equal terms."

The principle was clear, but what of its application? While hearing arguments, and in the written opinion itself, the court indicated its awareness of the "touchy" nature of the school segregation issue, of its "wide applicability" and "the great variety of local conditions." Consequently the cases remained on the docket for the next year, when the court would consider the problem of implementation. One year later, Warren delivered the second, or enforcement, decision on *Brown* v. *Board of Education.* Implementation would be gradual. He instructed lower courts to seek the end of segregation; yet the initial impetus should come from local school boards. A *start* had to be made, but once begun, "the courts may find that additional time is necessary to carry out the ruling." Nevertheless, the declared goal remained the admission of all children "to the public schools on a racially non-discriminatory basis with all deliberate speed."

Those who wished to preserve segregation seized upon the word "deliberate" and ignored the word "speed." The second decision of 1955, reasonable and well meaning though it was, bolstered segregationist hopes. Border state desegregation had gone well between 1954 and 1955, but the Supreme Court in providing loopholes all but ended any chance of rapid and voluntary desegregation in any part of the South. The constitutional rights of Negro schoolchildren had been affirmed; but at the same time they had been "postponed." Delay and resistance, not cooperation, became the hallmarks of white Southern response.

MASSIVE RESISTANCE

The nature of white Southern resistance to integration soon became clear. Southern politicians railed against the desegregation decisions as unwise, unwanted, unconstitutional, and "un-American." Georgia "nullified" the decisions, and other states talked of "interposition," invoking the Kentucky and Virginia Resolutions of a century and a half earlier. Such constitutional pronouncements tried to camouflage a serious attempt to block desegregation at the political and local level, part of a campaign Southern politicos proudly described as "massive resistance." Every possible roadblock to racial mixing went up: pupil placement laws, subsidization

of "private" schools (white public school systems turned over to private hands), and even closing the public schools.

Heartened by the slow pace of desegregation, the refusal of most Southern school districts to comply voluntarily, and by their own rhetoric, some white Southerners moved toward open defiance of federal policy. In the face of federal court orders to admit several black students to Central High School in Little Rock, Arkansas, Governor Orval Faubus in September 1957 decided to intervene on the side of segregation. He ordered units of the Arkansas National Guard to bar the Negro students' entry, and ignored additional court orders to remove the troops. President Eisenhower, who had never given his moral support to the cause of desegregation, reluctantly moved to uphold federal authority. After a fruitless conference with Faubus, the president had the courts prohibit further deployment of the guard. This left the black students at the mercy of a white mob near the school, so Eisenhower then dispatched U.S. Army troops to Little Rock to provide protection. Both the administration and the federal courts knew that to back down would have doomed any hopes for even gradual desegregation. Yet the "victory" did not represent a massive breakthrough against massive resistance. The presence of U.S. paratroopers at Little Rock's Central High School for two months did not achieve integration. Only a handful of black students had been involved; gradualism was still the court order of the day, and the battle for integrated schools would have to be refought in a thousand school districts.

Little Rock became a symbol of shame for most Americans, a symbol of manly resistance for others. Faubus continued to fight, threatening under a new law to close the schools, but the federal courts kept them open on a desegregated basis. When the next major school crisis erupted in New Orleans in 1960 over primary school desegregation, the Louisiana governor and legislature went through the prescribed racist motions, producing a flood of prosegregation laws, including one making it a crime for a public official to aid in desegregation, and seizing control of the city's schools. Eisenhower sent hundreds of U.S. marshals to New Orleans, who enforced the court orders without troops. The local federal judge dismissed interposition as "no more than . . . an escape valve through which the legislators blow off steam to reduce their tensions." In Virginia that same year, federal courts finally forced the state to reopen schools in one county which had been closed for several years rather than desegregate.

But the "escape valve" of interposition, though discredited legally, remained valuable to white politicians in the South. Governors Ross Barnett of Mississippi, George Wallace of Alabama, and as late as 1970 Claude Kirk in Florida symbolically stood "in the schoolhouse door" to stop desegregation, stepping aside only in the face of federal power and the threat of force. Many Southern voters fell for such political demagoguery, thinking resistance was feasible; and because the Supreme Court insisted on gradualism, little but token integration took place in the South. Its white population did not believe, or did not want to believe, that they would have to desegregate. Thus the first half dozen years of desegregation produced relatively little integration; most districts had done nothing, and in the others desegregation had gone little beyond tokenism.

The Limits of Civil Rights Progress

Despite these limited achievements, most Americans remained hopeful. They wanted an end to discrimination and legalized segregation. The stress was on lifting legal disabilities and expanding educational and job opportunities, and it resulted in renewed agitation for federal civil rights legislation. Truman's recommendations had been bottled up for years, but by the mid-1950s both political parties became more receptive. The legal rights of the Negro could no longer be safely ignored without imperiling the peace and health of the nation, and the growing power of the black vote made it politically dangerous to do so in most of the country.

In 1957 a mild civil rights bill, the first since Reconstruction, became law, and gave a bit more protection to Negro voting rights in the South, but Southern power in Congress remained strong enough to prevent passage of an effective law.

In 1960, however, Congress passed a civil rights act with some teeth in it: it called for federal registration of Negro voters, because experience proved that Southern officials would not apply the law fairly and were infinitely ingenious in devising ways to evade it. Senate majority leader Lyndon B. Johnson of Texas, seeking the Democratic presidential nomination, helped get this bill to the Senate floor, rather than blocking or watering it down as he had done with the civil rights bill of 1957.

The 1950s—the Eisenhower years—had been the decade of declaratory judgments on desegregation, years of much promise but limited accomplishment. Legalized discrimination seemed forever broken and a liberal solution to the race problem was at least possible. The president, mild and cautious, lacked a strong commitment to social justice that could be translated into government action. He reflected more old-fashioned attitudes, despite the fact that the necessary legal breakthroughs had taken place during his administration, and usually with government help. Yet Eisenhower, to the chagrin of the NAACP and liberal sentiment, declined to endorse the *Brown* decision, saying "it makes no difference whether or not I endorse it," an incredibly self-denying view of presidential influence. Strong words from him on the need for racial equality would have influenced, though perhaps not convinced, many people, especially in the South, where Ike was popular.

Instead, the president emphasized the need to win the "minds and hearts" of Americans to the goal of equality, a goal which he felt legislation could not impose. When violence erupted in a Texas town over school desegregation and the governor threatened to defy a federal court order, Ike called down plagues on "extremists on both sides" in a somewhat incoherent but revealing statement: "Now, there—the South is full of people that are adamant and are so filled with prejudice that they can't keep—they even resort to violence; and the same way on the other side of the thing; the people who want to have the whole matter settled today." On another unfortunate occasion, Eisenhower publicly referred to interracial marriage as "mongrelization." He would not actively oppose the drive for racial justice, but Dwight Eisenhower, who titled his World War II memoirs *Crusade in Europe,* was not the man to lead a civil rights crusade at home.

CHANGING THE GUARD: THE ELECTION OF 1960

In 1960 it became certain that the Eisenhower father figure would be replaced by a younger president. Vice-president Richard Nixon, then forty-six, easily obtained the Republican nomination, and on the Democratic side, John F. Kennedy, a forty-three-year-old senator from Massachusetts, ran a skillful and successful campaign. His principal rival at the Democratic convention, Senator Lyndon B. Johnson, a Texas conservative and one of the most powerful American politicians in the final years of the Eisenhower administration, surprised the country by agreeing to run for vice-president.

Although Kennedy criticized the drift and lethargy of the Eisenhower years, his strategy dictated the creation of a positive image rather than assault on the record of Eisenhower, who remained personally popular. Kennedy promised to do something about the low rate of economic growth and the rise in unemployment of the late 1950s; he also promised new federal programs for large-scale support of public education and Medicare for those over 65. "Vigor" was the key word in his appeal, the contention that the nation had to "move ahead," that it needed new, young blood. Kennedy also touched bases with the scattered elements of the Democratic coalition, some of whom had drifted away from the party. He matched traditional promises to labor and farmers with appeals to ethnic minorities through revision of the immigration laws, and shows of support for civil rights and desegregation.

In contrast, Nixon, though of the same generation as Kennedy, seemed old-fashioned. As Eisenhower's political heir he dutifully defended the Republican record, stressing prosperity and adding a few verbal feints in the direction of reform and welfare legislation. Essentially, however, Nixon's appeal lay with the contented—the wealthy and the lower middle classes who had an economic or psychological stake in conservatism and who believed that the American Dream worked, or would work for them if a businessmen's government ran things. Nixon opposed, for example, federal aid to education and Medicare, alleging they would lead to bureaucratic tyranny and socialized medicine.

The campaign produced one novelty, perhaps never to be repeated: the candidates appeared on the same platform four times for joint TV interviews. They were not debates, although each could comment on his opponent's previous answer to newsmen's questions, and no president running for reelection has since agreed to such appearances. Kennedy came off well, projecting just the image he considered vital to his success; he was articulate, displayed an engaging personality, and revealed a sense of humor and quick-wittedness. Nixon, who later admitted that the "debates" did him no good, predicted incorrectly: ". . . joint TV appearances of candidates at the presidential level are here to stay, mainly because people want them and the candidates have a responsibility to inform the public." (In 1968, Nixon and his "media" advisers would decide otherwise.)

Kennedy's Catholicism inevitably influenced the election. The percentage of Catholics in the American population had been growing steadily for a century. Much of the immigration of 1840–1920 had been Catholic; with a higher birth rate than Protestants, Catholics, though only 13 percent of the population at the close of the nineteenth century, made up almost 25 percent by 1960. Yet there had been a pronounced political lag behind this demographic expansion. True, Catholics ran many local and state machines, especially in the belt of industrial-urban states extending from New England to Illinois. But in the North and West, Protestant Republicans still worried about the power of the Church of Rome in American politics, as did Southern Democrats. Catholic Democratic bosses in the Northeast thus hesitated to push one of their own for the presidency, and the rout suffered by Al Smith in 1928 was so traumatic that American Catholic politicos despaired of electing a president.

Kennedy had to work hard against the Democratic leaders' fears about Protestant prejudices.

In 1956 when he first made moves for the nomination, JFK argued that in key industrial states his religion would help more than it would harm the Democrats. But not until he won several primaries in overwhelmingly Protestant states, such as West Virginia, did he make his point stick. Also, the Catholic vote was no longer so much of a *bloc* vote. Many Catholics (perhaps half in 1956) supported Eisenhower, so that Kennedy could not be sure of a massive outpouring of Catholic votes in his favor; this show of election day independence by Catholics helped to ease the fear among Protestants that nearly all Catholics would troop to the polls in unison, as part of a Popish Plot.

Kennedy confronted the religious issue openly, knowing that evasiveness would only reinforce prejudice against him. He declared his attachment to the separation of church and state at a dramatic meeting in Texas with Protestant ministers. To their credit, Republicans soft-pedaled the question, avoiding the low road offered by a whispering campaign or issuing anti-Catholic pamphlets through "independent" sources. But late in the campaign, the Catholic bishops of a U.S. territory, the Commonwealth of Puerto Rico, startled the nation by declaring that Puerto Rican Catholics (American citizens since 1917) could not in good faith support the party in power on the island and urging that they vote for a Puerto Rican Catholic party

(which got only 7 percent of the vote in November). Kennedy disavowed the bishops and Puerto Rican voters ignored their advice, but the damage had been done with Protestants, and Kennedy became convinced that the Puerto Rican affair cost him a million votes.

The election confirmed the shift to the right Dwight Eisenhower had first symbolized and later consolidated. Although the Democrats kept their hold on Congress, their majority party status did not extend automatically to the presidency. Kennedy won one of the slimmest victories in American history: of the nearly seventy million votes, he had only 113,000 more than Nixon, a margin of but .2 percent. JFK clearly won the personality aspect of the battle, but this advantage had nearly been offset by Protestant defections in the South's Bible Belt, where both the religious issue and Kennedy's support for Negro civil rights cut into Democratic votes. Unlike 1928, however, most of the South remained Democratic, demonstrating the wisdom of putting Lyndon Johnson on the ticket.

Kennedy's mandate was anything but overwhelming. According to one wit, whenever JFK saw a couple in the street he remarked: "One of them voted for me." But narrow victory or not, the president had promised to "move the country ahead," and to pay off the promissory notes accumulated in the 1950s when Americans had neglected their internal problems.

Chapter 36
The Politics of Deadlock

Eight years of Republican rule in the affluent 1950s soothed political tempers in the country after a generation of abrasive controversy generated first by the New Deal and then by a chronic crisis in world affairs. Under Ike, Republicans gave bipartisan legitimization to the Roosevelt Revolution of the 1930s at home, and to the Truman administration's policy of containing Communism abroad, despite the avowals of GOP spokesmen that things had changed. Still the world remained a dangerous place, balancing on the brink of thermonuclear destruction. The Cold War continued to consume huge chunks of the nation's resources, resources badly needed to satisfy growing human needs.

In the 1960s Americans increasingly came to question the price they were paying: high taxes spiraled even higher nearly every year, yet the physical decay of the American city proceeded at a galloping pace and so too did the pollution of the country's environment, its land, air, and water; and school systems, expanded hurriedly in the 1950s, began facing the impossible job of accommodating more students while their budgets failed to grow. Worst of all, Affluent America learned that it had earned its title in the 1950s only by sweeping large pockets of poverty under the rug, by pretending that several million desperately poor Americans did not exist—but in the 1960s this silent minority would be heard from.

Also in the 1960s Americans groped, without clear direction however, toward a way out of the Cold War and toward a more just social order. Though most Americans still prospered, the persistence of unemployment, the spread of depressed areas, and the periodic instability of the economy and its relatively low growth rate in the 1950s created pressures for new public policies. The inadequacies of a partial, outmoded, and hastily put together welfare system became more evident, crying out for overhauling and reconstruction. Moreover, Negro Americans refused to remain patient and passive any longer. The blacks revolted in city after city, making it tragically clear that America had barely begun to banish poverty and human blight from the urban ghettos. There may have been more poor whites than blacks, but poverty remained an overwhelming problem in the Negro community. Coupled with the reaction to racial discrimination, it made blacks more cohesive, more angry, and more disposed to revolt.

Americans confronted their domestic problems with uncertainty, recognizing the need for expansion of public services through more government spending, yet balking at the price. Increasingly people discovered that private consumption at the expense of public needs cheapened the quality of life for everyone, including the white middle class, the suburban commuters who lived in carbon-copy split-level homes and who saw life through a rosy picture window. Many sensed that something was wrong—black rioting gave all the proof needed—but few had ideas on *what* was wrong, let alone on how to correct the situation. A few on the far left identified the villain as capitalism, with its stress on materialism and individual competitiveness. But most Americans would not indict a system that had given them the highest standard of living in the world, even though some wondered why life even with affluence was so often joyless, especially on the job and in the schools.

Politicians sensed this national malaise but offered no fundamental remedies. In any case, sufficient popular support could not be generated for anything more than tinkering. Presidents Kennedy and Johnson expanded the welfare state and sought to bring the promise of American life within closer range of blacks, but in the mid-1960s the Cold War heated up again with disastrous results. The United States slipped into a major land war in Southeast Asia on the dubious assumption that national security required keeping Vietnam out of Communist hands. Such thinking failed to reflect the changed world of the 1960s. Red China had emerged as an abusive, provocative rival of Russia in the battle for leadership of the Communist world. The Soviets, facing dangers of Chinese aggression in the east, and secure in their western boundaries, hardly represented a menace to a revived and industrially strong Western Europe, the principal arena for Cold War defensive moves.

But the United States decided to hold Vietnam at all costs. After five frustrating years of guerrilla warfare in South Vietnam, in which half a million Americans with inexhaustible firepower and air supremacy could not stop the elusive enemy, most Americans concluded that their country was not all-powerful, and that Communist victory in Vietnam did not endanger vital American interests. Washington claimed otherwise, but people wondered why the United States had made such a colossal mistake. More than at any time since the isolation-intervention controversy of the late 1930s, Americans critically reexamined long-held axioms about foreign policy, especially the view that the United States must act as the world's policeman to curb any sign or hint of Soviet expansion.

Vietnam pointed up the fact that America had been neglecting its accumulating domestic issues. These problems seemed to make the country ungovernable, producing disorders, first in the ghettos, then on college campuses, and inspiring widespread distrust of politicians. Leaders in both parties tried to restore the legitimacy of public authority, some by calling for reason and self-sacrifice, others by threatening more repressive controls. But as the 1970s began, none had found a way to restore confidence, as of old, in the promise of American life.

NEW FRONTIER, OLD PROBLEMS

As the candidate of youth and energy, John Kennedy promised to get America moving again, to tackle the pressing national problems piling up after a decade's indifference. But in office, he soon ran into familiar roadblocks. Although most Americans accepted the New and Fair Deals and would back further extension of the welfare state, the political process, so long at dead center, resisted attempts to move it in a leftward direction. The supreme emergency of the Depression had forged a Democratic coalition of workers,

farmers, and segments of the middle class by uniting millions of Americans traditionally divided along ethnic, religious, and racial lines. That unity, based on economic deprivation and common class interests, weakened with the return of prosperity in the 1940s, as Truman learned after World War II; and Kennedy did not live long enough to find ways to overcome that factor.

Kennedy's "New Frontier" program—massive federal aid to education, medical care for persons over 65, and increased funds for public housing—immediately ran into opposition in Congress, where the coalition of Republicans and Southern Democrats sat on top of the legislative machine, and could, when necessary, block the will of the majority. Reform of the conservative-dominated House Rules Committee, which decided what bills reached the House floor for a vote, became a vital first step. After a long struggle, the administration forced the addition of some liberal congressmen to the committee and thereby weakened the conservatives' stranglehold over legislation.

The inconclusive outcome of the rules fight demonstrated that Kennedy was in no position to "boss" Congress. The Democratic majority included a large bloc of conservative Southerners and others who had won their seats by running ahead of the president on the party ticket. And nearly two dozen Democratic, Northern liberals, whose votes JFK had to have, lost reelection bids to Congress in 1960. Under the circumstances the administration had to settle for a few modest gains. Congress raised the minimum wage to $1.25 an hour, increased social security benefits, and went to the aid of "depressed areas" with federal money to stimulate the economies of such hard-hit areas as West Virginia's coal country, where miners had strongly backed JFK in his bid for the presidency.

But new programs got nowhere. The president and his brother, Attorney General Robert F. Kennedy, favored federal aid to education. The need was clear; across the nation attempts by school boards to raise their budgets ran into property tax payers' rebellions. Yet the connections between youth, undereducation, and unemployment were clear. Nearly 40 percent of those unemployed had had only eight years of schooling or less. With the bumper crop of post-war babies putting enormous strains on the capacity of schools and colleges to handle them, and with more and more jobs requiring a high level of literacy and technical training, youthful unemployment was bound to rise unless the government rushed to meet the crisis. Kennedy asked for federal money for school construction and to raise teachers' salaries. Congress would not budge. For two years running a compromise education bill passed in the Senate, but the more conservative House killed it. By 1963, Kennedy was willing to settle for any gains in education, but little got through.

Opposition came principally from two quarters. Roman Catholics, especially church leaders, insisted on receiving a share of any federal aid program for Catholic schools. This parallel, sectarian school system had also been tremendously expanded in the 1940s and 1950s. But as costs mounted, church leaders believed that only federal money could rescue them, since Catholic parents, already paying taxes for public schools and tuition for their children in parochial schools, could pay little more. Most Protestants and Jews objected, citing Supreme Court decisions defending separation of church and state. The religious deadlock produced a congressional deadlock. Democrats, dependent on big city Catholic constituencies, favored federal aid to education, but Catholic Democrats in Congress opposed any bill that excluded church schools. Kennedy's *negative* views on aiding the Catholic schools angered them further, since the first Catholic president took a harder line than had Eisenhower, a Protestant.

On top of the vexing religious problem, conservative Republicans, faithful to their party's opposition to the increase of federal spending and to the growth of new federal programs (except in national defense), argued that federal aid to schools, public and parochial, would mean federal controls. With the dollars would come directives, destroying the local autonomy of school districts as Washington bureaucrats tightened their grip. Though the pressures and need for federal assistance mounted in the 1960s, Kennedy failed to find a way to break the logjam. That became the task of his successors.

The same thing happened to Medicare. National health insurance had already been adopted by most European countries, but when Congress passed the Social Security Act in 1935, suggestions to include health insurance were postponed. Truman made health insurance a key part of his Fair Deal proposals. A well-organized campaign by the American Medical Association (AMA) doomed the idea. AMA propaganda warned that the federal government would dictate an individual's choice of doctors. Ike's election in 1952 killed any hopes of reviving the plan while he remained in office. Meanwhile, medical costs skyrocketed, partly as a result of advances in medicine. Millions of Americans obtained partial security against this increasing burden through voluntary health insurance plans, but old people, more prone to prolonged sickness and the crushing problem of rising costs, were generally left unprotected.

In 1960, Kennedy promised health insurance for persons over 65, an obvious compromise, but one that would give aid to the group most in need. Yet the doctors felt, perhaps with reason, that Kennedy's Medicare was the opening wedge for socialized medicine—full medical coverage through compulsory, prepaid, government insurance. Liberal Democrats hoped so, but in 1961–1962 they were politically wise enough to push aid for the aged and infirm, recalling no doubt the political storm Truman raised by advocating government health insurance. Even soft-pedaling tactics, however, failed to get Medicare through Congress.

The Kennedy Quandary

Kennedy accepted these and other defeats with calm resignation—too much calm, complained his critics. But whatever else the president may have been, he was no crusader; he would not play Don Quixote and "fight the unbeatable foe" on the latter's terms. He preferred to wait for the time when that same foe could be beaten. The "arithmetic of Congress" impressed Kennedy, and he placed little stock on attempts to *reform* the legislators and their procedures; voters would have to replace uncooperative congressmen with new men of different minds, or there would be no

New Frontier. This conviction kept Kennedy from going directly "to the people" with every issue. "There is no sense in raising hell and then not being successful," he observed cautiously. "There is no sense in putting the office of the presidency on the line on an issue, and then being defeated." Critics responded with variations on an old theme: nothing ventured, nothing gained.

The president reserved his big guns for a hit-and-miss battle with Big Business. Kennedy's father had become a millionaire in the stock market, but this brash Irish-Catholic from Boston never entered the inner sanctum of American business. Besides, the family was "too political," a fact confirmed by the older Kennedy's marriage to the daughter of the mayor of Boston, another Irish-Catholic nicknamed "Honey Fitz" Fitzgerald. John Kennedy grew up in wealth, but like FDR he never learned to admire monied men as such. His father's good relations with the New Deal (FDR appointed Joseph Kennedy ambassador to Britain in the late 1930s) and Boston Irish voting habits naturally inclined young Jack toward the Democratic party and its suspicion of GOP-dominated Big Business.

Like most presidents, and most Americans, Kennedy had a rudimentary knowledge of economics. He set out to learn, however, convinced that unless the nation raised its economic growth rate to at least 5 percent annually (it had fluctuated between 2 percent and 3 percent during the 1950s) and created more jobs, millions of adult Americans would face permanent unemployment. But sure-fire remedies were hard to come by. Economists recommended massive infusions of federal money to prime the economy, but without a depression, an "advantage" no president would wish on himself, such plans were idle dreams since Congress would ignore them.

Without a federal program the country would have to depend on American business to create sufficient jobs. Price stability seemed an indispensable precondition for higher levels of private investment. Kennedy watched steel, a bellweather industry, closely, and in his first year he urged anti-inflationary restraint on both the companies and the steelworkers' union. Steel profits were running high, so that the moderate wage-hike agreement signed in 1962 made price increases

unnecessary. When the president of U.S. Steel came to the White House to announce a $6 per ton increase in steel prices, nevertheless, Kennedy exploded: "My father always told me that all businessmen were sons-of-bitches, but I never believed it till now," a statement which got into the newspapers.

Kennedy decided to fight this issue, relying on the "arithmetic of public opinion." When most other steel companies followed U.S. Steel's lead, Kennedy publicly denounced them. A newsman asked him about the SOB remark; Kennedy replied that his father had been referring only to steel men. The president exerted every possible legal pressure against Big Steel—threats of anti-trust prosecutions, the loss of government contracts, and the dispatch of federal agents to snoop into company affairs. Kennedy's political stock rose, as public opinion backed him. In a few days the steel companies backed down, canceling their new price schedules.

Later, Kennedy tried to soothe hurt feelings, but the business community never forgave him. After eight years of Eisenhower Republicanism, they were unaccustomed to a president who was not their man. Kennedy did not wish to refight the battles of the 1930s, but he believed that the government *must* participate in key economic decisions, especially when the decisions of private enterprise seemed to jeopardize the national welfare. Although to many businessmen such ideas still smacked of bureaucratic tyranny, JFK, again like FDR, had no intention of engaging in direct government planning and control. And most Americans, though they might support presidential pressure for a "voluntary" reduction in steel prices, rejected the concept of recurrent government meddling in economic planning and decision-making. Kennedy's dramatic confrontation with Big Business could not obscure the fact that he still lacked a realistic plan for bolstering the economy and achieving full employment.

In view of the New Frontier's political and ideological limitations, the center of effective liberalism in American government remained outside of the White House. The Supreme Court, its members relatively free from *immediate* pressures of elections and public opinion by lifetime tenure, became the conscience of the nation. The

Warren Court, taking its name from the liberal Republican chief justice, followed up the desegregation decisions of 1954–1955 with further extensions of judicial protection for civil and minority rights. Similarly, civil liberties, especially the right of political dissent, advanced significantly. The court revolutionized due process in criminal cases: it ordered states to provide counsel for indigent defendants in *all* criminal cases, not merely those involving capital crimes. In addition, a defense lawyer had to attend pretrial questioning, and an arrested suspect had to be informed of his constitutional rights to remain silent and to obtain counsel. Most policemen argued that these decisions hamstrung them in fighting crime; some charged that they were Communist-inspired. In fact they extended to the poor protections enjoyed by the wealthy, but critics fashioned them into a convenient explanation for mounting crime rates which actually stemmed from poverty and alienation.

The court moved beyond the protection of individual liberties to democratize the political process itself. In 1960, and for generations before, representation in state legislatures failed to reflect population shifts caused by urbanization. Underpopulated farm areas had as much or more political power as highly populated cities. In short, cows were better represented than people. Although state laws, and even some state constitutions, required periodic reapportionment of legislatures to reflect shifts in population, legislators benefiting from overrepresentation did nothing, blocking reform through the established political process. In desperation, people turned to the federal courts. In *Baker* v. *Carr* (1962), the Supreme Court, though previously shying away from this "political" problem, ruled that failure to reapportion was unconstitutional, and warned that unless state legislatures themselves accomplished the redistricting, federal courts would do the job. Following this unprecedented intervention in state political matters, the court went on to outlaw Georgia's county unit system of voting, another device for favoring rural areas, and in 1965 it outlawed the poll tax and literacy tests for voters with at least a sixth-grade education.

These decisions, together with others restricting the leeway of officials and police to censor or suppress publications or shows which they considered pornographic, drew the wrath of many Americans on the court. Members of the Radical Right, represented most effectively and paranoically by the John Birch Society, singled out Chief Justice Warren for the foulest abuse. Billboards sprouted in the South and West proclaiming: "Impeach Earl Warren," who, according to the Birchites, was the international Communist conspiracy's chief agent within the American government.

BLACK REVOLUTION: NONVIOLENT AGITATION

No group in America had come to rely so much on the court to protect its fundamental rights than black Americans. During most of the 1950s the struggle for Negro equality and civil rights remained confined to the halls of justice. Then in the late 1950s the battle took to the streets and aroused the consciences of Americans to an extent unknown since Reconstruction days. Such outbreaks as Little Rock in 1957 had alerted Americans to the obvious: a radical racial "readjustment," or revolution, would not occur easily or peacefully; court orders would encounter defiance. Yet most liberal Americans remained optimistic, perhaps as much as a result of wishful thinking as of cool analysis. The court had clarified the "law of the land" and it now merely awaited application.

By 1960, however, reality had made a mockery of smug expectations. The Civil Rights Acts of 1957 and 1960 did not produce any fundamental changes. In the South, most school districts made no effort to desegregate; only 0.18 percent of the region's black school-age children were attending integrated schools. In the North, *de facto* segregation, the product of segregated residential patterns and gerrymandered school districts, still imprisoned black children in dead-end ghetto schools. Despite these disappointments, black civil rights activists clung to strict reliance on law and faith in the ultimate usefulness of the judicial process. Reaction to the *Brown* decision had reflected that faith, and the NAACP, a moderate and biracial organization that won the decision, patiently continued to file lawsuits.

In the early 1960s, however, black protest moved from a legalist-passive phase to a new campaign of aggressive nonviolence. The Montgomery bus boycott of 1955-1956 pointed the way. In that Alabama city, a black woman had refused to obey the city ordinance which required Negroes to ride at the rear of the bus. Following her arrest, Montgomery blacks launched a bus boycott until the city ended discrimination. Led by a young minister, Martin Luther King, Jr., they won after a six-month fight, withstanding threats and violence. King emerged as black America's most energetic and eloquent leader.

In 1960 black protest escalated spontaneously. Four black college students in Greensboro, North Carolina, broke the law by sitting at the lunch counter in the local Woolworth's and insisted that they be served milk shakes. The four young men sat at the counter and waited— they waited till closing time. Next day, seventy-five students joined them; and the sit-in movement was born, spreading quickly to other cities in the South. In some cases the sit-ins produced quick agreements to serve all comers; in others resistance proved prolonged; but the myth, long-nourished by white America, that Negroes were satisfied with their lot had been shattered. In particular, young blacks increasingly rejected the accommodating fatalism of many of their elders. Sensing that times had changed, in April 1960 some of them formed the Student Nonviolent Coordinating Committee (SNCC), or joined the older Congress of Racial Equality (CORE) to form a militant wing of the movement for racial justice. Aggressive nonviolence received an extended trial in 1961. CORE sponsored a bus tour through the South by "freedom riders" to test the ICC's ban on discrimination in interstate travel. In Alabama the riders ran into trouble. Mobs burned several busses, and rioting broke out in both Birmingham and Montgomery. When local and state police did nothing, President Kennedy sent hundreds of federal marshals to maintain order. His brother, the attorney general, explained: "We just can't afford another Little Rock or another New Orleans. For on this genera-

tion of Americans falls the full burden of proving to the world that we really mean it when we say all men are created free and are equal before the law."

These events put the civil rights spotlight squarely on the president. As a Massachusetts congressman, Kennedy had compiled a conventional Northern liberal's pro-civil rights record, though he never took the lead. Kennedy, who had received overwhelming Negro support in 1960, decided as usual to avoid a fight in Congress and within his party over a strong civil rights bill, and to concentrate instead on executive action. Even here he reconfirmed his cautiousness and infuriated civil rights leaders by delaying for nearly two years before signing an executive order prohibiting the use of federal money to construct segregated housing (though he had attacked Eisenhower for failing to do just that: to eliminate a major pocket of prejudice with one simple "stroke of a pen").

In 1962 and 1963, diehard white resistance to school integration in the Deep South forced the administration's hand. Mississippi, still convinced that General Lee had never surrendered, insisted that its state university remain all white. A young black, James Meredith, obtained a federal court order for admission, but Governor Ross Barnett, a slow-witted segregationist, said no. The White House tried unsuccessfully to reason with Barnett, then sent federal marshals, civilians armed only with tear gas, to the Ole Miss Campus to guard Meredith. This move cost two lives, since it took several hours for the federalized National Guard and the army to arrive and quell the inevitable riot.

Next year in Alabama, Governor George Wallace, a quick-witted segregationist, provoked another crisis. Wallace, short and pugnacious (a "cornpone Napoleon" to his many detractors), vowed: "I say segregation now, segregation tomorrow, segregation forever." But, he added significantly, "there will be no violence." Instead the governor went through a charade which stationed him at "the schoolhouse door" in defense of segregation when black students arrived, but after which he tamely retired from the field on orders from the commander of the federalized Alabama National Guard. Wallace achieved his primary goal, however, assuming leadership of anti-civil rights politicians. He would be heard from again.

Early in 1963, Kennedy spoke out loud and clear for civil rights, calling for new measures to make equality a reality. The recurrent school crises in the Deep South, the murder of the NAACP's leader in Mississippi, and most important the bombing of a church in Birmingham which killed four young black girls attending Sunday school disgusted most Americans and forced him to act. The president went on TV to condemn racism, urging passage of a tougher civil rights law. In August, a quarter million blacks and sympathetic whites staged a massive March on Washington. In front of the Lincoln Memorial, Martin Luther King surpassed his usual eloquence, evoking poetic images of an America free of race hatred: "I have a dream that one day . . . the sons of former slaves and the sons of former slaveowners will be able to sit down together at the table of brotherhood . . . —with this faith we will be able to hew out of the mountain of despair a stone of hope."

Earlier, King had predicted: "we will wear you down by our capacity to suffer. And in winning our freedom we will so appeal to your heart and conscience that we will win you in the process." But at that point, the autumn of 1963, no one knew how far white Americans, though obviously moved by events in the South, would commit themselves to racial equality. In October, a month before Kennedy's death, a House committee approved the new civil rights bill. On it rested many of the hopes and dreams of the black revolution's nonviolent phase.

KENNEDY AND THE WORLD

Foreign affairs dominated Kennedy's thinking. Here the president had far greater power to take the initiative than in domestic matters, where he needed the concurrence of Congress, and where he encountered so much frustration. The president's considerable popularity rested first on his personal attractiveness, and second on his handling of foreign policy.

At first, Kennedy offered no new directions.

As a candidate he sought to dispel Republican charges that Democrats were soft on Communism by sounding tougher and more hard-boiled than Ike and Nixon when it came to dealing with the Russians. The GOP, Kennedy charged, had permitted the Soviets to forge ahead of the United States in nuclear weapons and the means of delivering them, creating a "missile gap." Similarly, he sounded a belligerent note while castigating Ike for allowing the Communists to gain a secure foothold in the Western Hemisphere in Cuba.

Kennedy entered office determined to strengthen America militarily. He kept a tight personal reign over foreign policy, permitting no John Foster Dulles in his administration, and he appointed Republicans to important posts to assure a continuation of bipartisanship. Harking back to an earlier Cold War strategic maxim which held that the United States must always operate from "situations of strength" if it hoped to contain Soviet expansion, Kennedy pulled away from exclusive reliance on the nuclear balance of terror to a position combining nuclear deterrence and the capacity for resisting limited wars with conventional forces. Discovering that no "missile gap" existed, Kennedy felt freer to spend a larger part of the defense dollar on beefing up the army and the capacity to airlift American ground forces quickly to any world troublespot. "Massive retaliation," Dulles's policy that had proved ineffective in Indo-China, had been abandoned.

To balance massive retaliation the administration prepared for "counterinsurgency"—a fancy term for antiguerrilla warfare, on the assumption that the Communist world had shifted to "wars of national liberation" as an alternative to nuclear confrontation. A trial came during Kennedy's first year in office, when civil war in Laos threatened to throw that small and unstable Southeast Asian nation into Communist hands. But at the last minute JFK agreed to a settlement that called for neutralizing Laos.

Kennedy and Cuba

Kennedy's first major test came in Cuba. Since the Spanish-American War, the island had been an American-controlled, and largely American-owned, plantation. Heavy United States investments in Cuban sugar and mining interests were matched by an American military presence at the huge Guantánamo Bay naval base. The United States sugar quota gave the Cubans preferential treatment in the American market, but it also produced American domination of the Cuban economy. "The American Ambassador in Cuba," admitted a candid U.S. diplomat, "was the second most important man, sometimes even more important than the [Cuban] President."

The strongman of Cuban politics in the 1950s, an ex-army sergeant named Fulgencio Batista, tried to maintain the status quo — friendly relations with the United States, an attractive climate for foreign investment, and widespread illiteracy and poverty among the Cuban peasantry. Yet Cuba had abundant, fertile land, much of it unused. Some Cubans felt that peonage and economic misery were unnecessary, and they sought a radical solution. Their leader was a young middle-class lawyer, Fidel Castro, whom Batista had jailed after the failure of an abortive revolution in 1953. Castro gained his freedom in a general amnesty a year later and took to the mountains of eastern Cuba with a small band of revolutionaries, gradually gaining support among the peasants. Batista became more dictatorial and less popular each year and finally fell in 1959, leaving the country to the *fidelistas*.

Initially Americans hailed Castro's victory as the dawn of a new, democratic age for Cuba. But the U.S. government was less happy. Castro was nobody's man, whereas Washington was accustomed to calling the shots in the Caribbean. When the bearded Castro talked of social revolution, began nationalizing U.S.-owned property, and then finally contracted to sell sugar to Russia, Washington lashed back. It canceled the preferential sugar quota and in January 1961 Eisenhower, though about to leave office, broke off diplomatic relations. The American public did not know, and Kennedy soon learned, that Eisenhower had set in motion a CIA plot to invade Cuba by arming and transporting several thousand anti-Castro Cubans in exile.

Kennedy entered the picture with new rhetoric and old schemes. He ordered the CIA to keep the plan in motion. In March 1961 he cere-

moniously launched a new Latin-American policy, the Alliance for Progress, a proposal for a massive economic development program that promised to rescue Latin America from poverty, a Western Hemisphere counterpart to the Marshall Plan. Partnership was to be the keynote, and cooperation rather than intervention the means for cementing Western Hemisphere friendships. While Latin American diplomats applauded the message politely and skeptically, the CIA completed training of the Cuban exiles in Central America. Kennedy, pressed to guarantee that the United States would provide air cover and even troops, if needed, decided against direct American participation in the invasion.

Landing on the south coast of Cuba on April 16, at the Bay of Pigs, the exiles were quickly cut to pieces and forced to surrender. Their own air cover never materialized, nor did the hoped-for mass uprising against the Castro regime. Instead the dream of a quarter million Cuban exiles in Florida was grounded, and American prestige suffered around the world. "How could I have been so stupid to let them go ahead?" Kennedy later wondered. The success of a similar Guatemalan venture a few years before probably led him on, but even more important, the venture in Cuba also provided a chance to apply Kennedy's counterinsurgency strategy. But at the end of 1961, Castro, more entrenched than ever, declared himself a member of the Communist camp. Kennedy had been humiliated but not demoralized; his next venture in counterinsurgency would be carried out by American troops.

The Russians decided to probe United States determination on another front, a perennial sore spot in East-West relations — Berlin. The struggle over the German city proved the opener in a series of American-Soviet moves, in a diplomatic chess game with nuclear-tipped ICBMs as the pieces. Russia announced it intended to force the United States out of West Berlin by turning over control of access routes to the East Germans. The president stood his ground, preparing to mobilize army reserves, while Khrushchev's announced deadline drew closer. Each day thousands of East Germans were fleeing to the West. Suddenly the Communists threw up a wall between the Berlin sectors, effectively cutting off escape and easing tensions.

Kennedy reinforced the Berlin garrison but American troops made no attempt to knock down the wall. Construction of the wall achieved Russia's primary objective, propping up the East German regime, so Khrushchev withdrew his ultimatum.

THE MISSILE CRISIS

The missiles stayed on their launch pads and in the submarines on patrol, but Cuba remained a trouble-spot. It soon became the scene of nuclear confrontation. Castro, now firmly in the Communist camp, received substantial military aid from Russia. In the summer of 1962 the Soviets decided to put missiles in Cuba capable of hitting most Eastern and Midwestern American cities. Kennedy and his advisers huddled for a week, mapping out counterstrategy. The president knew he had to respond to the Russian probe but he also realized that rash action might explode into nuclear war. On October 22, Kennedy broke the story publicly in a tense TV address, calling the Russian action "a deliberately provocative and unjustified change in the status quo which cannot be accepted by this country, if our courage and our commitments are ever to be trusted by either friend or foe." Demanding removal of the missiles, he ordered a "quarantine" or blockade of Cuba which would stop missile-bearing Russian ships then steaming toward the island.

The United States and the Soviet Union stood confronting one another, in the phrase of that day, "eyeball to eyeball." A superpower such as Russia could not allow its ships to be stopped on the high seas without retaliating in some form. Washington suspected that the Soviets would make their long-feared move against West Berlin. After a tense week, and three days of shadowing by American ships and planes, the two dozen Russian freighters with their deadly cargoes had slowed down but still kept on course.

Khruschev soon realized that Kennedy would not retreat. The president insisted that the missiles in Cuba had altered the balance of power and that they had to go. Khrushchev backed down, or as a Kennedy aide put it smugly, "he blinked." The Soviet premier had gambled on narrowing the missile gap in one brilliant stroke: Cuban bases would have doubled Russian nuclear capacity against the United States, but with America still enjoying a two-to-one advantage. They would also have demonstrated Russia's ability to protect its first Western Hemisphere ally. Instead, Khrushchev lost all his bets. He mistakenly tried to leapfrog strategically by placing his weapons where they could not be defended with conventional arms, an error which contributed to his downfall a few years later.

Kennedy on the other hand came out of the missile crisis with high marks which all but erased the shame of the Bay of Pigs. He defended his actions as a moderate response to reckless Russian provocation, and by giving private assurances that the United States would not invade Cuba he made it easier for Khrushchev to recall his ships. Kennedy's firm resolve drew admiration from Americans and from most of the non-Communist world, and it sobered the Soviets.

The missile crisis was as much a psychological encounter as a strategic one. The presence of forty or so Russian missiles would not have altered the balance of power as much as Kennedy claimed. Yet the importance of *appearances* and the effect of psychological factors in influencing the balance of power always impressed him. The presence of missiles in America's backyard, in a country which three years earlier had been an American satellite, would have made the United States appear powerless.

Kennedy, holding all the high cards, won this test of strength. But the Cuban missile crisis made clear to both sides the necessity to reduce tensions and head off future nuclear confrontations that might end differently. Although the "victory" was exhilirating and politically profitable (Democrats gained a few congressional seats in the midterm elections), it solved none of the world's basic problems. Kennedy still sought an agreement with the Soviet Union, and he feared that Americans might interpret the missile crisis as proof that the Kremlin would always back down when confronted. In mid-1963 Kennedy sought tentatively to move in a new direction by advocating peaceful coexistence as the only alternative to mutual destruction. Khrushchev responded positively, and in June of that year both countries took the first step away from the balance of terror by signing a treaty to stop atmospheric nuclear explosions. The test-ban treaty ended nuclear pollution of the atmosphere, a danger that many scientists warned threatened human survival. But the post-Cuba thaw in East-West relations was clearly limited. Still committed to matching every Communist thrust with an American counterthrust, Kennedy stepped up policies that plunged the United States into an open-ended war in Indo-China.

VIETNAM

Kennedy's principal innovation in American strategic policy, the commitment to counterinsurgency as a means of fighting limited wars, ran smack into the Vietnamese civil war. Vietnam, which had been divided into a Communist North and a pro-American South under the Geneva accords of 1954, became the scene of renewed fighting. The American-supported dictator, Ngo Dinh Diem, refused to hold elections to unify the two sections as called for by the Geneva settlement; and the United States, in the words of *The Wall Street Journal,* was "in no hurry for elections" because we feared "the Red leader Ho Chi Minh would win." By the late 1950s, Communist guerrillas went on the offensive, benefiting from the increasing unpopularity of the corrupt and hard-fisted Diem regime. In 1963, the South Vietnamese army, with American backing, seized power and executed President Diem and members of his family.

Diem had been losing the battle against the insurgents. Yet even before his fall, the United States went openly to Diem's aid, fearing total collapse of the Western interests in Vietnam unless Americans intervened. First, Kennedy sent a trickle of advisers and plenty of military equipment. When these proved inadequate, more "advisers" went in, till their number reached 15,000. Washington now hoped that the new roster of generals who took over would stabilize the situation. Instead one general ousted another, producing near chaos in Saigon.

Despite the deteriorating military situation, the administration doggedly maintained that the tide had turned and that victory was around the corner. Kennedy's secretary of defense, Robert McNamara, sounding more and more like President Hoover during the Depression, claimed to see a military victory near at hand. His pet idea, the "strategic hamlet" program (or rounding up farmers and forcing them to live in fortified villages) failed miserably to curb the Vietcong guerrillas. Each American escalation merely increased the determination of the North Vietnamese to aid the guerrillas in the South, and although official American communiques continued to breathe optimism, the dispatches of a group of young reporters documented in undeniable detail an entirely different version of the war.

As the United States slid deeper into Vietnam, the president lost his early optimism. Yet Kennedy believed that South Vietnam was vital to American security, and in his mind Southeast Asia became another testing ground for American determination to maintain superpower supremacy. He thought America's will was being tested, as in Berlin and Cuba. Ever concerned with preserving the existing balance of power, Kennedy transformed the local struggle in Vietnam into part of the larger conflict with international Communism. Accepting the "domino theory," he argued: "for us to withdraw from that effort [in Vietnam] would mean a collapse not only of South Vietnam but Southeast Asia. So we are going to stay there." Kennedy also sensed the dangers of slipping into an exhausting land war in Asia, insisting that only the South Vietnamese could save themselves from Communist takeover, yet he pursued a contradictory policy of sending troops into Vietnam, knowing full well that the Saigon generals could not hold out alone. The trickle of American men would before long become a flood.

THE DEATH OF KENNEDY

After almost three years in office, John Kennedy had not been able to deliver on the promises of a New Frontier at home or a more stable international order abroad. In October 1963 he went on a fence-mending political tour of Texas. As he was riding in an open car through the crowded streets of Dallas, rifle shots fired from the Texas Book

Depository building killed the president and wounded the governor of Texas. For three days Americans sat glued in front of their TV sets watching the unfolding of a bizarre tragedy. Dallas police quickly arrested Lee Harvey Oswald, a young employee at the Depository. For two days hundreds of TV cameramen and reporters swarmed over the Dallas police headquarters, where Oswald was being held for questioning. The Dallas police chief failed to impose maximum security, to put it mildly, and as the police moved Oswald from the basement of police headquarters, a nightclub owner named Jack Ruby shot Oswald dead in full view of millions, since TV carried the murder "live."

Immediately countless theories sprang forth to explain the assassination. Some thought that Oswald had been part of a larger conspiracy, that the fatal bullets had come from more than one rifle; others argued that Oswald was an agent of Fidel Castro; and many believed that the CIA was involved in the business, that Ruby had been ordered to "execute" Oswald. Rarely had so many Americans come to doubt the validity of the official explanation that Oswald acted alone, and out of personal motives. To slow down the rumor mill, the new president, Lyndon Johnson, appointed Chief Justice Earl Warren chairman of an inquiry to determine the truth. The Warren Commission concluded, perhaps too quickly, that Oswald had indeed acted alone, and that this psychological dropout and ideological drifter had no previous connection with Jack Ruby. Ruby, a Kennedy admirer who was carried away by the postassassination shock and near hysteria, was also quoted as saying that he wanted "to prove that a Jew can have guts." The Warren Commission report still left many points unclarified and many persons unconvinced, but none of the countertheorists has thus far established a verifiable and convincing alternate version.

However one explained it, John Kennedy lay dead, the fourth American president cut down by an assassin. In death, Kennedy became a hero. His impressive funeral and burial at Arlington united the country more than at any time since FDR's death in 1945. Kennedy himself had recognized the limited extent of his accomplishments. The success of the New Frontier would depend, he thought, on his reelection and the election of a sympathetic Congress.

Kennedy had looked forward to the future. Unlike many presidents who have abandoned the White House with relief, he loved the job. He did much to revitalize the presidency, rescuing an institution mothballed during the Eisenhower years, Kennedy made government service seem more attractive, especially for bright young men, who in the 1950s preferred to make money in business. He also brought "the professors" back to Washington as advisers, and he established unprecedented links with the artistic and literary communities. To the New Frontiersmen, and especially to their ladies, the Kennedy administration—with its verve, wit, and lack of bureaucratic stuffiness—was "Camelot" with Jack Kennedy playing the lead. But many remained unimpressed. Left-wing intellectuals derided the Kennedy "style" as a papier-mâché façade, which obscured his failure to come to grips with the nation's problems. And older representatives of small-town, conservative America recoiled from the "dash" of Kennedy's Georgetown smart set; nor did they like "all that Mozart string music" being played at the White House.

Kennedy made his greatest impression on American youth. He gave them a cause, as the popularity of the Peace Corps demonstrated. Striving to create for America the "politics of modernity," Kennedy knew that America must master the problems of urban blight, unemployment, and racism, but these perceptions still left him a long way from finding workable solutions.

JOHNSON'S GREAT SOCIETY

Lyndon Johnson's first task was to convince Americans of the continuity of government. This meant persuading them that he could wear the mantle of Kennedy, the martyred president. A conservative Texan, Johnson had served as Senate majority leader in the 1950s, wielding more power than any other man in that body. Chosen by Kennedy to strengthen the ticket in the South, he did his job well and then settled into the vice-presidency, frustrated over his lack of power, uncomfortable amid the brash New Frontiersmen who held him at arm's length and laughed at his unpolished, Texas ways.

A month after becoming president, Johnson moved swiftly to make his presence felt as a new leader committed to pushing ahead from the New Frontier into the Great Society—to create an America in which the poor and the blacks would finally achieve social justice. A master of legislative tactics, Johnson pressed Congress to pass the stalled Civil Rights Bill as a memorial to JFK. Seeking to gain the confidence of the dominant liberal wing of the Democratic party, Johnson put himself on the line for civil rights: "We have talked long enough in this country about equal rights," he lectured Congress. "It is time to write the next chapter in the books of law." And he concluded, echoing the words of Martin Luther King, "We Shall Overcome."

Johnson's touch seemed magical. The Civil Rights Bill became law in 1964, impelled by presidential initiative and efficient pressure on Congress. "For thirty-two years," Johnson observed proudly, "Capitol Hill has been my home." And he demonstrated that he knew how to pull the legislative levers better than anyone else. He pushed through Kennedy's stalled tax reform bill, designed to stimulate economic growth, as well as the Economic Opportunities Act, a statute with which he promised to wage "war on poverty." Crowed the president: "This session has enacted more major legislation, met more national needs, disposed of more national issues than any other session of this century or the last."

The first six months of 1964 reconfirmed the fact that Lyndon Johnson knew how to work the machinery of Congress, even from "enemy headquarters," the White House. His congressional savvy worked fine on the Hill, and his fundamentalist preacher oratorical style worked well in Texas, but could he hold together the Democratic coalition, its Northern workers, its liberals, and its blacks, in the upcoming 1964 presidential election?

The Conscience of Conservatism

The Republicans seemed determined to help him. For the first time in a decade, the GOP's right wing made a serious challenge for party power. Republican moderates believed that Johnson (LBJ) could not be beaten, so they sat back apathetically. Conservative Republicans, buoyed by their political fundamentalism and preferring to be right than victorious, moved into the vacuum. When the moderates woke up, it was too late. Rightwing Senator Barry Goldwater of Arizona walked away with the GOP nomination.

Goldwater breathed old-fashioned Americanism from every pore. He opposed the New Deal, the Fair Deal—almost everything that would deal in the federal government, except the military establishment. He proposed to sell TVA to private interests, and he wanted social security made "voluntary," that is, available to those who could pay for it. He believed passionately that hard work was always rewarded, and that competitive individualism and private property must be free from government controls. The Goldwater forces made no effort to unite the GOP liberals behind them, for this time the Republican conservatives were determined to give America a "choice, not an echo," a choice between free enterprise and the welfare state. Not a John Birch Society member himself, Goldwater nevertheless refused to condemn the ultra-right-wing group, saying that he knew "many good Americans" who belonged. Goldwater proved popular in the South. Although the Republican platform supported the civil rights law, Goldwater had voted against it. Deploring racism, he still refused to accept federal "interference" in state and local affairs.

Goldwater's views on foreign policy became even more of a handicap. The Republican candidate did not believe in coexistence with Soviet Russia or any other Communist nation. His world view had no place in it for the stalemate created by nuclear weapons. Publishing a book disarmingly called *Why Not Victory?* (over Communism), Goldwater suggested that military field commanders, not solely the president, should decide when to use atomic weapons. He wanted the United States to withdraw from the United Nations and pursue all-out military victory in Vietnam. Dropping a "low-yield atomic bomb on Chinese supply lines in North Vietnam," he believed, would end the war quickly. These suggestions understandably disturbed many Americans, so the Republicans appealed to the sub-rational with the slogan: "In Your Heart You Know He's Right." The anti-Goldwater whispering campaign countered with: "In Your Guts You Know He's Nuts."

Johnson, confident of receiving all of the center and left vote, ran a relaxed, middle-of-the-road campaign. The country was prosperous and relatively at peace—and it was Goldwater who insisted on a greater military effort in Vietnam. Assured Johnson: "We don't want our American boys to do the fighting for Asian boys." He would not "play the war game of bluff and bluster"; it was too risky. The president, looking like a benevolent and self-assured uncle, went eagerly to meet the people, or as he put it, "to press the flesh." The voters got the message, burying Goldwater in a landslide unprecedented since 1936. Johnson carried 44 states with over 60 percent of the vote, and his party won a two-to-one majority in Congress. Some observers prematurely predicted the end of the Republican party.

Capitalizing on his landslide, in January 1965 Johnson proclaimed his vision of the Great Society. By mid-1965, Congress cooperated by approving massive federal aid to education and housing, including rent subsidies for the poor; a virtually airtight voting rights bill to enfranchise blacks; further tax reform; aid to Appalachia; and finally that stormy petrel of the Kennedy years, Medicare. Completely in control, with no effective political opposition, Johnson gave increasing attention to the long-festering war in Vietnam. Every previous American politician who had touched this problem had come away with burned fingers; Lyndon Johnson would be consumed.

WAR WITHOUT HONOR

Barry Goldwater's aggressive, hawklike statements in 1964 made the president look like a dovish peacemonger in *comparison,* yet Johnson had always been a hardline "hawk" on Vietnam. As vice-president he fully supported giving aid to the regime of President Diem whom he described as "the Winston Churchill of Asia." Two months after Kennedy's death, Johnson left no doubt as to where he stood: "Neutralization of South Vietnam would only be another name for a Communist takeover. Peace will return . . . just as soon as the authorities in Hanoi [North Vietnam] cease and desist from their terrorist aggression." During the election campaign, however, he played down his bellicose tendencies in public.

But escalation of the war lay ahead. In August 1964 Washington claimed that North Vietnamese gunboats had fired on two American destroyers, which then sank several of the attackers. The American ships were probably helping South Vietnamese ships raid North Vietnamese coastal installations, but the president labeled it simple "open aggression on the high seas" and ordered several retaliatory bombing attacks on North Vietnam. More important, he received a blank check from Congress to use U.S. military forces in Southeast Asia in whatever way he thought necessary. Although the president as Commander-in-Chief already had the constitutional power to so deploy the armed forces, the "Gulf of Tonkin Resolution" committed Congress beforehand to support presidential adventures in Asia. No representative, and only two senators, voted against the resolution. The influential Senator J. William Fullbright, though then warning against involvement in an Asia land war, supported it.

Johnson felt he now had indisputable mandates, domestic and foreign. Agreeing that Vietnam provided a testing ground for American resolve, and recognizing that the South Vietnamese government was near collapse, he decided to fight the war with American men. For years Washington had denied any intention of sending U.S. ground forces to wage an Asian guerrilla war. Johnson had promised: "I want to be very cautious and careful . . . when I start dropping bombs around that are likely to involve American boys in a war in Asia with seven hundred million Chinese." Careful or not, he decided to drop the bombs, though China had not come into the war directly, and though in early 1965 few North Vietnamese were fighting in the South. In February, in "retaliation" for a successful Vietcong guerrilla attack against an American base, continuous, massive bombing of the North began.

At the same time, the president began send-

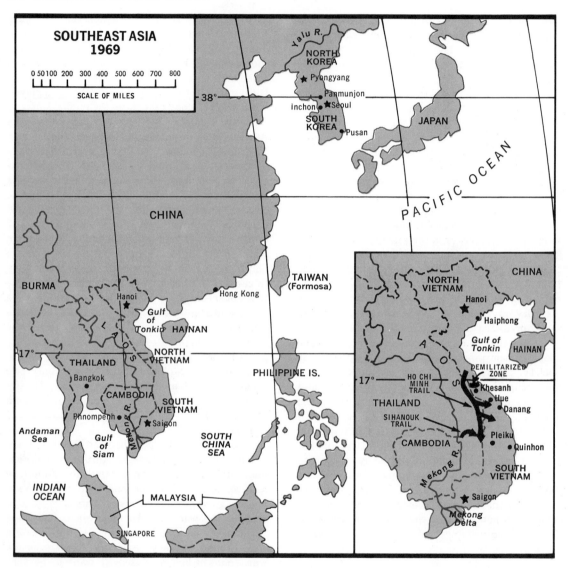

ing large numbers of U.S. troops to South Vietnam. "If we are driven from the field in Vietnam," he announced with gloomy determination in July 1965, "then no nation can ever again have the same confidence in American protection." By then, 75,000 Americans were in Vietnam; by the end of the year, 200,000; the number rose to more than 500,000 by 1967. Full-scale American intervention, according to the official explanation, was necessary to counter aggression by the North

Vietnamese, who allegedly had sent regular units to the South. Washington thereafter held stubbornly to this theory of invasion, denying the existence of a South Vietnamese civil war. But when Johnson decided to bomb the North and send in U.S. troops, few units from the North were then in the field fighting against the South Vietnamese. The charges of Northern infiltration provided the pretext for full-scale escalation; the real reason was the imminent disintegration of the South Vietnamese government. The war thus became overwhelmingly an American effort. Only two other foreign countries, Australia and South Korea, sent a handful of troops. The South Vietnamese Army, well equipped with American arms, was poorly trained and woefully lacking in morale and the will to fight. A new group of South Vietnamese generals did bring a measure of political stability to the country, however, and their rule had American blessing.

American men, planes, and supplies poured in, but the war went nowhere. If the Korean War had been frustrating, the war in Vietnam proved maddening. Shifting and slithering like drops of mercury, the many "war fronts" could hardly be identified, much less pinned down. The enemy was literally everywhere and nowhere; American soldiers did not know which of the "black pajama"-clad peasants tending the rice fields would become nightime Vietcong raiders. Soon many GIs came to regard all of the "gooks," and their families, as "Charlies" (Vietcong). At first, the American military tried to operate by the book, seeking out large enemy units, occupying this valley or capturing that mountain, but once the Americans withdrew Communist forces came back, though decimated by massive U.S. artillery and air strikes. North Vietnamese infiltrators and supplies, supposedly interdicted by the bombing which Johnson's advisers had assured him would humble the Reds in six months, continued to pour in. The American commander, General William Westmoreland, unable to crush the enemy, pressured Washington for another 100,000 troops or another dozen air squadrons although, given the small size of the country, South Vietnam seemed already saturated with well-equipped American fighting men.

Within the administration these frustrations led first to bewilderment, then to anger. The president's determination hardened. With no end in sight, and the war costing $30 billion a year, the predictably optimistic dispatches from Saigon became monotonous and unbelievable. Statistics on enemy casualties ("bodycount" in Pentagon jargon) quickly surpassed even the capabilities of American firepower; by 1967, claims of enemy dead reached 400,000, more than the entire strength of the North Vietnamese army. Johnson

and his supporters dismissed war critics as "nervous Nellies," bent on making the same mistakes isolationists committed in the 1930s when they urged appeasement of Hitler and the Nazis.

The Mounting Opposition

But bravado could not contain the growing opposition to the war. First, right-wingers criticized Johnson's "no-win" policy, demanding an even stronger military effort culminating in an invasion of North Vietnam and, if necessary, bombing of China. The strongest antiwar effort came, however, from liberal and left-wing circles, especially in the universities. Starting in 1965, when Johnson announced he would send an American army to Vietnam, "teach-ins" at the colleges examined and almost always condemned U.S. intervention in Southeast Asia. Protest spilled from the campuses to the streets and around military bases. Hundreds of young men publicly burned their draft cards, and several thousand fled to Canada to avoid conscription for a war they called stupid and immoral. Most young men accepted conscription fatalistically, however, but with no enthusiasm for the cause. A massive antiwar demonstration outside the Pentagon in 1967 made it painfully evident that an enormous gap existed between American policy and popular sentiment.

By 1968, Vietnam had poisoned American politics and derailed the Great Society. In Europe the Western alliance sagged, weakened by France's withdrawal from NATO. America's allies regarded the war as a self-inflicted wound, a problem they wanted no part of.

In other foreign policy areas Johnson ran into opposition. The Alliance for Progress remained largely an idea. Preoccupied with a Vietnamese war that cost billions, Congress would not appropriate sufficient money to help Latin America lift itself from economic backwardness. Instead of nurturing the alliance, the president reverted to strong-arm tactics. In 1965, following a revolution in the Dominican Republic, Johnson sent American troops into that Caribbean country in order to "protect American lives." Few Americans lived there, and all knew that Washington's real purpose was to prevent the emergence of a left-wing, pro-Castro, Dominican government. Earlier, when right-wing militarists seized power in Brazil, Johnson gave the army junta quick recognition and support.

Back home, civil rights leaders complained with increasing anger that the cost of the Vietnamese war had choked off funds for the war on poverty, that poor Americans—so many of them black—were being slaughtered in Vietnam and then neglected at home. Discontent over the negligible effects of civil rights legislation on black ghetto life exploded in city after city. The Watts section of Los Angeles, for all its vaunted sunshine, palm trees, and elbow room, burned down in three days of rioting in the summer of 1965. The burnings spread to Rochester, Newark, San Francisco, Detroit, Washington, and a hundred other places. Each "long, hot summer" became a time of particular tension, as Americans wondered where the next civil disturbance would erupt.

Established Negro leaders suddenly found themselves unable to lead the black masses. Martin Luther King, sensing the bankruptcy of legalism and nonviolence, began redirecting his energies in a campaign against ghetto blight. Militant groups like the gun-toting Black Panthers, though small in numbers, became large in importance as expressions of growing black rage.

With Johnson blindly groping for a way out of the war without disgrace, the Vietnamese Communists launched the Tet Offensive in January 1968. Attacking boldly in almost every province of South Vietnam, the Reds captured the major city of Hue and their commando units almost penetrated the American Embassy in Saigon. Though the Communists lost thousands of men, and though they had to fall back, the extent and ferocity of their attacks shocked Americans, and convinced them that military victory was impossible. From that point on, millions of Americans joined the many antiwar protesters in dismissing their own government's war communiques.

In the rubble of Tet lay the shattered remains of Lyndon B. Johnson's career, as well as the myth of American omnipotence. The Marines had landed in a tropical country, but the "natives" had not been pacified. "Armed peasants who are willing to die are a match for the mightiest power," observed Walter Lippman. "Elephants cannot clear mosquitoes from a swamp."

EXIT JOHNSON, ENTER NIXON

The Tet Offensive immediately undercut LBJ's chances for reelection. Senator Eugene McCarthy of Minnesota, a critic of the war, had decided to challenge the president for the Democratic nomination. Few took his bid seriously until the New Hampshire primary election. Coming shortly after the Tet debacle, the primary produced a new humiliation for the president when he almost lost to McCarthy, who had run an antiwar campaign staffed mainly by amateurs, many of them college students. McCarthy's "peace vote" of 42 percent could not be dismissed by those hoping to maintain the status quo.

Late in March, the president startled the world by announcing a halt in bombing of most of North Vietnam and calling for peace negotiations. But even more incredibly, this Texas political pro declared he would not run for reelection. Suddenly the Democratic nomination became a wide-open prize. After New Hampshire, former Attorney General Robert Kennedy, then a senator from New York, had entered the race, and Vice-president Hubert H. Humphrey joined in later with White House blessing. In the Republican camp, Richard Nixon, the new "Mr. Republican," had been waiting patiently in the wings for several years.

Then came the assassinations. Martin Luther King had gone to Memphis in April to support a strike by black garbagemen. A white gunman cut him down, touching off disorders in the black ghettos that lasted a week and hit dozens of cities. Troops patrolled the White House and Capitol Hill, as rioting spread through Washington, D.C. Meanwhile, Robert Kennedy had been running well in the primaries and California offered him his big chance. Kennedy, addressing himself particularly to the young and the underprivileged, hoped to shoulder aside McCarthy and present the Democratic bosses with a convention alternative of losing with Humphrey, Johnson's "heir," or winning with another Kennedy. Kennedy won the California test, but on his night of triumph another gunman (a young Palestinian immigrant angered over Kennedy's pro-Israel stand) altered the course of the campaign, and perhaps of the presidency as well, adding to the shock of an already traumatic year.

With the death of Kennedy, Vice-president Humphrey had clear sailing to the Democratic nomination. Humphrey, the talkative Democrat, became a political alchemist, trying to turn the dross of the now-discredited Johnson policies into the gold of a new and winning stance. Republican Nixon wanted to calm the electorate and presented a refurbished image, more relaxed and responsible, no longer that of the political gutfighter of the 1950s. The Vietnam War must be wound up, he agreed, but without humiliation for the United States. And as the campaign wore on, Nixon relied increasingly on the "law-and-order" theme, issuing appeals that both perturbed and promised to calm Americans. Street crime, ghetto rioting, and violent student protest disturbed and disgusted citizens of "Middle America," the majority of middle-class and prosperous working-class whites. Nixon called for more police protection, tougher treatment of lawbreakers. "The wave of crime is not going to be the wave of the future in the United States," he assured.

Since both candidates me-tooed each other, and with Vietnam hardly an issue between them, the "excitement" of the contest sprang mainly from dissident groups. First, the Democratic convention at Chicago became the scene of one of the wildest melees in American political history. Several thousand antiwar protesters had congregated in Chicago bent on provoking a confrontation with authority. When they would not leave a public park, or disperse before an unauthorized march, Chicago police waded in, completely out of control. Infuriated by the protesters' longhaired life-styles, and maddened by constant use of the word "pig" for "policeman," Mayor Richard Daley's cops began clubbing everyone in sight, including bystanders and newsmen. The day after Humphrey's nomination the police did behave like pigs, storming the McCarthy headquarters in the Conrad Hilton Hotel in a rage, indiscriminately clubbing the college students. Only McCarthy's hurried arrival at 5 A.M. prevented their arrest

and further manhandling. Later, an official investigation called the incidents "a police riot."

At the other end of the political spectrum stood Alabama's Governor George Wallace. The pugnacious segregationist who "stood in the schoolhouse door" in 1963 ran for president on the American Independent Party ticket. Campaigning in the North and West, as well as in his native South, Wallace hit the law-and-order issue hard, also attacking racial integration and failure to use maximum force in Vietnam. Nixon had made several concessions to the white South, agreeing that the snail's pace of school integration should be further slowed down, and that the Supreme Court needed more conservative justices, but he still feared Wallace's appeal to normally Republican right-wing voters, North and South.

The outcome, reflecting the absence of clear differences between the two major candidates, resulted once more in a political stalemate. Nixon with 43.4 percent of the vote and Humphrey with 42.7 percent had both called for peace in Vietnam, supporting negotiations with the North Vietnamese in Paris which began in May 1968, but they opposed immediate withdrawal; both called for law and order, the Democrat Humphrey putting heavier stress on the need for social reforms; and both urged the American people to unite, Nixon imploring leaders and dissidents to "lower their voices" and seek national harmony. Voter participation dropped to 61 percent of eligibles, despite the many disturbances of 1968 (in 1960 nearly 64 percent of eligibles had voted). The racist fringe expanded to 13.5 percent of the vote, but Wallace carried only five states, all in the Deep South.

For the first time in over a century an incoming president had failed to carry Congress for his party. Republican gains, a few seats in each house, still left them short of control. True, the Johnson administration had been utterly repudiated, but except in the South the Democratic coalition remained remarkably intact, though battered. Lackluster Hubert Humphrey nearly pulled victory out of the jaws of Johnson's defeat. Most of the traditional sources of Democratic strength, particularly organized labor and blacks, remained loyal. Although the Wallace vote confirmed that the country had lurched to the right,

Nixon had a tiny and tentative mandate. With Republicans still the minority party, Richard Nixon would have to work with a hostile Congress. Moreover, as head of a party suspicious of all government, and as self-appointed spokesman for the difficult-to-articulate yearnings of the Silent Majority, President Nixon faced seemingly intractable problems shorn of many of the political weapons he would need to fashion successful policies.

NIXON'S CONDITIONAL MANDATE

After a decade of disasters which eroded self-confidence and national unity, Americans yearned above all for harmony. Shortly after the election, President-elect Nixon adopted as his goal the motto held up by a teenager in Ohio during the campaign: "Bring Us Together." To dampen partisan spirit, Americans should work together. The call was both patriotic and politically expedient. As head of a minority party, and lacking control of Congress, Nixon would have to rely on continued support from nonaligned voters occupying the center of the political spectrum.

In practice the Nixon administration was anything but nonpartisan or unifying. The president chose only Republicans for his first cabinet, ignored blacks, and picked as secretary of labor the dean of the University of Chicago School of Business. After urging Americans to lower their voices, Nixon unleashed the strident Vice-president Spiro T. Agnew. The president took the high-toned road; Agnew took the partisan, political low road. Placed on the ticket to win Southern support, Agnew insulted one group after another. Himself of Greek descent, he referred to Polish-Americans as "Polacks," and to a Japanese-American reporter as a "fat Jap." As for blacks, Agnew demonstrated his customary insensitivity when he remarked with obvious disdain: "When you've seen one urban slum, you've seen 'em all." The vice-president later went on to attack newspaper and TV journalists as irresponsible, college students as long-haired bums, and intellectuals and professors as "effete, intellectual snobs." Nixon's double-barreled strategy thus sought votes from the center by appearing statesmanlike and moderate, while Agnew simultaneously cemented a Republican majority by courting Northern workers and suburbanites and white Southerners resentful of the new youth counterculture, the black revolution, and urban crime.

Agnew, formerly governor of Maryland, was part of a Republican "Southern Strategy." Nixon had hoped to carry most of the South in 1968, but the Wallace candidacy cost him five Southern states. Once elected, Nixon hoped to win the white South over to the Republican column and thereby forge a new GOP majority. As Southern white hatred for the Supreme Court had burned steadily since the desegregation decisions, Nixon promised more sectional and ideological "balance" on the court. When Chief Justice Earl Warren retired, the president replaced him with Warren Burger, a strict "law-and-order" federal judge who felt that the court had been overactive and too permissive. And when the next vacancy occurred, Nixon designated Clement F. Haynsworth, a South Carolina judge whose background generated attacks by civil rights and labor leaders. The Senate rejected Haynsworth, and then went on to veto Nixon's second choice, G. Harrold Carswell, a federal judge from Florida. Nixon, angered over these embarrassing slaps at his Southern Strategy, finally appointed a Northerner to the court.

On most other domestic issues, Nixon maintained the traditional Republican line. He severely cut the appropriations for Great Society programs and vowed to balance the budget. Yet he favored the development of a costly antiballistic missile (ABM) system. Without these missiles, designed to knock down enemy missiles in flight, argued the Pentagon and the White House, Russia or other nuclear powers possessing them could blackmail the United States. Critics replied that the ABM might not work, and that pressing ahead with ABM and a multiple warheads system for offensive missiles (MIRV) would open a Pandora's box of escalation in the nuclear arms race. After winning the first test in the Senate in November 1969 by one vote, the president announced that he would seek an expanded ABM system.

Although many scientists doubted the feasibility of ABM, a spectacular moonwalk in August 1969 made any technological achievement appear possible. The American space program had been accelerated following the Sputnik challenge in the late 1950s, and President Kennedy had promised that the first man to walk on the moon would be an American, and that he would do it before the end of the 1960s. With six months to spare Colonel Neil Armstrong made good on Kennedy's prophecy. The entire world applauded the amazing feat, even the Russians. When President Nixon welcomed the astronauts back to earth he told them: "This is the greatest week in the history of the world since the Creation." The televised moonwalk, exhilirating though it was, disturbed some Americans who wondered if it was worth the enormous expense considering other pressing needs at home. Urban blight, racial tensions, increasing unemployment, inflation—all these problems awaited solution while billions of dollars were poured into the space program. And even more billions continued to disappear down the Vietnamese rat-hole.

Nixon's War

During 1969–1970 the war "cooled off," but still it did not end. Peace negotiators had met fruitlessly in Paris since the spring of 1968, and after November 1968 Americans stopped bombing North Vietnam. The ground fighting also tapered off, punctuated from time to time by savage encounters which reminded the world that war still raged. In April 1969 U.S. deaths in Vietnam surpassed the death toll for the Korean War. Two months later, the president, though announcing coming reductions in the number of Americans in Vietnam, vowed that he would never accept outright defeat. Rapping the antiwar critics as "new isolationists," Nixon promised that the South Vietnamese would do more of the fighting. This policy of "Vietnamization" and gradual American pullout proceeded slowly. The first U.S. units withdrew in July, and by the end of 1969 American troop strength in Vietnam had been cut by about 60,000.

Vietnamization did not impress the war's critics, however. Calling the pullouts a "trickle" designed to divert attention and raise false hopes, they demanded immediate withdrawal. Revelations in late 1969 of a massacre by U.S. troops of civilians in a South Vietnamese village shocked Americans profoundly. Prodded into action by the news media, the army indicted a half dozen soldiers and suspended several more, including two generals, for trying to hush up the incident, but few men were brought to trial.

Then in the spring of 1970 the Cambodian incursion produced another profound shock. For years North Vietnam had been using Cambodia as a staging area and supply dump, the end of the Reds' "Ho Chi Minh Trail" from Hanoi through Laos and Cambodia. Nixon decided to attack these "sanctuaries," arguing that a successful sweep of the area would buy time and give Vietnamization a better chance to work. He promised that U.S. troops would be out of Cambodia in two months. But many Americans, recalling the piecemeal manner in which the United States became tangled in the Vietnam swamp, did not believe him. Antiwar protests flared anew, especially in the colleges. At Kent State University in Ohio, national guardsmen fired on demonstrators, killing four students. A few days later, Mississippi police killed several black students at Jackson State College. It seemed that the war had produced a new battle front, the college campus. Congress also reacted to Cambodia. In the Senate the number of war critics had grown. These Vietnam "doves" called for a quick end to the war through political settlement. Voting against any appropriation for war in Cambodia, they also repealed the Tonkin Gulf Resolution of 1968 and placed curbs on further expansion of the war. Most American politicians, like the president, balked at accepting defeat in Vietnam; however, Nixon's pullback from Cambodia on schedule and as promised helped him repel the doves' assault. As the congressional elections of 1970 approached it appeared that he had successfully neutralized the Vietnam issue, and that the popularity of troop withdrawals, partial though they were, might allow him to pull off the political coup he needed in order to govern effectively.

The Nixon administration's prospects depended on its ability to handle problems growing out of the Vietnam War. At home, the war produced the worst inflation since World War II, stemming from massive government spending without heavier taxations to cut back on purchasing power. Yet at the same time, the prosperity of the 1960s petered out and the country crept into a recession. By 1970, unemployment was as high as 11 percent in some parts of the country (nationally it averaged 6 percent), while prices still continued to surge. The president vacillated. An orthodox Republican, he rejected price controls to check inflation and favored reductions in federal spending to reduce demand. He cut back severely on Great Society programs and trimmed defense spending too, though the Vietnam War dragged on and kept the military budget high. The drop in government spending had little effect on inflation but caused increased unemployment and a deepening recession.

The Nixon Economy

Economic issues determined the outcome of the 1970 midterm elections. Attempting to divert voters' attention from their pocketbooks, Nixon and Agnew launched an unprecedented campaign to capture control of the Congress. They rested their hopes on inflammatory attacks on the Democrats as the party responsible for street crime, urban disorder, and student violence. The president went too far. He not only strained the credulity of the electorate, but he could not make people forget the condition of their finances. As a result Democrats retained control of both houses of Congress, and made huge gains in the state elections.

As Nixon looked ahead to 1972 and reelection, he had to abandon Republican orthodoxy and embrace Democratic fiscal policy. In January 1971 he announced a "full employment budget," a euphemistic phrase meaning deficit spending, which Republicans had condemned for a generation. Promising to stimulate the economy yet still combat inflation, Nixon also unveiled a program he described as the most revolutionary in decades. It included a proposal to reform welfare programs by guaranteeing poor families a minimum income; revenue sharing to return billions of tax dollars to the states and cities virtually bankrupt in the face of soaring costs for government services; and administrative reorganization to streamline the Washington bureaucracy. In mid-year, Nixon resorted to a 90-day wage and price freeze and further anti-inflationary government controls after that.

But the Vietnam War lurked in the background, haunting the president's hope for reelection in 1972. In 1969 he had proclaimed a "Nixon Doctrine," in which he promised that Asian allies would henceforth have to defend themselves. They could still count on American military supplies and economic assistance, but American troops would no longer be sent to the Asian mainland. Nearly all Americans welcomed the policy statement, but its implementation as something more than wishful thinking depended on the president's ability to extricate the United States from Vietnam.

With the economy faltering and the war still far from over (especially after a South Vietnamese invasion of Laos in February 1971, an incursion supported by American air power), some predicted that Richard Nixon would become the first president denied a second term since Herbert Hoover. The buoyed-up Democrats looked confidently ahead to recapturing the White House. Whatever happened, perceptive observers of American politics doubted that either party could achieve prosperity and social justice at home, and long-term peace abroad, without far-reaching shifts in public attitudes and national values that were nowhere in sight.

Chapter 37
Age of Anxiety

As Americans approached the two-hundredth anniversary of the founding of the Republic, it was painfully evident that they lacked much of the confidence and optimism that had inspired earlier generations. The first citizens of the United States were eighteenth-century revolutionaries; today Americans live in fear of twentieth-century revolution. Two hundred years ago the principles on which Americans founded their republic—the first nation conceived in liberty—inspired much of mankind in the Western world and liberated human aspirations in faraway places. Today few nations look to America for national ideals though they may envy its unparalleled prosperity. Two hundred years ago the United States was an untested, weak, new nation. Today it is the oldest republic in the world, and the most powerful nation on earth.

Yet, paradoxically, its future is in greater peril than at any time since the first decades of independence. Neither wealth nor power provide secure guarantees of survival in a world poised on the edge of nuclear extinction. Nor have affluence, military might, and world leadership given Americans a clear sense of purpose. Though Americans watched the landing on the moon with pride and with awe, this extraordinary technological feat, truly a monument to American science, technology, and wealth, stirred the nation's spirit briefly, but it could not by itself renew the people's faith in themselves.

THE SEARCH FOR VALUES

Somehow, somewhere, Americans sensed a loss of mastery, of national moorings and of direction. In the 1950s one of the country's leading philanthropic foundations established a commission to rediscover and articulate national goals. The effort proved little more than an expensive and fruitless exercise in self-scrutiny. Others responded to the sense of drift by seeking refuge in organized religion. Postwar America saw the makings of a religious "revival." By 1958 over 60 percent of the population claimed religious affiliation compared to 36 percent in 1900. Yet though churches and synagogues acquired new members, there was little evidence of renewed belief in the supernatural or of commitment to piety. The churches themselves became increasingly secularized, and what people wanted most from them was "peace of mind."

The most influential minister of the decade was the Rev. Norman Vincent Peale, who preached "The Power of Positive Thinking" as the sure way to success in business, romance, or anything else one desired in this world (Adlai Stevenson, ever ready with egghead quips which cost him so many votes, said of Peale: ". . . among the evangelists, I found Paul appealing, and Peale appalling"). Peale and his imitators, preaching smug versions of "self-help" and "peace of mind," had little or nothing to do with Judeo-Christian theology. Nonetheless, the religious revival revealed an uneasiness and a will to believe. "Our government makes no sense unless it is founded on a deeply-felt religious faith," said President Eisenhower, and he added characteristically, "I don't care what it is." As one shrewd observer of the religious revival explained: "The Faith is not in God but in faith; we worship not God but our own worshipping."

With neither politicians nor preachers offering Americans much to believe in, people turned inward. Adults retreated into the family, and sought refuge in consumption and escapist entertainment, especially television. And young people in the 1950s, especially middle-class youth, concentrated on getting ahead. The idealism people associated with the younger generation seemed to have disappeared. Instead the Silent Generation worked hard, conformed, and dreamed of carving out a mortgaged niche in the suburban afterlife.

Students of American national character detected a profound shift in personal values and behavior. The American model, they noted, had once been the rugged individualist. Now it was becoming the Organization Man. In the past

Americans navigated, or thought they navigated, through life on an internal gyroscope that made individuals willing to stand alone, to struggle for their beliefs, and compete for success. Now, critics argued, the American was becoming "other-directed," taking his cues from his fellows, unsure of his beliefs, fearful of offending anyone, attuning himself to prevailing wavelengths, shifting as they shifted. Conformity and caution seemed the safest course in an uncertain age, the best strategy for acquiring a share of the new affluence — the leisure, the creature comforts, and the privacy it made possible.

Then in the 1960s a revolution exploded in the United States. The complacency of the postwar years gave way to urgency over the unfinished business of American democracy—poverty, racism, urban and rural blight, pollution, and, above all, the quest for meaning in life. At one end of the social spectrum stood the poorest of the poor—America's twenty million black people. They wanted to share, too; their initial dream was little more than participation in the life-styles of the affluent but anxiety-ridden white middle classes. From peaceful protest to ghetto uprisings, the crusade for civil rights shifted by the end of the 1960s to a search for group identity through black power as the indispensable precondition for genuine racial progress. No group of white Americans empathized more with the blacks than middle-class white youth. They, too, protested against inequality, joined the March on Washington, and spent Freedom Summers in Mississippi.

But while their role in the black revolution at home and in the Peace Corps abroad gave evidence that youthful idealism remained alive in America, its principal manifestation took the form of an anti-middle-class cultural revolution in which millions of young people created new music, wore new hair styles, put on new clothing, and consumed new drugs, as they groped to discover who they were, what they wanted to become, and what sort of country they wished to live in. The Silent Generation of the 1950s gave way to the Now Generation of the 1960s, the gray flannel suit to blue jeans, the crew cut to shaggy locks, and the June-moon-spoon music of Frank Sinatra to hard and folk rock. To be sure, not all young people joined the "turned-on" generation, but

the new youth culture affected everyone, even the oldsters, to some degree. Young Americans were searching for new values that would give greater meaning to their lives than the privatism, conformity, and complacency of the 1950s had given to their elders.

In this new, more critical and dissenting mood, many realized that unprecedented affluence brought its own problems. Poverty and squalor, urban and rural, though it afflicted a minority, persisted to a greater degree in America than in any of the world's advanced industrial democracies. In the slums of New York and Chicago, in the cotton fields of Mississippi and Alabama, and on the giant farm-factories of California, millions remained trapped in poverty and apparent hopelessness. The affluent majority simply ignored the gross disparities existing in the world's richest nation. Since most people were doing well, the poverty of the urban ghetto or the migrant labor camp could be swept under the rug.

Moreover, the affluent felt new anxieties of their own. People fled to the suburbs from decaying central cities to escape, they thought, the disadvantages of urban life: its overcrowding, dirt, mediocre schools, and the tensions of multiethnic and biracial metropolises. Suburbia offered a chance to exchange the asphalt and concrete jungles of the Big City for a place where people had more room, some trees and grass, and a surrounding population of similar ethnic character and class status. Above all, suburbia provided a suitable setting in which home ownership and the accumulation of creature comforts gave tangible evidence of a family's achievement and status. Yet, once established in their suburban castles, the middle classes found that prosperity gave them no immunity from the smog that choked the atmosphere, the dreary real estate developments that marred the landscape, the traffic that jammed the highways, and the soaring crime rates that made life less secure for all.

And suburbia bred other characteristically middle class problems, especially the generation gap. A youth culture, already emerging in the 1920s, had grown by the 1960s into a counterculture. Young people, especially teen-agers, became an increasingly large and troublesome group. With life-styles that more sharply than ever set them off from their elders they began first to question, and then to dissent from, the morals, mores, and manners of their parents. Students charged them with favoring material values over human values, depriving people of meaningful work, dooming them to a world dominated by large, bureaucratic institutions—from the multiversity to the conglomerate giants of the corporate empire—and condemning them to a "rat race" in which people worked on a treadmill to make money to buy things and achieve status.

Parents and grandparents were bewildered by the attacks youth leveled against the system. The older generation of middle-class Americans was the first to enjoy the abundance and economic security provided by advanced technology, but their children, who never experienced economic deprivation, took the material achievements for granted. For an older generation which had known hard times, economic success was a source of pride and self-esteem. Yet whatever one's judgment, the Affluent Society was reshaping everyone's life in the last quarter century.

THE WELFARE OF THE AMERICAN PEOPLE

Measured by per capita income, Americans were materially better off than any other people in the world. The welfare of a nation, however, involves the distribution and allocation of its wealth, not merely the size of its GNP. The new American political economy, based on advanced technology, reliance on private ownership and management of the means of production, and partial public planning and control, gave the American people since 1945 a rising standard of living and unprecedented economic security. But by the 1960s many Americans began criticizing the performance of a productive system so efficient in producing goods yet so unresponsive to many glaring public needs.

Poverty remained a strange anomaly in a country capable of eliminating it. Between 20 and 25 percent of the population remained mired in poverty in the 1960s, a decline from the "one-third of a country" Franklin Roosevelt saw ill-fed, ill-clothed, and ill-housed in the mid-1930s, but

still a sizeable number. The persistence of poverty in an affluent society puzzled the prosperous, many of whom blithely cast blame on the poor for their misfortune. In fact, chronic poverty resulted from the social dislocations and social pathologies Affluent America seemed unable to cope with and which to some degree it had intensified. First, distribution of income remained lopsided, though somewhat less so than in the past. The top half of 1 percent owned 25 percent of all personal wealth in the 1950s, a decline from nearly 30 percent in the early 1920s. The most significant change occurred among the middle-income strata, whose share increased markedly. In contrast, families at the bottom very slightly increased their share, though the percentage at the very bottom declined.

Although the skilled, the educated, the organized did well in the Affluent Society, others fell behind, especially the aged, the black and Spanish-American minorities, small farm owners and agricultural laborers, and other unorganized, unskilled labor. Poor white farmers and black sharecroppers in Mississippi and Arkansas, for example, were pushed off the land, as planters consolidated their holdings and replaced labor with machinery.

Because of similar displacement elsewhere, millions migrated to the North and to the West in search of jobs and a new life. But rural folk— without skills and driven off the land into an unfamiliar urban environment—had difficulty getting good jobs. The wages they earned as garbage collectors, porters, dishwashers, and maids could not support a family (often a large family) decently. The Affluent Society had no plan for dealing with these social castoffs, victims of technological and entrepreneurial revolutions. Whole regions became depressed areas as the result of long-term shifts: the decline of coal mining left many thousands in the Appalachian mining country without jobs, and the continued movement of textile factories from the Northeast to the South created near ghost towns in New England.

Businessmen assumed no direct responsibility for the human wreckage that resulted from changes dictated by new profit opportunities, and the federal government did not step in until the

1960s. Often federal aid to hardship areas attempted to attract new industry to depressed counties but these efforts, and job retraining and remedial education programs for the poor, hardly made a dent in the problem. Even government help could not manufacture enough good jobs for the poor. Moreover, the poor were psychologically so beaten down and defeated, so immersed in a subculture of poverty, that it proved extremely difficult for them to escape from the cycle of poverty, through which one generation of poor bred the next.

The Affluent Society responded to poverty primarily with a jerry-built, inadequate system of public relief. Welfare kept the poor from starving, though hunger and malnutrition afflicted large numbers of them, especially in rural America, but it also perpetuated dependency. And while middle-class taxpayers complained about the growing burden of welfare costs, Americans produced no realistic plan for breaking the poverty cycle.

Private Wealth and Public Squalor

Equally disturbing, the Affluent Society failed to provide adequate public services neglected by the private sector. Americans spent more of their income on cars than on state and local governments. As a result of a preference for personal consumption, certain social needs were starved for funds. Americans, for instance, demanded and received more schooling than ever. An advanced technological society needed enormous numbers of engineers, technicians, and managers. Outlays for education rose especially in the 1960s when the federal government for the first time provided large-scale funding for education from kindergarten to graduate school. But the percentage of the GNP spent on education increased slowly and fell far short of need. Teachers remained underpaid, outdated school buildings survived long after they deserved to be scrapped, and many schools were jammed with students on double session. A massive increase in public higher education brought college within the reach of millions for the first time but the big state universities became giant educational factories, their students soon to complain vociferously of the impersonality of the system.

Urban growth created similar problems. The central cities decayed as the middle classes deserted them for the suburbs; the rural poor from all parts of the country poured into cities, whose slums spread like a terminal-stage cancer. Private enterprise failed to build new housing that low income groups could afford and the government's public housing proved woefully inadequate. Even the few low-cost units constructed were usually dreary, barrack-like stockades, clearly designed for society's failures. Slum clearance and mammoth urban renewal programs in the downtown areas made a start in the task of rebuilding America's cities but these projects replaced rundown poor areas with luxury apartment houses for the affluent and expensive office buildings for business. For the poor, urban renewal often meant their own removal, their forced transfer from one slum to another.

Americans had become so infatuated with the private automobile that they permitted mass transit systems to decay. But millions of miles of new freeways, including a 41,000-mile federal interstate highway program inaugurated in the 1950s, proved no substitute during rush hours for an efficient mass transit system in the cities.

Americans, however, preferred to spend their income privately rather than to pay higher taxes to buy better schools and nonpolluting transportation. Similarly, government stood by while rivers became fouled by waste from factories and sewage systems and automobile exhaust made city air unbreathable. Environmental pollution originated in unplanned growth—autos by the millions created smog, factories poured untreated wastes into local rivers, oil refineries blackened the atmosphere with putrid fumes. Cleaning up the air and water would cost billions of dollars. Until the late 1960s few Americans were aware of the deadly toll economic growth was taking on the environment. Then the results of a generation of neglect became apparent. But as awareness spread, it proved difficult to do anything because the polluters had a vested interest in polluting. It was cheaper to run a business or govern a city without respecting the environment. And while citizens unanimously clamored for clean air and pure water, only massive investments by business and government, and mandatory shifts in living patterns, could achieve such goals.

The neglect of the nation's environment, its cities, its schools, and its disadvantaged human beings ran parallel with neglect of its health needs. Despite dramatic, widely publicized advances in medical technology in the last twenty-five years, improvement in the health of the American people fell far short of what an affluent society could afford. Life expectancy increased and medicine made new conquests against diseases such as polio and measles. But compared to the other industrial nations of Western Europe, the United States slipped behind. With the sixth lowest infant mortality rate in 1950, the United States dropped to fourteenth in 1967, behind Communist East Germany. Yet during this period health care commanded a constantly growing percentage of the GNP and medical costs skyrocketed. A hospital bed which cost $15 a day in 1945 cost $60 a day in 1970. The country needed more doctors and dentists than were turned out by medical schools, shortages especially felt in small towns and rural areas.

Doctors became America's highest paid professionals but the system that sent them to the top financially did not serve the rest of the country so well. Operating on a fee-for-service basis, doctors were suspicious of the most efficient and effective health care systems since they feared that any alterations in private practice would cut into incomes and subject them to bureaucratic supervision. Organized medicine fought government-backed health insurance fiercely. Although most unionized workers and salaried employees obtained privately financed health insurance, it was expensive, rarely providing full coverage, and it left most of the unorganized low income groups uncovered. Finally in 1965 Congress adopted Medicare for persons over 65. As the cost of medical care advanced astronomically, middle-income families faced severe financial pressures despite their insurance coverage, creating new needs for a truly comprehensive system of national health insurance.

The niggardliness with which the Affluent Society funded public services contrasted sharply with the generosity with which it poured billions into national defense. Defense spending required huge federal budgets and high taxes and gobbled up the greater share—50 to 60 percent—of the revenues flowing into Washington. Although such expenditures were defended as a national necessity, and had served as a major prop behind postwar prosperity, they made it more difficult to rebuild the cities, clean the air, and improve the schools. Throughout the 1960s many Americans began to question the size of military budgets. Much military spending was wasteful and bought no national security. The Defense Department, for example, spent a billion dollars on the atomic plane before abandoning it as impractical, one of many such costly fiascos. The navy had stockpiled a hundred year's supply of canned hamburgers. With the federal government commanding the bulk of the scientific and engineering manpower for military purposes, the economy's private sector suffered neglect. Scientific solutions to the problems of mass transportation, inexpensive housing, efficient health care, and conservation of the environment were not pursued.

In like fashion, the money spent on the manned flight to the moon in 1969 could have given every teacher in America a salary raise of 10 percent annually, provided 200 small colleges with $10 million annually, financed seven-year fellowships for 50,000 scientists and engineers, built ten new medical schools, or erected and endowed complete universities in 53 nations, with money left over. In rebuttal the director of the National Aeronautics and Space Administration argued: "With a billion people already allied against us, and the uncommitted and emerging nations weighing events that will affect their own future welfare, the United States must present the image of a can-do nation, with which they can confidently align their futures."

Critics of military and space spending doubted the wisdom of the United States basing its international claims for leadership on military might and space achievements, while neglecting the needs of its own people. Such an arrangement of national priorities was not likely to impress the poor nations with two-thirds of the world's population—once the novelty of man-on-the-moon technology had passed. Two years and two more manned flights to the moon later, no "Third World" nation had aligned itself with the United States because of the moon walk. Moreover, within the United States, a generation of Americans was coming of age which adopted new life-styles and personal values profoundly at war with those that propelled the middle-class "straights" of the Affluent Society.

A NEW GENERATION

In August 1969 tens of thousands of young people from all over the country clogged every road leading to the tiny hamlet of Woodstock, New York. They came for three days to listen to rock music, to smoke marijuana, and make love, but above all, to find momentarily a new community built on the life-style and attitudes of their own generation. The "Woodstock Nation" gave dramatic witness to the emergence of an American youth culture in the 1960s. Huddled together among their own, they found temporary safety from the American institutions they considered oppressive, and from the hostile gaze of the older generation. Like the great religious revivals of the eighteenth and nineteenth centuries, Woodstock represented a search for a new community by those at odds with themselves and their society.

Woodstock had a history. Signs of revolt were already in the air by the 1950s. A small group of Beatniks proclaimed the moral bankruptcy of middle-class life, denounced materialism and the success ethic, and practiced new bohemianism based on art, drugs, mysticism, and sensuality. "Perhaps I could go to work selling soap or hair dye," asserted one Beatnik, "and in fifteen years work myself up to a $60,000 mortgage, and carry my wife's pocketbook for her through Europe. No thanks, I'd rather stick to my own mud puddle." Few took the Beatniks seriously—but in the next decade their message reached more receptive ears. Youth everywhere became more rebellious. The number of arrests of persons under eighteen was increasing far more rapidly than the growth of that age group. In 1964 students at the University of California in Berkeley brought that gigantic and prestigeous "multiversity" to a dead halt when hundreds of them sat-in at the administration building to protest restrictions on student political activity and the bureaucratization of higher education.

Meanwhile, young people were participating in a cultural revolution that was both a form of protest against their parents' world and an effort to create a new one of their own. The Flower Children of San Francisco, the advance guard of a new social type, the hippie, most sharply revealed the extent of the generation gap. Hippies were young people adrift. Some ran away from home; others simply "split" from their parents by mutual consent. All had dropped out of the "rat race," that treadmill to middle-class success which rewarded those who graduated from college, worked hard, and earned money to buy things and to achieve status. Hippie counterculture expressed in an extreme way the alienation millions of adolescents felt growing up in the 1960s, but who were unwilling to make a clean break. The hippies rejected a life of work for a life of play; they insisted on immediate gratification.

Millions imitated them, in varying degree. Drug use, especially of marijuana, became widespread in colleges and high schools. Drugs were an avenue of escape into new mind-expanding experiences which many found pleasurable. They enabled people to unblock, chemically, inhibitions kept tightly in check by man's powerful psychological mechanisms for repression. Paralleling the emergence of the drug culture that sought to heighten experience came new attitudes toward sensuality. The sexual revolution evident in the 1920s gained momentum among middle-class youth as more and more adopted freer attitudes toward sex which previous generations had labeled immoral and promiscuous. The development of birth-control pills had supposedly solved the physical problems of premarital sex. Yet illegitimate births among girls between 16 and 19 more than doubled between 1940 and 1960 though the number of persons in that age group increased only 10 percent, and the incidence of venereal disease rose sharply among young people.

A new music became the chief medium for the diffusion and celebration of the values of the youth culture. In the past, popular music flowed out of the Negro blues and jazz tradition, and from facile pens of commercial songwriters who found a thousand ways to write the same love song. Then in the late 1950s came rock-and-roll. Though it owed much to black music, rock-and-roll and its successors became media for expressing the alienation and the hopes of youth, white and black. The music of Elvis Presley, Little Richard, the Beatles, the Jefferson Airplane, the Rolling Stones, and others derived its power from a strong beat that moved people emotionally, from fresh melodic invention, and from lyrics which sometimes achieved poetic truth, as in the work of Simon and Garfunkel and Bob Dylan. Above all, rock was made by and for the Now Generation. Rock musicians wrote and performed their own music, giving authentic voice to the anxieties of adolescence.

> You who are on the road
> Must have a code
> That you can live by
> And so become yourself
> Because the past is just a goodbye.
>
> Teach your parents well
> Their children's hell
> Will slowly go by
> And feed them on your dreams
> The one they picks
> The one they know by*

The clothes, hair, music, and drugs turned off and frightened millions of older Americans. People who had struggled to acquire the material comforts of the affluent society could not understand why their children and grandchildren turned so rebellious or at least indifferent. Some politicians sought to capitalize on anxiety over campus unrest and the youth rebellion, further inflaming the generational conflict.

The Generation Gap

The generation gap existed for several reasons. First, America was becoming a younger nation. Because of the postwar population boom those under thirty became a majority by the 1960s. This sizable group, which in the past had carried on in the tradition of their fathers, now felt a sense of radical rupture with that past. Previous generations of middle-class Americans had disciplined their lives and found a sense of

---

* "Teach Your Children" (Graham Nash) © 1970 Giving Room Music, Inc. All Rights Reserved. Used by permission of Warner Bros. Music.

purpose by struggling for social respectability and material success. A man worked hard if only to give his children the opportunity to escape physical labor. But in Affluent America young Americans had wealth lavished on them. They became an important market in their own right for records, clothing, cosmetics, and other goods. At the same time, middle-class parents adopted more permissive child-rearing practices, in accordance with up-to-date psychological theories that held that a repressive atmosphere in the home impaired personality development and led to mental illness in later life. But the new permissiveness posed dangers. Not intended to give children license, permissiveness could easily become parental indifference or overindulgence. Advocates of old-fashioned parental discipline complained that American children were being "Spocked, not spanked," a derogatory reference to Dr. Benjamin Spock's influential baby- and child-care ideas. In any case, those growing up in America since 1945 had more opportunity, more security, more comforts than previous generations, but young people were also less certain of what they wanted.

Nowhere was the confusion more evident than in the colleges. In 1939 about 14 percent of those in the 18-to-21 age bracket went to college; by 1961 the figure had increased to almost 40 percent. Higher education, once the privilege of the affluent or lucky few, now became accessible to millions. Colleges expanded to meet the demand of affluent Americans for higher education. A complicated, technologically advanced society required more people with advanced training. The national defense enterprise, for instance, employed tens of thousands of scientists and technicians; the population explosion created a shortage of teachers at every level; and the expansion of government services opened new jobs in public employment.

Occupying a central role in higher education's expansion sat the multiversity, the state universities that grew enormously in the 1950s and 1960s. They combined traditional undergraduate with graduate instruction, and at the same time provided scholars with opportunities to engage in research as well as to put their expertise at the service of business and government. In these vast, often impersonal institutions, students complained that they were lost and ignored. Without clear career goals, many went to college looking for moral and ethical guidance professors could not supply. College training greatly prolonged the years of dependency, postponing the full assumption of adult responsibilities and independence. It also gave students a chance to reflect on life goals, and some rejected their fathers' vision of the good society.

The country fell far short of its declared standards. Whereas their parents were impressed with the strides the country had made *toward* achieving greater equality of opportunity and social justice, dissenting and absolutist youth pointed to the persistence of racism and poverty.

Though they did not reject the creature comforts that an advanced industrial society produced—the cars and the stereo sets—young people complained that man had become a prisoner of the machine and of corporate bureaucracies which manipulated him. They pointed to racial injustice, poverty in the world's richest nation, an endless arms race, and a brutal war in Indo-China as signs of decay. A minority turned to politics and radical confrontation to become part of the New Left, an amorphous coalition of radical groups, mostly young people, who identified capitalism as the source of their alienation, and the nation's problems. Racism and the Vietnam War, they argued, sprang inevitably from a system which liberalism had not fundamentally altered despite a generation of reform politics. The New Left revived Marxism, which in the 1950s had fallen into limbo—a casualty of the Cold War, of the brutality of Stalinist Russia, and of the loss of faith in the idea of progress. But the New Left could not agree either on a program or a strategy for remaking America, though their astringent criticism often hit home and reminded Americans of the gaps between the promise of American life and its shortcomings.

The Uncertain Future

The condition of America's twenty-five million blacks gave cogency to the younger genera-

tion's attacks. For almost 300 years the promise of American life remained an impossible dream for most black Americans. The civil rights movement of the 1950s and early 1960s began to change that, channeling black hopes into areas of peaceful protest. But though legal forms of discrimination fell before the civil rights crusade, by the mid-1960s rioting in most of the country's black ghettos dramatized the despair of the black urban masses. For them, racial integration—the goal of the civil rights movement—meant little. Their problems were economic: chronic poverty, unemployment, poor health, inadequate education, and family instability. The riots were the acts of desperate people whose hopes had first been raised by the struggle for racial justice, then dashed by its limited achievements.

Perceptive blacks and whites recognized that black rage also had its roots in a feeling of impotence, in a lack of self-confidence among Negroes. Until blacks could gain some measure of control over their own communities, it would be difficult to develop pride in themselves and difficult to believe in the beauty of blackness. And unless white America rooted out racism from the fabric of national life, it seemed unlikely that blacks could develop self-sufficiency and self-pride.

America thus seemed impaled on the horns on its own dilemma. The race problem had its roots in slavery, which arose when whites sought to increase their wealth and power at the cost of immeasurable human misery and at the cost of their own ideals. Now in the 1970s, over a century after the formal abolition of slavery, America had still not squared racial realities with national ideals. Though some said it could never be done without radical social transformation, most kept faith in the gradual betterment of the human condition in the United States. But all Americans—the Angry Minority and the Silent Majority—lived in anxiety.

Three and a half centuries ago men had crossed the Atlantic, hoping to gain greater control over their destiny and to build a better life in the New World. By the early 1970s, not even the world's most powerful nation, a nation whose citizens had been first to set foot on the moon, could look confidently to the future. The poet

W. H. Auden† spoke for silent multitudes who never heard his name:

> Our global story is not yet completed,
> Crime, daring, commerce, chatter will go on,
> But, as narrators find their memory gone,
> Homeless, disterred, these know themselves defeated.
>
> Some could not like nor change the young and mourn for
> Some wounded myth that once made children good,
> Some lost a world they never understood,
> Some saw too clearly all that man was born for.
>
> Loss is their shadow-wife, Anxiety
> Receives them like a grand hotel, . . .

The poet was certain of only one thing: "We must love one another or die."‡

SUGGESTIONS FOR FURTHER READING

Suggestions for further reading are highly selective. Works available in paperback editions are starred (*). For additional references, students should consult Carl N. Degler, *Affluence and Anxiety, 1945–Present* (1968)*.

INTRODUCTION

General Works on the Period Since 1945

John Brooks, *The Great Leap: The Past 25 Years in America* (1966)*; Herbert Agar, *The Price of Power: America since 1945* (1957)*; Eric F. Goldman, *The Crucial Decade, and After: America, 1945–1960* (1960)*.

CHAPTER 33

The New Confrontation

John W. Spanier, *American Foreign Policy since World War II* (1960)*; John A. Lucaks, *A History of the Cold War* (1961)*; Walter La Feber, *America, Russia, and the Cold War* (1967)*; William G. Carleton, *The Revolution in American Foreign Policy* (1954)*; Lloyd C. Gardner, *Architects of Illusion: Men and Ideas in American Foreign Policy, 1941–1949* (1970); Thomas G. Paterson (ed.), *Cold War Critics* (1971).

† From Sonnet XVI from "Sonnets from China." Reprinted from *Collected Shorter Poems, 1927–1957*. Copyright © by W. H. Auden. Reprinted by permission of Random House, Inc.

‡ From "September 1, 1939."

Cold War Origins

D. F. Fleming, *The Cold War and Its Origins* (2 vols., 1961); Martin F. Merz, *Beginnings of the Cold War* (1966); Herbert Feis, *Between War and Peace: The Potsdam Conference* (1960)*; Herbert Feis, *The Atomic Bomb and the End of World War II* (1966); Gar Alperovitz, *Atomic Diplomacy* (1965)*.

The Fair Deal

Cabell Phillips, *The Truman Presidency* (1966)*; Susan M. Hartmann, *Truman and the 80th Congress* (1971); Richard E. Neustadt, "Congress and the Fair Deal: A Legislative Balance Sheet," *Public Policy*, vol. 5 (1954); Barton J. Bernstein (ed.), *Politics and Policies of the Truman Administration* (1970)*; Allen J. Matusow, *Farm Policies and Politics in the Truman Years* (1969)*; William S. White, *The Taft Story* (1954); Karl M. Schmidt, *Henry A. Wallace: Quixotic Crusade, 1948* (1960)*; Curtis D. MacDougall, *Gideon's Army* (1965); Samuel Lubell, *The Future of American Politics* (1952)*.

Containment

George F. Kennan, *Memoirs, 1925–1950* (1967)*; Lucius D. Clay, *Decision in Germany* (1950); W. Phillips Davison, *The Berlin Blockade* (1958); Joseph Jones, *The Fifteen Weeks* (1955)*; Harry B. Price, *The Marshall Plan* (1955).

The NATO Alliance

Robert E. Osgood, *NATO: The Entangling Alliance* (1962); Dean Acheson, *Present at the Crea-*

tion (1969); Louis J. Halle, *The Cold War As History* (1967)*.

Asian Quagmire

Herbert Feis, *The China Tangle* (1953)*; Tang Tsou, *America's Failure in China, 1941–1950* (2 vols., 1963)*; A. Doak Barnett, *Communist China and Asia* (1960)*; David Rees, *Korea: The Limited War* (1964); Matthew B. Ridgway, *The Korean War* (1967)*; John W. Spanier, *The Truman-MacArthur Controversy* (1965)*; Courtney Whitney, *MacArthur* (1956); Kazuo Kawai, *Japan's American Interlude* (1960).

The New Red Scare

David A. Shannon, *The Decline of American Communism . . . since 1945* (1959); Max M. Kampelman, *The Communist Party vs. the C.I.O.* (1957); Robert Carr, *The House Committee on Un-American Affairs, 1945–1950* (1952); Walter Goodman, *The Committee* (1968); Earl Latham, *The Communist Controversy in Washington* (1966)*; Eleanor Bontecou, *The Federal Loyalty and Security Program* (1953); Walter Gellhorn, *Security, Loyalty, and Science* (1950); Edward A. Shils, *The Torment of Secrecy: The Background and Consequences of American Security Policies* (1956); Alan D. Harper, *The Politics of Loyalty: The White House and the Communist Issue, 1946–1952* (1969).

Richard H. Rovere, *Senator Joe McCarthy* (1959)*; Nelson W. Polsby, "Toward an Explanation of McCarthyism," *Political Studies*, vol. 8 (1960), pp. 250–271; William F. Buckley and L. Brent Bozell, *McCarthy and His Enemies* (1954); Michael Paul Rogin, *McCarthy and the Intellectuals* (1967)*; Robert Griffith, *The Politics of Fear: Joseph R. McCarthy and the Senate* (1970); Alistair Cooke, *A Generation on Trial* (1950)*; Whittaker Chambers, *Witness* (1952)*; Daniel Bell (ed.), *The Radical Right* (1963)*.

CHAPTER 34

General

Frederick Lewis Allen, *The Big Change* (1952)*; David M. Potter, *People of Plenty* (1954)*; Max Lerner, *America as a Civilization* (1957)*; John K. Galbraith, *The Affluent Society* (1958)*; Robert Theobald, *The Challenge of Abundance* (1961)*; David Riesman, *The Lonely Crowd*
(1950)*; Ruth S. Cavan, *The American Family* (1953).

Foundations of Affluence

Harold G. Vatter, *The United States Economy in the 1950's* (1963)*; Herman P. Miller, *Income of the American People* (1955); Vance Packard, *The Hidden Persuaders* (1957)*.

Giant Enterprise

Adolf A. Berle, Jr., *The 20th Century Capitalist Revolution* (1954); David E. Lilienthal, *Big Business: A New Era* (1953); Milton Friedman, *Capitalism and American Freedom* (1962); Edward S. Mason (ed.), *The Corporation in Modern Society* (1960); William H. Whyte, *The Organization Man* (1956)*; C. Wright Mills, *White Collar* (1951)*; Frederick Pollock, *Automation* (1957); Charles Silberman, *Myths of Automation* (1966)*; Francis Rourke and Glenn Brooks, *The Managerial Revolution in Higher Education* (1966).

The New Political Economy

Seymour Harris (ed.), *The New Economics* (1947); Joseph Schumpeter, *Capitalism, Socialism, and Democracy* (3rd ed., 1950)*; George A. Steiner, *Government's Role in Economic Life* (1953); John K. Galbraith, *American Capitalism: The Concept of Countervailing Power* (1952)*; James S. Dusenberry, *Income, Savings and the Theory of Consumer Behavior* (1949); Richard A. Lester, "The Economic Significance of Unemployment Compensation, 1948–1959," *Review of Economics and Statistics*, vol. 42 (1960), pp. 349–372; Henry S. Kariel, *The Decline of American Pluralism* (1961)*.

Interest Groups and Affluence

Daniel Bell, *The End of Ideology* (1960)*; C. Wright Mills, *The Power Elite* (1956)*; Robert A. Dahl, *Who Governs? Democracy in an American City* (1961)*; Edward Higbee, *Farms and Farmers in an Urban Age* (1963)*; Herbert J. Gans, *The Urban Villagers* (1962); Joel I. Seidman, *American Labor from Defense to Reconversion* (1953); Irving Bernstein, "The Growth of American Unions, 1945–1960," *Labor History*, vol. 2 (1961), pp. 131–157; C. Wright Mills, *The New Men of Power* (1948); Paul Jacobs, *The State of the Unions* (1963); John Hutchinson,

The Imperfect Union: A History of the Corruption in American Trade Unions (1970).

CHAPTER 35

General

Merlo J. Pusey, *Eisenhower the President* (1956); Sherman Adams, *First Hand Report* (1961)*; Emmet John Hughes, *The Ordeal of Power* (1963)*; Marquis W. Childs, *Eisenhower, Captive Hero* (1958); C. A. H. Thompson and F. M. Shattuck, *The 1956 Presidential Campaign* (1960); Samuel Lubell, *Revolt of the Moderates* (1956); Heinz Eulau, *Class and Party in the Eisenhower Years* (1962); Richard E. Neustadt, *Presidential Power* (1964)*; Herbert J. Muller, *Adlai Stevenson* (1964)*.

Dulles' Foreign Policy

L. Gerson, *John Foster Dulles* (1967); Norman Graebner, *The New Isolationism* (1956); Paul Peeters, *Massive Retaliation* (1958); Michael Howard, *Disengagement in Europe* (1958)*; David Green, *The Containment of Latin America* (1970); Ellen J. Hammer, *The Struggle for Indo-China, 1940–1955* (1966); Melvin Gurov, *The First Vietnam Crisis* (1967); Herman Finer, *Dulles Over Suez* (1964)*.

Revolution in Race Relations

Thomas F. Gossett, *Race: The History of an Idea in America* (1963)*; Leonard Broom and Norval Glenn, *Transformation of the Negro American* (1965); Richard M. Dalfiume, "The Forgotten Years of the Negro Revolution," *Journal of American History*, vol. 55 (1968), pp. 90-106; Ulysses Lee, *The U.S. Army in World War II: The Employment of Negro Troops* (1966); Richard M. Dalfiume, *Desegregation of the U.S. Armed Forces . . . 1939–1953* (1969); Henry Lee Moon, *Balance of Power: The Negro Vote* (1948); Samuel Krislow, *The Negro in Federal Employment* (1967); Louis Ruchames, *Race, Jobs, and Politics: The Story of the FEPC* (1953); Richard Bardolph, *The Negro Vanguard* (1959)*.

The Supreme Court and Segregation

Loren Miller, *The Petitioners . . . the Supreme Court . . . and the Negro* (1966)*; Albert P. Blaustein and Clarence C. Ferguson, Jr., *Desegregation and the Law* (rev. ed., 1962)*; Clement E. Vose, *Caucasians Only: The Supreme Court, the NAACP, and the Restrictive Covenant Clauses* (1967); John P. Roche, "Plessy vs. Ferguson: Requiescat in Pace?" *University of Pennsylvania Law Review*, vol. 103 (1954).

Massive Resistance

Numan V. Bartley, *The Rise of Massive Resistance: Race and Politics in the South During the 1950's* (1969); Benjamin Muse, *Virginia's Massive Resistance* (1961); Benjamin Muse, *Ten Years of Prelude . . . Integration Since the Supreme Court's 1954 Decision* (1964).

Election of 1960

Theodore H. White, *The Making of the President, 1960* (1961)*; James M. Burns, *John Kennedy* (1960)*; Richard M. Nixon, *Six Crises* (1962)*; V. O. Key, Jr., *The Responsible Electorate: Rationality in Presidential Voting, 1936–1960* (1966)*.

CHAPTER 36

General

James M. Burns, *The Deadlock of Democracy: Four-Party Politics in America* (rev. ed., 1968)*; Adam C. Breckenridge, *Congress Against the Court* (1970); Daniel P. Moynihan, "Politics as the Art of the Impossible," *American Scholar*, vol. 38 (1969).

New Frontier

Aida DePace Donald (ed.), *John F. Kennedy and the New Frontier* (1967)*; Theodore C. Sorensen, *Kennedy* (1965)*; Arthur M. Schlesinger, Jr., *A Thousand Days* (1965)*; Hugh Sidey, *John F. Kennedy, President* (1964); Richard E. Neustadt, "Kennedy in the Presidency: A Premature Appraisal," *Political Science Quarterly*, vol. 79 (1964), pp. 321-334; George Kateb, "Kennedy as Statesman," *Commentary*, vol. 44 (1966), pp. 54-60; Milton R. Konvitz, *Expanding Liberties* (1966)*; John P. Roche, *Quest for the Dream: The Development of Civil Rights* (1963)*; Archibald Cox, *The Warren Court* (1968); M. Lytle Clifford, *The Warren Court and Its Critics* (1968); L. Brent Bozell, *The Warren Court* (1967).

Black Revolution: Nonviolence

Louis E. Lomax, *The Negro Revolt* (1962)*; Charles E. Silberman, *Crisis in Black and White* (1964)*; Anthony Lewis, *Portrait of a Decade* (1964)*; James C. Wilson, *Negro Politics: The Search for Leadership* (1960)*; Everett Carl Ladd, Jr., *Negro Political Leadership in the South* (1966); Martin Luther King, Jr., *Why We Can't Wait* (1964)*; Howard Zinn, *SNCC: The New Abolitionists* (1964)*; Kenneth B. Clark, *Dark Ghetto: Dilemmas of Social Power* (1965)*; James Baldwin, *The Fire Next Time* (1962)*; Harold Cruse, *The Crisis of the Negro Intellectual* (1967)*; E. U. Essien-Udom, *Black Nationalism* (1962)*; *The Autobiography of Malcolm X* (1966)*.

Kennedy and the World

Roger Hilsman, *To Move a Nation* (1967)*; Robert F. Smith, *The United States and Cuba . . . 1917–1960* (1960)*; Theodore Draper, *Castro's Revolution: Myths and Realities* (1962)*; Tad Szulc and Karl E. Meyer, *The Cuban Invasion* (1962)*; Elie Abel, *The Missile Crisis* (1966); Robert F. Kennedy, *Thirteen Days* (1969).

The Death of Kennedy

William Manchester, *The Death of a President* (1967)*; Mark Lane, *Rush to Judgment* (1966)*; Edward Jay Epstein, *Inquest: The Warren Commission* (1966)*.

Johnson's Great Society

Theodore H. White, *The Making of the President, 1964* (1965)*; William S. White, *The Professional: Lyndon B. Johnson* (1964); Rowland Evans and Robert Novak, *Lyndon B. Johnson* (1966); Eric Goldman, *The Tragedy of Lyndon Johnson* (1969)*; Charles Roberts, *LBJ's Inner Circle* (1965).

War Without Honor

Philip L. Geyelin, *Lyndon B. Johnson and the World* (1966)*; John Bartlow Martin, *Overtaken by Events* [on Dominican intervention] (1966); George M. Kahin and John W. Lewis, *The United States in Vietnam* (1967); Robert Shaplen, *The Lost Revolution: The U.S. in Vietnam* (rev. ed. 1966)*; Bernard Fall, *Two Viet Nams* (rev. ed., 1967); Jean Lacoutoure, *Vietnam: Between Two Truces* (1966)*; Theodore Draper, *Abuse of Power* (1967)*; David

Halberstam, *The Making of a Quagmire* (1965)*; Douglas Pike, *Viet Cong* (1966).

Nixon's Conditional Mandate

Theodore H. White, *The Making of the President, 1968* (1969)*; Joe McGinnis, *The Selling of the President, 1968* (1969)*.

CHAPTER 37

General

John Kenneth Galbraith, *The Industrial State* (1967)*; David Bazelon, *The Paper Economy* (1963); Adam Yarmolinsky, *The Military Establishment* (1971); Arthur R. Miller, *The Assault on Privacy* (1971); Erik Barnouw, *The Image Empire . . . Vol. 3: From 1953* (1970); Marshall McLuhan, *Understanding Media* (1964)*.

The Search for Values

Andrew Hacker, *The End of the American Era* (1970); Norman Mailer, *Of a Fire on the Moon* (1970); Daniel J. Boorstin, *The Decline of Radicalism* (1969).

Poverty and Welfare

Gabriel Kolko, *Wealth and Power in America* (rev. ed., 1964)*; Michael Harrington, *The Other America* (1962)*; Jack Newfield, *A Prophetic Minority* (1966)*; Herman P. Miller, *Rich Man, Poor Man* (1964); Leon Keyserling, *Poverty and Deprivation in the United States* (1962); Robert Coles, *Uprooted Children: The Early Life of Migrant Farm Workers* (1970)*; John Kosa (ed.), *Poverty and Health* (1969); Jane Jacobs, *The Death and Life of Great American Cities* (1961)*; Mitchell Gordon, *Sick Cities* (1963)*; Edward C. Banfield, *The Unheavenly City . . . Our Urban Crisis* (1970).

A New Generation

David Riesman and Christopher Jencks, *The Academic Revolution* (1968); Charles E. Silberman, *Crisis in the Classroom* (1970); Jerome H. Skolnick, *The Politics of Protest* (1969)*; Sheldon S. Wolin and John H. Schaar, *The Berkeley Rebellion and Beyond* (1969)*; Lewis Feuer, *The Conflict of Generations* (1968); Kenneth Keniston, *Uncommitted: Alienated Youth in Amer-*

ican Society (1965); Henry Gross, *The Flower People* (1968)*.

Black Power

Stokely Carmichael and Charles V. Hamilton, *Black Power* (1967)*; Eldridge Cleaver, *Soul on Ice* (1968)*; Lewis M. Killian, *The Impossible Revolution?: Black Power and the American Dream* (1968)*; Alphonse Pinckney, *Black Americans* (1969)*; Nathan Wright, *Black Power and Urban Unrest* (1967); Robert Conot, *Rivers of Blood, Years of Darkness* (1967)*; Tom Hayden, *Rebellion in Newark* (1967); John Hersey, *The Algiers Motel Incident* (1968); Ben W. Gilbert, *Ten Blocks from the White House* (1969)*.

Appendix

The Constitution of the United States of America

Preamble

We the People of the United States, in order to form a more perfect Union, establish justice, ensure domestic tranquility, provide for the common defense, promote the general welfare, and secure the blessings of liberty to ourselves and our posterity, do ordain and establish this Constitution for the United States of America.

Article I

Section 1. All legislative powers herein granted shall be vested in a Congress of the United States, which shall consist of a Senate and House of Representatives.

Section 2. The House of Representatives shall be composed of members chosen every second year by the people of the several States, and the electors in each State shall have the qualifications requisite for electors of the most numerous branch of the State Legislature.

No person shall be a representative who shall not have attained to the age of twenty-five years, and been seven years a citizen of the United States, and who shall not, when elected, be an inhabitant of that State in which he shall be chosen.

Representatives and direct taxes shall be apportioned among the several States which may be included within this Union, according to their respective numbers, which shall be determined by adding to the whole number of free persons, including those bound to service for a term of years, and excluding Indians not taxed, three-fifths of all other persons. The actual enumeration shall be made within three years after the first meeting of the Congress of the United States, and within every subsequent term of ten years, in such manner as they shall by law direct. The number of representatives shall not exceed one for every thirty thousand, but each State shall have at least one representative; and until such enumeration shall be made, the State of New Hampshire shall be entitled to choose three, Massachusetts eight, Rhode Island and Providence Plantations one, Connecticut five, New York six, New Jersey four, Pennsylvania eight, Delaware one, Maryland six, Virginia ten, North Carolina five, South Carolina five, and Georgia three.

When vacancies happen in the representation from any State, the executive authority thereof shall issue writs of election to fill such vacancies.

The House of Representatives shall choose their Speaker and other officers; and shall have the sole power of impeachment.

Section 3. The Senate of the United States shall be composed of two senators from each State, chosen by the legislature thereof, for six years and each senator shall have one vote.

Immediately after they shall be assembled in consequence of the first election, they shall be divided as equally as may be into three classes. The seats of the senators of the first class shall be vacated at the expiration of the second year, of the second class at the expiration of the fourth year, and of the third class at the expiration of the sixth year, so that one-third may be chosen every second year; and if vacancies happen by resignation, or otherwise, during the recess of the legislature of any State the executive thereof may make temporary appointments until the next meeting of the legislature, which shall then fill such vacancies.

No person shall be a senator who shall not have attained to the age of thirty years, and been nine years a citizen of the United States, and who shall not, when elected, be an inhabitant of that State for which he shall be chosen.

The Vice President of the United States shall be President of the Senate, but shall have no vote, unless they be equally divided.

The Senate shall choose their other officers, and also a President *pro tempore,* in the absence of the Vice President, or when he shall exercise the office of President of the United States.

The Senate shall have the sole power to try all impeachments. When sitting for that purpose, they shall be on oath or affirmation. When the President of the United States is tried, the Chief

Justice shall preside: And no person shall be convicted without the concurrence of two-thirds of the members present.

Judgment in cases of impeachment shall not extend further than to removal from office, and disqualification to hold and enjoy any office of honour, trust or profit under the United States: but the party convicted shall nevertheless be liable and subject to indictment, trial, judgment, and punishment according to law.

Section 4. The times, places and manner of holding elections for senators and representatives, shall be prescribed in each State by the legislature thereof; but the Congress may at any time by law make or alter such regulations, except as to the places of choosing senators.

The Congress shall assemble at least once in every year, and such meeting shall be on the first Monday in December, unless they shall by law appoint a different day.

Section 5. Each house shall be the judge of the elections, returns and qualifications of its own members, and a majority of each shall constitute a quorum to do business; but a smaller number may adjourn from day to day, and may be authorized to compel the attendance of absent members, in such manner, and under such penalties as each house may provide.

Each house may determine the rules of its proceedings, punish its members for disorderly behaviour, and, with the concurrence of two-thirds, expel a member.

Each house shall keep a journal of its proceedings, and from time to time publish the same, excepting such parts as may in their judgment require secrecy; and the yeas and nays of the members of either house on any question shall, at the desire of one-fifth of those present, be entered on the journal.

Neither house, during the session of Congress, shall, without the consent of the other adjourn for more than three days, nor to any other place than that in which the two houses shall be sitting.

Section 6. The senators and representatives shall receive a compensation for their services, to be ascertained by law, and paid out of the Treasury of the United States. They shall in all cases,

except treason, felony and breach of the peace, be privileged from arrest during their attendance at the session of their respective houses, and in going to and returning from the same; and for any speech or debate in either house, they shall not be questioned in any other place.

No senator or representative shall, during the time for which he was elected, be appointed to any civil office under the authority of the United States, which shall have been created, or the emoluments whereof shall have been increased during such time; and no person holding any office under the United States, shall be a member of either house during his continuance in office.

Section 7. All bills for raising revenue shall originate in the House of Representatives; but the Senate may propose or concur with amendments as on other bills.

Every bill which shall have passed the House of Representatives and the Senate, shall, before it becomes a law, be presented to the President of the United States; if he approves he shall sign it, but if not he shall return it, with his objections to that house in which it shall have originated, who shall enter the objections at large on their journal, and proceed to reconsider it. If after such reconsideration two-thirds of that House shall agree to pass the bill, it shall be sent, together with the objections, to the other House, by which it shall likewise be reconsidered, and if approved by two-thirds of that House, it shall become a law. But in all such cases the votes of both Houses shall be determined by yeas and nays, and the names of the persons voting for and against the bill shall be entered on the journal of each House respectively. If any bill shall not be returned by the President within ten days (Sundays excepted) after it shall have been presented to him, the same shall be a law, in like manner as if he had signed it, unless the Congress by their adjournment prevent its return, in which case it shall not be a law.

Every order, resolution, or vote to which the concurrence of the Senate and House of Representatives may be necessary (except on a question of adjournment) shall be presented to the President of the United States; and before the same shall take effect, shall be approved by him or being disapproved by him, shall be repassed by two-thirds of the Senate and House of Representatives, according to the rules and limitations prescribed in the case of a bill.

Section 8. The Congress shall have power to lay and collect taxes, duties, imposts and excises, to pay the debts and provide for the common defense and general welfare of the United States; but all duties, imposts and excises shall be uniform throughout the United States;

To borrow money on the credit of the United States;

To regulate commerce with foreign nations and among the several States, and with the Indian tribes;

To establish a uniform rule of naturalization, and uniform laws on the subject of bankruptcies throughout the United States;

To coin money, regulate the value thereof, and of foreign coin, and fix the standard of weights and measures;

To provide for the punishment of counterfeiting the securities and current coin of the United States;

To establish post offices and post roads;

To promote the progress of science and useful arts, by securing for limited times to authors and inventors the exclusive right to their respective writings and discoveries;

To constitute tribunals inferior to the Supreme Court;

To define and punish piracies and felonies committed on the high seas, and offenses against the law of nations;

To declare war, grant letters of marque and reprisal, and make rules concerning captures on land and water;

To raise and support armies, but no appropriation of money to that use shall be for a longer term than two years;

To provide and maintain a Navy;

To make rules for the government and regulation of the land and naval forces;

To provide for calling forth the militia to execute the laws of the Union, suppress insurrections and repel invasions;

To provide for organizing, arming, and disciplining, the militia, and for governing such part of them as may be employed in the service of the United States, reserving to the States respectively, the appointment of the officers, and the authority of training the militia according to the discipline prescribed by Congress;

To exercise exclusive legislation in all cases whatsoever, over such district (not exceeding ten miles square) as may, by cession of particular States, and the acceptance of Congress, become the seat of the Government of the United States, and to exercise like authority over all places purchased by the consent of the legislature of the State in which the same shall be, for the erection of forts, magazines, arsenals, dock-yards, and other needful buildings;—And

To make all laws which shall be necessary and proper for carrying into execution the foregoing powers, and all other powers vested by this Constitution in the Government of the United States, or in any department or officer thereof.

Section 9. The migration or importation of such persons as any of the States now existing shall think proper to admit, shall not be prohibited by the Congress prior to the year one thousand eight hundred and eight, but a tax or duty may be imposed on such importation, not exceeding ten dollars for each person.

The privilege of the writ of habeas corpus shall not be suspended, unless when in cases of rebellion or invasion the public safety may require it.

No bill of attainder or ex post facto law shall be passed.

No capitation, or other direct, tax shall be laid, unless in proportion to the census or enumeration herein before directed to be taken.

No tax or duty shall be laid on articles exported from any state.

No preference shall be given by any regulation of commerce or revenue to the ports of one State over those of another: nor shall vessels bound to, or from, one State, be obliged to enter, clear, or pay duties in another.

No money shall be drawn from the Treasury, but in consequence of appropriations made by law; and a regular statement and account of the receipts and expenditures of all public money shall be published from time to time.

No title of nobility shall be granted by the

United States: And no person holding any office of profit or trust under them, shall, without the consent of the Congress, accept of any present, emolument, office, or title, of any kind whatever, from any King, Prince, or foreign State.

Section 10. No state shall enter into any treaty, alliance, or confederation; grant letters of marque and reprisal; coin money; emit bills of credit; make any thing but gold and silver coin a tender in payment of debts; pass any bill of attainder, ex post facto law, or law impairing the obligation of contracts, or grant any title of nobility.

No state shall, without the consent of the Congress, lay any imposts or duties on imports or exports, except what may be absolutely necessary for executing its inspection laws; and the net produce of all duties and imposts, laid by any State on imports or exports, shall be for the use of the Treasury of the United States; and all such laws shall be subject to the revision and control of the Congress.

No State shall, without the consent of Congress, lay any duty of tonnage, keep troops, or ships of war in time of peace, enter into any agreement or compact with another State, or with a foreign power, or engage in war, unless actually invaded, or in such imminent danger as will not admit of delay.

Article II

Section 1. The executive power shall be vested in a President of the United States of America. He shall hold his office during the term of four years, and, together with the Vice President, chosen for the same term, be elected, as follows:

Each State shall appoint, in such manner as the legislature thereof may direct, a number of electors, equal to the whole number of senators and representatives to which the State may be entitled in the Congress: but no senator or representative, or person holding an office of trust or profit under the United States, shall be appointed an elector.

The electors shall meet in their respective States, and vote by ballot for two persons, of whom one at least shall not be an inhabitant of the same State with themselves. And they shall make a list of all the persons voted for, and of the number of votes for each; which list they shall sign and certify, and transmit sealed to the seat of the Government of the United States, directed to the President of the Senate. The President of the Senate shall, in the presence of the Senate and House of Representatives, open all the certificates, and the votes shall then be counted. The person having the greatest number of votes shall be the President, if such number be a majority of the whole number of electors appointed; and if there be more than one who have such majority, and have an equal number of votes, then the House of Representatives shall immediately choose by ballot one of them for President; and if no person have a majority, then from the five highest on the list the said House shall in like manner choose the President. But in choosing the President, the votes shall be taken by States, the representation from each State having one vote; a quorum for this purpose shall consist of a member or members from two-thirds of the States, and a majority of all the States shall be necessary to a choice. In every case, after the choice of the President, the person having the greatest number of votes of the electors shall be the Vice President. But if there should remain two or more who have equal votes, the Senate shall choose from them by ballot the Vice President.

The Congress may determine the time of choosing the electors, and the day on which they shall give their votes; which day shall be the same throughout the United States.

No person except a natural-born citizen, or a citizen of the United States, at the time of the adoption of this Constitution, shall be eligible to the office of President; neither shall any person be eligible to that office who shall not have attained to the age of thirty-five years, and been fourteen years a resident within the United States.

In case of the removal of the President from office, or of his death, resignation, or inability to discharge the powers and duties of the said office, the same shall devolve on the Vice President, and the Congress may by law provide for the case of removal, death, resignation, or inability, both of the President and Vice President, declaring what officer shall then act as President, and such officer shall act accordingly, until the disability be removed, or a President shall be elected.

The President shall, at stated times, receive for his services, a compensation, which shall neither be increased nor diminished during the period for which he shall have been elected, and he shall not receive within that period any other emolument from the United States, or any of them.

Before he enter on the execution of his office, he shall take the following oath or affirmation: "I do solemnly swear (or affirm) that I will faithfully execute the office of President of the United States, and will to the best of my ability, preserve, protect and defend the Constitution of the United States."

Section 2. The President shall be Commander in Chief of the Army and Navy of the United States, and of the militia of the several States, when called into the actual service of the United States; he may require the opinion, in writing, of the principal officer in each of the Executive Departments, upon any subject relating to the duties of their respective offices, and he shall have power to grant reprieves and pardons for offenses against the United States, except in cases of impeachment.

He shall have power, by and with the advice and consent of the Senate, to make treaties, provided two-thirds of the Senators present concur; and he shall nominate, and by and with the advice and consent of the Senate, shall appoint ambassadors, other public ministers and consuls, judges of the Supreme Court, and all other officers of the United States, whose appointments are not herein otherwise provided for, and which shall be established by law: but the Congress may by law vest the appointment of such inferior officers, as they think proper, in the President alone, in the courts of law, or in the heads of departments.

The President shall have power to fill up all vacancies that may happen during the recess of the Senate, by granting commissions which shall expire at the end of their next session.

Section 3. He shall from time to time give to the Congress information of the state of the Union, and recommend to their consideration such measures as he shall judge necessary and expedient; he may, on extraordinary occasions, convene both houses, or either of them, and in case of disagreement between them, with respect to the time of adjournment, he may adjourn them to such time as he shall think proper; he shall receive ambassadors and other public ministers; he shall take care that the laws be faithfully executed, and shall commission all the officers of the United States.

Section 4. The President, Vice President and all civil officers of the United States, shall be removed from office on impeachment for, and conviction of, treason, bribery, or other high crimes and misdemeanors.

Article III

Section 1. The judicial power of the United States shall be vested in one Supreme Court, and in such inferior courts as the Congress may from time to time ordain and establish. The judges, both of the supreme and inferior courts, shall hold their offices during good behavior, and shall, at stated times, receive for their services, a compensation, which shall not be diminished during their continuance in office.

Section 2. The judicial power shall extend to all cases, in law and equity, arising under this Constitution, the laws of the United States, and treaties made, or which shall be made, under their authority; to all cases affecting ambassadors, other public ministers and consuls; to all cases of admiralty and maritime jurisdiction; to controversies to which the United States shall be a party; to controversies between two or more States; between a State and citizens of another State; between citizens of different States; between citizens of the same State claiming lands under grants of different States, and between a State, or the citizens thereof, and foreign States, citizens, or subjects.

In all cases affecting ambassadors, other public ministers and consuls, and those in which a State shall be party, the Supreme Court shall have original jurisdiction. In all the other cases before mentioned, the Supreme Court shall have appellate jurisdiction, both as to law and to fact, with such exceptions, and under such regulations as the Congress shall make.

The trial of all crimes, except in cases of impeachment, shall be by jury; and such trial shall be held in the State where the said crimes shall have been committed; but when not committed within any State, the trial shall be at such place or places as the Congress may by law have directed.

Section 3. Treason against the United States, shall consist only in levying war against them, or in adhering to their enemies, giving them aid and comfort. No person shall be convicted of treason unless on the testimony of two witnesses to the same overt act, or on confession in open court.

The Congress shall have power to declare the punishment of treason, but no attainder of treason shall work corruption of blood, or forfeiture except during the life of the person attainted.

Article IV

Section 1. Full faith and credit shall be given in each State to the public acts, records, and judicial proceedings of every other State. And the Congress may by general laws prescribe the manner in which such acts, records and proceedings shall be proved, and the effect thereof.

Section 2. The citizens of each State shall be entitled to all privileges and immunities of citizens in the several States.

A person charged in any State with treason, felony, or other crime, who shall flee from justice, and be found in another State, shall on demand of the executive authority of the State from which he fled, be delivered up, to be removed to the State having jurisdiction of the crime.

No person held to service or labour in one State, under the laws thereof, escaping into another, shall, in consequence of any law or regulation therein, be discharged from such service or labour, but shall be delivered up on claim of the party to whom such service or labour may be due.

Section 3. New States may be admitted by the Congress into this Union; but no new State shall be formed or erected within the jurisdiction of any other State; nor any State be formed by the junction of two or more States, or parts of States, without the consent of the legislatures of the States concerned as well as of the Congress.

The Congress shall have power to dispose of and make all needful rules and regulations respecting the Territory or other property belonging to the United States; and nothing in this Constitution shall be so construed as to prejudice any claims of the United States, or of any particular State.

Section 4. The United States shall guarantee to every State in this Union a republican form of Government, and shall protect each of them against invasion; and on application of the legislature, or of the executive (when the legislature cannot be convened) against domestic violence.

Article V

The Congress, whenever two-thirds of both Houses shall deem it necessary, shall propose amendments to this Constitution, or, on the application of the legislatures of two-thirds of the several States, shall call a convention for proposing amendments, which, in either case, shall be valid to all intents and purposes, as part of this Constitution, when ratified by the legislatures of three-fourths of the several States, or by conventions in three-fourths thereof, as the one or the other mode of ratification may be proposed by the Congress; provided that no amendment which may be made prior to the year one thousand eight hundred and eight shall in any manner affect the first and fourth clauses in the Ninth Section of the First Article; and that no State, without its consent, shall be deprived of its equal suffrage in the Senate.

Article VI

All debts contracted and engagements entered into, before the adoption of this Constitution, shall be as valid against the United States under this Constitution, as under the Confederation.

This Constitution, and the laws of the United States which shall be made in pursuance thereof; and all treaties made, or which shall be made, under the authority of the United States, shall be the supreme law of the land; and the judges in every State shall be bound thereby, anything in the Constitution or laws of any State to the contrary notwithstanding.

The senators and representatives before mentioned, and the members of the several State legislatures, and all executive and judicial officers, both of the United States and of the several States, shall be bound by oath or affirmation, to support this Constitution; but no religious test shall ever be required as a qualification to any office or public trust under the United States.

Article VII

The ratification of the conventions of nine States shall be sufficient for the establishment of this Constitution between the States so ratifying the same.

Done in convention by the unanimous consent of the States present the seventeenth day of September in the year of our Lord one thousand seven hundred and eighty-seven and of the Independence of the United States of America the twelfth. . . .

AMENDMENTS

Amendment I

Congress shall make no law respecting an establishment of religion, or prohibiting the free exercise thereof; or abridging the freedom of speech, or of the press; or the right of the people peaceably to assemble, and to petition the Government for a redress of grievances.

Amendment II

A well regulated militia, being necessary to the security of a free State, the right of the people to keep and bear arms, shall not be infringed.

Amendment III

No soldier shall, in time of peace be quartered in any house, without the consent of the owner, nor in time of war, but in a manner to be prescribed by law.

Amendment IV

The right of the people to be secure in their persons, houses, papers, and effects, against unreasonable searches and seizures, shall not be violated, and no warrants shall issue, but upon probable cause, supported by oath or affirmation, and particularly describing the place to be searched, and the persons or things to be seized.

Amendment V

No person shall be held to answer for a capital, or otherwise infamous crime, unless on a presentment or indictment of a grand jury, except in cases arising in the land or naval forces, or in the militia, when in actual service in time of war or public danger; nor shall any person be subject for the same offense to be twice put in jeopardy of life or limb; nor shall be compelled in any criminal case to be witness against himself, nor be deprived of life, liberty, or property, without due process of law; nor shall private property be taken for public use, without just compensation.

Amendment VI

In all criminal prosecutions, the accused shall enjoy the right to a speedy and public trial, by an impartial jury of the State and district wherein the crime shall have been committed, which district shall have been previously ascertained by law, and to be informed of the nature and cause of the accusation; to be confronted with the witnesses against him; to have compulsory process for obtaining witnesses in his favour, and to have the assistance of counsel for his defense.

Amendment VII

In suits at common law, where the value in controversy shall exceed twenty dollars, the right of trial by jury shall be preserved, and no fact tried by a jury, shall be otherwise re-examined in any court of the United States, than according to the rules of the common law.

Amendment VIII

Excessive bail shall not be required, nor excessive fines imposed, nor cruel and unusual punishments inflicted.

Amendment IX

The enumeration in the Constitution, of certain rights, shall not be construed to deny or disparage others retained by the people.

Amendment X

The powers not delegated to the United States by the Constitution, nor prohibited by it to the States, are reserved to the States respectively, or to the people.

Amendment XI

The judicial power of the United States shall not be construed to extend to any suit in law or equity, commenced or prosecuted against one of the United States by citizens of another State, or by citizens or subjects of any foreign State.

Amendment XII

The electors shall meet in their respective States, and vote by ballot for President and Vice President, one of whom, at least, shall not be an inhabitant of the same State with themselves; they shall name in their ballots the person voted for as President, and in distinct ballots the person voted for as Vice President, and they shall make distinct lists of all persons voted for as President, and of all persons voted for as Vice President, and of the number of votes for each, which lists they shall sign and certify, and transmit sealed to the seat of the government of the United States, directed to the President of the Senate. The President of the Senate shall, in the presence of the Senate and House of Representatives, open all the certificates and the votes shall then be counted. The person having the greatest number of votes for President, shall be the President, if such number be a majority of the whole number of electors appointed; and if no person have such majority, then from the persons having the highest numbers not exceeding three on the list of those voted for as President, the House of Representatives shall choose immediately, by ballot, the President. But in choosing the President, the votes shall be taken by States, the representation from each State hav-

ing one vote; a quorum for this purpose shall consist of a member or members from two-thirds of the States, and a majority of all the States shall be necessary to a choice. And if the House of Representatives shall not choose a President whenever the right of choice shall devolve upon them, before the fourth day of March next following, then the Vice President shall act as President, as in the case of the death or other constitutional disability of the President. The person having the greatest number of votes as Vice President, shall be the Vice President, if such number be a majority of the whole number of electors appointed, and if no person have a majority, then from the two highest numbers on the list, the Senate shall choose the Vice President; a quorum for the purpose shall consist of two-thirds of the whole number of Senators, and a majority of the whole number shall be necessary to a choice. But no person constitutionally ineligible to the office of President shall be eligible to that of Vice President of the United States.

Amendment XIII

Section 1. Neither slavery nor involuntary servitude, except as a punishment for crime whereof the party shall have been duly convicted, shall exist within the United States, or any place subject to their jurisdiction.

Section 2. Congress shall have power to enforce this article by appropriate legislation.

Amendment XIV

Section 1. All persons born or naturalized in the United States, and subject to the jurisdiction thereof, are citizens of the United States and of the State wherein they reside. No State shall make or enforce any law which shall abridge the privileges or immunities of citizens of the United States; nor shall any State deprive any person of life, liberty, or property, without due process of law; nor deny to any person within its jurisdiction the equal protection of the laws.

Section 2. Representatives shall be apportioned among the several States according to their respective numbers, counting the whole number of persons in each State, excluding Indians not taxed. But when the right to vote at any election for the choice of electors for President and Vice President of the United States, Representatives in Congress, the executive and judicial officers of a State, or the members of the legislature thereof, is denied to any of the male inhabitants of such State, being twenty-one years of age, and citizens of the United States, or in any way abridged, except for participation in rebellion, or other crime, the basis of representation therein shall be reduced in the proportion which the number of such male citizens shall bear to the whole number of male citizens twenty-one years of age in such State.

Section 3. No person shall be a Senator or Representative in Congress, or elector of President and Vice President, or hold any office, civil or military, under the United States, or under any State, who, having previously taken an oath, as a member of Congress, or as an officer of the United States, or as a member of any State legislature, or as an executive or judicial officer of any State, to support the Constitution of the United States, shall have engaged in insurrection or rebellion against the same, or given aid or comfort to the enemies thereof. But Congress may by a vote of two-thirds of each house, remove such disability.

Section 4. The validity of the public debt of the United States, authorized by law, including debts incurred for payment of pensions and bounties for services in suppressing insurrection or rebellion, shall not be questioned. But neither the United States nor any State shall assume or pay any debt or obligation incurred in aid of insurrection or rebellion against the United States, or any claim for the loss or emancipation of any slave; but all such debts, obligations and claims shall be held illegal and void.

Section 5. The Congress shall have power to enforce, by appropriate legislation, the provisions of this article.

Amendment XV

Section 1. The right of citizens of the United States to vote shall not be denied or abridged by the United States or by any State on account of race, color, or previous condition of servitude.

Section 2. The Congress shall have power to enforce this article by appropriate legislation.

Amendment XVI

The Congress shall have power to lay and collect taxes on incomes, from whatever source derived, without apportionment among the several States, and without regard to census or enumeration.

Amendment XVII

Section 1. The Senate of the United States shall be composed of two senators from each State, elected by the people thereof, for six years; and each senator shall have one vote. The electors in each State shall have the qualifications requisite for electors of the most numerous branch of the State legislatures.

Section 2. When vacancies happen in the representation of any State in the Senate, the executive authority of such State shall issue writs of election to fill such vacancies; *Provided,* That the legislature of any State may empower the executive thereof to make temporary appointments until the people fill the vacancies by election as the legislature may direct.

Section 3. This amendment shall not be so construed as to affect the election or term of any senator chosen before it becomes valid as part of the Constitution.

Amendment XVIII

Section 1. After one year from the ratification of this article the manufacture, sale, or transportation of intoxicating liquors within, the importation thereof into, or the exportation thereof from the United States and all territory subject to the jurisdiction thereof for beverage purposes is hereby prohibited.

Section 2. The Congress and the several States shall have concurrent power to enforce this article by appropriate legislation.

Section 3. This article shall be inoperative unless is shall have been ratified as an amendment to the Constitution by the legislatures of the several States, as provided in the Constitution, within seven years from the date of the submission hereof to the States by the Congress.

Amendment XIX

Section 1. The right of citizens of the United States to vote shall not be denied or abridged by the United States or by any State on account of sex.

Section 2. Congress shall have power to enforce this article by appropriate legislation.

Amendment XX

Section 1. The terms of the President and Vice President shall end at noon on the 20th day of January, and the terms of Senators and Representatives at noon on the 3rd day of January, of the years in which such terms would have ended if this article had not been ratified; and the terms of their successors shall then begin.

Section 2. The Congress shall assemble at least once in every year, and such meeting shall begin at noon on the 3rd day of January, unless they shall by law appoint a different day.

Section 3. If, at the time fixed for the beginning of the term of the President, the President elect shall have died, the Vice President elect shall become President. If a President shall not have been chosen before the time fixed for the beginning of his term, or if the President elect shall have failed to qualify, then the Vice President elect shall act as President until a President shall have qualified; and the Congress may by law provide for the case wherein neither a President elect nor a Vice President elect shall have qualified, declaring who shall then act as President, or the manner in which one who is to act shall be selected, and such person shall act accordingly until a President or Vice President shall have qualified.

Section 4. The Congress may by law provide for the case of the death of any of the persons from whom the House of Representatives may choose a President whenever the right of choice shall have devolved upon them, and for the case of the death of any of the persons from whom the Senate may choose a Vice President whenever the right of choice shall have devolved upon them.

Section 5. Sections 1 and 2 shall take effect on the 15th day of October following the ratification of this article.

Section 6. This article shall be inoperative unless it shall have been ratified as an amendment to the Constitution by the legislatures of three-fourths of the several States within seven years from the date of its submission.

Amendment XXI

Section 1. The eighteenth article of amendment to the Constitution of the United States is hereby repealed.

Section 2. The transportation or importation into any State, Territory, or possession of the United States for delivery or use therein of intoxicating liquors, in violation of the laws thereof, is hereby prohibited.

Section 3. This article shall be inoperative unless it shall have been ratified as an amendment to the Constitution by conventions in the several States, as provided in the Constitution, within seven years from the date of the submission hereof to the States by the Congress.

Amendment XXII

No person shall be elected to the office of the President more than twice, and no person who has held the office of President, or acted as President, for more than two years of a term to which some other person was elected President shall be elected to the office of the President more than once. But this Article shall not apply to any person holding the office of President when this Article was proposed by the Congress, and shall not prevent any person who may be holding the office of President, or acting as President, during the term within which this Article becomes operative from holding the office of President or acting as President during the remainder of such term.

Amendment XXIII

Section 1. The District constituting the seat of Government of the United States shall appoint in such manner as the Congress may direct:

A number of electors of President and Vice President equal to the whole number of Senators and Representatives in Congress to which the District would be entitled if it were a State, but in no event more than the least populous State; they shall be in addition to those appointed by the States, but they shall be considered, for the purposes of the election of the President and Vice-President, to be electors appointed by a State; and they shall meet in the District and perform such duties as provided by the twelfth article of amendment.

Section 2. The Congress shall have power to enforce this article by appropriate legislation.

Amendment XXIV

The right of citizens of the United States to vote in any primary or other election for President or Vice President, for electors for President or Vice President, or for Senator or Representative in Congress shall not be denied or abridged by the United States or any State for reason of failure to pay any Poll Tax or other Tax.

Amendment XXV

Section 1. In case of the removal of the President from office or his death or resignation, the Vice President shall become President.

Section 2. Whenever there is a vacancy in the office of the Vice President, the President shall nominate a Vice President who shall take the office upon confirmation by a majority vote of both Houses of Congress.

Section 3. Whenever the President transmits to the President *pro tempore* of the Senate and the Speaker of the House of Representatives his written declaration that he is unable to discharge the powers and duties of his office, and until he transmits to them a written declaration to the contrary, such powers and duties shall be discharged by the Vice President as Acting President.

Section 4. Whenever the Vice President and a majority of either the principal officers of the Executive Departments or of such other body as Congress may by law provide, transmit to the President *pro tempore* of the Senate and the Speaker of the House of Representatives their written declaration that the President is unable to discharge the powers and duties of his office, the Vice President shall immediately assume the powers and duties of the office as Acting President. Thereafter, when the President transmits to the President *pro tempore* of the Senate and the Speaker of the House of Representatives his written declaration that no inability exists, he shall resume the powers and duties of his office unless the Vice President and a majority of either the principal officers of the Executive Departments or of such other body as Congress may by law provide, transmit within 4 days to the President *pro tempore* of the Senate and the Speaker of the House of Representatives their written declaration that the President is unable to discharge the powers and duties of his office. Thereupon Congress shall decide the issue, assembling within 48 hours for that purpose if not in session. If the Congress, within 21 days after receipt of the latter written declaration, or, if Congress is not in session, within 21 days after Congress is required to assemble, determines by two-thirds vote of both Houses that the President is unable to discharge the powers and duties of his office, the Vice President shall continue to discharge the same as Acting President; otherwise, the President shall resume the powers and duties of his office.

Amendment XXVI

Section 1. The right of citizens of the United States, who are eighteen years of age or older, to vote shall not be denied or abridged by the United States or by any State on account of age.

Section 2. The Congress shall have power to enforce this article by appropriate legislation.

Index